EARLY

of

Eastern and
Southeastern Kentucky

And Their Descendants

By

WILLIAM C. KOZEE

Originally published: Strasburg, Virginia, 1961
Reprinted: Genealogical Publishing Co., Inc.
Baltimore, 1973, 1979, 1994
© 1961 Bessie M. Kozee
© transferred to Genealogical Publishing Co., Inc.
Baltimore, Maryland, 1973
All Rights Reserved
Library of Congress Catalogue Card Number 73-9089
International Standard Book Number 0-8063-0577-0
Made in the United States of America

PUBLISHER'S NOTICE

When *Early Families of Eastern and Southeastern Kentucky*
and *Pioneer Families of Eastern and Southeastern Kentucky*
were written, the intention of the author was to publish
them together, as complementary volumes. However, as each
volume is complete and independent of the other, we offer
them separately.

PREFACE

The two volumes, "Pioneer Families of Eastern and Southeastern Kentucky," published in 1957, and "Early Families of Eastern and Southeastern Kentucky and Their Descendants," as their titles infer, pertain almost exclusively to people—the early adventurers, explorers hunters, surveyors and first settlers and their descendants of the section of Kentucky which was originally included in the counties of Floyd (1799), Knox (1799), Greenup (1803) and Clay (1806) as formed by the General Assembly of Kentucky, which is the section of the state east and south of a line roughly drawn from the northwest corner of Greenup County on the Ohio River along the western boundary of that county, formerly Fleming County; thence with the present Rowan County line, a southerly direction to the original Floyd County line in the vicinity of present Yale, Bath County; thence a southerly course to the beginning corner of Clay County midway between the mouths of Ross's and Sturgeon Creeks on the Kentucky River; thence a westerly course to the corner of original Knox County which became the corner of Whitley County when formed in 1818, thence with the western line of original Whitley County, a southerly course to the Tennessee state line—the "Kentucky Highlands" or Mountain Section.

In the preparation of the books all known available source materials were examined which necessitated extensive research in person in large areas of Kentucky and Virginia and in the National Archives, the Library of Congress and other libraries in Washington, D. C.; also it was necessary to contact a great number of descendants of these early families for data relating to their respective families.

Many of the genealogies and biographies were prepared entirely from public records and data furnished by descendants; some of the genealogies however, which had been published many years previously, were supplemented and brought down to the present on the basis of public records and data furnished by descendants.

No similar book or books covering the entire mountain section of the state has been published. However, several excellent regional and county histories, some of which contain genealogies, have been published. Among others are Ely's The Big Sandy Valley, 1887; Jillson's The Big Sandy Valley, 1923; Hall's Johnson County, 1928; Scalf's Historic Floyd (1800-1950), 1950; and Biggs and Mackoy's History of Greenup County, 1951.

It has not been established as a fact that in all instances the coat-of-arms pertains to the branch of the family in connection with which it is reproduced herein.

I desire to express my thanks to the various county court clerks of the mountain section of Kentucky and of certain counties of Virginia and to those in charge of the National Archives and the Library of Congress, Washington, D. C., for courtesies shown while doing research in their respective offices; and I sincerely thank the many friends for their encouragement and interest and particularly for preparing and furnishing valuable biographical and genealogical data relating to their respective families.

WILLIAM CARLOS KOZEE

Washington, D. C., and
Cove Point Beach, Lusby, Maryland

June 1, 1957

TABLE OF CONTENTS

LIST OF ILLUSTRATIONS

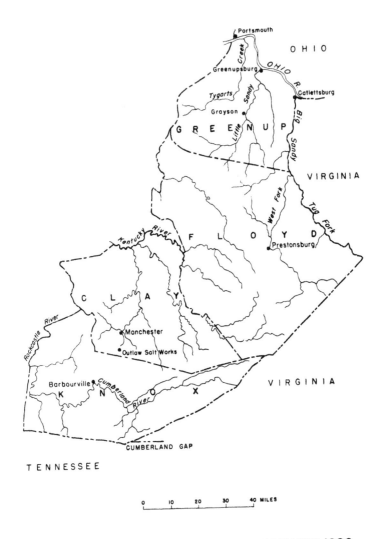

EASTERN AND SOUTHEASTERN KENTUCKY, 1809

C. M. Kozee, Sr., 1956

INTRODUCTION

The East Kentucky Pioneer Mountaineer—Race—Origin—Former Habitat—Class—Character and Characteristics.

The subject of mountain people of Kentucky has always been a fertile field for speculation on the part of the sociologists. They have been said to be descendants in a large measure of the younger children of the Virginia aristocracy; to be the Scotch-Irish of a later immigration than those settling in the Bluegrass; to be bluegrass settlers whom accident or stress of circumstances forced to settle in the mountains.

A Kentucky historian writing in the latter part of the 19th century said:

In the eastern mountainous region of Kentucky there are two classes of people growing up side by side. The larger and better class, constituting all but a few, are of English, Scotch-Irish and German origin; honest, courageous, kindly. A sombre-minded, liberty loving people, they kept retreating before advancing civilization until at last they lodged among the least accessible lands of the county * * * ; a hospitable gentle-mannered people yet fierce and reckless when thoroughly aroused. Many of them * * * bear the names and have in their veins the blood of statesmen and heroes who will be forever honored in the border history. * * * Latent in them are all the materials of a magnificent manhood. Only religion and literary culture are needed to call it forth. This class labors, is industrious, hardy, enterprising; a law-abiding and useful citizen. Of this class Boone, Kenton, Davy Crockett, Sam Houston, Andrew Johnson, John C. Calhoun, Lincoln and many others descended.

The second class of whom there are only a few in the Kentucky mountains are a sallow, gypsy-like people of unknown origin; idle and vicious. Whenever you read in the newspapers about these terrible vendettas which disgraced the country, you will, upon inquiry, find that nine out of every ten of them are traceable to this class or race of men. It was from these that the guerilla companies which infested the country during the Civil War were composed.[1]

In the ancestry of the East Kentucky mountaineers Scotch-Irish stock predominated and in successively smaller proportions there were families of English, German and French Huguenot blood. After the Revolutionary War the eastern seaboard states becoming thickly settled occasioned movements of great numbers of families Westward. Settlers came to the Kentucky mountains from central Pennsylvania, from Virginia, from North and South Carolina and a few from Maryland. The mountain people of today are a blend from the mingling of these several strains.[2]

It is generally agreed that the most outstanding trait of all the Southern Highlanders is a spirt of personal independence * * * for they are conscious of their rights as human beings, have serious self-respect and individual determination. Their dominant trait is independence raised to the fourth power. The Kentucky mountaineer is also characterized by physical courage. Facing a wild, natural environment that made all enterprise difficult and hazardous, the mountaineer was forced to face situations that constantly demanded an unbending courage.

Beside the personal independence and great courage, the Kentucky mountaineer is blessed with a third pioneer blessing—hospitality. The stranger need fear no refusal of food and shelter for the host is only too glad to give both for news of the outside world. Anything that might seem inhospitable is simply unthinkable.[3]

In the Civil War these honest, sturdy Kentucky mountaineers fought for the Union. Previous to that time they knew nothing of pistols and bowie-knives. The local war between them and the guerrillas, which raged at that time, first accustomed them to bloodshed; and the feuds then created by outrages perpetrated in the name of patriotism endured for many years.[4]

A distinguished lawyer and judge, a descendant of Eastern Kentucky mountain families, who knew the Kentucky mountaineer well, said: The mountain people are truthful and personally honest. In the United States Courts they do not equivocate; but even there they do not lie outright. They will not perjure themselves as people elsewhere often do. They try to conceal a fact, perhaps, and talk around a question, but even in a "moonshine" case, a witness will tell the truth in the main.[5]

Dr. Harvey W. Wiley said: "These Highlanders are not degenerates. On the contrary they are the best specimens to be found in the country, and probably in the world; they are the last remnant of the undefiled."

Woodrow Wilson said: "In these (Kentucky) mountains is the original stuff of which America is made."

Among the pioneer settlers of Eastern and Southeastern Kentucky were a very large number of Revolutionary War soldiers. Many of those from Virginia had received grants of land to be located in Kentucky in consideration of their services in the cause of American Independence; and they and almost all of the other pioneers came to Kentucky seeking good river and creek bottom lands on which to settle, establish homes and rear families. Probably they selected the mountain section of the State for the reason such lands were not then available in the Bluegrass section which had been settled for about a quarter of a century.

The eastern Kentucky mountain pioneer settlers were of the same class as the other people in the communities from which they came; and, therefore, of the same class—and often of the same family—as the pioneer Bluegrass settlers who came from these communities.

Early Kentuckians recognized no difference in the mountain population and that of Central Kentucky. Whatever difference that exists is due to the fact that the two sections have developed differently, economically, since their settlement.

In the trek Westward to Kentucky sometimes members of a family settled in the mountains while other members continuing on settled in the Bluegrass. A notable example: "Over a hundred years ago eleven Combs brothers, related to General Combs of the Revolutionary Army, came over the mountains from North Carolina. Nine of them settled along the North Fork of the Kentucky River in the mountains of Perry County; one went further down the stream into the rough hill country of Breathitt County; and the eleventh continued on his way till he came into the smiling region of the Bluegrass, and there became the progenitor of a family which represents the blue blood of the State, with all the aristocratic instincts of the old South * * * " •

Many of these pioneer families settled, first, in the Bluegrass; and subsequently they and/or their descendants settled in Eastern or Southeastern section of the State, among others, Capt. Elias P. Davis, the Gees, the Evermans, the Hords, Charles Nelms Lewis, Dr. A. J. Landsdowne, Capt. Thomas Scott, some of the Rices, the Wilhoits, a branch of the Ward family (Col. Joseph R. Ward) settled in Carter County; the Biggses, the Hockadays, the Howes, some of the Poages and the Warings settled in Greenup County; and the Hylton or Hiltons settled in Floyd County.

Among the pioneer families of the Little Sandy River valley were a number from Tidewater Virginia some of whom it is said descended from the Cavaliers who came from England to that section of Virginia in great numbers during the Civil War in Engand (1642-1649) and the reign of Cromwell. Some of these Tidewater Virginians had received large grants of land by reason of service of their forebears in the Revolutionary War; they established large plantations which were cultivated by their slaves, built fine homes and continued to live the life of the slaveholding, fox-hunting gentlemen as their forebears lived in Tidewater Virginia.

Of these Tidewater Virginians, the Carters, the Davises (Capt. E. P. Davis family), the Graysons, the Hords and the Landsdownes (Dr. A. J. Landsdowne family) came from Prince William County; the Lewises (Charles Nelms Lewis family) came from Richmond County; the Hortons originally came from Stafford County; and the

Browns (Judge George Newman Brown family), the Hamptons and the Peays (W. G. Peay family) came from King William County.

---

[1] The Story of Kentucky, by Emma M. Connelly, D. Lothrop Company, Boston, 1890.

[2] An Experimental Study of the East Kentucky Mountaineer, by Nathaniel D. Mittron Hirsch, Worcester, Mass., Clark University, 1928.

[3] Ibid.

[4] The Story of Kentucky, by Emma M. Connelly.

[5] Thomas F. Hargis, Judge and onetime Chief Justice of the Court of Appeals of Kentucky.

[6] The Anglo-Saxons of the Kentucky Mountains, by Ellen Churchill Semple. Reprinted from the Bulletin of the American Geographic Society, Vol. XLII, August 1910.

MEMBERS OF THE CONGRESS OF THE UNITED STATES WHO RESIDED IN AND WERE ELECTED FROM EASTERN OR SOUTHEASTERN KENTUCKY

HOUSE OF REPRESENTATIVES

ADAMS, GREEN, a Representative in Congress, was born at Barbourville, Knox County, Kentucky, August 20, 1812; pursued preparatory studies; studied law; was admitted to the bar and practiced his profession; was a State representative, 1839; president elector on the Whig ticket of Clay and Frelinghuysen, 1844; elected as a Whig to the Thirtieth Congress (March 4, 1847-March 3, 1849); was not a candidate for renomination, 1848; judge of the Circuit Court of Kentucky, 1851-56; elected as a candidate of the American Party to the Thirty-sixth Congress (March 4, 1859-March 3, 1861); was not a candidate for renomination in 1860; was appointed by President Lincoln as Sixth Auditor of the Treasury Department and served as such from April 17, 1861, to October 26, 1864, when he resumed the practice of law in Philadelphia; Chief Clerk of the U. S. House of Representatives during the Forty-fourth, Forty-fifth and Forty-sixth Congresses, (1875-1881); lived in retirement until his death in Philadelphia, January 18, 1884; interment in West Laurel Hill Cemetery. (Biographical Directory of the American Congress, 1774-1949, page 762.)

ADAMS, GEORGE MADISON, (nephew of Green Adams), Representative from Kentucky; born in Barbourville, Knox County, Kentucky, December 20, 1837; received private instructions from his father and attended Centre College, Danville, Kentucky; studied law; clerk of the Circuit Court of Knox County, Kentucky, 1859-1861; during the Civil War raised a company of volunteers and was Captain of Company "H", Seventh Regiment, Kentucky Volunteer Infantry, from 1861 to 1863; in 1864 was commissioned paymaster with rank of major; elected as a Democrat to the Fortieth and to the three succeeding Congresses (March 4, 1867-March 3, 1875); unsuccessful candidate for reelection in 1874 to the Forty-fourth Congress; elected Clerk of the National House of Representatives December, 1875, during the Forty-fourth Congress and served until the commencement of the Forty-seventh Congress December 5, 1881; appointed Register of the Kentucky Land Office by Governor J. Proctor Knott and served from 1884 to 1887; appointed Secretary of State for Kentucky by Governor Simon B. Buckner and served from 1887 to 1891; appointed State Railroad Commissioner in 1891; appointed United States Pension Agent at Louisville by President Cleveland and served from 1894 to 1898; after retirement he resided at Winchester, Clarke County, Kentucky, until his death, April 6, 1920; interment in Lexington Cemetery, Lexington, Kentucky. (Biographical Directory of the American Congress, 1774-1949, page 762.)

BATES, JOSEPH BENGAL, lawyer, sometimes teacher and public official, was born at Republican, Knott County, Kentucky, October 29, 1893, a son of Jesse and Hannah (Candill) Bates; attended the public school and the Mountain Training School at Hindman, Knott County; was graduated from the Kentucky State Teachers College at Richmond in 1916; studied law; taught in the rural schools of Knott County, 1912-1915; superintendent of the high school at Raceland, Greenup County, 1917-1919; served as clerk of the Greenup County Court, 1922-1938; elected as a Democrat to the Seventy-fifth Congress to fill the vacancy caused by the resignation of Fred M. Vinson; reelected to Seventy-sixth and to the six succeeding Congresses and served from June 4, 1938, to January 3, 1953; failed for renomination as a candidate in 1952, for the Eighty-third Congress; resumed the practice of law at Greenup, Kentucky, his home; married Virginia Rice, born at Wurtland, Greenup County, February 25, 1895, a daughter of Larkin Monroe and Annie Laurie (Myers) Rice. Children: Joseph Rice Bates and Becky Bates.

BATES, JOSEPH RICE, born December 7, 1916; educated in the public schools of Greenup County and University of Kentucky; presently employed in carrying the U. S. mails; married Jane Chamberlain of Watertown, New York, July 3, 1943. Their children are Alida Jane, Virginia Jo and Susan.

BATES, BECKY, born January 3, 1919; married William Shannon Vinson, June 26, 1943. Their children are Ann Randall, Carol Brooks and Josephine Rice.

Mr. Bates is a Democrat in politics and a Mason, a member of Greenup Lodge No. 89, F. and A. M.

BENNETT, JOSEPH BENTLEY. Greenup, Republican; elected to the Fifty-ninth, Sixtieth and Sixty-first Congresses, March 4, 1905—March 3, 1911. (See Bennett Family).

BOREING, VINCENT, London, Republican, born near Jonesboro, Washington County, Tennessee. November 24, 1839; moved with his father to Laurel County, Kentucky, in 1847; attended Laurel Seminary, London, Kentucky, and Tusculum College, Greenville, Tennessee; enlisted as a private in the Union Army during the Civil War, in Company A, Twenty-fourth Regiment, Kentucky Volunteers Infantry, November 1, 1861; was commissioned first lieutenant for meritorious conduct; was severely wounded in the battle of Reseca, Georgia, May 14, 1863; served as superintendent of public schools of Laurel County, 1868-1872; established the "Mountain Echo" at London in 1875, the first Republican Newspaper published in Southeastern Kentucky; served as judge of the Laurel County Court in 1866; president of the Cumberland Valley Land Company in 1887; president of the First National Bank of London in 1888; department commander of the Grand Army of the Republic in Kentucky in 1889; elected as a Republican to the Fifty-sixth, Fifth-seventh, and Fifty-eighth Congresses and served from March 4, 1899 until his death, September 16, 1903, in London, Laurel County; interment in Pine Grove Cemetery, London. (Biographical Directory of the American Congress, 1774-1949, p. 1868.)

COLSON, DAVID GRANT, born in Yellow Creek (now Middlesboro) Knox (now Bell) County, Kentucky, April 1, 1861; attended the public schools and the academies at Tazewell and Mossy Creek, Tennessee; was a student of law at the University of Kentucky at Lexington in 1879 and 1880; was admitted to the bar and commenced practice in Pineville, Kentucky; was an examiner and special examiner in the Pension Bureau, Department of the Interior, Washington, D. C., from September, 1882 to June 1886; returned to Kentucky in 1887; was a member of the State House of Representatives in 1887 and 1878; served as mayor of Middlesboro, 1893 to 1895; elected as a Republican to the Forty-fourth and Fifty-fifth Congresses, March 4, 1895-March 3, 1899; commissioned a colonel and commanded the Fourth Kentucky Regiment in the Spanish-American War; died in Middlesboro, September 27, 1904; interment in Colson Cemetery. (Biographical Directory of the American Congress 1774-1949, p. 1005.)

EDWARDS, DON CALVIN, born in Moulton Appanoose County, Kansas, July 13, 1861; moved to Erie, Neasho County, Kansas, with his parents in 1869; attended the public schools of Iowa and Kansas, and Campbell University, Holton, Kansas; engaged in banking and insurance business in Erie, Kansas, in 1883; moved to London, Laurel County, Kentucky, in 1892 and engaged in the manufacture of staves and in the wholesale lumber business; was president of the National Bank of London; served as clerk and master commissioner of the Laurel Circuit Court from 1898 to 1904; was chairman of the Kentucky State Republican convention in 1908; elected as a Republican to the Fifty-ninth, Sixtieth and Sixty-first Congresses (March 4, 1905-March 3, 1911); unsuccessful candidate for reelection 1910 to the Sixty-second Congress and resumed the lumber and banking business in London; was a delegate to the National Republican Convention at Chicago in 1912 which nominated the presidential ticket of Taft and Sherman; during the first World War he was a member of the State council of national defense; chairman of five Liberty Loan campaigns; fuel administrator for Laurel County in 1917 and 1918; unsuccessful candidate for nomination in

1918 to the Sixty-sixth Congress; died in London, September 19, 1938; interment in Pine Grove Cemetery. (Biographical Directory of the American Congress, 1774-1949, p. 1120.)

ELLIOTT, JOHN MILTON, Prestonsburg, Democrat; elected to the Thirty-third, Thirty-fourth, and Thirty-fifth Congresses (March 4, 1853-March 3, 1859). (See Elliott Family.)

FIELDS, WILLIAM JASON, Olive Hill, Democrat; elected to the Sixty-second and to the six succeeding Congresses and served from March 4, 1911, to December 11, 1923, when he resigned, having been elected Governor of Kentucky. (See Fields Family.)

FINLEY, CHARLES (son of Hugh Franklin Finley), born in Williamsburg, Whitley County, Kentucky, March 26, 1865; attended the public and select (subscription) schools, and Milligan College, Milligan, Tennessee; engaged in business as a coal operator, banker, and publisher; was a member of the State House of Representatives, 1894-1896; delegate to the Republican State Convention, 1895 served as Secretary of State of Kentucky, 1896-1900; chairman of the Republican executive committee of the Eleventh Kentucky Congressional District, 1912-28; elected as a Republican to the Seventy-first Congress to fill the vacancy caused by the resignation of John M. Robison; re-elected to the Seventy-second Congress and served from February 15, 1930, to March 3, 1933; was not a candidate for renomination in 1932; retired from business activities; died in Williamsburg, March 18, 1941; interment in Highland Cemetery, Williamsburg. (Biographical Directory of the American Congress, 1774-1949, p. 1157.)

FINLEY, HUGH FRANKLIN (father of Charles Finley) born at Tyes Ferry, Whitley County, Kentucky, January 18, 1833; attended the public schools, engaged in agricultural pursuits; studied law, was amitted to the bar in 1859 and commenced practice in Williamsburg; was a member of the State House of Representatives from 1861 to August, 1862, when he resigned; elected Commonwealths Attorney in 1862 and served until 1866, when he resigned; again elected in 1867 and reelected in 1868 for a six year term; unsuccessful candidate for election in 1870 to the Forty-second Congress; served in the State Senate, 1875, 1876, when he resigned; appointed in 1876 by President Grant as United States District Attorney for Kentucky and served until 1877; resumed the practice of law; was judge of the fifteenth judicial circuit, 1880-1886; elected as a Republican to the Fiftieth and Fifty-first Congresses (March 4, 1887—March 3, 1891); was unsuccessful candidate for renomination in 1890; resumed the practice of law and also engaged in coal mining; died in Williamsburg, October 16, 1909; interment in Woodlawn Cemetery. (Biographical Directory of the American Congress, 1774-1949, p. 1157.)

FITZPATRICK, THOMAS YOUNG, Prestonsburg, Democrat, elected to the Fifty-fifth and Fifty-sixth Congresses, (March 4, 1897—March 3, 1901). (See Fitzpatrick Family.)

GOLDEN, JAMES STEPHEN, lawyer and public official, was born in Barbourville, Knox County, Kentucky, September 20, 1891, a son of Benjamin Briston Golden, who was a captain in the Spanish-American War, and Elizabeth (Davis) Golden, and a grandson of Rev. Stephen Golden, a Baptist minister and a captain in the Union Army in the Civil War. He attended the graded school of Barbourville and pursued the high school course at Union College; was graduated from the University of Kentucky at Lexington with the degree of A. B., and from the University of Michigan at Ann Arbor with the degree of LL.B. While a student at Kentucky University he was junior class president of the Seventeen County Mountain Club. He was also president of the Union Literary Society.

Mr. Golden was elected county attorney of Knox County on the Republican ticket and served for four years. Subsequently and until his election to Congress, he engaged in general law practice in the State and Federal Courts. He was elected as a Republican to the Eighty-first Congress, November 2, 1948; reelected to the Eighty-second Congress, November 7, 1950 and to the Eighty-third Congress, November 4, 1952. He was not a candidate for renomination and election to the Eighty-fourth Congress.

Mr. Golden is a Republican in politics and a member of the Methodist Church, serving as chairman of the Board of Trustees; is a Mason and affiliated with several civic and fraternal orders, among others, the Phi Delta Theta law fraternity.

He is married to Ruth (Decker) Golden who was graduated from high school at Union College and was a student at Sullins College at Bristol, Tennesse. They have two sons, Richard Davis Golden, artist, a graduate of Yale University with degree of A. B., who had service overseas for four and one-half years in World War II; and Dr. James S. Golden, Jr, who was graduated from the University of Virginia with degrees of A. B. and M. D., and had service for two and one half years in World War II.

HAMILTON, FINLEY, born at Vincent, Owsley County, Kentucky, June 19, 1886; attended the public schools and Berea College, Berea, Kentucky; studied law, was admitted to the bar in 1915 and commenced practice in London, Laurel County, Kentucky; was with the Signal Corps, U. S. Army, with service in the Philippine Islands and Alaska, from 1907 to 1915, and during World War I enlisted, March 18, 1916; was commissioned a first lieutenant and later a captain and served in Company D, Three Hundred and Fifteenth Field Signal Battalion, Ninetieth Division, with service in France, until discharged, July 31, 1919; elected as a Democrat to the

Seventy-third Congress (March 4, 1933—January 3, 1935); was not a candidate for renomination in 1934; resumed the practice of law; died in London January 10, 1940; interment in Pine Grove Cemetery. (Biographical Directory of the American Congress, 1774-1949, p. 1257.)

HOPKINS, FRANCIS (FRANK) ALEXANDER, Prestonsburg, Democrat; elected to the Fifty-eighth and Fifty-ninth Congresses, (March 4, 1903—March 3, 1907); unsuccessful candidate for reelection in 1906 to the Sixtieth Congress. (See Lackey Family.)

HOPKINS, NATHAN THOMAS, born in Ashe County, North Carolina, October 27, 1852; moved to Pike County, Kentucky; attended the public schools; engaged in agricultural pursuits; ordained to the ministry in the Baptist Church in 1876 and actively engaged in ministerial work for half a century; served as assessor (Tax Commissioner) of Floyd County, 1878-1890; was a member of the State House of Representatives, 1893-1894; successfully contested as a Republican the election of Joseph M. Kendall to the Fifty-fourth Congress and served from February 18 to March 3, 1897; became a merchant, timberman, and farmer in Pike County, Kentucky; was unsuccessful candidate for election in 1900 to the Fifty-seventh Congress; was again a member of the State House of Representatives, 1923, 1924; engaged in agricultural pursuits near Yeager, Pike County, Kentucky; died in Pikesville, Kentucky, February 11, 1927; interment in Potter Cemetery at Yeager.

KENDALL, JOHN WILKERSON (father of Joseph Morgan Kendall), born in Morgan County, Kentucky, June 26, 1834; attended the public schools and Owingsville Academy, Owingsville, Kentucky; studied law; was admitted to the bar in 1854 and commenced practice at West Liberty, Kentucky; served as prosecuting attorney for Morgan County, 1854-1858; had service in the Confederate Army during the Civil War as first lieutenant and adjutant of the Tenth Kentucky Cavalry; was a member of the State House of Representatives, 1867-1871; served as Commonwealths Attorney for the thirteenth judicial district, 1872-1878; elected as a Democrat to the Fifty-second Congress and served from March 4, 1891, until his death, March 7, 1892, in Washington, D. C.; interment in Barber Cemetery, West Liberty, Kentucky. (Biographical Directory of the American Congress, 1774-1949, p. 1401.)

KENDALL, JOSEPH MORGAN (son of John Wilkerson Kendall), born at West Liberty, Morgan County, Kentucky, May 12, 1863; received his early education from private tutors and in the public schools; attended the State College of Kentucky (A. & M. College) at Lexington, and the University of Michigan at Ann Arbor; was examined by the judges of the Court of Appeals of Kentucky and was granted a license to practice law before he was of age; settled in Prestonsburg, Floyd County, Kentucky, was elected to the Forty-ninth and Fiftieth Congresses; elected as Democrat to the Fifty-second Congress to fill the vacancy caused by the death of his father, John W. Kendall, and served from April 21, 1892, to March 3, 1893; declined to become a candidate for renomination in 1892 on account of ill health; presented credentials as a member-elect to the Fifty-fourth Congress and served from March 4, 1895, to February 18, 1897, when he was succeeded by Nathan Thomas Hopkins who contested his election; resumed the practice of law at West Liberty, Kentucky; was a delegate to all Democratic State Conventions, 1884 to 1933; also engaged in agricultural pursuits at near Boonsboro, Clark County, Kentucky; died in West Liberty, Kentucky, November 5, 1933; interment in Barber Cemetery. (Biographical Directory of the American Congress, 1774-1949, p. 1401.)

KIRK, ANDREW JACKSON. Republican, Paintsville; elected as a Republican to the Sixty-ninth Congress to fill the vacancy caused by the resignation of John W. Langley and served from February 13, 1926 to March 3, 1927; unsuccessful candidate for renomination in 1926. (See Kirk Family).

LANGLEY, JOHN WESLEY (husband of Katherine Gudger Langley); born in Floyd County, Kentucky, January 14, 1868; attended the public schools; taught in the public schools for three years; attended the law department of the National, Georgetown, and Columbian (now George Washington) Universities, Washington, D. C., for an aggregate period of eight years; was an examiner in the Pension Office and a member of the Board of Appeals; law clerk for the General Land Office; disbursing and appointment clerk of the Census Office, 1899-1890, and was the caucus nominee fo his party, which was in the minority, for speaker of the House; was a delegate to three Republican National Conventions; elected as a Republican to the Sixtieth and the nine succeeding Congresses and served from March 4, 1907, until his resignation, January 11, 1926; resumed the practice of law in Pikeville, Kentucky, where he died January 17, 1932; interment in Langley Cemetery, Middle Creek, Floyd County, Kentucky. (Biographical Directory of the American Congress, 1774-1949, p. 1435.)

LANGLEY, KATHERINE GUDGER, (wife of John Wesley Langley) and daughter of James Madison Gudger, Jr., a representative in Congress from North Carolina, born near Marshall, Madison County, North Carolina, February 14, 1888; attended the public schools; was graduated from the Woman's College, Richmond, Virginia; attended Emerson College of Oratory, Boston, Massachusetts; taught expression at the Virginia Institute, Bristol, Tennessee; moved to Pikeville, Kentucky, in 1905; vice-chairman of the Republican State Central Committee of Kentucky, 1920-1922; served as the first Chairman of the Woman's Republican State Committee, 1920; alternate delegate to the Republican National Convention 1920 and delegate 1924; chairman of the Pike County (Kentucky) Red Cross Society during World War 1; elected as a Republican to the Seventieth and Seventy-first Congresses (March 4, 1927-March 3, 1931); unsuccessful candidate for reelection in 1930 to the Seventy-second Congress; served as railroad commissioner, third Kentucky district, 1939-1942; died in Pikeville, Kentucky, August 15, 1948; interment in Johnson Memorial Cemetery. (Biographical Directory of the American Congress, 1774-1949, p. 1435.)

LEWIS, WILLIAM, Republican of London; born at Cutshin, Leslie County, Kentucky, September 22, 1868; was reared on a farm and attended the public schools of Leslie and Perry Counties, Kentucky, and the Laurel County Seminary at London, Kentucky; was a student of law at the University of Kentucky at Lexington and at the University of Michigan at Ann Arbor; served as sheriff of Leslie County, 1891-1892; superintendent of public schools of Leslie County, 1894-1898; member of the State House of Representatives, 1900-1901; Commonwealths Attorney, 1904-1909; Circuit Judge of the twenty-seventh judicial district of Kentucky, 1909-1922 and 1928-1934; elected to the Eightieth Congress to fill the vacancy caused by the death of John Marshall Robinson and served from April 24, 1948, to January 3, 1949; was not a candidate for renomination to the Eighty-first Congress; resumed the practice of law in London, Kentucky, place of his residence.

MAY, ANDREW JACKSON, Democrat, of Prestonsburg; elected as a Democrat to the Seventy-second Congress and the seven succeeding Congresses, (March 4, 1931-January 3, 1947), unsuccessful candidate for reelection in 1946 to the Eightieth Congress.

MARTIN, JOHNSON PRESTON, Democrat, of Prestonsburg, (brother of Elbert Sevier Martin, a Republican in Congress from Virginia, and grandfather of George Brown Martin, a Senator in Congress from Kentucky); elected as a Democrat to the Twenty-ninth Congress, (March 4, 1845-March 3, 1847). (See Martin Family.)

MEADE, WENDELL HOWES, Republican of Paintsville; elected as a Republican to the Eightieth Congress (January 3, 1947-January 3, 1949); unsuccessful candidate for reelection in 1948 to the Eighty-first Congress. (See Meade Family.)

PAYNTER, THOMAS HANSON, Democrat of Greenup; elected as a Democrat to the Fifty-first, Fifty-second and Fifty-third Congresses, and served from March 4, 1889, until his resignation, effective January 5, 1895, having been elected to the Judiciary. (See Kouns Family.)

POWERS, CALEB, Republican of Barbourville; born near Williamsburg, Whitley County, Kentucky, February 1, 1869; attended the public schools, Union College, Barboursville, Kentucky, the University of Kentucky, Valparaiso University, Valparaiso, Indiana; attended West Point Military Academy, 1890 and 1891; studied law, was admitted to the bar in 1894 and commenced practice at Barbourville, Kentucky; superintendent of public schools of Knox County, Kentucky, 1894-1899; elected Secretary of State of Kentucky 1899 but was unseated after a contest; convicted of complicity in the assassination of Governor William Goebel in 1900 and sentenced to prison; was pardoned in 1908 by Governor A. E. Willson; author of "My Own Story" in 1905; elected as a Republican to the Sixty-second and the three succeeding Congresses (March 4, 1911-March 3, 1919); was not a candidate for renomination in 1918; delegate to the Republican National Convention at Chicago, 1912; moved to Washington, D. C., and served as assistant council for the Unitel States Shipping Board from 1921 until his death; died in a hospital in Baltimore, Maryland, July 25, 1932; interment in City Cemetery, Barbourville, Kentucky. (Biographical Directory of the American Congress, 1774-1949, p. 1699.)

PERKINS, CARL D., Democrat of Hindman, born at Hindman, Knott County, Kentucky, October 15, 1912, a son of J. E. and Dora (Calhoun) Perkins; educated in the Knott County Public Schools; at Hindman High School; and at Caney Junior College; studied law at Jefferson School of Law in Louisville, graduating in 1935, and began the practice of law; served as enlisted man in World War II and had service in the European Theatre, participating in battles of Northern France, the Ardennes, the Rhineland and central Europe.

He served unexpired term in 1939 as commonwealth attorney for the thirty-first judicial district; was a member of the Kentucky General Assembly from the ninety-ninth district in 1940; elected county attorney of Knott County, 1941, and reelected in 1945; resigned January 1, 1948, to become counsel to the Department of Highways at Frankfort; elected, November 2, 1948, as a Democrat to the Eighty-first Congress; reelected to the Eighty-second Congress; married Miss Verna Johnson of Knott County.

Mr. Perkins is a Democrat, a Mason, a Protestant and a member of the American Legion.

PUGH, SAMUEL JOHNSON, Republican of Vanceburg; born in Greenup County, Kentucky, January 28, 1850; moved with his parents to Lewis County, Kentucky, 1852; attended Chandler's Select School, Rand's Academy in Lewis County, and Centre College, Danville, Kentucky; studied law, was admitted to the bar and commenced practice at Vanceburg, Lewis County, Kentucky; served as City Attorney of Vanceburg, 1872-1873; master commissioner of the circuit court, 1874-1880; county attorney for Lewis County, 1878-1886; judge of the Lewis County Court, 1886-1890; delegate to the State Constitutional convention 1890-1891; member of the State Senate, 1893-1894; elected as a Republican to the Fifty-fourth, Fifty-fifth and Fifty-sixth Congresses (March 4, 1895-March 3, 1901; resumed his law practice at Vanceburg, Kentucky, and died there April 17, 1922; interment in Greenlawn Cemetery. (Biographical Directory of the American Congress, 1774-1949, p. 1708.)

RANDALL, WILLIAM HARRISON, Republican of London; born near Richmond, Madison County, Kentucky, July 15, 1812; completed preparatory studies; studied law, was admitted to the bar and commenced practice at London, Laurel County, Kentucky, 1835; served as clerk of the circuit court and county court of Laurel County, 1836-1844; elected as a Republican to the Thirty-eighth and Thirty-ninth Congresses (March 4, 1863-March 3, 1867); district judge of the fifteenth Kentucky district, 1870-1880; died at London, Kentucky, August 1, 1881; interment in the family cemetery there. (Biographical Directory of the American Congress, 1774-1949, p. 1716.)

RICE, JOHN McCONNELL, Democrat of Louisa; elected as a Democrat to the Forty-first and Forty-second Congresses (March 4, 1869-March 3, 1873); was not a candidate for renomination in 1872.

ROBSION, JOHN MARSHALL, Republican of Barbourville; born near Berlin, Bracken County, Kentucky, January 2, 1873; attended the public schools, the National Northern University, Ada, Ohio, and Holbrook College, Knoxville, Tennessee; was graduated from the National Normal University, Lebanon, Ohio, and from the law department of Centre College, Danville, Kentucky, 1900; taught in the public school of Kentucky for several years, and in Union College, Barbourville, Kentucky; was admitted to the bar, 1898, and commenced practice at Barbourville; president of the First National Bank of Barbourville, Kentucky; delegate to the Republican National Convention at Chicago, 1916; elected as a Republican to the Sixty-sixth and to the five succeeding Congresses and served from March 4, 1919, until January 10, 1930, when he resigned to serve as United States Senator; appointed to the Senate to fill the' vacancy caused by the resignation of Frederick M. Sackett and served from January 11 to November 30, 1930, when a duly elected successor qualified; unsuccessful candidate in 1930 for election to the vacancy and also for the full term; resumed the practice of law; elected to the Seventy-fourth and to the six succeeding congresses and served from January 3, 1935, until his death in Barbourville, Kentucky, February 17, 1948; interment in Barbourville Cemetery. He was an active member of the Christian (Disciples) Church; a Mason (32nd degree); J. O. U. A. M., I. O. O. F., and Knights of Pythias; married January 25, 1902, Lida Stanbury of Grays, Knox County, Kentucky, who resides in Washington, D. C. Two children were born to this union: Mrs. Daisy (Robsion) Bradshaw and John Marshall Robsion, Jr.

ROBSION, JOHN MARSHALL, JR., lawyer and civic leader, was born in Barbourville, Kentucky, but practically grew up in Washington, D. C.; his father being in Congress for many years; was educated in the public schools of Washington, at George Washington, Georgetown and National Universities in Washington; had many years experience in the Executive and Legislative branches of the Federal Government; was a Congressional secretary at the age of 18 and at 24 was Chief of the Law Division, U. S. Bureau of Pensions, the youngest chief of a major government division; served four years in World War II, of which two years were spent overseas in Africa, Italy and Austria, being on the staff of General Mark Clark a part of this time. Since his separation from the service he has been very much interested in veteran's affairs and is a past District Commander of the Veterans of Foreign Wars, a member of the American Legion, Disabled American Veterans, and other military organizations.

Mr. Robison established his home in Louisville in 1928 and began the practice of law there in 1935 and since the close of World War II he has practiced his profession with distinction and success and has served as special circuit judge by appointment of both Republicans and Democrats.

He was formerly General Council of the Republican Party in Kentucky; President of the Lincoln Club; President of the Highlands Men's Club, District Commissioner of the Boy Scouts of America and Commander of the Louisville Chapter, Military Order of World Wars.

He is a member of the Louisville Bar Association; the Board of the Salvation Army in Louisville; a Deacon and Secretary of the Official Board of the Crescent Hill Christian Church; and a member of the Louisville and Jefferson County Republican Executive Committees and several fraternal orders.

He was elected as a Republican to the Eighty-third Congress from the Louisville or First District and is presently serving as such.

Mr. Robsion is married to Laura Selinda Robsion who has an equally enviable record for church, social and civic works. They reside at 2011 Woodford Place, in Louisville.

SILER, EUGENE, Republican of Williamsburg; elected as Republican to the Eighty-fourth Congress, November 2, 1954. (See Siler Family.)

TAULBEE, WILLIAM PRESTON, Democrat of Salyersville; born in Morgan County, Kentucky, October 22, 1851; attended the public schools and was tutored by his father; was ordained to the ministry and admitted to the conference of the Methodist Episcopal Church,

South; was elected and served as clerk of the Magoffin County (Kentucky) Court, 1878, and reelected 1882; studied law and was admitted to the bar, 1881; elected as a Democrat to the Forty-ninth and Fiftieth Congresses (March 4, 1885-March 3, 1889); was not a candidate for renomination; was shot by Charles E. Kincaid in the Capitol Building, Washington, D. C., February 28, 1890, and died from the effects of the wound at Providence Hospital, in that city, March 11, 1890; interment in the family burying ground in Morgan County, Kentucky. (Biographical Directory of the American Congress, 1774-1949, p. 1897.)

TRIMBLE, DAVID, a Representative from Kentucky; born in Frederick County, Virginia, in July, 1782; was graduated from William and Mary College, Williamsburg, Virginia, in 1799; studied law, was admitted to the bar and commenced legal practice at Mt. Sterling, Kentucky; served in the War of 1812 as brigade quartermaster of the First Brigade, Kentucky Mounted Militia, and later as a private in the Battalion of Kentucky Mounted Infantry Volunteers commanded by Major Dudley; elected as a Democrat to the Fifteenth and the four succeeding Congresses (May 4, 1817-March 3, 1827) was an unsuccessful candidate for reelection to the Nineteenth Congress; died at Trimble's Furance, Greenup County, Kentucky, October 20, 1842. (Biographical Directory of the American Congress, 1774-1949, p. 1932.)

WHITE, JOHN, Whig, of Madison County; elected as a Whig to the Twenty-fourth and the four succeeding Congresses (March 4, 1835-March 3, 1845) and served as Speaker of the House of Representatives in the Twenty-seventh Congress. (See White Family.)

WHITE, JOHN DAUGHERTY, Republican of Manchester; elected as a Republican to the Forty-fourth Congress (March 4, 1875-March 3, 1877); declined to be a candidate for renomination; unsuccessful Republican candidate for the United States Senate in 1881; elected as a Republican to the Forty-seventh and Forty-eighth Congresses (March 4, 1881-March 3, 1885); declined to be a candidate for renomination in 1884 and resumed the practice of law in Louisville. (See White family.)

UNITED STATES SENATE

MARTIN, GEORGE BROWN, Democrat of Catlettsburg (grandson of John Preston Martin, a representative in Congress from Kentucky); appointed as a Democrat to the United States Senate to fill the vacancy caused by the death of Ollie M. James and served from September 7, 1918, to March 3, 1919; was not a candidate for reelection to the full term. (See Martin Family.)

STANFILL, WILLIAM ABNER, Republican of Hazard; born in Barbourville, Knox County, January 16, 1892; attended the public schools and Union College, Barbourville, Kentucky; was graduated from the law department of the University of Kentucky at Lexington, 1912; was admitted to the bar the same year and commenced practice in Barbourville; moved to Hazard, Perry County, Kentucky, 1916, and continued the practice of law; was a member of the board of regents of the Morehead State Teacher's College, 1927-1931; member of the board of governors of the Kentucky Children's Home at Lyndon, Kentucky, 1933-1936; chairman of the Republican State Central Committee, 1944-1948; appointed as a Republican to the United States Senate to fill the vacancy caused by the resignation of Albert B. Chandler and served from November 19, 1945, to November 5, 1946, when a successor was elected; was not a candidate for nomination in 1946 to the vacancy; resumed the practice of law and is a resident of Lexington, Kentucky. (Biographical Directory of the American Congress, 1774-1949, p. 1853.)

ROBSION, JOHN MARSHALL, Republican of Barbourville; appointed to the Senate to fill the vacancy caused by the resignation of Frederick M. Sackett and served from January 11, to November 30, 1930, when a duly elected successor qualified; unsuccessful candidate in 1930 for election to the vacancy and also for the full term. (Biographical Directory of the American Congress, 1774-1949, p. 1750.)

WILLIAMSON, BEN MITCHELL, Democrat of Catlettsburg; born at White Post, Pike County, Kentucky, October 16, 1864, son of Wallace J. and Columbia (Slater) Williamson; educated in the public schools of Kentucky and at Bethany College, Bethany, West Virginia, graduating in 1883; founder in 1886 and afterwards president of Ben Williamson and Company, wholesale hardware; engaged in banking and coal enterprises in eastern Kentucky and southern West Virginia; one of the founders of Williamson, West Virginia, and of the First National Bank at Williamson; was one of the founders of the Kentucky Crippled Childrens Commission, serving as president, 1924-1941; member of the Board of Charities and Corrections for the State of Kentucky, 1929-1930; served as a director of the International Society of Crippled Children; elected as a Democrat to the United States Senate November 4, 1930, to fill the vacancy caused by the resignation of Frederick M. Sackett and served from December 1, 1930, to March 3, 1931; was not a candidate for the full term; resumed the wholesale hardware business at Ashland, Kentucky, with residence in Catlettsburg; also interested financially in various other business enterprises. He died while a patient in a Cincinnati, Ohio, hospital, June 23, 1941; interment in Ashland Cemetery Mausoleum, Ashland, Kentucky; married January 19, 1887, Ceres Burgess Wellman. Children: Wallace J. Williamson, Geraldine Burgess Williamson (Mrs. Davis E. Gieger), and Ben Williamson, Jr. (Biographical Directory of the American Congress, 1774-1949, page 2022-3.)

GOVERNORS AND LIEUTENANT-GOVERNORS OF KENTUCKY WHO RESIDED IN THE EASTERN OR SOUTHEASTERN SECTION OF THE STATE:

LIEUTENANT-GOVERNORS

BLACK, JAMES DIXON, Democrat, of Barbourville; elected lieutenant governor of Kentucky, November, 1915, and served until May 18, 1919, when he resigned to become governor upon the resignation of Governor Augustus O. Stanley. (See Black Family.)

WORTHINGTON, WILLIAM JACKSON, Republican, of Greenup; elected lieutenant governor in November 1895, and served from December 10, 1895, to December 11, 1899, expiration of term. (See Worthington Family.)

TUTTLE, KENNETH, Republican of Barbourville; elected Lieutenant Governor, November 2, 1943, and served four-year term from December 1943 to December 1947.

GOVERNORS

BLACK, JAMES DIXON, Democrat; of Barbourville; appointed, May 19, 1919, to fill the vacancy caused by the resignation of Governor Augustus O. Stanley, and served the unexpired term which ended December 8, 1919. (See Black Family.)

FIELDS, WILLIAM JASON, Democrat, of Olive Hill; elected November 6, 1923; inaugurated December 11, 1923, and served until December 12, 1927. (See Fields Family.)

SAMPSON, FLEM D., Republican; of Barbourville, lawyer, judge and public official, a son of Joseph and Emoline (Kellums) Sampson, was born in London, Laurel County, Kentucky, January 23, 1875; educated in the public schools of Laurel County, at John T. Hays School, Union College, Barbourville, Kentucky, and Valparaiso University, Valperaiso, Indiana, from which latter institution, he was graduated with LL.B. degree in 1894; was admitted to the bar and commenced practice in Barbourville; elected judge of the Knox County Court, 1906, and served the four-year term ended 1911; elected judge of the Thirty-fourth Judicial District of Kentucky, 1911, and reelected 1915, for a six-year term; elected judge of the Kentucky Court of Appeals, Seventh Appellate District, 1916, and on January 1, 1923, became Chief Justice; reelected judge of the Court of Appeals without opposition 1924; elected governor of Kentucky, in November 1927; inaugurated December 13, 1927, and served the four-year term ended December 7, 1931; resumed the practice of law with Senator John M. Robsion in Louisville and

Barbourville; again elected Judge of the Thirty-fourth Judicial District.

Judge Sampson married Susie Steele in Knox County, September 20, 1899. Two children were born of this union: Pauline Sampson (Mrs. Gerrish) and Emolyn Sampson.

SIMEON S. WILLIS, lawyer, judge and one-time Governor of Kentucky, was born December 1, 1879, near Vesuvius Furnace, Lawrence County, Ohio, a son of John H. and Abigail (Slavens) Willis, the former of whom was born at Cross Roads, Jackson County, Ohio, and the latter at Franklin Furnace, Scioto County, that state. John H. Willis was one of the pioneer iron furnace men of Ohio where he was widely known because of his eminence in the charcoal-iron industry. The early American forebears of Governor Willis were residents of Virginia, emigrating to that colony before the Revolutionary War. The records reveal that forty-three Willises had service either as commissioned officers or soldiers in the Virginia Forces in the Revolutionary War.[1] Governor Willis' paternal grandparents were Captain William Willis and Elizabeth (Davis) Willis, the former of whom was born in Greenbrier County Virginia, (now West Virginia) in 1800, but during late middle life, removed to Ohio where he died in 1885. A staunch Union man, he had service in the Civil War as captain of Company "C", Fifth Regiment, West Virginia Infantry; and was with Gen. Philip H. Sheridan at Cedar Creek and with Gen. David Hunter in the "Raid on Lynchburg." His son, John H. Willis, the father of the Governor, was a corporal in his command.

Elizabeth (Davis) Willis, the Governor's grandmother, was born in Virginia, probably in Kanowha County. She was a daughter of Pleasant Davis and his wife, Sarah (Horton) Davis who was a grand daughter of Joseph Horton, a Revolutionary War soldier who had service in the Virginia Forces and settled in the Jackson County, Ohio, area, in pioneer days.

Governor Willis attended the public schools of Lawrence County, Ohio, until he was about ten years old when he removed with his father and mother from Ohio to South Portsmouth, a village known as Springville, on the Ohio River in Greenup County, Kentucky. He completed the "grades" in the public schools of Greenup County, and later took a teachers' course in a local private "Normal" school conducted by Prof. Wade. Here his formal education ended. He took a teachers' examination; was granted a teachers' certificate; and for the next three years he taught in the public schools of Greenup County, being employed as principal of the Springfield graded school before he was twenty years old. Not desiring to adopt teaching as a profession, he devoted the greater part of his out-of-school time while teaching, in studying law under Judge J. B. Bennett of Greenup; took a special course in law under William D. Corn and was admitted to the bar November 11, 1901. During this period he did some reporting for the old Portsmouth (Ohio) *Tribune* and contributed not a few Republican editorials for the *Greenup Gazette*.

In January 1902, Simeon S. Willis, then a stripling youth of twenty-two, opened a law office and began the practice of law in Ashland, Kentucky, with which progressive community he has ever since been closely identified as an outstanding lawyer, judge and citizen. Later he became associated with the law firm of Hager & Stewart of Ashland, one of the outstanding legal firms of Northeastern Kentucky. Entering the field of politics, he was the Republican candidate for City Attorney of Ashland in 1905 and was defeated. In 1918, when thirty-nine years old, he was elected for a four-year term as City Solicitor of the City of Ashland; and upon expiration of his term in 1922, he resumed the practice of law and rapidly rose in popular and professional esteem.

On January 1, 1928, Simeon S. Willis took his seat on the bench of the Court of Appeals of Kentucky, having been appointed to that position by Republican Governor Flem D. Sampson whose elevation to the office of Governor by the electorate at the previous November election had created the vacancy. In the Autumn of 1928, an outstanding and widely known Eastern Kentucky Republican, he was elected to fill the four-year unexpired term of Judge Sampson; and at the expiration of this period he was a candidate for re-election to the Court of Appeals of Kentucky but was defeated by Judge Alex Ratliff, a Democrat of Pikeville, in the Roosevelt landslide of 1932.

Again resuming his private law practice in Ashland, matured by his five years of experience as a member of Kentucky's Court of last resort, he brought back to his legal work a well-founded reputation as a learned and successful judge. New and important clients were attracted to him and within a very short time he became and was recognized as one of the outstanding lawyers of Northeastern Kentucky. Such was the position in private life that he occupied in mid-summer of 1943 when, at the insistence of many friends, he became the Republican candidate for Governor of Kentucky, to which office he was elected November 2, by a majority in excess of 8,600 votes over the Hon. J. Lyter Donaldson of Carrollton, Kentucky. Governor Willis was the sixth Republican to fill the office of Governor of Kentucky, the Hon. William O'Connell Bradley being the first.[2]

On the expiration of his term as Governor and on December 9, 1947, Governor Willis returned to his law office in Ashland and has practiced law continuously since with great distinction and success. In the meantime he has served and is presently serving as a member of the Constitution Review Commission by appointment of Governor Clements and reappointment of Governor Wetherby.

On April 14, 1920, Simeon S. Willis was married to Miss Ida Lee Millis, a daughter of Charles L. and Sarah S. (Ross) Millis of

Catlettsburg, Kentucky. Mrs. Willis was born December 25, 1897. They have one child, a daughter, Sarah Leslie Willis, who was born in Ashland July 16, 1922; educated in the public schools of Ashland; attended Margaret Hall Episcopal School, Versailles, Kentucky; and was graduated from the National Cathedral School for Girls, Washington, D. C., and Sarah Lawrence College, Bronxville, N. Y.; married, in December 1944, Henry Meigs II, lawyer. Mr. Meigs is a native of New York City; had service as captain in the Air Force during World War II; and is presently engaged in the practice of law in Frankfort, Kentucky, a member of the firm of Hobson & Meigs.

Mr. and Mrs. Meigs have one child, a son, Simeon Willis Meigs, born January 7, 1947. They reside at 130 W. State Street, Frankfort.

Mrs. Meigs is the author of a story "Another Spring, Another Song", published in *Colliers* in 1942.

Governor and Mrs. Willis are members of the Methodist Church and Republicans in politics. Governor Willis is a Knight Templar and Shriner of the Masonic fraternity and a member of the Benevolent and Protective Order of Elks. He is also a member of the Boyd County, the Kentucky State and the American Bar Association; and was a member of the State Board of Bar Examiners for five years. He is an honorary member of the Ashland Rotary Club. During his long residence in Northeastern Kentucky, he has served in many capacities in the public interest, among others, as appeal agent in the World Wars I and II for the Selective Service Board of Boyd County, Kentucky.

---

[1] Virginians in the Revolution, 1775-1783, by John H. Gwathmey, p. 834.

[2] Governor Simeon S. Willis, by Willard Rouse Jillson, Sc. D., The Register of the Kentucky State Historical Society, January 1944, Vol. 42, No. 138, pp 1-5.

JUDGES

MAJOR DRURY J. BURKETT, banker and agriculturist, was born in Floyd County, Kentucky, August 15, 1842, a son of Armsted and Rebecca (Pigg) Burchett, natives of Floyd County, and a grandson of Drury Burchett who was born in Rockingham County, Virginia, married Miss Elizabeth McCune of Virginia and came to Floyd County where he became extensively interested in farming. He was a devout Methodist and a Democrat. They were parents of eight children.

Armsted Burchett received a limited education and was reared and worked on a farm. After his marriage, he and his wife settled on a small farm in Floyd County but later removed to Louisa, Lawrence County, Kentucky, and there he died. He was a Republican in politics. They were parents of six children: Major Drury; Thomas, who lived in Johnson County; Sarah, who married L. M. Atkins and lived in Louisa; and Laura, who married a Mr. Holbrook. Probably the other two died young.

Major Drury J. Burchett's boyhood was spent on the farm. He was educated in the public schools. In 1849 he went with the family to Louisa where he continued to attend the public schools. A staunch Union man, he enlisted as a Private in Company "K", 14th Regiment Kentucky Volunteer Infantry, in 1861; was promoted to Captain, March 1, 1862; promoted to Major, September 29, 1864; and mustered out of the service at Louisa, January 31, 1865. (Report of the Adjutant General of Kentucky, 1861-1866, Vol. I, pp. 872 and 890.)

Returning to Louisa, he engaged in business there for a time during which he was nominated for Congress on the Republican Ticket but was defeated by only 129 votes in a strong Democratic district. He served as State representative from Boyd and Lawrence Counties. He was appointed by President Harrison as United States Marshall for Kentucky and served as such for four years and four months.

He organized a bank at Louisa and served as its president for 15 years when, in 1900, he removed to Mt. Sterling, Kentucky, and was induced to become interested in the Traders National Bank of which he was made president in 1912.

He was married, first, to Adelaide Jones, on March 15, 1865 Children: Mary R., married J. F. Ratliff; Emma, married George R. Vinson of Louisa (See Vinson Family.); John C., engaged in lumber business at Williamson, West Virginia, and Drury J., Jr., engaged in the coal business in Pike County, Kentucky.

Mrs. Burchett died February 12, 1890, and Major Burchett was married, secondly, on April 30, 1896, to Miss Annie Regan, who was born in Montgomery County, Kentucky, in 1847.

ALLAN N. CISCO, lawyer and judge, son of Hiram, a native of Scott County, Virginia and Sallie Ann (Nickell) Cisco of Morgan County, Kentucky, was born at West Liberty, Morgan County, Kentucky, January 1, 1866. He attended the rural public schools, West Liberty Academy, University of Kentucky for one year, Columbian University (now George Washington University) and was graduated from the National University Law School, Washington, D. C., with degree of LL.B., in 1894; admitted to the bar, 1894, and practiced law at West Liberty until November 2, 1915, when elected circuit judge of the 32nd judicial district; removed to Grayson, Kentucky, 1916, where he resided until 1922 while serving as judge of the Circuit Court. Judge Cisco served as U. S. Commissioner at West Liberty from July 26, 1901, to January, 1916, when he resigned to assume the duties of Circuit Judge. In 1922 Judge Cisco removed to Ashland, Kentucky, for the practice of his profession and was joined by his son, Byron R., who continued as a member of the firm of Cisco & Cisco until 1925, when he went to Florida.

On October 10, 1888, Judge Cisco was married to Miss Sarah C. Bays, daughter of John W. and Elizabeth (Spradlin) Bays of Floyd County, Kentucky.

Judge Cisco was a Republican and was a delegate to the National Republican Convention which met in Chicago in 1908 and nominated William Howard Taft for president and James Sherman for vice-president. He was a member of the Boyd County and the Kentucky State Bar Association, was affiliated with the Knights of Pythias and was a very active member of the First Christian Church of Ashland. Children: Morton L. Cisco, lawyer; was graduated from the law department of Transylvania College and was attorney for the U. S. Veterans Bureau at Louisville; married Miss Rena Rosenberg of the Shenandoah Valley of Virginia. Children: Morton, Jr., and Jack.

Stella May Cisco; married Daniel S. Henry, secretary and treasurer of McClintock-Field Company of Ashland. Children: John C., and Marylyn Mae.

Lilliam Russell Cisco; married Luther Blair, prominent merchant and also postmaster at West Liberty. Children: William Allen, Martha Carolyn and James Luther.

Byron R. Cisco, lawyer; educated in the public high schools and was graduated from the University of Kentucky with degree of LL.B.; practiced law at Ashland with his father from 1922 to 1925, when he went to Miami, Florida, where he continued to practice law; married Miss Goldie Smith of Huntington, West Virginia. Children: Betty Ann.

JUDGE J. MELVIN HALL, educator, sometime public official and civic leader, was born on Bobb's Branch in Johnson County, Kentucky, April 1, 1870, and died at his home near the Country Club on Davis Branch, that county, September 21, 1951, the only son of

Christopher Hall who migrated to Kentucky in early life from Grayson County, Virginia, and Ellen (Preston) Hall, daughter of William Preston, an early settler who lived near the mouth of Buffalo Shoal on the Big Sandy River. (See Moses Preston Family.)

Judge Hall's parents died early and he was compelled to rely on his own resources when very young but he managed to secure a good education: He attended the local public schools, the Normal School at East Point and Kentucky State University at Lexington. He had a successful career in public affairs for over 50 years and was widely known in the county and state. Beginning his public service as a school teacher, he taught in a majority of the school districts of the county and later in the schools of Paintsville. He served as supervisor of Johnson County schools for five years and subsequently was elected on the Democratic ticket and served as judge of the Johnson County Court for a term of four years, being the only Democrat ever having been elected to that office in Johnson County. During his terms of office many public improvements were made, including modernization of the county jail, practically all county roads constructed by the W. P. A., and the state highway underpass east of Paintsville on Route 40.

Judge Hall desired to retire to the quiet life of his farm near Paintsville upon completion of his term as judge, but always being an active worker in county, state and national affairs, he accepted an appointment as United States Commissioner for the Eastern Kentucky District and served in that capacity until 1941 when he retired.

Judge Hall loved his fellowmen and the welfare of the public always was first to him and above personal interest. The responsibility of his public positions, he always felt, and the results obtained confirmed the high opinion held of him by the people of the county and state. He was regarded as one of the ablest educators of his time and section of the State.

Judge Hall was married to Miss Ella Davis, member of a prominent pioneer family of Johnson County. To this union was born seven children, five sons and two daughters. A daughter, Neva, died at age of 19 years; Lenora married Mr. Gullett and is connected with the Paintsville Hospital. Three of the sons (and also two grandsons) are well-known surgeons and physicians; one is a professional engineer [1] and the other is a widely known minister of the Freewill Baptist Church.

1. Mitchel Hall, civil engineer, historian and author, was born at Paintsville, Kentucky, March 27, 1899; educated in the public schools of Johnson County, and the Paintsville High School; was graduated from Big Sandy Seminary, at Paintsville, with degree of B. S.; Georgetown College, Georgetown, Kentucky, with degree of B.S.; and School of Engineering, Milwaukee, Wisconsin, 1921. He is professionally a civil engineer and was connected with the Kentucky

State Highway Department, 1921-29; with the Missouri State Highway Department for some time and subsequently became head of an engineering staff of one of the major United States Air Commands. He served in World War I in the Infantry, U. S. Army.

Mr. Hall is the author of a History of Johnson County, Kentucky, 2 volumes, published by the Standard Printing Company, Louisville, 1928. He is actively interested in genealogy.

He is a Democrat and a Protestant; is a member of the Kentucky State Historical Society, Institute of American Genealogy, American Legion, and was appointed delegate to represent Kentucky on the pilgrimage to the birthplace of General George Rogers Clark, 1927.

Mr. Hall married, June 17, 1920, Miss Hester Rice of Paintsville.

STEPHEN GIRARD KINNER, lawyer and judge, was born on Bear Creek, Lawrence County, Kentucky, July 20, 1848, a son of W. H. and Mahala Kinner, who removed to Boyd County, Kentucky, durin his youth. He was educated in the public schools, at Centre College, Danville, Kentucky, and at Ohio Wesleyan University; studied law with Ireland & Hampton at Catlettsburg, Kentucky, and was admitted to the bar, 1872, and was almost immediately elected city attorney of Catlettsburg; was elected and served as county attorney of Boyd County, 1874; elected twice as commonwealths attorney for the sixteenth judicial district and on the expiration of the last term was elected judge of the newly formed twentieth judicial district. He served for three terms, declining to stand for reelection in 1910, thus closing an honorable career of thirty-six years in public office. Upon retirement from the bench in 1910, he resumed the practice of law and continued active herein until his death on July 8, 1913.

As a public prosecutor and a judge he stood high in the public regard.

On September 14, 1871, Judge Kinner was married to Miss Ceres Wellman, a daughter of Jeremiah and Zerilda (Bowen) Wellman. Four daughters were born to this union, the youngest of whom died at the age of nineteen while attending college. Mr. Kinner died June 2, 1918, and left three daughters surviving: Mrs. Murray Albert of Baltimore, Maryland; Mrs. W. P. Wheeler of Ashland; and Mrs. George Dismukes of Catlettsburg.

WILLIAM LEWIS, lawyer and judge, was born in Perry County, Kentucky, September 22, 1868, a son of Christopher Lewis, born in Perry County, 1844, and a grandson of Timothy and Nancy (Baker) Lewis, the former of whom was born in North Carolina, and the latter in Perry County. This branch of the Lewis family is of English extraction and settled in North Carolina in early Colonial days.

Christopher Lewis, farmer, clergyman of the Christian Church, and merchant, had service in the Union Army in the Three Forks

Battalion. He was a Republican in politics. He married Amy Templeton, who was born in Harlan County, 1841. They were the parents of nine children: Nancy, married Samuel Maggard, farmer and merchant of Leslie County; William; James H., resided in Leslie County where he was in the mercantile business; Felix, farmer, merchant and lumberman, resided in Leslie County; Matilda, married Elisha Pennington, a farmer of Leslie County; Malinda, married John York, farmer of Leslie County; Rhoda, married Grant Morgan, farm-owner of Leslie County and an employee of the Lexington & Eastern Railway Company; Wilson, a merchant of Leslie County; Katie, married James Browning, farmer and timberman of Leslie County.

Judge William Lewis was educated in the rural schools of Leslie County, attended the Laurel County Seminary and received private instruction; began teaching in the public schools of Leslie County when 16 years of age and continued for eight years, in the meantime studying law; admitted to the bar, 1895, and was actively engaged in practice of law at Hyden, Leslie County, 1898-1904.

A Republican in politics and a leader in the councils of his party, Judge Lewis held many public offices of honor and trust: Superintendent of public schools of Leslie County, 1894-1898; Sheriff, 1892-1893; State representative 1899-1900; Commonwealths Attorney, Twenty-seventh Judicial District, 1904 to May, 1909, when appointed Circuit Judge of the same district; elected Circuit Judge, November 1909 for six-year term; reelected, November 1915 for six-year term ended, 1922.

In 1904, Judge Lewis removed from Hyden, Leslie County, to London, Laurel County, where he subsequently lived. He was affiliated with the Masons, a member of McKee Lodge No. 144, F & A.M., London Chapter No. 103, Royal Arch, London Commandery No. 33, Knights Templar and Korsair Temple, Ancient Arabic Order of Nobles of the Mystic Shrine at Louisville. He was also a member of the I.O.O.F. Lodge and Knights of Pythias and the Kentucky State and American Bar Associations. He was a director of the Securities State Bank at Corbin and president of the Horse Creek Coal Company in Clay County. Both Judge and Mrs. Lewis were members of the First Presbyterian Church at London.

On November 9, 1893, Judge Lewis was married to Miss Alice Morgan, who died September, 1920, daughter of A. B. and Martha (Pace) Morgan. They were the parents of two children: Ona May, the eldest, married Hon. H. M. Brock of Harlan County. (See Brock Family.); and Ray C., lawyer at London, who attended Sue Bennett Memorial Institute and St. Mary's College near London; was graduated from the Law Department of Kentucky University with degree of LL.B and was a veteran of World War I.

JUDGE ROBERT TAYLOR PARSONS, onetime teacher, lawyer and public official, a son of Thomas and Chloe (Oney) Parsons, was born November 20, 1847, on Little Sandy River, Carter County, Kentucky. He was reared on his father's farm and attended the local rural public schools in his youth. On Octover 1, 1863, when 15 years of age he enlisted in the Union Army and served as a private in Company "D", 40th Kentucky Regiment, until December 29, 1864, when honorably discharged. His public school training was supplemented by a course at the National Normal University at Lebanon, Ohio, after which he engaged in teaching in Carter and Elliott Counties for 12 years in the meantime studying law. He was admitted to the bar in 1885 and practiced his profession at Sandy Hook, Kentucky, from 1885 to 1915. In 1916 he located at Greenup, Kentucky, where he continued to practice his profession until January 1, 1926, when he assumed the duties of Judge of the Greenup County Court, having been elected to that office the previous November for the four-year term ending December 31, 1930.

Judge Parsons was a Republican in politics and held many public offices of honor and trust. He was civil engineer (surveyor?) of Elliott County, 1880-1884; represented Carter and Elliott Counties in Constitutional Convention that formed the present constitution of the State; and served as judge of the Greenup County Court, 1926-1930.

On September 20, 1866, Judge Parsons was married to Miss Emily Ann Whitt, a daughter of Abijah and Nancy (Boggs) Whitt of Carter County. Mrs. Parsons died February 26, 1916.

Children: Elvira Josephine Parsons, born January 20, 1868; married B. B. Fannin, lumberman of Morgan County, Kentucky.

John Thomas Parsons, born April 2, 1870; married Miss Lucinda Flanery of Carter County. He was foreman for the C. & O. Railway Company at Ashland, Kentucky.

Edward Abijah Parsons, born March 6, 1873; married Miss Blanche Hall of South Portland, Maine. He was employed as agent at Galveston, Texas, for the Santa Fe Railway Company.

Laurenda Parsons, born February 16, 1876; married S. D. Click, furniture dealer of Ashland, Kentucky.

Charles Parsons born May 10, 1879; married Miss Ida Flanery of Carter County (a sister of Mrs. John Thomas Parsons). He engaged in farming in the vicinity of Wheelersburg, Ohio.

John Milton Parsons, born February 1, 1881, died October 11, 1904.

William Henry Parsons, born December 10, 1883; volunteered and served in World War I and was killed in action, October 28, 1917.

Roscoe Parsons, born March 11, 1888; married Miss Cleffie Holbrook of Elliott County; served as postmaster at Sandy Hook, Kentucky.

JOHN FREW STEWART, teacher, lawyer and public official, was born in Western Pennsylvania in 1833; educated at Westminister College, New Wilmington, Pennsylvania, completing a three year's course. Subsequently he engaged in teaching for six or seven years. Coming to Kentucky, he became principal of the Big Sandy Academy at Catlettsburg in October, 1857. Many of his pupils became prominent in Eastern Kentucky, among others, the Moors, the Richardsons, the Pritchards, the Burgesses and the Pattons. Judge S. G. Kinner also was a pupil in his school.[1]

John Frew Stewart began the study of law in the offices of Moore and Gallup at Louisa in 1859 and was admitted to the bar in 1860. He was elected county attorney of Lawrence County, 1862, and soon thereafter entered the Union Army; was enrolled November 18, 1862, and commissioned a second lieutenant of Co. "B", 39th Kentucky Volunteer Infantry; promoted to adjutant January 21, 1863; and commissioned a major, November 22, 1864, but never mustered as such; resigned February 2, 1865.[2]

Becoming a resident of Johnson County, he held many positions of honor and trust: deputy collector of Internal Revenue; United States Commissioner, School Commissioner of Johnson County and Judge of the Johnson County Court.

He was a Republican in politics and a member of the Methodist Episcopal Church. He was married but had no children.

JUDGE ROSCOE VANOVER, sometime teacher, lawyer and judge, son of John and Keziah (Landreth) Vanover, natives of Allegheny County, North Carolina, was born in Wise County, Virginia, September 7, 1863; attended the rural public schools, began teaching at the age of 18 years and continued for 14 years; studied law, admitted to the bar in 1895 and practiced law at Pikeville, Kentucky with success until 1919; elected judge of the Circuit Court of Pike and Letcher Counties in 1919 to complete the term of Judge John F. Butler, deceased.

Judge Vanover was a Republican in politics and an active and consistent member of the Christian Church. He was a Royal Arch Mason and a member of the Independent Order of Odd Fellows.

He married in Pike County, September 10, 1885, Miss Martha Potter, born 1868, daughter of Boone John Potter of Pike County. They were parents of thirteen children—seven sons and six daughters. Three sons and a son-in-law volunteered and had service in World War I; Roscoe, Jr., was commissioned a lieutenant, U. S. Army; Russell served in the Medical Department, U. S. Army; John was in training for a commission at Gettysburg and at Camp Greene, North Carolina, and son-in-law, F. F. Williams was in training for commission at Camp Green.

RUFUS HUMPHREY VAN SANT, sometimes public official, business man engaged in the lumber industry, was born in Morgan County, Kentucky, September 8, 1862, and died in Ashland, Boyd County, Kentucky, a son of William H. Van Sant who was born in Russell County, Virginia, October 15, 1819; was educated in the public schools of Scott County, Virginia; came to Kentucky when a young man and taught in the public schools of then Morgan, now Elliott County for five years, and was subsequently engaged in stock trading. He was possessed of fine literary attainments, was highly respected for his manly character and sound views on matters of public interest and wielded a healthful influence among his neighbors. He was a Union Democrat during the Civil War. He died in Elliott County, April 29, 1870, and was buried near Martinsburg. His father was one of the early settlers of Pennsylvania who migrated to Maryland and finally to Russell County, Virginia, where he died.

Rufus H. Van Sant's mother was Levisa Hunter who was born in Greenville, Tennessee; educated in Morgan County, Kentucky, public schools; married William H. Van Sant, December 24, 1841. She survived her husband 23 years, dying July 3, 1893. Her father, Benjamin Franklin Hunter, was born in Tennessee, in 1800; came to Morgan County and engaged in farming there until his death in 1875. He married Elizabeth Drake, born in Tennessee, in 1802, and died in Morgan County in February 1872. The Hunters were descendants of a highly respectable English family.

Rufus H. Van Sant was educated in Morgan County under the careful and able training of his father; was engaged in teaching in the public schools of Elliott County, 1870-1880; was deputy clerk of the Elliott County Circuit Court, 1880-1886; and was elected clerk of that court in 1886 and served until 1892; served as master commissioner of the Elliott Circuit Court, 1884-1895.

While serving as deputy circuit clerk in 1881, he became interested in the lumber industry at Leon, Kentucky, purchasing the lumber taken from the forests of Elliott County along the Little Sandy River. In this way he became an extensive lumber dealer and broker; and in 1894 he established his home at Ashland, Kentucky, where he formed and organized the lumber firm of which he was senior member and the energetic and capable manager.

Mr. Van Sant was a Democrat and was a leader and wise counselor, serving in many capacities, among others, as Chairman of the State Executive Committee. He was Knight Templar and Shriner and a member of the lumber association known as the "Concatenated Order of Hoo Hoo".

He married December 3, 1879, Anna W. Hannah, daughter of James W. Hannah of Elliott County. (See Hannah Family.) She was born in Kanawha County, West Virginia, September 12, 1862. Three children were born to this union: Mexie, born April 17, 1892;

Harold Henderson, born October 5, 1894; and a daughter who died in infancy.

JOHN WESLEY WOODS, lawyer and financier at Ashland, Kentucky, was born at Webbville, Lawrence County Kentucky, February 6, 1871, a son of William Henry and Mary Bentley Woods. William Henry Woods was a prosperous farmer and stock dealer at Webbville and served as judge of the Lawrence County Court for one term. He was born May 4, 1842, and died July 17, 1912. Mary Bentley Woods was a daughter of Benjamin and Elizabeth ,(Baker) Bentley, early settlers of Letcher County, Kentucky. She was born in 1851 and died in 1883.

John W. Woods was educated in the public schools of Lawrence County and was graduated from the A & M. College (now the University of Kentucky) with degree of A. B., 1896; studied law under the direction of Alexander Lackey of Louisa and in 1897 was admitted to the bar at Louisa where he practiced his profession until 1902 when he located at Ashland, Kentucky, where he continued practicing for a number of years. He was connected with the Third National Bank of Ashland and was president; aided in organizing the Ashland Building and Loan Association and was a director; and represented the Southern Securities Corporation of Ashland in a similar capacity.

A Democrat in politics, he served as county attorney for Boyd County, 1906-1910. He was a Mason and a member of the Kiwanis Club and the Sigma Chi, a college fraternity.

On June 29, 1909, Mr. Woods was married to Miss Frances Mills Peebles, daughter of Robert and Harriet (Boal) Peebles. Children: Mary Bentley Woods, born July 4, 1910; John Wesley Woods, Jr., born March 19, 1912; Robert Peebles Woods, born June 20, 1913; Frances Halstead Woods, born April 19, 1915; Harriet Boal Woods, born December 25, 1918; William Winston Woods, born July 15, 1920.

---

[1] William Ely, "The Big Sandy Valley", p. 86-88.

[2] Report of the Adjutant General of Kentucky, 1861-1866, Vol. II, p. 384-5.

ADAMS FAMILY OF MAGOFFIN COUNTY

The Adamses were numerous in Eastern Kentucky and South-eastern Kentucky in pioneer days. One WILLIAM ADAMS, second in descent from the early pioneer of his family, settled at Licking Station, present Salyersville, Magoffin County. He was a man of importance and prominence in his community. Not only was he a large farmer, but a merchant, manufacturer and hotel keeper. He conducted a large tannery, shoe shop, saddlery, flour mill, etc., with profit to himself, giving employment to many men.

William Adams' children and grandchildren have come to honor, and are prominent people. One son, Smith Adams, a captain in the Union Army during the Civil War, married Josophine Proctor.[1]

Among their children is Colonel Roscoe E. Adams, physician, born at Salyersville, Kentucky, April 5, 1877; educated in public schools of Magoffin County and was graduated from Magoffin County High School, 1894; student at Georgetown (Kentucky) College, pre-medical two years, (1894-95); M. D. Barnes Medical College, St. Louis, 1898.

Dr. Adams enlisted in the National (Kentucky) State Guard, 1908, was commissioned a second lieutenant; transferred to U. S. Medical Corps (Reserve), 1911, and commissioned first lieutenant; promoted to rank of captain, 1914; mustered into Federal service, 1916, and detailed to service on Mexican border; promoted to rank of major in 1917. Upon entry of the United States in World War I in 1917, he was sent to Camp Shelby and in 1918 was transferred overseas for service. In France he served with 22nd U. S. Engineers as lieutenant colonel; was promoted to lieutenant colonel in 1919.

Returning to the United States, Colonel Adams was transferred to the U. S. Health Department, receiving appointment of Designated Examiner, September 8, 1919; promoted to service with the U. S. Veterans Administration August 8, 1921; attained rank of Colonel, 1923, retired May, 1928. Colonel Adams married January 8, 1901, M. Lenore Patrick of Salyersville, daughter of Judge and Mrs. A. T. Patrick. They had one son, Richmond Adams.

In politics he is a Republican; in religion, a Methodist. Fraternities: Mason, Knight Templar, Shrine, a member of the Kentucky State Medical Association; National Association of Military Surgeons; Military Order of World War I.

---

[1] William Ely, "The Big Sandy Valley", 1887, pages 396-97.

ADAMS FAMILY OF PIKE COUNTY

CAPTAIN ALEXANDER E. ADAMS was born in Lee County, Virginia, August 15, 1835, and came to Whitesburg, Letcher County, Kentucky, at the age of ten years and was entered as "store boy" in the service of his brother-in-law, D. I. Vermillion, prominent merchant of that town. He became an expert in the fur trade and during the proper seasons traversed and bought furs for his employer in Letcher, Perry, and Harlan Counties, Kentucky, Lee County, Virginia, and Hancock County, Tennessee. Abandoning the fur trade, he attended a good country school in Lee County for a time and afterwards attended Sneedsville Academy, Sneedsville, Tennessee. His funds becoming exhausted, he returned to Whitesburg and again entered the service of his brother-in-law as a clerk in his store. Subsequently he was a student at Mossy Creek College in Tennessee and afterwards was graduated with honors from the Baltimore Commercial College in 1861.

Mr. Adams was a staunch Union man and was nominated for State representative at a convention of Union men at Pikeville, Kentucky, in 1861. He accepted the nomination but was defeated.[1] He recruited a company of soldiers for the Union Army and was made captain of Company "D", 19th Kentucky Volunteer Infantry. He was mustered in January 2, 1862, at Harrodsburg, Kentucky, and was mustered out March 19, 1863 (resigned).[2]

In 1863 Captain Adams married Miss Georgia A. Dils, eldest daughter of Colonel John A. Dils, Jr., of Pikeville. (See Dils Family.) Captain Adams held many offices of honor and trust: He was State representative from Pike County; was appointed United States Assessor of Pike County, but soon resigned; appointed assistant Marshall of Kentucky in 1870; was commissioned, April 3, 1870, by President Grant as Consul at Port Said, Egypt, but the Congress failing to make an appropriation, he resigned and came home. He was tendered the United States Marshalship of Kentucky, but declined; was State Senator, 1879. He was a delegate to the Republican National Convention at Chicago, June 1880, which nominated Garfield for President, and was, among others, presented a medal commemorative of the thirty-six ballots cast by the "Old Guard" for General Grant for President in that convention.

During a greater part of his career Captain Adams was engaged in mercantile pursuits.

Children and approximate dates of birth as shown by U. S. Census of Pike County for 1870:

Minnie H. Adams; born 1866.

John D. Adams; born 1868

---

[1] William Ely, "The Big Sandy Valley, pages 195-200.

[2] Report of the Adjutant General of Kentucky, 1861-1865   Vol. II, page 24.

AUXIER FAMILY OF BIG SANDY VALLEY

The Auxier family is of French descent. The progenitor of this family in Eastern Kentucky was MICHAEL AUXIER [1] who was born on the left branch of the Seine River in France near the town of Auxerre which is the French name for Auxier. He was a soldier in the French Army in the war of the Austrian Succession, 1748. After the war he went to the Rhine River Valley and married a woman of Holland (Dutch descent) who, it is said, lived on the Rhine River in Germany. Emigrating from the Rhine in Germany with his family to America in 1755 he settled in Pennsylvania where they lived until the close of the Revoluionary War. Subsequently certain members of the family migrated to Virginia and to Kentucky.

Children:

2. SIMON AUXIER, a soldier of the Revolutionary War, volunteering under General Washington at Cambridge, Massachusetts, in 1775, he was with Washington at the Battle of Trenton (December 25, 1776); with the Virginia troops sent to aid General Nathaniel Breen in the South (1780); at the Battle of Guilford Court House (March 15, 1781); and at the surrender of General Cornwallis at Yorktown (September 19, 1781). He died near the mouth of Big Sandy River, in 1825, aged ninety-nine years.

3. MICHAEL AUXIER; settled on Kinniconick Creek, Lewis County, Kentucky; died in Adams County, Ohio, at the age of ninety-nine years. The Rev. S. D. Grumbles is a descendant.

4. GEORGE AUXIER, a Revolutionary War soldier, settled on the Kanawha River in Virginia (now West Virginia).

5. ABRAHAM AUXIER settled on the Wabash River, in Indiana.

6. SAMUEL AUXIER. At the age of fifteen years he enlisted in the Army and served during the last three years of the Revolutionary War; migrated in 1791—apparently from Russell County, Virginia —to the Blockhouse bottom near the mouth of Johns Creek, Big Sandy River, then Mason county, Virginia, subsequently Floyd county, Kentucky, and was instrumental in the settling of Harman's Station near there; was killed in 1798 or 1799 by being thrown against a tree by his horse that he was riding on a Buffalo hunt; married, presumably in Virginia, in 1779, Sarah (Sallie) Brown (born about 1763, died about 1862), daughter of Nathaniel Brown, and niece of Thomas C. Brown, Revolutionary War soldier. After his death, his widow married ——— Kelly who was killed in the War of 1812. They had a son, Joseph Kelly, who resided at the Falls of Blaine, Lawrence County.

Children:

*7. Nathaniel (Nat) Auxier.
*8. John Auxier.
*9. Daniel Auxier.
10. Elijah; came to his death in a mysterious way; probably devoured by wild animals or taken by prowling Indians.
*11. Samuel Auxier.
*12. Nancy Auxier.
*13. Enoch Auxier.
*14. Mary (Polly) Auxier.
*15. Fannie Amelia Frances Auxier.

7. NATHANIEL (NAT) AUXIER; b. in Virginia. When only sixteen years of age he hunted with Daniel Boone and party when they were exploring and hunting on the upper waters of the Big Sandy River; m. ——— Beck.

Children:

16. Alfred Auxier.
17. Samuel Auxier; killed by fly-wheel of steamboat.
18. John (Jack) Auxier.
19. Mary Ann Auxier; m. William Rice (See No. 16 Rice Family).
20. Elizabeth (Betty) Auxier; m. George Washington Rice (See No. 14, Rice Family).
21. ——— Auxier; m. William Robinson. They migrated to Minnesota.
22. ——— Auxier; m. Henry Robinson of Magoffin County, Kentucky.
23. Ferina Lorena Rebecca Brown Auxier; m. Jefferson Conley.

8. JOHN AUXIER; owned and operated the first mills in Big Paint Creek, now Johnson county; m., in Floyd county, August 16, 1810, Jemima Remy (Ramey). They migrated from Johnson county to Missouri.

Children:

24. John Auxier.
25. Lucy Auxier.

9. DANIEL AUXIER; migrated to Illinois prior to the Civil War; married, in Floyd county, ------------, ------------ Sturgill.

Children:

26. Fletcher Auxier.
27. George Auxier; killed by saw log on John's Creek.
28. McKenzie Auxier.
29. Jemima Auxier; m. ——— Borders.
30. Emily Auxier; m. William (Billy) Burchett.

11. SAMUEL AUXIER; b. August 7, 1791, in Block-house bottom, near mouth of John's Creek, Big Sandy River; d. in 1883; an important personage in the settlement of what is now Johnson county; m. first, in Floyd county, October 1, 1812, Rebecca Phillips who d. September 20, 1835; and, secondly, Agnes Wells.

Children of Samuel Auxier and his wife Rebecca (Phillips) Auxier:

*31. Nathaniel Auxier.
*32. John B. Auxier.
*33. Jemima Auxier.
*34. George W. Auxier.
*35. Sarah B. Auxier.
 36. Joseph K. Auxier; b. December 25, 1822; m. Jane Waker.
*37. Samuel Auxier.
*38. Rebecca Auxier.
*39. Martha J. Auxier.
*40. Amanda Arminta Auxier.
*41. Henry Jefferson Auxier.

Children of Samuel Auxier and his wife, Agnes (Wells) Auxier:

*42. Margaret L. Auxier.
*43. Elijah Brown Auxier.
*44. William Lewis Auxier.
*45. James K. Polk Auxier.
*46. Susan Angeline Auxier.

12. NANCY AUXIER; m. ―――― Brown. They resided in Morgan county, Kentucky.

Children:

 47. Elijah Brown.
 48. William (Billy) Brown.

13. ENOCH AUXIER; lived to be nearly 100 years of age; possessed many souvenirs which Daniel Boone left the family while he and his party were exploring and hunting in the Big Sandy Valley in 1767 - 68; m. in Floyd county, December 22, 1833, Mary Van Hoose.

Children:

*49. Joseph Decab Auxier.
*50. Samuel Leonard Auxier.
*51. Nancy Ann B. Auxier.
 52. John Wesley Auxier.
 53. Grant Auxier.
*54. Sarah Malisa Jane Auxier.
*55. Lydia Jemima Auxier.
*56. Frances Emaline Auxier.
*57. Elizabeth Auxier.

14. MARY (POLLY) AUXIER; m. George DeLong.

Children:

58. George DeLong; m. Mary Moore.
59. James DeLong; m. "Betsy" Ward.
60. Samuel DeLong; m. —— Wells.
61. Sarah (Sallie) DeLong; m. Hiram McGinnis.
62. Nancy DeLong.

15. FANNY AMELIA FRANCES AUXIER; m. in Floyd county, April 27, 1820, Samuel Hanna (Hannah) Baptist minister; surveyor for Johnson county.

Children:

63. Emaline Hannah; m. Dock Goebel.
64. Minerva Hannah; m. Jasper Webb.
65. Margaret Hannah; m. William Hyden.
66. Jane Hannah; m. Abraham Goebel.
67. Samuel Hannah; m. —— Hammons; removed to Kansas.
68. Dr. Abram Hannah; m. Susanna Webb.
69. John Hannah; soldier in the Civil War; not heard of subsequently.

31. NATHANIEL AUXIER; farmer, b. April 14, 1815, d. January 24, 1865; m. in Floyd county, March 8, 1838, Hester Ann Mayo, (b. September 10, 1819, d. May 4, 1864), daughter of Louis Mayo.

Children:

70. Samuel Lewis Auxier; b. December 7, 1838; d. December 21, 1860.
*71. George W. Auxier.
72. Captain David V. Auxier; b. in 1840; enrolled and mustered in Company "A", 39th Kentucky Volunteer Infantry, at Louisa, Kentucky; promoted from 2d lieutenant to captain, February 24, 1864; k. in action October 4, 1864, at Saltville, Virginia.
73. Louisa Auxier; b. November 4, 1843.
*74. Andrew J. (Judge) Auxier.
75. Julia Auxier; b. July 2, 1847; m. James Cooley.
76. Thomas J. Auxier; b. 1849.
77. Martha Auxier; b. 1851; m. W. Theodore Hager; resided at Richhill, Mo.
78. Araminta Auxier; b. 1853; m. "Bud" S. Friend.
79. Angeline Auxier; b. 1855; m. John Layne.
80. James B. Auxier; b. 1857; lawyer.
81. Nathaniel D. Auxier; b. 1860; m. Margaret Prichard; migrated to Nebraska about 1880 where he became a prosperous farmer.
*82. Edward E. Auxier.

3. MAJOR JOHN B. AUXIER; man of affairs in his day; farmer, surveyor for Johnson county, 1845 - 1851; captain, Company "A", 39th Kentucky Volunteer Infantry, commissioned September 6, 1862; promoted to major December 22, 1863; resigned November 17, 1864; b. February 9, 1817 and d. ———; m., first, in Floyd county, May 30, 1839, Angeline Mayo, and secondly, Mary Tilsley.

Children of Major John B. Auxier and Angeline (Mayo) Auxier:
83. Henrietta Auxier.
84. Benjamin F. Auxier.
85. Rebecca Auxier.
86. Mariah Jane Auxier.
87. Angeline Auxier; m., first, Ballard Preston (See 28, Moses Preston Family), and secondly, David Curnutte.

Children of Major John B. Auxier and Mary (Tilsley) Auxier:
88. Sarah C. Auxier; m. Washington Pinson.
89. Samuel B. Auxier; m. Levina Webb.
90. A. Elijah Auxier; m. Louisa Ford.
91. Margaret Auxier.
92. H. J. Auxier.
93. Nathaniel L. Auxier.
94. James S. Auxier.

33. JEMIMA AUXIER; b. August 16, 1818; m. in Floyd County, November 29, 1838, John Prater, Jr.
Children:
95. Rebecca Prater; m. ——— Wilson.
96. Angeline Prater; m. George Auxier. (See No. 71 Auxier Family).
*97. Sarah Prater; m. Fleming Litteral.
98. Henry Prater.
99. Taylor Prater.
*100. Amanda Prater.
101. Samuel Prater.
102. Nancy Prater; m. Benjamin (Dock) Dixon.
*103. Thomas J. Prater.

34. GEORGE AUXIER; b. March 15, 1820; m. in Floyd county, October 3, 1839, Nancy Prater. They migrated to and resided in Missouri.
Children:
104. Samuel Auxier.
105. William Auxier.
106. George Auxier.
107. Thomas Auxier.
108. Carolina Auxier.
109. Mary Auxier.

35. SARAH B. AUXIER; b. November 2, 1821; m. first, in Floyd county, June 15, 1839, George Washington Mayo, secondly, Martin Leslie; and thirdly, James Denton.

Children of Sarah B. Auxier and George Washington Mayo:
*110. Thomas J. Mayo.
111. John Wesley Mayo.

Children of Sarah B. Auxier and Martin Leslie:
112. Amos Leslie; m. ———— Conley.
113. Dr. Samuel Leslie.
114. Robert Leslie; m. Molly Warnock.
115. Elizabeth Leslie; m. Benjamin Conley.
116. Araminta Leslie; m. Benjamin Conley.

37. SAMUEL AUXIER; b. November 1, 1824; m. in Floyd county, ———— Mayo.
Children:
117. Lewis Auxier.
118. Gertrude Auxier.
119. Margaret Auxier.
120. Adalaide Auxier.
*121. J. C. B. Auxier.

38. REBECCA AUXIER, b. January 8, 1827, married Thomas Prater.
Children:
122. John Prater.
123. Sarah A. Prater; m. Dr. W. T. Atkinson.
124. William Prater.
125. Louisa Prater.

39. MARTHA J. AUXIER; m. Henry Walker.
Children:
126. John Walker.
127. William Walker.
128. Rebecca Walker.

40. AMANDA ARAMINTA AUXIER; b. March 10, 1831; m. James Neibert.
Children:
*129. Martha Neibert.
130. Samuel Neibert.
131. "Took" Neibert.
132. Julia Neibert.
133. Araminta Neibert.
134. James Neibert.
135. Julia Neibert.

136. Joseph Neibert.
137. Benjamin Neibert.
138. John Neibert.

41. HENRY JEFFERSON AUXIER; b. May 2, 1833; m. Harriet Music.
Children:
139. Margaret Auxier.
140. Lucy Auxier.
141. Rebecca Auxier.
142. John Auxier.

42. MARGARET L. AUXIER; b. February 11, 1839; m. in Johnson county, May 2, 1855, Lorenzo Dow Chambers.
Children:
143. James Chambers.
144. Samuel Chambers.
145. Worland Chambers.
146. Otis Chambers.
147. Nancy Chambers.
148. Geneva Chambers.

43. ELIJAH BROWN AUXIER; b. November 12, 1840; m. Margaret Richmond, Daughter of James Richmond.
Children:
*149. Margaret Auxier.
*150. James W. Auxier.
*151. Anna L. Auxier.
*152. Samuel B. (Buck) Auxier.
153. John Auxier.
*154. Agnes Auxier.
*155. Dora B. Auxier.
*156. Charlie Auxier.

44. WILLIAM LEWIS AUXIER; b. October 26, 1842; m. Louisa Ford.
Children:
*157. Lucy Auxier.
158. Anna Lee Auxier.
159. William Auxier.
160. Eva Auxier; m. Edward Wharter.

45. JAMES K. POLK AUXIER; b. March 5, 1845; d. April 2, 1926; m. Emily Spradlin.
Children:
161. Agnes Auxier.
162. Ann Auxier; d. April 5, 1926.

*163. Jimmerson Auxier.
 164. Milton Auxier; m. Ann Music.
*165. Forrest Lee (Dick) Auxier.
 166. Robert Auxier.

46. SUSAN ANGELINE AUXIER; b. March 22, 1847; m. John Richmond, farmer, son of James Richmond.

Children:
*167. Margaret Richmond.
*168. James Richmond.
*169. Samuel B. Richmond.
*170. J. D. Richmond.
*171. E. B. Richmond.
*172. Henry Richmond.
*173. William R. Richmond.
*174. Lulu Richmond.
*175. Anna Richmond.

49. JOSEPH DECAB AUXIER; resided near East Point, Johnson county, and for many years was a prominent man in that county; m. Charlotte (Lottie) Spradlin, d. April 19, 1926.

Children:
 176. Mary Auxier; d. in infancy.
 177. Amanda Auxier; m. Ballard May; lived at Cliff, Floyd county.
 178. Binnie Auxier; d. young.
 179. Warren D. Auxier; m. Cynthia Davis. (See No. 107, Davis Family.)
 180. Anna Auxier; d. young.
 181. Tobe Auxier; m. Belle Preston. (See No. 176, Preston Family.)
*182. Harry Auxier.
*183. George Auxier.
*184. Samuel Auxier.
 185. Down Auxier; m. Frankie Davis. (See No. —, Davis Family.)
*186. Ethel Auxier.

50. SAMUEL LEONARD AUXIER; m. Jane Wellman.

Children:
 187. William Auxier; m., first, Mary Conley, and, secondly, ——— Miller.
 188. Samuel Auxier; migrated to Indiana.
 189. Belle Auxier.
 190. Thomas Auxier.
 191. James Auxier.

51. NANCY ANN B. AUXIER; m. Jacob Webb.
Children:
*192. Mary Margaret Webb.
193. Martha Ann Webb.
194. Andrew Auxier (Buddy) Webb; b. April 2, 1875.
*195. Dr. Tobe Turner Webb.

54. SARAH MALISA JANE AUXIER; m. Zion Stapleton.
Children:
196. G. B. (Mack) Stapleton, m. Emma Ward.
197. I. Grant Stapleton; m. Rose Pelphry.
198. Lydia Stapleton; m. Thomas Van Hoose.
Sarah Malisa Jane Auxier m. secondly Samuel Fannin.

55. LYDIA JEMIMA AUXIER; m. Rollin Pelphrey.
Children:
199. William Pelphrey; m. Elizabeth Honeycutt.

56. FRANCES EMALINE AUXIER; m. "Bud" Porter.
Children:
200. Maggie Porter; m. ——— Parker.

57. ELIZABETH AUXIER; m. Thomas Walker.
Children:
201. Martha Walker; m. first, Frank Kendrick, and, secondly,
Henry Hitchcock.

71. GEORGE W. AUXIER; b. November 10, 1841; d. April 21, 1895;
Sheriff of Johnson County for 9 years within the period 1876-1894;
enrolled April 25, 1863, and mustered in August 30, 1863, at Louisa,
Lawrence County, a corporal, Company "A", 39th Kentucky Volunteer Infantry; mustered out at Louisville, Kentucky, September 15,
1865; m. December 3, 1865, Angeline Prater (b. December 3, 1841),
daughter of John Prater.
Children:
*202. I. L. (Link) Auxier.
*203. Hester Ann Auxier.
*204. Samuel N. Auxier.
205. John D. Auxier; b. February 3, 1871.
*206. William A. Auxier.
207. Albert Auxier; b. March, 1876.
*208. Millard W. Auxier.
*209. Sarah J. Auxier.
*210. Martha Auxier.
*211. George G. Auxier.
212. Nora F. Auxier; b. August 19, 1883.

74. ANDREW J. AUXIER, lawyer, judge and sometime public official, was born in Johnson County, Kentucky, 1845, and d. at Pikeville, Pike County, Kentucky, August 5, 1905; attended the Johnson County public schools and studied law in the office of Judge James E. Stewart of Louisa; admitted to the bar, 1867, and located at Pikeville, Pike County. He held many public offices of responsibility and trust: County Attorney of Pike Court, Commonwealths Attorney and was U. S. Marshall of the Eastern District of Kentucky during the administration of President Arthur; was unsuccessful candidate for Congress; was appointed by Gov. Bradley to fill the unexpired term of Judge Patton as Circuit Court Judge and was subsequently elected and served a six-year term, 1898-1904.

Judge Auxier was a Republican in politics and an active member of the Presbyterian Church and was also influential in the founding and operation of the Pikeville College.

He married in Pike County, Elizabeth Scott, who was born on John's Creek, Pike County, 1848, a daughter of John and Martha Scott.

Children:

213. William M. Auxier; resided in Pikeville.

214. Rudolph R. Auxier, merchant at Pikeville; d. at age of 30 years; unmarried.

215. Hester Auxier; m. James Sowards.

216. Nathaniel J. Auxier, lawyer; graduated from Pikeville College; d. at the age of 40 years.

217. Andrew E. Auxier, lawyer, was born in Pike County, October 31, 1878; educated in the public schools of Pikeville and at Pikeville College; studied law in the office of his father and was admitted to the bar at the age of 21 years; commenced practicing law with his brother, Nathaniel J. Auxier, and after the latter's death, he organized the law firm of Auxier, Harmon and Francis, which firm continued practice at Pikeville. He was a State senator, 1920-1924. Mr. Auxier was a Republican and a member of the Presbyterian Church and of the local Sons of the American Revolution. He m. 1902, Emma Bell, daughter of William and Cordelia Bell of Cochranton, Pennsylvania. Children: Robert W. and Frank B.

82. EDWARD E. AUXIER; b. 1864; m. Lucy Pritchard, b. 1864; emigrated to and settled in Nebraska, where he became a banker, farmer and plantation owner and held several offices of honor and trust.

Children:

218. Mabel Auxier; m. G. H. Rice (See Rice Family).

97. Sarah Prater; b. 1844; m. Fleming Litteral, b. 1844, d. April 15, 1928.
Children:
219. Harry Litteral; lived at Oil Springs, Johnson county.
220. John Litteral.
221. George Ann Litteral.
222. Thomas Litteral; resided at Oil Springs, Johnson county.
223. Ida Litteral.
224. Newton Litteral.
225. Virginia Litteral.
226. Kate Litteral.
227. Hannah Litteral.
228. Susan Litteral.
229. Tallahassie Litteral.

100. AMANDA PRATER; m. Newton Adams.
Children:
230. Winnie Adams.
231. Helen Adams.
232. Nellie Adams.

103. THOMAS J. PRATER; m. Sarah Holderby.
Children:
233. Alma Prater.
234. Fanny Prater.

110. THOMAS J. MAYO, well-known and highly respected citizen, a leading figure in the business and political affairs of Paintsville for many years; m. in Johnson county, Elizabeth Leslie.
Children:
235. Washington Mayo.
236. J. J. C. Mayo; m. Alice Meek.
237. Victoria Mayo.
238. Robert Mayo; m. Nellie Osborn.
239. Milton Mayo.
240. Fannie Mayo; married Fred Atkinson (See Atkinson Family)
241. Leslie Marvin Mayo; d. in youth.

121. J. C. B. AUXIER; for many years a merchant in and near East Point, Johnson county, and Auxier, Floyd county; m. in Johnson county, Mollie Friend.
Children:
242. Anna Auxier.
243. Emma Auxier, d. at Grayson, Carter county, Kentucky; m. first, Alvin Luck, secondly, ———, and, thirdly, John M. Theobald, lawyer, Grayson, Kentucky (See Theobald Family).
244. Robert Auxier; migrated to, m. and resided in Oklahoma.
245. John Auxier.

129. MARTHA NEIBERT; m. Jesse Meek.
Children:
*246. James N. Meek.
247. Hattie Meek; m. ———Maynard.
*248. Mary Meek. (See Meek Family)

149. MARGARET AUXIER; b. March 5, 1863; m. Thomas May.
Children:
249. Anna May; m. David Richmond.

150. JAMES W. AUXIER; businessman; civic leader; b. at East Point, Johnson county, November 22, 1865; m. in Johnson county, October 2, 1889, Martha A. Stafford, daughter of William M. Stafford. Removing to Paintsville Mr. Auxier entered the grocery business there; became president of the Paintsville Grocery Company; trustee of the John C. C. Mayo College.
Children:
*250. Fannie M. Auxier.
*251. Margaret May Auxier.
252. Maxie Auxier, prominent in social affairs of Paintsville; m. Henry La Viers, civil engineer, graduate of the Ohio State University and sometime chief engineer for the North-East Coal Company.
*253. Leona Stafford Auxier.

151. ANNA L. AUXIER; b. January 1, 1867; m. Beverley C. May.
Children:
254. Charles May.
255. Margaret May; m. Crittenden Hall.
256. William May.
257. Tress May; married ——— Francis.
258. Anna Laura May.

152. SAMUEL B. (BUCK) AUXIER; b. February 18, 1869, farmer; resided near East Point, Johnson county; m., first, Laura Greer and secondly, Anna Stratton.
Children of Samuel B. (Buck) Auxier and Laura Greer:
259. Evert Auxier.
260. Ethel Auxier.
261. Dora Auxier.
262. Elijah Auxier.
Evert and Ethel were twins.
Children of Samuel B. (Buck) Auxier and Anna Stratton:
263. Clyde Auxier.
264. ———.

154. AGNES AUXIER; b. July 7, 1872; m. Alex Spradlin.
Children:
265. Alex Spradlin.

155. DORA B. AUXIER; b. May 9, 1874; m. John M.
Children:
*266. Cynthia May.
267. Elijah B. May; married —— Barney.

156. CHARLIE R. AUXIER; b. March 19, 1877; resided at Prestonsburg, Floyd County; chief electrician for the Eureka Coal Company
for some time; killed in automobile accident, October, 1925; m. Belle
Hall.
Children:
268. Estill Auxier.
269. Margaret Auxier.
270. ——.

157. LUCY AUXIER; m. William Hatcher.
Children:
271. Lucy Hereford Hatcher.
272. Meta Hatcher.
273. Totsie Hatcher.
274. "Bluebird" Hatcher.

163. JIMMERSON AUXIER; m. Angie Spradlin.
Children:
275. Wyonda Auxier.

165. FORREST LEE (DICK) AUXIER, farmer; resided on the Big
Sandy River just below East Point, Johnson county; m. Vada Music.
Children:
276. Margaret Auxier; m. June 20, 1928, Fred W. Harris of West
Point, Mississippi.
*277. Sallie Auxier.
278. J. K. Polk Auxier.
279. Morgan Auxier.

167. MARGARET RICHMOND; m. John Hager.
Children:
*280. Anna Hager.

168. JAMES RICHMOND: m., first, Sarah Wells.
Children:
281. Brooksie Richmond.
282. John Richmond.

    James Richmond m., secondly, —— ——, of Greenup
county, Kentucky.
Children:
283. —— ——.

169. SAMUEL B. RICHMOND; m. Unoka Clark.
Children:
284. Fannie Richmond; m. Benjamin Wells.
285. Susanna Richmond; m. ———— Wells.
286. William Richmond.

170. J. D. RICHMOND; m. Anna Elliott.
Children:
287. Galland Richmond.
288. Arthur Richmond; m. ———— ————.
289. Myrtle Richmond; m. ———— ————.

171. E. B. RICHMOND; noted for old-time fiddling; resided at the bend of John's Creek, Johnson county; m. Zora Webb.
Children:
290. Otis Richmond; m. ———— DeLong.
291. John D. Richmond.
292. Brownlow Richmond (a fiddler).
293. Abbie G. Richmond; m. Hobart Wells.
294. Jane Richmond.
295. Julia Richmond.
296. Fannie Richmond.

172. HENRY RICHMOND; resided on the old home farm at the bend of John's Creek, near Auxier, Floyd county; m. Lulu Porter.
Children:
297. Spillman Richmond.
298. Alice Richmond.
299. H. B. Richmond.
300. Anna Margaret Richmond.

173. WILLIAM R. RICHMOND, engineer, some time teacher in the rural schools of Johnson county; surveyor and engineer for Johnson county for many years, resided on his excellent farm one mile east of Paintsville; m. Alice Joseph.
Children:
301. Orville Richmond.
302. Estill Richmond.
303. John W. Richmond.
304. James G. Richmond.
305. Myrtle Richmond.

174. LULU RICHMOND; m. Watt Preston.
Children:
306. Claude Preston.
307. James Preston.
308. Lulu Grace Preston.
309. Willa Dene Preston.
310. Kathleen Preston.

175. ANNA RICHMOND; m. W. C. Sherman.
Children:
311. Arby Sherman.

182. HARRY AUXIER; resided on a farm at East Point, Johnson County; m. Miranda Music.
Children:
*312. May Auxier.
313. Virgil Auxier.
314. Lucy Auxier.
315. Octavia Auxier.
316. Junior Auxier.

183. GEORGE AUXIER; m. Nannie Baldridge.
Children:
317. ――― ―――

184. SAMUEL AUXIER; resided for a number of years at Burdine, Letcher county and at Weeksburg, Floyd county, where he was connected with coal-mining companies; m. Lulu King.
Children:
318. Evelyn Auxier.
319. Walton Auxier.
320. George Raymond Auxier.

186. ETHEL AUXIER; m. Gabriel Hughes.
Children:
321. Melva Grace Hughes.
322. Marzella Hughes.

192. MARY MARGARET WEBB, b. April 29, 1865; m. Frank Howe.
Children:
323. Edgar Howe; resided at Seco, Letcher county, where he was connected with the South-East Coal Company for a number of years.
324. Lawton Howe.
325. Burnard Howe.

195. DR. TOBE TURNER WEBB; b. November 29, 1879; practiced his prefession at Weeksbury, Floyd county; m. Hattie Spradlin, daughter of James Spradlin.
Children:
326. Girvis Webb.
327. Wilbur Webb; b. November 2, 1904.
328. Dora Webb; b. December 29, 1909.
329. Virgil Webb; b. March 31, 1912.
330. ――― ―――.

202. I. C. (Link) Auxier, b. November 19, 1866; life-long resident of Johnson county; resided on a farm near the family homestead prior to 1922, when he moved to Paintsville; held some local official position during the greater part of his adult life; married Jemima C. Wheeler (b. April 14, 1865), daughter of Martin Wheeler.

Children:

331. Fred Auxier; b. November 19, 1887, d. December 29, 1887.

332. Gertrude Auxier; b. February 24, 1889; m. P. T. Holbrook.

333. Earl M. Auxier; b. February 14, 1891; married Bessie Holbrook.

334. Julia Ann Auxier; b. January 12, 1893; m. A. G. T. Dorton.

335. Osa Ethel Auxier; b. May 4, 1895; m. G. H. Williams.

336. Mary Madaline Auxier; born July 7, 1897.

337. George W. Auxier; b. November 27, 1905.

203. Hester Ann Auxier; b. June 6, 1868; m. D. J. Van Hoose.

Children:

338. Dewey Van Hoose; m. Mary Castle.

339. Bessie Van Hoose; m. Buel Lemaster.

340. Myrtie Van Hoose; m. Frank Pelphry.

341. George W. Van Hoose; m. Addie Salyer.

342. Bert Van Hoose.

204. Samuel N. Auxier; b. September 17, 1869, carpenter and a contractor; removed to Chicago, Ill; m. Rosa Stapleton.

Children:

343. Mildred Auxier.

344. Elizabeth Auxier.

345. Rubie Auxier.

346. Earl Auxier.

347. Mrytle Auxier.

348. Samuel Auxier.

349. Irwin Auxier.

350. Truston Auxier.

351. Charles Auxier.

352. Church Auxier.

206. William A. Auxier; b. January 13, 1873, a contractor; resided at DeLand, Florida; m., first, Laura McKenzie; and secondly, Lolla Hannibal.

Children of William A. Auxier and Laura (McKenzie) Auxier:

353. Juanita Auxier.

208. MILLARD W. AUXIER; b. November 9, 1874; lived on a farm near Falls City, Nebraska; married Tessie Stapleton.

Children:
354. Sibyl Auxier.
355. Mollie Auxier.
356. Custer Auxier.
357. Lester Auxier.
358. Maude Auxier.
359. Marvin Auxier.

209. SARAH J. AUXIER; b. September 20, 1877; m. Wilson Rice, farmer, who lived on a farm on Barnett's Creek.

Children:
360. Mamie Rice.
361. Malta Rice.
362. Ella Rice.
363. Walter Rice.
364. Della Rice.
365. Martin Rice.
366. Dixie Rice.
367. Millard Rice.
368. Mary Rice.
369. Martha Rice.
370. Harry Rice.
371. Virgie Rice.
372. Anna May Rice.

210. MARTHA AUXIER; b. August 2, 1879; teacher in rural schools of Johnson county for many years; m. Henry Trimble.

Children:
373. Rexford Trimble; m. Bertha Blanton.
374. Victoria Trimble.

211. GEORGE G. AUXIER; b. March 25, 1881; a surveyor and businessman; surveyor for Johnson county, 1926 ———; m. Lulu Salyer.

Children:
375. Alka Auxier.
376. Cecil Auxier.
377. Hazel Auxier.
378. Ivy Joy Auxier.
379. Clerian Auxier.
380. Ruth Auxier.
381. Charlie Auxier.
382. G. G. Auxier, Jr.
383. Robert Auxier.
384. Paulina Auxier.
385. Irvine Auxier.

246. JAMES N. MEEK; m. Victoria Salyer.

Children:

386. Ernest Meek.
387. Walter Meek.
388. J. N. Meek, Jr.
(See Meek Family).

248. MARY MEEK; m. Harve Matney, sometime merchant at Thealka, Johnson county who subsequently conducted a taxi business at Paintsville.

Children:

*389. Katheryn Matney.

250. FANNIE M. AUXIER; b. July 27, 1890; m. at Paintsville, in November, 1910, Dr. Ernest E. Archer, surgeon, b. September 22, 1888, at Prestonsburg, Floyd county, son of George Preston Archer and Emma (Johns) Archer; attended the public schools of Prestonsburg and after completing the high school course, entered the University of Louisville where he completed his medical education and was graduated in 1810 with his degree. He immediately opened an office at Prestonsburg and within a year had established a satisfactory practice. He then took charge of the medical and surgical department of the North-East Coal Company, at Auxier, Kentucky, a position that gave him exceptional professional experience, and remained in that position from October 11, 1911, to August, 1917, when he entered for service in World War I, as a member of the Medical Corps of the Army, with the rank of captain. He had two years service, having served overseas from May, 1918, to March, 1919, and was honorably discharged April 3, 1919, at New York City, in the rank of major to which rank he had been promoted.

Returning to his home at Paintsville, Dr. Archer and associates formulated plans for and were instrumental in the organization of the Paintsville Hospital, one of the finest in Eastern Kentucky, with which institution he served as first president.

Children:

390. James W. Archer.
391. Mary Margaret Archer.
392. George P. Archer.
393. Martha Ann Archer.
394. Emma Elizabeth Archer; b. November 26, 1927.

251. MARGARET MARY AUXIER; m. Clarence Hager; sometime in wholesale business at Paintsville.

Children:

395. John Milton (Jack) Hager.
396. Helen Louise Hager.

253. LEONA STAFFORD AUXIER; m. John Gainey Newman, who was b. and reared in Frankfort, Kentucky; came to Paintsville and became connected with the Paintsville National Bank and subsequently Grocery Company; city clerk of Paintsville.

Children:

397. James Thomas Newman.

266. CYNTHIA MAY; m. Henry Stevens.

Children:

398. ——— ———.

277. SALLIE AUXIER; m. Milo Preston.

Children:

399. Mildred Lorraine Preston.

280. ANNA HAGER; m. Otto Bennington.

Children:

400. ——— ———.

312. MARY AUXIER; m. Burr Hereford, farmer, merchant, near Cliff, Floyd county.

Children:

401. ——— ———.
402. ——— ———.
403. ——— ———.

389. Katheryn Matney; m. Donald Foley.

Children:

404. ——— ———.

BAILEY FAMILY

1. CAPTAIN JOHN BAILEY was the ancestor of a large family of Baileys of Bath County, Kentucky, members of whom removed to Carter and Elliott Counties. He was born in North Carolina, probably in Orange County, and married Sarah Tatum in that state. He migrated to Lincoln County, Kentucky, with his family about 1772 and on March 29, 1780 he was commissioned a Captain, Virginia State Troops (Clark's Illinois Regiment [1]) and had service with his organization in the Revolutionary War. He was carried on the list at half pay dated April 13, 1782, and the Journal of the North West Commissioners shows that he was granted 4,000 acres of land on account of his military service in the Revolution.

Captain Bailey removed to Bath County, Kentucky, where he died in 1826. In his Will, probated in the Bath County Court at the June 1826 Term, he mentioned his wife, "Anna Jean"; sons John, Jesse L., Robert, Hiram, Warren, and Charles; and daughters, Elizabeth Rice, Sarah Davis, Nancy Clayton and Lucy. Children:

2. Elizabeth Bailey, m. Campbell Rice (See Rice family).

3. Sarah Bailey, m. Fleming Rice (See Rice family).

4. John Bailey.

5. William Bailey.

*6. Warren Bailey.

7. Jesse L. Bailey; m. in Bath County, November 23, 1816, "Caty Ewin" (Katie Ewing).

8. Nancy Bailey; m. in Bath County, July 7, 1821, Geo. Clayton.

9. Robert Bailey.

10. Hiram Bailey.

11. Charles Bailey; m. Martha England in Bath County, July 18, 1821.

12. Lucy Bailey; m. Zachariah Corbin in Bath County, January 18, 1819.

6. WARREN BAILEY, farmer, b. in Kentucky in 1804; m. in Bath County, February 21, 1832, Elizabeth Boyd, b. in Kentucky 1807. Children and their ages living at home in 1850 as shown by the U.S. Census of Bath County for that year:

13. John Bailey, aged 14.

14. Charles Bailey, aged 13.

15. Sarah Bailey, aged 11.

16. Swetnam Bailey, aged 9.

17. William Bailey, aged 5.

18. Nancy Bailey, aged 2.

---

[1] Historical Register of Virginians in the Revolution, by John H. Gwathmey, page 31.

BALLINGER FAMILY OF KNOX COUNTY

The Ballingers were among the most prominent and influential pioneer families of Southeastern Kentucky. They were farmers and slave holders; many held public office and some were lawyers.

*1. John, * 2. Richard, * 3. Edward and * 4. Franklin Ballinger, apparently brothers, migrated from North Carolina and settled in what is now Knox County, Kentucky, before the county was formed and organized.

1. JOHN BALLINGER was commissioned by Governor Garrard as one of the first Justices of Knox County, and took the oath of office June 23, 1800. He was a State representative from Knox County in 1806.

2. RICHARD BALLINGER was elected clerk pro tem of the Knox County Court on June 23, 1800, at the first session of the court. He was a slaveholder, having listed twelve negro slaves for taxation in 1810. He represented Knox County in the State Senate in 1821-26. One Richard Ballinger m. Millie Herndon in Knox County, June 21, 1810.

3. EDWARD BALLINGER m. Nancy Parker in Knox County, December 21, 1809.

4. FRANKLIN BALLINGER, lawyer; was Judge of the Knox County Circuit Court 1836-40.

Of this Ballinger Family, probably of the first generation born in Kentucky, was:

5. JAMES F. BALLINGER, b. in Kentucky, presumably in Knox County, in 1795. He was State representative from Knox County in 1819 and clerk of the Knox County and Circuit Courts for many years. He was "no doubt the best clerk in Kentucky." "(He) knew the forms of every judgment and order known to the Common Law and Equity practice; was counselor and transacted business for many of the county people in the mountains who had great confidence in him. His familiarity with Shakespeare led to his being given that as a nickname. Scott's novels and poetry were very familiar to him. (He) knew English history; read newspapers and (was) exceeding well informed on the history of the day."[1]

James F. Ballinger migrated to Iowa after his daughter, Lucy L. and her husband, Samuel Freeman Miller, subsequently justice of the Supreme Court, had settled at Keokuk, that State.

Children among others:

*6. William Pitt Ballinger.
*7. Lucy L. Ballinger.

The U. S. Census of Knox County for 1810 shows the following with respect to this family:

James F. Ballinger, 55, Circuit Court Clerk, b. in Kentucky.

Elizabeth J. Ballinger (apparently second wife), 38, b. in Kentucky.

8. Joseph Ballinger, age 19, student.

9. America Ballinger, age 15.

10. James Ballinger, age 14.

11. Randolph Ballinger, age 12.

12. Green A. Ballinger, age 10.

13. Elizabeth Ballinger, age 3.

6. WILLIAM PITT BALLINGER, lawyer, served under his father as deputy County Court Clerk of Knox County for a number of years and while so serving issued license, October 8, 1842, to Samuel Freeman Miller and Lucy L. Ballinger, the father, James F. Ballinger being present and consenting.

In 1843, William Pitt Ballinger migrated and settled in Texas. He served in the Mexican War and upon discharge and return home to Texas he was admitted to the bar. He became one of the most respected lawyers of the Southwest, and in 1874 was appointed judge of the Supreme Court of Texas, which office he promptly declined.

He was seriously considered by President Hayes in connection with the vacancy on the Supreme Court Bench in 1877.

7. LUCY L. BALLINGER was b. in Knox County, March 27, 1827, and d. of tuberculosis in Keokuk, Iowa, November 12, 1854; m. Samuel Freeman Miller in Barbourville, Knox County, Kentucky, November 8, 1842, by William T. Hopper, a Baptist minister of the locality.

SAMUEL FREEMAN MILLER, sometime physician, lawyer and jurist, was b. at Richmond, Kentucky, April 5, 1816, a son of Frederick Miller and Patsy Freeman, who were m. in 1815. Frederick Miller was of Pennsylvania German stock and had migrated from the vicinity of Reading, that State. Patsy Freeman was one of the 13 children of Samuel Freeman whose family had come from North Carolina prior to 1782.

Mr. Miller was reared on a farm and attended the academy in Richmond where, it is said, he stood at the head of his class and to have been particularly strong in English grammar and mathematics. His biographer [2] says that his mind bore no marks of the trammels of a formal education; that he had no predilections for manual labor;

that in later life he used to say that his motto was "never walk when you can ride; never sit when you can lie."

On leaving school Mr. Miller became clerk in the drugstore of Dr. Leverill, a relative of his mother, and then, as he later wrote, "at the age of eighteen began the study of medicine", and after several years of study which included two courses of lectures in the medical department of Transylvania University, at Lexington, he received the degree of MD. in 1838.

Between the first and second years at Transylvania University, Mr. Miller became a resident of Barbourville, County Seat of Knox County, a town of less than two hundred inhabitants. The population of the county was about seven thousand, of which less than one-tenth were slaves. In politics the county was overwhelmingly Whig. Thanks to the intellectual vigor of its citizens, Barbourville was later described somewhat expansively as having been the "Athens of the Kentucky Highlands from the early days until the railroad penetrated the county".

On May 27, 1837, Mr. Miller participated in the organization of the Barbourville Debating Society, and thereafter was the foremost participant in its encounters. Every Saturday "at early candlelight" a dozen or so of the young men of the town would meet at the courthouse and debate some question of current interest. When winter set in the Society disbanded, but reappeared in 1838 and 1839. Here Mr. Miller discovered his ability for effective public address and developed those traits which caused him to turn from medicine to law. As the journal of the Society [3] shows, he was an enthusiastic Whig, an advocate of constitutional revision which would put slavery in Kentucky in due course of extinction.

Mr. Miller's chief rival in debate was Green Adams.[4] Another was Joseph Eve.[5] A young lawyer named Silah Woodson [6] was another member of the Society. On April 4, 1864, when Montana was about to be organized as a territory, Mr. Miller recommended Woodson to President Lincoln for Chief Justice of the Territory, but a different selection was made. Apparently it was from Woodson's books that Mr. Miller did his first surreptitious reading in the law. The log cabin used by Woodson and Miller is still standing in Barbourville.

About 1845, as Mr. Miller later wrote of himself, he decided to change his profession, and after two years of study of the law with Judge Ballinger—probably 4. Judge Franklin Ballinger, a kinsman of Mrs. Miller and a member of the Debating Society, he was admitted to the bar of the Knox County Circuit Court, March 22, 1847, on motion of Silas Woodson.

Mr. Miller served as a Justice of the Peace of Knox County from

April 1, 1844, to August, 1849, when he resigned. He was an active emancipationist and aspired to a seat in the Constitutional Convention of 1849, but deferred to the claims of his friend, Silas Woodson, on the condition that the latter stand openly in favor of the gradual emancipation of slavery.

When Mr. Miller, whose antipathy of slavery went back to a day in childhood when he had seen his old negro "mammy" flogged, became satisfied that slavery would never be voluntarily abolished in a slave state, he decided to leave Kentucky and in the Autumn of 1849 first saw the town of Keokuk, Iowa, in a general tour of the Northwest. He decided to make that place his home and arrived there on the 7th day of May, 1850, with his family.

At Keokuk, Mr. Miller formed a partnership with Lewis R. Reeves, the best lawyer there and soon was engaged in a large and remunerative practice and took front rank among the lawyers of the State. Mr. Reeves died in 1854, and after the death of Mrs. Miller, November 12, 1854, Mr. Miller married Mrs. Reeves.

Mr. Miller took a leading part in organizing the Republican Party and was a candidate, sometimes active and sometimes passive, for high public office in his adopted State.

On June 16, 1862, President Lincoln named Mr. Miller as a Justice of the Supreme Court of the United States and he was confirmed by the Senate in half an hour without reference to committee, a courtesy usually reserved for persons who have been members of that body.

What Justice Miller regarded as his greatest opinion was in the case of the *United States vs. Lee* wherein specifically the judgement holds that an action of ejectment can be maintained against an officer in possession under claim of title in the United States, where the United States is not a party and has not consented to suit. As Justice Miller elsewhere related the facts, which gave the case its peculiar human interest, it "was a suit by Lee, who had married a descendant of Martha Washington, to recover the Arlington estate which had been seized by order of President Lincoln during the War, and part of it converted into a cemetery for the dead of our side. The officers of the Army set up the President's order as sufficient defense of their possession."

After holding the English cases on the immunity of the sovereign to be inapplicable to our form of constitutional government, and the American precedents to uphold the maintenance of the action, Justice Miller examined the question, "upon principle and apart from the authority of adjudged cases," and concluded : No man in this country is so high that he is above the law. No officer of the law may set the law at defiance with impunity. All the officers of the government from the highest to the lowest, are creatures of the law, and are bound to obey it.

Justice Miller lived for the greater part of his life in Washington, D. C., at 1415 Massachusetts Avenue, N. W. He died in 1890.

---

[1] The Ballinger Diary, Library of the University of Texas.

[2] "Mr. Justice Miller and the Supreme Court, 1862-1890", by Charles Fairman, Harvard University Press, Cambridge, Massachusetts, 1939.

[3] The Journal is still in existence, and was in the possession of Thomas D. Tinsley of Ashland, Kentucky, who found it lying in a heap of debris when the Knox County County House was being reconditioned.

[4] Green Adams was elected as a Whig to the Thirtieth Congress, (March 4, 1847-March 3, 1849) and elected as the candidate of the American Party to the Thirty-sixth Congress (March 4, 1859-March 3, 1861). (See Adams Family.)

[5] Joseph Eve, lawyer, held many public offices of honor and trust: State Representative from Knox County, 1810, 1811, 1815; State Senator 1817-1821; Major of the 29th Regiment Kentucky Militia, War of 1812; Judge of the Knox Circuit Court, 1826-1828. He married Betsey Withers, November 15, 1811.

[6] Silas Woodson, lawyer, was born in Kentucky, presumably in Knox County, in 1817. He held many public offices of honor and trust: County Attorney for Knox County; Commonwealth's Attorney for the Knox Circuit; State representative from Knox County, 1842, 1853-55; member of the Constitutional Convention of 1849 from Knox and Harlan Counties; was appointed as minister to the Republic of Texas. He married, first, in Knox County, Mary Jane Roberts, September 13, 1842, and, secondly, in that county, July 28, 1846, Oilvia Adams, born in Kentucky in 1829. Mr. Woodson migrated to Missouri and subsequently was elected and served as governor of that State, 1874-78. A third marriage was consumated in that State.

BENNETT FAMILY OF GREENUP COUNTY

Bennett

The name of Bennett originated from the personal name of Benedict. During the reigns of Edward II and III, the name is found m o d i fi e d, Fitz-Benedict, Benediscite, Benediste, Bendish, Bennett.

The f o u n d e r of the Bennett family, which has been a prominent one in America, particularly in the Southern States for many generations, was Richard. He was a nephew of Edward Bennett, a wealthy merchant of London, and a member of the Virginia Company.

Richard Bennett was identified in his adopted home, Virginia, with many public offices. He served as a member of the Council, 1642-1649. He later removed to Maryland, but returned to Virginia, and, in 1661, was appointed by Parliament one of the commissioners to reduce Virginia and Maryland. He was Governor of the Colony in 1652.

Robert Bennett, a brother of Edward Bennett of London, also came to Virginia, prior to 1623, and took up a grant of land in Nansemond County.

Descendants of this splendid family are now found in almost every Southern State and in the Far West.

Many members of the Bennett family settled in the New England Colonies.

1. THADDEUS BENNETT was the progenitor of the Bennett family of Greenup County, Kentucky. He was of Scotch-Irish extraction and a native of Virginia. When a child, he was taken by parents to a farm on the Genesee River in New York where he was reared. At the age of 16 he enlisted in the Continental Army and had service in the Revolutionary War. In 1818 he migrated with his family to Scioto County, Ohio, where he lived until his death at the age of 74 years.

Children, among others:

2. JOSEPH BENNETT, b. in Chemung County, New York, and d. April 30, 1868. He was a miller and operated a number of old water power flour mills; a minister of the Baptist Church and filled pastorates in Ohio, Kentucky, Virginia, and Michigan; had service in the War of 1812; a strong Union man; a Republican in politics; and

a justice of the peace. He married, first, Elizabeth Mills, a native of Havana, Schuyler County, New York, who d. July 12, 1862.

Children among others:

3. BENJAMIN FRANKLIN BENNETT, b. at Harrisonville, Scioto County, Ohio, October 11, 1829; managed his father's affairs while he was away from home and engaged in ministerial work; came to Kentucky in 1855 and purchased saw and corn mills at Globe Furnace on Tygarts Creek, Greenup County, which he improved and operated; purchased about 3,000 acres of land which he divided into small tracts and sold; served in the Union Army, Company "G", 56th Ohio Volunteer Infantry, and was discharged July 25, 1862, on account of disability; subsequently studied law; was admitted to the bar in March, 1866, and practiced at Greenup; was a Whig in politics and after the organization of the Republican party became a member of that organization; was appointed deputy provost marshal and special agent in 1863 and served as such until the close of the war; was a member of the State Constitutional Convention, 1890; and State representative, 1891, 1894; m. Miss Sarah Ann Snodgrass of Irish lineage, b. at Harrisonville, Ohio, December 12, 1830, daughter of John and Hannah (Titus) Snodgrass, the former a native of Virginia, and the latter of Ohio.

Children:

*4. Joseph Bentley Bennett.

5. Elizabeth Bennett; d. at age of 3.

6. Ruby Jane Bennett; d. at age of 6.

7. Mary Hannah Bennett; m. John Merrill of Greenup County.

8. Lucinda Bennett; m. Thomas Smith.

9. Isabel Bennett; m. W. B. Secrest of Greenup County.

10. Emily Bennett; m., first, George Wine and, secondly, Frank B. Bennett.

11. Sallie A. Bennett; m. Everett Taylor of Greenup County.

4. JOSEPH BENTLY BENNETT, lawyer, judge and legislator; b. at Bennetts Mills, Greenup County, April 21, 1859; educated in the public schools of Greenup County and at Greenup (Kentucky) Academy; engaged in teaching in the public schools of Greenup County for a time; studied law in the office of Judge Dulin, at Greenup, and admitted to the bar, August 30, 1878; engaged in merchandizing at Bennetts Mills, 1883-1894; subsequently practiced law at Greenup; unsuccessful candidate for County Attorney for Greenup County, 1882, 1886; elected and served as County Judge of Greenup County, 1896-1914; member of the Republican State Central Committee from 9th Congressional District, 1900 and 1904; elected

as a Republican to the Fifty-ninth, Sixtieth and Sixty-first Congresses and served as such from March 4, 1905, to March 3, 1911;[1] resumed the practice of law at Greenup and continued until his death, November 7, 1923. Interment Riverside Cemetery, Greenup; m. at Greenup, August 30, 1883, Miss Annie Louise Mytinger, b. at Maysville, Kentucky, May 27, 1861, and d. at Greenup, ———, daughter of Wharton and Josephine Eliza (Cole) Mytinger.

Children:

12. Chester Allen Mytinger Bennett, lawyer and connected with the U. S. Government at Washington, D. C., for a number of years; m. Esther M. Morton.

13. Frances Mytinger Bennett; m. Charles J. Geyer.

14. Kate Newman Bennett; m. Clement J. Hill.

15. Charles Bentley Bennett; one-time clerk of the Greenup Circuit Court; m. Lucille L. Wilson.

*16. Emmabel Bennett, teacher; m. Elmer D. Stephenson.

17. Julia Bennett; m. R. H. McWhortan.

18. Mary Louise Bennett; m. John Shaw.

19. Sallie Anna Bennett; m. Charles D. Jacobs, Jr.

20. Joseph Bentley Bennett, Jr.

16. ELMER D. STEPHENSON, lawyer and judge; b. in Greenup County, Kentucky. His ancestors in both paternal and maternal lines were pioneer settlers of North-eastern Kentucky. He was educated in the public schools of Greenup County; studied law; was admitted to the bar and in the early 1890s he located at Pikeville, Kentucky, for the practice of law in which profession he has attained high rank.

Judge Stephenson is a member of the Christian Church. A Democrat in politics, he has held many offices of honor and trust and has filled all of them creditably and well. He has served as judge of the Pike County Court, State Senator and is presently serving as Judge of the Circuit Court of his judicial district.

---

[1] "Biographical Directory of the American Congress, 1774-1949".

BIGGS FAMILY OF GREENUP COUNTY
BIGGE—BIGGS

The surname Bigge seems to be of Scandanavian origin. The name Robert Bigge is bourne on the Hundred Rolls of England.

The Biggs family of Greenup County, Kentucky, is of Scotch-Irish descent, being one of those families of Scotland that took up arms to defend the Presbyterian form of church government. They were persecuted and fled to Ireland for refuge. Three brothers Biggs emigrated from Ireland and settled at or near the present Brownsville, Pennsylvania, about the middle of the 18th century.

The Biggses served in all the early Colonial wars. Captain John Biggs was an Indian fighter and settled near present Zanesville, Ohio. He was killed in 1773 near Wheeling, Virginia, now West Virginia, along with Lieutenant Ashley. General Jack Biggs settled on the Miami River near Cincinnati. He also was in Indian wars. William Biggs of Virginia was with General George Rogers Clark at Fort Jefferson, 1780. General Benjamin Biggs was stationed at Fort Lawrence in 1773, when he was attacked by Indians and killed.

1. ANDREW BIGGS was the progenitor of the Biggs family of Greenup County, Kentucky. He was a son of William and Elizabeth Biggs. He was b. in 1769 and m. Judith Robertson of Bryans Station near Lexington, Kentucky, in 1795. Subsequently they lived at Mount Sterling where she d. in 1804. He m. again and in 1813 settled at Greenupsburg where he became a merchant and kept a tavern. Afterwards he removed to a farm on Smiths Branch, Greenup County, where he d. in 1827 and was buried.

Children:

THIRD GENERATION

2. Sallie Biggs; b. 1796.
3. Elizabeth Biggs; b. 1798; m. John Rice.
*4. William Biggs; b. 1800.
*5. Robinson or Robertson Biggs; b. 1802.

4. WILLIAM BIGGS, agriculturist and business man of many activities, was b. in Kentucky, presumably in Fayette County, in 1800, and was thirteen years of age when the family settled in Greenup County. He began his long business career very early in life. When but a mere boy he carried the U. S. mail on horseback between the Big Sandy River and Western part of Greenup County; at the age of 21 he was captain of a boat that was operated on the Big Sandy; and with Samuel Seaton he engaged in trade on the Ohio and Mississippi Rivers by flatboat. He operated a wood yard and landing where the Ohio river boats stopped for fuel.

He was a shrewd trader and became the owner of several fine farms in Greenup County as well as lands in Missouri and Arkansas.

He was interested in many enterprises: In 1854 he purchased a hotel in Portsmouth, Ohio, later known as the Biggs House, which was destroyed by fire in 1871 and rebuilt in 1872. He was in partnership with John Means and Samuel Cole of Ashland and John Peebles and Benjamin Gaylord of Portsmouth for the purchase of the Lexington and Big Sandy Railroad in 1864, and for the purchase also of the Ashland Coal and Iron Railroad sometime later.

William Biggs m. in Greenup County, October 15, 1827, Lucy Blakemore Davis, daughter of George Naylor Davis and Harriet (Bragg) Davis and granddaughter of Captain Thomas Bragg, Revolutionary War officer, and his wife, Lucy (Blakemore) Bragg.

Children:
FOURTH GENERATION

*6. Andrew Biggs.
*7. William Biggs, Jr.
8. Robinson Biggs.
*9. Thomas Naylor Biggs.
10. Susan Biggs.
*11. James Davis Biggs.
*12. George Nicholas Biggs.
*13. Dr. Romulus Culver Biggs.
*14. Lucy Biggs.
*15. Samuel Green Biggs.
*16. Lola Lloyd Biggs.
*17. Ann Eliza Biggs.

5. ROBINSON MILLS BIGGS; b. in Kentucky, presumably in Fayette County, in 1802; m. in Greenup County, Ann Culver, daughter of John Culver of Grays Branch.

Children:
FOURTH GENERATION

18. Robinson Mills Biggs; d. young.
19. Jane Biggs; m. ——— Young; reside in Ashland.
20. Elizabeth O. Biggs; m. ——— Farrell; reside in Ashland.

6. ANDREW BIGGS; m. in Greenup County, Maria Kouns, daughter of Major John C. Kouns. (See Kouns Family). They moved to Louisville.

Children:
FIFTH GENERATION

21. Mrs. Elizabeth Craveson.
22. Mrs. Mary Musselman.
23. William Biggs.
24. Mrs. Susan Tabler.
25. Mrs. Nancy Stallings.

7. WILLIAM BIGGS, JR., farmer; m. in Greenup County, Rebecca Ann King, daughter of Benjamin and Ann (Wurts) King of Laurel Furnace. They began housekeeping on his father's farm three miles below Greenup; and in 1866 moved to Mount Zion and lived for many years on the farm on which his brother, Thomas Naylor Biggs, had lived, known as the Gravenstein place on account of the large Gravenstein apple orchard thereon. This farm has been owned and operated by the Biggs family for over 100 years.

Children:

FIFTH GENERATION

26. Dr. Robinson Mills Biggs; d., unm.
*27. Maurice King Biggs.
28. Anna Wurts Biggs; d., unm.
29. Lucy Davis Biggs; m. Joseph Randolph of Siloam. They resided in Huntington, West Virginia.
30. Sarah Grandin Biggs; m. James Bullock of Louisville.
31. Helen Rebecca Biggs; d., unm.
32. Winifrede Biggs; m. Dudley Irwin Smith of Huntington, West Virginia; migrated to California. Late in life he retired from farming and she went to Huntington to live. Both were buried in Woodland Cemetery, Ironton, Ohio. Their son, Maurice King Biggs, assumed management of the farm and carried on until his death in 1937. His Widow, Nina,[1] continues to live there and manage the farm.

9. THOMAS NAYLOR BIGGS, farmer; m. Eleanor Humpheys of Carter County; began housekeeping on the farm at Zion which his father, William Biggs, Sr., had purchased from Pleasant Savage, and later moved to the old homestead of his father known as "Oak Lane" on the river three miles below Greenup which has been in the Biggs family since 1839.

Children:

FIFTH GENERATION

*33. William Alexander Biggs.
*34. John Humphreys Biggs.
*35. Ellen Humphreys Biggs.
*36. Lydia Connor Biggs.
*37. Thomas Naylor Biggs, Jr.
*38. Dr. James Davis Biggs.
*39. Romulus Culver Biggs.
*40. Royina Biggs.

11. JAMES DAVIS BIGGS, farmer; m. in Greenup County, Alice Wurts, daughter of George Wurts. They resided on the Wurts farm in the residence built by Hon. John McConnell (See biography in Lewis Family.) Later he purchased the farm and resided there all

his married life. He was a Presbyterian in religion and was a faithful member of the Greenup Union Presbyterian Church for 50 years. The church records as early as 1863 refer to him as ruling elder and frequent reference is made to him as moderator and as a delegate to annual meetings of the Presbytery.

Children: FIFTH GENERATION

*41. Mary Wurts Biggs.
*42. Sallie Russell Biggs.

12. GEORGE NICHOLAS BIGGS; m. Jane Elizabeth Bryson daughter of William and Elizabeth (Lawson) Bryson. They resided on the Bryson homestead until 1881 when they went to Huntington, West Virginia, where he engaged in merchandising.

Children: FIFTH GENERATION

43. Samuel Green Biggs.
44. James Davis Biggs.
45. Elizabeth Bryson Biggs Watts.

13. ROMULUS CULVER BIGGS, physician; practiced his profession in Greenup and in Ashland; m. Emma Brown of Wheelersburg, Ohio. Both were buried there. No children.

14. LUCY BIGGS; m. Dr. Andrew Beardsley of Huntington, West Virginia

Children: FIFTH GENERATION

46. Lola Beardsley; m. Elliott Northcutt, an attorney.
47. Willie Beardsley; m. Frederick McDonald of Huntington, West Virginia.

15. SAMUEL GREEN BIGGS; m. Agnes Peyton of Ripley, Greenbrier County, West Virginia, where they reside.

Children: FIFTH GENERATION

48. Lucy Biggs.
49. Charles Biggs.
50. Agnes Biggs.

16. LOLA LLOYD BIGGS; m. Judge William Thompson of Huntington, West Virginia; she d. young.

Children: FIFTH GENERATION

51. Lucy Thompson.

17. ANN ELIZA BIGGS; m. James Hockaday (See Hockaday Family.)

33. William Alexander Biggs; born in Greenup County, Kentucky, September 4, 1860; reared on a farm; attended public schools and followed agricultural pursuits until he reached the age of 19; removed to Arkansas, 1879, and for three years owned and operated a sawmill in Prescott. Returning to Greenup County in 1882, he resumed farming which he followed for nine years. In 1891 he removed to Greenup and opened a hardware store which he conducted in association with John Taylor Lawson until 1905, when he disposed of his interests to Mr. Lawson and then joined Robert E. Lee Mitchell in the milling business; m., February 18, 1887, Miss Maud Ellis Mitchell, daughter of Shadrack and Frances (Starks) Mitchell of Greenup County.

Mr. Biggs was a Democrat in politics, a member of the Presbyterian Church and affiliated with the Masonic fraternity.

Children:

SIXTH GENERATION

52. Irene Biggs; m. J. B. McCoy of Greenup. Children, Seventh Generation: James, Frances, William and Biggs.

53. Frances Biggs; m. Walter A. Boyer of Russell, Kentucky.

54. Thomas Carlisle Bibbs.

55. Eleanor Biggs; d. December 31, 1919.

56. William Alexander Biggs, Jr., m. Tabitha Blackburn of Williamson, West Virginia.

57. George Nicholas Biggs; m. Miss Martha Diehlman of South Bend, Indiana.

34. JOHN HUMPHREY BIGGS, lumberman, of West Virginia; m. his first cousin, Mary (Molly) Rucker: Children: Lucy, Easton, Lahoma, Maxine and Mabel.

35. ELLEN HUMPHRIES BIGGS; m. in 1884, John Taylor Lawson, farmer and hardware merchant at Greenup, a son of John Taylor Lawson, Sr., and Sarah (Gammon) Lawson. He was b. October 22, 1857; reared on the Lawson farm near Gray's Branch, Greenup County; and was educated at Ashland Academy, Ashland, Kentucky. Children: Katherine, Lucy Margaret, Mary Ellen, William Jacob, James Biggs, Robert Johnson and Winifred.

36. LYDIA CONNOR BIGGS; m. John Thompson Womack. (See Womack Family.)

37. THOMAS NAYLOR BIGGS, JR.; m. Mary De Bard of Greenup. Children: Dr. Alfred Biggs of Chicago; Naylor Biggs of Tiffin, Ohio; and Seaton Biggs, deceased.

38. DR. JAMES DAVIS BIGGS; resided and practiced his profession

in Williamson, West Virginia; m. Adelaide Burchett, daughter of Major D. J. Burchett of Louisa, Kentucky. (See biography of D. J. Burchett.)

39. ROMULUS CULVER BIGGS; studied law; d. in young manhood.

40. ROYINA BIGGS; m. James F. Taylor; resided in Columbus, Ohio. Children: Jack, James, Margaret Ellen and Mary Lou (twins).

41. MARY WURTS BIGGS; m. Harry Renick of Ashland.

42. SALLIE RUSSELL BIGGS; m. Sturdis G. Bates of Riverton, Kentucky, a son of Horace Watson Bates and Fannie (Goodwin) Bates, natives of Massachusetts. Horace Watson Bates came from Boston, Massachusetts, to Riverton, Kentucky, in 1868 to take over the general management and vice-presidency of the Eastern Kentucky Railway and lived at Riverton until his death in 1901. They were the parents also of Alice Bates, b. at Plymouth, Massachusetts, 1864; m. Joseph Kouns Pollock of Greenup in 1902. (See Kouns Family.) They resided in Cincinnati.

Sturgis Goodwin Bates was born in Cincinnati, Ohio, 1866; succeeded his father with the Eastern Kentucky Railway Company, in the same capacity and continued until the abandonment of the railroad in 1928. He was m. to Miss Sally Russell Biggs in 1899. They resided at Riverton for some time but finally removed to Ashland where they presently reside.

Children:

SIXTH GENERATION

58. Sturgis G. Bates II; b. at Riverton in 1907; is m. and resides in Atlanta, Georgia.

Children:

SEVENTH GENERATION

59. Sturgis G. Bates III.
60. Alice Bates.

---

[1] Nina Mitchell Biggs (Mrs. Maurice King Biggs) and Mabel Lee Mackoy are authors of an excellent History of Greenup County, Kentucky, published by the Franklin Press, Louisville, Kentucky, 1951.

BLACK FAMILY OF KNOX COUNTY

1. ALEXANDER BLACK was the ancestor of a branch of the Black family that settled in Knox County, Kentucky, in pioneer days. He was a native of Ireland of Scotch-Irish descent and was reared and educated in his native land from which shortly after his marriage he emigrated with his young wife to America and established his home in South Carolina where he continued associated with the farming industry. He removed to the eastern part of Tennessee and later came as a pioneer into Knox County, Kentucky. He instituted reclamation and development of one of the finest estates in Knox County; was influential in public affairs and general community life and was a commanding figure in connection with early stages of civic and material development and progress of Knox County where he continued to reside until the time of his death.

Children:

2. John C. Black, extensive and successful farmer; b. in South Carolina, 1804; d. in Knox County, Kentucky, 1876; originally a Whig in politics but later a Republican; was justice of the peace for several years, the only public office he ever held; m. in Clay County, Kentucky, Miss Clarissa Jones, b. in 1807 and d. in Knox County, 1862.

Children:

3. Permelia Black; b. 1827; m. Hiram Jones; lived in Laurel County, Kentucky.

4. Isaac J. Black, farmer; b. 1829; was a captain in a Kentucky regiment, Union Army in the Civil War.

5. Samuel Black, prosperous farmer; b. 1831; removed to Madison County, Kentucky, where he lived at time of his death in 1919.

6. Alexander Black, farmer; b. 1832; removed to Richmond, Kentucky.

7. Rhoda Black; b. 1834; m. Nathan McBee, farmer; resided in Laurel County Kentucky.

8. David Black, farmer; b. 1836; d. 1916; resided in Madison County, Kentucky.

9. Isabella Black; b. 1838; d. in Barbourville; m. John Brogan, who engaged in banking business in Oklahoma City, Oklahoma.

10. John A. Black, banker; b. 1842; resided in Barbourville where he was a leading merchant and was influential in reorganizing the private banking business founded by John A. Black into the National

Bank of John A. Black of which he became the first president and served for a number of years.

11. Hiram Black, farmer; resided in Knox County.

12. Alabama Black; m. William Hopper; farmer; resided and d. in Laurel County.

13. Hon. James Dixon Black, lawyer, and one-time Governor and Lieutenant-Governor of Kentucky, was b. September 24, 1849, on the old homestead of his father on Big Richland Creek, nine miles east of Barbourville, Knox County; educated in the public schools of Knox County, private schools in Barbourville and at Tusculum College in Tennessee from which he was graduated in 1872 with degree of Bachelor of Arts; taught in the public schools of Knox County for two years in the meantime studying law; admitted to the bar in August, 1874 and maintained a place of acknowledged leadership as a member of the bar in Eastern Kentucky, his practice being of representative order in connection with many civil and criminal cases of major importance and extended to the Court of Appeals of Kentucky and the U. S. District Courts.

A staunch Democrat, he was a leader in the councils and campaign activities of his party and was honored and elected by the people to many offices of honor and trust: He was State representative from Knox and Whitley Counties, 1876; served as School Commissioner of Knox County, 1884-5; president of Union College, 1911--12; first assistant Attorney General of Kentucky, 1912; Lieutenant-Governor of Kentucky, 1915-May, 1919; Governor of Kentucky, May 1919-Dec., 1919; Chief Prohibition Enforcement Officer, 1920.

Among the real estate holdings of Governor Black were his fine home property at corner of Main & High Streets in Barbourville and 2,000 acres of coal and other mineral lands in Whitley, Bell and Knox Counties. He was president of the National Bank of John A. Black for several years and a director of the Barbourville Cemetery Company.

Governor Black was a Democrat in politics and he and Mrs. Black were members of the Methodist Episcopal Church. He was a member of Mountain Lodge No. 187 F & A. M. of Barbourville — sometimes serving as Master; member of Barbourville Chapter No. 137, Royal Arch Masons; affiliated with the council of Royal and Select Masters, of London, Kentucky; affiliated with the Ryan Commandery No. 17, Knight Templars (York Rite) at Danville, Kentucky; was a member of Korsair Temple of the Ancient Arabic Order Nobles of the Mystic Shrine in Louisville.

JAMES DIXON BLACK was m. at Barbourville, December, 1875, to

Miss Mary Janette Pitser, daughter of T. J. and Mary (Gloss) Pitser from Virginia.

Children:

14. Pitser D. Black, lawyer; b. 1881; was graduated from Centre College with degree of A. B. and subsequently attended the law department of University of Virginia; was associated in law practice with his father.

15. Gertrude D. Black; was graduated from Woman's College at Danville Kentucky, with degree of A.B.

16. Georgia Black; was graduated from Woman's College with degree of A.B.; m. H. H. Owens, lawyer, of Barbourville.

BLAIR FAMILY OF PENNSYLVANIA, VIRGINIA, MARYLAND AND EASTERN KENTUCKY

The Blair family of the United States is of Scottish extraction. The Blars or Blairs may be traced back to the days of the turbulent feudalist wars between England and Scotland. Among them in Scotland are the Blairs of Agrshire, of Balthyock in Perthshire, of Wigton, and of Renfrew. Documentary evidence indicates that one William deBlair lived in 1205 during the reign of William the Lion. One genealogist has traced the Belairs from France to Scotland and believed they originated in France. Those were the day of royal fiefs, when nobles and ecclesiastics vied with each other for favors of the crown. The Blairs shared in some of these titles, and still point with pride to Blair castle in Perthshire. They were of midland Scottish blood and temperament, "bonnie fichters," and rebels. A Bryce Blair was treacherously slain by the English one year before King Edward called his Model Parliament; another Bryce Blair of high lineage escaped with his wife and daughter (1625) in a coal sloop to Ireland. There he possessed himself of a farm of four hundred acres near Carrickfergus. The Blairs led the inhabitants of Derry in the struggle against King James II, in 1689, until King William III gave them relief. Valiant Colonel Jamie Blair was there, and so was Lieutenant David Blair. The former emigrated to America and died in New England in 1773. In the rebellion of 1798 Samuel Blair led the sons of "Hearts O' Steel."

Descendants of the Blairs still live in Ireland, where, as Ulstermen, they staunchly oppose Home Rule.

One branch of the Blair family of the United States is traceable to the Bryce Blair who escaped from Scotland to Ireland in the coal sloop. During the first half of the 18th century one of these Blairs named Samuel became the father of many sons and daughters; sons, William, Samuel, John and James; and daughters: Elizabeth, Esther, Martha and Mary. These children were born in County Arenagh, Ireland, and were cousins to James Logan, Secretary to William Penn of Pennsylvania. Samuel Blair, the father, was, probably of Ballyvallough. Six of the children emigrated to America just when is not definitely known. Like many of their fellow countrymen, they followed the main tide of Scotch Irish migration to New York and Pennsylvania and sought their haven of prosperity in old Bucks County, Pennsylvania, where they were welcomed in the home of the scholarly Dr. William Tennent, a distinguished minister of the Presbyterian Church, and schoolmaster, who, in 1727, established the "Log College". Samuel Blair and John Blair became students at the Log College and subsequently became eminent ministers of the Presbyterian Church, and teachers.

1. REV. SAMUEL BLAIR was b. June 14, 1712; was educated at the

Log College; was licensed to preach in the fall of 1733, and preached in New Jersey. Six years later he established a seminary of learning at Fagg's Manor which he conducted to 1757, date of death. His descendants mainly remained in the East.

2. REV. JOHN BLAIR was b. in 1718; was educated at the Log College; was ordained to preach the faith of the New Lights (Presbyterian Church) in 1742 and preached in Pennsylvania and made expeditions to and organized churches in Virginia, in, among other places, Augusta county. At the death of his brother Samuel, he took charge at Fagg's Manor. He was called to the chair of divinity at Princeton, 1766, and taught and preached there and acted as vice-president of that university. Subsequently he accepted the pastorate of the Presbyterian Church at Walkkill (now Montgomery), New York, where he died December 8, 1771.

The Rev. John Blair married Elizabeth Durbarrow. To this union twelve children were born, one of whom was a son ———.

3. James Blair who was b. at Flagg's Manor in Pennsylvania in 1762. After receiving the best education which the early frontier schools and his scholarly father could give him, he became a student at Princeton; he read law; removed to Abingdon, Virginia, and practiced law there; was elected to the state Legislative Assembly as a member representing a western county; and became as active in the politics of his state as his location permitted.

Seeking better fields to the westward, he migrated over Boone's Wilderness Trail to Kentucky and established himself at Frankfort, the State Capitol, where he passed a perfunctory examination and was admitted to the bar. He served as attorney general for Kentucky for twenty years, 1796-1816.

While residing in Virginia James Blair m. Elizabeth Smith, one of the four daughters of Francis Smith and his wife, Ann (Preston) Smith, daughter of John Preston, the immigrant, a Virginia planter of Scotch-Irish extraction, founder of the famous Preston family, the history of which has been traced back in England to 1165, and is probably as pure Anglo-Saxon as any family in America. John Preston, the immigrant, m. in Ireland, Elizabeth Patton, sister of Colonel James Patton, wealthy ship-owner, who received a grant of 120,000 acres of land in Augusta county, Virginia. They had four children other than Ann: Colonel William Preston, who m. Susanna Smith of Hanover county, Virginia; Letitia Preston, who m. Colonel Robert Breckenridge of Virginia; Margaret Preston, who m. Rev. John Brown, a Presbyterian minister; and Mary Preston, who m. John Howard of Virginia. Some of these Prestons, Breckenridges and Browns emigrated to and settled in Kentucky and some of them became distinguished statesmen, diplomats, lawyers, judges, physicians, and preachers. Other Descendants of John Preston, the immigrant,

m. into the families of Marshall, Madison, Cary, Wallace, Lewis, Trigg, Peyton, McDowell, Floyd, Buchanan, Johnson, Carrington, Crittenden, Grayson, Gibson, Humphreys, Hart, Jessup, Gist, Lee, Taylor, Freemont, Randolph, Hampton, Wickliffe, Campbell, Porter, Cabell, Benton and many other prominent families of Virginia, Kentucky, Tennessee and the southern states.

3. JAMES BLAIR and his wife, Elizabeth (Smith) Blair, had seven children of whom a son ———.

4. FRANCIS PRESTON BLAIR, editor, politician and political writer, was b. at Abingdon, Washington county, Virginia, April 12, 1791. Owing to a deficiency in his vocal powers he did not follow in his father's footsteps and adopt the law as a profession. However, he studied law was admitted to the bar but never practiced. He distinguished himself as a student of rhetoric and as a linguist. He was educated at Transylvania University, Lexington, Kentucky, where he was graduated with honors in 1811. Having volunteered for service in the War of 1812, when Vincennes was reached on the march to the Canadian border, he became incapacitated for military service by reason of hemorrhage of the lungs and his commander, Governor Shelby, on whose staff he was serving, was forced to leave him behind. With a view of improving his health he settled on a farm on Bensons Creek, a small stream near Frankfort.

He had already formed definite conclusions on the political issues of the day and vigorously and ably supported these conclusions in phamphlets and in the press. He opposed the rechartering of the United States Bank; and he and his father, who was then attorney general of Kentucky, prepared the argument to sustain the state law passed to expel the United States Bank from Kentucky through state taxation. He affiliated with and vigorously supported the Relief Party (New Court Party) in the state and was chosen clerk of the new Court of Appeals which was established pursuant of an act of the Legislature which had, by legislative enactment, abolished the existing Court of Appeals. He seized and held for a time the records of the Court.

Having removed to Washington, D. C., in December, 1830, he founded *The Globe*, at Washington, which was made the Democratic party organ by President Jackson. He edited *The Globe* until the early days of President Polk's administration when he retired to his plantation home at Silver Spring, Maryland, near Washington, where he d. October 18, 1876, in his eighty-sixth year.

FRANCIS PRESTON BLAIR m. in the Governor's Mansion at Frankfort, Kentucky, Eliza Violet Gist, daughter of Colonel Nathaniel Gist of Kentucky, and granddaughter of Christopher Gist, noted pioneer. They had four children of whom two sons ———.

5. Montgomery Blair, lawyer, judge, statesman, was b. at Frankfort, Kentucky, May 10, 1813; educated in the public schools of Frankfort; entered Transylvania University, Lexington, Kentucky, but left before graduation and entered the military academy at West Point from which graduated in 1835 when he was commissioned a lieutenant in the Army to serve in the Seminole Indian war; resigned his commission in 1836 and reentered Transylania University to study law; entered the law office of Senator Thomas Hart Benton, at St. Louis, Missouri, 1837; was appointed United States Attorney General of Missouri, 1841; served as mayor of St. Louis, 1842-43; and judge of the Court of Common Pleas, St. Louis, during the Mexican War which position he resigned to practice law; removed to Washington, D. C. in 1853 to practice before the United States Supreme Court; represented Dred Scott before the Supreme Court (1857); was solicitor general of the United States Court of Claims, 1853; postmaster general in the cabinet of President Lincoln, 1861 to September 23, 1864, when his resignation was accepted by reason of pressure exerted by the radical element of the Republican party. He d. July 27, 1883.

6. Francis Preston Blair, Jr., soldier and statesman, was b. at Lexington, Kentucky, February 19, 1821; accompanied his parents to Washington, D. C. and was educated in the Washington schools; entered Princeton University in 1841 but left to study law; practiced law at St. Louis, 1842, with his brother, Montgomery; went West and was at Fort Bent when the Mexican War broke out and General Kearney appointed him the first attorney-general of New Mexico Territory; returning to Missouri he acted with the Free Soil Party and warmly supported Senator Benton; elected to the Missouri Legislature by the Free Soilers in 1852 and 1854; elected to the U. S. Congress from Missouri in 1856 and reelected in 1860; raised seven regiments and was commissioned brigadier-general in 1861 and major general in 1862, Union Army, and served under General Sherman; reelected to Congress in 1864; acted with the Democrats after the war and was unsuccessful candidate for president in the Democratic convention of 1868 but was nominated for vice president by the convention on ticket with General Horatio Seymour for president; again elected to the state Legislature of Missouri; and elected U. S. Senator from Missouri in 1871. He d. April 9, 1875. Missouri has placed his statue in the Hall of Fame, Washington, D. C., by the side of another great Missourian, Senator Thomas Hart Benton, his life-long friend and kinsman.

The descendants of (1). Rev. Samuel Blair and (2). Rev. John Blair have been scattered over the whole of the United States. The states of Kentucky, Virginia and Pennsylvania lead in the number of these descendants. Descendants other than (3). James Blair settled in southwestern, Virginia.

BLAIR FAMILY OF EASTERN KENTUCKY

Reputable genealogists and writers have stated that (*1) George Blair and (*2) Noble Blair, brothers, descendants of Rev. Samuel Blair or Rev. John Blair emigrated to Kentucky when young men and settled near the mouth of Big Mud Lick, Floyd county, now Johnson county. They are the progenitors of a large family of Blairs of Eastern Kentucky. George Blair purchased a large tract of land on Big Paint Creek opposite the present-day Paintsville. On this farm he erected a large hewn-log house on the bluff opposite the water-mill subsequently built by John Stafford. After conveying this land to the Staffords, George Blair and Noble Blair purchased all the land on the Middle Fork of Jennie's Creek, George taking the land on the upper reaches of the stream. Here near the head of the stream, about seven miles from Paintsville, he erected a large hewn-log house in which he lived practically the remainder of his life.

1. GEORGE BLAIR, farmer, was b. in Lee county, Virginia; migrated to Kentucky about 1816. He was a strong character, rugged and independent. In young manhood he possessed great physical strength and loved and participated in the rude sports of pioneer days. He descended from a long line of strict Presbyterians but there being no organization of that church in Eastern Kentucky, he united with the Primitive Baptist Church; and he followed Rev. Wallace Bailey in the secession movement which resulted in the formation of the United Baptist Church. Though a strict and honored member of the church, it is said that he sometimes drank whiskey sufficient in quantity to cause him to become boastful and jolly of which conduct he always repented in great humiliation when rebuked by his wife in the form of a curtain lecture which he dreaded more than any punishment that might have been inflicted.

George Blair m. in Floyd county, Mary Fairchild, daughter of Abiud Fairchild, a Revolutionary War soldier.

Children:

3. John Blair resided on the Louis Power farm at the ford of Licking River.

4. Levi Blair, m. in Floyd county, June 4, 1831, Rachel Cantrill. He was a shoemaker, trader in live stock, very thrifty and keen-witted; lived on the head of Barnett's Creek. They had a large family.

5. Brittain Blair, m. in Floyd county, August 26, 1841, Malinda Spradlin, daughter of the pioneer James Spradlin. He owned a large farm, opposite the farm of his father-in-law, where he d. and was buried. After his death his widow, Malinda, m. Dr. Isaac Rice.

6. WASHINGTON (WATT) BLAIR, m. in Floyd county, November 8, 1840, M. Spradlin, daughter of the pioneer James Spradlin. He lived on the head waters of Upper Twin Branch. It has been said that he was a genius and a sort of rustic Samuel Johnson whom he resembled in personal appearance as well as having similar mental traits; that he ate his meals with his hat on his head much as a sovereign wearing his crown; that he was brusque and contentious, often abrupt, over-bearing and imperious but that he had a kind heart and was fond of children; that he exacted implicit obedience of his children even after they had married, left home and established homes of their own, maintaining that such was in accordance with the teachings of the Bible; that he was, indeed, a patriarch, surrounded by a large family of married children, all paying him a sort of homage; that he was quaint and droll and in conversation eloquent and pleasing; that he did not talk much in public. His home was his castle.

7. JAMES BLAIR, emigrated to Minnesota and from thence to Washington state.

8. REBECCA BLAIR, m. in Floyd county, February 24, 1831, Henry Connelley (See Connelley Family).

9. WILLIAM BLAIR, Baptist minister, m. in Floyd county, March 26, 1835, Sarah Spradlin, daughter of the pioneer James Spradlin. He built a mill in the Licking River just above the present day Salyersville, Magoffin county, where he lived until the state purchased and removed the mill under the impression that the river would be made navigable. Subsequently he removed to the mouth of Rockhouse, Johnson county, where he died. After the death of his wife, Sarah, he m. Edith Montgomery.

10. NOBLE BLAIR, m. in Floyd County, July 10, 1840, Tillithy (Talitha) Stambaugh; lived on the head of Middle Fork of Jennies Creek. They had a large family.

11. CLARINDA BLAIR, m. in Floyd County, John Stambrugh, reputedly a very polite and well bred person. Issue: a son, Buchanan Stambaugh.

12. MARY BLAIR.

*13. ASA BLAIR, m. in Floyd County, Mahala Spradlin, daughter of Josiah Spradlin and grand daughter of the pioneer James Spradlin. Issue: Alexander Blair and Ellen Blair.

2. NOBLE BLAIR, m. ———.

Children:

*14. John Blair.

15. Hayden Blair, m. Mary Harve.

16. Margaret Blair, m., in Floyd County, March 14, 1839, John Conley.

14. JOHN BLAIR, m. ———.

Children:

17. Andrew Blair, m. ——— Phelphrey.

18. Frankie Jane Blair, m., first, ——— Fairchild, and, secondly, ——— Rowland. No issue.

19. ? Elizabeth Blair, m., in Floyd County, ——— William Adams. No issue.

20. ——— Blair, m. ———-Spears.

17. ANDREW BLAIR, m. ———.

Children:

21. John Milton Blair, m. Dicy Salyer Rice.

22. Sarah Blair, m. Caney Webb.

23. Pat. Blair, m. ——— Conley.

24. Artie Blair, m. Enoch Spears.

BOONE FAMILY OF GREENUP COUNTY

The Boones (Bohuns), Norsemen chiefs, carrying their arms, the White Swan crest above two Lions rampant, aided in founding dynasties in Normandy and England. Prominent in the conquest of England in 1066 by William the Conqueror, Boones became a ruling family in England. A branch of the family for three generations (1600-1717) lived in or near Exeter, Devonshire, England, where *1. George Boone III, son of George Boone, II and his wife, Sarah Uppey, was born at Stoak in 1666. He married, in 1689, Mary Maugridge of Bradnich, Devonshire, born in 1669, daughter of John Maugridge and Mary Milton, his wife. Their children, born in Bradnich between 1690 and 1711 were * 2. George IV, * 3. Sarah, * 4. Squire, (Daniel's father), 5. Mary, 6. John, 7. Joseph, 8. Benjamin, 9. James and 10. Samuel.

Always wanderers, members of the Boone family came to America in 1610 when Dr. Lawrence and Lord De La Ware reached Virginia. 2. George, IV, 3. Sarah and 4. Squire Boone were in America prior to 1713, but the parents of the other children did not arrive at Philadelphia until October 10, 1717. 1. George Boone, III, and family located at North Wales, Philadelphia County (now Montgomery County) becoming members of the Gwynedd Meeting of the Society of Friends. After three years they moved to Oley Township of Berks County, a part of which the Boones later organized and named Exeter Township of Berks County. He purchased lands six miles due east from Reading and in 1720 built a log house to which was added in 1730 a stone addition that is still in use. George Boone III purchased many tracts of land (as did his sons) extending their investments to Maryland and Virginia. He was part owner of Poole Forge, the first iron making in Pennsylvania. He and son, George IV built the first flour mill in Berks County. George Boone IV was especially prominent: teacher near Philadelphia for many years; a good mathematician and taught several branches of English learning; justice of the peace of Philadelphia County; surveyed many townships of Berks County.[1]

Daniel Boone's maternal grandfather was Edward Morgan of near Bela County, Merionshire, Wales. It is probable that his wife's name was Elizabeth. In 1691 he lived in Moyamensing District, Philadelphia, where his son, Daniel Morgan, who became a Quaker preacher, was born. About 1700 he moved to Towamencin Township near Gwynedd and joined the Quaker meeting of that name. His children were: 1. Morgan, 2. William, 3 Elizabeth, 4. Daniel, 5. Margaret, 6. John, 7. Joseph and 8. Sarah. Edward Morgan bought several tracts of land, as did his sons. All of them were farmers. An old record of the Gwynedd Meeting states that Sarah Morgan Boone was a "sister to the father of Col. Daniel Morgan of the Revolution Rifle Men", known to fame as General Daniel Morgan of the Virginia Line. The Morgans were substantial men of some means, doing their full share in the development of Pennsylvania.[1]

4. Squire Boone m. Sarah Morgan, October 4, 1720. Their children were: 5. Sarah, 6. Israel, 7. Samuel, 8. Jonathan, 9. Elizabeth, *10. Daniel, 11. Mary, 12. George, 13. Edward, 14. Squire, and 15. Hannah.

The first ten years of their married life were spent near Gwyneed; a part of it in Berks County, but in 1730 Squire Boone bought 250 acres of land in Exeter Township (then Oley) where he built a stone house.

Chronology of 10. Daniel Boone's Life

1734, b. in Exeter Township, Berks County, Pennsylvania, November 2, 1834 (new style); attended his uncle's school; was a hunter from childhood.

1750, May 1, moved with family to near Winchester, Virginia; in connection with hunting, explored the Blue Ridge Mountain region.

1753, moved with parents to a farm on the Yadkin River in Davidson County, North Carolina; hunted and explored along the border between Kentucky and Tennessee.

1755, joined Captain Dobbs' North Carolina Company in General Braddock's campaign against the Indians at Ft. Duquesne. Many of Braddock's men were massacred. Boone was a waggoner and escaped on one of his horses.

1756, August 14, m. Rebecca Bryan, b. January 9, 1739, daughter of Joseph Bryan of North Carolina.

1759, Due to Indian outbreak took his wife and two children to Virginia, near Fredericksburg. His parents went to Georgetown, Maryland, now District of Columbia, where they remained for three years.

1760. Joined Col. Hugh Waddell's North Carolina Regiment in War with Cherokee Indians. Peace resulting, he brought his family back to the Yadkin.

The Founding of Kentucky

1760, Joined Col. Hugh Waddell's North Carolina Regiment in War in Kentucky and Tennessee.

1764, Explored in Kentucky, reaching Rockcastle River.

1765, Explored the Altamaha River in Georgia; with his brother, Squire, and other hunters, he reached Pensacola, Florida, where he purchased a lot; his wife refused to go there.

1767, With William Hill and probably his brother, Squire, he explored the West Fork of Big Sandy River.

1768, In March, with Hill and Brother, Squire, he returned to the Yadkin where he met John Finley (or Findlay) an Indian trader who had been hunting in Kentucky. Boone and Findlay were companions in arms in Braddock's campaign against Ft. Duquesne.

1769, May 1st, taking with him John Finley, a brother-in-law, John Stuart (or Steward) and three other Yadkin settlers, Joseph Holden, James Mooney and William Cooley (or Cool), Boone left "the peaceful habitation" on the upper Yadkin and began the historic journey "in quest of the country of Kentucky". Probably their route lay across the Blue Ridge, Stone and Iron Mountains and through the valleys of the Holston and Clinch Rivers into Powells Valley, where they discovered Finley's promised trail through Cumberland Gap. Passing through this gap and along the Warriors' Path, they established their first permanent "station camp" on Red River in what is now Estill County, from which they hunted singly or in couples. On December 22nd, while returning from hunting, they were surprised and captured by a large party of Shawnees, led by Captain Will. The captives were forced to pilot the Indians to their main camp, where the savages, after robbing them of all their pelts and supplies and leaving them inferior guns and little ammunition, set off for the North, admonishing them not to come again to the Indians' hunting ground. Boone and Stuart retook two of the horses and fled with them at top speed. However, they were recaptured two days later and made to endure many humiliations. Subsequently, about January 4, 1770, they made good their escape by plunging into a dense cane brake.

Meanwhile Finley, Holden, Mooney and Cooley were homeward bound, convinced that Boone and Stuart had perished in their rash attempt to recover their property from the Indians. At the same time, Squire Boone, in company with Alexander Neely, whom he had accidently encountered while crossing the mountains, was hurrying Westward along the Warriors' Path bringing horses and supplies, as had been agreed. The two parties met not far from Cumberland Gap; and in view of the supposed death of Boone and Stuart, all six decided to return East without delay when the fugitives staggered into camp weary and famished and in tatters. Finley, Holden, Mooney and Cooley continued on their way to the settlements and the Boones, Stuart and Neely proceeded into the Kentucky wilderness and were soon afterwards building a new camp not far from the scene of the recent adventure.

From one of his long, solitary hunts, Stuart never returned; and it was not until five years later while cutting out the Wilderness Road for the Transylvania Company that Boone and his companions discovered, near the old crossing of Rockcastle River, in a standing hollow sycamore tree, a few human bones and a powder-horn marked with Stuart's name. The wilderness never gave up its tragic secret.

Soon afterwards Neely returned to the settlements satisfied with his share of the winter's hunting, leaving the Boones who continued to explore, hunt and trap. Subsequently due to the depletion of supplies, it was necessary for Squire Boone to return to the settlements twice for these necessities, leaving Daniel alone in the wilderness, who proceeded to make those remarkable solitary explorations of Kentucky—which gave him immortality—through the valley of Kentucky, the Licking and along the Ohio as far as the Falls, and the Big Bone Lick.

Perturbed after a time by Squire's failure to rejoin him at the appointed time on return from the second trip, Daniel started toward the settlements in quest of him, and was fortunate enough to encounter him on the trail; December, 1770. The Boones once more plunged into the wilderness determined to conclude their explorations by examining the regions watered by the Green and Cumberland Rivers and their tributaries. Authorities state that in the Green River region they encountered that party of hunters from Virginia known as the "Long Hunters" and spent some time with them. The Boones broke camp for the return to the Yadkin in March 1771, their horses laden with furs. The return trip was by way of the Warriors' Path, Cumberland Gap and Powells Valley. When in Powells Valley, a few miles from the westmost settlements they were captured by a war-party of Northern Indians and were robbed of all their pelts and guns and thereby left poorer than when the long hunt began two years before. But despite all his hardships and losses Boone had achieved the ambition of years: he had seen Kentucky which he "esteemed a second paradise". Another notable thing had been done: He and/or his brother Squire built a cottage. A stone marked "Squire Boone, 1770," found near Boonesborough, indicates that the cottage was at or near the site of the historic fort.

1771, Disposing of his property in North Carolina, Boone organized a colony of six families, including his own, and the families of Squire Boone (Daniel's brother), James, Morgan, Jr., and William Bryan, brothers, and Jonas Sparks; and on September 25, they left the Yadkin for Kentucky. In Powells Valley forty resolute men joined them and as the party neared Cumberland Gap a number who had fallen in the rear were fired upon (October 10th) by Indians and six killed, including Boone's young son, James. Boone and some others were in favor of going on to Kentucky, but a majority ruled against this and the entire party retraced their steps to the settlements on Clinch River where, according to some authorities, "the colony waited for two years before reaching its destination."

1774, Governor Dunmore of Virginia commissioned Daniel Boone to undertake a journey through the wilderness, and recall all hunters and surveying parties, in view of Indian hostilities. Boone selected Michael Stoner for his companion in this hazardous service. They set out in June; found Floyd surveying for Washington; sped on to where Harrod and his men were building Harrodstown; and reached Bullitt's party at the Falls of the Ohio, All these were gotten out except one man, Hancock Taylor, whom the Indians killed. Boone and Stoner returned undetected, having traveled 800 miles in sixty-two days. Boone was placed in command of More's fort in the Clinch River valley. He was not in the battle of Point Pleasant October 10th, but at the time was the commander of three frontier garrisons, believed to have been the three Greenbriar Forts.[2]

1775. Boone's discoveries and explorations aroused the interests of capitalists. In Virginia they were headed by Governor Dunmore and the statesman, Patrick Henry. A rival, the Transylvania Company, was organized by Judge Richard Henderson, of North Carolina, a friend of Boone and his lawyer in times of need. All these parties sought to secure title to the lands of Boone's explorations of 1769-71, the Governor by surveys and war and Henderson by purchase from the Indians. As representative of the Transylvania Company, Boone arranged a pow wow of 1200 Cherokee Indians, resulting in a treaty signed March 27th at Sycamore Shoals on the Wautaga River, a tributary of the Holston, in what is now East Tennessee, whereby the Cherokees sold to the Company for $50,000, paid in merchandise and supplies, all the lands south of the Kentucky River.

To meet the needs of the increasing colonies, Boone was chosen to select a seat of authority and to open a trace or road to it. He gathered around him a party, composed of Squire Boone, Richard Calloway, John Kennedy and eighteen others, and was joined by Captain Twetty, with eight men, making thirty in all. The trace or road began at a point on the Holston River. All went well until March 20th when the party had reached a point about fifteen miles south of Boonesborough when fired on by Indians. Captain Twetty and Felix Walker were badly wounded and a negro of the former was killed. On the 27th of March another attack was made on Boone's party, and five were killed and wounded. Captain Twetty died on the 28th of March. Proceeding, Boone and his men on April 1st reached the desired spot, believed by some authority to be that of his home of 1770, on the south bank of the Kentucky River and mouth of Otter Creek, and began the construction of Ft. Boonesborough. Judge Henderson and party arrived, April 26th and were "saluted with a running fire of about twenty-five guns, all there were then in the fort." On May 23rd, Henderson, as governor or proprietor, called a meeting of the first legislative assembly of the Western Territory to assemble at the capital, Ft. Boonesborough, to enact necessary laws. Boone was a member of this legislative assembly and when its session was over he hurried back to Clinch River for his famiy. They reached Boonesborough September 26th. With evident pride Boone records "My wife and daughter were the first white women to stand on the banks of the Kentucky River."

1776-1777, Boonesborough was constantly menaced and frequently attacked. On May 23rd a large party of Indians attacked the fort; three men were wounded but not mortally. May 26th a party went out to hunt for Indians.

Virginia recognized Captain Boone and sent him powder. Boone led the party of men in rescuing the two Calloway girls, and his daughter, Jemima, who had been captured by Indians on July 14th.

1777, April 24th Ft. Boonesborough was beseiged by 100 Indians under British direction. Boone was shot down with a bullet in his leg. His life was saved by Simon Kenton who carried him into the fort where he continued to direct the defense.

1778, In January Boone led a party of thirty men to make salt at Lower Blue Licks. Returning to the fort alone, he was captured by a large party of Indians who were marching against Boonesborough. Realizing that the fort was unprepared to resist, he offered to surrender the salt-makers. This strategy saved the fort. The captives were taken to the English fort for the offered bounty. Boone, whom the Indians refused to sell, was adopted as son by Chief Blackfish of the Shawnee tribe who named him Big Turtle and took him to the Indian camp. Although treated well he was guarded too closely to permit escape.

1779, In June the Indians assembled 400 of their best warriors to attack Boonesborough. On June 6th Boone started for the fort with the swiftest Indian runners at his heels and ran the intervening 160 miles in four days with but a single meal. Arriving at the fort, he took command and prepared for seige. On September 8th more than 400 trained Indian warriors led the seige. Captain De Quindre, a French officer, and the Indian Chief Blackfish led the attacking forces. The seige lasted for eleven days. Virginia honored Boonesborough with designation of "town for the reception of traders" and promoted Boone from Captain to the rank of major.

1780. On his way from Yadkin, North Carolina, to Richmond, Virginia, to purchase Kentucky land warrants, Boone was robbed of $20,000 in Continental script, his own money and that of others intrusted to him for investment. Though the loss was severe, Boone was appointed lieutenant colonel of the newly organized Fayette County, Kentucky; also was made deputy surveyor under Colonel Thomas Marshall. Edward Boone, his brother, was killed by Indians; Daniel escaped.

1781, Boone was elected to represent Fayette County in the Virginia General Assembly. In April Indians attacked Squire Boone's station, badly wounding Captain Squire Boone.

1782. August 15th British and Indians beseiged Bryan's Station for two days. Col. Boone led Boonesborough troops to the rescue. The Indians retreated to the Blue Licks, the troops following. Disregarding the warning of Colonel Boone, the Kentuckians followed the hot-headed officer, Major McGary, into an ambuscade, resulting in the killing of 70 men. Covering the retreat of others, Boone was the last to leave. His son, Israel, was slain while protecting his father. Col. Boone's appeal to the Governor of Virginia resulted in the expedition of Gen. George Rogers Clark against the Shawnee tribes and their confederates. Boone was a member of the expedition. Col. Boone erected Boone's Station near Athens, Kentucky, which he abandoned in December 1782, when he learned it was on the Madison Military Survey.

1783, He built another station on Marble Creek whence he moved in January.

1786, Col. Boone, having lost his lands in Kentucky, due principally to "claim-jumpers", he moved from Limestone (now Maysville) to Point Pleasant, Virginia, now West Virginia, about 1786, as is evidenced by a deed executed at that place by him and his wife on April 28, 1786. He probably moved up the river to site of Charleston about 1788 or 89. He lived on the south side of the river nearly opposite the original salt spring. On October 6, 1789, when Kanawha County was organized, he was made lieutenant colonel of the militia. He was elected as State representative from Kanawha County in 1791; attended the session at Richmond and returned on foot.[3] He did much surveying in 1791, 1795 and 1798, the last survey made in Kanawha County and probably the last ever made being on September 8, 1798.[4]

1799, Col. Boone left Kanawha County the latter part of 1798 or the early part of 1799 and moved to that part of Mason County, Kentucky, which was included in Greenup County on its formation in 1803. He bought land near present Riverton where he lived until the Fall of 1799 when he went to Missouri.[5]

1799, In September, on the invitation of the Spanish Government Boone moved to then upper Louisiana. He received from that government a grant of 1000 arpens (acres) of land in the Femme Osage district (now St. Charles County, Missouri). Here he built his final home, a modest cottage of logs. Spain having further honored Boone by appointing him synic (magistrate), he held court under a large elm tree known to history as "Boone's Judgement Tree." With the Louisiana Purchase by the United States, Boone again found his title to his land bad, but to the credit of the United States, on February 10, 1814, the Congress passed an act confirming the Spanish title.

His beloved wife Rebecca died March 18, 1814. After the death of his wife, Boone made his home with his daughter, Jemima, Mrs. Flanders Callaway, in Warren County, Missouri. Occasionally he visited his sons, Daniel M. and Nathan (both of whom reached the rank of colonel).

1820, On September 26, Daniel Boone died at the home of his son Nathan in St. Charles County, where he had arrived some days previously. He was laid to rest beside his wife. The Missouri Constitutional Convention, then in session, adjourned out of respect to his memory and the members thereof wore badges of mourning for thirty days.

A nephew who knew him well, describes Boone thus: He was five feet, eight or nine inches high, stout, strong made, light hair, blue eyes, wide mouth, thin lips, a nose a little on the Roman order.

Boone hunted all his life. Though strictly religious, he was a member of no church. His wife was a Baptist; his son Daniel Morgan was a Presbyterian. The only portrait of him is that painted by Chester Harding in 1820.

In 1845, the Missouri Legislature consenting, the State of Kentucky removed the remains of Daniel and Rebecca Boone to Frankfort, the capital, reinterring them in the State Cemetery on a high bank of the Kentucky River overlooking the capital.

In connection with the sesquicentennial of Boone's Wilderness Trace and the First Capital of the West, the Governor of Kentucky, Honorable William Jason Fields, wrote (March 18, 1925):

Although the body of the great pioneer Boone sleeps in our City of the Dead, beside the murmuring waters of the river he loved so well, his great spirit lives in the hearts of our people.

DANIEL BOONE m. in then Rowan County, North Carolina, August 14, 1756, Rebecca Bryan, b. January 9, 1739, a daughter of Joseph Bryan.[6]

Children:

11. James Boone, the eldest, killed by Indians in Powells Valley near Cumberland Gap in the Fall of 1773 when Boone and party were on the way to settle Kentucky.

12. Israel Boone, killed by Indians in the Battle of Blue Licks (August 2, 1782).

13. Susannah Boone.

14. Jemima Boone; m. in the fort at Boonesborough, Flanders Calloway, son of Richard Calloway.

15. Levina Boone.

16. Rebecca Boone.

17. Col. Daniel Morgan Boone; settled in Missouri before his father, Daniel, settled at Riverton, Greenup County Kentucky.

*18. Jesse Bryan Boone.

19. Col. Nathan Boone, the youngest; m. Olive Van Bibber, daughter of Mathias (Tice) Van Bibber; settled in Missouri.

20. William Boone.

18. JESSE BRYAN BOONE, farmer and public official was b. in Kentucky and d. in Missouri.

The record would seem to indicate that he lived in the same communities as his father until the migration of the latter to Missouri. He married, probably in what is now Kanawha County, West Virginia, Chloe Van Bibber, daughter of Mathias (Tice) Van Bibber. He was the first State Salt Inspector in what is now the Charleston, West Virginia, section of the Great Kanawha Valley. In the Fall of 1798 or the Spring of 1799, he removed to then Mason County Kentucky, now Greenup County, and settled near present Riverton. Here he became a farmer and slave holder (listing 12 negro slaves for taxation in 1810); and was prominent and influential in the early affairs of Greenup County.

Jesse Bryan Boone held many public local offices: He was commissioned (1804) and served as one of the first assistant judges of the Greenup Circuit Court and was again commissioned and held this office in 1805 and 1811; served as justice of the peace of Greenup County for many years; and was postmaster at Greenupsburg in 1814.

Disposing of his property in Greenup County and resigning the public positions he held, he migrated with his family to Missouri in 1819.

Children:

21. Col. Albert Gallatin Boone, explorer, was the first white man to camp on the site of present city of Denver, Colorado.

22. Harriet Boone.

23. Alphonso Boone.

24. Minerva Boone; b. in Greenup County, Kentucky; m. Winecup Warner.

25. Panthea Boone; b. in Greenup County.

26. Mattison Boone; b. in Greenup County.

Historians state that Jesse Bryan Boone was the grandfather of Governor Boggs of Missouri and Mr. Warner, a member of the U. S. House of Representatives from that state.

---

[1] "Outline of Ancestry and Life of Daniel Boone", by W. B. Douglass, LLM, 1925.

[2] Ibid.

[3] "Trans-Allegheny Pioneers," by John Peter Hale, 1885, p. 188.

[4] Ibid.

[5] Manuscript, prepared by Rev. James Gilruth and published in an Irontown, Ohio newspaper about 1879.

[6] Joseph Bryan was a son of Morgan Bryan and his wife, Martha (Strode) Bryan, whose other children were Samuel, James, Morgan, John, Elenor, Mary, William, Thomas, Sarah and Rebecca, the wife of Col Daniel Boone.

BORDERS FAMILY OF LAWRENCE COUNTY

1. JOHN BORDERS was the progenitor of the Borders Family of Eastern Kentucky. He was of German descent and came to America as a soldier in the British Army during the Revolutionary War and was with Cornwallis at the surrender of Yorktown (October 19, 1781). After the war he settled in Giles County, Virginia, from which county he migrated westward with his family in 1802 with intention of settling in the Scioto River Valley in Ohio. In the trek westward when he reached the Big Sandy River, in what is now Johnson County, Kentucky, he became ill and settled at the "Wild Goose Shoals" below the mouth of Toms Creek where he died, leaving a widow and eight children—four sons and four daughters. He married, presumably in Giles County, Virginia, Elizabeth Sellards, daughter of Hezekiah Sellards.[1]

Children:

*2. Michael Borders.

*3. John Borders, Jr.

*4. Hezekiah Borders.

*5. Archibald Borders.

6. Polly Borders; m. Isham Daniel in Floyd Co., August 15, 1809.

7. Betty Borders; m. Joseph Davis. (See Davis Family.)

8. Jennie Borders; m. Felty Van Hoose. (See Van Hoose Family.)

9. Katie Borders; m. John Brown.

2. MICHAEL BORDERS, farmer, was b. in Virginia, about 1787 and d. in Johnson County, Kentucky, 1882; m. in Floyd County, July 6, 1809, Christina Pack, b. in Virginia, about 1787. They lived on Georges Creek.

3. JOHN BORDERS, JR., farmer and minister of the Baptist Church, was b. in Virginia and d. in Johnson County in 1879 or 1880 at an advanced age; lived on Georges Creek; m. in Floyd County, June 13, 1814, Jincy or Jennie Nelson.

Children, among others:

10. Fannie Borders; m. Rhoderick Murray.

4. HEZEKIAH BORDERS, farmer and tavern keeper, was b. in Virginia about 1792; settled and lived at the mouth of Lost Creek on the Big Sandy River, present Lawrence County, at what is now and for over one hundred years has been known as Borders Chapel; m. in Floyd County, April 15, 1815, first, Fannie Davis, daughter of Joseph Davis, Jr.

Children:
11. Elizabeth Borders; m. W. H. Wheeler, September 17, 1829.
*12. Joseph H. Borders.
13. Sarah Borders; m. G. W. Price.   (See Price Family.)
*14. Archibald Borders.
15. Fannie Borders; m. ——— Hammond.
*16. William Borders.
17. Jane Borders.
18. John Borders.

4A. HEZEKIAH BORDERS m., secondly, in Johnson County, November 26, 1846, Jemima Lemaster, b. in 1815.

Children:
19. Emily Borders; m. ——— - Hammond.
20. ——— Borders; m. ——— Hammond.
21. Mary E. Borders; b. 1848.
22. Juliann Borders; b. 1850.

5. JUDGE ARCHIBALD BORDERS, farmer, merchant, public official and business man, was b. in Giles County, Virginia, in 1798, and d. in Lawrence County, Kentucky, November 12, 1886; m. in Floyd County, December 14, 1820, Jane (Jincy) Preston, b. in Bedford County, Virginia, 1799, daughter of Moses Preston, Revolutionary War soldier. (See Moses Preston Family.)

They settled near the White House Shoals on the Big Sandy River and later moved down the river to a farm in Lawrence County where Mr. Borders opened up a large plantation. Here he conducted a general store, shoe factory and saddlery. He also was one of the largest tan-bark and timber traders on Big Sandy.

In 1860 he built and for years operated on the Big Sandy River the steamer, Sandy Valley, a very superior boat for the time.

Judge Borders was very active in public and civic affairs. He was elected and served as justice of the peace of Lawrence County from 1834 to 1850 when he was elected Judge of the Lawrence County Court. He was reelected Judge in 1854 and served until 1858.

Judge Borders accumulated a vast amount of land and other property and was considered very wealthy for his day. He was a friend to the church and school and contributed liberally to their support. Yet, he never made a public confession of Christian faith until within a month of his death, when he united with the Methodist Episcopal Church, South.

Judge Borders was not only a man of great industry and business capacity but was a gentleman of refined tastes.

Children:

*23. John Borders.

*24. Arthur Borders.

25. David Borders; merchant, unm.

26. Allen P. Borders; m. a daughter of Lewis Mayo.

27. Julia Borders; m. J. W. Dillon, a business man of Catlettsburg.

12. JOSEPH BORDERS, farmer, b. 1818; m. in Floyd County, September 5, 1839, Julia A. Brown, b. 1820.

Children:

28. Joseph H. Borders, publisher, co-founder of the Advance at Paintsville in 1880, which in 1881 was published at Louisa by Borders alone; established the Chatteroi News in 1881; afterward became a banker in Kansas.

Children living at home and approximate dates of birth as shown by the U. S. Census of Lawrence County for 1850 and 1860:

29. Henry A. Borders; b. 1840.

30. Elizabeth E. Borders; b. 1842.

31. Frances Borders; b. 1844.

32. Maranda Borders; b. 1846.

33. Eda Borders; b. 1848.

34. Wallace Borders; b. 1850.

35. Nancy or Mary Borders; b. 1850.

36. Sarah Borders; b. 1855.

14. ARCHIBALD BORDERS, farmer; b. 1820; m. about 1848, Emmaline ———, b. about 1830.

Children living at home and approximate dates of birth as shown by the U. S. Census of Lawrence County for 1850:

37. Sarah F. Borders; b. 1849.

16. WILLIAM BORDER, farmer; b. 1827; m. in Lawrence County, July 30, 1945, Abigail Wheeler, b. 1826.

Children living at home and approximate dates of birth as shown by the U. S. Census of Lawrence County for 1850, 1860 and 1870:

38. John Borders; b. 1846.

39. Stephen Borders; b. 1848.

40. Jemima Borders; b. 1849.

41. Wallace Borders; b. 1851.

42. Matilda Borders; b. 1852.

43. Emily J. Borders; b. 1855.

44. Marion Borders; b. 1857.

45. Lavina Borders; b. 1859.

46. Fannie Borders; b. 1861.

18. JOHN BORDERS (believed to be identical with No. 18), farmer; b. 1824; m. in Lawrence County, December 29, 1842 (?), Zarilda Preston, b. 1828.

Children living at home and approximate dates of birth as shown by the U. S. Census of Lawrence County for 1850 and 1860:

47. Martin Borders; b. 1843.
48. Wallace Borders; b. 1845.
49. Matilda Borders; b. 1847.
50. Talitha Borders; b. 1849.
51. Louisa Borders; b. 1851.
52. Pricie Borders; b. 1853.
53. Julianna Borders; b. 1855.
54. Hester A. Borders; b. 1857.

23. JOHN BORDERS (believed to be identical with No. 23), was b. in 1821; m. in Lawrence County, March 6, 1838, Elizabeth Pack, b. in 1817.

Children living at home and approximate dates of birth as shown by the U. S. Census of Lawrence County for 1850 and 1860:

55. Hezekiah Borders; b. 1839.
56. Maryanna Borders; b. 1841.
57. David Borders; b. 1843.
58. Jane Borders; b. 1846.
59. Bartlett Borders; b. 1848.
60. Fanny Borders; b. 1849.
61. Joseph Borders; b. 1852.

24. ARTHUR BORDERS, farmer, b. 1822; m. Ann ———, b. in Pennsylvania, 1822.

Children living at home and approximate dates of birth as shown by U. S. Census of Lawrence County for 1850:

62. Henry H. Borders; b. 1841.
63. Leander C. Borders; b. 1843.
64. Alice Borders; b. 1846.
65. Mary Borders; b. 1849.

The Borders family supported the Union cause in the Civil War, but they were always conservative. After the War, Judge Borders and son, David, voted oftener for good men and measures than at the suggestions of the politicians.

BROCK FAMILY OF KNOX AND HARLAN COUNTIES

The name "Brock" is undoubtedly a "place name", as it appears to have originated from the residence site of the first Brock "by the Brook." The family is of English extraction. The old English spelling of brook was Broc, although the first to adopt the name spelled it "Brok". Early English records mention the name of William de la Brok in the Hundred Rolls of County Essex, A. D. 1273, Geoffrey de la Brok in the Rolls of County Kent, and Laurence Le Broc in the Rolls of Cambridge, A. D. 1275.

The name of Brock has long been established in the United States and is today found in almost every section of the country. There were "first settlers" of this name in both the Northern and Southern colonies. A great many who bear this name are today occupying positions of importance and trust in almost every phase of modern industry.

It is not definitely known when the first of the family of Brock crossed the mountains to Kentucky in the great Westward movement. However, John Brock was living in and was a tax-payer of Woodford County in 1790, and Henry Brock, Thomas Brock and another John Brock were living in and were tax-payers of Fayette County in the same year.

Jesse Brock, Revolutionary War soldier, was a progenitor of the Brock family of Southeastern Kentucky. His declaration for a pension filed October 16, 1833, in the Harlan Circuit Court—the Honorable Joseph Eve, Judge of the 15th Judicial District, presiding—discloses that he was born in Cumberland County, Virginia, December 8, 1752; that he enlisted at Guilford Court House, Guilford County, North Carolina (the year not remembered), for a term of three months in the North Carolina State Line, and served under General Alexander Martin, Colonel James Martin and Captain —— Roylston; that during this service he marched with his organization to Cross Creek in the State of North Carolina where, it was supposed, the British intended to land an army. Upon expiration of his enlistment he was discharged in the lower part of North Carolina; that he again enlisted in Guilford County for a term of three months in the North Carolina State Line during which enlistment he with other soldiers of his organization were detailed and marched and guarded wagoners and their wagons laden with provisions for the American Army stationed at Chartell (?) Court House, South Carolina. After performing this duty, he returned to Guilford Court House where, upon expiration of his enlistment, he was discharged; that he again enlisted in February, 1781, in Surry County, North Carolina, for a term of three months and served under Captain William Underwood, Lieutenant Joseph Porter and Ensign Richard Taliaferro, during which service he marched with his organization

to the Catawha River, arriving there a few days after the battle. Re-
turning to Surry County, he was subsequently ordered to Guilford
County at a place between Guilford Court House and the Yadkin
River, where he joined Colonel Thompson's Regiment of the North
Carolina State Line; that subsequently he was in skirmishes with
British and Tories at Albemarle Creek and at White's Mills, a few
days before the Battle of Guilford Court House (March 15, 1781).
Upon expiration of his enlistment, he was discharged near Guilford
Court House.[1]

Jesse Brock resided in Guilford County at his first enlistment and
he lived in Surry County when he enlisted for the third and last
time. In the Spring after the close of the War—probably 1782--he
removed to Guilford County and from there to Franklin County,
Virginia; then he went back to Guilford County; subsequently he
removed to Russell County, Virginia, where he lived for four years;
and finally, about 1797 or 1798, he emigrated to and settled in that
part of the Cumberland River Valley in Knox County, Kentucky,
which was subsequently (1819) embraced in the new county of
Harlan. Apparently he settled on Wallins Creek, as he entered,
patented and listed for purposes of taxation large tracts of land in
that vicinity.

None of the records that have been examined reveals whom, when
or where he married. However, his children were born in North
Carolina and it would seem logical to conclude that he was married
in that colony. In 1810—the earliest record—one son and three
daughters were living at home with him and his wife in Knox County.
At the same time, in Knox County, lived George Brock with his
family consisting of his wife, two sons and one daughter. Many other
Brock families lived near Jesse Brock—apparently his children or
grandchildren: (1) Aaron Brock, b. in North Carolina in 1786, m.
Elizabeth, (apparently his second wife), who was b. in 1842. In
1820 there were living at home six daughters; (2) Amon Brock, b. in
North Carolina in 1788, m., first, September 26, 1811, in Knox
County, Molly Osborn, who was b. in Virginia, in 1793. He m.,
secondly, presumably in Harlan County, Charity ———, who was
b. in North Carolina, in 1825. In 1830 five sons and one daughter
were living at home; (3) Hiram Brock, b. in 1800—presumably in
Knox County, Kentucky—m. Elizabeth ———, who was b. in 1805.
In 1830 two sons and two daughters were living at home; (4) Mahala
Brock, b. in Kentucky in 1814, m., in Harlan County, about ·———,
John Brummett, who was b. in Tennessee in 1810. Their children
were William, Amon, Peyton, Hiram, Chappell, James, Nancy, who
m. Hiram Osburn; Polly (Mary), who m. John Kozee; Elzira, who
m. Ned Brock; Jemima, who m. James Hylton, and Elizabeth, who
m. Gilbert Slusher. (5) Susannah Brock m. William Blanton in
Knox County, August 18, 1811;   (6) Polly (Mary) Brock m. Shad-

rack Helton in Knox County, May 24, 1809; (7) James Brock was living in Harlan County in 1820, with his family consisting of wife, one son and one daughter; (8) Jesse Brock, Jr., resided in Harlan County in 1820 with his family consisting of wife, three sons and three daughters. (9) William Brock was living in Harlan County in 1840 with his family consisting of wife, one son and one daughter.

Hiram Montgomery Brock, lawyer, at Harlan, Harlan County, Kentucky, is one of the outstanding descendants of Jesse Brock, the Revolutionary War soldier. He is a son of James Brock, a grandson of Aaron Brock, a great grandson of Amon Brock and a great, great grandson of the Revolutionary War soldier.

Mr. Brock is a Republican in politics and for many years has been an active and efficient party leader and a wise counselor in party affairs. He is a member of the Presbyterian Church. For many years he represented his district in the State Senate creditably and well. He married Ona May Lewis, a daughter of Judge William and Alice (Morgan) Lewis, of London, Laurel County. (See Judge William Lewis—Biography.)

BROWN FAMILY OF BOYD COUNTY

This branch of the Brown family is of English extraction and the records of the family have been preserved without a break as far back as 1609. Sir William Brown was the progenitor of this branch of the family. He was a native of England and was one of the original grantees under the Virginia charter of May 23, 1609, granted by King James I to Robert, Earl of Salisbury, and others of whom Sir William Brown was the fortieth on the list. Sir William Brown [1] had a son, Colonel Henry Brown,[2] member of the Virginia Council of 1642, who had a son, William Brown,[3] of Rappahannock County, Virginia, who was a member of the House of Burgesses from Surry County, 1659-1660. William Brown [3] had a son, Maxfield Brown,[4] of Richmond County, Virginia, b. 1675, d. 1745, who m. Elizabeth Newman and had a son, George Brown [5] of King George County, Virginia, whose son, George Newman Brown,[6] resided in Prince William County, Virginia, and was a soldier in the Revolutionary War, having participated in the battle and seige of Yorktown. He m. Sarah Hampton of Bloomsbury, a near relative of General Wade Hampton of South Carolina. (See H a m p t o n Family.) George Newman Brown [6] and his wife, Sarah (Hampton) Brown, had issue, among others:

*7. Henry Brown.

*8. Dr. Benjamin Brown.

*9. Richard Brown.

These three brothers migrated from their home in Prince William County, Virginia, in 1805, and settled in what was then a wilderness between the Guyandotte and the Great Tatteroi (now Big Sandy) Rivers, on lands known as the Savage Grant surveyed under Governor Dinwiddie's proclamation of 1754 and granted by Virginia in 1772 to Captain John Savage and his company of sixty men for services in the the French and Indian War. The Brown brothers settled on lands now included in the limits of the city of Huntington, West Virginia; and their log cabin home was displaced, in 1810, by a brick structure, the first built in Cabell County.

7. HENRY BROWN was one of the first justices of Cabell County and was the second sheriff of the county. He was a trustee of the town of Guyandotte. He was killed in the discharge of his official duty as sheriff, in 1810.

8. DR. BENJAMIN BROWN was b. in Virginia in 1786, and d. in Cabell County, Virginia, (now West Virginia) in 1848. He was a very successful physician and his practice extended over a large field. He m. Matilda Scales, b. in North Carolina, 1797, d. in Cabell

County, October 28, 1878, daughter of Nathaniel Scales, a Revolutionary War officer.

Issue:

10. James Henry Brown, lawyer and judge, was b. December 25, 1818, d. October 28, 1900; attended Marietta College and was graduated from Augusta College; studied law and was admitted to the bar in 1842; practiced in the circuit, Federal and appellate courts; served as Circuit Court Judge and was one of the first judges of the Supreme Court of Appeals of West Virginia and later president of the court. In 1848 he moved to Kanawha County and ever after made Charleston his home. Judge Brown opposed secession and played a very important part in the framing and adoption of the constitution and the organization of the new state of West Virginia. He m. Louisa M. Beuhring, daughter of George Lewis Beuhring. They had issue:

11. Vesta Brown, m. Albert Laidley. Their children were Alberta and John.

12. Ceres Brown, unm.

13. Josephine Brown, m. Rev. Robert Osborn, a Presbyterian minister.

9. RICHARD BROWN, m. Sarah Haney of Bourbon County, Kentucky. He sold his farm in Cabell County to his brother, Dr. Benjamin Brown; and about 1836, he moved to Lawrence County, Kentucky, and settled on a farm at the junction of the Levisa and Tug Rivers, the site of the present-day city of Louisa. He reared a large family, mostly daughters. Among his children were:

14. Mary Matilda Brown, m. in Lawrence County, March 19, 1840, Judge James M. Rice. (See Rice Family.)

15. Mrs. Hannah S. Gilbert, nee Brown, m. in Pike County, December 18, 1846, Samuel Robinson.

16. George N. Brown, lawyer and jurist, was b. September 22, 1822, on the site of Huntington, West Virginia; was educated at Marshall College, in West Virginia, and Augusta College, in Kentucky, graduating from the latter; studied law; was admitted to the bar in 1844; and locating at Pikeville, Kentucky, soon built up a good practice. In 1860, he moved to Catlettsburg, Boyd County, and at once became a leader at the bar. In 1880, he was elected circuit judge of the Sixteenth judicial district, defeating Judge John M. Burns, who, in turn, defeated him for the same office in 1886. Judge Brown justly bore the reputation of being one of the ablest and purest jurists of the Kentucky circuits; but largely extended that reputation by the firmness and integrity of his conduct and rulings in the celebrated murder cases of Ellis, Neal and Craft. Only his resolute determination to enforce the law in the face of the wild and infuriated

passions of the people, who were maddened to mob violence by the nature of the crimes committed and a belief in the guilt of the accused, secured the partial administration of the legal processes and punishments. By a like stern courage and inflexible will, the Floyd and Magoffin County frauds on the State treasury were discovered and arrested, a service for which the Auditor of the State, in his report for 1883, said that Judge Brown deserved the thanks of the State.

Judge Brown m., first, in Pike County, November 17, 1847, Sophia S. Cecil, daughter of Thomas Cecil and grand daughter of Kinzie B. Cecil, the first of the family to settle in Kentucky; and, secondly, Maria J. Poage, daughter of William Poage, of near Ashland, Kentucky.

Children:

17. Nancy F. Brown; b. in 1849.

18. Margaret M. Brown; b. in 1848.

19. Eliza Brown; b. in 1852.

20. Thomas R. Brown, b. in 1854, lawyer; was educated at the University of Virginia; m. a daughter of Greenville M. Lackey and grand daughter of General Alexander Lackey.

21. Lucy M. Brown; b. in 1863.

22. George N. Brown, Jr.; b. in 1865.

23. Sherar (?) E. Brown; b. in 1867.

Judge Brown was a successful business man and was considered wealthy in his day. In 1872-73 he was a member of a commission to expend seventy-five thousand dollars on improvements of the Big Sandy River.

In politics this branch of the Brown family were Whigs but on the organization of the Know Nothing Party in 1854, they affiliated with the Democratic party which they have since supported.

BROWN OF FLOYD AND JOHNSON COUNTIES

The Brown family of the Big Sandy Valley is of English origin. Their ancestors came to America before the Revolutionary War and settled on the North branch of the Potomac River. As early as 1789 Thomas C.[1] Brown and Nathaniel Brown, brothers, emigrated from that section to Kentucky and settled in Fleming county, but soon moved to the Sandy Valley, settling on the river, nearly opposite Paint Creek, now Johnson county. A daughter of Nathaniel Brown m. the pioneer Samuel Auxier. Very little has been learned of him.

1. THOMAS C. BROWN was b. in Hampshire county, Virginia (now West Virginia) in August, 1761; moved to Floyd county, Kentucky, about 1797, and d. in Johnson county, April 17, 1857. He was a soldier in the Revolutionary War and, in the Floyd County Court, on September 17, 1832, he filed a declaration in connection with his claim for a pension growing out of such service, wherein he states, among other things, that he enlisted in the Virginia state troops in the town of Rumney (Romney), Hampshire county, Virginia, in October or November, 1778, under Captain Peter Higgins, Lieutenant Patrick Johnston and Colonel Benjamin Williams; that he was ensign, or cornet, of the company which was a "horse" company and that the colonel (Benjamin Williams) directed it to remain in the county of Hampshire and at given times to patrol all that section of the county on the waters of Bull Pasture, Cow Pasture and the head waters of the South Branch of the Potomac and a portion of the county of Augusta, Virginia, for the suppression of the Tories; that his term of enlistment was for three years under the stipulation that the company should not be withdrawn from the state; that in the Spring of 1779 the company toured the country assigned for about 140 miles and had several engagements with the Tories on the South branch of the Potomac in which several Tories were killed and many taken prisoners and placed in the Rumney (Romney) jail; that about the first of October, 1781, the company marched, under orders, to Little York and remained there till Lord Cornwallis surrendered to the American Army and then marched to Winchester, Virginia, where they were discharged.

The name of Thomas C. Brown appears many times in the Floyd County Court order books, as he was very active and influential in public affairs, having held a number of county offices. He m. in Floyd county, December 15, 1831, Mary Brown, who apparently was not his first wife, and became the founder of a house noted in the annals of Big Sandy Valley.

Children:

*2. Francis Asbury Brown.

3. Sarah Brown; m. —— Auxier, and lived in Fleming county, Kentucky.

4. Daniel Brown; lived in Lawrence county, Kentucky.

2. FRANCIS ASBURY BROWN was one of the most distinguished members of the Brown family. He was a merchant and also active in the public affairs of the city (Paintsville) and county; and like his father, held offices of responsibility and trust in his county. He m., in Floyd county, June 1, 1811, Edy Preston, daughter of Nathan Preston, a Revolutionary War soldier and his wife, Elizabeth (Vaughan) Preston. They reared a large and respected family all of whom were successful in life.

Children:
*5. William Brown.
*6. Thomas S. Brown.
*7. Daniel Brown.
*8. Wallace W. Brown.
*9. Nathan Brown.
10. Julia Brown.
*11. Jefferson Brown.
*12. Edy Brown.
13. Lawrence Brown ?

5. WILLIAM BROWN (FRANCIS ASBURY, 2, THOMAS C., 2), a farmer and preacher in the Methodist Church; m. in Lawrence county, October 6, 1828, Julia Stafford, and lived in Morgan county, Kentucky.

Children:
14. Frank Brown; m. —— Ison?; removed from Morgan county to Salt Lake City, Utah.

15. John Brown; unm.

16. Thomas Brown; m. Elizabeth Hill and lived in Morgan county.

17. Foster Brown; m. Nancy Hill and lived in Johnson county, near the Morgan county line.

*18. William Brown.

19. Elizabeth Brown; m. James Ferguson and lived in Morgan county.

*20. Mary (Polly) Brown.

21. Sarah Brown; m. James Todd and lived in Fleming county, Kentucky.

*22. Amanda Brown.

6. THOMAS S. BROWN (FRANCIS ASBURY, 2, THOMAS C., 1) a merchant in Paintsville and a lawyer, but devoted little time to the practice of law; judge of the Johnson County Court for four years; and on the expulsion of John M. Elliott as State representative of the General Assembly of Kentucky, at the beginning of the Civil War, he was elected to fill the vacancy. While a member he made a speech against secession that was remarkable for brillancy as well as sound logic and carried all doubters with him. Subsequently, he was an unsuccessful candidate for Congress. He was for many years a preacher in the Methodist Church, but after his second marriage, he swerved from his ancient faith and joined the Latter Day Saints, or Mormons. He m. first, in Floyd County, May 7, 1835, Emaline Damron; and, secondly, Fanny Baldwin.

Children by the first wife:

*23. George Brown.

24. Arthur Brown.

*25. John M. Brown.

*26. Amanda Brown.

27. Angie Brown; m. Samuel P. Hager (See Hager Family).

*28. Mary Brown.

Children by the second wife:

29. Frank Brown.

30. Henry Brown.

31. Martin Brown.

32. Ella Brown; m. ——— Preston.

33. Lula Brown; m. ——— Stevens.

34. Rhoda Brown.

This family lived in Salt Lake City, Utah.

7. DANIEL BROWN (FRANCIS ASBURY, 2, THOMAS C., 1), was a preacher in the Methodist Church and lived in Lawrence County, Kentucky. He m. Ebbie Borders and they had children:

*35. Kye Brown.

36. Thomas Brown.

37. Washington Brown.

8. WILLIAM W. BROWN (FRANCIS ASBURY, 2, THOMAS C., 1), b. December 9, 1916, in Paintsville and d. there September 12, 1890. He was a farmer, merchant and lawyer; was elected to many public offices including that of county attorney for Johnson county, State representative and senator where he gained distinction in speeches pertaining to the Union, and the Confederacy during the Civil War. He

m., first, Nancy Hill, b. July 4, 1820, d. December 15, 1861; and secondly, Sarah Coleman.

Children by the first wife:

39. Selina Brown.
*40. Edgar Brown.
41. Sarah Brown; m. John D. Preston.
42. Frank A. Brown; m. M. Ella Preston.
*43. Thomas C. Brown.

Children by the second wife:

44. Annie Brown; m. Kid Moore.
*45. Evelina Brown.

9. NATHAN BROWN (FRANCIS ASBURY, 2, THOMAS C. 1), was a yer, sometime public official and a local preacher in the Methodist Church. He was judge of the Johnson County Court and held other offices of trust in Paintsville and Johnson county. He m. Elizabeth Hill and they had issue:

46. Sarah Brown.
*47. Leander Brown.
48. Edy Brown.
*49. Miranda Brown.

11. JEFFERSON BROWN (FRANCIS ASBURY. 2, THOMAS C., 1), was a farmer and carpenter and lived and d. in the Tom's Creek section of Johnson county. He m. Jane George and they had children:

50. C. Brank Brown.
51. Henry Brown.
52. Jefferson Brown.
53. Edy Brown.
54. ?

12. EDY BROWN (FRANCIS ASBURY, 2, THOMAS C. 1), lived and d. on Tom's Creek. She m. Jesse Van Hoose and they had issue:

55. John Van Hoose.
56. Wallace Van Hoose.
57. Oneida Van Hoose; m. Elliott Williams.
58. Martha Van Hoose.

18. WILLIAM BROWN (WILLIAM. 3, FRANCIS ASBURY, 2, THOMAS C., 1), lived in Boyd County, Kentucky, at the time of his death. He m. Sarah Seltzer and they had Children.

59. Sarah Brown.

60. George Brown.
61. Mildred Brown.
62. ?
63. Anglie Brown.

20. MARY (POLLY) BROWN (WILLIAM 3, FRANCIS ASBURY 2, THOMAS C. 1), lived in Morgan county. She m. Elliott Hill and they had children:
64. Leander Hill.
65. Wallace Hill.
66. William Hill.
67. Edward Hill.
68. Amanda Hill.
69. Sarah Hill.

22. AMANDA BROWN (WILLIAM 3, FRANCIS ASBURY 2, THOMAS C 1), lived in Morgan county. She m. John Phelfrey and they had issue:
70. William Phelfrey.
71. Edward Phelfrey.

23. GEORGE BROWN (THOMAS S. 3, FRANCIS ASBURY 2, THOMAS C., 1), lived near Paintsville on the "Sherman farm". He m. Eliza Sherman and they had children:
72. John Brown; m. Belle Layne.
73. Laura Brown; m. James Spradlin.

25. JOHN M. BROWN (THOMAS S. 3, FRANCIS ASBURY 2, THOMAS C. 1), lived and d. in Paintsville. He m. Martha Vaughan and they had children:
74. Edward Brown.
75. Jay Brown; m. ――― Salyer.

26. AMANDA BROWN (THOMAS S., 3, FRANCIS ASBURY, 2, THOMAS C., 1), d. in 1927; m. John Porter; resided in Boyd county, Kentucky.
Children:
76. Henry Porter.
77. ?
78. ?

28. MARY BROWN (THOMAS S., 3, FRANCIS ASBURY, 2, THOMAS C., 1), lived in Paintsville; m. Wayne Daniels and they had children:
79. Edward Daniels.
80. Fanny Daniels.

35. KYE BROWN (DANIEL, 3, FRANCIS ASBURY, 2, THOMAS C., 1), farmer, lived in Lawrence county, Kentucky. He m. Jane Auxier, daughter of Major John B. Auxier (See Auxier Family).

Issue:

81. Elijah Brown.

39. SELIMA BROWN (WALLACE W., 3, FRANCIS ASBURY, 2, THOMAS C., 1), m. Henry Preston; they resided in Paintsville and had children:

*82. Wallace Preston.

83. Forrest L. Preston; m. Della Maynard.

40. EDGAR BROWN (WALLACE W., 3, FRANCIS ASBURY, 2, THOMAS C., 1); merchant; lived in Morgan county, Kentucky, at date of his death; m. Violet Vertrice Hager.

Children:

84. Angie Brown; m. Leander Ferguson.

85. Ella Brown; m. Frank Williams.

86. Vertrice Brown; m. Ambrose Ferguson.

87. Nancy Brown; m. William Pelfrey.

*88. Wallace Brown.

89. Arthur Brown; killed in action in the Civil War.

43. THOMAS C. BROWN (WALLACE W., 3, FRANCIS ASBURY, 2, THOMAS C. 1), farmer; resided in Paintsville; m. Virginia Preston (see Preston family—Moses Preston, Jr. branch).

Children:

90. Lillian Brown.

91. Frank E. Brown; d. in 1901.

92. Nannie Brown, b. July 29, 1880; d. March 14, 1914.

93. Paul D. Brown, b. January 27, 1877; d. January 6, 1912.

*94. Marshall Brown.

*95. Flossie F. Brown.

45. EVELINA BROWN (WALLACE W., 3, FRANCIS ASBURY, 2, THOMAS C. 1); m. John Ramey and they lived in Mason county, Kentucky.

Children:

96. John Wallace Ramey.

97. Jesse Martin Ramey.

98. Venice Ramey.

47. Leander Brown (Nathan, 3, Francis Asbury, 2, Thomas C., 1); m. Lynchia Van Hoose; they resided in Kansas.

Child:

99. Edward Brown.

49. Miranda Brown (Nathan, 3, Francis Asbury, 2, Thomas C., 1); m. John B. Wheatley. John B. Wheatley, educator, was educated in the public schools and at National Normal University, Lebanon, Ohio. He was a noted teacher for many years, teaching very successfully in Johnson county schools, the Paintsville city schools and principal of the Willard (Kentucky) Graded School for a year.

Issue:

100. Heber Wheatley; resided in Paintsville where he sponsored a collection agency.

*101. Grant Wheatley.

*102. May Wheatley.

103. Virgil Wheatley; educated in the Paintsville City schools and was graduated from the Sandy Valley Seminary; resided in Paintsville.

104. John Brown Wheatley; m. Dicy Rice.

105. William Wheatley; m. Ora Sturgill.

82. Wallace Preston; m. ——— Prater.

Issue:

106. Ralph Preston.

107. Charles Preston.

88. Wallace Brown; m. ——— Hill.

Issue:

108. Ernest Brown.

94. Marshall Brown, civil engineer, m. Ollie Woods, who before her marriage was connected with business houses in Paintsville.

Issue:

109. Roger Brown.

95. Flossie F. Brown, b. May 3, 1884, d. June 30, 1920; m. Curt Preston, groceryman at Paintsville.

Issue:

110. Kenneth Preston.

111. Virginia Preston.

101. GRANT WHEATLEY, businessman at Paintsville and active in many business men's organizations; was manager of the Paintsville Light and Power Company for many years; m. Lorna Fairchild.

Issue:

112. John Grant Wheatley.

113. Mary Elizabeth Wheatley.

102. MAY WHEATLEY; m. James Layne, now deceased.

Issue:

114. Mildred Layne; m. Donald Pugh, December 31, 1927.

115. Mabel Layne.

116. Joe Layne.

117. Anna Laura Layne.

118. William Layne.

119. Elizabeth Layne.

121. John Layne.

BURGESS FAMILY OF LAWRENCE COUNTY

The Burgess family of the lower Big Sandy River region in Eastern Kentucky is of Scotch origin, the ancestors immigrating to America before the Revolutionary War. Edward Burgess I was the progenitor of this branch of the family. He was born, presumably in Virginia, circa 1744 and migrated with his family from Giles County, Virginia, to Floyd County, Kentucky, about 1806. He had service in the Revolutionary War and on the 15th day of June, 1818 filed in the Floyd County Court a declaration for a pension on account of such service wherein he stated, among other things, that he was 74 years of age and had resided in Floyd County about 12 years; that in 1779 he enlisted for 18 months in the company of Captain Newell under the command of Colonel "Bluford" (Buford) of the Virginia Regiment on the Continental Line; that he was in the battles at "Claps" Mills and Ramsour's Mill, North Carolina, and also was at Gates' defeat [at Camden, South Carolina, August 16, 1780] as a militiaman under command of Captain Thomas Williams; that he served out his enlistment and was honorably discharged at Hillsborough, North Carolina, in October, 1781.[1]

EDWARD BURGESS I. m., presumably in Virginia, Nancy ————, (surname not learned) who was b. about 1747 and d. in Lawrence County, Kentucky, at an advanced age.

Children:

*2. Edward Burgess II.

*3. William Burgess.

4. Clara Burgess; m. Edward Winfield.

5. Rebecca Burgess; m. Lewis Rigglesby in Lawrence County, December 21, 1826. They migrated to Kansas and prospered.

6. Permitta Burgess; m. John F. McClannahan in Lawrence County, January 4, 1831.

7. Mary Burgess; m. ———— Williams. They went West.

8. Sarah M. Burgess; m. ———— Donohoe. They migrated to Kansas and became wealthy.

2. EDWARD BURGESS II, farmer and large landowner, was b. in Virginia, about 1801. He served as sheriff of Lawrence County; m. Elizabeth ————, b. in Virginia, about 1810. They had, among other children, sons:

9. George Burgess, who m. into the prominent Johns family; was a man of great integrity and honor and reared a large family.

10. Edward Burgess III.

*11. Gordon Burgess.

Children living at home and approximate dates of birth as shown by the U. S. Census of Lawrence County for the years 1850 and 1860:

12. James E. Burgess; b. 1830.
13. William H. Burgess; b. 1833.
14. John F. Burgess; b. 1835.
15. Francis M. Burgess; b. 1837.[2]
16. Mary J. Burgess; b. 1839.
17. Julia Burgess; b. 1841.
18. Davis Burgess; b. 1843.
19. George Burgess; b. 1844.
20. Elizabeth Burgess; b. 1846.
21. Edgar L. Burgess; b. 1849.
22. G. C. Burgess; b. 1850.

3. WILLIAM BURGESS. Very little has been learned relative to him. It is known that among his children were:

*23. Reuben Burgess and

24. George R. Burgess, who m. a Spurlock. He was the best known representative of the family; was a justice of peace of Lawrence County for 40 years; and was State representative from Carter and Lawrence counties, 1850.

There is for consideration the fact that 2 Edward Burgess II, and 3, William Burgess, brothers, each had a son, George. Consequently there is much confusion arising from these similar christain names.

GEORGE R. BURGESS; farmer, b. in Kentucky, about 1815; m. Martha ———, b. in Virginia, about 1820.

Children living at home and approximate dates of birth as shown by the U. S. Census of Lawrence County for the year 1850 and for Boyd County for the years 1860 and 1870:

25. Octavia M. Burgess; b. 1837; m. George W. Andrews in Lawrence County, January 1, 1857.
26. Strother Burgess; b. 1839.
27. Sarah F. Burgess; b. 1841.
28. Goble Burgess; b. 1843.
29. Susan Burgess; b. 1845.
30. Virginia C. Burgess; b. 1847.
31. Charity C. Burgess; b. 1849.
32. Pamelia F. Burgess; b. 1850.
33. Catherine Burgess; b. 1852.
34. Martha A. Burgess; b. 1854.
35. George Burgess; b. 1857.
36. William Burgess; b. 1860.
37. John B. Burgess; b. 1861.

GEORGE R. BURGESS; farmer, a large landowner and wealthy for his day, was b. in Kentucky, about 1808; m. Emily ———, b. in Kentucky about 1812. Children living at home and approximate dates of birth as shown by the U. S. Census of Lawrence County for 1850 and 1860:

*38. Cornelius H. Burgess; b. 1833.

39. Thomas J. Burgess; b. 1835.

40. Mary J. Burgess; b. 1837.

41. Hester Ann Burgess; b. 1838, m. M. B. Goble, October 16, 1855.

42. Julia Ann Burgess; b. 1841.

43. Cynthia Ann Burgess; b. 1842.

44. Emily J. Burgess; b. 1843.

45. Isabel Burgess; b. 1847.

*11. GORDON C. BURGESS; farmer, was b. in Kentucky, about 1808; m. Louisa ———, b. in Ohio about 1819.

Children living at home and approximate dates of birth as shown by the U. S. Census of Lawrence County for the years 1850 and 1870:

46. Julia G. Burgess; b. 1842.

47. George T. Burgess; b. 1844.

48. Mary E. Burgess; b. 1853.

49. Louisa A. Burgess; b. 1856.

50. Francis E. Burgess; b. 1861.

*23. REUBEN BURGESS; farmer, b. in Kentucky, about 1813; m. Nancy ———, b. in Kentucky about 1821. Children living at home and approximate dates of births as shown by the U. S. Census of Lawrence County for 1850:

51. Strother Burgess; b. 1839.

52. William Burgess; b. 1841.

53. Sarah Burgess; b. 1843.

54. Emily Burgess; b. 1846.

55. George Burgess; b. 1848.

56. Elizabeth Burgess; b. 1850.

*38. CORNELIUS BURGESS; farmer, b. in Kentucky; m. Julia P. ———, b. in Kentucky, 1840. Children living at home and approximate dates of birth as shown by the U. S. Census of Lawrence County for 1870:

57. Alvy T. Burgess; b. 1866.

58. Nancy E. J. Burgess; b. 1869.

There were other Burgess families living in the Big Sandy Valley in pioneer days. The U. S. Census of Floyd County for 1810 bears the names of Garland, Henry and John Burgess. Garland Burgess m. Elizabeth Preston in Floyd County, February 22, 1810. Mrs. Elizabeth Burgess, sister to Moses Preston and Nathan Preston, Revolutionary War soldiers, gave her deposition in August, 1839, in the pension claim of Nathan Preston, stating she was 68 years of age. The U. S. Census of Lawrence County for 1860 bears the names of Henry Burgess, farmer, 87 years of age, b. in Virginia, Mary Burgess, aged 46, housekeeper, b. in Kentucky, and Elizabeth Chapman, boarder, aged 90.

The pioneer Burgesses were Methodists in religion. In politics they were divided. However, most of them were Democrats.

---

[1] Revolutionary War Soldier Pension Papers, The National Archives, Washington, D. C.

[2] One Francis M. Burgess had service in the Union Army during the Civil War. He was mustered into the service at Louisa, August 7, 1863, a second lieutenant, Co. "H", Fourteenth Kentucky Volunteer Infantry; died of wounds, August 10, 1864. (Report of the Adjutant General of Kentucky, 1861-65).

BURNS FAMILY OF GREENUP AND BOYD COUNTIES

The Burns family is of Scottish origin. Burn is the Scottish form of the Old English burne ("a brook, stream, river, fountain, well"). Burn as a prefix or suffix to place-names denotes that the places were located near a stream, e.g., Ashburn ("ash tree near the brook"). The surname Burn is also a variant of Bourne. In the Domesday Book (1086) we find "Godrick Burnes". One of the greatest bearers of the name Burns was Robert Burns (1759-1796), born near Ayr, Scotland of a long line of farmer ancestors, a plebeian background that did not seem to hinder him from becoming one of the finest and best beloved among the lyric poets.

Jeremiah Burns, a Revolutionary War soldier, was the progenitor of the Burns family of the Big Sandy Valley, Eastern Kentucky. His father and an uncle emigrated from Scotland and settled in Maryland. Jeremiah Burns married, first, presumably in Maryland, and from this union had two sons who migrated Southwest and became noted people. He emigrated to Virginia and lived in Franklin County, Bedford County and Monroe County (now West Virginia), that state; and finally he settled in Greenup County, Kentucky.[1]

On July 18, 1818, Jeremiah Burns appeared in the Greenup County (Kentucky) Circuit Court, Judge Willis presiding, and made declaration for the purpose of receiving a pension on account of his services in the Revolutionary War wherein he stated, among other things, that on the —— day of June, 1776, he enlisted in Bedford County, Virginia, for three years, in Captain George Lambert's Company, commanded by George Mathers (Colonel George Mathews?) of the 14th Virginia Regiment, Continental Line, subsequently consolidated with the 7th Virginia Regiment, under the command of General Green; that he continued to serve in various corps against the common enemy—being in the battles of Germantown (October 4, 1777,) and at Monmouth (June 28, 1778)—until the expiration of his enlistment when he again entered the service and served under General Greene until August, 1782, when he was discharged at Williamsburg, Virginia, by Captain Ross; that during this last enlistment he marched to Yorktown and was at the siege and surrender of General Cornwallis there (October 19, 1781).[2]

At another time, Jeremiah Burns appeared in court in Greenup County and made declaration in connection with his claim for pension stating, among other things, that he has a wife, aged 50 years, and six children living with him; three sons, whose ages are 11 years, 9 years and 27 years; and three daughters whose ages are 16 years, 14 years, and 5 years.

At various times Elizabeth Burns, widow, executed affidavits and made declarations in open court in connection with her claim for pension as widow of Jeremiah Burns, stating in that connection that she was born in 1772 and married the soldier in Franklin County, Virginia, March 20, 1794; that he died October 24, 1824.

1. JEREMIAH (or JERRY)BURNS; farmer and a noted Methodist preacher of his day, first saw his second wife, Miss Elizabeth Roland, at one of his great preaching-places, she being a devout worshiper at his meetings. A contemporary historian stated of her that in song she was wonderfully gifted; a brunette of the most perfect type; hair as black as a raven, heavy eye-brows, a curved lip, and a faultless figure.[3]

Reputable historians have stated that Elizabeth Roland was of a family made famous in French Huguenot history; and that the Burnses of the Big Sandy Valley "came along the same line of descent as Robert Burns, the illustrious poet".

Many of the descendants of Jeremiah Burns and Elizabeth Roland rose to distinction in law and theology and as public officials. Some of their children were born in Virginia, presumably Franklin County; others were born in Monroe County, Virginia, now West Virginia, where they had moved about 1800; and the younger ones were born near the mouth of the Big Sandy River.

Children:

2. —— Burns, a son, migrated to Missouri where his descendants held high official positions—one a representative in Congress.

3. —— Burns, a son, migrated to Oregon and his descendants rose to distinction.

4. —— Burns, a son, migrated to California and was a respected and influential citizen.

5. Jane Burns, m. Judge James M. Rice. (See Rice Family of Boyd County.)

*6. Roland T. Burns.

7. Juliann Burns, m. O. W. Martin, a lawyer from Virginia.

6. ROLAND T. BURNS; farmer, preacher, lawyer and sometimes a legislator, was born in Virginia and d. in what is now Boyd County, Kentucky, in 1834. He owned and lived on a farm on Bear Creek, Boyd County; practiced law over a large district; preached often and worked with his own hands on the farm. He was State representative from the Lawrence-Morgan district for two terms, 1828-1832. He m. Margaret Keyser.

Children:

*8. William Harvey Burns; m. Mary Sulser, July 14, 1834.

*9. John M. Burns.

10. Lafayette Burns, farmer; resided near the old homestead of his father and was greatly respected by his neighbors.

11. Roland T. Burns, Jr., an able lawyer, and also engaged in merchandising; resided at Louisa, Lawrence County.

12. Elizabeth Burns, m. Alexander Handley of Wayne County, West Virginia.

8. WILLIAM HARVEY BURNS; distinguished lawyer and judge; located at West Liberty, Morgan County, for the practice of his profession and engaged in the practice of law there until the commencement of the Civil War, in the meantime having been elected as circuit court judge of his district which position he was holding when the war broke out. Sympathizing with the Southern cause, he resigned his judgeship and removed to Lebanon, Russell County, Virginia, where he was very successful and acquired considerable property.

9. HON. JOHN M. BURNS, b. 1826; a lawyer and judge, studied law under the supervision of his brother, Judge William Harvey Burns at West Liberty, Kentucky; was admitted to the bar in 1851 and formed a partnership with his former preceptor and brother in the practice of their profession which continued for three years and covered Letcher, Perry and Breathitt Counties, Judge W. H. Burns residing at West Liberty and John M. Burns at Whitesburg, Letcher County during this period.

John M. Burns was elected as county attorney of Letcher County and served with ability as such until December, 1853, when his law partnership was dissolved and he removed to Prestonsburg, Floyd County, and formed a partnership with the lamented Judge John M. Elliott, which continued for six years. He was elected and served as State representative from the Floyd-Johnson district, 1857-1859; and in 1860 he was elected as State senator from the district composed of the Counties of Pike, Floyd, Johnson and Magoffin and served with marked ability for one month when it was discovered that, in the apportionment law enacted at a previous session of the Legislature, the Senate had in its membership too many members by one. Mr. Burns resigned his seat and delivered an amusing address which elicited laughter and praise from the members and the galleries.

Returning to his home at Prestonburg, Mr. Burns practiced his profession and lectured on education in Floyd County until 1864 when he moved to Catlettsburg, Boyd County. He served as school commissioner (county superintendent of schools) of Boyd County for two terms, lecturing on education in every school district of the county each year he held the office.

In 1867 he was a candidate for the office of Commonwealth's Attorney for the Sixteenth Judicial District against Judge James E. Stewart, and was defeated by a reduced political majority. In 1876 he again was unsuccessful candidate against Judge Stewart for the office of Judge of the Criminal Court of the same district. In 1880 he was a candidate for the office of Judge of Circuit Court of the same district against the Hon. George N. Brown and was again defeated. In 1886 he again was a candidate for the office of Judge of the Circuit Court, same district, against Hon. George N. Brown, the incumbent, who had incurred the enmity of many persons by reason of the trials of Neal, Craft and others, and after an active canvass of twenty-four days, was triumphantly elected.

JOHN M. BURNS m. in Lawrence County, Keziah Clay, April 24, 1843.

Children living in the household and ages in 1850 as shown by the U. S. Census of Letcher County for that year:

13. Rebecca C. Burns, aged 5.
*14. Roland C. Burns, aged 3.
15. Mary E. Burns, aged 1.

The records indicate there were other children:

16. Sophia A. Burns, b. 1852.
17. C. Burns, b. 1858.
18. Leonidas H. Burns, b. 1860.
19. Minnie K. Burns, b. 1861.

14. ROWLAND C. BURNS, lawyer, was b. about 1847 and d. at Catlettsburg, Kentucky, June 28, 1914; m. about 1866, Kennie Womack, b. about 1847, and d. in April, 1910, a daughter of James Allen Womack and his wife, Susan Anne (Lampton) Womack. (See Womack Family.)

Children:

20. John A. Burns; b. in 1867; d. in April, 1955; resided in Catlettsburg, Kentucky; unm.

21. James W. Burns; lawyer at Catlettsburg; b. 1869 and d. in December, 1954; m. Margaret Donaldson.

22. R. Clyde Burns, railroad employee, retired; b. in 1874; m. Hattie Sherritt; resides in Catlettsburg.

---

[1] William Ely, The Big Sandy Valley.
[2] The National Archives, Washington, D. C.
[3] William Ely, The Big Sandy Valley.

CAMPBELL, ARTHUR OF KNOX COUNTY

The famous Campbell family of the Scottish Highland was founded by Cailean Mor ("Colin the Great") who lived at Argyll near the close of the thirteenth century. The name Campbell, like Cameron, is derived from a nickname: "Caimbeul" meaning "Twisted mouth". The original form—Caimbeul— is from the Gaelic cam ("wry, twisted") and beul ("mouth"), supposedly an allusion to the personal appearance of an ancestor of the family. The principal Campbells of the Highlands came from the House of Argyll and from the Campbells of Breadalbane, Cawdor and Loudoun.

COLONEL ARTHUR CAMPBELL was one of the most distinguished pioneers of Southeastern Kentucky. He was of Scottish extraction and was born in Augusta County, Virginia, November 3, 1754, old style, and died at site of present Middlesboro, then Knox, now Bell County, August 8, 1811. He was a man of importance and very influential in the early affairs of Southwestern Virginia and Southeastern Kentucky. He represented Fincastle County in the first constitutional convention of Virginia 1776; was one of the first justices of the peace of Washington County, and of Fincastle County, 1773; was county lieutenant of Washington County; and was a lieutenant colonel of the (Washington County), Virginia militia.[1]

Colonel Campbell married his cousin, Margaret Campbell, daughter of Charles and sister to General William Campbell. In 1766 with his wife, he settled at Royal Oak, a mile east of present Marion, Smyth County, Virginia. Subsequently he settled on his plantation on Yellow Creek, site of present Middlesboro, Kentucky. He had acquired a very large estate of lands in Virginia, Tennessee and Kentucky, negro slaves and other personal property at date of death, which was bequeathed to his widow and their children by will which was proved in the Knox (Kentucky) County Court in 1811.

Children:

2. William Campbell

3. John B. Campbell. He was commissioned a lieutenant colonel, 19th Infantry, U. S. Army, March 12, 1812; promoted to colonel, 11th Infantry, April 9, 1814; died August 28, 1814, of wounds received in the battle of Chippewa, July 5, 1814, where he commanded the right wing of the army under Gen. Winfield Scott.[2]

4. Charles Lewis Campbell.

5. Arthur Lee Campbell.

6. James Campbell. He was a colonel in the War of 1812 and died in the service at Mobile, Alabama.

7. Elizabeth Campbell.

8. Margaret Campbell.

9. Mary Campbell Beard.[3]
10. Jane B. Campbell.
11. Martha C. Campbell.
12. Ann Augusta Campbell.

When Middlesboro first attracted the attention of the business people and was being developed, the grave of Colonel Arthur Campbell was discovered in an out-of-the-way place. The remains were removed by his Tennessee relatives and the grave newly marked. The grave was marked by an iron slab bearing the inscription:

"Sacred to the memory of Colonel Arthur Campbell, who was born in Augusta County, Virginia, November 3, 1754, old style, and after a well-spent life, as his last moments did and well could approve, of sixty-seven years, eight months and twenty-five days, ere a constitution, preserved by rigid temperance and otherwise moral and healthy, could but with reluctance consent.' The lamp was blown out by the devouring effects of a cancer on the eighth day of August, 1811, leaving a widow, six sons and six daughters to mourn his loss and emulate his virtues.

"Here lies, entombed, a Revolutionary sage,
An ardent patriot of the age.
In erudition great, and useful knowledge to scan—
In philanthropy hospitable, the friend to man,
As a soldier brave Virtue, his morality.
As a commander, prudent His religion, charity.
He practiced temperance to preserve his health
He used industry to acquire wealth.
He studied physic to avoid disease.
He studied himself to complete his plan.
For his greatest study was to study man.
His stature tall, His person portly,
His features handsome, His manners courtly.
Sleep, honored, sire In the realms of rest
In doing justice to thy memory, A son is blest.
A son is inheriting in full thy name,
One who aspires to all thy fame.

COLONEL ARTHUR CAMPBELL"[4]

---

[1] "Virginians in the Revolutionary War, 1776-1785", by John H. Gwathmey, pages 1924-5.

[2] Heintzman: "Historical Register of the U. S. Army, 1789-1903", Vol. 1, page 278.

[3] After the death of Mary Beard, her inheritance vested in her children, Arthur Beard and Margaret C. Beard.

[4] "History of Southwest Virginia, 1746-1786, Washington County, 1777-1870", by Lewis Preston Summers, 1903, page 463.

CARTERS OF VIRGINIA AND CARTER COUNTY KENTUCKY

Carter

This is a Welch and Gaelic occupational s u r n a m e, presumably from cart (small wagon), the designation of one who drives a cart. In medieval documents the name is written Carectar and Carectarius. There are many variations in spelling, such as Carteret, Cartier, Cartman and C a r t w r i g h t, this last signifying a mender or maker of carts.

In the year 1645, the English Parliament attempted to force Irishmen to take English names. Many of the McCartheys changed their name to Carter, but the change evidently was not a lasting one, for a century later the English authorities complained that "The Irish have become as Irish as ever."

The families of Carter were numerous in England in early days. The Hundred Rolls of Oxford County, 1273, bore the names of Jocius Caritarius and Nicholas le Carter. John le Cartere lived in Norfolk County in 1273 and Robert le Caretter and Margaret le Careter lived in Huntsford County, in 1273, as is evidenced by the Hundred Rolls of those counties. The poll tax rolls of Yorkshire County, 1379, bore the names of Ricardus Carter and Thomas Bell Carter.

There were several first settlers in America bearing the name Carter. Perhaps the first in the Virginia colony was John Carter who in 1649 was a member of the House of Burgesses from Upper Norfolk and in 1654 from Lancaster County. He was named commander in chief of the forces sent against the Indians in 1669.

It is now difficult to connect the many hundreds of branches of this splendid family. It has become wide-spread in the United States. It is a name that is esteemed everywhere for the substantial qualities of those who bear it.

Robert Wormely Carter and his family were among the first, if not the first, Carters to settle in Northeastern Kentucky. The records would seem to indicate that he was of the distinguished family of Carter of Tidewater Virginia of whom "King" Carter was the most noted. He married in Loudoun County, Virginia, in February, 1795, Hebe Smallwood Grayson, daughter of Colonel William Grayson (See Grayson Family). About 1808 the Carters and the Graysons (children of Colonel William Grayson) removed to and settled on lands granted to them by the Government on account of the military service of Colonel Grayson in the Revolution. They settled, at first, on the site of the present Grayson, Carter County, then Greenup County.

Hebe Carter, who had removed to Parish, Bourbon County, Kenutcky, in her will, probated in the Bourbon County Court, in November, 1818, bequeathed all her property to her six children (not giving their names), including the lands she owned in Kentucky, but excluding therefrom the interest she owned in the Little Sandy Salt Works and the 70,000 acres of land in Greenup County on which the Salt Works were located; also all lands in the States of Virginia and Maryland she had inherited from her uncle, "General" (Captain) Smallwood.

In a proceeding in the Jefferson County (Kentucky) Court, the court found and certified, January 6, 1829, that William G. Carter, Landon Carter, Alfred G. Carter and Hebe Carter were [then] the only children and heirs-at-law of Hebe Carter, deceased.

1. ROBERT WORMELY CARTER m. Hebe Smallwood Grayson in Loudoun County, Virginia, February, 1795.

Issue:

2. Colonel William Grayson Carter, planter and prominent citizen, was State senator from the district embracing Greenup, Lawrence and Lewis counties, 1834-38. During the last year of his term he was instrumental in the passage of the act establishing the County of Carter which was named in his honor. The seat of justice, Grayson, was named in honor of the Grayson family—the historian Collins states in honor of Colonel Robert H. Grayson, senator Carter's uncle.

Colonel Carter married Susan, the daughter of General Isaac Shelby, first and sixth governor of Kentucky. Mrs. Carter planned and had constructed on their plantation on the banks of the Little Sandy River about one-half mile from Grayson a fine dwelling house. The house was built of brick which were burned from clay on the site by the slaves on the plantation under the supervision of a Yankee overseer. Doors, mantels, staircases and other woodwork were hand-hewn. After having been furnished it was considered the finest mansion in all the countryside. In 1850 the Carters sold the plantation and mansion to Dr. A. J. Landsdowne who named the estate "Luck Enough" but soon thereafter changed it to Landsdowne Hall" which name it ever afterward bore. The house was razed in 1942.

In 1847 Colonel Carter removed to Arkansas. He died of cholera in Lexington, Kentucky, July 11, 1849, while on a visit there. About 1850 Mrs. Carter removed to her former home in the Bluegrass section. Colonel and Mrs. Carter had no children.

3. LANDON CARTER was graduated from the Military Academy at West Point. He d., unm., and was buried in the limits of Grayson in the rear of the dwelling built and occupied by the late Dr. William A. Horton. He was the only member of the Carter family who was buried in Carter County.

4. ALFRED G. CARTER removed to Mississippi. Very little has been learned concerning him.

5. HEBE CARTER; m. A. Dudley Mann of Virginia, Assistant Secretary of State in the administration of President Franklin Pierce.

6. COLONEL ROBERT GRAYSON CARTER, farmer, b. in Virginia Circa 1800; m. circa 1839 Sophia Berkeley, who was b. in Virginia circa 1810.

Children and ages as shown by the U. S. Census of Carter County for 1850, enumerated August 24, that year:

7. Robert G. Carter, age 10, b. in Virginia.

8. Hebe G. Carter, age 7, b. in Kentucky.

9. Susan Carter, age 5, b. in Kentucky.

These children removed to Ashland, Kentucky. Colonel Robert G. Carter lived in Grayson in a dwelling in the rear of the residence of the late Dr. William A. Hortan.

CECIL AND WITTEN FAMILIES OF VIRGINIA AND FLOYD COUNTY

These two families were so intermingled by intermarriage for several generations after they migrated to the Clinch River Valley, Southwestern, Virginia, that they are not considered separately previous to the migration to Eastern Kentucky.

The Wittens were of teutonic origin and founded the City of Wittenberg, Germany but left Saxony and migrated to England as early as the ninth century where they became identified with the Anglo-Saxons who had conquered the Britons and gave the name England to ancient Britain. The Cecils were of pure celtic blood and natives of the British Isles. Those of them who emigrated to America were lineal descendants of Sir William Cecil, Lord Burghley, who for forty years was the chief minister of England during the reign of Queen Elizabeth. Tradition and documentary evidence reveal that the progenitors of the Wittens and Cecils, in America emigrated from England to Maryland about 1634 with the Hon. Cecil Calvert, the second Lord Baltimore.

In 1766 Thomas Witten, Sr., and Samuel Cecil, his brother-in-law, migrated from Cecil County, Maryland, to Southwestern Virginia. Witten located temporarily on Walker's Creek in the present-day Giles county. Cecil settled where the present-day town of Dublin, Pulaski county, is located. Here he lived until his death in 1785 and here he and his wife were buried.

In the Spring of 1767 Thomas Witten, Sr., moved to and settled on the Crabapple Orchard tract of 1000 acres, on the Clinch River near the old Pisgah Methodist Church in what is now Tazewell county. His dwelling was, about 1772 or 1773, converted into a block house in order to safeguard his family and other oncoming settlers from depredations of hostile and marauding bands of Indians, and became known as Witten's Fort. With him to the Clinch River valley came his son-in-law, John Greenup, and five unmarried sons: Thomas, Jr., James, Philip, Jeremiah and William.

WITTEN

1. THOMAS WITTEN, SR., b. in Cecil county, Maryland, in 1719; d. in Tazewell county, Virginia, in 1794, m., in 1742, Elizabeth Cecil, sister of Samuel Cecil; served in Captain Daniel Smith's Company of Virginia Militia and fought at the battle of Point Pleasant (October 10, 1774), and was mustered into service on the Virginia Line during the Revolutionary War and served on the Virginia frontier against the Indians during 1776, 1777 and 1778.

Children:

2. John Witten, m. in Maryland previous to his father, Thomas Witten's migration to the Clinch River valley; settled near the Peaks of Otter, Bedford county, Virginia; and left many descendants in Bedford and Amherst counties, Virginia, who spelled their name "Whitten."

3. Elizabeth Witten m., John Greenup; removed to Kentucky in 1801. They had children, among others, (1) Thomas Greenup who, previous to going to Kentucky, had been commissioned a captain of the 2d Batallion of the 112 Regiment of Virginia Militia; and (2) Christopher Greenup who held many offices of honor and trust in Kentucky, among others, that of governor, 1804-08.

4. Thomas Witten, Jr., was b. in Maryland, January 23, 1753, and d. in Tazewell county, Virginia, about 1835; served in Captain Daniel Smith's Company of Virginia Militia and fought at the battle of Point Pleasant (October 10, 1774); also served in the Revolutionary War as ensign in the Washington county (Virginia) company of mounted riflemen under the command of then Colonel William Campbell, and fought at the battle of King's Mountain (October 7, 1780); was elected as one of the first members from Tazewell county to the General Assembly of Virginia and served as such from 1801-02 and 1802-03; m. his cousin, Eleanor Cecil, niece of his mother, Elizabeth (Cecil) Witten, and daughter of his uncle, Samuel Cecil. They had children, one of whom a daughter, Rebecca, m. John Graham and removed to Eastern Kentucky. (See Graham Family).

*5. James Witten.

6. Philip Witten, m. Ruth Dickerson and removed to Witten's Landing on the Ohio River.

7. Jeremiah Witten served as a private in Captain William Russell's Company of Virginia Militia and fought at the battle of Point Pleasant (October 10, 1774); m. and resided in Tazewell county where he left many descendants.

8. William Witten, m. and removed to the Sequatchie River valley in Tennessee.

5. JAMES WITTEN, famous woodsman, hunter and spy, was b. in in Maryland, January 7, 1757, and came with his father, Thomas Witten, Sr., to Southwest Virginia, when about fifteen years of age. Before he reached his majority he was recognized as the most skillful and daring scout employed by the military authorities against the Indians, and was regularly employed as scout from 1794 to 1796, operating in the vicinity of Witten's Fort which was located near present-day Tazewell Court House, Tazewell county, Virginia. In 1783 he m. his cousin, Rebecca Cecil, daughter of Samuel Cecil; and they left numerous descendants of whom there were sons:

9. Colonel Wilkinson Witten, soldier and legislator, b. August 12, 1807, d. March 26, 1876.

*10. Dr. William Witten; and probably sons:

11. Thomas Witten.

12. Jacob Witten who migrated to Kentucky and m., in Floyd county, April 18, 1820, Elizabeth Lester.

10. DR. WILLIAM WITTEN, migrated from Tazewell county, Virginia, and settled at Buffalo on John's Creek, then Floyd County, now Johnson county. He m., in Floyd county, October 24, 1819, Lockey Hackworth.

Children:

13. John Wesley Witten was a soldier in the Union Army during the Civil War.

14. Susan Witten, m. —— Howes.

*15. Isaac Quin Witten.

16. William Preston Witten was a soldier in the Union Army during the Civil War.

17. Rebecca Witten, m. —— Preston.

18. Thomas Floyd Witten was a soldier in the Union Army during the Civil War.

19. Limmie Witten, m. —— Preston.

20. Frank Witten was a soldier in the Union Army during the Civil War.

21. Nancy Witten, m. —— Mankins.

*22. George Hamilton Witten.

23. Frank Witten was killed in the battle of Kenesaw Mountain and was buried at Knoxville, Tennessee.

15. ISAAC QUIN WITTEN m. ———— ————.

Children:

*24. Charlotte Witten.

25. Susan Witten, m. ———— Bowe; resided at Sitka, Johnson county.

26. James Witten, resided at Thealke, Johnson County.

27. ———— Witten, m. John T. McKenzie; resided at Thealka, Johnson county.

28. ———— Witten, m. Schuyler Rice; resided at Volga, Johnson county.

22. GEORGE HAMILTON WITTEN, had service in the Union Army during the Civil War; served two terms in the Kentucky Legislature, one term previous to and the other soon after the Civil War; m. Martha Ann Butler; resided in Johnson county.

Children:

29. Frank Witten.

30. Martha Jane Witten, m. ———— Rice.

31. Florence Witten, m. ———— Burchett.

*32. Wilkinson (Wilk) Witten.

33. Mary Witten, m. ———— Stambaugh.

*34. Dr. George W. Witten.

24. CHARLOTTE WITTEN, b. April 28, 1826, d. June 30, 1926; m. first, Lee Dixon; resided in Johnson county.

Children:

35. ———— Dixon, m. A. E. Stambaugh.

36. ———— Dixon, m. U. G. Picklesimer.

37. ———— Dixon, m. E. H. Prater.

38. ———— Dixon.

24-A Charlotte Witten, m., second, John M. Williams, d. 1900.

Children:

39. ———— Williams, m. W. H. McKenzie.

32. WILKINSON (WILK) WITTEN, m. Rachel E. Witten ?; resided at Stambaugh, Kentucky.

Children:

40. Naomi Witten, m. ———— Stambaugh.

*41. Raleigh Hamilton Witten.

42. Anna Witten, m. ———— Arrowood; resided at Betsy Lane, Floyd county.

43. William Earl Witten; resided at Harrisburg, Illinois.

41. RALEIGH HAMILTON WITTEN, businessman, b. August 8, 1893, at Stambaugh, Johnson County; was for many years connected with the North-East Coal Company at Thealka and at White House, Johnson county; m., December 25, 1917, Virlia Johnson, b. March 27, 1895, daughter of Levi Johnson.

Children:

44. Raleigh Edwin Witten, b. October 14, 1920.
45. Wendell Witten, b. July 14, 1922.

11. THOMAS WITTEN migrated from Tazewell county, Virginia, to Eastern Kentucky, and m., in Floyd county, October 1, 1820, Polly (Mary) Lackey, daughter of General Alexander Lackey (See Lackey Family). They lived principally in Tazewell county, although Mr. Witten, for many years, was a businessman in Eastern Kentucky. They had two sons who were well educated in Tazewell county, and trained in mercantile affairs. The youngest son enlisted in the Confederate States Army and was killed in action. The other son, Green M. Witten, spent most of his youth and younger manhood in merchandizing at Prestonsburg, Kentucky, and subsequently he and his cousin, Josph M. Davidson of Prestonsburg commenced business in Catlettsburg, Kentucky, as private bankers. After two or three years Dr. Davidson withdrew from the firm and Mr. Whitten alone conducted the affairs of the bank until 1882 when he wound up its affairs and retired. Mrs. Polly (Lackey) Witten d. on her way to her home in Tazewell county, Virginia, from a visit to her friends in the Big Sandy Valley.[2]

34. GEORGE WASHINGTON WITTEN, physician, b. in Johnson County, Kentucky, January 15, 1854, and d. March 19, 1929; practiced medicine at various places in Eastern Kentucky for many years; m., December 25, 1878, Mary Williams, b. March 20, 1854, and d. November 21, 1933.

Children:

46. Noah Kendrick Witten; b. January 19, 1879; m., first, about 1901, Mollie Wellman who d., 1924. Children: Myrtle, Earl, Murl, Shurl and Roy Kendrick; m., secondly, 1929, Jennie Rice. No chidren. Mr. Witten is retired and resides on Route No. 1, Kenova, West Virginia.

47. John M. Witten, an employee of the C. & O. Railway Company, was b. November 26, 1882, and d. in Huntington, West Virginia, February 14, 1953; was a locomotive engineer on the C. & O. Railroad for many years; retired in 1951; m., November 26, 1906, Miss Eliza Jacobs, a lineal (direct) descendant of Roley Jacobs, a Revolutionary War soldier. She was the adopted daughter of Mrs. Elizabeth Adams of Willard, Kentucky. Children: Christine, May and John Ralph.

48. Foster Hamilton Witten, an employee of Veterans hospital, was b. July 11, 1888; served in World War I; m. 1919, Elsie Trott, Children: Foster, Jr., deceased, Mary Pauline and George.

49. Martha Jane Witten, sometime teacher and business woman, was b. December 18, 1890; taught in the public schools of Kentucky for four years and later did secretarial work and bookkeeping; is presently employed as bookkeeper for the Sheriff and the treasurer of Cobell County, West Virginia, in Huntington; unm.

50. Benjamin Franklin Witten, a Government employee, was b. February 23, 1892, and d. September 10, 1942; had service in World War I; m., June, 1929, Maude Easterday Manoor; no children.[3]

[2] The Big Sandy Valley, by William Ely.

[3] Dr. George W. Witten and His Wife Mary (Williams) Witten and Their Descendants (Manuscript), prepared by Martha Jane Witten, 512½ Fourth Street, Huntington, West Virginia, 1954.

CECIL

1. SAMUEL CECIL, brother-in-law of Thomas Witten, Sr., was b. in Maryland and was m. in that colony but the time or place of his marriage or name of his wife has not been learned. He d. in 1785 on the site of the present-day town of Dublin, Pulaski county, Virginia.

Children:

*2. William Cecil.

3. James Cecil, m. and settled at the head of Baptist Valley, Tazewell county. He left a large family of children.

2. WILLIAM CECIL m., about 1773, his cousin, Ann Witten, daughter of Thomas Witten, Sr. They had six daughters and two sons:

4. Susan Cecil m. Alex Sayers.

5. Rebecca Cecil never married.

6. Elizabeth Cecil m. William Price; they migrated to Missouri.

7. Linnie Cecil m. Crabtree Price; they migrated to Missouri.

*8. John Cecil.

9. Nancy Cecil m. Buse Harman.

*10. Samuel Cecil.

11. Sally Cecil m. James Caldwell; they migrated to Tennessee.

8. CAPTAIN JOHN CECIL was prominent in civil and military affairs of Tazewell county. For many years he was a member of the county court, and represented the county in the Virginia House of Delegates at the sessions of 1808-9, 1810-11 and 1811-12. While the

War of 1812 was in progress he raised a company of volunteers and was made captain of the company, but the Federal Government declined to muster the company into service. He m. Linnie Witten, his double first cousin and a daughter of James Witten, the scout. They acquired a beautiful and valuable farm on Little River, known as the Maiden Spring Fork of Clinch River, which was sold for Confederate money and thus lost.

10. SAMUEL CECIL, was b. in 1788 and d. in 1868. He m., in 1814, Sally Poston, and they built their fine home on the north side of and overlooking the Clinch River opposite the mouth of Plumb Creek which is still owned by descendants. Samuel Cecil did not care for public life and was never an office holder, civil or military, but was esteemed by all persons who came in contact with him.

Children among others:

12. Major William P. Cecil, b. April 9, 1820, and d. July 12, 1899, was prominent in the affairs of Tazewell county for many years as a lawyer and in an official capacity. He served several terms as commonwealth's attorney; delegate to the Virginia Secession Convention, 1861; member of the House of Delegates 1874-1877; commissioned Captain in the Confederate States Army and was promoted to major.

13. —— Cecil, a daughter, m. —— Pendleton and was the mother of William Cecil Pendleton, author of History of Tazewell County and Southwest Virginia, 1748-1920.

CECIL FAMILY OF BIG SANDY VALLEY
THE CECIL FAMILY OF EASTERN KENTUCKY

The Cecils of the Big Sandy Valley are of English Ancestry.

1. KINZY B. CECIL came in at a very early day and settled in the Johns Creek Valley where he reared a large family, the members of which have always held high standing in the business, political and social affairs of the country. When at an advanced age, he moved down in the Rockcastle country where he opened up a large plantation. Here he d. and his last resting place was marked by a stone tomb enclosing his grave erected by his dutiful sons.[1] He was a Virginian or Marylander and it is believed was of the family of Cecil of Southwestern Virginia.

Children, among others:

*2. William Cecil.

*3. Samuel Cecil.

*4. Colbert Cecil, Sr.

2. WILLIAM CECIL, farmer, and onetime public official was born in Virginia about 1803; elected and served as county judge of Pike County; m. in Pike County, May 8, 1828, Elizabeth Ratliff, daughter of Silas Ratliff.

Children living at home and approximate dates of birth as shown by the U. S. Census of Pike County for the years 1850 and 1860:

5. Colbert Cecil; b. 1837.

*6. Pauline Cecil.

7. John P. Cecil, merchant; b. 1844.

8. Crittenden Cecil, merchant; b. 1846.

6. PAULINE CECIL, b. about 1839 and d. 1905; m. in Pike County, Kentucky, Captain Orlando C. Bowles, farmer, lawyer, timber trader and sometimes legislator, b. at Sandusky, Ohio, 1839, and d. at Pikeville, Kentucky, March 7, 1895. He was well educated and was graduated from Oberlin College. He adopted the educator's profession and was so engaged at the outbreak of the Civil War when he was made captain (adjutant) of the 39th U. S. Infantry. He was in the Big Sandy River expedition under the command of Colonel, and afterwards General and President, James A. Garfield and was stationed at Piketon (Pikeville) when he was married. Settling at Pikeville after his marriage, he became interested and influential in the civic and business affairs of the community. He was a lawyer and for a time was a partner of Judge York; served on numerous occasions as special judge of the Circuit Court; served two terms in the Kentucky Legislature, 1865-69. In the business field he

dealt in timber and timber lands, floating logs down the Big Sandy and the Ohio Rivers to Cincinnati to market; and in his later life he engaged in merchandising at Pikeville. He was particularly active in and aided and encouraged the building of churches and schools.

In politics Captain Bowles was a Republican and he was affiliated with the Mason's Lodge in Oberlin, Ohio.

Children:

9. John C. Bowles; b. 1868; cashier of the First National Bank of Pikeville for many years.

*10. Colbert Cecil Bowles.

11. Roland Bowles, farmer, b. February 14, 1871; resided at Pikeville.

12. Malcolm Bowles; connected with the First National Bank of Pikeville.

13. Orlando Charles Bowles, Jr., farmer, and land owner; resided in Pikeville.

10. COLBERT CECIL BOWLES, b. at Pikeville, February 14, 1871; received his elementary education in the Pikeville schools, after which he attended Notre Dame University; was admitted to the bar in 1898 and practiced his profession at Pikeville; was county attorney of Pike County.

When still a youth he became interested in the wholesale grocery business and after reaching manhood he, with others, purchased a wholesale grocery business, of which he became secretary-treasurer. He was interested in and played an important part in the First National Bank of Pikeville and also a Bank in Ashland, Kentucky.

In politics a Republican, in religion a Presbyterian, Mr. Bowles affiliated with the Masons at Pikeville.

In 1896 he m. in Pike County, Miss Nona Connolly, daughter of Winston G. Connolly. (See Connelly Family.)

Children:

14. Charles W. Bowles, b. at Pikeville, 1897; graduated from Pikeville College; had two years in an agricultural college at Lansing, Michigan, where he entered Word War I to go in training for a commission; was sent to Saranac Lake, New York, by reason of tuberculosis, which, when arrested, he returned to his home at Pikeville, where he d. of typhoid fever, March 7, 1920.

15. Lilia L. Bowles; m. N. A. Christman.

16. Harrison C. Bowles; graduated in mechanical engineering at the University of Cincinnati.

17. Josephine Bowles; graduated from Pikeville College, 1921; attended Wesleyan College, Oxford, Ohio.

3. SAMUEL CECIL, farmer; b. in Virginia about 1811; m. Mary J. ——— b. in Virginia about 1827.

Children living at home and approximate dates of birth as shown by the U. S. Census of Pike County for 1850 and 1870:

18. Albert S. Cecil; b. 1847.

19. Thomas M. Cecil; b. 1849.

20. John George Cecil; b. 1853; was elected and serving as Register of the Land Office of Kentucky at the time of his death.

21. Palina Cecil; born 1857.

22. Melissa Cecil; b. 1859.

23. Polly Cecil; b. 1861.

24. Marion S. Cecil; b. 1863.

25. Rebecca Cecil; b. 1865.

26. David W. Cecil; b. 1869.

4. COLBERT CECIL, SR.; b. in Virginia about 1815; was a leading merchant at Pikeville for a time; a Democratic politician; held many local offices; removed to Catlettsburg, Kentucky, and engaged in banking and merchandising and amassed considerable real estate and personal property. He m. in Pike County, a daughter of (General) William Ratliff. The U. S. Census of Boyd County for 1870 shows the following with respect to him and his family:

Colbert Cecil, aged 57, b. in Virginia

Catherine, age 40, b. in Kentucky.

27. Colbert, age 32, dry goods merchant, b. in Kentucky.

28. Colbert, age 17, at school.

29. Sophie, age 15, at school.

Many other Cecil families lived in the Big Sandy Valley in the early and middle 1800's. Tradition has it that among the earliest settlers in the Upper Big Sandy were Kinsey B. Cecil, who settled on the Big Sandy near Pikeville between 1785 and 1790.[2]

The U. S. Census for Floyd County for 1820 shows one Kinsey B. Cecil over 45 years of age as head of a household of seven children and a female (apparently wife) between 26 and 45 years of age.

The U. S. Census discloses that other Cecil families resided in the Big Sandy Valley. In Floyd County, James W. Cecil in 1860;

William W. Cecil in 1860; Thomas Cecil, farmer, age 70 b. in Virginia; Jane, wife, age 70, b. in Virginia; daughters: Margaret, age 39, Sarah A., age 36; Susan, age 33 and Elizabeth age 31, all of whom were born in Virginia.

In Lawrence County in 1870, John Cecil, farmer, age 58, b. in Virginia, and wife, Margaret, age 54, b. in Virginia.

In Johnson County in 1850, Kinsey B. Cecil, farmer age 79, b. in Maryland (apparently the first to Kentucky) and Elizabeth, age 39, b. in Virginia.

One Kinsey B. Cecil m. Luvanna Helvy in Lawrence County, October 24, 1834, and one of the same name m. Elizabeth Muters (Mutters) in Pike County, April 5, 1849. Sophia Cecil, daughter of Thomas, m. Judge George N. Brown in Pike County, November 17, 1847. William N. Cecil m. Lucy Garrett in Floyd County, May 26, 1836.

---

[1] William Ely, The Big Sandy Valley, pages 193-4.

[2] William R. Jillson, Sc. D., The Big Sandy Valley, page 78.

CHANDLER FAMILY

Chandler

Chandler is an occupational name, meaning "the chandler"; a candlemaker; the official who attended to the lights in his lordship's household. The family is of English extraction and most of the pioneer Chandlers in the American Colonies came directly from England.

Major Job Chandler was a distinguished officer in the Maryland Provincial Forces, 1651-1656, Many of his descendants are now living in various states.

In the New England Colonies the Chandlers were represented by a number of early settlers. Edward Chandler settled at Plymouth in 1633 and was granted lands in Duxbury, Massachusetts, in 1640; John Chandler was a freeman in Concord, Massachusetts, in 1640; another John was a shoemaker in Portsmouth, New Hampshire, in 1659; Nathaniel Chandler was a settler in Duxbury, Massachusetts; Roger was a resident of Plymouth in 1633; William was an original proprietor in Andover, Massachusetts. Descendants of these men are living today in New England and great numbers of them pushed westward in the tide of immigration and are now to be found in the South, Middle West and Far West. The name is one that stands for stability and service in every field of endeavor.

The exact time that the first Chandler pushed over the mountains to Eastern or Southeastern Kentucky is not certainly known. The name does not appear on the first U. S. Census or the early tax lists of that section.

1. THOMAS CHANDLER was the progenitor of a large branch of the Chandler family of Cabell County, Virginia, and of the Big Sandy Valley in Eastern Kentucky. He was b., presumably in North Carolina, circa 1762 and d. in what is now Wayne County, West Virginia, in 1845 or 1846.

His declaration, filed in the Cabell County (Virginia) Court, October 22, 1827, in connection with his claim for pension,[1] discloses that he was then 65 years of age and his wife about 64 years old;

that he enlisted as a private for a term of three years or for the duration of the war on the — day of March, preceding Gates' defeat (at Camden, South Carolina, August 16, 1780), in the company of Captain William Lyttle in the Tenth Regiment, North Carolina Continental Line, commanded by Colonel Thaxton; that he served in the said Corps until after the surrender of Cornwallis when he was discharged near Camden, South Carolina.

Available records do not disclose when Thomas Chandler left North Carolina in the Westward movement. In the trek westward he stopped and lived for a time in both Wythe and Tazewell Counties, Virginia, after which, pushing over the mountains he settled about 1806, near the site of present Wayne Court House, Wayne County, West Virginia.

Other Chandlers, believed to have been children of the Revolutionary soldier, lived in Cabell County in Pioneer days:

2. Katie Chandler, the eldest or one of the eldest of the children, was b. in North Carolina or Virginia about 1785 and m. Giles Green (see Green Family).

*3. Abraham Chandler.

4. Sally Chandler, m. George Pyles in Cabell County, March 8, 1827.

5. Elizabeth Chandler m. Enoch Green in Cabell County and moved to Lawrence County, Kentucky (see Green Family).

6. Polly (Mary) Chandler m. William Jarrett in Cabell County, February 24, 1835.

*7. Henry Chandler, the youngest child.

3. ABRAHAM CHANDLER, farmer, was b. in Virginia in 1802; m. in Cabell County, Virginia, July 20, 1821, Susannnah Cox, b. in Virginia about 1802. Within the period 1831-1834 they removed to that part of Lawrence County, Kentucky, which was subsequently (1843) embraced in Johnson County upon its formation.

The U. S. Census of Johnson County for 1850-1860 shows their children with approximate dates of births as follows:

*8. William Chandler, farmer, b. in Virginia about 1826.

*9. Isaac Chandler, b. in Kentucky about 1828.

*10. Thomas Chandler b. in Kentucky about 1835.

11. Sarah J. Chandler b. in Kentucky about 1839.

12. Hannah Chandler b. in Kentucky about 1842.

13. Lydia Chandler b. in Kentucky about 1844.

14. George Chandler b. in Kentucky about 1846.

7. HENRY CHANDLER, the youngest of the children, a farmer, was b. in Virginia about 1816; came to the Big Sandy Valley when a young, unm. man; m. in Lawrence County, Kentucky, March 26, 1835, Jemima Wheeler, b. in Kentucky about 1818.

Children with approximate dates of birth as shown by the U. S. Census of 1850, 1860 and 1870 for Johnson County:

15. Elizabeth Chandler b. about 1837.
*16. James Chandler b. about 1838.
17. Nancy Chandler b. about 1839.
18. Pauline Chandler born about 1841. ⎱ Twins
19. Lovina Chandler born about 1841. ⎰
20. Catherine Chandler b. about 1843.
21. William Chandler b. about 1846.
22. Isaac Chandler b. about 1848.
23. John Chandler b. about 1850. ⎱ Twins
24. Katie Ann Chandler b. about 1850. ⎰
25. Joshua Chandler b. about 1852.

9. ISAAC CHANDLER, farmer, was b. in Kentucky in 1828; m. in Johnson County, September 29, 1848, Elzira Green, b. about 1826, daughter of Giles Green and his wife, Katie (Chandler) Green.

Children and approximate dates of birth as shown by the U. S. Census of Johnson County for the years 1850 and 1860:
26. Martha Chandler b. about 1849.
27. Susan Chandler b. about 1851.

10. THOMAS CHANDLER, farmer, b. in Kentucky about 1835, m. Mahala E. ———, b. about 1839.

Children and approximate dates of birth as shown by the U. S. Census for Johnson County for the years 1860 and 1870:
28. Sarah F. Chandler b. about 1861.
29. George W. Chandler b. about 1863.
30. Susan E. Chandler b. about 1865.
31. Martha A. Chandler b. about 1868.

8. WILLIAM CHANDLER, farmer, b. in Virginia in 1825 or 1826; m. in Johnson County November 20, 1852, Rachel F. O'Brien, b. about 1835.

Children and approximate dates of birth as shown by the U. S. Census of Johnson County for the year 1860:
32. James H. Chandler b. about 1854.
33. Gene (?) L. Chandler b. about 1859.

16. JAMES CHANDLER, farmer, veteran of the Civil War, b. in Kentucky in 1838; m. in Johnson County August 30, 1859, Catherine Daniel, b. in Kentucky, 1840.

Children and approximate dates of birth as shown by the U. S. Census of Johnson County for 1870:

*34. Lafayette Chandler b. about 1860.
*35. Amanda E. Chandler b. about 1866.
*36. Elizabeth J. Chandler b. about 1868.
*37. Columbus Chandler.
*38. H. G. Chandler.
*39. Jemima Chandler.
*40. Melvina Chandler.

34. LAFAYETTE CHANDLER, farmer, was b. in 1860 on the Rockhouse fork of Hood's ·Creek, Johnson County. He was always interested in the general welfare of his county, and was a staunch friend of education having served as local school trustee for twenty-five years. He married Amanda Green, daughter of Giles Green and his wife Margaret (Ghent) Yates. Children:

*41. Frank Chandler.
*42. S. F. Chandler.
*43. Sanford M. Chandler.
*44. J. M. Chandler.
*45. John H. Chandler.
*46. Elizabeth Chandler.
47. Emma Chandler.
48. Nora Chandler.
49. Irvin Chandler.
50. Mildred Chandler.
51. Laura Chandler.

35. AMANDA E. CHANDLER, b. 1876; m. Columbus Davis (see Davis Family).

36. ELIZABETH J. CHANDLER, b. about 1868; m. Wesley Davis.

Children:
52. A. J. Davis.
53. Boston Davis.

37. COLUMBUS CHANDLER m. Laura Lemasters. Children:
54. Bessie Lemasters m. Edford Davis.
55. Jessie Lemasters m. Artie Lemasters.

56. Letitia Lemasters m. Thomas Gibbs.
57. ―――――

38. H. G. CHANDLER m. Madge Davis. Children:
58. Earl Chandler.
59. May Chandler.
60. ―――――

39. JEMIMA CHANDLER m. Sherman McKenzie. Children:
61. Louvina McKenzie m. Louis Isaacs.
62. Lora McKenzie m. Nathan Castle.
63. Haskell McKenzie m. ――― Caudill.
64. Estill McKenzie.
65. William McKenzie.
66. Monroe McKenzie.

40. MELVINA CHANDLER m. Giles Wheeler. Children:
67. Virgie Wheeler m. Ellis Daniel.
68. Amanda Wheeler m. ――― Castle.
69. William Wheeler m. ――― Caudill.
70. Ida Wheeler m. Jesse Green.
71. Esta Wheeler m. ―――.
72. Frank Wheeler m. ―――.
73. (Son)
74. (Daughter)

41. FRANK CHANDLER, b. at Chandlerville, Johnson County; December 4, 1883; was educated in Paintsville Schools and Eastern Kentucky State Normal School at Richmond; taught in the public schools of Johnson County for thirteen years; was elected and served two terms as County Court Clerk of Johnson County, 1918-1926, after which he entered the employ of the Paintsville Bank and Trust Company, now the Second National Bank of Paintsville; married Mary J. Hamilton. Children:

75. Eseau Chandler.
76. Jessie Chandler.
77. Merle Chandler.
78. Emily Chandler.
79. James F. Chandler.
79½. Hazel Ruth Chandler, deceased.

42. S. F. CHANDLER m. Lou Fyle. Children:
80. Ruth Chandler.
81. Roy Chandler.

43. SANFORD M. CHANDLER was for many years connected with the firm of Oppenheimer and Flax at Paintsville and subsequently was traveling salesman for the Paintsville Grocery Company. He m. Maud Burton. Children:

82. Irene Chandler.
83. Homer Chandler.
84. Herold Chandler.
85. James Paul Chandler.

44. J. M. CHANDLER, m., 1919, Kennie Leray. Children:

86. (Son)

45. JOHN H. CHANDLER, b. March 31, 1895, d. August 19, 1938, was a merchant in Paintsville for several years and afterward he entered the employ of the Paintsville National Bank. He was a veteran of World War I; was very active in his local post of the American Legion that aided very materially in securing Paintsville's first fire department, of which he was the first chief. He m. Hazel Fannin, daughter of Bryant Fannin. Children:

87. Jack C. Chandler, b. April 30, 1921, d. in infancy.
88. Susan Chandler.
89. John E. Chandler.
90. Martha Jo Chandler.

46. ELIZABETH CHANDLER m. Lacy Chandler. Children:

91. Geneva Chandler.
92. Olive May Chandler.

Other Chandler families lived in Johnson County, Kentucky, who probably descended from Thomas Chandler, the Revolutionary War Soldier:

93. JAMES CHANDLER, farmer, b. in Virginia in 1817, m. in Lawrence County, Kentucky, August 13, 1835, Catharine Daniel, b. in Kentucky, 1822.

Children and approximate dates of birth as shown by U. S. Census of Johnson County for the year 1850:

94. Henry C. Chandler b. about 1837.
95. Lydia Chandler b. about 1840.
96. Sarah J. Chandler b. about 1842.
97. Martin L. Chandler b. about 1845.
98. Peter M. Chandler b. about 1849.

99. HENRY C. CHANDLER, farmer, b. in Kentucky about 1836; m. in Johnson County March 18, 1857, Perlina E. Grim, b. in Kentucky about 1832.

Children and approximate dates of birth as shown by the U. S. Census of Johnson County for year 1860:

100. James L. Chandler b. about 1858.
101. Charles J. Chandler b. about 1860.

ALBERT BENJAMIN CHANDLER, lawyer and State and Federal public official, was b. near Corydon, Henderson County, Kentucky, July 14, 1898, a son of Joseph S. and Callie (Sanders) Chandler, a grandson of Daniel and Mary (Terrel) Chandler, a great, great grandson of John and Elizabeth (Monroe) Chandler.

He attended the public schools; was graduated at Transylvania College, receiving an A. B. degree, in 1921, and received a LL.D. degree (honorary) from that college in 1936; was a student of law at Harvard University, 1921-22; was graduated at the University of Kentucky, receiving a LL.B. degree, in 1924, and received a LL.D. degree (honorary) from that university in 1937. He was admitted to the bar and began the practice of law at Versailles, Kentucky, in 1924. He served as attorney for the American Life and Accident Insurance Co., Louisville, from 1933 to 1935; was receiver of the Inter-Southern Life Insurance Co., Louisville, 1932; and for a time served as vice-president of the Costal State Life Insurance Co., Atlanta.

Governor Chandler is a Democrat in politics. He has held many high public offices of honor and trust and has always performed the duties pertaining thereto creditably and well. He was appointed Master Commissioner of the Woodford County (Ky.) Circuit Court in 1928; was elected a member of the Kentucky State Senate from the Twenty-second district in 1929; was elected Lieutenant-Governor of Kentucky in 1931 and served until 1935; was elected Governor of Kentucky in November, 1935, at the age of 37. (There has been only one governor of Kentucky younger than he at time of election.) He resigned the governorship, October 9, 1939, and was appointed U. S. Senator, October 10, 1939, to fill a vacancy caused by the death of Senator M. M. Logan; was elected in November 1940, to fill the remainder of the term which ended in January 1943; was reelected in November 1942, to the Seventy-seventh Congress for the six-year term ending in January 1949 and served until October 1, 1945, when he resigned. He was again elected Governor of Kentucky in November 1955, and is presently serving in that capacity.

Upon his resignation from the Senate, Senator Chandler became High Commissioner of Baseball and served in that capacity for several years when he resigned. He was for a time football coach at Centre College, Danville, Ky., and at Versailles (Ky.) High School; and is presently serving as president of the International Base Ball Congress, Wichita, Kansas.

He had service as a private, U. S. Army, in World War I, 1918-1919, and held reserve commission of captain, Judge Advocate General Corps for 25 years.

Governor Chandler's home is in Versailles, Ky. He is a member of St. John's Episcopal Church there and is a publisher of the *Woodford Sun*. He has served as Chairman of the Woodford County Democratic Executive Committee. He is a trustee of the Ty Cobb Memorial Foundation, a member of the American Legion, the Pi Kappa Alpha fraternity, the Lexington and Idle Hour Country Clubs, in Lexington, and is a 32° Mason (K. T. Shriner).

On November 12, 1925, he m. Mildred Watkins of Keysville, Va., a daughter of Marcellus Lee and Virginia (Stephenson) Watkins. Four children have been born to them:

Marcella Chandler (Mrs. Thomas D. Miller, Wilson, N. C.); Mildred Watkins Chandler (Mrs. J. J. Lewis, Versailles); Albert B. Chandler, Jr., and Joseph Daniel Chandler.

---

[1] Revolutionary War Soldier Pension Papers. The National Archives, Washington, D.C.

CHILDER'S FAMILY OF PIKE COUNTY

PLEASANT CHILDERS, Revolutionary War soldier, was the progenitor of a large branch of the Childers family of the Big Sandy Valley region of Kentucky. On the 19th day of October, 1818, he appeared before one of the Judges of the Floyd County (Kentucky) Circuit Court and filed a declaration for a pension on account of his services in the Revolution wherein he stated, among other things, that he was then fifty-seven years of age; that he enlisted in May, 1780, in Warren County, North Carolina, for nine month's service in Captain James Parker's Company of the Fifth Regiment, North Carolina Continental Line, commanded by Colonel Armstrong; that he served in said corps until May, 1781, when he was honorably discharged at Cross Creek (North Carolina) by Captain Armstrong; and that he was in the battles at Stono and Guilford Court House (North Carolina).[1]

1. PLEASANT CHILDERS was b. about 1761 and d. in Pike County, Kentucky, April 25, 1839. He m. in Buckingham County, Virginia, April 16, 1785, Sarah Jeffries, b. about 1765, and d. in Pike County, Kentucky, August 10, 1843.

Second Generation

Children:

*2. Nathaniel Childers.

3. Lucy Childers; m. Joseph Elswick; lived in Buchanan County, Virginia.

4. Elizabeth Childers; m. Levi Clevenger; lived in Pike County, Kentucky.

*5. Sally Childers.

6. Jesse Childers; m. Sally Belcher in Pike County, August 12, 1821.

*7. Pleasant Childers, Jr.

*8. Flemon Childers.

2. NATHANIEL CHILDERS, farmer; b. in Virginia, about 1804; m. Mary J. ———, b. in Virginia, 1816.

5. SALLY CHILDERS; b. in Virginia, about 1804; m. in Floyd County, January 6, 1820, Richard Ratliff, farmer, b. in Virginia, 1799. Children living in the household and approximate dates of birth as shown by the U. S. Census of Pike County for 1850 and 1860:

Third Generation

9. Thompson Ratliff; b. 1830.

10. Tiry (Tyre) Ratliff; b. 1832.

11. William Ratliff; b. 1834.
12. James Ratliff; b. 1835
13. Albin Ratliff; b. 1838.
14. Mary Ratliff; b. 1840.
15. Eliza Ratliff; b. 1842.
16. Richard Ratliff; b. 1847.

7. PLEASANT CHILDERS, JR., farmer, b. in Kentucky, 1806; m. in Pike County, November 30, 1837, Polly McClanahan, b. 1820, daughter of David McClanahan.

Children living at home and approximate dates of birth as shown by the U. S. Census of Pike County for 1860:

THIRD GENERATION

17. E. Jane Childers; b. 1840.
18. Lucy Childers; b. 1844.
19. Alex. Childers; b. 1846.
20. Pleasant Childers; b. 1848.
21. David Childers; b. 1849.
22. Patty Childers; b. 1851.
23. Louisa Childers; b. 1852.
24. Thompson Childers; b. 1854.
25. F. V. Childers (female); b. 1857.

8. FLEMON CHILDERS, farmer; b. in Ashe County, North Carolina (?) 1808; m. in Virginia about 1834, Charity Matney of Tazewell County, that state, who was b. 1810. Coming to Kentucky, he settled on Russell Fork of the Big Sandy, Pike County, where he owned a large tract of land. Later he moved to Marrowbone Creek. Here he d. in 1867 at the age of 74, and his wife d. at age of 68. He was a member of the Regular Baptist Church.

Children:
Third Generation

*26. Loven Childers; b. 1837.
27. Alexander Childers; b. about 1838.
28. John W. Childers; b. 1839.
29. William Childers; b. 1841.
30. Walter Childers; b. 1843.
31. Francis M. Childers; b. 1845.
*32. Flemon Childers, Jr.; b. 1852.
33. Jackson Childers.
34. Jane Childers.

26. LOVEN CHILDERS, farmer, a native of North Carolina, was b. in 1837 and d. in Pike County, Kentucky, in 1907. He had service in the Confederate Army and was taken prisoner and confined at Camp Chase, Ohio. After his release he returned to Pike County and engaged in farming until his death. He m. in Pike County, February 7, 1861, Rebecca Ratliff, a native of Virginia, b. in 1843 and d. in Pike County in 1900.

Mr. Childers was a Democrat in politics and he and Mrs. Childers were members of the Methodist Episcopal Church, South. They were parents of four sons and four daughters, of whom a son (fourth generation)—

35. JOEL EDISON CHILDERS, lawyer, judge and public official, was b. May 10, 1877, at the mouth of Elkhorn Creek near present Elkhorn City, Pike County, Kentucky. He is partially self-educated and attended the public school of Pike County and a private school at Dorton and began teaching in the rural schools prior to his 18th birthday. He was elected a justice of the peace of Pike County at the age of 21; studied law and was admitted to the bar in 1907. A brilliant speaker and possessed of inherent qualifications for the practice of law, he rose rapidly in his profession. A staunch Democrat, he is an active party worker and his party has had the use of his great oratorical powers in every national election from the Bryan campaign in 1896.

Judge Childers has held many public offices of honor and trust and filled all of them creditably and well. He served as Mayor of Pikeville; Presidential elector from the 10th Kentucky District on the Democratic ticket in 1912; served two terms as Circuit Judge of 35th Judicial District of Kentucky, composed of Pike and Letcher Counties; and served two terms as Commonwealth's Attorney of the same district.

Judge Childers is affiliated with the Masons and Independent Order of Odd Fellows .

He was m. in 1903 to Miss Kate M. Leslie, daughter of William Leslie in Pikeville, a lineal (direct) descendant of William Leslie, Revolutionary War soldier and the first settler in the Big Sandy Valley region. (See Leslie family).

Children:

Fifth Generation

36. Elmo Childers.
37. Madaline Childers.
38. Edison Childers.
39. Leslie Childers.
40. Rebecca Childers.
41. Donald Childers.
42. Houston Childers.

32. FLEMON CHILDERS, farmer, timber operator and businessman, was b. on Russell Fork of Big Sandy River near present Elkhorn City, Pike County, Kentucky, October 10, 1852; lived with his father until he was 21 years old and then engaged in farming until he accumulated enough money to buy a farm of his own on Marrowbone Creek, site of present Hellier; was engaged for many years in timber operations in Eastern Kentucky along the Big Sandy River and for twenty-one years rafted timber down that stream to market at points on the Ohio River.

He m., first, at age 21, Vandalia Belcher, daughter of David Belcher; she d. two years later.

Children: Fourth Generation

   43. Albert Childers.

32A. Flemon Childers m., secondly, in 1875, Louisa Spears, daughter of G. W. Spears; she d. in 1880.

Children: Fourth Generation

   44. William Childers.

32B. Flemon Childers m., thirdly, in 1881, Barbara Helton, daughter of Robert Helton. She was b. on Elkhorn Creek, Pike County, and was an active member of the Regular Baptist Church.

Children: Fourth Generation

*45. Adam Fonso Childers.

   46. Sabia Ellen Childers; m. K. Johnson of Greenville, Tennessee.

   47. A. Emile Childers; mine foreman of the Alleghany Mines at Hellier, Kentucky.

   48. Orpha Childers; m. Fred Browning of Hellier.

   49. Hattie Childers; m. William Lewis of Hellier.

   50. Bessie Childers; m. Marlow Stephens.

   51. Plenny Mae Childers.

45. ADAM FONSO CHILDERS, farmer, onetime public official, teacher and lawyer, was b. near present Hellier, Pike County, Kentucky, June 16, 1879; educated in the public schools of Pike County and engaged in teaching in that county for seven years; elected and served as Superintendent of Schools of Pike County, 1906-1910. While engaged in teaching he studied law, 1902-1906, and was admitted to the bar at Pikeville, 1906, and practiced his profession at Pikeville from 1910 to 1943, when he removed to a farm in Boone County, Kentucky, about 20 miles south of Covington, where he engaged in farming until 1948 when he removed to Ft. Pierce, Florida, and engaged in the growing of citrus fruits.

Mr. Childers is a Republican in politics and is a member of the Christian Church, having united with Pikeville Christian Church in 1910, when the late Rev. R. B. Neal was pastor.

Mr. Childers was m. at Pikeville, June 30, 1903, to Miss Kelsie Hildegard Phillips.

Children: Fifth Generation

*51. Leon Milton Childers.

*52. Helen Childers.

*53. Thomas Childers.

*54. Adam F. Childers, Jr.

*55. Joan Childers.

*56. Phyllis Jean Childers.

51. LEON MILTON CHILDERS, dentist, was b. at Ash Camp, Pike County, Kentucky, September 25, 1904; education (elementary and collegiate) Walton (Kentucky) High School, graduating in 1925; A. B., Transylvania College, Lexington, Ky., 1925. Education (Professional, dentistry) D.D.S., University of Louisville, School of Dentistry, 1931; and M.P.H., University of Michigan, at Ann Arbor, 1945.

Prior to his practicing dentistry, Mr. Childers was teacher and basketball coach at Burnside (Kentucky) High School, 1925-26; and at Pikeville (Kentucky) High School, 1926-27; was buyer in the music department of Sears Roebuck Company, Chicago and Minneapolis, 1927-28.

Dr. Childers engaged in dental practice in Lexington, Kentucky, in 1931 and continued for some time. Later he engaged in dental practice in Washington, D. C., and presently is chief dental surgeon in the Veterans Hospital, Coral Gables, Florida.

He is a member of the Bluegrass Dental Society (Secy.-Treas. 1935-36 and First Vice-President, 1934-35); Kentucky and American Dental Associations; Phi Kappa Tau Psi Omega; Elks; and Lexington Lions Club (President 1936, Vice President, 1935.)

Mr. Childers was m., September 7, 1928, to Beulah Roberts of Berea, Kentucky.

Children: Sixth Generation

57. Barry Philip Childers, who graduated from University of Kentucky in 1952, and presently is serving in the Air Force Intelligence, stationed in England.

58. Linda Bryan Childers; b. February 2, 1947.

52. HELEN CHILDERS, b. in Pikeville, February 28, 1907; graduated from Transylvania College, 1927, and taught in the public schools of Kentucky for about fifteen years; m. in 1928, John Meador of Hardinsburg, Kentucky.

Children: Sixth Generation

59. John Meador, Jr., b. 1936.

53. THOMAS CHILDERS; b. in Pikeville, June 4, 1910; educated in the public schools of Pikeville, graduating from the Pikeville High School. Later entered college and after about 2 years he enlisted in the U. S. Navy, serving for about 2 years. When World War II broke out he was living in New York City and employed by a construction company there. After registering for the draft, he went to Canada and was engaged in construction of the Alcan Highway, upon the completion of which he went to Alaska and was engaged in construction of air bases on the Aleutian Islands for many months. Subsequently he was engaged in construction work in Alaska and South America. He was m. in 1939, to Helen Waslick of North Hampton, Massachusetts.

Children: Sixth Generation

60. Roger Childers; b. 1942.

61. Anna Lou Childers (by a former marriage) graduated from University of Kentucky, 1951; m., 1952; resides in Indiana.

54. ADAMS F. CHILDERS, JR., b. in Pikeville, July 9, 1914; educated in the Pikeville public schools, graduating from the Pikeville High School; entered college and after about 2 years he enlisted in the U. S. Navy and served for four years, a part of the time being on foreign service in the Pacific at Okinawa and that area. He m., in 1951, Blanche Brittenhelm of Walton, Kentucky.

Children: Sixth Generation

62. Adam Fonso Childers, III.

55. JOAN CHILDERS; b. in Pikeville, March 18, 1923; educated in the Pikeville public schools, graduating from the Pikeville High School; received the degrees of A. B., 1943, and A. M. 1951, from University of Kentucky; m. Kenchin L. Harris, at Fort Pierce, Florida, in 1953; has been member of the Fort Pierce High School faculty for several years.

56. PHYLLIS JEAN CHILDERS; b. in Pikeville, October 10, 1925; educated in Pikeville public schools, graduating from the Pikeville High School; attended Pikeville College for two years; m. Lawrence Smith, a native of Pike County, Kentucky.

Children: Sixth Generation

63. Larry Scott Smith; b. 1946.

64. Hilda Jean Smith; b. 1948.

65. Barbara Smith; b. 1952.

66. Ricky Ashby (by a former marriage); b. about 1942.

---

[1] The National Archives, Washington, D. C.

CONLEY OR CONNELLY FAMILY OF FLOYD AND JOHNSON COUNTY

Connelly

Genealogists state that the Connelly family is descended from Milesius, King of Spain, through the line of his son, Heremon. The founder of the family was Eogan, ancestor of the Northern Hy Nials and son of Nial of the Nine Hostages, King of Ireland, A. D. 379. The ancient name was Conally and signifies "A Light". The names Connelly, Conally, Conneally, Connolly, Conneallan, O'Connell, and other names of Irish families, are derived from the ancient Milesian name, O'Conghalaigh.

The possessions of the clan were located in the present-day counties of Galway, Meath, and Donegal, Ireland. The Connellys were also chiefs in County Fermanagh, Ireland.

The Connelly family is southern in America. Thomas Connelly and his brother, Edmund, and perhaps two other brothers, John and Henry, emigrated from County Armagh, Ireland, and settled in the vicinity of present Charleston, South Carolina, about 1689. They were men of fortune and affairs; obtained large grants of land from the proprietors of the colonies, one grant, it is said, embracing a part of the site of present Charleston; engaged in town building and in traffic and merchandising by sea and also traded extensively with the the Creek and Cherokee Indians.

In the Revolutionary War the Connellys fought in the patriot armies of Virginia, the Carolinas and Pennsylvania. They served under Generals Washington, Greene, Morgan, Gates, Howard of Maryland, Lincoln, and Charles Cotesworth Pinckney. At the close of the Revolution many of them migrated West, South and Southwest to practically all parts of the United States. They have been exceedingly prolific. It has been estimated that Captain Henry Connelly who, after the Revolution removed from North Carolina to Virginia and thence to Kentucky, has at least one thousand descendants now living.

The name is now variously written but the tendency is to shorten it to Conley.

One of the most distinguished members of the family was Doctor Henry Connelly, late Governor of New Mexico, son of John

Donaldson Connelly of Virginia and brother or first cousin to Captain Henry Connelly, considered herein.

The Connellys have been men of fair fortune. They have been influential in every community in which they lived. Many of them have been possessed of fine literary taste—some of them of fair literary ability. They were in the advance guard in spreading civilization over the West and in a number of states they were pioneers.

1. HENRY CONNELLY of Ireland m. presumably in Ireland, but the name of his wife is not known.

Children:

*2. Edmund Connelly.

3. Thomas Connelly.

4. John Connelly.

5. Captain Henry Connelly, Sr.

2. EDMUND CONNELLY; m., in South Carolina, Mary Edgefield, who according to family tradition, was a daughter of Colonel Arthur Edgefield.

Children:

6. Harmon Connelly; removed to North Carolina where he had a large family of sons and daughters.

7. Thomas Connelly of Guilford County, North Carolina, d., probably in 1783; resided temporarily in Pennsylvania but returned to North Carolina; probably served in General Braddock's Army in its disastrous march on Fort Duquesne; served in the Revolutionary War during the winter of 1779-1780 in the First South Carolina Regiment, commanded by Colonel Charles Cotesworth Pinckney, in defense of Charleston; and according to family tradition he was wounded at King's Mountain (October 7, 1780); m. in Pennsylvania Mary Van Harlingen.

Children:

*8. Henry Connelly and other sons and also daughters.

8. CAPTAIN HENRY CONNELLY, b. in Chester County, Pennsylvania, May 2, 1752, d. in Johnson County, Kentucky, May 7, 1840. He migrated with his father from Pennsylvania to Guilford County, North Carolina and later removed to Kentucky, stopping first in what is now Letcher County, and finally settling in Johnson County. He had service in the Revolutionary War as Captain of a company of calvary, North Carolina Militia, from July 7, 1777 to 1782, serving under Colonels John Williams, John Paisley, John Taylor and William Washington; m., first, about 1774, Ann MacGregor, b.

February, 1756, daughter of Archibald, a member of the clan Mac-
Gregor; and, second, in Floyd County, March 8, 1832, Temperance
Hitchcock, widow of John Hitchcock, who had served in his company
in the Revolution.

Children:

9. Edmund Connelly, of Magoffin County, Kentucky, b. June 2,
1775, d. after 1865; m., in North Carolina, Lydia Joynes; lived and
d. at the head of the State-road Fork, Magoffin County.

*10. Thomas Connelly.

*11. Peggy Connelly.

*12. David Connelly.

13. Rachel Connelly, b. April 8, 1783; m. James Spradlin, one
of the pioneers of Eastern Kentucky; resided in Johnson County.

14. John Connelly, b. August 3, 1785; m. Leah Joynes; descendants lived in vicinity of Flat Gap and on Big and Little Paint
Creeks, Johnson County.

15. Henry Connelly, Jr., of Magoffin County; b. December 1,
1787; m. Mrs. Polly (McCarty) Jackson; lived on the left branch of
the State-road Fork of Licking River.

16. Elizabeth Connelly, b. April 8, 1789.

17. William Connelly, b. July 8, 1791; d., in Floyd County, unm.

18. Joseph Connelly, b. July 8, 1795.

10. THOMAS CONNELLY, b. in Guilford County, North Carolina,
June 25, 1777; m., in Wilkes County, North Carolina, Susan Joynes,
b. July 5, 1780, and d. in Johnson County, Kentucky, March 25,
1872. It is probable that they removed with his father, Captain
Henry Connelly, to Botetourt County, Virginia, where lived many
Connellys, and from there to Kentucky about 1809, where they
settled, first, in the Indian Bottom on the Kentucky River at the
mouth of Rock house Fork in what is now Letcher County. They
removed from there to Johnson County and settled on the main
branch of Jennie's Creek at mouth of Mill Creek where they opened
up one of the largest and best farms in the county. Finally they removed to what is known as the Preston farm at mouth of Miller's
Creek on Big Sandy, four or five miles above Paintsville.

Children:

19. Frances Connelly, b. in Wilkes County, North Carolina, 1880;
m. in Floyd County, February 15, 1821, Benjamin H. Salyer. (See
Salyer Family).

20. William Connelly, b. in Wilkes County, North Carolina, 1803,
and d. there.

*21. Constantine Connelly, Sr.

22. Celia Connelly, b. in 1806; m. Dr. Isaac Rice (See Rice Family).

*23. John Connelly.

*24. Henry Connelly.

*25. Thomas Connelly.

26. Nancy Connelly, b. 1813; m. Asa Fairchild, son of Abiud Fairchild, Revolutionary War soldier. (See Fairchild Family).

27. Susan Connelly, b. 1815; m. John Blair, son of Noble Blair. (See Blair Family).

11. PEGGY CONNELLY, b. August 8, 1779; m. Henry Cantrill.

Children:

28. Elijah Cantrill.

12. DAVID CONNELLY, b. June 24, 1781; m. Polly Howes.

Children:

29. Henry Connelly; m. ———— Davis.

30. Elizabeth Connelly; m. Rhodes Meade. (See Meade Family).

21. CONSTANTINE CONNELLY, SR., b. in Wilkes County, North Carolina, 1805; m. in Floyd County, June 26, 1828, Celia Fairchild, daughter of Abiud Fairchild, Revolutionary War soldier.

Children:

31. Hiram E. Conley; m. Clarinda Rice (See Rice Family).

*32. Jefferson Conley.

*33. Winston (Wince) Conley.

*34. Henry Conley.

*35. Asa J. Conley.

*36. Benjamin Conley.

*37. Amanda Conley.

38. F. Marion Conley; m. Elizabeth Rice. (See Rice Family).

23. JOHN CONLEY, b. 1808; m., in Floyd County, March 14, 1839, Mary Blair, daughter of Noble Blair.

Children:

39. James Hayden Conley; m. Cynthia Ellen Rice (See Rice Family).

*40. John Conley.

*41. Thomas Conley.

*42. William Conley.

43. H. Burns Conley of Hagerhill, Johnson County; m. ————.

44. Martin V. Conley.

*45. Amanda Conley.

*46. —— Conley.

*47. "Sis" (Jemima) Conley.

*48. Hiram Conley.

49. Julia Conley; m. Lewis Christian.

24. HENRY CONNELLY, b. in Letcher County, 1810, d. in Johnson County, July 20, 1877; lived on a large farm on Middle Fork of Jennie's Creek. He was a member of the United Baptist Church; m., in Floyd County, February 24, 1831, Rebecca Blair, b. March 6, 1815, d. April 19, 1862, daughter of George Blair. (See Blair Family).

Children:

*50. Constantine Connelly, Jr.

51. Celia Connelly, b. 1833; never m.

*52. Thomas Connelly.

53. William Connelly, b. 1835; d. at Lexington, K e n t u c k y, a private Company "A", 14th Kentucky Cavalry; was never m.

*54. Mahala Connelly.

55. Clarinda Connelly, b. 1839; m. Jeremiah Hackworth, son of Thomas Hackworth of Magoffin County. Jeremiah Hackworth had service in the Union Army during the Civil War as a private, Company "I", 14th Kentucky Volunteer Infantry.

56. Mary Connelly, b. 1841, d. April 13, 1862, unm.

57. Loucina Connelly, b. 1843; m. 1880, William Baldridge.

58. John Connelly, of Paintsville, b. 1845; m., in Johnson County, January, 1866, Matilda Long, daughter of Morgan Long, of North Carolina.

59. Ellen Connelly, b. 1847; m. Robert L. May.

60. Amanda Connelly, b. 1849; m. Thomas G. May.

61. Catherine Connelly, b. 1851; m. Andrew J. Rice, son of Martin R. Rice. (See Rice Family).

62. Cynthia Connelly, b. 1855; m. Rev. Lewis F. Caudill.

25. THOMAS CONNELLY, m., in Floyd County, September 12, 1833, Mahala Davis. (See Davis Family); resided on Abbot Creek in Floyd County.

*63. Matison Connelly.

32. JEFFERSON CONLEY; m. Irene Auxier.

Children:

64. Henry Connelly, m. —— Spradlin.

65. James Connelly, m. —— May.

66. Sherman Connelly.

67. Martelia Connelly.

68. Alice Connelly, m. Albert Burke.

69. —— Connelly, m. —— Middaugh.

33. WINSTON (WINCE) MAYS CONNOLLY, b. in Johnson County, in 1848, d. at Pikeville, Pike County, in 1897. He was reared to manhood on a farm, attended the public schools, and later studied law and was admitted to the bar. Subsequently he practiced his profession at Pikeville and rose to an honored position therein. He was one of the prime movers in the founding of the Pikeville College of which he was a constant and generous supporter throughout his life, and of which he was one of the first trustees, filling that office until the time of his death.

In his religious faith, Mr. Connolly was a Presbyterian, being one of the charter members and elders in the Pikeville Presbyterian Church. He d. in 1897.

Mr. Connolly m. Mary J. Ratliff, b. at Pikeville and d. in 1920 at the age of seventy years.

Children:

70. Nona Connolly; m. Colbert Cecil Bowles, lawyer and merchant at Pikeville. (See Bowles Family).

*71. William H. Connolly.

34. HENRY CONNELLY, m. Jennie Eastwood.

Children:

72. ——.

35. ASA J. CONLEY (the first of the family to spell the name "Conley") was born on Jennie's Creek, Johnson County, in 1838, and d. at Louisa, Lawrence County in 1911; m. Elizabeth Leslie, b. on Johns Creek, Pike County, September 12, 1845; d. January 25, 1882.

Mr. Conley sympathized with the Confederacy and served in the State militia or home guard. Soon after his marriage he established his residence at Louisa, Lawrence County, and here he held the position of wharfmaster in the meantime conducting a general store on a wharf boat. Subsequently he conducted a prosperous merchandise business on the Public Square at Louisa.

In politics Mr. Conley was a staunch Democrat and was prominent in public affairs of the local party and at one time served as a member of the Lawrence County Fiscal Court. He was a Mason and served as master of the local lodge, often representing it in the

Grand Lodge, and he passed the various chairs in the Louisa Chapter of Royal Arch Masons, including that of high priest.

Children:

73. Martin L. Conley.

*74. Milton F. Conley.

75. Mary Conley.

36. BENJAMIN CONNELLY; m. Mintie Leslie.

Children:

76. ———.

77. ———.

78. ———.

79. ———.

37. AMANDA CONNELLY; m. "Bud" Leslie.

Children:

80. ———.

81. ———.

40. JOHN CONNELLY, m. in Floyd County, March 14, 1839, Mary Blair.

Children:

82. William Connelly, m., first, ——— Lavendar; and, second, Mary Rice.

83. Sarah Margaret Connelly, m. Henry Arms.

84. Dennis Connelly, m. ——— Rice.

41. THOMAS CONNELLY, m. Sarah Reynolds.

Children:

85. Elisha Connelly, m. ——— Arms.

86. Phoebe Connelly.

87. Malinda Connelly.

88. Julia Connelly, m. Sandford Spradlin.

89. Lydia Connelly, m. Thomas Senters.

90. Della Connelly.

42. WILLIAM CONNELLY, m. Eliza Hitchcock.

Children:

91. Belle Connelly.

44. MARTIN V. CONNELLY, m. "Sis" ———.

Children:

92. Cynthia Connelly, m. Adrian Davis.

45. AMANDA CONNELLY, m. Milton Pelphrey.
Children:
93. Benjamin Pelphrey.
94. Smith Pelphrey, m., first, ———, and, second, ——— Adams.
95. Sherman Pelphrey.
96. Sarah Margaret Pelphrey, m. ———.
97. Clark Pelphrey, m. Dicie Schuyler.
98. Paris Pelphrey.
99. John Pelphrey, m. ——— Hall.
100. Daniel Pelphrey, m. ——— Phelps.
101. Milty Pelphrey, m. ——— McFarland.

46. ——— CONNELLY, m. Enoch Spears.
Children:
102. Wilbur Spears, m. Ella ———.
103. Edgar Spears, m. Vic McFaddin.
104. Marcus Spears, m. Ida McFaddin.

47. "SIS" CONNELLY, m. Green Hyden.
Children:
105. Mary Hyden.
106. Martha Hyden.

48. HIRAM CONNELLY, m. ———.
Children:
107. Hayden Connelly.

50. CONSTANTINE, CONLEY, JR. (first to so write the surname, shoe-maker and innkeeper; b. December 5, 1831 and d. April 5, 1904; served during the Civil War in the Union Army, his last service being in the Forty Fifth Kentucky Mounted Infantry, U. S. Volunteers; was thrice m., first, in Johnson County, June 9, 1854, to Rebecca Jane McCarty, b. January 14, 1837, d. November, 1862, daughter of John McCarty and his wife, Lydia (Burke) McCarty. John Mc-Carty was a great grandson of Captain Richard McCarty who had service in the Revolutionary War as captain in the Virginia line. Lydia Burke was a granddaughter of William Burke, private in General Henry "Lighthorse Harry" Lee's Legion, War of the Revolution; m., second, Artemisia May, daughter of Caleb May, who d. within a few months without children; and m., third, Charlotte Picklesimer, b. in Magoffin County, May 21, 1830, d. in Johnson County, February 11, 1907.

After the close of the Civil War, Mr. Conley removed to East Point, Johnson County, where he lived until his death in 1904.

50A. Children of Constantine Conley, Jr., and his wife, Rebecca Jane (McCarty) Conley:

*108. William Elsey Connelley (Conley).

109. Henry C. H. Conley, b. October 18, 1856; m. in Johnson County, January 17, 1877, Mrs. Catherine (Rice) May.

*110. Louisa Elizabeth Conley.

111. Martha Ellen Conley, b. July 19, 1860; m. in Johnson County, September 14, 1884, North J. Price, b. in Johnson County, March 4, 1855.

112. John Mason Conley, b. May 5, 1862; m. Mary ———. Resided at Little Rock, Arkansas, where he was a contractor in construction of railroads and levees.

50B. Children of Constantine Conley, Jr., and his wife, Charlotte (Picklesimer) Conley:

113. James M. B. Conley, b. November 20, 1866; m. Victoria Coleman.

114. Joseph Milton Conley, b. April 28, 1868; m. in Johnson County, July 31, 1892, Amanda Fitzpatrick, b. in Johnson County, June 27, 1869.

115. Sarah Conley, b. August 29, 1870; d., unm.

116. Mary Conley, b. June 5, 1873; m. in Johnson County, November 29, 1894, William R. Auxier.

117. Susan Conley, b. June 11, 1875; m. Thomas Luther, Louisa, Kentucky.

52. THOMAS CONLEY, m. ——— Conley.

Children:

118. ——— Conley.

54. MAHALA CONLEY, m., first, William Spradlin, and second, Nathaniel Picklesimer.

Children:

119. Clarinda Spradlin.

120. Mantford Spradlin.

63. MATISON CONLEY; m. Elizabeth Colvin.

Children:

121. John Milton Conley.

71. WILLIAM H. CONNOLLY, lawyer, b. at Pikeville, in 1872, and d. at that place in 1898; attended the public schools and then pursued a course in the Pikeville College. He was graduated from the University of Louisville, department of law, and began the practice at Pikeville in partnership with his father and later W. O. B.

Ratliff became associated with him with whom he remained until his death. He m. Hester A. Rolf, b. at Louisa, Lawrence County, who, after the death of Mr. Connolly, m. T. N. Huffman of Pikeville.

Children:

122. Winston M. Connolly, business man of Pikeville; educated in the pubilc schools of Pikeville, at Pikeville College, and an agricultural institution at Lansing, Michigan. He affiliated with the Masons.

123. Frank A. Connolly, business man of Pikeville; educated in the public schools and at Pikeville College; was connected with the Pikeville Ice Plant, acting as general manager. He affiliated with the I. O. O. F.

74. MILTON F. CONLEY, editor and publisher, banker and business-man, was born at Louisa, Lawrence County, Kentucky, June 13, 1868. After attending the public schools at Louisa and receiving private instructions under his maternal uncle, R. A. E. Leslie, then a teacher in the public schools at Prestonsburg, he left school at the age of fourteen and engaged in newspaper work. He began an apprenticeship in the office of Prestonsburg Banner, going later to the Lawrence County Index. With L. B. Ferguson he purchased the plant and business of the Louisa Index, the name of the publication afterward being changed to the *Big Sandy News* which became the leading newspaper in that section of the Big Sandy Valley. In 1901 he purchased a half interest in the *Ashland Daily Independent* at Ashland, Boyd County, and for two years he was editor of the paper while continuing similar service with the *Big Sandy News*. In 1904 Mr. Conley became associated with the organization and incorporation of the Louisa National Bank at Louisa and became its first cashier. He was likewise one of the organizers of the Louisa Fort Gay Bridge Company and became one of its directors. He was a member of the original Board of Trustees of the Big Sandy Valley Seminary at Paintsville, Johnson County, and it was he who suggested the name of the institution which title has since been changed to the John C. C. Mayo College, he continuing as a trustee of the college. He was a member of the Board of Trustees of Morris Harvey College at Barboursville, West Virginia.

In politics Mr. Conley was a Democrat. For many years he was a member and officer in the Methodist Episcopal Church, South, in his home city. He held public offices of honor and trust. He was postmaster at Louisa 1893-1897, and a member of the Kentucky State Prison Commission for four years under appointment of Governor McCreary.

In 1894 Mr. Conley m. Miss Willie Burgess, the daughter of Cornelius and Julia (McClure) Burgess and lineal descendant of

Edward Burgess, Revolutionary War soldier (See Burgess Family). Mrs. Conley was b. on a farm on the Big Sandy River, nine miles above Louisa, and her higher education was received at Bellewood Seminary at Anchorage, near Louisville, Kentucky.

Children:

Neil Burgess Conley; was a student in the engineering department of the University of Kentucky, when World War II broke out; enlisted in the Navy and was in training for a commission when armistice was signed; afterward he was associated with the Millers Creek Mining Company near Auxier, Floyd County.

Elizabeth Leslie Conley; attended Ward-Belmont College at Nashville, Tennessee, and thereafter completed a course of study at Gunston Hall, near Washington, D. C.

Emily Burgess Conley; student in Louisa High School.

108. WILLIAM ELSEY CONNELLEY, A. M., author, first of the family in Kentucky to write the surname "Connelley", b. in Johnson County, Kentucky, March 15, 1855; was principally self educated. A. M., honorary, Baker University, Baldwin, Kansas, 1911; taught school in Johnson County, Kentucky, 1872-1880, and in Wyandotte County, Kansas, 1881-1882; served as County Court Clerk of Wyandotte County, 1883-1887; in wholesale lumber business, Springfield, Missouri, 1888-1892; connected with banking interests, Kansas City, Kansas, 1892-1893; instrumental in organization of Kansas Oil Producers Association and initiated crusade which resulted in dissolution of the Standard Oil Company by the United States Supreme Court: Secretary of the Kansas State Historical Society; author: "The Provisional Government of Nebraska Territory," 1899; "James Henry Lane," 1899; "Wyandotte Folk-Lore," 1899; "Kansas Territorial Governors," 1900; "John Brown," 1900; "Life of John J. Ingalls," 1903; "An Appeal to the Record." 1903; "The Heckewelder Narrative" (edited), 1907; "Doniphan's Expedition," 1907; "Quantrill and the Border Wars," 1909; "Ingalls of Kansas," 1909; "Eastern Kentucky Papers," 1910; "Life of Preston B. Plumb," 1913; with Frank A. Root, "Overland Stage to California," 1901; "History of Kansas," 5 vols. 1917; with Judge Charles Kerr and E. M. Coulter, "History of Kentucky," 5 vols. 1922; contributor to scientific journals on folk-lore and ethnology of Wyandots, etc; prepared the first vocabulary ever written of the Wyandot language and made extensive investigations in language and history of the Delawares, Shawnees and other tribes.

William Elsey Connelley m., first, in Johnson County, Kentucky, February 18, 1874, Julia Frances Witten, b. in Johnson County, 1857, d. in that county April 9, 1881, daughter of William P. Witten and his wife, Mary Jane (Dixon) Witten; m., second, at

Council Bluffs, Iowa, January 13, 1885, Sarah Atalanta Fife, b. at Plymouth, Indiana, July 17, 1858, daughter of Thomas Fife, b. at Abbeville, South Carolina, December 12, 1811, d. at Plymouth, Indiana, August 21, 1882, m. November 9, 1837, Sarah Beatty Reid, b. at Connersville, Indiana, April 4, 1821, d. May 12, 1864.

Issue by first marriage:

124. Bernadette Connelley, b. in Johnson County, Kentucky, August 11, 1875; m., in Johnson County, James Coldiron.

125. Walter Constantine Connelley, b. in Johnson County, August 21, 1879; m., first, in Johnson County, Kentucky, Virgie Vincille, and, secondly, in Magoffin County, Kentucky, Mrs. Grace Bayes.

Issue by second marriage:

126. Elsie Louise Connelley, b. in Springfield, Missouri, November 28, 1890, d. at Beatrice, Nebraska, December 31, 1892.

127. Edith MacGregor Connelley, b. in Wyandotte County, Kansas, September 29, 1892; m. August William Ross of Topeka, Kansas.

110. Louisa Elizabeth Conley, b. May 26, 1858; m., first, Mantford Conley.

Children:

128. Flo. Virginia Conley, m. George Bayard.

*129. Dr. Edward Conley.

110A. Louisa Elizabeth Conley, m., secondly, John W. Columbus, a building contractor, who constructed some of the best buildings in the Big Sandy Valley.

Children:

130. John Columbus, architect, who experimented much with airplanes, electricity, etc.

121. John Milton Conley, m. Mary Woods; lived on Mud Lick Creek, Johnson County.

Children:

131. Forest Conley.

*132. Harry B. Conley.

*133. Ethel Conley.

*134. Evert Conley.

*135. Lillian Conley.

136. Ralph Conley.

137. Hobert Conley, m. Ethel Preston.

*138. William Conley.

139. Ivel May Conley.

129. Dr. Edward Conley, m. Ethel Williams; resided in Ashland, Kentucky.

Children:

140. Edward Conley.

132. Harry B. Conley, businessman of Paintsville; m. Bertha Barnett.

Children:

141. Irene Conley.

142. Charles Conley.

143. Harry Conley, Jr.

144. ——— Conley ⎱
145. ——— Conley ⎰ Twins

146. ——— Conley.

133. Ethel Conley; m. Homer Picklesimer.

Children:

147. Walter Picklesimer.

DAVIS FAMILY OF PRINCE WILLIAM COUNTY, VIRGINIA, AND CARTER COUNTY, KENTUCKY

Davis is a form of Davids, and means "Son of David". The name David, recurring often both as a personal name and as a surname, seems to have been a favorite name for many generations among the Welsh and Scots. The Biblical David means in Hebrew "beloved, dear". It was said of the great psalm writer: "All Israel and Judah loved David".

A pet name for David was Daw, from which came Daws and Dawson, both meaning "son of Daw", equivalent to Davidson. The name Davies is the fifth commonest name in England and Wales exceeded in frequency only by Smith, Jones, Williams and Taylor.

1. ELIAS DAVIS was the progenitor of a prominent and influential branch of the Davis family of Carter and Boyd Counties, Kentucky. He was a native of Wales and emigrated to Virginia before the Revolutionary War. His son, (second generation),

2. RICHARD DAVIS, farmer, was passionately fond of hunting and was known as "Hound Davis" on account of the number of fox hounds he kept. He m. in Prince William County, Virginia, Jane Reno. They migrated and settled in Fleming County, Kentucky, where he died in 1840. Their son (third generation):

3. ELIAS P. DAVIS, public official, was b. in Prince William County, Virginia, February 14, 1810; educated in the public schools of Prince William County; removed with his parents to Fleming County, Kentucky, where he resided for ten years when, in 1837, he removed to Carter County, Kentucky, where he rose to distinction as a public official and citizen. He held many positions of honor and trust and his performance of duty in all of them was very creditable. He served as Sheriff of Carter County, 1851; Circuit Court Clerk, 1851-1884; and County Court Clerk, 1854-1882.[1] A staunch Union man, he had service in the Union Army in the Civil War in Company "D", 40th Kentucky Volunteer Mt'd. Infantry; was enrolled March 28, 1864; mustered in a first lieutenant, April 12, 1864, at Lexington, Kentucky, for one year; promoted from first lieutenant to captain; and mustered out at Catlettsburg, Kentucky, December 30, 1864.[2]

Mr. Davis was a prominent Whig and subsequently was a member of the Republican party after its organization. He was a skillful politician, of pleasing personality and a colorful figure. He d. March 8, 1884. Interment at Grayson, Kentucky.

In 1836 Mr. Davis m. Myrtilla A. Winn, b. in Champaign County, Ohio, October 25, 1812, and d. at Grayson, Carter County, Kentucky, July 25, 1886. She was a devout member of the Christian

Church, a devoted wife and a woman of great influence and strength of character. Her father, Douglas A. Winn, a native of Virginia, migrated from that state to Champaign County, Ohio, and afterwards removed to Kentucky. Finally he removed to Calloway County, Missouri, where he died. He was a fine scholar, a noted mathematician, a professional teacher and a member of the Christian Church. He m. Elizabeth Trilby Rawlins, b. in Champaign County, Ohio, and d. in Calloway County, Missouri, 1876. Her mother was a Miss Trilby, a native of France.

The Davis and Winn families were originally from Wales.[2]

Children of Capt. Elias P. Davis and his wife, Myrtilla A. (Winn) Davis (fourth generation):

*4. Richard D. Davis.

*5. Elizabeth Davis.

*6. Watson A. Davis.

7. Mary ("Mallie") Davis.

4. RICHARD DOUGLAS DAVIS, lawyer, judge, public official and banker, was b. at Grayson, Carter County, Kentucky, September 22, 1844; educated in the public schools of Carter County and was well advanced in his studies when, in 1862, he was made deputy clerk of the Circuit and County Courts of Carter County. Later he served as deputy Circuit Court Clerk of Madison County, Kentucky, for 19 months; was for a short time in the office of the Collector of Internal Revenue at Richmond, Kentucky, and subsequently was in charge of the Circuit Court Clerk's office in Richmond, from February 20, 1865, to 1867, serving a part of that time as deputy clerk. Upon the resignation of the clerk, Mr. Davis was appointed to fill the vacancy and served until 1868 when, having been admitted to the bar, he returned to Grayson, Carter County, and began the practice of law in which he continued successfully until 1889.

Judge Davis was a Republican in politics. He was elected and served as county attorney for Carter County from September 1870 to August 1873, when he resigned, having been elected as State Representative from the Boyd-Carter district. He was elected and served as judge of the Carter County Court, October, 1881—September 1882. He organized the Second National Bank of Ashland in 1888 and was chosen president; and in 1889 he removed his family to Ashland where for many years he was considered one of its best and most enterprising citizens.

Judge Davis was a Mason, was affiliated with the Independent Order of Odd Fellows and was a member of the "Concatenated Order of Hoo Hoo" an association of railroad and lumber men.

Mr. Davis m., in Carter County, November 8, 1870, Miss Mary

Lewis, daughter of Charles Nelms Lewis II and his wife, L. A. (England) Lewis. (See Lewis Family).

Mary (Lewis) Davis was b. near Grayson, Carter County, May 25, 1851, and died, 1941; was a member of the Christian Church and was a lady of culture and fine personal appearance.

Both Judge and Mrs. Davis were interred in the Davis plot in the Grayson Cemetery at Grayson.

Children (fifth generation):

*8. Lewis N. Davis.

*9. Roscoe C. Davis.

*10. Myrtilla A. Davis.

*11. Richard D. Davis, Jr.

8. LEWIS NELMS DAVIS, bank cashier, was b. at Grayson, Kentucky, October 31, 1871; d., 1931; educated in the public schools of Ashland and at Notre Dame University; m. Nora Ringo.

Children (sixth generation):

12. Willis Davis; deceased.

13. Douglas Davis; deceased, 1913.

14. Robert Watson Davis; m. Helen Dickey.

9. ROSCOE CONKLING DAVIS, Navy officer, was b. at Grayson, Carter County, Kentucky, October 19, 1878; educated in the public schools of Ashland, Kentucky, graduating from the Ashland High School with the class of 1896; appointed Midshipman, U. S. Naval Academy, Annapolis, Maryland, 1898 and was graduated with the class of 1902; was commissioned ensign, U. S. Navy, 1904; lieutenant, 1906; lieutenant commander, 1916; commander, 1918; and captain, 1925; was retired from service, 1937 and 1945; served in World Wars I and II.

He was m., 1908, at Philadelphia, to Gettine Vroom, b. at Camden, New Jersey, 1889, daughter of Judge Vroom. Miss Vroom attended the Philadelphia School of Art and Design for Women. No children. Present address, 1626 Mt. Eagle Place, Alexandria, Virginia.

10. MYRTILLA ANN DAVIS; educated in the public schools of Ashland, Kentucky, and at Western College for Women, Oxford, Ohio; m. Daniel H. Holton; no children.

She is a member of the Colonial Dames and of the Daughters of the American Revolution, Huntington (West Virginia) Chapter, on the service records of her ancestors (maternal line) Captain Thomas Bragg and Captain George Neville, Revolutionary officers in the Virginia Forces.

Present address, 2188 Washington Blvd., Huntington, West Virginia.

11. RICHARD DOUGLAS DAVIS, JR., lawyer, was b. at Grayson, Carter County, Kentucky, July 15, 1885; educated, elementary, in the public schools of Ashland, Kentucky, collegiate, at Andover Academy and Yale University; legal, at University of Chicago and at University of Michigan, at Ann Arbor; m. Marjory Baker.

Children (sixth generation):

15. Richard S. Davis; m. Phyllis Beckwith.

16. Marianna Davis; m. Capt. Hewitt Larson.

5. ELIZABETH J. DAVIS was b. in Kentucky, probably Fleming County, 1837, and d. at Grayson, Carter County; m., in Carter County, 1958, George W. Littlejohn.

George W. Littlejohn, hotel keeper, was b. in Greenup County, Kentucky, 1835, and d. at Grayson, Carter County. He had service in the Union Army in the Civil War in the 40th Kentucky Volunteer Mt'd. Infantry; was mustered in March 30, 1864, at Lexington, Kentucky, for one year; promoted from first lieutenant, Company "E" to Regimental Quarter-Master; and was mustered out at Catlettsburg, Kentucky, December 30, 1864.[3]

Children (fifth generation):

17. Julia Littlejohn; b. at Grayson, 1859; educated in the public schools at Grayson and at Weirham, Massachusetts; unm.

18. Betty Littlejohn; d. in infancy.

*19. Myrtilla Littlejohn.

*20. John D. Littlejohn.

19. MYRTILLA LITTLEJOHN; m. Reese Dobyns.

Children (sixth generation):

21. Myrtilla Dobyns.

22. Emily Dobyns.

23. James Dobyns.

20. JOHN D. LITTLEJOHN, newspaperman; educated in the public schools of Grayson and at Bethany College, Bethany, West Virginia; publisher of the Grayson Tribune for a number of years; and was postmaster at Grayson for eight years; m. Catherine ("Katie") Giles.

Children (sixth generation):

24. Elizabeth Littlejohn; m. H. Wadsworth Hubbard, who is

connected with the Bell Telephone Company. They reside in Atlanta, Georgia.

25. Margaret Littlejohn; deceased.

26. Catherine Littlejohn; resides in Atlanta, Georgia.

27. Reese Littlejohn.

6. WATSON ANDREW DAVIS, public official, was b. at Grayson, Carter County, Kentucky, 1853; was deputy clerk of the Circuit and County Courts of Carter County for a number of years; elected and served as clerk of the Carter Circuit Court for many years; and was elected and served as judge of Carter County Court for one term, 1906-1910; m., February 27, 1872, Casteria Prichard, daughter of George W. Prichard (See Prichard Family). No Children.

7. MARY ("MALLIE") DAVIS; b. at Grayson, Carter County, Kentucky, 1843; m. Harrison B. Literal, who served in the Union Army during the Civil War as captain, Company "E", 40th Regiment, Kentucky Volunteer Mt'd. Infantry.[4]

[1] "Biographical Cyclopedia of the Commonwealth of Kentucky", compiled and published by John M. Gresham, Company, Chicago—Philadelphia, 1896.

[2] "Report of the Adjutant General of Kentucky, 1861-1866", Vol II, p. 430.

[3] "Report of the Adjutant General of Kentucky, 1861-1866", Vol. II. pp. 425, 432.

[4] "Report of the Adjutant General of Kentucky, 1861-1866", Vol. II, p. 432.

DAVIS FAMILY OF JOHNSON COUNTY

Davis is a form of Davids, and means "son of David". The name David recurring often both as a personal name and as a surname, seems to have been a favorite name for many generations among the Welch and Scots. The Biblical David means in Hebrew "beloved, dear". It was said of the great psalm writer: "All Israel and Judah loved David."

A pet name for David was Daw, from which came Daws and Dawson, both meaning "son of Daw", equivalent to Davidson. The name Davies is the fifth commonest name in England and Wales, exceeded in frequency only by Smith, Jones, Williams, and Taylor.

The Davis family of the Big Sandy Valley, Eastern Kentucky, is of Welsh ancestry. There are many branches of this family of whom James Davis left Johnson County and settled near West Liberty, Morgan County, Kentucky.

The ancestors of the Davis family of Johnson County came from either Tazewell or Augusta County, Virginia, probably from the latter.

1. RICHARD DAVIS, it would seem, was b. January 6, 1773, presumably in Virginia and d. in Johnson County, Kentucky, in 1873 at the age of 100 years; m., presumably in Virginia, Mary Fugett.

Children: Second Generation

2. Robert Davis.

3. Frank Davis; said to have been killed by being thrown from a horse.

*4. Henry Davis.

*5. Alfred Davis.

*6. Rachael Davis.

*7. James Davis.

*8. Elias Davis.

4. One HENRY DAVIS, m. in Floyd County, Kentucky, December 16, 1815, Polly (Mary) Waters.

Children: Third Generation

9. Thomas J. Davis.

5. ALFRED DAVIS; b. in Virginia; migrated to Kentucky and settled at Greenupsburg, (now Greenup) Greenup County; served in the Union Army during the Civil War and was killed while in the service; m., Matilda.

Children: Third Generation

10. Alfred Davis, Jr.

6. RACHAEL DAVIS, m. Allen Penix.

Children: Third Generation
*11. Henry Penix.

7. JAMES DAVIS, farmer and influential in civil affairs of Floyd
County in his time, having served as justice of the peace for several
years; lived for a time on Jennie's Creek, and was possessed of a
farm of 165 acres, nine horses and 176 head of cattle in 1837, as
shown by the tax lists of Floyd County for that year; removed to
near West Liberty, Morgan County, where many descendants reside;
was killed in 1860 at Ezel, Morgan County, at about the age of 80
years by Union soldiers returning his fire; m. Catherine Salyer.

Children: Third Generation
*12. Richard Davis.
*13. Mahala Davis.
*14. Joel Davis.
  15. Malinda Davis; m. Martin R. Rice. (See Rice Family.)
*16. Davidson Davis.
*17. Mary Davis.
  18. William R. Davis.
  19. James Davis.
*20. Kaley Davis.
*21. Alfred Davis.
*22. Amos Davis.
*23. Nancy Davis.
*24. Santford Davis.

8. ELIAS DAVIS, farmer; b. August 15, 1804, d. July 13, 1893; m.
in Floyd County, February 20, 1823, Elizabeth Curtis, b .October 30,
1803, d. March 22, 1887, daughter of James Curtis; lived near Fish
Trap Church, Johnson County, the greater part of their married
life.

Children: Third Generation
*25. Mary (Polly) Davis.
  26. Sarah Davis; b. February 20, 1826.
*27. James McHenry Davis.
*28. Anna Davis.
*29. Mahala Davis.
*30. Susan Davis.
*31. Lydia Davis.
*32. Bracken Lewis Davis.
*33. Davidson Davis.
*34. Elizabeth Jane Davis.

11. HENRY PENIX; m. in Floyd County, June 18, 1834, Rachael Jenkins?; resided in Magoffin and Morgan Counties, Kentucky.

Children: Fourth Generation
35. James Penix.
36. William Penix.
37. Martin Penix.
38. Allen Penix.

12. RICHARD R. DAVIS; m. in Floyd County, August 31, 1835, Ellen (Eleanor ?) Reed; resided on Little Paint Creek, Johnson County.

Children: Fourth Generation
39. Harvey Davis, m. ——— Howes.
40. John Davis; m. Lou Ann Webb.
41. Telitha Davis; d., unm.
42. Susan Davis; m. ——— Fairchild.
43. Hannah Davis; m. Shelby Baldwin.

13. MAHALA DAVIS; m., in Floyd County, September 12, 1833, Thomas Conley.

Children: Fourth Generation
44. Madison Conley.
45. Mary Conley.
46. Daniel Conley.
47. ——— Conley, m. ——— May.
48. James Conley.
49. ——— Conley, m. ——— Conley.
50. Marion Conley.
51. Harvey Conley.
52. Dicie Conley.
53. Benjamin ? Conley.
54. Ellen Conley.

14. JOEL DAVIS; m. Martha (Salyer) Conley; resided near West Liberty, Morgan County.

Children among others: Fourth Generation
55. William Davis.
56. Henry Davis, m. ——— May.
57. Santford Davis.
58. James Davis.
59. Ellen Davis, m. ——— Cottle.

16. DAVIDSON DAVIS, m. ———; lived in Carter, Elliott and Greenup Counties, Kentucky.

Children: Fourth Generation
60. John Davis.

17. MARY DAVIS; m., first, James Wheeler.
Children: Fourth Generation
  61. Henry Wheeler.
  *62. Martin Wheeler.
  *63. Louisna Wheeler.

17A. Mary Davis; m., secondly, John Colvin.
Children: Fourth Generation
  *64. Mantford Colvin.
  65. Alice Colvin; m. Milton McDowell, b. 1850. His opportunities in his youth for securing an education were limited but by working his way, he obtained his education wherever he could, attending such select schools as the county afforded at the time. He taught in the rural schools of Johnson County thirty-two years; served as county superintendent of schools of Johnson County for one term, 1906-1910, when he retired to his farm and afterwards devoted himself to farming and the raising of pure-bred live stock, mainly cattle and sheep.
  *66. Jefferson Colvin.

18. WILLIAM R. DAVIS, farmer and preacher; m. Elizabeth Wilson; resided on a farm on Red River at Adel, Morgan County, Kentucky.
Children: Fourth Generation
  67. James Davis.
  68. Henry Wise Davis.

20. KALEY DAVIS; m. William Wells.
Children, among others: Fourth Generation
  69. Mahala Wells; m. Robert Caudill.
  70. ――― m. John Caudill.
  71. Jefferson Wells.
    Here is the interesting case of twin sisters marrying twin brothers.

21. ALFRED DAVIS, m. ――― ―――.
Children:
  72. Jefferson Davis.

22. AMOS DAVIS, farmer and traveling salesman; interested in public affairs; defeated as Republican nominee for Congress from

the 10th Kentucky District by the Hon. Frank A. Hopkins, 1904; m. Mary Jane Henry; resided near West Liberty, Morgan County.

Children: Fourth Generation
73. Alice Davis.
74. John Davis.
75. Ellen Davis.
76. William Davis.

23. NANCY DAVIS, m. in Floyd County, July 14, 1841, Simpson Debord.

Children: Fourth Generation
77. Joel Debord; m. Alice Trimble.
78. James Debord.
79. William Debord.
80. John Debord.
81. Elizabeth Debord.

24. SANTFORD DAVIS; m. Matilda Perry.

Children: Fourth Generation
82. Mary Davis.
83. Thomas Davis.
84. Ida Davis.
85. Forrest Davis.
86. John Davis.

25. MARY DAVIS; b. July 8, 1824, at Fish Trap, Kentucky, d. April 7, 1897; m. James H. Blanton, farmer, b. January 25, 1820, d. August 5, 1905, son of George Blanton; resided on Blanton Branch, Johnson County.

Children: Fourth Generation
*87. Elias Blanton.
*88. George Washington Blanton.
*89. Martha Blanton.
*90. Anna Blanton.
*91. James (Mack) Blanton.
*92. John E. Blanton.
*93. Harmon Blanton.
*94. Mary Blanton.
*95. Sanford Lee Blanton.
*96. Lydia Blanton.
*97. William R. Blanton.
98. Benjamin Blanton, m. Cordelia Lemaster.

27. JAMES McHENRY DAVIS, farmer, respected citizen and faithful member of the United Baptist Church, acting as deacon for a

number of years; b. January 4, 1828, d. March 5, 1916; m. August 1, 1850, Naomi Price, b. November 13, 1835, d. May 28, 1890, daughter of George Washington Price.

Children: Fourth Generation
*99. George W. Davis.
*100. Sarah Davis.
*101. Elizabeth Davis.
*102. Emma Davis.
*103. Louise Davis.
*104. Roscoe Davis.
*105. Rheu Hemma Davis.
*106. Lorenda Davis.
*107. Cynthia Davis.
108. Ella Davis.
*109. Addie Davis.
*110. Minnie Davis.

28. ANNA DAVIS; b. April 14, 1830; m. Bracken R. (Life) Van Hoose.

Children: Fourth Generation
111. Amanda Van Hoose.
112. Malissa Van Hoose.
113. David Van Hoose.
114. Matilda Van Hoose.
115. Noah Van Hoose.
116. Sarah Alice Van Hoose.
117. Henry Van Hoose.

29. MAHALA DAVIS; b. April 13, 1832, d. March 13, 1914; m. Henry Conley, b. October 9, 1829, died June ?, 1879, son of David Conley and Polly (Howes) Conley; resided for a time in Johnson County; later in Greenup or Carter County; and finally at Webbville, Lawrence County, where he died.

Children: Fourth Generation
118. Mary Ann Conley; b. about September 1, 1850; m. a Fisher.
119. B. F. Conley; b. about February 4, 1852.
*120. Paulina Conley.
121. Harrison B. Conley; b. February 3, 1855.
122. Irene Conley.
*123. Redmond I. Conley.
124. Henrietta Conley.
125. Lizzie Conley.
126. Arch Conley.
127. Ollie Conley.
128. Rose Conley; m. a Withero.

30. SUSAN DAVIS; b. June 7, 1834; m. George Lemaster.

Children: Fourth Generation

129. Spencer Lemaster.
130. Kenas Lemaster.
131. Henry Lemaster.
132. Betsy Jane Lemaster.
133. Mahala Lemaster; m. James Day.
134. Oma Lemaster.
135. Paulina Lemaster.
136. Nannie Lemaster.
137. Mary Lemaster.

Mrs. Lemaster was reared on a farm near Fish Trap Church in Johnson County and d. from the infirmities of age on the Little Fork in Elliott County and is buried there on a Mr. Wheeler's farm. Mr. Lemaster was a farmer and had service in the Civil War for a short time.

31. LYDIA DAVIS; b. in Johnson County, April 6. 1836, and d. at the age of ninety-one at the home of a daughter. Mrs. E. W. Cleland, 1415 E. Tenth Avenue, Topeka, Kansas, and is buried in Lecompton Cemetery. She m., December 24, 1863, Alexander W. Nickell. of Scotch-Irish descent, a son of John and Civilar Jane Nickell. the former of whom came from Bath County, Kentucky, and the latter from the State of Illinois. Mr. Nickell served as sheriff of Johnson County.

Children: Fourth Generation

138. Amanda Elizabeth Nickell.
139. James Stewart Nickell; b. November 16, 1866; m. Pearl Banjour.
140. Mary Grant Nickell.
141. Susie Harriet Nickell.
142. Lydia Kathryn Nickell.
143. Cordelia Ann Nickell.
144. Rose Belle Nickell.

32. BRACKEN LEWIS DAVIS; b. September 11, 1838, d. December 1, 1921; m., first. Mary Elizabeth Conley, who d. March 16, 1908; m., secondly, Anna Moore.

Children: Fourth Generation

145. Mantford Davis; b. October 3, 1857, and d. July 16, 1859.
146. E. P. (Leck) Davis.
147. Lousine Davis.
148. James M. Davis.
149. Charlie Davis.
150. Julia Davis.

151. Mary Elizabeth Davis.
152. B. L. (Son) Davis; m. Zora Fitch.
153. Angie Davis.
154. Lon Davis.
155. Marie Alice Davis.

Mr. Davis lived the greater part of his life on a farm on the Big Sandy River at mouth of Buffalo Creek. He operated a ferry over the Big Sandy River; was an attorney at law and active in the political affairs of the county. He was a member of the United Baptist Church and is buried near Concord, Kentucky.

33. DAVIDSON DAVIS; b. in Johnson County, December 19, 1840, and d. near Topeka, Kansas, March 17, 1916; m. November 14, 1868, Civiliar King Nickell, b. April 1, 1849, d. November 30, 1900, daughter of Alex. Nickell of Flat Gap, Kentucky.

Children: Fourth Generation
156. Alexander Davis.
157. Elizabeth Katherine Davis.
158. Henry Powell Davis; b. July 12, 1868; m. Ida Sawyer; reside in Kansas City, Kansas.
159. Elias Monroe Davis.
160. James Edward Davis; b. July 8, 1872; m., first, Daisy Clark, and secondly, Mary ———.
161. Martila Isabel Davis.
162. Martha Ellen Davis.
163. Mary Alice Davis.
164. Mahala Angeline Davis.
165. Laura Maude Davis.
166. John Cleveland Davis; b. July 25, 1884; d. June 26, 1885.
Mr. Davis lived for a time on a farm, a part of which is now the east side addition to Paintsville. Later he went to Kansas and lived near Topeka. He is buried in Topeka Cemetery.

34. ELIZABETH JANE DAVIS; b. in Johnson County, April 3, 1843, or 1844; m. Isaiah Green, b. January 1, 1845, a son of Thomas and Jemima (Brown) Green, a grandson of Giles and Katie (Chandler) Green, and a great grandson of Thomas Chandler, Revolutionary War soldier. (See Green Family and Chandler Family.)

Children: Fourth Generation
*167. Christopher Green.
168. Elias Washington Green.
*169. Thomas L. Green.
*170. Elizabeth Green.
*171. James M. Green.
*172. Samantha Green.

62. MARTIN WHEELER; m. Julia Price.

Children: Fifth Generation
173. Lasco Wheeler; m. a Dee.
174. Mary Alice Wheeler; m. Sam Pelfrey.
175. Jemima Wheeler; m. Link Auxier.
176. Lula Wheeler; m. Ben Reed.

63. LOUISA WHEELER; b. October 29, 1845; m., first, Riley Colvin.

Children: Fifth Generation
177. Forest Colvin.

63A. Louisa (Wheeler) Colvin m., secondly, John Turner.

Children: Fifth Generation
178. Ray Turner.

64. MANTFORD P. COLVIN; m. Serena Reed; lived on Colvin Branch near Fish Trap Church in Johnson County.

Children: Fifth Generation
179. Wayne Colvin; m. Maude Rice.
*180. Ollie Colvin.
181. Roy Colvin; m. Daria Candill.
182. Bertie Colvin.

66. JEFFERSON COLVIN; d. 1956, aged 96, m. Mintie Pelfrey.

Children: Fifth Generation
183. Harry Colvin.
184. Hattie Colvin; m. a Callahan.
185. Hubert Colvin.
186. Walter Colvin.
187. ———— ————.
188. Charlie Colvin.
189. Mantford Clarence Colvin.

87. ELIAS BLANTON, a teamster who was engaged for many years in logging on Big Paint Creek; b. in November, 1843; m. Minerva McCarty, daughter of John McCarty of McCarty Branch, Johnson County.

Children: Fifth Generation
190. Mantford Blanton; m., first, Miranda Smith, and secondly, a Holbrook.
191. James Blanton; m., first, Mary Lemaster and secondly, Orgie Evans.
192. John Blanton; m. Alice Barker.
193. Henry Blanton; m. Rebecca (Williams) Fairchild.

194. Elzie Blanton; m. Mary Smith.
195. George Blanton; m. Ira Ferguson.
196. Hansford Blanton; m. Lucina Fairchild.
197. Dock Blanton; d. young.
198. Mary Blanton; m. Sam Tackett.
199. Martha Blanton; m. John Bradley.
200. Edward Blanton; m. Hattie Howard.

88. GEORGE WASHINGTON BLANTON, a timber man who engaged in marketing timber on Big Paint Creek; b. at Fish Trap Church, Johnson County, October 15, 1845; m. Angeline Nickell, a daughter of Alex Nickell.

Children: Fifth Generation
201. James Alex Blanton; m. Laura Sturgill.
202. Mary E. Blanton; m. G. B. Hitchcock.
203. Lurica Alice Blanton; m. C. C. Reed
204. 203 (Twins?)
205. Cora Blanton; m. John W. Jayne.
206. Stella Blanton; m. Garfield Hitchcock.
207. Missouri Blanton; d. in young womanhood.
208. Charlie Blanton; m. Rosa Tackett.
209. Lydia Blanton; m., first, Amos Williams and secondly, Sam McCane.
210. Ethel Blanton; m. Granville Williams.
211. Edgar Blanton; m. Lucy Tackett.
212. Gilla Blanton; m. Simon Tackett.

89. MARTHA BLANTON; m. Oliver B. McKenzie, son of David McKenzie.

Children: Fifth Generation
213. J. D. McKenzie; b. September 18, 1865; m. Laura Mahan.
214. John McKenzie; b. February 19, 1868; m., first, Phoebe Fairchild and secondly, Vertica (Williams) Reed.

90. ANNA BLANTON; m. D. J. McCarthy, son of John McCarthy.

Children: Fifth Generation
215. William McCarthy; m., first, Mary Clark and secondly, Ida Pennington.
216. John McCarthy; m. Lou Coldiron.
217. James McCarthy; m. Elizabeth Cantrill.
218. Paris McCarthy; m. Elvira McKenzie.
219. Rose McCarthy; m., first, Hardy McKenzie and secondly, Ollie McKenzie.
220. Susan McCarthy; d. young.
221. Martha McCarthy.
222. Mary McCarthy; m. John Curtis.

91. JAMES (MACK) BLANTON; Sarah McCarty, daughter of Nelson McCarty; resided on Big Paint Creek.

Children: Fifth Generation
223. Laura Blanton; m. James M. Lemaster.
224. Ella Blanton; m. Leslie Williams.
225. Lorenzo Blanton; m. Sallie Conley.
226. Oliver Blanton; m. Bessie Fairchild.
227. Alice Blanton; m. Lee Kimbleton.
228. Frank Blanton; m. Sallie Vincel.
229. Walter Blanton; m. Sallie Prichard.
230. Kendrick Blanton; m. Nola Lemaster.

92. JOHN E. BLANTON; m. Sarah Williams, a daughter of Luke Williams, who was killed while serving in the Confederate States Army.

Children: Fifth Generation
231. Blanch Blanton; m., first, Sarah Colvin and secondly, a Rice,
232. Julia Blanton; m. Forest Colvin.
233. Sanford Blanton; m. Hester Burchett.
234. Ora Blanton; unm.

93. HARMON BLANTON; m., first, Mintie Coldiron, daughter of Hiram Coldiron of Harlan County, Kentucky; resided at Fish Trap Church.

Children: Fifth Generation
235. James Blanton; m. Lulu Lemaster.
236. John W. Blanton; m. Virgie Williams.
237. Edward Blanton; d. at age of 16.
238. Alice Blanton; m. Sebastian McKenzie.
239. Dora Blanton; m. a McCreary.
240. Emma Blanton; m. Samuel Lyons; resided in Ashland.
241. Harry Blanton; d. at age 17.

93A. Harmon Blanton; m., secondly, Rose (McKenzie) Lemaster, daughter of Hiram McKenzie.

Children: Fifth Generation
242. Lura Blanton; d. at age of 5.
243. Fay Blanton.
244. Glenn Blanton.
245. Guy Blanton.
246. Hobart Blanton.

94. MARY BLANTON; m. James B. Gullett, son of Ira Gullett.
Children: Fifth Generation
247. Leck Gullett.
248. Cleffie Gullett; m. Thurman Cochran.

95. SANFORD LEE BLANTON; b. in Johnson County about April 1, 1858; served as justice of peace of Johnson County for eleven years, was a member of the Board of Education and has been active in local political affairs; m., February 13, 1879, Sarah Ann McKenzie, b. August 5, 1860, a daughter of Lafe McKenzie.

Children: Fifth Generation
249. George W. Blanton.
250. Harry Blanton.
251. Albert Blanton.
252. Mary Blanton.
253. Martha Blanton; b. January 13, 1887; d. May 10, 1887.
254. Willie Blanton.
255. John F. Blanton.
256. Virgie Blanton.
257. Oliver P. Blanton.
258. J. Kendrick Blanton.
259. Delia Blanton.
260. Bertha Blanton.
261. Lafe Blanton; b. March 17, 1902; d. March 18, 1905.
262. Verna Blanton; b. September 27, 1904; unm.

96. LYDIA BLANTON; m. William H. McKenzie, son of Lafe Mc-Kenzie; resided at Flat Gap, Johnson County.

Children: Fifth Generation
263. Forest McKenzie; m. Lou Grace.
264. Clinnie McKenzie; m. Lewis Blanton.
265. Mary McKenzie; unm.
266. Nola McKenzie; m. Victor Greene.
267. Malta McKenzie; m. Kendrick Salyer.

97. WILLIAM R. BLANTON; m. Julia McFarland, daughter of William McFarland of Fuget, Kentucky.

Children: Fifth Generation
268. Bessie Blanton; m. Crossford Blair.
269. Oscar Blanton; m. Carma Williams.
270. Bertha Blanton; d. of croup at age of 4.
271. Elizabeth Blanton; m. F. M. Tackett.
272. Carrie Blanton; m. Harry McKenzie.
273. Beulah Blanton; m. Herbert Lemaster.

99. CAPTAIN GEORGE WASHINGTON DAVIS was a "river man" all his life, hence the title of captain. He was well and favorably known on the Big Sandy from Pikeville to Catlettsburg and on the Ohio from Pittsburg to Cincinnati. During the latter years of his life he devoted most of his time to timber and real estate business in and around Fullerton, Kentucky, and Ironton, Ohio. Always success-

ful in business, he amassed considerable wealth. He was born July 21, 1851; m., first, Josephine Hager, b. November 10, 1854, and d. May 1, 1875, daughter of John Hager. (See Hager Family.)

Children: Fifth Generation

274. John F. Davis.

99A. Captain George Washington Davis m., secondly, January 1, 1879, Jennie Porter, who d. November 17, 1896, daughter of James A. Porter. Captain Davis d. February 24, 1922.

Children: Fifth Generation

275. Nora Lee Davis; b. at Paintsville, April 22, 1880; m., November 25, 1903, M. F. Forgey, b. March 28, 1876.

276. Glen F. Davis, civil engineer; b. on John's Creek, April 2, 1882; d. August 25, 1912; m. Laura Pugh.

277. Eugene Lawrence Davis, a brakeman and conductor on Big Sandy division of the C. & O. Railway Company, was b. March 14, 1884, and d. from injuries received from a slowly moving train at Shelby, Kentucky; m. Gertrude Kelly.

278. James Robert Davis; b. at South Point, Ohio, June 21, 1886; m. Lora Shea, July 13, 1913.

279. George W. Davis; b. August 9, 1888. He is an electrician; served for a time in the U. S. Army; m. February 14, 1924, Hazel Akers, b. October 31, 1903, daughter of John Akers; reside at Catlettsburg.

280. Harry Davis, electrician, at Catlettsburg; b. at South Point, Ohio, July 21, 1891; graduated from the Brooklyn Technical Institute; served in the U. S. Navy, 1909-1913; m., October 5, 1918, Virginia Eads, b. April 17, 1899, daughter of N. D. Eads of Catlettsburg.

281. Ernest P. Davis; b. at South Point, Ohio, June 14, 1893; served in the U. S. Navy for several years and was discharged on account of physical disability; m. Ruth Bennett, daughter of Dr. Bennett of Fullerton, Kentucky. Has resided at Fullerton or Greenup since discharge from the Navy.

100. SARAH DAVIS; b. May 25, 1858; d. June 5, 1890; m. January 6, 1874, Winfield Preston. (See Nathan Preston Family.)

101. ELIZABETH DAVIS; b. July 31, 1855; m. January 9, 1875, Martin Luther Ford who was b. March 28, 1854, and d. January 16, 1913, a son of Thomas Ford. This family resided on a farm below the mouth of Johns Creek on the Big Sandy River near East Point, Kentucky, in what was formerly a part of the Blockhouse Bottom.

Children: Fifth Generation

282. Mary Louise Ford; m. November 22, 1898, Elijah Auxier. (See Auxier Family.)

283. (Infant).

284. (Infant).

285. Clara Flossie Ford; b. May 6, 1878; d. at age of 15.

286. Lucy Hemma Ford; b. December 26, 1879; m., first, William Stratton; m., secondly, Proctor L. Clark.

287. James T. Ford; b. August 16, 1882; unm.

288. Frank Ford; d. young.

289. Ona Ford; b. March 28, 1891.

290. Hazel Elizabeth Ford, teacher; b. June 30, 1896; m. Thomas E. Moran, b. June 25, 1884, son of Thomas Moran. They reside at Auxier, Kentucky, where Mr. Moran conducts a theatre and confectionery.

291. M. L. Ford, Jr.; d. young.

102. EMMA DAVIS; b. April 15, 1857; d. July 15, 1890; m., May 24, 1883, William B. Borders, who d. July 22, 1890. (See Borders Family.)

103. LOUISE DAVIS; b. November 10, 1859; d. January 31, 1922; m. June 9, 1881, George Bascomb Vaughan. (See Vaughan Family.)

104. ROSCOE DAVIS, farmer and sometime timberman; b. November 25, 1861; m., August 31, 1895, Glennie Childers, b. August 16, 1876.

Children: Fifth Generation

292. Clarence Davis, timberman; b. in Johnson County, June 22, 1898; m. August 5, 1918, Exer Smith, b. March 1, 1899, daughter of William Smith.

293. Mary Oma Davis; b. July 7, 1903; m., March 1, 1923, Herbert Preston, b. December 13, 1902, son of Edward Preston of Graves Shoal.

294. Rhuie Davis; b. July 1, 1906.

295. Roscoe Davis, Jr.; b. January 13, 1909.

296. Bernard Davis; b. March 4, 1912.

105. RHEU HEMMA DAVIS; b. November 17, 1864; m. January 6, 1892, Press Childers, farmer, of Davis Branch, b. January 13, 1865, son of Russell and Pricy Childers.

Children: Fifth Generation

297. J. Russell Childers, an employee of the C & O. Railway Company for several years, who had service overseas for ten months in World War I, was born December 10, 1892; m. July 7, 1920, Lucy

Salyer, b. September 1, 1902, daughter of William and Matilda Salyer.

298. Press Honshell Childers; b. August 29, 1899.

299. Kit Elmon Childers; b. July 12, 1902; died October 9, 1903.

106. LORENDA DAVIS; b. November 17, 1865; m. James H. Spradlin who d. August 6, 1925.

Children: Fifth Generation

300. Frankie Davis Spradlin; b. May 7, 1888; m., December 23, 1908, Down Auxier, who was b. February 8, 1887.

301. Frances E. Spradlin; b. February 15, 1903; m. Henry Barber.

107. CYNTHIA DAVIS; b. June 20, 1867; m. January 1, 1895, Warren D. Auxier, who was b. May 22, 1873. (See Auxier Family.)

109. ADDIE DAVIS; b. July 14, 1872; m. August 21, 1890, C. C. Price, who was b. May 11, 1872.

Children: Fifth Generation

302. James M. Price; d. in infancy.

303. Robert W. Price; b. June 13, 1892.

304. (Infant).

110. MINNIE DAVIS; b. April 1, 1877; m. Robert W. Akers, teacher.

Children: Fifth Generation

305. Gertrude Akers; b. October 30, 1896; m., August 3, 1913, Jesse R. Piles, merchant, at Whites Creek, West Virginia.

306. Julian Virgil Akers; b. September 20, 1898; m. Helen Mary Cross, September 15, 1924.

307. Annie Lorinda Akers; b. April 14, 1900; m., June 14, 1919. Arnold Hamilton; reside at New Boston, Ohio.

308. Sibyl Davis Akers; b. April 10, 1902; m., November 24, 1920, Charles Burke Lawson; reside at New Boston, Ohio.

309-10. (Infants).

311. Lucy Akers; b. September 15, 1906; m. William Harr; reside at New Boston, Ohio.

312. Doxie Akers; b. July 18, 1904; d. September 6, 1904.

313. (Infant).

123. ISAAC REDMOND CONLEY; b. July 9, 1859; d. in 1937; m. March Sexton, b. in 1858 and d. in 1935, daughter of Enoch and Sarah (Mitchell) Sexton.

Children, among others: Fifth Generation

314. Sarah E. Conley; m. James B. Sparks. (See Sparks Family.)

315. Mahala Conley.

316. Bertha Conley.

167. CHRISTOPHER GREEN; m. Mary Webb; resided at Webbville, Kentucky.

Children: Fifth Generation
317. Lonnie Green.
318. Lloyd Green.
319. James Green.
320. Hillman Green.
321. ——— ———.
322. Ivory Jane Green.
323. Ilah Green; m. William Hensley.
324. Irena Green.
325. Blanche Green.
326. Paul Green.

169. THOMAS L. GREEN; m. Abbie Pennington; resided at Webbville, Kentucky.

Children: Fifth Generation
327. Lillian Green.

170. ELIZABETH GREEN; m. Samuel Ortes.

Children: Fifth Generation
328. Roscoe Ortes.
329. Bertha Ortes.
330. William Ortes.
331. Blanche Ortes.

171. JAMES M. GREEN, carpenter; b. April 7, 1875; m., first, May 5, 1904, Nora Adams, who d. July 19, 1905; no children; m., secondly, June 20, 1906, George Frazier, b. October 4, 1886.

Children: Fifth Generation
332. Fay Green; b. May 5, 1907.
333. Paul Green; b. July, 2, 1908.
334. Rebecca Green; b. April 24, 1912.
335. Tom Green; b. November 6, 1917.

James M. Green was connected with the Consolidated Coal Company both at Van Lear and Jenkins, Kentucky, for several years. He resided for several years at West Van Lear and was police judge of the town for a time.

172. SAMANTHA GREEN; m., first, Neil Webb.

Children: Fifth Generation
336. ——— ———.
337. ——— ———.

172A. Samantha Green; m., secondly, Lee Nickell.

Children: Fifth Generation
   338. ——— ———.
   339. ——— ———.

180. OLLIE COLVIN; m. Beecher Stapleton; resided in Paintsville for several years but later removed to a farm on Colvin Branch near Fish Trap Church and Mrs. Stapleton is a member of the United Baptist Church there. Mr. Stapleton was a teacher in the public schools of Johnson County for some time; was a traveling salesman, served as clerk of the Johnson County Court, 1914-1918, and judge of that court, 1922-1926.

Children: Fifth Generation
   340. Maxine Stapleton.
   341. Joe Stapleton.
   342. Kathleen Stapleton
   343. Christine Stapleton.
   344. Emma G. Stapleton.
   345. Ashley Ward Stapleton.
   346. Harold Beecher Stapleton.
   347. George Ben Stapleton.
   348. Irene Stapleton.

Other Davis families lived in Johnson County, Kentucky, in pioneer days. 1. A Joseph Davis came from Virginia and settled on the Big Sandy River at what is known as the Joe Davis Bend, in 1810. He was the ancestor of a prominent and honorable family. He married Elizabeth (Betty) Borders, daughter of John Borders. (See Borders Family.)

   Children:
   *2. William Davis.
   *3. John Davis.
    4. Fannie Davis; m. Jesse Murray.
    5. Elizabeth Davis; m. Henry Fannin.
   *6. Michael Davis.
    7. Theresa Davis.
    8. Betsy Davis.
    9. Mary (Polly) Jane Davis.
  *10. Joseph Davis, Jr.
   11. Hezekiah (?) Davis.
   12. Julia (?) Davis.

2. WILLIAM DAVIS, farmer and large land owner in Lawrence and Johnson Counties; m., first, Mary Borders.

Children:
13. Joseph Davis.
14. John Davis; resided on Hoods Fork of Blaine.
*15. Amos Davis.
*16. Louis Davis.
17. Mary Davis; m. John Wheeler. (See Wheeler Family.)
18. Julia Davis.
19. Jane Davis.
20. Fannie Davis.
21. Catherine Davis.
22. Elizabeth Davis.

2A. William Davis m., secondly, Dorcas Green.

Children:
23. William Davis, Jr.

2B. William Davis m., thirdly, Samantha Nickell.

Children:
24. Thursa B. Davis.

William Davis m., fourthly, a Bradley.

3. JOHN DAVIS; b. in Lawrence County; removed to Big Paint Creek, near mouth of Jennie's Creek, Johnson County. He was a leading businessman of Paintsville and one of the wealthiest men in the county. He married, June 28, 1840, Jemima Wheeler.

Children:
25. Elizabeth Davis.
*26. Dorcas Davis.
*27. Daniel Davis.
28. John W. Davis; m. Sarah Ellen Rule; no children.
*29. Catherine Davis.
30. Albert B. Davis.
31. Mary Allen Davis; m. Dock Nickels; no children.

6. MICHAEL DAVIS; m. ——— ———.

Children:
32. Mahala Davis; m. William Murray.

10. JOSEPH DAVIS; m. Vina Ward, daughter of Shadrack Ward. (See Ward Family of Johnson County).

Children:
33. Zina Davis; m. Henry P. Meade. (See Meade Family).

15. Amos Davis; m. Rhode ———. Descendants reside at Davisville, Johnson County.

Children:

*34. W. Columbus Davis.
35. Wesley Davis.
36. Charlie Davis.

16. Louis Davis; resided in Low Gap precinct, Johnson County; was an important citizen in his section of the county; m. ———.

Children:

37. John Davis.

26. Dorcas Davis; m. A. J. Fox.

Children:

38. ——— ——— (Infant).
39. John Fox.
40. Ella Fox.
41. Katherine Fox.
42. Don Fox.

27. Daniel Davis, a wealthy businessman and prominent Republican politician of Johnson County; m. Martha (Teass) Rule.

Children:

*43. Harry Davis.
44. Ray Davis.
*45. May Davis.
46. June Davis.
*47. Walter Davis.

29. Catherine Davis; m. James Foster Walker.

Children:

*48. Della Walker.
49. Fred Wade Walker; m. Anna Rice. (See Rice Family).
50. Dora Walker; m. John W. Wheeler. (See Wheeler Family).

34. W. Columbus Davis; m. Amanda Chandler. (See Chandler Family).

Children:

*51. Dr. A. M. Davis.
52. Lourenza Davis.
53. Proctor Davis.
54. Bessie Davis.

40. ELLA FOX; m. Tobe Dixon, farmer; resided on the Garrett Highway between Paintsville and Staffordsville, Kentucky.

Children:
55. Fanny Dixon.
56. Virginia Dixon.
57. Harriet May Dixon.
58. Andrew F. Dixon.
59. Della Marjorie Dixon.
60. Dorcas Eveline Dixon.

43. HARRY DAVIS, progressive farmer and businessman; resides on the old home farm and carries on the many things begun by his father; was a director in the Paintsville National Bank and connected with several business enterprises; m. Hazel Williams, a teacher.

Children:
61. Martha Elizabeth Davis; b. 1926.

45. MARY DAVIS; m. W. L. Gamble, a leading physician and surgeon of the Big Sandy Valley. He practiced his profession for many years in connection with the Consolidated Coal Company, both at Van Lear and at Jenkins, Kentucky, being in charge of the company hospital at Jenkins, after which he specialized and located at Ashland where he is regarded as one of the outstanding surgeons in the area.

Children:
62. John Davis Gamble.
63. Mary Marguerite Gamble.

47. WALTER DAVIS; m. Lou Segraves; resided at Pheonix, Arizona.

Children:
64. Daniel Scott Davis.
65. Joe Ann Davis.

48. DELLA WALKER; m., first, Milton Williams.

Children:
*66. K. B. Williams.
67. Everett Williams; killed by train on Beaver Creek.
68. Neva Williams; m. Irvin Rice. (See Rice Family).
*69. Ralph Williams.

Della (Walker) Williams m., secondly, John Dixon, a plumber of Paintsville.

55. FANNY DIXON; m. Toral Franklin.

Children:

70. James Herald Franklin.

Fanny and Toral Franklin were teachers in the rural schools of Johnson County for several years. They operated a general store at Staffordsville where they resided.

66. K.B. WILLIAMS; m., first, Tempa Powell.

Children:

71. Kenneth B. Williams.

He m. secondly, Mrs. John Williams; resided in Huntington, West Virginia.

69. RALPH WILLIAMS; connected with the Big Sandy Division of the C. & O. Railway Company, for many years; m. Lynchie Sublett.

Children.

72. Marjorie Lois Williams.

51. DR. AMOS M. DAVIS; b. at Chandlersville, Johnson County, Kentucky, April 5, 1883; educated in the public schools and taught in the public schools of Johnson and Lawrence Counties for eight years. Choosing the medical profession as a career, he entered University of Louisville, medical department, in 1907, from which he was graduated with degree of M.D. in 1911. He located at Denton, Kentucky, for practice of his profession in May, 1912, and continued practice there until 1919 when he located at Ashland, Kentucky, where he practiced with great success until 1942 when he retired on account of ill health. He died at Sebastian, Florida, November 4, 1950. Interment in Ashland Cemetery, Ashland, Kentucky.

Dr. Davis was interested in civic affairs. He served as alderman of Ashland for two terms and was a member of the school board of Ashland for several years.

On July 20, 1904, Dr. Davis was united in marriage with Miss Mary Jane Prose of Irad, Kentucky, a teacher in the public schools of Johnson County. They had no children. Mrs. Davis resides at 2816 Winchester Avenue, Ashland, Kentucky.

DILS FAMILY OF PIKE COUNTY

JOHN DILS, JR., was the first of the family of Dils to migrate and settle in Eastern Kentucky. He was born in Parkersburg, Virginia, now West Virginia in 1819. His father was John Dils II, and his grandfather was John Dils I who with his brother Henry migrated from Pennsylvania on the Monongahela River near Brownsville to then Virginia and settled in Wood County near Parkersburg in 1789.

Both John I and John II had service in the American Army in the Revolutionary War and were actively engaged with the Ohio settlers of Belpre and Marietta in the Indian troubles on the frontiers.

John Dils II was with the Wood County militia under Colonel Phelps who, under the proclamation of President Jefferson in 1806, undertook the arrest of Col. Burr and his associates on Blennerhasset Island but failing to find him on the island, Col. Phelps with part of his men hastened to intercept Col. Burr at the mouth of the Great Kanawha but Col. Phelps was again foiled by the wily foe.[1]

John Dils' sister had married R. D. Callahan in 1835 and in 1836 he went to Pikeville, Kentucky, with his brother-in-law. Here he taught two "subscription" (private) schools in 1840-1841. He entered the mercantile business in partnership with his brother-in-law, R. D. Callahan and John N. Richardson under the firm name of John Dils, Jr. and Company which in two years was changed to Richardson and Dils, and after about twelve years he purchased the interest of his partner, Richardson, and conducted the business until the Civil War.

John Dils, Jr., was captain of a company of soldiers recruited for service in the Mexican War, but the organization was never called into active service on account of being too remote for transportation. He was a staunch Union man and was arrested under orders of Col. John S. Williams, C. S. A.; and was taken to Richmond and confined in Libby Prison there. Returning to his home in Pikeville he recruited the 39th Kentucky Regiment Mounted Infantry of which he became the colonel. He was mustered into the service, February 16, 1863, at Peach Orchard and was discharged December 10, 1863.[2]

John Dils, Jr. m. in Pike County. November 6, 1842, Miss Ann Ratliff, third daughter of "General" (William) Ratliff. (See Ratliff Family).

Children living at home and approximate dates of birth as shown by U. S. Census of Pike County for 1860 and 1870.

Georgie A. Dils; b. 1844.
Mary E. Dils; b. 1846.
Augusta Dils; b. 1848.
Kate Dils; b. 1853.
John R. A. Dils; b. 1858.

[1] William Ely, The Big Sandy Valley, p. 45-55.
[2] Report of the Adjutant General of Kentucky, 1861-1865, Vol. II, page 384.

DIXON FAMILY OF JOHNSON AND LAURENCE COUNTIES

Dixon is a well known surname in Scotland, England and Ireland, as well as in the United States. In ancient records it is spelled in many ways, perhaps the first being the Scottish way, Dicksoune, Dickson and Dykysoun.

The chiefs of the clan Dickson are descended from the Keiths, Earls Marshall of Scotland, and a mighty power in themselves. It is said that a Keith could journey from the north to the south of Scotland and find shelter overnight in one of his own castles. Blind Harry, the ancient Scottish Minstrel, recounted the triumphs of Thom Dixon, the first eminent leader of this noted family. It was he whom the great Douglas sent through an enemy camp of 3,000 men bearing a message to Sir William Wallace. For this service Thom Dixon was awarded lands in County Lanark, King Robert Bruce indorsed the charter and also created him hereditary castellan of Douglas Castle.

In England where the name is not a clan name, it is spelled Dixon, and this spelling is used by many families in the United States. The name Dixon is well known in the Southern States, perhaps the most notable representative being Thomas Dixon, novelist, whose stories of post-Civil War days have been read from coast to coast.

The name Dixon and Dickson originated with the necessity of distinguishing father from son. Thus, Dick's son took unto himself the surname Dickson to be used by himself and his descendants for all time.

Henry Dixon was the ancestor of a branch of the family in the Big Sandy Valley. He was born, presumably in Grayson County, Virginia, in 1774 and died in Johnson County, Kentucky, in 1854. He and a brother came from Grayson County, Virginia, in 1814, and purchased and lived on the lands that embrace the site of present Paintsville. They were important and leading citizens of the community; purchased and owned large tracts of land, and were in easy circumstances.

Henry Dixon was a farmer; conducted a grist mill at the upper end of Paintsville; was a minister of the Baptist Church; and a fine violinist. It is related of him that he went to church to conduct services with his Bible under one arm and his violin under the other; and that he always opened and closed services with rendering several selections on the violin. He was an honored and respected pioneer citizen.[1]

1. HENRY DIXON m. Joyce Farmer—apparently in Grayson County, Virginia.

Issue:

*2. Andrew F. Dixon.

3. Elizabeth (Betty) Dixon m. Robert Herald in Johnson County, October 30, 1853.

*4. "Billy" Dixon (Note: It has not been definitely established that "Billy" was a son. However, the weight of evidence tends to show he was a son).

*5. Martin V. Dixon.

2. ANDREW F. DIXON; m. in Floyd County, March 2, 1834, Abigail Kelly.

Issue:

*6. Farmer Dixon.
*7. Sarah Dixon.
8. Joseph Kirker Dixon; m. Jemima Prince.
*9. Isaac Dixon.
10. Jack Dixon.

4. "BILLY" DIXON; m. ——— ———.

Issue:

*11. Thomas Dixon.

5. MARTIN V. DIXON, blacksmith and millwright; b. in Virginia 1805, and d. in Johnson County, Kentucky, 1885. He possessed great mechanical ability; constructed many mills in the Big Sandy Valley; m. Ruth A. Porter, daughter of Samuel Porter. (See Porter Family.)

Issue:

12. John Dixon.
13. Lee Dixon.
14. Isaac B. Dixon.
*15. Robert Dixon
16. Ariminta Dixon; m. John Abel.
17. James M. Dixon.
18. Sarah Dixon; m. Green George.

6. FARMER DIXON; m. Sarah Conley in Johnson County, 1858.

Issue:

19. John Dixon; resided at West Liberty, Kentucky.
20. Julia Dixon.
21. Fleming Dixon.

7. SARAH DIXON; m. ――― Rule.

Issue:

22. Hayden Rule; d. of tuberculosis.
23. Myrtle Rule; m. ――― McKinster.

9. ISAAC DIXON; m. Ella Margaret May.

Issue:

*24. Emma Dixon.
*25. Alonzo Dixon.
26. Tobe Dixon; m. Ella Fox.
*27. Clark Dixon.
28. Minnie Dixon.
29. Guy Dixon.
30. Erie Dixon; m. Warren Van Hoose. (See Van Hoose Family).
*31. Don Dixon.
*32. Dutch Dixon.
33. A. C. Dixon.
*34. Dolly Dixon.

11. THOMAS J. DIXON; b. in 1841 and d. June 15, 1926; served in Union Army during the Civil War; volunteered November 8, 1861; served three years and honorably discharged January 31, 1865. He was kind and considerate and beloved by all; m. Eliza J. McFarland, 1872.

Issue:

35. Lou Dixon.
36. Mantford Dixon.
37. Edward Dixon; resided at Oil Springs, Johnson County.
38. Will Dixon; resided in Ashland, Kentucky.

15. ROBERT DIXON, businessman of many activities, was b. August 7, 1858, on Paint Creek, near Paintsville, Johnson County, Kentucky; educated in rural schools of Johnson County, and among his teachers was the noted William Elzy Connelley. At the age of 20, with a capital of $600, be began the mercantile business at Charley, Lawrence County, which he afterwards sold to his brothers and he removed to Louisa, Lawrence County. In 1890 he was nominated as candidate by the Democratic party and was elected County Court Clerk of Lawrence County and by subsequent elections served for twelve years. Subsequently he served as Treasurer of Lawrence County for three terms; and served as postmaster of Louisa for six years under President Wilson. After retiring from the clerk's office, he engaged in many business enterprises. He was one of the organizers of the firm of Watson & Dixon, wholesalers at

Louisa, of the Dixon and Moore Wholesale Grocery Company; of the First National Bank of Louisa and also of the Louisa National Bank. He was active in organizing the Louisa and Fort Gay Bridge Company.

Mr. Dixon was a Democrat and affiliated with the Masons and Independent Order of Odd Fellows. In Masonry his affiliations included membership in the Chapter of the Royal Arch Masons at Louisa.

He m., in 1883, Miss Sadie Borders, daughter of Arthur Borders. (See Borders Family).

Issue:

39. Frederick Dixon, jeweler at Louisa.

40. Lawrence Dixon; associated with father in business at Louisa.

41. Roberta Dixon; m. Fred M. Vinson. (See Vinson Family).

42. Robert Dixon, Jr., Assistant Secretary of State of Kentucky for two years in the administration of Gov. W. J. Fields.

24. EMMA DIXON; m. Marion Van Hoose; lived on Toms Creek, Johnson County, near Mingo, the first settlement of the Van Hooses on Toms Creek.

Issue:

43. Stella Van Hoose; m., first, Elbro Van Hoose.

44. Rascus Van Hoose; m. Virgie Stapleton.

45. Ella Van Hoose; m. Bascom Van Hoose.

46. Hoy Van Hoose; m. Minnie McKenzie.

47. Sallie Van Hoose; m.

48. Madgie Van Hoose; m. Ely Stapleton.

49. Minnie Van Hoose.

24A. Emma Van Hoose m., secondly, Harry Van Hoose.

Issue:

50. Gladys Van Hoose, Mingo, Kentucky.

25. ALONZO DIXON; m. Mary Hays, daughter of Andrew Hays; resided on head of Rush Fork of Toms Creek.

Issue:

51. Arla Dixon.

52. Rollie Dixon; m. Lillian Conley.

53. Hascie Dixon; m. Lexie Conley.

54. Hester Dixon; m. Carlie Davis.

55. Elmer Dixon; m. Bessie Conley.

27. CLARK DIXON; m. Mintie Rice; resided at Buchanan, Lawrence County, Kentucky.

Issue:

56. Mitchell Dixon.
57. Marion Dixon.
58. Golda Dixon.
59. Thelma Dixon.
60. Eunice Dixon.
61. Ruth Dixon.
62. John Dixon.
63. Mary Dixon.
64. Paul Dixon.
65. Jack Dixon.

29. GUY DIXON; m. Margaret Slane; resided on Rush Fork of Toms Creek.

Issue:

66. Roy Dixon.
*67. Sherlie Dixon.
68. Merlie Dixon.

31. DON DIXON, building contractor; m. Emma Hays; residence, Ashland, Kentucky.

Issue:

69. Bruce Dixon; m. Geneva Miranda.
70. Rexford Dixon; m. Olive Parker.
71. Ralph Dixon.
72. Clemmons Dixon.
73. Archie Dixon.
74. Ella Louise Dixon.
75. Carl D. Dixon.
76. Pauline Fay Dixon.
77. Donald B. Dixon.
78. Edith Dixon.
79. Mildred Dixon.
80. Calvin Eugene Dixon.

32. DUTCH DIXON; m. James McKenzie, son of John T. McKenzie; resided on Rush Fork of Toms Creek.

Issue:

81. Ernestine Dixon.
82. Glenn Dixon.
83. Kenneth Dixon.
84. Roy Dixon.

34. DOLLY DIXON; m. J. Langley Preston; legal residence on a farm on Rush Fork of Toms Creek. Mr. Preston spent much time in Paintsville, he being a public official: clerk of the Johnson Circuit Court for six years. He was an efficient official and a very popular citizen.

Issue:

85. Olive Preston.
86. Irma May Preston.
87. Edith (Maxine) Preston.
88. Agnes Preston.
89. Iva Preston.
90. Hermalee Preston.
91. Dixie Fay Preston.
92. James Heber Preston.
93. Erie Kathleen Preston.

67. SHERLEY DIXON; m. Jesse Wilcox; resided on the original "Bud" Witten farm on Rush Fork of Toms Creek.

Issue:

94. Augustus Roy Wilcox.
95. Ernest Lowell Wilcox.

DUPUY FAMILY OF GREENUP COUNTY

This family is of French Huguenot extraction.

1. BARTHOLOMEW DUPUY was the progenitor of the Dupuy family of Northeastern Kentucky. He was born in 1652 in the province of Languedoc, France. At the age of 18 he enlisted in the army and continued service for fourteen years, holding the rank of lieutenant and assigned to the King's (Louis XIV) household when he retired in 1684. He then purchased a chateau and vineyard in Velours and married Countess Susanna Lavillon.

Religious persecutions of the Huguenots breaking out afresh and Bartholomew Dupuy still being in the good graces of the King, was given a chance to abjure Protestantism. He and his wife refused to become Catholics.

However, the King gave him a document granting him protection until the end of the year 1685. He immediately began carrying out his plan to leave France by disposing of his property. This done, and dressing himself as a King's guardsman and his wife as a page, and having in his possession the King's guarantee of protection, they began the flight from France and reaching the frontier in eighteen days, they entered Germany where they remained for fourteen years when they went to England in 1699.

In England they joined that small band of Huguenots who came to America about 1700 with the purpose of settling in North Carolina. Upon reaching Virginia means of transportation to Carolina failed and, sponsored by William Byrd III, they settled at Manakin Town, present Goochland County, on the James River about twenty miles above Richmond. Here Bartholomew Dupuy died in 1743.

Children:
*2. Peter Dupuy.
3. John James Dupuy; m. Susan Levilain.
4. Martha Dupuy; m. ———— Chastain.
5. Philippa Dupuy; m. John Levilain in 1730.

2. PETER DUPUY; m. Judith Lefevre, 1772. He was the ancestor of the Dupuys of Greenup County, Kentucky.

Children among others:
6. Peter Dupuy; m. Elizabeth Malone.

Children among others:
*7. William Dupuy, the eldest son.
*8. Jesse Dupuy.

7. WILLIAM DUPUY; m., first, Elizabeth Fuqua, and secondly, Peggy Littlejohn. According to historians he was a captain in the

Revolution. He emigrated from Pittsylvania County, Virginia, to near Wheelersburg, Ohio, and settled on the "French Grant" and from there removed to Springville (South Portsmouth), Greenup County. He was a farmer and slaveholder.

Children of William Dupuy and his wife, Elizabeth (Fuqua) Dupuy:

9. Moses Fuqua Dupuy, the eldest son, b. 1799, d. 1889; m. Phoebe Stephenson, 1818.

Children:

10. Albert Gallatin Dupuy, the fourth son, b. 1829; m. Ann B. Lee, 1862.

Children:

11. Agnes Mary Dupuy; m. William J. Stevens of Titusville, Pennsylvania, and resided there.

12. Samuel Edward Dupuy; m. Anna Bell Athey; migrated to Colorado.

*13. Rosswell Dupuy.

14. William Dupuy; m. Gertrude Humphreys who d. in 1946. He resided in California.

*15. Ernest Richard Dupuy.

16. Bessie Dupuy; deceased.

13. ROSSWELL DUPUY; m. Virginia B. Hardman; resided on Tygarts Creek. He was killed in an automobile accident near his home, 1945, and she d. of heart failure a week later.

Children:

17. Raymond Dupuy; migrated to Texas.

18. Essie Marie Dupuy; deceased.

19. Clifford Hardman Dupuy; m. Sally Roberts.

20. Virgil Dupuy; deceased.

21. Rosamond Dupuy; m. Niles Greenslate; resided in Russell.

22. Kenneth Dupuy; deceased.

23. Mary Agnes Dupuy; m. William Miller.

24. Mildred Dupuy; m. Herman Webb.

15. ERNEST RICHARD DUPUY; m. Beulah Jayne; resided on Tygarts Creek.

Children:

25. William Jayne Dupuy; m. Josephine Jeffers.

26. Ernestine Dupuy; m. W. V. Howland.

27. Richard Dupuy; m. Mary Inez Mosely.

28. Robert Dupuy; m. Mondalia Boggs.

8. JESSE DUPUY; m. Ann Stewart; they settled on Tygarts Creek; were members of the Christian Church at Siloam and are buried in the churchyard there.

Children:

*29. John M. Dupuy.

*30. Wesley M. Dupuy.

*31. Thomas J. Dupuy.

29. JOHN M. DUPUY; m. Ann Blair.

Children:

32. Louisa M. Dupuy; m. George Reeg; and they had a son:

33. Arthur Reeg.

30. WESLEY M. DUPUY; m. Mary Conway.

Children:

34. Henrietta Conway, a teacher in the Portsmouth, Ohio, High School.

31. THOMAS J. DUPUY; m. Sarah Hicks.

Children:

35. Paul Hicks Dupuy; m. Dorothy Wright; and they are the parents of:

36. Paul H. Dupuy, Jr.

37. Mary Martha Dupuy.

38. James W. Dupuy and

39. Richard E. Dupuy, all of whom reside in Portsmouth, Ohio.

DYSART FAMILY OF CARTER AND GREENUP COUNTIES

Dysart is a place name from the town of Dysart in Fife, Scotland. Walter and Gaffrid de'Dysert are mentioned in an instrument of 1427 by Thomas Maule of Panmure. Michael Disard appears in the records in 1527. Katherine Dysart became the spouse of John Calve in Newburgh, 1560. John Dysart was admitted burgess of Aberdeen in 1569.[1]

The name Disart appears in the records of England during the reign of King Henry (1114-15). The Scottish Dysart is of different origin.[2]

The name Disart or Disert is derived from Izzards, a local name of Normandy, France. The name D'Izard appears on the roll of the Battle Abbey[3] and apparently members of the family came from France to England with William the Conqueror (1066) and were in the battle of Hastings. It is believed that this family settled in Wales.

Dysart Castle in Ireland was the seat of a powerful family of Dysarts in early times.

Captain James Dysart was the first of the name to come to Kentucky. He was living in the Valley of Virginia at the breaking out of the Revolutionary War. He was one of the first justices of the peace of Washington County, Virginia; the first sheriff of the county; and was a captain of the (Washington County) Virginia Militia. He commanded a division in the battle at Kings Mountain (October 7, 1781), where he was wounded.[4]

After the close of the Revolution, Captain Dysart settled in Rockcastle County, Kentucky. He patented several large tracts of land in Rockcastle and Jefferson Counties. Very little has been learned concerning him after his coming to Kentucky. He was a State representative from Rockcastle and Lincoln Counties. The records of Rockcastle County would seem to indicate that members of his family migrated to and settled in Missouri.

Captain Johnston Dysart, believed to be a son of Captain James Dysart, married in Pulaski County, Kentucky, Polly Cowan, February 13, 1817. He served in the War of 1812 as captain of Dysart's Company, Kentucky Mounted Volunteer Militia, in Col. Williams' Regiment; and was State representative from Rockcastle County, 1814; Samuel Dysart was a private in his company.[5]

DYSART FAMILY OF CARTER AND GREENUP COUNTIES, KENTUCKY

Isaac G. Dysart, a son of Jacob Dysart, was the progenitor of the branch of the family that settled in Greenup County in the early 1800s. He came in from what is now Greenbriar County, West Virginia. Tradition and documentary evidence reveal that the family had previously lived at Altoona, Pennsylvania.

1. Isaac G. Dysart was b. in Virginia, presumably in Greenbriar County in 1803. He was living with his family in Greenup County in 1820, his wife being between twenty and thirty years of age.

Children living at home and approximate dates of birth as shown by the U. S. Census of Greenup County for 1850:

2. Jane Dysard; b. 1830.

*3. William Dysard.

4. Elizabeth Dysard; b. 1835.

5. Harriet Dysard; b. 1837.

6. Sarah A. Dysard; b. 1839.

7. Angeline Dysard; b. 1843.

8. Rebecca Dysard; b. 1845.

All children were born in Kentucky. Wife was not listed in above census; she died sometime between 1840 and 1850.

The 1870 census of Greenup County shows that Isaac G. Dysard, wagonmaker, was then living in the home of Irwin and Jane Brown (his daughter.)

Apparently Isaac G. Dysard had other children. The 1870 U. S. Census of Greenup County shows:

9. Newton Dysard, farmer, aged 42, b. in Kentucky.

10. Arminta Dysard, wife, aged 38, b. in Kentucky.

Children:

11. William Dysard, aged 16.

12. Elizabeth Dysard, aged 11.

13. Edward Dysard, aged 6.

14. Alfred Dysard, aged 4.

15. Jane Dysard, aged 1.

3. William Dysard, farmer, was b. in Greenup County, Kentucky, in 1834, and d. at Charlotte Furnace, Carter County, 1907; had service in the Union Army during the Civil War as private,

22nd Kentucky Cavalry; m. in Carter County, Nancy Fults, who
d. 1913, a daughter of Wesley Fults of Carter County.

Children:
16. Martha Dysard; m. E. A. Zarnes.
17. Leonard Dysard; m. Hattie Huff.
*18. H. R. Dysard.
19. Mary Dysard, teacher in the public schools of Carter County;
m. George B. Gannon, teacher and merchant at Grayson.
20. Annie Dysard, teacher; m. Robert Whitt.
21. Naomi Dysard; m. Henry Kotcamp.
22. Nora Dysart; m. Roscoe McGlone.

18. HENDERSON RICHARDSON DYSARD, lawyer, one time teacher and
public official, was born at Charlotte Furnace, Carter County, October 2, 1875. His boyhood was spent on his father's farm. He was
educated in the public schools at Charlotte Furnace and at the
National Normal University at Lebanon, Ohio, where he was
prepared for teaching. He taught in the public schools of Carter
County from 1896 to 1901. Choosing the legal profession as a
career, he studied law and was admitted to the bar in 1896 and afterwards pursued his law studies at Columbian University Law School,
Washington, D. C., and at Valparaiso University, Valparaiso, Indiana. He did not enter upon the practice of law until 1901 when
he opened an office at Grayson, Kentucky, where he practiced for the
succeeding eight years, when in 1909 he located at Ashland, Kentucky, for the practice of his profession. He soon attained and ever
since has maintained high rank as an attorney at the Boyd County
Bar and elsewhere.

A Republican in politics and always interested in public affairs,
he was nominated on the Republican ticket and elected judge of the
Carter County Court for the term 1902-1905, inclusive, at the expiration of which he was elected and served as county attorney for
Carter County for the term, 1906-1909, inclusive. He was elected
and served as mayor of Ashland for the term, 1917-1921. During
his administration the city water works were built, Central Park
lighted and the highway to Russell paved to the city limits. Subsequently he was appointed and confirmed as State Tax Commissioner
but did not accept. He served for two years as examiner of applicants for license to practice law.

Judge Dysard m., first, in Carter County, in 1902, Miss Jessie
Strother, daughter of Dr. J. W. Strother and his wife, Amanda
(Horton) Strother, of Grayson. (See Strother Family.) Judge
Dysard m., secondly, Mrs. Maud Tinsley Marcum, daughter of Judge
W. W. Tinsley of Barbourville, Kentucky. She was b. June 25,

1877, and d. June 28, 1953. Interment at Ashland, Kentucky. No children.

Children of H. R. Dysard and Jessie Strother Dysard:

23. William Henderson Dysard, lawyer, junior member of the law firm of Dysard and Dysard, Ashland, Kentucky, b. at Grayson, Carter County, Kentucky, January 31, 1909; educated (elementary and academic) in the public schools of Ashland, at Greenbrier Military School, and at the University of Kentucky, Lexington, graduating with degree of A. B. He received his legal education at the University of Kentucky from which he graduated with degree of LL.B. in 1932; was a member of the Order of the Coif in law school; and admitted to the bar in 1932, and immediately began and has since continued the practice of law at Ashland in partnership with his father; had service in World War II as Captain in the Air Force, 1942-1945, during which service he was Recorder of the Aircraft Scheduling Unit at Wright Field, Dayton, Ohio; since September 1951, has been consultant on production for the Air Force at Wright Field; m., June 3, 1939, Geneva B. Bushey.

Children:

24. Geneva Anne Dysard; b. July 9, 1945.

25. Amanda Mary Dysard; b. December 4, 1949.

---

[1] "The Surnames of Scotland" by George Fraser Black, Ph.D., The New York Public Library.

[2] "Family Names", by Baring Gould.

[3] "British Family Names", by Rev. Henry Barber, M.D., F. S. A., London, 1903.

[4] "Virginians in the Revolutionary War", 1775-1783, by John H. Gwathmey, p. 245.

[5] "Soldiers of the War of 1812, from Kentucky, as reported by the Adjutant General of Kentucky, 1891."

ELLIOTT AND PRICHARD FAMILIES OF CARTER AND ELLIOTT COUNTIES

Eliot is another diminutive form of Elias. The name Elias is from Hebrew Elijah meaning "Yahweh is my God". The names Ellet and Eliot also occur in the forms Allott and Aliot. Eliot may sometimes be from Elliston, signifying "town of St. Elias". Elliott is also a famous Scottish clan name.

The name first made its appearance in England with William the Conqueror (1066) who had a follower called William Aliot, although some authorities claim that the name originated with the clan Eliot in Scotland. There is a locality by the name of Eliot in the region of Dundee, Scotland.

Families of Eliot or Elliott settled and lived in all the thirteen original American colonies in early colonial days and were numerous in some of them, particuarly in New Hampshire, Massachusetts, Connecticut, New York, Pennsylvania, Virginia, South Carolina and North Carolina.

The Elliotts of England who emigrated to the United States are all descendants of Henry Algernon Elliott, Esq., of the British Navy. He, according to tradition and some authorities, descended from the valiant knight, Sir William de Aliot, who came to England with William the Conqueror. The Irish branch's first definite line is Edwin Elliott who lived and died and is buried in Fincastle, Donegal County, Ireland. The Elliotts in the south of England (Cromwell) embrace the Earls of Germanes from which the family of the Apostle to the Indians sprang.[1]

1. COLONEL RICHARD ELLIOTT was the American progenitor of a large branch of the Elliott family who settled in Eastern Kentucky. He served in the Virginia Forces in the Revolutionary War as did sixty other Elliot, Elliote and/or Elliotts.[2] He was b. at sea; m. Mary Stewart; migrated to and d. in Montgomery County, Ky., in 1799. They had a son.

2. JAMES ELLIOTT, b. 1770, who m. Miss Hannah Scott, daughter of Benjamin Scott who resided on the South branch of the Potomac River in Hardy County, Virginia, now West Virginia. Authorities state that she was a cousin to Gen. Charles Scott, Governor of Kentucky, 1808-1812, and of General Winfield Scott of the U. S. Army.

James and Hannah (Scott) Elliott had a son.

3. CAPTAIN JOHN LISLE ELLIOTT, farmer, surveyor and sometime legislator, who was b. in Hardy County, Virginia, now West Virginia, September 30, 1799, and d. at his home "Highland Forest," in Elliott County, Kentucky, in 1855. He m. in Russell County, Virginia, about 1878, Miss Jane Richie, b. February 24, 1795, d. at her home, "Highland Forest", in Elliott County, Kentucky, June 13, 1870, daughter of Samuel Ritchie of Russell County, Virginia, and, according to some authorities, a cousin to Thomas Ritchie, editor of Richmond (Virginia) Enquirer, who, in his time, was called the "Napoleon of the American press".

Authorities state that John L. Elliott came from Russell County, Virginia, with his family and settled on the North Fork of the Licking River in Morgan County in 1824. However, he settled in what is now Morgan County at an earlier date as is evidenced by the fact that when Morgan County was organized (at the house of Edward Wells) on March 10, 1823, John Elliott, Esq. was recommended to the Governor as a proper person to fill the office of surveyor of the county. He moved and settled on the Maggard farm in the central part of present Elliott County about 1838. Subsequently he entered and patented several tracts of land aggregating 1800 acres on Big Sinking, Gimlet and Caney creeks in Carter and/or Morgan Counties; and acquired other tracts of land in other localities.

John L. Elliott was one of the outstanding men of his time and section of the State. He was an honored and respected citizen; and held many offices and positions of honor and trust and filled all of them creditably and well. He was a captain of the Virginia militia in the War of 1812 and commanded a company for one tour of 90 days. Under contract with the Carter County Court, he built the first court house and jail at Grayson, 1841-2; was State representative from Lawrence County, 1836-1837, and State senator from the district composed of Lawrence and Morgan Counties, 1851-1853.

Elliott County was named for him.

Children:
*4. Samuel R. Elliott.
*5. James Winfield Scott Elliott.
*6. Leonidas Hamilton Elliott.
*7. John Milton Elliott.
*8. Ephraim Blaine Elliott.
*9. William Kendall Elliott.
*10. Benjamin F. Elliott.
*11. Amanda S. Elliott.
*12. Mary Jane Elliott.

4. SAMUEL R. ELLIOTT, farmer; b. in Scott County, Virginia, 1812, and d. in Elliott County, Kentucky; was State representative from Carter County, 1855-57; had service in the Confederate Army,

a private in 5th Regiment Kentucky Infantry Volunteers; m. about 1840, Minerva (surname not known), b. in Kentucky 1817.

Children living in the household and approximate dates of birth as shown by the U. S. Census of Carter County for 1860 and 1870:

13. John M. Elliott; b. 1841.
14. James H. Elliott; b. 1843.
15. Mary A. Elliott; b. 1845.
16. Edmund O. Elliott; b. 1852.
17. Delila E. Elliott; b. 1857.

5. JAMES WINFIELD SCOTT ELLIOTT; b. in Scott County, Virginia, 1815 and d. in Carter County, Kentucky, September 2, 1857.[2] He was m. about 1846 to Julia A. Richards, daughter of John and Rebecca (Power) Richards, and sister to Jeremiah Power Richards who m. Mr. Elliott's sister Amanda.

Children:

18. Rebecca J. (Jennie) Elliott; b. 1845, d. at Owingsville, Bath County, Kentucky, at an advanced age; unm.

19. John L. (Jack) Elliott; b. 1847; was a prosperous merchant at Owingsville, head of the firm of Elliott & Goodpaster. He m., but the name of his wife is not known. They were the parents of four children: Julia, m., first, Horrst Gee of Grayson, Kentucky, and they had a son, Elliott; m., secondly Mr. Tebo.

Coleman S. Elliott, banker of Owingsville.

William Elliott.

Jack Elliott.

6. LEONIDAS HAMILTON ELLIOTT; b. in Scott County, Virginia, 1818; served in the Confederate Army; was commissioned captain, Company "C", 5th Regiment Infantry Kentucky Volunteers, October 19, 1861, and was killed in action at Princeton, Virginia, May 16, 1862. Very little has been learned concerning him. His heirs received land grants for 3800 acres on Sinking and Caney Creeks in Carter County.

7. JOHN MILTON ELLIOTT, lawyer, judge and legislator, was b. May 16, 1820, on the Clinch River in Scott County, Virginia, and came to then Morgan County, Kentucky, with his family about 1822; was educated in the public schools and at Emory and Henry College, Emory, Virginia, in which he studied law and was graduated about 1842, standing high in his class; was admitted to the bar in 1843 and began his legal career at Prestonsburg, Kentucky, in partnership with the Hon. Henry C. Harris. In 1847 he was elected State representative from the district composed of the counties of Johnson, Floyd and Pike. In 1853 he was elected to Congress from the 6th

District then known as the Gibraltar Whig district, defeating Dr. Pierce of Garrard County by 881 votes; reelected in 1855, defeating George W. Dunlap, Know Nothing candidate by 1357 majority; reelected in 1857, defeating John A. Moore of Rockcastle County by a majority of 1775. After the close of this term he was elected (1861) State representative from the Floyd County district without opposition and was expelled, December 21, 1861, for being connected with, or giving aid to the Confederate Army, he having enlisted October 19, 1861, in the command of then Captain John S. Williams, "Old Cerodo Gordo" and later resigned to enter the Confederate Congress. He represented the 6th Kentucky district in first and second sessions of the Confederate Congress. After the close of the Civil War he established himself at Owingsville, Bath County, for the practice of law; and in 1868 he was elected judge of the thirteenth Kentucky Judicial district, defeating Benjamin Gudgell of Bath County by a majority of 2400. In 1876 he was elected judge of the Court of Appeals of Kentucky and was serving as such when on June 6, 1879, he was assassinated at the side door of the old Capital Hotel, Frankfort, by Thomas Buford, because, he claimed, the court had made an unjust decision against his sister, causing her to lose $20,000.

Judge Elliott was interred in the State Cemetery at Frankfort. He married in Johnson County, September 23, 1848, Miss Sarah Jane Smith, daughter of William Smith whose Virginia ancestors served in the Revolutionary War. Judge and Mrs. Elliott had no children.

A statue of him was erected by his widow on the court house yard in Catlettsburg.

8. EPHRAIM BLAINE ELLIOTT, farmer and public official, was b. in Kentucky, presumably Morgan County, 1829. He was clerk of the Carter County Court, being the first elected under the Constitution of 1849; represented Carter County in the State House of Representatives, 1855-57; m. about 1853, Susan A. (surname not known), b. in Kentucky, 1832.

Children:

20. Volney H. Elliott; b. about 1854.
21. John L. Elliott; b. about 1856.
22. Frances J. Elliott; b. about 1859.
23. Amanda Elliott; b. about 1864.

Very little has been learned concerning E. B. Elliott's descendants. However, a grandson, John Smith, presently resides on Lancaster Avenue, Richmond, Kentucky, and a grandson, Roy Elliott Smith resides in Tyler, Texas.

9. WILLIAM KENDALL ELLIOTT; b. in Kentucky, 1831; enlisted in

the Confederate Army, October 19, 1861, a third sergeant, Company "C", 5th Regiment Infantry Kentucky Volunteers; was commissioned a second lieutenant in Fields' company of Partisan Rangers, October 28, 1862; and was killed in action; m. in Carter County, February 28, 1856, Delila A. Vincent, b. in Shenandoah County, Virginia, July 29, 1832, a daughter of John F. and Sarah (Hoke) Vincent. (See Vincent Family.)

10. BENJAMIN F. ELLIOTT, farmer and school teacher; b. January 4, 1834, on his father's estate, "Highland Forest" in Elliott County; served in the Confederate Army, a private, Company "C", 5th Regiment Infantry Kentucky Volunteers; m. Nancy Mary Kigley in Carter County, August 12, 1858, who was b. December 18, 1840, at Wytheville, Virginia.

Children living in the household and approximate dates of birth as shown by the U. S. Census of Carter County for 1860 and 1870:

24. Rachel C. Elliott; b. 1860.
25. Amanda Elliott; b. 1863.
26. John Elliott; b. 1865.
*27. Mary Elliott; b. 1867.
28. Minerva Elliott; b. 1869.

There were other children:

29. Ephraim B. Elliott.

11. AMANDA S. ELLIOTT; b. in Scott County, Virginia, 1824; d. in Missouri, September 22, 1872; educated at a young ladies school, Shelbyville, Kentucky; m. in Carter County, February 6, 1842, Jeremiah P. Richards.

JEREMIAH POWER RICHARDS, farmer, sometime businessman and stock trader, son of John Richards of Scott County, Virginia, and Rebecca Power of Lexington, Kentucky, and grandson of James Anderson Richards, (born 1726) and Mary Burbridge, was b. September 15, 1816, on Triplett Creek in Fleming County, Kentucky, now Rowan County, and d. at his home "Walnut Grove", near Soldier, Kentucky, July 9, 1913 at the age of 96 years, 9 months and 24 days.

Prior to the Civil War Mr. Richards became one the the leading farmers and traders of the State, having commercial houses at Morehead, Olive Hill, West Liberty and Walnut Grove. He drove and sold horses, cattle and hogs to Virginia, the Carolinas, Tennessee and lower Kentucky. When the war broke out, robbers, pretended Union men, looted the stores, despoiled the plantations and drove away the herds, all of which hastened Mr. Richards' enlistment in the Confederate Army. He served throughout the war during which all his property was swept away except his lands and these were involved in debt on behalf of his friends. Being aged and broken in fortune and the society of his native hills so wrecked that it was impossible to resume the life of his former years with the ardor and success with which he had pursued it, he went to Illinois with his family and remained four years and thence to Renick, Missouri. Here his wife died in 1872. His daughter, Zarelda, who had married J. A. Dunlap, died in Illinois. He returned to his home, "Walnut Grove" where he lived until his death.

Eleven years after the death of his wife, Mr. Richards was married to Mrs. Henrietta Connell, an estimable and cultured lady of Trimble County, Kentucky, with whom he lived most happily until her death a few years later. There were no children by this marriage.

He was an ardent Democrat and for many years was a consistent member of the Christian Church. For more than sixty-one years he was a member of Trimble Lodge No. 145, F. & A.M. at Grayson which attended the funeral in a body and in every way showed all the honor due its oldest member and also its last charter member who had aided in establishing the lodge many years before.

Children—one son and seven daughters:

30. Jane M. Richards; b. 1843; d. in infancy.

31. Rebecca Susan Richards; m. James A. Vincent. (See Vincent Family.)

*32. John William Richards.

33. Zerilda E. Richards; b. 1849; m. J. A. Dunlap; d. in Illinois.

*34. Mrs. R. E Dunlap

35. Lucy Richards.

36. Julia Richards; m. Stuart L. Vincent. (See Vincent Family.)

*37. Eliza Hamilton Richards.

32. JOHN WILLIAM RICHARD, farmer ,was b. June 5, 1847, at "Highland Forest", then Carter, now Elliott County, the home of his maternal grandfather, Capt. John L. Elliott, and d. February 7, 1918, at his home near Soldier, Kentucky. He was admitted to the bar but did not actively engage in the practice of law. He was a man of wonderful memory; was widely read; and was familiar with the Bible, Shakespeare and other classics. He was perhaps the best posted historian of his time in the county.

John William Richards was m. to Miss Alice Vincent on February 13, 1873. (See Vincent Family.)

38. Blake Richards.

39. Erie Richards, teacher.

40. Helen Richards.

41. Lottie Richards.

34. MRS. ROBERT E. DUNLAP, distinguished church worker, was born at the Richards home "Walnut Grove" near Soldier, Carter County, Kentucky, and died in Tacoma, Washington, at the age of 88 years. She married in October 1871, Robert E. Dunlap, a minister of the Christian Church. She was active in all lines of church work with her husband. She was one of the organizers of the Seattle Y. W. C. A., and devoted much volunteer time to its work. Her efforts there also included organizing the Missionary Social Union of which she was president for seven years. This organization was the predecessor of the Woman's Council of Churches.

ROBERT E. DUNLAP, minister of the Gospel, evangelist, prohibition advocate, was born in Illinois, 1849, died at Tacoma, Washington, June 1, 1938, in his eighty-ninth year; educated at Transylvania University, Lexington, Kentucky; taught school and preached in Kentucky; served the state board of Kentucky, was sent on missionary service to Montana, serving in Deer Lodge, Bozeman, and other places; became pastor of the First Christian Church, Seattle, Washington, 1891, and organized the University Church in that city in 1899. For 21 years his headquarters were in Seattle; and for 14 years he served as state secretary and evangelist in Arizona. He labored in Idaho and was twice a candidate for governor of the State on the Prohibition ticket.

Both Rev. Dunlap and Mrs. Dunlap died at the home of their daughter, Mrs. Eugene White, Tacoma. Both were interred on Vashon Island.

Children:

42. Mrs. Eugene White, Tacoma, Washington.

43. William Dunlap, of Vashon, Washington, who was the father of William Dunlap, Jr., Robert Dunlap and Mrs. Stanley Youngs of Seattle.

37. ELIZA HAMILTON RICHARDS was born at "Walnut Grove", near Soldier, Kentucky, May 1, 1856, and died at Soldier, August 7, 1928. She was educated in the schools of Sangamon County, Illinois, and the public schools of Kentucky, attending the Morehead public school when 15 years of age, of which Robert E. Dunlap, her brother-in-law, was the principal. She was married to John Quincy Adams of Soldier. Both were consistent members of the Christian Church.

Children:

44. Amanda Adams.

45. Jeremiah Adams.

46. Waller Adams.

47. Elsie Adams.

48. Carrie Adams.

12. MARY JANE ELLIOTT, b. in Kentucky about 1830, d. at Clarendon, Arkansas; was educated at a young woman's school at Shelbyville, Kentucky; m. about 1843, Littleton T. Harris; lawyer. (See Harris Family.)

27. MARY ELLIOTT, teacher, journalist, active in political circles, patriotic organizations, civic and social activities, was b., 1867, on her grandfather, Capt. John L. Elliott's estate, "Highland Forest", in Central Elliott County. She was educated in the public schools, private schools and attended Barbourville College, Huntington, West Virginia, and University of Kentucky at Lexington. Having acquired a thorough education, she engaged in teaching in the public schools of Carter and Elliott Counties for a time. At Limestone, Carter County, on June 28, 1893, she was united in marriage with William Harvey Flanery, then a student of law at the University of Michigan, Ann Arbor. She spent some time in Ann Arbor with her husband. They went to housekeeping at Pikeville, Kentucky, where Mr. Flanery began the practice of law.

While engaged in rearing her family she became interested in newspaper work and from 1904 to 1926 she was one of the able writers c o n s t i t u t i n g the editorial staff of the *Ashland Daily Independent*.

The Flanerys moved to Catlettsburg, Kentucky, and lived in the beautiful home that had been bequeathed to Mrs. Flanery by an aunt, the widow of the late Judge John Milton Elliott.

Mrs. Flanery was an ardent suffragist and had a predilection for politics. She was a delegate to the Democratic National Convention at Madison Square Garden, New York City, in 1928; was State representative from Boyd County in 1920, being the first southern woman to be so honored by her State. She was a member of the Daughters of the American Revolution on the record of Colonel Richard Elliott and served as regent of Poage Chapter at Ashland for three years; was a member of the Order of the Eastern Star and during 1911 was worthy matron of Anna O. Young Chapter No. 28 at Pikeville; was director of the Brookover School of Music of Ashland and Catlettsburg and an associate member of the Civic Music Association in the latter city; was chairman of the legislative board of the Ashland Woman's Club and also connected with the Woman's Literary Club of Catlettsburg.

WILLIAM HARVEY FLANERY, lawyer, was b. at Sandy Hook, Elliott County, Kentucky, November 10, 1865; educated in the public schools; attended University of Kentucky three years and was graduated from the National Normal University, Lebanon, Ohio, with degree of I. S. and B. S., in 1889; engaged in educational work for a time, proving a capable instructor and conductor of teacher's institutes; entered the law school of the University of Michigan, Ann Arbor, and was graduated with degree of LL.B. in June 1895, and immediately returned to Kentucky; began his professional career at Pikeville, Kentucky, where he continued for 17 years, representing, among other clients, the Northern Coal & Coke Company, of which the late John C. C. Mayo was president. He moved to Catlettsburg in 1912 where he continued the practice of law with success.

He was a Mason, being a member of Hampton Lodge No. 235; was a member of the Methodist Episcopal Church, South, and gave his allegiance to the Democratic Party. He was appointed by the City Council of Catlettsburg to fill a vacancy caused by death of James H. McConnell, judge of the Police Court, in the Spring of 1925 and at once took a determined stand for a rigid enforcement of law, thereby incurring the enmity of the criminal element who at 1:30 in the morning of August 7, 1925, dynamited his home. He continued his activities against the violators of the law and success at length crowned his efforts.

Children:

49. Merle Flanery; educated in the public schools and was graduated from the Castle, a select school conducted by Miss Mason; m. Davis M. Howerton, lawyer at Catlettsburg; residence—Catlettsburg.

50. Dew Flanery; educated in the public schools and was guaduated from Smith College, Northhampton, Massachusetts; m. W. H. Haffler.

51. Dawn Flanery; m. H. Leslie Parker.

52. Elliott Flanery; graduated from Staunton Military Academy at the age of 16, and studied law and military science at the University of Kentucky at Lexington, where he was a member of Kappa Alpha.

53. Sue Elliott Flanery; b. at Pikeville; d. at age of 3 years.

---

1 Genealogy of the Elliott Family, by Leon D. Elliott.

2 Virginians in the Revolutionary War, 1775-1783, by John H. Gwathmey, p. 253.

3 Vital Statistics of Carter County, Kentucky, 1852-1862.

EVERMAN FAMILY OF CARTER COUNTY

According to family tradition supported by some documentary evidence 1. WILLIAM EVERMAN, who was b. in England and emigrated to Virginia in the early days, was the progenitor of a branch of the Everman family who settled in Greenup County, Kentucky, in pioneer days. He m. Margaret French who was b. in Wales; and they migrated from Virginia to the Bluegrass region of Kentucky, probably Harrodsburg, where they lived for a number of years. Margaret (French) Everman d. and was b. in the Bluegrass section of Kentucky.

Children, among others:

Second Generation

2. John Everman, farmer and man of affairs, was b. at "Potomac", Virginia, in 1777 and d. in Carter County, Kentucky, March 11, 1855, aged 78 years. His father was William Everman and his mother was ——— (name not of record).[1] He m. Sarah Clark, b. in Virginia, 1787, and d., 1857. She is said to have been of the same family as General George Rogers Clark. About 1808 John Everman brought his family and his father and settled on Barretts Creek at mouth of Smiths Creek, about five miles west of present Grayson, then Greenup County. Here he built his home of great yellow poplar logs, hand hewn to about six inches thick and "lock notched". All lumber was hand-sawed and brick for the chimneys was burned on the farm. Here his father, William, d. and was b. near the home in what has since been known as the Everman graveyard.

John Everman was one of the prominent and influential pioneers and was active in the early affairs of Greenup County.

Children:

Third Generation

*3. Samuel Everman.

*4. William Everman.

5. Martha Everman; m. Elzaphan Offill, September 26, 1829.

6. Malinda Everman; m. Jacob Kibbey, in Greenup County, June 9, 1824. (See Kibbey Family.)

3. SAMUEL EVERMAN, SR., farmer, was b. in Kentucky, 1805; m. first, Miss Barnes, and after her death, m., secondly, in then Greenup County, December 12, 1825, Phoebe Skidmore, b. in Virginia, 1809. He established his home on Smith's branch about two miles above the mouth where, about 1830, he built a double hewn log house of two large rooms about eight feet apart, between which a large "stick and clay" chimney was built, thus giving each room a fire

place. The roof was of shaved shingles, probably chestnut, which remained on the house until about 1895.

Children of Samuel Everman, Sr., living at home and approximate dates of birth as shown by the U. S. Census of Carter County for 1850 and 1870:

Fourth Generation

   7. Brunetta Everman; b. 1831.
   8. William Everman; b. 1832.
   9. Joseph Everman; b. 1838.
  10. Samuel Everman; b. 1857.
  11. George Everman; b. 1862.

   4. WILLIAM EVERMAN, farmer and one-time public official, was b. in Greenup County, Kentucky, April 26, 1808, and d. in Carter County. He served as justice of the peace of Carter County, 1869; m. in then Greenup County, September 29, 1829, Elizabeth Toler, b. February 22, 1813, in Virginia. They 'built and ever afterwards lived in their home on Barretts Creek about one-half mile east of the mouth of Smith's branch.

Children as shown by the U. S. Census of Carter County for 1850, 1860 and 1870:

Fourth Generation

 *12. John Everman.
  13. Samuel Everman.
 *14. Washington Everman.
  15. William Everman; b. 1837; unm.
 *16. Henry Everman.
 *17. James S. Everman.
 *18. Charles Everman.
 *19. Francis Marion Everman.
 *20. Lafayette Everman.
  21. Margaret Everman.
 *22. Sarah Ann Everman.

  12. JOHN EVERMAN, farmer, b. February 13, 1831; served in Union Army in Civil War, m. Nancy Biggs. They were the parents of six children:

Fifth Generation

  23. Lizzie Everman; m. Thomas James and they had fourteen children (sixth generation).
  24. George Everman; m. Lyda Davis and they had nine children (sixth generation).
  25. Martha Everman; m. Frank Rice and they had four children (sixth generation).

26. Thomas Everman; m. Susie Hudson and they had two children (sixth generation).

27. Willie Everman d. young; unm.

28. Millard Everman d. young; unm.

13. SAMUEL EVERMAN, farmer; b. April 12, 1832; served in Union Army in Civil War; m. Catherine Hord, daughter of Philip B. Hord. (See Hord Family).

They were the parents of twelve children (fifth generation):

29. William B. Everman; m. Lizzie Brown and they had six children (sixth generation).

30. Wadsworth Everman; m. Malissa Rice and they had eight children (sixth generation).

31. Ulysses Everman, known throughout the West as "Salt Lake Jack", never m.

32. Robert Everman; m. Mattie Witherow and they had four children (sixth generation).

33. Lizzie Everman; m. Henry Bowers and they had five children (sixth generation).

34. Florence Everman; m. William Cook and they had five children (sixth generation).

35. Katharine Everman; m. Chris. Rupert; they had five children (sixth generation).

36. Charles Everman; m. Hattie Gosney and they had six children (sixth generation).

37. George Everman; m. Carrie Hensley and they had three children (sixth generation).

38. Rosie Everman; m. Robert Nipp and they had three children (sixth generation).

40. Ida Everman; m. Roy Gosney and they had two children (sixth generation).

14. WASHINGTON EVERMAN, farmer, b. September 24, 1833; served in Union Army in Civil War; m. Emma Roberts. They were the parents of ten children.

Fifth Generation

41. Mollie Everman; m. Nelson Messer. They were the parents of five children (sixth generation).

42. Lillie Everman m. Forrest Bowling. They were the parents of five children (sixth generation).

43. Carrie Everman; m. Bruce D. Smith; no children.

44. George D. Everman went West in the late 1870s or early 1880s and nothing more is known concerning him.

45. Annie Everman.
46. Jennie Everman.
47. Charles Everman.
48. Andrew Everman.
49. Elizabeth Everman, never m.

16. HENRY EVERMAN, farmer, b. December 20, 1839; served in the Union Army in Civil War; m. Brintha Gee, b. 1842, daughter of David P. and Sarah Gee. (See Gee Family). They were the parents of one child (fifth generation):

50. Sallie Everman, known as "Little Sallie".

17. JAMES SANDERS EVERMAN, farmer and minister of the Christian Church for about 64 years, was b. on his father's farm on Barrett's Creek, November 20, 1842, and d. March 18, 1929; m. in Carter County, December 9, 1869, Mary A. Gee, b. September 7, 1849, d. December 1, 1927, daughter of Micajah and Martha Belle (Shelton) Gee. (See Gee Family). He had service in the Union Army during the Civil War.

They lived for a time on Smiths branch, Carter County; later in Lewis County and in Greenup County about two miles west of Old Town and finally came back to Carter County and lived on a farm about two miles east of present Charlotte Furnace until Mrs. Everman's death. Subsequently Mr. Everman lived most of the time with his son George on Evermans Creek until his death.

Children:

Fifth Generation

51. Anthony Wayne Everman; b. March 5, 1871, and d. May 14, 1904; m. Jennie Kiser, b. 1873. They were the parents of four children (sixth generation).

52. Ella Eliza Everman; b. March 17, 1873, d. May 1, 1891.

53. George J. Everman, farmer and minister of the Christian Church; b. January 5, 1876; d. July 22, 1932; m. Dicie Kiser, b. 1877. They were the parents of eight children (sixth generation).

54. William H. Everman, b. February 12, 1877; m. Effie A. Canterberry, b. 1876. They were the parents of ten children (sixth generation).

*55. Walter Everman.

56. Samuel J. Everman; b. May 17, 1882; m. Laura Huffman, b. 1887. They were the parents of twelve children (sixth generation).

57. Bettie W. Everman; b. September 4, 1884; m. Arch A. Nipp, b. 1874. They were the parents of five children (sixth generation).

58. Martha B. Everman; b. December 15, 1886, d. September 23,

1943; m. Charles E. Davis, b. 1877. They were the parents of six children (sixth generation).

59. Truman Everman; b. January 8, 1893; had service in World War I; m. Bessie Craycraft. They are parents of twelve children (sixth generation).

18. CHARLES EVERMAN; b. December 31, 1846; served in Union Army in Civil War; m. Mahala Rice. They were the parents of eight children.

Fifth Generation

60. Mariam Everman; m. Davy Jones; they had eight children (sixth generation).

61. Andrew ("Buddy") Everman; m. Rose Stamper; they had five children (sixth generation).

62. Lafe Everman; m. Etta Pope; they had two children (sixth generation).

63. William Everman; m. Cynthia Yates; they had one child (sixth generation).

64. Washington Everman; m. Flora Yates; they had thirteen children (sixth generation).

65. James Everman; m. Nora James; they had four children (sixth generation).

66. Irene Everman; unm.

67. Annie Everman; m. Joseph Stapleton; they had eleven children (sixth generation).

68. Sallie Everman; m. Garfield Patrick; they had thirteen children (sixth generation).

69. Gracie Everman; m. C. Gibson; they had two children (sixth generation).

70. John Everman; m. Gertie Davis; they had four children (sixth generation).

19. FRANCIS MARION EVERMAN, farmer; b. May 8, 1850; m., first, Katharine Armstrong. Children:

Fifth Generation

71. John Everman; m. Minnie Kozee; no children. (See Kozee Family).

72. Eunice Everman; m. Shade Stamper; they had fourteen children (sixth generation).

73. Albert Everman; m. Bertha Kozee; they had five children (sixth generation). (See Kozee Family).

19A. Francis Marion Everman; m., secondly, Sarah Reeves. Children:

Fifth Generation

74.Frank Everman; m. Maude Drumright; they had ten children (sixth generation).

75. Ora Everman; m. John Williams; they had one child (sixth generation).

20. LAFAYETTE EVERMAN, farmer; b. November 20, 1853, died July 30, 1942; m., June 20, 1880, Victoria Lee, b. February 14, 1861, d. December 30, 1942, whose father is said to have been a first cousin to General Robert E. Lee. Children:

Fifth Generation

76. William Lafayette Everman. b. March 28, 1881; m. Myrtie Bailey; they had ten children (sixth generation).

77. Saunders Washington Everman, b. May 11, 1883; m. October 2, 1912, Marcina Conley; they had seven children (sixth generation).

78. Mary Elizabeth Everman, b. January, 3, 1888; m. November 22, 1927, Thomas Prater; no children.

79. James Nelms Everman, b. April 23, 1885; m. March 9, 1906, Chloe Criswell, d. October 2, 1951; they had ten children (sixth generation).

*80. Ella Belle Everman.

81. Francis Marion Everman, b. July 1, 1896; m. July 11, 1919, America Jackson; they had two children (sixth generation).

82. Tivis A. Everman, b. September 4, 1889; m. May 20, 1915, Eva Justice; they had six children (sixth generation).

83. Emma Boone Everman; b. July 17, 1900; m. July 26, 1919, Richard Ratcliff; they had five children (sixth generation).

22. SARAH ANN EVERMAN, b. January 19, 1857; m. Alfred D. Buckley.

Children: Fifth Generation

84. James Buckley; m. Eliza Maddox; they had ten children (sixth generation).

85. Etta Buckley; m. Isaac Stamper; they had ten children (sixth generation).

55. WALTER EVERMAN, soldier, was b. on Smiths branch of Barretts Creek, Carter County, November 5, 1879; served in the U. S. Army for a period of 24 years and three days; enlisted May 16, 1899, and served to July 28, 1916 in Companies "D" and "H", 14th Infantry, reenlisted July 28, 1916 and served to July 11, 1917 in Supply Co. 14th Infantry; served from July 11, 1917 to February 4, 1918 in Supply Co. 44th Infantry; served from February 4, 1918 to February 1, 1919, in Ordnance Department; served from February

1, 1919 to September 11, 1919 in the Quartermaster Corps; reenlisted and served from September 11, 1919, to May 18, 1923 in the Ordnance Department. He was retired from the service, May 18, 1923, and held at different times during his service the grades of corporal, sergeant, company quartermaster sergeant, first sergeant, post ordnance sergeant and quartermaster sergeant, Q. M. Corps.

He was on foreign service for six years, serving in the Philippine Insurrection and the Boxer Rebellion in China. He took part in several skirmishes and engagements in the Philippines and was one of the men who scaled the wall that surrounded the city of Pekin, China (August, 1900) and is said to have been the second white man to cross a small bridge leading to the Forbidden City. He was at the assault and capture of the Forbidden City, Pekin, August 15, 1900).

He was on police duty—in charge of China Town—in San Francisco, California, in 1906 during the earthquake. After retirement and his return home, he served as City Marshal of Grayson, Kentucky, 1926. He m. Miss Lula M. Wade, who was b. January 13, 1877, and d. April 18, 1951; no children.

80. ELLA BELLE EVERMAN, one time teacher, church and civic worker, was b. September 1, 1893, on her father's farm on Barrett's Creek, Carter County, Kentucky; was educated in the public schools of Carter County and took a teacher's course, preparing for teaching; taught in the rural public schools of Carter County for a year; m. August 16, 1913, Roscoe C. Littleton.

Mrs. Littleton has devoted much of her time and energies to the church and its auxiliaries and to civic organizations and clubs. She is a member of the First Christian Church of Grayson and has taught a class in its Sabbath school for many years and is also an active member of its Missionary Society. She is a member and has served as Worthy Matron of the Grayson Chapter of the Order of Eastern Star; a member and has served as president of the Women's Club of Grayson; a member of the Garden Club and Parent-Teacher Association. She served as president of the local Woman's Christian Temperance Union and district president of that organization. For seven years she was in charge of the local Girl Scout Troop.

Mrs. Littleton is a Republican in politics and active in all party affairs.

ROSCOE CONKLING LITTLETON, one-time teacher, public official, lawyer and judge, was b. near Fultz, Carter County, Kentucky, February 2, 1892, educated in the public school of Carter County and was graduated from the Grayson (Kentucky) High School; taught in the rural public schools of Carter County for three years; attended the Law School of Kentucky University at Lexington; was admitted to the bar in June, 1914, and began the practice of his profession at Grayson where he has continued to practice when not in conflict with his official duties.

By close and continuous application to his profession, he rose to, and has ever maintained, a high place as a successful and competent lawyer and judge.

A Republican in politics and always deeply interested in public affairs, Mr. Littleton entered the field of politics early in life. He has held many positions and offices of honor and trust and has filled all of them creditably and well. He was county attorney of Carter County for eight years and three months, two terms by election and three months by appointment; served as Master Commissioner of the Carter (County) Circuit Court; clerk of the Carter County Quarterly Court; and was elected and served as Circuit Judge of the 37th Judicial District for two terms or twelve years.

In addition to and contemporaneous with his official and other duties, he served as president of the Frst National Bank of Grayson, 1933-1940, when he resigned, having been elected Circuit Judge. He was a member of the Republican State Central Committee for four years.

Judge Littleton is a member of Trimble Lodge No. 145, F. & A.M, at Grayson and served as Master for four years; is a member of the Rotary International and also served as Governor of that organization one year. He is a member also of the local Rotary Club; served as its president and later served as District Governor of the organization.

Children:

Sixth Generation

86. June Portia Littleton; b. at Grayson, June 5, 1915; educated in the public schools of Grayson, graduating from the Grayson High School; m., February 6, 1934, Darrell H. Savage. Children (seventh generation): Gary Arlen Savage, b. March 20, 1936, and Robert Conkling Savage, b. December 20, 1937.

87. Maurice Martin Littleton; b. at Grayson, June 27, 1916; educated in the graded and high schools of Grayson and was graduated from Kentucky University at Lexington; was employed at the Atomic plant at Oak Ridge, Tennessee, during World War II; presently is living in Carter County and engaged in agricultural pursuits; m. February 11, 1937, Blanche Stovall. Children (seventh generation): Charles Stovall Littleton, b. March 17, 1941, and Gary Lee Littleton, b. September 14, 1943.

88. Annie Lee Littleton; d. in infancy.

89. Roscoe C. Littleton; d. young.

90. Kenneth Claude Littleton; d. young.

91. Olive Belle Littleton; b. January 5, 1922; educated in the graded and high school of Grayson and was graduated from the Kentucky State Teachers' College at Richmond; was employed at the Atomic plant at Oak Ridge, Tennessee, during World War II; mar-

ried William E. Tewes at Oak Ridge, where they reside. Children (seventh generation): Madeline Leigh, Amelia Ann and Ellen Claire.

92. Alene Elizabeth Littleton; b. March 2, 1923; was educated in the graded and high schools of Grayson; was a student for two years at Kentucky State Teachers' College at Richmond; and subsequently was graduated from the College of Commerce at Ashland; was employed for a time at the American Rolling Mills Company at Ashland; m. Edward H. Ratcliff, an employee of the A R M C O. Children (seventh generation); Edward H., Jr., and Vicki Jean.

Other Everman families lived in Greenup and/or Carter Counties in pioneer days, who might or might not have been of the same family as John Everman, the pioneer who settled on Barretts Creek about 1808.

1. JACOB EVERMAN settled at site of Hopewell, Greenup County, about 1800 or earlier. He m. Martha Deering of that vicinity, a daughter of William Deering and granddaughter of Richard Deering. In his will, probated in the Greenup Court in September, 1812, he mentions his wife, Rebecca; his sons *2 Moses and 3 William; daughter 4 Barbara and her two children; and Riley a son or grandson. Probably he had other daughters who had already married:

Ann Everman m. Walke Cummings in Greenup County, December 22, 1806.

Elizabeth Everman m. John Leaton in Greenup County, October 29, 1807.

Mary Everman m. William McGlothin in Greenup County, November 28, 1807.

Katie Everman m. David Frame in Greenup County, July 15, 1808.

2. MOSES EVERMAN, farmer, was b. in Kentucky, 1797, and d. in Carter County within the period 1850-1860; m. Eleanor Virgin, b. in Virginia or Pennsylvania, 1795, a daughter of Captain Rezin Virgin, a Revolutionary War officer who settled in Greenup County in pioneer days. (See Virgin Family.)

Children living in the household and approximate dates of birth as shown by the U. S. Census of Carter County for 1850 and 1860:

5. Rebecca Everman; b. 1828.
6. Delila Everman; b. 1830.
*7. Tignal Everman.
8. Caroline Everman; b. 1837.
9. Nancy Everman; b. 1844.

7. TIGNAL EVERMAN, farmer and school teacher, was b. in Kentucky, 1832; m. Ollevia ———, b. in Kentucky, 1838.

---

[1] Vital statistics of Carter County, Kentucky, 1852-1862.

FAIRCHILD FAMILY OF JOHNSON COUNTY

ABIUD FAIRCHILD, a Revolutionary War soldier, was the progenitor of one branch of the Fairchild family of Eastern Kentucky. On February 18, 1834, he appeared in open court before the justices of the Floyd County (Kentucky) Court and filed his declaration for a pension on account of his services in the Revolutionary War,[1] wherein he stated, among other things, that he was born in Westmoreland County, Virginia, in 1762, and that he removed to and lived in Wilkes County, North Carolina, until about 1808 when he removed to Floyd County, Kentucky; that he first entered the service as a drafted soldier on or about October 10, 1778, in a company of North Carolina Militia of which John Robbins was Captain; and that he joined his company at Wilkesborough, Wilkes County, North Carolina; and Captain Robbins not joining, William Gillery, the Lieutenant of the Company took command and commanded the Company throughout the whole tour, William Sutton the ensign acting as lieutenant, and the sergeant, whose name to the best of his recollection was James Lewis, acting as ensign; that from Wilkesborough he marched with his Company via Salisbury, Charlotte and Camden, South Carolina, to Perosburg, South Carolina, where they remained for about six weeks, Colonel John Brevard (Prevard) being the Colonel commanding the regiment to which his company was attached; that from the encampment at Perosburg they marched up the Savannah River to Three Sisters at which place his company under Captain Gillery left the other troops and marched down the river about three miles to White House where they remained on garrison duty to guard a ferry on the Savannah River for about six weeks when they marched to Turkey Hill where they were discharged on April 10, 1779, Captain or Lieutenant Gillery signing his discharge; that from April 10, 1779 to June 1, 1780, he served as a volunteer on short excursions under orders of Colonel Benjamin Cleaveland to proceed in pursuit of the Tories and to report as to their strength, etc.; that in the latter part of June or the first of July, 1780, he volunteered and joined for duty under Colonel Benjamin Cleaveland at Wilkesborough, North Carolina, and was placed in a company by Colonel Cleaveland, the names of the officers not remembered; and that in July, 1780, the company, Colonel Cleaveland commanding, marched to Ramsour's Mills (North Carolina), arriving there after the battle (June 20, 1780) between the Mecklenburg troops and the Tories was over, and the Tories defeated; that from Ramsour's he returned home to his residence in Wilkes County, having been in the service about two weeks; that he next volunteered and served in the company under Captain William Jackson, Colonel Cleaveland being the commanding officer, joining his company for duty at Wilkesborough on or about September 1, 1780. From Wilkesborough he marched with his company in the direction of Kings Mountain and while on the march they fell in with the Virginia troops under the command of Colonel William Campbell, which troops were mounted; that Colonel Cleaveland with all the mounted troops under his command proceeded with Colonel Campbell to Kings Mountain, leaving the footmen, including this soldier, to follow with all possible expedition; that the footmen reached Kings Mountain, October 8, 1870, the day after the battle; that he returned to Wilkes County and received a discharge signed by Captain Jackson for a three months' tour; that he next volunteered and served under Captain John Cleaveland, son of Colonel Benjamin Cleaveland, reporting for duty at Wilkesborough on or about March 3, 1781; that he marched with his company—there being about forty of them under Captain Cleaveland—to the old Trading Fort on the Yadkin River in Rowan County, and returned from the expedition about April 25, 1781.

Abiud Fairchild, the Revolutionary War soldier, removed from Wilkes County, North Carolina, to what is now Johnson County, Kentucky, in 1808, and settled on Big Paint Creek near Fish Trap Meeting House, a famous Baptist Church building about six miles from Paintsville. He m., apparently in Wilkes County, North Carolina, Rebecca Johnson. He died in Johnson County, Kentucky, in 1848.

1. Abiud Fairchild, m. Rebecca Johnson. Children:

2. Asa Fairchild, m. Nancy Conley; lived and d. on Jennie's Creek near Denver Post Office, Johnson County.

*3. Sarah Fairchild.

*4. Mary Fairchild.

*5. Enoch Fairchild.

5½. Celia Fairchild, m. Constantine Conley. (See Conley family.)

3. SARAH FAIRCHILD, b. 1784 and d. 1865; m. first, James Curtis in 1802, and second, John Colvin.

Children of Sarah Fairchild and James Curtis:

6. Elizabeth Curtis, b. 1803 and d. 1887; m. Elias Davis in 1823. (See Davis family).

6½. James Curtis.

4. MARY FAIRCHILD, m. George Blair. (See Blair Family.) Children:

7. Asa Blair, m. Mahala Spradlin daughter of Josiah Spradlin and granddaughter of James Spradlin the pioneer.

5. ENOCH FAIRCHILD, blacksmith, mechanic, gunsmith and manufacturer of violins, removed from North Carolina and settled near

Paintsville, Johnson County, Kentucky. He m., apparently in North Carolina but the name of his wife has not been learned. Children:

   *8. William Fairchild.

   8. WILLIAM FAIRCHILD, blacksmith at Paintsville, was b. on Jennie's Creek, Johnson County, in 1835 and d. March 21, 1926; served in the Union Army during the Civil War in the 14th, the 39th and the 45th Regiments, Kentucky Volunteer Infantry. Married, first, Alva Estep. Children:

   *9. Mary Fairchild.
  *10. Dr. J. R. Fairchild.
  *11. Minta Belle Fairchild.
   12. Arla Fairchild, m. Randolph Salmons.
   13. Jessie Fairchild, m. North J. Price.

   8A. William Fairchild m., second, Laura Spradlin. Children.

   14. William Fairchild, Jr.

   9. MARY FAIRCHILD, b. in Magoffin County, Kentucky, November 14, 1864; m. January 13, 1879, Francis Marion Bayes (b. July 11, 1853, d. December 17, 1921), physician and businessman at Paintsville. When a young man he removed from Magoffin County to Johnson County where he studied medicine under Dr. Marion Picklesimer until his marriage. Subsequently he was graduated from the Louisville College of Medicine and practiced his profession in Johnson County. He was a charter member of the I. O. O. F. Lodge at Paintsville and was its first Noble Grand; was a Mason and served as Worshipful Master of the F. & A. M. Lodge No. 381 at Paintsville; and was a member of the Christian Church. Children:

   15. Malta Bayes, m. Judge J. F. Bailey.
  *16. Murah Bayes.

   10. DR. J. F. FAIRCHILD, physician, sometime school teacher and public official, was b. October 7, 1865; m. in 1886, Sue Allen, daughter of Captain Jack Allen. Dr. Fairchild began his career by teaching in the public schools of Johnson County. He was graduated from the Medical Department of the University of Louisville in 1892 and immediately established himself in a general practice at Inez, Martin County, where he enjoyed a lucrative practice. In the meantime, he was elected and served as assessor and as county court clerk of Martin County. In politics he was a Republican and was one of the leaders of his party in Martin County. Children:

   17. Lorna Fairchild, m. Grant Wheatley. (See Brown family).
   18. Fred Fairchild.
   19. Willie Fairchild.

11. MINTA BELLE FAIRCHILD, b. January 20, 1862; m. October 15, 1887, Dr. W. F. Fairchild, b. January 20, 1862, died 1927, son of Isaiah Fairchild and Susanna (Miller) Fairchild.

Dr. Fairchild received his early education in the public schools of Kentucky and was a teacher therein for a number of years. He was graduated from the Louisville Medical College and in 1901 he attended post graduate clinics and received the degree of Doctor of Surgery. For a period of 27 years he was surgeon for the B. & O. Railway Company.

In 1891 Dr. Fairchild removed with his family to Flora, Illinois, where he became influential in the affairs of the city and a leader in church. Children:

20. Effie Fairchild, b. December 5, 1888, m. Dr. R. D. Finch.

16. MURAH BAYES, b. December 16, 1893; m. March 12, 1914, Dr. H. G. Hazelrigg, b. May 4, 1889.

Dr. Hazelrigg was b. in Mason County, Kentucky. He went to Magoffin County and after finishing his education he removed to Paintsville and established an excellent practice in dentistry. Children:

21. Mary Frances Hazelrigg, b. January 29, 1917.

22. William Bayes Hazelrigg, b. November 18, 1918.

---

[1] Revolutionary War Soldier Pension Papers, The National Archives, Washington, D. C.

FAIRCHILD FAMILY OF THE VICINITY OF MUDDY BRANCH, JOHNSON COUNTY, KENTUCKY

1. JOSEPH FAIRCHILD, m. Katherine Lark. He was b. in Tennessee or Virginia from whence he removed to Kentucky and settled at Paintsville, Johnson County. Probably he was not related to Abiud Fairchild, the Revolutionary soldier. Children:
  *2. Abner Fairchild.
   3. Nancy Fairchild, m. James Pennington.
   4. Fanny Fairchild, m. Henry Cantrill.

   2. ABNER FAIRCHILD m. Lucinda Salyer. Children:
  *5. Lou Ann Fairchild.
  *6. Joe Fairchild.
   7. William Fairchild.
   8. Katie Fairchild.
  *9. Nancy Fairchild.
 *10. Phoebe Fairchild.
  11. Frank Fairchild m. Minnie Hawk; lived near Huntington, West Virginia. Children:
  12. John Henry Fairchild m. Vina Horner; lived at Van Lear, Johnson County.
  13. Cyrus Fairchild m. Cora Castle, daughter of Moses Castle; lived in West Virginia.

   5. LOU ANN FAIRCHILD m. Gardner Salyer. Children:
  14. Ben Salyer.
  15. Julia Salyer.
  16. Hadley Salyer, m. ―――― Johnson.
  17. Laura Salyer, m. ―――― Pelphrey.

   6. JOE FAIRCHILD, m. first, Atha Preston. Children:
  18. Lawrence Fairchild, m. ―――― Van Hoose.
  19. Lora Fairchild, m. Leon Laniel.
  20. Alda Fairchild, m. "Pug" Daniel.
  21. Flora Fairchild.

  6A. Joe Fairchild, m., secondly, Sarah Van Hoose. Children:
  22. George Fairchild.

   9. NANCY FAIRCHILD, m. Mont Van Hoose. Children:
  23. Irvin Van Hoose.
  24. Lofty Van Hoose.
  25. Phoebe Van Hoose, m. Florida Borders.
  26. Chlora Van Hoose, m. ―――― Arrowood.
  27. Stella Van Hoose, m. Robert Dale.
  28. Pearl Van Hoose, m. Dewey Croce.

  10. PHOEBE FAIRCHILD, m. John C. McKinsey. Children:
  29. Roy McKinsey, m. Maud Rice.
  30. Cynthia McKinsey, m. ―――― Lark.
  31. ―――― McKinsey, m. ―――― Salyer.

FIELDS FAMILY OF CARTER AND BOYD COUNTIES

This is a local or place name 'at the field', from residence in or by a field. The family is of English extraction and was seated in Engand in early days as is evidenced by the Hundred Rolls and other records of England which bear the names of—

Thomas atte Felde, 1301
William de la Felde, County Gloucester
John de la Feld, County Oxford
Linot ate Feld, County Oxford, 1273
William a la Feld, County Somerset, 1273
John in the Feld, County Somerset
Stephen atte Feld, County Somerset.

Families of Field or Fields settled and lived in all the thirteen original colonies in early colonial days; and they were numerous in many of these colonies, particularly in Rhode Island, Massachusetts, Vermont, New York, Maine, Maryland, Pennsylvania, North and South Carolina and Virginia.

1. ANDERSON FIELDS was the ancestor of a large branch of the Fields family of Northeastern Kentucky. The weight of authority and family tradition is that he was born in Raleigh, North Carolina, in 1795; m. Elizabeth Manis in that State about 1818; went to East Tennessee where a majority of his children were born; and came to Carter County, Kentucky, about 1840. Some authorities claim that he was born in Pennsylvania in October, 1789; removed to Tennessee in 1804 and was engaged in farming near Nashville; and that he came to Carter County, Kentucky, in 1858.' However this may be, the records show that his wife, Elizabeth (Manis) Fields, daughter of Seth and Susan Manis, was b. in North Carolina in 1794 and d. in Carter County, Kentucky, November 13, 1859, aged 65 years.²

ANDERSON FIELDS d. in 1878 and was buried on the point above Hitchings brick plant. He and his wife were Methodists in religion and he voted the Democratic ticket for nearly 70 years.

Children:

*2. William Jason Fields.

*3. James M. Fields.

4. Hiram Fields; m. and settled in Ohio. He was a captain in the Union Army in the Civil War.

*5. Anderson Fields, Jr.

6. Susan Fields m. Clinton Manis, her first cousin. Children: Bige, Jane, Mary Ann.

*7. Mary Fields.

8. Sallie Fields; m. Lewis Minor. Children, among others, Anderson Minor.

2. WILLIAM JASON FIELDS, farmer, public official and officer in the Confederate Army, was b. in East Tennessee, February 25, 1819. When seventeen years of age—about 1836—he migrated to the vicinity of Fielden, present Elliott County, Kentucky, then Lawrence County, and about three years later he m. in that County, Rebecca Boggs, b. in Kentucky in 1827, daughter of James Boggs. Soon after marriage he located on the Boggs farm near present Hitchins, Carter County, and two years later he purchased for the sum of $400 a one thousand acre tract of land on "Lick Branch" (being practically all the land on the branch) near Reedville, Carter County. Here he built his permanent home and here he lived until he entered the Confederate Army in 1862. The stream was called Fields Branch after Mr. Fields, the first permanent settler, which name it has since borne.

William Jason Fields became interested in Carter County politics early in life and was elected and served as Sheriff of Carter County for four terms, three of which were successive. He was defeated for a fourth term by one Stephen England. However, after the expiration of Mr. England's term he was again elected and was serving as Sheriff when the Civil War broke out. A Democrat in politics, Sheriff Fields acquiesced in the policy of neutrality adopted by the State with respect to secession and endeavored, in good faith, to remain neutral in the great conflict and to continue to perform his official duties of Sheriff, but the bitterness engendered by the local strife of the times decreed a different fate for Sheriff Fields. Three companies of 22nd Kentucky Volunteer Infantry (Union) were recruited and organized at Grayson (1861), the seat of justice of Carter County. The captain of one of these companies demanded of Sheriff Fields that he resign his office and enlist in the company, informing him that if he did not enlist voluntarily he would force him to do so. Sheriff Fields replied, cooly and firmly, so it was reported, in the presence of many persons that his people were in the South, his sympathies with the South, and that he would not take up arms against the land of his birth; that if he was forced into the war he would cast his fortunes with the Confederacy. He returned to his home on Fields Branch that afternoon; and that night, near the midnight hour, he was awakened from sleep by the barking of the family dog and the clatter of horses' hoofs. Knowing full well the meaning of this alarm, he sprang from his bed, grabbed his shoes with one hand and his clothes with the other and hurriedly made his exit through the rear door into the night just as a musket was fired at the dog which had challenged the invaders' right to enter its master's home. Returning to the house after the Union soldiers had searched it and departed, he bade his family goodbye, saddled his favorite horse and rode to the home of his brother-in-law, Absolam Rucker; and from thence he went to Camp Mocassin in Virginia, where, on March 22, 1862, he was commissioned a 2nd Litutenant,

Company "G", 5th Regiment Kentucky Volunteers (consolidated). Later resigning his commission, he returned to Eastern Kentucky and recruited Fields' Company of Partisan Rangers, C. S. A., of which he was made the captain. The organization served under Gen. Humphrey Marshall in the Big Sandy River and Southwest Virginia campaigns.

In 1863 while in East Tennessee, Captain Fields was taken a prisoner by the Union forces and sent, first, to Louisville, Kentucky, then to Camp Chase, Ohio, and finally to Fort Delaware on the island in the Delaware River. Here on or about July 2, 1864, Captain Fields and about 2,400 other Confederate prisoners died of smallpox. They were buried in a "trench" on the New Jersey shore of the river. A monument erected on the site by the Daughters of the Confederacy recites these facts.

The sureties on Sheriff Field's official bond were Samuel McDavid, Absolom Rucker, John Jordan and John Armstrong, who took over his Little Fork lands. The sheriff's default was never pressed by the State owing to the extenuating circumstances.

One daughter and five sons were born to Captain William Jason Fields and his wife, Rebecca (Boggs) Fields:

9. Matilda Fields, b. in Carter County, in 1845; m., first, James Dickinson, and they had one child, "Sissie" Dickinson. After his death she m., secondly, Charles Fowler. They migrated to Washington State and she d. at Everett, that State, December 22, 1930, at the advanced age of eighty-six years.

*10. Christopher Columbus Fields.

*11. James A. ("Captain") Fields.

*12. Walter A. Fields.

*13. Elihu N. ("Boone") Fields.

*14. Leander Calloway Fields.

10. CHRISTOPHER COLUMBUS FIELDS, farmer b. in Carter County, in 1847; m. in Carter County, about 1873, Alice Rucker.

Children:

*15. William Jason Fields.

*16. Mollie Fields.

*17. Rebecca Fields.

18. Nannie Fields; m. Lee Fuller.

19. Robert Fields; went South in young manhood and later to Washington or Oregon.

20. Ettie Fields, teacher, deceased; unm.

*21. Thomas Austin Fields.

22. Eva Fields, m. Frank Fleming; reside in Ashland.

23. Earis Fields, farmer, sometime postmaster at Johns Run and merchant, m. Mary Adams; daughter of James and Sallie Adams.

15. WILLIAM JASON FIELDS, farmer, lawyer, legislator and public official, was b. near Willard, Carter County, Kentucky, December 29, 1874; educated in the public schools of Carter County and at Kentucky University, Lexington; was a commercial traveler for wholesale groceries and dry goods, 1899-1910; elected to the 62nd Congress from the 9th Kentucky District, 1911, and reelected and served through the succeeding Congresses until December 1923; when he resigned to assume the office of Governor to which he had been elected the previous November for the term, 1924-27, inclusive; was appointed and served as Commonwealth's Attorney for the 37th Kentucky District, 1932-3.

Governor Fields was a true friend of the public school system and of education and earnestly advocated the construction of more and better public roads and a revision of the State's financial system. During his administration the States financial system was so revised and improved that State warrants that were frozen assets at the beginning of his term were currently cashed by all banks at face value at close of his administration, resulting, among other things, in making certain payment of teacher's salaries when due for the first time in the history of the State. During his administration State Normal Schools at Morehead and Murray were established and extensive improvements made on the Eastern and Western State Normal Schools, at Richmond and Bowling Green, and the State University at Lexington, including the purchase of the much-needed farm for agriculture experiments; the public health service was extended more than it had been from the date of its establishment; over 1000 miles of State roads were graded and hard surface placed on most of it; and the State debt was reduced by $2,000,000.

Governor Fields was a Democrat in politics, a Methodist (Methodist Episcopal, South) in religion and a member of the Masonic fraternity. He m., in Carter County, October 28, 1893, Miss Dora McDavid, of Rosedale, Carter County, daughter of Samuel McDavid.

Governor Fields d. at Stovall Memorial Hospital at Grayson, October 21, 1954.

Children:

24. Forrest Fields; m. Althea Scott, daughter of William H. Scott of Olive Hill. (See Scott Family.)

25. Robert Forde Fields; m. Nora Patton.

26. Everett E. Fields; m. Stella Buck.

27. Frank C. Fields.

28. William Earl Fields.

29. Elizabeth Alice Fields; m. Mr. Johnson.

16. MOLLIE FIELDS; m. Samuel McDavid of Rosedale, Carter County.

Children among others:
30. Nora McDavid.
31. Leslie McDavid.
32. Myrtle McDavid.
17. REBECCA (RHEA) FIELDS; m. William Deal of Willard.
Children:
33. Clyde Deal; m. Gretchen Coffee.
34. Adria Deal; m. George Lambert; reside in Louisville.
35. Roy Deal; m. Agnes Bingham; reside in Ashland.
36. Hazel Deal; resides in Louisville.
37. Althea Deal; m. Samuel Martin; reside in Louisville.
38. Virginia Deal.

21. THOMAS AUSTIN FIELDS, lawyer, was b. near Willard, Carter County, Kentucky, February 7, 1884, and d. at Grayson, Carter County, 1944. He was educated in the rural public, graded and high schools of Carter County; was graduated from Holy Family Business School, Ashland, Kentucky; and was graduated from the George Washington Law School, Washington, D. C., with degree of LL.B. In young manhood he engaged in teaching in the rural schools of Carter County for a time. Later he became a traveling salesman; and in 1911 he became secretary to his brother, W. J. Fields, Congressman from the 9th Kentucky District. Resigning his position, he located in Texas where he practiced law for a time. Abandoning the practice of law in Texas due to ill health, he returned to Carter County and subsequently established a home and continued the practice of law at Grayson where he lived until his death.

In Kansas on August --, 1912, Mr. Fields was united in marriage with Miss Stella May, b. March 23, 1889, d. February 2, 1936, daughter of Thomas Green May, a native of Johnson County, Kentucky.
Children:
39. Jean Fields, b. August 7, 1923, m. Keith M. Huffman, June 3, 1943. Children: Keith Martin Huffman, Jr., b. September 2, 1944, and Ann Fields Huffman, b. February 24, 1947.
40. Ruth Fields, b. September 7, 1923; m. Charles R. Sickafus, August 23, 1946. No children.

11. JAMES ANDERSON ("CAPTAIN") FIELDS, farmer; b. in Carter County, 1849, d. 1907; m. in Carter County, Mary F. Jacobs.
Children:
41. Julia Fields; m. Mr. Cook.
42. Lulu Fields.
43. Emma Fields.
44. Carlos Fields.
45. Jason Fields; m. Cora Horton. (See Horton Family.)
46. Jasper Fields.

12. WALTER A. FIELDS, farmer; b. in Carter County, 1851, d. 1913; m. Amanda Banfield. No children. They adopted and reared Myrtle who m. Will Bellomy.

13. ELIHU N. ("DANIEL BOONE") FIELDS, traveling salesman for many years; postmaster at Olive Hill, Kentucky, b. in Carter County, 1858, d. at an advanced age; m. Elizabeth Jessie.

Children:

47. Florence Fields, b. January 24, 1880, d. 1954; m. 1958, at Ironton, Ohio, Mr. Hoover of Van Wert, Ohio. No children.

48. Ethel Fields, b. August 23, 1882; m., first, Ted Jarvis and after his death, m., secondly, Mr. Shepherd.

49. Charlotte Fields, b. September 20, 1885; m. in Huntington, West Virginia, John Holley, who d. 1914.

50. Georgia Fields, b. August 19, 1889; m. Harry Kearns, telegrapher, C. & O. Railway Company, deceased.

51. Wayne Fields, b. March 10, 1892; resides in Cleveland, Ohio.

52. Carrie Fields, b. October 6, 1894; m. in Carter County about 1922, Frank Burton; reside in Birmingham, Alabama.

14. LEANDER CALLOWAY FIELDS, farmer, b. in Carter County, 1860; m. Maggie Browning, daughter of Thomas Browning. Both are buried in the Womack graveyard at Reedville.

Children:

53. Lee Fields.

54. Ennis Fields.

3. JAMES M. FIELDS, farmer, was b. in Tennessee, March 10, 1820. He came to Carter County, Kentucky, in the 1840's, leaving his three oldest children there until after the close of the Civil War when they were brought to Carter County by his brother Anderson. They were:

*55. James Ervin Fields.

56. Melville Fields, b. in Tennessee in 1849.

57. Inez Fields; b. in Tennessee.

JAMES M. FIELDS m. in Carter County, Kentucky, December 19, 1852, Mrs. Mary Ann Boggs (nee Mary Ann Eastham), born in Boyd County, Kentucky, August 12, 1823, widow of Ephraim Boggs. They removed to Boyd County, Kentucky, in 1879.

Children:

58. William C. Fields, b. in Kentucky, 1853; m. ———— Fannin.

59. George N. Fields, b. in Kentucky, 1858.

60. Elizabeth Susan Fields, b. in Kentucky, 1860; m. John Mc-Whorter.

*61. Robert A. Fields.

62. Cecil Edward Fields, b. in Kentucky, 1869.

55. JAMES ERVIN FIELDS, farmer, was b. in Tennessee, 1846 or 1847; m. in Carter County, about 1868, Elizabeth Savage, b. in Kentucky, 1851.

Children:

63. Mary ("Mollie") Fields; b. 1869; m. Hiram Pope.
*64. George W. Fields.
65. Will Fields; m. Laura Womack.
66. John Fields; m. Betty Mannin.
67. Fred Fields; unm.
68. Bertha Fields; m. Ned Wilburn.
69. Mabel Fields; m. Jerome Blankenship.

64. GEORGE W. FIELDS, traveling salesman; m. Helen Vincent. (See Vincent Family.)

Children:

70. Claude Fields.
71. Gladys Fields.
72. Glen Fields; m. Margaret Mitchell; reside in Ashland.

61. ROBERT A. FIELDS was b. in Carter County, Kentucky, August 1, 1862. His great-grandfather on the maternal side, Hartwell Eastham, a native of Virginia, was a farmer in Boyd County, Kentucky, where he d. in 1850. He m. Iby McGuire.

Robert A. Fields was educated in the schools of Grayson, Kentucky, and Catlettsburg, Kentucky, and finished his education at National Normal University, Lebanon, Ohio. He taught in the schools of Cannonsburg and Sandy City for five years; was elected superintendent of public schools of Boyd County in 1890 and was reelected in 1893 without opposition. He was a member of the Knights of the Golden Eagle and the Mutual Protective Association.

On June 12, 1889, Mr. Fields was m. to Rebecca Ann Moore, daughter of Enoch Moore. Miss Moore was b. in Lawrence County, Ohio, March 31, 1861, and was educated at Ironton and Ada, Ohio.

Children:

73. Marie Fields; b. July 17, 1890.
74. Robert Arnold Fields; b. December 9, 1891.
75. Vernon C. Fields; b. December 11, 1892.
76. Esther Fields; b. November 4, 1894.[3]

5. ANDERSON (OR ANDREW) FIELDS, farmer was b. in Tennessee 1826; m. about 1858, Lucinda ———, b. 1835.

Children living in the household and approximate dates of birth as shown by the U. S. Census of Carter County for 1870:

77. Sarah Fields; b. in Tennessee, 1859.
78. Susan Fields; b. in Tennessee, 1861.

79. Christopher Fields: b. in Tennessee, 1863.

80. James Fields; b. in Tennessee, 1865.

81. John Fields; b. in Tennessee, 1866.

82. McClelland Fields; b. in Kentucky, 1869.

7. MARY FIELDS; b. in Tennessee, about 1825: d. in Carter County, Kentucky, at an advanced age; m. in Tennessee about 1848, Andrew Lawson, farmer, b. in Tennessee, 1826, who, while serving in the Confederate Army and at home on leave of absence, was assassinated or killed by "bushwhackers" on or about February 28, 1864. In 1866 Mary Fields Lawson came to Carter County, Kentucky, with her children, where they afterward made their home.

Children:

83. Solomon Lawson, b. in Tennessee, January 21, 1849, d. in Carter County, 1927; m., first, Dinah Bush and secondly, Minnie Offard.

84. Preston Lawson, b. in Tennessee about January 18, 1850; m. Jane Fraley.

85. Susan Lawson, b. in Tennessee, May 8, 1855; m., first, April 1866, Martin Justice, and after his death, she m. April 18, 1876, Robert Rucker, b. October 10, 1850, and d. October 28, 1935.

86. Elizabeth (Betty) Lawson, b. in Tennessee, 1857, d. 1918; m. William ("Bud") Rucker.

87. William Jason Lawson, b. in Tennessee, 1859; m. Nellie Rucker.

88. Emaline Lawson, b. in Kentucky, June, 1860; m., first, James Rucker; were divorced and she m., secondly, James Van Horn.

89. Anderson Lawson, b. 1861, d. 1880.

90. Alice Lawson, b. February 28, 1864; m. El. Canor Horton. (See Horton Family.)

R. MONROE FIELDS, lawyer, judge; b. on Kings Creek, Letcher County, Kentucky, January 24, 1881, a son of Matthew C. and Rachel (Musslewhite) Fields; educated in the public schools of Letcher County and the University of Louisville, Department of Law, class of 1903-4; was County Attorney of Letcher County, 1912-21; Commonwealth's Attorney, 35th Judicial District, 1912-21; resigned in 1921 and practiced law at Whitesburg, Kentucky, until 1928; Circuit Judge of the 35th Judicial District from 1928 until his death.

Judge Fields was a Republican in politics, a Methodist and a member of the Kentucky State Bar Association.

He m. Florence Tyree of Whitesburg, August 20, 1905. Children:

Glenn T. Fields (a U. S. Mail pilot killed in a crash on Little Kennesaw Mountain, Georgia, in a fog, January 20, 1933; Mrs. Joseph M. Graham of Pittsburg; Mrs. Arthur C. Smith of Pittsburg; and Hazel Fields.

---

[1] Biographical Cyclopedia of the Commonwealth of Kentucky, John M. Gresham Company, Chicago—Philadelphia, 1896, p. 16.
[2] Vital Statistics of Carter County, Kentucky, 1852-62.
[3] Biographical Cyclopedia of the Commonwealth of Kentucky, John M. Gresham, Company, Chicago—Philadelphia, 1896, p. 16.

FITZPATRICK FAMILY OF FLOYD AND LETCHER COS.

The Fitzpatricks came from Virginia and settled in Floyd County, Kentucky, in early pioneer days—the exact time not definitely known —but prior to 1810, as is evidenced by the U. S. Census of Floyd County for that year which bears the names of four Fitzpatricks as heads of families: (1) John, Sr., b. about 1775; (2) John, b. about 1785; (3) John, b. about 1795; and (4) Thomas, b. about 1787.

Early marriages of the members of the Fitzpatrick family in Floyd County:

John Fitzpatrick and Fanny Rice, May 17, 1811.
William Fitzpatrick and Patsy Blair, May 8, 1813.
Sally Fitzpatrick and David Hamilton, July 27, 1813.
Jacob Fitzpatrick and Sally Hamilton, August 21, 1813.
Levisa Fitzpatrick and Robert Spradlin, April 15, 1816.
Betty Fitzpatrick and Lewis Haywood, September 24, 1816.
Jacob Fitzpatrick and Rainey Haywood, November 18, 1817.
Jonathan Fitzpatrick and Agnes Haywood, November 26, 1818.
Margaret Fitzpatrick and John Spradlin, May 4, 1820.
"Betsy" (Elizabeth) Fitzpatrick and Avery Keesee, August 10, 1820.
Susanna Fitzpatrick and Nathaniel Crank, August 20, 1820.
Ruth Fitzpatrick and George Sheets, August 7, 1821.
Mollie Fitzpatrick and John Hitchcock, November 21, 1822.
Sally Fitzpatrick and Thomas Conley, January 8, 1824.
Jeremiah Fitzpatrick and Lucinda Blair, October 2, 1829.
Nancy Fitzpatrick and Samuel Evans, June 28, 1832.
James Fitzpatrick and Sarah Caudill, February 1, 1836.
Thomas Fitzpatrick and Nancy Nesterson (Kesterson), February 7, 1837.
Sarah Fitzpatrick and James Milton Rule, November 4, 1839.

1. One JACOB FITZPATRICK came from Virginia and acquired a large landed estate in Southeastern Floyd County, Kentucky, which was confiscated by the Federal Government at the time of the Civil War. He was a lawyer; was b. in Virginia about 1805 and had m. in Virginia, Pauline ————, b. about 1803.

Children among others:

*2. James B. Fitzpatrick.

3. Honorable Thomas Young Fitzpatrick, a lawyer, was b. near Prestonsburg, Floyd County, Kentucky, September 20, 1850; attended the public schools of Floyd County; studied law; was admitted to the bar, 1877, and practiced his profession; was judge of the Floyd County Court, 1874-75; State representative, 1876-7; County Attorney for Floyd County, 1880-84; presidential elector on the Democratic Ticket of Cleveland and Hendricks in 1884; elected as a Democrat to the Fifty-fifth and Fifty-sixth Congresses (March

4, 1897-March 3, 1901); d. at Frankfort, Kentucky, January 21, 1906; interment in the Frankfort Cemetery.[1]

2. JAMES B. FITZPATRICK, lawyer and teacher, was b. on Middle Creek, Floyd County, in 1837 and d. in Letcher County, Kentucky, in 1901. He acquired a liberal education, mainly by his own efforts, and was a successful teacher in the public schools of Floyd County and at Hazard, Perry County. While teaching at Hazard he studied law with Judge John Dishman; was admitted to the bar and became a successful lawyer. Leaving Hazard, he located at Whitesburg, Letcher County, and in 1872 he represented that district in the State House of Representatives. He had service in the Confederate Army; entered the service October 18, 1862, at Whitesburg as 2nd Lieutenant, Company "I", 13th Regiment Kentucky Volunteers; promoted to First Lieutenant, same organization; was captured at Gladeville, Virginia, July 7, 1863,[2] and was held a prisoner of war two years on Johnson's Island in Lake Erie. He m. Josephene Godsey, who was born on Carr's Fork, Letcher County. Her family came from Scott County, Virginia.

In politics Mr. Fitzpatrick was a Democrat.

Children:

*4. Dr. John D. Fitzpatrick.

5. Mollie Fitzpatrick; m. Elisha Blair, newspaperman, who was connected with the publishing of the Mountain Eagle at Whitesburg.

6. Thomas Fitzpatrick d. at age of ten.

7. Pauline Fitzpatrick; d. in childhood.

4. DR. JOHN D. FITZPATRICK, M. D., was born at Whitesburg, September 28, 1880; attended Whitesburg schools until the age of thirteen and during the succeeding three years he continued his studies at Prestonsburg, Kentucky. At the age of sixteen he began teaching in the public schools and for three years was principal of the Whitesburg schools during which period he worked evenings in the County Court Clerk's office, thereby supplementing his salary sufficiently to defray his expenses in the Medical Department of the University of Louisville from which he was graduated at the age of twenty with second highest honors of his class. Upon graduation he established himself in active general practice at Whitesburg and soon had, and has since maintained, a large practice, never failing to respond to all calls whether from rich or poor.

Dr. Fitzpatrick is a Democrat and has served as judge of the Letcher County Court. He is a member and has served as President of the Letcher County Medical Society; a Mason, Blue Lodge and Chapter of the Scottish Rite; and a member of the Junior Order of the United American Mechanics. In religion he is a Presbyterian.

In 1914, Dr. Fitzpatrick m. Miss Eunice Baker, of Hazard, Kentucky.

Children :
8. James Fitzpatrick.
9. Pauline Fitzpatrick.
10. Josophene Fitzpatrick.
11. John Fitzpatrick.
12. Thomas Fitzpatrick.

---

[1] Biographical Directory of the American Congress, 1774-1949, page 1162.

[2] Report of the Adjutant General of Kentucky, Confederate Kentucky Volunteers, 1861-1865, Vol. II, pages 158-9 and 172-3.

FLAUGHER FAMILY AND TYREE FAMILY OF CARTER COUNTY

1. CHRISLEY FLAUGHER was the ancestor of the Flaugher family of Northeastern Kentucky. He was apparently of German origin. He lived near present Hitchens, Carter County, Kentucky; and d. April 18, 1855, aged 81 years.[1] He m. Margaret Swetnam.

Children among others:

*2. James Flaugher; b. in Greenup County, Kentucky, March 24, 1824, and d. in Carter County; m. in Carter County, June 27, 1844, Margaret McGuire.

*3. Eliza Flaugher.

2. JAMES FLAUGHER was born in Greenup County, Kentucky, March 24, 1824, and died in Carter County; married presumably in Carter County, June 27, 1844, Margaret McGuire.

Children:

*5. James Polk Flaugher.

6. Eliza Flaugher; b. September 18, 1847.

7. Chrisley C. Flaugher; b. August 17, 1849.

*8. Lafayette Flaugher.

*9. George W. Flaugher.

10. W. J. Flaugher; b. February 10, 1856.

*11. Sidney Flaugher.

12. Martha Flaugher, b. May 20, 1860.

13. Nancy C. Flaugher; b. July 20, 1862.

5. JAMES POLK FLAUGHER, farmer, was b. in Carter County November 22, 1845, and d. at Willard, that county, April, 1935; had service in the Union Army in the Civil War; m. Ann Catherine Shearer, b. December 25, 1848, and d. at Willard, 1915, a daughter of Rev. Walter Shearer and his wife, Nancy B. (Rice) Shearer. (See Rice Family.)

Children:

14. J. Walter Flaugher; b. October 13, 1868; m. Sarah B. (Ducie) Graham, daughter of James K. P. and Nancy (Pennington) Graham. They reared a large family.

15. W. LaFayette Flaugher; b. July 2, 1871; m. May Graham, daughter of James K. P. and Nancy (Pennington) Graham. They reared a family.

16. Nancy Lee Flaugher; b. January 16, 1872, and d. in November 19—; m. Murray Fleming. No children.

17. D. W. Flaugher; b. and d. March 10, 1873.

*18. Margaret Flaugher.

19. Ida Florence Flaugher; b. December 12, 1875, and died, 1949; m. Mr. Greer; resided at New Castle, Pennsylvania. No children.

*20. Ione Lake Flaugher.

18. MARGARET FLAUGHER was b. at Willard, Kentucky, August 27, 1874; m. Walter W. Walls who came with his parents from near Saltville, Virginia, to Carter County, Kentucky, in his youth. He engaged in the timber and lumber business for a number of years; and subsequently the family went to New Castle, Pennsylvania. Mr. Walls was very much interested in education and was active in school affairs in his community. Their daughter, Rae, married a Mr. Rice, son of James Rice of Rosedale, Kentucky, (See Rice Family) whose daughter Rose married A. J. Everett who resides at King Street, Littleton, Massachusetts.

20. IONE LAKE FLAUGHER; b. at Willard, May 6, 1879, and d. at Boca Grande, Florida, March 18, 1950. Interment at Huntington, West Virginia; m. July 3, 1902, Battie Barnard Gilbert, born at Aden, Kentucky, February 11, 1879, and died at Russell, Kentucky, May 29, 1934, a son of Tom T. and Del Sena (Wilcox) Gilbert of Aden, Kentucky.

Mr. Gilbert had service in both the Spanish-American War in Cuba and the Philippine Insurrection in the Philippine Islands. He was a passenger conductor on the C. & O. Railway for about 28 years.

Mr. and Mrs. Gilbert lived at various places; Clermont, Florida; Huntington, West Virginia; Ashland, Kentucky, and Russell, Kentucky. They were members of the Central Christian Church in Huntington, West Virginia. Both were interred in Rose Hill Cemetery, Ashland.

Children:

*21. Lelia Eliza Gilbert.

*22. Rachel Ione Gilbert.

*23. Virginia Catherine Gilbert.

21. LELIA ELIZA GILBERT; b. at Willard, May 11, 1903; educated in the public schools of Huntington, West Virginia, graduating from the Huntington High School; was graduated from the Teacher's College of Marshall College, Huntington, West Virginia, in August, 1923; and was a student at Ohio State University, 1928; taught in the public schools of Logan, West Virginia, 1923-1925; in Williamson, West Virginia, public schools, 1925-1927; and in Chardon (Ohio) public schools, 1928-1932; m. August 10, 1926, Ober Carter Slotterbeck of Bloomdale, Ohio, then teacher of chemistry in the Williamson (West Virginia) High School. Mr. Slotterbeck is descended on the paternal side from the early German settlers of the Toledo, Ohio, area, and on the maternal side from the Dale family of Weston, Vermont, and the McConnell family of Salem, Massachusetts. He was graduated from the Ohio State University, receiving

degree M. Sc. in 1931; degree Ph.D. in chemistry, 1936; and degree of Doctor of Philosophy, 1936. He taught in the high school, Williamson, West Virginia; was principal of the Chardon (Ohio) school for a time and, removing to Oxford, Ohio, in September, 1933, he taught in Miami University there; and became principal of the training school of McGuffey High School of Miami University in the Fall of 1935. In November, 1936, he accepted a position as organic chemist with the Standard Oil Company of New Jersey. He has been granted about 50 patents in the field of chemistry. Mrs. Slotterbeck accepted a position as teacher during World War II and is presently a teacher in the Charles H. Brewer School at Clark, New Jersey. She has been very active in civic affairs, serving as clerk of the Parent Teacher Association for 2 years, a member of the board of that organization and chairman of the Teenagers program committee.

Dr. and Mrs. Slotterbeck are members of the First Presbyterian Church at Rahway, New Jersey. Residence 18 Ridge Road, Clark, New Jersey.

They have one child, a daughter, Oberta.

Oberta Slotterbeck was b. at Christ Hospital, Cincinnati, Ohio, Friday, July 3, 1936; was educated in the public schools of Clark, New Jersey and was graduated June 23, 1954, from the Jonathan Dayton High School, Springfield, New Jersey, as valedictorian of her class of 245, having made an "A" average for the four year's college preparatory course by reason of which she was awarded the 1954 scholarship. She is presently a student at the New Jersey College for Women (New Brunswick, New Jersey) of Rutgers University, majoring in Dramatic Art and English, and studying voice under a private teacher. She is an accomplished dancer; has danced in several New Jersey night clubs and has appeared on the stage in several civic group players shows, the latest being in May, 1954, with the Elizabeth Civic Players in "Desert Song" directed by the well-known Broadway and Millburn Play House singer, Donald Gage. Her ambition is to go on the stage.

22. RACHEL IONE GILBERT was b. at Ashland, Kentucky, December 10, 1905; was educated in the public schools of Huntington, West Virginia, graduating from the Huntington High School; and was graduated from Marshall College at Huntington; married, first, July 6, 1926, James Lee McCaffrey, Sr., student and football star at Marshall College. After graduation from Marshall both Mr. and Mrs. McCaffrey taught school for several years at Echols, West Virginia. Mr. McCaffrey served in World War II in the South Pacific area; and, sustaining an injury incident to his war service, he is presently confined to Veterans' Hospital, Chillicothe, Ohio. They have one child, a son, James Lee McCaffrey, Jr., born at Russell, Kentucky, September 28, 1928. He was educated in the

public schools of Huntington, West Virginia, graduating from the Huntington High School; and subsequently he attended Marshall College. In February, 1950, he m. Carolyn Cook of Cleveland, Ohio. They have two children: Linda Ann, born January 1951, and Linda Catherine, b. October, 1952. He is employed by an aircraft manufacturer in Cleveland where they reside.

After divorce from James Lee McCaffrey, Sr., in 1931, Rachel (Gilbert) McCaffrey taught in the schools of Russell and Catlettsburg, Kentucky, and Fort Myers and Branton, Florida. In October, 1952, she married James Pearly Staley of Huntington, West Virginia, where they resided for the succeeding two years, after which they went to Key West, Florida, where Mrs. Staley is engaged in teaching.

23.   VIRGINIA CATHERINE GILBERT was b. in Huntington, West Virginia, June 6, 1908; educated at Marshall College, Morehead (Kentucky) State Teacher's College; and at the University of Florida at Gainsville; taught in the public schools of Russell, Kentucky, for several years.

In 1947 Miss Gilbert accepted a position as teacher in the public schools of Boca Grande, Florida, going there to live accompanied by her mother, Ione Lake (Flaugher) Gilbert, who died in her home from heart attack in 1950. Resigning her position as teacher in 1950, she accepted a position in the Boca Grande post office and is presently filling that position.

Miss Gilbert is a civic leader, taking an active part in the many and various activities of her community. While teaching, she coached the girl's basketball team of the Boca Grande High School. A charter member of the Boca Grande Woman's Club, she has held at one time or another every office of the organization except that of president, which she has steadfastly refused. She has charge of the girl scouts and directs the activities of the Student Community House.

She is an active member of the Methodist Church.[2]

6.   ELIZA FLAUGHER; b. at Willard, Carter County, September 18, 1847, and d. in Huntington, West Virginia, April, 1937; m. in Carter County about 1868, Jesse Adams, who served in the Union Army in the Civil War. He was wounded in battle from the effects of which he d. about 1877. He was a son of Pleasant Adams.

Children:

24.   Maggie Adams, a teacher; b. at Willard, 1869, and d. at Denton, Kentucky, 1894; m. Roland Prichard of Denton. (See Prichard Family) No children.

*25.   George W. Adams.

*26.   Laura Adams.

25. GEORGE W. ADAMS, farmer; b. at Willard, November 1871, and d. at his home on his farm near Willard, April 12, 1929; m., July 1, 1890, Miss Martha McDavid, only daughter of Daniel and "Betty" (Sturgill) McDavid.

Children:

27. Betty Adams; m. Harry Walker, a teacher and farmer. Children: Arlene, Shirley, Wilbur, Calvin, Edgar and Leonidas.

28. Milton Adams; m. Opal Bays. Children: Mary Martha, Leonard Russell, Milton, Jr., Nina and George.

29. Homer Adams; m. Dolores Cook. No children.

30. Watt Adams; m. Gladys Rucker. One child, Jennie.

31. Russell Quin Adams; m. Rose Sevettic. Children: Martha Katherine and Carolyn.

32. Mary Adams; deceased; m., first Arthur Stevens. Children: Billie George.

Mary Adams m., secondly, Pete Acton. No children.

33. Charles Adams; m., first, Mabel Heaberlin; and after he was divorced, he m., secondly, Sadie Harper. (See Harper Family.) Children: Audrey and Ernest.

34. Jessie Adams; m. Roy Fraley. Children: Laura Ethel, Dorothy, Irene, Bobby and Quinn.

35. Frank Adams; m. Arva Kitchen. Children: Maurine and Lowel, deceased.

36. Jennie Adams; m. Dewey Johnson. Children: Shirley Marie, Edna, Howard and George.

26. LAURA ADAMS; b. at Willard, May 2, 1875; m. at Willard January 15, 1899, Milton S. Duke, a locomotive engineer, b. in Carter County, 1869, and d. in Huntington, West Virginia, November 16, 1924.

Children:

*37. Milton Rankins Duke.

*38. Martha Elizabeth Duke.

39. Gertrude Imogene Duke.

27. MILTON RANKINS DUKE; b. at Greenup, Kentucky, October 15, 1901, and d. in Huntington, West Virginia, February 18, 1943; m. February 18, 1923, Ruth Christine Miller, daughter of William Jacob Miller and Jershua (Hague) Miller of Guyandotte, West Virginia. Children: Charles William Duke; m. Billie Rosamond Bryant. They have three children. Dorothy Ann Duke m. Thomas Mearl Jeffrey. They have two children. Joe Raymond Duke, unm.; and Milton Lee Duke, unm.

38. MARTHA ELIZABETH DUKE; b. at Willard, August 9, 1906; m. first, Earl Scanlon Fullerton, son of Mr. and Mrs. Ezekiel Fullerton of Huntington, West Virginia. Children: Betty Lee Fullerton; unm.

Earl Milton Fullerton; m. Sallie Watson. They have one child.
Carolyn Maude Fullerton; m. Harold Basil Jordan. They have two
children. Jo Ann Fullerton, unm.
  Earl Scanlon Fullerton d. at Huntington, December, 1938; and
his widow, Elizabeth, m. Marvin Allen. They had two children.
Marvin and Elizabeth Allen were divorced and Elizabeth later m.
Norman Collins, son of Mr. and Mrs. Elijah Collins of Huntington.
They have one child.

  39. GERTRUDE IMOGENE DUKE; b. at Willard, December 21, ——,
and d. at Huntington, December, 1931; m. Raymond Blain, son of
Mr. and Mrs. Frank Blain. No children.

  8. LAFAYETTE FLAUGHER; b. 1852 at Mt. Savage, Carter County,
Kentucky; m. Matilda Kennedy, daughter of Milton and Eleanor
(Boggs) Kennedy; migrated to and lived in Oklahoma. Children:
Drew, Roscoe, Sibyl, Huxley, Leydon and Opal.

  9. GEORGE W. FLAUGHER; b. at Willard, April 13, 1853, and d.
at Willard, April 20, 1925; m., first, January 1, 1874, Lucinda Kennedy, b. May 9, 1851, and d. March 6, 1896, daughter of Milton
and Eleanor (Boggs) Kennedy. Children: Thomas W., went west
when a young man; unm. Lottie; d. in young womanhood; Ily, m.
a Mr. Gilbert. Raymond Quimby (Quinn), teacher and traveling
salesman; d. in young manhood; m. ——— ———, Earl; Herbert;
Dexter, m. Miss Webb of Webbville, Kentucky; Aurora; m. Raymond
Hunter, son of Jesse and Jennie (Bowling) Hunter of Willard.

  9A. GEORGE W. FLAUGHER m., secondly, May 5, 1897, Lacy Triplett,
b. August 24, 1865, and d. January 16, 1929. Children: Kroler,
Edith, Lowell, Eureka, Buenos and Hazel.

  11. SIDNEY FLAUGHER; b. March 10, 1857; m. John J. Swetnam, b.
November 9, 1849, and d. February 24, 1917. John J. Swetnam was
a son of Zephaniah Swetnam who lived and d. in Iowa. After his
death John J. Swetnam was brought to Lawrence County, Kentucky,
and was reared by an uncle, Neri Swetnam. (See Swetnam Family.)
Children: E. Leslie Swetnam; teacher; b. at Blaine, Lawrence
County, Kentucky, November 2, 1876; educated in the public schools
of Lawrence County, Blaine (Kentucky Normal School, and Valparaiso Normal College, now Valparaiso University; taught in the
public schools of Carter, Lawrence and Letcher Counties, Kentucky; was principal of the Grayson Graded School and the Jenkins
High School. Webb Swetnam; Norman Swetnam; Elizabeth Swetnam; Ruby Swetnam, who m. a Mr. Moore and reside at Plain City,
Ohio; Martha Swetnam; Morton Swetnam; Zephaniah Swetnam who
lives in Colorado; and Opal Swetnam.
  3. ELIZA FLAUGHER; b. in Kentucky, 1814; m. in then Greenup

County, Kentucky, August 17, 1832,[2] Zachariah Tyree, a minister of the Methodist Church and an official of the Carter County (Kentucky) Court in early days. He was b. in Virginia—apparently in the Shenandoah County area about 1806, a son, it is believed of 1. William and Nancy Tyree, pioneer settlers in Greenup County, Kentucky. The records would seem to indicate that he had a sister, Mrs. Mary Ann Bacook who was b. in Shenandoah County, Virginia. and d. in Carter County, Kentucky, April 3, 1853, age 57 yrs.[3] The records show that one Zachariah Tyree m. Barbara Gollihue in then Lawrence County, Kentucky, August 9, 1827. According to tradition he was the identical Zachary Tyree here under consideration. Children living in the household, September 16, 1850, and approximate dates of birth as shown by the U. S. Census of Carter County for 1850:

3. Elzira Tyree; b. 1833.

4. Sarah Tyree; b. 1835.

5. Chrisley Tyree; b. 1838.

6. William Tyree; b. 1840.

7. James Tyree; b. 1854.

*8. John Tyree.

9. Jerome Tyree; b. 1856.

10. Perry Tyree; b. 1858.

11. Lafayette Tyree; b. 1860.

There were other sons:

12. Frank Tyree of Olive Hill, a contractor and for many years a justice of the peace in Carter County.

13. Gaines Tyree; recruited a company of soldiers for service in the Spanish-American War and served as captain of the company in that war.

One of the daughters m. Rev. Zimmerman of Olive Hill.

8. JOHN MILTON TYREE, hotel keeper at Grayson and Olive Hill, was b. 1854; served in the Union Army in the Civil War; served as second lieutenant, Company "E", 40th Kentucky Volunteer Infantry, and was mustered out at Catlettsburg, Kentucky, December 30, 1864; m. Temperance Osenton, daughter of Henry Kelly Osenton and his wife, Sciotha (McAllister) Osenton. (See Osenton Family.)
Children:

14. Frederick Warner Tyree, physician and surgeon; practiced medicine in the Grayson area for several years and later established his home at Hitchens; was surgeon for the C. & O. Railway Company; m. Martha Washington Partlow, daughter of Mr. and Mrs. J. W. Partlow of Willard. Children: Ralph Bonfield, deceased, Isabelle and Frank.

15. Frank Herman Tyree; was connected with the U. S. Secret Service for a number of years, acting as the personal bodyguard of

President Theodore Roosevelt for a time. Subsequently going to Huntington, West Virginia, he was elected and served as sheriff of Cabell County, West Virginia; m. Clara Burdick. Children: Frederick Quintin and Harold B.

Harold B. Tyree m. Miss Greene and they are the parents of one child, Thomas Green Tyree. Mr. Tyree is interested in genealogy and has prepared valuable manuscripts on the genealogy of the Tyree and Osenton families. Residence: 2000 Second Avenue, Detroit, Michigan.

16. Gertrude Thorndale Tyree; lived in the Tyree home in Grayson; unm.

17. Mary Sunshine Tyree (adopted daughter) resides in Grayson.

---

[1] Vital Statistics of Carter County, Kentucky, 1852-1863.

[2] James Flaugher and His Descendants as shown by Old Embroidered Sampler in the possession of Ann Catherine (Shearer) Flaugher, wife of James Polk Flaugher. The Descendants of James Flaugher and his Wife, Margaret (McGuire) Flaugher (Manuscript) prepared by Lelia Eliza (Gilbert) Slotterbeck (Mrs. Ober Carter Slotterbeck) 1954.

[3] Vital Statistics of Carter County, Kentucky, 1852-1862.

FUSON FAMILY OF BELL COUNTY

The Fuson family is of French origin. The family lived for a number of generations in Scotland. Emigrating to America, they first settled in Virginia and subsequently at Nashville, Tennessee, where many of the family presently reside. In various generations there have been lawyers, physicians and planters.

1. THOMAS FUSON was the immediate ancestor of the Fusons of Southeastern Kentucky. He migrated from Tennessee to present Bell County, Kentucky, coming over the mountains as companion of Daniel Boone. He settled at head of Bear Creek near present Chenoa. In his old age while attempting to visit his relatives in Tennessee, he was frozen to death on Log Mountain.

Children, among others:

2. James R. Fuson; b. near Nashville, 1822; m. Lucinda Evans, b. February 15, 1819, at the Fuson settlement in present Bell County.

Children:

3. James A. Fuson, farmer; lived on his farm in the Fuson settlement; was one of the first surveyors of Bell County; d. September 28, 1918.

4. Letitia Fuson; m. James Smith.

5. William Lafayette Fuson.

*6. John Thomas Fuson.

7. Beth A. Fuson, merchant at and prominent in the public affairs of Pineville, Bell County; served as County Judge of Bell County. Subsequently resided in Indianapolis, Indiana.

8. Henry Jeff Fuson.

9. Eliza Jane Fuson.

6. JOHN THOMAS FUSON; b. in the Fuson settlement in present Bell County, 1854, m. Sarah Jane Lee, b. on Big Clear Creek, Bell County, 1856, a member of the distinguished Lee family of Virginia, being a grand daughter of Hancock Lee, founder of Lee's Station near Frankfort. She was the fifth child of Philip and Mary (Bray) Lee. Her father d. at the age of 82 and her mother at the age of 45. Her brother, James Lee, was a school teacher and surveyor and was well educated. He was the first County Court Clerk of Bell County, 1867; served as private in the Union Army in the Civil War and was in the battle at Lookout Mountain and with Sherman in the March to the Sea.

Children:

*10. Henry Harvey Fuson.

11. Thomas Sewell, physician at Cumberland Gap, Tennessee.

12. Cora Lucinda; d. of typhoid at age of 18.

13. Mary Lee; m. Willet Almy; d. at birth of her first child, Lee Almy.

14. Bertha Letitia; m. D. H. Howard of Harlan County.
15. Arthur Luther, physician of Cumberland Gap, Tennessee.
16. Verda Ray; resides in New Mexico.
17. Van Whorton, farmer; resides on the paternal farm.
18. Effie; m. Morris Adler of Indianapolis.
19. Clara; teacher at Harlan, Kentucky.

10. HENRY HARVEY FUSON, educator, historian, writer and poet, was b. August 21, 1876, on his father's farm on Little Clear Creek, Bell County, Kentucky; worked on his father's farm until 18; attended the public schools, 1883-1894, and then attended the Williamsburg (Kentucky) Institute one short session; attended the Pineville High School, 1895-1897, and then attended Cumberland College at Williamsburg the winter and spring terms, 1895-1905, usually teaching during the fall terms, and was graduated with degree of B. S., 1905. Never regarding his education as complete and while holding many important responsible positions, he continued his studies both privately and in higher institutions: He was a student at the University of Tennessee during the summer of 1912; and at University of Cincinnati from which he was graduated with degree of B. S., 1920, and subsequently received from that institution twelve credits leading to the A. M. degree.

Mr. Fuson taught in the rural public schools of Bell County, 1895-1901; served as County Superintendent of Public Schools of Bell County, 1902-1910; was superintendent of the Pineville City Schools, 1911-1912; principal of a district school in Covington, Kentucky, 1912-1914, and in 1914 became principal of the First District School of that city.

Aside from his educational work he had many business interests in Bell County and Southeastern Kentucky. He was Secretary-Treasurer of the Central Coal Company, 1907-1910; Secretary of Martin Fork Coal Company, 1911-1921; Secretary-Treasurer and General Manager of the Fort Branch Coal Company of Fusona, Perry County, 1917-1918.

During the last two years of World War 1, Mr. Fuson was a private in the Military Training Camps assigned to the Division of Southern Ohio, and from 1918 until muster out in 1921, he was a private, corporal or sergeant in Company "D" of the Kentucky State Guards.

He affiliated with the Junior Order of United American Mechanics at Covington, Lodge No. 109, F. & A. M., at Covington, the Folk Lore Society, Covington Industrial Club, Covington School Masters Club and Parents and Teachers Association of the First School District. He was one of the organizers in 1907 of the County Superintendent Section of the Kentucky Educational Association. He is a Republican and a member of the First Baptist Church at Covington.

Mr. Fuson is a great hunter and fisherman and has written more than 80 poems largely dealing with mountain scenery and pioneer events and personalities, and is a collector of materials bearing on the history and legends of Southeastern Kentucky. He is the author of History of Bell County, Kentucky.

At the Phoenix Hotel in Lexington, Kentucky, on May 25, 1906, Mr. Fuson was married to Sara Ellen Watson, daughter of John Watson, a resident of Somerset, Kentucky, and one-time sheriff of Pulaski County, Kentucky. For ten years prior to marriage, Mrs. Fuson was a successful teacher in Southeastern Kentucky, teaching in Pulaski and Whitley Counties.

Children:

20. Ruth Maurine Fuson.

FUQUA FAMILY

This family is of French Huguenot extraction; and after the revocation of the Edict of Nantes (1685) by Louis XIV, King of France, members of the family fled from France to England on account of religious persecution. They were of that party of French refugees who were induced to emigrate from England to North Carolina. Upon reaching Virginia, means of transportation failed, and, sponsored by William Byrd III, of Virginia, they settled at Manakin Town on the James River about twenty miles above Richmond.

1. CAPTAIN MOSES FUQUA was the ancestor of the Fuquas who settled in present Greenup County, Kentucky, then Mason County. He was the son of William Fuqua of Lunenburg County, Virginia, and descended from the French Huguenot Gilliame Fouquet of Henrico County, that state. He was born in 1738; had service in the Revolutionary War as Captain of the Virginia Militia. In 1759 he m. Judith Woodson, daughter of Obadiah Woodson and his wife, Constance (Watkins) Woodson. The Woodsons descended from Dr. John Woodson who came with Governor Yeardley to Jamestown in 1619.

About 1797 or 1800 Captain Fuqua purchased a tract of over 1300 acres of land in then Mason County, now Greenup County, Kentucky, along the Ohio River, extending from Mt. Zion to Tygarts Creek and brought his family and slaves from Campbell County, Virginia, and settled there. His wife had died in Virginia and he died in Greenup County, about 1814. In his will, dated 1808, and a codicil dated 1811, probated and recorded in the Greenup County Court, he mentions

Children:
*2. Obadiah Fuqua.
*3. Sally Fuqua.
*4. William Fuqua.
*5. Nancy Fuqua.
*6. Samuel Fuqua.
7. David Fuqua.
*8. Lavinia Fuqua.
*9. Elizabeth Fuqua.
*10. Moses Fuqua, Jr.
11. Mary (Polly) Fuqua.
All these children did not migrate to Kentucky.

2. OBADIAH FUQUA, b. in Virginia in 1760; m. Mary Morton, daughter of Captain John Morton of Prince Edward County, Virginia. They settled on the Kanawha River, then Virginia, now West Virginia.

3. SALLY FUQUA; b. in Virginia, 1762; m. Benjamin Cook of

Franklin County, Virginia. They never came to Kentucky, but a daughter

12. Nancy Cook; m. Thomas B. King and came to Kentucky as his wife.

4. WILLIAM FUQUA; b. in Virginia, 1764; m. Sarah Morton, 1789. Children:

13. William Fuqua, Jr.; farmer and slaveholder, m. in Greenup County, April 21, 1823, Lydia Waring, daughter of Thomas G. Waring. (See Waring Family). They migrated to Missouri.

14. Martha M. Fuqua; b. in 1798; m. Samuel Wilson Gammon in 1818.

15. Mary M. Fuqua; b. 1802; m. in 1821 Rival D. Jones of Tygarts Valley.

16. Richard Fuqua; b. 1804; m. Mary Hollyday Waring in 1831. (See Waring Family.)

5. NANCY FUQUA; b. in Virginia, 1766; m. Josiah Morton in 1790.

6. SAMUEL FUQUA; b. in Virginia in 1769; m. Polly Armistead in Franklin County, Virginia, 1797. Probably they remained in Virginia.

8. LAVINIA FUQUA; b. in Virginia, in 1776; m. John Mackoy in Campbell County, Virginia, 1795.

9. ELIZABETH FUQUA; b. in Virginia, 1776; m. William Dupuy in Campbell County, Virginia.

10. MOSES FUQUA, JR., b. in Virginia in 1778; large landowner and slave holder. He was very prominent in county affairs; was one of the first justices of Greenup County, 1804, and was sheriff of the county, 1813. He served in the War of 1812 as a private in Captain Gaines' Company of Colonel John Poage's Kentucky Mounted Volunteer Militia. He d. in 1834 and was buried on the old home farm near Mt. Zion.
Children:
*17. John Fuqua.
18. Mary Fuqua; m. Anthony Thomson.
19. Sarah Fuqua; m. Asbury Ware.
20. Catherine Fuqua; m. Andrew Thomson.
21. Martha Fuqua; m. Stephen Smith.
22. Cynthia Jane Fuqua; m. James Morton.
23. Lavinia Fuqua; m. Benjamin Rankins.
24. Louise Fuqua; m. Julius B. Higley.

17. JOHN FUQUA inherited the home farm on condition "that he

help his mother, Cynthia (Collins) Fuqua, rear the young daughters, Catherine, Martha, Cynthia Jane, Marie and Louise". He m. Lydia Stephenson in Greenup County in 1813.

Children:

25. Martha Fuqua; m. Elijah P. Davenport.

Children:

26. Alvin Terry Davenport; m. Nancy Boynton.
27. Anthony Preston Davenport; m. Lola Tooley.
28. Eva Davenport; d. 1892.
29. Gertrude Davenport; m. Orville Smith.
30. Dora Davenport; m. Frederick Rigrish.
31. Elijah Davenport; m. Jennie Schultz.
32. Lennis Davenport; d. young.
33. Belle Davenport; d. young.

GARRARD FAMILY OF CLAY COUNTY

Daniel Garrard was the ancestor of the Garrards of Southeastern Kentucky. He was a son of James Garrard, second Governor of Kentucky, and his wife, Elizabeth (Montjoy) Garrard, and a grandson of Col. William Garrard and his wife Mary (Lewis) Garrard.

1. DANIEL GARRARD was b. in Stafford County, Virginia, November 10, 1870, and was brought to Kentucky by his parents when three years of age. In 1806 he went to what is now Clay County for the purpose of developing the salt industry on a 500-acre tract of land which had been surveyed for and patented by his father in 1798. He established a furnace at Buffalo Salt Lick where he produced salt until his death, when his son, Gen. T. T. Garrard, took over the industry and continued operations until his death.

Daniel Garrard was one of the most enterprising, prominent and influential citizens of Clay County. He amassed a large estate in lands and personal property including 25 negro slaves; held many public offices of honor and trust; and defended his country in War. He was State representative from Clay County, 1822, 1855-57; State Senator. 1813-17; 1825-27; and served in the War of 1812 as Captain of the First Company of the 2nd Regiment of Kentucky Militia.[1]

He m., first, in Mobile, Alabama, February 21, 1808, Lucinda Jane Toulmin, who d. April 10, 1849, a daughter of Hon. Harry Toulmin, Secretary of State in the administration of Gov. Garrard.[2]

Children:

*2. James H. Garrard.

*3. Gen. T. T. Garrard.

4. Daniel Garrard, Jr.; served in the Union Army in the Civil War; was Captain of Company "F", 22nd Kentucky Volunteer Infantry; mustered in at Louisa, Kentucky, January 10, 1862; residence, Frankfort, Kentucky, was killed in action in the battle of Chickasaw Bluffs, Mississippi, December 29, 1862.[3]

Other children of Daniel Garrard and his wife, Lucinda Jane Toulmin, living at home and approximate dates of birth as shown by the U. S. Census of Clay County for 1850:

5. Catherine Garrard; b. 1826.

6. Sophia Garrard; b. 1830.

7. Paulina Garrard; b. 1833.

8. Lucinda Garrard; b. 1836.

Daniel Garrard m., secondly, October 16, 1855, Mary F. Adkins of Knox County. He was then 75 years of age and she 24. No children. He died at his home in Clay County, September 20, 1866.

2. JAMES H. GARRARD, salt manufacturer, was born in Clay County, 1811; accumulated a large estate in lands and personal property including 16 negro slaves; was representative from Clay

County, 1836; member of the Constitutional Convention of 1849; and Treasurer of the State of Kentucky for six years.

He m., apparently in Clay County, about 1837, Letitia J. ———, b. in Kentucky, 1821.

Children living at home and approximate dates of birth as shown by the U. S. Census of Clay County for 1850:

9. Toleman (Toulmin) Garrard; b. 1838.

10. Daniel Garrard; b. 1841.

11. Matilda Garrard; b. 1843.

12. James L. Garrard; b. 1848.

3. GENERAL THEOPHILUS TOULMIN GARRARD, farmer, salt manufacturer, legislator and soldier, was b. at Union Salt Works, Clay County, Kentucky, June 7, 1812; was State representative from Clay County, 1843, 1844; State Senator, 1857-61; was commissioned a captain, 16th U. S. Infantry, April 16, 1847; had service in the Mexican War; honorably discharged, August 5, 1848; commissioned a colonel, 7th Kentucky Infantry, September 22, 1861; promoted to brigadier-general of Volunteers, November 29, 1862; honorably mustered out, April 4, 1864 (d. March 15, 1902). He commanded the Union forces at "Wild Cat" Kentucky, and defeated the Confederates.[4]

He m. Lucy B. Lee of Mason County, Kentucky, about 1851. Children living at home and approximate dates of birth as shown by the U. S. Census of Clay County for 1860 and 1870:

13. Joseph Garrard; b. 1852.

14. Gilbert Garrard; b. 1854.

*15. Belle (Isabella) Garrard; b. 1855.

16. Mary Garrard, b. 1857.

17. Kate Garrard; b. 1859.

18. Sophia Garrard; b. 1861.

19. Daniel Garrard; b. 1864.

20. Emma L. Garrard; b. 1869.

15. BELLE OR ISABELLA GARRARD; m. Col. C. B. Lyttle. (See Lyttle Family.)

---

[1] Report of the Adjutant General of Kentucky, Soldiers of the War of 1812, 1891, p. 59.

[2] Harry Toulmin was born at Taunton, Somersetshire, England, in 1766, and died in Mobile, Alabama in 1823. Arriving in Kentucky, he was elected, February 1794, president of Transylvania University at Lexington; was appointed Secretary to the Commonwealth of Kentucky, and served from June 1, 1796 to 1804; was appointed, 1804 Judge of the Superior Court for the Eastern district of Mississippi (later part of Alabama). He was author of many legal studies; his name was identified with three formal state codes.

[3] Report of the Adjutant General of Kentucky, 1861-1866, Vol. II, page 112.

[4] Historical Register and Directory of the United States Army by Francis B. Heitman, 1903, Vol. I, page 448.

GARRED FAMILY OF LAWRENCE COUNTY

David Garred was the first of the family to settle in Eastern Kentucky; and he was the immediate ancestor of a very large and prominent branch of the family. The surname of the family was always spelled "Jarrett" and David Garred was the only member among the pioneers of the family to change and spell the name "Garred".

David Garred was b. on the Greenbriar River near the village of Pent Springs, Greenbriar County, Virginia. He was a son of David Jarrett, Sr., who lived at Wolfe Creek Fort during the Revolutionary War, which was one of the three forts on the Virginia frontier commanded by Daniel Boone during Dunmore's War and at the time of the Battle of Point Pleasant (October 10, 1774).

DAVID JARRETT, SR., migrated from Greenbriar County, Virginia, now West Virginia, and settled on the Kanawha River about eight or ten miles above present Charleston. His son, David Jarrett (Garred) Jr. moved from the Kanawha River and settled in the vicinity of the Falls of Tug River near the post office, Clifford, Kentucky. Here he acquired a large tract of land, became an extensive agriculturist, utilizing the services of his large number of slaves; and engaged in the timber and mill business. Disposing of his property, he moved and settled on the first Garred location in Kentucky—on the Big Sandy River about ten miles above the present city of Louisa. Here he acquired a large tract of land and developed an extensive farm property utilizing the labor of his many slaves in its operation. He was buried in a stone vault constructed of native stone above ground on a point overlooking the Garred home.

David Garred, Jr., m. in Virginia circa 1792, Jane Graham, daughter of Captain James Graham and his wife, Florence Graham, who was a daughter of James Graham and his wife, Florence Graham.

James Graham, a Scotchman, left his native country and went to the north of Ireland (Ulster) to escape religious persecution. Later he imigrated to America and settled in Virginia. He served as a captain of the Virginia Forces in the Revolutionary War.

1. DAVID GARRED, JR., and his wife, Jane (Graham) Garred were the parents of three sons and ten daughters:

First Generation In Kentucky

*2. Jane Garred.
*3. Hannah Garred.
*4. Elizabeth Garred
*5. Flora Garred.
*6. Mary (Polly) Garred.
*7. Minerva Garred.

*8. Ulysses Garred.
*9. James Garred.
*10. David W. Garred.
*11. Sarah Ann Garred.
12. Rebecca Garred.
13. Nancy Garred.
14. Margaret Garred.

2. JANE GARRED; m. in Lawrence County, 1826, Harvey Ratcliff; moved to Kansas City, Missouri. in 1821; thence to Springfield, Missouri, and finally to Careltac, Arkansas.

Children:

Second Generation

15. William Ratcliff.
16. Harvey Ratcliff.
17. Minerva Ratcliff; m. ——— Gimler; went to State of Washington.
18. ——— Ratcliff, a daughter; m. ——— Franchier.
19. ———, a daughter; m. ——— Cardwell.

3. HANNAH GARRED; m. Charles Wilson.

Children:

Second Generation

20. James Wilson.
21. David Wilson.
22. Jane Wilson.
23. Mordecai Wilson.
24. Ramsey Wilson.
25. Grimes Wilson.
26. Jack Wilson.
27. Sarah Wilson.
28. Flora Wilson.

4. ELIZABETH GARRED; m. Ira W. Goff.

Children:

Second Generation

29. Elizabeth Goff; m. David See.
30. David Goff; m. Mary Harris.
31. John Bee Goff; m. Mary Small.
32. Felix Goff; m. Elizabeth Randall.
33. Jane Goff; m. ——— Hale.

5. FLORA GARRED, b. in Virginia about 1797, and d. in Lawrence County, Kentucky; m. Garred See, farmer; b. in Virginia, about 1786; and d. in Lawrence County.

Children:

Second Generation

34. Jane See; m. Jacob Peters, October 19, 1837.
35. Emily See; m. William Short in Lawrence County, March 13. 1832.
36. Fannie See; m. Lincoln Burk.
37. Michael See; m. Elizabeth Peck, December 22, 1859.
38. Florence See; m. James Wellman.
*39. John See; m. Sarah Wellman.
*40. David See; m. Elizabeth Goff.
*41. William See; m. Kizzie Wellman.
42. Garred See, Jr.; m. Katy Maynard, August 31, 1857.
43. Felix See; m. ——— Shannon.

6. MARY (POLLY) GARRED; m. Richard Chambers.

Children:

Second Generation

44. Margaret Chambers; m. William Vinson (See Vinson Family).
45. James Chambers.
46. David Chambers.

7. MINERVA GARRED; m. Chanoe Kise.

Children:

Second Generation

47. Benjamin Kise; m. Belle Maynard.
48. Thomas Kise; m. Lizzie Deskins.
49. Rebecca ("Becca") Kise; m. Mr. Ramsey.
50. David Kise; m. Annie Ramsey.
51. Lizzie Kise; m. Frank Dixon.
52. Minerva Kise; m. Mr. Stafford.
53. Ulysses ("Lyss") Kise; m. Miss McClure.

8. ULYSSES GARRED, farmer, was b. in Virginia about 1813; engaged in timber business; represented Lawrence County in the State House of Representatives for two terms from 1872. He and his brother, David W. bought all the other heirs' interests in the David Garred, Jr., homestead and he built a fine stone mansion thereon. Ulysses Garred afterward lived and also died on his one-half of the homestead.

Ulysses Garred m. in Johnson County, Kentucky, about January 13, 1853, Lyda Stafford, b. in Kentucky about 1830, daughter of John Stafford. (See Stafford Family).

Children:

Second Generation

54. Millard Garred; m. Julia Borders. No issue.
*55. Jane Garred.
*56. Calista Garred.
57. Emma Garred; m. Victor Muncy. No issue.
58. Johnny Garred; d. young.
59. David Garred; d. young.

9. JAMES GARRED, farmer; b. in Virginia about 1793; m. Mary (Polly) Wilson, b. in Virginia about 1819.

Children:

Second Generation

*60. Anderson Garred.
61. James Garred.
62. Ulysses Garred.

10. DAVID W. GARRED, farmer; b. in the Tug Falls district of Virginia, now West Virginia, in 1822, and d. on his homestead in Lawrence County, Kentucky, (the original Garred homestead in Kentucky) in 1907, at the age of 85 years. After his marriage, he came to Lawrence County, Kentucky, and established his home on the Levisa Fork of the Big Sandy River about eight miles above Louisa where he acquired a large acreage of land, including one-half of his father's homestead, and developed an extensive farm property, utilizing the labor of his many slaves in its operation. He also engaged in the timber business and owned and operated the steamboats "Dew Drop" and "Sam Cravins".

He was one of the honored and substantial citizens of the county; served as a member of the local militia; was a stalwart Democrat in politics and an active member of the Methodist Episcopal Church, South.

David W. Garred m. in Lawrence County, March 18, 1847, Nancy Woolbright Dyer, b. in Kentucky about 1832, and d. at her home on a part of the original Garred homestead in Lawrence County at a very old age.

Children:

Second Generation

63. Isadore Monroe Garred, captain, steamboats "Dew Drop" and "Sam Cravins", m. Erma Thompson; no issue.
*64. Onolda Garred.
*65. Owen Garred.
66. Corilda Garred; d. at age of 3 years.
*67. Arnoldus Garred.

*68. Dr. Bernard Pogue Garred.
*69. Michael William Garred.
*70. Alvin Hatton Lee Garred.
*71. Ulysses Anderson Garred.
72. Felix Garred; m. Ellen Penelle.

11. SARAH ANN GARRED.

39. JOHN N. SEE, farmer; b. in Kentucky, about 1817; m. Sarah Wellman, b. in Virginia, about 1840.

Children living in the household and approximate dates of birth as shown by the U. S. Census of Lawrence County for 1860 and 1870:

Third Generation

73. David G. See; b. 1858.
74. Amanda See; b. 1860.
75. Julia M. See; b. 1862.
76. James E. See; b. 1865.
77. Mary J. See; b. 1866.
78. Montraville See; b. 1869.

40. DAVID SEE, farmer; b. in Kentucky, 1823; m. Mary Elizabeth Goff, b. in Tennessee, 1833.

Children living in the household and approximate dates of birth as shown by the U. S. Census of Lawrence County for 1860 and 1870:

Third Generation

79. Margaret Lee See; b. 1849.
80. Elizabeth See; b. 1852.
81. Felix See; b. 1854.
82. John B. See; b. 1856.
83. Emily M. See; b. 1857.
84. Fanny See; b. 1861.
85. William D. See; b. 1863.
86. Mary E. See; b. 1865.
87. Nancy L. See; b. 1867.
88. Ulysses Lee See; b. 1869.

41. WILLIAM SEE, farmer; b. 1829; m. Kizzie Wellman, b. in Virginia, 1833.

Children living in the household and approximate dates of births as shown by the U. S. Census of Lawrence County for 1860 and 1870:

Third Generation

89. Samuel See; b. 1851.
90. Louisa V. See; b. 1853.
91. Garred See; b. 1856.
92. Corilda See; b. 1859.

93. John C. See; b. 1861.
94. Rebecca See; b. 1862.
95. Margaret See; b. 1864.

55. JANE GARRED; m. Joseph McClure.

Children:

Third Generation

96. Dr. Ulysses ("Lyss") McClure; m. Ethel Quinn.

56. CALISTA GARRED; m. Daniel Reece.

Children:

Third Generation

97. Francis Garred Reece.
98. Emma Muney Reece.

60. ANDERSON GARRED; m. Elizabeth Dyer.

Children:

Third Generation

99. Wiley Garred; migrated to Washington State.
100. James Garred; migrated to Oregon.
101. Becca (Rebecca) Garred; m. ——— Bell.
102. Joseph Garred; migrated to Washington State.
106. Add. Garred; migrated to Oregon (54 years old, 1926).
104. Charles Garred (62 years old, 1926.)
105. George Garred.
106. Add. Garred; migrated to Oregon (54 years old, 1926).

64. ONALDA GARRED; m. T. J. Burgess.

Children:

Third Generation

*107. Malcomb Burgess; m. Victoria Elam.
*108. Corilda Burgess; m. Dr. O. W. Thompson.
109. Julia Burgess; m. ——— Francis.
*110. Willie Burgess; m. Dr. T. D. Burgess.
111. T. J. (Jeff) Burgess; m. Addie Gilkerson

65. OWEN GARRED; m. Lou McClure.

Children:

Third Generation

112. Lyda Garred; m. Frank Boggess.
113. Alex. Garred.
114. George Garred.
*115. Nina Garred; m. Edgar Crow.
*116. David Garred; m. Mary Forsyth.

117. Nellie Garred; m. Herman E. Giskie.
118. Vinson Garred; m. Ina Mae Cochran.

67. ARNOLDUS GARRED, lawyer; b. July 24, 1856, on his father's farm on the Levisa fork of the Big Sandy River eight miles above Louisa; was graduated from the University of Kentucky; served as county attorney of Lawrence County; and m. Jennie Vinson, daughter of Richard R. Vinson of Louisa. (See Vinson Family.)

Children:

Third Generation

*119. Richard V. Garred.
*120. Victoria Garred.

68. DR. BERNARD POGUE GARRED; graduated from Baltimore School of Medicine; m. Hester Selby.

Children:

Third Generation

121. Dr. Herbert Garred; graduated from Baltimore School of Medicine; m. Louisa Lang.
122. Felix Garred, deceased (1946); unm.
123. Mildred Garred; m. ——— Harshburger.
124. Marguerite Garred; m. Mr. Tulkason.
125. Robert Garred; m. Margaret ———.
126. Owen Garred.

69. MICHAEL WILLIAM GARRED; m. Zella De Jarnett.

Children:

Third Generation

*127. Beulah Garred; m. ——— Hammond.
128. Ray Garred; m. Ethel ———.
129. Jennie Lee Garred.
130. Mary Frances Garred.
131. Avonell Garred.

70. ALVIN HATTON LEE GARRED; m. Jennie Elam.

Children:

Third Generation

*132. Dr. Ulysses V. Garred; m. Florence Kathryn Phillips.
*133. Emily Rebecca Garred.
*134. Nancy Onolda Garred.
*135. Benard Poage Garred.
*136. Dr. Matthew David Garred.
*137. Dr. Isadorre Garred.
*138. Bella Kathryn Garred.

139. Lou Ella Garred; d., 1918.
*140. Dr. Emery William Garred.

71. ULYSSES ANDERSON GARRED; m. Elizabeth Handy.
Children:

Third Generation

141. Nancy Garred; m. ——— Sexton.

107. MALCOMB BURGESS; m. Victoria Elam.
Children:

Fourth Generation

142. Willie Jane Burgess.
143. Julia Burgess.
144. Emily O. Burgess.
145. Thomas Burgess.
146. Dr. Francis Burgess; graduated from the College of Medicine,
Louisville.
147. Lola Burgess.

108. CORILDA GARRED; m. Dr. O. W. Thompson.
Children:

Fourth Generation

148. John Jeff Thompson.
149. Burgess Thompson.

110. WILLIE BURGESS; m. T. D. Burgess, M. D.
Children:

Fourth Generation

150. Elizabeth Burgess.
151. Neal Burgess.
152. Julia Jane Burgess.
115. NINA GARRED; m. Edgar Crow.
Children:

153. Edgar Crow m. Ola Richards, 1927.

Fourth Generation

154. David Owen Crow.
155. Wyatt Allen Crow.
156. Frank Boggess Crow.

119. RICHARD V. GARRED; m. Ollie May Clark.
Children:

Fourth Generation

157. ——— Garred.
158. ——— Garred.
120. VICTORIA GARRED; m. Lynden Irvin Brode.
Children:

Fourth Generation

159. Linnie Brode.
160. ——— Brode.

127. BEULAH GARRED; m. ——— Hammond.
Children:

Fourth Generation

161. Margaret Hammond.

132. DR. ULYSSES V. GARRED, dentist; graduated from Kentucky
University with degree of B. S. M. E., 1920, and for a time was
consultant engineer in New York City; was graduated from the
School of Dentistry, University of Louisville, 1934, and for a number
of years practiced his profession in Ashland, Kentucky; removed to
Whiting, Iowa, 1952, where he continued to practice his profession;
m. Florence Kathryn Phillips, daughter of John Christian Phillips
and Viola Elizabeth (Mickle) Phillips. Florence Kathryn Phillips
was educated at Syracuse University; was graduated from Columbia
University, New York City, with degree of B. S. and was a teacher
in the School of Music.

Children:

Fourth Generation

162. John Lee Garred, M. D., Lieutenant, jg., U. S. Navy, resides
and practices medicine at Whiting, Iowa.
163. William Phillips Garred, M. D., School of Medicine Northwestern University, Chicago, resides and practices medicine at Whiting, Iowa.

133. EMILY REBECCA GARRED; m., first, Fred Blair, M.D., No issue;
m. secondly, Dr. J. C. Sandlin, dentist.

Children:

Fourth Generation

164. Margarite Jane Sandlin; educated at Ward-Belmont College,
graduating with honors, and at George Washington University, Washington, D. C. Emily Rebecca Garred m., thirdly, Rice K. Broley; no
issue.

134. NANCY ONOLDA GARRED; m. Robert L. Denues.

Children:

Fourth Generation

165. Dorothy L. Denues, a graduate of the University of Kentucky.
135. BENARD POGUE GARRED; m. Lewis Cass Richmond, M.D., a
graduate of School of Medicine, University of Louisville.

Children:

Fourth Generation

166. Lewis Cass Richmond.

167. Lee Richmond.

136. MATTHEW DAVID GARRED, M. D., graduated from the School of Medicine, University of Louisville; was a major, U .S. Army, World War II; m. Lottie May Rogers.

Children:

Fourth Generation

173. David Carleton Garred.

174. Lee Ann Garred.

70-A. JENNIE (ELAM) GARRED, wife of Alvin Hatton Lee Garred, was a daughter of Matthew M. Elam, who served in Union Army in the Civil War and his wife, Emma G. (Botner) Elam and a grand-daughter of Oliver Botner, who served in the Union Army in the Civil War, and his wife Jane Stafford. (See Stafford Family.) Other Children of Matthew M. Elam and Emma G. (Botner) Elam were:

175. Oliver Elam, lawyer.

176. Victoria Elam.

177. Arthur Elam, a graduate of the College of Dentistry, Columbus, Ohio, and B.S.M.E., University of Kentucky.

178. Emery Elam.

179. Botner Elam, a graduate of the College of Dentistry, Columbus, Ohio. ("Family Tree of the Garred and Some Related Families", prepared by Dr. Ulysses V. Garred, 1947, 2820 Moore Street, Ashland, Kentucky.)

GEE FAMILY OF CARTER COUNTY

This is an old Colonial family in America; and were numerous in Maryland, Virginia, North Carolina and New York prior to the establishment of the Federal Government. In Virginia, they lived principally in Mecklenburg and Shenandoah Counties. Col. Richard Gee lived in the latter county. Eight Gees served in the Virginia Forces in the Revolutionary War.[1]

James Gee probably was the first of the family to settle in Kentucky. He was a tax-payer in Lincoln County, May 11, 1790.

1. HENRY GEE was the ancestor of the Gees of Northeastern Kentucky. Apparently he was a native of Virginia and m. in that colony "Polly" (surname not known). However, there is a family tradition that he came from Scotland to America and that he and his wife Polly came to Kentucky in 1825.

Children among others:

2. Robert Gee; b. in Virginia March 11, 1767, and d. in Carter County, Kentucky, at an advanced age. He was living in the home of his son-in-law, Ira Jacobs, in 1860 at the age of 97 years. He m. Elizabeth Waters, who was b. in Kentucky, October 12, 1780, and d. in Carter County, Kentucky, within the period, 1850-1860.

Children:

3. Henry Gee; very little has been learned about him. Probably he was b. about 1803. His daughter Sarah m. George Nethercutt.

*4. Champness Gee.

5. Mary Gee; b. February 25, 1806; m. George Martin, January 13, 1839.

6. Martha Gee; b. January 19, 1808; m. Asa Bellew, July 21, 1837.

7. Margaret Gee; b. November 10, 1808; m. John Gilkey, in Greenup County, August 10, 1829.

8. Sally Gee; b. July 12, 1811; m. David DeVore in Greenup County, January 26, 1828.

*9. David P. Gee.

*10. Macager (Micajah) Gee.

*11. Robert Anderson Gee.

12. William Gee; b. June 26, 1820; m. Sarah McCarthy; migrated to Oklahoma and from thence to Texas.

13. Elizabeth Gee; b. January 12, 1831.

4. CHAMPNESS M. GEE, farmer, was b. in Kentucky, presumably in Jessamine County, August 30, 1804, and d. in Carter County, December 4, 1881; m. April 25, 1827, Nancy (surname not known), b. in Kentucky, March 19, 1812, and d. in Carter County, April 27, 1883.

Children:

14. Henry Gee; b. April 14, 1830.
15. Asa Gee; b. September 6, 1832.
16. Mary Elizabeth Gee; b. November 17, 1835, and d. April 27, 1883; m. James Walton, November 15, 1849.
17. Icybindy Gee; born February 24, 1838, and d. September 17, 1889; m. Mr. Prophet.
18. John W. Gee; b. February 13, 1840.
19. Robert Gee; b. December 26, 1842.
20. Margaret Gee; b. July 30, 1845.
21. Martha Gee; b. 1847 or 1848.[2]

9. DAVID PALMER GEE, farmer; b. in Jessamine County, Ky., February 13, 1813, and d. in Carter County, December 6, 1861;[3] m. about 1833, Sarah James, b. in Kentucky, 1812, daughter of John W. James, who organized the Barretts Creek Christian Church, September 3, 1803.[4]

Children living in the household and the approximate dates of birth and marriages as shown by the U. S. Census of Carter County for 1850 and the marriage records of that county:

22. Martha Gee; b. 1834; m. Ira Jacobs. (See Jacobs Family.)
23. Champness Gee; b. 1836; m. Amanda Littleton, October 5, 1856.
24. Mary Gee; b. 1838; m. Camillus ("Cam") Biggs.
*25. Robert Gee; b. 1839.
26. Rintha Gee; b. 1842.
27. Macager (Micajah) Gee; b. 1844; m. Elizabeth Jane Jordan, July 1, 1866.
28. David Gee; b. 1847; m. Louisa James, November 30, 1865.
29. Myrtilla Gee; b. 1849; m. Francis M. Jacobs. (See Jacobs Family.)
30. Dudley Gee.
31. William Gee. One John William Gee m. Lenah A. James, December 5, 1869.

10. MICAJAH GEE, teamster, b. in Kentucky, 1817; m. about 1846 Martha (surname not known), b. 1831.

Children among others:

32. William Gee; b. about 1847.
33. Mary A. Gee; b. about 1847; m. Sanders Everman. (See Everman Family.)

11. ROBERT ANDERSON GEE; b. in Kentucky, October 26, 1817; m. in Greenup County, November 15, 1836, Theresa Williams, b. in Kentucky, 1818.

Children living in the home and approximate dates of birth as shown by the U. S. Census of Carter County for 1850:

34. Thompson Gee; b. 1840.
35. Elizabeth Gee; b. 1842.
36. Lewis Gee; b. 1845.
37. Roxey A. Gee; b. 1847.
38. Henry Gee; b. 1849.

25. ROBERT GEE, farmer, sometime blacksmith and merchant and a minister of the Christian Church, was b. in then Greenup County, 1839; m., first, in Carter County, December 26, 1860, Celetha Jacobs, daughter of William Wood and Rhoda (Pruit) Jacobs and a great grand-daughter of William Jacobs, Revolutionary War soldier. (See Jacobs Family.)

Children:

*39. William David Gee.
40. Rose Gee; m., first, Theodore Gantz and secondly, Thomas Eifort.
41. Virginia Gee; m. "Bud" Williams.
42. Champness Gee; killed in explosion of mill; unm.
43. Frank Gee; m. Lucy Johnson. Their daughter Bessie m. Charles Johnson.
44. Lillie Gee; d. in infancy.
45. John Gee; m. Martha Tarr.
46. Sara Celetha ("Sallie") Gee; m., first, Peter Brawner. Children: William Dudley Brawner and Ella R. Brawner who m. Norman Green; m. secondly, Thomas Harvey Morefield. Children: Clarence Morefield, who m. Ada Miller; Lawrence Morefield, who d. in infancy; Charles Morefield who resides in Ashland and is yard master of the C. & O. Railway Company there; and Thomas Harvey Morefield. Jr., who m. Grethen (surname not learned).

25-A. Robert Gee m., secondly, March 29, 1883, Ella Elizabeth Eifort, b. March 4, 1857, and d. July 27, 1930.

Children:

47. Harry Gee; d. young.
48. Mary C. (Mollie) Gee; m. Stephen Stamper.
49. Lewis Hurst Gee; b. March 13, 1888, and d. January, 1955; m., first, Julia Elliott (See Elliott Family.) Children: Dr. Elliott Gee, surgeon, presently serving in the U. S. Navy stationed in Cuba in the rank of Commander.

Lewis Hurst Gee m., secondly, Carrie Buck. Children: Kathleen, head nurse at Stovall Memorial Hospital at Grayson; Genevieve, deceased, m. Robert Staton; Robert Henry; Arthur Elbert, a sergeant, U. S. Army, presently stationed in Germany; m. a German girl; Walter Gee; m. Ramona Sexton; Joseph Gee; m. Katie (surname not learned).

50. Charles Northcott Gee; b. March 24, 1890, one-time teacher, merchant, and for many years postmaster at Willard, Kentucky, m.

June 10, 1914, Kyon Peay, teacher, b. February 23, 1885, daughter
of William George and Willie Hamilton (Elliott) Peay. (See
Elliott Family.) Children: Thelma Anita (June), b. March 11,
1915; unm.; Kyon Josephine (Jo), teacher and presenty a supervisor in the Carter County schools, b. July 27, 1921; m. Harold H.
King. (See King Family and Prichard Family.); Charles Northcott
Gee, Jr., b. July 11, 1924; m. Elaine Miller, daughter of Jonnie
McDavid Miller and Bert Miller. He is serving in the U. S. Army
stationed in Germany.

51. Jessie Gee; m. Milford Littleton.

52. Bradley Gee, farmer.

53. George Gee; m. Loraine Ruley; reside in Roanoke, Virginia.

54. Goldie May Gee; d. in infancy.

55. Leo Ebert Gee. deceased. Children: Philip. who resides in
North Carolina and Brad'ey JI, who resides in Charleston, West
Virginia. Both are m.

Robert Gee was a consistent member and minister of the Barretts
Creek Christian Church for over half a century. He united with
that church October 17, 1857, and was elected clerk in 1871 and
served as such until his death. He was ordained a minister of the
Gospel in the Christian Church, October 22, 1877, at Cora Hill, Kentucky, by Elders M. L. Maddix, H. L. Forrest and B. F. Bowling.
He served in the Middle Kentucky Christian Conference as Secretary from 1871 to 1890, when he was elected Secretary of the Kentucky State Christian Conference which position he held until his
death.

The Barretts Creek Christian Church was organized, September
3, 1803, by Robert Gee's grandfather, John W. James, was represented in the first session of the Kentucky Conference which met
in 1804.

Robert Gee's grandfather, John W. James, was present at the
conference held in the old Lebanon Church, Surry County, Virginia,
in 1794, when all human names were rejected and the name "Christian" accepted.

For many years Robert Gee had it in his heart to build a meeting
house on the site of the original church, which hope was realized during the latter part of his lifetime by the building and dedication of
the Robert Gee Memorial Church.

39. WILLIAM DAVID GEE, one-time public official and blacksmith,
was b. at Barretts Creek, Carter County, Kentucky, September 22,
1861, and d. at Grayson, Kentucky, January, 1929. Interment in
Gee cemetery at Gregoryville. He was a Republican in politics, a
member and Elder in the Presbyterian Church at Grayson and was
affiliated with the Masonic fraternity, a member of Trimble Lodge
No. 145, F. & A.M. at Grayson. serving as Master several years, a
member of Greenup Chapter and a Knight Templar of the Ashland,

Kentucky, organization; was elected and served as sheriff of Carter County, 1910-1914; m. at Little Sinking, Carter County, January 29, 1882, Miss Rebecca Elizabeth Mitchell, b. September 4, 1864, daughter of Thomas Jackson and Arias (King) Mitchell. Mrs. Gee is living in her home in Grayson at the advanced age of 91 years, in full possession of all her faculties.

Children:

56. Walter Gee; b. September, 1883; d. in May, 1904; unm.
57. Alva Gee; b. 1885; d. in 1932; unm.
58. Robert Gee; b. 1887; m. Miss Amelia Hutchinson.

Children: Billy Elizabeth Gee; m. Elmer Gunther. Their children are John David and Jack Gunther; Berton Eldridge Gee m. Mary Alice Gibbs. Their children are Daniel Joseph and Richard Berton; Geneva Gee m. Elwood Gunther. Their children are Jo Lynn, William David and Michael: Marguerite Gee m., first, James Gunther. Children: a son, Robert Frederick. She m., secondly, Milton Glower. Children: Ella and Michael; Robert Gee, Jr., unm.; Blanche Gee; unm; Thomas Gee, m.; two children; resides in Detroit.

59. Clara Gee; m. Earl Robert Johnson, an employee of the N. & W. Railway Company; residence Roanoke, Virginia. Children: Majorie Ann Johnson; was graduated from Mary Washington College, Ferdericksburg, Virginia; taught in the Arlington County (Virginia) schools; m. Dr. Robert Walter, chemist; resides at Hopewell, Virginia. Children: Margaret Ellen.

Dr. Earl Robert Johnson, Jr., was graduated from University of Virginia, 1950, and from Medical College, 1954; is presently an interne at University Hospital at Charlottesville and on July 1st goes to the University of North Carolina at Chapel Hill as resident physician and to specialize in internal medicine; m. Nancy B. Taylor, April 2, 1955.

60. Arthur Gee, Vice President and cashier of the Commercial Bank of Grayson; was born at Sinking, Carter County, Kentucky, April 23, 1889; attended the Grayson public schools; was clerk in clothing store in Grayson in his youth; served as deputy sheriff of Carter County, 1909-1913, under his father, W. D. Gee, Sheriff; accepted a position in the Commercial Bank of Grayson as assistant cashier, 1915, and is presently serving as Vice President and Cashier of that institution; m. July 3, 1941, Miss Paulina Burton, b. January 9, 1903, daughter of Isaac and Mary Ball (Rice) Burton. No children.

61. Ora Gee, teacher; b. July 11, 1891; educated in the Grayson public schools; taught in the Carter County public schools for a short time; m. July 3, 1913, William Craycraft, merchant, b. July 17, 1892. Children: Helen Gee Craycraft; b. September 9, 1914; m., 1932, Howard Readmon, printer. No children.

William Arthur Craycraft; b. May 16, 1918; m., first, Glima
Steele. They had one child (son) William Arthur, Jr., b. September, 1949; m., secondly, Martha Trent. Children: Honey, b. August,
1950; Warren Allen, b. September, 1951 and Jane Ann, b. November,
1953.

Robert Alva Craycraft; b. July 18, 1921; m. Betty Jo Brown,
June, 1951. Children: Robert Matthew, b. January 1946 and
Rebecca Sue, b. February 1954. Clayton Brown Craycraft; b. November 9, 1922; m. Evelyn Lunsford, September 1941. No children.

62. Floris Gee, teacher; b. December 9, 1897; educated in the
public schools of Grayson, graduating from High School, 1916;
was graduated from University of Kentucky, 1932, with degree of
A. B.; began teaching in 1919, and has continued teaching for 33
years—in the Raceland, Louisiana schools, 1919-1920; the Ashland
(Kentucky) schools, 1923-32, and the Grayson (Kentucky) graded
and high schools, for 23 years and is presently teaching in the
Prichard High School at Grayson; unm.

---

[1] Gwathmey, "Virginians in the Revolutionary War, 1775-1862", p. 301.

[2] The Gee Family Bible.

[3] Vital statistics of Carter County, Kentucky, 1852-1862.

[4] David Palmer Gee and His Descendants (Manuscript), prepared and furnished by
Floris Gee, Grayson, Kentucky, 1955.

GRAHAM FAMILY OF FLOYD COUNTY

GRAHAM

Ancestors of the Graham family seem to have wandered from England into Wales and afterward into Scotland. The name is derived from the Old English personal name Grim or Graeme ("fierce, warlike"). In Wales the Graemes founded the town of Graemsport ("harbor of Graeme"), later known as Groomsport. In Scotland, Graham is one of the Highland clan-names; and the first definite appearance of the name of Graham in Scotland is about the year 1143 when "William of Graham" signed the Holyrood Charter. In the following centuries many members of the Graham family became distinguished in Scottish history.

John Graham, farmer, surveyor, soldier, merchant, banker and public official, was the progenitor of a large family of Grahams of the Big Sandy Valley, Eastern Kentucky. He was of Scotch-Irish extraction and was b. in Augusta County, Virginia, January 1, 1765. His father, David Graham, b. in Augusta County, Virginia, 1742, d. in February or March, 1768, was a soldier in Captain William Preston's Company of Rangers in the French and Indian War in 1758, and m. Jane Armstrong in 1764. His grandfather, William Graham, Sr., b. in Donegal County, Ireland; emigrated to America in 1741 and settled on Calf Pasture River about 1742; d. in Augusta County, Virginia, April ———, 1740, and m. Jane ———.

1. JOHN GRAHAM received a good education in Virginia, probably at Augusta Seminary and later while still a youth, had service in the Revolutionary War in the Eighth Virginia Regiment, Continental Line. Subsequently, after coming to Kentucky, he had service in the Kentucky Militia under Captain William Price in the Indian campaign of 1788.

John Graham came to Kentucky when still a young man. He entered lands on the waters of Red River in 1784 and explored the headwaters of the Big Sandy River about 1787. About this time he was employed to survey a vast boundary of 100,000 acres of new and first class land on the headwaters of the Big Sandy River which had been entered in 1787 for Colonel John Preston. In 1797 he made his first survey covering the site of the present city of Prestonsburg, and soon thereafter surveyed for his own homestead, a 2,000-acre tract extending along the waters of the Levisa Fork of Big Sandy all the bottom land on each side of the river from Cliff to mouth of Beaver Creek.

At the close of the century his surveys of the Preston lands being well advanced, and having purchased land and having become a resident of the section, then Mason County, and the new county of Floyd having been established thus making possible local self government in Eastern Kentucky, John Graham went back to Virginia where he m., February 16, 1803, in Tazewell County, that State, Rebecca Witten, whom he had met and wooed in her home while contemplating settling in Kentucky. Rebecca Witten, b. in Washington County, Virginia, January 29, 1775, d. in Floyd County, Kentucky, August 28, 1843, was a daughter of Thomas Witten, Jr., Revolutionary War soldier, and his wife, Eleanor Cecil,[1] and a first cousin to Governor, Christopher Greenup of Kentucky, and a lineal or direct descendant of William Cecil, Lord Burghlev or Burleigh, who for forty years was Prime Minister of England during the reign of Queen Elizabeth. (See Witten and Cecil Families).

After their marriage John Graham and his wife lived in Tazewell County for a year or so. About 1805, their new home of hewn logs on the Big Sandy having been completed, they with their infant son, Thomas, moved with their slaves and household effects to Kentucky. Their first cabin stood close to the river, about three miles below Beaver Creek, near the present hamlet of Emma, Floyd County. Here a year or so later, John Graham erected the first fine home in all the country side. The dwelling immediately attained wide fame for it contained twelve rooms, had four huge brick chimneys and in appearance, inside and out, resembled the ample and picturesquely designed plantation homes of Eastern Virginia. Here John Graham and Rebecca (Witten) Graham spent the remainder of their lives and in this home their six daughters were b. and lived until their marriage.

As the years passed John Graham prospered in lands and chattels and grew in public esteem. He became the outstanding leader in the upper Big Sandy Valley and held many public offices of honor and trust. Upwards of 150,000 acres of land were surveyed by him, much of it passing by title through his hands. He became the leading merchant and was the first banker of the community. He was elected and served as the first State representative from his district, then Mason County, 1799-1800 and was instrumental in securing passage of the act forming and establishing Floyd County. He served as surveyor of Floyd County for many years; and in 1808 and again in 1814 he was chosen as one of the Assistant Judges of the Floyd County Circuit Court.

Judge Graham died April 20, 1835 "and was simply buried on a low timbered knoll near his home above the quiet waters of the Big

Sandy River." In his will executed April 19, 1835, and probated in the Floyd County Court. at the June Term, 1835. he bequeathed to his wife and their six daughters over 5,000 acres of land and a large estate of personal property, including 14 negro slaves; and emancipated one negro slave.

Children of Judge John Graham and his wife, Rebecca Witten Graham:

2. Thomas Witten Graham, the eldest child, b. in Tazewell County, Virginia, January 19, 1804, and d. in Floyd County, Kentucky, October 23, 1833; unm.; served as sheriff of Floyd County, from April 15, 1829 to May 15, 1831.

*3. Rebecca Graham, b. 1807.

*4. Dorothy Graham, b. 1809.

*5. Eleanor Graham, b. 1810.

*6. Tabitha Graham, b. 1812.

*7. Eliabeth Graham, b. 1819.

8. Sophia Graham, m., in Floyd County, Kentucky, December 28, 1832, William H. Layne.

3. REBECCA GRAHAM m., in Floyd County, December 14, 1826, Jacob Mayo, farmer, b. in Kentucky, 1800.

Children and approximate dates of birth as shown by the U. S. Census of Floyd County for the year 1850:

9. William Mayo, b. 1830.

10. Susan Mayo, b. 1833.

11. Tabitha Mayo, b. 1836.

12. Juliann Mayo, b. 1837.

Apparently there were other children.

4. DOROTHY GRAHAM m. in Floyd County, July 22, 1827, Edwin Trimble, b. in Kentucky, 1808, Deputy Clerk of the Floyd County Court for many years and County Attorney for Floyd County, August 19, 1833, to October 11, 1840.

Children and approximate dates of birth as shown by the U. S. Census of Floyd County for the year 1850:

13. James Trimble b., 1830.

14. Edwin Trimble b., 1837.

15. William Trimble b., 1840.

16. Josephine Trimble b., 1843.

17. Thomas G. Trimble b., 1848.

18. Robert Trimble b., 1850. } Twins
19. Meggy Trimble b., 1850.

5. ELEANOR GRAHAM m. in Floyd County, ———, 1825, David Morgan, Jr., farmer, b. in Kentucky, 1805.

Children and approximate dates of birth as shown by the U. S. Census of Floyd County for the year 1850:

20. Thomas Morgan b., 1830.
21. Rebecca Morgan b., 1832.
22. Eleanor Morgan b., 1834.
23. David Morgan, Jr., b., 1836.
24. William Morgan b., 1838.
25. Dorothy Morgan b., 1842.
26. James K. Polk Morgan, b., 1844.
27. John B. Morgan b., 1847.

6. TABITHA GRAHAM m. in Floyd County, June 25, 1835, John B. Harris, farmer, b. in Kentucky, 1811.

Children and approximate dates of birth as shown by the U. S. Census of Floyd County for the years 1850 and 1860:

28. Andrew J. Harris b., 1836.
29. Edwin Harris b., 1837.
30. William J. Harris b., 1839.
31. Thomas M. Harris, b., 1841.
32. James P. Harris b., 1844.
33. John Q. Harris b., 1848.
34. California Harris b., 1850.
35. Beunavista Harris b., 1853.
36. Newton P. Harris b., 1856.

7. ELIZABETH GRAHAM, m., in Floyd County, March 8, 1838, Thomas P. Johns, farmer, b. in Kentucky, April 2, 1816, and d. ———, 1865.

Children and approximate dates of birth as shown by the U. S. Census of Floyd County for the years 1850 and 1860:

37. John Johns b., 1840.
38. Rebecca Johns, b., 1843.
39. Julia A. Johns, b., 1846.
40. Mary Johns b., 1848.
41. Elizabeth Johns b., 1849.
42. Thomas Johns b., 1852.

Many descendants of John and Rebecca Graham are residents of Kentucky, Missouri, Oklahoma and Texas.

---

[1] Antecedents and Descendants of John Graham and Elizabeth Witten, 1719-1843, by Dr. Willard Rouse Jillson, The Register of the Kentucky Historical Society, April, 1939, Vol. 37, No. 119, pages 117-126.

GILBERT FAMILY OF LEE COUNTY VIRGINIA, AND CARTER COUNTY, KY.

Gilbert

Apparently the Gilbert families in the United States are of English extraction. Gilbert is an ancient Saxon name which means "bright pledge". The name, it seems, originated from a shortened form of the personal name Giselbertus introduced into England at the time of the Norman Conquest (1066). The name is found in the Doomsday (or Domesday) Book compiled A. D. 1086, and the Patent Rolls of Hertsfordshire dated 1320 contain the name Gibbessone. The name Gilbert was sometimes bestowed in honor of Saint Gilbert of Sempringham (c. 1085 - 1187) English ecclesiastic founder of the order of Gilbertines.

This name not only is itself a common surname in many countries, but has given rise to many diminutives, such as Gibb, Gibbes, Gibbard, Gibbings, Gill, Gilpin, Gibson, and many others.

The earliest known ancestor of the family was Gilbert of Compton, parish of Marldon, County of Devon, in the thirteenth century. The homes of the families in England are mainly in Cornwall, Devonshire, Kent, Leicestershire, Rutlandshire, Lincolnshire, N o r f o l k, Northamptonshire, Staffordshire, Warwickshire, and Worcestershire.

One of the first of the Gilbert family to come to America was Jonathan who was b. in England in 1617. With him came his brothers, Thomas and John. Jonathan settled at Hartford, Connecticut, where he became a land owner and the chief inn keeper. He was prominent in the affairs of the community, serving as deputy to the General Court from Hartford. His brother Thomas settled at Springfield, Massachusetts.

By the time of the breaking out of the Revolutionary War, Gilberts had settled in all the original thirteen colonies and were numerous, particularly, in the colonies of Massachusetts, New York, Pennsylvania, Maryland, North Carolina, and Virginia.

The Gilbert family of Southwestern Virginia descended from Samuel Gilbert, a Revolutionary War soldier, who was b. about 1761, apparently in Virginia. On the 18th day of February 1833, he appeared in the Lee County (Virginia) Court and filed a declaration in connection with his claim for a pension growing out of his service in the Revolutionary War, from which declaration it appears he was then a resident of Lee County, 72 years of age, and that in May 1776, he enlisted for a term of six months in a company of rangers commanded by Captain James Crabtree, Humberson Lyon being the lieutenant and Philemon Higgins, the ensign, under the command of Colonel Arthur Campbell of Washington County. Virginia, an officer of the Virginia Militia. He served in this organization for a period of five months as a spy against the Indians and in guarding the frontier of the then county of Washington, now Russell County. which was then the Southwestern frontier of Virginia. At the end of five months and about the 1st day of Nov., 1776, he was discharged by Captain Crabtree at Jeremiah Harrison's Fort in Washington county.

He again entered the service, probably in 1777, and served a six months' tour against the British at Williamsburg, Virginia, in a company commanded by Captain John Canifax, Samuel Gilbert, a relative, being the lieutenant. The names of the other officers were not remembered he being only sixteen years of age at the time.

In July 1780, he again enlisted in Washington county in a company of Militia commanded by Captain James Montgomery, Samuel Newell, lieutenant, and James Sims, ensign, and with his company marched to the Lead Mines on New River, operating against the Tories, and joined some regular troops there under the command of Colonel Jeremiah Pearce of the Militia. He was engaged in this campaign for a little over two months when, after causing several Tories to enlist in the regular service, dispersing all other Tories, and procuring a large quantity of lead for the protection of the frontiers, the troops were permitted to return to their homes.

After his return from the Lead Mines and in June 1781, he again enlisted as a spy for a term of seven months under Captain James Crabtree, making Harrison's Fort his place of rendezvous from which place, at short intervals, and with other spies, he coursed the wilderness under great privations and dangers for the period of his enlistment of seven months, spying upon the Indians who were making frequent incursions into the settlements and doing a great deal of mischief in their sanguinary mode of warfare. During this enlistment, he together with his organization was in an expedition commanded by Colonel Arthur Campbell, aided by troops under Captains Sevier and Clark against the Cherokee Indian towns on the Tennessee River and at Tellico and Hiawassee; and after having destroyed the Indians' towns and killing and taking many prisoners with the loss of only one white man killed, the troops returned after a service of three months.

Just prior to the surrender of Cornwallis, he substituted for a six months' tour to guard New London, Virginia, under the then captain Samuel Gilbert, his relative, Arch Moon, lieutenant, in the regiment commanded by Colonel Stiff, and had served for a period of eight weeks when the news of the surrender was received and he was discharged at Williamsburg, Virginia.[1]

After the close of the Revolutionary War, Samuel Gilbert settled in Washington County, Virginia. Subsequently he removed to Lee County in which county he resided until his death which occurred about 1845 at the advanced age of about 84 years. Exhaustive research has not disclosed whom he married, nor the time or place of his marriage. Public records disclose, however that in 1810, his family at home, consisted of a wife and eight children. Of the children, three were daughters and five were sons whose names apparently were *2. Nathan or Nathaniel, 3. William, *4. Benjamin, 5. James, and 6. Thomas P. The records would seem to indicate that he died in the home of his son Thomas P. Gilbert.

Many—probably a great majority—of Samuel Gilbert's descendants of the early generations lived in Southwestern Virginia. However, some settled in Southeastern and in Eastern Kentucky and others migrated and settled in Missouri.

2. NATHANIEL GILBERT, who the records indicate was one of the oldest sons, was b. in 1788, presumably in Washington County. He m., presumably in Lee County, Rebecca Creech. The Cheeches were among the earliest settlers in Southwestern Virginia and Southeastern Kentucky.

Nathaniel Gilbert and his wife migrated to Carter County, Kentucky, about 1858 and lived in that county until their deaths, his on September 1, 1859, at the age of 71 (Vital Statistics of Carter County, 1852-1862), and hers about 1869.

Children among others:

7. Samuel Gilbert, farmer, who was b. in Lee County, Virginia, in 1827, preceded his parents to Carter County and on September 1, 1849, m. Nancy W. Jacobs, b. in 1824, daughter of William W. Jacobs and his wife, Rhoda (Prewitt) Jacobs.

Children, all of whom were b. and m. in Carter County:

*8. Elizabeth Gilbert.

9. William Nathaniel Gilbert; b. in 1850; and d. 1915; m. Jane Dailey. They reared a large family.

*10. Rhoda Caroline Gilbert.

*11. James Carter Gilbert.

*12. John Franklin Gilbert.

13. Martha Ellen Gilbert; m. Judge John Green Morris. (See Morris Family.)

14. Jackson Harrison Gilbert; b. September 24, 1863 and d. in 1898; unm.

7-A. NANCY (JACOBS) GILBERT d. at the birth of her son, Jackson Harrison Gilbert, and subsequently Samuel Gilbert m. in Carter County, Eliza Fraley. Children, all of whom were b. in Carter County:

15. Annie Laurie Gilbert; m. Robert McClurg.
16. Flora Belle Gilbert; unm.
17. Andrew Jackson Gilbert; unm.
18. Elijah Gilbert; m. Vicie Bear (Baer).
19. Malissa Gilbert; m. ——— Hollister.
20. Walter Gilbert; unm.

8. ELIZABETH GILBERT; b. in Carter County, Kentucky, in 1842; d. in Oklahoma, 1923; m. in Carter County, Burrell Burchett, b. in Carter County in 1844, son of Burrell and Sarah Burchett. (See Burrell Burchett Family.) He was sheriff of Carter County; migrated to Oklahoma and was elected and served as sheriff of Kingfisher County, that state. They reared a family of children of whom one, a daughter,
21. Rhoda Burchett m. Burrell Morris. (See Morris Family.)

10. RHODA CAROLINE GILBERT; b. in 1852, and d. 1934; m. Dock Boggs.
Children:
22. Samuel Boggs; m. ——— Bear or Baer.

11. JAMES CARTER GILBERT, farmer; b. in 1854 and d. December 7, 1933; m. Martha Stallards.
Children:
23. Watt Gilbert.
24. Pearl Gilbert.
25. Clyde Gilbert.

12. JOHN FRANKLIN GILBERT, merchant and postmaster at Soldier, Kentucky, was b. November 1, 1856, and d. at Soldier, December 28, 1930; m. December 4, 1880, Martha Underwood, b. August 22, 1861, and d. June, 1936. Both were buried in the Ashland Cemetery, Ashland, Kentucky.

Children:
26. Pearl Gilbert; b. August 22, 1881, and died October 31, 1896; unm., was buried at Soldier and later was reburied in Ashland Cemetery.
27. Wilford A. Gilbert, merchant at Soldier, was b. November 11, 1882; m. March 15, 1942, Mrs. Lulu (Patton) Clifton, b. in Floyd County, Kentucky, July 7, 1899; no children.
28. Earl Gilbert; b. May 6, 1887; m. Fannie Ratcliff.

4. BENJAMIN GILBERT; was b. in 1791; m.. presumably in Lee County, Virginia, Levisa Hunt, b. in 1795. He was a miller and built the first water mill in Lee County—on the Powell River.
Children:
*29. William P. Gilbert.
30. John Gilbert; settled in Harlan County, Kentucky.

31. Samuel Gilbert; settled in Harlan County, Kentucky.
32. Jesse Gilbert; settled in Harlan County, Kentucky.
33. Elizabeth Gilbert.
34. Rebecca Gilbert.
35. Martha Gilbert.
36. Jane Gilbert.

29. WILLIAM P. GILBERT was b in Lee County, Virginia, November 25, 1817, and d. October 3, 1863; m. in Lee County, Elizabeth Thompson, b. in Lee County, April 27, 1820, and d. April 19, 1909.[2]

Children:

37. Rosina Gilbert; m. James Arnold who d. in prison at Camp Douglas.
38. Leander Gilbert; m., first, Clarinda Creech and secondly, Mollie Bowen.
39. Margaret Gilbert; m. Charles Short; settled in Harlan County, Kentucky.
40. Polly (Mary) Gilbert; m. Alexander Morris, a Union soldier in the Civil War.
41. William Gilbert; m. Jane Kelley; settled in Harlan County, Kentucky.
42. Lucy Gilbert; m. John Cox.
43. Alfred Gilbert; m. Rebecca Ann Kelley; settled in Harlan County, Kentucky.
44. Cynthia Gilbert; m. in Lee County, Campbell Thompson; settled in Missouri.
45. Rebecca Gilbert; m. in Lee County, John Lucas.
*46. Elbert Martin Gilbert.

46. ELBERT MARTIN GILBERT, the youngest child, farmer, stock-raiser, dealer in real estate and merchant, was b. in Lee County, March 31, 1862, and d. in that county, September 15, 1942; m. in Lee County, Minnie Belle Crabtree[3] who was b. in Lee County, December 25, 1871.

Children:

47. Frank Clark Gilbert, merchant; b. September 17, 1891; educated in the public schools of Lee County and at Big Stone Gap, (Virginia) Normal School; served for approximately one year in World War I; m. Thelma Cooney, teacher in the public schools of Lee County.
48. Roy Gilbert, farmer, telegrapher and agent, Louisville and Nashville Railway Company; b. April 15, 1893; educated in the public schools of Lee County and at Big Stone Gap (Virginia) Normal School; m. Mattie Burke.
49. Kittie Gilbert; b. November 30, 1895; educated in public Schools of Lee County and was graduated from State Teachers' Col-

lege at Radford; teacher in the public schools of Lee County for several years; m., June 8, 1921, Silas James Shelburne, farmer, sometime teacher; veteran of World War I; and Superintendent of public schools of Lee County for several years.

50. Joe Wheeler Gilbert, telegrapher, Louisville and Nashville Railway Company, farmer and merchant; b. July 14, 1897; educated in public schools of Lee County and at Dryden (Virginia) High School; m. Mary Lynn Wolfe, a teacher in Lee County public schools.

51. Dana Shelburne Gilbert; b. February 14, 1899; educated in the public schools of Lee County; early in life became an employee of the Louisville and Nashville Railway Company and was a conductor at age of 21; veteran of World War I.

52. Sada Lee Gilbert, teacher; b. January 24, 1904; educated in the Lee County public schools, graduating from the Dryden High School; and was graduated from State Teachers' College at Radford in 1927; teacher in the graded and high schools of Lee County for many years; m. Clyde H. Bishop, a contractor.

53. Luther Crabtree Gilbert, teacher; b. August 6, 1911; educated in Lee County public schools and at Emory and Henry College, Emory, Virginia, graduating in 1933; was a teacher (principal) of St. Charles (Virginia) High School and of Pennington Gap and Elkknob schools.

---

[1] The National Archives, Washington, D. C.

[2] The Thompsons were among the earliest settlers in Lee County. On Powell River a short distance west from the town of Dryden is the old family burying ground and inscriptions, now almost obliterated, on the tombstones indicate that W. S. Thompson and his wife, Elizabeth (Thorpe) Thompson, were the first to be buried there and that W. C. Thompson, apparently their son, b. July 15, 1785 and d. March 18, 1864, who m. Elizabeth (———) Thompson, b. March 22, 1788, and d. September 18, 1857, were among the earliest buried there.

The Children of W. C. Thompson and Elizabeth (———) Thompson were (1) Mary Thompson Tritt, b. July 23, 1809; (2) Alfred Thompson, b. February 10, 1811; (3) Annie Thompson, b. November 21, 1812; (4) Jackson Thompson, b. April 1, 1816; (5) William S. Thompson, a justice of the peace for Lee County, was b. January 11, 1818; (6) Elizabeth Thompson, b. April 27, 1820, d. April 19, 1909, m. William P. Gilbert; (7) Campbell Thompson, b. June 26, 1882; (8) Sarrilda Thompson Arnold, b. September 27, 1826; (9) Catharine Thompson, b. April 27, 1828; and (10) B. F. Thompson, b. May 24, 1834.

[3] Among the earliest pioneer settlers of Southwestern Virginia were the Crabtrees. James Crabtree had service in the Revolutionary War as an ensign and as a captain in the Washington County (Virginia) Militia. Abraham Crabtree and Jacob Crabtree were Revolutionary War soldiers and subsequent to the close of the war resided in Lee County.

On Powell River a short distance west of the town of Dryden, Lee County is the old burying ground of the Crabtree family. From the inscriptions, now illegible, on the tombstones, it appears that Job Crabtree, b. in 1766 and d. January 12, 1828, and his wife, Rebecca (———) Crabtree, b. June 25, 1775, d. April 19, 1864, were the first to be buried there. Their son, G. A. Crabtree, who d. at White Water, Kansas, m. Ann Garrett, b. in 1814 and d. in 1883. Their son, James Crabtree, m. Susan Parsons, a daughter of Jack Parsons and Rebecca (Pennington) Parsons. Their daughter, Minnie Belle Crabtree, b. December 25, 1871, m. Elbert Martin Gilbert.

GRAYSON FAMILY OF PRINCE WILLIAM COUNTY VIRGINIA AND CARTER COUNTY, KENTUCKY

The Grayson family of Virginia and Kentucky is of English or Scottish extraction. Yorkshire, England, appears to be the true early home of the family. However, members of the family lived in Scotland. The poll tax lists of Yorkshire, England, as of the year 1379, bear the names of Thomas Graysson, Johannes Grayfson, Thomas Grayfson. Emma Grefeson, Mary Grayson and George Grayson resided at Salwicke, England, in 1639 and John Greason lived at Leonaster, England, in 1637.

1. BENJAMIN GRAYSON was the first of the name who emigrated to the American colonies of which there is any known record. He was believed to have come from Scotland. He settled in Prince William County, Virginia, where he was a merchant and acquired great wealth. He m., first, Susan or Susanna Monroe, a daughter of Andrew Monroe and great aunt of President James Monroe, and m., secondly, Mrs. Linton, a widow.

Children of Benjamin Grayson and his wife, Susan Monroe:
2. Benjamin Grayson, Jr.
3. Spence Grayson.
*4. William Grayson.
5. Susan Monroe Grayson.

4. WILLIAM GRAYSON was b. in Prince William County, Virginia, in 1726; was graduated from the College of Philadelphia in 1760 and is said to have studied law at the Temple in London. Entering the service of his country during the Revolutionary War, he was aid-de-camp to General Washington in 1776; was commissioned colonel on the Continental Line in 1777; and later, in 1779, was one of the Commissioners of the Board of War. He was elected as a member of the Continental Congress in 1784 and was president of that body in 1788. Upon the organization of the Federal Government, he was chosen by Virginia as one of the two first United States Senators—Richard Henry Lee being the other one.

Colonel Grayson m. Eleanor (Hebe) Smallwood, one of the five sisters of Captain Heaberd Smallwood of Charles County, Maryland. Captain Smallwood had service in the Revolutionary War on the Maryland State Line.

Children of Colonel William Grayson and his wife, Eleanor Smallwood:
6. William Grayson d. without issue.
*7. George W. Grayson.
*8. Robert H. Grayson.
9. Heaberd S. Grayson. Very little has been learned concerning him.

*10. Alfred Grayson.

*11. Hebe Smallwood Grayson; m. Robert Wormerly Carter of Loudoun County, Virginia. (See Carter Family).

These children and/or their descendants received from the United States Government large tracts of land in Kentucky, Virginia and Maryland by reason of the military service of their father, Colonel Grayson, and their uncle, Captain Smallwood. In the early 1800's they migrated to and entered large tracts of land under the Grayson grant on the little Sandy River at the present Grayson, Kentucky, then Greenup County, now Carter County.

7. GEORGE W. GRAYSON was enumerated in the U. S. Census of Greenup County for 1810 as head of family and as owning five negro slaves. Apparently he subsequently returned to tidewater Virginia as he d. in Fauquier County, Virginia, sometime prior to March 27,. 1832, leaving three children:

12. Frances Grayson; m. Richard H. Foote.

13. George W. Grayson, Jr.

14. William Grayson.

8. ROBERT H. GRAYSON, lawyer, large landowner and slaveholder, owning the greatest number of slaves of any person (49) in Greenup County in 1810; m., September 3, 1809, Miss Sophonisba Cabell, daughter of Joseph Cabell of Virginia.

Issue:

15. William Preston Grayson.

16. Hebe C. Grayson; m. Preston Smith.

17. Ellen S. Grayson.

The records indicate that this family removed to Henderson County, Kentucky.

10. ALFRED W. GRAYSON; m. October 26, 1804, Miss Letitia P. Breckenridge, daughter of Hon. John Breckenridge, of Fayette County, Kentucky, Attorney General in the administration of President Jefferson. Miss Breckenridge was aunt of General John Cabell Breckenridge, Vice-President of the United States in administration of President Buchanan and sometime Secretary of War in administration of Jefferson Davis.

Alfred W. Grayson removed to Washington County, Arkansas, where he died in 1816 or 1817. His widow, Letitia, m. at Princeton, N. Jersey, October 16, 1818, Major General Peter B. Porter, U. S. Army, of New York.

Children of Alfred W. Grayson and Letitia P. Breckenridge:

18. John C. Breckenridge Grayson. He was captain, major and lieutenant colonel in U. S. Army in the Mexican War; was a brigadier-general in the Confederate Army in the Civil War; and d. October 21, 1861.

GREEN FAMILY OF JOHNSON AND CARTER COUNTIES

This is a local name, "at the green" from residence thereby; a grassy plat used by the village as a common. As every village in England had its green or common it is not surprising that modern directories teem with the name.

The family Green is of English extraction. The Hundred Rolls of England, 1273, bear the names of Robert de la Grene and Warin de la Grene and the Poll Tax list of Yorkshire, England, 1379, bear the names of Petrus del Grene, Adam del Grene and Willemus del Grene.

The family was numerous in the New England and Southern colonies at an early date.

THE GREEN FAMILY OF JOHNSON AND LAWRENCE COUNTIES, KENTUCKY

* 1. Giles Green and * 2. Enoch Green, brothers, were ancestors of a branch of the Green family who settled in the Big Sandy Valley region, Eastern Kentucky.

*1. GILES GREEN, farmer, was b. in Virginia in 1800 and d. in Johnson County, Kentucky, circa 1876. He m., first, in Virginia, presumably in Cabell County, about 1817 or 1818, Katie Chandler, b. in North Carolina or Virginia about 1795 and d. in Johnson County, Kentucky, about 1844. According to family tradition she was a daughter of Thomas Chandler, a Revolutionary War soldier. (See Chandler Family). He m., second, in Johnson County, Kentucky, March 14, 1846, a widow, Margaret Yates, nee Ghent, who was b. in Virginia in 1807 and d. in Johnson County, Kentucky.

By conveyance dated April 11, 1826, Giles Green transferred to John M. McConnell of Greenup County, Kentucky, and others a 175-acre tract of land situated on Twelve Pole Creek, Cabell County, Virginia; and soon thereafter, about 1827, he removed with his family to that part of Lawrence County, Kentucky, which was subsequently, in 1843, included in Johnson County. In 1832 he patented 200 acres of land on Hoods Fork of Blaine, Lawrence County; also 100 acres on Rockhouse Fork, that County, in 1833; and in 1841 he purchased of Avery Keezee and others lands situated on Hoods Fork of Blaine, same county.

Children of Giles Green and his wife, Katie (Chandler) Green with approximate dates of their birth as shown by the U. S. Census of Johnson County for the years 1850, 1860 and 1870:

*3. Thomas Green.

4. Elias Green; b. in Kentucky, 1831. One Elias Green m. Annie Bevins in Lawrence County, March 18, 1851.

    5. William Green; b. in Kentucky, 1833.
 *6. John Green; b. 1838 or 1839.
    7. George W. Green; b. 1841.
    8. Patsy (Martha) Green; m. John Wheeler.
 *9. Judy or Judith Green; m. William Wheeler.
*10. Elzira Green; m. Isaac Chandler.
  11. Sarah Green; m. E. P. S. Hylton (see Hylton Family).
*12. David Green.

*1-A. Children of Giles Green and his wife, Margaret (Ghent) Yates Green living at home and approximate date of birth as shown by U. S. Census of Johnson County for 1850 and 1860:
  13. Enoch Green; b. 1847.
*14. Marcus L. Green; b. 1849.
  15. James M. Green; b. 1852.

In the household of Giles Green in 1850 lived "Judea" Green (apparently his mother), age 91 years, b. in Virginia.

3. THOMAS GREEN, farmer, was b. in Cabell County, Virginia, now Wayne County, West Virginia, 1820. He m. in Johnson County, Kentucky, February 1, 1844, Jemima Brown, b. in Johnson County, 1822, daughter of John Brown. They purchased and removed to a farm on Lick Creek, near Webbville, Lawrence County, where they d. and were buried.

Children living at home and approximate dates of birth as shown by U. S. Census of Lawrence County for 1850, 1860 and 1870:
  16. Isaiah Green; b. in Johnson County, 1845; m. Jane Davis.
  17. George W. Green; b. in Johnson County, 1846, and d. near Willard Carter County, July, 1929; m. Sarah Clark, b. 1846 and d. July, 1921, daughter of Joseph Clark.
  18. John W. Green; b. in Johnson County, 1848; m. Susan Vanbibber.
  19. Giles Green; b. Johnson County, August 17, 1849, and d. at Webbville, Lawrence County, April 12, 1929; m. Eliza Kitchen, daughter of Lewis and Jane Kitchen.
  20. Catherine Green; b. 1851 and d. October 2, 1947; m. David Simpson.
  21. Julia A. Green; b. 1852, and d. November 23, 1946; m. James Rice.
  22. William M. Green; b. March 3, 1854; m. Verna Pennington.
  23. Samantha Green; b. December 20, 1855; m. Frank Spears.
  24. Harman Green; b. July 23, 1857, and d. 1928; m. Mary Webb.
  25. Elizabeth Green; d. 1943; m. Monroe Cunningham.
  26. Mary Green; b. 1860; m. Elisha Wellman.
  27. Rosa Green; b. December 11, 1870; m. Oscar Riley.
  28. ———— Green; daughter; d. in infancy.

6. John Green, farmer; b. about 1839; m. in Johnson County, Jemima ———, b. 1846.

Children living at home and approximate dates of birth as shown by U. S. Census of Johnson County for 1870:
29. William P. Green; b. 1866.
30. Mahala A. Green; b. 1868.
31. Cynthia S. Green; b. 1870.

9. Judy or Judith Green; b. 1835; m. in Johnson County, November 14, 1853, William Wheeler, farmer, b. 1832.

Children living at home and approximate dates of birth as shown by U. S. Census of Johnson County for 1870:
32. Nina E. Wheeler; b. 1855.
33. Melvina Wheeler; b. 1856.
34. Nancy E. Wheeler; b. 1858.
35. Jemima Wheeler, b. 1860.
36. Sarah Wheeler, b. 1862.
37. Pricy D. Wheeler; b. 1863.
38. Ezra K. Wheeler; b. 1865.
39. Jasper Wheeler; b. 1869.

10. Elzira Green; b. 1826; m. in Johnson County, November 29, 1848, Isaac Chandler, b. 1828.

Children living at home and approximate dates of birth as shown by U. S. Census of Johnson County for 1850:
40. Martha Chandler; b. 1849.

12. David Green; m. in Johnson County, October 2, 1847, Lucinda Barnhardt, b. 1832. The record indicates that he d. about 1868.

Children living at home with mother and approximate dates of birth as shown by U. S. Census of Johnson County for 1870:
41. Sarah A. Green; b. 1856.
42. Nancy E. Green; b. 1859.
43. Julina Green; b. 1862.
44. Amanda Green; b. 1867.

14. Marcus L. Green, farmer; b. 1849; m. Mary ———, b. 1848.

Children living at home and approximate dates of birth as shown by U. S. Census of Johnson County for 1870:
45. Amanda J. Green; b. 1868.
46. Colister M. Green; b. 1869.

2. Enoch Green, farmer and Baptist preacher, was b. in Virginia in 1812 and d. in Lawrence County, Kentucky, about 1885. He m. in Cabell County, Virginia, April 17, 1831, Elizabeth Chandler, "after one publication according to law," the Rev. Stephen Spurlock, officiating. She was b. in Virginia, presumably in Cabell County, in

1811, a daughter of Thomas Chandler, Revolutionary War soldier (see Chandler Family).

By conveyance dated November 28, 1840, Enoch Green transferred his farm situated on Camp Creek of Twelve Pole, Cabell County, Virginia, to one John Bailey; and soon thereafter, about 1841, he removed with his family to Lawrence County, Kentucky.

Children of Enoch Green and his wife, Elizabeth (Chandler) Green, and approximate dates of their birth as shown by the U. S. Census of Lawrence County for the years 1850, 1860, and 1870:

47. Amosa Green, daughter; b. in Virginia, 1831.
*48. Andrew J. Green; b. in Virginia, 1832
49. George W. Green; b. in Virginia, 1834.
*50. Burwell Green; b. in Virginia, 1835.
51. Abigail Green; b. in Virginia, 1837.
52. John F. Green; b. in Virginia, 1840.
53. Mary Green; b. 1858.

The U. S. Census of Lawrence County for 1880 shows the following with respect to Enoch Green and family:

Enoch Green, aged 68, farmer, b. in Virginia.
Elizabeth (apparently second wife), aged 41.
54. Clayton Green, aged 5.
55. Etta N. Green, aged 4.
56. Anna C. Green, aged 3.
57. B. Enoch Green, aged 1.

48. ANDREW J. GREEN; m. Dorcas Jayne in Johnson County, November ———, 1856. She was born 1837.

Children living at home with mother and approximate dates of birth as shown by U. S. Census of Johnson County for 1870:

58. Emma Green; b. 1857.
59. Alexander Green; b. 1860.
60. Amanda Green; b. 1861.

50. BURWELL GREEN; m. Phoebe Cordell in Lawrence County, April 14, 1857. She was b. 1833.

Children living at home and approximate dates of birth as shown by U. S. Census of Lawrence County for 1860 and 1870:

61. Jane E. Green; b. 1859.
62. Samantha Green; b. 1861.
63. George G. Green; b. 1864.
64. Nancy E. Green; b. 1866.
65. Enoch C. Green; b. 1868.

HAGER FAMILY

The Hager family is of German descent. The progenitor of this family in Eastern Kentucky, was John Hager, Sr.[1], who was b. in Hesse Cassel, Germany, December 26, 1759; emigrated to America as a British subject during the Revolutionary War; and subsequently having been converted to the cause of American independence, joined the colonists in the Revolution, serving as a soldier under the command of General Thomas Sumter of South Carolina. At the close of the war he settled near the present-day Lynchburg, Virginia, then Amherst county, where he m., in 1785, Mary Schrader or Schaefer, who was b., apparently in Virginia, in 1755, and d. in Johnson county, Kentucky, 1847.

Emigrating to Kentucky about 1806 with his wife and some of his children, including sons James and Daniel, he settled at the mouth of Beaver Creek, Floyd county, Kentucky, and soon thereafter removed down the Big Sandy River to the mouth of John's Creek, then Floyd county subsequently Johnson county where he lived until his death in February, 1819.

According to tradition, John Hager, Sr.[1], had two brothers, one of whom (Jonathan) settled Hagerstown, Maryland, and the other Hagerstown, Indiana.

Children:

*2. John Hager.

*3. George Hager.

*4. Katherine Hager.

5. William Hager; b. in Virginia, May 5, 1790; migrated from that state to Murfreesboro, Tennessee, where he d. in 1833, at the age of forty-three years, leaving a family there.

6. Elizabeth Hager; b. in Virginia, March 4, 1792; m., in Floyd county, Kentucky, August 22, 1811, John McKee; emigrated to and lived in Mississippi until her death.

7. Katie Hager; m. James Layne.

8. Henry Hager; b. in Virginia, January 20, 1794; migrated from that state to Nashville, Tennessee, where he engaged in merchandising until his death in 1847, at the age of fifty-three years.

*9. James Hager.

*10. Daniel Hager.

2. JOHN HAGER; b. in Virginia, October 13, 1786; migrated to Kentucky from Amherst county, Virginia some years after his father's emigration, and lived in Floyd and Johnson counties until his death in the latter county in 1868 at the age of eighty-two years; m., in Virginia, Elizabeth Johnson.

Children:

11. Elizabeth Hager; m. Daniel Wheeler. (See No. 12, Wheeler Family.)

12. Martha Hager; m. Jesse Fortune.

13. Jane Hager; m. Madison Howes.

14. Katherine Hager; m. Horace Roberts.

*15. Eliza Hager; m. Edward Lavender.

16. Nancy Hager; m. Kendrick Sunday.   Their descendants lived at Portsmouth, Ohio.

17. Amanda Hager; m. Ralph Stafford.   (See No. 15, Stafford Family.)

18. James Hager.

19. Samuel Hager; minister of the Gospel; m. ——— Clark; emigrated to Texas; killed by runaway horse.

20. John Hager.

21. Eldridge Hager; descendants lived in Southwestern Virginia, chiefly at Max Meadows that section.

3. GEORGE HAGER, b. in Virginia May 18, 1788; migrated to Kentucky about the same time as his brother John (2) and settled in what is now Johnson county; subsequently removed to Cabell or Wayne County, West Virginia, and died in Boyd county, Kentucky, in 1884, at the age of ninety-six years; member of the Methodist Church and very religious; m. in ——— county, ——— Porter.

Children:

22. Harman Hager; lived at East Point, Johnson county.

23. Mary Hager; m. ——— Van Horn.

4. Katherine Hager; m. in Amherst County, Virginia, James Layne.   (See No. 2 Layne Family.)

Children:

24. Judge Lindsay Layne.

25. Nancy Layne; m. ——— Honaker.

26. Arminta Layne; m. ——— Boyd; lived in Bath county, Kentucky.

27. ——— Layne; m. ——— Boyd.

9. JAMES HAGER; b. in Virginia March 2, 1800; came with his father, John Hager, Sr.,[1] to Kentucky and lived in Floyd county until his death in 1868 at the age of sixty-eight; m. in Floyd county, September 2, 1819, Susanna Porter, daughter of Patrick Porter, (a Revolutionary War soldier) and his wife Martha (Hutchinson) Porter.

Children:

28. ——— Hager; m. Peter Wells (see Wells Family).

29. Richard Hager.

30. Katherine Hager; m. ——— Sammons.

31. Elizabeth Hager; m. ——— Sparks.

32. Sarah Hager; m. ——— Porter.

33. Morgan Hager.

10. DANIEL HAGER, farmer, merchant, hotel-keeper, brigadier-general of the Kentucky militia for many years, first sheriff of Johnson county, state representative, was b. in Virginia November 15, 1801; d. at Paintsville, Johnson county, Kentucky, July 5, 1887; youngest child of John Hager, Sr.[1], was about five years old when they came to Kentucky; m. in Floyd county, January 31, 1822, Violet Vertrees Porter, b. in Russell county, Virginia, February 4, 1804, d. in Johnson county, Kentucky, February 22, 1877, a daughter of John Porter (Revolutionary War soldier) and his wife, Elizabeth (Pendleton) Porter.

Children:
*34. John Jackson Hager.
*35. Henry George Hager.
*36. William James Hager.
*37. Mary Jane Hager.
38. Martha Ann Hager; m. William Stafford (see No. 16 Stafford Family).
*39. Amanda Burns Hager.
*40. Samuel Patton Hager.
41. Emily Elizabeth Hager; m. Frank Preston (see No. 23 Preston Family).
*42. Daniel Marion Hager.
43. Louisa Hager; m. Moses Preston (see No. 20 Preston Family).
*44. Benjamin F. Hager.
45. Violet Vertrees Hager; m. Edward Brown (see No. 40 Brown Family).

General Daniel Hager, by reason of his energy and superior mental endowments, ranked as the leader of the Hagers of his time. He became comparatively wealthy and did well by his children, not so much in a pecuniary sense as in rearing them to think and act independently. He was one of the great pioneers who did much to develop the Big Sandy Valley and to make it a place of wealth and culture. He was a life-long Democrat, as were the Hagers generally voted for Andrew Jackson, in 1824, and was neutral in the Civil War, but sympathized with the South. In religion, he was a member of the Methodist Episcopal Church, South.

15. ELIZA HAGER; m. Edward Lavendar.
Children:
46. Kittie Lavendar; m. George W. Preston (see Preston Family).
47. John William Lavendar; m. Susie Webb.
48. James Lavendar; d. in infancy.
49. Marietta Lavendar; m. F. M. Stafford (see Stafford Family).

34. JOHN JACKSON HAGER, farmer and blacksmith; b. December 6, 1822; d. February 6, 1864, in Wythe county, Virginia, caused by falling from a moving train while in the Confederate Army during the

Civil War; m., February 20, 1844, Rhoda Godsey (b. February, 1821), daughter of John Godsey and his wife Julia A. (Jett) Godsey.

Children:
*50. Julia Hager.
51. D. Martin Hager.
*52. Lou Hager.
53. ——— Hager; m. ———; lived in Lawrence county.
*54. James Henry Hager.
55. Josephine Hager; m. G. W. Davis (see Davis Family).
*56. John J. Hager.
57. Frances Hager; m. Oliver Loar; lived in Lawrence county.

35. HENRY GEORGE HAGER, merchant and steamboat-owner, b. March 12, 1824, d. January 11, 1869; m., first, Nancy Jane Franklin, b. October 4, 1825, d. June 30, 1856, and secondly, Mrs. Caroline Mayo Jaqueth (d. 1862 or 1863), daughter of Jonathan Mayo, of Paris, Illinois.

Children of Henry George Hager and Nancy Jane Franklin:
*58. Mary Hager.
*59. James Hager.
*60. John F. Hager, Sr.
*61. Daniel Milton Hager.

Children of Henry George Hager and Caroline Mayo Jaqueth:
62. Harry Hager.
63. Frank Hager.
They resided in Paris, Illinois.

36. WILLIAM JAMES HAGER, b. January 22, 1826, d. March 21, 1903; m., March 16, 1853, Phoebe Ann Roach, of Gallia County, Ohio, who d. October 29, 1904. They lived in Salyersville, Kentucky.

Children:
*64. Fanny Hager.
*65. Samuel Wilbur Hager.
66. Edward Hager; resided in Salyersville.
67. Warren Hager; m. ———. No children.

37. MARY JANE HAGER, b. February 27, 1828, d. in 1908; m., April 22, 1857, Dr. J. W. Martin. They resided in Ashland, Kentucky.

Children:
68. Daniel Martin.
69. Charley Martin.
70. Sarah Martin.
71. Lulu Martin.
72. Frank Martin.
73. Dr. Harry Martin.

39. AMANDA BURNS HAGER; m. Captain Reuben Patrick, of Magoffin county, Kentucky (see Patrick Family).

40. SAMUEL PATTON HAGER, sometime merchant, insurance man, b. in Floyd County, May 22, 1834, d. in Ashland, Kentucky, December 12, 1926, aged ninety-two years; educated in the rural schools; entered his father's store, at Paintsville, as salesman in 1852 and continued as such until 1856; merchant at Paintsville 1856-1857; engaged in merchandising at Tinneys Grove, Ray county, Missouri, from the Fall of 1857 to April, 1859, when he returned to Paintsville and resumed merchandising and engaged in steamboating until 1881, when he removed to Ashland where he became identified with many of the business enterprises of that city; was senior member of Hager & Hager, insurance; a promoter, director and stockholder in many other Ashland enterprises; partner in the firm of S. P. Hager and Brother, at Paintsville. Subsequent to March, 1886, he devoted most of his time to the insurance business.

On November 21, 1860, in Johnson county, Samuel Patton Hager, m., Angie R. Brown, daughter of Thomas S. Brown and his wife, Emaline (Damron) Brown.

Children:

*74. Wilbur C. Hager.

*75. Harry H. Hager.

76. Fred Hager; d. in infancy.

77. Edgar B. Hager; junior member of the firm of Hager & Hager, insurance, succeeded to, and operated the business after the death of his father.

*78. John S. Hager.

79. Freddie Hager; d. September 19, 1870.

80. Paul Verner Hager; d. in infancy.

42. DANIEL MARION HAGER, merchant, in Paintsville; b. July 19, 1840; d. ———; m., in Johnson county, ——— 1866, Mary L. Borders (d. May 27, 1871), daughter of Joseph Borders.

Children:

*81. George W. Hager.

82. Samuel Patton Hager, Jr.; m. ——— Prichard; removed to Huntington, West Virginia, and engaged in merchandising there.

83. Bennie B. Hager; d. July 7, 1871.

42. DANIEL MARION HAGER; m., first, Jessegat T. Vaughan, b. February 11, 1859, d. September 17, 1886, and, secondly, Jane Melvin.

Children of Daniel Marion Hager and Jessegat T. Vaughan:

84. Eugene Hager.

85. Virgie Hager.

86. Robert Hager.

Children of Daniel Marion Hager and Jane Melvin:

87. Russell Hager.

88. Jane Hager.

44. BENJAMIN F. HAGER, businessman of Paintsville; vice president of the Paintsville Grocery Company at time of his death; also active in church work, was superintendent of Sunday School of the Methodist Episcopal Church, South, for twenty-seven years; b. July 10, 1845; d. December 31, 1921; m. ——, 1866, Julia Sherman.

Children:

*89. Frank P. Hager.
90. Forrest Hager; deceased; unm.
*91. Ada Hager.
92. Edward Hager.

Fourth Generation

50. JULIA HAGER 4 (John Jackson Hager 3, General Daniel Hager 2, John Hager, Sr., 1,); m. Henry Jayne (see No. 12, Jayne Family).

51. D. MARTIN HAGER 4 (John Jackson Hager 3, General Daniel Hager 2, John Hager, Sr. 1), farmer, local preacher in the Methodist Episcopal Church, South, b. October 20, 1846; m. January 30, 1867, Elizabeth May, b. October 27, 1849, d. September 16, 1908.

Children:

93. Laura Hager; m. Martin Music.
94. John Hager; m., first —— Richmond, and, secondly, Mrs. Winston Conley.
95. Rhoda Hager; m. Dr. William Patrick.
96. Fanny Hager; m. William Greenway.
97. Gertrude Hager; m. Scott Smith.
98. Mary Hager; d. in infancy.

52. LOU HAGER 4 (John Jackson Hager 3, General Daniel Hager 2, John Hager, Sr. 1); m. J. Foster Walker.

Children:

99. Lillie Walker; m. John Hampton.
100. Esta Walker.

54. JAMES HENRY HAGER 4, (John Jackson Hager 3, General Daniel Hager 2, John Hager, Sr. 1); b. December 20, 1849; d. September 8, 1895; m. Martha Dixon b. March 12, 1853, d. December 14, 1921. They lived near West Van Lear, Johnson county.

Children:

101. Ben Hager; m. Exer Childers.
102. Fred Hager; m., first, Missouri Rice, b. October 14, 1879, d. May 12, 1898; secondly, Digie Arrowood, b. May 22, 1872, d. March 14, 1909; and thirdly, Sallie Bagett.

56. JOHN J. HAGER 4 (John Jackson Hager 3, General Daniel Hager 2, John Hager, Sr. 1); m. —— Reynolds, in Tennessee. They lived in Bristol, Virginia-Tennessee.

Children:
103. ——— lived in Philadelphia.
104. ——— lived in Chicago.

58. MARY HAGER 4 (Henry George Hager 3, General Daniel
Hager 2, John Hager, Sr. 1); m. Captain John Milton Atkinson.

59. JAMES HAGER 4 (Henry George Hager 3, General Daniel
Hager 3, General Daniel Hager 2, John Hager, Sr. 1); m. Emma
Prudy. They lived at Kingfisher, Oklahoma.
Children:
105. Milton Hager.
106. Laura Hager.

60. JOHN F. HAGER, SR. 4, (Henry George Hager 3, and his wife,
Mary Jane (Franklin) Hager, General Daniel Hager 2, John Hager,
Sr. 1), lawyer, was b. in Floyd County, K e n t u c k y, March 16,
1853, and d. in Ashland, Kentucky. His mother d. in 1856 and at
the age of 11 he went to Ashland, Kentucky, where he attended a
private school for two years conducted by J. B. Powell. Afterward
he attended school at Catlettsburg for a year and Masonic Academy
at Louisa for another year. In his boyhood when not in school he
worked on Big Sandy River steamers, serving as cabin boy, cook,
watchman and "cub" pilot. At the age of 15 he was employed by
his uncle, S. P. Hager, a general merchant, at Paintsville, and remained there for four years except a part of one year when he attended school at Paris, Illinois. At the age of 19 he was appointed
deputy clerk of the Magoffin Circuit Court, receiving one-third of the
fees of the office for his services, at the same time reading borrowed
law books and qualifying himself for examination for license to
practice law. He was admitted to the bar at West Liberty, Kentucky, November 13, 1873, being then under 21 years of age; and soon
afterward returned to Ashland and formed a partnership with John
W. Hampton for the practice of law in place of William C. Ireland
who had been elected judge of the sixteenth circuit. This partnership continued until 1880 when Mr. Hampton removed to Texas.
Subsequently he formed a partnership with John W. M. Stewart, and
the firm practiced for many years with great distinction and success.
    Mr. Hager was recognized as one of the great lawyers of the
state. He was well versed in the history of his state and especially
of his native section and its people.
    He served as Commissioner from Kentucky under appointment
by Governor Buckner at the celebration of the Centennial of the
Federal Constitution at Philadelphia in September, 1887; served as
Commissioner from Kentucky to the Centennial Exposition at Cincinnati in 1888; served as Railroad Commissioner of Kentucky from
May, 1888, to August, 1891, when he resigned several months before
the expiration of his term; served as one of the Commissioners in

charge of the State Treasury after the defalcation and flight from the country of the Treasurer J. W. Tate. He was twice elected City Attorney of Ashland, in 1878 and 1886, and with these exceptions was never a candidate for or held public office.

On December 22, 1881, Mr. Hager was m. to Margaret Elizabeth Maupin. Children:
107. Lawrence Hager.
108. Adell Hager; m. William H. Harrison, Jr.
109. ———— ————.
110. Peggy Hager; m. ———— Wilson.
*111. John F. Hager, Jr.

61. DANIEL MILTON HAGER 4 (Henry George Hager 3 and his wife Nancy Jane Franklin, General Daniel Hager 2, John Hager, Sr. 1); proprietor of the Hager Hotel, Paintsville, for many years; m., first, Jessie Booton and, secondly, Ida Leo Green, b. 1889.

Children of Daniel Milton Hager and Jessie Booton:
112. Henry Hager.
113. Paul Hager; businessman of Paintsville; former clerk of the Johnson County Court.

Children of Daniel Milton Hager and Ida Leo Green:
114. Clarence Hager; m. Margaret Auxier. (See Auxier Family).
115. Mary Hager; m. Tobe Davis Vaughan. (See Vaughan Family).
116. Anna Hager; m. Alexander Cameron, of Ashland, Kentucky.
*117. D. Milton Hager.

64. FANNY HAGER 4 (William James Hager 3, General Daniel Hager 2, John Hager, Sr. 1); m. D. M. Atkinson. They lived at Salyersville.

Children:
118. Emma Atkinson.
119. Ernest Atkinson.

65. SAMUEL WILBUR HAGER 4 (William James Hager 3, General Daniel Hager 2, John Hager, Sr. 1), newspaper publisher and public official, was b. on his father's farm near Gallipolis, Gallia County, Ohio, December 19, 1858, and d. in Owensboro, Kentucky, December 27, 1918; removed with his parents to Salyersville, Kentucky, when a child; attended the public school and engaged in teaching for a time; was graduated from the University of Kentucky; engaged in merchandising at Salyersville, but in 1887 went to Ashland, Kentucky, and became associated with an uncle in business.

A Democrat in politics, Mr. Hager held many public offices of honor and trust: He served as judge of the Boyd County Court, 1896-1899; Treasurer of Kentucky, 1900-1903; Auditor of Kentucky, 1904-1907. He was unsuccessful candidate for Governor,

1907. He served as a member of the Workman's Compensation Board.

He purchased the Owensboro Enquirer in 1909 which he edited and published until his death. He was a member of the Christian Church and was affiliated with the Masons.

On June 30, 1888, Mr. Hager was m. to Elizabeth Woods White of Clay County, Kentucky, sister of Hon. John D. White, M. C. (See White Family.)

Children:

120. William Bruce Hager.

121. —— Hager.

122. Lawrence White Hager, newspaper publisher and civic worker; b. at Louisville, Kentucky, May 28, 1890; attended the public schools; was graduated from Centre College with degree of A.B., 1909, and with degree of A. M., 1910; editor and publisher of the Owensboro (Kentucky) Enquirer, 1910, and the Owensboro Messenger, 1929; president of the Owensboro Publishing Company which publishes both papers; appointed postmaster at Owensboro, 1935; served as officer, Finance Department. U. S. Army, in Argonne offensive, World War I; member of Owensboro Chamber of Commerce; Owensboro Y. M. C. A. (director 14 years); a Democrat; member of the Christian Church; a Mason (K. T.). Clubs: Owensboro Investigators, Rotary (president, 1922), Owensboro Country (director, 1920), Kentucky Postmasters Association (president 1935-6); founder of Goodfellow Club which furnished necessities to needy children at Christmas time.

On June 25, 1921, Mr. Hager was m. to Martha Augusta Brown of Parkersburg, West Virginia. Children: Lawrence White, Jr., and John Stewart.

74. WILLIAM C. HAGER 4 (Samuel Patton Hager 3, General Daniel Hager 2, John Hager, Sr. 1); m. —— ——.

Children:

123. Hazel Hager; m. Edward Berger.

75. HARRY H. HAGER 4 (Samuel Patton Hager 3, General Daniel Hager 2, John Hager, Sr. 1); d. ——, 1909; m. ——.

Children:

124. —— ——.

78. JOHN S. HAGER 4 (Samuel Patton Hager 3, General Daniel Hager 2, John Hager, Sr. 1); m. Genevieve Braham.

Children:

125. —— ——.

126. —— ——.

127. John S. Hager, Jr.

81. GEORGE W. HAGER 4 (Daniel Marion Hager 3, General Daniel
Hager 2, John Hager, Sr. 1); merchant, at Paintsville; m. Sarah
———.
Children:
128. George Hager, Jr.

81-A. George W. Hager; d. March 11, 1926; m. Ida Gullett.
Children:
129. Georgen Hager.
130. Daniel Marion Hager.
131. Mariana Hager.
132. Samuel Patton Hager.

84. EUGENE HAGER 4 (Daniel Marion Hager 3 and his wife, Jessegat T. Vaughan, General Daniel Hager 2, John Hager, Sr. 1); traveling salesman, merchant at Paintsville; local politician; m. Alice
Perry, daughter of John C. Perry.
Children:
133. Eugene Hager, Jr.; m. Annebelle Kise.
134. Steplun Hager.

85. VIRGIE HAGER 4 (Daniel Marion Hager 3, and his wife Jessegat T. Vaughan, General Daniel Hager 2, John Hager, Sr. 1); m.
O. Cook Geiger.   They resided in Paintsville.
Children:
135. Marion Geiger; sometime professor of chemistry, Georgetown
College, Georgetown, Kentucky.
*136. Dorothy Geiger.

86. ROBERT HAGER 4 (Daniel Marion Hager 3 and his wife Jessegat T. Vaughan, General Daniel Hager 2, John Hager, Sr. 1); engaged in business at Louisa, Kentucky; subsequently went West and
became a successful business man; m., in Greenup county, Kentucky,
———————.
Children:
137. ——— ———.
138. ——— ———.

87. RUSSELL HAGER 4 (Daniel Marion Hager 3 and his wife, Jane
Melvin, General Daniel Hager 2, John Hager, Sr. 1); businessman;
conducted Hager Drug Company, Paintsville; m. Dawson Halstead,
of a well-known family of Bardstown, Kentucky.
Children:
139. Nat Halstead Hager.

89. FRANK P. HAGER 4 (Benjamin F. Hager 3, General Daniel
Hager 2, John Hager, Sr., 1); sometime traveling salesman; busi-

nessman, Paintsville; local politician; unsuccessful candidate for Secretary of State of Kentucky on the Democratic ticket in 1927; m. Callie Preston.

Children:

140. Frank Hager, Jr.

91. ADA HAGER 4 (Benjamin F. Hager 2, General Daniel Hager 2, John Hager, Sr. 1); m. John Prindible, a surveyor and engineer. They resided for a time in Paintsville but went East.

Children:

141. Loretta Prindible.
142. John Prindible.

111. JOHN F. HAGER, JR. 4, (John F. Hager, Sr. 3, Henry George Hager 2, and his wife, Nancy Jane Franklin, John Hager, Sr. 1); of Ashland, Kentucky; m. ——— ———.

Children:

143. Betty Bransbury Hager, who was killed August 26, 1927, aged five years, by an automobile.

Fifth Generation

Children:

117. D. MILTON HAGER 5 (Daniel Milton Hager 4, and his wife, Ida Leo Green, Henry George Hager 3 and his wife, Nancy Jane Franklin, General Hager 2, John Hager, Sr. 1); of Ashland, Kentucky; m. Helen Russell.

Children:

144. D. Milton Hager, III.

136. DOROTHY GEIGER 5 (Virgie Hager 4 and her husband, O. Cook Geiger, Daniel Marion Hager 3 and his wife Jessegat T. Vaughan; General Daniel Hager 2, John Hager, Sr. 1); m. Lee Marsh of Paintsville.

Children:

145. Janet Louise Marsh; b. June 12, 1927.

HACKWORTH FAMILY OF FLOYD COUNTY

This is a local surname, 'of Hackworth', that is, the worth of the farmstead of Hake. The family is of English extraction and was seated in England in very early times as is evidenced by the Hundred Roll which bears the names of Peter de Hakeworth and John de Hakeworth, County Devon, 1273. Members of the family emigrated from England to Virginia in early Colonial days and were numerous in Bedford County, that colony in the middle 1700s. In Virginia they defended the colony in all its wars and supported the cause of American Independence.

Augustine Hackworth and William Hackworth had service in Thomas Buford's Company of Bedford County (Virginia) militia and were in the battle at Point Pleasant (October 10, 1774) between the Virginia troops under General Andrew Lewis, and a strong Indian Army led by the Shawnee chief, Cornstalk. Thomas Hackworth had service in the Revolutionary War in Captain Trigg's Company of militia.

THE HACKWORTH FAMILY OF EASTERN KENTUCKY

Members of the Hackworth family migrated and settled in Eastern Kentucky in early pioneer days, the exact time not certainly known. The earliest available records, the U. S. Census of Floyd County for 1810, bear the names of John Hackworth and Jeremiah Hackworth as heads of families. John Hackworth and his wife were then over 45 years of age; and living in the household were eight sons and three daughters. Jeremiah Hackworth and his wife were then between 26 and 45 years of age; and living in the household were their two sons. Apparently John Hackworth was the ancestor of a great many of the Eastern Kentucky Hackworths.

Members of the Hackworth family married into some of the import and influential pioneer families of Eastern Kentucky, among others, the Haywoods, the Laynes, the Meades, the Pattons, the Ratliffs and the Wittens. The family became numerous and spread over the entire Eastern section of the state.

MARRIAGES OF THE PIONEER HACKWORTHS
Floyd County

Hackworth, Thomas—Jenny Preece, November 5, 1816.
Hackworth, John—Betsy Allen, February 2, 1829.
Hackworth, George—Elizabeth Franklin, January 17, 1830.
Hackworth, Abner—Doris Patton, May 11, 1831.
Hackworth, George—Polly Hansbrun, October 15, 1833.
Hackworth, Thomas—Lucretia Spradlin, July 26, 1839.
Hackworth, Elizabeth—John W. Walker, January 29, 1835.

Hackworth, Lockey—William Witten, October 24, 1819.
Hackworth, Polly—Moses Meade, October 4, 1810.

Pike County

Hackworth, Tolbert—Lelia Trent, August 31, 1826.
Hackworth, Pleasant—Rachel Ratliff, September 25, 1827.
Hackworth, Preston—Nancy Branham, February 19, 1828.
Hackworth, Jesse—Polly Ratliff, October 7, 1830.
Hackworth, Piety—William Layne, April 24, 1823.

Greenup County

Hackworth, Nancy Ann Elizabeth—William B. Boley, October 29, 1836.
Hackworth, Narotha—John Dixon, May 26, 1838.

THOMAS HACKWORTH, Revolutionary War soldier, appeared in the Bedford County (Virginia) Court on April 11, 1833,[1] and made declaration for a pension on account of his war services, wherein he stated, among other things, that he was 70 years of age; that he entered the service in March 1781, under Captain Alexander Clemins and Lieutenant Conrad Speece as a drafted militiaman; that he left his home in Bedford County, Virginia, and reported at New London for duty to guard magazines there; and was in the service for three months when he was discharged in June, 1781; that he was again drafted for service in July or August, 1781, and served in Captain John Trigg's company of the regiment commanded by Colonel Tucker; that he marched to Yorktown, Virginia and guarded prisoners surrendered there as they were being taken from place of surrender to Winchester, Virginia; that he was discharged in October, 1781, and subsequently returned to his home in Bedford County. Other records show that Thomas Hackworth removed from Bedford County, Virginia, to Greenup County, Kentucky, in November, 1837, for the reason his children had previously removed to that state.

The U. S. Census of Greenup County for the year 1850 shows the following with respect to John Hackworth, apparently a son of Thomas Hackworth, Revolutionary soldier:

HACKWORTH, JOHN, aged 41; farmer, b. in Virginia. Sarah Hackworth (wife) aged 40; b. in Virginia.

Children:

William T. Hackworth, aged 22; b. in Virginia.
Tabitha Hackworth, aged 18; b. in Virginia.
James Hackworth, aged 13; b. in Virginia.
Reuben Hackworth, aged 12; b. in Kentucky.
Charles Hackworth, aged 8; b. in Kentucky.
Joseph Hackworth, aged 5; b. in Kentucky.
Elias Hackworth, aged 7 months; b. in Kentucky.

GREEN HAYWOOD HACKWORTH, lawyer and jurist; b. near Prestonsburg, Floyd County, Kentucky, January 23, 1883, son of Jonathan T. and Lydia (Haywood) Hackworth and grandson of Benjamin and Mahala (Tussey) Hackworth; educated at Willard (Kentucky) graded and high schools; Valparaiso University, LL.B., and A. B.; Doctor of Laws of Universities of Kentucky and (honorary) Valparaiso.

When in young manhood he completed a commercial course at Valparaiso University and for some time thereafter he engaged in business activities at Huntington, West Virginia. He passed a Civil Service examination and was appointed a clerk in the Civil Service Commission. Washington, D. C., that year when he removed with his family to Washington. was admitted to the bar of the District of Columbia and of the Supreme Court of the United States, 1915; appointed attorney, Department of State, Washington, D. C. 1916; was Assistant Solicitor, same department, 1918-1925; counsel for the United States, 1922-1925, in all matters coming before the International Joint Commission under the Boundary Waters Treaty of 1909, between the United States and Great Britain; on special mission to Lausanne, Switzerland, 1923, to assist the American delegation in drafting the treaty between the United States and Turkey, and to Madrid, same year. to negotiate treaty of commerce between the United States and Spain; appointed Solicitor of the Department of State. August, 1925: United States delegate to the Hague Conference on the codification of international law, 1930; appointed legal adviser to the Secretary of State, July 1, 1931.[3] serving as such until March, 1946; United States delegate to the eighth International Conference of American States, Lima. 1938; and to the eighth Scientific Congress of American States, Washington. 1940; adviser to the Secretary of State at the second meeting of Ministers of Foreign Affairs, Havana, 1940; United States delegate to the Inter-American Marine Conference, Washington, 1940; accompanied the Secretary of State to the Moscow Conference, 1943: was a member of the United States delegation at the Dumbarton Oaks Conference on international organization, Washington, 1944; adviser to the United States delegation at the Conference of American States on problems of war and peace, Mexico City, 1945; Chairman of the United Nations' Committee of Jurists which met in Washington in April, 1945. to prepare a draft of the Statute for the International Court of Justice; adviser to the United States delegation at the United Nations Conference on international organization, San Francisco, April-June, 1945; senior Advisor of the United States delegation at the first part of the First Session of the General Assembly of the United Nations, London, 1946.

On the 6th of February, 1946, Judge Hackworth was elected a Judge of the International Court of Justice by the General Assembly and the Security Council of the United Nations and was chosen by lot drawn by the Secretary-General for a six year term[4] upon the expiration of which he was reelected for a full term of nine years.

He has contributed articles on international and constitutional law to various periodicals, and is the author of a *"Digest of International Law"*, 8 volumes, (1944).

He is a member of the American Society of International Law, the American Bar Association and the Permanent Court of Arbitration.

He has been a member of the Christian (Disciples) Church since boyhood and presently is a member of the National Christian Church, Washington, D. C.

Green Haywood Hackworth m. at Huntington, West Virginia, April 30, 1908, Miss Clara E. Christy, b. June 28, 1890, daughter of Charles C. and Susan B. Christy. Home: 3714 Morrison Street, N. W., Chevy Chase, D. C. Two children were b. to this union: Earl Christy and Helen Mary.

EARL CHRISTY HACKWORTH, lawyer, was b. in Washington, D. C., August 15, 1909; educated in the Washington schools, graduating from the Central High School, 1928; was graduated from George Washington University, A. B., with honors, 1934, and from Harvard University, LL.B., 1938; was admitted to the bar, 1938; entered U. S. Government service, Department of Commerce, Legal Office, 1939; later transferred to Department of State and was promoted to Assistant Chief of the Economic and Financial Division, 1940, which position he was holding at time of his death, June 14, 1946. Interment Lincoln Memorial Cemetery, Washington, D. C. area; unm.

HELEN MARY HACKWORTH was b. in Washington, D. C., October 30, 1914; educated in Washington schools, graduating from Western High School, 1933, and later attended George Washington University for two years; was m. June 8, 1936, to Robert L. Swope, Treasurer, Southern Oxygen Company, b. August 1, 1913. Two children have been b. to this union: Robert H. Swope, student, b. February 21, 1938, and Richard E. Swope, student, b. May 8, 1941.

Residence 4 East Blackthorn Street, Chevy Chase, Maryland.

---

[1] "The National Archives", Washington, D. C.

[2] Ibid.

[3] "Who's Who in Kentucky, 1936", edited by Mary Young Southard and Ernest C. Miller, The Standard Printing Company, Louisville, Kentucky, p. 172.

[4] Year Book, International Court of Justice, 1946-1947", pp. 45-46.

HAMPTON FAMILY OF PRINCE WILLIAM CO., VA., AND BOYD COUNTY, KY.

This is a local or place name, 'of Hampton'. There are at least thirteen parishes of this name in England, representing the dioceses of Worcester, London, Hereford, Oxford, Exeter and Lichfield.

The Hundred Rolls and other records of England bear the names of—

John De Hampton, Co. Somerset, 1273.
William deHampton,Co.Huntington, 1273.
Nicholas de Hampton, Co. Wiltshire, 1273.
Philip de Hampton, Co. Cambridge, 1273.
Geoffrey de Hampton, Co. Lincoln, 1273.
A marriage license was issued to John Hampton in London, 1575.

1. One WILLIAM HAMPTON was the progenitor of a large family of Hamptons some descendants of whom settled in Northeastern Kentucky about 1800. He was b. in England in 1586 and d. in Gloucester County, Virginia, in 1682. He was a member of the ancient family of Hampton of Middlesex and Stafford Counties, England, and came to Virginia in 1620 on the ship Bono Novo and was followed the next year by his wife, Joan, and their three children who came over on the ship Abigail.

William Hampton had a son, 2. Thomas, b. in Virginia. pril 16, 1623, and d. in James City County, that colony, who was an Episcopal minister and whose eldest son, 3. lived at Hampfield in Gloucester County and moved to King William County, Virginia, where he d. in 1718. His son, 4. John, Jr., b. June 3, 1683, was the ancestor of General Wade Hampton of South Carolina. 4. John Hampton, Jr., had a son,5. Henry, b. October 5, 1721, in King William County, d. at his home at Buckland, Prince William County, March 27, 1778, who was half-brother of Sarah, the wife of Judge George Newman Brown (See Brown Family of Boyd County, Kentucky). 5. Henry Hampton acquired an interest in the Savage Grant. In his will he refers to "800 acres of soldiers land which I purchased", already allotted, being upon the Sandy Creek below the mouth of the Great Kanawha. This interest was devised to a son, 6. Dr. Cary Henry Hampton, b. November 16, 1754, d. in August, 1840, who came out to the lands about 1802. (He dropped the name Cary after his father's death.) He had service in the Revolutionary War as assistant surgeon or surgeon's mate.[1] Fifteen Hamptons had service as officers or soldiers in the Virginia Forces in the Revolution.[2]

Dr. Hampton began to dispose of this land very early and the last portion of tract 38 was sold in 1821. He had his home on the Ohio River East of 16th Street, Huntington, on the high ground on which Marshall College is now located, and his grandson, Oliver Hampton, who attended that college in 1850 said that at that time some remains of the old house were still noticeable, as well as some of the snags of the cedar trees that had stood in front of it

The Hamptons were among the earliest pioneers of Northeastern Kentucky and have always been regarded as one of the most notable families of that section. They are of English descent; some of them came to America before the Revolutionary War and have spread from New York and Pennsylvania all over the Southern and Western States.[3]

    6. DR. HENRY HAMPTON reared a large family of sons:
*7. Anthony Hampton.
*8. William Hampton.
    9. Dr. Hampton; migrated to California.
10. Dr. Hampton; migrated to Texas.
11. ———— Hampton, son; migrated to Iowa.
*12. Levi J. Hampton.

    7. DR. ANTHONY HAMPTON, physician, was b. in Virginia about 1787; m. Susanna ————. b. in Virginia, about 1788.

Living in the household, apparently children, in 1850 as shown by the U. S. Census of Wayne County, Virginia, for that year were:
13. Eliza E. Hampton, aged 42.
14. Helen M. Hampton, aged 20.
15. William Hampton, aged 17.
16. John D. Hampton, aged 14.

A daughter of Dr. Anthony Hampton m. Col. John L. Zeigler who was living on Doc's Creek taking care of his aged in-laws when the Civil War broke out. Doc's Creek, formerly known as White's Creek, empties into the Big Sandy not far from Neal's station. Dr. Henry Hampton disposed of his holdings in the Catlettsburg area and spent his last days with his son, Dr. Anthony Hampton, on Doc's Creek.

    8. WILLIAM HAMPTON, farmer, minister of the Methodist Church and man of affairs generally, was b. in Cabell County, Virginia, now Wayne County, West Virginia, in 1808, and d. in Boyd County, Kentucky. He was one of the most useful and honorable citizens of the Catlettsburg area. For nearly fifty years he was a useful lay preacher of the Methodist Church. He m., first, Sarah Buchanan, b. in Kentucky, 1808, d. in Boyd County, Kentucky, 1874 who descended from an ancient and honorable family of Scotland and was of the same lineage as President James Buchanan. After her death Mr. Hampton m., secondly, Mrs. Salena Mason. There were no children by this second marriage.

Children of William Hampton and his wife, Sarah (Buchanan) Hampton, living in the household and approximate dates of birth as shown by the U. S. Census of Greenup County for 1850 and of Boyd County for 1860:
*17. George S. Hampton; b. 1831.

*18. William O. Hampton; b. 1835.
 19. Joseph N. Hampton; b. 1837.
 20. Eliza M. Hampton; b. 1839.
*21. John W. Hampton; b. 1842.
*22. Charles H. Hampton; b. 1845.
*23. Wade Hampton; b. 1848.
*24. Frances C. Hampton; b. 1851.

12. LEVI J. HAMPTON, tradesman, was b. in Virginia in 1817. He went to Brown County, Ohio, where he m. Elizabeth Henderson, b. in Ohio, 1820. He soon afterward returned to the Catlettsburg, Kentucky area and ever afterward made the place his home, being sometimes engaged in timbering, timber-dealing, general trading and conducting a hotel.

He was a man of ardent temperament, of determination and pursued with all his might any course decided upon. A staunch Whig in politics, he was equally ardent in his support of Southern institutions. A great admirer of the statesman, Henry Clay, in a meeting of the stockholders of the Kentucky Iron, Coal and Manufacturing Company held on April 7, 1854, he moved that present Ashland, Kentucky, just then laid out, be named for the home of the great statesman, which motion was carried by the vote of a majority of the stockholders.[4] When the issue of secession was raised in the South he declared for the Union and was enrolled in the 39th Kentucky Regt. Volunteer Infantry October 27, 1862; was made adjutant of the regiment; and was killed in action, December 4, 1862, in Floyd County.[5]

Children living at home and approximate dates of birth as shown by the U. S. Census of Greenup County for 1850 and of Boyd County for 1860:
*25. Julia Hampton; b. in Kentucky, 1840.
*26. Amelia Hampton; b. 1843.
*27. Mary Hampton; b. 1845.
*28. Millard F. Hampton; b. 1849.
*29. Elizabeth Hampton; b. 1854.

17. George S. Hampton; migrated to Missouri where he engaged in agricultural pursuits.

18. WILLIAM OLIVER HAMPTON, lawyer, public official and timber dealer, was b. in Catlettsburg, Kentucky, March 25, 1835, and d. in Ashland, June 3, 1905; educated in the public schools of Catlettsburg and at Marshall College, Huntington, West Virginia; served as clerk of the Boyd (County) Circuit Court from 1865 to 1875; established and laid out Hampton City which was later embraced by Catlettsburg; m. at Grayson, Kentucky, May 21, 1862, Mary Adaline Ward, b. near Grayson, October 31, 1841, and d. at Catlettsburg, April 27,

1886, daughter of Jackson Brown Ward and his wife, Louisa Ward. (See Ward family of Carter and Greenup Counties.)
Children:
30. Louisa Adeline Hampton; b. October 2, 1867; d. at age of four.
31. William Jackson Hampton, abstracter of land titles, was b. at Catlettsburg, Kentucky, December 28, 1874, and d. at his residence in Ashland, Kentucky, April 10, 1938; m. at Grayson, Kentucky, January 1, 1919, Miss Mary Quince Stovall, daughter of Dr. J. Q. Stovall and his wife, Mary (Watts) Stovall, who moved from Beckley, West Virginia, to Grayson, Kentucky, in May 1891. Mary Quince Stovall was b. in Beckley, West Virginia; educated principally in the public schools of Carter County, Kentucky, and for a number of years was engaged in teaching in that county. After the death of her husband, she continued abstracting land titles for a time. No children were b. to this union.

32. SALLIE BUCHANAN HAMPTON was b. in Catlettsburg, Kentucky, September 2, 1876, and d. in Ashland, Kentucky, April 8, 1920; m., September 7, 1897, Wallace Hankes, a minister of the Gospel.
Children:
——— Hankes; d. in infancy.

FRANCIS HAMPTON HANKES, b. in Ashland, Kentucky, November 3, 1900; m. August 26, 1931, Mabel Irene Lewis, b. at Berea, Kentucky, March 9, 1899.
Children:
Betty Jane Hankes; b. in Oakland, California, November 24, 1939.
Lewis Hampton Hankes; b. in Washington, D. C., March 27, 1942. They reside in Falls Church, Virginia.
33. Frances Barnett Hampton was b. at Catlettsburg, Kentucky, July 30, 1880; m. Duncan D. McCosh of Toronto, Canada, September 22, 1919. Residence, Toronto, Canada. No children.

21. JOHN W. HAMPTON, lawyer and minister of the Methodist Episcopal Church, South; b. at Catlettsburg, Ky., May 6, 1842, d. January 19, 1912, and was buried at Ashland, Ky.; practiced law with great success until 1882 when he abandoned the legal profession and entered the ministry of the Methodist Episcopal Church, South; filled the pulpits of that church at Charleston, West Virginia, and other places with great acceptability and was the popular pastor of the M. E. Church, South, in Ashland; m. at Ashland, July 4, 1871, Louisa Virginia Ireland, b. May 5, 1849, and d. April 7, 1911, daughter of Judge William C. Ireland.
Children:
34. Ireland Hampton, b. in Ashland, Kentucky, April 6, 1872. d. July 6, 1943, and was buried at Ft. Worth, Texas; m. in 1897, Marion Kager, of Fort Worth, who d. November 11, 1910, and was b. there.

Children:

(a) John Howard Hampton, b. at Ft. Worth, Texas, January 16, 1898; m. August 26, 1929, Valvera Moore of Lott, Falls County, Texas, who was b. at Lott, Texas, February 14, 1906. Their daughter, Marian Elise Hampton, was b. in Dallas, Texas, August 20, 1935. They reside at Lubbock, Texas, and he owns and operates a ranch of registered hereford cattle in San Miguel County, New Mexico.

(b) Ireland Hampton, Jr., was b. at Ft. Worth, Texas, December 23, 1902, and d. December 27, 1943; m. Annie Laurie Brown of Houston, Texas. Two children were b. to this union:

Annie Laurie Hampton, b. September 23, 1935, and Lee Hampton, b. November 22, 1936, both of whom reside with their mother in Ft. Worth.

35. PAMELIA HAMPTON was b. in Kentucky, August 19, 1877, and d. at Thomas, West Virginia, June ——, 1925; m., June 3, 1902, Dr. Joseph Lyon Miller, b. in Mason County, West Virginia, in 1875.

Children:

Henderson Hampton Miller, b. at Thomas, West Virginia, February 18, 1903; m. Helen Sherman in 1926. Residence, New York City. No children.

Ireland Fielding Miller (the other twin) was b. at Thomas, West Virginia, February 18, 1903; has been m. twice; no children; resides in Wichita, Kansas, and is employed by the Chelcott-Watnor Pharmaceutical Laboratories there.

John Hampton Miller, physician, was b. in Ashland, Kentu ky April 12, 1906. He is a heart specialist and is connected with the Laconia Clinic at Laconia, New Hampshire; twice m.; his second wife being Frances Mansfield Taylor. One child, Henderson Ireland Miller, b. April 26, 1940. Residence, Laconia, New Hampshire.

22. CHARLES H. HAMPTON, capitalist and trader, particularly in timber, was b. at Catlettsburg, Kentucky, December 8, 1844, and d. in that city, February 16, 1889; m., March 20, 1866, Lucy Mead, b. 1845, d. at Asheville, North Carolina, May 30, 1909.

Children:

36. Edgar Mead Hampton; b. December 13, 1866, and d. at Huntington, West Virginia, July 9, 1933; m., August 17, 1920, Beatrice Wilson Riley of Lawrenceburg, Ohio. No children.

37. John W. Hampton; b. December 11, 1867; m. Betty Berry at Abilene, Texas, August 24, 1892; one child, James Miller Hampton; b. December 22, 1893, resides at 1100 Page Street, Berkeley, California.

38. Sarah Elizabeth Hampton; b. March 22, 1870, and d. October 3, 1890; m. Harry Hager, March 19, 1889. Their only child, Harry Hampton Hager, was b. December 22, 1889, and d. July 26, 1892.

39. James Miller Hampton; b. May 2, 1872, and d. November 13, 1890.

40. Jennie Cook Hampton; b. January 28, 1877, and d. September 27, 1904; m. Will R. Howard, September 9, 1897. Their only child, Elizabeth Naomi Hampton, b. June 20, 1900, m. December 23, 1923, Horton Lisenby, a graduate of Tulane University. They have two adopted daughters : Marie, aged 10 and Ann, aged 9. Residence, Panama City, Florida.

41. Kate Honshell Hampton; b. November 10, 1880, and d. at Russell, Kentucky, March 13, 1895.

42. Charles H. Hampton, Jr., b. March 8, 1882, and d. at Asheville, North Carolina, December 7, 1909.

43. Joseph Hall Hampton; b. September 4, 1884, and d. at Catlettsburg, Kentucky, October 14, 1884.

23. WADE HAMPTON, the youngest son, migrated to Missouri, where he engaged in agriculture.

24. FRANCES (FANNIE) C. HAMPTON; b. at Catlettsburg, Kentucky, February 22, 1851; and d. September 2, 1881; and was b. at Catlettsburg; m., September 8, 1869, Dr. William C. Barnett, b. in Kentucky, July 2, 1842; d. April 4,1865; and was buried at Catlettsburg.

Children:

44. William A. Hampton; b. June 24, 1870; d. February 17, 1890; unm.

45. Harry Hampton; b. October 1, 1871; d. July 23, 1872.

46. Frank B. Hampton; b. August 3, 1875; d. June 7, 1876.

47. ——— Hampton, son; moved to Tennessee where he reared a family.

25. JULIA HAMPTON; m. Henry J. Whitman, a merchant of Omaha, Nebraska.

26. AMELIA HAMPTON; m. O. P. Hawes, a lawyer and member of the U. S. House of Representatives from Omaha.

27. Mary Hampton; m. Capt. Matthew Scovill, steamboat operator and owner of the steamboat "Shreveport".

28. MILLARD F. HAMPTON; graduated from Asbury College (now Depauw University); engaged in merchantile pursuits for a time; subsequently was deputy clerk of the Boyd Circuit Court under his cousin, William O. Hampton, and succeeded him in that office, serving for twelve years; member of the Independent Order of Odd Fellows; active member of the Presbyterian Church; a Democrat in politics; m. the eldest daughter of Capt. Washington Honshell, steamboat operator.

29. ELIZABETH HAMPTON; m., went West and prospered.

1 John H. Gwathmey, Historical Register of Virginians in the Revolution, 1775-1783, p. 343.
2 Ibid.
3 William Ely, The Big Sandy Valley, pp. 171-177.
4 Minute Book of the Kentucky I. C. and Mf'g. Co.
5 Report of the Adjutant General of Kentucky, 1861-1866, Vol. II, pp. 384-5.

HANNAH

1. JAMES W. HANNAH, lawyer, was the ancestor of a branch of the family of Elliott County, Kentucky. He was b. in Virginia in 1824; came to Kentucky and studied law in the office of and under the supervision of Judge James M. Rice of Louisa, Lawrence County; was admitted to the bar and located at Martinsburg, county seat of Elliott County, for the practice of his profession. When Elliott County was formed and organized, he was appointed county attorney for the county. He m. Elector ———, b. in Virginia in 1836.

Children living at home and approximate dates of birth as shown by the U. S. Census of Elliott County for 1870:

2. Rice Hannah; b. in Virginia, 1856.

*3. Jefferson B. Hannah; b. in Virginia, 1859.

4. Anna W. Hannah; b. in Kanawha County, W. Va., 1862; m. Rufus H. Van Sant.

3. JEFFERSON B. HANNAH, lawyer and judge, was b. in Virginia, probably in Kanawha County, now West Virginia; studied law; was admitted to the bar and practiced his profession for many years with distinction and success at Martinsburg, the county seat of Elliott County.

Judge Hannah was a Democrat and held many public offices of honor and trust and filled all of them creditably and well. He served as county attorney of Elliott County; represented Carter, Elliott and Greenup Counties in the State Senate; was elected and served as Circuit Judge of the 32nd Judicial District for several years and was judge of the Court of Appeals of Kentucky for a time.

Judge Hannah located at Ashland, Kentucky, and resumed the practice of law during the latter period of his life. He m. Miss Henry of Morgan County, Kentucky.

HARKINS FAMILY, OF FLOYD COUNTY

1. HUGH HARKINS was the ancestor of the Harkins family of Eastern Kentucky. He was b. in Pennsylvania in 1809 and migrated and settled at Prestonsburg, Floyd County, Kentucky, in the 1830's. He received a good English education in his youth and learned the saddlery trade but having an aptitude for the legal profession, he studied law and in 1857 was admitted to the bar at Prestonsburg where he practiced his profession and worked more or less at his trade during his long life. He was a man of refinement and considerable reading and was much respected for his many good qualities as neighbor, businessman and citizen. He d. in 1869. He was a justice of the peace of Floyd County, 1835, and county attorney, 1863. He m. Maranda James in Floyd County, September 26, 1835.[1]

Children and approximate dates of birth as shown by the U. S. Census of Floyd County for 1850 and 1860:

*2. John Harkins; b. 1836.
3. Elizabeth Harkins; b. 1839.
4. Emily Harkins; b. 1841.

2. JOHN HARKINS, lawyer, was b. at Prestonsburg in 1836. He was well educated and being especially endowed with mental qualifications requisite for the legal profession, he studied law and was admitted to the bar at Prestonsburg in 1860, where he almost immediately took high rank as an attorney. From that time until the commencement of the fatal malady which ended his short but busy and useful life, August 25, 1871, he constantly rose in the estimation of the people as one of the brilliant lawyers of his time and place. He was an ardent Republican in politics,[2] and was Master Commissioner of the Floyd Circuit Court. His son:

5. Walter Scott Harkins, lawyer, was born at Prestonsburg, Kentucky, September 25, 1857; educated in the public schools of Prestonsburg and at Centre College, Danville, Kentucky; studied law in the office of the late John F. Hager, Ashland, Kentucky; admitted to the bar in 1877, and locating in his home town of Prestonsburg, he practiced his profession with great distinction and success in the State and Federal Courts of Kentucky for over forty years. Serving one term as county attorney for Floyd County, he never thereafter sought political office but devoted his time and energies to his profession and other activities. He organized the Bank of Josephine at Prestonsburg in 1891 (named in honor of his wife) and was its first president and continued in that position until his death. He was among the earliest to realize the prospective values of the hidden mineral wealth in the hills of his section and with prudent foresight accumulated large ownership of timber, coal, oil and gas lands and rights therein. He was associated with the late Col. John C. C. Mayo in developing

the mineral resources of Eastern Kentucky. He was public-spirited and fostered every movement calculated to advance the material prosperity and well-being of the Big Sandy Country. To this spirit more than any other contributing cause the people of Prestonsburg owe the beautification of their city in the fine building of the Bank of Josephine, the number of fine residences (including his home which cost about $65,000) and the handsome church edifice of the Methodist Episcopal Church, South, where he and those of his spiritual faith worshipped.

Mr. Harkins was hospitable without limit, of a kindly disposition and uniformly courteous to all. He d. February 20, 1920. Interment at Prestonsburg.

Mr. Harkins was m. at Prestonsburg in 1880 to Josephine Davidson, daughter of Joseph Morgan and Mary Amanda (Hatcher) Davidson. (See Davidson in Lackey Family.) Josephine Davidson was b. at Prestonsburg, July 27, 1859; was educated in the public local school and figured prominently and wielded great influence in the intellectual, moral and social affairs of her home city.

Children:

*6. Joseph Davidson Harkins.

7. Mary Elizabeth Harkins; m. Dr. G. L. Howard; residence Huntington, West Virginia.

8. Josephine Anna Harkins; m. I. B. Browning of Ashland. She is a talented musician; and for many years has given of her time, talents and energy to the advancement of the Order of the Eastern Star and presently is Right Worthy Grand Trustee of the General Grand Chapter of the organization.

*9. Walter Scott Harkins, Jr.

6. JOSEPH DAVIDSON HARKINS, lawyer, was b. at Prestonsburg, April 24, 1884; educated in the public schools of Prestonsburg; at Hogsett Military Institute, Danville, Kentucky; at Randolph Macon Academy, Bedford, Virginia; was graduated from Centre College, Danville, Kentucky, 1904; and from the University of Virginia with degree of LL.B. in 1906; was admitted to the bar and formed a partnership with his father with whom he was associated until the death of the latter. He is a wise and reliable counselor and an able and skillful advocate.

Aside from his legal practice, he engaged in many business activities: Vice-president of the Bank of Josephine. In 1920 he organized and financed the Pennsylvania Oil and Gas Company, capitalized at $3,000,000 and was elected its vice-president. He constructed a pipe line from Sitka, Johnson County, to Maytown, Floyd County, by which means all the gas in the Beaver Creek district was made available for use in Louisville. The business was sold to the Louisville Gas and Electric Company.

Mr. Harkins is a member of the Methodist Episcopal Church, South; is affiliated with the Elks Lodge at Catlettsburg and is a Mason, being a member of Zebulon Lodge No. 273, F. & A. M. at Petersburg, Pikeville Chapter, Ashland Commandery and Covington Shrine and Consistory. He organized the Rotary Club at Prestonsburg and was its president for first ten years.

On January 1, 1908, Mr. Harkins was m. to Miss Reca Baker, daughter of George W. Baker of Mt. Vernon, Kentucky.

Children:

10. Joseph Davidson Harkins, Jr.
11. Walter Scott Harkins, III.

9. WALTER SCOTT HARKINS, JR., was b. at Prestonsburg, July 3, 1898; educated in public schools of Prestonsburg and at Kentucky Military Institute, Prestonsburg; attended school in Lexington, Kentucky, and was student at Centre College; later entered Harvard Law School but was called home owing to illness of his father. In 1917 he volunteered for service in World War I and was sent to an officers' training camp near Chicago; was commissioned a second lieutenant of the army and assigned to duty as instructor of Students' Army Training Corps at Butler University, at Indianapolis.

Mr. Harkins m. Miss Margaret Fox of Danville, Kentucky.

Children:

12. Montgomery Scott Harkins.
13. William Fox Harkins.

---

[1] William Ely, "The Big Sandy Valley", pp. 247-249.
[2] Ibid.

HARRIS FAMILY OF FLOYD COUNTY

1. EDWIN LANIER HARRIS, a native of Georgia, was the ancestor of a branch of the Harris family, members of whom settled in Floyd County, Kentucky. His mother was a Lanier of the same family as the Southern poet, Sidney Lanier. On the paternal side he was of the same family as Isham G. Harris, Governor of Tennessee.

Edwin Lanier Harris m. Elizabeth Logan, daughter of Col. John Logan and Jane (McClure) Logan. Col. John Logan was a brother to General Benjamin Logan, pioneer settler and Indian fighter who settled at St. Asaphs in Kentucky. Jane McClure was of a large Scotch-Irish family that settled in the Valley of Virginia.[1]

Children:
*2. Henry Clay Harris.
*3. Littleton Tazewell Harris.
*4. Harriet Harris.
*5. Lucretia Harris; m. Dr. McMillan of Lexington, Kentucky.

2. HENRY CLAY HARRIS, lawyer and legislator, a man of "naturally good and sprightly mind", settled at Prestonsburg, Kentucky, in the early 1820s for the practice of law. He represented Floyd County in the State House of Representatives, 1834, 1835, 1838 and in the State Senate from 1843 to 1847, when he removed to Covington, Kentucky, and there practiced law until his death. He m. Rhoda Harmon Davis, daughter of John L. Davis and his wife Louisa (Harmon) Davis.

Children:
6. Letitia Harris; m. Robert Richardson of Covington who became distinguished. He served in the Mexican War as private in Cassius M. Clay's Company of Col. Humphrey Marshall's Regiment; practiced law in Covington; was State Representative, 1855-57; and was Superintendent of Public Instruction of Kentucky, 1859-63. He was a life-long Democrat. His father, Samuel Q. Richardson, an able lawyer, was assassinated in the prime of life by John U. Waring. His mother was a daughter of Robert Carter Harrison of Fayette County, Kentucky, whose wife was a sister of the wife of the Hon. John Breckenridge, Attorney General in President Jefferson's cabinet, and a daughter of Col. Joseph Cabell of Virginia. The father of Robert Carter Harrison was Carter Henry Harrison, a younger brother to the signer of the Declaration of Independence, Benjamin Harrison. The wife of Carter Henry Harrison was one of the daughters of Isham Randolph of Dungeness and sister to President Jefferson's mother.

3. LITTLETON TAZEWELL HARRIS, lawyer, was b. in Florida, 1822, and d. at Memphis, Tennessee, 1882. He settled at Prestonsburg,

Floyd County, Kentucky, and about 1843 he m. Mary J. Elliott, daughter of Capt. John Lisle and Jane (Richie) Elliott. (See Elliott Family.)

MARY J. ELLIOTT was b. in 1829 in Kentucky, presumably in Morgan County, and died at Clarendon, Arkansas, at the advanced age of ninety years. She was educated at a young ladies school, Shelbyville, Kentucky. In the 1850s the Harrises went to New Orleans and they resided most of their married life in the South, principally in New Orleans and later at Memphis, Tennessee, Mr. Harris becoming an outstanding lawyer. Both Mr. and Mrs. Harris were interred in a cemetery at Memphis.

Children:

7. Amanda J. Harris; b. in Kĕntucky, 1844.
8. Julia C. Harris; b. in Kentucky, 1848.
9. Ione Harris; b. in Kentucky, 1850.
10. Edwin Lanier Harris, planter and businessman, was b. at Hallettsville, Texas, November 28, 1853, and d. at Clarendon, Arkansas, February 25, 1919. Interment in Elmwood Cemetery, Clarendon. At an early age he moved to Tunica, Mississippi, where he resided until he was thirteen years of age, when he removed to Arkansas. He was a cotton merchant and owner of large plantation and was wealthy for his time and place.

Children:

11. Littleton Tazewell Harris, who resided at Clarendon, Arkansas.
12. Mrs. Julia Houston, who resided at Tunica, Mississippi.

4. HARRIET HARRIS; m., first, Mr. Goodloe.

Children:

13. John Kemp Goodloe; served in the Mexican War in the command of Col. Humprey Marshall; represented Woodford County in the State House of Representatives, 1855 to 1861, and in the State Senate, 1861 to 1865. He was a staunch Union man. Removing to Louisiana, he was appointed United States Attorney for that state which position he held for many years. Returning to Kentucky, he engaged continuously in the practice of law until his death.

4-A. After the death of her husband, Mr. Goodloe, Harriet (Harris) Goodloe m. secondly, Mr. Izett.

Children:

14. Harriet Izett, who m. Rev. A. D. Madeira, a minister of the Presbyterian Church.

---

[1] "The Big Sandy Valley", by William Ely.

HATCHER FAMILY OF FLOYD COUNTY

Although not among the first settlers in the Big Sandy Valley, the Hatchers were by no means late arrivals. James H. Hatcher m. a Miss Peery of Tazewell County, Virginia, and settled at mouth of Mud Creek about 1830. They had a large family of sons who early developed into businessmen and occupied a conspicuous place in the mercantile affairs of the valley. By the mother's side they were connected by consanguinity with many of the leading families of the valley: Mrs. David Borders (see Borders Family); Mrs. "Coby" (Moses, Jr.) Preston, afterward Mrs. Dr. Strong (see Moses Preston Sr. Family); Mrs. K. N. Harris; and Mrs. Arthur Preston (see Moses Preston, Sr. Family). The Hatchers have always been identified with the Methodist Church and most of the family are active members of the Methodist Episcopal Church, South. In politics they are Democrats.[1]

1. JOHN HATCHER was the ancestor of the Hatcher family of the Big Sandy Valley. Migrating from Bedford County, Virginia, he settled in then Floyd County, Kentucky, in the early 1800s. He was a farmer and held public offices of honor and trust, serving as Sheriff of Floyd County from May 16, 1831 to June 16, 1833. He m., presumably in Bedford County, Virginia. However, the name of his wife has not been learned.

Children, among others:

2. JAMES G. HATCHER, was b. in Floyd County, in 1805. He was a farmer and merchant, conducting general stores in several localities. He served as deputy clerk of Floyd County, 1833. He m. Christina Perry of Tazewell County, Virginia, who was b. in Virginia about 1810 and d. in Floyd County. After the death of her husband, she continued to operate the several general stores.

Children living at home and approximate dates of birth as shown by the U. S. Census of Floyd County for the years 1850 and 1860:

*3. A. J. P. Hatcher; b. in Kentucky, 1832.
4. John L. Hatcher; b. 1834.
5. Eleanor L. Hatcher; b. 1836.
6. James H. Hatcher; b. 1838.
7. Kenas Hatcher; b. 1841.
8. George M. Hatcher; b. 1843.
9. Ferdinand C. Hatcher; b. 1848.
10. Isabella Hatcher; b. 1852.

In the household also lived in 1850 David M. Hatcher, farmer, b. in Virginia, 1831.

3. ANDREW J. HATCHER, farmer and merchant was b. in Floyd County. He was a partner of his father in general merchandising and after death of father he became associated with his mother in that

business. He m. in Floyd County, Mary C. Layne, b. in Kentucky, 1838, d. in Floyd County about 1876, daughter of John L. Layne and his wife, Elizabeth (Priest) Layne.

Andrew J. Hatcher was a Mason and affiliated with Zebulon Lodge No. 375, F. & A. M. at Prestonsburg. The family were members of the Methodist Episcopal Church, South.

Children:

11. John Hatcher; lived in Pikeville.

*12. James Hatcher.

13. Richard Hatcher, farmer; lived at Williamsburg, Ohio.

14. Lizzie Hatcher; m. James Trimble, a banker of Washington, D. C.; d. at age of 28.

12. JAMES HATCHER OF PIKEVILLE; businessman of many activities; largest individual land owner in Pike County and prominent figure in business affairs in the Big Sandy Valley, was b. at mouth of beaver Creek in Floyd County, September 22, 1859; resided in Pikeville; educated in the public schools of that city; went into business for himself at age of 18; owned wholesale house at Pikeville; interested in building steamboat; exploration of timber resources on the Big Sandy River and floated hundreds of rafts of timber down the Big Sandy to the markets at Cincinnati, Louisville and Evansville; owned 3,700 acres of coal lands at Big Shoals where he operated the James Hatcher Coal Company. He built the Pike Hotel at Pikeville in 1916; sold it afterwards built the James Hatcher Hotel in same city.

In religion Mr. Hatcher was a Methodist; in politics a Democrat. He was elected and served as County Court Clerk of Pike County, 1902-1906. He m. in 1889, Miss Octavia Smith, daughter of Jacob Smith. She d. May 2, 1891, on her 21st birthday; interment at Pikeville.

Children:

15. Jacob Hatcher; d. in infancy.[2]

Other Hatchers lived in the Big Sandy Valley:

George F. Hatcher m. Amanda Burns in Floyd County, August 4, 1831. One George F. Hatcher was deputy County Court Clerk of Floyd County in 1833.

John G. Hatcher m. Thursa Stratton in Floyd County, March 1, 1832.

Peggy Hatcher m. Harrison Ratliff in Floyd County, February 22, 1840. (See Ratliff Family.)

Thursa Hatcher m. John W. Powell in Floyd County, September 22, 1843.

John L. Hatcher m. Elizabeth Weddington in Pike County, February 6, 1855. (See Weddington Family.)

[1] William Ely, "The Big Sandy Valley, p. 205.
[2] "History of Kentucky", by Charles Kerr (Editor), Vol. IV, pp. 358-9

HOCKADAY FAMILY OF GREENUP COUNTY

Hockaday is an old Colonial family of Virginia, members of whom came from Virginia to Clark County, Kentucky, in early days. 1. Isaac Hockaday and son *2. John, came to what is now Greenup County, then Mason County, Kentucky, before the county was established and organized. Isaac Hockaday was the first acting clerk of the Greenup County Court, having been appointed clerk pro tem by the justices of peace of the county on February 1, 1804, when the county was organized. John Nichols and Jesse Boone were sureties on his official bond. On the same day and at the same session of the court, on motion of Isaac Hockaday, Clerk of the Court, John Hockaday was permitted to take the necessary oath (as clerk?) with John Nichols, Moses Fuqua and William Lowery as sureties on his official bond. Nothing further is known of Isaac Hockaday. It is presumed that he returned to Clark County. John Hockaday was the first clerk of the county. The Rev. James Gilruth wrote concerning him: "Next above Boone (Daniel) settled John Hockaday. He came to these parts a single man, not far from 1804 or 1805. He was said to possess $3,000 in cash. He kept school for one term in an old cabin between Thomas Hood's and Jesse Boone's. He bought a tract of improved land (I think it was part of the Boone tract), built a hewed log double house with an open entry between nearly as wide as either end was long, shingle roofs and brick chimneys. I mention these things because brick chimneys and shingle roofs were not yet common in these parts and the plan of the house was rather novel. Hockaday obtained the Clerkship of the Court of Greenup County, kept his office in his own house a few miles above Greenupsburg. After living here some years he m. Margaret Donathan, a young lady of good family and of respectable character. On settling here Hockaday commenced improving his land in which he succeeded to a considerable extent. He was considered a good shot with the rifle and enjoyed as a gentleman the chase and the fishing rod, but did not let them interfere with business. He owned some slaves and was never known to use his tongue or his talents to the injury of others. Few men sustained a more amiable and worthy character than John Hockaday." (See Gilruth manuscript herein.)

2. JOHN HOCKADAY m. Margaret Donathan. They purchased a from from Jesse B. Boone lying on the Ohio River above Greenupsburg at present Riverton, the terminal of the Eastern Kentucky Railroad. It is said that Mrs. Juliet Collins, a descendant, is in possession of the deed to the land from Boone to Hockaday, dated 1807, and also of another deed, from the same party, dated 1817 (just before Jesse B. Boone went to Missouri). John and Margaret Hockaday were buried in cemetery on the farm at Riverton and the land has been in possession of the Hockaday family ever since that early day.

Children, among others, of John and Margaret (Donathan) Hockaday:

3. Edwin Hockaday. He lived on the Boone farm. The Eastern Kentucky Railway station was on this land. His children were:

*4. George Hockaday.

*5. James Hockaday.

6. Edwin Hockaday; m. Rebecca Seaton, daughter of John and Mary E. (Rice) Seaton.

7. Martha Hockaday; m. Jefferson McComas of West Virginia.

8. Eugene Hockaday; m. Frances Lake; migrated to Mississippi.

4. GEORGE HOCKADAY; m. Minnie Kouns, daughter of William Smith and Caroline (Van Bibber) Kouns. (See Kouns Family.)

Children:

*9. May Hockaday.

10. Carrie Hockaday; m. Ezekiel Shackleford of Mt. Sterling, Kentucky.

11. Walter Hockaday; m. Julia Dorsey.

12. Edwin Hockaday, Jr., m. Mary Anderson.

13. Juliet Hockaday; m. William Collins, son of Nathaniel and Lydia (Daugherty) Collins.

5. JAMES HOCKADAY; m. Ann Eliza Biggs, daughter of William and Lucy (Davis) Biggs.

Children:

14. Irvine Hockaday; m. Mintie Weddington of Pikeville, Kentucky. (See Weddington Family.)

15. Lucy Hockaday, m. Cyrus Van Bibber, son of Charles and Caroline Van Bibber. They resided in Huntington, West Virginia.

9. May Hockaday, musician and artist; m. Morris Reid, son of Adolphus and Henrietta Reid; resided at Grayson, Kentucky, where Mr. Reid was a merchant and where he died. After his death, Mrs. Reid continued to live at Grayson for some time and taught painting and music. She was a member of the Grayson Christian Church and was one of its most active members. Later she removed to Ft. Pierce, Florida, with her unm. children.

Children:

16. Amelia Reid; member of the Christian Church and for many years organist of the Christian Church at Grayson, Kentucky, and at Ft. Pierce, Florida; unm.

17. Aline Reid; m. John Errett, now deceased, son of Isaac Errett, owner and publisher of the Christian Standard, Cincinnati, Ohio.

18. George Reid.

19. Robert Reid.

20. Julian Reid.

HOOD FAMILY OF GREENUP COUNTY

1. Jasper Hood was the ancestor of the Hood family of Berkeley County, Virginia, (now West Virginia) and of Bourbon, Clark, Montgomery, Mason and Greenup Counties, Kentucky.[1] The place of his birth is not known; nor is anything known concerning his parents. The marriage records of the old Dutch Reformed Church of New York City reveal that he married Tryntje Lucas (Luykas), alias Catrina Andries[2] in June 1696. She was the eleventh of fourteen children baptized in this same church by their parents, Lucas Andrieszen and Aefje Laurens. In the baptismal register of this old church are the baptismal records of five of their children:

Second Generation

2. Jan (John), April 1697.
*3. John (Jan), February 1699.
4. Aefje, February 1701.
*5. Luykas, October 1708.
6. Thomas, August 1711.

It is possible that other children were b. between 1701 and 1708. There is no further record of Thomas Hood. Presumably the first son, John, d. in infancy.

3. John Hood m. Rachel, daughter of Tunis Eliaszen van Benschoten and Gerritje Gerrits, at Kingston, N. Y., October 27, 1718. They migrated to Virginia and were of the 70 families that founded Hopewell Friends Meeting House in Frederick County in 1735. They received land grants in 1772 in that part of Frederick County which was subsequently included in Berkeley County (now West Virginia) when formed in 1772. On June 14, 1744, Rachel Hood qualified as administratrix of the estate of John Hood, deceased. On August 7, 1771, Tunis Hood "sole surviving son and heir of John Hood, deceased" sold to John Pearce 130 acres, being a part of 1175 acres granted to John Hood, Sr., lying along the Potomac River at the mouth of Back Creek. Tunis Hood then moved to Mecklenberg County, North Carolina.

Children: (Third Generation)

7. Theunis (Tunis) Hood, b. at Kingston, N. Y., February 22, 1719.
8. Johnasses Hood, b. at Kingston, N. Y., January 8, 1721.
9. Jacobus Hood, b. at Kingston, N. Y., December 25, 1721.
10. Gerritjen Hood, b. at Kingston, N. Y., January 8, 1727.

The records indicate that there was a daughter Rebecca who m. John Johnson prior to 1757.

5. Lucas Hood followed his brother John to Virginia and also settled in that part of Frederick County that was included in Berkeley

County when formed in 1772. The first record of him found in Frederick County is a promisory note dated November 7, 1760. He patented 133 acres of land on Sleepy Creek, August 26, 1765. His will dated November 13, 1770, and proved May 7, 1771, names "Joanna my beloved wife whole and sole executrix".

The marriage record of Lucas Hood has not been found. However, other records reveal that he m. Johanna van Stockholm.

Children: (Third Generation)

11. Aaron Hood, baptized at Readington, N. J., October 31, 1742.
12. John (Jan) Hood, baptized at Readington, N. J., February 3, 1745.

Other children mentioned in Lucas Hood's will, proved May 7, 1771, sons:

13. Luke Hood.
*14. Andrew Hood.
15. Thomas Hood (youngest); and daughters:
16. Cattren Smith.
17. Leora Francis (also called Lena).
18. Margaret Hood.
19. Hannah Hood.

No further records have been found of son 15 Thomas or of the four daughters. Son Lucas (13 Luke) was paying taxes on 133 acres in Berkeley County and son 12 John on 300 acres as late as 1801.

THE HOOD FAMILY OF KENTUCKY

14. ANDREW HOOD, SR., was b. about 1745 and m. Massa Sudduth prior to 1770. He migrated to Pennsyvania in 1774 and from thence he went to Kentucky about 1784 and settled in that part of Bourbon County (then Fayette) that was included within the boundary of Clark County upon its formation in 1792. He served 18 days in the Revolutionary War as a private under Gen. George Rogers Clark. He was known as Major Hood. However, it is not believed that such rank was bestowed by reason of military service.

Andrew Hood's first appeared on the tax list of Bourbon County May 25, 1787; he was on the tax lists of Clark County from 1793 to 1795 and on the tax lists of Mason County from 1799 to 1803 when Greenup County was formed. He owned 1000 acres on Fox Creek in Fleming County and 250 acres on the Ohio River on which tract he built his home and lived about one half mile above the mouth of Little Sandy River. The local courts were organized and held their sessions for a time in a rough plank shed attached to the north end of Major Hood's home; also in a shed attached to his house Benjamin Chinn kept the first dry goods store on either side of the Ohio River between the Big Sandy and the Big Scioto Rivers.

Major Hood was a respected and good citizen. He took an active part in organizing Greenup County and establishing the county seat, Greenupsburg. He served on the first grand jury empaneled for the county and was appointed a reviewer of the first public road of the county—from a point on the Ohio River opposite the mouth of the Scioto River to the mouth of the Big Sandy River.

Children of Maj. Andrew Hood and his wife Massa (Sudduth) Hood:

Fourth Generation

*20. Lucas Hood, b. in Berkeley County, Virginia, (now West Virginia), July 4, 1770, d. in Clark County, Kentucky, September 30, 1843; m. about 1790, Frances Wills, b. June 25, 1774, d. December 21, 1841, a daughter of Frederick Wills. Both are buried in well-marked graves in the Hood-Ramsey burying ground about four miles from Winchester on Ecton pike on the Joe Stevenson farm. The inscription on the monument marking his grave states that he was in Gen. Harmar's army at its defeat by the Indians (near the site of Ft. Wayne, Indiana in 1790); that he was a spy under Gen. "Mad Anthony" Wayne and was in the battle of August 21, 1794, (on the Maumee River near the site of Toledo, Ohio), where the Indians were completely defeated. He was on the tax lists of Bourbon County for 1792.

21. Lewis Hood. He was on the tax list of Clark County for 1793. The U. S. Census for 1810 shows that he was married, and the head of a house and had several children. He may have been the father of George Hood who m. Susannah Hardman in Clark County, October 25, 1810. One Lewis Hood m. Betsy Railstock in Clark County, September 9, 1842. This could have been a second marriage or the marriage of his son. He d. subsequent to 1831 as he appears on the tax lists for that year.

22. John Hood; m. Margaret Sudduth in Clark County, December 29, 1794, a daughter of Ann Sudduth, who gave her consent to the marriage. He was security on several marriage bonds between 1794 and 1802 and d. pior to 1804.

Apparently he was the father of Ann Hood, who m. James Cast, November 19, 1817, and of Mariah Hood.

23. Sarchet ("Sybbee") Hood; m. Jesse Griffith, October 26, 1796.

*24. Thomas Hood; m. Sarah Pickey; d. about 1825; was on the tax lists of Mason County for 1801, 1802 and 1803 along with his father; he had several children. (See further for children.)

*25. Andrew Hood, Jr., farmer, b. in Kentucky in 1784; lived to an advanced age—some say to 100 years, others to 115. He was buried in the Collins Cemetery on East Fork of Little Sandy; m. in Greenup County, October 19, 1807, Polly (Mary) Cain, b. in Virginia in 1788, a daughter of Jacob Cain. They were parents of fourteen children. (See further.)

26. Rachel Hood; m. Joseph Howe in Greenup County, December 10, 1810. (See Howe family.)

27. Henry Hood; m. Margaret Cain in Greenup County, September 17, 1811. She was a daughter of Robert Cain.

28. Elizabeth Hood; m. Solomon Brown in Greenup County, January 27, 1811.

29. Peggy Hood; m. Cary Clark in Greenup County, August 28, 1818.

30. Martha Hood; m. James Howe in Greenup County. (See Howe Family.)

31. Catharine Hood; m. Solomon Brown in Greenup County, November 3, 1826.

20. CHILDREN OF LUCAS HOOD AND FRANCIS (WILLS) HOOD:

Fifth Generation

*32. Andrew Hood; b. March 31, 1796, d. November 16, 1859 of heart disease; m., first, June 3, 1819, Mariam White, who was b. November 27, 1801, and d. November 30, 1830; m., second, May 12, 1832, Hannah Kerley, who was b. January 16, 1804, and d. September 11, 1848; and m., third, April 9, 1850, Mrs. Ellen McAdams. Andrew Hood was a physician, a member of the Constitutional Convention of 1849-50 and was affiliated with the Masons.

*33. John W. Hood; physician, b. January 1, 1798, d. November 30, 1852; m. Theodosia French, daughter of the pioneer James French.[3] (See further for children.)

*34. William S. Hood, physician; m. Mary Smith, a daughter of Nelson Smith and his wife, Sarah Kirr and granddaughter of David Kirr and his wife Dorothy Rodes. Dorothy Rodes was a daughter of Clifton Rodes, Sheriff of Albemarle County, Va., in 1782, and his wife Sarah Waller, and a granddaughter of Sir Humphrey Waller, Crown Judge of Albemarle County, Va.

35. Frances Hood; m. Dr. Alexander Ramsey, who was b. July 8, 1784, and d. June 5, 1845. Children:

Sixth Generation

35a. John H. B. Ramsey, who d. July 11, 1846, aged 26 years.

35b. Frances Margaret, who m. Seneca Clark and d. November 9, 1846, aged 22 years, 1 month and 21 days.

35c. Mariam E., b. March 23, 1829, d. February 26, 1845.

24. CHILDREN OF THOMAS HOOD AND SARAH (PICKEY) HOOD:

Fifth Generation

39. Elizabeth Hood; m. Eli Piggott in Greenup County, February 10, 1831.

40. William Hood; m. Matilda Horn in Greenup County, December 13, 1831. The U. S. Census for Carter County, 1850, shows William P. Hood aged 45 years; Matilda Hood 44 years; and children

(Sixth Generation) :
40a. James Hood, aged 17.
40b. Charles Hood, aged 15.
40c. Martha Hood, aged 13.
40d. Sarah Hood, aged 11.
40e. Mary Hood, aged 9.
40f. Nancy Hood, aged 6.
40g. William Hood, aged 2.

25. CHILDREN OF ANDREW HOOD, JR., AND MARY (CAIN) HOOD:
Fifth Generation
41. Matilda Hood, b. July 2, 1806; m. Jesse Davidson, April 14, 1826.
42. Jacob Hood, b. July 11, 1808; m., first, Joanna Lewis, November 20, 1829, and second, Phoebe Barker, November 7, 1842.
The U. S. Census of Greenup County, 1850, shows the following concerning his family:
Children—Sixth Generation:
42a. Hezekiah Hood, aged 16.
42b. Nancy A. Hood, aged 13.
42c. Pleasant Hood, aged 10.
42d. "Tabithy" Hood, aged 6.
42e. Bluford Hood, aged 4.
Nancy Barber, aged 72, b. in Virginia, was living with the family.
43. Andrew Hood, b. May 20, 1810.
44. Massa Hood, b. April 7, 1812; m. Robert McGuire, October 11, 1830.
45. Lukus Hood, b. Feb. 14, 1814; m. Zerelda Shropshire, April 26, 1834. The U. S. Census of Greenup County, 1850, shows the following concerning this family:
Elizabeth A. Hood, wife, aged 24.
Children (Sixth Generation)
45a. Charles Hood, aged 8.
45b. John Hood, aged 5.
45c. Nancy J. Hood, aged 3.
46. Thomas Hood, b. January 2, 1816; m. Minerva Piggot, June 1, 1835.

The U. S. Census, 1850, shows the following:
Children (Sixth Generation)
46a. William Hood, aged 13.
46b. Mary J. Hood, aged 10.
46c. Charles Hood, aged 8.
46d. Sarah A. Hood, aged 6.
46e. Eli R. Hood, aged 3.
46f. Martha F. Hood, aged 1.

47. Mariah Hood, b. May 2, 1818; m. John Collins in Greenup County, April 27, 1833. Their daughter

47a. Helen Collins (Sixth Generation) married George Kidd in 1870 and their daughter

47b. Inez Kidd (Seventh Generation) m. Albert Hales, a minister of the Christian Church. After marriage they went to Liverpool, England, where he was pastor of a church on Beaumont Street, that city. When World War I broke out Mrs. Hales returned to the United States and Mr. Hales continued his pastoral work for a time. Subsequently he returned to the United States and was pastor for a church at West Liberty, Ky., for three years and afterwards was pastor of a church at Jackson, Ky. Mrs. Hales lives on a farm on East Fork of Little Sandy.'

48. Sarah Hood, b. June 25, 1820; m. John Akin in Greenup County, May 10, 1836.

49. Mary Ann Hood, b. April 19, 1822; m. Bellas Martin, February 16, 1837.

50. Catharine Hood, b. June 2, 1824; m. L. D. Stewart, December 25, 1838.

51. Alma D. (Amy) Hood, b. July 10, 1826; m. John W. Adams, November 22, 1847.

52. Jesse Hood, b. August 18, 1828.

53. Francis Hood, b. April 27, 1830.

54. William H. O. L. Hood, b. June 11, 1834.

32. Children of Dr. ANDREW HOOD AND MIRIAM (WHITE) HOOD:

Sixth Generation

55. James M. Hood, b. March 30, 1820; m. Louisa Embry, January 11, 1844, d. November 5, 1859.

56. Thomas Jefferson Hood, b. September 26, 1821; m. March 19, 1851, Mary A. Turner, eldest daughter of Maj. S. Turner; d. July 10, 1854. He was a lawyer, and along with his father, a member of the Constitutional Convention of 1849-50. The U. S. Census of Carter County for 1850 shows that he was living in the home of Robert G. Carter of Grayson that county. He wrote his will the day he died and mentioned his children in it but did not name them.

57. Andrew L. Hood, b. February 15, 1823, d. September 25, 1827.

58. William Kerley Hood, b. September 20, 1825; m. October 20, 1846, Elizabeth Simpson; d. February 18, 1890. They had three children, names not known.

Seventh Generation

58a. ———— Hood.

58b. ———— Hood.

58c. ———— Hood.

59. Frances (Fanny) W. Hood, b. September 6, 1827; m., August 5, 1847, Lewis Hampton, son of George and Routt Hampton; d. November 10, 1849.

Children: Seventh Generation

59a. Andrew Hood Hampton, who was the father (Eighth Generation) of Andrew Hood Hampton, Jr., Catherine W. Hampton, b. June 6, 1848, and Miss Fannie Hood Hampton of Winchester, Ky.

Children of DR. ANDREW HOOD AND HANNAH (KERLEY) HOOD:
Sixth Generation

60. Nancy K. Hood, b. June 17, 1833; m. November 26, 1850, W. R. Embry.

61. Miriam W. Hood, b. January 20, 1835; d. September 29, 1915; m. Col. Joseph Thomas Tucker, a lawyer from Vermont.

Children Seventh Generation

61a. Hood Tucker, b. May 22, 1859, who m. Margaret Allen.

61b. Nannie Hood Tucker, b. June 13, 1860, d. 1951, unm.

62. Lucas Andrew Hood, b. October 25, 1836; m. March 7, 1861, Cornelia Chism of Tipton, Mo., where he d. October 20, 1920.

Children (eight) Seventh Generation

62a. Matt Embry Hood; d. at Tipton, Mo., March 3, 1869, aged 3 years and four months. Surviving children mentioned in obituary:

62b. Rev. J. Turner Hood of Geneseco, Ill.

62c. Mrs. A. L. George of Tipton, Mo.

62d. Mrs. R. H. Whittaker of Twin Falls, Idaho.

62e. Mrs. J. S. McLain of Red Rock, Okla.

63. John K. Hood, b. November 22, 1839, d. March 11, 1877.

64. Joseph T. Hood, b. March 28, 1842, d. May 20, 1890; m. a Miss Million. He was a physician, a graduate of Jefferson Medical College of Philadelphia.

Children (Seventh Generation) Names not known

64a. ——— Hood.

64b. ——— Hood.

65. Dr. Richard French Hood, b. June 14, 1844, d. February 11, 1910. No mention in obituary of wife or children but mentions that he was a Mason.

33. Children of DR. WILLIAM S. HOOD AND THEODOSIA (FRENCH) HOOD:
Sixth Generation

*66. Gen. John Bell Hood.

67. William A. Hood; m. in 1855, Susan J. Howell, daughter of David and Rachel Ann Howell, who was b. near Casey Lick, Montgomery County, Ky., May 3, 1838, and d. July 19, 1888. They lived near Mt. Sterling until they moved to Hendersonsville, Tenn., in 1881. They moved to Nashville in 1883.

*68. James Hood.

69. Olivia or Keziah; m. George Owens Graves and lived in Winchester until she d. in 1913.

Children Seventh Generation

69a. Mary Hood Graves; m. a Squires.

69b. Theodosia Graves; m. a Tebbs.

69c. Dr. Spenser Coleman Graves, a physician of St. Louis and one time a professor at University of Pennsylvania, d., unm.

69d. Julia Graves who resided at 273 S. Main St., Winchester, Ky.

34. Children of Dr. William S. Hood and Mary (Smith) Hood: Sixth Generation

70. Dr. William Nelson Hood; m. Clara Hickman; moved to Matagorda Plantation, Washington County, Miss., when he retired in 1841; was killed in explosion of the steamboat "James Jackson" when he was only 49 years old.

71. Dr. Thomas Howard (?) Hood; m. Kate Cummingham; d. in Harrison County, Ky., in 1900.

72. Elizabeth Waller Hood; m. Dr. William R. Fleming; d. in Lexington, Ky., in 1864.

66. John Bell Hood, Confederate soldier, was b. at Owingsville, Bath County, Ky., June 1, 1831, and d. at New Orleans, La., August 30, 1879. Against the wishes of his father, who wished him to study medicine, he entered West Point in 1849 and was graduated, after an indistinguished career as cadet, forty-fourth in a class of fifty-two that included Sheridan, McPherson and Schofield. After brief garrison duty at Ft. Columbus, N. Y., he served two years in California as 2nd Lt. in the 4th Inf., and was transferred to Texas to join the 2nd Cav., then under the care of Lt. Col. Robert E. Lee. Wounded in a scouting expedition against Indians, he was partially incapacitated for two years.

In April 1861, he received his commission; joined the Confederacy and was sent as a 1st Lt. to Yorktown, Va., where Gen. John B. Magruder put him in charge of the Cavalry attached to his forces. By rapid promotions he became a brigadier-general on March 2, 1862, and took command of the Texas Brigade. These troops, which he personally led into action at Gaines Mill, broke the Federal line on June 27, 1862, and won high reputation, which they confirmed by hard successful fighting at Second Manassas and Sharpsburg (Antietam). Following the Maryland campaign, he was promoted a major-general October 11, 1862, partly at the instance of "Stonewall" Jackson and his troops became the first division of Gen. Longstreet's corps. At Gettysburg he was badly wounded in the arm on the afternoon of July the 2nd and before he fully recovered he rejoined his men, enroute to Georgia, and at Chickamauga (September 19-20, 1863), he distinguished himself while directing Longstreet's corps and three divisions of the army of the Tennessee.

Another wound, which necessitated the amputation of the right leg, deprived him of further part in the campaign.

General Hood was made a lieutenant-general on February 1, 1864. to date from the battle of Chickamauga. Crippled as he was, he went to Dalton, Ga., a few days later to take command of one of the corps of the army under Gen. Joseph E. Johnston. Trained to the offensive, he had now to fight under a general who held to the defensive. Previously he had been successful in all his operations but in every battle thereafter he met defeat. In the neighborhood of Marietta, Ga., in the latter half of June, there were a series of fierce contests, and the Union forces were successful. The Confederates were beaten back, but succeeded at last in repulsing a gallant charge at Kenesaw Mountain. By the middle of July, Gen. Johnston reached Atlanta, having conducted his orderly retreat in a masterly manner. President Davis, demanding an aggressive policy, relieved Gen. Johnston, on July 18, 1864, and put Gen. Hood in command. Hood urged the President to defer the order of Johnston's removal until the impending battle at Atlanta was over, but Davis refused. Johnston left Army headquarters and Hood struck promptly against Sherman on July 20th and 22nd. Failing to drive back his adversary, he had to submit to seige in Atlanta, where he was forced to retire on September 1st. After the battle of Jonesboro it was made clear that Sherman would soon envelop him.

Sherman was strong enough to detach Thomas and Schofield, with a stronger force than Hood commanded, while the remainder of the Federal army rested preparatory to the march to the sea which Hood did not anticipate. Hood moved into Tennessee abandoning the campaign against Sherman and amid misgivings of Pres. Davis and Gen. Beauregard who had been given general supervision of the operations, launched operations against Thomas and Schofield. At Franklin, Tennessee, November 30th, Hood fought a sanguinary drawn battle with the advanced portion of Thomas's army under Schofield. He encountered Thomas himself in the great battle of Nashville, December 15th and 16th in which his army was routed and scattered.

General Hood asked to be relieved and on January 23, 1865, he said farewell to his troops. On the way to the Trans-Mississippi Department with orders to collect troops, learning of the surrender of Gen. Lee, he rode into Natchez and surrendered on May 31, 1865. Going to Texas, which he regarded as his adopted state, he was able to make good business connections and soon established himself as factor and commission merchant in New Orleans and seemed to be very successful but unwise ventures soon reduced him to poverty.

In physique Gen. Hood was commonding and dignified with ample ability to impress soldiers. As a commander he undoubtedly deserved the reputation he won in Virginia as "a fighting general and admirable leader of a brigade or a division in action"; but if he possessed the higher military qualities, they were marred by irrepressible rashness.

Gen. Hood m. Anna Marie Hennen in New Orleans, in 1868, who d. August 24, 1879, presumably of yellow fever. Gen. Hood and several of his family were stricken and he and his eldest daughter d. on August 30, 1879. He was buried in New Orleans. Ten children survived him among them twins three weeks old.[5]

Children of GEN. JOHN BELL HOOD AND ANNA MARIE (HENNEN) HOOD:

Seventh Generation

73. Lydia Marie Hennon Hood.
74. Anna Belle Hood.
75. Ethel Genevieve Hood.
76. John Bell Hood.
77. Duncan Norbert Hood.
78. Marian Marie Hood.
79. Lillian Marie Hood.
80. Odile Musson Hood.
81. Ida Richardson Hood.
82. Oswald Hood.
83. Anna Gertrude Hood.

68. JAMES HOOD, lawyer, b. in Montgomery County, Kentucky, about 1829; m. about 1851 Emily C. Gatewood of Montgomery County, who was b. about 1832 and d. subsequent to 1863 as her youngest child, Asa, was b. that year.

James Hood lived and practiced law in Mt. Sterling, Ky., for several years after marriage. He and some of his French family relatives became very much interested in the legendary Swift's Silver Mines which according to tradition are in Carter County, Kentucky. About the early 1890's he went to Willard, Carter County, and for several years searched for the mines near that town but without success. He purchased a small tract of land on the headwaters of Johns Run, built a small house and lived there several years. Here he was joined by sons, Asa and Dr. John who lived with him for a short time. He spent the latter part of his life in the home of his son Asa in Willard.

Children of JAMES HOOD AND EMILY (GATEWOOD) HOOD and approximate dates of birth as shown by the U. S. Census of Montgomery County, Kentucky, for the years 1860 and 1870:

Seventh Generation

84. Catherine (Kate) Hood, b. 1852.
85. Charles Hood, b. 1856.
86. Jennie B. (Genevieve) Hood, b. 1858. (She m. ——— Isted.)

87. John Hood, b. 1860. (He was a physician and never m.)

*88. Asa B. Hood, b. 1863.

The U. S. Census of Montgomery County for 1870 shows that Charles, John and Asa Hood were living at that time in the home of F. C. Barnes, a retired merchant, probably of Mt. Sterling.

88. Asa B. Hood was b. in Mt. Sterling, Ky., about 1863. He owned and operated a laundry prior to his coming to Willard, Carter County, which he subsequently leased to his sister Genevieve. After locating at Willard, he engaged in general merchandising in the town.

He m. Miss Viola Adams, daughter of Daniel and Nancy (Triplett) Adams of Willard. After living at Willard and vicinity for several years, the family went to California where they have since resided.

Children of Asa B. Hood and Viola (Adams) Hood:

Eighth Generation

89. Genevieve Hood, b. at Willard; d. young.

90. Carl Gatewood Hood, b. at Willard, went with the family to California; dec'd.

91. Rollo Hood, b. at Willard; went with family to California.

92. Emma Hood; went with family to California.

93. Ruth Hood; lives in California.

---

[1] The Ancestry of John Bell Hood by W. T. Black, the Register of the Kentucky Historical Society, Frankfort, Kentucky, October 1953, Vol. 51, No. 177, pp. 305-314.

[2] The Early Dutch, who settled New Amsterdam (New York City), for the most part, did not use surnames (family names) ; instead they used patronymics and aliases. A child was given a baptismal name ; for a second name it could take its father's first (christen) name and, in case of a son, add "zen" to it, signifying "son of". A girl would sometimes use her father's second (surname) name for her second name. Married women continued in most cases, to use their own names. Both men and women used aliliases to some extent.

[3] James French was born in Prince William County, Va., November 1756, and died in Montgomery County, Ky., April 1, 1835. He married Keziah Calloway, a daughter of Elizbaeth Calloway who died December 13, 1813, aged 80 years. Keziah (Calloway) French was born in Virginia in 1769, and died in Montgomery County, Ky., September 26, 1845.

Children of James French and Keziah (Calloway) French were, among others,

1. Richard French, b. June 20, 1792, d. May 1, 1854. He was a lawyer, judge and Congressman and selected his nephew, John Bell Hood, as cadet to West Point.

2. Susan French, b. July 25, 1795, d. March 5, 1866 ; m. Kenaz Farrow, a distinguished lawyer and jurist who was b. in Virginia, December 23, 1794, and d. in Montgomery County, Ky., August 31, 1864.

3. Stephen French, lawyer, b. July 9, 1798, d. May 3, 1827.

4. Theodosia French, b. June 16, 1801, d. January 12, 1886 ; m. Dr. John W. Hood (33).

5. Keziab French, b. March 18, 1804, d. November 13, 1827 ; m. ——— Prewitt.

6. Mary T. French. b. November 19, 1805, d. February 14, 1886.

[4] History of Greenup County, Kentucky, by Nina Mitchell Biggs and Mabel Mackay, 1951.

[5] "Directory of American Biography", Charles Scribner's Sons, New York, 1932, Vol. 9, pp. 194-5.

HORD FAMILY OF VIRGINIA AND CARTER COUNTY, KENTUCKY

Coat of Arms
English Ancestry of the Hord Family of Virginia

The lineage of the Hord family of England has been traced to Richard Hord, Shropshire, 1275 A. D. In 1553, Alan Hord 9 (John 8, Thomas 7, Richard 6, Thomas 5, Richard 4, Richard 3, John 2, Richard 1, 1275 A. D.) a member of the Shropshire family and a Bencher of the Middle Temple, London, purchased the Manor of Cote, Oxfordshire, where the family continued to reside until it became extinct in the main line in 1840.

Younger branches of the family of Alan Hord of the Middle Temple removed to London, to Ewell, in Surry and to the southern and southwestern counties of England.

Research recently made in England and in Virginia indicate that the Hord family of Virginia is descended from the family of Alan Hord of the Middle Temple, whose grandfather, Thomas Hord 7, was Attorney General during the reign of Henry VII.

May 22, 1650, "Aalan Hoord" came to Virginia with Colonel Moore Fauntleroy; and his name appears as head-right in the patent granted to Moore Fauntleroy for land in what is now the county of Richmond in the Northern Neck of Virginia.

May 27, 1654, "Elias Hoard" came to Virginia and was headright in the patent of Captain John West, a relative of Lord Delaware.

August 1, 1708, John Hord, who came from England, was living at this time in Christ Church Parish, Middlesex county, Virginia. His eldest son, Thomas Hord, proved his importation into the colony, April 15, 1740, in the Essex County Court, Virginia.

First Generation

John Hord and his eldest son, Thomas Hord, styled "Gentlemen" in the Virginia county records (relatives of Alan Hord and Elias Hord, who came to Virginia at an earlier date) were the immigrant ancestors of this branch of the Virginia family, as proved by the oath of Thomas Hord in the Essex County Court, Virginia, April 15, 1740, in which he stated that he "came into this colony to dwell in the year 1737 and this is the first time of proving his importation either by himself or his parents."

John Hord was an English gentleman. He was b. in Ewell, England, December 29, 1664 and was baptized there the following January 19th. He came to Virginia in 1685, and it is supposed that he was engaged in the rebellion of the Duke of Monmouth against King James II, and came to America after the defeat of the former at the battle of Sedgemoor (1685). It is a well-known fact that several other members of the family were engaged in this rebellion and a record still exists showing that Thomas Hord, Esq. of "Cote House", the head of the family at that time, was imprisoned in Oxford Castle for this offense.

Coming to Virginia, John Hord purchased a large tract of land in what is now Caroline county, on the Rappahannock River, which he named "Shady Grove". His house was brought from England in sections and in its day was considered a very handsome one, but is so badly in need of repairs that it is now uninhabitable. It is located two miles south of the Rappahannock River, and eight miles below the village of Port Royal. It is a large, double mansion, with a spacious hall ten feet in width running through the center, having on each side rooms twenty feet square. In the middle of the hall is an archway handsomely carved. The entire building is massive and substantial, having hardwood floors, tall white mantels and handsomely panelled doors. It is two stories high, built of massive timbers, with brick foundations and chimneys. Here John Hord lived and died. By will, probated in Essex county, November 21, 1749, he gave to son Ambrose Hord "the land and houses whereon I now live after my son William has had the use of it for one year, also the land that my son Thomas Hord escheated for me x x x". He bequeathed 1000 acres of land in King George county to sons Thomas, Peter, James, and William Hord; and made other bequests to son John Hord, grandsons Mordecai Hord and William Hord, (son of William) and to William Miller "that marry'd my daughter Jane".

JOHN HORD m., in Virginia, Jane ———, and they had issue:

Second Generation

*2. Thomas Hord, b. in England September 7, 1701.

3. Elizabeth Hord baptized in Christ Church, Middlesex county, December 22, 1703.

4. Susannah Hord baptized in Christ Church, April 7, 1706.

*5. John Hord baptized in Christ Church, August 1, 1708.

*6. James Hord baptized in Christ Church March 21, 1713.

*7. Peter Hord.

*8. William Hord.

9. Ambrose Hord.

10. Jane Hord.

*11. Mordecai Hord.

Third Generation

2. THOMAS 2 HORD (John 1), was b. in England September 7, 1701; m., June 24, 1726, Jane Miller, daughter of Captain Simon Miller, who was a son of Captain John Miller, a noted shipbuilder of old Rappahannock county. Thomas Hord[2] is described as "gentleman" in the court records. He was sub-sheriff and surveyor of highways of Essex county. Subsequently he removed to King George county, living on an estate bequeathed to him by the will of his

father, in which county he was inspector. By his will, proved in King George county, September 4, 1766, he bequeathed his plantation in King George county to his wife; mentions granddaughter Betty Hord, grandson John Hord, sons James Hord, Rhodin Hord, Thomas Hord, Jesse Hord and daughters, Aggy Hord, Molly Hord, Betty Hord, Betty Withers and Suckey Shelton.

Issue of Thomas Hord:

*12. Thomas Hord, b. July 11, 1727; d. May 11, 1778.

13. John Hord, b. March 27, 1729; no issue.

14. Elizabeth Hord, b. September 22, 1732; m. William Withers, of Stafford county. Issue.

*15. James Hord, b. January 22, 1736.

16. Jane Hord, b. May 8, 1738.

17. Rhodin Hord, b. May 4, 1740.

18. Susan Hord, b. April 23, 1742; m. John Shelton. Issue.

19. Mary Hord, b. September 27, 1744; m. Killis Hord (36).

20. Agnes Hord, b. October 22, 1747; m. (1) William Hord (41) and (2) Anthony Sale, of Essex county.

*21. Jesse Hord, b. October 31, 1749; m. Anthret Hord (39).

5. JOHN HORD 2 (John 1), was an appraiser of Essex county in 1734 and was a resident of Prince William county in 1741 and subsequently removed to Culpeper county where he died. His will, proved in Culpeper county July 21, 1783, bequeaths half of the negroes "left me by my brother Ambrose Hord to my son Ambrose Hord" and the "other half of the negroes left me by my brother Ambrose Hord to my daughter Fanny Watts" and to daughter Fanny Watts also "the remainder of my estate". He married Sarah Redd and they had issue:

22. Thomas Hord.

23. James Hord.

24. Frances Hord m. Barnett Watts.

25. Ambrose Hord was a private in Captain William Henderson's Company, Ninth Virginia Regiment, Colonel George Matthews, commanding, April 10, 1776-October, 1777. He m. Margaret Sherrill.

26. Elizabeth Hord.

6. JAMES HORD 2 (John 1), was bequeathed an estate of 250 acres in King George county by his father. He is styled "gentleman" in the county records; was surveyor of highways and inspector in King George county; m. Margaret Miller, sister of Captain Simon Miller, of the Fauquier county Militia, and a daughter of John Miller, a noted shipbuilder of old Rappahannock county.

They had issue:

27. James Hord probably was the James Hord who had service as ensign, King George county Militia, in the Revolutionary War.

28. Thomas Hord.
29. Ambrose Hord.
30. William Hord.
31. John Hord.
32. Jane Hord; m. John Sherrill.
33. Mildred Hord; m. Rev. Aaron Bledsoe, of Orange county, son of William Bledsoe.
34. Sarah Hord; m. James Hord (58).
35. Isabella Hord.

7. PETER HORD 2 (John 1), was a resident of Essex county in 1736 and subsequently removed to King George county to occupy an estate of 250 acres left him by the will of his father. Issue:
*36. Killis Hord, b. in 1745; d. in 1815; m. Mary Hord (19).
37. Reuben Hord.
38. Peter Hord; m. (1) Honor Wheatley and (2) Rebecca Wilkenson, of Maryland, and had issue by both wives. He was a resident of Stafford county in 1785.
Robert Hord states in his manuscript (1838) that he was a soldier in the Revolution and "lost an eye and a leg in the War."
39. Anthret Hord; m. May 7, 1772, Jesse Hord (21).
40. Sarah Hord; m. Rhodin Hord (17).

8. WILLIAM HORD 2 (John 1), was many years a resident of King George county, in which his father bequeathed him an estate of 250 acres which he sold to his brother James Hord in 1760. Subsequently he removed to Caroline county. He m. Lucy Norvell, and they had issue:
*41. William Hord; m. Agnes Hord (20).
*42. John Hord; m. (1) Anne Peyton and (2); Margaret Hawkins.
*43. James Hord, an ensign, Seventh Virginia Regiment, and a captain of Virginia Militia, in the Revolutionary War; m. Nancy Curd.
*44. Jane Hord; m. James Fletcher, of Charlotte county.
*45. Sarah Hord; m. Colonel Gilbert Hunt, of Charlotte county.
*46. Thomas Hord, captain, Sixth Virginia Regiment, Continental Army, in the Revolution; m. ——— Turner.
*47. Richard Hord, captain, Caroline County Militia, in the Revolution.
48. Frances Hord.

11. MORDECAI 2 HORD (John 1), a captain and a wagonmaster in General Braddock's Army, in the French and Indian War, in 1755; m. Sarah Carr, daughter of "Captain William Carr, Gentleman" justice of Caroline County, 1740, and granddaughter of "Thomas Carr, Gentleman," justice, 1702, and high sheriff, 1708-1709, of King William county. He removed from Louisa county to Henry county,

Virginia, in 1770, and subsequently purchased 1750 acres of land in the latter county from Walter King of Great Britain. On March 30, 1780, he conveyed 350 acres to Patrick Henry, the great orator, (for whom the county was named) who removed to and made that county his home for a number of years. On November 26, 1781, a land warrant for 2383½ acres of land in Henry county was granted to him, apparently for his services in the French and Indian War. On September 11, 1786, for a consideration of £2970, he conveyed to General Campbell (who commanded the Virginia troops in the battle of Kings Mountain October 7, 1780 and brother-in-law of Patrick Henry) 900 acres of land in Henry county, 50 head of horned cattle, 600 bushels of Indian corn, ten thousand weight of tobacco, one wagon, five horses and slaves, Margery and her seven children. Mordecai Hord d. at his seat "Hordsville", Henry county. His will, proved in that county, June 29, 1789, shows that his personal property amounted to $9,045.03; he had 32 slaves valued at $175 each. Besides the valuable property on which he lived which was abundantly stocked with horses and cattle he owned vast tracts of land in Powell's Valley, or on the Western Waters, as he referred to them in his will. His executors were his "friends (Governor) Patrick Henry, Colonel George Waller, his brother-in-law and Edmund Lyne."

Issue:

49. Mordecai Hord.

*50. William Hord, called "Colonel"; was a member of the Tennessee Legislature from Hawkins county.

51. John Hord, b. December 1, 1766; d. August 3, 1803.

52. Stanwix Hord.

53. Mary Hord; m. Thomas Jett, of Henry county.

54. Jane Hord; m. John Fleming.

Fourth Generation

12. THOMAS 3 HORD (Thomas, 2, John 1), of King George county, was b. July 11, 1727; m. Charity McLane, October 10, 1753; d. May 11, 1778. He is frequently described as "gentleman" in the records. He was a corporal in the Prince William County Militia during the French and Indian War, serving "66 days at 22 lbs. of tobacco per day" receiving "1452 lbs. of tobacco" for his full term of service. He was inspector for Falmouth, King George county, in September, 1753; a "Gentleman Justice" of that county from 1767 to 1772; and a vestryman of Brunswick Parish, in June, 1771.

Issue:

56. Susannah Hord, b. August 14, 1754; m. James Withers.

57. Jane Hord; m. Robert Sale.

58. James Hord, moved to Fauquier county. He married (1) Sarah Hord (34) and (2) Agatha Sinclair. He owned two estates in Fauquier county, known as "Elk Marsh" and "Knox Hill". His

will, proved in Fauquier county, July 22, 1822, mentions sons Thomas and James and daughter "Margit" and divides fifteen negroes among them.. These were children by the first wife. Land was devised to second wife; and children by her—Enos Hord, Ambrose Hord, William Hord and Charity Hord—were mentioned. The inventory of the estate shows books, silver and forty-one slaves.

59. Elizabeth Hord; m. Austin Bradford, son of Alexander Bradford, b. in 1728.

60. Mary Hord.

61. Thomas Hord.

15. JAMES 3 HORD (Thomas 2, John 1), b. January 22, 1736; m. Susan Miller, daughter of Simon Miller, of Culpeper county, who conveyed to him by deed dated September 17, 1767, 200 acres of land in St. Mark's Parish, that county. He owned land also in Spottsylvania county. His will, proved in Culpeper county, December 14, 1804, mentions issue:

62. James Hord who seems to have removed to Spottsylvania county.

63. Jane Hord; m. Thomas Brooks.

64. Frances Hord; m. —— Slaughter.

65. Anne Hord; m. James Withers, son of James Withers, Sr., who was a Burgess, of Stafford county, in 1692.

21. JESSE 3 HORD (Thomas 2, John 1), b. October 31, 1749; m. May 7, 1772, Anthret Hord (39). He was a resident of Stafford county in 1785; was an officer in the Virginia Militia during the Revolution and after the close of the war, in 1786, emigrated to Kentucky and settled on Mill Creek, in Mason county, where he d. in 1814. He was a famous hunter and Indian fighter.

October 1. 1796, Jesse Hord, Alexander K. Marshall (brother of Chief Justice John Marshall), De Vall Payne, William Triplett are described as "gentlemen and Trustees of Lewisburgh", Kentucky. On September 29, 1812, he purchased 200 acres of land in Mason county of Alexander K. Marshall. In a deed of September 12, 1814 (shortly before his death), he mentions his children and distributes thirteen negroes among them:

Issue:

*66. Elias Hord, b. in Virginia, March 9, 1773; m. Ann Triplett, daughter of Colonel Francis Triplett, of Fauquier County, Virginia.

67. Edward Hord, b. in Virginia, November, 1784; d. October 2, 1823; a Captain, Seventh, United States Infantry, from May 3, 1808, to January 1, 1810; m. in 1812, Eliza Benson, daughter of Thomas Benson, of Virginia.

68. Jesse Hord; m. Mary Triplett, daughter of William Triplett.

69. Thomas Hord, m. Sarah Conway, daughter of Judge Miles Withers Conway, of Mason County, Kentucky, who with Daniel

Boone was trustee of Washington, one of the earliest settlements and the first county seat of Mason county.

*70. Jane Hord, b. in Virginia, May 8, 1776; m. John McIlvane.
71. Ann Hord.
72. Isabella Hord.
73. Susannah Hord, b. in Virginia, May, 1778; m. John Brickley.
74. Lucy Hord; m. Dr. McGready.

36. KILLIS 3 HORD (Peter 2, John 1), was b. in 1745 and d. in 1815; m. Mary Hord (19). He is described as "Killis Hord, Gentleman" in the Stafford county, (Virginia) records. He was a "Gentleman Justice" of Stafford county, 1806-1809.
Issue:
*75. Edwin Hord.
76. Alexander Hord; resided in Culpeper county.
77. Lewis Hord, of Culpeper county.
78. Daniel Hord, of Culpeper county.
79. Thomas Hord; left no issue.
80. Peter Hord; left no issue.
81. Minnie Hord; m. John Cross.

41. WILLIAM 3 HORD (William 2, John 1), m. Agnes Hord (20) and resided in Caroline county, Virginia. His will was proved May 13, 1777. His widow m. Anthony Sale, of Essex county.
Issue:
*82. Willis Hord.
83. Lucy Norvell Hord; m. Major William Taylor, brother of Commodore Richard Taylor, of the Virginia Navy, during the Revolution.
84. Elizabeth Hord; m. Hancock Taylor, brother of President Zachary Taylor, and son of Colonel Richard Taylor, who made the first recorded trading voyage down the Ohio River and settled at Louisville, Kentucky.

42. JOHN 3 HORD (William 2, John 1), had service in the Revolutionary War as lieutenant, Fourth Dragoons, Continental Army, January 20, 1777 to ———; ensign in Captain Stern's company of Caroline County Militia, January 8, 1778 to ———; and Captain in Lee's Light Dragoons from 1779 to ———. He owned and lived at "Shady Grove", Caroline county, the ancestral home of the Hords. He m. (1) Annie Peyton and (2) Margaret Hawkins, of Essex county.
Children by first wife:
85. Sarah Hord; m. in 1797, Gabriel Slaughter, b. in Virginia in 1767; emigrated to Kentucky at an early period; was frequently a member of the State Legislature; commanded a regiment of Kentucky troops at the battle of New Orleans (January 8, 1815);

elected lieutenant-governor of Kentucky in 1808 on the ticket with Governor Charles Scott; and again elected lieutenant-governor in 1816 on the ticket with Governor George Madison, upon whose death, October 14, 1816, he became acting seventh governor 1816-1820).

86. Frances Hord; m. Edward Rowzee, of Essex county.

87. William Hord.

Children by second wife:

88. John Hord.

89. Hiram Hord; m. Catharine Hedgman, daughter of "John Hedgman, Gentleman," who was the son of "Peter Hedgman, Gentleman", vestryman and justice of Stafford county; Burgess, 1748; Burgess of Prince William county, 1736-1738.

90. James Hord.

91. Hawkins Hord.

92. Thomas Hord; m. Catharine Stuart.

93. Robert Hord: m. Celia Jane Stuart Foote, sister of Governor Henry S. Foote, eighteenth governor of Mississippi (1852-1854). He was author of the manuscript of the Hord family written in 1838; was b. at "Shady Grove", March 4. 1795: and was a member of the House of Delegates of Virginia, 1834-1835.

43. JAMES 3 HORD (William 2, John 1), was a resident of Caroline county. He had service in the Revolution as ensign, Seventh Virginia Regiment, February 13, 1777 to March 7, 1778, and subsequently as captain in the Virginia Militia. He was a trustee of the town of Newmarket, Virginia, in 1786, the town site of which was purchased from John Curd, whose daughter Nancy was his wife. After the close of the Revolution, he went west and settled in Jessamine county, Kentucky, where he died January 3, 1815. He was the first to discover salt water on the Kanawha River, and made the first effort to procure it by boring.

Issue:

94. Lucy Norvell Hord; m. John Fishback.

95. Francis P. Hord.

46. THOMAS 3 HORD (William 2, John 1), had service in the Revolutionary War as second lieutenant, Tenth Virginia Infantry, in 1776; first lieutenant, in 1777; captain-lieutenant, Sixth Virginia Regiment, in 1778; captain, in 1781. He was wounded and taken prisoner at Charleston, May 12, 1780, and was a prisoner on Parole at the close of the war. He was with the army during the winter encampment at Valley Forge, 1777-78, serving under Colonel John Green in the Tenth Virginia Regiment. In 1783, he received a land grant of 5221 acres for services in the Revolution, and in 1808 he received another grant of land for ten months' service in excess of seven years in the Revolutionary War.

Thomas Hord was a resident of Caroline county, Virginia, and subsequent to the close of the Revolution, he held commissions as major and captain in the militia of that county. He was a member of the Virginia Society of the Cincinnati.

Thomas Hord m. Miss Turner, of Caroline county, and settled on the Rappahannock River, where he died about 1810.

Issue:

96. Elizabeth Hord: m. Edmund Taylor, son of Colonel John Taylor, and d. without issue. Handsome oil paintings of Colonel John Taylor, President Zachary Taylor and other members of this family were in the possession of Mr. Augustine Fitzhugh Turner, of Port Royal, Caroline county, Virginia.

47. RICHARD 3 HORD (William 2, John 1), was a captain of the Caroline County Militia during and also after the close of the Revolutionary War. On December 14, 1786, he took the oath of a deputy sheriff of Caroline county. He m. Miss Turner and they had issue:

97. George T. Hord; removed to Yellow Banks, Kentucky, and d. without issue.

Fifth Generation

66. ELIAS 4 HORD (Jesse 3, William 2, John 1), was b. in Virginia, March 9, 1773, and moved to Mason county, Kentucky. He was a captain of Scouts in the regiment commanded by Colonel Richard M. Johnson; participated in the battle of the Thames (October 5, 1813) and, in company with Colonel Devall Payne, he pursued and overtook the carriage of the British General Proctor after his defeat at the battle, capturing and taking from it the general's compass. In the inventory of his estate, dated December 21, 1821, on file in the Mason County Court House, is mentioned a compass (probably General Proctor's), a tomahawk and other articles used by the early pioneers of Kentucky. He m., in Mason county, Kentucky, September 15, 1786. Ann Triplett, (b. in Virginia November 27, 1774; d. in Mason County, Kentucky, March 14, 1866), daughter of Francis Triplett, and granddaughter of Thomas Francis Triplett, Esquire, the first of the family in Virginia. Her father, Francis Triplett, was b. in Fauquier county, Virginia, about 1728. He was a Captain, Major and Colonel; served in George Washington's regiment in the French and Indian War; and participated, among others, in the battle of Cowpens (January 17, 1781) and for his services received a sword from Congress. He m. Benedite ———; d. in January, 1794, leaving, among other property, 37,000 acres of land in Kentucky to his children.

Elias Hord and Ann (Triplett) Hord had issue:

*98. Francis Triplett Hord; b. September 19, 1797; d. May 20, 1866.

99. Thornton Hord, b. March, 1799; d. December 6, 1854; m. Ann Bowling, August 6, 1821, who was b. in Alexandria, Virginia, May 10, 1801.

100. Abner Hord, b. June 10, 1801; d. June 9, 1873.

101. Caroline Hord; m. John Sinclair, of Scott county, Kentucky.

102. Annie Hord; m. Belville Moss, son of Kendal Moss.

103. Eliza Hord.

104. Lewis Hord; d. near Vicksburg, Mississippi, in 1837.

82. WILLIS HORD 4 (William 3, William 2, John 1), b. April 17, 1769: m. January 2, 1793, Polly Buckner, b. February 16, 1778, daughter of Captain Philip Buckner and his wife, Tabby (Daniels) Buckner.

Willis Hord was the first clerk of the Bracken (Kentucky) county court. He was a man of wide influence and high standing, a true type of the early Kentuckian. strong intellectually and physically; and left the impress of his strong personality upon society and civilization. He moved to Jefferson county, Kentucky and from there to Greenup county, now Carter county, that state, and settled on the Little Sandy River, near the present-day city of Grayson, in 1816. He was thrown from his carriage and killed, September 28. 1828, while on a visit to Jefferson county, and was buried at Middletown, that county. His widow lived and reared her family on the plantation on Little Sandy River. the crossing of which has always been known as "Hord's Ford". She was a proud, aristocratic woman; and lived to be eighty-seven years old, retaining her physical and mental faculties to the end.

Issue:

105. William Hord. b. June 10, 1794; d. in infancy.

106. John Taylor Hord, b. January 6, 1795; d. in infancy.

*107. Thomas Todd Hord.

*108. Lucy Norvelle Taylor Hord.

*109. Robert Craddock Hord.

*110. Philip Buckner Hord.

*111. John Nicholas Hord.

112. Laura Agnes Hord, b. November 27, 1810.

113. Polly Willis Hord, b. January 17, 1814; m. James Clark, of Clarke county, Kentucky.

*113a. Betsy Taylor Hord.

44. LUCY FLETCHER 4 (Jane Hord 3, William 2, John 1), m. Thomas Ewell, son of Lord Darleigh, of Scotland.

Issue:

114. Sarah, d. without issue.

115. Jane, m. Winston Henry, son of Patrick Henry, the great Virginia orator.

45. ELIZABETH HUNT 4 (Sarah Hord 3, William 2, John 1), m.
Fayette Roane, son of Judge Roane, and grandson of Patrick Henry,
the great Virginia orator. They moved to Kentucky and settled in
Mercer county, where Fayette Roane d. about 1822.
Child:
116. Sarah Anne Roane, m., first, Thomas J. Thorpe; secondly, J.
M. Mattingly. Elizabeth Hunt Roane m., secondly, Dr. Bigbee, by
whom she had several children—names unknown.

50. THOMAS HORD 4 (William 3, Mordecai 2, John 1), m. Miss
Mary McCulloch, daughter of Benjamin McCulloch, of Rutherford
county, Tennessee. She was a lineal descendant in an unbroken line
of Sir Cullo O'Neal, who was knighted for gallantry on the field of
battle by Edward De Bruce, of Scotland, in 1316, and was made
"Laird of Myrton", "Captain of Horse" and his "Standard Bearer".
She evidenced in her gentle, aristocratic bearing the true nobility
of her descent. Thomas Hord m., secondly, Mrs. La Foute, a widow;
of Shrevesport, Louisiana.
Issue of first marriage:
117. Sarah Hord, m. Mr. Bibb, of Alabama.
118. Ada Hord, m. J. W. Ewing, son of Hon. Edwin H. Ewing, of
Tennessee.
119. Jane Hord, d. without issue.
120. Benjamin M. Hord, m. Miss Annie Warner, of Nashville,
Tennessee.
121. Alice Hord, m., J. H. Warner, of Chattanooga, Tennessee.
122. Eldridge Hord, d. without issue.
123. Ellen Hord, m. William Wendell, of Murfreesboro, Tennessee.
124. Mary Hord, d. without issue—a child six years old.
Issue of second marriage:
125. Mildred Hord, m. Frank Washington, of Nashville, Tennessee.
126. Thomas Hord, m. Miss Sikes, of Rutherford county, Tennessee.

75. EDWIN HORD 4 (Killis 3, Thomas 2, John 1), emigrated to
Kentucky and settled in Mason county. He was a noted Indian fighter and pioneer. He participated in General Harmar's campaign of
1790; in those of Generals Scott and Wilkinson; was with General
St. Clair in 1791; and with General Wayne (Mad Anthony) in 1794.
He m. a daughter of Henry Lee, of Woodford county.
Issue:
127. Willis Hord; d. in Missouri.
128. Alfred Hord; resided in Fleming county, Kentucky.
129. Marcus D. Hord; m. Mary Parker.
130. Sarah Hord; resided in Mason county, Kentucky.
131. Ellen Hord; m., first, Mr. Green; and secondly, Dr. Ephraim
McDowell, of Kentucky.
132. Thomas Hord m. ——— ———; and d. in 1834.

70. JANE HORD 4 (Jesse 3, Thomas 2, John 1) was b. in Virginia, May 8, 1776, and d. in Washington county, Missouri; m. John McIlvane, February 14, 1799. He was b. May 8, 1777.

Issue:

133. Jesse Hord McIlvane.

134. Marie Emaline McIlvane, b. July 21, 1802; m. Colonel Archibald Yell, who was governor of Arkansas, 1840-44; member of Congress, 1835-39 and 1845-46; colonel of an Arkansas regiment of cavalry during the Mexican War; and was killed at the battle of Beuna Vista, (February 23, 1847) by being run through the mouth by a Mexican lancer.

135. Eveline Anthoret McIlvane; m. Dr. John Gano Bryan.

136. Isabella McIlvane; m. Mr. McGready.

137. Lucy McIlvane; m. Israel McGready.

138. Orville McIlvane; b. June 22, 1809.

139. Cynthian McIlvane; m. Firmin R. Desloge.

140. Narcissa McIlvane; m. Mr. Payen.

141. Susan McIlvane; m. Mr. Smith.

Sixth Generation

98. FRANCIS TRIPLETT 5 HORD (Elias 4, Jesse 3, Thomas 2, John 1), of "Beechland", near Mavsville, Mason county, Kentucky, was b. September 19, 1797 and d. May 20, 1869. In early manhood he was a surveyor; studied law, was admitted to the bar and became "one of the leaders of the Kentucky bar", ranking with the first men of his state. He held the office of circuit judge. He m., September 20, 1826, Elizabeth Scott Moss, daughter of Kendal Moss and his wife, Ann (Grant) Moss.

Issue:

142. Mary Hord, b. August 10, 1827.

143. Oscar B. Hord, b. August 31, 1829; attorney-general of Indiana, 1862-64.

144. William Taliaferro Hord, b. March 3, 1832; medical director of U. S. Navy; d. April 1, 1901.

145. George Moss Hord, b. August 24, 1833.

146. Francis Triplett Hord, b. November 24, 1835; attorney-general of Indiana, 1882-86.

147. Elias Hord, b. June 27, 1838.

148. Kendal Moss Hord, b. October 20, 1840; resided at Shelbyville, Indiana; judge of the Circuit Court, 1876-88.

149. Josephine Hord, b. December 13, 1845.

150. Henry C. Hord.

107. THOMAS TODD HORD 5 (Willis 4, William 3, William 2, John 1), was b. December 15, 1796 and m., March 16, 1823 in Greenup county, Clarinda Kibbey, daughter of Moses Kibbey. He settled on Everman's Creek, Carter county; was very successful farmer and

trader and amassed a large fortune. He d. in Grayson, Kentucky,
September 11, 1851, of Cholera. His widow, Clarinda, d. January
26, 1869.

Children:
151. Willis Kibbey Hord.
*152. Mary Ann Hord.
*153. Mildred Lewis Hord.
*154. Moses Pendleton Hord.
*155. Sarah Thomas Hord.

108. Lucy Norvelle Taylor Hord 5 (Willis 4, William 3, William 2, John 1), was b. August 28, 1799; m. Jefferson Bell, and moved
from Jefferson county to Oldham county. Many of their descendants
lived in Oldham and Shelby counties, Kentucky.

Children:
156. Mary Bell.
157. Willis Bell.
158. Agnes Bell.

109. Robert Craddock Hord 5, (Willis 4, William 3, William 2,
John 1,) was b. October 15, 1803; m. November 24, 1824, in Greenup county, Kentucky, Julianna Pickett. Just prior to the marriage he was appointed Miss Pickett's guardian as is evidenced by
the following order entered by the Jefferson (Kentucky) County
Court, a copy of which is attached to the marriage bond:
"Order of the Jefferson County Court, November, 1824: On
motion of Sarah Mayfield (the mother), the court appoints Robert
C. Hord, guardian to Julian Pickett, infant orphan of John Pickett,
deceased; whereupon he gave bond in the penalty of four thousand
dollars with Thomas Parker, William Sale and Hancock Taylor, his
sureties, according to law.
A copy Teste:
Worden Pope, C. J. C.
By Robert Tyler, D. C. J. C. C."
They resided in Jefferson county, Kentucky.

Children:
159. Mildred L. Hord.
160. Lucy N. Hord.
161. Hancock Taylor Hord.

110. Philip Buckner Hord 5 (Willis 4, William 3, William 2,
John 1), b. October 27, 1804; d. April 10, 1886; m. July 18, 1829, in
Greenup county, Miss Catharine England.

Children:
162. William Taylor Hord; d. in infancy.
*162. Hebe Susan Hord.
*164. Mary Catharine Hord.

111. JOHN NICHOLAS HORD 5 (Willis 4, William 3, William 2, John 1), b. February 3, 1806; m., December 27, 1828, Ann Lewis Beckwith, granddaughter of Councillor Carter, of Virginia.

Children:
165. Lewis Beckwith Hord.
166. Mary Willis Hord.
*167. Bainton Matilda Hord.
168. Arthur Almerin Hord; b. April 9, 1838, d. October 8, 1856.
*169. John Willis Hord.
*170. William Thomas Taylor Hord.
*171. Frank Joyce Hord.

113-A. BETSY TAYLOR HORD 5, (Willis 4, William 3, William 2, John 1), b. August 30, 1808; m. George Roberts.

Child:
172. Lucy Mary Roberts; m. John Vincent; and they emigrated West.

32-B. JESSE BLEDSOE (Elizabeth Sherill 4, Jane Hord 3, James 2, John 1), lawyer, legislator, was b. in Culpeper county, Virginia, April 6, 1776. In spite of delicate health and weakness of the eyes he succeeded, by the most persevering industry, in acquiring a good education, and in time became one of the most eminent lawyers of the West. Having emigrated to Kentucky, he was elected repeatedly to the state legislature, and in 1808 was secretary of state in the administration of Governor Charles Scott. In 1812 he was a member of the state legislature; was elected to the U. S. Senate in 1813, serving, until 1815; state senator from 1817 to 1820; was appointed circuit judge of the Lexington district, 1822; elected professor of law, Transylvania University, 1822; returned to the practice of law and in 1833 removed to Mississippi, two years later going to Texas where he was engaged in collecting historical material at the time of his death which occurred near Nacogdoches, June 30, 1837.

Children:
173. Joseph Bledsoe, Shelbyville, Kentucky.
174. Jane Bledsoe, New Orleans.
175. Mary Bledsoe; m. H. J. Bodley, Lexington, Kentucky.

Seventh Generation

152. MARY ANN HORD 6 (Thomas Todd Hord 5, Willis 4, William 3, William 2, John 1), b. August 15, 1825; m. Dr. A. J. Landsdowne, May 13, 1842. Dr. Landsdowne was b. in Prince William County, Virginia, October 20, 1814. He was a near relative of Lord Landsdowne of England. He was well educated and intelligent and inherited a fine estate to which, with great energy and successful management, he added greatly until he became wealthy. His home "Luck Enough" afterward called Landsdowne Hall) near Grayson,

Kentucky, was known far and wide for its hospitality where many of the distinguished men and women of his time were entertained until the Civil War when all his property was swept away but the land. Dr. Landsdowne d. April 15, 1873. His widow survived him eight years. She was a lovely Christian woman of intelligence and social qualities.

Children:

176. Lucy Landsdowne; b. March 4, 1843; m. Louis J. Goble.

177. Daisy Landsdowne; b. November 11, 1844; m. George N. Osenton. (See Osenton Family.)

178. George Landsdowne; m. Helen Bayless.

179. Juliet Landsdowne, civic leader, was b. at "Landsdowne Hall", near Grayson, Kentucky, January 20, 1852, and d. at Grayson, April 7, 1947; m. at "Landsdowne Hall", July 2, 1879, Frank Powers, who was b. at Wheelersburg, Ohio. September 17, 1852, a son of Ezekiel and Sarah (Dean) Powers. He was educated in the Wheelersburg public schools and in 1873, when a young man of 21 years, came to Grayson, Kentucky, as general agent for the Eastern Kentucky Railway Company. He filled the position until 1884 and afterwards studied law in the office of Judge James R. Botts at Grayson and in 1895 was admitted to the bar. In the same year he formed a partnership with Judge Botts under the firm name of Botts and Powers which existed until 1910. He devoted considerable time to the management of his real estate and mine holdings. From 1879 to 1882 he operated a charcoal pig iron furnace called the Iron Hills Furnace which was one of the last furnaces of this sort operated in the county. In 1884 he was the Democratic candidate for Congress and was defeated by Gen. William H. Wadsworth of Maysville. He was a Democrat in politics and was a member of the Episcopal Church, South. He served as Master Commissioner of the Carter (County) Circuit Court for 15 years and was Chairman of the Democratic Committee of Carter County for 30 years. Interment in Grayson County.

Mrs. Powers was a civic leader, being interested and active in all moral, educational and social activities of the community. She was a member of the Daughters of the American Revolution, Philip Buckner Chapter at Augusta, Kentucky, a member of the Woman's Christian Temperance Union for many years and in this capacity appeared on public platforms all over the State. She was also a member of the John D. Gordon Chapter of the Daughters of the Confederacy. She was a member of the Episcopal Church, South.

Mr. and Mrs. Powers had no children but left surviving an adopted daughter, Mrs. Lula Stewart of Grayson.

153. MILDRED LEWIS HORD 6 (Thomas Todd Hord 5, Willis 4, Willliam 3, William 2, John 1), b. June 3, 1830 and d. May 29, 1868; m., March 16, 1852, Dr. William D. Jones of Pennsylvania, who was

b. September 10, 1829, and d. at Grayson, Kentucky, October 7, 1876. Dr. Jones was a leading physician in the Grayson area for a number of years. Mrs. Jones was a bright, dashing woman, charming in conversation and agreeable in manners. They entertained lavishly.

Children:
*180. Thomas Hord Jones.
*181. Sallie Mildred Jones.

180. THOMAS HORD JONES, liveryman, at Grayson; m. Miss Virgin.

Children:
182. Sallie Jones; m. Mack McAllister.
183. William D. Jones; m. Emma Seaton. (See James Seaton Family.)
184. Minnie Jones; m. John M. Theobald, attorney, at Grayson. (See Theobald Family.)
185. Elton Jones.

181. SALLIE MILDRED JONES; m. John G. Ault, a merchant at Grayson for many years.

Children:
186. Allie Ault.
187. William A. Ault.
188. John G. Ault, Jr.

154. MOSES PENDLETON HORD 6 (Thomas Todd Hord 5, Willis 4, William 3, William 2, John 1), b. July 7, 1832; m. Mary Frizzell; removed to Fleming County, Kentucky, and d. there, February 27, 1871.

Children:
189. Lizzie Hord.
190. Lyde Hord.
191. Mildred Hord.
192. Moses Hord.

155. SARAH THOMAS HORD 6 (Thomas Todd Hord 5, Willis 4, William 3, William 2, John 1), b. May 11, 1840; m. twice before she was 21 years of age, first, Lafayette Burrows, who d., leaving a child, a son; m., secondly, in April 1861, Hugh Nelson Richards and went on a visit to his family at Warm Springs, West Virginia, where she d., December 7, 1861.

Child:
193. Thomas Hord Burroughs.

163. HEBE SUSAN HORD 6 (Philip Buckner Hord 5, Willis 4, William 3, William 2, John 1), b. October 4, 1835; m. November 29, 1855, John Z. Duley of Fleming County, Kentucky.

Children:

194. Florence Duley, b. September 20, 1856; m. George Willis. Children: William, Bert, Minnie and Ollie.

*195. Jennie Duley.

196. Aurora Duley, b. April 4, 1860; m. William Carroll. Children: Calvin, Frank and Hattie.

197. John Duley, b. July 17, 1862; m. Della Canterberry. Children: Grace Duley, m. Ellis Stewart.

198. Schuyler Duley, b. October 12, 1867; m. Carrie Crawford. Children: Nora, Hord, June and Crawford.

199. William Duley, b. May 4, 1870; m. Clara Campbell. Children: Joseph and Irvin.

195. Jennie Dudley, b. July 13, 1858; d. in Washington, D. C., November 20, 1941. Interment in Lincoln Memorial Cemetery, in Washington area; m., first, George Craycraft. Children: Hebe and Elmer.

195-A. Jennie (Duley) Craycraft m. secondly Isaiah H. Jones, a native of Lee County, Virginia, who was b. May 10, 1856, and d. in Carter County, Kentucky, September 23, 1924. Children: Mae Jones, Federal employee and one-time teacher; b. near Grayson, Kentucky, October 15, 1901, educated in the public schools of Carter County, Kentucky, and at Southern Brothers Business University, Ashland, Kentucky, taught in the public schools of Carter County for two years and was employed as stenographer in Ashland for a time; accepted a position with Veterans Administration, Washington, D. C., on November 20, 1931, and is presently an employee of that Administration; m. July 20, 1940, Worth Sauls; no children.

164. MARY CATHERINE HORD, b. July 17, 1842; d. in 1894; m. Samuel Everman. They were parents of thirteen children; lived near Grayson, Kentucky. (See Everman Family.)

167. BAINTON MILDRED HORD 6 (John Nicholas Hord 5, Willis 4, William 3, William 2, John 1), b. July 21, 1834; d. November 17, 1880; m. William Cutter Mitchell of Pennsylvania.

Children:

200. Lewis B. Mitchell, b. October 21, 1860; unm.

201. Annie E. Mitchell, b. March 25, 1862; m. May 20, 1886, H. G. Van Arsdale of Owen County, Kentucky, resided in Lexington, Kentucky.

202. Mary Statina Mitchell, b. January 27, 1871.

203. William Hord Mitchell, b. January 1, 1873; m. Minnie Prater of Grayson.

204. Hebe Hilton Mitchell, b. February 1, 1875.

169. JOHN WILLIS (JACK) HORD 6 (John Nicholas Hord 5, Willis, 4, William 3, William 2, John 1), farmer and stock raiser, was b. December 6, 1844 in the ancestral home on Little Sandy River near Grayson built by Willis Hord in 1816. He d. November 6, 1927. Isterment in the Hord cemetery on the farm. He was a successful farmer and livestock dealer, made wise investments and amassed considerable wealth. On June 21, 1901, he was m. to Miss Edith Spangler at her home at Sharpsburg, Virginia.

Children:

205. John Frank Hord, farmer and stock raiser, was b. on the ancestral Hord farm, September 29, 1903; educated in the public schools of Grayson, graduating from Prichard High School and was graduated from Millersburg, Kentucky) Military Institute with the class of 1923; m., October 20, 1927, Miss Margaret Ann Woolery, daughter of Charles and Emma (Hatchett) Woolery of Grayson.

Children:

John Willis Hord, b. July 21, 1936.
Dorothy Mary Hord, b. August 30, 1942.

170. WILLIAM THOMAS TAYLOR HORD 6 (John Nicholas Hord 5, Willis 4, William 3, William 2, John 1), farmer and banker, was b. on the ancestral Hord farm, January 8, 1849, and d. at Greenup, Kentucky, August 4, 1924. Interment in Ashland Cemetery, Ashland, Kentucky. He was one of the organizers of the First National Bank at Greenup, Kentucky, and was its president at the time of his death. He m. Jennie Geiger of Ashland. No children.

171. FRANK JOYCE HORD 6 (John Nicholas Hord 5, Willis 4, William 3, William 2, John 1, farmer and stock raiser, was b. on the ancestral Hord farm, August 2, 1856, d. May 30, 1936, and was buried in the Hord Cemetery on the farm; m. Geneva Duke. No children.

HORTON AND KING FAMILIES OF CARTER AND ELLIOTT COUNTIES

This is an old English local name, 'of Horton', from a township in the parish of Bradford, Yorkshire; from a township in the parish of Gisburn, Yorkshire; and from Horton-in-Ribblesdale, near Settle, County Yorkshire.

The family was seated in England in early days as is shown by the following names borne on the Hundred Rolls and other records:

Thomas de Horton, county Devon, 1273.

William de Horton, county Kent, 1273.

Adam de Horton, county Cambridge, 1273.

Emma de Horton, 1379.

The Hortons emigrated to America in early colonial days and were numerous particularly in Virginia and the Carolinas.

The Hortons came to Virginia about the middle of the seventeenth century. They were Royalists and apparently Cavaliers and settled in the tidewater region where they acquired vast landed estates and became planters of importance.

1. John Horton, Sr., was the early American progenitor of the branch of the Horton family that settled in the Little Sandy River valley, Eastern Kentucky. He was b., presumably in Overwharton parish, Stafford County, Virginia, and m., probably in that county, Sarah ——— (family name not learned).

Children:
Second Generation

2. John Horton, Jr., (probably there were other children), b. December 23, 1749, apparently in Stafford county, Virginia; m. Isabel Kendrick, b. in Russell County, Virginia, in 1754, daughter of Patrick Kendrick, a Scotchman.[1]

Children:
Third Generation

*3. Lettice Horton.

4. Sarah Horton; m. John Bradshaw.

5. Elizabeth Horton; m. Elijah Sargent; migrated to Kentucky.

6. Dicie Horton; m. Mashak White.

7. Lucy Horton; m. William Sargent; migrated to Kentucky.

8. John Horton; settled in Ohio.

9. Enoch Horton; migrated to then Texas Territory. The town of Horton, that State, was named for his family. His daughter, Sallie, m. Cochrell and lived in Dallas, that State.

10. Robert Horton; resided in Russell County, Virginia.

*11. Travis Horton.[2]

3. Lettice Horton; m., apparently in Russell County, Virginia, William Horton, her cousin, onetime sheriff of that county.

Children: Fourth Generation

*12. Daniel Horton.
*13. Rhode Horton.
 14. Robert Horton; m. ——— Howard; removed to Kansas about 1860.
 15. C. Horton; b. in Russell County, Virginia, November, 1809.

12. DANIEL HORTON, b. in Russell County, Virginia, in 1812; m. Susan Kendall.

Children: Fifth Generation
 16. W. D. or D. W. Horton; m. Jane Meeks.
 17. Julia F. Horton; m. Christopher H. Vincent. (See Vincent Family.)
 18. Mary Horton; m. William Hickenbottom.
*19. Lettice Horton; m. William Weddington.
 20. Lucy Horton; m. Oscar Hickenbottom.
 21. John Horton; m. Amanda Redwine. (See Redwine Family.)
 22. Benjamin Horton; m. ——— Meeks.
 23. A. H. Horton.
 24. Ren. Horton; m. ——— Meeks, daughter of Jesse Meeks.

13. RHODE HORTON; m., first, ——— Davis; removed to Joplin, Missouri, about 1885.
The U. S. Census, 1870, for Elliott County, shows the following concerning this family:
Rhode Horton, age 56, farmer, b. in Virginia.
Rachel Horton, age 32, b. in Virginia.

Children: Fifth Generation
 25. Sarah, age 22, b. in Virginia.
 26. David, age 17, b. in Kentucky.
 27. Phoebe, age 14, b. in Kentucky.
 28. Catherine, age 11, b. in Kentucky.
 29. Lavegal (?), age 9, b. in Kentucky.
 30. Margaret, age 8, b. in Kentucky.
 31. William, age 7, b. in Kentucky.
 32. Elbert, age 5, b. in Kentucky.
 33. Nancy L., age 3, b. in Kentucky.
 34. Genevera (?), age 10 months, b. in Kentucky.
The records would seem to indicate that there was another son by the first marriage.

19. LETTICE HORTON; m. William Weddington.
Children: Sixth Generation
 35. Mollie Weddington; m. George Whitt.
 36. J. H. Weddington; m. Nannie Duvall.

37. Dora Weddington; m. Wylie Duvall.
38. James Weddington; m. Paulina Whitt.
39. Charles Weddington; m. Ollie Duvall.
40. Reba Weddington; m. George Bailey.
41. Julia Weddington; m. William Elliott.

11. TRAVIS HORTON, farmer and sometime local public official, was b. in Stafford County, Virginia, May 5, 1779, and d. in then Carter, now Elliott County, Kentucky, August 13, 1848. He migrated to Russell County, Virginia—time not known—where he lived several years. Later and within the period from 1820 to 1830, he removed with his family to Lee County, Virginia, where he and his family became acquainted with one Henry Cox [3] and his family. Subsequently four of his sons m. four of Henry Cox's daughters. Finally he and his family migrated to Kentucky, tarrying for a time on the Big Sandy River, probably in Pike County, and about 1830 or 1835 he settled at Bushy or Horton Flats, near Bruin, then Greenup, subsequently Carter and now Elliott County. Here he lived until his death and here he was buried. He m., October 4, 1805. Rebecca Arthur Lester, b. in Virginia, February 9, 1780, d. in Carter County, Kentucky, June 28, 1854. There is documentary evidence showing that he was of the upper class of land owners in Virginia and was a man of influence and importance in his community. He was surety on the bond of William Horton, brother-in-law, and Sheriff of Russell County. The records show that soon after settling in Kentucky there were surveyed for him on land warrants and he acquired three tracts of land aggregating 800 acres on Little Sandy River and Clifty Creek in then Carter County. He was elected and served as justice of the peace of Carter County for several years; and had service in the Mexican War as wagon master in the company of Captain John S. Williams.

Children of Travis Horton and his wife, Rebecca (Lester) Horton:

Fourth Generation

42. Lettice Horton, b. in Virginia, April 9, 1803; m., probably in Pike County, Kentucky, John Kelley; lived in Letcher County, Kentucky.

43. Sarah Horton, b. in Virginia, December 25, 1807; m. Hiram Ely; settled in the vicinity of Soldier, Carter County, Kentucky.

*44. Isabel Horton.

45. Patsy (Martha) Horton; b. in Virginia, December 23, 1815; m. Silas Flanery; resided in Virginia.

*46. Elijah Sargent Horton.

*47. Reese Duff Horton.

*48. Travis Horton, Jr.

*49. John Thompson Horton.

Travis Horton had another daughter,

50. Elizabeth, the eldest child, b. February 29, 1800; m. James Herrell.

44. ISABEL HORTON, b. in Russell County, Virginia, January 18, 1809, and d. in Carter County, Kentucky; m., presumably in Virginia, about 1831, Elias King, farmer, b. in Virginia about 1805 and d. in Carter County.

Children:

Fifth Generation

51. Cana King; d. at age 21.
*52. F. Marion King.
*53. Joseph Newton King.
*54. Van Buren King.
*55. Houston King.
56. Sabra King; m. Samuel Mobley. (See Mobley Family.)
*57. Sarah King; m. Robert Rose.
58. Calla King; m. James Elliott; migrated to Kansas.

52. FRANCIS MARION KING, farmer, b. in Virginia, about 1834; m. about 1858, Rebecca Whitt, b. in Virginia about 1835. He had service in the Confederate Army during the Civil War as corporal, Fifth Regiment, Infantry, Kentucky Volunteers.

Children:

Sixth Generation

*59. Isabel King.
60. James M. King; architect, Ashland, Kentucky.
61. Van King.
62. Florence King; m. John McGuire.
63. Bertha King; m. ——— Epperson; lived in Australia.
64. Edd. King, farmer; one-time State representative from Carter and Elliott Counties; m. Mellie Mobley, daughter of Harris W. Mobley. (See Mobley Family.)
65. Bige King.
66. Sallie King, teacher; d. of typhoid.
67. Alice King; m. ——— Hunter; d. in Wisconsin, 1935.

59. ISABEL KING; m. John S. Sloan, farmer, who died August, 1937.

Children:

Seventh Generation

68. Nora Sloan, teacher, deceased; unm.
69. Mayme Sloan, teacher.
70. Ethel Sloan; m. Herbert Criswell.
71. Carrie Soan; m. Cecil Walker.
72. Eva Sloan; m. Leonard Walker.
73. Frances Sloan; m. J. W. Bowling.
74. Watt Sloan; m. Judy Lewis.

53. JOSEPH NEWTON KING, farmer and merchant; resided at Newfoundland, Elliott County; m. Lina Green; d. at age of 73.

Children:

Sixth Generation

75. John B. King, manager of the Kitchen-Whitt Grocery Company, Ashland, Kentucky; d. July 1937.

76. William N. King, farmer, merchant and businessman; b. at Newfoundland, Elliott County, June 17, 1879; engaged in merchandizing at Soldier Carter County, for 15 years; purchased farm of 458 acres seven miles south of Lexington, the old Robert Todhunter farm, where he engaged in the operation of a limestone quarry and crushing and grinding limestone for agricultural and industrial purposes; also a stockholder in a tobacco warehouse and a general farmer; m. in 1900 Effie W. Kitchen, daughter of Charles and Loretta Kitchen and great-granddaughter of James Kitchen, Revolutionary War soldier, who came with his family from Greenbrier County, Virginia, now West Virginia, and settled near present Willard, Carter County, in the early 1820s. Children: Justine and William N. (Billy), Jr.

77. James Elias King, businessman; b. at Newfoundland, Kentucky, September 3, 1884; educated in public schools of Newfoundland; was a student at Marshall College, Huntington, West Virginia, for two years and later pursued a business course; was clerk and traveling salesman for Kitchen-Whitt Company for several years and afterwards became interested in many business activities: He was associated with N. T. Fannin in conducting a men's furnishing establishment in Ashland, was assistant cashier in the Second National Bank, Ashland; coal mining operator; director of wholesale grocery firm of Kitchen-Whitt, at Ashland; and a real estate operator.

On November 4, 1909, he was m. to Miss Lula B. Kitchen, daughter of Charles and Lauretta (Mobley) Kitchen, a granddaughter of Major Andrew J. and Winnie Kitchen and a great-granddaughter of James Kitchen, Revolutionary War soldier. Children: a son, Charles Newton King, b. November 21, 1910.

Mr. King was a Democrat, a member of the Chamber of Commerce; was affiliated with the Masons and the Elks and was a member of the Bellefonte Country Club.

78. Sarah King; m. John A. Gray, lawyer. Mr. Gray served as county attorney of Elliott County.

54. VAN BUREN KING, farmer and merchant at Counts Cross Roads, Carter County; m. Nannie (Nancy) Counts in Carter County, January 8, 1893.

Children: Sixth Generation

79. Lillie King; m. William H. Scott, merchant, Olive Hill, Kentucky. (See Scott Family.)

80. Bertha King; for many years cashier of the Carter County Commercial Bank, Olive Hill.

81. Letha King, a school teacher.

82. Wattt King.

*83. Herbert H. King.

84. Cena King.

85. Ruby King.

55. HOUSTON KING, farmer, b. in Tennessee, about 1837; m. about 1858, Elizabeth Mobley, daughter of Samuel and Talitha (Thompson) Mobley. (See Mobley Family.) He served in the Confederate Army during the Civil War; and was appointed and served as the first circuit court clerk of Elliott County.

Children and approximate dates of birth as shown by the U. S. Census of Elliott County for the year 1870:

Sixth Generation

86. Belle King; b. in 1859; unm.

87. Sarah King; b. in 1861.

88. Julia King; b. in 1867; m. John M. Williams.

89. Eliza King; b. in 1869; m. Jesse Robinson.

90. "Tom" King; m. Charles Evans.

91. Lula King; m. in the West; husband's name unknown.

92. William King; m. Mintie Evans.

57. SARAH KING; m. Robert Rose.

Children: Sixth Generation

93. Belle Rose; m. William Holbrook.

94. Francis Rose; m. Missouri Walker.

95. Sabra Rose; m. Dr. Wales B. Brown.

83. HERBERT H. KING, farmer; b. at Counts Cross Roads, Carter County, September 25, 1883; m. Carolyn Prichard, b. August 22, 1885, daughter of Leander Cox Prichard. (See Prichard Family.)

Children: Seventh Generation

96. Prichard King, teacher; m. Mona Caudill.

97. Watt King; m. Thelma Gollihue.

98. Harold King, teacher; has been engaged in teaching for several years and presently is superintendent of the Hitchins High School at Hitchins, Carter County; m. Josephine Gee, daughter of Charles and Kyon (Peay) Gee. (See Gee Family.) Mrs. King has engaged in educational work for several years and presently is a supervisor of the rural schools of Carter County.

99. Charlotte King; m. Raymond Isaac.

46. ELIJAH SARGENT HORTON, farmer and sometime public official, was b. in Russell County, Virginia, May 21, 1811, and d. in Carter County, Kentucky. He m. in Lee County, Virginia, about 1837, Nancy Cox, b. June 20, 1814, daughter of Henry Cox and his wife, Rebecca (Flanery) Cox. Soon after marriage he removed with his family to and settled on the little Sandy River about 12 miles from Grayson, Kentucky, the seat of justice of Carter County, where he lived until his death. He was elected and served as assessor (commissioner of revenue) for Carter County for the four-year term from 1851 to 1854, inclusive.

Children: Fifth Generation

*100. Henry Cox Horton.

101. Travis D. Horton; b. July 2, 1840; unm.

102. Rees Duff Horton; b. May 14, 1842; served in Confederate Army; m. Sarah Ballard.

103. David L. Horton, b. August 29, 1846, and d. March 29, 1847

104. Phoebe Horton, b. June 7, 1849; m. Alfred G. Rice. (See Rice Family.)

105. Amanda R. Horton; m. Dr. J. W. Strother. (See Strother Family.)

*106. Rebecca E. Horton; m. James D. Jones.

*107. William C. Horton.

100. HENRY COX HORTON, farmer and sometime public official, was b. in Carter County, August 26, 1838, and d. at Grayson, that county, March 13, 1914; m. in Carter County, January 11, 1860, Thursa Blankenbeckler, b. in Smyth County, Virginia, May 17, 1835, and d. December 5, 1927.

Henry C. Horton had service in the Confederate Army during the Civil War as a private in Fields' Company of Rangers and as second sergeant, Company "R", 5th Regt., Infantry, Kentucky Volunteers, C. S. A. He served as police judge of Grayson and for a number of years was a justice of the peace of Carter County.

Children: Sixth Generation

*108. Sarah Elizabeth Horton.

109. Travis M. ("Matt") Horton, b. July 16, 1863; m. Bettie Mc-Whorter.

*110. William A. Horton.

*111. Nancy R. ("Recie") Horton.

112. Phoebe J. Horton, b. December 14, 1870; d. ———, 1880.

113. John Elijah Horton, druggist at Grayson; b. March 20, 1874; m., first, April 10, 1898, Carrie Hubbard, b. November 30, 1869, and d. January 25, 1949, and m., secondly, December 15, 1949, Lela Holbrook, b. April 7, 1895. No children by either of these marriages.

114. Henry ("Harry") A. Horton; b. March 6, 1877; m. Gertrude Cheap.

108. SARAH ELIZABETH HORTON; b. October 18, 1860, and d. December 11, 1900; m. in Carter County, July 26, 1888, George Moses T. Botts, grocer, at Grayson, b. March 6, 1858, and d. February 2, 1927.

Children:
Seventh Generation

115. Roy Sellards Botts, b. May 22, 1889; m. Lillian Davis of Pocatello, Idaho.
116. Phoebe Leota Botts, b. February 17, 1891; m. Watt A. King.
117. William O'rear Botts, b. December 27, 1892; m. Ercel Gifford.
118. Mary Horton Botts, b. January 22, 1895.
119. Recie Botts, b. April 4, 1897.
120. George Wesley Botts, b. February 7, 1899; m. Louella Callihan.

110. WILLIAM ANDREW HORTON, physician, at Grayson; was b. in Carter County, Kentucky, December 11, 1865, and d. at Grayson, February 19, 1931. He was graduated from the Medical College of the University of Cincinnati in 1891 and immediately thereafter began the practice of his profession at Grayson and continued until his death. Aside from his profession, Dr. Horton was a businessman of many activities: He owned and operated a fine farm near Grayson; organized the Horton Drug Store at Grayson in 1889 which subsequently was reorganized as the Horton Brothers Drug Store upon the admission of his brother, J. E. Horton, as a partner. He was one of the original stock holders of the Commercial Bank of Grayson and for many years was chairman of the official board of that institution.

Dr. Horton was a Democrat in politics and was long a consistent member of the Christian Church at Grayson, serving as deacon for many years.

Dr. Horton m. at Grayson, December 28, 1892, Mollie Lewis, teacher, b. near Lee's Summit, Missouri, October 14, 1869, and d. at Grayson, October 30, 1942, a daughter of Charles Nelms Lewis III, and his wife, Phoebe (Stewart) Lewis. (See Lewis Family.)

Children:
Seventh Generation

121. William Lewis Horton, b. at Grayson, February 9, 1894; was educated in the graded and high schools of Grayson, graduating from the latter in 1913, graduated from Christian Normal Institute; (now the Kentucky Christian College); attended Transylvania College, Lexington, Kentucky, and Fuggazzi School of Business, that city; was a traveling salesman for many years; an employee of the Office of Price Administration in the regional offices of Lexington, Louisville and Cincinnati; and an employee of the Kentucky Division of Motor Transportation during the administration of Governor Earle C. Clements. He was appointed acting postmaster at Grayson, January 1, 1949, which appointment was confirmed by the U. S.

Senate in July, 1951. He has been a director of the Commercial Bank of Grayson since 1927; is a member of the First Christian Church of Grayson and has served as deacon since 1931. He m. Miss Bess Marie Stidham of Grayson, daughter of E. L. Stidham, merchant and businessman of Grayson. No children.

122. Thursa Horton; teacher of music; b. at Grayson, January 20, 1898; educated in the public schools of Grayson, graduating from Grayson High School in 1916; graduated from the Christian Normal Institute (now Kentucky Christian College) in 1925; attended Hamilton College at Lexington, Kentucky, and the College of Music at Cincinnati; taught piano at the Christian Normal Institute for several years and is presently engaged in private piano teaching.

Miss Horton became a member of the Christian Church at Grayson early in life and has been an active worker ever since; she was chosen church pianist at the age of 12 and is presently church organist.

123. Phoebe Horton was b. at Grayson, December 14, 1899; m. Arthur Huff, December 28, 1921. Mr. Huff is a native of Carter County; was educated in the public schools and attended the Grayson (Kentucky) Normal School where he was trained for teaching; taught in the common and graded schools for several years; engaged in the mercantile business at Grayson for a time; and deals in real estate. He is an active member of the First Christian Church at Grayson and frequently fills the pulpit in the absence of a regular pastor.

124. Blanche Horton, b. at Grayson, December 20, 1908, and d. May 4, 1917.

111. Nancy R. (Recie) Horton, teacher, was b. June 30, 1868; m. Peter Brown, Jr., of Grayson. Peter Brown, farmer and sometimes a local public official, was b. January 19, 1870. He was long a deputy Sheriff of Carter County and served as master commissioner of the Carter (County) Circuit Court.

106. Rebecca Elizabeth (Coba) Horton was b. February 15, 1857, and d. July 18, 1940; m. James Dunlap Jones, who was a grandson of Evans Jones and Ann Griffith, who were b. in Wales, and a son of Griffith Jones and Elizabeth Ann Dunlap, the former of whom was b. in Wales and d. in Carter County, Kentucky, April 18, 1857, and was buried at Lindsay Chapel, near Grayson; and the latter of whom was b. 1805, in Washington County, Pennsylvania, a daughter of William and Ann Dunlap who emigrated from Ireland.

The other children of Griffith and Elizabeth Ann (Dunlap) Jones were: (a) Dr. William Dunlap Jones who m. Mildred Hord. They were the parents of Thomas Hord Jones and Mrs. Sallie J. Ault. (See Hord Family.) (b) Martha Ann Jones who m. William Bowling. They were the parents of Elizabeth who m. Dr. D. B. Wilcox;

Mary P. Bowling; Mildred Bowling; Kate who m. Mr. Stewart; and Sallie who m. Mr. Lukens.

Dr. D. B. Wilcox was a native of Carter County, Kentucky. In young manhood he engaged in teaching in the public schools of Carter County. Later he was graduated in medicine and began the practice of his profession at Grayson and continued with success until his death. He was a Republican in politics; was an active worker and wise counselor; and served his party in many capacities, among others, that of Chairman of the County Committee.

Dr. and Mrs. Wilcox were the parents of two children—daughters: Lelia Wilcox was educated in the graded school of Grayson and the Grayson Normal School where she was trained for teaching; taught in the Grayson schools; was elected on the Republican ticket and served as Superintendent of the Public Schools of Carter County for a term; m. Mr. Peters.

Helen Wilcox was educated in the public schools of Grayson; m. Elbert S. Reeves. Mr. Reeves is a native of Carter County and descended from pioneer families of Northeastern Kentucky—on the maternal side from the Williams family of present Boyd County. He was educated in the public schools of Carter County and at Grayson (Kentucky) Normal School where he was trained for teaching; taught in the public schools of Carter County for a time, mostly as principal of the Denton and the Hitchens Graded Schools. Later he entered the insurance business in connection with the Inter-Southern Insurance Company with offices in Ashland, Kentucky. Resigning his position with the Inter-Southern, he became connected with a large insurance company of the South and is presently a regional director of that company with offices in the Atlanta, Georgia, area.

James Dunlap Jones, lawyer and sometime public official, was b. at Louisa, Lawrence County, Kentucky, December 12, 1835, and d. at Grayson, Kentucky, February 15, 1901; educated in the Owensboro (Kentucky) Schools; studied law and was admitted to the bar; was appointed and served as the first county attorney of Boyd County. Removing to Grayson, he continued in the practice of law; and served as county attorney of Carter County, 1884-1888.

Children of James D. and Rebecca Elizabeth (Horton) Jones:

Sixth Generation

125. Maud Horton Jones, teacher; b. July 21, 1879, d. December 23, 1947; educated in the schools of Grayson and Southern Normal School at Bowling Green, Kentucky; taught in the public schools of Carter County for 30 years; m., November 25, 1903, Millard Goble Porter, son of Frank and Harriet (Goble) Porter. They were the parents of two children—daughters (Seventh Generation): Harriet Rebecca, who m. Delmar C. Little, and Blanche, who m. Arnold Counts.

126. Bettie C. Myra Jones, teacher, b. April 11, 1881, d. October

5, 1940; m. Edward or Edwin Crawford, son of John and Alice (Duncan) Crawford. They were the parents of one child—a son (Seventh Generation), Thornton Jones Crawford, b. July 28, 1915, who m. Eloise Triplett, daughter of Charles and Carrie (Houck) Triplett.

127. Nannie Joe Jones, b. February 20, 1883, d. October 28, 1905, unm.

128. James Henry Jones, b. December 12, 1884, d. April 26, 1919.

129. Ella Jones, teacher, b. October 14, 1886, d. October 27, 1918; m. Ray Loyal Forrest. They were the parents of four children (Seventh Generation): Claudia F., who m. Mr. Reynolds; Bess, who m. George Cooksey; Jack; and Louise, who m. Orville Montgomery.

130. Mary Travis Jones, teacher, b. August 28, 1889, d. October 25, 1918; m. Clarence W. Henderson, undertaker at Olives Hill, a son of Robert and Sarilda (Armstrong) Henderson. They were the parents of one child, a daughter (Seventh Generation), Mary Elizabeth, b. December 12, 1912, who m. Clyde Maggard.

131. Mattie Tom Jones, b. January 26, 1893; has been employed as clerk in the Commercial Bank of Grayson since 1915.

132. William Horton Jones, b. February 4, 1895, d. December 26, 1951; m. Charlene Montgomery. No children.

133. John Strother Jones, b. August 16, 1897; m. Bess Lyle Hall; employed by the American Rolling Mills Company; resides in Ashland, Kentucky.

107. WILLIAM C. HORTON, farmer, miller and merchant, at Rosedale; b. June 22, 1844; m. Mildred Whitt.

Children:
                    Sixth Generation

134. Elijah E. Horton, traveling salesman; m. Elsie McDavid; resided in Ashland.

135. Reese Duff Horton; resided at Russell, Kentucky.

136. William C. Horton, Jr.; b. 1901, d. at Ashland, June 8, 1926; m. Beadie Mobley. Children (Seventh Generation): William Thomas Horton and Laura Mildred Horton.

137. Florence Horton; m. Herbert McDavid; resided in Pasadena, Calif.

138. ——— Horton, daughter; m. John L. Kitchen; resided at Versailles, Kentucky.

139. Adeliade Horton; m. Mr. Piphey; resided in Oakland, California.

47. REESE DUFF HORTON, farmer; b. in Russell County, Virginia, November 18, 1813, and d. in Carter County, Kentucky, in 1871; m. May 16, 1839, Susan Cox b. in Lee County, Virginia, October 6, 1822, and d. in Carter County, Kentucky, April 22, 1903, daughter of Henry Cox and his wife, Rebecca (Flanery) Cox. He served in

the Confederate forces during the Civil War as a second corporal, Company "B", 5th Regiment, Infantry, Kentucky Volunteers.

Children:

Fifth Generation

140. Martha Horton, b. March 24, 1839; m. Harris Mobley. (See Mobley Family.)

*141. Elizabeth Horton.

*142. James K. Polk Horton.

143. Travis Horton; b. 1845.

*144. William Lester Horton.

*145. Flanery Horton.

*146. Rebecca Susan Horton.

147. Elijah Horton; b. 1854, m. (last) Mildred Whitt Horton, widow of William C. Horton.

*148. Mima Sarah Horton.

149. John Horton; b. 1859.

150. Reese Duff Horton, b. 1863; killed by explosion in a quarry near Greenup while engaged in construction work on the C & O Railroad.

141. ELIZABETH HORTON; b. 1841; m. John Elliott; removed to Wisconsin about 1895 with whole family.

Children:

Sixth Generation

151. Samuel Elliott.

152. Minerva Elliott.

153. Reese Elliott.

154. Edd. Elliott.

155. James K. Polk Elliott.

156. Martha Elliott.

157. Thomas Elliott.

158. Rebecca Elliott.

159. Amanda Elliott.

144. WILLIAM LESTER HORTON (Curly Bill) was b. March 18, 1847; m., March 22, 1867, Ellen Hood, b. October 30, 1847.

Children:

Sixth Generation

*160. Susan Alice Horton.

*161. Eliza Elizabeth Horton.

162. Samantha Isabel Horton, b. August 8, 1871, d. young.

163. Reese Theodore Horton, b. November 6, 1873, d. at the age of 5 years.

164. Sarah Loretta Horton.

165. Maggie Florence Horton; b. December 3, 1879; m. John Stump.

*166. John William Horton.

*167. Rebecca Ethel Horton.
168. Pearl Geneva Horton; b. August 21, 1886; m. Dalton Kitchen.
*169. Louisa Ellen Horton.

160. SUSAN ALICE HORTON; b. April 26, 1868; m. Alex. (Eck) Williams.

Children:
Seventh Generation

170. Dora Williams; m. Dillard Dykes.
171. Leonard Williams; m. Nancy Crowe.
172. Bertha Williams; m. John Cales.
*173. Lonnie Williams.
174. Retta Williams; m. Gus Shafer.
175. Estille Williams; m. Velma ———.
176. Edward Williams; m. Agnes Jones.
177. Laura Williams; m. Charles Blossom.

161. ELIZA ELIZABETH HORTON, b. November 26, 1869; m. William Lowe Mobley.

Children:
Seventh Generation

*178. Charles Lester Mobley.
179. James Arval Mobley; m. Letha Kitchen.
180. Earl Thompson Mobley; m. Theorie Barker.
*181. Malinda Ellen Mobley.
*182. Goldie Alice Mobley.

William Lowe Mobley was twice married. He m., first, Arminta Whitt, daughter of J. (Jack) P. Whitt, merchant, and Missouri (Cox) Whitt; and they were the parents of Julia Mobley, who m. Charles McCoy, and John Harris Mobley, merchant at Olive Hill, who m. Clara Shumate.

166. JOHN WILLIAM HORTON; b. June 25, 1881; m. Laura Mobley.

Children:
Seventh Generation

183. Lou M. Horton; b. November 7, 1902.
184. William L. Horton; b. November 12, 1908.
185. Charles O. Horton; b. September 25, 1911.
186. Estill Horton.

167. REBECCA ETHEL HORTON; b. March 3, 1884; m. Charles Thornsberry.

Children:
Seventh Generation

187. Glenn H. Thornsberry; m. Virginia Kearns.
188. Madge Thornsberry; m. William Rice.

169. LOUISA (LULU) ELLEN HORTON; b. February 28, 1889; m. Britt Ison.

Children:

Seventh Generation

189. Opal Ison.
190. Burrell Ison.
191. Faye Ison.

173. LONNIE WILLIAMS; m. Ada Wolfe.

Children:

Eighth Generation

192. Ruby Williams.
193. Edith Williams.

178. CHARLES LESTER MOBLEY; m. Sarah Creech.

Children:

Eighth Generation

194. Herston Mobley.
195. Esther Mobley.
196. Throne Mobley.
197. Arval Mobley.
198. Woodrow Mobley.

181. MALINDA ELLEN MOBLEY; m. Charles B. Wallace.

Children:

Eighth Generation

199. Linda E. Wallace.
200. Arval E. Wallace.

182. GOLDIE ALICE MOBLEY; m. Lonnie Howerton.

Children:

Eighth Generation

201. Christine Howerton, b. March 27, 1920.
202. Carl L. Howerton, b. October 27, 1921.
203. Lonnie Howerton, Jr., b. February 15, 1928.

142. JAMES K. POLK HORTON, b. 1843; m. October 9, 1867, Mrs. Elizabeth Boggs, b. Elizabeth Green, who m. a Mr. Boggs who was killed in the Civil War. They were the parents of Sallie Boggs, who m. Flanery Horton, brother to James K. Polk Horton.

Children:

Sixth Generation

204. William (Billie) Horton.
205. Rebecca Horton; m. Floyd Greene.
206. Minerva Horton; m. James Robinson.
207. James K. Polk Horton, Jr.
208. Eliza Belle Horton; m. James Robinson after the death of his wife, her sister, Minerva.

145. FLANERY HORTON; b. June 15, 1849, d. at Elton, Wisconsin, March 4, 1935; m. Sarah Boggs, who d. January 8, 1935, aged 80.

Children:

Sixth Generation

209. Nelson Boggs Horton; m. Dollie Rice.
210. Leota Horton; m. Joseph Powers.
211. Mary Susan Horton; m. Jasper W. Roe.
212. Maude Horton.
213. Belle Horton; m., first, Mr. Armstrong, and secondly, Dr. Voss.
214. Florence Horton; m. Fred Carrier.
215. Evaline Horton.
216. Sarah Horton.

146. REBECCA SUSAN HORTON, b. 1851, d. May 2, 1930; m. Daniel Sparks who d. in 1929. They removed to Ephrata, Wisconsin, about 1905.

Children:

Sixth Generation

217. John Sparks, d. 1899; m. Mollie Osborn.
218. Reese Duff Sparks; m. Lizzie Elkins; resided at Covington, Ky.
219. Jesse Sparks; m. Nola Gambill.
220. William Flanery Sparks; m. Goldie Lee Bowling; resided in Ashland, Kentucky.
221. James Sparks; m. ——, deceased, resided at Bluefield, West Virginia.
222. Alcia Susan Sparks; m. Thomas Baker; resided at Wanatcha, Washington. No children.
223. Martha Sparks; m. Thomas Purdy; resided at Roland, Washington.
224. Eliza Sparks; d. at age of 18.
225. Virginia Sparks; m., first, Bernard Rankins of Spokane, Washington, and after his death she m., secondly, Thomas Baker, who after her death in 1918, m. her sister, Alcia Susan (See No. 222). Children of Virginia Sparks and Bernard Rankins (seventh generation) were Hoyt Rankin and Daniel Rankin.

148. MIMA SARAH HORTON; b. 1857; m. Gus Ratcliff.

Children:

Sixth Generation

226. Johnny Ratcliff.
227. Susan Ratcliff; m. Green Adkins.
228. Cora Ratcliff; m. Nelson Whitt.
229. Missouri Ratcliff.
230. Elijah Ratcliff.
231. Leota Ratcliff.

232. Oscar Ratcliff.

233. Harris Ratcliff; was killed at Lexington by C & O Railroad train.

234. Richard (Dick) Ratcliff.

235. Gus Ratcliff, Jr.; had service in World War II and was killed in action.

48. TRAVIS HORTON JR. was b. in Russell County, Virginia, November 30, 1818; m. in Carter County, Kentucky, December 24, 1841, Rebecca Cox, b. in Russell County, Virginia, a daughter of Henry Cox and his wife, Rebecca (Flanery) Cox. He had service in the Confederate Army.

Children:

Fifth Generation

236. Elijah Horton served in the Confederate Army; was promoted from fifth sergeant to second Lieutenant, Company "D", 5th Regt. Infantry, Kentucky Volunteers, at Prestonsburg, October 19, 1861. In the fall of 1864 he was shot under orders of Gen. Stephen G. Burbridge, then commanding the Union Forces in Kentucky, for the reason, allegedly, he had engaged in guerilla warfare. Efforts by his relatives to save him were unavailing. He was interred in the State Cemetery at Frankfort.

*237. John T. Horton.

238. Phoebe ("Dollie") Horton; b. 1849.

239. Eliza ("Coot") Horton.

*240. Travis R. Horton.

237. JOHN T. HORTON, farmer; b. August 15, 1843, d., 1907; m. in Carter County, September 15, 1870, Lovinia Rice, b. 1850, d. 1944, daughter of Nelson T. and America (Richards) Rice' and great-granddaughter of Captain John Bailey and Charles Rice, both of whom had service in the Virginia Forces (Clark's Illinois Regiment) in the Revolutionary War. (See Rice Family and Bailey Family.)

Children:

Sixth Generation

241. Nelson T. Horton, farmer; b. December 12, 1871, d. February 12, 1950.

242. Bertha M. Horton, teacher; b. April 29, 1874, d. December 31, 1942; m. James B. Mobley. (See Mobley Family.)

*243. Mary L. (Mollie) Horton.

*244. John H. Horton.

*245. Goldie Horton.

*246. Eliza Alford (Alie) Horton.

243. MARY L. (MOLLIE) HORTON, teacher, local public official, postmaster and business woman, was b. at Bruin, Elliott County, Kentucky, December 20, 1876; was educated in the public schools of

Elliott County—completing the eighth grade; attended the Holbrook Normal School at Newfoundland which was equivalent to high school; and was a student for more than two years at Morehead (Kentucky) College; began teaching in 1894, at 18 years of age and continued teaching in the rural schools of Carter, Elliott and Greenup Counties for the nine succeeding years; was elected on the Democratic ticket and served as superintendent of public schools of Elliott County for three terms, twelve years—from 1906 to 1910 and from 1926 to 1934; served as chairman of the Elliott County Democratic Executive Committee, 1933-1934 when she resigned to accept appointment as postmaster at Sandy Hook, serving from December, 1934, to December, 1943, when she resigned so as to give personal attention to her general store at Sandy Hook.

In June, 1907, Mollie Horton was united in marriage with John Will Greene. They established and maintained their home at Sandy Hook (Martinsburg) county seat of Elliott County. Being in complete agreement with respect to the important things in life, they worked together very effectively in all matters pertaining to public schools and education, politics and civil affairs. They entertained in their home and consulted and advised with important people who came to the community on business and/or political affairs. Aside from and in addition to her many public duties, Mrs. Greene was interested in and gave considerable time to the Church and to the social and civic activities of the town, particularly to the Church and its activities, teaching classes of both adults and teen-agers in Sunday School.

John Will Greene, sometime teacher, traveling salesman and merchant at Sandy Hook, son of James and Mary (Day) Greene, was b. in Elliott County, Kentucky, December 23, 1873, and d. at Sandy Hook, August 23, 1933. Interment in Rose Hill Cemetery, Ashland, Kentucky. His mother d. when he was a youth, thus throwing him more or less on his own resources. He received very little formal education. However, by utilizing his spare time he managed to obtain sufficient education to begin teaching school in 1896. He was a thorough, painstaking teacher.

In 1899 he entered Bowling Green (Kentucky) Business University from which he was graduated in 1900. Subsequently he taught school for two years and then became a traveling salesman and continued as such for six years. Soon after his marriage in June, 1907, he located permanently at Sandy Hook. Here he went into the department mercantile business which he conducted successfully until his death.

Aside from conducting his extensive mercantile business, he was an active worker in the Democratic party and actively supported all educational and progressive movements in his county, particularly that of highway improvement. He was of pleasing personality, forceful, magnetic and influential in his county.

Children:

Seventh Generation

247. John Woodrow Green; b. December 30, 1916.

244. JOHN H. HORTON; b. April 12, 1880, d. December 1, 1932; m., March 1915, Essie Justice.

Children:

Seventh Generation

248. Nelson T. Horton; b. December 21, 1915.
249. Irene Horton; b. February 6, 1917.
250. Justice H. Horton; b. October 28, 1923.

245. GOLDIE HORTON, teacher, was b. at Bruin, Elliott County, September 2. 1881. She attended the local public school at Mouth of Bruin in her girlhood days; and during the long interims between sessions of school she read in the library at home the Bible, Ridpath's U. S. History (complete), Marvin's Travels and high school text books of an uncle who had attended a high school in Virginia. In due course of time two older sisters became old enough to and began teaching in the public schools. They subscribed for four or five educational journals which were read with avidity by sister Goldie, creating in her a desire to become an efficient teacher. Her schooling and study at this point was supplemented by a three-month's course at Prof. Holbrooks' Normal School at Newfoundland, Elliott County, where she was trained for teaching. At the close of the course she entered a teacher's examination, was granted a first class certificate and entered upon her long successful career as teacher. She was engaged in teaching in the public schools of Carter, Elliott, Greenup and Lawrence Counties for 37 years, retiring in 1948.

Miss Goldie Horton was m. to Mr. Oscar Johnson. No children. She is presently living in the ancestral home at Bruin.

240. TRAVIS R. ("LITTLE TRAV.") HORTON; b. March 27, 1857, d. at Portsmouth, Ohio, October 24, 1929; m., July 19, 1885, Martha Lee Rose.

Children:

Sixth Generation

*251. Charles C. Horton.
252. James W. Horton; b. December 3, 1887.
253. Rebecca Horton; b. September 25, 1889; m. Mr. Heaberlin.
254. Ora Horton; b. November 13, 1891; m. Mr. Tamme.
255. Eliza Horton; b. October 22, 1895; m. Mr. Roberts.
256. Henry Horton; b. 1900.
257. Faye Horton; b. March 2, 1904; m. Mr. Andrews.
258. Jessie Horton; b. July 19, 1908; m. Mr. Stewart.

251. CHARLES C. HORTON; b. June 15, 1886; m., February 6, 1913, Emma Crabtree.

Children:

Seventh Generation

259. Roy Horton; b. August 12, 1913.

260. Ned Horton; b. December 24, 1917.

261. Ada Horton; b. April 17, 1921; d. April 20, 1921.

49. JOHN THOMPSON HORTON, farmer and sometime local public official, was b. in Russell County, Virginia, July 15, 1821, and d. in Carter County, Kentucky, June 27, 1898; m. in Carter County, January 10, 1849, Elizabeth Cox, b. in Lee County, Virginia, October 26, 1826, and d. in Carter County, daughter of Henry Cox and his wife, Rebecca (Flanery) Cox. John T. Horton was for many years a justice of the peace of Carter County. He had service in the Confederate Army during the Civil War as second corporal and second lieutenant, Company "D", 5th Regiment Infantry, Kentucky Volunteers.

Children:

Fifth Generation

*262. Travis Henry ("Riggs") Horton.

263. Rebecca Jane Horton, b. September 19, 1852; m. Richard ("Dick") Williams, July, 1871.

264. Leander C. Horton, b. July 13, 1855, and d. September 20, 1858.

265. Nancy Susan Horton, b. July 13, about 1857, and d. July 9, 1892.

266. Phoebe Ann Horton, b. April 30, 1859, and d. October 10, 1859.

267. Martha T. Horton, b. October 16, 1861, and d. October 8, 1879.

268. Johnny Elizabeth Horton, b. January 14, 1864, and d. May 4, 1889.

269. Elijah H. Horton, b. March 29, 1866, and d. April 1, 1866.

270. Beulah Lee Horton, b. December 28, 1868, and d. April 5, 1869.

John T. Horton was the father of other sons:

*271. Lorenzo Dow Horton.

*272. El Canor (Elkanah) Horton.

262. TRAVIS HENRY ("RIGGS") HORTON, farmer, b. November 7, 1849, and d. May 4, 1923; m. July 11, 1871, Talitha E. Mobley, b. about 1855, daughter of Harris W. and Malinda Lowe Mobley. (See Mobley Family.)

Children:

Sixth Generation

*273. John Dallas Horton.

274. Harris Ward Horton, twin brother of John Dallas Horton, b. December 22, 1872, and d. May 7, 1892.

275. Elijah Horton, b. March 21, 1878, and d. October 13, 1927.
*276. Malinda Susan Horton.

273. JOHN DALLAS HORTON, farmer, b. December 22, 1872; m., first, March 4, 1900, Rosa Myrtle Greene, d. July 3, 1909.

Children:
Seventh Generation
*277. Elizabeth (Bettie) Horton.
278. William W. Horton, b. March 20, 1905; m., February 9, 1929, Ada Cassidy.
*279. John T. Horton.

273-A. John Dallas Horton, m., secondly, Florence Craig, October 28, 1911.

Children:
Seventh Generation
*280. Wick Ford Horton, b. September 26, 1912.
281. Charles Wayne Horton, b. January 12, 1914.
282. Hazel W. Horton, b. January 8, 1916.
283. Ralph Henry Horton, b. May 28, 1918, and d. December 6, 1930.
284. Glen Fleming Horton, b. December 14, 1920.
285. Mary Katharyn Horton, b. March 1, 1923.
286. Reece Homer Horton, b. February 24, 1925.
287. Marvin Vaughan Horton, b. May 14, 1927.
288. Frank Kenneth Horton, b. October 22, 1929.
289. Donald Rex Horton, b. July 28, 1933.
290. Reba June Horton, b. June 23, 1935.

277. ELIZABETH (BETTIE) HORTON; b. September 8, 1903; m. Henry Thomas. Children: (eighth generation): Ronald Wayne, David Cleve, Henry Horton and Leonard Earl.

279. JOHN T. HORTON; b. June 20, 1907; m. Della Dinkins. Children (eighth generation): Dallas, Gladys Faye, and Myrtle Ann.

280. WICK FORD HORTON; b. September 26, 1912; m. Jewel Gearhart. Children (eighth generation): Nancy Sue and Hazel, who m. Max E. Calhoun.

276. MALINDA SUSAN HORTON; b. October 19, 1875, d. February 5, 1909; m. Conn Harper, August 3, 1895. They were the parents of Loretta Harper (seventh generation) b. May 24, 1896, who m. Lewis Fargo, May 28, 1915, and whose son (eighth generation) is John William Fargo, b. January 16, 1916.

271. LORENZO DOW HORTON, farmer and old-time school teacher; b. February 16, 1844; served in the Confederate Army as private, Company "B", 5th Regiment Infantry, Kentucky Volunteers; m., March 28, 1866, Amanda Melvina Coburn, b. August 17, 1847.

Children:
Sixth Generation
291. John Horton; b. 1867.
292. Elijah J. ("Jake") Horton; b. 1870.
He was for many years agent and telegrapher for the E. K. Railway Company, at Willard, Kentucky, and later auditor for the company in the main office at Riverton, Kentucky; m. in Carter County, March 17, 1893, Lybb Fleming, b. 1873. No children.
293. Robert Lee Horton, one-time teacher, farmer and stock raiser; unm.
L. D. Horton lived on Bells Trace, Carter County, about four miles south of Willard.

272. EL CANOR (ELKANAH) HORTON, farmer; b. in Carter County, Kentucky, May 4, 1849, and d. at Johns Run, that county, November 3, 1934; m. in Carter County, April 3, 1879, Alice Lawson, b. in Tennessee, February 28, 1864, d. at Johns Run, a daughter of Andrew and Mary (Fields) Lawson. (See Fields Family.)
Children:
Sixth Generation
*294. Cora Horton.
*295. Aaron Horton.
*296. Gertie Horton.
*297. Tessie Horton.
*298. Walter B. ("Watt") Horton.
*299. Dorcie Horton.
*300. Herman Horton.

294. CORA HORTON; b. January 23, 1880, d. July 20, 1916; m., first, May 20, 1900, Jason Fields, who d. October 5, 1909. (See Fields Family.)
Children:
Seventh Generation
301. Herbert Fields; b. February 24, 1901; m. Lillie Ferrell.
302. Lura Fields; b. June 4, 1903.
303. Orbie Fields; b. January 19, 1906.
304. Edgar Fields; b. December 25, 1908.

294-A. Cora Horton Fields m., secondly, Robert Waddell, October ——, 1910.
Children:
Seventh Generation
305. Alma Waddell; b. March ——, 1913.
306. Jesse Canor Waddell; b. February ——, 1915.

295. AARON HORTON; farmer; b. March 29, 1882, d. near Cascade Caves, Carter County, 1942; interment in Snodgrass Cemetery at

Grayson. He enlisted in the U. S. Army in young manhood and had service in the Phillipines. He m. Minnie Bush, daughter of Fayette Bush of Lost Creek, near Willard.

296. GERTIE HORTON; b. June 10, 1885; m. Allen Crawford, March 5, 1905.

Children:

Seventh Generation

307. Raymond Julian Crawford; b. September 25, 1906; m. July 13, 1927, Beulah Adams. b. September 24, 1906.

308. Russell Bertrand Crawford; b. August 9, 1909; m., September 24, 1931, Arlene Walker, b. June 22, 1912.

309. Dorcie Maude Crawford; b. November 20, 1913; m., December 7, 1927, Charles Kelley, b. April 16, 1906.

310. Adah Alene Crawford; b. April 16, 1915.

311. Kenneth Horton Crawford, b. November 6, 1918, d. June 23, 1919.

312. Arville Leslie Crawford, b. August 27, 1924.

297. TESSIE HORTON; b. November 4, 1890; m. Clarence Bush, son of Fayette Bush.

298. WALTER BROUGHTON ("WATT") HORTON; b. May 28, 1893; m., first, October 16, 1913, Nannie Bays, who d. December 23, 1921. No children. He m., secondly, Leatha Adams, November 10, 1922.

Children:

Seventh Generation

313. Garnet Alene Horton.

314. Ellis Horton; b. July 24, 1925.

315. Watt Horton. Jr., b. January 6, 1928.

316. Mary Lois Horton; b. January 19, 1933.

299. DORCIE HORTON; b. August 11, 1898; m. Sherman Adams.[5]

300. HERMAN HORTON, teacher and public official; b. at Johns Run, Carter County, Kentucky, November 10, 1901, d. at Grayson, Kentucky, September 16, 1938; attended the Carter County rural school; graduated from the high school at the Christian Normal Institute at Grayson and attended Junior College at C. N. S.; was graduated from the Eastern Kentucky Teachers' College at Richmond with degree of A. B., May, 1930; and attended Kentucky University at Lexington, 1937. He began teaching in the Carter County rural schools in 1920 and taught almost continuously in the rural, graded and high schools until 1934; was elected Superintendent of the Carter County schools in 1934 and was serving as such at date of his death, September 16, 1938.

On August 18, 1929, Mr. Horton was united in marriage with Miss Grace Leavett Sanders at Jellico, Tennessee. Miss Sanders was

b. December 18, 1908, at Bondville, Mercer County, Kentucky; attended the Mercer County rural schools; was graduated from the Harrodsburg High School, 1926; attended Centre College at Danville, Eastern State Teachers' College at Richmond and Morehead State College at Morehead, taught in the rural schools of Mercer County, 1927-1930, and in the Grahn Graded and High Schools, at Grahn, Carter County, 1931-1935. In 1938 she was selected as Clerk and Treasurer of the Carter County Board of Education, and in 1939 as Attendance Officer of the Carter County schools and Treasurer of the Carter County of Education which positions she is presently holding.

Children:

Seventh Generation

317. Carol Lynn Horton (son), b. November 7, 1930, at Grahn, Carter County.

318. Alice Lee Horton, b. December 26, 1936, at Grayson, Carter County.

319. Joel Thomas Horton, b. April 13, 1938, at Grayson.

---

[1] In his will, probated in the Russell County (Virginia) Court, September 10, 1903, Patrick Kendrick bequeathed his property to his children: William, Jane Lock, Frances Richie, Patrick, Rachel Johnson, George, Molly Horton, Isbel Horton.

[2] The Horton Family Bible in possession of E. J. Horton, Grayson, Kentucky.

[3] Henry Cox, b. June 14, 1776, d. 1837; m., 1802, Rebecca Flanery, b. April 29, 1787. They settled in Lee County, Virginia. He was a son of David C. Cocke, who d. July 10, 1827, and Jemima (Leece) Cocke, who d. January 15, 1834. David C. Cocke had service in the Revolutionary War. The spelling of the surname "Cocke" was changed to "Cox" about 1840 by the Legislature of Virginia on the application of one of Henry Cox's brothers. Henry Cox and Rebecca Flanery were the parents of ten children: (a) Phoebe Cox married John Bailey and they were the ancestors of the Baileys of Rosedale and Grahn communities in Carter County. (b) Jemima Cox married George Wallace and they were the ancestors of the Wallaces of the Leon community in Carter County; (c) John Cox m. Lina Whitt; (d) David Cox remained in Virginia; (e) Henry Cox married Eleanor Roe; (f) Adam Cox married Sidney Roe and they were the parents of Elijah, Henry, Mrs. J. W. Whitt and others; (g) Nancy, (h) Susannah, (i) Rebecca, and (j) Elizabeth married, respectively, Elijah, Reese, Travis and John Horton, brothers.

[4] The Horton Family (Manuscript), prepared by Goldie Horton Johnson, Bruin, Ky.

[5] The Horton Family Genealogy (Manuscript), by Herman Horton, Grayson, Kentucky

HOWE FAMILY OF GREENUP COUNTY

This surname, originally spelled Hoo, is traced to ancient France, where it signified in those times, a high place—a hill. It later took on the Norman form "de la Hoo" and "de la Howe," meaning people who lived on a hill. The name was introduced into England at the time of the Norman conquest (1066), and has been consistently spelled Howe in that country. In the New England States in America it was spelled How until comparatively recent times.

John How, the immigrant ancestor of a large number of families of this name in America. is thought to have descended from John Howe, of Warwickshire, England, and to have been a grandson of John Howe of Hodin-hall. This line has been traced back to Sir John How of Lancaster, who lived during the reign of Charles I.

John How, the American founder, was among the earliest settlers of Watertown, Massachusetts.

A branch of the English family of Howe settled in the North of Ireland and the name is well scattered throughout that country. Francis Howe, of the Irish branch, came to America as a child with his widowed mother and located at Stonington, Connecticut. There is a tradition that he was of the same branch of the family as Sir William Howe and Lord Howe, who led the British forces in the American Revolution.

The progenitor of the Howe family in Northeastern Kentucky was John W. How or Howe. a Revolutionary War soldier. He was b. in Virginia, probably Fincastle county, in 1753, and migrated with his family and settled in then Mason county, Kentucky, now Greenup county, probably in the 1780's. He was elected as State representative from Mason county, 1796. and was a farmer, a slave holder, and a man of importance in the early affairs of Greenup county. On June 3. 1833, he appeared in the Greenup County Court and made declaration in connection with his claim for pension growing out of his service in the Revolutionary War wherein he stated, among other things, that in the Fall of 1775 he enlisted in the Army and served in Captain William Campbell's Company, a rifle company, of the First Regiment of the Virginia State Line, commanded at first by Colonel Patrick Henry and after his resignation by Colonel William Christian; that when enlisted he resided in that part of Fincastle county, Virginia, which was embraced within the boundary of Montgomery county upon its formation; that he did not engage in any regular battles but was in a number of skirmishes and that he was engaged mostly in guarding the coasts: that he rendezvoused at New London and marched to Williamsburg and from there to points on the coast and then returned to Williamsburg where he was discharged after having served about twelve months.

He stated further that in the Spring of 1778 he was appointed by Colonel William Preston as a spy for a term of two years and served as such for at least six months of each year in Captain Cloyd's Company.

He stated further that he volunteered for military service in Montgomery County, Virginia, in 1774, and served under Captain James Robinson; that he was stationed at Woods Fort and rendezvoused at Camp Union subsequently called Louisburg (Lewisburg) and with his organization marched to the mouth of Kanawha River [Point Pleasant] and arrived there the night of the day [October 10, 1774] the battle was fought.

In a deposition made March 16, 1841, by Mary Ann Howe, widow, she stated that she was 75 years old; that she married John W. Howe in Montgomery county, Virginia, September 19, 1782, and that he died April 30, 1835. Elizabeth Howe, daughter-in-law of John W. Howe, gave her deposition, March 17, 1841, in the claim for a pension of the widow, and filed as an exhibit thereto, a flyleaf taken from a volume of the "History of Scotland" whereon John W. Howe had entered the names and dates of birth of his children:

2. Joseph How, b. September 12, 1783.[1]
3. Rebecca How, b. May 22 [1784?] [2]
4. Eleanor How, b. April 11, 1785.[3]
5. Sarah How, b. February 20, 1787.[4]
6. William How b. January 20, 1789 (or 1791).
7. Daniel Lynham How, b. March 22, 1793.[5]
8. John Nelson How, b. November 3, 1795.

In his will probated in the Greenup County Court, June 1, 1835, John W. Howe mentions his wife, Mary Ann and children: son Joseph and his seven children, John, Nelson, William, George, Andrew, Henry and Joseph. Jr.; son, John, deceased, and his six children, Melcenia[6], Milton, John, David, Minerva and one, name not recalled; son William's five children Eleanor, Mary Ann and three, names not recalled. He mentions also granddaughter, Elizabeth, daughter of son, Daniel, deceased, and Thomas Haney, son-in-law and husband of his daughter Sally.

Historians and genealogists[7] state that John W. Howe had another son: 9. James Howe who was b. in Montgomery County, Virginia, in 1774; was a major in the War of 1812 and was at the Battle of New Orleans; that he m. in Greenup County, Martha Hood, sister to Andrew Hood, Jr. (See Hood Family); that they lived for a time above Greenupsburg and then removed to Old Town to a plantation which they called "Willow Grove" on which they built a brick house said to be the first in Greenup County; that James Howe donated the ground for the log church house which stood at Old Town for many years—the site of the present Methodist Church; that he d. about 1843 and probably was buried at Old Town.

In this connection there is for consideration the fact that John W. Howe did not mention a son James in his will or list such a son in his record of births and names of his children; nor did the Rev. Gilruth mention a son James. (See Gilruth papers.) If there were a son James obviously he was by an earlier and former marriage of John W. Howe. One James Howe was a pioneer settler of Greenup county as is evidenced by the U. S. Census of that county for the year 1810 and was the first Commissioner of the Revenue of Greenup County.

Children of James Howe and his wife, Martha (Hood) Howe:

10. Elizabeth Ann (Betsy) Howe; m. Daniel Clifton.
11. John Howe; m. Sarah Dickerson.
12. George Howe; m. Sarah Fannin.
13. Mary J. Howe; m. John Montgomery.
14. Martha Howe; m. William Hood.
15. Rebecca Howe; m. James William Warnock (See Warnock Family).
16. Adalaide Howe; m. Henry Stark.
17. Martha Ann Howe; m. William Hunt.
18. James Andrew Howe; m. Malvina (Cameron) Craycraft, a widow.

Children of James Andrew Howe and his wife, Malvina (Cameron) Craycraft Howe:

19. Lucinda Howe.
20. Anna Howe.
21. Alexander Howe.
22. Walker Howe.
23. Simon Howe.
24. Dolly Howe.

---

[1] Joseph Howe married Rachel Hood, sister to Andrew Hood, Jr.

[2] Rebecca Howe married James Warnock (See Warnock Family).

[3] Eleanor Howe married Rowland Cornelius in Greenup County, October 6, 1804.

[4] Sarah (Sally) Howe married Thomas Haney.

[5] One Daniel L. Howe married Angeline Ellison in Greenup County, March 12, 1828.

[6] Melcena Howe m. Joseph B. Puthuff in Greenup County, May 23, 1838.

[7] History of Greenup County, Kentucky, by Nina Mitchell Biggs and Mabel Lee Mackoy. The Franklin Press, Louisville, Kentucky, 1951.

HOWES FAMILY OF JOHNSON COUNTY

This is a local surname, 'at the house', from residence in some large hall or mansion as servant or retainer; possibly it might represent the proprietor himself.

House is an old English family as is evidenced by the Hundred Rolls of England which bear the names of

Geoffrey de la House, County Hants, 1273.

William de la House, County Hants, 1273.

Richard de la Huse, County Berks, 1273.

Jacob Huse, County Somerset.

Families of Howes, Howse, House lived in all the thirteen original colonies in early colonial days.

Chares Howes was the progenitor of the Howes family of Eastern Kentucky. The records indicate that he was a native of Maryland and that he migrated and settled in Clay County, Kentucky, in pioneer days. In his will, dated March 9, 1821, and probated in the Clay County Court, May 14, 1821, he bequeathed lands and personal property to his wife, "Anny", sons William, John, and Elexious and to Samuel St. John (relationship, if any, not disclosed).

1. ELECTIOUS (ELEXIOUS) HOWES was the ancestor of the Howes family of the Big Sandy Valley. He was b. in 1789—presumably in Maryland; and in company with two brothers, William and John, he migrated from Maryland in 1809 or 1810 and settled in Floyd County, Kentucky, now Johnson County. William Howes and John Howes settled in Clay County, Kentucky.

Elexious Howes was a farmer and acquired large tracts of land on Rockhouse Creek, Johnson County, where he d.; a minister of the Methodist Church and organized many churches of that denomination in the section of the country of his residence; and a public official, serving as one of the first justices of the peace of Johnson County, 1844. He m., presumably in Maryland, Sallie Hudson, b. May, 1794.

Children:

*2. Claiborne Howes.

3. Wiley Howes.

4. Matthew Howes.

5. Sarah Howes, m., first, Anthony Baldwin, Jr., and secondly, James Trimble.

2. CLAIBORNE HOWES, b. in Johnson County, February 18, 1825, d. in 1863; m. in Johnson County, May 10, 1854, Delilah Baldwin.

Children:

*6. John Howes.

*7. Henry S. Howes.

*8. Paulina Howes.

8½. (Infant).

6. JOHN HOWES, a minister of the Methodist Episcopal Church, a lawyer and a county official, serving as the first county court clerk of Johnson County, from June, 1844, to September, 1866; m., in Floyd County, October 13, 1835, Jane Young.

Children:
*9. Pennelia Howes.
*10. Elexious Fremont Howes.
11. Julia Howes (See Buckingham and Wells Families.)
*12. Josephine J. Howes.
*13. Charlie J. Howes.
*14. George Winn Howes.
*15. Millard Howes.
*16. —— ——?
17. ——?, m. Sandy Vaughan.

7. HENRY S. HOWES, b. in Paintsville, April 4, 1859, d. August 6, 1924; educated in the schools of Paintsville and for a time taught in the rural schools of Johnson County; appointed deputy sheriff of Johnson County, February 7, 1879; appointed sheriff, January 5, 1891, and subsequently was elected to that office and served until 1894. While acting in an official capacity, Mr. Howes studied law and was admitted to the bar in 1895. Subsequently he was appointed U. S. Commissioner for his district and after serving as such for one year, he began the practice of law at Paintsville and continued until his death, and acted on numerous occasions as special judge; and his rulings were marked by fairness and sound judgment. He was associated at various times with members of his profession in practice, among others, S. Kirk, H. S. Vaughan, a son, Clarence W., and a cousin Frederick Howes. The law firm was known and styled Howes & Howes.

Judge Howes was also a businessman and was president of the Paintsville Bank and Trust Company during the later years of his life.

Henry S. Howes m., first, in Johnson County, Sarah Fitzpatrick, secondly, Sip (Rule) Bays, and thirdly, Mollie Whitaker.

Children of Henry S. Howes and Sarah (Fitzpatrick) Howes:
18. Clarence W. Howes.
19. Beulah Howes, m. Dr. Floyd G. Meade. (See Meade Family.)
20. Mary Evalyn Howes.

8. PAULINA HOWES, d. in 1915; m. Henry Huff; resided on a farm on Big Sandy River.

Children:
21. Roy Huff; m. Ethel Davis.
22. Hattie Huff, m. Cassius M. Whitt.
23. Louise Huff, deceased.
24. John Huff, m. —— Hazelett.

9. PENNELIA HOWES, m. Frank Spradlin; resided on what is known as the Mayo Farm.
Children:
*25. John Spradlin.
26. Benjamin Spradlin.
27. Fannie Spradlin, lived in Newport, Kentucky.
28. Alphonso Spradlin.
*29. Genova Spradlin.
30. Robert Spradlin was killed at Huntington, West Virginia.
*31. Martha Spradlin.

10. ELEXIOUS FREMONT HOWES, realtor at Paintsville and public official, b. December 8, 1849, served as county court clerk of Johnson County for two terms, from 1879 to 1886; served as master commissioner of the Johnson Circuit Court for six years; m., first, June 6, 1870, Cynthia Preston, daughter of Eliphus Preston, and secondly Sarah E. Dollarhide. Children of Elexious Fremont Howes and his wife, Cynthia (Preston) Howes:
*32. John Howes.
*33. Will Howes.
34. Fred Howes, m. Amanda Allen. (See Rice Family.)
*35. Charles J. Howes.
36. Albert Howes, m. Fannie Rice. (See Rice Family.)
37. Gypsie Howes, m. Elmer F. Ramey, son of Jasper N. Ramey, b. in Rowan County, Kentucky, teacher, and County Superintendent of Schools of Carter County, 1890-1895; and his wife, Millie (Fenwick) Ramey, b. in Bath County, Kentucky. Elmer F. Ramey and Gypsie (Howes) Ramey resided in Portsmouth, Ohio.
38. Edgar Howes, veteran, World War 1.
*39. Fannie Howes, d. in young womanhood.
40. Eulastie Howes.
41. Preston Howes.

Children of Elexious F. Howes and Sarah E. (Dollarhide) Howes:
42. Richard G. Howes, served in the U. S. Navy during World War I, making many trips across the ocean in the transport service. After returning to Paintsville from his service, he entered politics and was elected police judge of Paintsville at the age of twenty-two.
43. James Layne Howes.

12. JOSEPHINE J. HOWES; b. in Johnson County, Kentucky, January 21, 1857; d. in Ashland, Kentucky, September 7, 1922; m. in Johnson County, October, 1878, Noah Kendrick Williams.

Noah Kendrick Williams, physician, was b. in Carter County, Kentucky, February 14, 1849, and d. in Catlettsburg, Kentucky, October 2, 1905; was graduated from the Kentucky School of Medicine at Louisville in 1889 and practiced his profession at Flat Gap, Johnson County, Willard, Carter County and Catlettsburg, Boyd County; m., first, in 1871, Levina Castle; no children; m., secondly, Josephine J. Howes, October 1878.

Children:

Madge Williams; b. at Flat Gap, August 8, 1879, and d. in Louisville, Kentucky, May 5, 1943; m., first, Dr. J. B. Watson, b. at Willard, Kentucky, 1876, and d. (street car accident) in Chicago, March 26, 1916. Children: James Kendrick Watson, b. April 19, 1897. Madge (Williams) Watson m., secondly, Harry Skelly; no children.

Blanche Williams; b. at Flat Gap, January 20, 1882; educated at Willard (Kentucky) graded and high school and at Parochial Business College, Ashland, Kentucky, was an employee of the A. C. & I. Company, Ashland, for a number of years; m., December 17, 1905, Wade Clay, merchant at Ashland, who was b. July 12, 1879, and d. February 3, 1938. Children: Mary Maxine Clay, teacher, was educated in the Ashland public schools and at Marshall College at Huntington, West Virginia, and is presently engaged in teaching.

Goldie Katherine Williams, b. at Flat Gap, February 17, 1886, and d. at Ashland, September 11, 1919; m. Harry Poor, merchant at Ashland, who was b. in 1878, and d. in 1924. Children: A son who d. in infancy and a daughter, Mrs. Josephine (Poor) Brown.

Sandy Williams; b. at Flat Gap, March 23, 1892; m. Agnes O' Kelly.

Children: Clay Watson Williams.

Bruce Williams; b. at Willard, Kentucky, October 14, 1893; d. September 30, 1945; unm.

13. CHARLIE J. HOWES, a minister of the Methodist Episcopal Church; m. Mollie Bronson.

Children:
44. John Howes, m. ——— ?
45. George Howes, m. Neva Howes.
46. Lou Howes.
47. Harry Howes.

14. GEORGE WINN HOWES, a lawyer; practiced his profession for a time; entered the ministry and became an able preacher in the Methodist Episcopal Church; and was pastor of a church at Newton, Kansas, at the time of death; m., first, ——— Borders, and secondly ———?

Children of George Winn Howes and ——— (Borders) Howes:
48. Neva Howes, m. George Howes.
49. Evert Howes.
50. Jane Howes.

15. MILLARD HOWES, educator, active member of the Methodist Episcopal Church at Paintsville; b. June 24, 1855, d. at Paintsville, April 23, 1904; m. Mary Kennard, b. March 24, 1864.
Children:
51. Harry Howes, resided at Lexington, Kentucky.
52. ———? Howes.

16. ———? HOWES, m. William Childers, a minister of the Methodist Church, who d. at Covington, Kentucky.
Children:
53. George Childers.

25. JOHN SPRADLIN, m. Rose Stafford.
Children:
54. Anna Spradlin, m. Oscar P. Williams.
55. ———? Spradlin, m. Bruce Wiley.
56. ———? Spradlin, m. Arzie Conley.
57. Frank Spradlin, m. ———? Taylor.

29. GENOVA SPRADLIN, d. in 1927; m. Cassius M. Cooper, d. in 1927.
Children:
*58. Frank S. Cooper.
59. Olga Cooper.

31. MARTHA JANE SPRADLIN, m., first, Richard, (Dick) Stafford, and, second, Marcus Davis; resided at Paintsville.
Children of Martha Jane Spradlin and Richard Stafford:
*60. Leona Stafford.

32. JOHN HOWES, a lawyer who devoted much time to abstracting; in politics a Democrat who served his party as county chairman and committeeman; and a public official of Paintsville who served his city well; m. Maud Castle, daughter of John Castle.
Children:
61. Virginia Howes, m. S. H. Jett who was connected with the oil supply business at Paintsville for several years. They removed to Winchester, Kentucky.
62. Christine Howes, a graduate of the John C. C. Mayo College, a musician and sometime teacher in the city schools of Paintsville; m. Carmel Murray who was engaged in the automobile business at Paintsville.

33. WILL HOWES was connected with the North-East Coal Company at Thealka, Johnson county, for some time and subsequently became a coal operator at Betsy Lane, Floyd county. He removed to Greenville, North Carolina; m. Victoria Lane.
Children:
*63. Oneida Howes, m. Jack Williams.
64. James Berry Howes.

35. CHARLES J. HOWES, politician, sometime public official, was b. in Paintsville, Johnson county, Kentucky, —— —— ——, and d. at —— —— ——; m. Blanche C. Hill.

Mr. Howes never affiliated with the party of his fathers—the Republican party, but in youth he began serving the Democratic party and his services were of inestimable value to his party.

Below are given excerpts from newspapers regarding Mr. Howes:

"Since 1896 Mr. Howes has been serving the Democratic party. In that year as a boy he took the stump and began a career that has been of inestimable value to his party. In 1910 and 1912 he was reading clerk at the House of Representatives under the late James Stone, a foremost authority on parliamentary law. He has served his fourth consecutive session as chief clerk of the House and at the last session was elected by acclamation without a dissenting voice or any opposition. He has been attached to virtually every department of the State government since his early youth and is as familiar with the organization and operation of the State's business as any official in Frankfort.

"Serving as chief clerk of the House, Mr. Howes guides the deliberations of the law-makers in the proper channels of parliamentary procedure. His knowledge of parliamentary law and wide experience in this field is most valuable to the speaker, the presiding officer. There is no parliamentary tangle too difficult for Mr. Howes to unravel and speakers of the House have become accustomed to depend upon him for advice and assistance.

"Because of his intricate knowledge of parliamentary law and his ability as a parliamentarian, Mr. Howes has virtually written the rules of the House for the past several sessions. The changes that have been made were suggested by him, and the Kentucky House of Representatives is operating under a system of rules that is second to none of any legislative body. He has drawn several rules, innovations in parliamentary law, that facilitate the business of the House and prevent the possibilities of dreaded filibusters.

"Mr. Howes' service to his State is also a record of valuable service to his party. He has been a delegate to every Democratic convention since his early youth and Secretary to all State conventions for many years.

"In addition to other qualifications to fill the important post of clerk, the vocal capacity of Charlie Howes has become famous. He has a voice that carries an accurate enunciation to the remotest corner of any large hall. It is not a voice that is deafening or splits the eardrums, but rather without effort Charlie Howes sends fourth a call that is clear, definite, and altogether pleasing. When the clerk calls the roll or reads a bill it can be understood with ease above the noise and confusion of the legislative hall.

"Mr. Howes is a native of Paintsville, but for a number of years has been living in Frankfort. He is highly popular with his colleagues at Frankfort, and is conceded to have the post of chief clerk of the House of Representatives as long as he wants it. With the duties of his office engrossing all his time and that of a large staff during the session of the Legislature, Mr. Howes is never too busy to confer with legislators and give them advice and instruction on the proper method of completing some given task."

39. FANNIE HOWES, d. ——— ———; m. Earl Holcomb, d. ——— ———, son of W. C. Holcomb and his wife, Millie (Armstrong) Holcomb of Grayson, Carter county, Kentucky.

Children:

65. ——— Holcomb.

58. FRANK S. COOPER, lawyer; for many years practiced as member of the firm of Howes & Howes, Paintsville; m. Corine Dempsey. They had children whose names have not been learned.

60. LEONA STAFFORD, businesswoman in Paintsville; m., first, Bird Webb, and second, Asberry Patrick.

Children of Leona Stafford and Bird Webb:

66. Richard Webb, a physician.
67. Wendell Webb.

63. ONEIDA HOWES, m. Jack Williams, a jeweler. They removed to Greenville, North Carolina.

Children:

68. ——— Williams.

HYLTON FAMILY OF FLOYD, JOHNSON AND CARTER COUNTIES

Hilton

The exact origin of the name Hilton is lost in the clouds of antiquity, but it is known that this is one of the oldest families entitled to bear arms in Great Britain. It is certain that the house of Hilton existed and flourished in great splendor at the time of the Norman conquest (1066), and under the feudal system of the country enjoyed the rank and reputation of barons, by tenure, a title which, after the decline of the family, was constantly attributed to the chiefs of the name by popular courtesy.

Hilton is a "place name" and means literally "men of the hills or on a hill". Authorities have stated that the name Hilton is from a town in Derbyshire, situated on a hill. There are several parishes and places in England bearing this name, as well as a number of distinct families. Hylton or Hilton Castle in Durham is an ancient family seat of the English Hiltons. It is there the Hilton arms were found sculptured on the walls. The Hiltons quartered their arms with the families of Nevill, Skirlow, Percy, Washington and many others.

The American immigrant representing the Durham branch of the family was Edward Hilton who came to New Hampshire and settled in a place that was called Hilton's Point (now the town of Dover). There are many descendants of Edward Hilton living in various sections of this country today.

The Hiltons became numerous in the "Appalachian Highlands" and other sections of the country as is evidenced by the naming for the family settlements, villages and postoffices, among others: Hylton, Pike County, Kentucky, Texas; Hilton, California, Georgia, Nebraska and New York; Helton, Leslie County, Kentucky, and Ashe County, North Carolina; Hiltonian, Perry County, Kentucky; Hiltons, Scott County, Virginia; Hilton Village, Warwick County, Virginia; Heltonsville, Indiana; Hiltonhead, South Carolina.

The first of the family of Hilton, of whom there is any available record, to pass the mountain barriers to Kentucky in the great Westward movement were

1. JOHN HILTON and his son * 2. Jesse Hilton. The records tend

to show that they were Virginians and came from Bedford County. The exact time they settled in Kentucky is not certainly known, but obviously it was prior to 1786 as Benjamin Hilton, Jesse's son, was b. in Kentucky, March 13, 1786. Both John and Jesse Hilton were residents and tax-payers of Madison County, Kentucky, as of April 7, 1789. Available records disclose nothing futher concerning John Hilton.

2. JESSE HILTON was b., presumably in Virginia, about 1755, and d. in Floyd County, Kentucky, within the period 1830-1840. He m., presumably in Bedford County. Virginia, about 1775, Juda Wright. About 1800 they removed from Madison County, Kentucky, to Floyd County, Kentucky, in which county in 1810 there were living at home with them one son under ten years of age and one daughter over ten and under sixteen years of age. It is definitely known that there were other children—two sons at least:

*3. Roderick B. Hylton.
*4. Benjamin Hylton.

Though not definitely established, the record would seem to indicate that there were other daughters:

5. Eliabeth Hilton who m. William Ward in Floyd County, September 5, 1818.

6. Nancy Hilton, who m. John Lester in Floyd County, January 24, 1820.

There were other Hilton or Hylton families living in the Big Sandy Valley contemporaneously with Jesse Hilton and his family who might or might not have been descended from or related to him:

Roberson H. Hilton who m. Ailsey Castle in Floyd County, August 3, 1834.

William Hylton who m. Katharine Griffiths in Lawrence County, February 19, 1829.

Jesse Hilton who m. Elizabeth Ball in Lawrence County, November 10, 1831.

Letish Hylton who m. John Brown in Lawrence County, July 17, 1834.

Susannah Hylton who m. Andrew Daniel in Lawrence County, July 17, 1834.

James Hylton who m. Susan Griffith in Pike County, October 20, 1850.

James Hilton who m. Minta Coleman in Pike County, October 21, 1852.

Charles Hylton who m. Elizabeth Sweeney in Pike County, February 15, 1855.

Hiram Hylton who m. Elizabeth Gibson in Pike County, June 1, 1860.

Malinda Hylton who m. Gideon May in Pike County, December 30, 1830.

Margaret Hylton who m. David Maynard in Pike County, December 22, 1841.

Elizabeth Hylton who m. Alex. Ratliff in Pike County, August 13, 1837.

Delila Hylton who m. James Smith in Pike County, March 25, 1838.

Cynthia Hylton, daughter of William, who m. Wylie Rowe in Pike County, December 13, 1849.

3. RODERICK HYLTON, apparently the eldest child, was b. in Virginia in 1776 and died in the home of his nephew, E. P. S. Hylton, near Willard, Carter County, Kentucky, November 10, 1859.'. He m., presumably in Floyd County, Kentucky, and in 1810 was living in that county with his family which consisted of a wife, two sons and three daughters, all the children then being under ten years of age. The U. S. Census of Carter County for 1850 shows that Roderick Hylton, aged 74, b. in Virginia, and Nancy Hylton, aged 50, b. in Virginia, were living in the home of Hervy M. and Mary A. Skaggs.

4. BENJAMIN HILTON, farmer and stonemason, was b. in Kentucky, presumably in Madison County, March 13, 1786, and d. in Johnson County, Kentucky, June 4, 1856. He m. in Floyd County, Kentucky, about 1803, Nancy Preston, b. in Bedford County, Virginia, in October, 1781, d. June 28, 1871, in the home of her son, E. P. S. Hylton, near Willard, Carter County, Kentucky. She was buried in near-by graveyard at mouth of Hylton branch. She was the eldest child of Nathan Preston, Revolutionary War soldier, and his wife, Elizabeth (Vaughan) Preston. (See Nathan Preston Family.)

Children:

*7. Nathan Preston ("Press") Hylton.

8. Elizabeth Hylton; m. Charles Jefferson Grim in Floyd County, May 6, 1824.

9. Leah H. Hylton; m. James Corder in Floyd County, August 22, 1832. They migrated to Missouri.

10. Louvina Hylton; m. Charles W. Young, Jr., in Floyd County, May 11, 1834. They migrated to Texas.

11. Anna Hylton; m. James Wright in Floyd County, February 13, 1840.

*12. Eliphaz (Eliphus or "Life") Preston Shelton Hylton.

7. NATHAN PRESTON HYLTON, farmer, was b. in Floyd County, Kentucky, 1816, and d. in Johnson County, Kentucky, subsequent to 1880 (his name appears on the U. S. Census for that year); m., first, in Lawrence County, Kentucky, August 5, 1832, Mary (Polly) Meek, who d. about 1842, a daughter of William and Julia (Poplar)

Meek; (See Meek Family), m., secondly, in Lawrence County, February 2, 1843, Frances Yost, b. 1823.

Children living at home and approximate dates of birth as shown by the U. S. Census of Lawrence County for 1850, 1860, 1870 and 1880:

13. Charlotta Hylton, b. 1838; m. Eliphus Stapleton.
14. Jeffrey Hylton; b. 1840.
15. Charles Hylton; b. 1844.
16. Elizabeth Hylton; b. 1846.
17. Levina Hylton, b. 1848; m. Isaac Stapleton.
18. Leah Hylton; b. 1850.
19. Sarah Hylton; b. 1852.
20. Louisa Hylton; b. 1857.
21. Julia Hylton; b. 1865; m. Bascom Van Hoose.
22. Frances Hylton, b. 1866.

12. ELIPHAZ PRESTON SHELTON HYLTON, farmer, old-time school teacher and Baptist (United) preacher, was b. in then Floyd County, Kentucky, February 28, 1820. and d. and was buried at Cherokee, Lawrence County, Kentucky, in February 1896. He had service in the Union Army duing the Civil War, having enlisted at Grayson, Kentucky, September 26, 1863, as a private in Company "C", 40th Kentucky Regiment of Volunteers, and was honorably discharged a corporal at Catlettsburg, Kentucky, December 30, 1864, by reason of expiration of enlistment. He m., first, in Johnson County, September 19, 1844, Sarah Green, b. in 1824, and d. about 1853, daughter of Giles Green and his wife, Katie (Chandler) Green who was a daughter of Thomas Chandler, Revolutionary War soldier. (See Chandler and Green Families). He m., secondly, in Lawrence County, November 8, 1855, Nancy Castle, b. in 1824 and d. near Willard, Carter County, and was buried in graveyard at mouth of Hylton branch.

Children of E. P. S. Hylton and Sarah (Green) Hylton:
*23. Willson (or William) Preston Hylton.
*24. Selina Jane Hylton.
25. Nancy G. Hylton, b. in Johnson County, Kentucky, September 12, 1849, and d. near Willard, August 20, 1929; m. James Leadingham, son of Jacob and Frances (Watson) Leadingham. Children: Ida and Nathan.
*26. Nathan Hylton.

12-A. Children of E. P. S. Hylton and Nancy (Castle) Hylton:
*27. Victoria Hylton.
*28. Douglas A. Hylton.

23. WILLIAM PRESTON HYLTON, farmer, b. in Johnson County, Kentucky, in 1846, d. in Lawrence County, at the age of 88 years; enlisted at Grayson, Kentucky, September 26, 1863, and served as

private, in Company "C", 40th Regiment, Kentucky Infantry Volunteers until December 30, 1864, when he was honorably discharged at Catlettsburg, Kentucky, by reason of expiration of enlistment; m. in Carter County, April 25, 1867, his cousin, Nancy Wright, daughter of James Wright and Anna (Hylton) Wright. They reared a large family of children in the Cherokee (Kentucky) locale, among others, Benjamin F., Sarah Ann, Eliphus (Life), George, Barbara, Thomas, Elijah.

24. SELINA JANE HYLTON was b. in Johnson County, Kentucky, January 20, 1847, and d. in Ashland, Kentucky, August 5, 1931. Interment in Webbville (Kentucky) Cemetery; m., first, in Lawrence County, about 1866, Calvin Wright and secondly, in Carter County, June 5, 1873, George W. Kozee. (See Kozee Family.)

Calvin Wright, farmer, Webbville, Kentucky, was b. in Virginia in 1826, d., 1872, and was buried in Webbville Cemetery.

Children:
*29. Giles Wright.
*30. Sarah Wright.
31. Trinvilla Wright; b. at Webbville, August 2, 1871; d. in Ashland, July 5, 1951, and was buried in Triplett family graveyard near Willard; m. at Willard, April 25, 1888, Oscar Tripett. No children.

29. GILES WRIGHT, lumberman, was b. at Webbville, Kentucky, January 6, 1867; d. in Ashland, July 5, 1947. Interment in the Kitchen family mausoleum, Ashland Cemetery; attended the public schools of Carter County and when in his early teens was caretaker of the property of one J. M. Bent near Willard who undertook development of cannel coal industry on the Little Fork above Willard. Later he became a lumber inspector in the employee of Leatherbee, Slade and Skelton, Parkersburg, West Virginia, under the supervision of H. H. Case. Subsequently going in the lumber business, he moved and located in Ashland where he was one of the organizers of the Wright-Kitchen Lumber Company which engaged in the manufacture and sale of lumber for a number of years.

He m. at Leon, Kentucky, September 27, 1891, Mollie Lee Kitchen, b. in Carter County, June 15, 1871, and d. in Ashland, August 2, 1932. Interment in Kitchen family mausoleum, Ashland Cemetery. She was a daughter of Charles and Lauretta (Mobley) Kitchen and a lineal (direct) descendant of James Kitchen, Revolutionary War soldier, and his wife, Jane (Patterson) Kitchen.

Children:
32. Lena Mabel Wright; b. at Leon, February 14, 1893; d. in Ashland, April 16, 1904. Interment at Leon.
*33. Charles Kitchen Wright.
*34. Lauretta Florence Wright.
*35. Giles Edward Wright.
*36. Mary Lee Wright.

33. CHARLES KITCHEN WRIGHT; b. at Leon, October 1, 1894; d. in Ashland, September 24, 1948; was educated in the public schools of Ashland; m. in Ashland, January 9, 1914, Mary Jane Richardson.

Children:

37. Giles Calvin Wright was b. in Ashland, May 7, 1916; was educated in the public schools of Ashland, graduating from the Ashland High School; and at Washington and Lee University where he was a member of the Phi Kappa Phi fraternity; was on the staff of the Ashland Daily Independent when, on December 18, 1941, he enlisted in the Air Corps, U. S. Army; received his primary training at Pine Bluff, Arkansas, and basic training at Randolph Field, Texas; was given his wings and commissioned, August 8, 1942, and was soon thereafter commissioned a first lieutenant; had everseas service during World War II and was awarded the Air Medal with Three Oak Leaf Clusters for meritorious achievement while participating in aerial flights against the enemy in European theater of operations; m. Nancy VanSant of Ashland, a daughter of W. R. VanSant of that city. She was educated in the Ashland public schools, graduating from the Ashland High School, and at the Holy Family Business School and has held responsible positions with the Kentucky—West Virginia Gas Company; and was a member of the Woman's Club. Residence: Houston, Texas.

34. LAURETTA FLORENCE WRIGHT was b. at Leon, October 29, 1899, and d. June 21, 1933; m. Clifford L. Smith, January 29, 1921.

Children:

38. Billy Marsh Smith; b. August 5, 1925.
39. Mary Lee Smith; b. March 11, 1930.
40. Barbara Jane Smith; b. April 2, 1932.

35. GILES EDWARD WRIGHT, newspaperman, was b. in Ashland, June 8, 1907; educated in the public schools of Ashland, graduating from the Ashland High School, and attended Washington and Lee University. In his youth he was a reporter on the Ashland Daily Independent. Later removing to Los Angeles, California, he accepted a position on the Los Angeles Examiner and is presently holding that position. He m. Gladys Carlisle of Cincinnati, Ohio. No children. Residence: 209 N. Sycamore Drive, San Gabriel, California.

36. MARY LEE WRIGHT was b. in Ashland, April 12, 1909; m., October 26, 1929, James William Kendall, businessman, presently a traveling salesman.

Children:

41. James William Kendall, Jr., b. in Ashland, June 9, 1932; educated in the public schools of Ashland and Indianapolis and at Depauw University—having been awarded a scholarship—where he

took the R. O. T. C. course; was commissioned a lieutenant, U. S. Air Force; m. at the Irvington Presbyterian Church in Indianapolis, June 26, 1955, Miss Mary Smith, daughter of Mrs. Albert Dickinson Smith of Indianapolis.

42. Charles Edward Kendall, student; b. in Ashland, October 23, 1939.*

30. SARAH WRIGHT; b. at Webbville, October 4, 1869, d. in Florida, in August, 1947, and was buried in Rude Cemetery at Flatwoods, Boyd County; m. at Willard, in January, 1890, Henry Alphonso Pennington, who d., 1932, son of James Pennington of Willard.

Children:

43. Mollie Pennington; m. ——— Buckley.

44. Verle Pennington; b. near Willard, April 15, 1893, and d. in 1949; m. December 27, 1911, Rev. E. L. Gallion. Children: Lena May, b. 1913, d. September 19, 1923, and Ruth Ann, b. 1916.

45. James Pennington; m. and reared a family of children of whom John is one.

46. Charles Pennington.

47. Jennings Pennington; d. young.

48. Edy Pennington; d. young.

49. Ercel Pennington.

50. Ray Pennington.

51. Edith Pennington.

52. Ruth Pennington.

53. Mary Lee Pennington.

26. NATHAN HYLTON, farmer; b. in Johnson County, Kentucky, October 29, 1851, and d. near Riverton, Greenup County, at the age of 91 years; m. in Carter County, near Webbville, May 4, 1873, Violet Pennington, b. April 30, 1855, and d. May 20, 1895, daughter of Henry Pennington and Sally (Gullett) Pennington. He lived in the Webbville area until about 1905 when he removed to Greenup County where he lived until his death.

Children:

*54. Martin Hylton.

55. Mary Hylton; m. John Johnson; removed to Ohio where they reared a large family.

*56. Jesse Hylton.

57. Martha Hylton; m. James Stuart. (See Stuart Family.)

58. Giles Hylton; m. Agnes ———; lived at Sciotoville, Ohio, and reared a family.

54. MARTIN HYLTON, farmer; b. near Willard; m. Viola (Ola) Wright; removed to Greenup County where they reared a family. A son 59. Everett, formerly a teacher in Greenup County, is presently

connected with the Department of Education at Frankfort, Kentucky.

56. JESSE HYLTON, farmer; b. near Willard, Kentucky, January 30, 1880; m. May 28, 1899, Maude Wright, who was b. in Boyd County, Kentucky, December 20, 1876, and d. in Greenup County, Kentucky, September 5, 1947.
Children:
*60. Estill R. Hilton.
*61. Ethel Hilton.
 62. William Stanley Hilton.
*63. Hargis Lee Hilton.
*64. Charles Woods Hilton.
*65. Giles Hilton.
*66. Viola Hilton.
*67. John Milton Hilton.

60. ESTILL R. HILTON; b. near Willard, Kentucky, March 26, 1900; educated in the rural public schools; is presently employed by the Chesapeake and Ohio Railway Company, at Raceland, Greenup County, Kentucky, and is State representative from Greenup County and has so represented Greenup County for a number of terms; m., December 24, 1921, Ethel Webb of Webbville, Kentucky.

Children:
68. Marie Hilton; b. at Raceland, January 31, 1923; educated in the Raceland public schools; at Ashland (Kentucky) Junior College; and at Eastern (Kentucky) State College, Richmond, Kentucky; m. December 20, 1943, Edwin M. Ellington of Ashland, Kentucky. Children: Stephen Perry, b. October 27, 1948, and Judith Carroll, b. March 7, 1952.

69. Anna M. Hilton; b. at Raceland, August 13, 1924; educated in the Raceland public school, graduating from the Raceland High School; m. October 3, 1944, James E. Short of Raceland. Children: James E. Short, Jr., b. August 17, 1945, in California.

70. Frances E. Hilton; b. at Raceland, September 16, 1925; educated in the Raceland public schools and was graduated from Berea College with degree of B. S. (Home Economics); taught in the public schools for six years; m. November 18, 1950, Joseph T. Hunt of Bloomfield, Kentucky. Children: Joseph Hilton Hunt, b. at Bloomfield, February 8, 1952.

71. James Estill Hilton; b. at Raceland, November 10, 1929; educated in the Raceland public schools and at Eastern State College at Richmond; later had service in U. S. Air Force, stationed in Korea; unm.

61. ETHEL HILTON; b. near Willard, November 26, 1901; educated

in the public schools; m. in Carter County, February, 1925, Norman Porter.

Children:

72. Dorothy Mae Porter; b. in Ashland, January 25, 1926; educated in the Ashland public schools, graduating from Ashland High School; m. Charles Rischer, Columbus, Ohio, December 16, 1946. No children.

73. Claudine Porter; b. in Ashland, December 15, 1927; educated in the Ashland public schools and at Ashland Junior College; presently employed in the office of the American Rolling Mills Company at Ashland.

74. Betty Ruth Porter; b. in Ashland, February 27, 1930; educated in the Ashland public schools and at Ashland Junior College; presently employed in the office of the Ashland Oil and Refining Company at Ashland.

75. Helen Louise Porter; b. in Ashland, July 31, 1932; educated in Ashland public schools, graduating from Ashland High School; presently employed in office of American Rolling Mills Company at Ashland.

76. Carl Lee Porter; b. in Ashland, September 18, 1934; educated in Ashland schools.

62. WILLIAM STANLEY HILTON; b. near Willard, October 2, 1903; attended the public schools; presently employed as clerk, Chesapeake and Ohio Railway Company at Russell; unm.

63. HARGIS LEE HILTON; b. near Willard, January 28, 1907; attended public schools; engaged in farming and resides at Marengo, Ohio; m. Della J. Boggess at Ashland, December 22, 1928.

Children:

77. Edna Lorene Hilton; b. in Boyd County, November 26, 1929; d. August 13, 1944.

78. Bill Eugene Hilton; b. in Carter County, November 22, 1931; educated in public schools, graduating from High School; presently serving in U. S. Navy.

79. Geneva Loretta Hilton; b. in Carter County, April 12, 1936; student in High School, Sparta, Ohio.

80. Robert Lee Hilton; b. at Sparta, Ohio, October 9, 1947.

64. CHARLES WOODS HILTON; b. near Willard, December 20, 1908; educated in public schools; resides and is engaged in farming at Centerburg, Ohio; m. Virgie Dudley, July 8, 1931, in Laurel County, Ohio. Children: Charles Raymond Hilton; b. in Knox County, Ohio, May 29, 1946.

65. GILES HILTON; b. near Willard, December 23, 1910; attended the public schools; resides and is engaged in farming at Centerburg, Ohio; m. Clara Mathews at Mt. Vernon, Ohio, October 2, 1939. No children.

66. VIOLA HILTON; b. near Willard, March 24, 1915; educated in public schools; m. David Burrell Robinson. (See Robinson Family.)

67. JOHN MILTON HILTON; b. near Willard, January 23, 1917; attended the public schools; resides and is engaged in farming at Johnstown, Ohio; m. Mary Paynter at Johnstown, January 14, 1942. Children: Julia Lee Hilton, student; b. in Licking County, Ohio, September 20, 1942; and John Stanley Hilton, student; b. in Licking County, Ohio, March 10, 1945.[3]

27. VICTORIA HYLTON; b. in Johnson County, Kentucky, 1856; m. in Carter County, Kentucky, Levi Pennington, farmer. Children: Faris, m. Miss Hall; Lindsey, m. Miss Creech; Lillie, m. Martin Hicks; Charles, m. Rebecca Blevins; Morton; Vallas, m. Fronie Barker; Annie May, m. Willie Sloas; Pearl, m. a Matthews.

28. DOUGLAS A. HYLTON, farmer; b. in Carter County, Kentucky, in the early 1860s; m. Sarilda Maggard; lived on the Little Fork near Willard. Children: Rosa, m. Jackson Sizemore; Nancy, m., first, a Salyer and, secondly, Sam Leadingham; Norman, m. Miss McDavid; Missouri, m. Will Simpson; Dennis, m. Miss McDavid; Alice, deceased; unm.; Minnie, m. Mont McDavid; Bessie, m. Ellis Maggard; Watt, m. Ollie Blevins.

[1] Vital Statistics of Carter County, Kentucky, 1852-1853.

[2] The Family Tree of Giles Wright and Mollie Lee (Kitchen) Wright, prepared by Mrs. Mary Lee (Wright) Kendall, Indianapolis, Ind., 1952.

[3] Descendants of Jesse and Maude (Wright) Hilton (Manuscript), prepared by Estill R. Hilton, Raceland, Kentucky, 1952.

JACOBS FAMILY OF FLOYD AND CARTER COS.

*1. Rolev Jacobs and *2. William Jacobs, brothers and Revolutionarv War soldiers, were the progenitors of large branches of the Jacobs Family of Eastern and Northeastern Kentucky.

1. ROLEY JACOBS, a resident of Floyd County, Kentucky, personally appeared in the Floyd County Circuit Court, on October 19, 1818, and filed his application for a pension growing out of his services in the army wherein he stated among other things, that he was 65 years old: that he enlisted for one year at Winchester, Virginia, on or about January 25. 1774, and served in the command of Daniel Morgan, afterwards Gen. Morgan, and was attached to the Rifle Regiment at Boston. commanded bv Gen. Arnold; and from thence he marched to Quebec where he was taken prisoner and remained a captive for nine months; that he served until about the 1st of January, 1776, and owing to his captivity he never received a discharge from his enlistment: that on Januarv 21, 1777, he enlisted again for three years under Captain Charles Porterfield and was attached to the Rifle Regiment of Col. Daniel Morgan, which last enlistment was at Winchester, Virginia; that he served until February 9, 1780, and was honorably discharged by Col. B. Ball.[1]

The above statements were corroborated by William Jacobs, a brother and Revolutionary War soldier. Roley Jacobs d. February 19, 1825. Carter H. Jacobs was his executor.

2. WILLIAM JACOBS, aged 63 years. on October 19, 1818, personally appeared before Judge Benjamin Mills, Judge of the Floyd County (Kentucky) Circuit Court, and filed his application for a pension growing out of his services in the army during the Revolutionary War, wherein he stated. among other things, that he was then a resident of Clay County. Kentucky; that on or about January 15. 1776, he enlisted at Winchester, Virginia, for one year's service in the Revolutionary War. in Captain Thomas Perry's Company of the Eighth Virginia Regiment, commanded by Col. Muhlenburg; that before the expiration of his enlistment he reenlisted for three years in Captain Westfall's Company of the same regiment; and that he continued to serve in said corps until the expiration of his enlistment when he was honorably discharged in Frederick County, Virginia, in 1782, by Gen. Daniel Morgan.[2]

William Jacobs' statement was corroborated by Roley Jacobs, a brother and Revolutionary War soldier.

The Jacobs family is of Scotch-Irish descent. The earliest ancestor of record in Kentucky is William Wood Jacobs, Sr., who may have been identical with the William Jacobs who was at Fort Pitt in 1760 with his wife Elizabeth and daughter Margaret. He probably was related to a Christopher Jacobs who was licensed as an Indian trader in 1747; and to William Woods, who was killed by Indians in

1763 or 1764. Apparently he was a native of Frederick County, Virginia, where the Wood family was very prominent in those days. He received from Virginia a warrant for 100 acres of land in consideration of his services for three years as a soldier in the continental line. It is not known what disposition he made of this land warrant.

William Jacobs was b. in Virginia about 1755 and lived to be nearly one hundred years old. It has not been established whom he married. However, one William Jacobs m. Lydia Suttle in Frederick County, Virginia, April 3, 1787.

The records would seem to indicate that Roley and William Jacobs settled in Floyd County, Kentucky, in the early 1800s.

Though not definitely established by records, the facts and circumstances strongly indicate that William Jacobs had children and/ or grandchildren as follows:

*3. Elizabeth Jacobs.
*4. William W. Jacobs.
*5. Madison G. Jacobs, Sr., b. August 15, 1813.
6. John M. Jacobs, born January 21, 1815.
7. Celetha Ann Jacobs; b. May 9, 1825; m. a Bryan.

3. ELIZABETH JACOBS; b. in Virginia, 1792 and d. in Carter County, Kentucky, February 27, 1865; m. Benjamin Morris in Floyd County, March 27, 1808. (See Morris Family.)

4. WILLIAM W. JACOBS, farmer; b. in Virginia March 6, 1808, d. in Carter County, June 25, 1893; m. Rhoda Pruitt, b. in Virginia, February 2, 1805, and d. in Carter County, August 25, 1870.

Children (fourteen):

7. Nancy Jacobs; b. November 25, 1824, and d. August 15, 1863; m. Samuel R. Gilbert, September 1, 1849. (See Gilbert Family.)

8. William Jacobs; b. September 6, 1826, and d., November 21, 1869; m. Nancy Cornett, January 13, 1853.

*9. Ira Jacobs; b. December 16, 1827; m. Martha Gee, December 4, 1856. (See Gee Family.)

10. Carter H. Jacobs; b. September 20, 1829; m. Nancy Roe, March 22, 1853.

*11. Hiram Jacobs; b. December 22, 1831, and d. December 20, 1916; m. Elvira Counts, October 12, 1856. She d. August 29, 1869.

12. John W. Jacobs; b. January 16, 1833; m. Susan Burton, February 26, 1861.

13. Celetha Ann Jacobs; b. September 25, 1834; m. Robert Gee, December 25, 1860. (See Gee Family.)

14. Lydia Jacobs; b. April 16, 1836, and d. November 19, 1839.

15. Madison G. Jacobs; b. December 16, 1837; d. November 18, 1839.

16. Jackson H. Jacobs; b. January 17, 1840; m. Frances ("Fanny") Stephens, February 23, 1868.

17. Rhoda Jacobs; b. August 22, 1842; m. M. G. Morris, February 27, 1861.

18. George W. Jacobs; b. August 22, (1842?), and d. October 7, 1852.

19. Mahala Jacobs; b. February 24, 1847, and d. June 9, 1848.

20. Francis M. Jacobs; b. December 13, 1848; m. Myrtilla Gee, October 11, 1875. (See Gee Family.) *

5. MADISON G. JACOBS; went to Texas with Fannin's men to fight for Texas independence from Mexico; was captured with others at Goliad but escaped the massacre by pretending to be dead and fled during the night; received grant of a large tract of land (16,000 acres) from the State of Texas on account of his war services on which he lived (P. O. Hackheim) until his death, December 18, 1881. He left a widow and ten children.

9. IRA JACOBS, farmer; lived the latter part of his life at present Jacobs post office, Carter County.

Children:

21. GEORGE W. JACOBS, a merchant, first at Jacobs and afterwards at Grayson; and sheriff of Carter County, 1910-1914; m. Minerva Porter, teacher, a granddaughter in the maternal line of William T. and Amanda S. (Elliott) Mobley, a great-granddaughter of Samuel R. and Minerva Elliott and a great-great-granddaughter of Captain John Lisle and Jane (Ritchie) Elliott. (See Elliott and Mobley families.)

Prior to her marriage Mrs. Jacobs was a teacher in the public rural schools. She is a Republican in politics and is a competent organizer and an active worker in local party affairs. Residence Grayson, Kentucky.

Children: Martha, Edna, Bessie and Jack.

22. Charles Jacobs, a merchant, first at Jacobs, afterwards at Grayson and finally at Olive Hill; m. Sarah Porter, a sister of Minerva (Porter) Jacobs. Children: Virgil and Orval.

23. James W. Jacobs, farmer; resided at Lawton; m. Ellen Underwood. Children: Viola, a teacher; resides in the ancestral home; unm.

24. Lizzie Jacobs; resides at Lawton; is of advanced age; unm.

25. Robert Jacobs, farmer; resides at Jacobs; m. Miss Porter; reared a family.

26. Frank Jacobs, farmer at Jacobs; m. Hebe Porter, a sister of Minerva (Porter) Jacobs. Children: a daughter.

27. Laura Jacobs, deceased; m. Charles Mabry, a teacher. Children: a daughter, Ottie, a teacher.

11. HIRAM JACOBS; resided in Western part of Carter County.

Children:

28. Robert Jacobs; m. Mary Jane Olive, an Englishwoman.

*29. Lewis Jacobs.

*30. Madison Jacobs.
*31. Mordecai Jacobs.
32. Harrison (Harry) Jacobs; d. at age of 13.
29. LEWIS JACOBS; m. Susanna Burchett. Children: Burrell and Lula, who is m. and resides at 324 N. 83rd Street, East St. Louis.
30. MADISON JACOBS; b. July 22, 1862, and d. January 10, 1935; m. January 22, 1892, Ollie Jacobs, b. April 30, 1862, d. April 22, 1951, daughter of John S. and Susan (Morris) Jacobs. Children:
33. Fred Jacobs; b. January 6, 1883; m. Minnie Selinger, April 10, 1912. Children: Olive, b. March 12, 1916; Harold, b. July 5, 1917; Evelyn, b. August 15, 1918; and John, b. October 15, 1919.
34. Claud W. Jacobs; b. July 25, 1885; m. Katherine Klassen, December 30, 1908. Children: Claud H., b. June 28, 1916, and Lucille, b. December 27, 1917.
35. Maud Jacobs, teacher; b. July 25, 1895; resides at 732½ N. 5th Street, Springfield, Illinois.
36. Albert Jacobs; b. February 19, 1888; m. Eudena Patnode, June 25, 1908. Children: Luella, b. June 28, 1910; Maurine, b. July 29, 1913; Arthur, b. December 27, 1915; Russell, b. May 1, 1919; Evelyn, b. May 15, 1921; and Kathryn, b. September 29, 1922.
37. Minnie Jacobs; b. June 30, 1892; m. Henry Groesch, October 30, 1912. Children: Madeline, b. September 4, 1913; Edgar, b. April 19, 1918; commissioned a lieutenant, U. S. A. A. F.; lost in the Mediterranean, April 2, 1944; Robert, b. March 3, 1925.
38. Russell Jacobs; b. February 10, 1895, and d. July 4, 1940; m. Bernice Jones, December 11, 1922. Children: Vernon, b. March 5, 1923; Walter, b. November 16, 1924, and killed in automobile accident, July 4, 1940; and James, b. November 7, 1926.
39. Darrell Morris Jacobs; b. February 25, 1897; m. Mary Cox, September 2, 1924. Children: Eileen, b. December 2, 1925, and d. June 13, 1951; Lyle, b. April 14, 1927; Darrell H., b. October 31, 1931; Keith, b. June 25, 1934; Willis, b. April 28, 1936; Michael, b. January 5, 1944; and Judith, b. February 5, 1950.
40. Pearl Jacobs; b. June 23, 1899; m. Rodney Borusky, October 29, 1925. Children: James, b. August 3, 1926, and Clarice, b. October 7, 1927.
41. Eugene Jacobs; b. August 16, 1901; m. Evelyn Carlson, December 12, 1922, Children: Gloria, b. May 17, 1927; Eugene H., b. February 12, 1932; and Patricia Ann, b. February 22, 1940.
42. Paul Jacobs; b. September 8, 1908, and d. June 9, 1925.
31. MORDECAI JACOBS; m. Laura Floyd. Children: Effie, b. June 16, 1891; Anna, b. June 29, 1893; and Ruth, b. August 10, 1895.[4]

[1] The National Archives, Washington, D. C.
[2] Ibid.
[3] The William W. Jacobs Family Bible.
[4] The Descendants of William W. Jacobs (Manuscript), prepared by Maud Jacobs, 732½ N. 5th Street, Springfield, Illinois, November 28, 1954.

JAYNE FAMILY OF JOHNSON COUNTY

William Jayne was the progenitor of the Jayne family of Johnson County, Kentucky. According to authorities he migrated from Scott County, Virginia, to the Big Sandy Valley, Eastern Kentucky. He m., presumably in Scott County, Virginia. However, the name of his wife has not been learned.

1. WILLIAM JAYNE; m. ———— ————.
Children:
*2. Henry Jayne.
*3. Daniel Jayne.
 4. Susan Jayne, m. Thomas Conley. (See Conley Family.)
 5. ———— Jayne, m. William Wheeler.

2. HENRY JAYNE; settled at Flat Gap, Johnson County, Kentucky, about 1832. He m. Sarah Sparks in Lawrence County, December 25, 1824.

Children:
*6. Daniel Jayne.
*7. William Jayne.
*8. Martha Jayne.
*9. Elizabeth Jayne.
 10. Sarah Jayne, m. David Daniel.
 11. Eleanor Jayne, m. Isom Daniel in Lawrence County, May 5, 1842.
*12. Henry Jayne; m. Julia Hager, daughter of John Jackson Hager. (See Hager Family.)
*13. Phoebe Jayne.
 14. Mary Jayne; m. Henry Hill; removed to and lived at Topeka, Kansas.

3. DANIEL JAYNE; settled at Flat Gap, present Johnson County, about 1832; m. Civilar Nickell?

Children:
 15. Daniel Jayne; m. Irene Salyer.
 16. Henry Jayne.
 17. Thomas Jayne.
 18. William Jayne; m. ———— Layne.

6. DANIEL JAYNE; m. Mary Ross.
Children:
 19. Stephen Jayne; d. in young manhood.
 20. Verlina Jayne; m. ———— Keaton.
 21. Sarah Jayne.

7. WILLIAM JAYNE, teacher and minister of the Baptist Church, was educated in the public schools of Johnson County and completed a high school course at and was graduated from Georgetown College, Georgetown, Kentucky. After graduation returning to his home in Johnson County, he devoted practically his long life to teaching and preaching. With Elder T. J. Rigg he established and organized the first Baptist Church (Missionary) of Johnson County—Liberty Church at Denver, in 1869. He established the Enterprise Academy at Flat Gap, Johnson County, and was its principal teacher for many years. The academy was the first training school for teachers in Johnson County.

Prof. Jayne d. at Lake City, Florida, December 22, 1917, at an advanced age. Children:

22. William Legrand Jayne, educator; was educated in the public school of Johnson County; at Enterprise Academy at Flat Gap; and was graduated from Georgetown College, Georgetown, Kentucky; taught in the public schools of Boyd County, Kentucky, for a number of years; was instructor in teachers' institutes; was a professor in Eastern Kentucky State Normal School at Richmond and in Morehead State Teachers' College at Morehead.

Prof. Jayne was a Baptist in religion and a Republican in politics. He was elected on the Republican ticket and served as superintendent of public schools in Boyd County for two terms.

8. MARTHA JAYNE; d. March 26, 1893; m., 1853, David Ross, b. 1823, d. January 5, 1897; descendants live in Flat Gap section, Johnson County.

Children:
23. Daniel Ross; b. 1855; m. Ellen Fannin.
24. Sarah Ross; b. 1856; m. Clark Fairchild.
25. Elizabeth Ross; b. 1858; m. Thomas M. Bailey.
26. James Ross; b. 1859; migrated and lived in Texas.
27. Joe Ross; b. 1861; unm.
28. William Ross; b. 1862; m. Rhoda McKenzie.
31. Eliphus Ross; b. 1869; m. Cora Grimsley.
29. Jefferson Ross; b. 1864; unm.
30. David Ross; b. 1866; m. Elizabeth Fairchild.
32. Plyman Ross; b. 1870.
33. Phoebe Ross; b. 1872; m. William Shavers.
34. Stephen Ross; b. 1874; m. Mollie Kazee.
35. Alminta or Almeda Ross; b. 1876; m. Harry Sagraves.

9. ELIZABETH JAYNE; m. John Kazee.
Children:
36. Wise Kazee.

37. John Kazee.
38. Daniel Kazee; m. Louise Johnson, daughter of Levi Johnson.
———— Kazee; d. in young manhood.

12. HENRY JAYNE; farmer and influential citizen; m. Julia Hager. (See Hager Family); lived and d. at Flat Gap.

Children:
39. Irvin Jayne.
40. Ernest Jayne.
41. Augusta Jayne.

13. PHOEBE JAYNE; m. Colsby Lyons.

Children:
42. Henry Lyons; m. Cora Sagraves.
43. Alonzo Lyons; m. ———— Sparks.
44. William Lyons; m. Mary Daniels.
45. Cora Lyons; m. Morton Sparks.
46. Mary Lyons; m. Jefferson Stafford.

JOHNS FAMILY OF FLOYD COUNTY

Thomas Johns was the ancestor of the Johns family of the Big Sandy Valley, Eastern Kentucky. He came in from Virginia at an early day and helped to clear the forests and make the valley a fit dwelling place for man. His descendants spread along the river from Pikeville to Louisa and all have occupied high positions in life.[1]

1. THOMAS JOHNS, farmer, was a resident of Amherst County, Virginia, and m., presumably in that county, Nancy Layne, daughter of William S. Layne. He was therefore brother-in-law of the pioneers, John Shannon Layne and Tandy Stratton. (See Layne and Stratton Families.)

Thomas Johns served in the Virginia forces in the Revolutionary War.

Children:

2. John Johns, a merchant, at Prestonsburg.

3. Daniel Johns was nominated by a committee of Whig-American Party and elected State representative, being the first representative from the then new district composed of Boyd and Lawrence Counties. Soon after the expiration of his term, he removed to Minnesota where he held official positions.

4. James Johns; resided in Louisa.

5. Harvey Johns.

Early marriage records of the Big Sandy Valley show marriages of members of the Johns family as follows:

Frances Johns and Pleasant Childers, in Pike County, March 28, 1828.

Elizabeth Johns and Tandy M. Layne, in Floyd County, April 21, 1831.

Elizabeth Graham and Thomas P. Johns, in Floyd County, March 8, 1838. She was the daughter of Judge John Graham (See Graham Family).

Martin H. Johns and Mary L. Goble, in Lawrence County, November 12, 1847.

Christina Johns and Booker Elkins, in Pike County, January 25, 1861.

Dan W. Johns and Annie Adkins, in Pike County, December 25, 1824.

---

[1] William Ely, "The Big Sandy Valley," p. 214.

KEESEE, KOZEE FAMILY

KEESEE, KESEE, KEEZEE, KEZEE,
KISSEE, KAZEE, KOZEE

According to tradition Jacques La Caze, a French Huguenot, was the progenitor of the Keesee or Keezee family of the Virginia colony. He was of that large company of French Huguenot refugees who emigrated from England or France about 1700 and, sponsored by William Byrd III, settled at Manocantown, Henrico County, (now Mankin, Goochland County) about twenty miles up the James River from present Richmond. At this time Jacqques La Caze was thirty-one years of age and unmarried. Research has disclosed nothing concerning his marriage.

Not long after Manocantown was erected into a parish, the parishioners were assembled to erect a vestry and Jacques La Caze was elected as one of the twelve vestrymen. He was reelected and served as vestryman many years.[1]

In anglicizing the name the "La" was dropped and the "Caze" was pronounced as two syllables and spelled Keesee, Keysee, or Keezee. Subsequently the name has been spelled many other ways: Kesee, Kezee, Kissee, Kazee, Kozee.

With respect to the progenitor of the Keesee family in America, it was stated by Olivia (Simmons) Keesee (Mrs. Charles Blackwell Keesee), prominent in the Daughters of the American Revolution, that a George Keesee, Huguenot, who came to Henrico County, Virginia, about 1700, was the founder of the family in America. However that may be, it is agreed by all authorities that all Keesees of Virginia were of the same family, descending from a common ancestor.

Many of the descendants of the first immigrant remained in Henrico County; others spread out westward and southwestward and by the year 1800 they were numerous, particularly in the counties of Campbell, Charlotte, Halifax and Pittsylvania. At this period families of the name lived in the Carolinas. Members of the family migrated and settled in Tennessee, Arkansas, Mississippi, Oklahoma, Kentucky, West Virginia, Colorado and Missouri and probably other states.

The records indicate that prior to the Civil War, the Keesees of Eastern and Southern Virginia were generally planters or farmers, owning large plantations on which tobacco was cultivated, principally by their slaves. Some of them, however, were professional men and others held public office. The records do not disclose that any member of the family had service in the armed forces in the Revolutionary War. However, the records show that on August 10, 1781, the Commissioners of Pittsylvania County assessed one Jesse Keesee four pounds and one John Kessee forty-two pounds for provisions for the

Revolutionary Army. Arthur Keesee and Richard Keesee's service in the Revolutionary War was civil as distinguished from military. However, the descendants of Jesse, John, Arthur and Richard Keesee would be eligible to membership in the D.A.R. and S.A.R. by reason of this support and service rendered to the cause of American Independence.

THE KEESEES OF HENRICO COUNTY, VIRGINIA OF TENNESSEE AND OF ARKANSAS

1. GEORGE KEESEE II, a son of George Keesee I, the immigrant, was the ancestor of a large branch of the family of Henrico County, Virginia. He was b. in 1755 and d. in 1840. He is said to have had brothers and sisters: 2. Charles Keesee who m., first, Rebecca Smith and secondly, Lucy ———; 3. Thomas Keesee who m., first Elizabeth Burton and, secondly Nancy Obey; 4. Mildred Keesee who m. a Norment; 5, a sister, christian name not known, who m. Dano Roper; and * 6. John Keesee.[2]

George Keesee m. in Henrico County, Fanny (Frayser) Price, widow of John Price, a daughter of William Frayser II and his wife, Martha Burton (daughter of John Burton) and a granddaughter of William Frayser I of Scotland and his wife, Hannah, who settled in Henrico County about 1700.

Fanny (Frayser) Price Keesee had brothers and sisters: William Frayser, III, m. Mollie Hale; Jackson Frayser m. Mildred Hobson; Lucy Frayser m., first, William De Priest, and, secondly, William Young; Jesse Frayser m. Keziah Hobson; and Andrew Freyer m. Rebecca Marshall.

Children of George Keesee II and Fanny (Frayser) Price Keesee:[1]

*7. Jesse Frayser Keesee.

*8. John William Keesee.

9. Thomas Colin Keesee; m., first Nancy Sharp and, secondly, Lucy Childry.

10. Elizabeth Keesee; m. Caleb Frayser.

6. JOHN KEESEE; m. Lucy Brightwell, daughter of Reynolds Brightwell.

Children:

11. Millie Keesee; m., first, Henry Mellert in Henrico County, Virginia, June 28, 1804, and, secondly, a Nowlan.

12. Nancy Keesee; m. William Talbot in Pittsylvania County, 1807.

*13. John Keesee.

14. Blackwell Keesee; moved to Tennessee.

15. Charles Keesee; moved to Missouri.

13. JOHN KEESEE; b. November 15, 1783, Richmond, Virginia, went to Pittsylvania County, Virginia, and thence to Caswell County, North Carolina; had service in the War of 1812; d. May 18, 1848; m. March 7, 1811, Mary John Dupuy, b. November 17, 1793, d. October 5, 1866, a daughter of John and Mary (Watkins) Dupuy.

Children:

*16. John Dupuy Keesee.

17. Louisa Turner Keesee; b. November 17, 1812, d. March 5, 1836; m., December 24, 1829, William Y. Stokes.

18. Paulina A. Keesee; b. August 29, 1818; m. William Anderson, minister of the Methodist Church.

16. JOHN DUPUY KEESEE was b. in Caswell County, North Carolina, February 5, 1816, and d. in that county, January 6, 1891; m. January 26, 1854, Jane E. Johnston, b. December 13, 1831, d. March 1, 1899, a daughter of Lancelot Johnston and Matilda (Simpson) Johnston.

Children:

19. Dr. John Johnston Keesee; b. July 8, 1855, d. October 11, 1907; unm.

20. Louisa Matilda Keesee; b. April 20, 1857, d. July 24, 1930; m. November 28, 1875, Rufus L. Rawleigh.

21. Frances Turner Keesee; b. January 26, 1859, d. April, 1896; m. November 27, 1892, J. A. Swann.

*22. Charles Blackwell Keesee.

23. Elbert Dupuy Keesee; b. October 31, 1864; d. July 17, 1865.

22. CHARLES BLACKWELL KEESEE, banker, industrialist, philanthropist and civic leader, was b. at Oak Lawn, Caswell County, North Carolina, October 21, 1861, and d. at Martinsville, Henry County, Virginia, February 1940.

Mr. Keesee was a businessman of many activities. A banker, he was president of the Peoples National Bank at Martinsville and was interested in and owned considerable stock in the American Furniture Company, the Bassett Furniture Company and the North Carolina Granite Company.

In his will, probated in the Henry County (Virginia) Circuit Court in February, 1940, he disposed of an estate valued at $685,000 of which $30,000 was represented by real estate and the remainder personal property. He bequeathed to his nephew, John Raleigh, 4,000 shares of common stock in the American Furniture Company and to R. H. Simmons 5,000 shares of the same stock. He provided for a trust fund founded on 4,000 shares of American Furniture Company stock, the income from which was to go to two family servants, Elvira Zeigler and Martha Kate Spencer, the principal ultimately to go to the Salem (Virginia) orphanage. He provided for a trust fund composed of 150 shares of Bassett Furniture Company preferred stock, 200 shares of North Carolina Granite Company stock, 150 shares of American Furniture Company preferred stock and 20,000 shares of common stock of the American Furniture Company, the income from which was given in equal parts to four nieces, Mrs. A. K. Walker, Mrs. R. A. Stokes and the Misses Janie and Ruth Raleigh for their lives and ultimately to revert to the estate. He bequeathed all the residue of the estate to his widow, Olivia (Simmons) Keesee, one half in fee simple and the remaining one-half to be administered by the trustees of the estate who were to pay the income therefrom to Mrs. Keesee. He made provisions for the establishment of the Keesee Educational Fund for the benefit of the youths of the Baptist Church.

Mr. Keesee was a consistent member of the Baptist Church and was a generous contributor to it and its auxiliaries.

He m. Olivia Helm Simmons, October 14, 1897, who was b. at Brookhurst, Floyd County, Virginia, December 4, 1873. She was educated by governess and at Oxford Academy, Floyd Court House, Virginia. She was a member of many patriotic societies, among others, Daughters of the American Revolution, in which she was prominent and influential and held many high positions, including that of State Regent of the Virginia Society and Corresponding Secretary General of the National Society.

In her will, Mrs. Keesee disposed of an estate valued at $834,000. She bequeathed to nieces and nephews incomes for life from rental property, and the home on Church Street, Martinsville, was left to the First Baptist Church for use as a parsonage at the death of a sister, Mrs. Mattie S. Marshall, and a niece, Miss Alice Simmons, who were given a life estate in home. The Virginia Baptist Orphanage at Salem, Virginia, was bequeathed $70,000 with which to construct a Keesee Memorial Recreation Building; and the bulk of the estate of $834,000 was eventually to pass into the Charles D. Keesee Educational Fund.

Mr. and Mrs. Keesee left no children. Residence "Chaskeeookee" Hunt Street, Martinsville, Virginia.

7. JESSE FRAYSER KEESEE, farmer, was b. in Virginia, August 11, 1799, and d. in Richmond, August 25, 1881. He served Henrico County in the capacity of sheriff, tax collector and coroner and the city of Richmond as assistant treasurer; m., in Henrico County, November 20, 1822, Cynthia Bullington, b. in Virginia about 1802, daughter of Josiah and Marie (Hobson) Bullington. Issue:

24. Elizabeth Keesee, b. in 1823, d. in 1887; m. Elisha Straughan Turpin. Children: John B. Turpin, Florence L. Turpin, Fannie Keesee Turpin, George Wilmer Turpin and Elisha Straughan Turpin.

25. Emma Bullington Keesee, b. in 1824, d. in 1892; m. 1850,

Augustus B. Clarke.   Children: G. Harvey Clarke, Arthur B. Clarke and John Stanley Clarke.

26. George Keesee.

27. Maria Frances Keesee, b. in 1827, d. in 1892; m. George A. Hundley.   Children: Sallie Lee Hundley.

28. George William Keesee, a Baptist minister, b. about 1831; was pastor of the Baptist church in Goldsboro, North Carolina.

29. Ann Judson Lipscomb Keesee.

30. Sallie Giles Keesee.

31. Cynthia Cary Keesee, b. in 1837, d. in 1914; m., 1860, William Russell Jones.   Children: George William Jones, Charles Lawrence Jones, Jesse Keesee Jones, Mary Porter Jones, John Marshall Jones and Fannie Cary Jones.

32. Josiah Thomas Keesee, b. in 1840, d. in 1912; m., 1863, Lucy Nelson.   Children: Jessie Clair Keesee, Erle Keesee and Page Nelson Keesee.

33. Jesse Mercer Keesee, b. in 1842, d. ———; m., in 1882, Mary Izilla Haynes.   Children: Carrie Belle Keesee, Lucy Gay Keezee, Fannie Emma Keesee, Jesse Sanford Keesee, Mary Elizabeth Keesee, and Mabel Mercer Keesee.

34. Mary Lucy Keesee, b. in 1844, d. in 1892; m. 1866, Ezekiel W. Brooking.   Children: Peyton Brooking, Keesee Brooking and Hugh Brooking.

8. JOHN WILLIAM KEESEE; m. Martha Woodfin.

Children:

35. Mary Jane Keesee; m. Mr. Cameron of Richmond.

*36. Thomas Woodfin Keesee.

37. Julia Ann Keesee; m. Daniel Pleasants.

36. COLONEL THOMAS WOODFIN KEESEE, Confederate States Army, was b. in Virginia, August 21, 1816, and d. in Columbia, Tennessee, in 1886.   In young manhood he felt the impulse to go West and he migrated to Maury County, Tennessee and settled at Columbia, that county, where he lived until his death in 1886.   He m., first, in Columbia, November 1, 1837, Marie Louise Bolling Cross, b. in Overton County, Tennessee, February 17, 1819, and d. at Columbia, Tennessee, in November, 1839, daughter of John Bolling Cross and his wife, Elizabeth (Armstrong) Cross.   They had one child:

*38. Captain John William Keesee.

Colonel Thomas Woodfin Keesee m., secondly, Elvira Narcissa Nelson of Columbia, Tennessee.   He held offices of honor and trust and was respected and admired by all who knew him.

38. CAPTAIN JOHN WILLIAM KEESEE, Confederate States Army, was b. at Columbia, Tennessee, August 8, 1838; was educated at Jackson College.   At the breaking out of the Civil War he entered the

Confederate States Army and served therein until the close of the war. At first he served under the great cavalry leader, General N. B. Forrest. Subsequently, having been transferred to the West, Mississippi Division, he was Adjutant of Major General Dobbins' brigade, following which he was staff officer with the rank of captain on the staff of General Hindman.

Captain John William Keesee m., first, at "Fairfield" near Clarksville, Tennessee, February 15, 1859, Louisa D. Drane, b. in Montgomery County, Tennessee, December 24, 1834, and d. at "Cypress Plains", Phillips County, Arkansas, September 5, 1862, daughter of Dr. and Mrs. W. H. Drane. They had issue:

*39. Eliza Jane Keesee.

*40. Thomas Woodfin Keesee II.

38-A. Captain John William Keesee m., secondly, January 25, 1866, Susan Reynolds Johnson of Lawrence County, Tennessee, daughter of George Reynolds Johnson and his wife, Martha (Ernel) Johnson of Alabama.

Issue:

*41. John William Keesee, Jr.

*42. Annie Sue Keesee.

43. Florence Johnson Keesee, d. at age of 17 without issue.

*44. Morris Johnson Keesee.

39. ELIZA JANE KEESEE, b. in 1860, m., April 27, 1882, Walter Parish Woldridge of Columbia, Tennessee. They had one child, Louise Woldridge, who m., June 29, 1904, Rev. Walter Branham Capers, of Jackson, Mississippi, son of Rt. Rev. Bishop Ellison Capers and grandson of Rt. Rev. Bishop William Capers. They had two children, Walter Capers, Jr., deceased, and Charlotte Capers who resides in Jackson, Mississippi.

40. THOMAS WOODFIN KEESEE II, (Woody); b. July 10, 1861; m., January 13, 1887, Susan Huntington Polk, daughter of Allen Jones Polk and his wife, Anna Clark (Fitzhugh) Polk, of Helena, Arkansas.

Colonel Allen Jones Polk was son of Dr. William Polk and his wife Mary Polk of Columbia, Tennessee, and a nephew of Rt. Rev. Bishop Leonidas Polk of Louisiana, the "fighting bishop", and lieutenant-general of the Confederate States Army, who fell with his face to the foe in the battle on Pine Mountain, Georgia. The Polks of Columbia, Tennessee, who were, in their day, the first citizens of Maury County, were descended from a long line of ancestors who were illustrious in the history of both North Carolina and Tennessee. The ancestry of Mrs. Mary (Long) Polk, the mother of Colonel Allen James Polk, was equally distinguished.

Children of Thomas Woodfin Keesee II and his wife, Susan Huntington Polk:
*45. Zelda Polk Keesee.
*46. Thomas Woodfin Keesee III.
47. Allen Polk Keesee; b. October 1, 1896. No children.

41. JOHN WILLIAM KEESEE II was b. in Phillips County, Arkansas, August 3, 1869; m., June 8, 1908, Hettie Johnson Scaife. Children: Martha Scaife Keesee, John William Keesee III, Fred Scaife Keesee and Susan Johnson Keesee, all of whom lived at Lakeview, Arkansas.

42. ANNIE SUE KEESEE was b. at "Beechlands", Phillips County, Arkansas, December 25, 1875; and d. in Helena, Arkansas, February 18, 1935; m. February 1, 1894, Dr. Willis Moss Richardson.
Children: Annie Keesee Richardson, b. June 16, 1895; m., August 28, 1917, Lewis Williamson Cherry, Jr., No children; John William Richardson m. Katherine Lee and they had two sons, Thomas Lee Richardson and John William Richardson, Jr., who m. Martha Nelson, reside in Dallas, Texas, and have a son.

44. MORRIS JOHNSON KEESEE; b. October 25, 1884; m. May 11, 1910, Margaret McKenzie of Mississippi; reside in Helena, Arkansas. Children: Morris Johnson Keesee, Jr., Thomas McKenzie Keesee and Lillian McKenzie Keesee.

45. ZELDA POLK KEESEE was b. January 31, 1889; m. William J. O'Brien of Olean, New York. Children: Zelda Keesee O'Brien, b. August 7, 1913; Elizabeth Pointer O'Brien, b. December 24, 1914; Susan Polk O'Brien, b. September 1, 1920; resides in Memphis, Tennessee.

46. THOMAS WOODFIN KEESEE III, was b. at Helena Arkansas, July 13, 1891; m., November 12, 1913, Gladys Key, daughter of Marshall Keith Key and his wife, Susan Joyce (Humphreys) Key.
Issue:
*48. Thomas Woodfin Keesee IV.
49. Gladys Key Keesee, b. October 9, 1916.
50. Allen Randolph Keesee, b. April 19, 1919; m. Miss Miles; lives in Helena, Arkansas.
51. Keith Keesee; lives in Maryland.

48. THOMAS WOODFIN KEESEE IV, lawyer; member of the firm of Simpson, Thacher & Bartlett, New York City, was b. in Helena, Arkansas; was graduated from Duke University in 1935 and from Harvard Law School in 1938; m. April 6, 1940, in the Protestant Episcopal Church of St. James, New York City, Miss Patricia Peale, daughter of Mr. and Mrs. Rembrandt Peale, Jr., of Greenwich, Connecticut, and granddaughter of Mrs. Rembrandt Peale of 510 Park Avenue, New York City, and the late Mr. Peale and of Mrs. Thomas F. Daly of Denver, Colorado, and the late Mr. Daly.[3]

KEESEES IN THE WESTWARD MOVEMENT

Just before the breaking out of the Revolutionary War and Boone's first attempt to settle Kentucky, the first of the family Keesee, so far as there is any record, crossed the Blue Ridge mountains and settled on the Holston River. On May 5, 1782, there were surveyed for one George Keesee 190 acres on Moccasin Creek in then Washington County, now Scott County, Virginia, actual settlement of which was made in 1772. On June 20, 1796, 100 acres were surveyed for Elias Keesee on Reedy Creek, actual settlement of which was made in 1774. During the period from 1797 to 1799, Charles Keezee and his wife, Mary, and Avery M. Keezee and his wife, Jennie, lived in Russell County, Virginia, as is evidenced by the purchase and/or sale of lands on Glade branch and Sinking creek tributaries of the Clinch River and on Little Cedar and Big Moccasin Creeks, tributaries of the North Fork of the Holston River.

Richard Keezee was the progenitor of a large family in Eastern Kentucky and, so far as the records disclose, was the first of the family Keesee to cross the Allegheny Mountains in the Westward Movement. He was b. in Virginia—presumably in Pittsylvania County—about 1760 and m. in that State about 1784, Sallie (surname not known). In the early 1800s he, with his family and slaves, settled on or near the mouth of Pigeon Creek on the Tug Fork of Big Sandy River in then Cabell County, Virginia. It is not known whether he came from the Holston or Clinch River settlements in Southwestern Virginia where the Keesees had settled about a quarter of a century before or from Eastern or Southern Virginia where the family had been seated for about a century. It is definitely known, however, that Richard Keezee was of the host of settlers who came in via the Great Kanawha River and settled Cabell County in the early 1800s.

Richard Keezee acquired by assignment considerable acreage in a tract of 11,065 acres of land situated on the Tug Fork and Pigeon Creek, then Cabell County, Virginia, which he had surveyed into small farms and conveyed in 1812 to Richard Ferrell, John Safford, Vincent Grant, Elijah Donothan, Ferrell Ivins and others. It is not known when he removed from Cabell County to Kentucky. However, he was a resident of Floyd County, Kentucky, in 1810 and soon afterwards purchased and patented several tracts of land in that county. He finally settled on Hood's fork of Big Blaine on the line between Lawrence and Johnson Counties.

1. RICHARD KEEZEE was b. in Virginia about 1760 and m. in that State about 1784, Sallie (family name not known).

Children:

2. Dorina (or Derinah) Keezee, b. in Virginia in 1786, d. in Carter County, Kentucky, May 3, 1861,[5] m. Henry Bear (Baer or

Bayer) farmer, b. in Tennessee in 1785. They left many descendants in the Little Sandy River region in present Elliott County, Kentucky.

3. Charles Keezee, farmer, b. in Virginia in 1790; m. in Lawrence County, June 24, 1824, Barbara Elain, b. in Virginia in 1790. The U. S. Census of Lawrence County for 1840 shows that they had five sons and two daughters then living at home and such census for 1860 shows that Charles Kezee, age 70, his wife, Barbara, age 70, and Jesse Kesee, age 24, apparently son, were boarding in the home of William and Amanda Elam.

*4. Elias Keezee.

*5. Jesse Keezee.

*6. Avery Keezee.

7. Nancy Kezee; m. Charles Staton in Floyd County, August 13, 1820.

8. Elizabeth Keezee; m. Allen Sparks in Floyd County, June 27, 1822.

4. ELIAS KEEZEE, farmer and Baptist preacher, was b. in Virginia in 1798; m. in Floyd County, Kentucky, October 29, 1819, Mary Curnutte, b. in Virginia about 1793.

Children living at home and approximate dates of birth as shown by the U. S. Census of Lawrence County for the year 1850:

9. Cynthia Keezee, b. 1826.

10. Jane Keezee, b. 1827.

11. Sarah Keezee, b. 1829.

12. Harvey Keezee, b. 1832.

13. Elias Keezee, Jr., b. 1835.

14. Jarred Keezee, b. 1843.

15. Reuben Keezee, b. 1846.

16. Rufus Keezee, b. 1849.

5. JESSE KEEZEE, farmer; b. in Virginia, 1803, and d. in Carter County, Kentucky. He m., first, in Floyd County, August 8, 1821, Sarah Elizabeth Kitchen, b. in Greenbrier County Virginia, 1803, and d. in Carter County, Kentucky, February 4, 1852, daughter of James Kitchen, Revolutionary War soldier, and his wife, Jane (Patterson) Kitchen; and m., secondly, in Carter County, January 31, 1856, Nancy Ward.

Children of Jesse Keezee and Sarah Elizabeth (Kitchen) Keezee:

17. William Patterson Kozee; migrated to Missouri. Children: Judd Kozee and Joe Kozee.

*18. Andrew J. Kozee.

19. Allen Wylie Kozee; b. in Carter County, 1837; d. at Grayson, Kentucky, January 5, 1909. He taught in the public schools of Carter County for a time and was a bank clerk and a deputy clerk of

the Carter County Court for several years. He was the first to write the family surname "Kozee".

20. Sarah Elizabeth Kozee; b. in Carter County, 1841; m., first, B. Lansdown and, secondly, Thomas Copeland.

21. John L. Kozee; b. in Carter County, 1846; had service in the Union Army; mustered in at Grayson, Kentucky, September 28, 1863, a private Company "E", 40th Kentucky Volunteer Mounted Infantry, and d. at Paris, Kentucky, April 15, 1864.

22. Mary A. Kozee; m. ——— Murphy, went West.

23. Rebecca Kozee; m. ——— Burton.

24. Granville Kozee; b. 1857.

25. Roland Kozee; b. 1859.

Children of Jesse Kozee and Mary Frances (Ward) Kozee:

26. G. G. Kozee; lived in Ohio.

27. W. R. Kozee; lived in Cabell County, West Virginia.

28. Sally Kozee; m. Jesse Ward.

18. ANDREW JACKSON KOZEE, farmer; b. in Carter County, 1834, and d. October 6, 1907; m. in Carter County, June 23, 1853, Susan Kozee, b. 1825.

Children:

29. Green Kozee.

30. Millard Kozee.

31. James Kozee.

32. Trinvilla Kozee; m. ——— Hardy.

33. America Kozee; m. Lon Ingalls.

34. Jack Kozee.

35. Thomas Kozee.

36. Hugh Kozee.

37. Minnie Kozee; m. John Everman (See Everman Family.)

38. Bertha Kozee; m. Albert Everman (See Everman Family.)

6. AVERY KOZEE, farmer; b. in Virginia, 1803; d. in Carter County, Kentucky, within the period 1870-1880; m. in Floyd County, August 10, 1820, Elizabeth (Betsy) Fitzpatrick, b. in Kentucky, 1806, and d. in Carter County subsequent to 1880. She was a daughter of John Fitzpatrick of Floyd County, Kentucky.

Children, among others:

*39. John Kozee.

40. Sarah Kozee; b. 1834.

41. Levisa Kozee; b. 1839.

42. Phoebe J. Kozee; b. 1841.

43. Susan Kozee; b. 1846; m. George Griffith.

44. George W. Kozee; b. 1848; unm.

45. Avery Kozee, Jr.; b. 1855.

46. Martha Kozee; m. Martin Johnson, December 7, 1849.

39. JOHN KOZEE, farmer; b. in Lawrence County, Kentucky, about

1830, and d. at Willard, Carter County, Kentucky, May 1909; m. in Johnson County, Kentucky, August 25, 1848, Mary (Polly) Brummett, b. in Harlan County, Kentucky, in 1832 and d. in Willard, January 15, 1925, a daughter of John Brummett and his wife, Mahala (Brock) Brummett and a great-granddaughter of Jesse Brock, Revolutionary War soldier. (See Brock Family.) Soon after marriage they moved to Harlan County, where they lived until after the close of the Civil War. John Kozee had service in that war from October 13, 1862, to January 13, 1863, as a private, Company "G", Harlan County Battalion.

Children:

47. William Harrison Kozee; b. 1849; m. Louisa Grim, daughter of Charles and Elizabeth (Hylton) Grim. (See Hylton Family). They lived in Johnson County. Children: John, Charles, Elizabeth, Mary, Lottie and Bessie.

*48. George W. Kozee.

49. Mahala Kozee; b. 1856; m. Jasper Reeves. No children.

50. John Kozee; b. 1857; m., first, America Grim, daughter of Charles and Elizabeth (Hylton) Grim. Children: William Sherman, Sam, Jeanette, Geneva and Lessie. He m., secondly, Nancy Ward and they had one child: Annie.

51. Nancy Kozee; b. 1858; m. William Maddox. Children: Fred, Edward and John.

52. David Kozee; b. 1861; m., first, Lou Herrald. No children. He m., secondly, in Minnesota. They had a daughter, Mary.

53. Jemima Kozee; b. 1864; m. Troy Holbrook. Children: Fred, Dova, Cam, Murray and Martha.

54. Lewis (Luke) Patterson Kozee; b. 1869; m. Rhoda Jacobs. Children: Sheridan and Goldie.

*55. Sam Kozee.

56. Greenville Kozee; b. 1874; d. November 1951; m. Martha Knipp.

Children: Russell, Mary and Estie.

48. GEORGE WASHINGTON KOZEE, farmer; b. in Lawrence County, Kentucky, January 22, 1851, and d. in Ashland, Kentucky, December 25, 1936. Interment in "Fairview" graveyard near Willard; m. on Bells Trace, near Webbville, Kentucky, June 5, 1873, Mrs. Selina Jane (Hylton) Wright, b. in Johnson County, Kentucky, January 30, 1847, and d. in Ashland, Kentucky, August 5, 1931. Interment in Webbville Cemetery. She was a daughter of E. P. S. Hylton and his wife, Sarah (Green) Hylton, and a great-granddaughter of Nathan Preston, Revolutionary War soldier. (See Hylton Family and Nathan Preston Family.)

Children:

*57. Lindsey Lester Kozee.

58. Mary Alice Kozee; b. January 10, 1876; m., August 31, 1898,

James W. Montgomery, a coal operator, of West Virginia, who finally became a realtor in Ashland, Kentucky, where he resided during the later part of his life and d. April 25, 1931. Interment at Ashland. They had no children but adopted a daughter, Mrs. Willie Wheatley, wife of Hobart Wheatley of Ashland.

*59. William Carlos Kozee.

60. Martha Belle Kozee; b. August 9, 1880, d. June 27, 1901. Interment in Fairview graveyard; unm.

61. Infant son, b. and d. March 24, 1888.

57. LINDSEY LESTER KOZEE: b. at Webbville, Lawrence County, April 30, 1874, and d. at Willard, June 28, 1910. Interment in "Fairview" graveyard; m. Ethel Graham.

Children:-

62. Rex Kozee; b. near Willard, February 3, 1907; educated in the Ashland (Kentucky) Graded and High Schools; was employed by the American Rolling Mills Company of Ashland, March 5, 1924, as a laborer; promoted to roll foreman in 1939 and is presenty employed as such; m. at Columbus, Ohio, July 3, 1933, Edna Virginia Rolle, who was b. at Frontenac, Kansas, July 17, 1903; was graduated from the Frontenac High School; attended Pittsburg Business College; and has held positions with the Girard Publishing Company, Girard Kansas, the Ashland Daily Independent, Ashland, Kentucky, the Ashland Traffic Bureau and the American Rolling Mills Company. No children.

63. Goldie Kozee; d. young.

59. WILLIAM CARLOS KOZEE, lawyer, sometime teacher and public official, Federal employee, historian and genealogist; b. near Webbville, Lawrence County, Kentucky, February 4, 1878; educated in the Willard (Kentucky) Graded, High and Normal Schools; at Central Normal College, Danville, Indiana, at Kentucky University (now Transylvania College) at Lexington; was graduated from Bryant and Stratton Business College, Louisville, 1915; took law course by correspondence with the Indianapolis College of Law; and was graduated from the National University Law School, Washington, D. C., with degree of LL.B. in 1927; began teaching in the rural schools of Carter County, Kentucky, in July, 1896, and continued in educational work in that county for the succeeding twenty years except for two years; taught in rural schools five years and was principal of graded schools for nine years—five years at Willard, two years at Grayson and two years at Denton; was admitted to the bar at Greenup, Kentucky, July 17, 1903, and practiced law at Grayson for a time and at Pikeville, Kentucky, as junior member of the firm of Vanover and Kozee. 1906-7; was appointed superintendent of public schools of Carter County, June 2. 1908, vice Dr. Hardin Gilbert, resigned; was elected in November, 1908 to serve the unexpired term; and was re-elected in November, 1909, and served a

term of four years ended December 31, 1913; accepted a position
with the Federal Trade Commission, Washington, D. C., November
1, 1916; transferred to the Office Auditor for the War Department,
August 1, 1917, and was assigned to the military claims division as a
claims adjustor; was promoted to Claims Reviewer and was serving
as such when the General Accounting Office was formed and organized
by consolidation of the Office Auditor for the War and other agencies;
was promoted, 1936, to Chief Review Examiner of claims filed against
the Government in the U. S. Court of Claims and the U. S. District
Courts; and continued to serve in that capacity until retirement from
the Government service, March 1, 1948.

Mr. Kozee was m. at Catlettsburg, Kentucky, November 7, 1907,
to Miss Bessie Myrtle Morris, eldest daughter of Judge John G., and
Mrs. Martha E. (Gilbert) Morris of Grayson. (See Morris Family
and Gilbert Family.) Mrs. Kozee was b. at Smoky Valley, Carter
County, Kentucky, February 4, 1886; educated in the Grayson Graded
and High Schools and at the Morehead (Kentucky) Normal School;
taught in the public schools of Carter County for four years.

Both Mr. and Mrs. Kozee united with the Christian Church in
their youth and are presently active members of the National City
Christian Church, Washington, D .C. They were initiated in the
Grayson Chapter, Order of the Eastern Star in 1904, and Mrs. Kozee
is a charter member of Miriam Chapter O. E. S., Washington, D. C.

Mr. Kozee is a Republican in politics and was made a master
mason in Willard Lodge, No. 626, F. and A. M., February 22, 1902.
He affiliated with the Independent Order of Odd Fellows and Junior
Order of American Mechanics and is a member of the Sons of the
American Revolution, District of Columbia, the National Geneal-
ogical Society, Washington, D. C., and the Kentucky State Historical
Society, Frankfort, Kentucky, and a Kentucky Colonel.

Children:
*64. Karl Morris Kozee.

65. George Joseph Kozee; b. at Grayson, Kentucky, February 15,
1916, and d. in Washington, D. C., November 18, 1920. Interment
in Glenwood Cemetery, Washington, D. C.

66. Mary Grace Kozee; b. at Grayson, December 20, 1917, and
d. in Washington, D. C., September 26, 1924 (automobile accident).
Interment in Glenwood Cemetery.

64. KARL MORRIS KOZEE, Federal employee, was b. at Grayson,
Kentucky, June 13, 1911; educated in the Washington, D. C. schools;
was graduated from the Columbia School of Technology, Washington, D. C., and did post graduate work in George Washington University; entered the Government service in 1934 and is presently a
Scientific Illustrator in the Interior Department; m., first December
6, 1931, Jeannette Dulin. Children: 67. Karl Morris Kozee, Jr., b.
in Washington, D. C., March 3, 1934; educated in the public and

parochial schools of the Washington area, graduating from high school, 1952; became a student at Mount St. Mary's College, (Maryland) 1953.

64A. Karl Morris Kozee again m. at Wade, North Carolina, on December 24, 1944, Margaret (Partridge) Erskine, daughter of Albert Eugene and Megnotie Jane (Ferrell) Partridge of Wade, North Carolina.

Children:
68. Martha Jane Kozee; b. in Washington, D. C., May 14, 1950.

Margaret F. Partridge was b. at Zebulon, North Carolina, October 9, 1921, and was educated in the rural and high schools of North Carolina. She m., first, Raymond E. Erskine. Children: Raymond E., Jr., b. 1938, d. 1938; and Dorcas Anne, b. November 18, 1942.

55. SAM KOZEE; farmer, b. January 1, 1872, d. March 22, 1916; m. December 9, 1900, Frances Skaggs, b. February 15, 1877; resided at Johns Run, near Willard, Kentucky.

Children:
*69. Ercel Kozee.
70. Pearl Kozee, b. February 23, 1902; m. William Burns, November 8, 1921.
71. Ray Kozee, b. January 16, 1906; m. Sena Flanagan, December, 1938.
72. Lionel Kozee, b. July 24, 1908, d. July 3, 1912.
73. Beecher Kozee, b. July 12, 1913; m. Ruby Pennington, September, 1938.
74. Hansel Kozee, b. September, 1915; m. Sue Helen McDavid, September, 1940.

69. ERCEL KOZEE, teacher and sometime public official, was b. at Johns Run, near Willard, Carter County, Kentucky, October 18, 1903; educated in the public schools of Carter County; was graduated from the Kentucky Christian College at Grayson; and attended Eastern (Kentucky) State College at Richmond; began teaching in the public schools of Carter County in early manhood and has taught for 19 years in the Carter County School System; is presently a supervisor of the Carter County schools; was State representative from Carter County in the General Assembly, 1948; m. July 2, 1943, Miss Clara Elizabeth Robinson, teacher, daughter of Burrell and Edna (Walker) Robinson. (See Robinson Family.) Mrs. Kozee was b. at Willard, September 18, 1918; was educated in the public schools of Carter County; graduated from the Prichard High School at Grayson, 1936, attended the Kentucky State Teachers' College at Morehead for two years, and was graduated from the University of Kentucky, Lexington, in June, 1940; has taught for 10 years in the Carter County School System.

Children: 75. Lionel Burrell Kozee, b. March 15, 1946. Residence: Willard, Kentucky.

THE KEESEE FAMILY OF WESTERN KENTUCKY, COLORADO AND NEW MEXICO

According to family tradition one John Keesee was the ancestor of a branch of the Keesee family who settled in Western Kentucky. He was b. in Virginia, 1760, and d. in Richmond in 1830. He m. Adeline Brusch, b. April 22, 1760, on her uncle General Francis Marion's farm in South Carolina. Her mother, Martha Caroline Marion, a sister of General Francis Marion, was b. at Georgetown, South Carolina, January 19, 1744, d. at Lovelaceville, Ballard County, Kentucky, in 1848; m. in 1759, John Jacob Brusch, a captain in the Cherokee Indian War, b. at Georgetown, South Carolina, June 27, 1742, and d. there in 1794.'

1. JOHN KEESEE m. Adeline Brusch. Children, among others:
*2. Charles Keesee.
3. Martha Caroline Keesee.
4. Adeline Keesee.
5. Charity Keesee.

2. CHARLES KEESEE; b. in Richmond, Virginia, September 22, 1799, d. at Lovelaceville, Ballard County, Kentucky, May 15, 1892; m., June 18, 1835, in Kentucky, Sallie McGrew, b. May 18, 1822, and d. in 1847.

Children among others:
6. William Mathias Keesee, the oldest of eight children, was b. April 16, 1836, and d. in the Confederate States Home, Pewee Valley, Kentucky, at an advanced age. He is said to have been a captain in General Robert E. Lee's army. He m., in Ballard County, Kentucky, August 22, 1866, Anna Ritta Hall, b. August 14, 1848, d. at Las Cerrillas, New Mexico, August 14, 1892, a daughter of Charles Hall, (b. in Devonshire, England, d. December 2, 1892, at Trinidad, Colorado) and of his wife, Mary Jane Sloan who was a daughter of Dr. Sloan of Kentucky.

Children:
7. Alta M. Keesee.
8. Charles Jackson Keesee.
9. Mary Vietta Keesee.
10. Minnie L. Keesee.
11. Lula Emma Keesee, poet and author of "William Keesee and His Descendants"; m. Mr. Evarts and resided in Oklahoma City, Oklahoma.

George Hugh Keesee, banker, was b. in Richmond, Virginia, December 2, 1878, a son of Dr. George Fish Keesee, who was b. in Richmond, Virginia, September 15, 1842, where he lived all his life and where he d. in October, 1924, at the age of 82 years. Dr. Keesee was graduated from the Baltimore College of Dentistry in 1869 as valedictorian of his class and immediately began the practice of his profession in Richmond. He rapidly became one of the most prominent and best beloved dentists in the Richmond area. He was prominently identified with and instrumental in the organizing of both the Virginia State Dental Association and the Richmond Dental Society; served as president of both organizations and served as secretary of the State Association for more than 50 years. Both associations presented him with large silver loving cups in recognition of his fifty years active leadership in his chosen profession.[5] Throughout his long and useful adult life, he was very active in his profession, the Church (Methodist) and Masonry until within a few months of his death in October, 1924.[6] He was the father of five children—four daughters and a son, George Hugh Keesee, the subject of this sketch.

George Hugh Keese was educated in the public schools of Richmond, graduating at the age of 16 from the Richmond High School (now known as the John Marshall High School). Soon after graduation he became a messenger in one of the smaller banks in Richmond and continued in the banking business in one capacity or another until retirement in 1946.

When a very young bank clerk, Mr. Keesee began studying banking in evening classes and was instrumental in associating several other young bank employees in the study of banking and commercial law, particularly as applied to the business of banking. Since the organization of the American Institute of Banking in 1901, which has long been recognized as the educational branch of the American Bankers Association, he has been active and is a charter member of the local Richmond Chapter formed in 1902. By several years he was the first and only A.I.B. graduate in Virginia, having pursued the course of study by correspondence with New York headquarters. During the period 1915-1921, he taught "Banking" in evening classes in Richmond, the classes varying from 40 to 85 students.

Mr. Keesee was employed in different clerical positions in several Richmond banks prior to 1903 when he was appointed assistant cashier of the Merchants National Bank of Richmond in which capacity he served until he was elected Secretary of Federal Reserve Bank of Richmond upon its organization in November, 1914.

Throughout his long banking career, Mr. Keesee was active in the American Institute of Banking, having served the National organization as a Vice Chairman, a member of its Committee on Arrangements. a member of its Executive Committee. 1907-1908, and a member of its Executive Council, 1913-1916. He is an honorary life member of both the National and local organizations. Becoming interested in Masonry in early manhood, he has long been a 32° Mason: has served as Master of his lodge, High Priest of Royal Arch Chapter, Commander of his Commandry of Knights Templar and Potentate of Acca Temple Shriners. For many years he has been a Trustee of the Grand Lodge of Masons of Virginia, of the Grand Royal Arch Chapter of Virginia and of the Scottish Rite Bodies; and is presently the active Secretary-Treasurer of the Knights Templar Education Foundation which grants loans to needy college students.

For many years Mr. Keesee was one of the youngest to hold membership in the old Westmoreland Club, now consolidated with the Commonwealth Club. He is a member of the Commonwealth Club, Virginia Boat Club, Country Club of Virginia and the Hermatage Golf Club.

Mr. Keesee was married to Miss Virginia Sheppard Taylor, a great-great-granddaughter of Nathaniel Fox, who served on General George Washington's Staff during the Revolutionary War. She d. in 1951. They had no children; and the only member of Mr. Keesee's immediate family bearing his name is a grandnephew, George Keesee Tyler, a great-grandson of President John Tyler.

CURTIS GORDON KEESEE, Federal employee, son of Samuel and Lottie (Love) Keesee and grandson of Isaac A. and Virginia (Motley) Keesee, was b. at Gretna, Pittsylvania County, Virginia, September 28, 1899; educated in the public schools of Pittsylvania County; engaged in farming, was a traveling salesman and an assistant rural mail carrier for a time; entered the U. S. Government service May 6, 1936, as clerk in the National Archives, Washington, D. C.; was promoted and appointed Superintendent of Mails of that department, May 16, 1942, and is presently serving in that capacity; m. at Gretna on Setember 1, 1926, Miss Uva Bennett, b. February 9, 1907, daughter of Charles and Mary (Ramsey) Bennett. Mrs. Keesee was educated in the public schools of Pittsylvania County, graduating from the Gretna High School, 1925. She entered the U. S Government service, February 15, 1943, as clerk in the Internal Revenue Department and was transferred to the Air Force, November 17, 1953, where she is presently employed. She is of an old Colonial family of Bennett of which Captain John Bennett, who had service in the Revolutionary War, was one of the most prominent.

Both Mr. and Mrs. Keesee are active members of the Methodist Church. Mr. Keesee is a Mason, a member of Anderson Lodge No. 258, F. & A.M., at Gretna, Virginia, Chatham Royal Chapter No. 52 at Chatham, Virginia, Brightwood Commandery No. 6 and Almas Temple, Washington, D. C.

Mr. and Mrs. Keesee are the parents of two children (sons): Curtis Gordon Keesee, Jr., and Larry Bennett Keesee, student, b. in Washington, D. C., May 30, 1944. Curtis Gordon Keesee, Jr., was b. at Gretna, Virginia, October 31, 1928; was educated in the public schools of Washington, D. C., graduating from the Eastern High School, 1947; was graduated with distinction from American University, Washington, D. C., with degree of Bachelor of Science in

Social Science, June, 1951; and from Westminster Theological Seminary, Westminster, Maryland, with degree of S. T. B. in May, 1955. Mr. Keesee is a second lieutenant of the 125th AAA Battalion of the National Guard of Virginia.

He was m., at Gaithersburg, Maryland, on June 12, 1954, to Miss Gloria Walker, daughter of Grover K. and Marian (West) Walker. Mrs. Keesee was b. December 6, 1930; was graduated from the Gaithersburg (Maryland) High School, 1948; from Southern Seminary and Junior College, Buena Vista, Virginia, 1950, and attended the University of Maryland where she was a member of Alpha Delta Pi Sorority.

Buell H. Kazee, a minister of the Baptist church and a professor in a Bible college, is a grandson of Rufus Kazee, b. in 1849, and Frances (Sparks) Kazee, a great-grandson of Elias Keezee, a Baptist preacher, and Mary (Curnutte) Keezee and a great-great-grandson of Richard Keesee or Keezee, the Kentucky ancestor of the family in Eastern Kentucky.

In 1930, Rev. Buell H. Kazee was selected as pastor of the Morehead, (Kentucky) Baptist Church in which capacity he served the church for the succeeding twenty-two years or until 1952 when he became a professor in the Lexington Bible College, Lexington, Kentucky. He is presently teaching the Old Testament in that college. Residence, 1625 Danzler Court, Lexington, Kentucky.

EARLIEST MARRIAGES OF KEESEES PITTSYLVANIA COUNTY, VIRGINIA

Keesee, Elizabeth—Clabourn Hicks. November 19, 1787.
Keesee, John—Betsy Parsons, December—, 1787.
Keesee, Jesse—Elizabeth White. November 26, 1794.
Keesee, Amey—Thomas G. Turley, January 5, 1799.
Keesee, Nancy—Charles Bazzell, April —, 1800.
Keesee, Richard—Jean McMurray. August 17, 1803.
Keesee, Patsy—Jacob Croft, December 23, 1801.
Keesee, Jensey—William Taylor ——— — 1804.
Keesee, Anna—Solomon Pickerel, November 13, 1805.
Keesee, Nancy—William Talbot, ——— — 1807.
Keesee, Nancy Parsons—George Dalton, January 10, 1808.
Keesee, James—Sally Parker, June 13, 1810.
Keesee, John—Polly Dupuy, ——— — 1811.
Keesee, Sally—James Arthur, February 10, 1814.
Keesee, George—Lettice Taylor, ——— — 1811.
Keesee, Dorcas—Humphrey Thacker, December 7, 1815.
Keesee, Booker—Jane Dove. March 10, 1814.
Keesee, Milly—Michael Huffman. February 24, 1816.
Keesee, Sarah B.—David H. Grubb, January 23, 1821.
Keesee, William—Anna Pickeral, December 28, 1826.

Keesee, George W.—Judith Coleman, October 11, 1859.
Keesee, Tabitha—Robert Martin, April 25, 1789.
Keesee, Peniah—Kinsley Marlow, January 13, 1791.
Keesee, Mary—Lewis Dalton, November 21, 1797.

ABSTRACT OF EARLY WILLS, CHRONOLOGICALLY ARRANGED

Pittsylvania County, Virginia

Arthur Kezee. Will dated January 15, 1789; proved in court, May 18, 1789; mentions wife, Tabitha; and bequeaths estate, consisting of land and slaves, to her and children: Jesse, Stovall, Jeremiah, Phoebe, Benjamin, George, John and Betty Burton.

Richard Keesee. Will dated March 9, 1789; proved in court, January 20, 1794; mentions wife, Ann, and bequeaths all property to her for life or widowhood and then to children: Mary, George, Charles, John, Jesse, Jeremiah and Ann.

John Keesee. Will dated October 17, 1810; proved in court June 15, 1812; mentions wife, Mary; and bequeaths lands in Pittsylvania and Halifax Counties to her and to sons, John, Charles and Blackwell, and remainder of estate to daughters, Nancy Talbott and Melly Mellert, and to three sons above mentioned.

John Keesee. Will dated October 17, 1810; proved in court October 20, 1823; mentions and bequeaths land and slaves to daughters, Polly Shenault, Sally Woosley, Dorcas Thacker and Nancy Bazzell and to sons, James, Richard and George.

Jeremiah Keesee, Sr. Will executed March 5, 1824; probated in court, January 17, 1825; mentions and bequeaths land and slaves to daughters, Ella Arnold, Jinsey Taylor, Anna Turley and Sally Grubbs, and to sons, Arthur, Benjamin B., and Jeremiah, Jr.

Jesse Keesee. Will executed February 18, 1829; probated in court March 16, 1829; bequeaths to wife land and house and two slaves and balance of estate to nine children: Amy Green, Polly Dalton, Avery M. Richard, Maryann Walden, Anna Pickerel, Sally Pickerel, Booker and Millie Hoffman.

George William Keesee. Will executed April 24, 1861; probated in court October 20, 1862; bequeaths all his property to wife, Judith T. Keesee, after payment of debts.

William Keesee. Will executed December 5, 1892; probated in court, August 19, 1901; mentions and bequeaths property to children: Susan C. Haynes, Martha F. Mayhew, Isaac A. Keesee, Elizabeth Dove, and W. T. Keesee; and to wife, Elizabeth M. Keesee; to children of Sarah J. Dalton and to granddaughter, Carrie Lee Keesee.

Peyton Clay Keesee. Will executed August 24, 1908; probated in court, June 23, 1909; leaves f rm at Peytonsburg to wife, Sally

Green Keesee, and to sons, George Keesee, W. R. Keesee and John C. Keesee. Dr. C. W. Pritchett, executor, Keeling Post Offiec. Isaac C. Keesee. Will executed May 9, 1911; probated in court Octoberr 8, 1921; bequeaths all his property to wife, Virginia G. Keesee, for her life and then to son, Samuel W. Keesee.

Sumner County, Tenn.

George F. Keesee. Will, dated July 5, 1825, probated November, 1825, bequeaths lands and personal property, including 44 negro slaves, to wife and children, Laree (Laura?) Smith, Patience Smith, Rhoda McKnight, Thomas, Agnes Lyons, Nancy Henry, George F., Jane, Champness, and to grandsons Champness Ball and George Saunders.

ABSTRACTS OF CENSUS RECORDS—HEADS OF FAMILIES—KEESEE

Halifax County, Virginia, State enumeration, 1782 and 1785: Kesee, John.

Pittsylvania County, Virginia, State enumeration, 1782 and 1785: Keezee, Charles; Keezee, Jeremiah; Keezee, Jesse; Keezee, Richard.

Greenville County, South Carolina, U. S. Census, 1790: Keesee, George.

Pittsylvania County, U. S. Census, 1820: Keesee, James; Keesee, Jeremiah; Keesee, John; Keesee, Jesse; Keesee, Booker; Keesee, Richard; Keesee, Charles.
    U. S. Census, 1830: Keesee, William; Keesee, Mildred; Keesee, George P.

Henrico County, Virginia, U. S. Census, 1810. Keesee, George.
    U. S. Census, 1820: Keesee, Thomas; Kezee, William; Keesee, George; Keezee, Jacob.
    U. S. Census, 1830: Keesee, Jesse F.; Keesee, Thomas C.; Keesee, George; Keesee, William G.; Keesee, Martha A.; Keesee, Jacob B.

[1] Collections of the Virginia Historical Society, New Series, Vol. 5, page 70, by R. A. Brock, Richmond, Virginia, 1886.

[2] George Keesee, Huguenot, the Immigrant and Some of His Descendants (Manuscript) prepared by Olive (Simmons) Keesee (Mrs. Charles Blackwell Keesee), 193—.

[3] The Keesee Family Chart, prepared by Mrs. Ann R. Cherry, 2 Sunset Circle, Little Rock, Arkansas. The Bullington Family Chart, Public Library, Richmond, Virginia. The Family Chronicle and Kinship Book, by Mrs. Octavia Zollicoffer Bond.

[4] William Keesee and His Descendants, by Lulu Evarts, Oklahoma City, Oklahoma, 1918.

[5] Vital Statistics of Carter County, Kentucky, 1852-1862.

[6] Life and Character of George Fish Keesee, by Harry Bear, Philadelphia, 1925. Reprint from the Dental Cosmos, July, 1925. Read before the Virginia State Dental Association at Staunton, April 28, 1925.

KIBBEY FAMILY OF CARTER AND GREENUP COS.

The Kentucky ancestor of the Kibbe or Kibbey family who lived in Greenup and Carter Counties in pioneer days, was

1. MOSES KIBBE. In his will, probated in the Greenup County Court in March, 1832, he bequeathed a large estate in lands and personal property, including eleven negro slaves.

Children, among others:

Second Generation

*2. Jacob Kibbey.

3. Clarinda Kibbey; m. Thomas T. Hord in Greenup County, March 13, 1823. (See Hord Family.)

4. Jacintha Kibbey; m. William Womack in Greenup County, December 29, 1829. (See Womack Family.)

5. Delila Kibbey; m. George W. Rigg, in Greenup County, July 6, 1832.

2. JACOB KIBBEY, farmer, was b. in Kentucky, 1804; m. in Greenup County, June 9, 1824, Malinda Everman, b. in Kentucky, 1807, a daughter of John Everman and his wife, Sarah (Clark) Everman. (See Everman Family.)

Children living at home and approximate dates of birth as shown by the U. S. Census of Carter County for 1850:

Third Generation

*6. William Kibbey; b. 1831.

7. Harriet Kibbey; b. 1833; m. in Carter County, August 20, 1840, John T. Shepherd, b. 1824, a school teacher, who was living in the household of Jacob Kibbey in 1850.

8. John Kibbey; b. 1835.

9. George Kibbey; b. 1838.

10. Samuel Kibbey; b. 1840.

11. Francis Kibbey; b. 1842.

12. James Kibbey; b. 1844.

13. Mildred Kibbey; b. 1847.

6. WILLIAM E. KIBBEY; b. in Greenup County, Kentucky, in 1830 or 1831, and d. May 15, 1883; m. at Estill Flats. Kentucky, October 30, 1860, Edy McGlone, b. in Greenup County, October 5, 1835, and d. July 27, 1908.

Children living in the household and approximate dates of birth as shown by the U. S. Census of Carter County for 1870:

Fourth Generation

14. Eli Kibbey; b. 1855.

15. George Kibbey; b. 1857.

*16. Samuel Kibbey; b. 1864.

17. Harriet Kibbey; b. 1870.
It is believed there were other children.

16. SAMEL E. KIBBEY, farmer and for many years a justice of the
peace of Carter County, was b. at Iron Hill, Carter County, October
23, 1864, and d. at Rooney, Carter County, August 5, 1951, at the age
of 86 years. Interment in the Kibbey Cemetery; m. at Cox, Kentucky, February 23, 1893, Sarah Clemmer Ames Crawford, b. December 12, 1876, and d. June 15, 1946, a daughter of L. H. and Mary
S. (Hargett) Crawford.

Children:
Fifth Generation
*18. Delbert V. Kibbey.
19. Alma E. Kibbey, deceased; m. Charles Stallard; no children.
20. Faye Kibbey, teacher; m. Robert Cargo; no children.
21. William O. Kibbey; m. Blanche Underwood. Children (Sixth
Generation): Helen Perry and Alma Grace Moore.

18. DELBERT V. KIBBEY, lawyer, one time teacher and public official, was b. at Rooney, Carter County, Kentucky, December 1, 1893;
educated in the public schools of Carter County and at the Grayson
(Kentucky) Normal School where he received training for teaching;
attended College of Law, University of Kentucky, 1916-17; began
teaching in the public schools of Carter County in 1912 and continued teaching for five years; served in World War I; was commissioned a second lieutenant, Infantry, U. S. Army, August 26,
1918, and served in France from August, 1918, to April 1919, when
honorably discharged. Returning to his home in Carter County, he
established his home at Grayson and began the practice of law there,
he having been admitted to the bar in 1917.

A staunch Republican in politics, Mr. Kibbey has been an active
party worker since his youth and is a leader and wise counselor in
local party affairs. Always deeply interested in pubic affairs, he has
held many offices of honor and trust and has filled all of them with
credit to himself and to the satisfaction of the public. He served as
Commissioner of Revenue of Carter County, 1920-1922; Superintendent of Public Schools of Carter County, 1922-1926; was elected
County Attorney of Carter County, 1949; reelected, 1953; and is
presently serving in that capacity.

At Catlettsburg, Kentucky, on March 20, 1918, Mr. Kibbey was
married to Miss Susie H. Robinson. Mrs. Kibbey is a daughter of
William E. and Lucy (Morris) Robinson. (See Robinson and Morris
families.) She was b. near Willard, Kentucky, June 21, 1896; educated in the public schools of Carter County, and at the Grayson
(Kentucky) Normal School; began teaching in the public schools of
Carter County, 1917, and has been so employed for 19 years. She is

a Republican in politics and an active party worker; and is a consistent member of the Baptist Church at Grayson.

Children:

Sixth Generation

22. Jack Robinson Kibbey, lawyer; b. at Grayson, Kentucky, December 29, 1918; educated in the public schools of Grayson, graduating from Prichard High School, 1937; was graduated from University of Louisville, Law School, 1949; admitted to the bar, 1949, and is presently residing and practicing law at Vanceburg, Lewis County, Kentucky; m., December 29, 1939, Miss Ruby Perry, daughter of William Perry. Children (Seventh Generation): Mary Sue, b. June 5, 1942, and Linda Faye, b. December 29, 1953.

23. William C. Kibbey, lawyer; b. at Grayson, September 6, 1922; educated in the public schools of Grayson, graduating from Prichard High School; was graduated from University of Louisville Law-School, 1949; admitted to the bar, 1949; and is presenlty practicing law at Grayson; m. Marie Fosson. No children.

24. Samuel Frederick Kibbey, lawyer; b. at Grayson, September 5, 1925, educated in the public schools of Grayson, graduating from Prichard High School; was graduated from the University of Louisville Law School, 1949; admitted to the bar, 1949, and is presently residing and practicing law at Grayson; m. Edith Thomas. Children (Seventh Generation): Carol Ann, b. October 22, 1954.

25. Marcella Kibbey (Seventh Generation) (granddaughter of and being reared by Mr. and Mrs. D. V. Kibbey, a daughter of Jack), student, was b. at Grayson, December 5, 1935; educated in the public schools of Grayson, graduating from Prichard High School, 1953; entered Georgetown College, Georgetown, Kentucky, 1953, and is presently a sophomore in that institution.

Other Kibbe families lived in Greenup County in pioneer days who may or may not have been of the same family of the pioneer, Moses Kibbe.

1. Amos Kibbe was listed in the U. S. Census of Greenup County for 1810 as being the owner of twelve negro slaves.

KIRK FAMILY OF JOHNSON AND MARTIN COS.

It would seem that this family is of Scottish extraction. The surname Kirk was commonly characteristic of the Lowland Scottish border counties, particularly Berwickshire, Roxburgshire and Dumfriesshire. The name was originally used to designate a resident by a Kirk (a church).

The word Kirk is derived from the Gaelic "cearcall" meaning a circle. The primitive places of worship among the Celts were round, a symbol of eternity and the existence of the Supreme Being, without beginning or end.

The ancient seat of the Kirks in Scotland was at Whitehough Hill, in Derbyshire. There were many distinguished men of the name who added luster to the already shining pages of English and Scottish history. Sir David Kirke (the English spelling usually retained the e) was Governor of Newfoundland; Lewis Kirke was Governor of Canada; Captain Thomas Kirk was vice admiral of the English fleet and was in the engagements which resulted in victory over the French and the capture of Canada.

The first appearance of the name in America was in 1665 with Henry Kirk, a resident of Dover, New Hampshire. Zacheriah Kirk is recorded as an inhabitant of Boston, Massachusetts, in 1686.

William Burns Kirk, son of Jesse Kirk, was b. in Scotland in 1799. He came to America with two brothers and located at Fishkill, New York, where he became a wheelright. He was a thrifty man and prospered in his trade, accumulating a large amount of property. In 1826 he bought the John Garrison Tavern, on the site of a popular present-day city block in Syracuse, N. Y. He became a very influential man in Syracuse and was active in securing a charter for the city.

The records indicate that the Kirks had settled in all the American colonies at the time of the Revolutionary War. They were numerous in New York, Pennsylvania, Maryland, Virginia and the Carolinas.

The Kirk family intermarried with some of the most distinguished families and there is a long line of descendants who have contributed much to the communities and to the Nation.

Three brothers Kirk lived in Mason County, Kentucky, in pioneer days—Thomas, Benjamin and William.

Thomas Kirk had service in the Revolutionary War. He appeared in the Mason County Court on October 8, 1832, and made declaration in connection with claim for a pension on account of his services wherein he stated, among other things, that he served in the Maryland militia under the command of Philip Marooney, Lieutenant Elisha Bell, Ensign William Beatty in the regiment of Colonel Charles Griffith and Lieutenant-Colonel Scioc (?); that he volunteered in Frederick County, Maryland, in June 1776; that he was in the battle at York Island and at White Plains and was honorably discharged at Philadelphia by Captain Elisha Bell by reason of expiration of six months tour of duty.

One Nathaniel Kirk m. Dorcas Madden in Mason County, February 6, 1800. The records would seem to indicate that the first of the family to settle in the Big Sandy Valley were John Kirk and Thomas Kirk, brothers. * John Kirk settled on a farm near the site of present-day Warfield, Martin County, then Floyd County.

1. JOHN KIRK m., in Floyd county, September 26, 1821, Clara Marcum. He and his brother Thomas were ministers of the Primitive Baptist Church and were prominent in the organization of several churches of that denomination in Eastern Kentucky.

Children of John Kirk and Clara (Marcum) Kirk:

*2. Joseph M. Kirk.
*3. James T. Kirk.
*4. Thomas Kirk.
*5. Elsie Kirk.
*6. Cynthia Kirk.
*7. Vasti Kirk.
*8. Pricie Kirk.
*9. ———— ————?

2. JOSEPH M. KIRK was a man of importance in Martin County. He served in the Union Army during the Civil War as captain, Company I, 39th Kentucky Infantry. He m. in Lawrence county, October 26, 1843, Nancy Dingus.

Children:

*10. J. D. Kirk.
*11. John L. Kirk.
*12. William R. Kirk.
*13. Joseph M. Kirk, Jr.
*14. Thomas S. Kirk.
*15. Andrew J. Kirk.
16. Wilda Kirk; m. Andy Spradlin.
*17. Mary (Polly) Kirk.

3. JAMES T. KIRK; b. in 1826; d. in 1883; coal operator at Warfield, Martin county and also manager of the Salt Works at that place; jailer of Martin county for one term; active in politics and the Church; m., first ——— Maynard, and secondly, Sarah C. Mash, who was b. in North Carolina; emigrated to Kentucky in 1867, and d. in Martin county at the advanced age of eighty-two years.

Children of James T. Kirk and ——— (Maynard) Kirk:

18. Amy Kirk.
19. Martha Kirk.
20. Ella Kirk.
21. John F. Kirk.
22. Pricie Kirk.
23. George W. Kirk.

Children of James T. Kirk and Sarah C. (Mash) Kirk:

*24. McClellan C. Kirk.

25. Nora Kirk; m. Peter C. Ward.

26. Lee Kirk; m. Argie Copley.

27. Effie Myrtle Kirk; m. W. H. Barchus.

4. THOMAS KIRK; m. Sibyl Workman.
Children:

28. Samuel Kirk.

29. W. Sherman Kirk.

5. ELSIE KIRK; m. James Smith. They resided in West Virginia.
Children:

30. Masion Smith.

31. Ira Smith; m. ——— Vinson.

32. Lindsey Smith.

33. Albert Smith.

34. Wayne Smith.

35. Thomas Smith.

36. Jeanette Smith; m. Gideon Damron.

37. Laura Smith; m. ——— ———.

6. CYNTHIA KIRK; m. Martin Weddington.
Children:

38. John Weddington.

39. William Weddington.

40. Frank Weddington.

41. Augustus Weddington.

42. Josie Weddington.

43. John Weddington.

44. Laura Weddington; m. Dr. ——— Daniel.

45. ——— Wedington; m. Thomas Marcum.

7. VASTI KIRK; m. J. Augustus Payne.
Children:

46. Lucian B. Payne; m. Niza Vinson.

47. Laura B. Payne.

8. PRICIE KIRK; m., first, William Davis, and, secondly, Rush Floyd.
Children of Pricie Kirk and William Davis:

48. Emma Davis.
Children of Pricie Kirk and Rush Floyd:

49. Lucian Floyd.

9. ——— KIRK; m. ——— Spalding.
Children:

50. John Spalding; m. Mary Vermillion.

51. William Spalding; m. ———.

52. Jackson Spalding; m. Alice Estice.

53. Marion Spalding; m. ——— ———.

54. ——— Spalding; m. ——— Romans.

10. J. D. KIRK served in the Union Army in the Civil War and was wounded in action. He was thrice married—first, to Holly Scoffield, secondly, to Elizabeth Preston and thirdly, to Mahala Ward.
   Children of J. D. Kirk and Holly Scoffield:
   55. Millard Kirk; m. ——— Cassady.
   56. Jennie Kirk; m. ——— Algo.
   57. Alwilda Kirk; m. ——— Payne.
   Children of J. D. Kirk and Elizabeth Preston:
   58. Mary Kirk; m. ——— Ratliff.
   11. JOHN L. KIRK; m. Alice Cain.
   Children:
   59. Edgar Kirk; m. ———Cassady.
   60. Lucian Kirk; m. ——— Hopson.
   61. Walter Kirk; m. Nora Copley.
   62. Evert Kirk; m. ——— ———.
   63. Carl Kirk; m. ——— Cassady.
   64. Frank Kirk.
   65. Norma Kirk; m. George Hale.
   66. Elmer Kirk.
   12. WILLIAM R. KIRK resided in Martin county; m., first, Florence King, and, secondly, Cordelia Borders.
   Children of William R. Kirk and Florence King:
   67. Albert Kirk; m. Alice Weddington.
   68. Mathew Kirk; m. Jennie Starr.
   69. Charles A. Kirk; m. Mabel Preston (See Preston Family).
   70. James Kirk; m. ——— Mason.
   71. Hessie Kirk; m. Wade Hampton.
   Children of William R. Kirk and Cordelia Borders:
   72. McKinley Kirk.
   73. Fannie Kirk.
   74. Mark Kirk.
   13. JOSEPH M. KIRK, JR.,; m. Talitha Lawson.
   Children:
   75. Thomas Kirk.
   14. THOMAS S. KIRK; prominent Republican politician; state senator and leader of his party in the Senate during the Goebel-Taylor contest for the governorship; lived in Paintsville; m. Edna J. Harris.
   Children:
   *76. Rushie Kirk.
   77. James Darwin Kirk.
   78. Thomas Lawton Kirk.
   15. ANDREW J. KIRK, lawyer, judge, public official, b. in Martin county, March 19, 1866; d. in Paintsville, Johnson county, ——— ———; educated in the public schools of Martin county and was graduated from the law school of Valparaiso (Indiana) University in 1890 and began the practice of his profession in Martin county

but soon entered the political field and was elected as a Republican, successively, to the office of county attorney of Martin county; commonwealth's attorney of the 24th Judicial District; Circuit judge of the 24th Judicial District; Representative in Congress from the 10th Kentucky District.

Judge Kirk removed with his family to Paintsville; and in addition to his public services he engaged in the practice of law there and was chief counsel for the Consolidation Coal Company, at Jenkins, Kentucky, just prior to his death.

In December, 1888, in Martin county, Judge Kirk m. Elizabeth Goble, daughter of Drury Goble.

Children:
*79. Conrad Kirk.
 80. Garnet Kirk; m. Tobe Rule.
 81. Laban T. Kirk; m. Mollie McWhorter.
 82. Ethel Kirk; m. Charles York.
*83. Andrew J. Kirk, Jr.
 84. Chester Kirk.
 85. Louis Kirk.
 86. Alice Kirk.

 17. MARY (POLLY) KIRK; m. Washington Findley.

Children:
 87. Minnie Findley.
 88. Ida Findley.
 89. Millard Findley.

24. McCLELLAN CALVIN KIRK, lawyer, public official, civic leader was b. on a farm near Warfield, Martin county, on which farm also were born his father, James T. Kirk (No. 3) and his grandfather, John Kirk (No. 1). Left as the chief support of his mother and younger brothers and sisters by the death of his father when he was but a youth, he was employed by the Peach Orchard Mining Company and at the end of two years was manager of its mines. Consequently his early educational advantages were very limited. Subsequently he was graduated from the law schools of Valparaiso (Indiana) University in 1894 and entered upon the practice of law at Inez, Martin county, where he was associated in practice with his cousin, Judge Andrew J. Kirk (No. 15) for six years.

A Republican in politics, Mr. Kirk was elected and served as police judge of Inez for four years (1895-1899); postmaster of that city for twelve years; and state representative in the General Assembly of Kentucky.

Mr. Kirk was a man of domestic tastes and devoted to his family. However, he enjoyed the companionship of his fellows and was a member of the Independent Order of Odd Fellows; the Knights of Pythias; the Benevolent and Protective Order of Elks; Inez Lodge No. — F. & A.M. of which he was Master for five years—having been a mason at the age of twenty-one years; Louisa Chapter, R.A.M.; Ashland Commandery, K. T.; and Covington Consistory R. and S.M. He belonged to the Shrine at Ashland.

Removing from Martin county to Paintsville, Mr. Kirk acquired much real estate in that city; and with his sons he operated three large fruit farms in Florida and shipped to New York City more fruit than any single fruit grower in that state.

In addition to a large clientele which covered the entire Big Sandy Valley, he was counsel for the Chesapeake & Ohio Railway Company in Johnson, Floyd, Pike and Lawrence counties, and counsel for the Mrs. John C. C. Mayo Company, the Consolidation Coal Company, the North-East Coal Company and many other important business enterprises.

In Martin county, ———— ————, McClellan C. Kirk m. Bessie Cassady, daughter of Benjamin Cassady.

Children:
*90. K. Russell Kirk.
*91. W. H. Kirk.

76. RUSHIE KIRK; active in womens organizations in Paintsville; m. Arthur Phillis, mechanic, who has held responsible positions with the Consolidation Coal Company, and the Chesapeake & Ohio Railway Company.

Children:
92. Patsy Phillis.
93. Philip Phillis.

79. CONRAD KIRK; attorney-at-law, Paintsville; m. Mildred Powell.

Children:
94. Tommy Jean Kirk.
95. Betty Kirk.

88. ANDREW J. KIRK, JR.; electrician and in business in Paintsville; m. Peggie Williams, a former school teacher in the Johnson county schools.

Children:
96. Garnet Louise Kirk.

90. K. RUSSELL KIRK; operates an orange farm in Florida where he spends the winters. He returns to and spends the summers in Paintsville; m. Mary Langley.

Children:
97. Russell Langley Kirk.

91. W. HOLMES KIRK; resides in Paintsville during summer season where he is engaged in real estate; operates orange farm in Florida during winter; m., first, Cathleen Preston, who d. in 1924, secondly Josephine Bowles, daughter of C. C. Bowles, Pikeville, (See Bowles Family).

Chidren of W. Holmes Kirk and Cathleen (Preston) Kirk:
98. Mary Cathleen Kirk.

KOUNS FAMILY OF GREENUP COUNTY

1. JACOB KOUNS was the first of the name to settle in what is now Greenup County, Kentucky. He mgirated from Pennsylvania in 1792. He was a farmer and slaveholder and a man of importance in the early affairs of Greenup County. He was a member of the commission appointed by the court, July 7, 1806, to let contract for and to superintend construction of a temporary court house on the public square in Greenupsburg. He served as deputy sheriff of Greenup County, 1812-13, and was sheriff of the county, 1814-15.

It has not been learned whom, when or where he married.

Children, probably among others of Jacob Kouns:

2. Sallie Kouns; m. Jacob Neal in Greenup County, September 6, 1804.

3. Major John C. Kouns, inn-keeper and public official, was b. in Pennsylvania, circa 1787; m. in Greenup County, November 21, 1818, Elizabeth Smith. In 1827 he built and began conducting in Greenupsburg the Kouns House which for many years was the chief hotel in the town. He had service in the War of 1812 as major, First Kentucky Regiment, and served on the staff of General Jackson at the Battle of New Orleans (January 8, 1815). He was a justice of the peace of Greenup County in the early days; a State representative from Greenup County, 1828-31; sheriff of the county, 1836-37; and was State senator from Greenup and Lewis Counties, 1850.

Children:

*4. Dr. William Smith Kouns.

*5. Elizabeth Kouns.

*6. Sarah A. Kouns.

7. Nancy Kouns; m. John Winn.

8. Maria Kouns; m. Andrew Biggs. (See Biggs Family.)

4. WILLIAM SMITH KOUNS, physician and druggist; resided in Greenup where he was a druggist for many years; m. in Greenup County, October 21, 1841, Caroline Van Bibber, b. about 1822.

Children:

9. Minnie Kouns; m. George Hockaday. (See Hockaday Family.)

10. Maria Kouns; m. John P. Sidenstricker; migrated to Tennessee.

11. Elizabeth Kouns; m. John Ball; migrated to Georgia.

12. William Kouns, druggist; proprietor of Kouns Drug Store in Greenup; m. Fannie Roberts.

13. Anna Kouns.

5. ELIZABETH KOUNS; m. John Hollingsworth in Greenup County, December 1, 1845. He was a justice of the peace of Greenup County in the late 1820's and again in the late 1830's; and was State rep-

resentative, 1834-35. They lived in the old Kouns homestead in Greenup.

Children:

14. John Hollingsworth; m. Julia Hager, daughter of George and Miranda Hinton Hager.

15. Mary Hollingsworth; m. William Sands, lawyer.

6. SARAH ANN KOUNS; m. in Greenup County, October 20, 1850, Joseph Pollock, b. in Washington County, Pennsylvania, in 1812, son of John and Ann (Donohoe) Pollock of Scotch-Irish ancestry. He migrated to Greenup County in 1843. He became a merchant and after the Civil War disposed of his mercantile business and engaged in the banking business in which he continued until 1885.

Children:

*16. John Edward Pollock.
*17. Joseph Pollock, Jr.
*18. Elizabeth Pollock.

16. JOHN EDWARD POLLOCK; educated in the schools of Greenup County; Clerk in the office of the Eastern Kentucky Railway Company at Riverton for seven years; partner of Milton Stevens in the hardware business in Greenup, 1877-93; and one of the organizers of the Farmers and Merchants Bank in Greenup, which in 1904 was merged and/or organized as the First National Bank with which he was connected until his death. He m. Laura Williams Van Dyke in 1883.

Children:

19. Louise Van Dyke Pollock.

20. Augustus Van Dyke Pollock; connected with the First National Bank; m., first, Clotine McClure, and they had a son:

21. Joseph Pollock.

Augustus Van Dyke Pollock m., secondly, Winifred Paynter Lawson.

17. JOSEPH POLLOCK, JR., was employed in the office of the Eastern Kentucky Railway, at Riverton, for some years; m. Alice Bates; and subsequently removed to Cincinnati, Ohio.

18. ELIZABETH POLLOCK m. Thomas H. Paynter.

Honorable Thomas Hanson Paynter, lawyer, judge, legislator, was b. on a farm near Vanceburg, Lewis County, Kentucky, December 9, 1851; was educated in the public schools of Lewis County; at Rand's Academy, that county; and at Centre College, Danville, Kentucky; studied law, admitted to the bar in 1872 and commenced practice at Greenup, Kentucky; was county attorney for Greenup County by appointment, 1876-78, and by election, 1878-82, after which he resumed practice of the law at Greenup; elected as a Democrat to the Fifty-first, Fifty-second and Fifty-third Congresses and served from March 4, 1889, until resignation effective January 5, 1895; elected and served as judge of the Court of Appeals of Kentucky from January 1895, to August, 1906, when he resigned because of election to the U. S. Senate; elected as a Democrat and served as Senator from March 4, 1907, to March 3, 1913, expiration of term.

Judge Paynter was not a candidate for reelection to the Senate in 1912. In 1913 he removed to Frankfort and continued the practice of law there; also he became interested in agricultural pursuits. He d. in Frankfort March 8, 1921. Interment in State Cemetery there.

Children:

22. Winifred Paynter; m. Morton Yonts; resided in Louisville.

23. Pollock Paynter; resided in Frankfort. (Biographical Directory of the American Congress, 1774-1947).

Other Kouns families lived in Greenup County in pioneer days. The U. S. Census of the county for 1810 shows two John Kouns, one of whom owned ten slaves.

LACKEY, DAVIDSON AND HOPKINS FAMILIES OF FLOYD COUNTY

GENERAL ALEXANDER LACKEY was the founder of the family Lackey of Eastern Kentucky. He was b. in Virginia, 1772, and migrated from Pittsylvania County, that state, in 1804 and settled at the forks of Beaver Creek in Floyd County, Kentucky. Bringing with him from his home in Virginia his slaves and considerable property and selecting one of the richest tracts of land for his plantation, he began life in the new country under very favorable auspices; and being of clear judgment and iron will, he soon rose to distinction both as a successful businessman and as a public official.[1] He held many offices of trust and honor both county and State. He was an assistant judge of the Floyd County Circuit Court; State representative in the Kentucky Legislature from Floyd County, 1816, 1817, 1818, 1825, 1826, 1830, 1831, 1840; State senator, 1819-23; sheriff of Floyd County, 1827-29; school commissioner (Superintendent of Schools), 1838; tax commissioner (assessor), 1827, 1840; and a brigadier-general of the State Militia.

General Lackey m., in Virginia, Mary Morgan, b. in Virginia, 1781, daughter of David Morgan, a relative of General Daniel Morgan, who distinguished himself in the Revolutionary War, particularly at the battle of the Cowpens (January 17, 1781). He reared and educated in the best schools available, a family of sons and daughters who added luster to the name they bore.[2]

Children:

2. Morgan Lackey, merchant at Prestonsburg, was a member from the Pike-Floyd-Johnson district which formed the third constitution of Kentucky, 1849, and filled many local offices, civil and military, with honesty and fidelity. He led the fight which resulted in making illegal the sale of intoxicating liquors in Floyd County. Mr. Lackey never married.

*3. Greenville M. Lackey.

4. Elizabeth Lackey, m. Hon. John P. Martin. (See Martin Family.)

*5. Judith Lackey; m. Samuel Davidson.

6. Polly Lackey m. Thomas Witten. (See Witten Family.)

7. James M. Lackey, merchant; b. in Kentucky, 1802.

3. GREENVILLE M. LACKEY, merchant at Louisa, Kentucky, was b. in Kentucky, 1807; m. Rebecca W. ———, b. in Kentucky, 1819. Children living in the household and approximate dates of birth as shown by the U. S. Census of Lawrence County for 1860 and 1870:

8. James Q. Lackey; b. 1851.

9. Alexander Lackey; b. 1853.

10. Sarah A. Lackey; b. 1855.

11. Mary Lackey; b. 1858.

5. JUDITH LACKEY; b. in Kentucky, 1810; m. in Floyd County, about 1828, Samuel P. Davidson, farmer; b. in Virginia, 1800. Children living in the household and approximate dates of birth as shown by the U. S. Census of Floyd County for 1850 and 1860:

12. Alexander A. Davidson; b. 1829.
13. Mary M. Davidson; b. 1832.
14. Elizabeth J. Davidson; b. 1834.
*15. Joseph M. Davidson; b. 1837.
16. Martha Davidson, b. 1839.
17. Greenville Davidson; b. 1842.
18. Andrew J. Davidson; b. 1845.
18. Andrew J. Davidson; b. 1845.
19. Victoria Davidson; b. 1848.
20. John Davidson; b. 1850.
21. Samuel Davidson; b. 1852.

Samuel P. Davidson d. prior to 1860 as his widow, Judith, was head of the household in that year. Her father, Alexander Lackey, aged 88, was living in her home. She listed as personalty 16 slaves for taxation purposes.

15. JOSEPH MORGAN DAVIDSON, sometime public official and businessman of many activities was b. in Floyd County, Kentucky, June 25, 1837, and was of Scotch lineage. Handicapped in youth by lack of advantages, he managed to secure a good education and the exercise of effort developed his latent powers, enabling him to achieve prominence both in business and public affairs. He was a merchant and trader of great prominence and for a time a banker in connection with his cousin, Green M. Witten at Catlettsburg. He was a large land-owner in his county and took a deep interest in the county's welfare. Soon after the close of the Civil War he was elected sheriff of Floyd County and afterwards served two terms in the State Legislature, being Speaker of the House for one term; and at the time of his death on September 9, 1882, he was a candidate for Congress. He was a staunch Democrat and a leader in state politics. A man of strong physique, he was six feet, four inches in height, large in mind as well as in stature; and his integrity was never questioned.

Mr. Davidson m. in Floyd County, Mary Amanda Hatcher.

Children:

22. Mary Sally Davidson m. H. H. Fitzpatrick. (See Fitzpatrick Family.)
*23. Josephine Davidson; m. Walter Scott Harkins. (See Harkins Family.)
*24. Alice Gray Davidson; m. Hon. F. A. Hopkins.
25. ——— Davidson, a daughter; m. Mr. Schmacker.

24. ALICE GRAY DAVIDSON was b. at Prestonsburg, November 23, 1857. She acquired, partly through her own efforts, a liberal edu-

cation. She was educated in the public schools of Floyd County; at a female seminary at Stubenville, Ohio; at a school at College Hill near Cincinnati; and at Glendale Seminary. She was an active member of the Methodist Church.

Miss Davidson m. at Prestonsburg, in November, 1876, F. A. Hopkins.

HON. FRANCIS (FRANK) A. HOPKINS, lawyer and public official, was a native of Virginia of Colonial ancestry. He was b. at Jeffersonville, now known as Tazewell, in Tazewell County, Virginia, May 27, 1853. His grandfather, John Hopkins, m. Mary Turner, a daughter of Rev. James Turner, a noted Presbyterian minister of Bedford County, Virginia. Mary Turner's mother was Sallie Leftwich, a daughter of William Leftwich who was a lieutenant colonel in the American forces during the Revolutionary War and also a captain of militia during the Colonial wars. His father was John Calvin Hopkins.

F. A. Hopkins was educated in the Tazewell (Virginia) High School. In January, 1874, he moved from Tazewell to Prestonsburg, Kentucky, where he was soon admitted to the bar and subsequently became one of the leading attorneys of Eastern Kentucky.

From the beginning of his career in Kentucky, he was before the public in one or another capacity and filled all positions of trust creditably and well. He was Superintendent of Schools of Floyd County, 1882-6; a member of the Constitutional Convention of Kentucky from Floyd, Knott and Letcher Counties, 1894, in which body he was the moving spirit in having incorporated into the constitution a section forfeiting all claims under the Old Virginia Land Grants for failure to list for taxation, thereby removing the clouds upon the titles of the land owners of Eastern Kentucky. He was a member of the Board of Trustees of the University of Kentucky for a number of years; and in 1902 was elected as a Democrat to the Fifty-eighth Congress, and in 1904 was reelected to the Fifty-ninth Congress, but failed of reelection in 1906 to the Sixtieth Congress.

Mr. Hopkins was a Mason of high standing. He d. at Prestonsburg June 5, 1918, and was buried there.

Children:

26. Joseph Davidson Hopkins; b. October 13, 1877; d. June 30, 1879.

27. Elizabeth Ann Hopkins; b. May 17, 1879; educated in the public schools of Prestonsburg and at Glendale Female College, Gendale, Ohio; m. December 29, 1898, William Henry Layne of Prestonsburg. (See Layne Family.)

28. Mary Martha Hopkins; b. March 30, 1882; d. June 5, 1882.

*29. John Calvin Hopkins.

30. Josephine Davidson Hopkins; b. at Prestonsburg, September

8, 1885; educated in the Prestonsburg public schools; and at Hamilton and Campbell-Hagerman Colleges, Lexington, Kentucky; m., September 7, 1904, Thomas Edward Dimick of Prestonsburg, son of G. H. Dimick, a pioneer oil and gas man of Pennsylvania, who came to Kentucky in 1889.

29. COL. JOHN CALVIN HOPKINS, lawyer; b. in Prestonsburg, June 25, 1883; educated in the public schools of Prestonsburg; attended Hogsett Military Academy, Danville, Kentucky; the Randolph-Macon Academy, Bedford, Virginia, and finished literary training in Centre College, Danville, Kentucky, receiving the degree of A. B. in 1904; studied law at Washington and Lee University at Lexington, Virginia, with class of 1906; admitted to the bar that year and at once began practice at Prestonsburg where he rose to a high place in his profession but was forced to discontinue his professional career owing to ill health and subsequently devoted himself to managing his personal and his mother's extensive interests. On December 28, 1915, he was appointed as aide-de-camp on the governor's staff, with rank of colonel by Gov. A. O. Stanley; was appointed Government Appeal Agent for the local board of Floyd County and served until March 31, 1919; was appointed and served as a member of the Legal Advisory Board of Floyd County and was relieved, March 31, 1919.

He was associated with many companies engaged in the development of the mining industry in Floyd County and Eastern Kentucky.

Becoming a Mason just after reaching his majority, he rapidly rose through the York Rite, the Commandery and through the Scottish Rite to the thirty-second degree. He was a member of the Mystic Shrine.

Col. Hopkins m., December 15, 1909, Miss Valentine Pieratt of Mt. Sterling, Kentucky, granddaughter of Hon. John Wickliffe Kendall, M. C., of West Liberty. (See John Wickliffe Kendall in List of Members of Congress.)

Children:

31. John Calvin Hopkins, Jr., b. July 22, 1918.

---

[1] "The Big Sandy Valley", by William Ely, Central Methodist, Catlettsburg, Kentucky. 1887, pages 124-5-6.

[2] Ibid.

LANE FAMILY

Lane is an ancient English name that originally indicated one who lived in a lane, a narrow way between hedges, afterwards an alley, a narrow street. Early English records include such forms as "John in ye Lane". After the tenth century, Norman influence led to the use of the French "de" before the surname, a custom that may account, in some instances, for the name "Delaney", although that name may have other sources. Lane may sometimes be Gaelic from "Llane" ("a plain, narrow lands"), or French from "le aine" ("the old one").

1. WILLIAM S. LAYNE, of Amherst County Virginia, was the progenitor of the Layne family of the Big Sandy Valley region in Eastern Kentucky. Some of his children settled in present Floyd County, then Mason County, Kentucky, in the late 1790s:'

*2. James Shannon Layne.

3. Mildred Layne; m. Tandy Stratton (See Stratton Family).

*4. Nancy Layne; m. Thomas Johns (See Johns Family).

Early marriages of members of the Layne Family:

Floyd County

James Layne and Nancy Solomons, October 22, 1809.
James Layne and Polly Walker, February 20, 1817.
Sally Lane and George Pack, September 27, 1819.
Jenny Lane and Solomon Stratton. November 20, 1820.
Samuel Layne and Judith Elkins, February 28, 1825.
John L. Layne and Elizabeth Priest, May 12, 1829.
Tandy M. Layne and Elizabeth Johns, April 21, 1831.
William Layne and Sophia Graham, December 28, 1832.
James H. Lane and Sarah M. May, April 29, 1836.
John N. Layne and Polly M. Stratton, October 22, 1836.
Lindsey Layne and Edy Meade, August 5, 1834.
Jane Layne and William G. Porter, November 26, 1840.
Mary Layne and Cyrus Boyd, January 14, 1843.
Nancy Layne and Thomas D. Honaker, February 15, 1843.
Lucy Layne and William Collier, March 19.

Pike County

William Layne and Piety Hackworth, April 24, 1823.
Austin Layne and Catherine Ratliff, January 20, 1839.
Merida Layne and Margaret Phillips, November 13, 1839.
Nancy Layne and Joel Church, Jr., February 10, 1837.
William Layne and Sarah Ratliff, January 6, 1843.
John N. Layne and Mary Honaker, October 10, 1842.
Malinda Layne and John Lee, October 16, 1843.
Nancy Jane Layne and Martin Smith, June 15, 1845.
John L. Layne and Sarah Walters, June 16, 1855.
Daniel Layne and Polly Robinette, June 12, 1851.
Meredith Layne and Daisy Blankenship, September 17, 1854.

John Layne and Elizabeth McCoy, June 29, 1848.

Thomas Layne and Angeline Weddington, July 30, 1860.

*2. JAMES SHANNON LAYNE migrated from Amherst County, Virginia and settled near the present Betsy Layne, present Floyd County, about 1796. He had m. in Amherst County, Virginia, "Caty" (Katy) Hager, daughter of John Hager, who migrated to Floyd County a few years later. (See Hager Family.)

Children, among others:

5. W. H. Layne, who was probably only a child when brought to Kentucky. His children, among others, were:

6. Dr. John Witten Layne; b. on the Big Sandy River near mouth of Beaver Creek in 1837 and resided at Prestonsburg. He engaged in many undertakings. He recruited a company of soldiers that had service in the Union Army during the Civil War; conducted the Bonanza Hotel at Prestonsburg for years; was postmaster at Prestonsburg for twelve years; studied dentistry under Dr. Work and practiced for many years; and was a merchant.

Dr. Layne m. Angeline Auxier, b. 1852 and d. 1915, daughter of Nathaniel and Hester (Mayo) Auxier. (See Auxier Family.)

*7. Will H. Layne.

8. Anna Layne; m. Joseph M. Davidson who was connected with the Bank of Josephine at Prestonsburg.

9. John Layne, Secretary and General Manager of Kentucky Solvay Co. at Ashland.

10. Grace Layne; d. in childhood.

11. James Trimble Layne; d. at age of thirty-two years.

7. WILL H. LAYNE, lawyer and coal operator, was b. at Prestonsburg, March 10, 1874; educated in Prestonsburg schools: taught one term following which he commenced studying law in the office of Judge Goble at Prestonsburg: was admitted to the bar, 1896, and was associated with Senator Dingus for a time and for many years was engaged in civil practice alone or until 1920 when his office and library were destroyed by fire. Subsequently he was interested in coal mining and was Secretary-Treasurer and General Superintendent of the Anchor Coal Company.

Mr. Layne was Master Commissioner of the Floyd Circuit Court for six years; also was Special Master Commissioner for several years; member of the City Council and Mayor of Prestonsburg.

In 1908 he m. Elizabeth Hopkins, daughter of Hon. Frank A. Hopkins.

Children:

12. Elizabeth Layne.　　　　14. Frank H. Layne.

13. Grace Layne.　　　　15. Angelina Layne.

In politics he is a Republican; in religion a Presbyterian; and affiliated with the Masons and Odd Fellows.[2]

---

[1] Henry P. Scalf, "Historic Floyd," 1800-1950.
[2] "History of Kentucky," by Charles Kerr (Editor), Vol. IV, pp. 468-9.

LESLIE FAMILY OF PIKE AND GREENUP COUNTIES

The Leslie family is of Scottish or Scotch-Irish extraction. William Robert Leslie was the progenitor of the Leslie family of Eastern Kentucky. He and his brother John emigrated from Scotland to New York City. Here they became separated and never saw each other again. William Robert migrated to Pennsylvania where he m. Elizabeth Buchanan, b. about 1765. They migrated to Augusta County, Virginia, where four children were born. William Robert Leslie was a Revolutionary War soldier.[1]

This Leslie family attempted to make a settlement at the mouth of Pond Creek on the Tug River, then Mason County, in 1789 but were driven out by Indians. They returned in 1791 but instead of stopping at Pond Creek, they went on to Johns Creek and founded what to this day is known as the Leslie Settlement. The Leslies must have been the earliest permanent settlers in the Big Sandy Valley region.[2]

According to some authorities William Leslie migrated to and settled in what is now Pike County, Kentucky, in 1802.[3] He d. at the age of 73 years. Ely in "The Big Sandy Valley", p. 211, describes his casket and burial as follows:

"In early days when the plank in the upper Johns Creek country was sawed by hand, and used as fast as sawed, William Leslie d. at seventy-three, and no plank could be procured to make a coffin to bury him in. Nor could a whipsaw be procured to saw enough. His relatives and friends were determined to give him a decent burial; so they had a nice poplar tree cut down and chopped off a log of proper length, squared it up, and with ax and adze, shaped it into a coffin, digging out a trough. They took clapboards and shaved them, with which they made a nice lid for the trough-like casket; and in this unique case the remains of William Leslie of Johns Creek were consigned to mother earth."

Children, among others:

2. Robert Leslie; b. in Augusta County, Virginia, 1763, and d. in Pike County, Kentucky, 1822; m. Elizabeth Compton. They were the parents of fifteen children—eight sons and seven daughters, among whom the records would seem to indicate were:

3. Allen Leslie, farmer; b. in Virginia, 1793, m. Elizabeth ——, b. in Virginia, 1794.

4. Jemima Leslie; b. in Virginia, 1801.

5. Esther Leslie; b. in Virginia about 1802.

*6. Pharmer Leslie.

*7. Martin Leslie.

*8. John P. Leslie.

6. PHARMER LESLIE, farmer, was b. in then Floyd County, now Pike County, Kentucky, in 1802 or 1803, being the first male white

child b. on Johns Creek. He became one of the most prominent citizens of the Big Sandy country. He was a model farmer and grew wealthy at farming, stock raising and timbering. He m. in Pike County, July 12, 1829, Mary J. Bevins, b. in Kentucky, 1813, daughter of John Bevins. Pharmer Leslie d. in 1883.

Children living at home and approximate dates of birth as shown by U. S. Census of Pike County for 1850 and 1860:

9. Robert W. Leslie; b. 1831.
10. John E. Leslie; b. 1833.
11. James K. Leslie; b. 1835.
12. Esther M. Leslie; b. 1837.
13. Addison N. Leslie; b. 1838.
14. Elizabeth Leslie; b. 1840.
15. Kenas F. Leslie; b. 1842.
16. Samuel Leslie; b. 1846.
17. Victoria A. Leslie; b. 1848.
18. Araminta R. Leslie; b. 1851.
19. Amos Leslie; b. 1856.

7. MARTIN LESLIE, farmer, was b. in Pike County, 1807; m. Sarah Auxier Mayo, b. in 1821, or 1822.

Children living at home and approximate dates of birth as shown by U. S. Census of Pike County for 1850 and 1860:

20. Thomas J. Leslie; b. 1842.
21. John W. Leslie; b. 1844.
22. Rebecca E. Leslie; b. 1846.
23. Amos S. S. Leslie; b. 1849.
*24. Martin Samuel Leslie; b. 1852.
*25. Robert A. E. Leslie; b. 1854
26. Trmines (?) Leslie; b. 1856.

8. JOHN P. LESLIE, farmer; b. in Virginia (?) 1810; m. about 1836, Jane ———, b. in Ohio, 1813.

Children living at home and approximate dates of birth as shown by the U. S. Census of Lawrence County for 1850:

27. Elizabeth Leslie; b. 1837.
28. Martha Leslie; b. 1839.
29. David K. Leslie; b. 1843.
30. Eliza M. Leslie; b. 1849.

24. MARTIN SAMUEL LESLIE, physician, was b. in Pike County, Kentucky, March 19, 1852, and d. February 17, 1904; studied medicine in Lexington, Kentucky, and located in Greenup, Kentucky, in 1882 for the practice of his profession; m. soon thereafter Florence Hunt of Lexington, b. December 31, 1859, and d. July 10, 1946.

Children:

*31. Phillip Jones Leslie.
*32. Samuel Thurman Leslie.

*33. Ralph Hunt Leslie.
*34. Robert Gladstone Leslie.

25. ROBERT ALLEN ENGLISH LESLIE, farmer and teacher, was b. in Pike County, Kentucky, 1854; removed to Greenup County, Kentucky, and was m. to Mary Frances Womack of Old Town, that county; taught in the public schools of Greenup County for a number of years; resided for the greater part of the time in the Big Sandy Valley in Kentucky and in Viginia. He d. in Burkesville, Virginia, in 1926, and his wife in 1943. Both were interred in Riverside Cemetery at Greenup.

Children:
35. June Leslie.
36. Mary Leslie.
37. Robert Leslie.
38. Guy Womack Leslie.
*39. Ruth Cleveland Leslie.
*40. G. W. Leslie.

39. RUTH CLEVELAND LESLIE; resides in the Washington, D. C. area.

40. GEORGE WASHINGTON LESLIE was b. May 5, 1891, in Montague County, Texas, during the temporary residence of his parents in that state; attended the public schools of Pike County, Kentucky, and became a student in the Pikeville High School, but left before graduating to accept a position with the Chesapeake and Ohio Railway Company, which position he filled for three years when he resumed his education; attended Milligan College, Lexington, Kentucky, 1910-1911, and then became chief clerk of the Chesapeake & Ohio Railway Company at Cannel City, Morgan County, Kentucky; was promoted to auditor and treasurer in 1907.

Mr. Leslie is a Democrat in politics and is a member of the Christian Church.

He was m., May 29, 1912, at Cannel City, to Miss Bertha C. Jones, daughter of Thomas A. and Julia (Park) Jones.

Children:
41. Elizabeth Frances Leslie.

31. PHILLIP JONES LESLIE, druggist at Greenup; b. October 24, 1900 and d. at Greenup, July 9, 1954; educated in the Greenup (Kentucky) public schools, graduating from the Greenup High School; m., December 3, 1920, Edith Doran who was b. August 2, 1894; and educated in the Greenup Graded and High Schools.

Children:
42. James Robert Leslie, bank teller; b. April 5, 1926; educated in Greenup public schools, graduating from the Greenup High School in 1944; student at Duke University, Durham, N. Car.; m. July 20, 1946, Doris Anne Cole, who was graduated from the Ashland High

School in 1944; was a student in Ashland (Kentucky) Junior College one year; and attended graded schools in Ashland, Kentucky, and in Asheville and Raleigh, North Carolina. Children: Philip Bruce, b. June 24, 1947, and Anne Elaine, b. November 16, 1950.

43. Mary Alice Leslie; b. December 25, 1928; educated in the Greenup public schools, graduating from the Greenup High School in 1946; was a student in University of Cincinnati for a year; m., December 3, 1947, Riley F. Stultz who was educated in the Russell (Kentucky) public schools, graduating from the Russell High School in 1946. Children: David Riley Stultz, b. February 12, 1949, and Thomas Joseph Stultz, b. July 28, 1951.

32. SAMUEL THURMAN LESLIE, druggist; b. November 21, 1895; educated in the Greenup (Kentucky public schools, graduating from the Greenup High School; and the Louisville School of Pharmacy; m., June 10, 1925, Jeanette Cole, who was b. June 29, 1902, and educated in Greenup (Kentucky) graded and High School.

Children:

44. William Hunt Leslie; b. September 8, 1926; educated in the Greenup Graded School and the Ashland High School.

45. Florence Reid Leslie; b. February 11, 1934; educated in the Greenup Graded School and graduated from the Ashland High School in 1952; and is presently a student in Centre College, Danville, Kentucky.

46. Barbara Jane Leslie; b. November 15, 1927, and d. November 19, 1927.

33. RALPH HUNT LESLIE, druggist, b. January 2, 1888; educated in the Greenup Graded and High Schools and in University of Cincinnati, School of Pharmacy; m. November 3, 1909, Mattie Collins, who was b. May 21, 1887, and educated in the Wurtland Graded and the Greenup High Schools.

Children:

47. Lois Leslie, b. December 28, 1914; educated in the Greenup Graded and High Schools, graduating from the latter in 1930; was student at University of Kentucky, 1931-1932.

34. ROBERT GLADSTONE LESLIE, dentist; b. December 23, 1897; educated in the Greenup Graded and High Schools; at Staunton Military Academy, Staunton, Virginia, and at University of Louisville, College of Dentistry; m., April 5, 1945, Elizabeth Boehm, b. May 4, 1907, who was educated in the Graded and High Schools of Greeley, Pennsylvania, and was a student at Columbia University, New York City.

[1] John H. Gwathmey, "Virginians in the Revolution, 1775-1783", page 469.
[2] William Ely, "The Big Sandy Valley", page 11.
[3] Nina M. Biggs, "History of Greenup County, Kentucky", page 65.

LEWIS FAMILY OF FLEMING, CARTER AND GREENUP COUNTIES

Lewis

According to tradition the progenitors of the Lewis family of Virginia were first of the Louis family of France who fled to Wales during the Huguenot persecutions. Some authorities have discredited this theory, but, however that may be, most of the first Lewises in America, and particularly in the Southern colony, came from Wales.

One tradition which has continued in the family says that their progenitors in Wales were two of four brothers, Samuel, William, Robert, and John; that Samuel migated to Portugal, William died in Ireland and that Robert and John migrated to America and established homes in Virginia early in the eighteenth century.

John Lewis was b. in Ireland in 1678; m. Margaret Lynn. In 1720 he killed an Irish landlord, fled to America and finally settled near the town of Staunton, Augusta County, Virginia. He had many conflicts with the Indians and built his dwelling house with portholes through which he could fire on the savages and so protect his family. He d. in 1762 in his 84th year, leaving a large family of whom General Andrew Lewis was the most distinguished.

The Robert Lewis family m. into the Warner family of Virginia, from which comes the notable "Warner Hall" Lewises of Gloucester County. This branch also became connected with the Washington family through the marriage of General Fielding Lewis to Betty Washington, sister of General George Washington.

The Descendants of the Virginia Lewises are very numerous and have a creditable record for the distinguished services of its members in all the major conflicts of this nation.

Another well-known and interesting Lewis family in America is the Pennsylvania house, which traces descent from Ellis Lewis, who was b. in Wales in 1680. He came to Kennett Township, Pennsylvania, and established his home in 1708. His father was Owen Lewis of Wales. This family has preserved an unbroken chain showing descent from Lord of Nanan, Wales, who was descended from Cynfyn, Prince of Powys and King of Wales who d. in 972.

Lewis Family of Northeastern Kentucky

1. PETER LEWIS was the Virginia ancestor of a branch of the Lewis family that settled in Fleming County, Kentucky, in pioneer

days. He m. Hannah (surname not known). They lived in North Farnham Parish, Richmond County, Virginia. Issue: Among other children, a son.

2. JAMES LEWIS, farmer and slave holder, was b. in North Farnham Parish, Richmond County, Virginia, 1725, and d. in Fleming County, Kentucky, 1819; m., August 25, 1772, in North Farnham Parish, Richmond County, Virginia, Ailsey Forrester, daughter of Robert and Bridget Forrester. Family tradition and documentary evidence would seem to indicate that this branch of the Lewis family is descended from the "Warner Hall" Lewises of Gloucester County. Some of James and Ailsey Lewis' children settled in that part of Mason County which was embraced in Greenup County upon its formation in 1803 and included within the boundary of Carter County upon its formation in 1838.

In his will, executed September 10, 1819, and probated in the Fleming County Court, May 1, 1820, James Lewis leaves bequests to this wife (Ailsey) and to his children:

*3. Charles N. Lewis.
4. Betsey Bell.
5. Bridget Lewis Gault.
6. Ailse Hawkins.
7. Fanny Goodard.
8. Nancy Ringo.
9. James R. Lewis.
10. Peter B. Lewis.
11. Robert G. Lewis.
12. William D. Lewis.

He named as executors his wife and sons, Peter B. Lewis and Robert G. Lewis.

3. CHARLES NELMS LEWIS I was b. in Virginia, June 26, 1773, and d. of cholera in Frankfort, Kentucky, in 1813, while attending a session of the Kentucky Legislature as senator from Greenup and Lewis Counties. He was one of the outstanding pioneers of his time in his section of the State and was a man of affairs, generally. He was a farmer and slave-holder, having listed for taxation 20 Negro slaves in 1810. He was commissioned by Governor Garrard as one of the first justices of the peace of Greenup County in 1803, and in 1813 he was elected State Senator from the district composed of the counties of Greenup and Lewis and was serving as such at date of his death.

Charles Nelms Lewis I m. in Mason County, November 17, 1801, Miss Eliza (Betsy) Bragg, who was b. in 1782 and d. in what was then Greenup County, now Carter County, in 1832. She was a daughter of Capt. Thomas Bragg, Revolutionary War officer.

Issue:
13. Dr. Harvey Lewis; m. Miss Elizabeth Leathers.

14. Lucy Bragg Lewis; m. John M. McConnell.[1]
15. Sidney Lewis; m. Washington Ward.
16. John Milton Lewis; unm.
17. Adelaide Lewis; m. Joseph R. Ward. (See Ward Family.)
*18. Charles Nelms Lewis II.

After the death of Charles Nelms Lewis I, his widow m. James Ward, Jr. They had issue:

19. Harriet Ward; m. Richard D. Womack, in Greenup County, February 28, 1833. (See Womack Family.)
20. George Ward.

Charles Nelms Lewis I was interested in the salt works near Grayson, Kentucky. On November 24, 1804, an Act was passed by the General Assembly of Kentucky for opening the road (The Lexington Tunpike) suitable for horsemen and drivers from Thomas Green's farm near mouth of Triplett's Creek, in Fleming County, to the Big Sandy River at the junction of a road opened by Virginia, which Act was amended, December 9, 1806, requiring the road to be fit for wagons and carriages. Subsequent Acts of the General Assembly authorized commissioners named therein to erect turnpike gate on the road and to let to some person, bound by bond with security to put road in good repair and to keep in good order during term of years, during which time he was to keep the turnpike gate and take toll from passengers allowed by law.

Pursuant to these Acts the turnpike was let to Charles Nelms Lewis I for a long term of years, probably 16 years, he owning at the time a farm of 145 acres on the road known as Barns old place on which he erected a turnpike gate on the hillside west of "Tignets" (Tygarts?) creek on which tract there was a tavern at the turnpike gate. He was operating the turnpike at date of his death; and subsequently, early in 1815, his personal representatives, Amos Kibbe and Eliza Lewis, his widow, assigned the turnpike contract and leased the farm and tavern to one John Jouett for the unexpired term for consideration of $400 annually together with stipulations concerning repairs, etc. Jouett and/or his assignees defaulted in performance and on September 16, 1818, Lewis' Administrators filed suit against Jouett and Others in the Montgomery (County) Circuit Court for failing to keep the road in repair and were awarded judgment. Subsequently, on November 21, 1826, suit, involving this contract and lease, was filed in the Greenup Circuit Court which suit was transferred to the Bourbon Circuit Court, and final decree rendered by that court, August 25, 1837, the commissioners having reported settlement.

A great number of pioneers living along the turnpike appeared in this long, drawn-out litigation either as witnesses, administrators or bondsmen:

Administrators of Lewis: Amos Kibbe, Eliza Lewis (widow) and

James Ward, Jr., jointly, succeeded by George Washington Ward who was succeeded by Thomas Scott. Edward Stockton and Landon Jouett, jointly, for John Jouett.

Bondsmen (sureties): Jesse B. Boone, Sarah Stratton, William Lowery, John Everman, Thomas Ward on the bond of James Ward, Jr., guardian of Lewises and Ward. Thomas Moseley and Levi Stewart for Jouett.

Witnesses (depositions): Joseph Boudurant of Montgomery County; Rowland Burns of Greenup County; Nathaniel Dawson of Greenup County; James Gatewood of Montgomery County; William Hayden of Montgomery County; Robert Henderson of Greenup County; Joshua Kemp of Greenup County; John Moseley of Greenup County; William Norris of Greenup County; James Offett of Greenup County; Lewis Reason of Greenup County; Burtis Ringo of Fleming County; Thomas Scott of Greenup County; Thomas Triplett of Bath County; James Trimble of Bath County; Edward Young and Senate Young of Bath County; James Ward, Sr., of Greenup County; William Yocum of Montgomery County.

18. CHARLES NELMS LEWIS II, farmer, was b. near Grayson, then Greenup, now Carter County, Kentucky, December 29, 1812, and d. in Carter County, June 20, 1892; m. in Greenup County, January 9, 1834, Louisa Ann England, who was b. in Bath County, Kentucky, December 20, 1815, and d. in Carter County, January 19, 1892.

Issue:
*21. Jesse England Lewis.
22. Sarah Ann Lewis; m. Levi Owings, August 25, 1868.
*23. Charles Nelms Lewis III.
24. Lucy Lee Lewis; m. Charles D. Corey, May 14, 1866.[2]
25. Harvey Lewis; unm.
26. Mary Lewis; m. Richard D. Davis. (See Davis Family.)
*27. William Jackson Lewis.
28. Robert C. Lewis; unm.

23. CHARLES NELMS LEWIS III, farmer, was b. near Grayson, Kentucky, September 25, 1845, and d. in Grayson, November 6, 1933; m. in Carter County, December 22, 1867, Miss Phoebe Stewart, who d. December 29, 1912.

Issue:
29. Anna Lewis; d. in infancy.
30. Mary (Mollie) Elizabeth Lewis; m. Dr. William A. Horton. (See Horton Family.)
31. Edith Lewis was b. near Lee Summit, Missouri, January 4, 1871; m. at Grayson, December 28, 1892, Edward Lewis Ault, merchant at Grayson, b. near Shrewsberry, West Virginia, April 5, 1860.

Children:
Richard Lewis Ault, b. December 9, 1893, educated in the public

schools of Grayson; served in World War I, serving 16 months overseas; d. October 22, 1922.

Virginia Elizabeth Ault, teacher, b. January 13, 1901; educated in the public schools of Grayson; received A. B. degree in Commerce, College of Commerce, Bowling Green, Kentucky, and did post graduate work at University of Kentucky at Lexington; taught in the Marlinton (West Virginia) High School, 1923-1933; in the Catonsville (Maryland) High School, 1933-1934; and in Spencer (West Virginia) High School, 1934-1943. She is presently secretary of the J. Q. Stovall Memorial Hospital at Grayson.

Mary Louise Ault, b. July 26, 1907; lives at Grayson.

32. Lucy Nelms Lewis, teacher, b. February 10, 1881, d. 1954: educated in the public schools of Carter County and at Morehead (Kentucky) Normal School; taught in the public schools of Carter County for several years; m. Dr. Watts Stovall.

JAMES WATTS STOVALL, physican and surgeon, a son of Dr. John Quincy and Mary (Watts) Stovall, who migrated from Beckley, Raleigh County, West Virginia, and settled at Grayson, Carter County, Kentucky, where Dr. Stovall continued the practice of his profession until his death, February 8, 1917. Mrs. Stovall d. at Grayson, March 12, 1908.

Dr. James Watts Stovall was b. at Beckley, West Virginia, April 26, 1882; was educated in the public schools of Beckley and Grayson, Kentucky, and at Morris Harvey College, Barbourville, West Virginia, from which he was graduated with degree of A. B. in 1899. In September, 1899, he enlisted in the U. S. Army and served in the Forty-sixth Regiment, U. S. Volunteers Infantry, in the Philippines at Manila and on Luzon Island until May 30, 1901, when he was honorably discharged. Returning to the United States after the close of the war, he entered Kentucky University, now the University of Louisville, Medical Department, from which he was graduated with degree of M. D. in 1905. Returning to his home in Grayson, he formed a partnership with his father with whom he was associated in the practice of medicine until 1916. On May 1, 1927 he established a hospital in Grayson, thoroughly modernized in all its appointments, which became the "J. Q. Stovall Memorial Hospital" in honor of his father. He is presently superintendent of and surgeon at the hospital.

Aside from his professional activities, Dr. Stovall has been interested and influential in the business and political affairs of the community. He was president of the Grayson Garage Company for a time; was a director of the Ramsey-Gatlin Construction Company of Ashland and of the Commercial Bank of Grayson. An influential factor in State politics, he served as chairman of the Democratic Committee of Carter County for many years. He has served as vice-president of the Kentucky State Board of Health since 1926; trustee of Prichard High School at Grayson; president of the Kentucky State Medical Association, 1945; is a member of the American Hospital Association; Southern Medical Society; and Carter County Medical Society. He is affiliated with the Masons—a member of Trimble Lodge No. 145, at Grayson, and a Noble of the Mystic Shrine (York Rite); a member of the Rotary Club at Grayson and a Kentucky Colonel.

Residence, 915 Hord Street, Grayson.

Children:

Mary Lewis Stovall; m., first, 1930, Hubert Chaffin of Louisa, Kentucky, who d., 1947. He had service in World War II. No children. Mrs. Chaffin m., secondly, in 1949, Stuart W. Heard of Center Sandwich, New Hampshire, who had service in World War II. Residence, Center Sandwich.

Mildred Watts Stovall; m. in Los Angeles, California, 1941, Sidney Taylor of Greenville, Kentucky who was then serving in World War II. They are the parents of three children: Mary Nelms Taylor, b. 1943; Martha Lynn Taylor, b. 1944; and Margaret Bee Taylor, b. 1948.

Blanche Bee Stovall; m. Maurice Littleton, son of Judge Roscoe Conkling and Ella Belle (Everman) Littleton. (See Everman Family.) Both Mr. and Mrs. Littleton are graduates of University of Kentucky. They are parents of two children: Charles Stovall Littleton, b. 1941, and Gary Lee Littleton, b. 1943.

27. WILLIAM JACKSON LEWIS, farmer, b. December 30, 1852, d. September 7, 1939; m., October 15, 1879, Miss Maud Mary Botts, b. December 17, 1852, d. February 23, 1935, a daughter of Judge J. R. Botts of Grayson.

Issue.

*33. Bertha Lee Lewis.

34. Sallie C. Lewis, b. November 3, 1884; m. September 14, 1911, Charles C. Poppleton, who d. November 1922.

35. James Harvey Lewis, farmer, b. September 25, 1886; m., October 8, 1913, Miss Maude Alice Gilbert, teacher.

36. Charles Nelms Lewis IV, farmer; b. January 21, 1890; m., March 1923, Miss Bessie Everman.

37. Anna Mary Lewis, b. October 20, 1892; unm.

33. BERTHA LEE LEWIS, teacher, b. near Grayson, Kentucky, January 30, 1881; educated in the public schools of Carter County; at Transylvania College, Lexington, Kentucky, and was graduated from Morehead (Kentucky) State Teachers College with degree of Bachelor of Arts in education in 1939; began teaching in the public schools of Carter County early in life and continued teaching in that county and in West Virginia for fifteen years, when, in 1918, she

accepted a position as teacher in the public schools of Ashland (the Wylie school) where she taught for the succeeding twenty-nine years. She retired in 1951. Miss Lewis was married to Mr. T. A. James, September 7, 1910.

Mrs. James is a member of the Professional Woman's Club, the Ashland Educational Association, the Eastern Kentucky Educational Association, the Kentucky Educational Association and the National Educational Association; served as treasurer of the Wylie Parent-Teacher Association for twenty-six consecutive years. She is a member of the First Christian Church of Ashland; and a member of the Daughters of the American Revolution on the military records of her ancestors, Capt. Thomas Bragg and Capt. George Neville, both of whom had service in the Virginia Forces during the Revolutionary War.

THOMAS ARTHUR JAMES, general insurance, Ashland, Kentucky, son of J. H. and Jane (Bane) James, natives of England, was b. at Frostburg, Maryland, 1876; came with his parents from Pennsylvania to Grahn, Carter County, Kentucky, when about nine years of age; attended the public schools of Louisville; taught in the rural public schools of Carter County for a time and was principal of the Grayson (Kentucky) Graded School for two years and was examiner of applicants for teacher's certificates of Carter County. He was manager of the Fire Brick Works at Grahn, Kentucky, for 14 years. Later he accepted a position with the Inter-Southern Life Insurance Company, and subsequently he went to Ashland and established a general insurance business and is presently conducting that business.

Mr. James m., first, Miss Georgia Littleton, a teacher of Carter County. Two children, daughters, were born of this union: Nellie, who m. Mr. Gus Parsons and Mable, a business woman of Ashland.

21. JESSE ENGLAND LEWIS; b. about 1837; m. Mary Frances Bagby, a daughter of Willis Bagby and his wife ——— (Thompson) Bagby, and a sister of the late James Bagby of Grayson.

Children, among others:

38. Robert Franklin Lewis, b. November 9, 1867, and d. July 23, 1923, at Grayson. He engaged in the tobacco industry for a time. A staunch Democrat in politics, he was an enthusiastic local party worker. He m., at Willard, Kentucky, Coney Kitchen, a daughter of William R. and Nancy Elizabeth (Shearer) Kitchen. She is a lineal (direct) descendant of Charles Rice and Capt John Bailey, both of whom had service in the Revolutionary War. (See Bailey and Rice Families.)

CONEY KITCHEN, civic and social worker and political leader, was b. at Willard, Kentucky, December 25, 1879; educated in the Willard Graded, High and Normal Schools, Christian Normal Institute (now Kentucky Christian College) at Grayson and Boothe Business College at Huntington, West Virginia.

The Lewises lived in Grayson and Mrs. Lewis has been active in the social and civic and the political affairs of the city and county for many years. She is a consistent member of the First Christian Church at Grayson and has been a member of the Christian Church from young girlhood. A Democrat in politics, she has served her party faithfully and well in many capacities. She was postmaster at Grayson for several years. In July, 1936, she was appointed Field Worker in the Kentucky Department of Welfare, Division of Public Assistance (now Department of Economic Welfare), and served for many years and until her retirement recently.

Children:

39. Jesse Kitchen Lewis, lawyer and sometime public official; b. at Grayson, April 15, 1900; educated in the graded and high schools of Grayson; was graduated from Transylvania University with degree of A. B., 1924, and from the University of Kentucky with degree of LL.B., 1931; admitted to the bar and practiced law at Grayson for a time. Mr. Lewis is a staunch Democrat and has always been very active and is a leader in his party. He served as City Attorney of Grayson, 1931-1937; Assistant Attorney General of Kentucky, 1937-1944; member of the Public Service Commission of Kentucky, 1946-1948. Since 1949 he has practiced law in Lexington, Kentucky where he resides.

Mr. Lewis has been a very active member of the Christian Church from youth. While living in Frankfort he was a member of the Frankfort Christian Church, serving as Chairman of the Official Board, 1940-1944. He is presently a member and elder in the Woodland Christian Church, Lexington, and serving as Chairman of the Board of Elders.

In 1933, Mr. Lewis was united in marriage with Miss Emily Fortune, daughter of Dr. and Mrs. A. W. Fortune of Lexington. No children. Dr. Fortune, now deceased, was an eminent minister in the Christian Church.

40. William Riley Kitchen, civil engineer b. at Grayson, December 21, 1902; educated in the public schools of Grayson and at Tri-State College, Angola, Indiana; served in World War II as Chief Petty Officer, U. S. Navy, 1943-1945; had foreign service; presently and for many years an employee of the Kentucky Highway Department; m., first, November 13, 1927, Ruby Moore and secondly, June 23, 1933, Lillian Emmons. Children: a daughter, Mrs. J. F. (Roberta) James, Ft. Wayne, Indiana. Mr. Lewis resides at Flemingsburg, Kentucky, and is a member of the Christian Church there.

41. Fay Francis Lewis; b. at Grayson, November 6, 1905; educated in the Grayson public schools and at Hamilton College at Lexington, Kentucky; m., August 8, 1925, Elwood Lewis, deceased, who was cashier of the Peoples Bank at Olive Hill, Kentucky; members of the Olive Hill Christian Church.

Children: Robert Fielding Lewis, b. January 23, 1929; educated in the Olive Hill public school and was graduated from Transylvania College with degree of A. B.; is presently serving in the U.S. Air Corps; is a member of the Christian Church.

Charles Shearer Lewis, b. September 27, 1933; educated in the Olive Hill public schools and the Erie High School and is presently a student at Transylvania College; is a member of the Christian Church.

42. Dorothy Joy Lewis; b. at Grayson, September 27, 1916; educated in the Grayson and the Lexington public schools, at Kentucky University, and was graduated from Transylvania College with degree of A.B.; m., August 30, 1941, Lieutenant David B. Knox; members of the Christian Church. Children: David Lewis Knox, b. August 10, 1942, and Susan Fay Knox, b. February 3, 1948.

---

[1] John M. McConnell, lawyer and sometime public official, was of Scotch-Irish descent and was b. in Western Pennsylvania, circa 1790. He received a good education before he attained his 16th year when he was apprenticed to a tailor and draper. While engaged in his regular work he spent his spare time in pursuing a course of study previously decided upon; and living in a college town, Cannonsburg, he pursued and completed a college course at home, encouraged and assisted by the students and the professors of the college so that when his apprenticeship expired at the age of 21 he had completed his education.

In 1812 his employer gave him twenty-five dollars, a horse, bridle and saddle, a large pair saddle bags and a new suit of broadcloth clothes; and he left his native state and started to Kentucky which he reached opposite Portsmouth, Ohio. He rode to Greenupsburg Court House where he tarried for a time. Subsequently he went to Woodford County, Kentucky, but soon returned to Eastern Kentucky and went to Prestonsburg where he taught school and studied law with Robert Walker, one of the early lawyers of that town. About this time he married Miss Lucy Brag Lewis and settled in Greenup County where he lived the remainder of his life.

From his entrance upon the practice of law until his death, John M. McConnell stood at the front rank in his profession and was considered as one of the most eloquent men on the stump and brilliant conversationalist of his time in the State. Enjoying a large and lucrative practice and making wise investments in the infant industries of his county which yielded large returns, he became wealthy for his day; and being a gentleman of taste and culture, he set up an establishment comparable to any in the older settlements at that time. He purchased a large boundary of land fronting the Ohio River four miles above Greenupsburg where he laid out a four-acre plot, fronting the bank of the river, and in the center erected a splendid two-story brick mansion which he furnished with the most skillfully wrought furniture. He landscaped the lawn, planted shrubbery and laid out flower beds; built his law office and negro quarters; and when ready to occupy the premises, without any apparent sickness, he died July 5, 1834, at the age of 43. His widow, Lucy Brag Lewis McConnell, died about 1854.

During his busy career Colonel McConnell was interested also in politics. He was elected and served as State representative from Greenup County, 1822, 1824, 1825; and as State senator from Greenup and Lewis Counties, 1826-30.

Commencing his adult life with comparatively nothing, he accumulated and left his widow and children what was considered in his day a large estate—over $50,000 in money, lands and negro slaves. His will, dated June 23, 1834, and probated in the Greenup County Court, August 4, 1834, leaves his property to his widow, Lucy B. and to their children, Charles, Mary Ann, Caroline, Elizabeth and Harriet; and recommends that the children be educated at Marietta, Athens and/or Oxford (Ohio) Colleges.

[2] Charles D. Corey was the editor of the **Herald**. "He was a very amiable and brilliant young man, a New Yorker, bought the outfit used by the **Advocate** and ventured on the **Herald** in 1863. Mr. Corey was a Democrat and made his paper at first mildly Democratic; but as it grew in age it also grew to be a stalwart Democratic organ, even in time of war. Mr. Corey was a genius; he was a photographer, printer, poet, painter, and a good prose writer. He made a good paper. He m. a beautiful young lady of Grayson— Miss Lucy Lewis, the daughter of Hon. Nelms Lewis. But the married life of the handsome pair was cut short by the death of the husband whose physical nature was almost ethereal, so delicate was he. The young, loving wife would not be comforted after her 'Charley's' death, and she soon joined him in the land of pure delight. The connubial love of this beautiful couple for each other was more than human." (Ely, "The Big Sandy Valley", p,. 329.)

LYTTLE FAMILY OF CLAY COUNTY

The Lyttle family is of Scotch-Irish origin and the founders of the American Branch of the family settled in Virginia in the Colonial period.

1. HARRINGTON LYTTLE was the ancestor of the branch of the family that settled in Southeastern Kentucky. He passed his entire life in Lee County, Virginia; was a successful planter and a citizen of prominence and influence. He was a resident of and d. at Jonesville, county seat of Lee County. His son—

2. HON. DAVID YANCEY LYTTLE, lawyer, was b. in Lee County, Virginia, in 1821; was educated in Virginia and about 1846 came to Kentucky and established residence at Harlan (then Mt. Pleasant), Harlan County, whence in 1856 he removed to Manchester, Clay County, and engaged in the practice of law, besides becoming the owner of the nearby Cedar Craig farm which he developed into one of the fine properties of that section of the State. Here he spent the remainder of his long and worthy life and here he d. in 1907. He became one of the distinguished members of the Kentucky bar and for many years controlled an exceptionally large and representative law business.

He was a leader in the councils of the Democratic party in his section of the State but preferred to devote himself to his profession rather than to hold public office. However, he represented Clay County in the State Senate, 1867-71.

He m., first, in Harlan County, Kentucky, Miss Drucilla Brittain, b. in Harlan County, in 1823 and d. at the Cedar Craig homestead, Clay County, in 1863.

Children:

3. Prof. G. Brittain Lyttle, educator, a man of high intellectual attainments who achieved special pedagogic distinction as a teacher of Spanish languages in the schools of Knoxville and New Orleans as well as in various other communities.

4. Dale C. Lyttle, farmer, resided near Manchester; d. in 1882.

*5. Col. C. B. Lyttle.

6. Louisa Lyttle; d. in infancy.

7. William Lyttle; d. in infancy.

8. Nancy Lyttle; m. A. J. Hecker, attorney of Manchester; both d. at Manchester.

9. James Lyttle; merchant in Topeka, Kansas; d. there in 1901.

10. Sallie Lyttle; m. Harvey L. Hatton of Barboursville, Kentucky.

11. Robert Lee Lyttle; resided in Harlan County; d. in 1891.

2. COLONEL DAVID YANCEY LYTTLE; m., secondly, Miss Ellen Jett, who was b. in Breathitt County, Kentucky, in 1830, and d. at the old homestead, Cedar Craig, in Clay County.

Children:

12. Malva Lyttle; m. D. K. Rowlings and d. at the homestead, Cedar Craig, in 1884. Mr. Rowlings was engaged in the practice of law at London, Laurel County, at the time of his death.

13. Cassie Lyttle, resided at Versailles, Kentucky; m. B. White, Jr. a farmer by vocation who was assassinated in the Spring of 1921.

14. Lenora Lyttle; m. Frank P. Milburn, architect; resided in Washington, D. C.

15. Margaret Lyttle; b. at Manchester, Clay County, Kentucky, and d. at her home in the 6200 block, Thirty-third Street, Washington, D. C.; burial was in Fort Lincoln Cemetery; m. in 1898 George W. Combs and came to Washington with her husband in 1909. Mr. Combs is a Washington newspaper correspondent and has been a member of the Baltimore Sun staff since 1909.

Children:

16. William Edgar Combs of Washington.
17. Mrs. Ethel C. Luening of Washington.
18. Mrs. Claude W. Leathers of Chatham, New Jersey.
19. Mrs. J. Hugh Green of Falls Church, Virginia.

5. COL. C. B. LYTTLE, lawyer, received his early education in the public schools of Manchester and thereafter was a student for four terms in the University of Kentucky at Lexington. He prepared himself for his profession under the tutorship of Hon. W.C.P. Breckenridge and John T. Shelby, distinguished lawyers of Lexington, Kentucky. Prior to his taking law course he had so far advanced his technical knowledge as to prove himself eligible to the bar to which he was admitted in 1871, when he engaged in practice at Manchester and where he continued for many years. He resided on his beautiful surburban homestead, Brooks View, one-fourth mile west of Manchester.

In politics Col. Lyttle was a Democrat. Both he and his wife were members of the Presbyterian Church at Manchester.

Col. Lyttle served as county attorney for Clay County for three terms, twelve years; was President Elector, 11th Congressional District, in President Wilson's first election; and was a colonel on the staff of Governor Black.

He m. in 1878, Miss Belle or Isabella Garrard, daughter of Gen. Theophilus T. Garrard and his wife Lucy (Lee) Garrard. (See Garrard Family). Miss Garrard was educated among other institutions of learning, at Loretta College and at Ben Franklin school at Frankfort.

Children:

20. John Dishman Lyttle; d. at the paternal home when 21 years old.

21. Theophilus T. Lyttle, b. 1881; prosperous lumber dealer at Manchester and also identified with important coal mining operations in his section of the State.

22. David Y. Lyttle, lawyer, b. in 1882; professionally followed in the footsteps of his father and grandfather; resided on the farm.

23. Emma Lyttle m. John Lucas, coal operator; resided in East Manchester.

24. James M. Lyttle, lumber dealer and coal operator; resided in Manchester.

25. Lucy Lyttle; m. C. B. Donnelly who operates a part of the Garrard homestead, Cedar Craig. He was secretary to Hon. John M. Robison, U. S. House of Representatives, in 1921.

26. Carl Lyttle; d. in infancy.

27. Helen Lyttle; m. J. M. Kieth, who engaged in the insurance business in Knoxville, Tennessee.

28. Drucilla Lyttle; m. John C. White, Jr., prosperous farmer, near Park Valley, Clay County.

MARTIN FAMILY OF FLOYD AND BOYD COUNTIES

COLONEL JOHN P. MARTIN, lawyer, legislator and politician, was the founder of one branch of the Martin family of Eastern Kentucky. He was b. in Lee County, Virginia, October 11, 1810, and d. at Prestonsburg, Kentucky, December 23, 1862. In 1828, he removed to Harlan County, Kentucky, and when only nineteen years of age, he was a candidate for State representative against one John Bates who was elected by thirty-seven votes, much less than the usual majority. In 1835, he removed to Floyd County where he lived until his death. He was elected a State representative in 1841 and 1843 and on February 23, 1842, he cast a solitary vote for Judge Richard French for U. S. Senator in opposition to John J. Crittenden, and was hissed for such action. He was elected to Congress for one term, 1845-47, defeating Adams and McKee, in a district that was normally 3,500 against him; in 1848 he was defeated for Congress by Judge Daniel Breck by only 900 votes—having reduced the Democratic majority from 3,500 to 900. In 1848, as the Democratic candidate for lieutenant-governor he was defeated by John C. Helm by a much smaller majority than his distinguished co-nominee for governor, Lazarus W. Powell, was defeated by John J. Crittenden. He represented Floyd, Morgan, Johnson and Pike Counties in the State Senate 1855-59, having been elected by over 2,000 majority. In 1856 he was a delegate from the state at large to the Democratic national convention at Cincinnati, and advocated the claims of his warm personal friend Linn Boyd, for the presidency in preference to James Buchanan. His efforts and influence turned the tide in the mountains of Eastern Kentucky against Know-Nothingism. In 1860, he was on the Democratic ticket for the Peace convention and canvassed a large portion of the State and then returned to his home and quietly observed the logic of events until his death in 1862.

Contemporary historians have stated that Col. Martin was a gentleman of high social qualities, fine intellect, extensive information, and generous heart; that few men had so great influence with the masses, and none equaled him in personal popularity in the Eastern or mountain region of Kentucky.

In Floyd County, on May 24, 1835, Col John P. Martin m. Elizabeth Lackey, daughter of General Alexander Lackey (See Lackey Family). They had two daughters and one son:

2. ——— Martin, a daughter, m. in Floyd County, ——— Trimble, who d. during the Civil War, leaving two sons:

(1) Malcolm Trimble, merchant at Prestonsburg; d. in 1885.

(2) James Trimble, merchant at Prestonsburg for a time and then removed to Catlettsburg and when the Catlettsburg National Bank was established there he was given a position in the bank.

Several years after the war, Mrs. Trimble m. a Mr. Armstrong, a lawyer, and they removed to Missouri.

3. Mousie Martin m. Capt. John C. Hopkins of a prominent family of Tazewell County, Virginia. He was a lawyer by profession but engaged principally in steamboat business on the Big Sandy River. The family lived at Catlettsburg.

4. ALEXANDER LACKEY MARTIN, lawyer, was b. at Prestonsburg, Floyd County and d. there in 1877. He was a State representative from Floyd County, 1867-69 and a State senator, 1871-75. He m. in Floyd County, Nannie Frances Brown, daughter of Judge George N. Brown. See Brown Family of Boyd County.)

Issue:

5. George Brown Martin, lawyer and U. S. Senator, was b. at Prestonsburg, Floyd County, Kentucky, August 18, 1876, and d. at Catlettsburg, Kentucky.

After his graduation from the Catlettsburg High School in 1889, he became a student in Central University, Richmond, Kentucky—since removed to Danville, Kentucky—from which institution he was graduated with the degree of A. B. in 1895. In 1900 he was admitted to the bar and entered into the general practice of law at Catlettsburg, a member of the prominent law firm of Brown & Martin, which firm, by reason of its important cases and the able manner of conducting them, became known all over Kentucky; and many of its cases attracted wide attention.

From early manhood Senator Martin took a deep interest in public affairs and held many public offices of honor and trust and discharged the duties of all of them with ability. Before entering upon the practice of law he served as deputy sheriff of Boyd County; was deputy Circuit Court Clerk; and served as judge of the Boyd County Court, 1904 and 1905. Upon the death of U. S. Senator Ollie James, he was appointed Senator, September 7, 1918, to serve the unexpired term which ended March 3, 1919. Soon after the outbreak of World War I, he was called, first to the office of the Judge Advocate General of Kentucky, with the rank of major and then was commissioned a major in the Judge Advocate Office at Washington, D. C. Subsequent to 1918 he was a member of the National Conference of Commissioners of various states to bring about uniform state laws.

Senator Martin was a member of the Masons, the Elks and of his college Greek Letter society, the Delta Kappa Epsilon. He was a valued member of many professional organizations, including the Boyd County, Kentucky State and American Bar Associations. He was reared as a Presbyterian. He never married.

MAY FAMILY OF FLOYD COUNTY

There are a number of possible sources for the name May. Children born in the month of May were sometimes named May. The Old English word may mean a "flower, a daisy". The Middle English may denoted a "maiden". May is also a shortened form of Matthew, abbreviated from the Old French name Mahieu (Mayhew). The form Mayes signifies "son of May". Sometimes May is shortened from the Irish Mayo (local from County Mayo in Connaught). May is also one of the Scottish clan names; the May clan of the Highlands was affiliated with the clan MacDonald. The May family of the Big Sandy Valley, Eastern Kentucky, was among the early pioneers, coming in from Virginia about 1796.

1. THOMAS MAY was the first, or at least among the first of the family, settling on Shelby Creek, then Mason, now Pike County. Contemporary historians state that he was a jovial man, fond of "fiddling" and dancing and very popular with his neighbors; that he was the largest slave holder of his time or afterwards in the Sandy Valley, having been possessed of seventy-one negro slaves.

Other branches of the May family settled further down the river, mostly at Prestonsburg. They spread over a half dozen counties in the Sandy Valley and adjacent section.

From the beginning the family became prominent and influential, many of them served as county officers and as members of the Legislature. Many of them were local preachers in Methodist Episcopal Church, South; some have been lawyers and judges. In politics the Mays of the immediate Sandy Valley were and are Democrats, but some of them in other counties were Republicans.[1]

2. COLONEL ANDREW JACKSON MAY, lawyer, was b. in Prestonsburg, Kentucky, January 28, 1829; was admitted to the bar; began the practice of the law in Prestonsburg and became one of the best barristers of the place and period; m., first, in 1855, Matilda Davidson, b. 1830, d. 1896, and secondly, Nell Davidson, of Prestonsburg, b. 1880, d. 1918.[2] He served with distinction in the Confederate States Army; was appointed or commissioned, May 26, 1861, at West Liberty, Kentucky, a captain, 5th Regiment, Infantry, Kentucky Volunteers; C. S. A.; assigned to duty as lieutenant-colonel, November 17, 1861; promoted to colonel, April 18, 1862; resigned on account of ill health and resignation accepted, November 14, 1862.[3]

After the close of the war, Colonel May located for and resumed the practice of law at Tazewell Court House, Tazewell County, Virginia, where he had an honorable career at the bar. He d. in 1903 and was buried in Tazewell County.

3. REUBEN MAY was the ancestor of a branch of the Mays in Floyd County. He migrated from Scott County and settled on

Beaver Creek, Floyd County, about 1820. He m. Sally Allen in Floyd County, November 27, 1825. The land on which they settled is still in the possession of their descendants. Reuben May had service in the Mexican War and the family were Southern sympathizers during the Civil War. They were prominent and consistent members of the Christian Church and as a family they organized the Reuben May Chapel of that denomination.

Issue:

*4. John May.
*5. George May.
6. Samuel May.
7. Wesley May.
*8. William H. May.

4. JOHN MAY was b. December 13, 1831, and lived to a ripe old age. He m. at the age of 17 or 18 years, Dorcas Conley, b. 1827, and d. 1914, daughter of Sampson Conley. The Conleys came in from Virginia and North Carolina and settled in what is now Knott County. John May and Dorcas Conley lived together as man and wife for over 60 years. He had no educational advantages whatever so far as schools were concerned. After marriage a neighbor taught him to read and write. He became a prolific reader and fitted himself for the duties and responsibilities of a citizen. For twenty-five years he was deputy County Court Clerk of Floyd County and his records are a model for neatness and accuracy.

Issue:

9. B. L. C. May, farmer and coal operator at Alphoretta, Floyd County; owner of 1100 acres of the old Stephens tract at the forks of Beaver.

10. Felix T. May, farmer and lumberman, d. at Prestonsburg at the age of forty-eight.

11. David Crockett May, farmer; lives on the old homestead.

*12. William H. May.
*13. Andrew J. May.

12. WILLIAM H. MAY, onetime teacher, lawyer and judge, was b. on Beaver Creek, near present Langley, Floyd County, June 24, 1875; educated in public schools of Floyd County, at the Prestonsburg Normal School and for several years engaged in farming and teaching in the Floyd County Schools. At the age of 27 (in 1902) he entered Cumberland University, Lebanon, Tennessee, where he completed a classical course and law studies; was admitted to the bar there and had some experience in practice.

Returning to Prestonsburg in 1899, he was admitted to the bar, September 9, 1899, and formed a partnership with his brother, A. J. May, under the firm name of May and May. He served his judicial district as commonwealth's attorney for ten years and was the logical candidate for the office of circuit judge without opposition at the date of his death, February 20, 1921. During the last five years of his life, he was attorney for the Consolidated Coal Company at Jenkins, Kentucky.

In politics, Mr. May was a Democrat. He was affiliated with the Masons (a Knight Templar).

13. ANDREW JACKSON MAY, lawyer and U. S. Representative from Kentucky; b. on Beaver Creek, near Langley, Floyd County, Kentucky, June 24, 1875; attended the public schools; taught in the public schools of Floyd and Magoffin Counties, Kentucky, for five years; was graduated from the Southern Normal University Law School, Huntington, Tennessee (later Union College, Jackson, Tennessee) in 1898; was admitted to the bar same year and commenced practice in Prestonsburg, Kentucky; county attorney of Floyd County, 1901-1909; special judge of the circuit court of Johnson and Martin Counties in 1925 and 1926; also engaged in agricultural pursuits and coal mining; elected as a Democrat to the Seventy-second and to the seven succeeding Congresses (March 4, 1931—January 3, 1947); unsuccessful candidate for reelection to the Eightieth Congress; resumed the practice of law in Prestonsburg, Kentucky, where he now resides.[4]

On July 17, 1901, Andrew J. May m. Julia Grace Mayo, b. —— and d. ——, daughter of John D. Mayo.

Mr. May is a Democrat in politics, is affiliated with the Masons, and he and Mrs. May are members of the Missionary Baptist Church and he is a deacon and trustee of that church.

Issue:

14. Olga H. May.
15. Andrew J. May, Jr.
16. Robert Vernon May.

A Mr. May represented Floyd County in the State House of Representatives, 1822. Samuel May represented Floyd and Pike Counties in the State House of Representatives, 1832-33 and represented the same district in the State Senate, 1834-39. David May represented Pike County in the State House of Representatives, 1861-63 and was expelled August 29, 1862, for joining or giving aid to the Confederate Army.

Other May families, apparently descendants of 1. Thomas May, the first settler, lived in Pike and Floyd Counties:

1. WILLIAM MAY, farmer; b. in Virginia, 1800; m. Susannah ———, b. in Virginia, 1800.

Children and others living in the household and approximate dates of birth as shown by the U. S. Census of Pike County for 1850:

2. Rebecca May; b. in Virginia, 1825.
3. Mary May; b. in Virginia, 1828.
4. Joseph May; b. in Virginia, 1832.
5. Alexander May; b. in Kentucky, 1834.
6. William C. May; b. in Kentucky, 1834.
7. Sarah May; b. in Kentucky, 1835.
8. Joseph May; b. in Kentucky, 1849.
9. Sarah May; b. in Virginia, 1775.
10. Martha May; b. in Virginia, 1770.

11. DAVID MAY, farmer; b. in Kentucky, 1807; m. Nancy ———,
b., 1810. Children living in the household and approximate dates
of birth as shown by the U. S. Census of Floyd County for 1850:
12. Joseph May; b. 1835.
13. Clarinda May; b. 1836.
14. William May; b. 1840.
15. Cynthia May; b. 1841.
16. John W. May; b. 1844.
17. Mary May; b. 1845.
18. Naomi May; b. 1848.
19. Emily May; b. 1850.

20. BLAIR MAY, farmer; b. in Virginia, 1808; m. Sarah (or Sally)
Adams in Floyd County, May 17, 1829; she was b. in Kentucky 1815.
Children living in the household and approximate dates of birth
as shown by the U. S. Census of Floyd County for 1850:
21. William May; b. 1834.
22. Harvey May; b. 1836.
23. Henry May; b. 1836.
24. Robert W. May; b. 1840.
25. Samuel May; b. 1842.
26. Dial May; b. 1844.
27. Stephen L. May; b. 1846.
28. Rebecca May; b. 1850.

29. HARVEY MAY, farmer; b. in Kentucky, 1825; m. Louisa ———,
b. 1826. Children (U. S. Census, Floyd County, 1850):
30. Mary May; b. 1847.
31. Theodore May; b. 1849.

1 William Ely, "The Big Sandy Valley", p. 82.

2 Henry Preston Scalf, "Historic Floyd, 1800-1950."

3 Report of the Adjutant General of Kentucky, Confederate Kentucky Volunteers, War
of 1861-1866, Vol. II, pp. 142-177.

4 "Biographical Directory of the American Congress, 1774-1949".

MAYO FAMILY OF FLOYD COUNTY

The surname Mayo originated in the Gaelic "Moy", meaning a river or plain. There is a town in Ireland called Moy.

In New England the Mayo family was represented as early as 1638 by John, who was a resident of Boston. He was the first minister of North Church, Boston. Another John Mayo emigrated from County Kent, England, to Roxbury, Massachusetts, in 1682.

The above coat-of-arms was found on the tomb of one Joseph Mayo of Powhatan, Virginia. He is recorded as a "Gentleman, born in Somersetshire, England, 1693, d. 1740". The arms are also found on the tomb of his son, George Mayo, who was b. on the Isle of Barbados in 1717 and who d. in Virginia in 1739. Joseph Mayo emigrated from Barbados to Virginia about 1723 and established his home at Powhatan, near Richmond. He was one of the first justices of Goochland County and served as a surveyor in running the dividing line between Virginia and North Carolina.

Joseph Mayo served the colony in other public capacities and was active in military affairs. He held the rank of colonel of Goochland County Militia in 1740.

THE MAYOS OF THE BIG SANDY VALLEY, EASTERN KENTUCKY

The Mayos were among the early pioneers in the Big Sandy Valley.

*1. Jacob Mayo came from Fluvanna County, Virginia, and was appointed clerk of the Floyd Circuit Court in 1800. *2. Harry B. Mayo and *3. Wilson Mayo came later. *4. Lewis Mayo came to the Valley in 1837.

The Mayos were industrious, of good morals and intelligent. The various branches of the families have spread to all parts of the Big Sandy Valley.[1]

Anticipating that the new Floyd County would need a scholarly man for clerk, General Alexander Lackey requested 5. William James Mayo, brother of 2. Harry B. Mayo, to emigrate to that county. Soon after his arrival, William James Mayo became clerk.[2] He was b. in Virginia, presumably in Fluvanna County, in 1779, and d. in Floyd County, Kentucky, in 1849. He was the first County Court Clerk of Floyd County, serving from 1800 to September 25, 1825. The records would seem to indicate that he was a competent official.

1. ONE JACOB MAYO was deputy clerk of Floyd County in 1817, and served as County Court Clerk from September 26, 1825, to April 12, 1839. One Jacob Mayo, b. in Kentucky, 1800, m. Rebecca Graham, daughter of Judge John Graham. (See Graham Family.)

2. ONE HENRY B. MAYO (probably identical with 2. Harry B. Mayo) was a deputy County Court Clerk of Floyd County in October, 1809; deputy sheriff, November 25, 1811—September 26, 1814; and School Commissioner (County Superintendent) in 1838. He m. Peggy McGuyer in Floyd County, January 14, 1818.

3. WILSON MAYO m. Jenny Stratton in Floyd County, September 24, 1818.

4. LEWIS MAYO was well educated and was employed practically all his adult life in teaching school. He reared a family of sons and daughters who maintained the fine reputation of the house of Mayo. Members of his family married into some of the prominent families of the Big Sandy Valley.

The U. S. Census of Johnson County, Kentucky, for 1850, and the marriage records show the following with respect to Lewis Mayo and his family:

Lewis Mayo, aged 54, farmer, b. in Virginia.

6. Mariah L. Mayo (wife), aged 52, b. in Virginia.

7. Maranda L. Mayo, aged 22; m. Lorenzo Dow Walton in Johnson County, November 22, 1850.

8. Rebecca Mayo, aged 20.

9. Mariah Mayo, aged 16.

10. John W. Mayo, aged 14.

11. Cynthia Mayo, aged 9; m. Hon. James E. Stewart. (See James Stewart Family.)

According to historians [3] there were other children. Some of them, however, might be identical with some named above:

12. ——— Mayo, a daughter; m. Harry Davis who lived at mouth of Johns Creek.

13. ——— Mayo. a daughter; m. William Borders of Paintsville. It is noted that a Sarah J. Mayo m. William Borders in Johnson County, July 10, 1849.

14. ——— Mayo, a daughter; m. Allen P. Borders.

15. Lewis Mayo, a son, was a merchant.

Other Mayo families lived in the Big Sandy Valley as shown by the U. S. Census:

MIAL MAYO, farmer, b. in Virginia about 1795; m. Susanna Matthews in Floyd County, October 10, 1816. A daughter, Elizabeth, b. in Kentucky, 1819, was living in the household in Floyd County in 1850.

WINSTON MAYO, farmer, b. in Virginia, 1814; m. Cynthia S. Friend in Floyd County, January 24, 1834. She was b. in Virginia, 1815.

Children living in the household in Johnson County in 1850 and ages as of that date as shown by the U. S. Census of that county for that year:

Charles L. Mayo, aged 14.

Henry H. Mayo, aged 13.

Susan R. Mayo, aged 11.

Mildred Mayo, aged 11 months.

WILLIAM J. MAYO, farmer, b. in Kentucky, 1821; was living in Floyd County in 1850 with members of his household as shown by the U. S. Census of Floyd County for that year:

Rhoda, aged 16; Mial M., aged 14; Solomon, aged 12; Martha J., aged 3.

LEWIS P. MAYO, farmer, b. in Kentucky, 1825, was living in Floyd County in 1850 with the following persons in his household as shown by the U. S. Census of Floyd County in 1850:

Ann Mayo, wife, aged 22, b. in Kentucky.

Jane, aged 16, Jacob, aged 8; Jane, aged 2; Mary E., aged 1 month.

JOHN CALDWELL CALHOUN MAYO, industrialist, was b. in Pike County, Kentucky, September 16, 1864, and d. in Paintsville, Johnson County, Kentucky, May 11, 1914. When four years of age his parents, Thomas Jefferson Mayo and Elizabeth (Leslie) Mayo moved to Johnson County. He attended the public schools in Johnson County and in 1883 was graduated from Kentucky Wesleyan College then located at Millersburg, now at Winchester. He worked his way through that institution by teaching mathematics. Afterwards he engaged in teaching in the rural schools of Johnson and Pike Counties. Even when a student he had decided ideas regarding the development of the natural resources of Eastern Kentucky; and as is admitted by all, he became prominent in the development of the coal industry in that section of the state.

Having taken options on vast quantities of coal lands, he consumated his first important deal in the development of his coal properties when in 1901 he effected the organization of the Northern Coal & Coke Company. Subsequently he organized other companies. In 1913 the Elkhorn Fuel Company was organized and took over several of the holdings of these other companies. Later the Elkhorn Coal Corporation was organized which took over the holdings of the Elkhorn Fuel Company and other companies which Mr. Mayo had acquired. He was interested in the Williams Coal & Coke Corporation, the Toms Creek Coal Company and had other holdings at the head of the Kentucky River. Finally a number of corporations in which he was interested were combined under the name of the Kentucky River Coal Company. The agreements for this merger were made before his death but illness prevented his signing the final papers.

Mr. Mayo was a dominant figure in the Democratic party in Kentucky but he never sought public office. He was National Committeeman from Kentucky at date of death.

He m. Miss Alice Meek, daughter of Green Meek, a well-known timberman of Paintsville and owner of a line of steamboats operating on the Big Sandy River. Two children were born to them: John C. C., Jr., and Mary Margaret.

Mr. Mayo passed away May 11, 1914, and he was buried in Paintsville. Many distinguished men attended the funeral which was the largest and most notable ever held in Eastern Kentucky.

[1] William Ely, "The Big Sandy Valley," p. 83.
[2] Scalf, "Historic Floyd, 1800-1950", p. 27.
[3] William Ely, "The Big Sandy Valley", p. 83.

MEADE FAMILY OF JOHNSON COUNTY

Meade

This name was taken from the old Anglo-Saxon "maed," which meant "mowed or cut down—a meadow". The Meades of Ireland trace the name to the old Irish "Meagh." The family of Meades were seated in the county of Cork, Ireland, for many centuries. At Meadstown, in that county, there was formerly a great castle built by the Meades.

The first of the family in America was Andrew Meade of County Kerry, Ireland. He landed in New York where he met and married Mary Latham of Flushing, Long Island. Five years afterward he removed to Virginia and settled in Nansemond county. He left two children, a son and a daughter. David, the son, m. Susanna Everard, daughter of Governor Everard of North Carolina.

Richard Meade, the son of Edward, the immigrant, was aide to General Washington during the Revolution. He was with the commander in chief in all the important battles, and it is recorded that the great general held him in high esteem and warmest affection. At the close of the war, on taking leave of his soldiers, he said to Colonel Meade: "Friend Dick, you must go on a Virginia Plantation. You will make a good farmer and an honest foreman of the grand jury of your county." This advice was followed and the prediction verified.

Families of Mead, Meade, Meed, lived in all the thirteen original colonies in early days.

The Meades intermarried with some of the most outstanding families of America.

The Meade Family of the Oil Springs vicinity, Johnson county, Kentucky.

The progenitor of this branch of the Meade family was Samuel Meade who probably was b. in Scotland and was of Scottish extraction. He emigrated from Scotland and settled in Floyd county, Kentucky. He m.—the name of his wife not learned.

1. SAMUEL MEADE, m. ——— ———.
Children:
*2. Samuel Meade.
*3. Robert Meade.
   Keziah Meade, m. in Floyd county, April 24, 1823, Thomas
Blackburn Akers.
*5. Thomas Meade.
*6. Rhoades Meade.
7. Elizabeth Meade, b. 1802, d. 1870; m. John Baldridge.
8. Katy Meade, b. 1804; m. ——— Cannady. (Kennedy?)
9. Ibby Meade, b. 1806.

2. SAMUEL MEADE, b. in South Carolina in 1794; m. in Floyd
county, Kentucky, August 5, 1813?, Prica Hall.
Children:
10. Zilpha Meade.

3. ROBERT (BIG BOB) MEADE, b. 1796, d. 1869; m. in Floyd
county, July 6, 1823, Susie Clark, daughter of Samuel Clark.
Children:
11. Polly Meade, b. 1826; m. 1844; d. 1865.
12. Peggie Margaret Meade, m. James Williams (See Williams
Family).
13. Katy Meade. b. 1830: d. 1900.
14. Leanna Meade, b. 1832; d. 1863.
*15. Samuel Meade.
16. John Meade. b. 1836; m. 1867; d. 1895.
17. Hulda Meade, b. 1838; m. 1862; d. 1895
*18. Robert Meade, Jr.
*19. Rhoades Meade.
20. Joe Meade. b. 1846; d. February 18, 1869.
21. James K. P. Meade, b. 1844; d. 1865.
*22. Leeash B. Meade.
23. Susie Meade, b. 1850; d. 1864.
24. Elizabeth Meade, b. 1852; d. 1870.

5. THOMAS MEADE, b. in Floyd county in 1798; m. Mary (Polly)
Hall, daughter of Samuel Hall.
Children:
25. Rhoades Meade.
26. Ruby Meade.
27. Madison Meade.
28. Riley Meade.
29. Albert Meade.
30. Christena Meade.
31. Kate Meade.

32. Polly Meade.
33. Rachel Meade.

6. RHOADES (BIG RHOADES) MEADE, b. in Floyd county 1800, d. 1865; m., Sarah (Sally) Richardson, daughter of Daniel Richardson.

Children:
34. Robert Meade.
35. Lemuel Meade.
36. Mack Meade.
37. Rhoades Meade, Jr.
38. John P. Meade.
39. Thomas Meade.
40. Kate Meade, m. Fred Williams (See Williams Family).
41 Ibby Meade.

15. SAMUEL MEADE, b. in Floyd county, in 1832; m., Polly Gearhart, daughter of Robert Gearhart.

Children:
*42. George Meade.
43. Robert Meade, m. ——— Thompson.
44. Mary Meade, m. Frank Parsons.
45. Jane Meade, m. Jack Hale.
46. Susie Meade, m. William Parsons.
47. Nannie Meade, m. ——— Gross.

18. ROBERT MEADE, JR., b. 1840; m. 1864, Catherine Litteral, daughter of Horton Litteral.

Children:
48. Florence Meade, b. 1865; m. James Murphy.
49. Elizabeth Meade, b. 1867; m. Jack George.
50. Cynthia Meade, b. 1869; m. Elliott Gullett.
51. Molly Meade, b. 1873; m. Ben F. Mahan
52 Kate Meade, b. 1875; m. Fred Williams.
*53. Linzie Meade.
*54. John R. Meade.

19. RHOADES MEADE, b. in Floyd county, 1842; m., 1866, Elizabeth Conley, b. 1845, daughter of David Conley.

Children:
*55. John C. Meade.
56. Sam Meade, b. 1869.
57. Mahala Meade, b. 1871; m. Isaac Conley.
58. Barnes Meade, b. 1873.
*59. Crate Meade.
*60. Leck Meade.
61. Susie Meade, b. 1879; m. Manford Conley.

22. LEEASH B. MEADE, b. in Floyd county, October 7, 1848; m. in 1870, Ellen Howard, b. March 17, 1853, daughter of William Howard.

Children:
62. Jacob Meade, b. November 11, 1870; d. October 12, 1878.
63. Susie Meade, b. March 15, 1874; d. June 5, 1890.
64. Augie Meade, b. November 24, 1877; m. William T. Pelfrey.
65. Eunice Meade, b. May 4, 1881; d. December 4, 1894.
*66. Joe Meade.
*67. Bradley Meade.
68. Terman Meade, b. March 7, 1890; m. ——— Hall.
69. Henry Meade, b. March 10, 1901; m. Sarah Gipson.
*70. Kate Meade.
71. Robert Meade, b. October 28, 1906.

42. GEORGE MEADE, m. Sip Harkins.
Children:
72. Joe Meade.
73. Crate Meade.
74. Eunice Meade.
75. James Meade; m. ——— Stambaugh.

53. LINZIE MEADE, m. Mary Coldiron.
Children:
76. Ora Meade, m. John Strator.
77. Robert Meade, m. Mamie Ferguson.
78. Hagar Meade.
79. Mabel Meade.
80. Guy Meade.

54. JOHN R. MEADE, m. Katy Litteral.
Children:
81. Frank Meade.
82. Jennie Meade, m. ——— Nickel.
83. Mamie Meade.
84. Anna Meade

55. JOHN C. MEADE, m. Mary Estep.
Children:
*85. Wannie Meade.
86. Rhoades Meade, m. Ann Williams.
87. Andrew Meade, m. ——— Cooper.
88. George Meade, m. ——— Williams.

59. CRATE MEADE, a successful farmer; resided on Jennie's Creek, two miles from Paintsville; and prospered by the oil development in the county; b. in 1875, d. June, 1928; m. Minta Lemaster.

Children:
89. Taylor Meade, m. ———— Witten.
90. Hobert Meade, m. Edna Mae Spears. (See Preston Family).
91. Carmina Meade, m. Raymond Conley.
92. Polk Meade.
93. ———— Meade.

60. Leck Meade, m. Julia Howard.
Children:
94. Fred Meade, m. ———— Caudill.
95. Evert Meade.
96. Joe Meade.
97. Nancy Meade, m. Holly Lemaster.

66. Joe Meade, b. in Magoffin county, July 14, 1885; m. Nannie Wheeler.
Children:
98. Arnold Meade.
99. Beulah Meade.
100. Eugene Meade.
101. Lydia Meade.
102. Robert Meade.

67. Bradley Meade, b. in Magoffin county, September 22, 1888; m. Nona Williams, daughter of Steve Williams.
Children:
103. Verlie Meade.
104. Hazel Meade.

70. Kate Meade, b. in Morgan county, Kentucky, December 18, 1903; m. ———— 1923, Rutherford Price, son of G. W. Price.
Children:
105. Mary Lou Price, b. 1924.
106. Marion Lee Price, b. 1926.

85. Wannie Meade, m. Mary Wheeler.
Children:
107. Roly Meade.
108. Tally Meade.
109. Lloyd Meade.

Meade family of the vicinity of Greasy Creek, Johnson county, Kentucky.
1. Fielden Meade, m. ———— Thacker.
Children:
*2. Henry P. Meade.

2. Henry P. Meade, b. at Castlewood, Russell county, Va., d. in Johnson county, Kentucky in 1860; m. Elizabeth Hicks, d. in 1896, daughter of Charles Hicks.

Children:
3. Charles Meade, m. —— Hofferlin.
4. Fielden Meade, m. Nancy Osborn.
5. W. R. Meade, m. Nancy Ghost.
6. Cree Meade, m. Ellen Willis.
7. Thomas Meade, m. —— Ghost.
*8. Henry P. Meade.
*9. T. J. Meade.
10. Martha Meade, m. John Pack.
11. Elizabeth Meade, m. Ransom Ward. (See Ward Family).

8. Henry P. Meade, b. at Castlewood, Russell county, Virginia, in 1846, d. in Johnson county, Kentucky, January 23, 1919. He had service in the Confederate Army and soon after the close of the War, in 1867, he removed from Virginia to Johnson county, Kentucky, and settled on Greasy Creek where he subsequently lived and died. He was a successful school teacher. In 1871, in Johnson county, he m. Zina Davis, b. 1854, daughter of Joe Davis.

Children:
*12. Dr. Paris P. Meade.
13. Dr. Joseph D. Meade, a poet; m. Jemima Price
*14. Walter Meade.
*15. Dora Meade.
*16. Dr. Lloyd G. Meade.
17. Elizabeth Meade.
18. George C. Meade.
10. Vina Meade.
20. May Meade.
21. Byron Meade, d. 1904.

9. T. J. Meade, b. in Virginia, 1850, d. in Johnson county, 1928; m. Rittie Boyd. When a boy he, accompanied by two brothers, came from Russell county, Virginia, to Johnson county, Kentucky, and settled on Greasy Creek, that county.

Children:
22. —— Meade, m. C. C. Ward.
23. W. R. Meade
24. Nollis Meade, m. —— Ward.
25. G. B. Meade.

12. Dr. Paris P. Meade, a physician of Flat Gap, Johnson county, b. at Ward City, Johnson county; m., in 1895, Tera Webb, daughter of Crate Webb of Flat Gap.

Children:

26. Neva E. Meade, sometime teacher in the common schools of Johnson county; m. Dr. Proctor J. Evans, a graduate of the Sandy Valley Seminary at Paintsville, and of the School of Dentistry of the University of Louisville at Louisville.

27. Dr. Walter W. Meade.

14. WALTER MEADE, merchant in Indianapolis, Indiana; b. at Ward City, Johnson county; m. in 1900, Lora Grimsley, daughter of Felix Grimsley.

Children:

28. Vera Meade, m. William Lane.

29. Walter E. Meade.

15. DORA MEADE, b. at Ward City, Johnson county; m. B. F. Conley, son of Daniel Conley of Flat Gap, Johnson county; resided at Flat Gap.

Children:

30. Lexie Conley.

31. Herschel Conley.

32. Ray Conley.

33. Fern Conley.

34. Hazel Conley.

35. Merle Conley.

16. DR LLOYD G. MEADE, dentist and businessman, b. at Boons Camp, Johnson county, November 9, 1883; was educated in the common schools of Johnson county and was graduated from the School of Dentistry of the University of Louisville in 1907. Upon graduation he began a successful practice of his profession at Paintsville and also became financially interested in the oil and gas development of Johnson county, and in real estate. He m., in 1905, Beulah Howes, daughter of Henry S. Howes of Paintsville.

Children:

*36. Wendell Howes Meade.

37. Sipp H. Meade.

36. WENDELL HOWES MEADE, lawyer; b. in Paintsville, Johnson County, Kentucky, January 18, 1912; attended the Paintsville schools and was graduated from the high school department of Kentucky Military Institute at Lyndon, Kentucky, in 1929; attended Western State Teachers College, Bowling Green, Kentucky, 1930-1933; engaged in the banking business from 1933 to 1936; graduated from the University of Louisville, Law School, in 1939; was admitted to the bar the same year and commenced practice in Paintsville; during World War 11 served as a lieutenant, U. S. Navy, from Novem-

ber 1943, until January, 1946, of which service twenty months was in the South Pacific; resumed the practice of law; elected as a Repubican to the Eightieth Congress (January 3, 1947—January 3, 1949); unsuccessful candidate for reelection to the Eighty-first Congress; resumed the practice of law in Paintsville. (Biographical Directory of the American Congress, 1774-1949, p. 1553.

FRED MEADE, teacher and public official, was b. at Oil Springs, Johnson County, Kentucky, June 3, 1880; attended the public schools at Oil Springs, East Point and Paintsville and the Eastern Kentucky State Normal School at Richmond; commenced teaching in the public schools of Johnson County at the age of 18 years and continued for 12 years when, in November, 1910, he was elected superintendent of the public schools of Johnson County. He was reelected three times, serving four consecutive terms or 16 years. He dedicated himself to the advancement of the standard of education in the county and his objectives and administration of school affairs were approved by the people as is attested by his long tenure of such an exacting and difficult office.

In 1900 Mr. Meade was united in marriage with Miss Lula M. Butler, a teacher. Children: Augustus E., b. September 26, 1901; Gladys, b. December 24, 1902; June, b. June 1, 1904, m. Crate Rice; Ruth, b. August 6, 1905; May, b. May 6, 1907; Georgia Lee, b. March 8, 1909; Hannibal, b. May 21, 1911; Evert Bruce, b. June 1, 1913; Eloise, b. October 29, 1914; Betty Lou, adopted when three years old, August 5, 1927.

Mr. and Mrs. Meade are members of the Christian Church. Mr. Meade is a Republican in politics and is affiliated with the local lodge of Maccabees. They resided in Paintsville for a time and afterward at Staffordsville, Johnson County.

MEEK FAMILY OF LAWRENCE COUNTY

The Meek family is of Scotch-Irish descent. In 1765 a number of Meek families emigrated from Ulster (Northern) Ireland, landing at Charleston, South Carolina. With these families came other families including Andrew Jackson, Sr. and his wife Elizabeth (Hutchison) Jackson, parents of President Andrew Jackson, both of Scotch-Irish descent.

Reputable historians have stated that Adam Meek was a soldier of the American Revolution, serving in Captain Baker's Company under Colonel Francis Marion of South Carolina. The records show that Moses Meek had service in the Revolutionary War as a private in Captain William Alexander's Troop in the Regiment of Light Dragoons commanded by Lieutenant-Colonel Wade Hampton of South Carolina.

The U. S. Census of South Carolina for 1790 bears the names of Captain Adam Meek, James Meek, Sr., James Meek, Jr., John Meek, Thomas Meek, Athi Meeks, Jesse Meeks and Littleton Meeks.

According to family tradition James Meek and his brother William migrated from North Carolina to the Big Sandy Valley about 1800 and settled in the vicinity of the present-day Offutt, Johnson county.

1. ADAM MEEK; m. ——— ———.

Children:
*2. James Meek, Sr.

2. JAMES MEEK, SR., One James Meek m. Malinda Price in Floyd County, September 7, 1815.

Children:
*3. William Meek.
*4. James Meek, Jr.

3. WILLIAM MEEK; m. Julia Poplar; resided near the mouth of Greasy Creek, Johnson county.

Children:
*5. Isaac Meek.
6. William Meek. One William Meek m. Peggy McCord in Floyd County, January 24, 1820.
7. ——— Meek; m. Jackson White.
8. Polly Meek; m., August 5, 1832, Preston Hilton (See Hilton Family).
9. George Meek; m. Amelia J. ———.
10. Richard Meek.

4. JAMES MEEK, JR., m., firstly, ——— ———, in ——— county,

—— Hilton; and, secondly, —— ——, in Lawrence County, —— ——.

Children of James Meek, Jr., and —— (Hilton) Meek:
11. Lucinda Meek; m. James (Whitehead) Ward. (See Ward Family).
*12. Ellen Meek.
13. Elizabeth Meek; m. William Ward, Sr. (See Ward Family).
14. Malinda Meek; m. Jonathan Ward, brother of James Ward (See Ward Family).
*15. William Meek.

Children of James Meek, Jr., and —— ——.
16. Jesse Meek, Jr.
*17. —— Meek.
18. Jacob Meek.
19. John Meek.
20. Richard Meek.

5. ISAAC MEEK; m., in Floyd County, June 19, 1828, Sally Ward; lived and d. near the mouth of Toms Creek.
Children:
21. Juda Meek; m. Charles Hilton (See Hilton Family).
*22. William Meek.
23. Zephaniah Meek.
24. Pauline Meek.
25. Zinia Meek.
26. Shadrack Meek.
27. Sallie Meek; m. C. C. Price (See Price Family).
*28. Jesse Meek.
29. Greenville Meek, b. 1847, d. 1901; m. Hulda Price (See Price Family).
30. Vinnier Meek.
31. Exer Meek; m. M. L. K. Wells (See Wells Family).

12. ELLEN MEEK; m., firstly, Andrew Francis; and secondly, —— Johnson.
Children of Ellen Meek and —— Johnson:
*32. Epperson Johnson.

15. WILLIAM MEEK, m., in Lawrence county, September 5, 1833, Elizabeth Mollett.
Children:
33. Rev. Nathan Meek; m. Columbia Webb.
34. Susan Meek; m. Richard Wells. (See Wells Family).
35. Ellis Meek.
36. Mary Meek; m. Marion Booth.
37. Elizabeth Meek; m. William Ward. (See Ward Family).

38. John Meek.
39. Julia Meek; m. Preston Hall.
40. Davis Meek.
41. Jane Meek; m. Moses Stepp of Martin county.

17. ——— Meek; m. ——— Lauhon.
Children:
42. Tot Lauhon; m. Mayme Elliott.

22. William Meek; m. ——— ———.
Children:
43. Zephaniah Meek; m. Elizabeth Osborn.

23. Rev. Zephaniah Meek, D.D., distinguished minister of the Methodist Episcopal Church, South, and publisher, was b. in Johnson county in 1833. Having in his boyhood days but few opportunities to procure an education, he used these the best he could, and supplemented the lack of high-schools and academies by reading and studying the best books obtainable by loan or purchase. By systematic study, consecutively pursued, he was at thirty superior in knowledge and mental culture to almost any of his age in his native county. In early life he taught school, like most men who have come to prominence; acted as county and circuit court clerk for Johnson county and for some years engaged in mercantile business and speculated in oil and made considerable money; removed to Catlettsburg, Boyd county, in 1865 and made investments there; established, in the Spring of 1867, edited and published at Catlettsburg the *Christian Observer,* subsequently called the *Central Methodist,* a sixteen-page paper, as the organ of his Church; published for the author, William Ely, history of the "Big Sandy Valley", 1887.

Rev. Meek received the degree of D.D. from the Kentucky Military Institute, Farmdale, Kentucky, in 1885. He m., in Johnson County, *November, 18, 1854,* Mary Jane Davis.
Children:
44. Rev. LaFayette Meek, minister of the Methodist Episcopal Church, South; educated in East Kentucky Normal School, Millersburg College and Vanderbilt University, finishing the course in the School of Theology in the latter; entered the ministry in Tennessee where he was stricken with Typhoid fever; returned to Catlettsburg, Kentucky, where he d. October 2, 1885, at the age of thirty-one years.
45. Davis Meek; resided at Catlettsburg.
46. ——— Meek.
47. Hessie Meek.

28. Jesse Meek, b. 1842; m. Martha Neibert, b. 1849, daughter of James Neibert; resided for many years at White House, Johnson

County, where he engaged in farming and "Steamboating" until the construction of the railroad up Big Sandy when he removed to near Paintsville at the mouth of Big Paint Creek.

Children:

*48. James N. Meek.
49. Hattie Meek, d. January 2, 1928, m. Jasper Maynard.
50. Green Meek.
*51. Mary Meek.

32. EPPERSON JOHNSON, m. ———; resided for a number of years near the Concord Church, Thelma, Johnson county.

Children:

*52. John Johnson.
53. ——— Johnson.
54. Gladys Johnson; m. Homer Castle.

48. JAMES N. MEEK, sometime teacher and college professor, merchant and coal operator, b. in Johnson county, March 17, 1870; began his career of teaching in the rural schools of Johnson county and subsequently was an instructor in Marshall College, Barbourville, West Virginia; conducted a general merchandise store at White House, Johnson county, later moving to Thealka, that county, where he operated a store until about 1922. Becoming interested in coal mining, he opened up and operated for a number of years a coal mine at the mouth of Greasy Creek, Johnson county, and later acquired and operated some coal mines on Beaver Creek, Floyd county.

Mr. Meek served as mayor of Paintsville, was active in politics for some time and was a leader of the Democratic party.

He m., in Johnson county, in 1905, Victoria Salyer, daughter of William Salyer.

Children:

55. Ernest Meek.
56. Walter Meek.
57. J. N. Meek, Jr.

51. MARY MEEK; m. J. H. Matney. They owned and operated a general store at Thealka for many years and, disposing of the store, they moved to Paintsville where Mr Matney conducted a taxi and bus service.

Children:

58. Mary Catherine Matney; m. ——— Foley.

52. JOHN JOHNSON; m., firstly, ———.

Children:

59. Inez Johnson.
60. Mary May Johnson.
61. John Johnson, Jr.

John Johnson, m., secondly, Lyda (Preston) Stambaugh.

MOBLEY FAMILY OF CARTER AND ELLIOTT COUNTIES

Samuel Mobley was the ancestor of the Mobley family of Northeastern Kentucky. Family tradition supported by some documentary evidence is that in the early 1820s three brothers Mobley left Pennsylvania for Frankfort, Kentucky, to visit an uncle who, according to the information available and obtained, was Gen. John Adair, the then Governor of Kentucky. They travelled by flatboat down the Ohio River and when Catlettsburg, Kentucky, was reached, one of the brothers, Samuel, left the boat and decided and proceeded to finish the journey to Frankfort on foot so as to get a better view of the famous Bluegrass region. On reaching the site of present Willard, he stopped as snow about four feet deep had just fallen, which made further travel impossible. By the time the snow had cleared away he had been employed by the parents of the community to teach a three-month subscription (select) school; and while so engaged, he met, wooed and married Elizabeth Talitha Thompson. He never finished the journey to Frankfort nor heard from his brothers again.

1. SAMUEL MOBLEY, farmer and teacher, was b. in Pennsylvania about 1804 and d. in Carter County, Kentucky, in 1839 at the age of 35 years. He m. Elizabeth Talitha Thompson in Lawrence County, now Carter County, Kentucky, August 16, 1822. Soon after marriage they settled on a grant of land in present Carter County on the Little Sandy River near the mouth of Bruin. The records disclose that Samuel Mobley, Talitha Mobley and Samuel Mobley's heirs received grants of five tracts of land, aggregating 1563 acres, situated on the Little Sandy River and on Clifty and Big Sinking Creek in Carter County. The original homestead is in possession of their descendants.

TALITHA (THOMPSON) MOBLEY was b. in Kentucky, 1804 or 1805, and d. in Carter County in 1850 or 1851 at the age of 46 years.

Children (Second Generation):

*2. Harris W. Mobley.
*3. William Mobley
*4. Thomas T. Mobley.
*5. Samuel Mobley.
*6. Elizabeth Mobley.

2. HARRIS W. MOBLEY, (MOBBERLY), farmer, was b. in Lawrence County, August 8, 1828, and d. in Carter County, December 9, 1901. He was thrice m., first in Carter County, July 17, 1849, to Malinda Lowe, b. 1833, daughter of William Lowe.

Children (Third Generation):

7. Talitha Mobley; b. about 1855; m. Travis Henry ("Riggs") Horton. (See Horton Family.)
8. William Mobley; b. 1857; m. Eliza Horton, daughter of William L. and Ellen Horton. (See Horton Family.)

9. James Mobley; b. 1860; m. Cena Kitchen, daughter of Major Andrew J. Kitchen and granddaughter of James Kitchen, Revolutionary War soldier who came with his family from Greenbrier County, Virginia, (now West Virginia) and settled near present Willard, Carter County, in the early 1820s.

10. Sarah Mobley; b. 1863; m. David Walker.

HARRIS W. MOBLEY, m., secondly, Mary Miller, daughter of Harvey Miller. Children (Third Generation):

11. Mellie Mobley; m. Edd. King, son of Marion King. (See Horton Family.)

HARRIS W. MOBLEY m., thirdly, Martha Horton, daughter of Reese and Susan Horton. (See Horton Family.)

Children (Third Generation):

12. Thompson Mobley; m. Laura Davis, daughter of John and Sarilda Davis.

13. Charles Mobley; m. Tishie Green, daughter of W. W. (Wag) Green.

*14. Lucy Mobley; m. George B. (Bud) Harper.

3. WILLIAM T. MOBLEY, farmer, surveyor and for many years a justice of the peace of Carter County, was b. about 1835 and d. at an advanced age; m. in Carter County, December 10, 1855, Amanda S. Elliott, daughter of Samuel R. and Minerva Elliott and granddaughter of Capt. John Lisle Elliott. (See Elliott Family.)

Children (Third Generation):

15. Samuel Mobley, farmer, justice of the peace and one time an employee at the Kentucky Penitentiary at Frankfort, m. Laura Cole, daughter of Sampson Cole. Children, among others (Fourth Generation): Roy Mobley and Maud Mobley. Late in life, Samuel Mobley with his family went to Oregon.

*16. Thomas T. Mobley.

17. Mary Mobley; m. John B. Reeves.

18. Martha Mobley; m. George E. Green.

19. Nerva Mobley; m. Leander Binion.

20. Talitha Mobley; m. John Porter.

4. THOMAS T. MOBLEY, farmer; b. 1832; had service in the Confederate Army; was made a third corporal October 19, 1861; promoted to lieutenant of Captain Blevins' Company, January 17, 1862, and promoted to Captain, Company "K", 5th Regiment Kentucky Infantry (consolidated) October 20, 1862; m. about 1855 Elizabeth (Betty) Gillespie, b. 1836.

Children and approimate dates of birth as shown by the U. S. Census of Elliott County for 1870, and other records. (Third Generation):

21. Winston Mobley; b. 1856.

22. Talitha Mobley; b. 1864; m. James Duvall.
23. Mary Mobley; b. 1866; m. William Clark.
24. Reese Mobley; b. 1869; m. Carrie Miller.
26. Charles Mobley; unm.
27. Lec. Mobley, dec'd; unm.

5. SAMUEL MOBLEY, farmer; b. 1826; m. Sabra King, b. about 1823, daughter of Elias King.

Children and approximate dates of birth as shown by the U. S. Census of Carter County for 1860 and 1870, and other records. (Third Generation):
28. Sarah Mobley; b. 1858; m. John Kitchen.
29. Susan Mobley; b. 1860.
30. Malinda Mobley; b. 1864.
31. Mary Mobley; b. 1866; m. Robert Green.
32. Loretta Mobley, b. about 1848; m. Charles Kitchen.
*33. James Mobley; m. Bertha Horton. (See Horton Family)

6. ELIZABETH MOBLEY; b. 1834; m. Houston King, son of Elias King. (See Elias King in Horton Family.)

14. LUCY MOBLEY m. George B. (Bud) Harper, a son of James and a grandson of Davy Harper who came from Virginia and settled in Carter County. He had one son and two daughters: (a) Louisa Harper m. James Tolliver; (b) "Tude" Harper m. a Mr. Burton; and (c) James Harper; m. Polly Lowe, daughter of William and Martha Lowe; and they had seven children: Con Harper who m. Susan Horton, daughter of Travis Henry (Riggs) and Talitha Horton; Willie Harper who m. Goldie Fraley, daughter of Fulton and Mary (Green) Fraley; Martha Harper who m. John Blankenbeckler; Mandy Harper who m. Charles Goodman, son of Louis and Sarah Goodman; Lulu Harper who m. Dee Whitt, son of Ned and Mary Whitt; Dollie Harper who d., unm.; and George B. (Bud) Harper.

The children of George B. (Bud) Harper and Lucy (Mobley) Harper are:
*34. Ernest W. Harper.
35. James Ray Harper who m. Beatrice McDavid, daughter of Jesse and Rebecca McDavid.
36. Teddy D. Harper who d. December 4, 1953, at age of 51 years; unm.
37. Charles Thompson Harper who d. January 28, 1933, at the age of 22 years, unm.
38. Ralph Edward Harper.
39. George B. Harper, Jr.; d. July 22, 1950, at the age of 33 years; unm.
40. Sadie B. Harper; m. Charles Adams, son of George W. and Martha (McDavid) Adams.

41. Myrtle Harper; m. James S. Hudgins, son of Thomas W. and Florence (Porter) Hudgins.

42. Dorothy Fay Harper; m. Thomas W. Hudgins, Jr., son of Thomas W. and Florence (Porter) Hudgins. Thomas W. Hudgins, Sr., was a son of Dr. Thomas W. Hudgins I and his wife, Lee (Loving) Hudgins.

43. Martha Sue Sarper; m. Clyde Williams, son of Daw and Ella Keeton Williams.

34. ERNEST W. HARPER, onetime teacher, traveling salesman and a businessman, was educated in the rural schools of Carter County and at the Grayson (Kentucky) Normal School where he was prepared for teaching; began teaching in the public schools of Carter County in 1912 at the age of 18 and continued until he entered the military service in World War I. After discharge from the army he entered the employ of the Liggett & Myers Tobacco Company as traveling salesman and continued in that capacity until 1948 when he organized and established a wholesale tobacco business in Ashland, Kentucky, incorporated as the Ohio Valley Tobacco Company. He has since conducted the affairs of the company.

Mr. Harper never married. His present business address is 1308 Greenup Avenue, Ashland, Kentucky.

16. THOMAS THOMPSON MOBLEY, farmer, onetime teacher and public official, was b. at Bruin, Carter County, Kentucky; was educated in the public schools and began teaching at the age of sixteen and taught in the public schools of Carter and Elliott for a number of years. He is a Democrat in politics and during a long life he has been active and influential in local political affairs. He has held many public offices of honor and trust and filled all of them creditably and well. He served as superintendent of public schools of Elliott County; was sheriff of the county; and represented the Carter-Elliott district in the State House of Representatives.

Mr. Mobley was m. to Rachel R. Reeves, b. March 4, 1870, a daughter of James Franklin and Mahala (Haney) Reeves. (See Reeves Family.)

Children. Fourth Generation:

44. Bessie Mobley, teacher, now retired; b. at Bruin, Kentucky, March 12, 1890, educated in the public schools and at the Grayson (Kentucky) Normal School where she was prepared for teaching; taught in the public school for many years; m. J. T. Parsons.

45. Walter Elliott Mobley, onetime teacher, public official and lawyer, was b. at Bruin, Kentucky; educated in the pubic schools and the Grayson (Kentucky Normal School; was graduated from the University of Louisville Law School; taught in the public school for a time; admitted to the bar and practiced law at Sandy Hook, Kentucky.

Mr. Mobley is a Democrat and is an active worker and wise counselor in local political affairs. He served as county attorney of

Elliott County for two terms after which he accepted appointment as attorney in the Office of the General Counsel, General Accounting Office, Washington, D. C., and served in that capacity for several years when he retired from the service.

Upon retirement Mr. Mobley returned to his home at Bruin in Elliott County; and since was appointed an attorney in the Kentucky State Highway Department and is presently serving in that capacity. Mr. Mobley never was married.

46. Ellen Mobley, State employee; b. April 19, 1894; educated in the public school and Grayson (Kentucky) Normal School; m. Charles C. Rose, now deceased; presently is an employee of the Kentucky State Highway Department at Frankfort.

47. Harve Weddington Mobley; b. at Bruin, Kentucky, November 22, 1899; educated in the public schools and at the Grayson (Kentucky) Normal School; graduated at University of Kentucky, with degree of A.B., 1924, and degree of M.A., 1926; teacher in the Kentucky schools, 1926-1933.

For many years Mr. Mobley has held responsible positions in the Federal government: U. S. Department of Agriculture, 1935-1937; Social Security Board, 1937-1951. He has held administrative and/or clerical positions in connection with the U. S. Congress since 1952 and is presently with the Hon. Carl D. Perkins, M. C., from 9th Kentucky district.

On September 19, 1926, Mr. Mobley was m. to Miss Mary Alice Greene who was b. at Versailles, Kentucky, January 28, 1907, a daughter of E. L. and Laura Elizabeth (Toll) Greene. Mrs. Mobley was educated at Linlee School at Greendale, Kentucky; the Russell Cave High School; the Picadome High School at Lexington, graduating in 1924; and at the University of Kentucky (1924-25-26).

48. Lena Mobley, teacher; b. at Bruin, Kentucky; educated in the public school and graduated from University of Kentucky with degree of A. B.; has taught in the Kentucky public schools since 1928 and is presently principal of the Hazard (Kentucky) Central Graded School; m. to Joe Foley.

49. Joe V. Mobley; b. at Bruin, Kentucky, August 9, 1907; educated in the public schools and graduated at University of Kentucky with degree of A. B., 1927; presently is State employe, serving in the Internal Revenue Department at Frankfort; m. Lillian Redwine.

50. Ruth Mobley, postmaster at Sandy Hook; b. at Bruin, Kentucky, February 3, 1913; m. John A. Keck.

John A. Keck, lawyer and judge; was graduated from the University of Louisville Law School; admitted to the bar and located at Sandy Hook for the practice of his profession; was appointed and served for some time as head of the Kentucky State Highway Department; resigned; was elected Circuit Judge of his judicial district and is presently serving in that capacity. Judge Keck is a Democrat in politics.

MOORE FAMILY OF LAWRENCE COUNTY

1. FREDERICK MOORE was the progenitor of a branch of the Moore family of Big Sandy Valley in Eastern Kentucky. He was of Teutonic (ancient Germanic) origin. His ancestors settled in or near Philadelphia before the Revolutionary War. Here he was born in 1782. When a young man he married a Miss Van Hoorn, born in 1795, a sister of John Van Horn, well and favorably known on the lower Big Sandy River.

Frederick Moore established and operated a nail factory in Philadelphia which business was disrupted by the War of 1812, when he purchased a stock of goods in Philadelphia, hired his brother-in-law, John Van Horn, as clerk, and leaving his wife and children with relatives in the East, came to present Louisa, Kentucky, in 1815, and became identified with the development of the community. He purchased a large tract of land on which Louisa is situated. Subsequently he purchased a much larger tract on the Virginia side of the Big Sandy which included the site of present Cassville, West Virginia. On this tract about one-half mile below the forks of the river, he built a large brick house as his home. Here his wife and children rejoined him in 1818.

Mr. Moore was prominent and influential in the affairs of the community. He was a farmer, merchant, tanner, saddler, shoemaker and for a short time a distiller. In politics he was a Whig, but was never an office seeker. However, he served as colonel of the State militia, justice of the peace and State representative in the Virginia Legislature. He d. in 1874, aged 92. His wife d. in 1881, aged 86[1]

Children:
*2. Sarah Moore.
*3. Frances Moore.
4. W. F. Moore, the oldest son, was of literary tastes, of extensive reading, and one of the most scientific farmers of Boyd County.
5. Frederick Moore, Jr., the youngest son, was a farmer and lived in Lawrence County.
*6. Laban T. Moore.
7. ——— Moore, a daughter; m. Talton Everett of Guyandotte, Virginia. They reared a large family.
*8. Mary Moore.
*9. Mrs. C. M. Sullivan.
*10. Rebecca A. Moore.

2. SARAH MOORE was b. in Pennsylvania, 1812; m., first, John Poage, iron manufacturer. (See Poage Family.)
Children:
11. ——— Poage, a daughter; m. H. C. Gartrell. Sarah Moore Poage m., secondly, Pleasant Savage, merchant, b. in Virginia, 1789.
Children living at home and approximate dates of birth as shown by U. S. Census of Lawrence County for the year 1860:

12. Mary Savage; b. 1850.
*13. Samuel S. Savage; b. 1852.
14. Alfred Savage; b. 1853; was a contractor.
15 Franklin Savage; b. 1855; was a banker for sometime and then engaged in merchandising in Cincinnati.
16. Sarah Savage; b. 1857.

3. FRANCES MOORE; m. W. T. Nichols, a prominent businessman, first at Louisa, and then at Catlettsburg and finally at Ashland.
Children:
────── Nichols, a daughter, who m. a gentleman who resided in Brooklyn, New York.

6. HONORABLE LABAN THEODORE MOORE, lawyer, was b. in Wayne County, Virginia (now West Virginia), near Louisa, Kentucky, January 13, 1829; attended Marshall Academy now Marshall College) and was graduated from Marietta College, Marietta, Ohio; attended Transylvania Law College, Lexington, Kentucky; was admitted to the bar in 1849, and commenced practice at Louisa; was unsuccessful candidate on the Whig ticket for State representative, 1857; elected as a National American to the Thirty-sixth Congress (March 4, 1859-March 3, 1861); was not a candidate for re-nomination in 1860; during the Civil War raised and enlisted the Fourteenth Regiment, Kentucky Volunteer Infantry of which he was elected colonel, November 19, 1861, and resigned, January 1, 1862; located at Catlettsburg in 1863 where he resumed the practice of law; became a Democrat after the Civil War, having voted for McClelland for President in 1864; was a State senator in 1881 and a member of the State Constitutional Convention, 1890-91; d. in Catlettsburg, Kentucky, November 9, 1892; interment in Ashland Cemetery, Ashland, Kentucky.[2]
Colonel Moore m. Sallie E. or Sarah Everett, b. in Virginia, 1828 or 1829, daughter of Colonel John Everett of Guyandotte, Virginia.
Children living at home and approximate dates of birth as shown by U. S. Census for Lawrence County for 1860 and Boyd County for 1870:
18. Felicia E. Moore; b. 1851.
19. Mary F. Moore; b. 1853.
20. Lida G. Moore; b. 1855.
21. Minnie H. Moore; b. 1857.

8. MARY MOORE; b. in Virginia, 1817 or 1818; m. Thomas Wallace, merchant and trader, b. in Ohio, 1812.
Children living at home and approximate dates of birth as shown by U. S. Census of Lawrence County for 1850 and 1860:
22. Eleanor R. Wallace; b. 1833.
23. Elizabeth C. Wallace; b. 1835.
24. Permelia A. B. Wallace; b. 1842.

*25. Fred R. W. Wallace; b. 1844
26. Charity A. Wallace; b. 1847.
27. Elvessa Wallace; b. 1849.
28. Frances Wallace; b. 1851.
29. Eugene Wallace; b. 1853.
30. Grace Wallace; b. 1858.

9. —— Moore; m. Rev. C. M. Sullivan, distinguished minister of the Methodist Episcopal Church, South, who died soon after the close of the Civil War. They had three sons, and resided at Louisa.

10. Rebecca A. Moore, the youngest daughter, b. in Virginia, 1834; m. about 1853, George W. Gallup.

GEORGE W. GALLUP, lawyer, was b. in New York, about 1829, and located at South Point, Ohio, in 1850, where he engaged in teaching school; subsequently he located at Louisa, Kentucky, where he studied law, was admitted to the bar and formed a partnership for the practice of his profession with his brother-in-law, Laban T. Moore, which partnership continued until 1861. A strong Union man during the Civil War, he was made regimental quartermaster of the Fourteenth Kentucky Regiment, Volunteer Infantry, when the regiment was formed in October, 1861; was promoted to lieutenant-colonel, May 11, 1862; promoted to colonel, January 13, 1863.[3]

Returning home to Louisa after the close of the War, Col. Gallup did not engage in the practice of law, but engaged in the milling and lumbering business. He removed to Catlettsburg and became a contractor in construction of the Chesapeake and Ohio and the Keys Creek Mining Railroads; was appointed postmaster at Catlettsburg by President Hayes and was serving as such at time of his death in 1881.

Colonel Gallup acted with the Democrats for a short time after the Civil War. He was defeated on the Democratic Ticket for State senator and subsequently acted with the Republicans. He was a member of the Methodist Church, South, and was affiliated with several benevolent orders.

Children living at home and approximate dates of birth as shown by U. S. Census of Boyd County for 1860:

31. Henry M. Gallup; b. 1854.
32. Frederick B. Gallup; b. 1855; succeeded his father as postmaster at Catlettsburg.

(Gallup, Kentucky, Lawrence County, is named for this family.)

13. SAMUEL S. SAVAGE, lawyer; after death of his father, Pleasant Savage, at Louisa in 1862, removed with the family to Catlettsburg, where he studied law, practiced for several years and served as police judge. He removed to Ashland; was elected as a Democrat and served as judge of the Boyd County Court; and was a prominent and influential citizen. A wife and several children survived him.

1 William Ely, "The Big Sandy Valley," pages 28-44.
2 Biographical Directory of the American Congress, 1774-1949, page 1592.
3 Report of the Adjutant General of Kentucky, 1861-1865, Vol. I, page 872.

MORRIS FAMILY OF FLOYD AND CARTER COS.

There have been many explanations propounded to account for the name Morris. Some authorities claim it is derived from the personal name Maurice; others that is comes from Moorish, and originally indicated a person of dark complexion, like a Moor; and yet others, probably the majority, claim that the name is derived from the Welsh word mawr-rhys (mawr meaning great and rhys, a warrior) which denotes a great hero. Although the name may have originated in Wales, the family of Morris has been well established in England, Scotland, and Ireland for many generations and were numerous in all the American colonies prior to the Revolutionary War.

The Morris Family of Eastern Kentucky

According to family tradition a John Morris was the progenitor of a branch of the Morris Family of Eastern Kentucky. Apparently he was of Scotch-Irish extraction. He m. at Limerick, Ireland, Mary McCloud. Soon after marriage he and his wife emigrated from Ireland to America and settled in Patrick County, Virginia. Subsequently members of the family migrated to Floyd County, Kentucky.

The earliest available records of Floyd County show a large family of Morrises living in that county. Mary Morris, head of a household and apparently a widow, was living in Floyd County in 1810 with her four children—two sons and two daughters. She was then over 45 years of age. Apparently other of her children had already married and established homes of their own.

1. MARY MORRIS, b. in Virginia, about 1760, d. in Floyd County, Kentucky, within the interim 1820-1830; m. in Virginia about 1774, John Morris (probably). The records would seem to indicate that they had seven children:
  *2. Benjamin Morris.
  *3. Ezekiel Morris; m. Mary Rose, June 17, 1809.
  *4. John Morris.
  *5. Daniel Morris.
   6. Isaac Morris; m. Peggy Oney, July 30, 1826.

7. Elizabeth Morris; m. Isaac Briggs, March 23, 1823.
8. William Morris.

2. BENJAMIN MORRIS was b. in Virginia about 1775 and d. in Carter County, Kentucky, about 1855. He was residing in Prestonsburg, Floyd County, in 1810, when there were only six residents of the town. In 1816 he purchased a tract of land on the Jones fork of the Right Hand fork of Beaver Creek, that county, and subsequently lived there. He m., in Floyd County, March 27, 1808, Elizabeth Jacobs, b. in Virginia, about 1792, d. in Carter County, Kentucky, February 27, 1865, daughter of William Jacobs, Revolutionary War soldier. William Jacobs gave his written consent to the marriage of his daughter, March 25, 1808, and the ceremony was performed by James Patton, a justice of the peace, "according to the rights and privileges of the Christian Church". (See William Jacobs Family.)
Children, among others:
9. Elizabeth Morris; m. James Easterling, September 18, 1829.
10. Ezekiel Morris, b. in Floyd County, Kentucky, about 1812, was emancipated by his father, Benjamin Morris, August 2, 1831, so that he might engage in business for himself.
*11. Henry Cloud Morris.
*12. Louanna Morris.
13. William Morris; b. about 1820.
13½. Elizabeth Morris; b. 1834.

4. JOHN MORRIS, b. in Virginia in 1782, d. in Floyd County, Kentucky, about 1864. He was a farmer, a good citizen, and for many years was a highly respected preacher in the Baptist Church. He m., first, in Floyd County, May 9, 1811, Mary Gearhart. The records would seem to indicate that he m., secondly, Naomi ———, b. in Virginia about 1805.
Children living at home in 1850, as shown by the U. S. Census of Floyd County for that year:
14. Zachariah Morris, b. about 1830.
15. Sarah Morris, b. about 1832.
16. Seatta Morris, b. about 1834.
17. Amy Morris, b. about 1837.
18. Biddy Morris, b. about 1839.
19. Ezekiel Morris, b. about 1843.

11. HENRY CLOUD MORRIS, a farmer and Baptist preacher, was b. in Floyd County, Kentucky, on Friday, February 6, 1825, and d. at Jacobs, Carter County, Kentucky in 1907. He had service in the Union Army in the Civil War as a corporal, Campany "I", 22nd Kentucky Infantry. He m., first, in Carter County, Kentucky, September 3, 1852, Nancy Eddington Burchett, b. January 15, 1835, and d. in Carter County, March 17, 1865, a daughter of Burrell Burchett and his wife, Sarah (Easterling) Burchett.[1] After her death he was

thrice married. He m., secondly, April 25, 1867, Mrs. Margaret McKinney, who d. November 4, 1883; third, May 16, 1884, Mrs. Margaret A. Underwood, who d. February 26, 1896; and, fourth, September 28, 1896, Mrs. Annie Wells. There were no children by these marriages.

Children:
*20. William Morris.
*21. John Green Morris.
*22. Burrell Morris.
23. Lucy Morris; m. William E. Robinson. (See Robinson Family.)
*24. Elizabeth Morris.
25. Annie Marie Morris, b. February 21, 1865, d. February 28, 1865.

18. WILLIAM MORRIS, farmer, sometime school teacher and a minister of the Baptist Church, was b. in Carter County, Kentucky, July 29, 1853, and d. in Iowa in October, 1901. In young manhood he was engaged for a short time as teacher in the public schools of Carter County. He m., in 1879, Lourana (or Lou) Martin of Morehead, Rowan County, Kentucky, and the following year he migrated with his family to Colyer, Trego County, Kansas, where he took up a homestead. While perfecting title to his homestead, he engaged in teaching school at Colyer. Later he removed with his family to Holton, Jackson County, Kansas, where his wife d. in May, 1889. Subsequently he removed to Iowa where he lived until his death in October, 1901.

Issue: Five Children:
*26. Melvina Genoa Morris.
*27. Benjamin Frederick Cloude Morris.
*28. Florence Anne Morris.
*29. William Alexander Morris.
*30. Maude Irene Morris.

26. MELVINA GENOA MORRIS, artist and poet, was b. at Holton, Kansas, January 13, 1881. After her mother's death she lived in the home of a maternal uncle, William Martin, at Holton. She was graduated from the Holton (Kansas) High School in 1897, and later studied art at Campbell College, Washburn College and Kansas University. From 1908 to 1911, she was an instructor and head of the department of art at Campbell College. In 1911, she removed to Oklahoma City, Oklahoma, and established and has since conducted a studio of painting there.

In June, 1941, Miss Morris had published by Henry Harrison, Publisher, New York, first edition of her poems in book form entitled "This Is Quivira." The collection includes certain poems which had appeared in various magazines, newspapers and anthologies and others theretofore unpublished. Ten of the poems have received first awards in state and national contests; and the volume of poems has received highly favorable reviews by newspaper and magazine book critics throughout the nation.

Miss Morris is an active member of the Oklahoma Artists' Association, the National League of Penwomen, the Oklahoma Writers and the Oklahoma Poetry Society.

27. BENJAMIN FREDERICK CLOUDE MORRIS, businessman and civic leader, was b. at Colyer, Kansas, November 28, 1882. His family removed to Holton, Kansas, when he was very young; and after the death of his mother, he went with his father to Iowa. He was educated at the Benton County (Iowa) School and at the Madison School at Cedar Rapids. During his youth from his twelfth to his seventeenth year he engaged in various kinds of work: harvest hand, was foreman of culvert construction crew and a bridge carpenter. During this period he became a champion corn-husker; and, in the field of sports, he excelled in boxing and wrestling.

When about 18 years of age, Mr. Morris left the farm and accepted a position as traveling salesman and for the next sixteen years he was traveling salesman for two Kansas City hardware firms, being high salesman for ten years of his last employer.

Entering the business field, in 1917, Mr. Morris organized the Morris Manufacturing Company, taking over in the organization, the One Minute Washer Company of El Reno, Oklahoma. In 1920 he purchased the largest vegetable forcing greenhouse in the Southwest —located at Oklahoma City—operating it successfully until his retirement from active business in 1932. During this period of business activities, he was a director and the treasurer of the Pominok Corporation, a seven and one-half million dollar corporation of Chicago, and a director of the Incubator Manufacturers Association of America. He has served, also, on the Board of Directors of the Oklahoma City Chamber of Commerce.

In religion, Mr. Morris is a Baptist and a member of the First Baptist Church, Oklahoma City. He has served as trustee, deacon and treasurer of his church and has contributed liberally to religious and civic welfare. He has been active in promoting the State Gideons, and for a time he was a Rotarian.

Mr. Morris m., March 11, 1907, Miss L. May Stone of El Reno, Okla., daughter of the late Mr. and Mrs. James K. Stone, Eighty-Niners and granddaughter of Colonel Andrew Austin, Missouri Legislator, who was killed in action at the battle of Wilson's Creek (Missouri).

Children:

31. Robert James Morris was b. in Oklahoma City, May 2, 1908; was graduated from Oklahoma University; m., in June, 1929, Miss Martha Elizabeth Ham, daughter of Dr. M. F. Ham, then minis-

ter of the First Baptist Church at Oklahoma City; d. in Little Rock, Arkansas, at the early age of twenty nine when acting as secretary and business assistant to Dr. Ham, who then was engaged in evangelistic work. They had one child, Robert James Morris, Jr.

32. Eva May Morris was b. in Oklahoma City, Nov. 17, 1910; was graduated from the Oklahoma City High School at the age of 15, and subsequently graduated from Oklahoma City University, the State University (O. U.) at Norman, Oklahoma, and from Miss Mason's School, "The Castle," at Tarrytown, New York. An outstanding student of piano, she rendered a program of ten numbers when only ten years of age. Later she studied under Miss Faye Frumbell for many years; m., in October, 1931, Louis Keith Schaetzle. They reside in Wichita, Kansas, where Mr. Schaetzle is president of the Kansas Morris Plan Bank. Children: Two daughters, Norine and Holly, and a son, Louis Keith, Jr.

33. Adeline Lorraine Morris was b. in Oklahoma City, December 8, 1913; was educated at Classen High School, Oklahoma City, and at Oklahoma City University; m. in June, 1933, Karl Joseph Sladek, a graduate of Oklahoma City University. They live in Centralia, Illinois. Children: Karel Lou and Karl Joseph III.

34. Virginia Morris was b. in Oklahoma City, August 29, 1917; was graduated from the Classen High School, Oklahoma City; m. Joseph Cromwell, only son of Joseph I. Cromwell, Oklahoma oil man. They live in San Antonio, Texas, where Mr. Cromwell is engaged in the oil industry. Children: Joseph Austin, who d. in infancy, and Robert Owen.

35. Benjamin Frederick Cloude Morris, Jr., was b. in Oklahoma City, June 17, 1921; educated in the high schools of Oklahoma City and at the University of Southern California. While a student in high school he evinced and developed talent for dramatic art, winning the annual award for acting and oratory among the high school students of the State. While a senior he was chosen as the best male contestant in the local (State) Gateway to Hollywood but his age (seventeen) prevented his competing in the National try-outs. About this time he became an announcer for W.K.Y. radio station and continued as such for some time except for the summer of 1941 when he was in New York City, acting in coast-to-coast plays over the Columbia Broadcasting System. He m., May 6, 1943, Betty Ann Alexander. Children: Claudia, b. November 30, 1946, and Nancy, b. January 18, 1949.

36. Claude Frederick Morris (son by a former marriage, the mother dying at childbirth), was b. January 28, 1905. He and wife, Ruth, reside in Houston, Texas. No children.

28. FLORENCE ANNE MORRIS was b. at Holton, Kansas, May 22, 1885. She was educated in the Jackson and county schools and at Campbell College. After teaching in the public schools for three

years she took a nurse's training course. For many years she was secretary to the president of the Morris Manufacturing Company, El Reno; m., in 1909, W. D. Fugate of Hannibal, Missouri. Children: Dorothy and Benjamin. Dorothy Lorraine Fugate was b. in Hannibal, Missouri, December 23, 1913. She was educated in the El Reno, Oklahoma, schools, graduating with honors from the high school of that city. She was versatile and talented, particularly in esthetic dancing and amateur dramatics; m., in 1933, Otto C. Kreipke. They reside in San Antonio, Texas. Children: Lorraine, Dorothy Marie, Patricia and Otto.

BENJAMIN FUGATE was b. December, 1910, in Hannibal, Missouri. Going to Oklahoma in 1913, he lived, first, at Edmond and later in El Reno where he was graduated from the high school, being president of his class. Later he attended Oklahoma City University for two years and then entered Oklahoma State University from which he was graduated with both A. B. and B. S. degrees. After teaching for three years, he went to Los Angeles, California, to complete Ph.D. degree, majoring in administrative education. Subsequently he was principal of the Red Mountain (California) High School; m. in 1940, Margaret ———.

29. WILLIAM ALEXANDER MORRIS, was b. at Colyer, Kansas, July 14, 1886. He went with his family to Holton, Kansas, in October, 1898, and joined his father and brother in Iowa in 1891 where he lived until 1919 when he went to Oklahoma. He was connected with the Morris Manufacturing Company, El Reno, until his death in October, 1940. He was an invalid for many years; m., in Cedar Rapids, Iowa, Anna Nestril. Children: a son, William Arlen, b. August 6, 1911, educated in the public schools of Cedar Rapids and El Reno, graduating from the high school of the latter city. He was graduated from the medical school of Oklahoma University in June, 1937, and after internship in the Cedar Rapids and Wichita (Kansas) hospitals, he travelled for a year as ship's surgeon on a Pacific passenger steamer. Subsequently he became a member of the staff of the Los Angeles County (California) hospital; m., in 1936, Pearl ——— Children: twins, William and Linda Anne.

30. MAUDE IRENE MORRIS was b. at Colyer, Kansas, March 27, 1888. When an infant she was taken to Holton, Kan., where she was reared by grandparents. She was educated in the Jackson County (Kansas) public schools and for three years was a primary teacher in those schools. Later she removed to and resided in Kansas City, Missouri.[2]

21. JOHN GREEN MORRIS, lawyer, judge and public official, was b. on Stinson Creek, near Grayson, Carter County, Kentucky, September 7, 1855; educated in the public schools of Carter County and attended a private school conducted by Prof. Friend, a resident of

Prestonsburg, Kentucky; taught in the public schools of Carter County for a number of years in the meantime studying law; was admitted to the bar and began the practice of law at Grayson where he continued until his death, January 25, 1921.

Entering the field of politics, he was elected Judge of the Carter County Court, November 6, 1894; was reelected and served a second term upon the expiration of which he was elected county attorney for Carter County and served a term of four years.

Judge Morris was a Republican in politics, a member of the Christian Church and was affiliated with the Masons, a member of Trimble Lodge No. 145, F. and A. M., at Grayson and of the Royal Arch at Greenup.

He m. in Carter County, October 21, 1880, Martha Ellen Gilbert, b in Carter County, March 15, 1860, and d. in Arlington County, Virginia, December 14, 1943, a daughter of Samuel and Elizabeth (Jacobs) Gilbert, and a lineal (direct) descendant 'of Samuel Gilbert, Revolutionary War soldier. (See Gilbert Family.)

Judge and Mrs. Morris were interred in the family plot in Grayson Cemetery.

Children:

*37. Henry Claude Morris.

*38. William Samuel Morris.

39. Bessie Myrtle Morris; m. William C. Kozee. (See Kozee Family.)

40. Albert Ernest Morris; b. June 26, 1888, and d. October 3, 1911; unm.

*41. Gracia May Morris.

*42. John Green Morris, Jr.

37. HENRY CLAUDE MORRIS; b. at Smoky Valley, Carter County, Kentucky, Sept. 13, 1881; d. in Ashland, Kentucky, March 3, 1941; interment in the Morris family plot in Grayson Cemetery; m. at Willard, Carter County, Dorcie Lake Adams, b. October 27, 1887, and d. in hospital, Ashland, Kentucky, August 29, 1925; interment Mannin graveyard, Jacobs, Kentucky. She was a daughter of Lieutenant Daniel and Nancy (Triplett) Adams.

Children:

43. Edgar Herbert Morris; b. at Willard, November 6, 1902, and d. in hospital at Frankfort, Kentucky, July 31, 1951; interment in Morris family plot in Grayson Cemetery; unm.

44. Ethel Viola Morris, b. at Grayson, March 14, 1905; m., June 24, 1925, Cornelius Sherman Reeves.

Cornelius Sherman Reeves, son of J. Franklin and Correlda (Holbrook) Reeves, was b. near Willard, September 1, 1901; educated in the common and graded schools of Carter County and at the Christian Normal Institute at Grayson; held for several years a responsible executive position with the American Rolling Mills Company at Ashland, and also operated his cattle farm at Denton, Kentucky, raising pedigreed Hereford cattle. Children: a daughter Delores Evelyn, b. in Ashland, April 24, 1932; educated in the public schools of Ashland, graduating from the Senior High School in May, 1950; and was a student at Ashland Junior College, 1951; accepted a position in U. S. Government, Washington, D. C., in June, 1951; m., August 30, 1952, Jack Larkie of Chicago, noncommissioned officer, Medical Department, U. S. Navy. They reside in the Washington, D. C. area.

45. Martha Elizabeth (Betty) Morris, Federal employee; b. at Grayson, June 29, 1906; educated in the graded and high schools of Grayson and was graduated from Strayers Business College, Washington, D. C., 19—; m., first, in Washington, D. C., June, 1931, Henry C. Nestor of Omaha, Nebraska. Children: a daughter, Dorcie Mae, b. in Washington, D. C., January 12, 1935; m. in Washington, James Heffner, Federal employee. Children: a daughter, Lisa Ann Heffner, b. April — 1953.

45A. Martha Elizabeth Morris m., secondly, in Washington, Russell H. Evanson, Federal employee, a native of Wisconsin. Children: a daughter, Margaret (Peggy) Elizabeth Evanson, b. in Washington, July 4, 1945. Mrs. Evanson is an employee of the General Accounting Office, Washington, D. C.

46. John Green (Jay) Morris; b. at Enterprise, Kentucky, June 27, 1908.

47. Ernest Daniel Morris; b. at Enterprise, Kentucky, January 24, 1912.

48. William Claude Morris, Federal employee; b. at Enterprise, Kentucky, June 4, 1920; educated in the schools of Washington, D. C., and of Arlington County, Virginia, graduating from the Washington and Lee High School, Arlington County, in 1939; entered the Columbus University Law School (now Southeastern University) but soon thereafter, December 15, 1941, volunteered and enlisted in the U. S. Army and had service therein until September 24, 1945, when honorably discharged at Sioux Falls, South Dakota; served overseas in England from August 6, 1942, to June 15, 1945; accepted a position in the General Accounting Office, Washington, D. C., November 1, 1945, and is presently a special transportation reviewer in that office; m. in Norwick, England, June 19, 1943, Barbara Claire Kingsland, b. at Worthington, England, June 6, 1923. Children: Elaine Elizabeth Morris, b. at Hempnall, England, August 18, 1944, and John Daniel Morris, b. at Washington, D. C., July 12, 1947.

49. Bobby Jack Morris; b. and d., October 28, 1924.

34. WILLIAM SAMUEL MORRIS, grocer, b. at Smoky Valley, Carter County, Kentucky, August 7, 1883; received a common school education in the public schools of Grayson; was employed by the Eastern Kentucky Railroad Company in young manhood and con-

tinued in such employment and with the Chesapeake and Ohio Railway Company for 15 years. Later, in 1920, he went in the grocery business at Russell, Kentucky, and subsequently at Ashland and is presently conducting such business at 2301 Carter Avenue, Ashland; m. December 21, 1910, Mary E. Thompson, b. June 20, 1893, daughter of George and Dora B. Thompson of Greenup County. Children: a son, Clifford Murl.

50. CLIFFORD MURL MORRIS, pharmacist, was b. at Riverton, Greenup County, September 26, 1911; educated in the public schools of Russell, Kentucky, graduating from the Russell High School in 1929; and was graduated from the Louisville College of Pharmacy in 1934; was employed as pharmacist by the Steel Drug Company of Ashland for a number of years; and presently is representative of the Abbott Laboratories of Chicago over a large area of Northeastern Kentucky; m. in Ashland, August 9, 1936, Miss Hope Garner, teacher, who was b. at Millersburg, Ohio, May 26, 1911, and was educated in the public schools of Ashland, graduating from the Senior High School in 1929, and at Marshall College, Huntington, West Virginia, graduating in 1938. Children: Sharon Ann, b. August 7, 1940, and Jack William, b. October 6, 1950.

37. GRACIA MAY MORRIS, teacher, civic and church leader; b. at Smoky Valley, Carter County, Kentucky, December 31, 1890; educated in the graded and high schools of Grayson and at Morehead (Kentucky) Normal School, graduating with the class of 1908; began teaching in the public schools of Carter County in 1908, and continued until 1914; m. Joseph Ewalt Shawhan at Grayson, December 26, 1914. They immediately went to Washington, D. C. to live, Mr. Shawhan having previously entered the Government service there. In 1925 they built and established their home at 723 N. Ivy Street, Arlington, Virginia, where Mrs. Shawhan now resides. She was a substitute teacher in the Arlington public schools for a number of years.

Mrs. Shawhan united with the Christian Church at Grayson, Kentucky, her home town, in 1902; was a member of the "H" Street and/or the Ninth Street Christian Church, Washington, D. C., while residing in that city; was a member of the Wilson Boulevard Christian Church, Clarendon, Virginia, for a number of years and is presently a member of the Pershing Drive Christian Church, Arlington, Virginia. During this period of over fifty years she has given of her time, energy, talents and means to her church and its auxiliaries, serving faithfully and well in many and various capacities.

Mrs. Shawhan became a member of Grayson (Kentucky) Chapter Order of the Eastern Star in 1908; was a charter member of Mariam Chapter, Washington, D. C., and is presently a member of Mary Washington Chapter No. 50, in which she has creditably filled practically all offices and/or positions, serving as Worthy Matron, 1939.

JOSEPH EWALT SHAWHAN [3] was b. on Wilson Creek, Carter County, Kentucky, July 27, 1883; attended the public schools of Carter County; enlisted in Company "E", 18th Regiment Infantry, U. S. Army, March 24, 1905, and served until June 5, 1907, when honorably discharged at Ft. Leavenworth, Kansas; reenlisted June 6, 1907; had foreign service in the Philippines from November 3, 1907, to October 10, 1909, and was in the engagement at the camp on the Ramain River East of Lake Lanas, Mindanao May 22, 1909, repelling an attack by hostile Moros; was honorably discharged, at Ft. Mac-Kenzie, Wyoming, June 5, 1910; reenlisted at Ft. Thomas, Kentucky June 9, 1910, and served in Company "B", 2nd Regiment Infantry, until May 22, 1913, when honorably discharged at Ft. Mc-Dowell, California, a Quartermaster sergeant; accepted a position in the Bureau of Engraving, Washington, D. C., July 1914; was an employee of the U. S. Navy Yard, Washington, for two years from 1920-1922; and accepted a position, February 16, 1922, in U. S. Park Police, Public Buildings and Grounds, Corps of Engineers, War Department, and continued to serve in that department until his death on April 15, 1944.

Mr. Shawman was a member of the Christian Church and was affiliated with the Masons—a member of Trimble Lodge No. 145; F. and A.M., at Grayson, Kentucky, Interment in National Memorial Cemetery, Arlington, Virginia.

Children:

51. Daniel Green Shawhan, executive, was b. in Washington, D. C. July 29, 1918; educated in the public schools of Arlington County, Virginia, graduating from the Washington and Lee High School in 1936; entered the Virginia Polytechnic Institute at Blacksburg, September, 1936, and was graduated therefrom in June, 1940, in civil engineering; was commissioned, July 20, 1940, a second lieutenant, Officers Reserve Corps, Corps of Engineers; was called to and reported for active duty, January 17, 1941; promoted to first lieutenant, February 1, 1942; to captain December 15, 1942; and to major February 1944; was commissioned a lieutenant colonel, Officers Reserve Corps, January 6, 1946; and was separated from active service, April 27, 1946; was on active duty overseas from October 14, 1944, to January 1, 1946.

Col. Shawhan accepted a position, April 16, 1946, as construction engineer with the Standard Oil Company. Subsequently he was promoted to a high executive position, and is presently employed in that capacity with offices in Baltimore. He m., November 6, 1943, Miss Jessie Lee Austin, a daughter of Joseph B., and Laura Katherine Austin of Roanoke, Virginia. Miss Austin was b. in Roanoke, January 10, 1921, and was educated in the public schools of that city, graduating from the Roanoke High School.

Children:
Katherine Grace Shawhan, b. March 17, 1945.
Laura Lee Shawhan, b. April 13, 1947.
Ann Morris Shawhan, b. November 22, 1951.
Daniel Joseph Shawhan, b. January 26, 1954.
Col. and Mrs. Shawhan reside on Lawyers Hill Road, Elkridge, Maryland.

28. JOHN GREEN MORRIS II, Federal employee and sometime teacher, was b. at Smoky Valley, Carter County, Kentucky. May 18, 1894; educated in the graded and high school of Grayson, Kentucky; at Bryant and Stratton Business College, Louisville, Kentucky, and at George Washington University Law School, Washington, D. C.; engaged in teaching in the public schools of Carter County, Kentucky, 1912 to 1917, when he accepted a position in the Office of the Auditor for War, Washington, D. C.; was assigned to the Claims Division and was claims adjuster and/or reviewer, when, in August, 1921, the General Accounting Office was organized, taking over, among others, the functions of the Auditor for the War; continued as claims reviewer until he was promoted and appointed Assistant Chief of Service claims in which position he was serving on June 1, 1949, when he retired from the Government service.

After retirement, Mr. Morris owned and operated The John G. Morris Apartments at 1112 N. Stafford Street, Arlington, Virginia. He d. January 3, 1955. Interment in Kozee family plot, Glenwood Cemetery, Washington, D. C.

20. BURRELL MORRIS, farmer; b. on Stinson creek, near Grayson, Carter County, Kentucky, October 11, 1857; m. in Oklahoma, Rhoda Burchett, daughter of Burrell and Rhoda (Gilbert) Burchett. (See Gilbert Family.) Children:
52. Estelle Morris.
20-A. Burrell Morris m., secondly, in Carter County, Kentucky, Noda Pelfrey. They removed to Wisconsin where they reared a family. Mr. Morris was killed in automobile accident.

22. ELIZABETH MORRIS; b. on Stinson creek, near Grayson, Carter County, Kentucky, April 22, 1862, and d. at Smoky Valley, Carter County, October 9, 1919; m. George W. Hall, b. in Floyd County, Kentucky, March 12, 1859, and d. at Upper Tygart, Carter County, March 20, 1945. He was a farmer and served as deputy assessor and deputy sheriff of Carter County for some time.
Children:
*53. Henry Cyrus Hall.
*54. Verdie Hall.
*55. Bessie M. Hall.
*56. Dennie H. Hall.

53. HENRY CYRUS HALL, farmer and miner; b. at Smoky Valley, Carter County, Kentucky, December 27, 1895; served as member of the Carter County Board of Education two terms; m., in 1921, Elsie Porter.

Children: Edgar L., b. and d. September 17, 1922; Flora Elizabeth, b. August 9, 1923; Lucille M., b. June 29, 1926; George, C., b. July 4, 1928, and d. in Berlin, Germany, September 5, 1949.

54. VERDIE HALL; b. at Smoky Valley, January 8, 1898; m. Henry Harman of Betsy Lane, Floyd County, Kentucky.

Children: James Arthur, Byrtle and Emogene.

55. BESSIE M. HALL; b. at Smoky Valley, September 27, 1901; m. James Gilliam of Smoky Valley. Children: Lodena.

56. DENNIE H. HALL, public official and contractor, was b. at Smoky Valley, September 27, 1907; educated in the public schools of Carter County and at Morehead Normal School, now Morehead State Teachers College; was elected clerk of the Carter (County) Circuit Court, 1939, and reelected, 1945, and 1951; was m., January 31, 1931, to Loraine Coleman, daughter of Edward R. and Mary (Boggs) Coleman of Olive Hill, Kentucky. Mrs. Hall was b. at Olive Hill, October 10, 1912; was educated in the public schools of Olive Hill; was appointed deputy clerk of the Carter Circuit Court, 1942, and is presently serving in that capacity and in charge of the office.

Mr. Hall is a Republican in politics, a member of the Baptist Church and a Mason, a member of Trimble Lodge No. 145, F & A. M., at Grayson, which he has served as Worshipful Master. He has served as Patron of Grayson Chapter No. 10, Order of Eastern Star and as Deputy Grand Patron of District No. 4. He is also a member of the Scottish Rite.

Children: Phyllis Ann, b. September 27, 1931; Conrad Coleman, b. February 21, 1938; and Dennie Herbert, Jr., b. June 20, 1952.

12. LOUANNA MORRIS; b. in Floyd County, Kentucky, about 1815, and d. in Carter County subsequent to 1860; m. her cousin, John Morris, a son of Ezekiel and Mary (Rose) Morris. John Morris d. in Carter County prior to 1850.

Children:

*57. Amy Morris.

58. Martha Morris; b. 1835; m. Mr. Welch.

59. Madison Green Morris, b. 1837; m. Rhoda Jacobs.

60. Susan Morris; b. September 6, 1839; m., first, John S. Jacobs and, secondly, George W. Evans.

61. Elizabeth (Betty) Morris, b. 1841 or 1842.

62. James (Jimmie) Morris, b. January 4, 1845.

57. AMY MORRIS; b. at Grayson, Carter County, Kentucky, September 28, 1832, and d. at Sedan, Kansas, July 9, 1900; m. April

6, 1851, William Chauncey Adams, b. in Portage County, Ohio, December 21, 1827, and d. at Gunniston, Colorado, October 16, 1896, a son of Samuel Adams and his wife, Orra Ann (Hard) Adams.

WILLIAM CHAUNCEY ADAMS had service in Company "E", 2nd Kentucky Regiment Volunteer Cavalry in the Civil War. He was mustered in as sergeant, September 9, 1861, at Muldraugh's Hill (Kentucky) for three years; promoted from sergeant to second lieutenant, May 3, 1863; and was mustered out of the service at Maysville, Alabama, November 23, 1863.[4]
Children:
*63. Orra Ann Adams.
64. Martin R. Adams; b. at Star Furnace, Kentucky, 1854.
65. Clarence Devore Adams; b. at Grayson, Kentucky, September 2, 1859, and d. July 8, 1939; m. Ethel Miller.
66. Grace Mary Adams; b. at Grayson, 1866, d. December 21, 1931; m. Sylvester J. Miller.
67. Charles Elmer Adams; b. at Topeka, Kansas, February 14, 1869; d. June 7, 1940; m. Meta Gibbs, September 19, 1893.

63. ORRA ANN ADAMS; b. at Star Furnace, Carter County, Kentucky, January 4, 1852, and d. at Sedan, Kansas, July 24, 1934; m. at Grand Creek, Kansas, November 25, 1872, Orange Vanderveer Lemon Jones, b. July 30, 1846, at Jonesborough, Trash County, Indiana, and d. April 28, 1898, at Sedan, Kansas, a son of Jacob Jones and his wife, Hester (Beuoy) Jones.
Children:
*68. Loreno Avis Jones.
69. Otha Clyde Jones; b. at Hartford, Indiana, February 15, 1877, and d. May 24, 1945; m. Gwendolyn Jones.
70. Amy Alta Jones; b. Chautauqua, Kansas, February 18, 1880; m. Charles Lester Conner.
71. Grace Gertrude Jones; b. Chautauqua, Kansas, December 6, 1882; m. Edward LeRoy Sharpless, July 16, 1905.
72. William Cecil Jones; b. at Sedan, Kansas, June 12, 1886, and d. April 14, 1941; m. Mabel Howell.

68. LORENO AVIS JONES; b. at Grand Creek, Chautauqua County, Kansas, September 27, 1873; m. March 18, 1893, Julian Harkness Colyar (Collier), b. in Scotland County, Missouri, March 9, 1870, and d. in Salt Lake City, Utah, December 31, 1951, a son of Jonathan Pierson Colyar (Collier) and his wife, Olive Marie (Shelton) Colyar.
Children:
73. William Chauncey Colyar; b. at Sedan, Kansas, December 20, 1893; m. Sadie Stark, May 5, 1915.
74. Clarence Cebert Colyar; b. April 17, 1900; m. Alice Bernice Porter, November 4, 1920.

75. Kenneth Colyar; b. at Humphrey, Nebraska, August 8, 1902, and d. October 3, 1902.

76. Maurice Clyde Colyar; b. at Columbus, Nebraska, August 28, 1903; m. Alice M. Peterson, September 26, 1928.

77. Amy Catherine Gertrude Colyar; b. at Sedan, Kansas, February 28, 1906; m. Warren Clark Zimmerman, April 2, 1926.

78. Helen Virginia Colyar; b. at Bingham Canyon, Utah, July 1, 1911; m. Elmo Nester, August 6, 1929.

79. Robert Raymond Colyar; b. at Bingham Canyon, Utah, August 7, 1908; m. Beth Hintze, March 18, 1944.

80. Charles Newton Colyar; b. at Bingham Canyon, Utah, February 17, 1916, and d. July 9, 1916.[5]

---

[1] Burrell Burchett, farmer and blacksmith, was b. about 1805 in Virginia—probably in Wythe County; m. in Lawrence County, Kentucky, June 20, 1825, Sarah Easterling, b. about 1807; resided on Stinson Creek near Grayson, Carter County. Children living in the household and approximate dates of birth as shown by the U. S. Census of Carter County for 1950:
2. John Heron Burchett; b. 1826. He was a farmer and lawyer; served as County Attorney of Carter County for one term.
3. Elizabeth Burchett; b. 1831.
4. Benjamin Burchett; b. 1833. He m. a Bond.
5. Nancy Burchett; b. 1835; m. Henry Cloud Morris.
6. Thomas Burchett; b. 1837.
7. Silas Burchett; b. 1840.
8. Drewry Burchett; b. 1842.
9. Burrell Burchett; b. 1844; m. Elizabeth Gilbert (See Gilbert Family); served as sheriff of Carter County; removed to Kingfisher County, Oklahoma, and served as sheriff of that county.
10. Ann Burchett; b. 1847.
11. Susanna Burchett; b. 1849; m. Samuel Reeves (See Reeves Family).

[2] The Descendants of William Morris and His Wife, Lourana (Martin) Morris (Manuscript), prepared by Melvina Genoa Morris, Oklahoma City, Oklahoma.

[3] Joseph Ewalt Shawhan, 7, descended from the Bedfords, Cantrills, Ewalts and Shawhans, prominent pioneer families that settled in the Bluegrass region of Kentucky in early days. His father, Daniel Shawhan, 6, was b. at Shawhan's Station, Harrison County, Kentucky, and d. in Carter County, Kentucky. He m. Elizabeth Norval Bedford, b. in Bourbon County, Kentucky, November 2, 1854, and d. in Carter County, a daughter of Capt. Harry Poval Bedford and Mary Susan (Ewalt) Bedford who was b. in Bourbon County, January 29, 1831. Capt. Harry P. Bedford was b. in Bourbon County, April 10, 1826, and d. in Carter County at an advanced age. He was a captain in the Mexican War. Interment in Paris (Kentucky) Cemetery.
The children of Daniel Shawhan and Elizabeth Bedford Shawhan were Harry Bedford Shawhan, who m. Margaret Nanny; John Hunt Shawhan, who m., first, Kate Carey and, secondly, Byrd Adams; Pugh Miller Shawhan, who m. Rachel Adams; and Joseph Ewalt Shawhan, who m. Gracia May Morris.
Daniel Shawhan and Elizabeth Bedford Shawhan were interred in the Paris (Kentucky) Cemetery.
Daniel Shawhan was a son of Major John Shawhan, 5, and Talitha (Rust) Shawhan who was a daughter of George and Jane Anderson Rust. Major John Shawhan was b. near Mt. Carmel Church, Bourbon County, Kentucky; enlisted in the Confederate States Army at Cynthiana, September, 1861; was commissioned a captain, Company "A", First Battalion Calvalry, Kentucky Volunteers; was promoted from captain to major and held commission as colonel to recruit a full regiment; was killed or assassinated by "bushwhackers" on Callihan's Creek, Rowan County, Kentucky, September, 1862. (Report of the Adjutant General of Kentucky, 1861-1865).
Major John Shawhan was a son of Joseph Shawhan, 4, and his wife, Sarah Ewalt. (Henry Shawhan, the oldest son of Joseph Shawhan and Sarah Ewalt Shawhan, was b. November 20, 1805, and d. March 4, 1882. He was a farmer and banker. He m., November 7, 1844, Sallie Cantrell, who was b. December 28, 1807, and d. November 18, 1857. Both were interred in Battle Grove Cemetery, Cynthiana, Kentucky.)
Joseph Shawhan was a son of Daniel Shawhan, 3, and his wife, Margaret Bell. Daniel Shawhan, 3, was son of Daniel Shawhan, Sr., 2, and his wife, Jeannetta ———— (surname not known).
Daniel Shawhan, Sr., was a son of Darby Shawhan 1, and his wife, Sarah ———— (surname not known).

[4] Report of the Adjutant General of Kentucky, 1861-1865, Vol. I, p. 54.

[5] Louanna Morris and Her Descendants (Manuscript), prepared by Robert Raymond Colyar, Salt Lake City, Utah, 1952.

OSENTON FAMILY OF CARTER AND GREENUP COS.

The progenitor of the Osenton family of Northeastern Kentucky has been traced in England to:

1. Henry, b. about 1725. His son 2. Henry, b. 1750, settled at Cliffe in Kent when a young man where he followed the trade of thatcher. He m. Hannah Evrett, October 12, 1773, and they had issue: 3. James, b. 1775; 4. Henry, b. 1778, d. January 26, 1836, while psalm singing in the Cliffe church; 5. George, b. 1781, m. Anne Peters, 1804; *6. Samuel and 7. Sarah who m. a Mr. Carr.

6. SAMUEL OSENTON, carpenter, was b. at Cliffe, County Kent, England, 1783. He moved to High Halstow in Hundred Hoo, which is situated on a neck of land lying between the mouths of Midway and the Thames Rivers about three miles east of Cliffe. Here he m. Charlot Webb and here their son *8. James was b. on "February 17, 1812, at six minutes to 3 o'clock in the morning".[1] Charlot Osenton d. at the age of 20 years and baby James was taken to his Uncle. 5. George in Cliffe.

When James Osenton was three years old, the father, Samuel, decided to emigrate to America. Under the laws and/or regulations then obtaining children were not permitted to board ocean vessels; and Samuel, being unwilling to leave son James in England, and being a skillful carpenter, having served seven years apprenticeship in England, constructed an elaborate tool chest with a false bottom in which to conceal son James. In the top of the chest Samuel stored a full set of carpenter's tools, weighing nine hundred pounds. He sailed from England with the tool chest and contents arriving at New York in 1815 after a safe voyage. From New York he went to Philadelphia with son James and his carpenters' tools where he remained for about a year and disposed of three hundred pounds of the tools. From thence he began the trek Westward with son and the balance of tools, passing through Pittsburg and down the Ohio River to Greenupsburg (now Greenup). Here he boarded son James with various families, trying to give him a proper education.

In August, 1819, Samuel Osenton m., secondly, Emzy Downs. They purchased a farm at Old Town, Greenup County, and son James' formal education ended. About the time the Lexington turnpike was under construction from Lexington to Catlettsburg, he removed to Olive Hill, Carter County, where he built a home, still standing, and kept a hotel and public house. He d. in April, 1856, and his wife, Emzy, d. in 1864. Both were buried at Old Town.[2]

Issue:

9. Lucy Osenton; m. Allen Womack (See Womack Family).

10. Sarah Ann Osenton; m. Judge Joseph H. Strother. (See Strother Family).

*11. Henry Kelly Osenton.

*12. John Thomas Osenton.
*13. Samuel Osenton.
*14. George Nicholas Osenton.

8. JAMES OSENTON, farmer, worked on his father's farm when a boy but while still a youth he became a teamster in his own right and engaged in digging and delivering iron ore to the iron works at Hunnewell and Argelite, Greenup County. He had already begun to show signs of that thrift, industry, perseverance and saving by which he became one of the most wealthy men of his time and community. It has been said that he would dig ore at night so as to procure enough for a day's hauling and delivery.

During the depression of 1837 the iron works were closed, leaving Mr. Osenton without employment or a home. With his savings of the prior eight years and taking advantage of depression prices, he purchased a 691-acre farm at Pactolus, Carter County, where he lived for sometime.

He m., first, in Carter County, in 1853, Maria Sophia Goble.
Issue:
15. Martha Osenton; m. Merritt Megan. She d. at Pactolus and was buried beside her mother in the Plummer graveyard in Carter County.
8A. James Osenton m., secondly, Elizabeth Apple.
Issue:
16. Lafayette Osenton; b. 1866; d. 1886; unm.
*17. Laura Osenton.
*18. Amanda Osenton.
*19. Minnie Osenton.
*20. Martha Osenton.
*21. James Osenton.

17. LAURA OSENTON; b. 1868; d. 1911; m. Jacob Kern in 1892.
Issue:
22. James Kern; d. in infancy.
23. Betty Kern; m., first, —— Bursick. Issue: Elmer Bursick. She m., secondly, Webb Kidd.
24. Marie Kern; m. William Weisback.
25. Myrtle Kern; m., first —— Messner. Issue: Ruth Messner. She m., secondly, —— Anderson. Issue: Mary Lou Anderson.
26. Maude Kern; m. Thomas Tudor. Issue: Ina Tudor.
27. Russell Kern.

18. AMANDA OSENTON, b. 1871, m. Samuel Shivel at Grayson, Kentucky, in 1894.
Issue:
28. Harry Shivel; m. Ercille Blankenship. Issue: Jo Ann Shivel.
29. Victor Shivel; m. Faustine Pauley.

30. Wilma Shivel.

31. Carmen Shivel; m. Charles Dennues. Issue: Billy Lee Dennues.

19. Minnie Osenton; b. 1876, d. 1931; m. R. M. Bagby at Grayson in 1896.

The Bagby family settled in Greenup County in pioneer days. R. M. Bagby located at Grayson with his parents in his youth and became a jeweler. Subsequently he engaged in many business activities: the lumber business, real estate and banking. He is a Methodist. A democrat in politics, he represented his district in the State Senate for a term.

Issue:

32. Lilliam Bagby; m. W. F. Wollin, 1923. Issue:

33. Dorothy Mary Wollin, Editor of "Profile of the Osenton Family".

34. Aurella Wollin.

20. MARTHA OSENTON, b. 1877; m., 1896, Russell W. Botts, druggist of Grayson.

Issue:

35. Ruth Botts; m., first, —— Bonnell. Issue: Ruth Anna Bonnell who m. Charles Queen; m., secondly, Frank Kennedy.

36. Elizabeth Botts; m. John Watters. Issue: Charlene Watters who m. —— Simmons; and William Watters.

37. Russell Botts; m. —— Carroll. Issue: Phyllis Ann Botts, Brenda Joyce Botts and Sandra Lee Botts.

38. Mody Botts; m. Lillian Crawford. Issue: Margaret Ann Botts and Bonnie Joe Botts.

21. JAMES OSENTON, b. 1884; m., 1908, Mrs. Etta Wiles.

Issue:

39. Malcomb Osenton; m. Barbara Carpenter. Issue: Roberta Denny Lee Osenton and Joe Mid Osenton.

40. Robert Osenton; m. Iona Gannon. Issue: Bobbie Gannon Osenton and Mary Judith Osenton.

41. Vernal Osenton; m. Ann Messersmith.

11. HENRY KELLY OSENTON, farmer and blacksmith; b. 1821; m. in Carter County about 1845, Sciotha McAllister, b. 1828.

Issue:

*42. Lucy Ann Margaret Osenton.

*43. Temperance Osenton; b. 1848; m. John Milton Tyree. (See Flaugher Family.)

*44. Joseph Osenton; b. 1853.

*45. William Osenton.

*46. John Osenton.
*47. Kate Osenton.
*48. Carrie Osenton.
49. George Osenton.
*50. Emily Osenton; b. 1854 (twin to Emzy).
51. Emzy C. Osenton; b. 1854; m. William Ward.
52. Elizabeth Osenton; b. 1849.

42. LUCY ANN MARGARET OSENTON, b. 1846; m. James Hatchet.

Issue:

53. William Wirt Hatchet.

54. James Howard Hatchett; m. Elizabeth Kentner; reside in Huntington, West Virginia. Issue: James Hatchett, who married Miss Wallace.

55. Emma Hatchet; m. Charles Woolery. Issue: Emily Lucille Woolery; m. Frank Malone. Issue: Betty Lou Malone and Carol Ann Malone.

Margaret Ann Woolery m. John Frank Hord. Issue: Jack Willis Hord and Dorothy Mary Hord. (See Hord Family.)

Daniel Woolery m. K. Jepson. Issue: Suzanne Jepson and Charles H. Jepson.

56. Charles Watson Hatchet m. Bernice Hall. Issue: Charles Roe Hatchet; m. Louise Prichard, daughter of Belvard (Bell) Prichard (See Prichard Family). Issue: James Lee Prichard and Anna Laura Prichard.

James Hall Hatchet.
Mary Floyd Hatchet; m. J. Lefebre.
Fred Lacy Hatchet.

44. JOSEPH OSENTON; b. 1853; m. ——— Phillips.

Issue:

57. Ollie Osenton; m. William Greer.

58. Mary Osenton; m. E. Newcomb. Issue: Lillian Newcomb, Merrill Newcomb, and Frank Newcomb.

59. Ella Osenton.

60. Steph. Osenton.

61. Henry Osenton; m. Norma ———. Issue: LeRoy Osenton, Betty Joe Osenton and Billy Jean Osenton.

62. Baynard Osenton.

63. Cleveland Osenton; m. C. DeHart. Issue: Gertrude Osenton, Ruby Osenton and Virginia Osenton.

64. LeRoy Osenton.

45. WILLIAM OSENTON, b. 1855; m. Maggie Rupert. Issue: Ebert Rupert, bank cashier, deceased; unm.

46. JOHN OSENTON, b. 1857; m. Illinois ————. Issue: Harley Shelby Osenton, Ferne Osenton, Reed Osenton and Mary Ellen Osenton.

47. KATE OSENTON; m. J. Gilbert. Issue: Roy Gilbert and Lloyd Gilbert.

48. CARRIE OSENTON; m. F. Corbin. Issue: Marie Corbin, Roscoe Corbin, Emma Flo Corbin, Charles Corbin and Willie Corbin.

50. EMILY OSENTON, b. 1854; m. I Halsted. Issue: Sciotha Halsted and Harry Halsted.

12. JOHN THOMAS OSENTON; b. December 19, 1828, and d. July 2, 1868; m. January 7, 1855, Katherine Cameron.

Issue:

65. William E. A. Osenton; d. in infancy.
66. Mary Belle Osenton; d. in infancy.
67. Ida Mae Osenton; m. James Watt Womack. (See Womack Family.)
68. John Thomas Osenton; b. March 16, 1862, and d., 1939; m. Araminta Atkins. Issue: Mabel Osenton, m. O. W. Stennett. Issue: Ida Louise Stennett.
69. George E. Osenton; b. March, 1864, and d., 1930; m. Verda Cox. Issue: Willie Osenton, Clyde Osenton, Forrest Osenton and Lola Osenton.
70. Samuel T. Osenton; b. September 23, 1866.

13. SAMUEL OSENTON; b. July 3, 1834, and d. at Grayson, Kentucky, 1878; m. in Carter County, January 1, 1857, Sallie Scott.

Issue:

71. Robert Osenton; b. September 28, 1858; m. Annie Lape. Issue: Elizabeth Osenton, m. Roy Parish. Issue: Earl Osenton Parrish who was killed in action in Sicily in 1944 while serving with the Rangers in Africa, World War II.
72. Henry Kelly Osenton; b. March 28, 1862.
73. Jennie Scott Osenton; b. December 6, 1864.

14. GEORGE NICHOLAS DUKE OF CUMBERLAND OSENTON, businessman of many activities and fine violinist, was b. at Old Town, Greenup County, Kentucky, December 12, 1842; was educated in the public schools of Greenup County and at Owingsville (Kentucky) Academy, receiving a good education. He was employed by Dr. A. J. Landsdowne at the salt works near Grayson, Carter County, for a time; was engaged with Robert G. Carter in business in Ashland, Kentucky; opened and conducted a general store and lumber business in Ceredo, West Virginia; and during the latter part of his life he was associated in business with Thomas P. Brown in Portsmouth, Ohio.

While in the employ of Dr. Landsdowne, he met, wooed and afterwards married Dr. Landsdowne's daughter, Daisy, June 23, 1861, at the Biggs House in Portsmouth, Ohio. Miss Ann Strother was her bridesmaid and Mr. Peck Henry was his groomsman. They resided at Old Town and Grayson until 1862. Later they lived in Ashland, Kentucky, and at Ceredo, West Virginia; and finally returned to Kentucky and moved to the Landsdowne farm, a part of which she had inherited from her father. She maintained Landsdowne Hall as her home as long as she lived. Although she spent some time with her children, who lived in various sections of the county.

DAISY LANDSDOWNE OSENTON was b. in Carter County and was educated by governesses and in public schools of Carter County. She d. January 1, 1923, while on a visit to the home of her son, Charles Wilson Osenton, at Kanawha Falls, West Virginia. George Nicholas Osenton d. November 29, 1904, in Nicholas County, West Virginia. Through a mistake in a telegram his body was not returned to Kentucky for burial. He was b. in the Alderson cemetery, Alderson, West Virginia.

Issue:

*74. Blanche Osenton.

*75. Charles Wilson Osenton.

76. Juliet Osenton; b. at Ceredo, West Virginia, 1868; m. Frank O. Harbeson. Issue: (a) Gartrell Harbeson who m. Carrie ———. Issue: Adele Harbeson. (b) Thomas Tomb Harbeson.

77. LANDSDOWNE OSENTON; b. 1871; m., first, Clara Given of Webster County, West Virginia. Issue: Desha Breckenridge Osenton and Bartlett Osenton. Landsdowne Osenton m., secondly, Elizabeth Patterson of Scotland. Issue: Lillian Osenton, m. ——— Eames. Issue: James Eames, Robert Eames and Virginia Eames.

78. Amy Lee Osenton; b. 1876; m. John G. Matthews. Issue: (a) Paul Matthews, m. Diane ———; (b) Hayden Matthews; (c) John Gill Matthews, Jr., m. ——— Hamlin. Issue: Bonnie Matthews; (d) Landsdowne Matthews and (e) Julian Matthews.

74. BLANCHE OSENTON was b. at Old Town, Greenup County, June 1, 1862, and d. May 4, 1938; m. Hallock Hayden Case, lumberman, b. at Glenville, Kentucky, August 2, 1856, and d. April 7, 1944. Issue: (a) Mary Hord Case, d. in infancy; (b) Lacon Manning Case, b. 1889, m. Elaine Kersley; (c) Margaret Nelson Case, b. at Flat Woods, West Virginia, m. David Alston. Issue: Lelia May Alston; (d) Edwin Hayden Case, b. October 30, 1894; m. at Grayson, Kentucky, July 14, 1919, Maude Webb, b. June 1, 1890, daughter of Benjamin Franklin Webb, merchant at Webbville, Kentucky, b. November 22, 1855, and d. January 6, 1897, and of Emma (Rad-

cliff) Webb, b. near Carter City, Kentucky, February 10, 1860, and d. September 30, 1893. Both the Webbs and Radcliffs were prominent pioneer families of Northeastern Kentucky.

Issue: Edwin Thomas Case, teacher; b. in Ashland, Kentucky, July 7, 1920; educated in the schools of Ashland and was graduated from the Morehead (Kentucky) State Teachers' College; and is presently principal of the Adelaide School, Bountiful, Utah; m., December 27, 1947, Dorothy Sessions, b. September 5, 1918. Children: Leland Stuart Case (stepson), b. September 28, 1943; Mary Elizabeth Case, b. June 6, 1949; Edwin Sessions Case, b. October 30, 1951; and Brent Steven Case, b. September 28, 1953.

75. CHARLES WILSON OSENTON, lawyer, businessman and politician; b. at Grayson, Kentucky, 1865; accepted a position in the U. S. Government, Washington D. C., in young manhood and after serving several years, he resigned and located at Kanawha Falls, West Virginia. He became outstanding as a businessman and politician, and amassed considerable wealth. He was interested and engaged in development of the mineral resources of West Virginia, particularly coal mining. A staunch Democrat and skillful politician, he represented his party on the National Committee. He m., first, Kate Cappela. Issue: Daisy Rebecca, Eugenia, Jennings, Charles J. and Katherine. He m., secondly, Mrs. Williamson. No issue.

---

[1] Charlot Webb's Bible.

[2] "Profile of the Osenton Family", edited by Dorothy Mary Wollin, 1946.

PARSONS FAMILY

1. WILLIAM PARSONS was the ancestor of a large branch of the Parsons family some descendants of whom finally settled in Northeastern Kentucky. According to family records he had service in the Revolutionary War in the South Carolina forces under General Francis Marion. Authorities state that one William Parsons served in the South Carolina forces during the Revolutionary War.[1]

William Parsons lived in Rutherford County, North Carolina, and m., presumably in that county, Polly Craig.

Children. Second Generation:

2. Solomon Parsons, b. 1778, d. 1861; lived in Alleghany County, North Carolina.

3. Robert Parsons, b. 1776, d. 1865; lived in Grayson County, North Carolina.

*4. Hezekiah Parsons.

5. William Parsons.

6. James Parsons.

7. Edmund Parsons.

4. HEZEKIAH PARSONS; b. in North Carolina; m. Leah DeBord; removed to Washington County, Virginia, about 1830 where the family remained until about 1860 when Mr. Parsons, his wife and five of their children came to Carter County, Kentucky, and settled on a farm on the Little Sandy River at the mouth of Deer Creek. He d. in Carter County in October, 1869, and his will is recorded in the Will Book 2, page 92, Carter County Court records.

Children. Third Generation:

*8. John F. Parsons.

*9. Ferdinand Parsons.

10. Stephen J. Parsons; b. 1835; d. 1897; lived in Russell County, Virginia.

*11. George B. Parsons.

12. James Parsons; b. 1838; lived in Russell County, Virginia.

13. Joseph Parsons; b. 1840; lived in Russell County, Virginia.

14. Mary Parsons; m. Faris McFarland of Carter County.

*15. Naomi Parsons.

16. Ephraim Parsons; lived in Virginia.

8. JOHN F. PARSONS; b. in Virginia, July 26, 1834; d. in Carter County, Kentucky, January 3, 1897; m. Sarah Jane Walker in Carter County, 1863. Children. Fourth Generation:

17. James F. Parsons; m. Phoebe Carroll, September 26, 1888.

18. Nancy Parsons; m. William Lowe, 1884.

19. Mary Parsons; m. John Carroll.

20. Ephraim Parsons; m. Fannie Sexton, July 25, 1900.

21. Fanny Parsons; m. D. B. Skaggs, January 26, 1898.

22. Amelia Parsons; m. Robert Bear, November 8, 1902.

9. FERDINAND PARSONS; b. in Virginia, 1835; d. in Rowan County, Kentucky, 1911; m. Amelia (or America) Tackett.
Children. Fourth Generation:
23. Robert Parsons; m. Nancy Blevins, August 18, 1891.
24. Ferrell (Dock) Parsons; migrated to Texas.
25. Hezekiah (Carr) Parsons; m. Eliza DeBord, November 18, 1900.
26. Stephen Parsons.
27. John Parsons; m. Daisy James, December 26, 1900.
28. George Parsons; m. Lizzie Taylor, December 22, 1909.
29. Alfred Parsons; m. Mary Richwood, April 19, 1919.
30. Leah Parsons; m. David Parker.
31. Sarah Jane Parsons; m. George Barbour, April 17, 1909.
32. Ann Parsons.

11. GEORGE B. PARSONS; b. in Washington County, Virginia, 1836; d. in Carter County, Kentucky, 1912; m. Malissa Sturtevant ' in Virginia about 1862; came with his father's family to Carter County during the Civil War.
Children. Fourth Generation:
*33. Henry Parsons.
*34. Joseph Parsons.
*35. John M. Parsons.
36. Mary Jane Parsons; m. Alex Sturgill.
37. Sarah Parsons; b. January 11, 1865; m. William Holbrook.
38. Malissa Parsons; m. James J. James, October 18, 1888.
39. George B. Parsons; m., first, Elizabeth Harper and thirdly, Rhoda Thompson.
40. George Anna Parsons; m. Robert Young.
41. Stephen Parsons.
42. Phoebe Parsons; m. Lewis H. Stephens.
43. Ephraim Parsons, d. young.
44. David C. Parsons; m. Nora McGuire, June 24, 1907.

15. NAOMI PARSONS; m. William Leadingham, b. 1826, son of Peter Leadingham, Sr., and Sally Hamilton Leadingham who lived near Willard, Carter County.
(See note No. 3, in Robinson family.)
Children. Fourth Generation:
45. Elisabeth Leadingham.
46. Angeline Leadingham.
47. Leah Leadingham.
48. Peter Leadingham.
49. Hezekiah Leadingham.
50. Louisa Leadingham.
51. Jesse C. Leadingham.
52. William Leadingham, Jr.
53. Robert Leadingham.

33. HENRY PARSONS; b. in Scott County, Virginia, 1856; d. in Carter County, Kentucky, 1930; m., first, Margaret Holbrook, d. 1877; secondly, Belle Maddox and, thirdly, Lucy Carter.

Children of Henry Parsons and Margaret (Holbrook) Parsons. Fifth Generation:

54. John Parsons; b. 1879; d. 1933; m. Chloe J. Lee, February 10, 1900.
55. Willis Parsons; b. 1881; d. 1927; m. Fanny Alfred, March 28, 1902.
56. Albert Parsons; b. September 15, 1883; m. Martha Adkins, May 12, 1906.
*57. William Parsons; b. June 22, 1885; m. Olivia Messer, January 14, 1908.

33A. Henry Parsons m. Belle Maddox, August 29, 1888.

Children. Fifth Generation:

*58. George Parsons; b. March 15, 1895; m. Linnie Evans, December 11, 1912.
*59. Grover Cleveland Parsons; b. June 18, 1893; m. Sarah Adkins, January 13, 1911.
*60. Thomas Allen Parsons; b. June 4, 1895; m. Eula Van Hoose, November 24, 1915.
61. Luther Parsons; b. February 25, 1897; d. 1901.

33B. Henry Parsons m. Lucy Carter, November 7, 1900.

Children:

62. Sally Parsons; b. November 1, 1901; m. Oscar Van Hoose, May 23, 1915.
63. Taylor Parsons; b. April 16, 1903.

34. JOSEPH WILLIAM PARSONS; b. January 28, 1863; d. at Charlotte Furnace (Iron Hill), Carter County, December 1, 1944; m. Cora Belle Colley, January 20, 1887.

Children. Fifth Generation:

*64. Charles Harold Parsons.
65. David Leonard Parsons; b. February 11, 1891; m. Georgia Faulkner, November 18, 1916.
66. William Arthur Parsons; b. April 28, 1893; m. Belle Wyth Shivel, December 30, 1914.
67. Rosa Belle Parsons; b. January 2, 1895; m. Charles Craycraft, January 13, 1914.
68. Lewis Wayne Parsons; b. November 16, 1896; m. Clara Glass, March 25, 1918.
69. Dovie Meek Parsons; b. November 7, 1898; m. Corum Hannah, July 29, 1920.

70. Gus James Parsons; b. July 13, 1900; m., May 11, 1924, Nellie James, daughter of T. A. and Georgia (Littleton) James. (See Lewis Family.)

71. Melissa Alice Parsons; b. July 19, 1902; m. Clyde B. Womack March 14, 1919.

72. Ella Beed Parsons; b. April 7, 1905; m. Albert W. Cooper, May 12, 1923.

73. Joseph Wheeler Parsons; b. September 4, 1908; m., first, Mildred Callahan and, secondly, Opal Taber.

74. Edith Marie Parsons; b. March 18, 1910; m. Orville Blankenship, May 6, 1929.

35. JOHN M. PARSONS; b. September 25, 1864; d. December 23, 1933; m. Effie Bush.

Children. Fifth Generation:

75. Mary Parsons.
76. Ellis Parsons.
77. William Parsons.
78. Clark Parsons.

57. REV. WILLIAM PARSONS; b. June 22, 1885; m. Olivia Messer, January 14, 1907.

Children. Sixth Generation:

79. Homer Parsons; b. September 29, 1908.
80. Herdie Parsons; b. December 14, 1909.
81. Catherine Parsons; b. July 26, 1912.
82. Hurst Parsons; b. December 1, 1913.
83. Clayton Parsons; b. January 21, 1915.
84. Lucy Parsons; b. October 21, 1916.
85. Troy Parsons; b. October 16, 1918.
86. Luther Parsons; b. November 10, 1919.
87. Blanche Parsons; b. May 11, 1922.
88. Maxine Parsons; b. October 9, 1923.
89. Clyde Parsons; b. December 13, 1925.
90. Willis Parsons; b. October 22, 1929.
91. Chloe Parsons; b. March 4, 1932.

59. REV. GROVER CLEVELAND PARSONS; b. June 18, 1893; m. Sarah Adkins, January 13, 1911.

Children. Sixth Generation:

92. Lonnie Parsons; b. April 18, 1912.
93. Eula Parsons; b. January 2, 1914.
94. Irene Parsons; b. June 2, 1916.
95. Buell H. Parsons; b. September 8, 1918.
96. Garnet Parsons; b. August 6, 1920.

97. Ercle Parsons; b. July 8, 1922.
98. Alma Parsons; b. August 2, 1924.
99. Betty Parsons; b. June 9, 1927.
100. Garland Parsons; b. September 7, 1930.
101. John W. Parsons; b. June 8, 1935.
102. Charles E. Parsons; b. November 1, 1938.

58. GEORGE W. PARSONS: b. March 10, 1890; m. Lena Evans.
December 11, 1912.

Children. Sixth Generation:
103. Noble Parsons; b. September 2, 1913.
104. Ruth Parsons; b. March 7, 1915.
105. Emily Parsons; b. February 28, 1917.
106. George Parsons; b. July 28, 1920.
107. Clarice Parsons; b. June 27, 1922.
108. Roy Parsons; b. May 31, 1924.
109. Lona Parsons; b. November 26, 1925.
110. Calvin Parsons; b. April 24, 1927.
111. Anna Parsons; b. September 8, 1929.

60. THOMAS ALLEN PARSONS; b. June 4, 1895; m. Eula Van
Hoose, November 25, 1915.

Children. Sixth Generation:
112. Edith Marie Parsons; b. November 1, 1916.
*113. Charles Woodrow Parsons.
114. Dennis Herman Parsons; b. April 3, 1920.
115. Anna Lois Parsons; b. April 15, 1922.
116. Nell Alene Parsons; b. November 6, 1925.
117. William Thomas Parsons; b. February 24, 1928.
118. Shirley Parsons; b. September 16, 1930.

64. DR. CHARLES HAROLD PARSONS, onetime dentist and progressive businessman at Ashland, Kentucky, was b. at Saulsberry, Carter
County, Kentucky, January 27, 1888; was reared on his father's
farm and attended the rural public school of the vicinity in his youth.
After completing a course in the Grayson (Kentucky) High School,
he entered the dental department of the University of Louisville
from which he was graduated in 1916. He located at Ashland, Kentucky, for the practice of his profession and after three years of
successful practice he entered the commercial field in Ashland in
1919, becoming the owner of the department store conducted by the
Bigbee-Carden Company, on Winchester Avenue. He reorganized
the business and it is now controlled by the C. H. Parsons Company
of which he is president.

Dr. Parsons is a Democrat in politics and a member of the First
Presbyterian Church of Ashland, serving as elder. He is a mem-

ber, serving as a director, of the Ashland Chamber of Commerce. He is a member of the various Masonic bodies and a worthy exemplar of the order and is affiliated with the local Kiwanis Club of which he has served as president.

On October 18, 1916, Dr. Parsons was m. to Miss Elizabeth Potts, a daughter of James L. and Eliza Belle (Burns) Potts of Grayson, Kentucky. To this union two children were born (sixth generation):

119. Mary Elizabeth Parsons, b. September 15, 1917.
120. Elenore Burns Parsons, b. August 15, 1921.

113. CHARLES WOODROW PARSONS; b. March 15, 1918; m. Valcia Taylor, September 15, 1941.

Children. Seventh Generation:

121. Charles Elwood Parsons; b. June 20, 1942.
122. Carol Ann Parsons; b. March 29, 1946.
123. Michael Ray Parsons; b. July 2, 1947.

---

[1] "South Carolina in the Revolution" (Supplement), compiled by Sara Sullivan Ervin, 1949, p. 109.

PATRICK FAMILY OF MAGOFFIN COUNTY

1. HUGH PATRICK, a Marylander, was the progenitor of the Patrick family of Eastern Kentucky. He had a son.

2. JEREMIAH PATRICK who m. Sallie Blair and migrated from Maryland to Giles County, Virginia about 1790. In 1810 he moved from Giles County to Russell County, Virginia, and from there to Floyd, now Magoffin County, Kentucky, in 1822 where he d. and was buried on the Middle Fork of Licking River.[1]

Issue:

3. William Patrick; m. Mollie Raines; migrated from Giles County, Virginia, to what is now Magoffin County, Kentucky.

Issue:

*4. Meredith Patrick.
5. Reuben Patrick.
6. John Patrick.
7. Jeremiah Patrick.
8. Jincy Patrick.
9. Richard Patrick.
10. William Patrick.
11. Nancy Patrick.
12. Polly Patrick.

4. Meredith Patrick; b. in Magoffin County, Kentucky; was one of the largest landowners, possessing between 2500 and 3000 acres; was active in local politics; served as justice of the peace; was an important and influential citizen; active member of the Methodist Episcopal Church; sympathized with the North in the Civil War; m. Rebecca Cope.

Issue:

13. Herod Patrick; lived to an old age and d. at Bloomington, Kentucky.
14. Elijah Patrick; served in the State Senate following the close of the Civil War; was a merchant whose trade extended over a large territory, including Breathitt and surrounding counties. One Elijah Patrick m. Louise Rule in Johnson County in 1856.
*15. Reuben Patrick.
16. Serena Patrick; m. Neri Swetnam. (See Swetnam Family.)
*17. Wiley C. Patrick.
18. Alexander Patrick; d. in Morgan County where he had resided for some time.

15. REUBEN PATRICK was b. December 15, 1830, and d. October 14, 1902. A Republican in politics, he served as School Commissioner (County Superintendent of Schools) of Magoffin County for many

years; served in the Kentucky General Assembly; and was a deputy collector of internal revenue during three National Administrations. He served with distinction in the Union Army in the Civil War.[2]

After the close of the war he returned to a farm near Salyersville, Magoffin County, and became one of the largest land-owners of that section.

Reuben Patrick m. in Johnson County, November 11, 1851, Amanda Burns Hager, b. April 4, 1832, d. April 14, 1914, daughter of General Daniel Hager. (See Hager Family.)

Issue:

19. Salena H. Patrick; b. 1852; m. James Connoy.
*20. Robert A. Patrick.
21. Susan E. Patrick; m. Robert Hurt.
22. Franklin M. Patrick; m. ——— Hammonds.
23. Annie Patrick; b. 1856 and d. 1934; m. Madison Monroe Walter. (See Walter Family.)
*24. Mattie Patrick.
*25. Dennis B. Patrick.
*26. Catherine Patrick.
*27. Katherine Patrick.
28. Grant Patrick; unm.
29. Maud Patrick: m. D. B. Salyer; lived in Owingsville, Kentucky.
30. Jacob Patrick; unm.
31. June Patrick; m. Richard Millard.
32. Henry W. Patrick; m. Jessie Arnett.
33. Benjamin B. Patrick.

20. ROBERT A. PATRICK, b. October 19, 1861; was reared on Burning Fork of Licking River; began his career as traveling salesman; was manager of one of his father's stores; served as clerk of the Magoffin County Court during which period he studied law; was admitted to the bar at Paintsville. 1880 and engaged in practice for a time; became associated with John C. C. Mayo, having full charge of the surveys and abstracts of that industrialist; served as police judge of Paintsville; was a director of the Second National Bank, Paintsville, for a number of years and his wise counsels and splendid business judgment were always highly valued by his associates; was a member of Paintsville Lodge No. 381, F. and A.M., for about fifty-four years and served as master and filled numerous other offices. For over fifty years he was a devout Christian and member of the Methodist Episcopal church, giving liberally of his time and means. He served as a member of the church board for many years and for nearly a quarter of a century was the teacher of the Ladies' Bible class.

ROBERT A. PATRICK m. in Johnson County, February 22, 1882, Collista A. Stafford, b. November 24, 1862, daughter of Francis M. Stafford. (See Stafford Family.)

Issue:

34. Bertha Patrick; m. Harry C. Howes. (See Howes Family.) Resides in Lexington, Kentucky.

35. Beulah Patrick; (deceased), m. Dan Wheeler. (See Wheeler Family.)

36. Gertrude Patrick; resides in Paintsville.

37. Nora Patrick; d. in infancy.

24. MATTIE PATRICK; m. Augustus R. Arnett; residence, Salyersville.

Issue:

38. Florence Arnett; m. Rowland Menix.

39. Fannie Arnett; m., first, Benjamin Johnson and, secondly, John Adams.

40. Ernest Arnett.

41. Maud Arnett; m. Chester Back.

42. Julia Arnett; m. William Patrick.

43. Lilly Mae Arnett; m. Abijah Wells.

44. Clarence Arnett; m. ——— Duff.

45. William Arnett.

46. Arby Arnett.

47. Thelma Arnett.

48. ——— Arnett (?)

25. DENNIS B. PATRICK; m., first, ——— Salyers; residence, Salyersville.

Issue:

49. ——— Patrick (?)

50. ——— Patrick, a daughter; m. Brownlow Keaton.

Issue:

51. Alfred Patrick.

25A. Dennis B. Patrick; m., secondly, ——— Patrick.

Issue:

52. ——— Patrick, a daughter; m. John ———.

53. ——— Patrick; m. ——— Patrick.

27. KATHERINE PATRICK; m. M. M. Salyer.

Issue:

54. John Salyer.

17. WILEY C. PATRICK; m. in Johnson County, in 1856, Mary Huff, daughter of German Huff of Paintsville. He served with dis-

tinction in the Union Army in the Civil War. He was enrolled for service at Louisa, Kentucky, February 7, 1863, a lieutenant, Company "I", 14th Kentucky Vol. Infantry; promoted from first lieutenant to captain, the same day; killed in action near Altoona Mountain, June 2, 1864.[3]

From the day of the coming of the elder Patrick to the present time, the family has held a high rank in the social, intellectual, material and church affairs of the country.[4]

The Patricks were old-time Whigs in politics and are now Republicans. They are members of the Methodist Episcopal Church; and are an aggressive and forceful people.[5]

---

[1] Mitchell Hall, "History of Johnson County, Kentucky", 1928, Vol. II, p. 363.

[2] At about the time of the Battle of Middle Creek (January 10, 1862) between then Col. James A. Garfield's command and Gen. Humphrey Marshall's command, Reuben Patrick stole in the nighttime a cannon from Gen. Marshall's army, which later was taken to his home at Salyersville. Subsequently the cannon was placed in the Armory at Frankfort but finally, at the urging of "Jake" Patrick, it was restored to the Patrick family and placed in the keeping of Ernest Arnett at Salyersville, a grandson of Reuben Patrick.

[3] Report of the Adjutant General of Kentucky, 1861-1866, Vol. I, pp. 872-893.

[4] William Ely, "The Big Sandy Valley", p. 395.

[5] Mitchell Hall, "History of Johnson County, Kentucky", Vol. II, p. 363.

POAGUE OR POAGE FAMILY

This family is of Scotch or Scotch-Irish extraction and migrated from Scotland to Ireland, probably to Ulster, Northern Ireland, and thence to the American colonies about 1738. Colonel Robert Poague, the immigrant, with his wife and nine children came to the Virginia colony by way of Philadelphia and on the 22nd day of May, 1740, he appeared in the Orange County (Virginia) Court to prove the importation of his family in order to obtain land. He settled on a plantation of 772 acres about three miles north of present Staunton, then Orange County, subsequently Augusta County, apparently purchased from William Beverley, as the land was in Beverley Manor.[1] He acquired other land directly from the Government as is evidenced by a patent issued to him by Governor Gooch, July 30, 1742, for 306 acres in Orange County on the west side of Blue Ridge.

Colonel Poague m., in Ireland, Elizabeth Preston, sister to John Preston, the Scotch-Irish immigrant [2] who settled in Augusta County Virginia, and was the ancestor of many distinguished families of Virginia and Kentucky. (See Preston Family.) Upon the organization of Augusta County, Colonel Poague was commissioned as one of the first magistrates. He was also commissioned a captain of the Virginia militia in November 1761. He d. March 1774.

1. COLONEL ROBERT POAGUE m., in Ireland, Elizabeth Preston.
Issue:
*2. John Poague, b. in Ireland.
3. Robert Poague, b. in Ireland.
4. George Poague, b. in Ireland.
*5. William Poague, b. in Ireland.
*6. Thomas Poague, b. in Virginia.
7. Elizabeth Poague, b. in Ireland; m. in Virginia, —— Crawford.
8. Margaret Poague, b. in Ireland; m. in Virginia, —— Robertson.
9. Martha Poague, b. in Ireland; m. in Virginia Archibald Woods.
10. Mary Poague, b. in Ireland; m. Colonel Robert Breckenridge (his first wife). She d. quite young, leaving two sons, Robert and Alexander, who became noted citizens.
11. Sarah Poague, b. in Ireland; m. Thomas Gordon.[3]

2. MAJOR JOHN POAGUE 2 (Colonel Robert Poague 1, and his wife Elizabeth Preston) was a vestryman of Augusta Parish; deputy surveyor of Augusta County; became High Sheriff of the county, March 17, 1778, and the next day he qualified as surveyor. Probably he acquired lands in Greenbriar County, Virginia, now West Virginia, as is evidenced by a survey of 420 acres of land in that county on April 27, 1752, for one John Poage of Augusta. His

will dated February 16, 1789, proved in court April 22, 1789, mentions his wife, Mary (Blair) Poage, and his seven children:

12. Robert Poage qualified June 16, 1778, as assistant surveyor to Thomas Lewis, surveyor of Augusta county. He m. Martha Jane Hopkins.

13. James Poage m. his cousin, Mary Woods, daughter of Mrs. Martha Woods and granddaughter of Robert Poague, the immigrant; removed to Kentucky and was a member of the Kentucky Legislature in 1796; had two sons, Andrew and George, both Presbyterian ministers; and two daughters, Margaret, who m. Rev. T. S. Williamson and Sarah, who m. Rev. G. H. Pond.

14. John Poage, Jr., succeeded his father as surveyor of Augusta County; resided on a farm near Mawrys Mill about five miles north of Staunton; d. in 1827, leaving several children, most of whom went West. His son James, who remained in Augusta County, d. in 1876.

15. Thomas Poage, a minister; m. Miss Jane Watkins; d. in 1793.

16. Elizabeth Poage m., August 23, 1783, Rev. Dr. Moses Hoge, who for many years was president of Hampden-Sydney College. She d. June, 1802. Their three sons were eminent ministers—Rev. Dr. James Hoge, at Columbus, Ohio; Rev. John Blair Hoge, who d. young at Martinsburg, Virginia; and Rev. Samuel Davies Hoge who also d. young and was the father of Rev. Moses D. Hoge of Richmond, Virginia.

17. Ann Poage; m. Rev. James Blair.

18. COLONEL GEORGE POAGE, SR., 3 (John Poage 2, and his wife, Mary Blair, Colonel Robert Poague 1, and his wife, Elizabeth Preston) was b. in Augusta County, Virginia, March 28, 1754, and d. in Greenup County, Kentucky, September 6, 1821. He and his family were the first of the Poages to migrate to Northeastern Kentucky. They acquired a vast tract of land about 1790 between the Big Sandy and Little Sandy Rivers along the Ohio and extending back from the river. Colonel Poage built his home and lived in the limits of the present Ashland, being the first resident of the area. He m. Ann Allen, b. January 25, 1757, and d. August 6, 1835, daughter of Captain James Allen and his wife, Margaret (Anderson) Allen.

Issue—Thirteen children:

*19. John Poage.
*20. Allen Poage.
21. Margaret Poage m. ——— Campbell.
22. Mary Poage m. Robert Poage.
23. Elizabeth Poage m. ——— Johnson.
24. George W. Poage m. Martha ———.
*25. William Poage.
26. James Allen Poage m. Sarah ———.
27. Thomas Hoge Poage m. Nancy Allen Frame in 1817.
*28. Robert C. Poage.

*29. Hugh C. Poage.

30. Ann K. Poage m. ――――― Burton.

*31. Jane Trimble Poage [4]

19. "GENERAL" JOHN POAGE had service in the War of 1812, as colonel commanding Poage's Regiment, Kentucky Volunteers, rendezvousing at Newport, August 31, 1813. He m. his cousin, Ann Poague daughter of 5. William Poague and his wife, Ann (Kennedy) Wilson Poague.

20. ALLEN POAGE was b. in Greenbriar County, Virginia, now West Virginia, January 23, 1778, and migrated to Kentucky in 1799; m., first, Susan Caroline Frame and m., secondly, in Greenup County, Kentucky, June 2, 1806, Margaret Terrill, who was b. in Greenbrier County, Virginia, August 18, 1790. They removed to Vermillion County, Illinois in 1825.

Issue:

32. Malinda Poage, b. October 11, 1807; m. in Greenup County, February 7, 1824, Simpson C. Head.

33. Alpheus Poage; b. July 9, 1809, d. young.

34. Nicholas Poage, b. February 23, 1811, d. at Mary, McDonald County, Missouri.

35. Louann Poage, b. November 13, 1813; m. John Bailey. Both d. in Iowa.

36. William B. Poage, b. November 21, 1814; removed to Johnstown, Bates County, Missouri.

37. Robert T. Poage, b. November 22, 1819; d. young.

38. Rebecca T. Poage, b. November 22, 1819.

39. George Terrill Poage, b. October 30, 1822; removed to Exoria, Audubon County, Iowa.

40. Margaret Poage, b. August 12, 1824; m. Nathaniel Hamlin, Draytown, Iowa.

41. John P. Poage, b. October 22, 1827; unm.

42. Mildred Poage, b. November 14, 1828; m. Thomas Simpson, b. October 22, 1827. She d. at Lebanon, Indiana.

43. Thomas Poage, b. November 25, 1832; d. at Decatur, Georgia, while serving in the Federal Army.

44. James Poage, b. February 22, 1835.

25. WILLIAM POAGE was b. in Virginia, presumably in Greenbriar County, February 2, 1788, and d. in Greenup County, Kentucky, September 3, 1836; m. in Lawrence County, Kentucky, March 5, 1822, Eliza Van Horn, b. in Pennsylvania, July 16, 1797, and d. in Greenup County, Kentucky, May 26, 1854, daughter of John Van Horn.

In his will, probated November 4, 1836, in the Greenup County (Kentucky) Court, William Poage names as executors his widow Eliza M. and H. A. Poage, but if incapacitated, then his brother,

"General" John Poage, Thomas H. Poage and brother-in-law, F. Mose; and mentions his children, as follows:

    45. Estill Poage.

  *46. George B. Poage.

    47. Permelia Ann Poage; b. March 18, 1835; m. Daniel Miller.

  *48. Theodore Moore Poage.

    49. Maria Jane Poage who m. in Pike County, Kentucky, November 16, 1857, Judge George N. Brown. (See Brown Family of Boyd County.)

    50. Sarah Frances Poage who m. in Lawrence County, Kentucky, November 25, 1852, Judge John M. Rice. (See Rice Family of Boyd County.)

  *51. Elizabeth Poage, b. June 28, 1834; m. ———— Apple.

    46. GEORGE BERNARD POAGE, minister of the Methodist Episcopal Church, b. January 18, 1823; m. July 19, 1846, Lucy Jane Eubank; was elected and served as clerk of the Lawrence County Court; removed to Bracken County, Kentucky, in 1862 and was elected County Court Clerk of that county.

    48. Theodore Moore Poage, tobacco planter; b. July 21, 1827; removed to Bracken County, Kentucky, and m. Miss Holton there.

    28. ROBERT CYRUS POAGE, agriculturist and miller; was b. at Poage's Landing, now Ashland, October 12, 1815, and d. in Ashland, April 17, 1904. He was educated in the local pioneer schools and in the schools of Cincinnati, Ohio. In 1854 when Ashland was organized, he sold his farm which was laid out in town lots; and a few years before the Civil War he erected a flour mill in Ashland, afterward installing the best machinery obtainable and conducted a milling business until his death after which the business was conducted by a grandson under the style R. C. Poage Milling Company. He m. December 24, 1839, Miss Ann Gallaher, daughter of James and Sarah (Craut) Gallaher of Guyandotte, West Virginia.

    Issue: Four children, one of whom d. in infancy.

  *52. James Harvey Poage.

  *53. Ashland Poage.

    54. Louella Kemper Poage; resided in the Poage home, 1016 Winchester Avenue., Ashland; unm.

    52. JAMES HARVEY POAGE; b. in Ashland, October 31, 1840, and d. in Huntington, West Virginia, September 16, 1916. For a number of years he was associated with his father in the milling business in Ashland and afterward in the transfer business, becoming manager of Wharf boats. He went to Cabell County, West Virginia, in the 1850's where he m. Miss Mary C. Haskall, a native of Ohio.

    Issue:

    55. Nettie Poage; m. F. J. Duesler of Ashland.

    56. Mary Poage; d. in infancy

    57. Evaline Poage; m. A. R. Lawrence of Peru, Indiana.

58. Louis Kemper Poage; d. young.
59. Anna Poage; m. Alexander Poage.
60. Harriet Poage.
61. Robert Poage.

53. ASHLAND POAGE, was b. June 16, 1854, the day Ashland was organized and was the first child born in the town for which he was named. He was educated at Beach Grove Academy. At the age of eighteen, he became associated with his father and brother in the milling business in which he continued until his death on October 16, 1886, at the age of 32. He m. Miss Nellie May Flye of Maine.
Issue:
*62. Edwin Flye Poage.
63. Robert Cyrus Poage; d. in infancy.
64. Helen Marguerite Poage.

62. EDWIN FLYE POAGE was reared to the age of 8 years in Ashland; grew to manhood and was educated in Maine; and after completing his education, he returned to Ashland. In 1907 he was elected president of the R. C. Poage Milling Company. He m. Miss Virginia McCready Savage of Ashland, daughter of Samuel S. Savage, onetime County Judge of Boyd County, Kentucky.
Issue:
65. Edwin F. Poage, Jr., d. in infancy.[5]

29. HUGH CALVIN POAGE m. Miss Sarah E. Davenport, b. at Jonesville, County Seat of Lee County, Virginia, which town was named for her grandfather, Wylie Jones, who gave the ground for the public buildings.
Issue:
66. Judge Hugh William Poage m. Lausetta Shaw: was Judge of the Boyd County Court.
67. Nannie Rebecca Poage d. in infancy.
68. M. Emma Poage m. John H. Elba.
*69. Col. M. Annie Poage.
70. Dr. Thomas Hoge Poage; m. M. Josephine Kleinman, businesswoman of Chicago.
71. Judge James H. Poage m. Gertrude Skelley; was onetime clerk of the Boyd County Court, and First Assistant City Attorney of Chicago.
72. Virginia S. Poage; m. Frank R. Henderson.
73. Catherine Crawford Poage; m. Ernest H. Townsend.
74. Robert Hamlin Poage m. Josephine Everett.
75. Louise Poage; unm.

69. COL. M. ANNIE POAGE, journalist, publicist, club woman, civic worker; was educated in the public schools of Ashland, at the Ashland Normal School and at Professor Sopher's School of Oratory at the Atheneum in Chicago, being the valedictorian of her class. She never engaged in teaching, the profession for which she was educated

but always engaged in journalism. She was a member of the staff of the Ashland Daily Independent for a number of years and subsequent to retirement from that position in 1921, she was engaged in writing newspaper and magazine articles as well as in club, church and civic work.

Miss Poage was commissioned a colonel on the staff of Gov. Black which she considered a great honor. She was an active member of the Kentucky Press Association, the Ashland Womens' Club, the Three Arts Club of Ashland, the Altrusa Club, the Business and Professional Woman's Club, the Y. W. C. A., the D. A. R., and the Daughters of the War of 1812. In politics she was a staunch Democrat.

31. JANE TRIMBLE POAGE, b. at Staunton, Virginia, in 1800, d. at Point Pleasant, Virginia, now West Virginia, 1854; m., first, Alphonso B. Hawkins and after his death m., secondly, at Point Pleasant, Virginia, November 12, 1835, Jacob Knopp, b. October 11, 1815, at Letart, Ohio, and d. September 19, 1900.

Issue:

76. John Allen Knopp, b. July 10, 1836, in Mason County, Virginia, and d. September 18, 1903, at Alderson, West Virginia.

77. Sarah Leonard Knopp, b. at Portsmouth, Ohio, May 13, 1842, d. September 9, 1909, at Alderson, West Virginia; m., 1860, at Collegeville, West Virginia.

5. WILLIAM POAGUE, 2 (COL. ROBERT, 1) was b. in Ireland about 1726; m. in Augusta County, Virginia, in 1762, Mrs. Ann Wilson, nee Kennedy; resided a while near Natural Bridge in Rockbridge County; removed to near present Abingdon, Virginia, then Fincastle, now Washington County, in 1774. William Poague had service in the French and Indian War as sergeant in command of Ft. Russell.

In company with the families of Colonel Richard Calloway and John B. Stagner, William and Ann Poague migrated to Kentucky and settled in the fort at Boonesborough on September 26, 1775. In the following February they went to Harrodstown and in the spring of 1776, Poague cleared ground and planted corn about two miles from the fort. On September 1, 1778, a company of 16 white men, including Poague, while going from Harrodstown to St. Asaphs, were fired upon by Indians when near the site of present Danville and all escaped unhurt except Poague who was mortally wounded. He was rescued by his friends but d. the next day. His horse, on which he had escaped from the Indians, was given to his son, Robert, then 12 years old.

According to the historian Collins, William Poague had great mechanical skill and during two or three years made all the wooden vessels used by the people in the fort at Harrodstown; he also made the wood-work of the first plow used in Kentucky, and the first loom on which weaving was done in the State.

After the death of William Poague, his widow, Ann, m., in 1781, Captain Joseph Lindsay who was killed in the battle with the Indians at Blue Licks (the last battle of the Revolution, August 19, 1782). Subsequently she became the wife of James McGinty.

According to the historian Collins, Ann (Kennedy) Poague-Lindsay-McGuinty was a woman of rare energy and ingenuity; and brought the first spinning-wheel to Kentucky, and made the first linen manufactured in the country from the lint of nettles and the first linsey from Nettle-lint and buffalo wool.

Children of William Poague and his wife, Ann (Kennedy) Wilson Poague:

78. Elizabeth Poage, b. in Virginia, September 4, 1764; d. October 10, 1850; m. Capt. John Thomas.

*79. "General" Robert Poage, b. in Virginia, September 6, 1766.

80. Joseph Poage, b. in Virginia, May 8, 1770.

81. Martha Poage, b. in Virginia, June 5, 1772.

82. Mary Poage, b. in Virginia, March 10, 1775.

*83. Ann Poage, b. in Kentucky, August 12, 1777.

84. Amaziah Poage, b. in Kentucky, August 17, 1778.

The Poages of Cincinnati, Ohio, are descendants of William and Ann (Kennedy) Wilson Poague.

79. "GENERAL" ROBERT POAGE, 3 (William Poage 2, and his wife Ann (Kennedy) Wilson, Colonel Robert Poage, 1 and his wife, Elizabeth Preston) was b. in Virginia September 6, 1766. The records indicate that "General" Robert Poage, with associates, Robert Campbell, General Thomas Bodley, and one Hughes, purchased 10,-000 acres of rich cane lands in the Mayslick (now Maysville) neighborhood, Mason County. Apparently General Poage established his home on this land. Robert Poage was a lieutenant colonel of Poage's Regiment of Kentucky Militia in the War of 1812. He rendezvoused with his regiment at Newport, Kentucky, August 27, 1812. He also served in the Indian Wars under General Wayne and was in the Battle of Fallen Timbers in Ohio, 1794.

"General" Poague m. Jane Hopkins, daughter of Captain John Hopkins, Revolutionary War officer, of Rockingham County, Virginia.

Children:

*85. William Lindsay Poage.

86. Jane Poage; m. November 1823, William Mackey, merchant.

87. Ann Poage.

88. Amanda Poage; m. Dr. J. A. McDowell of Fleming County; she d. January 1827.

85. WILLIAM LINDSAY POAGE, ironmaster; b. in Kentucky, 1794; m. in Greenup County, Kentucky, November 8, 1824, Ann Mc-Cormick. He received by deed from his father, "General" Robert Poage, a 80,000-acre tract of land on Tygarts Creek and its tributaries, Three Prong, Bushy, Buffalo, Smith and Grassey Creeks.

This land extends into present Carter County and embraces Carter Caves and was sold in small tracts, the first of 3,000 acres near the mouth of Buffalo Creek was sold to Peter Duzan in 1824. Eli Cooper, who had come from Orangeburg, Mason County, m. in Greenup County, August 17, 1824, Rachel, daughter of Peter Duzan, and acquired a 200-acre tract at present Kehoe.

William L. Poage patented many acres in Northeastern Greenup County. He built Amanda Furnace, named for his daughter, Amanda, who m. John Paull Jones. In 1826 he organized a company with William Paul, George Paull Walker and others to build Bellefonte Furnace. A large brick house was built on the bank of the Ohio River for use of the furnace manager and his family. It had folding doors and an underground passage where the supplies for furnace use were stored. It has been said that Confederate soldiers were cared for in the underground passage during the Civil War.[6]

Of the William L. Poage family.

89. Ann Poage; m. Samuel Garrison; lived in the extreme western part of Greenup County at present Garrison.

90. John Poage; m. Ann Moore.

91. Eliza Poage; m. —— Gartrell.

92. Harriet Eleanor Poage; m. Ranson W. Cooper.

The Poage home is still standing below Ashland and is owned by Dr. Kyle J. Kinkead, a surgeon of Birmingham, Alabama, who descends from the Poage or Pogue family.

Much of the Poage land has been sold to the American Rolling Mill Company; other parts of it are included in the Bellefonte subdivision and in the property of the Ashand Country Club.

83. Ann Poage was b. in the fort at Harrodstown, August 12, 1777 and is claimed by reputable historians to have been the fourth white child b. in Kentucky. She m. her cousin, "General" John Poage, (See No. 19, Poage Family) and was a resident of Greenup County, Kentucky from the Spring of 1802 (when there were only six families in what is now Greenup County) until her death April 24, 1848.[7]

6. THOMAS POAGUE 2, (COL. ROBERT POAGUE 1, and his wife Elizabeth Preston) was the youngest and only child of Colonel Robert Poague, the immigrant, b. in America. He inherited and lived on the old homestead in Beverley Manor near Staunton; m. Polly McClannahan, daughter of Robert and Jane McClannahan. His will proved in court, January 14, 1803, mentions his eight children:

93. Elijah Poague; m. July 3, 1787, Nancy Gratton, daughter of John. They migrated to Kentucky.

94. Robert Poague; m. Martha Crawford, September 15, 1791. They migrated to Kentucky.

95. John Poague; m., November 27, 1792, Mrs. Rachel Crawford, widow of John Crawford of Augusta County and daughter of Hugh Barclay of Rockbridge County. They resided in Rockbridge County

and were the grandparents of Colonel William T. Poage of Lexington, Virginia.

96. William Poage, the youngest son of Thomas, Sr., was a major in the Revolution; lived many years in the ancestral home; m., first, Betsy, daughter of Col. Andrew Anderson, who d. without issue, and m., secondly, Peggy Allen, who had many children. A son, Thomas, a lawyer who resided in Southwestern Virginia, was colonel of the 15th Virginia Regiment, Confederate States Army and was killed on the Blackwater in February, 1863. A daughter m. General James A. Walker, one-time Lieutenant Governor of Virginia.

97. Ann Poague; m. March 5, 1789, Col. Archibald Woods of Botetourt County, son of Mrs. Martha Woods, daughter of Col. Robert Poague, Sr., removed to Ohio County, Virginia, now West Virginia; d. in 1846. A son, Thomas, was cashier of the North Western Bank of Virginia at Wheeling and was father of Rev. Edgar Woods of Pantops Academy, Albemarle.

98. Elizabeth Poague; m. Rev. William Wilson of Augusta County.

99. Polly Poague; m. Thomas Wilson, lawyer and congressman. They lived at Morgantown, Virginia, now West Virginia. A son, Rev. Norval Wilson, was a prominent minister of the Methodist Episcopal Church, and a daughter, Mrs. Louise Lowrie, was a missionary in India. Among the grandsons was Bishop Alpheus Wilson of the Methodist Episcopal Church.

100. Agnes Poague; d., unm.

According to tradition and documentary evidence, Colonel Robert Poague, the immigrant, had a brother, John, who settled in Rockbridge County, Virginia and m. Jane Somers (Summers) of that county. They had ten children and were a noted family.

The Poage or Poague families furnished a comparatively large number of commissioned officers and enlisted men in defense of their country in the French and Indian War, the Revolutionary War [8] and the War of 1812. Generally they were planters and slave-holders. However, some were public officials and ministers of the Gospel; and many of them were businessmen: bankers, merchants, millers and iron masters. Generally they were Democrats in politics and Presbyterians in religion. Some of them were considered wealthy in their day.

---

[1] "Robert Poage or Poague (father of William Poague) and his wife Ann Kennedy", by Martha R. Thomas Nuckols, 1915.

[2] Virginia Magazine of History and Biography.

[3] "Annals of Augusta County, Virginia, 1776-1871", by Joseph A. Waddell, Second Edition, pp. 258-261.

[4] "Poague or Poage Family" (manuscript), in Library of the Kentucky State Historical Society, Frankfort, Kentucky.

[5] "History of Kentucky", by Temple Bodley and Judge Samuel M. Wilson, the S. J. Clarke Publishing Company, Chicago - Louisville, 1928.

[6] "History of Greenup County, Kentucky", by Nina M. Biggs, 1957.

[7] Collins, "History of Kentucky."

[8] "Virginians in the Revolutionary War 1775-1783", by John H. Gwathmey, page 629.

PRICE FAMILY OF JOHNSON COUNTY

This is a well-known Welsh name formed by the joining (alphesis) of elements in the patronymic "Ap Rice" (son of Rice). Previous to the time of Henry VIII, there were no fixed Welsh surnames in the usual sense of the word. A man simply prefixed "Ap" (son of) to his father's baptismal name. Thus if the father's name was Thomas the son's might be Ap Thomas, whilst the grandson's might be John Ap John. But after that time the father's name or the name of some earlier ancestor began to be adopted as a permanent surname. After the surname became permanent, it soon underwent another change by the absorption of the prefix "Ap". The name Powell arose from Ap Howell; Price from Ap Rhys; Prichard from Ap Richard; Preece from Ap Reese, the modern form of Rhys; Pugh from Ap Hugh, etc. In all such cases the modern form of the name originates from a baptismal name.

The Price families are numerous and large and are found in all parts of the United States. Most of them originated in Wales and doubtless have a common origin. The Welsh family of Price was an important one, famous for its soldiers and statesmen.

The Maryland Prices descended from a Captain John Price who, in a colony of twenty-four families, was the first to arrive there. In Pennsylvania there were two separate colonies of Prices: one Philip Price came from Wales with the first colony, and another family of German extraction whose surname, being similar to Price, was changed to Price. A John Price, member of the Jamestown (Virginia) colony, was the ancestor of the largest Price family in the United States. Most of the Prices in Virginia, Tennessee, Kentucky and Missouri are of this family.

The Progenitor of the Price family of Eastern Kentucky has not been definitely determined. However, it would seem from exhaustive research that one Thomas Price was the founder of this branch of the family. He was b. in Culpeper county, Virginia, about 1738, presumably a son of Kalem (or Calem) Price, and resided for a time at Elk Garden, now Russell county, Virginia. He was in Lord Dunmore's War against the Indians in 1774, having enlisted and served in Captain John Lewis' Company of the Augusta County(Virginia) Regiment commanded by Colonel Charles Lewis. He was at the battle of Point Pleasant (October 10, 1774). He had service in the Revolutionary War and was at the battle of King's Mountain (October 7, 1780). He migrated and settled in Kentucky prior to 1793, as a son, John A. Price, was b. in Kentucky in 1793. He had other children—five came with him to Kentucky—one of whom, William m. ——— Eaton about 1800. It is believed that another son was named Jesse.

Thomas Price and sons, William (and his family) and John A., removed to Posey county, Indiana, prior to 1814, where Thomas

Price d. November 12, 1824, "aged ninety years or upward." Apparently his other children remained in Kentucky.

1. JESSE PRICE, b. in Tazewell county, Virginia, m., in Floyd county, Kentucky, December 29, 1808, Lynchie Preston, d. in 1870's daughter of Moses Preston, Revolutionary War soldier, and his wife, Fanny (Arthur) Preston. They resided for a time at Graves Shoals on Big Sandy River; later near the mouth of Buffalo Creek and finally, after 1873, at Paintsville where they died. They had issue —fourteen children—eleven sons and three daughters:

Second Generation

*2. George Washington Price.
*3. Moses Price.
*4. Thomas Jefferson Price.
*5. John Price.
*6. William Price.
*7. Jesse Price, Jr.
*8. Harrison Price.
*9. A. Jackson Price.
*10. David Price.
*11. Frank Price.
*12. Columbus Price.
*13. Louisa Price.
14. Betsy Ann Price, m. Redford Preston (See Preston Family).
*15. Kesiah Price.

2. GEORGE WASHINGTON PRICE, b. in Floyd county, Kentucky, January 31, 1811, d. in Morgan county, Kentucky, September 20, 1889. He was a farmer, a hotelkeeper at Paintsville where he resided for a longtime, and a distinguished minister of the United Baptist Church, being pastor of seven churches at the time of his death. He m., first, in Floyd county, in 1832, Sarah Borders (b. 1816, d. September 1, 1870) daughter of Hezekiah Borders, and, second, Lucinda Clark of Pike county.

Children of George Washington Price and his wife, Sarah (Borders) Price:

16. Hamilton Price.
17. Naomi Price, m. James M. Davis. (See Davis Family).
18. Lorenda Price, m. Montraville Preston. (See Preston Family).
19. Elizabeth Price.
20. Anderson Price, d. at age of 19 years.
21. Fannie Price.
22. Sophie Price.
23. Julina Price, m. Hereford Preston. (See Preston Family).
24. Martin Luther Price.
25. Ellen Price, d. at the age of 17 years.

26. Jemima Price.
27. Louisa Price.
28. Sarah Price, d. in infancy.

Children of George Washington Price and wife, Lucinda (Clark) Price:

29. Rosa Price, d. in young womanhood.
30. Sallie Price, m. Dock Ison.
31. Vasti Price, d. in young womanhood.
32. James Price, d. in young manhood.
33. George W. Price, Jr., m. Sallie Smith of Morgan county.
34. Thomas Price, m. ——— Keaton.
35. Tamar Price, d. in young womanhood.

3. MOSES PRICE, b. in Floyd county, in 1809, d. in Lawrence county, August 20, 1829, m. Sarah Van Hoose.
Children:
36. Boham Price.
37. Louisa Price.
38. Martin Price.
39. Lent Price, m. ——— Van Hoose.

4. THOMAS JEFFERSON PRICE, m., in ——— county, ———, Susan Ward.
Children:
40. Bishop Price.
41. Logan Price.
42. Jane Price, m. Adam Stacy.
43. Clara Hall Price.
44. Margania Price.
45. Hemma Price, m. ——— Brown.
46. Angie Price, m. John Spradlin.
47. Dicy Price, m. ——— ———.

5. JOHN PRICE, m. Sarah Fitch.
Children:
48. Frank Price.
49. David Price.
50. Jesse Price.
51. Jefferson Price.
52. Telitha Price.
53. Betsy Ann Price.
54. Lynchie Price.

6. WILLIAM PRICE, m., in Floyd county, August 8, 1838, Polly Preston, daughter of Jeffrey Preston.
Children:
55. Kenis Price.
56. Jane Price.

7. JESSE PRICE, JR., Baptist preacher; had service in the Union Army during the Civil War; b. 1826; m. Dicie Salyer, daughter of David Jesse Salyer.

Children:
57. Trinvilla Price, m. John Riley Akers.
58. Delila Price.
59. David Price.
60. Henry Price.
61. Betsy Ann Price.
62. Lynchie Price.
63. Noah K. Price.
64. Rosella Price.

8. HARRISON PRICE, settled on the head of Buffalo Creek, Johnson county. It is said that he migrated to Texas; m. Zina Ward.

Children:
65. Harlan Price, m. ——— Daniel.
66. Lynchie Price.
67. Emma Price, m. ——— Weddington.

9. A. JACKSON PRICE, b. in Floyd county, in 1820; m. Jemima Osborn, b. in 1827, d. 1899.

Children:
68. North J. Price, m., first, Martha Clark; second, ——— Conley; and, third, Mrs. Jenny Bays.
69. Hulda J. Price.
70. Julia Ann Price.
71. Winfield Price.
72. Fairway Price.
73. Daniel Price.
74. M. L. Price.
75. King F. Price.
76. Alice Price, m. Cyrus Preston (See Preston Family).
77. Crosford Price.

10. DAVID PRICE, m. Delilah Mankins, b. 1829. They began housekeeping on a farm in Johnson county but removed to Kansas and from thence to Oklahoma.

Children:
78. Harlan Price.
79. David Price, Jr.
80. ——— Price.

11. FRANK PRICE, m. Sarah Huff, daughter of German Huff.

Children:
81. Flora Price, m. ——— Hood.
82. Laura Price.

83. Jerome M. Price, m. ——— Zeigler.
84. Evert Price.
85. Stella Price, m. ——— Jones.
86. Victor Price.

12. COLUMBUS PRICE m. Sarah Meek.

Children:

87. Malcolm Price.
88. Henry Price.
89. Laura Belle Price.
90. Ella Price.
91. C. C. Price, m. Addie Davis. (See Davis Family).
92. John Price.
93. Virgie Lee Price.
94. Isaac Stewart Price.
95. Wilson Clark Price.

13. LOUISA PRICE, m. Valentine Van Hoose.

Children:

96. Harry Van Hoose.
97. Jasper Van Hoose.
98. Lafayette Van Hoose.
99. Jesse Van Hoose.
100. John Van Hoose, m. Susan Brown.
101. Frank Van Hoose, m. Louisina Pelphrey.
102. Martin Van Hoose.
103. Ruhemma Van Hoose.
104. Lynchie Van Hoose, m. Leander Brown.
105. Julia Van Hoose, m. Harvey B. Rice. (See Rice Family).

15. KESIAH PRICE, m. Hudson Keaton; lived in Morgan county, Kentucky.

Children:

106. Movetta Keaton.
107. Rhuhemma Keaton.
108. Harve Keaton.
109. Lynchie Keaton.
110. Martin Keaton.
111. Jefferson Keaton, m. Cecelia Smith.

MOSES PRESTON, SR., FAMILY

Moses Preston, Sr., was b. in Virginia, presumably in Bedford county, in 1763 and d. in Lawrence County, Kentucky, April 18, 1842. In the Fall of 1779 or the Spring of 1780, he enlisted as a private for a term of eighteen months in the Virginia Line of Infantry and served under Major Hill and Colonel Abraham Buford; and, under orders, was marched to Hillsborough, North Carolina, where General Cornwallis had retired with the British Army after his repeated failures to overtake General Greene as he retreated across the Carolinas after the disastrous defeat of the British Army under Colonel Tarleton at the Cowpens. He served also under Captain "Boyers" (Bower?) in a regiment commanded by Colonel William Campbell in the Army commanded by General Horatio Gates subsequently commanded by General Nathaniel Green. He was in the battles and/or engagements at Guilford Court House (March 15, 1781); at Camden (August 15, 1780); and at Ninety-six (June 29, 1781); and continued in the service until the close of the War at which time he was guarding the home of General Hugar near the Eutaw Springs, South Carolina. He was honorably discharged in South Carolina in 1783, by Captain Crawford, a regular officer; and received a certificate for his bounty lands which, as he stated in his declaration for a pension, he "sold for 20 or 25 dollars."

Returning to his home in Bedford County, Virginia, Moses Preston, on the 9th day of July 1783, in that county, m. Fanny Arthur, b. in 1764, daughter of Captain Arthur. Emigrating to the Big Sandy Valley in 1800, in the Great Westward Movement, he settled on the Morgan farm, Floyd county. From there he moved to the Forks of Beaver Creek, that county; and finally settled on a farm at the mouth of Georges Creek, then Floyd now Lawrence county, where he lived and d. He was a farmer.

Children of Moses Preston, Sr., 1, and Fanny (Arthur) Preston, his wife:

Second Generation

*2. Isaac Preston.
*3. Stephen Preston.
*4. Moses (Coby) Preston.
*5. John Preston.
*6. Henry Preston.
*7. Arthur Preston.
*8. Susan Preston.
*9. Linda or Lynchie Preston.
*10. Polly Preston.
*11. Jane or Jency Preston.
*12. Betty Preston.

2. Isaac Preston 2, (Moses, Sr. 1), farmer, paymaster of the

98th Regiment of Kentucky Militia, in 1819, m., February 1, 1812, Polly Sloan, of Pike county, Kentucky. They lived all their life on a farm in the vicinity of Peach Orchard, Lawrence county, where he d. at the age of seventy-six and she at eighty-five.

Children:

*12½ ——— Preston.

*13. Thomas Preston.

3. STEPHEN PRESTON 2, (Moses, Sr. 1), farmer; m., in Lawrence county, January 14, 1824, Pricilla (Pricie) Miller. They resided on a farm near Peach Orchard where he d. at the age of seventy-four and she at an advanced age.

Children:

14. Robert M. Preston.

4. MOSES (COBY) PRESTON 2, (Moses Sr. 1), the most prominent of his family and one of the outstanding businessmen of Eastern Kentucky of his time, a farmer, merchant; dealer in tan bark and timber, was b. in Bedford county, Virginia, May 2, 1797, and d. November 28, 1867, from the kick of a horse; m., first, presumably in Floyd county, Elizabeth Haney, b. in 1797, d. February 25, 1845; and secondly, Nancy Peery, b. June 4, 1814, d. May 26, 1883; daughter of David Peery, of Tazewell county, Virginia. Soon after his first marriage he and his young wife removed to the Scioto River (Ohio) region, but returning to the Big Sandy Valley, settled on the Spencer farm, now the Kise farm, some miles below the mouth of Georges Creek, Lawrence county, where they lived until about 1843, when they moved to the mouth of Paint Creek, about one-half of a mile from Paintsville, Johnson county. They maintained residences at both places.

Issue of Moses (Coby) Preston and Elizabeth (Haney) Preston, his wife.

*15. James (Cobe) Preston.

16. Redford Preston; b. in 1820, d. in 1906; m. in Johnson County, December 9, 1845, Betsy Ann Price.

*17. Greenville Preston.

*18. William Preston.

*19. Martin Preston.

*20. Moses Preston.

*21. Angeline Preston.

*22. Montraville Preston.

*23. Frank Preston.

*24. Henry Preston.

25. Thomas J. Preston; b. in 1841, d. in 1847.

*26. John D. Preston.

Issue of Moses (Coby) Preston and Nancy Peery, his wife.

27. Winfield Scott Preston.

*28. George Ballard Preston.

29. Infant.
30. Infant.
*31. M. Ella Preston.
*32. Josie Preston.
*33. Louisa Preston.

5. JOHN PRESTON 2, (Moses Sr. 1), m. in Lawrence county, October 27, 1842, Koeziah (Kizzie) Fitzpatrick. They reared a large family—of sons and one daughter.

6. HENRY PRESTON 2, (Moses Sr. 1), farmer; m. in Lawrence county, January 18, 1827, Betty Cains. They settled on a farm on Nat's Creek, where they resided until death—he at age of seventy-two and she at the age of eighty-six.
Children:
34. Sarah Preston; m. in Lawrence county, August 31, 1843 Wells Ward.
35. Stephen Preston; m. ——— Meade.
36. Arminta Preston; m. Nathan Ward.
*37. Madison Preston.
38. Jane Preston; m. in Lawrence county, December 25, 1853 William Warnock.
39. Rinda Preston; m. Noah Meade.
*40. Hiram Preston.
41. McDonald Preston; m. ——— Borders.
42. Amanda Preston; m. ——— Childers.
43. Caroline Preston; m. ——— Fitch.
44. William Preston; emigrated to Oregon.
*45. Julia Preston.

7. ARTHUR PRESTON 2, (Moses, Sr. 1), farmer and stockraiser, m., first, in Lawrence county, October 26, 1828, Nancy Miller, d. 1852; and secondly, Sarah Poory, d. 1881, daughter of David Peery of Tazewell county, Virginia. He first settled on Rockcastle creek, Martin county, but soon moved to Tygarts Valley, Greenup county. Subsequently, he returned to the Big Sandy Valley and settled on a farm at Graves Shoals, Lawrence county, where he d. in 1884. They left a large number of descendants near the old home-place.

8. SUSAN PRESTON 2, (Moses, Sr. 1); m., presumably in Floyd county, Abraham Mead. They lived on a farm on Mead Branch where she d. in 1847. They left numerous sons and daughters.

9. LINDA (LYNCHIE) PRESTON 2, (Moses Sr. 1); m., in Floyd county, December 29, 1808 or 1809, Jesse Price (See Price Family).

10. POLLY PRESTON 2, (Moses, Sr. 1); m. in Floyd county, November 7, 1809, John Hawes (See Hawes Family).

11. JANE (JINCY) PRESTON 2, (Moses, Sr. 1); m. in Floyd county, December 14, 1820, Archibald Borders (See Borders Family).

12. BETTY PRESTON 2, (Moses, Sr. 1); m. in Lawrence county, December 25, 1823, Abraham Childers.   They lived the greater part of the time on the Big Sandy River near Richardson, Lawrence county, but spent some time on Rockcastle Creek, Martin County.

Children:

45¼. Winston Childers.

Third Generation

12½. ——— PRESTON 3, (Isaac 2, Moses, Sr. 1).

Children:

45½. Milton T. Preston; merchant; lived near Peach Orchard, Lawrence county.

13. THOMAS PRESTON 3, (Isaac 2, Moses, Sr. 1).

Children:

46. Isaac (Red Ike) Preston; lived on Toms Creek, near Nippa, Lawrence county.

47. Sam Preston.

48. Patrick J. Preston.

49. Nancy J. Preston; m. Epp. Combs.

15. JAMES (COBE) PRESTON 3, (Moses (Coby)2, and Elizabeth Haney, his wife, Moses, Sr. 1); was b. in 1819 and d. in 1860; m., in Lawrence county, March 12, 1840, Levina Murray.

Children:

50. Elizabeth Preston; m. Winfield Walters (See Walters Family).

51. La Favette Preston.

52. Exer Preston; m. Martin Luther Price (See Price Family).

53. Nancy V. Preston; m. James Elliott.

*54. Samuel Preston.

55. Roscoe Preston; m. Josephine Porter.

56. Susie Preston; m. Winston Childers. (See No. 45¼.)

57. James Clayton Preston; m. Caslista Ward.

17. GREENVILLE PRESTON, 3 (Moses (Coby) 2, and Elizabeth Haney. his wife, Moses, Sr. 1), b. in 1821, d. in 1905; m., first, Exer Ward; and secondly, ——— Davis.

Children:

58. Levina Preston; m. Daniel Pelfrey, 1868.

59. ——— Preston m. John Dobbins.

60. Mace Preston m. a Golden.

61. Shade Preston (killed) m. Fanny Ward.

62. Greenville Preston.

63. James B. Preston m. Amanda Van Hoose.

64. Redford Preston.

65. Jeff Preston.

66. Isaac Preston m. Jemima Spears.

18. WILLIAM PRESTON 3, (Moses (Coby) 2, and his wife, Elizaabeth Haney, Moses, Sr. 1), farmer; owned a large boundary of land;

an important man in the county during his time; was born in Johnson county, December 20, 1823, d. January 12, 1896; lived at Thelma, Johnson county; m. in Lawrence county, November 25, 1845, Susan Murray, b May 3, 1828, d. January 10, 1912, daughter of Samuel Murray.

Children:

*67. Jeff Preston, b. February 15, 1850, d. January 28, 1873; m. Mary Williams.
*68. James Hereford Preston.
*69. Martin Preston.
70. Kennis Preston, b. in 1858; d. at age of 25.
*71. Sanford Preston.
*72. McClelland Preston.
73. Fanny Preston (infant).
*74. Martha Jane Preston.
75. Ellen Preston, b. March 25, 1852, d. July 5, 1881; m. Christopher Hall.
*76. Vina Preston.
*77. Angie Preston.
*78. Trinnie or Trinvilla Preston.
79. Elizabeth Preston.

19. MARTIN PRESTON 3, (Moses (Coby) 2, and his wife Elizabeth Haney, Moses, Sr., 1), b. January 8, 1828, d. June 4, 1891; m. (1) ——— Lord; (2) May 29, 1854, Nancy M. Brown, b. in Tazewell county, Virginia, in 1832, d. August 21, 1864; and (3) Rachael King.

Children of Martin Preston and his wife, Nancy M. Brown:

80. South G. Preston, noted minister of the Methodist Church and writer, m. Frona Dixon.
81. Angeline Preston; m. ——— Coleman; emigrated to St. Louis Missouri.
82. Frank Preston; emigrated to Utah.
83. Thomas Preston; m. Virginia Spradlin. Their daughter, Beatrice, m. J. H. Cooper, of Paintsville.

Children of Martin Preston and his wife, Rachael King:

84. Calla Preston.
85. James Preston; m. ——— Conley.
86. Cleveland Preston.
87. Addie Preston.

20. MOSES PRESTON 3, (Moses (Coby) 2, and his wife, Elizabeth Haney, Moses, Sr., 1), b. December 28, 1830, d. July 11, 1869; lived in Paintsville; m., first, Mary Jane Perry; and secondly, Louisa Hager.

Children of Moses Preston and his wife, Mary Jane Perry:

*88. Mary Jane (Mollie) Preston.

89. Virginia (Jenny) Preston; m. Thomas C. Brown (See Brown Family).

90. John Preston; m. Amanda Huff.

Children of Moses Preston and his wife, Louisa Hager:

*91. Morrell G. Preston.

*92. Daniel E. Preston.

93. Willie W. Preston, b. July 3, 1868, d. October 6, 1872. After his death, Mr. Preston's widow, Louisa, m. Dr. I. R. Turner.

21. ANGELINE PRESTON 3, (Moses (Coby) 2, and his wife, Elizabeth Haney, Moses, Sr., 1), b. in 1833; d. in 1858; m. Colonel Nathan Preston, son of Jeffrey Preston and his wife, Jane (Jency) Burgess.

Children:

*94. Theresa Preston.

95. Millard Preston; m. Amanda Preston, daughter of Eliphus Preston.

22. MONTRAVILLE PRESTON 3, (Moses (Coby) 2, and his wife, Elizabeth Haney, Moses, Sr., 1), farmer, prominent in the Big Sandy Valley and played a large part in its development in pioneer days; b. May 2, 1835, d. April 20, 1906; m. Lorenda Price, b. October 7, 1836, d. November 16, 1904.

Children:

*96. Paris F. Preston.

*97. George W. Preston.

*98. Samantha Preston.

*99. Anderson Bee Preston.

100. Elizabeth Preston; m. Charles Stafford.

*101. Warren L. Preston.

*102. Gayland Preston.

23. FRANK PRESTON 3, (Moses (Coby 2), and his wife, Elizabeth Haney, Moses, Sr., 1), merchant, lumberman, owner and operator of the steamboat "Frank Preston", president of the Sandy River Transportation Company, which operated several boats on the Big Sandy, successful in business and wealthy, was b. January 7, 1837, d. April 14, 1890; m. in Johnson county, January 28, 1857, Emily Hager, daughter of General Daniel Hager.

Children:

*103. Cyrus M. Preston.

*104. D. Lynn Preston.

*105. Caroline Preston.

*106. James Henry Preston.

107. (Infant).

108. (Infant).

109. Vertriece Preston, b. May 2, 1865, d. June 26, 1886; m. Charles M. Keyser; lived at Catlettsburg. No issue.

*110. Charles A. Preston.

*111. Ben F. Preston.

112. Fanny E. Preston, b. September 18, 1876, d. March 5, 1896; m. George H. Dimick, Jr.

24. HENRY PRESTON 3, (Moses (Coby) 2, and his wife, Elizabeth Haney, Moses, Sr., 1), b. November 25, 1839, d. January 8, 1881; m.; first, Selina J. Brown, b. January 25, 1843, d. May 11, 1878; and, secondly, Louisa E. Atkinson. Children of Henry Preston and his wife, Selina J. Brown:

113. Wallace Preston; m. ——— Prother.

114. Forrest Preston; unm.

Children of Henry Preston and Louisa Elizabeth Atkinson:

115. ——— Preston; d. in infancy.

26. JOHN D. PRESTON 3, (Moses (Coby) 2, and his wife, Elizabeth Haney, Moses, Sr., 1), proprietor of the Preston Hotel, at Paintsville, b. May 29, 1844, in Paintsville, d. May 13, 1925; m., in Johnson county, February 22, 1866, Sarah A. Brown, b. October 28, 1846, d. August 31, 1920, daughter of Hon. Wallace W. Brown.

Children:

*116. Frank H. Preston.

*117. Lina V. Preston.

*118. William M. Preston.

119. Edward Preston, b. July 25, 1876; m. September 19, 1903, Blanche Roe, b. December 1, 1881.

*120. Ethel Preston.

*121. Thomas C. Preston.

122. Paul Preston; d. in infancy.

123. Nannie Preston; d. in infancy.

28. GEORGE BALLARD PRESTON 3, (Moses (Coby) 2, and his wife, Nancy Peery, Moses, Sr., 1), farmer; resided on a farm at the mouth of Big Paint Creek, near Paintsville; b. September 6, 1851 and d. June 24, 1889; m., in Johnson county, Angelina Auxier.

Children:

*124. Laura Preston.

125. John Preston; m. Elizabeth Montgomery.

*126. Warren H. Preston.

*127. Hopkins Preston.

*128. James Preston.

129. Lula Preston.

31. M. ELLA PRESTON 3, (Moses (Coby) 2, and his wife Nancy Peery, Moses Sr., 1), b. in 1854 and d. in 1902; m. Frank A. Brown. They resided in Paintsville where Mr. Brown owned considerable real estate and was well-to-do.

Children:

130. Josephine Brown; m. John Preston.

131. Wallace W. Brown; m. Julia Allen.
132. Augusta L. Brown, b. September 23, 1882, d. September 6, 1908; m. Frank Allen.
133. Virginia Brown, b. September, 1885, d. December 1907.
134. Blanche F. Brown, b. July 4, 1889, d. December 22, 1912; m. William Thomas Roberts.
135. Captain Everett Brown; m. Jessie Vaughan.
136. Vertriece Brown.
137. (Infant).

32. JOSIE PRESTON 3, (Moses (Coby)2, and his wife, Nancy Peery, Moses, Sr., 1), b. in 1857; d. in 1909; m., first, T. B. Strong; and, secondly, George McDonald.

Children of Josie Preston and T. B. Strong:
138. James Strong.
139. Grace Strong.

33. LOUISA PRESTON 3, (Moses (Coby) 2, and his wife Nancy Peery, Moses, Sr., 1), b. in 1859; m. (1) John Strong; (2) John Barton; and (3) Arthur Preston, Jr. She lived on a farm near Graves Shoal and life many descendants there.

37. MADISON PRESTON 3, (Henry 2 and his wife, Betty Cains, Moses, Sr., 1) m. Dixie Taylor.
Children:
140. Virgie Preston; m. M. H. Robinson.
After Mr. Preston's death, his widow, Dixie, m. B. P. Porte..

40. HIRAM PRESTON 3, (Henry 2, and his wife, Betty Cains, Moses, Sr., 1), m. ——— Myers.
Children:
142. John W. Preston; lived at Paintsville; member of firm of Copley, Ward and Preston; m. Pauline Walker.

45. JULIA PRESTON 3, (Henry 2, and his wife, Betty Cains, Moses, Sr., 1), m. Hamilton Preston:
Children:
143. Curtis Preston.

13. SAMUEL (COONIS) PRESTON 3, (Isaac 2, and his wife, Polly Sloan, Moses, Sr., 1), farmer; lived on Toms Creek, Lawrence county; m., in Johnson county, August 8, 1854, Mahala Ward.
Children:
*144. Jonathan Preston.
*145. Rhoderick Preston.
*146. James M. Preston.
*147. George Preston.
148. Sarah Preston; m., first, James George; and, secondly, Shade Daniel.
*149. L. T. Preston.
*150. LaFayette Preston.

Fourth Generation

51. LA FAYETTE PRESTON 4 (James Cobe 3, and his wife, Levina Murray, Moses (Coby) 2, and his wife, Elizabeth Haney, Moses, Sr., 1), m., first, in ——— county, Eleanor Wheeler, and secondly, in ——— county, Malaney Van Hoose, daughter of Thomas Van Hoose.

Children of LaFayette Preston and Eleanor Wheeler:
*151. J. Henry Preston.
*152. Elizabeth Preston.
*153. Mary Susan Preston.
154. James (Coby) Preston.

Children of LaFayette Preston and Malaney Van Hoose:
155. Edward Preston.
*156. Cyrus Preston.
157. Forrest B. Preston.
*158. Thomas Preston; m. Angelee Spencer; lived in Idaho.
159. Guy Preston.
160. Kittie Preston.
*161. Eugene Preston.
*162. Maggie Preston.
163. E. Herschell Preston.

Lafayette Preston lived on a farm on the Big Sandy River, near Thelma, Johnson county.

54. SAMUEL (BUFFALO) PRESTON 4, (James Cobe 3, and his wife, Levina Murray, Moses (Coby) 2, and his wife, Elizabeth Haney, Moses, Sr. 1), farmer and a preacher in the United Baptist Church; lived on a large farm on Buffalo Creek, Johnson county; m. in Johnson county, ———, Elizabeth Murray.

Children:
164. Jesse Preston; m. Alvine Murphy; d. February 10, 1928.
165. Tip Preston; m. Virgie Price.
*166. James C. (Cobe) Preston; m. Zilpha Ward.
167. Susie Preston; d. in infancy.
*168. Lestie Preston; m. Bethel Murray.
169. Jenny Preston; m. E. Miller, a merchant; lived at forks of Buffalo Creek.
170. Martela Preston; m. John Price.

67. JEFF PRESTON 4, (William 3, Moses (Coby) 2, and his wife, Elizabeth Haney, Moses, Sr. 1), b. February 15, 1850; d. January 28, 1873; farmer; lived on Big Mud Lick Creek, Johnson county; m. Mary Williams.

Children:
171. Hansford Preston; m. Exer Walters; lived in the West.

68. JAMES HEREFORD PRESTON 4, (William 3, and his wife, Susan Murray, Moses (Coby) 2 and his wife, Elizabeth Haney, Moses, Sr.

1), b. in 1844; farmer; resided for a time on a farm on the Big Sandy River below Paintsville and subsequently on a farm on Big Paint Creek, near Volga; m., first, Julina Price, daughter of G. W. Price, and secondly, Julina Porter, daughter of Canada Porter. Children of James Hereford Preston and Julina Price:

172. Lassie Preston; d. at age of 15.
173. Susie Preston.
*174. Edgar Ted Preston.
175. Lyda Preston.
*176. Belle Preston.

Children of James Hereford Preston and Julina Porter:

*177. Ben Preston.
*178. Susie Preston.
*179. Martin L. Preston.
180. Murah Preston; m. Albert Stambaugh; live on Toms Creek.

69. MARTIN PRESTON 4, (William 3, Moses (Coby) 2, and his wife, Elizabeth Haney, Moses, Sr. 1), b. in 1854; m. Anna Webb.
Children:
181. Mahama Lee Preston.

71. SANFORD PRESTON 4, (William 3, Moses (Coby) 2, and his wife, Elizabeth Haney, Moses, Sr. 1), b. in 1856; m. Mary Van-Hoose.
Children:
*182. William Preston.
*183. George Preston.
184. Myrtie Preston; m. Millard Akers.
185. Hereford Preston; killed by a falling tree at age of 23.

72. McCLELLAND PRESTON 4, (William 3, Moses (Coby) 2, and his wife, Elizabeth Haney, Moses, Sr. 1), b. in 1866; merchant; resided for a time near Offutt, Johnson county; subsequently moved to Paintsville; m. Vina Ward, who d. December 8, 1927.
Children:
*186. Sallie Preston.
*187. Susie Preston.
*188. Eulah Preston.
189. Deekle Preston.

74. MARTHA JANE PRESTON 4, (William 3, Moses (Coby) 2 and his wife, Elizabeth Haney, Moses, Sr. 1), b. in 1842; m. Harry Litteral.
Children:
190. Willie Litteral; m. Ann Davis.
191. Henry Litteral.
192. Ella Litteral.

76. VINA PRESTON 4, (William 3, Moses (Coby) 2, and his wife, Elizabeth Haney, Moses, Sr.1), b. in 1860; m. W. J. Mayo, son of Lewis Mayo, of Floyd county.

Children:

193. Grover Mayo.
194. Lora Mayo; m. Challie Patrick.
195. LeGrand Mayo; m. ——— Clark.
196. Earl Mayo; m., first, ——— McKenzie, and, secondly ———.
197. Anna Mayo; m. Everett Daniels.

77. ANGIE PRESTON 4, (William 3, Moses (Coby) 2, and his wife, Elizabeth Haney, Moses, Sr. 1), b. in 1862; m. L. G. Chatfield of South Point, Ohio.

Children:

198. Paul Chatfield; d. in infancy.
199. Stella Chatfield; m. ——— Conley; resided in Huntington, W. Va.

78. TRINNIE PRESTON 4, (William 3, Moses (Coby) 2, and his wife, Elizabeth Haney, Moses, Sr. 1), b. in 1864; m. Nathan Stapleton.

Children:

200. Maude Stapleton.
201. Vineta Stapleton.
202. Paul Stapleton; d. in infancy.
This family lived in California.

79. ELIZABETH PRESTON 4, (William 3, Moses (Coby) 2, and his wife, Elizabeth Haney, Moses, Sr. 1), b. December 19, 1869; d. July, 1908; m. Lloyd Clay, traveling salesman, grocer at Paintsville and postmaster of that city for a term.

Children:

203. Virginia Clay.
204. Elizabeth Clay.

84. CALLA PRESTON 4, (Martin 3, and his wife, Rachael King, Moses (Coby) 2, and his wife, Elizabeth Haney, Moses, Sr. 1), m. F. P. Hager (See Hager Family).

Children:

205. Frank Hager.

88. MARY JANE (MOLLIE) PRESTON 4, (Moses 3, and his wife, Mary Jane Perry, Moses (Coby) 2, and his wife Elizabeth Haney, Moses, Sr. 1), b. October 16, 1860; d. September 27, 1927; m. December 15, 1878, Henry Stafford, a businessman of Paintsville.

Children:

206. Don G. Stafford.

91. MORRELL G. PRESTON 4, (Moses 3, and his wife, Louisa Hager, Moses (Coby) 2, and his wife, Elizabeth Haney, Moses, Sr. 1); m. Ida Walker.

Children:
207. Redmond Preston; b. June 30, 1886; d. May 7, 1911.
*208. Marshey Preston.
209. Glenn Preston.
210. Charles Preston.
211. Darwin Preston.
212. Gertrude Preston.

92. DANIEL E. PRESTON 4, (Moses 3, and his wife, Louisa Hager, Moses (Coby) 2, and his wife, Elizabeth Haney, Moses, Sr. 1); m. ——— (?)

Children:
213. Sylvia Preston.
214. James Preston.
215. Willa Mae Preston; m. Herbert Wheeler.
216. Richard Preston.
217. Theresa Preston.

94. THRESA PRESTON 4, (Angeline 3, and her husband, Col. Nathan Preston, Moses (Coby) 2, and his wife, Elizabeth Haney, Moses, Sr. 1); m. Edward Brown.

Children:
218. Virgie Brown; m. Leander Ferguson.
219. Wallie Brown.
220. ——— ———.
221. Arthur Brown.
222. ——— ———.
223. ———; m. ——— Pelphrey.

96. PARIS F. PRESTON 4, (Montraville 3, and his wife, Lorenda Price, Moses (Coby) 2, and his wife, Elizabeth Haney, Moses, Sr. 1), b. in 1857; m. (1) Lou J. Dixon, b. January 27, 1863; d. January 30, 1893, and (2) Roxie Cline.

Children of Paris F. Preston and Lou J. Dixon:
224. Quincy Preston; b. October 28, 1882; d. September 30, 1903.
225. Ida Preston; m. Edward Preston.
226. Cecil Preston; m. ———.
227. Anna Preston; m. Eugene Daniel.
*227½. Hazel Preston.
228. Mont. Preston; m. Jenny Maxler.

Children of Paris F. Preston and Roxie Cline:
228. Mary E. Preston.
229. Frances Ruth Preston.
230. Paris F. Preston, Jr.
231. Martha Preston.

232. Sarah Price Preston.

Paris F. Preston, Sr., had service in the Spanish-American War and removed to Warren County, Ohio.

97. GEORGE W. PRESTON 4, (Montraville 3, and his wife, Lorenda Price, Moses (Coby) 2, and his wife, Elizabeth Haney, Moses, Sr. 1), businessman of Paintsville; timberman; stockholder and vice-president of the Paintsville National Bank; b. April 1, 1859; m., first, Kate Lavendar, and, secondly, Talitha Childers.

Children of George W. Preston and Kate Lavendar:

*233. George Herschel Preston.
*234. Ernest R. Preston.
235. (Infant).
236. Arthur L. Preston; b. October 27, 1896; d. February 18, 1900.
237. Mariam Preston; b. March 16, 1900; d. August 13, 1900.

98. SAMANTHA PRESTON 4, (Montraville 3, and his wife, Lorenda Price, Moses (Coby) 2, and his wife, Elizabeth Haney, Moses, Sr. 1), b. in 1861; d. in 1887; m. Greenfield Adams.

Children:

238. Helen Adams; m. Dwight Rogers.
239. Anna Adams; m. Howard Estill.
240. Will Mont Adams; m. ———.

99. ANDERSON BEE PRESTON 4, Montraville 3, and his wife, Lorenda Price, Moses (Coby) 2, and his wife, Elizabeth Haney, Moses, Sr. 1), farmer and merchant, m. Kate Howard and lived at Wheelersburg, near Portsmouth, Ohio.

Children:

241. Samantha Preston; m. John Ginheimer.
*242. Clarence C. Preston.
243. Mitchell Preston.
244. Howard Preston; m. Edith Wilson.
*245. George A. Preston.
*246. John Harper Preston.
*247. Lorenda Preston.
247½. Arthur Preston; m. Barbara Montgomery.

101. WARREN L. PRESTON 4, (Montraville 3, and his wife, Lorenda Price, Moses (Coby) 2, and his wife, Elizabeth Haney, Moses, Sr. 1), was for a number of years associated with his brother, George W. Preston, in the timber and lumber business; minister of the United Baptist Church; m. Laura Preston, daughter of Jesse Preston.

Children:

248. Geneva Preston; m. Virgil D. Picklsimer.
249. Elizabeth Preston; m. J. E. Russmisel, Welch, West Virginia.
250. Roberta Preston, m. Henry Zeigler, New York City.
251. Alene Preston; m. James Mitchell, of Richmond, Virginia.
252. Warren L. Preston, Jr., d. at age of 18.

253. Mariam Preston.
254. Charles Clay Preston.
255. Chester Preston.
256. Eloise Preston.
257. Gayland Preston.

102. GAYLAND PRESTON 4, (Montraville 3, and his wife, Lorenda Price, Moses (Coby) 2, and his wife, Elizabeth Haney, Moses, Sr. 1), lived for a number of years on the old home farm in Johnson County, later removed to and lived on a farm in Scioto County, Ohio; m. Nora Van Hoose.
Children:
258. Mont Oral Preston.

103. CYRUS M. PRESTON 4, (Frank 3, and his wife, Emily Hager, Moses (Coby) 2, and his wife, Elizabeth Haney, Moses, Sr. 1), b. November 14, 1857, in Paintsville, where he lived for a time; removed to Ashland, Kentucky, and engaged in the flour milling business there; post master, Ashland, for two terms (8 years) after the expiration of which he moved to a farm near Winchester, Clark County, Kentucky; m. (1) in 1878, Alice Price, b. in 1858, daughter of Jackson Price, and (2) Minnie J. Hurt, b. in 1857, daughter of Dr. Robert, of Middlesburgh, Kentucky.
Children of Cyrus M. Preston and Alice Price:
259. Ora Preston; single; instructor in music; in charge of the music department of the John C. C. Mayo College, Paintsville, for a number of years.
260. Frankie Preston; m. Frank C. Malin, attorney, Ashland.
261. (Infant).
262. (Infant).
263. (Infant).
Children of Cyrus M. Preston and his wife, Minnie J. Hurt:
264. Roger L. Preston; b. May 1895.
265. Clarence Ray Preston; b. October 5, 1900.
266. Esther Preston; b. in 1903.

104. D. LYNN PRESTON 4, (Frank 3, and his wife, Emily Hager Moses (Coby) 2, and his wife, Elizabeth Haney, Moses, Sr. 1); b. in 1860; reared in Paintsville, and was engaged in the steamboat business while living there; subsequently he moved to Ashland where he lived until his death; m. Sarah F. Brown.
Children:
*267. Beulah Preston.
*268. Mabel Preston.

105. CAROLINE PRESTON 4 (Frank 3, and his wife, Emily Hager, Moses (Coby) 2, and his wife, Elizabeth Haney, Moses, Sr. 1), m. Robert Barton.

Children:
269. Zella Barton; m. Claude Mitchell.
270. Frank Barton; m. Maude ———.
271. Virginia Barton; m. Douglas Barnett.
272. Robert Barton, Jr.
273. Clara Barton; m. William Summerall.

106. JAMES HENRY PRESTON 4, (Frank 3, and his wife Emily Hager, Moses (Coby) 2, and his wife Elizabeth Haney, Moses, Sr. 1); resided in Ashland; m. Allie Miller, of Millersburg, Kentucky.
Children:
274. Fanny Preston; m. Harry Hatcher.
275. Bruce Preston; m. ——— Vaughan.

110. CHARLES A. PRESTON 4, (Frank 3, and his wife Emily Hager, Moses (Coby) 2, and his wife, Elizabeth Haney Moses, Sr. 1), b. in 1867; d. in 1900; m. Amanda Kamitz.
Children:
276. Walter Preston.
277. ——— ———.
278. Frieda Preston.

111. BEN F. PRESTON 4, (Frank 3, and his wife, Emily Hager, Moses (Coby) 2, and his wife, Elizabeth Haney, Moses, Sr. 1), b. in 1874; d. in 1903; m. Victoria Dixon; lived in Paintsville and resided in Frankfort, Ky., for a time.
Children:
279. Fanny Preston; m. Harry Scott.

116. FRANK H. PRESTON 4, (John D. 3, and his wife, Sarah A. Brown, Moses (Coby) 2, and his wife, Elizabeth Haney, Moses, Sr. 1), b. in Paintsville, December 18, 1866; m. January 15, 1896, Mollie Rolland, b. December 14, 1872, daughter of Joe L. Rolland; resided in Huntington, West Virginia.
Children:
280. Mary Mildred Preston; b. May 9, 1900; m. D. Z. Lowry.
281. E. Ernestine Preston; b. November 26, 1902; m. Elgin Evans.
282. Lillian L. Preston; b. January 24, 1905; m. James S. Alexander.
283. Frank Henry Preston; b. April 25, 1908.
284. John Lloyd Preston; b. April 29, 1911.

117. Lina V. Preston 4, (John D. 3, and his wife, Sarah A. Brown, Moses (Coby) 2, and his wife, Elizabeth Haney, Moses, Sr., 1), b. in Paintsville, March 3, 1869; m. November 22, 1893, Lee Tate, b. June 13, 1867, son of J. P. Tate; resided in Huntington, West Virginia.
Children:
285. Mamie Ruth Tate; b. October 15, 1895; m. R. C. Smith.

118. WILLIAM M. PRESTON 4, (John D. 3, and his wife, Sarah A. Brown, Moses (Coby) 2, and his wife, Elizabeth Haney, Moses, Sr. 1); b. in Paintsville, July 12, 1871; m. August 1, 1891, Lorenda Price, b. in 1871, daughter of Hamilton Price; lived in Paintsville.

Children:
286. Eunice Preston; b. in 1892; m. Henry Pfening.
287. Winifred Preston; b. in 1893; m. Arthur J. Archer.
288. Marshall P. Preston; b. April 28, 1895; d. September 24, 1917.
289. Kathleen Preston; b. 1897; m. Holmes Kirk.
290. Frank Preston; b. in 1899; m. Clara Terry.
291. John H. Preston; b. in 1904; m. Margaret Mathews.
292. William Martin Preston; b. 1906.
293. William Moses Preston, Jr.

120. ETHEL PRESTON 4, (John D. 3, and his wife, Sarah A. Brown, Moses (Coby) 2, and his wife, Elizabeth Haney, Moses, Sr. 1), b. in Paintsville, August 22, 1880; m. September 17, 1902, Clarence W. Howes, b. July 27, 1880, d. May 15, 1913, who was an attorney of Paintsville.

Children:
294. Anna Wallace Howes; b. February 26, 1911; m. R. G. Sager.

121. THOMAS C. PRESTON 4, (John D. 3, and his wife, Sarah A. Brown, Moses (Coby) 2, and his wife, Elizabeth Haney, Moses, Sr. 1), b. in Paintsville, September 14, 1882; m. September 26, 1906, Lottie Walker, b. May 14, 1884, daughter of Electious Walker; resided in Huntington, West Virginia.

Children:
295. Ruth Lyon Preston; b. April 6, 1913.

124. LAURA PRESTON 4 (George Ballard 3, and his wife, Angelina Auxier, Moses (Coby) 2, and his wife, Nancy Peery, Moses, Sr. 1); m. Charles Smith.

Children:
296. Frankie Smith; m. Samuel Lockwood, a conductor on the Big Sandy Division of the Chesapeake and Ohio Railroad.

126. WARREN H. PRESTON 4, (George Ballard 3, and his wife, Angelina Auxier, Moses (Coby) 2, and his wife, Nancy Peery, Moses, Sr. 1); lived in Paintsville, and was for many years express agent for the C & O Ry. Co.; m. Elizabeth Reynolds.

Children:
297. Russell Preston; m., first, Ruth Ward, and Secondly, ———.
298. Earl Preston; m. Ruth Butler.
299. Virginia Preston.
300. Gertrude Preston.

127. Hopkins Preston 4, (George Ballard 3, and his wife, Angelina
Auxier, Moses (Coby) 2, and his wife, Nancy Peery, Moses, Sr. 1),
resided in Paintsville where he was connected with the Paintsville
Grocery Company; m. Josie Ward, sometime teacher in the common
schools of Johnson County.

Children:
301. Charles Lee Preston.
302. Anna Louise Preston.

128. James Preston 4, (George Ballard 3, and his wife, Angelina
Auxier, Moses (Coby) 2, and his wife, Nancy Peery, Moses, Sr. 1),
resided in Paintsville, and for a number of years was connected with
the Paintsville Grocery Company there; m. Susie Walters, sometime
teacher in the common schools of Johnson County.

Children:
303. Rubie Preston.
304. James W. Preston.
305. George Russell Preston.

Fifth Generation

144. Jonathan Preston 5, (Samuel (Coonis) 4, and his wife,
Mahala Ward, Thomas 3. Isaac 2, and his wife, Polly Sloan; Moses,
Sr., 1); m., first, Mary Howe.

Children:
*306. Lynn Preston.
144-A. M., secondly, ———— ————.

Children:
307. Gartha Preston; m., first, James B. Castle, secondly, Moreta
Brown.
308. Costetta Preston; m. J. Travis.

144-B. M., thirdly, Puss Castle.

Children:
309. Asa Preston; m. ———— Caudill.
310. Arthur Preston.
311. Samuel Preston.
312. Emma Preston.

145. Rhoderick Preston 5, (Samuel (Coonis) 4, and his wife,
Mahala Ward, Thomas 3, Isaac 2, and his wife, Polly Sloan, Moses,
Sr., 1); m. ———— Ward.

Children:
313. Sarah Preston; m. ———— Caudill.
314. Mary Preston; m. D. Salyers.

146. James M. Preston 5, (Samuel (Coonis) 4, and his wife,
Mahala Ward, Thomas 3, Isaac 2, and his wife, Polly Sloan, Moses,
Sr., 1); m. Mary Lemaster.

Children:

*315. Jethro Preston.
*316. Theodore Preston.
317. Sipora Preston; m. Harry VanHoose.
318. J. Langley Preston.
319. Guy W. Preston.
320. Beulah Preston; m. ——— DeMoss.

147. GEORGE PRESTON 5, (Samuel (Coonis) 4, and his wife, Mahala Ward, Thomas 3, Isaac 2 and his wife, Polly Sloan, Moses, Sr. 1); m. Elizabeth Meek.

Children:

321. Samuel Preston; m. Collista Ward.
322. Monroe Preston; m. Mary Ward.
323. Elliott Preston; m. Bette Preston.

149. L. T. PRESTON 5, (Samuel (Coonis) 4, and his wife, Mahala Ward, Thomas 3, Isaac 2 and his wife, Polly Sloan, Moses, Sr., 1); m. Julia Fannin.

Children:

324. Rutherford Preston; m. Mary Salyers.

150. LaFAYETTE PRESTON 5, (Samuel (Coonis) 4, and his wife, Mahala Ward, Thomas 3, Isaac 2, and his wife, Polly Sloan, Moses, Sr., 1); m. Julia Pack.

Children:

325. Calla Preston; m. Dr. Avery Lewis.
326. Tilda Preston; m. Josh Daniel.
327. L. T. Preston; m., first, ——— Clay; secondly, ——— ———, and thirdly, ——— Clark.
328. F. B. Preston.
329. N. M. Preston; m. Rose Daniel.
330. I. D. Preston; m. Malta Howe
331. Mahala Preston; m. Frank Daniel.
332. Charlie Preston; m. Lestie Preston, daughter of James "Cobe" Preston.

151. J. HENRY PRESTON 5, (LaFayette 4, and his wife, Eleanor Wheeler, James Cobe 3, and his wife, Levina Murray, Moses (Coby) 2, and his wife, Elizabeth Haney, Moses, Sr., 1); lived at Louisa, Lawrence county; m., first, Nancy Hayes, and, secondly, Julia Fitzpatrick.

Children of J. Henry Preston and Julia Fitzpatrick:

333. Ellen Preston.
334. Beulah Preston.
335. Elizabeth Preston.

152. ELIZABETH PRESTON 5, (LaFayette 4, and his wife, Eleanor Wheeler, James Cobe 3, and his wife, Levina Murray, Moses (Coby) 2, and his wife, Elizabeth Haney, Moses, Sr. 1); m. London Stapleton.
Children:
336. Claude Stapleton.
337. Edna Stapleton.
338. Henry Stapleton.
339. Arthur Stapeton.
340. Clyde Stapleton.
341. James Stapleton.
342. Charles Stapleton.

153. MARY SUSAN PRESTON 5, (Lafayette 4, and his wife, Eleanor Wheeler. James Cobe 3, and his wife, Levina Murray, Moses (Coby) 2, and his wife, Eizabeth Haney, Moses, Sr., 1); m. Isaac Ward.
Children:
343. Ethel Ward; m. Junior Hinkle.
344. Ellen Ward; m. ———— Clifton.
345. Lafe Ward; m. Ella Ward.
346. Hester Ward; m. Conrad Hutchins.
347. William J. Ward. Jr.; m. Gladys Ratliff.
348. Samuel George Ward.

156. CYRUS PRESTON 5, (LaFavette 4. and his wife. Malaney Van-Hoose, James Cobe 3, and his wife, Levina Murray, Moses (Coby) 2, and his wife, Elizabeth Haney, Moses, Sr. 1); m. Belle Cunningham.
Children:
349. Delmas Preston.
350. Ernest Roy Preston.

157. FORREST B. PRESTON 5, (LaFayette 4, and his wife, Malaney VanHoose, James Cobe 3, and his wife, Levina Murray, Moses (Coby) 2, and his wife, Elizabeth Haney, Moses, Sr. 1); m., first, ———— Leslie, and secondly, Grace Rice, daughter of Clinton Rice.
Children of Forrest B. Preston and ———— Leslie:
351. Thomas Preston.
352. ———— ————.
353. ———— ————.
Children of Forrest B. Preston and Grace Rice:
354. Jack Preston.
Mr. Preston was a coal operator and for many years operated mines at Emma, Floyd county, and at Denver, Johnson county.

161. EUGENE PRESTON 5, (LaFayette 4, and his wife, Malaney Van-Hoose, James Cobe 3, and his wife, Levina Murray, Moses (Coby) 2, and his wife, Elizabeth Haney, Moses, Sr. 1); lived at Wenatchee, Washington; m. ———— Walker, daughter of Fred Walker.

Children:
355. Helen Jane Preston.

162. MAGGIE PRESTON 5, (LaFayette 4, and his wife, Malaney Van-Hoose, James Cobe 3, and his wife, Levina Murray, Moses (Coby) 2, and his wife, Elizabeth Haney, Moses, Sr. 1); lived at Dairytown, Pennsylvania; m. Daniel Ward.
Children:
356. Howard Purcell Ward.
357. Roberta Ward.

166. JAMES C. (COBE) PRESTON 5, (Samuel (Buffalo) 4, and his wife, Elizabeth Murray, James Cobe 3, and his wife, Levina Murray, Moses (Coby) 2, and his wife, Elizabeth Haney, Moses, Sr. 1; farmer, active member of the United Baptist Church; lived on Buffalo Creek, near Mealey post office; m. Zilpha Ward.
Children:
358. Leslie Preston who m. Charles E. Preston.

168. LESTIE PRESTON 5, (Samuel (Buffalo) 4, and his wife, Elizabeth Murray, James Cobe 3, and his wife, Levina Murray, Moses (Coby) 2, and his wife, Elizabeth Haney, Moses, Sr. 1); m. Bethel Murray.
Children:
359. Arbie Preston who m. ——— Preston.

174. EDGAR (TED) PRESTON 5, (James Hereford 4, and his wife, Julina Price, William 3, and his wife Susan Murray, Moses (Coby) 2, and his wife, Elizabeth Haney, Moses, Sr. 1); lived in Mason county, Kentucky; m. Laura Ward.
Children:
*360. Gertrude Preston.
361. Sarah Preston who m. George Turner.
*362. Jeff Preston.
*363. John Preston.
364. Anna Lee Preston.

175. LYDA PRESTON 5, (James Hereford 4, and his wife, Julina Price, William 3, and his wife, Susan Murray, Moses (Coby) 2, and his wife Elizabeth Haney, Moses, Sr. 1); m. John Stambaugh, farmer and one-time sheriff of Johnson county.
Children:
365. Garfield Stambaugh.
366. Theodore Roosevelt Stambaugh.
367. Rosebelle Stambaugh.
After separation, Mrs. Stambaugh m., secondly, John Johnson.

176. BELLE PRESTON 5, (James Hereford 4, and his wife, Julina Price, William 3, and his wife, Susan Murray, Moses (Coby) 2, and

his wife, Elizabeth Haney Moses, Sr. 1); m. Tobe Auxier; resided near East Point, Johnson county.

Children:
368. Beatrice Auxier.
369. Joe D. Auxier.
370. Richard (Dick) Auxier who m. Sarah Stapleton.
371. Lydia Auxier who m. ——— Conley.
372. Samuel Auxier.
373. Hereford Auxier.
374. Lotta Auxier.
375. Frank Auxier.
376. Edgar Auxier.

177. BEN PRESTON 5, (James Hereford 4, and his wife, Julina Porter, William 3, and his wife, Susan Murray Moses (Coby) 2, and his wife, Elizabeth Haney, Moses, Sr. 1); telegrapher, Chesapeake & Ohio Rv. Co., for a number of years; m. Nannie Fannin (Pinson).

Children:
377. James Donald Preston.
378. Billie C. Preston.

178. SUSIE PRESTON 5, (James Hereford 4, and his wife, Julina Porter, William 3, and his wife, Susan Murray, Moses (Coby) 2, and his wife, Elizabeth Haney, Moses, Sr. 1); m. Hobart Osborn.

Children:
379. Elizabeth Osborn.

179. MARTIN L. PRESTON 5, (James Hereford 4, and his wife, Julina Porter, William 3, and his wife, Susan Murray, Moses (Coby) 2, and his wife Elizabeth Haney, Moses, Sr. 1); telegrapher; served in the American Expeditionary Forces in France and in the Army of Occupation in Germany in the first World War; m. ——— Reed, daughter of Samuel Reed, of Caney, Kentucky.

Children:
380. ——— ———.

182. WILLIAM PRESTON 5, (Sanford 4, and his wife, Mary Van-Hoose, William 3, and his wife, Susan Murray, Moses (Coby) 2, and his wife, Elizabeth Haney, Moses, Sr. 1); m. Linnie Ward.

Children:
381. Sanford Preston.
382. Nancy Preston.
383. Jimmy Preston.
384. ——— ———.
385. ——— ———.
386. ——— ———.
387. ——— ———.

183. GEORGE PRESTON 5, (Sanford 4, and his wife, Mary VanHoose,

William 3, and his wife, Susan Murray, Moses (Coby) 2, and his wife, Elizabeth Haney, Moses, Sr. 1) ; m. —— Wells.
Children:
388. ——— ———.
389. ——— ———.
390. ——— ———

186. SALLIE PRESTON 5, (McClelland 4, and his wife, Vina Ward, William 3, and his wife, Susan Murray, Moses (Coby) 2, and his wife, Elizabeth Haney, Moses, Sr. 1) ; m. Logan Akers.
Children:
391. Clyde Akers.

187. SUSIE PRESTON 5, McClelland 4, and his wife, Vina Ward, William 3, and his wife, Susan Murray, Moses (Coby) 2, and his wife, Elizabeth Haney, Moses, Sr. 1) ; m. Madison Smith; resided at Wheelersburg, Ohio.
Children:
392. Neva Smith.

188. EULAH PRESTON 5, (McClelland 4, and his wife, Vina Ward; William 3, and his wife, Susan Murray, Moses (Coby) 2, and his wife, Elizabeth Haney, Moses, Sr. 1) ; m. Major Cornett; resided at Dawson Springs, Kentucky.
Children:
393. (Son).

208. MARSHEY PRESTON 5, (Morrell G. 4, and his wife, Ida Walker, Moses 3, and his wife, Louisa Hager, Moses (Coby) 2, and his wife, Elizabeth Haney, Moses, Sr. 1) ; m. Samuel Copley, senior member of the firm of Copley, Ward and Preston, in Paintsville.
Children:
394. Clarence Copley.
395. James T. Copley.
396. Robert Walker Copley.

227½. HAZEL PRESTON 5, (Paris F. 4, and his wife, Lou J. Dixon, Montraville 3, and his wife, Lorenda Price, Moses (Coby) 2, and his wife, Elizabeth Haney, Moses, Sr. 1) ; m. Stewart Ball, one time official of the Chesapeake & Ohio Ry. Co. They resided in Ashland, Kentucky.
Children:
397. Charles Ball.

233. GEORGE HERSCHEL PRESTON 5, (George W. 4, and his wife, Kate Lavendar, Montraville 3, and his wife, Lorenda Price, Moses (Coby) 2, and his wife, Elizabeth Haney, Moses, Sr. 1) ; farmer and lived on a farm in Custer county, Oklahoma; m. Eunice Combs.
Children:
398. Dorothy Evelyn Preston.

399. George Charles Preston.
400. Kitty Lenore Preston.
401. Betsy Ruth Preston.
402. Mary Grace Preston.

234. ERNEST R. PRESTON 5, (George W. 4, and his wife, Kate
Lavendar, Montraville 3, and his wife, Lorenda Price, Moses (Coby)
2, and his wife, Elizabeth Haney, Moses, Sr. 1); farmer and resided
in Custer county, Oklahoma; previously had service with the United
States Shipping Board during World War I; m. Virgie Brown.
Children:
403. Arthur L. Preston.
404. Frank B. Preston.

242. CLARENCE C. PRESTON 5, (Anderson Bee 4, and his wife, Kate
Howard, Montraville 3, and wife, Lorenda Price, Moses (Coby) 2,
and his wife, Elizabeth Haney, Moses, Sr. 1); connected with the Big
Sandy Hardware Co., at Paintsville, for some time; subsequently
moved to and lived on a farm near Loveland, Ohio; m. Zora Daniel
who was an active worker in the United Baptist Church.
Children:
405. Katherine Preston.

245. GEORGE A. PRESTON 5, (Anderson Bee 4, and his wife, Kate
Howard, Montraville 3, and his wife, Lorenda Price, Moses (Coby)
2, and his wife, Elizabeth Haney, Moses, Sr. 1); m. Minnie Burns.
Children:
406. John H. Preston.

246. JOHN HARPER PRESTON 5, (Anderson Bee 4, and his wife, Kate
Howard, Montraville 3, and his wife, Lorenda Price, Moses (Coby)
2, and his wife, Elizabeth Haney, Moses, Sr. 1); m. Eunice ———?
Children:
407. Mitchel W. Preston.

247. LORENDA PRESTON 5, (Anderson Bee 4, and his wife, Kate
Howard, Montraville 3, and his wife, Lorenda Price, Moses (Coby)
2, and his wife, Elizabeth Haney, Moses, Sr. 1); m. Frank Lallow.
Children:
408. Frank Lallow, Jr.

267. BEULAH PRESTON 5, (D. Lynn 4, and his wife, Sarah F. Brown,
Frank 3, and his wife, Emily E. Hager, Moses (Coby) 2, and his
wife, Elizabeth Haney, Moses, Sr. 1); m. Sidney A. Webb, some
time proprietor of the Webb Hotel, Paintsville, and realtor. Mrs.
Webb was active in social circles there.
Children:
409. Gordon Webb.
410. Sidney Webb.

411. Aleene Webb.
412. Lynn P. Webb.

268. MABEL PRESTON 5, (D. Lynn 4, and his wife, Sarah F. Brown, Frank 3, and his wife, Emily E. Hager, Moses (Coby) 2, and his wife, Elizabeth Haney, Moses, Sr. 1); m. Charles A. Kirk, civic leader of Paintsville and owner, editor and publisher of the Paintsville Herald in that city.
Children:
413. Raymond L. Kirk.
414. Georgiene Kirk.

Sixth Generation

306. LYNN PRESTON 6, (Jonathan 5, and his wife, Mary Howe, Samuel (Coonis) 4, and his wife, Mahala Ward, Thomas 3, Isaac 2, and his wife, Polly Sloan, Moses, Sr. 1); m. Maxie Dale.
Children:
415. Craig Preston.
416. Easter Preston.

315. JETHRO PRESTON 6, (James M. 5, and his wife, Mary Lemaster, Samuel (Coonis) 4, and his wife, Mahala Ward, Thomas 3, Isaac 2, and his wife, Polly Sloan, Moses, Sr. 1); m., first, Louella Van-Hoose; and their children were:
417. Vella Preston who m. Jeff Grimm.
418. Glance Preston who m. ――― Hughes.
419. Vivian Preston.

315-A. JETHRO PRESTON; m., secondly, Susan Banks.
Children:
420. Roosevelt Preston.

Mr. Preston formerly lived on Tom's Creek, Johnson county. The family removed to Weleetka, Oklahoma, and he was one time mayor of that city

316. THEODORE PRESTON 6, (James M., 5, and his wife, Mary Lemaster, Samuel (Coonis) 4, and his wife, Mahala Ward, Thomas 3, Isaac 2, and his wife, Polly Sloan, Moses, Sr. 1); physician; resided at Weleetka, Oklahoma, and he was health officer of that city; m. Della Daniel.
Children:
421. Ollie Preston.

360. GERTRUDE PRESTON 6, (Edgar (Ted) 5, and his wife, Laura Ward, James Hereford 4, and his wife, Julina Price, William 3, and his wife, Susan Murray, Moses (Coby) 2, and his wife, Elizabeth Haney, Moses, Sr., 1); b. January 1, 1886, in Johnson county; m. April 1, 1909, Guy W. Preston, b. December 31, 1889, a minister of the Baptist Church; connected with the North-East Coal Company,

at Threlka, for a number of years and subsequently entering the business field became one of the leading stockholders in the Mountain Furniture Company at Paintsville.

Children:

422. (Infant).
423. James Edgar Preston; b. April 16, 1915.
424. Imogene Preston; b. July 5, 1920.

362. JEFF PRESTON 6, (Edgar (Ted) 5, and his wife, Laura Ward, James Hereford 4, and his wife, Julina Price, William 3, and his wife, Susan Murray, Moses (Coby) 2, and his wife, Elizabeth Haney, Moses, Sr. 1) ; m. Myrtle List.

Children:

425. Cecil Preston.
426. Elwood Preston.

363. JOHN PRESTON 6, (Edgar (Ted) 5, and his wife, Laura Ward, James Hereford 4, and his wife Julina Price, William 3, and his wife, Susan Murray, Moses (Coby) 2, and his wife, Elizabeth Haney, Moses, Sr. 1) ; m. Elizabeth List. The family resided in Illinois.

Children:

427. Fay Preston.
428. (Infant).
429. Freeda Preston.
430. Elmer Preston.
431. ——— ———?
432. ——— ———?

NATHAN PRESTON FAMILY OF FLOYD AND JOHNSON COS.

This is a place or local name, 'of Preston'. The family is English and there are no less than 24 parishes situated in every part of England which bear the name. The Hundred Rolls of 1273 bear the names Laurence de Preston, Lincolnshire county; Alice de Preston, Northampton county; Adam de Prestone, Salop county; John de Prestone of Preston, Somerset county. The tax lists of 1379 bear the names Isabella de Preston and Johnanna de Pryston of County Yorks.

The family of Preston was numerous in all the original thirteen colonies.

Reputable historians and writers have stated that the early progenitors of the Prestons of the Big Sandy Valley, in Eastern Kentucky, were Francis Preston, Charles Preston, William Calvert Prestonton and Robert Preston, all of whom emigrated from England and settled in Maryland.

The first Preston of whom there is any record that emigrated to and settled in Maryland was Richard Preston. He received a grant of a large tract of land on the Patuxent River from Charles I of England on which he built his manor house called Charles' Gift. Here during the religious wars of 1653-1661, and the reign of Cromwell in England, were held the sessions of the Legislature and the public business of the province conducted. The services of Richard Preston are commemorated by a marker erected at the village of Lusby, Calvert county:

"Preston on Patuxent, Home of Richard Preston, Commander of the north bank of the Patuxent River, 1649. The seat of the Puritan Government of Maryland where the colonial records were kept, 1653-1657."

Moses Preston and Nathan Preston, brothers, and Revolutionary War soldiers, and their sister, Mrs. Elizabeth (Preston) Burgess, were the first of the family of Preston to emigrate and settle in the Big Sandy Valley, Eastern Kentucky, in the Great Western Movement. These brothers were the progenitors of a relatively large number—if not all—of the Prestons of Eastern Kentucky. They emigrated from Bedford county, Virginia, and settled in Floyd county about 1800. Prior to that time a large family of Prestons had lived in Bedford county, of whom David, Moses and Philip were privates in the Bedford County Militia and had service in the French and Indian Wars during the year 1758.

1. NATHAN PRESTON was b., presumably in Bedford county, Virginia, in 1761. In January, 1777, in Bedford county, he enlisted as a private for a term of three years in Captain George Lambert's Company of the 14th Virginia Regiment on the Continental Line under the command of Colonel Charles Lewis and Lieutenant Colonel

Abram Buford; fought in the battles of Brandywine (September 11, 1777) and Germantown (October 4, 1777); encamped at Valley Forge during the Winters of 1777-78; served his enlistment of three years and was honorably discharged at Philadelphia, Pennsylvania, January ——, 1780; when, as he stated in his declaration for a pension on account of such service, he received "the paltry sum of ten dollars, which was the whole sum he received for his service."

Soon after his discharge from the service, he returned to his home in Bedford county and in August, 1780, in that county, he m. Elizabeth Vaughan, b. about 1760, "by publication three times at church by the Rev. Mr. Ramsay".

It appears from an affidavit executed by Jeffrey Preston, a son, that eight children were b. to Nathan Preston and Elizabeth (Vaughan) Preston, his wife. However, only six children were mentioned in said affidavit, as follows:

2. Nancy Preston; m. Benjamin Hylton (See Hylton Family).
3. Edy Preston; m. Francis Asbury Brown (See Brown Family).
*4. Jeffrey Preston.
5. Matilda Preston; b. in Bedford conuty, Virginia; m., in Floyd county, Kentucky, December 23, 1819, Bracken Lewis.
*6. Eliphus Preston.
*7. Elizabeth Preston.

4. JEFFREY PRESTON, farmer; b. in Bedford county, Virginia, about 1792; m. in Floyd County, Kentucky, about 1814, Jane (Jincy) Burgess, b. in Virginia in 1796, daughter of Garland Burgess.

Children:
*8. Burgess Preston.
*9. Col. Nathan Preston, Jr.
*10. Eliphus Preston, Jr.

Genealogists have stated that other children of Jeffrey Preston and Jane Burgess were:
*11. Mrs. Henry Sherman.
*12. Mrs. William Randolph.
13. Mrs. Mace Mahan.
*14. Mrs. John H. Ward.

United States Census, Johnson county, 1850, show children of Jeffrey Preston and Jane (Burgess) Preston, then living at home, as follows:
15. Charlotte Preston, age 20 years.
16. Edy Preston, age 18 years.
17. Sarah Preston, age 16 years.
18. Frances Preston, age 15 years.
19. William Preston, age 13 years.
20. Benjamin Preston, age 11 years.
21. Amanda Preston, age 7 years.

6. ELIPHUS PRESTON, farmer; b. in Bedford county, Virginia,

about 1795; m., in Floyd county, Kentucky, December 10, 1815, Annie Pelphrey, daughter of John Pelphrey. The records would seem to indicate that children of Eliphus Preston and Annie (Pelphrey) Preston were, among others:

23. Atchison Preston; b. in 1825.
24. Harrison Preston; b. in 1835.
25. Leah J. Preston; b. in 1839.

United States Census, Johnson county, 1860, shows that there were then living in the household of Jeffrey Preston, the following:

26. LUCINDA PRESTON—apparently second wife, b. in Kentucky in 1827—and their children:

27. Thomas Jefferson Preston; b. in 1847.
28. Julia A. Preston; b. in 1848.
29. Mary J. Preston; b. in 1849.
30. Matilda Preston; b. in 1851.
31. Cynthia A. Preston; b. in 1853.
32. James L. Preston; b. in 1857.
33. Isaac L. Preston; b. in 1859.

7. ELIZABETH PRESTON; b. in Bedford county, Virginia, m., in Floyd county, Kentucky, September 25, 1811, James VanHoose, Sr., farmer; b. in North Carolina, about 1791. Children living at home in 1850 as indicated by the United States Census, Johnson county, for that year:

34. Nathan VanHoose; b. in 1829.
35. John VanHoose; b. in 1832.
36. Henry J. VanHoose; b. in 1835.
37. Eliphus Preston VanHoose; b. in 1837.

8. BURGESS PRESTON 3, (Jeffrey 2, and his wife, Jane Burgess, Nathan 1); farmer; b. about 1817; d. 1875; m. Elizabeth Porter, b. 1821, d. 1885, daughter of Samuel Porter and his wife, Anna (Hanes) Porter; colonel of Militia in the Union Army in the Civil War; b. on a farm opposite Paint Creek and moved to and lived on a farm near the mouth of Millers Creek.

Children:

38. Samuel W. Preston, soldier; b. in 1844; had service in the Union Army and was killed in the engagement at Cynthiana (Ky.) with Morgan's men.
*39. Helen Preston.
*40. Winfield Scott Preston.
*41. John H. Preston.
*42. Alice Preston.
*43. Clayton Preston.
*44. Josie Preston.

39. HELEN PRESTON, b. March 1, 1847; d. January 11, 1910; m. William A. Webb.

Children:

45. Burgess Webb.

46. Sidney Webb; proprietor of the Webb Hotel, Paintsville, for a number of years and a realtor; m. Beulah Preston, active in social circles.

47. Allie Webb; m. Frew S. VanHoose, a minister of the Free Will Baptist Church; engaged in lumber and planing mill business in Paintsville.

40. WINFIELD SCOTT PRESTON; b. January 27, 1850 and d. January 2, 1926; truck-farmer; lived near the mouth of Millers Creek; m., first, Sarah Davis, b. May 25, 1858, and d. June 5, 1890, daughter of James McHenry Davis and his wife, Naomi Price, daughter of G. W. Price; and m., secondly, on November 9, 1892, May Marshall. Children of Winfield Scott Preston and his wife, Sarah (Davis) Preston:

48. Virgie Preston.

49. Norma Preston.

50. Bert Preston.

51. Ernest Preston; b. November 14, 1875 and d. December 22, 1896.

52. Carson Preston; b. August 6, 1877 and d. June 28, 1890.

53. Burnard Preston; b. January 18, 1880 and d. May 31, 1882.

40A. Children of Winfield Scott Preston and his wife, May Marshall:

54. Clyde Preston; m. Alma Rice, daughter of Nathaniel Jackson Rice and his wife, Katharine Louise (McCloud) Rice.

41. JOHN H. PRESTON, merchant, first at McDowell, Floyd county, and subsequently at Paintsville; b. December 9, 1853; m. in 1891, Vine Gibson, daughter of D. B. Gibson, of Floyd county.

Children:

*55. McKinley Preston.

42. ALICE PRESTON; m. Millard Rule. They resided at Paintsville.

Children:

56. C. T. Rule.

57. Ora Rule; m. ——— Shannon.

43. CLAYTON PRESTON, truck-farmer; lived on a part of the home farm about the mouth of Millers Creek; m. Pricilla Elliott.

Children:

58. Otto Preston.

59. Milo Preston; m. Sallie Auxier, daughter of Forrest Lee Auxier and his wife, Vada Music.

Children:

60. Mildred Loraine Preston.

44. JOSIE PRESTON; m. B. L. Spradlin.

Children:

61. Josaphine Spradlin.

55. McKINLEY PRESTON 4 (John H. 3, and his wife, Vine Gibson, Burgess 2, and his wife, Elizabeth Porter, Nathan 1); business-

man, Paintsville; m. Lydia Nunnery, prominent in social circles there.

Children:
    62. Billie Marie Preston.
    9. COLONEL NATHAN PRESTON, JR., 3, (Jeffrey 2, and his wife, Jane Burgess, Nathan 1), b. about 1820; merchant; colonel of Militia in the Union Army during the Civil War; m. Angelina Preston, b. in 1832.
    10. ELIPHUS PRESTON, JR., 3, Jeffrey 2, and his wife, Jane Burgess, Nathan 1), farmer; b. about 1821; m. Nancy ———, b. about 1830.
    Children living at home in 1860 as indicated by the U. S. Census of Johnson county for that year:
    63. Jeffrey Preston; b. 1847.
    64. Charles Preston; b. about 1848.
    65. John F. Preston; b. 1850.
    66. Laura (?) Preston; b. 1852.
    67. Francis M. Preston; b. 1855.
    68. William W. Preston; b. 1857.
    69. Amanda Preston; b. 1848.
    11. MRS. HENRY SHERMAN (MATILDA PRESTON ?) 3 (Jeffrey 2, and his wife, Jane Burgess, Nathan 1); m., December 1, 1831, Henry Sherman, farmer; b. in Tennessee in 1808.
    The United States Census, Johnson county, 1850 and 1860, indicate that their children then living at home were as follows:
    70. Eliza A. Sherman; b. in 1835.
    71. William Sherman
    72. Jefferson Sherman   Twins; b. in 1836.
    73. Catherine Sherman; b. 1840.
    74. Nathan Sherman; b. 1841.
    75. Nancy J. Sherman; b. 1843.
    76. Julia F. Sherman; b. 1846.
    77. Winfield S. Sherman; b. 1849.
    78. Lewis C. Sherman; b. 1852.
    79. Henry C. Sherman; b. 1854.
    80. James H. Burns Sherman; b. 1857.
    12. MRS. WILLIAM RANDOLPH (MARY PRESTON ?) 3, (Jeffrey 2, and his wife, Jane Burgess, Nathan 1); b. about 1820; m. William Randolph, school teacher; b. about 1824, in Virginia.
    The United States Census, Johnson county, 1860, indicates that their children then living at home were as follows:
    81. Burgess J. Randolph; b. 1848.
    82. Angeline A. Randolph; b. 1850.
    83. John R. Randolph; b. 1856.
    14. MRS. JOHN H. WARD (NANCY PRESTON ?) 3, (Jeffrey 2, and his wife, Jane Burgess, Nathan 1); b. about 1826; m. John H. Ward, farmer; b. about 1824, in Kentucky.
    Children living at home in 1860:
    84. Lovina Ward; b. in 1859.

PORTER FAMILY OF JOHNSON COUNTY

1. SAMUEL PORTER was the ancestor of a large branch of the Porter family. He was among the early settlers of the Big Sandy Valley. He m. into that very large prominent family of the Damrons who lived in the valley region from Pike County to Twelve Pole in what is now Wayne County, West Virginia. He was a shrewd businessman and was one of the largest land owners of his time, owning the entire valley of Miller's Creek, in what is now Johnson County, many acres on Little Paint Creek in Floyd County and a large boundary on Big Sandy River. He was jovial and took great delight in horse racing and other sources of amusement. He reared a large family of children who became prominent in the valley.[1]

Children:

*2. James Porter.

*3. Walker Porter.

*4. John Porter.

*5. Logan Porter.

6. —— Porter, daughter; m. a son of Edward Burgess. (A Martha Porter m. James E. Burgess in Johnson County, October 18, 1859.)

7. Elizabeth Porter; m. Burgess Preston in Johnson County, April 3, 1844.

8. Ruth A. Porter; m. Martin V. Dixon (See Dixon Family.)

9. Canada Porter; m. Polly Crum in Johnson County, August 19, 1853; lived on Miller's Creek, Johnson County, where they reared a large family.

2. JAMES PORTER was a member of the State House of Representatives from Floyd and Johnson Counties; lived for a time on Miller's Creek; later moved to Kenova, West Virginia. A daughter

10. Jennie Porter, m. G. W. Davis.[2]

3. WALKER PORTER lived in Prestonsburg. His daughter,

11. —— Porter, m. "Dick" (Richard) Mayo. (See Mayo Family.)

4. JOHN PORTER lived for a time just above the mouth of Miller's Creek where he carried on farming on an extensive scale. Later he removed to Catlettsburg where he conducted a hotel. He m. Amanda Brown, daughter of Judge Thomas Brown of Paintsville. (See Brown Family of Johnson County.) A son,

12. Henry Porter was accidently shot with a pistol in 1885 and was thereafter a cripple. A daughter,

13. —— Porter, (the oldest) m. Glenn Ford, only child and son of James R. and Sally Ford.

5. LOGAN PORTER lived on John's Creek where he was a farmer and conducted a general store.

[1] William Ely, "The Big Sandy Valley", pages 400-402.
[2] Mitchel Hall, "History of Johnson County, Kentucky". Vol. II, pp. 373-374.

PRICHARD FAMILY

Pritchard

This is an old Welsh surname and is derived from the name Richard, being a contraction of "Ap Richard". John Ap Richard in ancient Welsh vernacular meant "John, the son of Richard." This system of naming was greatly simplified when the use of surnames became popular.

The coat of arms here illustrated is borne by the Pritchards, or Prichards, of Tresgawen, Angelsey, Wales, and their descendants.

Some of the early settlers in the New England colony bearing the name Pritchard were Hugh Pritchard of Wales who came to Gloucester, Massachusetts, and later established his home in Roxberry; Richard who lived at Yarmouth, Massachusetts in 1643, and later (1660) lived in Charlestown, Massachusetts; Roger, who was a settler in Springfield, Mass., in 1643, removed to New Haven where he d. in 1671; and William Pritchard who settled in Lynn, Mass in 1645 and later went to Brookfield.

Another family of Pritchard is represented in America by those of Maryland, Pennsylvania and Ohio, many of whom trace ancestry to John Pritchard who was b. in Wales in 1775, the son of Jesse Pritchard. John emigrated to America with his father in 1785, settling at Frederick, Maryland. In 1795 he moved to Uniontown, Fayette County, Pennsylvania, and from there to Cadiz, Ohio.

William Prichard was the progenitor of the Prichard family of Northeastern Kentucky. He was of Welsh extraction and was b. in Wales circa 1730. According to tradition he and his brother, John, were kidnapped in Wales and brought to near Norfolk, Virginia, about 1744, when William was about 14 years of age. Here the owner of the ship on which they were transported apprenticed them to Virginia planters for a term of years the consideration being the cost of their passage across the ocean.

1. WILLIAM PRICHARD migrated from Norfolk to Russell County, Virginia, and from thence to Greenup County, Kentucky, about 1811. He m., probably in Russell County, Virginia, Dorcas Glover or Lunsford, who, after the death of her husband, m. in Lawrence County, February 10, 1825, Solomon White. She d. in 1839 at the home of her son, James Prichard, on Bolts Fork, in then Greenup County, now Boyd County.

Children of William Prichard and his wife Dorcas (Lunsford) Prichard:

Second Generation

*2. James Prichard.
3. John Prichard.
*4. Lewis Prichard.
*5. Elizabeth Prichard.

2. JAMES PRICHARD, b. in Virginia, May 3, 1796, and d. in Boyd County, Kentucky, September 21, 1877. He served as sheriff and justice of the peace of Lawrence County and justice of the peace of Boyd County: and served in the War of 1812; m., December 5, 1818. Elizabeth Stewart, b. in Giles County, Virginia, July 26, 1802, daughter of Absolem and Tabitha (Clay) Stewart.

Children:

Third Generation

*6. George W. Prichard.
*7. William Allen Prichard.
8. James Prichard; b. September 3, 1825, and d. June 27, 1826.
*9. Wylie Prichard.
*10. Lewis Prichard.
*11. Martha Prichard.
*12. John Wesley Prichard.
*13. Kenaz Farrow Prichard.
*14. Charles Napoleon Prichard.
*15. Noah Phichard.
*16. Jerome T. Prichard.

4. LEWIS PRICHARD, farmer, b. in Russell County, Virginia, June 12, 1800, and d. November 23, 1879; migrated with his parents to Greenup County, Kentucky, when he was eleven years of age, their first home being on the waters of Rush Creek, present Lawrence Co., a short distance from their last and permanent home; m. Lucy Toler, d. December 30, 1883, in her 82nd year.

Children:

Third Generation

17. ——— Prichard, a son who d. in infancy.
*18. Sarah Prichard.
19. Mary Ann Prichard, b. May 16, 1824, and d. September 17, 1846, unm.
*20. William Prichard.
*21. Andrew Jackson Prichard.
*22. Lucinda Prichard.
*23. Joseph Prichard.
*24. Lewis Prichard, Jr.
*25. James Prichard.
*26. Robert H. Prichard.
*27. Columbus Prichard.
*28. Richard J. Prichard.

6. George W. Prichard, farmer; b. April 29, 1821, and d. in 1901; m. in Lawrence County, Kentucky, September 21, 1843, Olivia A. Bolt, b. July 27, 1827. They resided at Grayson, Carter County, for many years.

Children:

Fourth Generation

29. Mary E. Prichard; b. October 7, 1844.
*30. Leander ("Bud") C. Prichard.
31. Casteria V. Prichard; m. W. A. Davis. (See Davis Family.)
*32. Greenville Prichard.
*33. Cerena Prichard.
*34. Belvard ("Bell") Prichard.
*35. Clinton T. ("Babe") Prichard.
*36. Annie Prichard.
*37. Martha Prichard.
*38. George W. Prichard, Jr.

7. William Allen Prichard, physician; b. in Lawrence County, Kentucky, August 9, 1823, and d. in Boyd County, that State, February 2, 1900; was graduated from the Electric Medical College, Cincinnati, and in 1854 began the practice of medicine at Garner, Boyd County, where he lived and enjoyed a large and lucrative practice until his death; m. November 12, 1850, Samantha Jones, b. September 17, 1830, daughter of Stephen and Mary (Parsons) Jones of Lee County, Virginia.

Children:

Fourth Generation

*39. James Marion Prichard.
*40. Louvernia Prichard.
41. Belvard Jones Prichard.
42. Mary Elizabeth Prichard, b. December 7, 1858, and d. June 23, 1871.
*43. Samantha Helen Prichard, b. August 22, 1883.
*44. Robert Allen Prichard.

9. Wylie Prichard, farmer and businessman of many activities; b. May 25, 1827, and d. April 13, 1896; m. in Lawrence County, July 25, 1855, Elizabeth Bolt, b. June 23, 1839, and d. April 29, 1900; resided at Mount Savage, Carter County.

Children:

Fourth Generation

*45. Celeste Prichard.
*46. Roland Prichard.
*47. Kenton Prichard.
*48. William Prichard.
*49. Annie Laurie Prichard.
*50. Samantha Prichard.
*51. Watt Lemuel Prichard.

10. LEWIS PRICHARD, physician; b. September 16, 1829, and d. November 29, 1889; was graduated from the Electric College of Medicine, Cincinnati, in 1856, and began practice of his profession in Northeastern Kentucky, but soon thereafter removed to Cloverdale, Indiana, where he continued practice until his death; m. November 23, 1858, Joanna Ross of Cloverdale.

Children:

Fourth Generation

52. Walter K. Prichard.
53. May Alma Prichard.

11. MARTHA PRICHARD; b. January 5, 1832, and d. August 25, 1893; m., August 16, 1849, Chrisley Perry Banfield, farmer, who d. September 10, 1878.

Children:

Fourth Generation

*54. Allen Prichard Banfield.
*55. John Milton Banfield.
*56. Camillus Jefferson Banfield.
*57. Sidney Ann Banfield.
*58. Columbia Banfield.
*59. James Crittenden Banfield.
*60. Charles Henry Banfield.
*61. Kenaz Farrow Banfield.
*62. Elizabeth Catherine Banfield.
*63. William Lewis Banfield.

12. JOHN WESLEY PRICHARD, farmer; lived in Greenup County; b. June 12, 1834, and d. March 9, 1896; m., first, Sarah Jane Mobley who d. in 1876; m. secondly, Susan A. Hulett, September 18, 1879.

Children of John Wesley Prichard and Sarah Jane (Mobley) Prichard:

Fourth Generation

*64. Hannah Elizabeth Prichard.
*65. Lewis Napoleon Prichard.
*66. Samantha Ellen Prichard.
*67. John Guerney Prichard.

Children of John Wesley Prichard and Susan A. (Hulett) Prichard:

Fourth Generation

*68. Nettie Prichard.
*69. Ollie Prichard.
*70. Hester Prichard.
*71. Henry Prichard.
72. Corbet Prichard.

13. KENAZ FARROW PRICHARD, lawyer; b. December 1, 1836, and

d. October 29, 1887; studied law under supervision of Frank Canterberry of Louisa, Kentucky, and was admitted to the bar in 1858; served as State Senator, 1869, and was clerk of the Senate; m., August 29, 1859, Amelia C. Stewart.

Children:

Fourth Generation

73. Clara Glenwood Prichard, b. July 5, 1861; m. Earl Stockwell.
74. Annie Lee Prichard, b. January 29, 1864.
75. Stella Prichard, b. September 13, 1866; d. in her 18th year.
76. Henry Prichard, b. May 21, 1869.

14. CHARLES NAPOLEON PRICHARD, farmer, b. on Bolts Fork, June 5, 1839, and d. September 12, 1904; m. July 13, 1864, Sarah A. Smith, d. January 6, 1905.

Children:

Fourth Generation

*77. Gertrude Prichard.
*78. Minnie Lee Prichard.
*79. Hallie Prichard.

15. NOAH PRICHARD, farmer; b. October 14, 1841, and d. March 19, 1908; m. November 6, 1862, Ariminta Reeves, b. August 18, 1844.

Children:

Fourth Generation

80. Martha Prichard, b. December 24, 1863.
81. Emma Prichard, b. December 24, 1865, and d. July —, 1885.
82. John Milton Prichard, physician, b. February 19, 1868. He had a general practice at first and later specialized in ear, nose and throat at Ashland; m., September 11, 1895, Ida Lillian Cyrus, b. October 24, 1863. No children.
83. Jerome Cornelius Prichard, b. April 3, 1870; unm.
84. Mary Prichard, b. July 30, 1872, and d. June, 1891.
*85. James Prichard.
86. Kenaz F. Prichard; b. March 29, 1877; m. and resided in West Virginia; nothing further has been learned concerning him.
87. Maude Prichard; b. March 11, 1880.
88. Ralph Prichard; b. April 12, 1882.
89. Samantha Prichard; b. September 21, 1884.
90. Henry Prichard.
91. Braxton B. Prichard; b. May 17, 1891.

16. JEROME T. PRICHARD, farmer; b. May 30, 1844, and d. March 3, 1932; educated in the public schools of Boyd County; engaged in farming and stockraising; elected as a Democrat and served as State Senator from the Boyd-Lawrence-Elliott district, 1910-1914; life-long resident of Bolts Fork, Boyd County; m. in Lawrence County, October 14, 1866, Olivia Bolt, b. July 14, 1849, d. March 13, 1919, daughter of Judge M. F. Bolt.

Children:
Fourth Generation
*92. James Allen Prichard.
93. Henry Greenville Prichard; b. September 8, 1869, and d. September 18, 1869.
94. Carl L. Prichard; b. October 29, 1870; m. Elizabeth Christine Hatcher, July 22, 1907.
*95. Leonidas Montraville Prichard.
*96. Millard F. Prichard.
*97. Annie Elizabeth Prichard.
*98. Sophia Earle Prichard.
99. Frank Prichard; b. January 13, 1880, d. August 6, 1893.
100. Charles D. Prichard; b. March 12, 1882; m., November 4, 1909, Carrie Queen.
*101. Watt M. Prichard.
102. Lula Prichard; b. October 31, 1889, and d. April 3, 1911; unm.
18. SARAH PRICHARD; b. in Lawrence County, Kentucky, May 4, 1823, and d. in Richardson County, Nebraska, July 27, 1898; m. in Wayne County, Virginia, January 26, 1846, Abraham Vaughan.
Children:
Fourth Generation
103. Tabitha Vaughan; b. in Wayne County, Virginia, December 16, 1847, and d. in Hamilton County, Ohio, November 10, 1858.
*104. Lewis Preston Vaughan.
105. Christopher Columbus Vaughan; b. in Wayne County, Virginia, January 21, 1852, and d. in Richardson County, Nebraska, November 8, 1877; unm.
*106. Andrew Jackson Vaughan.
107. Thomas Jefferson Vaughan; b. in Lawrence County, Ohio, October 3, 1856, and d. in Richardson County, Nebraska, November 24, 1877; unm.
*108. Sarah Ann Vaughan.
109. Abraham Girard Vaughan; b. in Lawrence County, Ohio, in 1861, and d. in infancy.
110. Laura Lucinda Vaughan; b. in Lawrence County, Ohio, January 24, 1864; m. in Lawrence County, February 21, 1881, Leander C. Prichard, son of William Prichard. No children.
20. WILLIAM PRICHARD, farmer; owned and resided on a farm on the Big Sandy River in Boyd County; b. June 9, 1827, and d. February 12, 1906; m., March 15, 1853, Caroline Newman, d. January 10, 1881.
Children:
Fourth Generation
111. Leander C. Prichard, b. in then Lawrence County, now Boyd County, January 15, 1854; m., February 21, 1881, Laura Lucinda Vaughan of Richardson County, Nebraska; resided at Falls City,

Nebraska. No children.

*112. Columbus B. Prichard.

113. James Prichard; b. 1859, and d. January 8, 1881; unm.

114. Laura Annie Prichard; b. in Boyd County, January 24, 1862, d. January 8, 1881; unm.

*115. Virginia A. Prichard.

*116. Robert L. Prichard.

21. ANDREW JACKSON PRICHARD, farmer; b. September 28, 1828, and d. February 6, 1868; lived near his birthplace on Big Sandy River about eight miles from Catlettsburg; was State representative from Lawrence County, 1855-1857; m. in Lawrence County, April 17, 1856, Nancy Jane Burgess, b. February 17, 1837, and d. January 21, 1878. (See Burgess Family.)

Children:

Fourth Generation

117. George A. Prichard; b. July 11, 1857, and d. August 19, 1857.

*118. Thomas Jefferson Prichard.

*119. Emily Lucy Prichard.

*120. James Lewis Prichard.

*121. Alice Lee Prichard; b. January 2, 1866, and d. January 27, 1866.

122. Jenkins Ann Prichard.

22. LUCINDA PRICHARD; b. March 13, 1834; m., April 30, 1857, William Ballard Faulkner who d. July 21, 1873; lived on a farm near Mt. Savage, Furnace, Carter County. After death of her husband, Mrs. Faulkner continued to live on this farm for a time, but finally moved to the home farm in order to care for her mother.

Children:

Fourth Generation

123. Mary Elizabeth Faulkner; b. November 11, 1859; d. December 15, 1863.

124. Lucinda Faulkner; b. May 23, 1860; d. August 10, 1887; m., February 12, 1882, William Hornbuckle. Children (fifth generation): Lueffie Hornbuckle, b. December 3, 1884; m., October 18, 1903, Herman Lakin who was b. November 4, 1873. Children (sixth generattion): Lucinda Lakin, b. August 3, 1904; Hazel Lakin, Henrietta Lakin, b. May 12, 1906; a n d Carrie Amelia Laken, November 11, 1907.

125. George B. Faulkner, farmer; b. October 1, 1861; m., December 10, 1900, Anna Belle Alley of Boyd County; resided near Catlettsburg; no children.

126. Samantha Jane Faulkner; b. December 8, 1863; d. July 12, 1887; unm.

127. Andrew Jackson Faulkner; b. July 12, 1865; d. September 16, 1906; m. July 10, 1891, Cora Bromfield; resided in Ashland. Children (fifth generation): Edith L. Faulkner, b. January 22, 1894;

Georgia O. Faulkner, b. May 15, 1896; and Karl P. Faulkner, b. June 15, 1899.

128. Lewis Faulkner; b. July 19, 1868; resided with his mother on home farm; assisting in the work and management of the farm and dealing in live stock; weighed 375 pounds; unm.

129. Oscar Faulkner; b. May 8, 1870; d. September 30, 1872.

130. Emily Faulkner; b. February 7, 1872; m., October 18, 1893, Hugh M. Smith, mail carrier, of Pueblo, Colorado, b. November 28, 1867. Children (fifth generation): James Ballard Smith, b. December 6, 1894; Lucinda Irma Smith, b. March 18, 1902; and Mabel Fern Smith, b. May 12, 1906.

131. William Ballard Faulkner; b. December 10, 1874; lived with his mother on farm, directing the active work with his brother, Lewis; unm.

23. JOSEPH PRICHARD; b. in Lawrence County, November 3, 1836; m. in Wayne County, Virginia, Caroline Compton. He was a blacksmith. About the close of the Civil War he migrated to Richardson County, Nebraska, where he purchased a farm and became well to do. He was an upright and respected citizen.

Children:

Fourth Generation

132. Pheribe Prichard; b. in Lawrence County, Kentucky, August 14, 1862; m. in Richardson County, Nebraska, October 24, 1883, Nathaniel D. Auxier. Children (fifth generation): Walter Talmage Auxier, b. October 31, 1887; Edward Elmer Auxier, b. October 15, 1889; Maud Ethel Auxier, b. March 15, 1891; d. December 26, 1893; and Ruth Edna Auxier, b. August 16, 1892; d. December 26, 1893.

133. Mary Lucy Prichard; b. in Lawrence County, June 6, 1864; m. in Richardson County, Nebraska, February 13, 1887, Edward Everett Auxier. Children (fifth generation): Mabelle Auxier, b. December 12, 1887; Homer Joseph Auxier, b. February 24, 1891; Grace Auxier, b. April 30, 1892; Ethel Ernest Auxier, b. January 19, 1896; Edward Jennings Auxier, b. January 10, 1899; and Cloyd Raymond Auxier, b. July 8, 1900.

134. Cora Lutitia Prichard; b. in Richardson County, Nebraska, March 20, 1868; m., January 19, 1896, Clinton Hiram Simpson. Children (fifth generation): Irl Dean Simpson, b. April 8, 1900; and Cliver Clinton Simpson, b. June 9, 1905.

135. Hubert Joseph Prichard; b. in Richardson County, Nebraska June 27, 1871; m. Ada E. Kimmel, November 15, 1893. Children (fifth generation): Alberta Prichard, b. August 20, 1894; and Wilbur Joseph Prichard, b. February 4, 1898.

136. Jacob Prichard; b. November, 1873, and d. September 27, 1878.

137. George W. Prichard; b. in Richardson County, Nebraska, April 29, 1876; m., first, in that county, February 17, 1897, Pink Bloomer,

who d. February 17, 1909; m., secondly, October 18, 1910, Otie Fisher of Falls City, Nebraska. Children (fifth generation): Harry Hubert Prichard, b. January 26, 1899, and Guy Jennings Prichard, b. July 7, 1901.

24. LEWIS PRICHARD, physician and surgeon, banker and business-man, was b. January 19, 1839, on his father's farm on the Big Sandy River about 12 miles above Catlettsburg, Kentucky, in then Lawrence now Boyd County, Kentucky. He worked on his father's farm to manhood; attended the rural public schools and taught one term. Early in life he began dealing in timber, buying standing trees and floating the logs down the Big Sandy to market by which he earned money to continue his education. Subsequently he attended the public schools of Catlettsburg for a time. In 1858 he was a student at Marshall Academy, now Marshall College, at Huntington, West Virginia. He attended school at Decatur, Ohio, and at South Salem, Ohio; and finally he entered the National Normal University at Lebanon, Ohio, and was a student there when Lincoln was assassinated and due to sectional feeling he returned home. In 1865 he entered the Medical Department of the University of Michigan, remaining two years, when he graduated with honors.

In the Spring or early summer of 1867, Dr. Prichard began the practice of medicine at Grayson, Carter County, Kentucky, being associated with William D. Jones, then the leading physician in the county. Not long afterwards Dr. Jones retired from active practice, leaving his large and growing practice to Dr. Prichard, who, by untiring devotion to duty, steadily arose in his profession until he was acknowledged to be the leading physician and surgeon in Northeastern Kentucky.

On January 7, 1868, Dr. Prichard was m. to Miss Sarah Belle Meade, daughter of Armistead Meade, who lived near Russell, Greenup County, Kentucky. Twenty-six dollars was the sum of all of his wealth at the time, of which sum he gave fifteen dollars to the Rev. John T. Johnson of the Methodist Church, South, who performed the marriage ceremony. During the first few months of their married life, Dr. and Mrs. Prichard lived in the home of Capt. E. P. Davis of Grayson. In the course of the six months following their marriage, Mrs. Prichard's father gave her sums of money aggregating about $1250 which she turned over to her husband. About two months after marriage Dr. Prichard purchased a small cottage and about 15 acres of land on the outskirts of Grayson. Here all their children were born. He planted orchards of apples and peaches and cultivated the farm at such times as he was not attending to his professional duties while Mrs. Prichard did all her house work including washing, mending and caring for the children. By economy and industry, their property steadily increased and Dr. Prichard dealt considerably in real estate; owned a brick building on Main Street in which he conducted a drugstore and a small banking business.

In the latter part of 1875, Dr. Prichard went to New York for a post graduate course in surgery. He disposed of his banking business to James Osenton, who became president, C. C. Magann, Merritt Magann and E. B. Wilhoit.

In 1884 Dr. Prichard became one of the charter members and organizers of the Charleston National Bank of Charston, West Virginia, which was promoted by his brother-in-law, Charles P. Mead, who became president and served as such until his death in 1888. Dr. Prichard succeeded him as president of the bank under whose wise management the bank grew from a capital stock of $50,000 to one of the largest in the area. Dr. Prichard owned about one-half of the capital stock besides large blocks of stocks in about 15 other banking institutions. He acquired about 20,000 acres of coal lands in West Virginia besides considerable other property and became one of the wealthiest men of the area in which he lived, all of which attest to his enterprising spirit, industry and great business abilities. In 1889 Mrs. Prichard joined him in Charleston. Here they established their home and afterwards lived.

Children:

Fourth Generation

138. Henry Lewis Prichard; b. at Grayson, Kentucky, December 25, 1868; was graduated from Notre Dame University in June 1890; was connected with the Charleston National Bank for many years; m., October 16, 1895. Emma Elizabeth Walker, b. August 6, 1871, daughter of Henry S. Walker, the great orator. Children (fifth generation); Henry Lewis, b. September 9, 1903; Frederick Walker, b. December 26, 1906.

139. Frederick Charles Prichard; b. at Grayson, Kentucky, March 1, 1874. Never idle, he worked on farm, in tobacco warehouse and at various occupations in his youth. He was a student at Notre Dame University for four years, graduating in Civil Engineering. Subsequently going to Charleston, West Virginia, he was employed in and about that city for eight years; in a bank, a wholesale grocery; and in conducting a retail business. In 1899 he became first superintendent of the White Oak Fuel Company of Fayette County, West Virginia; became interested in other mines and mining properties.

Mr. Prichard removed to Huntington, West Virginia, in 1909 and became one of the outstanding businessmen of that city, particularly in building and real estate. He was associated with Houghton A. Robson in business; and they erected the Robson-Prichard building and many other buildings in Huntington.

On October 24, 1894, Mr. Prichard was m. to Alice Claire Wilson, b. August 31, 1873, daughter of Hardy Wilson, of LaPorte, Indiana. No children.

140. Armsted Mead Prichard; b. at Grayson, Kentucky, September 9, 1875; educated at Notre Dame University (September, 1889—

February, 1896); studied law in Charleston and then at University of West Virginia (September, 1896—June 1897) from which he was graduated with degree of LL.B.; admitted to the bar June 21, 1897, and practiced law until August, 1910, when he became connected with the Charleston National Bank as assistant cashier; m., first January 7, 1902, Lydia Bahlmann Robson, b. November 1, 1880, in Fayette County, West Virginia, d. in Charleston, June 19, 1910. Children (fifth generation): Belle Mead, b. August 15, 1905; Lydia Robson, b. January 4, 1908. He m., secondly, October 10, 1911, Betty Douglas Robson, at the home of her parents in Culpeper County, Virginia.

25. JAMES PRICHARD, merchant and trader in livestock and lands, was b. October 16, 1841, and d. December 3, 1910; m., August 10, 1870, Henrietta Smith, at residence of her father, Lindsey Smith, at Round Bottom (now Prichard), West Virginia. No children.

26. ROBERT H. PRICHARD; b. February 28, 1844; d. June 17, 1899; m. January 16, 1873, Mary Elizabeth Campbell at the residence of her uncle, H. A. Mead in Greenup County; resided in Catlettsburg. Mr. Prichard was a timber dealer for a time.

Children:

Fourth Generation

141. Colbert Cecil Prichard, b. November 10, 1873, d. February 19, 1875.

142. Mary A. Prichard, b. November 19, 1875, and d. November 19, 1875.

143. Lucy Prichard, teacher; graduated at Vassar College, June 1899; taught in the Hampton City schools and was principal of the High School there.

144. Karl C. Prichard; b. June 23, 1879. Education: Was graduated from Lafayette College with degree of Ph.D. and from Jefferson College of Medicine; was connected with the Easton (Pennsylvania) Hospital; and subsequently removed to Huntington, West Virginia, and practiced his profession; m., June 2, 1908, Elizabeth Ann Morrison, daughter of Charles A. Morrison of Easton, Pennsylvania.

27. COLUMBUS PRICHARD; b. September 16, 1846; engaged in wholesale grocery business in Catlettsburg; later lived in Ashland; m. Virginia Caroline Burgess, b. March 12, 1847, and d. July 5, 1902. Children (fifth generation): Taylor Bascom, b. May 6, 1873, and d. December 15, 1874; Charles Hampton, b. January 25, 1876; m., 1900, Ceres Kinner of Catlettsburg, b. August 22, 1881.

28. RICHARD J. PRICHARD; b. April 11, 1850, and d. August 21, 1903. He was a merchant at Louisa, Kentucky, for many years; and was affiliated with the Masonic fraternity (a Knight Templar, etc); m., January 30, 1878, Victoria Vinson of Louisa, b. June 28, 1860. (See Vinson Family) Children (fourth generation): Lucille Vinson Prichard, b. January 13, 1879, and d. January 20, 1902; m. Edgar Brown Hager of Ashland, b. December 6, 1868. Children (fifth

generation): Edgar B., Jr., b. December 2, 1899; Virginia Patton, b. March 23, 1901; Georgia Finley, b. July 3, 1887 and d. February 26, 1888. (See Hager Family.)

5. ELIZABETH PRICHARD; b. June 20, 1809, d. July 1, 1892; m., August 20, 1825, Samuel White, b. May 29, 1801, d. July 24, 1888. Children:

Third Generation

145. William White; b. July 5, 1826.

146. Alfred White; b. October 13, 1830.

147. Mary Ann White; b. June 29, 1833; m., April 5, 1860, James Lakin. Children (fourth generation): Elizabeth Lakin, b. April 8, 1861; Catherine Lakin, b. May 22, 1862; m., Charles Higgins, Children (fifth generation): Frederick Higgins, d. February 3, 1897; Effie Elizabeth Higgins, b. December 8, 1885; m., January 10, 1907, Clem Atkins; Sallie Ann Higgins, b. May 21, 1888; m., November 22, 1906, Oscar Riffle. Children (sixth generation): George W. Riffle, b. January 1, 1909; Delbert Higgins, b. February 1, 1890; Pearl H. Higgins, b. October 10, 1891; Sophia Ethel Higgins, b. April 26, 1895.

148. Sarah White; b. October 18, 1835.

149. James White; b. March 1, 1838.

150. Bethany White; b. November 30, 1839.

151. Susan White; b. February 24, 1843.

152. Elizabeth White; b. September 30, 1845.

153. Henry White; b. April 8, 1848; m., August 31, 1882, Arletta Campbell. Children (fourth generation): Walter White, b. September 1, 1883, and d. August 3, 1885; Charles White, b. August 24, 1884, and d. January 13, 1894; Zella E. White, b. September 2, 1886; Bernard White, b. April 18, 1888; Mary E. White, b. September 6, 1889; Martha J. White, b. June 28, 1891; m., June 30, 1907, Dode Fields. Children (fifth generation): Two who d. in infancy, May 8, 1909, and February 22, 1910, respectively; Sarah A. White, b. February 16, 1893; Emily F. White, b. July 4, 1895; Albert White, b. February 25, 1897; America White, b. October 21, 1899; Bascom White, b. November 15, 1902; Harry White, b. November 28, 1904; Russell White, b. January 25, 1908, d. February 12, 1908.

154. Robert White; b. September 27, 1850.

155. Lindsey (Lenzy) White; b. October 3, 1852.

30. LEANDER ("BUD") COX PRICHARD, farmer; b. July 3, 1847; d. July 15, 1932, and was buried in Kitchen graveyard near Willard, Kentucky; resided at Sandy Hook, Elliott County, for many years; represented Carter, Elliott and Lawrence Counties in the State Senate, 1910-1914; m., first, September 13, 1871, Caroline Kitchen, b. March 4, 1848, d. April 19, 1886, daughter of William Kitchen of Sandy Hook; m., secondly, June 16, 1887, Nancy Belle Kitchen, b.

January 6, 1867, d. August 9, 1940, daughter of Lewis and Jane (Bays) Kitchen of Willard. Mrs. Prichard was buried in Kitchen graveyard near Willard.

Children of Leander C. and Caroline (Kitchen) Prichard:

Fifth Generation

156. Laura S. Prichard, teacher, b. August 8, 1872; m. February 15, 1898, Henry Clay Turner, farmer and realtor. Children (sixth generation): Louise, b. December 4, 1890; m. Allen Cloyd; Carolyn, b. March, 1901; Elizabeth, b. August 19, 1902, m. Charles Brown; and Henry Clay, Jr., b. March 28, 1905.

157. William Allen Prichard, teacher; b. December 1, 1873; m., Janury 13, 1910, Tisha Adkins. Children (sixth generation): Kathleen, who m. Boyd Blair; and Leander.

158. George Walter ("Watt"), Prichard, merchant; b. February 10, 1876; m., November 10, 1909, Bernice Womeldorf. Children (sixth generation): Henry Lee; Watt, Jr.; Charles Frederick; Jean.

159. Lewis Napoleon Prichard, farmer; b. January 17, 1878; m., March 11, 1909, Laura Hunter. Children (sixth generation): Carolyn, m. Winford Crosswaite; Frances, m. Ray Brown; Lewis Curtis, m. Ruth Ison; Isabel.

160. John Barber Prichard; b. May 20, 1880; deceased.

161. Nancy Olivia Prichard; b. June 19, 1882; m. Emory Beecher Greene, merchant. Children (sixth generation): Emory Lee Greene; m. Reba Fannin.

162. Charles Fleming Prichard, farmer; b. August 22, 1885; m. Mary Virginia Kitchen. Children (sixth generation): Georgia Belle Prichard; Carolyn Prichard, m. Edward Davis; James Prichard, m. Jean Rogers; Herbert Prichard; Harlan Prichard; Dorothy Prichard; Lawrence Prichard; Allen Lewis Prichard.

163. Carolyn S. Prichard; b. August 22, 1885; m. Herbert King, b. September 25, 1882. (See King Family in Horton Family.) Children (sixth generation): Prichard King, m. Mona Caudill; Watt King, m. Thelma Gollihue; Harold King, m. Josephine Gee (See Gee Family); Charlotte King, m. Raymond Isaac.

Children of Leander C. and Nancy Belle (Kitchen) Prichard:

Fifth Generation

164. Janie F. or Jennie Prichard; b. November 10, 1888; m. William Caskey, merchant. Children (sixth generation): William Prichard Caskey, m. Osha Wingo; Robert Caskey, m. Helen Elam; Georgia May Caskey, m. Woodrow Stamper; Isabelle Caskey.

165. Georgia Prichard; m. Allie Logan Kitchen, farmer.

32. GREENVILLE PRICHARD, farmer; b. December 29, 1852; m. Miss Jessee; lived on a farm on Little Sandy River above Grayson where they reared a family.

33. CERENA PRICHARD; b. August 25, 1855; m., October 27, 1886, Robert Franklin Elam of West Liberty, Kentucky, who was b. December 6, 1846, and d. July 23, 1904. Children (fifth generation): William Prichard Elam, b. April 6, 1888; m., 1904, Georgia Lillian Thomas. Children (sixth generation): Robert Thomas Elam, b. October 12, 1904. Maude L. Elam; b. December 24, 1889; m., February 5, 1911, Samuel Carter at Morehead.

34. BELVARD ("BELL") PRICHARD; b. March 7, 1858; m. January 5, 1910, Laura Ethel Barnhill. They reared a family of whom a son, Curtis Randolph, the eldest was b. January 19, 1911.

35. CLINTON T. ("BABE") PRICHARD; b. April 9, 1860; m., October 15, 1890, Olive A. Proctor, b. November 24, 1871. Children (fifth generation): Rebecca Aline, b. September 17, 1891; Myrtilla Alva, b. May 3, 1893; Proctor Leander b. April 27, 1895; Mary Ethel, b. December 24, 1896; George William, b. January 16, 1899; Elizabeth Adella, b. January 4, 1903; Oliva Maria, b. July 27, 1905; Paul Clifton, b. October 3, 1909.

36. ANNIE PRICHARD; b. April 18, 1862; m., June 29, 1904, Daniel Boone Lacy, b. July 22, 1860.

37. MARTHA PRICHARD; b. April 10, 1865; m., June 1, 1893, H. C. Simpson. Children (fifth generation): Beryl Brentano Simpson, b. March 9, 1894, and Thomas Belvard Simpson, b. May 19, 1895.

38. GEORGE W. PRICHARD; b. April 21, 1867; m. Effie Colley. No children.

39. JAMES MARION PRICHARD, physician; b. in Carter County, August 31, 1851; graduated from Marshall College and afterwards from the Electric Medical College at Cincinnati; m., March 21, 1900, Mary Bailey of Lee County, Virginia; lived and practiced his profession at Orlinger, Virginia. Children in 1912 (fifth generation): Allen Bailey Prichard, b. January 17, 1901.

40. LOUVERNIA PRICHARD; b. in Carter County, March 16, 1854; m., March 16, 1871, James W. Mullen of Boyd County, who d. April 1, 1904; resided in Catlettsburg. Children (fifth generation): Howard Mullen, b. May 25, 1873; Edward Mullen, b. May 25, 1873; m., 1902, Lottie Blackburn, b. 1876. Children (sixth generation): Louise, b. November 25, 1902; Janet, b. April 30, 1904; Alice Mullen, b. March 20, 1876, d. June 12, 1906; Lee Mullen, b. August 22, 1879, d. October 18, 1880; Lucille Mullen, b. September 14, 1881; Belva H. Mullen, b. 1883.

41. BELVARD JONES PRICHARD, lawyer; b. in Carter County, June 10, 1856; educated at Centre College, Danville, Kentucky, and at University of Louisville Law College; editor of the "Hancock Democrat", published at Greencastle, Indiana; located at Wayne, West Virginia, for practice of law; elected State senator from the fifth Senatorial district of West Virginia, and served from 1888 to 1892;

served as president of the Wayne County Bank; m., first, September 23, 1880, Kate D. Finley and after divorce m., secondly, May 2, 1903; Etta Rucker of Huntington.

Children, first marriage (fifth generation):

166. Edmund Finley Prichard; b. September 14, 1881; m. May 30, 1904, Frances Miller Davis of Catlettsburg. Children (sixth generation): Louise Beuhsing, b. at Catlettsburg, May 16, 1907.

167. Stella May Prichard; b. May 22, 1885; m., June 16, 1906, Edward Gordon Davis of Huntington. Children (sixth generation): Edward Gordon, Jr., b. at Huntington, May 3, 1907; Catherine Elizabeth, b. at Winchester, Kentucky, April 27, 1909.

168. Oscar B. Prichard; b. October 9, 1886, m. at Catlettsburg, January 7, 1909, Hattie Huntington Wash. Children (sixth generation): George Finley Prichard, b. at Huntington, October 16, 1907, d. April 14, 1909.

169. Sallie Louvernia Prichard; b. April 5, 1888; m., May 17, 1909, Clarence William Harp.

170. Albert Courtland Prichard; m. January 14, 1905, Violet Pruett. Children, second marriage: Fifth generation.

171. Belvard Rucker Prichard; b. at Wayne Court House, West Virginia, May 30, 1904.

44. ROBERT ALLEN PRICHARD, physician; b. in Boyd County, Kentucky, July 15, 1864; graduated at Electric Medical College at Cincinnati; practiced his profession in Boyd County; m., first, February 18, 1886, Sophia Fannin, who d. October 17, 1886, without issue; m., secondly, May 30, 1889, Florence Reese of Lee County, Virginia. Children (fifth generation): Virginia Lee Prichard, b. March 7, 1890; m., September 16, 1908, Garrett D. Davis of Kentucky; Philip Howard Prichard, b. September 22, 1904.

43. SAMANTHA HELEN PRICHARD; b. in Boyd County, August 22, 1862; m., December 20, 1882, Samuel Dempsey Finley. Children (fifth generation): James Albert Finley; b. January 20, 1884; m., July 30, 1907, Zella A. Dorsey, b. April 22, 1887; resided in Huntington. Mr. Finley was a well-known painter by trade; no children. Allen Finley; Alexander Altsman Finley, b. October 14, 1892; Elijah Earl Finley, b. June 13, 1898.

45. CELESTE PRICHARD; b. near Olive Hill, Kentucky, July 20, 1856, d. in Ashland, June 6, 1903; m., March 7, 1878, Dr. Alexander Taylor Henderson, b. near Olive Hill, December 21, 1846. Children (fifth generation): Edna Earl Henderson, b. at Willard, Kentucky, April 19, 1880; m., June 6, 1900, W. Frank Therkildson, b. July 25, 1879. Children (sixth generation): Earl Lee, b. March 21, 1901; Thelma Celesta, b. May 6, 1903; W. Frank, Jr., b. June 6, 1908.

OSCAR PRICHARD HENDERSON; b. at Willard, April 26, 1882; m.

November 24, 1909, Ella V. Calame of Birmingham, Alabama; resided at Birmingham.

WATT ALEXANDER HENDERSON; b. at Denton, Kentucky, December 14, 1884; m. December 6, 1908, Sarah Valentine Hardin of Tuscaloosa, Alabama; resided at Tuscaloosa. Children (sixth generation): Valoris Alene, b. September 14, 1909.

Alberto Henderson; b. at Denton, January 7, 1887, d. March 9, 1888.

Norman Claude Henderson; b. at Denton, July 13, 1891.

Paul Russell Henderson; b. at Denton, December 6, 1893.

46. ROLAND PRICHARD. farmer; b. June 24, 1858; m., first, Maggie Adams, teacher; no children. (See Flaugher Family). Married, secondly, at St. Louis, September 27, 1897, Nancy (Nannie) Carroll, teacher, b. September 27. 1877. Children (fifth generation): Wylie Reid, b. March, 1904; Marie ("Wayda"), b. November 9, 1909.

47. KENTON PRICHARD, businessman; b. August 13, 1860; resided at Denton for many years where he was superintendent of the Straight Creek coal mines for several years, which he finally purchased and operated for a time; removed to Ashland in later life where he made investments particularly in connection with real estate; m. at Grayson, Kentucky, December 11, 1895, Elizabeth Caroline Malone, daughter of William D. Malone of Grayson. Children (fifth generation): Leda Lucille, b. January 2, 1897; Kenton Malone, b. March 13, 1905.

48. WILLIAM PRICHARD, farmer; b. July 23. 1862; m. February 29, 1892, Hattie Polhamus, daughter of John Polhamus of Grayson. No children.

49. ANNIE LAURIE PRICHARD; b. November 2, 1874; m. November 29, 1894, John Robert Graner, b. November 12, 1867; resided at Covington, Kentucky. Children (fifth generation): Ernest Victor, b. January 31, 1896, d. August 10, 1897; John Forrest, b. May 23, 1900; Hazel May, b. July 1, 1902.

50. SAMANTHA PRICHARD; b. January 27, 1867; m., June 1, 1892, O. F. L. Beckett, b. October 1, 1862. Mr. Beckett was agent for the C & O Railway Company at Denton for a time and afterwards went to Ashland where he engaged in the lumber business. No children.

51. WATT LEMUEL PRICHARD, educator; b. December 9, 1874; educated in the public schools, at National Normal University, Lebanon, Ohio, and was graduated from Harvard University; taught in public schools of Carter County for a short time; instructor at Puget Sound University, Tacoma, Washington, and was president of Clemson College.

54. ALLEN PRICHARD BANFIELD, physician and surgeon; specialist,

eye, ear, nose and throat; b. June 16, 1850; had special professional training in Europe; resided in Catlettsburg and in later life in Ashland; unm.

55. JOHN MILTON BANFIELD; b. August 7, 1852, d. July 1, 1853.

56. CAMILLUS JEFFERSON BANFIELD; b. January 5, 1854; d. November 5, 1877; m. September 21, 1876, Jacintha Elizabeth Kouns, b. March 10, 1857, in Boyd County, Kentucky. Children (fifth generation): Louella C., b. July 11, 1877; unm. 1912 and residing in Ashland.

57. SIDNEY ANN BANFIELD; b. August 16, 1850; m., June 2, 1881, Francis Marion Newman, farmer; b. February 14, 1846; resided on Big Sandy River about ten miles above Catlettsburg. Children (fifth generation): Elba, b. June 3, 1889; d. June 3, 1899; Lena Rivers, b. September 8, 1891.

58. COLUMBIA BANFIELD; b. May 7, 1858, d. December 9, 1891; m. February 23, 1881, John J. Turman, farmer; b. May 11, 1858; resided on farm on Big Sandy River near Kavanaugh. Children (fifth generation): Perry C., b. December 23, 1882, d. December 23, 1882; Ida, b. January 16, 1884, d. January 17, 1884, twin to Ison, b. January 16, 1884, d. January 17, 1884.

59. JAMES CRITTENDEN BANFIELD, physician and surgeon; b. April 21, 1859; resided and practiced his profession in Huntington; m. August, 1904, Alice Crum, widow of E. D. Crum, deceased. Children (fifth generation): James Crittenden, Jr., b. November 5, 1905.

60. CHARLES HENRY BANFIELD; b. August 9, 1861, d. April 14, 1899; m., May 28, 1890, Flora May Lark of Portsmouth, Ohio. Children (fifth generation): Arthur Perry, b. March 30, 1891; Clyde Lark, b. September 5, 1892.

61. KENAZ FARROW BANFIELD; b. March 27, 1863, d. 1911; m. May 3, 1890, Sophia Fannin, who d. September 1, 1898. Children (fifth generation): Joseph, b. July 6, 1892, d. January 6, 1907; Delbert, b. June 21, 1894, d. August 6, 1897; Frederick, b. March 18, 1897.

62. ELIZABETH CATHERINE BANFIELD; b. April 24, 1866; m., November 4, 1888, William R. Selbee (or Selby). Children (fifth generation): Beulah Eugie, b. December 23, 1889; Earl Banfield, b. March 18, 1893; Lucille Margaret, b. February 21, 1897; Chester Perry, b. May 4, 1900; Martha Marie, b. March 12, 1908.

63. WILLIAM LEWIS BANFIELD; b. July 1, 1870; m., November 7, 1893, Emma Clay, b. April 20, 1874; resided at Wayne Court House, West Virginia. Children (fifth generation): Elba M., b. May 7, 1896, d. July 30, 1896; Virgil, b. February 27, 1898; Reba, b. March 27, 1901; Eril, b. December 13, 1904; Golden, b. January 20, 1906; Lelia, b. August 24, 1908.

64. HANNAH ELIZABETH PRICHARD; b. 1867, d. July 22, 1909; m., 1887, James Monroe Adams. Children (fifth generation): Maude Adams, b. 1888; m., 1907, Warren Simmons. Children (sixth generation): Pauline, b. 1908; Evelyn, b. 1909.

65. LEWIS NAPOLEON PRICHARD; b. 1869.

66. SAMANTHA ELLEN PRICHARD; 1871; m., 1890, William Dempsey. Children (fifth generation): Florence.

67. JOHN GURNEY PRICHARD, farmer, teacher and public official; b. February 7, 1874; taught in the public schools of Greenup County; was elected on the Democratic ticket and served as Superintendent of public schools of Greenup County, 1910-1913, inclusive, and was Clerk of the Greenup County Court, 1916; m., January 22, 1905, Hyrtleline Moore. Children (fifth generation): John Gurney, Jr., b. August 28, 1908.

68. NETTIE PRICHARD; m. Richard Perry.

69. OLLIE PRICHARD; m. Tilden Edmonds of Portsmouth, Ohio.

70. HESTER PRICHARD; m. Mr. Shartneck of Wayne, West Virginia.

71. HENRY PRICHARD, dec'd; unm.

77. GERTRUDE PRICHARD; b. April 6, 1865; m., March 25, 1891, John A. Lair of Goshen, Rockbridge County, Virginia. Children (fifth generation): Hallie May, b. June 21, 1893, d. at age of 14 months; Florence Gertrude, b. September 18, 1895; John Prichard, b. April 13, 1905.

78. MINNIE LEE PRICHARD; b .May 6, 1867; m., March 18, 1885, Hugh Marshall Mitchell of Shelocta, Indiana County, Pennsylvania. Children (fifth generation): Hugh Kenton, b. December 23, 1885, m., April 21, 1907, Carolyn Kerr; Leonidas James, b. April 30, 1888; Minnie Nadine, b. December 28, 1891, d. October 8, 1008; Marshall Clyde, b. November 25, 1893, d. August 30, 1894; Collis P. Huntington, b. August 14, 1895; Lawrence Napoleon, b. August 8, 1900; Paul Prichard, b. December 14, 1905.

79. HALLIE PRICHARD; b. October 31, 1869, d. May 6, 1893.

85. JAMES PRICHARD; b. December 25, 1874; m. August 8, 1900. Children (fifth generation): Ethel, b. July 15, 1901; Mary, b. September 23, 1902; James, b. November 22, 1904.

92. JAMES ALLEN PRICHARD; b. September 8, 1867; m. March 31, 1909, Laura Compton. Children (fifth generation): Marion Compton, b. June 16, 1910.

95. LEONIDAS MONTRAVILLE PRICHARD, physician; b. October 10, 1872; m., August 14, 1899, Josephine Phillips; practiced his profession at Rush, Kentucky. Children (fifth generation): Carl Hildred, b. December 30, 1901.

96. MILLARD F. PRICHARD; b. September 1, 1874; m., March 30, 1903, Mary Robinette. Children (fifth generation): Thelma, b. July 5, 1904; Joseph, b. November 17, 1906; Edgar Malcom, b. June 5, 1909.

97. ANNIE ELIZABETH PRICHARD; b. May 19, 1876; m., December 31, 1893, George W. Chapman, educator. Mr. Chapman was a native of Lawrence County, Kentucky, of a prominent pioneer family of the Big Sandy Valley and engaged in educational work practically all his adult life. He was educated in the public schools of Lawrence County, at the National Normal University, Lebanon, Ohio, and received his Ph.D. degree in middle life. He taught in the public schools of Lawrence County for a time and was superintendent of city schools, among others, the public schools of Paris, Kentucky. He was an instructor of teachers' institutes. Children, among others, (fifth generation): Georgiana, b. August 22, 1894, d. August 23, 1894; Beatrice Sophia, b. December 14, 1895; Lillian Jerome, b. June 6, 1897; Louise Blanche, b. January 1, 1901; George Prichard, b. December 19, 1908.

98. SOPHIA EARLE PRICHARD; b. January 14, 1878; m., October 4, 1903, Charles W. G. Hannah of Greenup, b. May 29, 1881. Children (fifth generation): James Prichard, b. May 24, 1905; Charlotte Ruth, b. July 9, 1907; Mark Bradley, b. January 8, 1909.

101. WATT MONROE PRICHARD, lawyer and judge; b. at Bolts Fork, Kentucky, January 8, 1885; educated in the public schools of Boyd County; in the Greenup (Kentucky) High School; and at the Southern Normal School at Bowling Green, Kentucky; studied law; was admitted to the bar and began practicing at Catlettsburg in partnership with the late Judge S. G. Kinner; served as city attorney of Catlettsburg, 1914-1916; was chairman of the District Draft Board, Eastern District of Kentucky, 1917-1918, during World War I; was Commonwealths Attorney, Thirty-second Judicial District, 1925-1928; was elected on the democratic ticket, November 1933, Circuit Judge of the Thirty-second Judicial District and since has been renominated and reelected practically without opposition from either of the two major political parties, and is presently filling the office with distinction—all of which attest to his ability, integrity and fairness as a judge.

Judge Prichard is a Democrat in politics, a member of the Methodist Church and is affiliated with the Kiwanis and the Masonic fraternity (Shriner, York Rite). On July 8, 1925, he was m. to Miss Bess Iris Kitchen, b. September 6, 1890, a daughter of James and Florence (Pope) Kitchen, of Ashland; a granddaughter of Charles and Loretta (Mobley) Kitchen of Ashland, a great-granddaughter of Major Andrew I. and Winnie Kitchen and a great-great-granddaughter of James Kitchen, Revolutionary War soldier, and his wife, Jane

(Patterson) Kitchen of Greenbrier County, Virginia (Now West Virginia), who settled in then Lawrence County, Kentucky, near Willard in the early 1820's.

Children (fifth generation): James Jerome Prichard; b. November 12, 1926; m., November 27, 1947, Sharon Thomas, b. September 2, 1926; Nancy Florence Prichard; b. October 9, 1929; m., August 19, 1953, Lewis Edward Davis, b. September 16, 1924.

104. LEWIS PRESTON VAUGHAN; b. in Wayne County, Virginia, March 10, 1850; m. at Brownsville, Nebraska, June 21, 1883, Lillie Wayne. Children (fifth generation): Grover, b. in Hodgeman County, Kansas, June 22, 1884; Lloyd Thomas, b. in Hodgeman County, June 6, 1886; George Lewis, b. in Hodgeman County, October 31, 1888, m., September 23, 1909, Pearl Frances Wagoner of Richardson County, Nebraska; Clarence Leslie, b. in Hodgeman Co., Kansas, November 30, 1890; Edna May, b. in Hodgeman County, May 22, 1893; Jesse Delbert, b. in Payne County, Oklahoma, April 28, 1900.

106. ANDREW JACKSON VAUGHAN; b. in Wayne County, Virginia, October 1, 1854; m. in Richardson County, Nebraska, July 3, 1879, Clara Louise Bennett. Children (fifth generation): Florence Mabelle, b. August 18, 1880; m. at Liberal, Kansas, October 2, 1909, Dr. Frank Vest Coson; George Franklin, b. February 2, 1882; Rolla B., b. July 5, 1884; m. at Phoenix, Arizona, January 27, 1909, Teresa Leasenfelt.

108. SARAH ANN VAUGHAN; b. in Lawrence County ,Ohio, January 28, 1859; m. in Richardson County, Nebraska, May 21, 1878, George Thomas Jones. Children (fifth generation): James Herbert, b. May 9, 1879; m. in Pawnee County, Nebraska, May 21, 1901, Birdie May King. Children (sixth generation): Eva Merlo, b. March 14, 1902 and Frances Mildred, b. June 2, 1906; Laura Delphia, b. January 14, 1881; m. in Pawnee County, Nebraska, March 19, 1901, George Francis King; Lewis LeRoy; b. October 10, 1888.

112. COLUMBUS B. PRICHARD; b. October 4, 1856; m., March 14, 1878, Alice Newman, of Wayne County, West Virginia; removed to Neosho County, Kansas, when he d., November 27, 1879. Children (fifth generation): Clyde C.; b. December 23, 1878, and d. at Portsmouth, Ohio, December 14, 1908; m., October 30, 1904, Annie L. Staley of Catlettsburg. Children (sixth generation): Lois Alice, b. at Portsmouth, February 19, 1906.

115. VIRGINIA A. PRICHARD; b. in Boyd County, July 1, 1864, and d. in Wayne County, West Virginia, February 25, 1894; m., October 23, 1891, Hamilton M. Bloss of Huntington. Children (fifth generation): Virginia Alice Bloss; b. day of mother's death, February 25, 1894, in Wayne County.

116. ROBERT L. PRICHARD; b. in Boyd County, August 4, 1866; m. at Ironton, Ohio, April 4, 1890, Belle Lona.

118. THOMAS JEFFERSON PRICHARD, physician; b. December 25, 1858, and d. October 6, 1904; studied medicine under his uncle, Dr. Lewis Prichard at Grayson, Kentucky, and afterwards completed a course and was graduated in medicine; located at Huntington for practice and became an eminent physician and surgeon; m., November 5, 1889, Marianne Fretwell of Paris, Kentucky. Children (fifth generation): Edward Fretwell, b. May 20, 1891; Thomas Taylor, b. May 15, 1893.

119. EMILY LUCY PRICHARD; b. February 23, 1881, m. Watson L. Andrews; resided in Ashland. Children (fifth generation): Ernest Bickmore, b. November 8, 1883; Watson L. Jr., b. October 7, 1887; Jack, b. January 14, 1897.

120. JAMES LEWIS PRICHARD; b. May 16, 1863, and d. November 25, 1907; resided in Huntington where he was a successful businessman; m., January 21, 1895, Fannie Marr, daughter of Thomas Marr of Catlettsburg. Children (fifth generation): Pauline, b. October 1, 1896; Thomas Jefferson, b. February 26, 1898; Fannie Belle, b. May 5, 1901; Matilda Jane, b. March 2, 1903.

122. JENKINS ANN PRICHARD; b. February 15, 1867; m., November 4, 1891, George Washington Calvin who was b. June 2, 1866. Children (fifth generation): Vincent, b. March 14, 1896; Emily Elizabeth, b. February 15, 1904.[1]

---

[1] "Descendants of William Prichard", by A. M. Prichard, Charleston, West Virginia.

RATLIFF FAMILY OF PIKE COUNTY

1. JAMES RATCLIFF or RATLIFF was the ancestor of the Ratliffs of the Big Sandy Valley. He was a Virginian and migrated from Henry County, that State, and settled in what is now Pike County, Kentucky, in 1787. He was a man of strong convictions and was always on the side of virtue and morality. The family has spread over the entire Big Sandy region and embraces a host of people, many occupying prominent places in the affairs of life. Firmness and decision of character, with great individuality, are family characteristics.[1]

James Ratliff m. Marybee, ——— b. in Virginia in 1774.

Children, among others:

*2. Caroline M. Ratliff.

*3. "General" (William) Ratliff.

2. CAROLINE M. RATLIFF was b. in Floyd County, now Pike Co., 1816; m. in Pike County, April 20, 1840, John N. Richardson, merchant, b. in Pennsylvania, 1812. They moved to Catlettsburg, Kentucky.

Children living at home and approximate dates of birth as shown by the U. S. Census of Pike County for 1850 and Boyd County for 1860:

4. Marybee Richardson; b. 1841.

5. Jane Richardson; b. 1843.

6. James Richardson; b. 1845.

7. William Richardson; b. 1846.

8. Katherine Richardson; b. 1847.

9. John C. Richardson; b. 1848.

10. Robert Richardson; b. 1853.

11. George Richardson; b. 1855.

3. "GENERAL" (WILLIAM) RATLIFF was b. near present Shelby Junction, then Mason, now Pike County, Kentucky, in the early 1790s, and d. at Shelby Gap, Pike County. He was a man of great mental vigor and strong will. For twenty years he was sheriff of Pike County and held other positions of honor and trust.[2] He had service in the War of 1812 and also in the Confederate Army in the Civil War. He m. in Floyd County, June 27, 1813, Elizabeth Ford, b. in Tennessee, 1793. Both were members of the Christian Church. All his long life "General" Ratliff was a strong supporter of the principles and candidates of the Democratic Party.

Children, among others:

12. Mrs. Cobb Cecil, Sr. (See Cecil Family.)

13. Ann Ratliff; m. John Dills, Jr. (See Dills Family.)

*14. William Harrison Ratliff.

Chidren living at home and approximate dates of birth as shown by the U. S. Census of Pike County, for 1850:

15. Katherine Ratliff; b. 1831.

16. Thomas J. Ratliff; b. 1832.
17. James S. Ratliff; b. 1834.
18. Joseph E. Ratliff; b. 1835.

14. WILLIAM HARRISON RATLIFF was b. in what is now Pike County, 1814, and d. in Sullivan County, Tennessee, while on a visit to his son W. O. B. Ratliff, then serving in the Confederate Army in General Morgan's command. He m. in Floyd County, February 27, 1840, Margaret Hatcher, b. 1818, and d. 1900 at the advanced age of 82 years.

Children:
*19. William O. B. Ratliff.

20. James G. Ratliff, lawyer, b. in Pike County, 1855, and d. at Tacoma, Washington, 1918.

21. Nancy Ratliff: b. in Pike County; m. in Pike County, March 20, 1856, Tyre Ratliff, a member of another family, b. in Tazwell County, Va., son of Richard Ratliff. They removed to Carter County Kentucky.

22. Virginia Ratliff; m. T. L. Sowards.
23. Ann Ratliff; m. John N. Ferguson.
24. Mary Ratliff; m. W. M. Connolly of Pikeville.

19. JUDGE WILLIAM ORLANDO BUTLER RATLIFF, lawyer, timber dealer, and sometime public official, was b. on a farm about two miles below Pikeville, July 24, 1844, and d. at Pikeville, March 14, 1908. He attended the private school at Coal Run conducted by White Reynolds. In September 1861 he enlisted in Company "C", Tenth Kentucky Infantry, Confederate States Army, commanded by General Humphrey Marshall and later by General John S. Williams. He participated in a number of General John Morgan's raids; was wounded in the engagement at Mount Sterling and was captured at Georgetown and taken to Camp Morton, Indiana, where he was held as prisoner of war until March 25, 1865.

Returning to his home in Pike County, he studied law in the office of Judge Rowland T. Burns at Pikeville, and was admitted to the bar in 1870. Like his father and grandfather, he was a man of influence and prominence in his community. He was appointed sheriff of Pike County in 1886 to fill out an unexpired term of two years. In 1902 he was elected as Judge of the Pike County Court and served as such until the expiration of the term in 1906.

In addition to handling a large and important general legal practice in the courts, Judge Ratliff engaged in the lumber business, operating in partnership with John G. Cecil and Captain O. C. Bowes of Pikeville, floating timber down the Big Sandy and Ohio Rivers to Cincinnati.

In 1875 Judge Ratliff was m. to Mary Elizabeth Coates, b. at

Prestonsburg, August 5, 1855, and d. at Pikeville, daughter of Aaron T. Coates of Athens, Ohio.

In politics Judge Ratliff was a Democrat; was affiliated with the Masons; and was a very active member of the local Presbyterian Church, not only serving it as elder, but was largely instrumental in securing the location of the College at Pikeville which institution he generally supported until his death.

Children:
25. Virginia Lee Ratliff.
*20. Abert Sidney Ratliff.
27. Mayme Hopkins Ratliff; m. Arthur Hardwick, d. at Pikeville, 1913.

26. ALBERT SIDNEY RATLIFF; lawyer, sometime teacher and businessman, was b. at Pikeville, February 14, 1878; was educated in the public schools of Pikeville and was graduated from Pikeville College in 1898, after which he engaged in teaching for a time. Choosing the legal profession as a career, he studied law in the offices of his father, Judge Ratliff, at Pikeville, and was admitted to the bar in 1900. For the next succeeding fifteen years, he was engaged in a valuable law practice at Pikeville, but in 1915 he became interested in coal mining and has since devoted himself to furthering the interests of the Keel Coal Company of which he acted as secretary.

In religion, Mr. Ratliff is a Presbyterian. He is a Master and Chapter Mason; and is a staunch Democrat, the value of his services to his party having been recognized by his appointment as supervisor of the U. S. Census for the Tenth Kentucky District, 1920.

On September the 9th, 1907, Mr. Rtliff was m. to Katherine Matney, daughter of James Matney of Pikeville.

Children:
28. Marion D. Ratliff.
29. Katherine Ratliff.
30. Imogene Ratliff.

JUDGE ALEX L. RATLIFF; lawyer, judge, was b. at Ash Camp, Pike County, Kentucky, December 20, 1884, and d. at Frankfort, Kentucky, a son of Marion and Polly (Francisco) Ratliff; educated in Pikeville High School and Pikeville College; LL.B., University of Louisville, College of Law, 1910; unm.; began practice of law at Pikeville, 1910; City Attorney for Pikeville, 1918-25; Democratic nominee for Congress, 7th District, 1924; elected Judge of the Court of Appeals of Kentucky, 1932, for an eight year term.

Judge Ratliff was a Democrat in politics, a Presbyterian in religion and was affiliated with the Masons.

---

[1] William Ely, "The Big Sandy Valley", pages 97, 98.
[2] Ibid.

REDWINE FAMILY

1. ALBERT T. REDWINE was the progenitor of the Redwine family of Eastern Kentucky. He was b. in Virginia in 1825 and d. in Elliott County, Kentucky, in 1920. He was a farmer and merchant. The records indicate that in the trek westward, he tarried and lived for a time in Harlan County, Kentucky. About 1851 he m. in Virginia, Mary Pace, who was b. in Virginia in 1830 and d. in Elliott County in 1907.

Issue :

2. WILLIAM B. REDWINE, b. 1852; d. 1940; m. Addie Lytton who d. 1930. They were the parents of six children, one of whom, James, resided in Ashland, Kentucky.

*3. Matthew Marion Redwine.

*4. David B. Redwine.

*5. John S. Redwine.

6. Amanda Redwine, b. 1858, and d. 1925; m. Nelson Pennington.

Six children.

*7. Albert T. Redwine, Jr.

*8. Amos P. Redwine.

9. Mary Redwine; b. 1865, d. 1918.

10. Lucy M. Redwine; b. 1868; d. 1935.

3. MATTHEW MARION REDWINE, lawyer, judge and public official, was b. in Harlan County, Kentucky, February 13, 1853, and d. at Sandy Hook, Elliott County, Kentucky, December 4, 1946; interment Redwine cemetery at Sandy Hook; educated in the public schools and a private school conducted by Prof. Friend, a resident of Prestonsburg, Kentucky; studied law under Col. Z. T. Young at Morehead, Kentucky, and was admitted to the bar May 22, 1877; engaged in teaching in the rural public schools for five years. Entering politics, he was elected and served as County Attorney of Elliott County, 1881-1885; Commonweaths Attorney, 13th Judicial District, 1886-1892, and after the state was redistricted Commonwealth's Attorney, 20th Judicial District, 1892-1893; Circuit Judge, 1906; later judge of the 37th Judicial District; State Representative from the Carter-Elliott district, 1905-6, at which session he introduced and was instrumental in passage of the Redwine-McCormick Local Option Bill under which 92 counties adopted local option.

After the expiration of his term as circuit judge, Judge Redwine resumed the practice of law at Sandy Hook. Subsequently he was elected and served as county attorney of Elliott County.

Judge Redwine was a Democrat in politics; was affiliated with the Masonic fraternity and was a member of the Methodist Church. On August 7, 1877, he was united in marriage with Isabelle (Belle) Green, b. July 7, 1860, and d. 1952, daughter of W. W. Green of Elliott County.[1]

Issue:

11. Leonidas Young Redwine, lawyer and judge; b. at Sandy Hook, Kentucky, 1878, and d. in Lee County, Florida, 1950; practiced law at Sandy Hook and Jackson, Breathitt County, Kentucky; was elected and served as Circuit Judge of the 37th Judicial District of Kentucky. Locating at Ft. Myers, Florida, he was subsequently elected and served as County Judge of Lee County, that State; m. Leonabelle Carter. No children.

12. Virgil Homer Redwine, lawyer, of Sandy Hook; b. at Sandy Hook, 1883; has served as County Attorney of Elliott County for many years and is presently holding that position; m. Effie M. Sparks, b. 1889. They are the parents of Ethel Isabel Redwine, b. 1919 and d., 1953, m. James D. Ishmael, b. 1920. They are the parents of James D. Ishmael, Jr., b. 1947.

Virgil Homer Redwine, Jr., lawyer; b. at Sandy Hook, 1909; m. Bessie Turner, b. 1912. Residence 1710 Windsor Place, Louisville, Kentucky. Children: Patricia L., b. 1936, and Isabel A., b. 1941.

Fred B. Redwine, lawyer; b. 1912; m. True Culbertson, b. 1909. No children.

James L. Redwine, farmer; b. 1917; m. Joella Perryam, b. 1918. Children: Joseph, b. 1952 and Fred T., b. 1948 and d. 1955.

13. Stella A. Redwine; b. at Sandy Hook, 1886; m. Guy M. Strayhorn, who served as Circuit Court Clerk of Elliott for a time; subsequently went to and lived at Ft. Myers, Florida. Children: Norwood, an attorney, and Orville, a rancher.

14. Edgar O. Redwine; b. at Sandy Hook, 1888 and d. 1915; m. Clara Thornberry. Children: Opal, b. 1910, and Delma, b. 1912.

15. Talmage B. Redwine, farmer and merchant; b. at Sandy Hook, 1892 and d. 1951; m. Faye Green, b. 1895. Children: John, a farmer; Carl, a merchant; Guy, a mechanic; and Hazel (deceased) a teacher.

16. John Tennyson Redwine, lawyer; b. at Sandy Hook, 1895; m. Mollie Davis, b. 1898. Children: Eloise, a teacher, and Edgar O., a chemical engineer.[2]

4. DAVID BOWLING REDWINE, lawyer and judge; b. in Elliott County, Kentucky, December 6, 1855, and d. at Jackson, Breathitt County, Kentucky, February 25, 1913; member of the General Assembly, 1885-1886; elected County Attorney for Breathitt County, 1890, and served two years when he resigned; elected Circuit Judge of his judicial district in 1891 and served the six-year term; re-elected in 1897 and served until 1903; again elected in 1909 and was serving in that capacity at date of death, February 25, 1913; m., August 19, 1904, Nelle Hurst of Wolfe County, Kentucky, who was b. March 11, 1886, and d. March 20, 1954.

Issue:

Elsie Hurst Redwine; b. at Jackson, Kentucky, February 23, 1908; m. December 3, 1929, William Guy Bush, owner and operator of the Bush Insurance Agency, Lexington, Kentucky, who was b. at Jackson, Tennessee, September 25, 1904.

Isabelle Duff Redwine; b. at Jackson, Kentucky, April 2, 1911; m. October 16, 1954, Robert Graves Goodwin, farmer of Fayette County and U. S. Tobacco Inspector, who was b. in Fayette County, Kentucky, October 1, 1912.[5]

5. JOHN SMITH REDWINE, physician; b. March 23, 1865; practiced his profession in Elliott, Breathitt and Fayette Counties, Kentucky; superintendent of the Insane Asylum, Lexington, Kentucky, for eight years; physician of the L. & N. Railway for several years; and was medical examiner for Draft Board in World War I; m. Deborah Adeline Combs.

Issue:

Meredith Montague Redwine, electrical engineer; m. Hattie Belle Ewen.

Bertha Redwine, music teacher; m. Hiram June Jett.

May Redwine, music teacher at one time and later owner and operator of Children and Ladies' Ready-to-Wear shop at Jackson; unm.

Jean Redwine, owner and operator of Children and Ladies' Ready-to-Wear shop for a time and later owner and operator of jewelry store at Jackson; unm.

John Smith Redwine, Jr., mechanical and electrical engineer, b. March 1910, was an employee of the Clarage Fan Company in Cleveland, Ohio, and later in New York City and is presently an employee of the Alcola Aluminum Company, at Alcola, Tennessee; m. Elizabeth Pickens.

Mattie Lee Redwine; b. June 16, 1913; was an accountant, U. S. Navy Department, Washington, D. C., for several years; owned and operated jewelry store at Jackson for a time; and is presently in charge of the department of music in the Breathitt County public schools; unm.[4]

7. ALBERT T. REDWINE, JR., lawyer, and sometime public official; b. October 12, 1860, and d. October 30, 1925; practiced law at Sandy Hook and served as County Attorney of Elliott County three terms; m. Estella Waters, b. 1871, and d. 1951. Children: Ruth, deceased; Lucille, deceased; Samuel Lowell, merchant; m. Effie Johnson. They were the parents of five children, of whom Samuel, Jr., an architect, was one; Lillian Redwine; and Marcus Carlisle Redwine, lawyer; b. at Sandy Hook, December 10, 1893; educated in the public schools of Sandy Hook and was graduated from the Eastern Kentucky State Normal School at Richmond, 1914; was principal of the

Bridgeport High School for two years; enlisted in the U. S. Army, April, 1918; and was honorably discharged November, 1918, and then entered the University of Kentucky from which he was graduated with degree of LL.B. in 1919; was admitted to the bar and located at Winchester, Kentucky; taught political science and economics at Kentucky Wesleyan College, 1919-20.

In 1920, Mr. Redwine began his career as a lawyer. He formed a partnership with his cousin, Judge Leonidas Y. Redwine, with whom he was associated from May, 1921, to May, 1923, when the partnership was dissolved. He continued the practice of law at Winchester.

He is a Democrat and served as City Attorney of Winchester; is a Mason, a member of the Kiwanis Club of Winchester and the Clarke County and Kentucky Bar Association. He m. Mary ———. They are the parents of Marcus C., Jr., an attorney at Winchester, and Betty.[5]

8. AMOS P. REDWINE, farmer; b. 1872; m. Kansas Stegall; reside at West Point, Mississippi. Children: Jack and Helen.

---

[1] Who's Who in Kentucky, 1936. ·

[2] The Descendants of Albert T. Redwine and his Wife, Mary (Pace) Redwine (Family Tree) prepared and furnished by Virgil Homer Redwine, Louisville, Kentucky, 1955.

[3] The Descendants of Judge David Bowling Redwine and his Wife, Nellie (Hurst) Redwine (Manuscript) prepared and furnished by Elsie (Redwine) Bush (Mrs. William Guy Bush), 1461 Creek Pike, Lexington, Kentucky, 1955.

[4] The Descendants of Dr. John Smith Redwine and his Wife, Deborah Adeline (Combs) Redwine, (Manuscript) prepared and furnished by Miss Mattie Lee Redwine, Jackson, Kentucky, 1955.

[5] Who's Who in Kentucky, 1936.

REEVES FAMILY OF CARTER COUNTY

Although these names are represented by separate and distinct families in many sections of Great Britain, the United States, and other parts of the world, they have undoubtedly a common derivation. The name originated in the ancient word "reve", meaning a bailiff, provost or steward.

In the feudal days of Britain almost every manor of consequence had its "reve" whose authority was to levy the lord's rent, to set to work his servants, to superintend his dominions to his best profit and to govern his tenants in peace as well as to lead them forth to war when necessity required.

After the Normans invaded England (1066) the name "reve" was changed to "bailiff". In later times the word "sheriff" (shire-reve) came into use designating the principal Governor over the English shire or county.

Robert Reve of Blandford, County Dorset, was the earliest known ancestor of the English family of Reve, Rives, or Ryves. He was b. about 1490. At his death in 1551, he was buried in the Church of Saints Peter and Paul in Blandford Forum where the coat of arms here reproduced was found in the north window.

William Rives who settled in Virginia was the founder of Rives, Ryves family in the Southern States of America. He was a son of Timothy Rives of Oxfordshire, England, and came to Virginia about 1653 as records of him are found in Surry County about that time. The family has spread over almost every section of the United States and are either descendants of William, the immigrant, or of related families.

One William C. Rives, b. 1793, d. 1868, represented Virginia in the U. S. Congress as a Democrat from 1823 to 1829. While Minister to France from 1829 to 1832 he negotiated the Indemnity Treaty of 1831. He was a U. S. Senator from 1833 to 1834, and from 1836 to 1845; Minister to France from 1849 to 1853, and a Confederate Congressman from 1861 to 1864. He wrote an elaborate life of President James Madison.

1. BARRTLETT REEVES was the Kentucky ancestor of a branch of the Reeves family that settled in Northeastern Kentucky in pioneer days. It is believed that he was a descendant of or related to William Reeves the first of the family to emigrate to Virginia. He or his father migrated from Ashe County, North Carolina, and settled in then Mason County, now Greenup County, Kentucky, apparently in the Tygart Valley area. He m. Mahala (Matilda) Warnock, daughter of Samuel and Rachael Warnock, and granddaughter of William James and Eizabeth (Carlisle) Warnock, the first of the family to settle in Kentucky. (See Warnock Family.)

Bartlett Reeves, farmer, purchased all the land (about 407 acres) on what was afterwards called Reeves Branch, a tributary of Lost Creek, near Willard, Carter County, the consideration being one horse. Here he established his home, lived and died.

Children:
2. Jasper Reeves; m. Mahala Kozee. No children.
*3. James Franklin Reeves.
4. Holton Reeves; unm.
*5. Samuel L. C. Reeves.
6. Elizabeth Reeves; m. Casanter Blankenship.
7. Miriam Reeves; m. William S. Rice.
8. Sarah Reeves; m. Marion Everman. (See Everman Family.)
9. Matilda Reeves; unm.

3. JAMES FRANKLIN REEVES, farmer, b. April 22, 1828, d. February 6, 1921; m. Mahala Haney, b. April 28, 1834, d. March 31, 1895. He acquired one-half of his father's farm on Reeves branch where he lived, reared his family and died.

Children:
10. Mary Jane Reeves; b. February 1, 1853, and d. February 19, 1937; m. George W. Webb.
11. Samuel L. Reeves; b. January 4, 1857, and d. October 28, 1866.
12. James Holton Reeves; b. May 13, 1859; d. about 1949; m. Eliza Ratcliff.
13. Sarah Elizabeth Reeves; b. October 27, 1861; d. October 17, 1923; m. John H. Thomas, a minister of the Christian Church.
14. Eliza Ellen Reeves; b. July 24, 1864; d. October 9, 1896; m. Martin V. Webb.
15. John B. Reeves; b. February 15, 1867; m. Mary Mobley, daughter of William T. and Amanda S. (Elliott) Mobley. (See Mobley Family.)
16. Rachel R. Reeves; b. March 4, 1870; m. Thomas T. Mobley. (See Mobley Family.)
17. Nancy Reeves; b August 18, 1873; m. Daniel J. Kiger.
*18. Joseph Reeves.
19. Amanda Reeves; b. April 3, 1878; m. ———— Sammons.[1]

18. JOSEPH REEVES, one-time teacher, postmaster, merchant and Federal employee, was b. on his father's farm on Reeves branch, December 14, 1875; worked on the farm in his youth; was educated in the public schools of Carter County and at Willard (Kentucky) Normal School where he was prepared for teaching; and was graduated from the Business Department of Valparaiso University, Valperiso, Indiana; taught in the rural public schools of Carter and Lawrence Counties during the period from 1893 to 1907 and taught for a term of three months in the Metropolitan Business College at Aurora, Illinois, immediately after graduation from Valparaiso Uni-

versity; served as postmaster at Olioville and at Ratcliff, Kentucky, for periods aggregating five and one half years; was a merchant at Ratcliff for some time and was bookkeeper for the McDavid-Smith Wholesale Grocery Company at Hitchens, Kentucky, for a short time.

In December, 1913, Mr. Reeves was appointed and accepted a position in the Treasury Department, Washington, D. C., was transferred to the Office Auditor for the War Department; was assigned to duty in the Audit Division and was serving as an auditor in 1921, when the General Accounting Office was established by consolidation of the Auditor for the War and other Government Agencies. Subsequently he served as auditor, assistant chief and in other high and responsible positions in the General Accounting Office until his retirement from the service, October 1, 1942.

Mr. Reeves m. Miss Cora Jones, a daughter of Isaac M. Jones, who d. in 1916, and his wife, Josephine (Duvall) Jones, b. November 28, 1845, and d. 1917. Both the Joneses and Duvalls were natives of North Carolina.

Mr. and Mrs. Reeves have been consistent members of the Christian Church in the various communities in which they have lived for over 50 years. Mr. Reeves united with the Sand Hill (Kentucky) Christian Church when about 25 years of age. About this time he began a systematic and intensive study of the Bible, supplemented by commentaries thereon, with the result that he became one of the best informed men in the local brotherhood on religious matters. For over 50 years he has given of his time, talents and means in support of the Church and its auxiliaries; and at one time or another filled, creditably and well, practically every position or place in the Church and Sunday School of which he was a member.

5. SAMUEL L. C. REEVES, farmer; asquired one-half of his father's farm on Reeves branch where he lived and d.; m. Susan Burchett, b., 1849 or 1850, daughter of Burrell and Sarah (Easterling) Burchett.

Children:

20. Burrell Reeves; m. Julia Fauson.
21. Mary Reeves; m. a Viers.
22. Sarah Reeves.
23. Ann Reeves; m. August Fauson.
*24. James Franklin Reeves.
25. Wesley Reeves; m. Miss Houck.
26. Henry Reeves; unm.
27. Martha Reeves; m. W. W. Keller.
28. Lucy Reeves; m. Charles Buck.
29. Benjamin Reeves.
30. Robert Roy Reeves; m. Miss Marcum.

24. JAMES FRANKLIN (FRANK) REEVES, farmer and teacher; m.

Corrilda Holbrook. Children: Sherman, who m. Ethel Morris (See Morris Family); Goldie, who m. Edward Polhamus; Ruby, who m. Harve Burton; and Edith.

Other Reeves families lived in Mason County in early days as is evidenced by the marriage records of that county as follows:

Reeves, Eli and Sarah Ann Redman, 1790.
Reeves, Benjamin and Nancy Reeves, 1790.
Reeves, Spenser and Susannah Reeves, 1791.
Reeves, Samuel and Elizabeth Melton, April 7, 1800.
Reeves, Nancy and Joseph Chilton, August 26, 1799.
Reaves, Elizabeth and Samuel Jones, 1790?
Reeves, Sarah and Abraham Mahan, April 11, 1795.

---

[1] Descendants of Bartley Reeves and his wife, Matilda (Warnock) Reeves, (Manuscript) prepared by Joseph Reeves, 2219 High Street, Ashland, Kentucky, 1955.

RICE FAMILY OF BOYD CO., KY.

1. JAMES M. RICE, lawyer, judge and sometime legislator, was b. near Guyandotte, Virginia, now West Virginia, in 1802, and d. at Catlettsburg, Boyd County, Kentucky, October 24, 1870. His father migrated from Eastern Virginia in 1799 and settled near Guyandotte, Virginia, where he m. in 1800. His grandfather emigrated to America before the Revolutionary War and fought in that war for American independence. Judge Rice's father removed with his family to what was known as the Toler farm adjoining Coalton, then Greenup County, now Boyd County.

In his youth Judge Rice attended the public schools in the settlement when he could be spared from work on the farm. However, every book procurable by his scanty means was diligently studied and mastered by him. Before he was twenty years of age he left his father's home and farm and secured work at the salt-wells on the Little Sandy River near the present-day Grayson, Carter County, Kentucky, and continued his studies by reading at night by the light of the salt furnace. By the time he had reached man's age, he had so improved his time in study that he was known and recognized as one of the best scholars of his time in the surrounding country. At this period of his life the distinguished John M. McConnell, lawyer and then state senator was attracted to him as a young man of great intellectual endowments and invited him to study law under his supervision in his office. Accepting the invitation he entered upon the study of law in Senator McConnell's office at Greenup, Kentucky, and was admitted to the Bar about 1823.[1]   Soon after his admission to the Bar, Judge Rice settled at Pikeville, Pike County, for the practice of his profession and practiced there for six years when he removed with his family to Louisa, Lawrence County, continuing the practice of law there. In 1860 he removed with his family to Catlettsburg, Boyd County, where he lived until his death.

In politics Judge Rice was a Democrat and was strongly Southern in his feelings, but at the same time declared secession of the Southern States to be heresy. He was a State senator, 1838-1842 and 1846-1850; and served as circuit judge of his circuit by appointment.

On September 23, 1823, in Lawrence County, Judge Rice m., first, Jane H. Burns, daughter of Rev. Jerry Burns, a Revolutionary War soldier, and his wife, Elizabeth Roland, after whose death, he m., secondly, in Lawrence County, March 19, 1840, Mary Matilda Brown, daughter of Richard Brown and sister of Judge George N. Brown. (See Brown Family of Boyd County.) There were no children by this second wife.

Children of James M. Rice and his wife, Jane H. (Burns) Rice:

*2. Jacob (Jake) Rice.

3. Amanda Rice, m. ——— Cutler; migrated to Florida.

4. Elizabeth Rice, m. September 11, 1845, Samuel Short of Law-

rence County. No issue, but they adopted a daughter who became the wife of F. F. Freese of Louisa.

5. —— Rice, a daughter; m. John Jones, son of Daniel Jones, prominent citizen of Prestonsburg, Floyd County.

*6. John McConnell Rice.

2. JACOB (JAKE) RICE, lawyer, a Mason and onetime Grand Master of the Grand Lodge of Kentucky; a Methodist who frequently preached as a lay member of the Methodist Episcopal Church; a State representative from the district composed of the counties of Lawrence and Boyd, 1884; was b. in 1826.

From childhood Mr. Rice was troubled with obesity which grew with his age, not only hindering locomotion but depressing his naturally bright intellect. Notwithstanding this drawback he was a good lawyer, a popular orator and one of the most genial of men. He d. from paralysis, commencing at Frankfort while he was attending a session of the General Assembly as State representative, and terminating in his death at his home near Louisa in 1884.[2]

On August 8, 1850, in Lawrence County, Jacob Rice m. Adelaide Crabtree, b. about 1835.

Children of Jacob Rice and his wife, Adelaide (Crabtree) Rice, living at home in 1860 and/or in 1870 as evidenced by the U. S. Census of Lawrence County for said years:

7. Jane H. Rice, b. about 1851.
8. John C. Rice, b. about 1853.
9. James M. Rice, b. about 1855.
10. Elizabeth C. Rice, b. about 1857.
11. Mary M. Rice, b. about 1859.
12. Eureka Rice, b. about 1862.
13. Jake Rice, Jr., b. about 1864.
14. Rodger B. G. Rice, b. about 1867.
15. Jay N. Rice, b. about 1869.

6. JOHN McCONNELL RICE, lawyer, judge and public official, was b. at Prestonsburg, Floyd County, Kentucky, February 19, 1831; received a limited schooling; was graduated from a Louisville(Kentucky) law school in 1852; was admitted to the bar in 1853 and commenced practice at Pikeville; served as Superintendent of public schools of Pike County, 1854; elected prosecuting attorney of Pike County, 1856; member of the State House of Representatives in 1858; removed to Louisa, Kentucky, 1860; again a member of the State House of Representatives in 1861; elected as a Democrat to the Forty-first and Forty-second Congresses (March 4, 1869-March 3, 1873); was not a candidate for renomination in 1872; resumed the practice of law at Louisa; appointed judge of the Lawrence County Criminal Court in 1883; was elected to the same office in 1884; re-elected in 1890 and served in that capacity until his death in Louisa, September 18, 1895; interment in Pine Hill Cemetery, Louisa, Kentucky.[3]

Judge Rice was a Democrat in politics. He was m. about 1853 to Miss Sarah F. Poage, b. about 1832, daughter of William Poage of Greenup County, Kentucky.

Children living in the household and approximate dates of birth as shown by the U. S. Census of Lawrence County for 1860 and 1870:

16. Eliza J. Rice, b. 1854.

17. Ida Rice, b. 1856.

18. Ada Rice, b. 1858.

19. Willie Rice, b. 1861.

20. John Rice, b. 1864.

One daughter m. James H. McConnell, grandson of the distinguished lawyer, John M. McConnell. (See biography of John M. McConnell in Lewis Family.) James H. McConnell resided in Catlettsburg, Kentucky, and was postmaster of that city. Another daughter m. James Q. Lackey of Louisa, Kentucky, and other daughter m. Benjamin Thomas, civil engineer. One son m. Miss Abbott; the other son was employed in the revenue service.[4]

---

[1] William Ely, "The Big Sandy Valley", pp. 55-66.

[2] Ibid.

[3] Biographical Director of the American Congress, 1774-1949, page 1734.

[4] William Ely, "The Big Sandy Valley," pp. 55-66.

RICE FAMIILY OF BATH, CARTER AND ELLIOTT COS.

1. CHARLES RICE, a Revolutionary War soldier, was the progenitor of a branch of the Rice family that settled in Bath County, Kentucky, members of whom removed to Carter and Elliott Counties. He was b. in Virginia, presumably in Powhatan County, in 1749, and m. Molly Tony or Toney in that State. He served in the Revolutionary War as private in the Virginia State Troops (Clark's Illinois Regiment [1]). After the close of the war he removed to Bath County, Kentucky, where he lived and d. at the age of 89 years. Issue:

*2. Campbell Rice.
3. Nelson Rice.
4. Holman Rice.
*5. William Rice.
*6. Fleming Rice.
7. Charles Rice.
8. Nancy Rice, m. William Boyd, probably in Madison County, Kentucky.[2]

2. CAMPBELL RICE, a minister of the Methodist Church, was b. in Powhatan County, Virginia. November 17. 1778, and d. October 12, 1846, and was buried at Willard, Carter County, Kentucky. He was sheriff of Carter County, 1844. He m., probably in Madison County, Kentucky, Elizabeth Bailey, who was b. in Orange County, North Carolina, January 20, 1781, and d. in present Elliott County, Kentucky, about 1874. She was a daughter of Captain John Bailey (See Bailey Family), and came to Lincoln County, Kentucky, with her family when seven years of age. Issue:

*9. Fleming B. Rice.
10. Alford G. Rice, m. Malinda Richards of Bath County, May 26, 1829; lived in Owen County, Kentucky. Issue: Mary, m. a Mr. Honaker; Eliza, m. Mr. Yarborough; and Marcus died young.
11. William Rice, local politician in Bath County, Clerk of the Bath County court; m. Martha Thompson. Issue: Mary Rice.
*12. Nelson T. Rice.
13. John Holman Rice; m. in Bath County, June 29, 1839, Margaret Ann Richards. Issue: Sarah, m. a Mr. Morris; Eliza, d. young; Amanda d. young; and Charles.
14. Charles Rice, lawyer; m. Nancy Hensley; d. young; no children.
*15. Sarah Rice.
*16. Nancy Rice.
*17. Mary Rice.

9. FLEMING B. RICE, farmer, b. in Bath County about 1804, m. in that county November 12, 1829, Eliza Shumate, b. in Virginia

about 1807. Children and approximate dates of birth living at home
in 1850 as shown by the U. S. Census of Carter County, Kentucky,
for that year:

18. Hiram A. Rice; b. 1831; was a lieutenant in Confederate
Army.

19. Jefferson Rice; b. 1835.

20. Campbell Rice; b. 1837.

21. Berryman S. Rice; b. 1840; was a prominent physician in
Catlettsburg, Kentucky; unm.

22. Caroline Rice; b. 1845; m. a Mr. Wilson.

23. Thomas S. Rice; b. 1848.

12. NELSON T. RICE, farmer and teacher, b. in Bath County, April
13, 1811; m. in Owingsville, that county, March 23, 1836, America
Frances Richards, b. in Bath County, November 11, 1819, and d. in
present Elliott County. She was a daughter of Elzaphan Richards.
(See Richards Family.) Children and approximate dates of birth
as shown by the U. S. Census of Carter County for the years 1860
and 1870:

*24. James Holman Rice; b. about 1837.

25. Alford Grayson Rice; b. about 1839; d. 1892; m. Phoebe Horton. (See Horton Family.)

26. Elzaphan Campbell Rice; b. about 1841; d. 1923; m. Emma
Black.

27. Zachary Taylor Rice; b. about 1847; d. 1934; m. Vicey Fraley.

28. Lovenia Margaret Rice; b. 1851, d. 1944; m. John T. Horton.
(See Horton Family.)

29. Walter Fleming Rice; b. about 1853; d. 1928; m. Mary Lewis.

24. JAMES HOLMAN RICE, farmer resided near Rosedale post office,
Carter County; m. Julia Green, daughter of Thomas and Jemima
(Brown) Green and granddaughter of Giles and Katie (Chandler)
Green, who was a daughter of Thomas Chandler, Revolutionary War
soldier. (See Green and Chandler Families.)

Issue:

30. Rosa Belle Rice; b. 1874; d. 1917; m. Ed. Bowling. They
were parents of five children.

31. Cornelius Taylor Rice; b. 1876; d. 1885.

32. Elizabeth Frances Rice; b. 1878; m. Oscar Marcus Fraley.
They are the parents of ten children.

33. Vena Amanda Rice; b. 1880; m. James K. Polk Horton; three
children. (See Horton Family.)

34. Thomas G. Rice; b. 1883; m. Sarah Maggard; eight children.

35. Geneva Florence Rice; b. 1885; d. 1948; m., first, Nelson Horton; secondly, Edward Elliott; thirdly, a Mr. Miller; and fourth, a
Mr. Dickow.

*36. Walter Alford Rice.

37. William Lovie Rice; b. 1891; m., 1st, Nellie Porter, and secondly, Thelma ———; two children by second marriage.

38. James Franklin Rice; b. 1895; m. Myrtle McDavid; four children.

36. WALTER ALFORD RICE; b. 1887; m. Nellie Rae Walls, daughter of Walter W. and Margaret (Flaugher) Walls. (See Flaugher Family.)

Issue:

(a) Victor Elmer Rice; b. October 4, 1912; m. Madeline Rosina Schmitt. Children: James Holman Rice, b. March 23, 1940, and David Walter Rice, b. January 14, 1943.

(b) Hazel Frances Irene Rice; b. August 27, 1914; m. Raymond Robinson. No children.

(c) Eleanor Rose Rice; m. Adrian J. Everett. No children.

15. SARAH (SALLY) RICE; b. in Kentucky, 1799; m. in Bath Co., Kentucky, December 12, 1822, Rev. John M. Yarbrough (sometimes spelled "Yarborough"), who was b. in Kentucky, 1797.

Issue:

Children living in the household and ages in 1850 as shown by the U. S. Census of Jeffersonville Township, Clarke County, Indiana, for that year:

*39. Nelson Yarbrough, 18, b. in Indiana.
*40. Fleming Yarbrough, 16, b. in Indiana.
*41. Spencer Yarbrough, 14, b. in Indiana.
*42. Holeman Yarbrough, 13, b. in Indiana.
*43. Sarah A. Yarbrough, 10, b. in Indiana.
*44. Adaline Yarbrough, 7, b. in Indiana.

Other children who had apparently married prior to 1850 were:

45. James Yarbrough.
46. Elizabeth Yarbrough; m. Pern Carr; resided in Jeffersonville, Indiana.
*47. John B. Yarbrough.
48. Milton Yarbrough; d. young.
49. Rachel Yarbrough, d. young.

39. NELSON K. YARBROUGH; m. Eliza Rice, daughter of Alfred G. Rice; resided at Harmony, Owen County, Kentucky.

40. FLEMING RICE YARBROUGH; m. America Wilson; resided near Owensboro, Daviess County, Kentucky.

41. SPENCER YARBROUGH; m. Elizabeth Southworth; resided at Harmony, Owen County, Ky.

42. HOLEMAN YARBROUGH; d. young.

43. SARAH (SALLIE) A. YARBROUGH; m. Dr. G. R. Lee; resided at Harmony, Owen County, Ky.

44. MARY ADELINE YARBROUGH; m. Dr. R. L. Sparks; resided at Stamping Ground, Kentucky.

47. JOHN B. YARBROUGH; b. in Kentucky, apparently in Bath County, January 6, 1824; d. in Clarke County, Indiana, January 10, 1895; m. Parthena Morris, b. in Indiana, August 3, 1827, and d. May 18, 1911, daughter of Richard and Nancy (Stenson) Morris of Clark County, Indiana.

Issue:
*50. Enos Yarbrough.

51. Merritt Yarbrough; b. 1856; d. 1937; m. Sarah E. Summit.

52. Franklin Yarbrough; b. June 7, 1857; d. February 17, 1872.

53. Alexander Yarbrough; b. about 1859; d. about 1933; m. Mollie Gaskins.

54. Jesse Yarbrough; b. April 14, 1863; d. about 1940; m. Harriet Marmaduke.

55. 55. Adelia Mary Yarbrough; b. about 1865; d. November 4, 1921; m. Robert Morgan Lee.

56. Aaron Yarbrough; b. about 1867; d. 1935; unm.

57. Nannie Yarbrough; b. September 13, 1872; d. February 9, 1941; m. John Alexander.

50. ENOS YARBROUGH; b. in Floyd County, Indiana, July 7, 1849; d. May 23, 1931: m. first, Frances Catherine Drury, and after her death, m., secondly, Mary Elizabeth Drury (half sister of first wife), b. in Martin County, Indiana, October 22, 1859, and d. April 23, 1952, aged 92 years, a daughter of Washington and Lydia (Walton) Drury. They were parents of 13 children.

Issue:
58. Charles Augustus Yarbrough; b. March 27, 1878; m. Louise Swartz, who d. May 16, 1916.

*59. John Washington Yarbrough.

60. Olie Elizabeth Yarbrough; b. April 15, 1882; d. June 27, 1954; m. Chester O. Smith, April 26, 1904.

61. Thomas Enos Yarbrough; b. October 16, 1883; m. Geneva Calloway.

62. William Russell Yarbrough; b. November 16, 1885; m. Carrie H. Stall.

63. Seth Yarbrough; b. August 16, 1887; m., first, Ada M. Reister, who d. March 14, 1920, and m., secondly, Rachel Wallace.

64. Maudie Ray Yarbrough; b. November 16, 1889; m. Leo Andrew Greenwell, who d. January 4, 1954.

65. Laura Ellen Yarbrough; b. December 14, 1891; m., first, Marion E. Alford, who d. August 11, 1944, and m., secondly, John Cleveland.

66. Glen Yarbrough; b. March 22, 1893; m. Edith Leonard.

67. Leo Joseph Yarbrough; b. December 25, 1895; m. Della Kitterman, now deceased.

68. Mary Agnes Yarbrough; b. July 10, 1896; d. July, 1896.

*69. Parthena Yarbrough.

70. Lydia Louvern Yarbrough; b. July 26, 1902; m. Robert Lee Foster.

59. JOHN WASHINGTON YARBROUGH; b. in Washington Township, Washington, Indiana, February 7, 1880, and d. April 1, 1937; m. Lue Purcell, May 5, 1904. He was a prominent Washington (Indiana) citizen: a worker in community affairs: served as city councilman and manager of the water works plant; was an employee and manager of the Bell Telephone Company. He served as a private in Co. "D", 159th Regiment, Indiana Volunteers, in the Spanish-American War.

Issue:

71. Charles John Yarbrough.

72. Helen Glen Yarbrough.

73. Robert Burke Yarbrough.

69. PARTHENA YARBROUGH; b. in Washington, Indiana, June 29, 1898; m. Otis T. Jones, b. in Loogootee, Indiana, June 12, 1893, a son of Richard W. and Ella (Greenwell) Jones of the Bramble community, Loogootee, Indiana. Mr. Jones had service in the U. S. Navy during World War I. Mrs. Jones is presently an employee of the U. S. Government in Washington, Residence: Apt. 104, 704 N. Wayne Street, Arlington, Virginia.

Issue:

74. Donald R. Jones; b. in Indianapolis, Indiana, June 24, 1920; had service in the U. S. Navy in World War II and is presently a commander, U. S. Navy; m. Evelyn Edith Beamer. Children: Donald R., Jr., and Evelyn Cecilia.

75. Carl Thomas Jones; b. in Indianapolis, Indiana, October 31, 1923; had service in U. S. Navy in World War II; m. Doris Lawson. Children: Sharon Ann and Carl Thomas, Jr.[3]

16. NANCY BAILEY RICE; b. in Bath County, Kentucky, April 17, 1822, and d. at Willard, Carter County; m. in Carter County, July 16, 1840, Rev. Walter Shearer, a minister of the Methodist Church, who was b. in Kentucky, presumably in Wayne County, September 13, 1813, and d. in Lawrence County, Kentucky, at an advanced age. They resided near Willard, Kentucky.

Issue:

76. Sarah J. Shearer; b. May 7, 1841; m. James Rucker.

77. Charles W. Shearer, a minister of the Methodist Church, b. June 5, 1843; m. Paulina Pennington, a daughter of James Pennington of Willard. They resided at Barbourville and other places in West Virginia where Rev. Shearer was pastor of the local Methodist Church.

*78. Nancy E. Shearer.

79. Ann Catherine (Kate) Shearer; b. December 25, 1848; m. James Polk Flaugher. (See Flaugher Family.)

80. Eliza C. Shearer; b. December 9, 1858; m. Joseph Bowling.

*81. Mary W. Shearer.

82. Alfred W. Shearer; b. October 20, 1865.

78. NANCY ELIZABETH SHEARER; b. near Willard, Kentucky, April 21, 1846; m. in Carter County, October 11, 1866, William R. Kitchen, a lineal (direct) descendant of James Kitchen, Revolutionary War soldier, and his wife, Jane (Patterson) Kitchen who migrated from Greenbrier County, Virginia, (now West Virginia) to Scott County, Virginia, and from there to Lawrence County, Kentucky, in the early 1820s.

WILLIAM R. KITCHEN was a good citizen and a leader in civic affairs. He was a general merchant in the Willard community for many years; was a consistent member and leading worker in the Christian Church. Deeply interested in education and good schools, he was influential in establishing and organizing the Willard Graded School, the first of such a school in Carter County.

Issue:

83. Robert Hayden Kitchen; m. Miss Mary Bellomy.

84. Charlotte (Lottie) Kitchen; m. John M. Saulsberry.

85. Gilby Kitchen; d. young.

86. Tracy S. Kitchen; m. Miss Belle Pennington, daughter of Dr. A. Pennington of Willard.

87. Coney Kitchen; m. Robert F. Lewis. (See Lewis Family.)

88. Ennis Kitchen; m., first, —— and secondly, Mrs. Belle Lemaster (nee Belle Chapman).

89. Fay Kitchen; m. Ad Hardy.

81. MARY W. SHEARER; b. August 7, 1856; m. in Carter County, June 13, 1871, John M. Kitchen (brother of W. R. Kitchen). Mrs. Kitchen was sister of Mrs. W. R. Kitchen. John M. Kitchen and family lived at Willard for many years, but rather late in life they removed to Argillite, Greenup County.

Issue:

90. Sopha Kitchen, teacher; taught in the public schools of Carter and Greenup Counties for many years; was elected on the Democratic ticket and served as Superintendent of public schools of Greenup County for a term of four years; unm.

91. Quinn Kitchen, farmer.

17. MARY RICE; m. Rev. Samuel Kelly.

Issue:

92. Rev. Gilby Kelly.

93. Florence Kelly; m., first, a Mr. Lockhart and, secondly, a Mr. Clary; descendants reside in Bourbon County, Kentucky.

94. Virgil Kelly.
95. Samuel Kelly.

5. WILLIAM RICE; m. Sarah Lynam in Bath County, Kentucky, January 1, 1827.
Issue:
96. David Rice.
97. Nelson Rice.
98. Hezekiah Rice.
99. Linda Rice.
Very little information has been secured concerning this family. However, it is known that the sons settled in Estill County, Kentucky, where probably their descendants live.

6. FLEMING RICE; b. in Powhatan County, Virginia, in 1780 or 1781; d. in Bath County, Kentucky, in 1807 or 1808, aged 27 years; m. Sarah Bailey, daughter of Capt. John Bailey (See Bailey Family). After Fleming Rice's death, his widow m., secondly, a Mr. Davis of Bath County. There is no known record of their descendants.

Issue:
100. Jefferson Rice; b. in Bath County, Kentucky, June 14, 1806, and d. in that county, March 5, 1898; m. in Bath County, first, April 6, 1829, Nancy Richards, b. November 3, 1813, and d. January 15, 1850, a daughter of Elzaphan and Elizabeth (Hazelrigg) Richards (See Richards Family). He m., secondly, in Bath County, March 18, 1856, Mrs. Amanda (Richards) Thompson, b. April 27, 1827, and d. December 5, 1912, a daughter of Elzaphan and Elizabeth (Hazelrigg) Richards. (See Richards Family.) There were no children by this second marriage. However Amanda Richards m. first, a Mr. Thompson; and they had a daughter, Mary, who m. James Hall Bean, whose descendants live in Winchester, Kentucky.

JEFFERSON RICE was one of the outstanding citizens of Bath County for many years prior to his death. He was a very large land owner; was respected by all; and his family, together with the families into which they m., was one of the most respectable and useful body of citizens in the State.
Issue:
*101. Eliza Rice.
102. Fleming Rice; b. December 23, 1831; settled in Missouri.
103. Elzaphan Rice; b. January 1, 1834; unm.
*104. James Harvey Rice.
105. Salem Rice; b. June 10, 1838; unm.
*106. Sarah E. Rice.
*107. William Holman Rice.
*108. Emma Frances Rice.
*109. Mary E. Rice.

*110. Miranda Taylor Rice.

111. Caroline Rice; b. September 1, 1849; d. in infancy.

All sons and daughters of Jefferson and Nancy (Richards) Rice, except Holman, lived in Bath, Montgomery and nearby counties in Kentucky.

101. ELIZA RICE; m. Jefferson Dawson.

Issue:

112. Mary Pillow Dawson (1846-1922); m. James Ficklin; no children.

*113. John Dawson.

*114. Emma Dawson; m. Hodge Arnold.

115. Joe Dawson (1857-1923); unm.

116. Jennie Dawson (1860-1932); m. Lewis Young; no children.

*117. Jefferson Dawson.

*118. Ella Dawson.

*119. Sallie Dawson.

120. George Dawson (1877-1921); unm.

113. JOHN DAWSON; m. Alice Young.

Issue:

121. Ashby Dawson; m. Carrie Conner. Issue: Marian Dawson; m. Dod Best. Issue: Caroline, b. about 1940, and Kathryn, b. about 1944.

122. Elbert Edwin Dawson; b. October 15, 1874; d. October 12, 1921; m. Myrtle Maxey, June 26, 1901.

Issue:

(a) Arnold Maxey Dawson; b. April 16, 1902; m. Thelma Coliver, February, 1937; no children.

(b) John Kenneth Dawson; b. July 17, 1904; m. Mary Skinner. Issue: Mary Berta Dawson, b. February 2, 1949.

(c) Ashby Alexander Dawson; b. November 11, 1905; m., first, Edna Smith, 1946. Issue: John Daniel Dawson, b. June 26, 1947, and Sandra Lee Dawson, b. April 14, 1949. He m., secondly, 1952, Dulia McDaniel. Issue: Rose Etta Dawson, b. December 21, 1953.

(d) Sarah Elberta Dawson; b. March 17, 1908; m. C. Frank Daily, June 13, 1931. Issue: Saramay Daily, b. September 30, 1933; Emily Bruce Daily, b. October 26, 1936; and Mary Elberta Daily, b. August 9, 1939.

(e) Lewis Caldwell Dawson; b. August 10, 1910; m. Mary Bruce Daily, September, 1939; no children; adopted boy and girl (John King and Sandra Lee).

123. Mary Dawson; m. Oscar Brother. Issue: John W. Brother; m. (whom not learned); Issue: John W. Brother, Jr., b. 1832.

124. Lyda Dawson; unm.

125. Jane Dawson; m. W. B. Kincaid. Issue: Burrell Kincaid, Jr., b. about 1920. Unm.

126. Stella Dawson; m., first, Rev. J. Tyler Davis. Issue: Alice

Young Davis; m. (whom not learned); two children; and Dawson Young Davis; m. (whom not learned); two children.

117. JEFFERSON DAWSON; m. Mary Warner. Issue: (a) Warner Dawson; b. 1902; m. (whom not learned); two daughters, one born about 1930 and other about 1932. (b) Sallie Dawson; b. 1901; unm.

114. EMMA DAWSON; m. Hodge Arnold, November 25, 1875. Issue: William Benjamin Arnold; b. February 20, 1877; resides in Owingsville, Kentucky, no descendants.

118. ELLA DAWSON; m. Walter Harper. Issue: Kelly Harper, b. 1898; m. Clara Frye. Issue: Kelly Harper, Jr., b. 1937.

119. SALLIE DAWSON; m. Robert Brother. Issue: (a) J. Dawson Brother; m. Elizabeth Prewitt in 1928. Issue: a son, Jeff, b. 1938.

(b) Ida Belle Brother; m. in Mt. Sterling, Kentucky, in 1923, Stanley E. French. Issue (a) Sara Kathryn French; b. 1929; m. Dr. Bobly Brown in 1951. Issue; Peter Brown, b. September 23, 1952, and Beverly Brown, b. August 17, 1954. Residence Burlingame, California. (b) Dawson French b. 1932; unm.

104. JAMES HARVEY RICE; m. Amanda Cook.

Issue:

127. Thomas Jefferson Rice.

128. Giles Fleming Rice.

129. Elzaphan (Elza) Rice; d. in infancy.

130. Mary Ensor Rice; m. Henry Worthington.

131. Nannie Margaret Rice: m. a Mr. Bullock.

132. Amanda Cook (Ada) Rice; m. William Walker.

133. John Young Rice.

133½. Alica Dee Rice; m. Dr. Stevenson.

134. Salem Jewel Rice; b. April 19, 1877; resides in Lexington, Kentucky.

135. Charles Homer Rice.

136. Ethel Agnes Rice; m. Walter Worthington.

137. Frank Holman Rice.

138. William Harvey Rice.

All the sons and daughters of James Harvey Rice and Amanda (Cook) Rice, except Salem Jewel Rice, are deceased.

106. SARAH E. RICE; m. James T. Crooks.

Issue:

139. Emma Crooks; b. March 17, 1862, and d. January 2, 1944; m. Price Calk.

140. James Crooks (1864-1909); unm.

141. Ida Crooks; b. September 1, 1866, and d. November 1946; m. a Mr. Heath.

142. Fannie Crooks; b. August 27, 1868, and d. January 15, 1952; m. O. M. Jones.

143. Alfred Crooks; b. November 13, 1870, and d. October 16, 1944.

144. Mary Crooks; b. February 2, 1872; m. a Mr. Paynter; resides at 216 9th Street, San Bernadino, California.

145. Samuel Crooks; b. September 21, 1874; resides in Owingsville, Kentucky.

146. Robert Crooks; b. April 18, 1876; resides in Owingsville, Kentucky.

107. WILLIAM HOLMAN RICE; m. Mary Belle Wright, b. May 9, 1861, and presently resides at 135 N. Maysville Street, Mt. Sterling, Kentucky.

Issue:

147. Benjamin Holman Rice; b. July 25, 1884; d. June 16, 1914; no children.

148. Nancy Catherine Rice; b. July 29, 1892; no children.

108. EMMA FRANCES RICE; m. in Bath County, Kentucky, September 10, 1860, William Atchinson Hodge, a son of Samuel Dunlap Hodge and his wife, Elizabeth (Atchinson) Hodge.

Issue:

149. Willie Hodge (daughter) b. June 23, 1865; d. January 16, 1954; m., December 1886, John Sinclair Wyatt, Jr., son of John Sinclair Wyatt and Elizabeth (O'Rear) Wyatt of Montgomery County, Kentucky.

Issue:

150. Jefferson Rice Wyatt; b. November 8, 1887; m., May 17, 1932, Vera Broughton de Jarnette, Richmond, Kentucky, who was b. April 13, 1903. Issue: Martha Rice Wyatt, b. September 10, 1936.

151. Emily Hodge Wyatt; b. September 14, 1890; m., February 7, 1910, Norman Horton, Mt. Sterling, Kentucky, who was b. July 16, 1888. Issue:

(a) James Horton; b. January 17, 1913; d. September 24, 1954; m., June 9, 1945, Eva Marie Garrison, Winchester, Kentucky. Issue: Pamela Wyatt Horton, b. June 14, 1945.

(b) John Courtney Horton; b. September 26, 1917; d. July 10, 1946; m., November 10, 1943, Cynthia Margaret Chandler, Mt. Sterling, Kentucky; she was b. July 2, 1920. Issue: John Courtney Horton, Jr., b. November 22, 1944.

152. Nettie Reid Wyatt; b. May 16, 1895; m., June 4, 1917, William Oates Caraway of Clayton, Barbour County, Albama, who was b. September 17, 1894. Issue: William Hodge Caraway; b. February 2, 1919; resides in San Francisco, California.

153. Luther Buford Wyatt; b. December 16, 1897; m. in Baltimore, Maryland, August 30, 1950, Loretta Cassily, who was b. August 19, 1911; no children.

154. Mary Willie Wyatt; b. August 10, 1907; m. February 27, 1927, James Kendrick Baldwin of Arlington, Kentucky, who was b. October 7, 1902. Issue: (a) James Granville Baldwin; b. May 16, 1930; m., June 8, 1953, Carol Bertine Wells, Great Falls, Montana, who was b. April 10, 1935. Issue: Hayden Lee Baldwin, b. May 15, 1954, and Wendy Kay Baldwin, b. January 13, 1955.

(b) William Hayden Baldwin; b. December 8, 1933; unm.[4]

[1] Gwathmey's "Virginians in the Revolutionary War" 1775-1783, p. 660.

[2] Descendants of Charles Rice and his Wife, Molly (Tony) Rice (Manuscript) prepared by Goldie Horton Johnson, Bruin, Kentucky, 1952.

[3] Descendants of Rev. John M. Yarbrough and his Wife, Sarah (Sallie) Rice Yarbrough (Manuscript), prepared by Parthena Yarbrough Jones (Mrs. Otie T. Jones) 704 N. Wayne Street, Arlington, Virginia, 1955.

[4] Descendants of Jefferson Rice and his Wife, Nancy Richards Rice (Manuscript), prepared by William Oates Caraway, Sugar Land, Texas, 1955.

RICE FAMILY OF JOHNSON COUNTY

Rice

The Rice family is of Welsh descent and the name is another form of the old Welsh name Rhys, anglicized Rees. From this name also comes the nace Price which is the combination of the Welsh "ap" meaning "son of" and Rhys— Thomas ap Rhys— "Thomas the son of Rhys" became too awkward so "ap Rhys" was shortened to Price. This does not mean, however, the Rice and Price families are necessarily connected by ties of blood, although there may have been relationship in that far-off time when surnames were first adopted. The meaning of the name is "to rush", figuratively, a dashing young man. Another variant of the name is Reese.

The family of Rice was seated in England at an early date, the records showing that there lived in that country:

Powell Rice or Rise, 1570.

Thomas Rice of Great Saughall, 1605.

Henry Rice, County Carmarthen, 1607.

Evans Rice of Harwarden, 1693.

Winn Rice.

Rice families resided in all the original thirteen colonies in early colonial days and were numerous, particularly in the New England and in the Middle colonies.

DEACON EDMUND RICE, one of the first of the family to immigrate to America, was b. in Buckinghamshire, England, about 1594. He m., firstly, Tamazine or Thomasine ———— and came with his wife and seven children and another child born during the voyage to America and settled at Sundbury, Massachusetts, in 1638. He was a son of Thomas Rice, b., probably in 1555, and grandson of William Rice of Boemar, Buckinghamshire, who was granted a coat of arms by Queen Mary of England in 1555 and who was a son of Sir Rice ap Griffith and Lady Katharine Howard, his wife. A John Rice and his wife, Rebecca, lived in Rappahannock county, Virginia, in 1687, as is evidenced by deeds executed by them as of that year. Their coat of arms is the same as that of the Rice family of County Kerry, Ireland, which possessed land in County Cork, Ireland, also in the time of Edward III, and was descended from Sir John Rice.

John Rice of Welsh descent, came from England to Rhode Island, in 1661. Robert Rice was in Boston in 1634.

The name Rice is now represented in almost every section of the

United States, and those who bear it are honored for their personal worth and for the rich heritage of a distinguished name.

The ancestor of this branch of the Rice family has not been definitely determined. However, according to family tradition one John Rice was the progenitor of this branch of the family. It is stated that he was born in England and emigrated from Dover, England, and settled near Roanoke, Virginia, about 1780; that he had service during the latter part of the Revolution, and subsequently was killed near Roanoke by Indians in a raid on white settlers.

1. JOHN RICE probably was twice m., firstly, probably to Patsy Fleming. The name of the second wife, if any, is not known. After John Rice's death or separation, Patsy (Fleming) Rice m., secondly, Samuel Cox who, about eight months later, went on a hunting expedition from which he never returned. Subsequently she m., thirdly, John Fitzpatrick.

Children of John Rice and Patsy (Fleming) Rice:
*2. Martin Rice.
*3. Fanny Rice.
*4. John Rice.

Children of John Rice and his second wife according to family tradition:
*5. Samuel Rice.

2. MARTIN RICE; m. ———— ————?

Children:

6. William Marsh Rice; m., firstly, Miss Bremond, of Houston, Texas; and, secondly, ———— ————? Martin Rice's descendants went to New York. A William Marsh Rice d. in New York City in 1900 under suspicious circumstances which led to the indictment of his valet and a New York lawyer, Albert T. Patrick. The valet turned State's evidence and Patrick was convicted of the murder of Mr. Rice and sentenced to be electrocuted. The sentence was commuted to life imprisonment and afterwards he was given a full pardon.

Mr. Rice's will was probated in New York and Texas. He left an estate of several millions of dollars which passed under his will to an educational corporation created under the laws of Texas, located in the city of Houston and known as the Wm. M. Rice Institute for the Advancement of Literature, Science and Art.

3. FANNY RICE; m., in Floyd county May 17, 1811, John Fitzpatrick (See Fitzpatrick Family).

Children:
7. Civilian Fitzpatrick.
8. Henry Fitzpatrick.
9. William Fitzpatrick.

4. JOHN RICE, farmer, violinist; was b. in Virginia, in 1786. There is a family tradition that he was captured by Indians when a young man and was taken by them to their camps in Tennessee to make music for them; then upon release he returned to his home which was said to have been in the vicinity of Roanoke, Virginia. Migrating to Kentucky with his family, accompanied by two brothers and a sister, he settled, in March, 1815, first, on Middle Creek and subsequently on the head of Jennie's Creek, now Johnson county.

Mr. Rice prospered as a farmer. The tax lists of Floyd county for the year 1837 show that he had property as follows: 350 acres of land on Jennie's Creek, 4 slaves and 400 head of cattle. He m. Nancy Davis (d. 1854), daughter of John Davis, of Cumberland Gap, whom, according to family tradition, he met when on his trips to Tennessee as a musician (fiddler).

Children:
10. Joseph Rice; d. in infancy.
*11. Martin R. Rice.
12. Malinda Rice; m. Payne Patrick.
*13. Samuel Rice.
*14. George Washington Rice.
15. Mahala Rice; m. Johnson Adams.
*16. William Rice.
*17. Andrew Jackson (Black Jack) Rice.
18. Cynthia Rice; m. Robert Prater, son of John Prater, and they resided at Bloomington, Kentucky.

Children:
19. John Prater; migrated to Missouri.
20. Wiley Prater; migrated to Missouri.
21. William Prater; migrated to Missouri.
22. Mary Elizabeth Prater; m. Captain Jeff Prater. She lived a long life of usefulness spent in the service of her friends and neighbors and will long be remembered, especially by traveling salesmen, for the very efficient manner in which she conducted the Prater Hotel of which she was in charge for many years.

5. SAMUEL RICE, farmer, was b., according to the opinion of his descendants, in what is now Letcher county, Kentucky; settled on Jennie's Creek, then Floyd now Johnson county; reputed to have had service in the War of 1812; m. in Floyd county, December 24, 1815, Phoebe Hitchcock, daughter of John Hitchcock.

Children:
*23. Margaret (Peggy) Rice.
*24. John Rice.
*25. Dr. Isaac Rice.
*26. Samuel K. Rice.
*27. George Washington Rice.

*28. Jackson Rice.
*29. W. B. (Wal) Rice.
30. William Rice; m. ——— Meade.
31. Marion Rice; m. ——— Meade.

11. MARTIN R. RICE, farmer; was b. February 16, 1810, near Cumberland Gap in either Southwestern Virginia or Northeastern Tennessee and d. in Johnson County, Kentucky, in 1897; migrated to Kentucky with his parents and settled March 16, 1815, on a farm on the head of Jennie's Creek, now Johnson county; prominent citizen of his community—being mentioned many times in the older records of the county; large landowner. The tax list of Floyd county for the year 1837 shows that he was possessed of 183 acres of land on Jennie's Creek, 4 horses and 75 head of cattle; m., first, in Floyd county, April 21, 1831, Malinda Davis (d. 1847), daughter of James Davis; and, secondly, in Johnson county, December, 1848, Mary Hannah, daughter of John S. Hannah.

Children of Martin R. Rice and his wife Malinda (Davis) Rice:
*32. Harrison Rice.
*33. Elizabeth Rice.
*34. John R. Rice.
*35. Samuel J. Rice.
*36. Wiley Rice.
*37. Nancy Jane Rice.
*38. Catherine Rice.

Children of Martin R. Rice and his wife, Mary (Hannah) Rice:
*39. Lydia M. Rice.
*40. Andrew J. Rice.
*41. Harvey Burns Rice.
*42. Elliott M. Rice.
43. Cynthia E. Rice (See Price Family).
*44. Sarah Ann Rice.
*45. George B. Rice.
46. Smith Rice; m. Katherine Price, daughter of Hamilton Price (See Price Family).
*47. Sherman Rice.

13. SAMUEL RICE; lived on the Burning Fork of Licking River, near Salyersville, Magoffin county; m., first, ——— Bays.
Children:
48. Robert Rice; lived at Irvington, Kentucky.
49. Jack Rice.
50. Elelyn Rice; m. ——— Patrick.
51. Martin Rice.

13-A. SAMUEL RICE; m., secondly, Jencie Patrick.

Children:
52. Newton Rice.
53. Berg Rice.
54. Clay Rice.

14. GEORGE WASHINGTON RICE; d. 1907; m., in Floyd county, September 26, 1839, Elizabeth (Betty) Auxier, daughter of Nathaniel (Nat) Auxier and his wife ——— (Beck) Auxier. (See No. 7, Auxier Family). They and their descendants lived near Gifford post office, in Magoffin county.
Children:
*55. John Jackson Rice.
56. William Marion Rice, b. September 18, 1843; reputed to have had service in the Union Army in the Civil War.

16. WILLIAM RICE, farmer, stock-dealer; b. February 16, 1815 on Jennie's creek, now Johnson county and d. July 5, 1886; an upright citizen; member of the United Baptist Church and very religious; m., first, in Floyd county, August 27, 1835, Dicy Prater, daughter of Elijah Prater, of Magoffin county; and, secondly, in Johnson county, Mary Ann Auxier (d. March 20, 1883), daughter of Nathaniel (Nat) Auxier and his wife, ——— (Beck) Auxier.
Children of William Rice and his wife, Dicy (Prater) Rice:
57. Nancy Jane Rice.
*58. Clarinda Rice.
Children of William Rice and his wife, Mary Ann (Auxier) Rice:
*59. John Rice.
*60. Cynthia Ellen Rice.
*61. Louise Elizabeth Rice.
*62. Samuel Rice.
63. William Rice.
*64. J. Payne Rice.
*65. Nathaniel Jackson Rice.
*66. Charley Rice.
*67. James Harvey Rice.
*68. Sarah Trinnie Rice.

17. ANDREW JACKSON (BLACK JACK) RICE; b. November 14, 1822; m., first, in Johnson county, September 19, 1844, Phoebe Fairchild (b. September 30, 1823); and, secondly, in Johnson county, Nancy Jane Fairchild.
Children of Andrew Jackson Rice and his wife, Phoebe (Fairchild) Rice:
*69. John Henry Rice.
*70. Martha Susan Rice.

*71. Benjamin Franklin Rice.
*72. Nancy Rice.
*73. Henry Harmon Rice.
*74. Alex. Hamilton Rice.
*75. William Wiley Rice.
*76. Elizabeth Rice.
*77. George P. Rice.

Children of Andrew Jackson Rice and his wife, Nancy Jane Fairchild:

*78. Mintie A. Rice.
*79. Julia Rice; b. August 10, 1879; m. Hargis Conley; lived at Riceville.
*80. Lou Emma Rice; b. November 25, 1881; d., unm.
*81. Myrtle Rice.

23. MARGARET (PEGGY) RICE; m., first, Elijah Bays and, secondly, —— Justice.

Children of Margaret Rice and Elijah Bays:

82. Samuel Bays; m. —— Morgan.
83. William Bays.
84. Joshua Bays; m. Margaret Slone.
85. Mary Bays; m. Jasper Slone.

Children of Margaret Rice and —— Justice:

86. Margaret Justice; m. Jesse Daniel.

24. JOHN RICE; m. in Floyd county, August 30, 1840, Nancy Jane Mollett.

Children:

87. William M. Rice; d. July 18, 1864, at Nashville, Tennessee, while serving in the Union Army, a private, Co. "D", 14th Ky. Vol. Inf.
88. Julia Rice; d., unm.
89. Nathan Rice; d. in infancy.
90. Lydia Rice; m. Wyatt W. Daniel of Johnson county.
91. Samuel Rice; had service in the Union Army during the Civil War, a private, Company "D", Fourteenth Kentucky Volunteer Infantry; transferred to 14th Ky. Vet. Inf.; m. Lydia Huffman of Carter county.
92. Henry Rice; m., first, Malissa Clay, and, secondly, Nancy J. Wheeler.
93. John Elliott Rice; m. Elizabeth Daniel. (See No. ———, Daniel Family).
94. Mary Rice; m. Plyman Daniel.
95. Ruth Rice; m. Buchanan Wood of Lawrence county.
96. T. J. Rice; d. in infancy.

97. James M. Rice; m. Elizabeth Ferguson.
98. Benjamin M. Rice; m. Louisa Elkins.
99. Nancy Jane Rice; m. John Vest of Morgan county.
100. George W. (Gallop) Rice; migrated to Montana.
101. H. Grant Rice; m. ———— Lemasters.

25. DR. ISAAC RICE; m., in Floyd county, March 29, 1839, Celia Connelly, daughter of Thomas Connelly.
Children:
102. Phoebe Rice.
103. Alex. Rice.
104. Samuel M. Rice.
105. Andrew W. Rice; m. Dicy Salyer, daughter of David Salyer.
106. James Rice; m. Nancy Rice.
107. Thomas Rice; m., first, Elizabeth J. Caudill, and, secondly, Mary Witten, daughter of Thomas Witten.
108. Clinton C. Rice.
109. Susan Ann Rice; m. Andrew Rivers.

26. SAMUEL K. RICE; had service in the Union Army during the Civil War, a private Company "I", Fourteenth Kentucky Volunteer Infantry; m., first, ———— Reed, daughter of Asa Reed; secondly, Mrs. Adams; and, thirdly, ———— Leek.
Children of Samuel K. Rice and his wife ———— (Reed) Rice:
110. Jesse Rice.
111. Nancy Rice; m. James Rice.
112. Kale Rice.
113. Samuel Rice.
114. David Rice; m. ———— Price (See No. ——, Price Family).
115. William Rice; m. ———— Blair.
116. Lydia Rice.
Children of Samuel K. Rice and his wife, Mrs. ———— Adams Rice:
117. Sheridan Rice; m. ———— Baldridge.
118. Mintie Rice; m. Thomas Burke.

27. GEORGE WASHINGTON RICE; had service in the Union Army during the Civil War, a private, Company "A" Thirty-Ninth Kentucky Volunteer Infantry; mustered in February 16, 1863, at Peach Orchard, Kentucky; mustered out September 15, 1865, at Louisville, Kentucky; m. Mary Emily Ramey, daughter of Judge Ramey.
Children:
119. Lidda Rice; m, first, Green P. Salyer, and, secondly, ———— Litteral.
120. William Jasper Rice.

121. Cynthia Rice; m. Wick Holbrook; they resided in Washington, D. C.

122. Mollie Rice; m. Elijah Gamble.

123. George Winton Rice; m. Maggie Osborn.

124. Belle Rice; m. J. H. Gamble.

125. James A. Rice; m. Dollie Crislipp.

126. Emma Rice.

127. Louis Rice; m. Louisa Akers.

28. JACKOSN RICE; m. —— Lemasters, sister of Elijah Lemasters.

Children:

128. Samuel Rice.

129. John Rice.

130. James Hayden Rice.

131. ——, daughter; m. William Jayne.

132. ——, daughter; m. —— Taylor.

29. W. B. (WAL) RICE; had service in the Union Army during the Civil War, a corporal, Company "I", Fourteenth Kentucky Volunteer Infantry; mustered in December 10, 1861, at Louisa, Kentucky; mustered out January 31, 1865, at Louisa; resided on Mud Lick Creek, Johnson county; was a plain-spoken, honest and respected citizen and reared a family of honorable citizens; d. at the age of eighty-nine years, four months and four days; m., first, —— Castle, and secondly, Mary (Sis) Butler.

Children of W. B. (Wal) Rice and his wife, —— (Castle) Rice:

133. Vina Rice.

134. Charles Rice.

135. Will Rice.

136. Kittie Rice.

137. Schuyler Rice.

Children of W. B. (Wal) Rice and his wife, Mary (Sis) (Butler) Rice:

138. Jane Rice; m. Burns Conley.

32. HARRISON RICE; b. March 6, 1832; d. January 14, 1922; lived on the Middle Fork of Jennie's Creek in Johnson county; m., first, Sallie Rollin and, secondly, —— Lemaster.

Children of Harrison Rice and his wife, Sallie (Rollin) Rice:

139. Armstrong Rice.

140. Martin N. Rice.

141. Patrick G. Rice.

142. Mary Eizabeth Rice.

143. Linda Alice Rice.

144. Julia Rice.

33. ELIZABETH RICE; b. September ——, 1833; d. 1925; m. Jackson M. Patrick; resided on Jennie's Creek in Johnson county.
Children:
145. Jane Patrick.
*146. Leander Patrick.
*147. Samuel H. Patrick.

34. JOHN R. RICE; b. October 13, 1835; d. about 1918; m. Jennie Adams; lived on main Jennie's Creek in Johnson county.
Children:
*148. Malinda Rice.
*149. Greenville Rice.
150. Jane Rice.
151. Samuel J. Rice; m. Sarah Trin Rice.
152. Elec Rice.

35. SAMUEL J. RICE; b. February 6, 1838; d. 1906; m. Sarah Powers, daughter of Judge Holly Powers.
Children:
153. Franklin Rice.
154. Wiley Rice, hotel-keeper at Salyersville, Magoffin county.
155. John Rice.
156. Harlan Rice.
157. Mollie Rice.
158. Charlie Rice.
159. Curtis Rice; m. —— Williams, daughter of Powell Williams.
160. Lillie Rice.
161. Perlie Rice.

36. WILEY RICE; b. August 24, 1840; m. Martha Fairchild.
Children:
162. German W. Rice.
163. Ettie Rice: m. John W. Watkins.
164. Elizabeth Rice: m. William Goble.
165. Ella Rice; m. Benjamin Candill.
166. Mintie Rice; m. "Yank" Rice.

37. NANCY JANE RICE; b. March 2, 1844; d. 1889; m. "Captain" George Jack Allen, farmer, merchant at Paintsville, who was mustered in at Peach Orchard, Kentucky, February 16, 1868, a first lieutenant, Company "F", Thirty-Ninth Kentucky Volunteer Infantry, and resigned November 14, 1864.
Children:
167. Amanda Allen.
168. Lizzie Allen.
169. Kate Allen.
170. Lucy Allen.

171. Susan Allen.
172. Florence Allen.
173. Martin R. Allen.

38. CATHERINE RICE; b. February 12, 1847; m., first, John White
May; resided in Magoffin county.
Children:
174. Ulysses G. May, contractor, Huntington, West Virginia; m.
Lou Roberts.
175. Maude May; m. Harlan Rice of Riceville, Johnson county.
176. Emma May; m. R. C. Patrick of Riceville, Johnson county.
177. Sallie May; m. Charles Rice.
178. Frank May; d. at the age of 13 years.

38-A. CATHERINE (RICE) MAY, m., secondly, January 17, 1877, Henry
C. H. Conley, b. October 18, 1856, d. 1925. (See Conley Family.)
Children:
179. John Conley; m. Gertrude Spencer.
180. Stella Conley.
181. Heber Conley; m. Julia Hazlett.
182. May Conley.
183. Virgie Conley; m. John D. Steele.

39. LYDIA M. RICE, b. February 16 (?), 1850, d. March 17, 1887;
m. William J. P. Blair, b. 1834, d. July 16, 1901, son of "Noby"
Blair.
Children:
184. Cynthia Blair.
185. Sarah C. Blair.
186. Dora Blair.
This family lived on a farm on Jennie's Creek.

40. ANDREW J. RICE, b. June 10, 1852; m. November 22, 1873,
Katheryn Conley, b. July 22, 1851, d. September 12, 1911, daughter
of Henry Conley.
Children:
187. Fred M. Rice.
188. Mary L. Rice, b. October 13, 1876; m. F H. Williams, July 14,
1895.
189. Millard B. Rice.
190. Allie Rice.
191. Rebecca Rice.
192. Pearl H. Rice.
193. Bernice G. Rice.
This family lived for a time on Jennie's Creek and afterward
moved to Boyd County.

41. HARVEY BURNS RICE, sometime teacher, businessman and public

official, was b. on Jennie's Creek, Johnson County, Kentucky, January 11, 1854, and d. at Paintsville, March 9, 1923. Interment at Paintsville; educated in the public schools of Johnson County; at the University of Kentucky (A. & M. College) at Lexington; and at National Normal University, Lebanon, Ohio, where he was trained for teaching; taught in the public schools of Johnson County for a time and afterwards engaged in numerous business enterprises: engaged in merchandising for seventeen years at Paintsville with his brother, Elliott M. Rice; was one of the organizers of the Paintsville Bank & Trust Company (now the Second National Bank) and was cashier of the institution for six years. Later in life he organized an insurance business under the name of H. B. Rice & Co., which business he conducted at Paintsville until his death.

Mr. Rice was a Republican in politics and served his county faithfully and well in public office. He was elected and served as Circuit Court Clerk of Johnson County for two terms (1882-1894) and served as judge of the Johnson County Court for one term (1902-1906).

On September 23, 1880, Mr. Rice was m. to Mary L. Hurt, b. February 4, 1857, a daughter of Robert Hurt.

Children:

*194. J. Verne Rice.
*195. Heber H. Rice.
*196. Edgar P. Rice.
*197. Garland Hurt Rice.
*198. Martin Robert Rice.
*199. Francis Lester Rice.
200. Lucille Esther Rice; b. September 4, 1889.

42. ELLIOTT M. RICE, merchant, b. July 24, 1855, and d. in May, 1895; m. Ella Borders, daughter of Joseph Borders. They resided in Paintsville where Mr. Rice was a successful merchant.

Children:

201. Guy M. Rice.
202. Bert Rice.
203. Bob Rice.
204. Mabel Rice.

44. SARAH ANN RICE; b. December 4, 1859; m. Charles M. Patrick; resided at Denver, Kentucky. Mr. Patrick was a farmer and owned and operated a large farm at Denver.

Children:

205. Willie Patrick; taught in the public schools of Johnson County for some time and subsequently became a physician; m. Rhoda Hager.

206. Challie Patrick; b. December 17, 1882; m., 1905, Lora Mayo, b. December 18, 1882; lived at Auxier, Kentucky, for a number of years and subsequently at Van Lear; reared a large family.

45. GEORGE B. RICE, farmer, merchant and dealer in lumber and real estate; b. at Denver, Kentucky, November 7, 1861; m., first, November 15, 1888, Janettie Stafford, b. February 28, 1862, d. April 22, 1918, daughter of William M. Stafford.

Children:

207. Willie S. Rice, b. November 20, 1889; m. December 1, 1923, —— ——.

208. Anna Rice; b. March 11, 1892; m. July 19, 1917, Howard C. Sale. They resided for several years in St. Petersburg, Florida, but returned to Dawkins Station, Johnson County; reared a family.

209. George D. Rice; b. March 8, 1894; unm.

George B. Rice m., secondly, Minnie Fulinister.

47. SHERMAN RICE, farmer, merchant and businessman; b. June 28, 1867; m. June 22, 1889, Emma Price, b. October 7, 1868; resided on a large farm which is a part of the Martin R. Rice estate on the main fork of Jennie's Creek.

Children:

210. Prudence Rice; b. April 21, 1891, at Riceville, Kentucky; m. March 28, 1918, Oscar Rice, b. September 19, 1890, son of G. W. Rice of Asa, Kentucky; resided at West Van Lear, Johnson County. Children: Edna, Earl Rice, Marvin Rice and Edwin Rice.

211. Kathryn Rice; b. August 9, 1893; unm.

212. Earl Rice; b. May 11, 1895, d. April 5, 1914.

213. Myrtle Rice; b. November 1, 1897; m. Sherwood K. Fidler, October 16, 1922.

214. Lucy Rice.

215. Mary Evelyn Rice; b. March 21, 1904; m. Maurice Backer, June 22, 1925.

216. Gladys Rice; b. March 26, 1908.

217. Sherman Rice, Jr., b. May 26, 1910.

218. Ruth Linell Rice; b. July 30, 1912.

55. JOHN JACKSON RICE; b. January 3, 1841; m. Sarah Colvin, daughter of Abiud Colvin; resided at Gifford, Kentucky.

Children:

219. Marie Rice; b. May 4, 1859, in Magoffin County; m. J. B. Millard, son of Abraham Millard; lived at Bloomington, Kentucky. Children: Minnie Millard, Maud Millard, d. young; Ella Millard and Fred Millard.

220. George Wash Rice; b. in Magoffin County, June 26, 1860; m. Martha May, daughter of William Smith May. Children: Virgie Rice, Grace Rice, Rose Rice, Goldie Rice, Georgia Rice, Luther Rice, Millard Rice and Roy Rice.

221. Willie Rice; b. October 31, 1862; d. February 12, 1925; m. Fanny Johnson. Children: Beulah Rice, Raleigh Rice, Marvin Rice and Retta Rice, who m. Martin Lindom. This family lived at Daysboro, Kentucky.

222. Henry C. Rice; b. June 23, 1864; m. Mary May, daughter of William Smith May; resided at Salyersville, Kentucky. Children: Ida Rice, Edgar Rice and Mabel Rice.

223. Johnie Rice; b. September 24, 1866; m. Leotha Adams, daughter of James Adams; resided at Iola, Kansas. Children: Maude Rice, m. Proctor Patrick, Myrtle Rice, Maggie Rice; Windel Rice and Wayne Rice.

224. Fairlena Rice; b. December 3, 1871; d. young.

225. Lou Dora Rice; b. March 28, 1874; m. S. D. May, son of Samuel May; resided at Salyersville, Kentucky. Children: Berry May, Prudence May, Sylvia May, Ollie May, Earl May, Myrtle May, Edna May and Alta May.

226. H. B. Rice; b. October 25, 1876; m. Callie Wilson, daughter of John Wilson, resided at Middletown, Ohio. Children: Ethel Rice, Jessie Rice, Gifford Rice, Herold Rice and Jenny Rice.

227. Bernice Rice; b. June 15, 1879; d. young.

58. CLARINDA RICE; m. Hiram E. Conley.

Children:

228. Frank P. Conley; m. Mary Dixon, daughter of Henry Dixon. (See Dixon Family.) Children: Eugene Conley m. Mabel Rice; Lillie (Shug) Conley m. Clyde Hazelett.

229. John Eliott Conley, a minister of the Freewill Baptist Church; resided at Thealka, Kentucky; m. Susan James of Virginia. Children: Claude Conley m. Mima Burk; Laura Conley m. Peter Dixon; Smith Conley m. Grace Preston; Hattie Conley m. W. I. McCloud; Everett Conley; Jennie Conley; May Conley m. Buck Sherman; Alfred Conley m. Fanny Dixon; Grace Conley m. a Blair.

230. Mantford Conley; resided at Paintsville; m. Lou Conley, daughter of Constantine Conley. Children: Ed Conley, dentist at Ashland, Kentucky; m. Ethel Williams; Robert Conley; Bessie Conley, m. a Chandler, no children.

231. H. B. (Burns) Conley); resided in Paintsville where he managed several hotels and was interested in several business enterprises; a leading minister in the Freewill Baptist Church; was elected and served as judge of the Johnson County Court one term; m. Mintie Jane Rice, daughter of W. B. Rice. Children: Theodore Conley d. at age of 20; Virgie Conley; Herbert Conley m. Jessie Atwood; Mamie Conley.

232. George W. Conley; lived on Jennie's Creek; was found dead in the woods December 28 ,1924; probably frozen to death; m. Mintie Rice, b. in October, 1868, daughter of John Rice. Children: Eunice Conley, Morris Conley, Burnice Conley m. Fanny McCloud; Myrtle Conley m. Troy Fairchild.

233. S. Bascom Conley; lived at Denver, Kentucky; m. Maggie Blair, daughter of Pyrtle Blair. Children: Kirk Conley, Orville Conley and Alvin Conley.

234. Fred W. Conley.

235. Albert Conley; lived on Middle Fork of Jennie's Creek; m. Ida Blair, daughter of Ned Blair. Children: Raymond Conley, teacher, m. Carmie Meade; Hazel Conley, teacher, m., first, Emerson Picklesimer and secondly, Richard Conley.

236. Cyrus Conley, b. July 16, 1878; lived on a farm near Paintsville and was employed at the shipping yards at the Paintsville depot; m., January 1, Elizabeth McCloud, b. September 7, 1879. Children: Maxie Conley, Vern Conley and Elvin Conley.

237. Den B. Conley; lived on Middle Fork of Jennie's Creek for many years, later moving to Paintsville where he was mail carrier for the local post office; m. to Mintie Fairchild, daughter of Levi Fairchild. Children: Mabel Conley m. Work Hazelett; Mattie Conley m. Earl McCloud; Dorothy Conley.

238. Emily Conley; m. Calfax Butler, a minister; resided at Staffordville. Children: Ruth Butler m. Earl Preston; John Butler.

59. JOHN RICE; b. January 5, 1841; resided on Jennie's Creek; m. Mariam Fitch.

Children:

239. William Elzie (Dick) Rice; b. June 7, 1873; lived at Collista, Kentucky; m., December 23, 1892, Allie Webb, b. July 11, 1877. Children: Mintie Rice, b. April 8, 1894; m. December 22, 1913, Hebern Fitch.

240. McKinley Rice, b. August 7, 1896, and d. November 5, 1920.

241. Missouri Rice, b. July 27, 1899, m., July 18, 1917, Brookie Sublett.

242. Daisy Rice, b. February 7, 1901, m., June 20, 1917, Grant Johnson.

243. Paris Rice, b. September 4, 1904, d. September 9, 1905.

244. Walter Rice, b. August 21, 1907.

245. Gladys Rice, b. July 8, 1911, d. December 26, 1913.

246. Russell Rice, b. May 25, 1913.

247. Mildred Rice, b. October 25, 1915.

60. CYNTHIA ELLEN RICE; m. James Hayden Conley, son of John Conley, lived on Rockhouse Creek, about three miles from Paintsville.

Children:

248. Louise Conley; m. John Reynolds. Children: Laura Reynolds m. Sulvon Lewis; Leslie Reynolds; William Reynolds m. a Sturgill; Robert Reynolds d. young; Eugene Reynolds.

249. Millard V. Conley; m. Lou Johnson, daughter of William H. Johnson; resided in Paintsville. Children: Roy Conley; Buell Conley; Everett Conley, physician, resides in Cleveland, Ohio; Carmel Conley; Brooks Conley m. a Meade; Norma Conley; Opal Conley d. young.

250. John Clint Conley; m. Helen Johnson; resided at Hagerhill, Kentucky. Children: Troy Conley m. an Adams; Dollie Conley m. Ott Taylor; Mason Conley m. a Fairchild; Linzie S. Conley m. Hazel Conley; Charles Conley was killed in World War I while serving in the army; ——— Conley m. a Horne.

251. Sola Gertrude Conley; m. William Trimble; resided at Barnetts Creek, Kentucky. Children: Paris L. Trimble m. Lucinda Fannin; James Trimble m., first, a Caudill and secondly ——— (?); Myrtle Trimble m. a Reed; Theodore (Ted) Trimble; John Trimble; Gillie Trimble (female).

252. Lindsey S. Conley; b. on Rockhouse Creek, January 11, 1871; m., December 26, 1894, Emma C. McFarland, b. December 12, 1877. Children: Curtis M. Conley, killed November 4, 1918 in World War I; Teria E. Conley; Erie Conley; Ora Conley; Wayne Conley; Flora Conley; Lindsey Conley, Jr., d. in infancy.

253. Charles F. Conley; m. Rose McFarland; resided at Paintsville. Children: Roy Conley; Rhuie Conley m. Roby Horne; Earl Conley m. a Fairchild; ——— Conley m. a Dixon; James Conley.

254. A. F. Conley; m. Phoebe Rice; resided in Paintsville. Children: Elmer Conley m. a Conley; Hazel Conley m. Rodney Picklesimer; John Conley m. a Fairchild.

255. Frank J. Conley, teacher and businessman, b. December 17, 1882; educated in the Paintsville City Schools, the Sandy Valley Seminary and the State Normal School at Bowling Green, Kentucky; was principal of the Van Lear schools for four years after which he taught for a year in Oklahoma. Returning to Johnson County, he taught two years in the rural schools after which he became an employee of the North-East Coal Company at Thealka. In 1919 he and some of his associates severed their connections with the coal company and organized the Paintsville Furniture Company of which he was manager; m., in 1911, Clara Mollett, daughter of John R. Mollett. Children: Alice Vivian Conley; Frances Ellen Conley; Rubie Virginia Conley; Joanna Conley.

256. Genoa Coney; m. Lonzo (Stapleton) Conley. Children: ——— (name not learned).

257. Virgie Lee Conley; m. Ray Turner, businessman at Paintsville; resided in their beautiful country home at the intersection of the Garrett Highway and Mayo Trail near Paintsville. Mr. Turner was a coal dealer for a number of years; later was associated with the Paintsville Bank and Trust Company as assistant cashier and cashier. Severing his connection with the bank, he became associated with J. K. Butcher & Company. Children: Ruth Turner, m. C. W. Compton, September 15, 1927; John W. Turner.

61. LOUISE ELIZABETH RICE; b. on Jennie's Creek, July 3, 1844; m., November 21, 1861, F. Marion Conley, b. November 6, 1836, d.

January 28, 1892, son of Constantine Conley, Sr.; lived near Hagerhill.

Children:

258. German Conley; b. June 15, 1863; d. April 10, 1920; m. April 18, 1891, Colista Carroll, b. January 14, 1873, daughter of William Carroll of Wise County, Virginia; lived on the Lick Fork near Hagerhill. Children: Forest Conley, b. January 21, 1892; Nora Conley; Mary Conley; Hobert (?) F. Conley; Loretta Conley; Susie Conley, b. January 10, 1901, m. Bud Butcher; German A. Conley; Mildren Marie Conley and Harry Conley, b. June 17, 1906.

259. Mary Conley; b. January 9, 1866; m. George Burchett.

260. Jesse Conley; m. Dora Ratliff. Children: Jesse Conley, b. October 4, 1891; Oliver Conley, b. November 9, 1892; Willie Lee Conley, b. March 13, 1895, m. Anna Wells; Mazzie Conley, b. June 28, 1897, m. Charlie Castle; Alka Conley, b. April 10, 1899, and Ollie Conley, b. December 9, 1900.

261. Leonard Conley; b. March 30, 1868; m. Elizabeth Robinson. Children: Okie Conley, m. Norse Kesner; Ida Conley; Frank Conley, m. Linda Likens; Sidney Conley, m. Georgia Ann Cantrill; Luther Conley and Grace Conley.

262. Charlie W. Conley; b. June 12, 1870; m. ——— Music. Children: Oliver Conley, m. Lydia Auxier; West Conley m. Kimbert Oliver; Moonie Conley, m. John Spradlin; Oscar Conley.

263. Josie Conley; b. March 30, 1872; m. "Red" Picklesimer. Children: Bessie Picklesimer, m. Ben Stambaugh; June Picklesimer, m. John Flannery; Charlie Picklesimer.

264. William Lewis Conley; b. April 27, 1874; m. Oma Friend; operated a bus and taxi service in Paintsville and over the Mayo Trail from Paintsville to Ashland. Children: Presley Conley, m. Marie Daniels; Edwin Conley, m. Opal Prose; Hope Conley; Tave Conley.

265. Kate Conley; b. September 2, 1876; m. Tilden Harrod. Children: Willie Harrod; Fanny Harrod, m. Harry Hale; Reuben Harrod; Gladys Harrod, m. Ray Salyer; Arthur Harrod.

266. Laura Conley; b. April 3, 1879; m. Charlie Friend; resided at West Van Lear where Mr. Friend was a general merchant. Children: Garland Friend; Virgie Friend, m. Newt Fannin; Russell Friend; Mary Friend; John Friend; Bob Friend.

267. Nora Conley, b. April 6, 1882.

268. Grover C. Conley, b. November 6, 1884; d. August 29, 1885.

269. Worth Conley, onetime teacher and afterwards a truck farmer; b. September 29, 1886; m. Suda Lowe. Children: Virgil Conley.

62. SAMUEL RICE; b. April 5, 1846; m., first, October 21, 1868, Elizabeth Huff, b. February 19, 1884.

Children:

270. Lou Ella Rice; m. Harry Taylor. Children: William Taylor; Douglass Taylor; David Taylor.

271. John W. Rice; m. Ella Lyons. Children: Birdie Rice; Minnie Rice; ——— (name not learned); John Kinkaid Rice.

272. Julia Rice; m. William Taylor; lived on Big Mud Lick Creek near Staffordsville. Children: Morris Taylor; Bert Taylor; Gypsie Taylor, m. Paris Fackett, lived on Barnetts Creek; Emory Fay Taylor, m. a Stafford, lived at Russell, Kentucky; Willie Curtis Taylor; Rubie Gordon Taylor; Mary Ellie Taylor.

273. Mary (Mollie) E. Rice; b. April 22. 1877, on Jennie's Creek; m. May 10, 1896. Ernest (Dick) Turner, b. February 14, 1873, son of John W. and Frances (Lyon) Turner; lived near Paintsville on Turner Branch on the Mayo Trail. Mr. Turner was a building contractor in Paintsville. Children: Fay Carroll Turner, b. March· 27, 1897; m. October 17, 1917. Clyd Hatfield, b. October 27, 1896, son of Anderson Hatfield of Catlettsburg. Children: a daughter, Imogene Hatfield, b. February 19, 1919. Residence, Charleston, West Virginia. Frankie Turner, b. March 3, 1903, m. September 2, 1922, William Schluneger, a native of Switzerland who resided in Texas. Residence, Tulsa, Oklahoma. Dixie Ray Turner, b. March 2, 1919.

274. German W. Rice.

275. Laura Rice; m. Camel Williams. Children: Millegen Williams; Myrtle Williams.

62-A. Samuel Rice m., secondly, April 27, 1888. Dolly Stafford; resided on a farm near the forks of Jennie's Creek.

Children:

276. Ben H. Rice; m. a Hoffman; lived near Columbus, Ohio.

277. Carl F. Rice; lived in Los Angeles, California.

278. Estill Rice, deceased.

279. William R. Rice, m. ——— Clay; lived at Rock Camp, Ohio. Children: ——— Rice (name not learned).

280. Dewey Rice, m. Myrtle McFaddin.

281. Maude Rice; m. a Clannahan.

282. Arthur Rice.

64. J. PAYNE RICE; b. February 11, 1850, and d. January 2, 1925; m. in March 1874, Frances Elizabeth (Puss) Sublett, b. March 31, 1849, and d. October 13, 1899.

Children:

283. Infant (name not learned).

284. Jennie Rice; m. Tobe Wiley. Children: Hansel Wiley.

285. Monroe Rice; b. Febrary 26, 1876, and d. January 10, 1881.

286. Mary Rice; b. November 17, 1878; m. Ernest Van Hoose.

287. Fanny Rice; b. March 18, 1883; m. Albert Howes, d. in 1915, son of E. F. Howes. Children: Harold Howes, b. September 2, 1908.

288. Eva Rice, social leader in Paintsville, b. September 3, 1887; m. G. E. Clark, October 31, 1920.

J. Payne Rice resided in Paintsville where he conducted a furniture store for many years. He was a good and respected citizen. He m., secondly, "Siss" Elliott. Interment in Paintsville Cemetery.

65. NATHANIEL JACKSON RICE; b. in Johnson County, May 21, 1852; d. February 28, 1926; m. January 26, 1893, Catherine Louise McCloud, b. March 25, 1874, and d. November 12, 1920, daughter of George and Angeline McCloud; lived on a farm at the mouth of Jennie's Creek.

Mr. Rice received his education in the public schools of Johnson County and attended Normal schools in Paintsville. He was a teacher in the rural schools for a short time and conducted a general merchandising business at his place of residence. Mrs. Rice was b. on Jennie's Creek. She cared for her younger brothers and sisters after the death of their mother; cooperated with her husband in carrying on the general store and was much attached to him; was kind to and thoughtful of her children's needs and willing to make any sacrifice to promote their happiness and welfare. Both Mr. and Mrs. Rice were buried near their home at Collista.

Children:

289. Chloe Rice, teacher; b. in Johnson County, December 8, 1893; m. January 26, 1916, Bert Watkins, b. November 29, 1895, son of Henry Watkins. Mr. Watkins was b. on a farm near Denver, Kentucky. When a young man he went to Russell, Kentucky, where he was connected with business houses. Returning to Johnson County, he was employed by the Consolidation Coal Company at Van Lear in a sub-station and a general store there for a number of years, after which he and some associates organized a general merchandise store, Bert Watkins & Company at West Van Lear, of which he became the head.

Mr. Watkins is an aggressive businessman and he and Mrs. Watkins are active members of the Missionary Baptist Church at West Van Lear and leaders in the affairs of their community. Children: Walter Clifton Watkins, b. April 18, 1908; Katherine Louise Watkins, b. August —, 1921; Henry Nathan Watkins, b. May 5, 1928.

290. Alma Rice; b. in Johnson County, May 11, 1896; m., December 18, 1917, Clyde Preston, b. December 7, 1894, son of Winfield S. Preston. Mr. Preston was b. on a farm on the Big Sandy River near Van Lear; was educated in the rural schools; volunteered and had honorable service throughout World War I; had overseas service and was wounded on the battlefields of France. Returning home after close of the War he was employed by the Big Sandy Division of the

Chesapeake & Ohio Railroad for a time, but being unable tb perform his duties on account of injury received, he severed his connection with the railroad and afterwards did such farm work as his condition would permit.

Mrs. Preston was educated in the rural public schools of Johnson County and the Sandy Valley Seminary at Paintsville, and taught school for a number of years previous to her marriage. She is an attractive woman and popular with her friends. Residence—mouth of Miller's Creek, near West Van Lear. Children: Anna Marguerite Preston, b. February 27, 1920; Kenneth Clyde Preston, b. February 27, 1922; Jackie Winfield Preston, b. August 21, 1927.

291. Hester Rice, teacher; b. in Johnson County, January 15, 1898; educated in the public schools; attended the Paintsville High School and John C. C. Mayo College, at Paintsville, where she pursued normal courses for teachers; taught in the public schools of Johnson County several years; m., June 17, 1920, Mitchell Hall. Children: Maurice Mitchell Hall, b. December 31, 1921. (For a biographical sketch of Mitchell Hall see biography of Judge J. Melvin Hall.)

292. John Russell Rice; b. December 18, 1902; m. January 2, 1925, Osa Taylor, b. February 19, 1908, daughter of John M. Taylor of Siloam, Kentucky.

Mr. Rice was reared on Jennie's Creek. Leaving Johnson County after the death of his mother, he became an employee of railroad companies first at Cincinnati, next at Waverly, Ohio, and then at Tongs, Kentucky. He has held many responsible positions of trust with the railroads. He met Miss Taylor while working at Tongs. Her people live in the vicinity of Portsmouth, Ohio. Children: Evelyn Louise Rice, b. December 29, 1926.

66. CHARLEY RICE, farmer and stock raiser; b. March 3, 1854; m. April 24, 1879, Mary Jane Webb, b. December 1, 1856; lived on a farm at the intersection of the Lick and Middle Forks of Jennie's Creek.

Children:

293. Malcolm Rice; m. Calla Lee Rice.

294. Lonzo Rice; b. on the Lick Fork, September 6, 1881; d. February 3, 1927; m. December 21, 1904, Laura Blair, daughter of Harry Blair; lived near the Forks of Jennie's Creek the greater part of his life. Children: Norma Rice, b. October 25, 1905, m. Sandy Ramey; Fanny Rice, b. August 24, 1907; Herschell Rice, b. February 13, 1909; Myrtle Rice, b. December 31, 1910; Erskine Rice, b. October 4, 1912, d. November 13, 1913; Marie Rice, b. August 18, 1914; Hansel Rice, b. May 17, 1918; Vernon Rice, b. October 4, 1921; Anna Rice, b. October 10, 1923; Ed. Eugene Rice, b. February 16, 1925.

295. Mary Rice; b. April 23, 1883; m. June 23, 1904, William Conley, b. March 5, 1874. Children: Lowe Conley, dec'd; Geneva Conley, m. Walter Lester, April 24, 1922; Genoa Conley; Alvin Conley; Ernest Conley; Marie Wilson Conley.

296. Alex Rice; b. August 9, 1890; m. Grace Conley.

297. Martha Rice; b. June 28, 1884; d. September 13, 1884.

298. Bertha Rice; b. July 2, 1885; d. October 18, 1886.

299. Lora Rice; b. July 25, 1888; d. August 12, 1903.

300. Heber Rice; b. April 4, 1894; m. October 21, 1921, Hattie Spears; lived near home-place at mouth of Middle Fork; served in World War I. Children: Mattie Rice, d. young; Nancy May Rice, b. March 13, 1924.

301. Katherine Rice; b. August 16, 1892; m. Jesse Horne, July 22, 1915; lived on Rockhouse Creek near Paintsville. Children: Virginia Horne.

302. Hobart Rice; b. May 13, 1896; d. June 28, 1923; m. Pricilla Blair.

303. Dewey Rice; b. July 22, 1898; m. Ollie Conley, June 7, 1922; two children.

304. John Walker Rice; b. September 20, 1901; d. October 11, 1901.

67. JAMES HARVEY RICE, farmer; b. November 14, 1857; d. November 25, 1925; lived on a farm on the main fork of Jennie's Creek about three miles from Paintsville; m., February 20, 1884, Julia Van Hoose, b. February 29, 1894.

Children:

305. Warren Rice; b. January 2, 1885; served in World War I; was killed in action, July 18, 1918, while serving as captain in the American Expeditionary Forces in France.

306. Irvin Rice; b. November 26, 1886; m. Neva Williams, June 5, 1907.

307. Alka Rice; b. February 22, 1889; m., first August 4, 1907, Jack Milum, d. October 12, 1913. Children: Mildred Milum, b. July 15, 1912; James Patrick Milum, b. March 18, 1914.

Alka Rice Milum m., secondly, February 21, 1917, John Baldwin. She d. November 16, 1925. Children. William Edward Baldwin, b. December 8, 1917; Everett Rice Baldwin, b. January 15, 1920; Neva Jean Baldwin, b. August 10, 1922; Thomas Baldwin, b. November 1, 1924.

308. Everett Rice; b. July 27, 1900; m., November 18, 1922, Hazel Lester, daughter of Charley Lester of Denver, Kentucky; lived at Smalley, Floyd County, for a time and subsequently in Paintsville. Children: Charles Harvey Rice, b. September 10, 1923; Warren L. Rice, b. July 7, 1925.

309. Bertha Mae Rice; b. October 3, 1901; m. Jay Wilson, October 19, 1920; resided in West Virginia. Children: James Milton Wilson, b. September 12, 1921; Fred Carroll Wilson, b. January 8, 1923; Julia Frances Wilson, b. June 24, 1925.

310. Mabel Rice; b. October 3, 1903; m. Eugene Conley, January 15, 1924.

311. Harva Lee Rice; b. June 8, 1906.

68. SARAH TRINNIE RICE; b. July 18, 1860; m. July 27, 1888, Samuel Rice, b. February 13, 1866.

Children:

312. Alta Rice; b. June 17, 1889; d. July 31, 1909.

313. Curtis Rice; b. January 4, 1891.

314. Clyde Rice; b. January 18, 1893; d. July 4, 1913.

315. Hazel Rice; b. October 11, 1895.

316. John R. Rice; b. July 17, 1897.

317. Willie Rice; b. February 11, 1899.

318. Ellis Rice; b. September 29, 1901.

319. Everett Rice; b. September 29, 1901; d. February 28, 1903.

Mr. and Mrs. Rice lived on Jennie's Creek, Johnson County, for a number of years after which they moved to Big Sandy Junction near Catlettsburg where Mr. Rice was killed by a train. Later Mrs. Rice and the children made their home in Ashland.

69. JOHN HENRY RICE; b. October 28, 1845; m. Mary A. May, daughter of David May.

Children:

320. Emma Rice; dec'd; unm.

321. Hallock J. Rice; dec'd; unm.

322. Sheridan Rice; dec'd; unm.

323. Nannie Rice; dec'd unm.

324. Frank Rice; dec'd; unm.

70. MARTHA SUSAN RICE; b. August 18, 1847; m. Thomas Green May, son of David May of Salyersville.

Children:

325. James Franklin May, physician; m. Charlotte Sagraves, teacher.

326. Samuel David May; m. Emma Hammond.

327. Reuben May; m. Bomma Kimbler.

71. BENJAMIN FRANKLIN RICE; b. August 11, 1849; m. Emily May, daughter of David May of Salyersville.

Children:

328. Harlan Rice; m. Maude Robinson.

329. Alice Rice; m. Edgar Hurt.

330. Willie Rice; d., unm.

331. Frea Rice; m. Trinnie Fairchild.

332. Charlie Rice; m. Dessa May.

333. Rose Rice; m. Frank Caudill.

334. Virgie Rice; m. Dr. Sanford Wright.

335. Harry Rice; m. Chloe May.

336. Bertha Rice; m. Lester May.

72. NANCY RICE; b. December 5, 1851; m. Samuel Jackson May, son of David May of Salyersville.

Children:

337. E. Dee May; m. Louise Wheeler.

338. Sola May; m. a Day.

339. Frank May; m. Roslie Preston.

340. Fred May; m. a Harrod.

341. Mintie May; m. a Cooper.

342. Laura May; m. a Salyer.

343. Samuel J. May, Jr.

73. HENRY HARMON RICE, farmer and minister of the Baptist Church; b. June 14, 1854; m. June 14, 1879, Nancy J. Hackworth, b. November 7, 1854; lived on a farm on Jennie's Creek, Johnson County, for a number of years and afterwards moved to Potters, Boyd County, and resided on a farm on the Midland Trail.

Children:

344. Burris Rice; b. in Johnson County, January 26, 1880; m. September 2, 1916, Clara Lee Woods of Boyd County; lived in Boyd County. Children: Carl Wood Rice, b. August 24, 1917; Claudie Burris Rice, b. June 17, 1920.

345. Calla Lee Rice; b. March 18, 1882; m. October 15, 1919, Malcolm Rice, soldier, a son of Charley Rice (See No. 66); served in the U. S. Army for 27 years. He served on the Mexican border and with the First Division in World War I; was in several major battles and was decorated by the United States government and several foreign governments because of bravery in action; attained the rank of captain; remained in the service several years after the close of the war and was stationed at several camps, among others, Ft. Benning, Georgia; d. September 4, 1927, as a result of intestinal operation; no children.

346. Daisy Denning Rice; b. in Johnson County, August 8, 1884; d. January 31, 1907; m. September 4, 1901, H. C. Vanover of Johnson County. Children: Virgil Francis Vanover, b. October 18, 1902, m. March 7, 1924, Della Sue Green; Paul Joe Vanover, b. February 11, 1905.

347. Joe J. Rice; b. January 15, 1887; d. while serving in World War I, at Camp DeSouge, France, October 15, 1918; m. Nona Leslie Reynolds.

348. Jake Rice; b. February 28, 1890.

349. Barney B. Rice; b. October 28, 1892; d. December 15, 1911.

350. Fannie Marie Rice; b. April 1, 1895; m. Allen H. Turman, April 1, 1925.

74. ALEX HAMILTON RICE; b. May 5, 1857; m. Elizabeth May, daughter of William May of Prestonsburg.

351. William J. Rice

352. Laura Belle Rice.
353. Cynthia Rice.
354. Martha Rice.
355. John Harmon Rice.
356. May Rice.
This family resided in Seattle, Washington. All the children m. and reared families.

75. WILLIAM RILEY RICE; b. October 13, 1859; m. Nola Hamilton, daughter of John Hamilton of Flat Gap.
Children:
357. Elma Rice; m. Grant Barber.

76. ELIZABETH RICE; b. May 19, 1862; m. James Howes, son of Wiley Howes of Salyersville.
Children:
358. Ida Howes; m. Riley Hackworth.
359. Anna Howes; m. Miles Conley.
360. Molly Howes; m. John Collins.
361. Henry Howes; d. young.
362. Carl Howes; m. a Patrick.
363. Emma Howes; m. John Sparks.
364. Norman Howes; m. a Conley.
365. Ina Howes.
366. Lou Howes; m. a Patrick.

77. GEORGE P. RICE; b. July 29, 1865; m. Mary May, daughter of James L. May, of Ivyton.
Children:
367. Cora Rice.
368. Luther Rice.
Both children married and reside in the State of Washington.

78. MINTIE A. RICE; b. October 19, 1877; m. Amos Conley; resided at West Van Lear. Mr. Conley was interested in lumber and planing mill for several years.
Children: Alta, unm.; Osa m. Russell Akers; John; May m. Luther McCloud; June m. a Corder; Victor; Vertrice; Maxine.
79. JULIA RICE; b. August 10, 1879; m. Hargis Conley; resided at Riceville.
80. LOU EMMA RICE; b. November 25, 1881; d., unm.
81. MYRTLE RICE; m. Asa Ramey; resided at Riceville. Children: Bessie, Ora and Genoa.

24. JOHN RICE; m. Nancy J. Mollett, August 30, 1840.
Children:
369. William M. Rice; d. while serving in the army during the Civil War.
370. Julia Rice; d.; unm.
371. Nathan Rice; d. young.

372. Lydia Rice; m. Wyatt W. Daniel, a son of David Daniel of Johnson County. He was long a minister of the United Baptist Church; d. at the home of his daughter, Mrs. Ben Van Hoose, at Thealka, and was buried near the Sugar Grove Church on Hood's Fork of Blaine, his old home. Children: W. M., a jeweler, of Prestonsburg; Dr. Harman of Wolfpit; Martha who married Campbell Howard and resided at Paintsville; Mrs. George Boyd of White House; Mrs. Ben Van Hoose of Thealka; Winston of Sitka; Mrs. Rebecca Mollett of White House; and Rev. John A. of Nippa.

373. Samuel Rice; had service in Company "B", 14th Kentucky Infantry, during the Civil War; m. Lydia Huffman of Carter Co.; resided at Grayson.

374. Henry Rice; m., first, Malissa Clay, and secondly, Nancy J. Wheeler.

375. John Elliott Rice; m. Elizabeth Daniel.

376. Mary Rice; m. Plyman Daniel.

377. Ruth Rice; m. Buchanan Wood of Lawrence County.

378. T. J. Rice; d. in infancy.

379. James M. Rice; m. Elizabeth Ferguson.

380. Ben M. Rice; m. Louisa Elkins.

381. Nancy Jane Rice; m. John Vest.

382. George W. (Gallup) Rice; m. ———?, went to Montana; dec'd.

383. H. Grant Rice; m. a Lemaster.

25. Dr. Isaac Rice; m. March 29, 1839, Celia Connelley, daughter of Thomas Connelley.

Children:

384. Phoebe Rice; m. Rev. Samuel Picklesimer.

Children: I. J., m. Mandy Colvin; Mary m. S. T. Bayes; John W. m. a Trimble; Ben F. m. a Pelphrey; Nathaniel m. a Rice; Celia m. a Colvin; Tom m. a Young; Martha m. Harry Van Hoose.

385. Alex Rice m. Lucy Barnett. Children: "Bud" Rice.

386. Samuel M. Rice; b. December 31, 1843; served in Company "I", 14th Kentucky Infantry during the Civil War; m., 1866, Martha J. Witten, b. November 7, 1849, daughter of George H. Witten. Children: George Lincoln (Link) m. Katherine Powell; Celia Ann, m. Fred W. Walker; Isaac G., one-time farmer, lawyer and oil man; held many public offices in Johnson County: served as commonwealths attorney for a term and also represented his district in the General Assembly; m. Della Caudill, March 31, 1903; Dora m. Valentine Daniel, no children; Phoebe m. Phonso Conley; Jane, unm.; Artie m. A. M. Shepherd; Proctor W. lived in Spokane, Washington; John D. served in the U. S. Army for twenty years and held the rank of captain during World War I; resided on Long Island, New York, and was paymaster for the Cosmopolitan Shipping Company; m. Minnie Slitz; and Gustava died at age of 14.

387. Andrew W. Rice; m. Dicy Salyer, daughter of David Salyer.

388. James Rice; m. Nancy Rice.

389. Thomas Rice; m., first, Elizabeth Caudill and, secondly, Mary Witten, daughter of Thomas Witten.

390. Clint C. Rice; m. Alice Johnson; resided on Rockhouse Creek, near Paintsville. Children: Mose, m. Mattie Watkins; Emma, teacher, connected with the city schools at Jenkins; Grace; Erie, teacher, connected with city schools at Jenkins; and Crate, m. June Meade.

391. Susan Ann Rice; m. Andrew Rivers.

26. Samuel K. Rice; served in the Union Army during the Civil War; m., first, —— Reed, daughter of Asa Reed.

Children:

392. Jesse Rice.

393. Nancy Rice; m. James Rice.

394. Kale Rice; m. a Watkins.

395. Samuel Rice.

396. Dave Rice; m. a Price.

397. William Rice; m. a Blair.

398. Lydia Rice.

26A. Samuel K. Rice; m., secondly, a Mrs. Adams.

Children:

399. Sheridan Rice; m. a Baldridge.

400. Mintie Rice; m. Tom Burke.

27. George Wash Rice; served in the Union Army during the Civil War; m. Mary Emily Ramey.

Children:

401. Lidda Rice; m., first, Greene P. Salyer and secondly, a Litteral.

402. William Jasper Rice; m. Eloise McGuire; resided at Paintsville for several years where he published a religious publication. He d. at Atlanta, Georgia; Mrs. Rice d. at Laredo, Texas.

Children:

403. Alfred Elmer Rice; resided in Houston, Texas.

404. Arthur Rice; m. in New York.

405. Elbert Rice; m. in Oklahoma; resided in Mexico City.

406. Carroll Rice; resided in Dayton, Ohio.

407. Virginia Rice; m. Free Boord; resided in Wilmington, Delaware.

408. Vivian Rice; m. a Stephens; resided in Hollywood, California.

409. Willa Louise Rice; m. a Flynn; resided in Laredo, Texas.

410. Richard Rice; d. in France during World War I.

28. Jackson Rice; m. a Lemasters, a sister of Elijah Lemasters.

Children:

411. Samuel Rice.

412. John Rice.

413. James Hyden Rice.
414. —— Rice; m. Will Jayne.
415. —— Rice; m. a Taylor.

29. W. B. (WALL) RICE; m., first, a Castle; lived on Mud Lick Creek.
Children:
416. Vina Rice; m. George Melvin. Children: James, Ben and Lyda, who m. B. McKenzie.
417. Charles Rice; m. Sola May. Children: Milburn, ——, m. a Bailey and ——, m. George Daniel.
418. Will Rice; m., first, Anna Akers. Children: "Dugan", —— Rice, name not known. He m., secondly, —— Stambaugh and, thirdly, —— Picklesimer. They had three children, names not known.
419. Kittie Rice; m. Eugene Preston; lived at Paintsville; Children: Harper Preston.
420. Schuyler Rice; m. Rosa Witten. Children: "Kittie" Rice, m. a McKenzie.

29A. W. B. (Wall) Rice; m., secondly, Mary (Sis) Butler; served in the Union Army during the Civil War; d. about 1927 at the age of eighty-nine years, four months and four days.
Children:
421. Jane Rice; m. Burns Conley.

32. HARRISON RICE; b. March 6, 1832; d. January 14, 1922; m. Sallie Rollin.
Children:
422. Armstrong Rice; m. Nan Rice, daughter of Alex Rice; resided in South Ashland, Kentucky. Children: Pearlie, Myrtle, Allie, Bee and Alox.
423. Martin N. Rice; m. —— Fairchild, daughter of Asa Fairchild of Asa's Creek. Children: Martin, ——, m. a McFadden, —— m. a Ratliff, ——, —— m. a Ratliff.
424. Patrick G. Rice; m. Mary Rice, daughter of Alex Rice. Children: Deshia, Cora, Sarah, Ross, Don, Elmer and Clay.
425. Mary Elizabeth Rice; m. Abram Fitch; lived on the Middle Fork of Jennie's Creek. Children: Beulah, Carl, Rusha and Roxie.
426. Linda Alice Rice; m. Sam Hayden; resided in Fletcher Gap, near East Point. They had two children—names not known.
427. Julia Rice; b. December 3, 1863, on Middle Fork; m. in 1890, H. C. May, b. April 16, 1861, son of J. L. May of Magoffin County. Children: Leonard Rice May; m. Nancy Wallace of Ashland; Guy May m. Priscilla Haskins, daughter of Robert; Paris May, born February 22, 1893; Ellis May, m. Maggie May, daughter of Harman of Salyersville; Elizabeth May, b. January 14, 1897; m. December 11, 1924, Glen Powell, b. December 23, 1899; Gertrude May, m.

Charles H. Caudill; Ottie May, b. April 15, 1906; Rice May, b. April 23, 1909, m. Joy Litteral, November 25, 1927.

146. LEANDER PATRICK; m. Elizabeth Price.
Children:
428. Hazel Patrick.
429. Hebron Patrick.

147. SAMUEL H. PATRICK; m. Mintie Patrick; lived on Jennie's Creek near the Beach Wall Church where Mr. Patrick conducted a general merchandizing business.
Children:
430. Herschell Patrick.

148. MALINDA RICE; m. Malcolm Price.
Children:
431. Proctor Price.

149. GREENVILLE RICE; m. Jane Cunningham, daughter of Timothy and Elizabeth Spears lived on the Middle Fork of Jennie's Creek. After the death of Mr. Rice, Mrs. Rice and daughters moved to Paintsville.
Children:
432. Nora Rice.
433. Bessie Rice; m. Den Conley of Hagerhill, Kentucky.
434. Bertha Rice; m. J. F. Blair; lived at West Van Lear where Mr. Blair was a merchant.
435. Luther B. Rice.
436. Jennie Rice; m. Darwin J. Long; lived in Paintsville where Mr. Long was an automobile salesman.
437. Elizabeth Rice; employee in Paintsville post office; prominent in Paintsville society.
438. Hazel Green Rice; teacher for a time in the schools of Paintsville and was also connected with the Federal Public Utilities Company of the city; m. February 19, 1828, D. T. Blakeway, salesman, from Fort Worth, Texas.

167. AMANDA ALLEN, b. in Paintsville; m. December 24, 1897, Fred Howes, lawyer, of Paintsville. (See Howes family.)

194. J. VERNE RICE, physician; m. Edith V. Hand of Philadelphia; resided in Arkron, Ohio. Children: John Edgar Rice and Mary Elizabeth (Betty) Rice.

195. COL. HEBER HOLBROOK RICE, lawyer; b. at Paintsville, Kentucky, December 17. 1882; attended the public schools of Paintsville; B. S., cum laude, University of Kentucky, 1904; LL.B., Harvard University, 1907; LL.D., Athens College, 1944; admitted to the Kentucky State bar, 1907; West Virginia bar, 1908; Tennessee bar, 1919, District of Columbia bar, 1922 ;U. S. Court of Claims, 1923; and Supreme Court of the United States, 1928; practiced law at

Huntington, West Virginia, 1908-11; was assistant prosecuting attorney for Cabell County West Virginia, 1909-11; counsel for the Government in marital law litigation, 1914-15; attorney for Old Hickory Powder Plant, Nashville, Tennessee, 1919-21; attorney; later special assistant to U. S. Attorney General, Washington, 1921-34; also special assistant to U. S. Attorney General Washington, 1922-23; attorney for H. O. L. C., Washington, 1934-40, supervising 150,000 land law suit proceedings in all the 48 states, head attorney, ton, 1934-40, supervising 150,000 land law suit proceedings in all the 1943-44; served on the general counsel staff of the Comptroller General of the United States, Washington, from May, 1944, to retirement; served as major, U. S. Army on the Mexican border and in World War I, 1916-18; lieutenant colonel, Judge Advocate General, War Department, World War II, 1940-42; served on staff judge advocate and chief of legal division, Huntsville, Alabama, Arsenal, 1942-43; reverted to inactive status, December, 1943; promoted to colonel, inactive Reserves, 1945.

He is a member of the American Bar Association, American Law Institute, American Society of International Law, Inter-American Bar Association, Federal Bar Association, United Nations League of Lawyers; and is a member of the University of Kentucky Alumni Association, Columbia Historical Society, West Virginia Society of D. C., Judge Advocates Association, American Legion, Military Order of World Wars, Reserve Officers Association, Sigma Alpha Epilson. He is a Methodist and a Mason (Shriner) and a member of the Harvard Club. He is author of "Collected Speeches", published in 1947, "U. S. Land Law Procedural Map" and articles "Behind the Iron Curtain", etc. He has been a contributor to law journals.

On September 6, 1917, Heber Holbrook Rice was married to Ruth Straughan of West Virginia. Children: Heber H., Jr., and Craig Shelby.

Residence 3807 Taylor Street, N. W., Chevy Chase, Maryland.

196. EDGAR P. RICE, civil engineer; educated in the public schools of Paintsville and University of Kentucky; had service in World War I; lived in Huntington, West Virginia; m. Nellie Willis of Catlettsburg, Kentucky. Children: Robert Harvey and Donald Willis.

197. GARLAND HURT RICE, businessman of Paintsville; b. October 24, 1886, educated in Paintsville public schools and business college in Louisville. Early in life he became associated with his father in the insurance firm of H. B. Rice & Company, and finally became head of the firm; served as vice-president of the Second National Bank at Paintsville and president of the Paintsville-Van Lear Rotary Club; m. Mabel Auxier of Richardson County, Nebraska, who is an active member of several local civic and charitable organizations and is prominent in social affairs. Children: Mary Grace.

198. MARTIN ROBERT RICE; b. October 7, 1892; educated in the public schools of Paintsville and was graduated from University of Kentucky; served with honor in World War I as major and after the close of the war continued as instructor in rank of captain, being assigned as professor of military science, first, at Cornell University and next at Purdue University. Leaving the military service, he became connected with a public utilities company at Carrollton, Kentucky.

Mr. Rice was married to Opal Temple, daughter of C. D. Temple.

199. FRANCIS LESTER RICE; b. June 21, 1895; attended the public schools of Paintsville and University of Kentucky after which he became connected with the Consolidation Coal Company of Jenkins, Kentucky, as civil engineer. Here he met and married Miss Burnetta Redmond of Paintsville who was employed by the National Bank at Jenkins.

Residence, Pikeville, Kentucky.

RICHARDS FAMILY OF BATH, CARTER AND ELLIOTT COUNTIES

1. SILAS RICHARDS was the ancestor of a branch of the Richards family of Bath County, Kentucky, members of whom removed to Carter and Elliott counties. Very little has been learned concerning him. He migrated to Kentucky in early pioneer days and was slain by Indians.

Children:

2. ELZAPHAN RICHARDS; m. Elizabeth Hazlerigg, daughter of Joshua and Frances (Wright) Hazlerigg. According to genealogists Elzaphan Richards was first cousin to Colonel Richard M. Johnson, U. S. Senator and Vice President of the United States. Elzaphan Richards died in 1835; and in his will, probated at the September, 1835, term of the Bath County Court, he mentioned his wife without giving her christian name, his oldest daughter, Eliza Hazlerigg, and other children: Nancy Rice, James H., America, Margaret, Sarah, Amanda, Betsy, Elzaphan W., and Caroline. James Richards and John Burbridge witnessed the signing of the will and Jefferson Rice was named as executor.

Children:

3. Eliza Hazlerigg Richards; m. ——— Roe.

4. Harvey Richards; d. young.

5. Nancy Richards; m. Jefferson Rice in Bath County, April 6, 1829.

6. Margaret Ann Richards; m. John Holdman Rice in Bath County, June 29, 1839. (See Rice Family).

7. Amanda Richards; m. ——— Rice.

8. Dr. Walter Richards; m. Miss Kimbrough of Owingsville.

9. Elizabeth Richards; m. ——— Hazlerigg.

10. Caroline Richards; m. ——— Hardin.

11. Sarah Jane Richards; m. Randall Scott in Bath County, April 25, 1842.

12. America Frances Richards; m. Nelson T. Rice (See Rice Family).

13. James H. Richards; m. Eliza Shroutt in Bath County, February 27, 1838.

14. Elzaphan W. Richards.

ROBINSON FAMILY OF CARTER COUNTY
ROBINSON, ROBESON, ROBERTSON

Robinson

These surnames meaning "son of Robert" are all derived from Rob (Robin), the nickname for Robert. Other pet-forms of Robert are: Robbie, Bob, Bobbie and Bobby.

The ancient English name Robert is of Saxon origin. It signifies: "bright fame", from the old English rod ("Praise, fame") and beorht ("bright, shining").

Robinson families lived in all the American colonies in early colonial days and were numerous in the Carolinas, Maryland, Pennsylvania and Virginia. One hundred ninety-four Robinsons, Robesons and/or Robertsons had service in the Revolutionary War of which number six were James "Robinsons" and eleven James "Robertsons".[1]

According to family tradition supported by some documentary evidence, a 1. James Robinson was the ancestor of a branch of the Robinson family of Carter and Elliott Counties. He was a Virginian; served in the Revolutionary War; foretold the exact date of his death; died at the advanced age of 116 years; and m. Sally Townsley.

Children:
Second Generation
2. John Robinson.
3. James Robinson, Jr.
4. William Robinson, a lawyer and judge in Virginia.
*5. Ezekiel Robinson.
6. Sally Robinson; m. Austin Hicks. They had one child, (third generation), Hiram Hicks.
*7. Delilah Robinson.

5. EZEKIEL ROBINSON; b. in Virginia, 1775; m. in Jonesboro, Washington County, Tennessee, Sabra Castner, b. in Tennessee, 1777, daughter of Jacob Castner, a Revolutionary War soldier.[2]

Children:
Third Generation
8. Isaac Robinson; m. but name of wife not learned; no children.
*9. Jacob Robinson.
*10. James Castner Robinson.
11. Sally Robinson.

12. Betsy Robinson.
13. Polly Robinson.
14. Charity Robinson.
15. Peggy Robinson.
16. Nancy Robinson.

7. DELILAH ROBINSON; b. in Tennessee, 1800; m. Joseph Langley, farmer, b. in North Carolina, 1795. They settled in Floyd County, Kentucky; and their children living at home in 1850 and approximate dates of their birth as shown by the U. S. Census of Floyd County for that year were:

Third Generation

17. Mary Langley; b. 1832.
18. Matthew Langley; b. 1834.
19. Joseph Langley, Jr., b. 1836.

The Hon. John W. Langley of Prestonsburg and Pikeville, Congressman from the 10th Kentucky District for a number of years was a descendant of Joseph and Delilah (Robinson) Langley. (See John W. Langley in List of Members of the House of Representatives, this work.)

9. JACOB ROBINSON, farmer, b. in Virginia, 1812; m. Malinda Mullens, b. in Kentucky, 1822. They reared a large family of children.

10. JAMES CASTNER ROBINSON, or ROBERTSON, farmer; b. in Kentucky, 1824; m. in Carter County, August 17, 1853, Hettie Leadingham, b. 1820, daughter of Peter Leadingham.³

Children:

Fourth Generation

20. America Robinson; d. at the age of 5 years.
⁴21. William Ezekiel Robinson.
22. Nancy Jane Robinson; m. George Wells; no children.

21. WILLIAM EZEKIEL ROBINSON, farmer, teacher and one-time public official, was b. near Willard, Carter County, Kentucky, July 3, 1856, and d. at Grayson, Kentucky, in 1920; educated in the public schools of Carter County and attended a private school conducted by Prof. Edward Friend of Prestonsburg; began teaching in the public schools of Carter County in 1872 at the age of 16 and continued in educational work for nearly 50 years, until his death, February 20, 1920; was elected and served as Superintendent of Schools of Carter County, 1914-1918.

Mr. Robinson was a Democrat, a member of the Baptist Church and was affiliated with Willard Lodge No. 626, F. and A. M., serving as master at one time. He m., May 30, 1878, Lucy Mary Morris, b. March 15, 1860, d. in 1940, daughter of Henry Cloud Morris and his wife, Nancy Edington (Burchett) Morris. (See Morris Family.)

Children:
Fifth Generation
*23. America Edington Robinson.

24. Hattie Elizabeth Robinson, teacher, b. May 4, 1881; d. February 14, 1947; m. Andrew Jackson Alexander, 1930; no children.

*25. Nancy Eliza Robinson.

*26. James Henry Robinson.

*27. Burrell Adelbert Robinson.

28. Clara Mabel Robinson, teacher, b. March 25, 1889; d. February 28, 1945, educated in the public schools of Carter County; at Christian Normal Institute (now Kentucky Christian College) at Grayson; and at Kentucky State Teachers College at Morehead; taught in the public schools of Carter County and in Grayson Graded and High Schools for a number of years; unm.

*29. Nellie Grace Robinson.

*30. William Ezekiel Robinson, Jr.

31. Susie Helena Robinson; m. Delbert V. Kibbey. (See Kibbey Family.)

32. John Green Morris Robinson.

*33. George Frederick Robinson.

23. AMERICA EDINGTON ROBINSON, teacher; b. April 18, 1879; m. March 19, 1902, William Wellington Green, who was a traveling salesman for a number of years and served as clerk of the Elliott County (Kentucky) Court for a term.

Children:
Sixth Generation
34. Thelma Edington Green, teacher; b. at Sandy Hook, Kentucky, December 12, 1903; m. December 30, 1926, Haskell Roland Estep, presently Jailer of Boyd County, Kentucky; no children.

35. Delma Opal Green; b. at Sandy Hook, December 14, 1904; d. October 17, 1910.

36. Lucy Virginia Green; b. at Willard, Kentucky, March 8, 1907; m. February 16, 1924, T. J. Bingham; no children.

37. William Wellington Green, Jr.; b. at Willard, August 9, 1908; m., September 21, 1931, Dora Virginia Urban.

Children:
Seventh Generation
William Wellington Green III, b. December 19, 1936, **and Michael** Lewis Green, b. December 15, 1941.

38. Sally Mae Green, b. at LaLande, New Mexico, May 3, 1910, d. August 14, 1950; m. May 13, 1926, Walter Clyde Razor; no children.

39. John Paul Green; b. at Willard, January 11, 1912; m., January 3, 1933, Cora Lee Wilson.
Children:
Seventh Generation
Walter Clyde Green; b. August ——, 1933; d. at birth;
John Paul Green, Jr.; b. February 25, 1939;
Sharon Lou Green, b. January 15, 1947.
40. Oswald Meredith Green; b. in Ashland, Kentucky, November 8, 1914; m., September 12, 1937, Georgia Webb.
Children:
Seventh Generation
Nancy Sue Green, b. January 27, 1939, d. April 9, 1944.
Stephen Gregory Green, b. August 2, 1946.
Thelma Diane Green, b. September 2, 1952.
41. Susie Helen Green, b. in Ashland, November 16, 1916; m. August 8, 1937, John Berton McClanahan.
Children:
Seventh Generation
John Berton McClanahan, Jr., b. April 26, 1947;
Barbara Sue Green McClanahan, b. November 21, 1950.
42. Morris Robinson Green, b. in Ashland, November 17, 1921; m. February 4, 1945, Dorothy Childers.
Children:
Seventh Generation
Morris Robinson Green, Jr., b. May 24, 1946.
Peggy Jo Green, b. March 21, 1949, and d. October 14, 1953.
25. NANCY ELIZA ROBINSON, teacher; b. June 3, 1883; m., June 10, 1908, John Mark Hillman, farmer and teacher, b. April 15, 1877, d. January 23, 1936, son of Robert A. Hillman and his wife, Sabra Ellen (Berry) Hillman.
Children:
Sixth Generation
43. Paul Hillman; b. in Elliott County, Kentucky, June 1, 1909; m. May 7, 1933, Garnet Mae Gibson.
Children:
Seventh Generation
Joyce Elaine Hillman, b. February 24, 1934.
Dwight Emerson Hillman, b. January 18, 1936.
Judith Ann Hillman, b. October 2, 1938.
44. Lucy Hillman; b. in Elliott County, October 22, 1910; m. December 2, 1929, Jason C. Daniels.
Children:
Seventh Generation
Charles Jason Daniels, b. October 5, 1930; m. Geneva Hackworth, March ——, 1949. Their children are (Eighth Generation): Jona-

than Lee Daniels, b. August 29, 1952, and Jeffrey Wayne Daniels, b. May 9, 1950.

Betty Jane Daniels, b. September 28, 1932; m. January 13, 1950, Donald Edwin Hill. They have one child (Eighth Generation): Carl Jason Hill, b. October 30, 1950.

Phillip Gail Daniels; b. April 23, 1935.

Robert Denver Daniels; b. May 15, 1938.

45. Sabra Hillman; b. in Elliott County, October 15, 1912; m. August 12, 1933, Jason Louis Holbrook. They had seven children (seventh generation):

Loretta Ann Holbrook; b. March 6, 1935, d. April ——, 1935.

Ralph Dan Holbrook; b. August 11, 1936.

Alma Sue Holbrook; b. June 24, 1938.

Novella Holbrook; b. March 15, 1942.

Jason Lewis Holbrook, Jr., b. August 19, 1944.

William Mark Holbrook; b. August 16, 1951.

Virginia Karen Holbrook; b. February 23, 1952.

46. William Allen Hillman; b. in Elliott County, August 20, 1914; m. Helen Haflich. They have one child (seventh generation): Mary Ellen Hillman, b. June 10, 1951.

47. Robert Ezekiel Hillman; b. in Elliott County, August 31, 1916; m. May 28, 1949, Helen Frances Moore. They have one child (Seventh Generation): John Robert Hillman; b. January 29, 1951.

48. George Hillman; b. in Elliott County, March 19, 1919; m. March 15, 1950, Helen Vargo. They have one son (seventh generation): George Michael Hillman, b. December 29, 1950.

49. Eliza Pauline Hillman; b. in Elliott County, June 16, 1921; m. December 13, 1941, Edgar Lester. They have one child (seventh generation): Eliza Pauline Hillman, b. May 23, 1943.

26. JAMES HENRY ROBINSON, farmer; b. March 28, 1885; m. March 4, 1908, Myrtle Boggess, teacher, daughter of Sherman and Melissa (Sloas) Boggess.

Children:

Sixth Generation

50. Belva Robinson; b. March 18, 1910 and d. April 7, 1936; m. Ercel Barber, February 10, 1931. Children (Seventh Generation):

Lucille Barber; b. May 30, 1933;

Lorene Barber; b. March 20, 1936, and a daughter who d. in infancy.

51. Glen Robinson; b. June 2, 1912; m., June 9, 1949, Corabelle Becraft. They have one child (seventh generation): Anna Lee Robinson, b. July 31, 1950.

52. Ercel Robinson; b. at Willard, April 23, 1919; m. in England, December 12, 1945 Margery Macro. Children (seventh generation):

Lindsey Guy Robinson; b. September 2, 1948.

Desmond Phillip Robinson; b. September 1, 1949.

Amoret Browyn Robinson; b. February 23, 1952.

53. Beecher Robinson; b. at Willard, January 31, 1921; m. December 24, 1951, Lucy Mae Coburn. They have one child (seventh generation): Randall Keith Robinson; b. October 23, 1953.

54. Raymond Robinson; b. November 7, 1914; d. December 10, 1917.

27. BURRELL ADELBERT ROBINSON, traveling salesman; b. May 3, 1887, and d. August 25, 1925; m. June 30, 1907, Edna Mae Walker, b. October 10, 1886, and d. September 15, 1949.

Children:

Sixth Generation

55. Gladys Gertrude Robinson; b. March 31, 1908; m., June 18, 1922, Dennis Morton Gollihue, b. February 27, 1900. Children (seventh generation):

Elmer Burns Gollihue; b. January 17, 1924; m. September 15, 1947, Zona Bragg. Children (Eighth generation): Edna Fay Gollihue; b. October 18, 1949; Larry Frederick Gollihue; b. May 12, 1951; Charlene and Charles Gollihue, twins; b. May 2, 1952.

Evadeen Gollihue; b. November 24, 1925; m., February 1, 1947, Frederick Watson Minifee; no children.

John Burrell Gollihue; b. February 12, 1928.

Christine Gollihue; b. October 8, 1932; m. October 9, 1951; Jay D. Stewart. They have one child (eighth generation): Euthania, b. November 1, 1952.

Mary Lucy Gollihue; b. February 24, 1934.

56. BUEL ARTHUR ROBINSON; b. July 27, 1909; m., August 10, 1928, Mabel Elizabeth Wilcox, b. December 22, 1911.

Children:

Seventh Generation

William Burrell Robinson; b. August 18, 1930.
John Leslie Robinson; b. September 18, 1932.
Ronald Keith Robinson; b. July 17, 1934.
Anna Mae Robinson; b. January 31, 1936.
Lena Joy Robinson; b. October 11, 1939.
Rita Frances Robinson; b. April 28, 1941.
Harry Hudson Robinson; b. November 22, 1944.

John Leslie Robinson enlisted in the U. S. Army, January 10, 1949, at age of 16; received his basic training of ten weeks at Camp Breckinridge, Kentucky, and then was sent to Camp Lewis, Washington, for further training; left for foreign service in Korea, July 20, 1950, landing at Pusan, Korea, two weeks later when he went into combat; was captured by the Chinese, November 30, 1950, and held in prison camps for the succeeding 38 months; was among the first to be exchanged, having been released April 19, 1953. Due to his serious physical condition he remained in hospital at Tokyo for two weeks after exchange and before return to the United States. After having been returned to the United States, he was hospitalized at San Francisco, Dayton Ohio, and at Phoenixville, Pennsylvania. His sight, hearing and speech are greatly impaired, all resulting from malnutrition caused by starvation diet while he was in Chinese prison camp for 29 months.

57. BLANCHE WARD ROBINSON; b. August 12, 1911; m., March 19, 1927, Herbert A. Gollihue.

Children:

Seventh Generation

Althea Mae Gollihue; b. May 1, 1928, m. David Smith, December 20, 1951. Their daughter (eighth generation), Linda Frances Smith, was b. November 6, 1952, and a son, Donald Keith Gollihue was b. July 18, 1933.

58. David Burrell Robinson; b. June 3, 1913; m., April 12, 1931, Viola Hilton, b. March 24, 1915. Children:

Seventh Generation

Edna Lucille Robinson; b. October 26, 1931.

Galbie David Robinson; b. November 12, 1933.

59. William Ernest Robinson; b. October 3, 1915, m., February 28, 1939, Beatrice Clark, b. December 26, 1913. Children:

Seventh Generation

James Morris Robinson; b. January 9, 1941.

Jack Clark Robinson; b. July 4, 1953.

60. Clara Elizabeth Robinson; m. Ercel Kozee (See Kozee Family).

61. Helen Grace Robinson; b. March 1, 1921; m., December 31, 1952, Haskell Riffe, b. January 7, 1911. Their daughter (eighth generation), Sharon Riffe, was b. October 14, 1953.

62. Harry Greene Robinson; b. March 1, 1921; m. December 29, 1948, Evelyn Elsie Hankes, b. 1921. Their daughter (eighth generation), Helen Diana Robinson, was b. in 1950.

63. Charles Hudson Robinson; b. December 7, 1924; m. January 27, 1949, Mary Adeline Recco, b. June 25, 1927. Their son (eighth generation), Charles Dominick Robinson, was b. January 3, 1952.

64. James Frederick Robinson; b. July 3, 1927; m. August 19, 1950, Dorcas Jeannette Ratcliff, b. September 26, 1928.

30. WILLIAM EZEKIEL ROBINSON, JR., farmer, was b. April 6, 1893; m. October 25, 1911, Mary Lee Boggess, daughter of Burney and Margaret (Jackson) Boggess. They live on the W. E. Robinson homestead on the Little Fork about four miles above Willard, which has been owned and occupied by the Robinson family for several generations.

Children:

Sixth Generation

65. Burris Robinson; b. November 25, 1913; m. Evelyn Miller, 1945. Their son (seventh generation) Marlin Robinson, was b. August 28, 1947.

66. Grace Robinson; b. October 18, 1915; m., 1933, Ossie Wells. Their children (seventh generation) are:
Phillis Wells, b. September 2, 1934.
Calvin Wells, b. May 1, 1938.
Wilbur Wells, b. June 28, 1941.
Helen Wells, b. February 7, 1950.

67. Geneva Robinson; b. April 1, 1926; m., 1948, Thomas Parsons. Their son (seventh generation), Stanley Lee Parsons, was b. November 18, 1953.

68. Russell Robinson; b. March 14, 1919.

69. Ruby Robinson; b. October 21, 1932.

70. Billy Robinson; b. July 5, 1935.

71. Hattie Robinson; d. in infancy.

29. NELLIE GRACE ROBINSON, teacher, was b. near Willard, Carter County, Kentucky, July 8, 1891, and d. at Waverly, Ohio, August 1, 1944; educated in the public schools of Carter County and at the Christian Normal Institute at Grayson, Kentucky; engaged in teaching in the public schools of Carter County and of Pike County, Ohio, for a number of years; m. at Grayson, Kentucky, November 17, 1917, Elijah H. Jackson.

ELIJAH H. JACKSON, teacher, sometime merchant and public official, was b. in Elliott County, Kentucky, April 16, 1890; educated in the public schools of Elliott County, Kentucky; at Morehead (Kentucky) Normal School; Christian Normal Institute, Grayson, Kentucky, and Eastern Kentucky State Normal School, Richmond, Kentucky; taught in the public schools of Elliott and Boyd Counties, 1908-1916.

Mr. Jackson moved to Stockdale, Ohio, in 1915 and continued his education and, among other activities, engaged in teaching in the public schools. He was graduated from the Waverly (Ohio) High School and was a student at Wilmington College, Wilmington, (Ohio); was principal of the Stockdale elementary school, 1917-1920 and served as principal of the elementary schools in the central rural district, Pike County, 1935-1945; owned and operated a farm at Stockdale for several years; elected County Recorder of Pike County and removed to Waverly, the county seat, in October, 1923 and after serving two terms, operated a furniture store in Waverly for two years.

In politics Mr. Jackson is a Democrat and for several years was president of the Pike County Democratic Publishing Company which published the *Waverly Watchman*. (On January 1, 1954, a controlling interest was sold to Charles Sawyer, former Secretary of Commerce and Ambassador to Belgium, who is now president of the publishing company. Mr. Jackson is presently a director.) Mr. Jackson was appointed acting postmaster at Waverly, in October, 1945, and on March 26, 1949, was commissioned by President Truman as postmaster and is presently serving as such.

Children:

Sixth Generation

*72. Jay Greene Jackson.

*73. Opal Lorraine Jackson.

*74. William Thomas Jackson.

*75. Grace Romaine Jackson.

72. COL. JAY GREENE JACKSON, radio and television announcer and moderator, was b. at Stockdale, Pike County, Ohio, November 4, 1918; educated at Miami University, Oxford, Ohio, (1935-37) and at Ohio State University, Columbus, Ohio (1938-1940). He became engaged in radio work early in life; and was employed by WCOL Radio Station, Columbus, Ohio, 1937-1838 and by WBNS Radio Station, Columbus, Ohio, 1938-1942. He had service in the U. S. Army during World War II from 1942 to 1946, serving overseas in India and Burma as manager of Armed Forces Radio Station VU2ZV in Chabua, India, 1944-1946. Subsequent to discharge from the service and return to the United States, he was staff announcer, WOR-Mutual, New York City, 1946. Since 1947 he has been a free-lance announcer and moderator on various network radio and television programmes in New York City and currently is moderator on "Twenty Questions" program (Mutual Network—Radio; Dumont Network-Television) and announcer on Philco Television Playhouse, Omnibus and others.

On August 26, 1953, Lawrence W. Wetherby, Governor of Kentucky, commissioned Mr. Jackson a Colonel on his staff.

Colonel Jackson m., 1941, Elizabeth Ann Rodgers of Columbus, Ohio.

Children:

Seventh Generation

76. Jay Stephen Jackson, b. December 24, 1941.

77. Sally Dee Jackson, b. October 7, 1946.

Residence—3 Knolls Lane, Manhasset, Long Island, New York.

73. OPAL LORRAINE JACKSON, teacher; b. at Stockdale, Ohio, November 24, 1919; educated in the public schools of Pike County, Ohio, and was graduated from the Kentucky State Teachers' College, at Morehead with A. B. degree in 1943; teacher in the Waverly (Ohio) schools since 1939; m. Charles Cutler Brown, August 2, 1946.

Children:

Seventh Generation

78. Linda Kay Brown; b. February 3, 1949. Present address 108 E. 4th Street, Waverly, Ohio.

74. WILLIAM THOMAS JACKSON, educator; b. at Stockdale, Ohio, May 10, 1923; educated in the public schools of Waverly, Ohio, graduating from the Waverly High School in 1941; received degree of Bachelor of Science in Education from Ohio State University, 1947; Master of Science degree in Botany, University of Tennessee; 1949; Ph.D., Duke University, 1953.

Mr. Jackson had service in the U. S. Army in United States and in Europe, 1943-1946, but has devoted practically all his time to research and teaching. He taught science in the Stockdale High School, 1945-1946, while on convalescent furlough from the Army; was graduate assistant in botany at the University of Tennessee, 1947-49; staff forester for T. V. A., summer of 1949; instructor in botany at West Virginia University, 1949-50; graduate assistant in botany at Duke University, 1950-51; associate professor of botany in Clemson College, February, 1952-February, 1953; research assistant in botany at Duke University, February, 1953—September, 1953; and is presently a plant physiologist at Yale University in the Osborn Botanical Laboratory. He has specialized in plant and soil water relationships; and has prepared for publication (with Dr. Paul L. Kramer of Duke University) a paper on "Flooding of Tobacco". His current research activities are concerned with physiology of isolated roots in sterile culture.

He is a member of several fraternities and societies: Phi Kappa Phi, Phi Epsilon Phi, Biologia, American Society of Plant Physiologists, American Botanical Society, Sigma Xi, Association Southeastern Biologists.

He was m., March 10, 1949, to Muriel Corinne Shy, b. February 26, 1927, daughter of Herman and Elizabeth Moore Shy. Their daughter (seventh generation), Nancy Lynne Jackson, was b. August 10, 1950.

75. GRACE ROMAINE JACKSON, teacher; b. at Waverly, Ohio, February 14, 1929; educated in the public schools of Waverly and was graduated from Ohio State University in 1951 with degree of B. Sc. in Education; taught in the Sandusky (Ohio) public schools from September, 1951, to June, 1953; m., December 20, 1952, Cecil Eugene Knoder of Columbus, Ohio. Present address Route 5, Athens, Ohio.

32. JOHN GREENE MORRIS ROBINSON, lawyer; b. near Willard, Carter County, Kentucky, June 12, 1898; educated in the public schools of Grayson, Kentucky, graduating from the Grayson High School; student at George Washington University Law School, Wash-

ington, D. C., and was graduated from University of Louisville with degree of LL.B., 1923; admitted to the bar 1923 and began practice of law in Ashland, Kentucky, in partnership with Bunion S. Wilson; appointed by Judge Watt M. Prichard as Master Commissioner of the Boyd Circuit Court; commissioned a lieutenant commander, U. S. Navy, and had service in World War II; and after discharge from the service resumed the practice of law and duties of master commissioner at Ashland and has since continued in these activities.

Mr. Robinson is a Democrat in politics, is affiliated with the Masons and is a member of the Boyd County and the Kentucky State Bar Associations.

He m. at Grayson, May 21, 1926, Mary Lucille Williams, dec'd, daughter of Edward R. and Carmie (Cassidy) Williams.

Children:

Sixth Generation

79. Nannette Robinson; b. at Ashland, December 15, 1929; m. September 11, 1948, Eugene Prata.

Children:

Seventh Generation

80. Lucy Prata; b. July 11, 1949.

81. Michael Green Prata; b. May 30, 1951.

33. GEORGE FREDERICK ROBINSON, banker; b. near Willard, Carter County, Kentucky, June 26, 1900; educated in the Grayson (Kentucky) graded and high schools; selected president of the First National Bank of Grayson, 1940, and has since served as such; m., July 12, 1928, Miss Anna Giles, daughter of James Tandy and Ida (Webb) Giles of Webbville, Kentucky.

Children:

Sixth Generation

82. Giles Frederick Robinson; b. at Grayson, August 1, 1930; educated in the public schools of Grayson; was graduated from Millersburg (Kentucky) Military Institute, Junior School, 1944; Prichard High School at Grayson, 1948; A. B., Centre College, Danville, Kentucky, 1952; and A. M., University of Southern California, 1954.

---

1 "Virginians in the Revolution, 1775-1781", by John H. Gwathmey, The Dietz Press, Richmond, Va., 1938, pp. 670-673.

2 Jacob Castner had children other than Sabra Robinson, viz: Jacob, Jr., Isaac; Polly and Nancy.

3 "Peter Leadingham was b. in South Carolina and d. in Carter County, Kentucky, March 2, 1856, aged 65; his father ——— Leadingham (christian name not given), his mother, Eliza Leadingham". (Vital Statistics of Carter County, Kentucky, 1852-1862.)

Peter Leadingham m. Sally Hamilton and was among the first settlers of Licking Station, near present Salyersville, Kentucky. They finally settled in the Bend of the Little Fork above Willard, Carter County. Their children other than Hettie (Leadingham) Robinson were:

Jacob or "Jake", b. 1816; m. Frances Watson, b. 1821;
Jesse, b. 1824; m. Eliza ———, b. in Virginia, 1828;
William, b. 1826; m. Naomi Parsons;
Thomas, b. 1828; m. Polly (Mary) Justice, b. in Virginia, 1837;
Polly, b. 1820; m. Harvey Sturgill;
Sarah, b. 1832; unm.; and
Nancy, b. 1834; m. David Lester.

RUPERT FAMILY OF CARTER COUNTY

1. JOSEPH RUPRECHT (RUPERT) was the progenitor of the Rupert family of Northeastern Kentucky. He was of German extraction and was b. in Baden, Germany, in 1821; m. in Germany circa 1843, Mary ———, b. in Germany, 1820. Soon after marriage they emigrated to America and settled near Chillicothe, Ohio. Here he was engineer for an iron furnace for a number of years and finally migrated to Kentucky and settled on a farm near Grayson, Carter County, where he lived until his death, March 5, 1894. His wife d. November 4, 1898.

Children:

*2. John Rupert
3. Conrad Rupert; b. in Ohio, January 20, 1846.
4. George Rupert; b. in Ohio, May 1, 1848.
*5. Elizabeth Rupert; b. in Ohio, September 19, 1849.
6. Joseph Rupert; b. in Ohio, July 22, 1851.

Other children and approximate dates of birth as shown by the U. S. Census of Carter County for 1870:

7. William Rupert, b. in Ohio, 1852.
*8. Michael Rupert; b. in Ohio, 1854.
9. Christian Rupert; b. in Ohio, 1856.
10. Andrew Rupert; b. in Ohio, 1857.
*11. Margaret Rupert; b. in Ohio, 1862.
*12. Henry C. Rupert; b. in Ohio, 1864.

2. JOHN RUPERT, farmer, was b. January 1, 1844, near Chillicothe, Ohio, where he was reared and followed the business of contractor in the ore-mining industry; served in the Union Army during the Civil War in the First Ohio Heavy Artillery from which he was discharged a sergeant; m., first, Minnie Chester, b. in Germany, 1847, d. at Grayson, Kentucky, 1881, daughter of Fred Chester, Sr., a farmer, who lived and died near Chillicothe, Ohio.

Children:

*13. Joseph Rupert, Jr.
14. Emma Rupert; m. James T. Crawford, farmer, who resided near Grayson.

2-A. John Rupert moved to the vicinity of Grayson in 1875 and was identified with farming until his death, December 17, 1917.

He m., secondly Miss Carrie Botts, daughter of Judge J. R. Botts of Grayson.

Children:

15. Betty Rupert; m. Owen Stewart. Owen Stewart, farmer and teacher, was educated in the public schools of Carter County and at the Southern Normal School at Bowling Green, Kentucky; engaged

in teaching in his youth and taught for a number of years in the common and graded schools of Carter County.

16. Ottie Rupert, teacher, m. John Hubbard, Jr., d., 1920.
17. Luther Rupert, farmer.
18. Chester Rupert, farmer.
19. Jennie Rupert; m. Strother Womack. (See Womack Family).
20. Mary Rupert.

13. JOSEPH RUPERT, JR., businessman of many activities and sometime public official, was b. near Chillicothe, Ohio, 1867; educated in the public schools of Carter County, Kentucky, and at a Seminary at Ironton, Ohio, leaving school at the age of 15 and subsequently for 18 years was a clerk in his father's general store at Grayson; located at Frankfort, Kentucky, in 1900 and established a wholesale grocery business which, in 1901, was incorporated as the Rupert Grocery Company of which he was president, H. C. Rupert, vice president, and W. J. Lang, secretary and treasurer.

Mr. Rupert served as mayor of Frankfort, 1913-1917, and for four years was a member of the City Council. He was a Democrat in politics, a member of the Frankfort Chamber of Commerce, a member of the Methodist Episcopal Church, South, and was affiliated with Trimble Lodge No. 145, F. and A. M., at Grayson, serving as master for two terms, Greenup Chapter, R. A. M., Ashland Commandery No. 28, K. T., and Frankfort Lodge No. 530, of the Elks.

He was m. at Frankfort, Kentucky, in June, 1903, to Miss Frederika Weisenburg, daughter of L. B., and Frederika (Kaltenbrum) Weisenburg, of Frankfort. (History of Kentucky by Charles Kerr (Editor), 1922, Vol. V, p. 186.)

5. ELIZABETH RUPERT; b. in Ohio, September 19, 1849; m. Charles Cricher of Ironton, Ohio.

Children, among others:

21. Emma Marie Cricher; m. at Williamson, West Virginia, October 15, 1908, William Nuckles Doak.

WILLIAM NUCKLES DOAK, labor leader, was b. near Rural Retreat, Wythe County, Virginia, December 12, 1882, son of Canero Drayton and Elizabeth (Dutton) Doak, and a descendant of David Doak, who came to America from North Ireland (Ulster) about 1740 and settled at first in Chester County, Pennsylvania, subsequently removing to what is now Wythe County, Virginia, where he patented a large tract of land.

Mr. Doak was educated in the public school and was graduated from a business college. He entered employ of the Norfolk and Western Railway Company as yardman at Bluefield, West Virginia, in 1900 and was promoted to conductor and assistant yardmaster. His career as a labor leader began with his election to membership in the Brotherhood of Railroad Trainmen in 1904. Subsequently he held many high positions in the Brotherhood, among others, that of National Legislative Representative. On November 28, 1930, he was appointed by President Hoover, as Secretary of Labor and served as such until his death, October 23, 1933. Interment, temporarily, was in the Abbey Mausoleum, near Arlington Cemetery, and later in a private mausoleum in Marvin Churchyard on Reed Creek near his paternal home in Wythe County Virginia.

Mr. and Mrs. Doak purchased property at the end of Chain Bridge, the site of a Union Civil War fort, in Arlington County, Virginia, where they built their fine home, Notre Nid, "Our Nest." They had no children.

12. HENRY C. RUPERT, farmer and businessman of many activities, was b. near Chillicothe, Pike County, Ohio, in 1864; came with his father's family to Carter County, Kentucky, and lived and engaged in agricultural pursuits at Pactolus near Grayson until 1920 when he was chosen president of the citizens Bank of Grayson (now the First National Bank) when he removed to Grayson.

Aside from his agricultural activities he engaged in many business enterprises: He was one of the organizers and a stock-holder of the Rupert Wholesale Grocery Company of Frankfort and was its vice president; was one of the organizers of the Betterman-Rupert Coffee Company of Ashland and the Consolidated Grocery Company of that city.

He m., in 1888, Louella Virgin, a daughter of Lemech and Jane (Curry) Virgin, and probably a lineal (direct) descendant in the fifth generation of Captain Rezin Virgin, who had service in the Virginia Forces in the Revolutionary War.

Mr. Rupert d. in 1934 and Mrs. Rupert in 1944.

Children:

22. Irene Rupert; b. ——; d. 1948; m. Calhoun B. Wilhoit. (See Wilhoit Family.)

23. HAZEL RUPERT; m. C. E. Anglin.

Children:

24. John Clay Anglin.

25. Jane Elizabeth Anglin.

SALYER FAMILY OF JOHNSON COUNTY AND MAGOFFIN COUNTIES

The Salyer family is of French extraction and had its earliest home in the southern part of France where generations of them have lived for centuries. Authorities claim that the name goes back 2000 years, to the time of Julius Caesar, when the "Salye" tribe resisted the conqueror, holding that part of France known as Provence, despite the valor of Caesar's legions.

The history of the Salyer family in America begins with Benjamin K. Salyer, a French Huguenot who emigrated from his native land and settled in or near Charleston, South Carolina, about 1700. In the course of time he became a wealthy planter in South Carolina. He seems also to have acquired land in the colony of North Carolina, having died at Guilford Court House, that colony in 1754. There is some definite information with respect to at least two of his sons who have numerous descendants in Virginia and Kentucky and scattered throughout the southern and western states. One of these sons, Benjamin Salyer, Jr., b. in 1730, was a soldier in the Revolutionary War under General Greene and was wounded during Greene's retreat from the Dan River in Virginia. Another son, Zachariah Salyer, also had service during the Revolutionary War and was with Washington at Valley Forge during the winter of 1776-7.

The Salyer family is very numerous in Eastern Kentucky and is found mostly in Johnson and Magoffin counties.

1. BENJAMIN K. SALYER d. at Guilford Court House, North Carolina, in 1754; m. ———— ————. Children:
   *2. Benjamin Salyer, Jr.
   *3. Zachariah Salyer.
   4. John (?) Salyer.
   *5. Isaiah Salyer.

2. BENJAMIN SALYER, JR., b. 1730; m. ————. Children:
   *6. Zachariah Salyer.
   *7. William Salyer.

3. ZACHARIAH SALYER; m. ———— ————. Children:
   *8. Samuel Salyer.

5. ISAIAH SALYER, migrated from Virginia, probably Wise County, to the Big Sandy Valley, Eastern Kentucky; m. ———— McCarty (or Carter). Children:
   *9. David Jesse Salyer.
   10. Zachariah Salyer. A daughter m. Dr. Ray.
   *11. Thomas Salyer.
   12. Dicy Salyer; m. Jesse Price, Jr. (See Price Family).
   13. Tilda Salyer; m. ———— Hickman of Lawrence County, Kentucky.

14. Vina Salyer; m. ——— Berry; lived near the mouth of Rich Creek on Big Blaine.

*15. Anna Salyer.

6. ZACHARIAH SALYER lived in Virginia, probably Wise County; m. Elizabeth Dunn. Children:

*16. Benjamin Salyer.

*17. John Salyer.

7. WILLIAM SALYER, farmer and stockdealer; b. in Virginia; settled on Copper Creek, Scott County, Virginia; removed to Kentucky in 1818 and settled on the Cumberland River where he remained for several years; removed to Breathitt County, Kentucky, on the Kentucky River, and finally to Floyd County, Kentucky, where he lived until his death; m. ——— Ramey of Johnson County, Kentucky.

Children:

*18. Samuel Salyer (The Legislator).

*19. Abner Salyer.

8. SAMUEL SALYER lived in Russell County, Virginia, m. ———. Castle, daughter of Joseph Castle one of the "Long Hunters" in Kentucky, 1773, and who it is said was the founder of Castlewood, Virginia, about 1767. Children:

*20. Samuel Salyer, Jr.

9. DAVID JESSE SALYER, b. 1818 in Virginia, probably Wise County; d. in Johnson County, Kentucky, January ———, 1893; m. Mary Burton. Children:

21. "General" Salyer; d. while serving in the Army.

*22. Sophia Salyer.

*23. Lucina Salyer.

24. Zachariah Salyer; d. while serving in the Army.

*25. Malissa Salyer.

*26. Thomas Salyer.

27. Dicie Salyer, b. 1848; m. A. W. Rice.

*28. David Jesse Salyer, Jr.

*29. B. F. Salyer.

30. Mary Salyer; d. in infancy.

11. THOMAS SALYER, m. ——— ———. Children:

*31. William Salyer.

32. Samuel Salyer, lived at Pikeville, Kentucky, where he conducted insurance business.

15. ANNA SALYER, m. ——— Miller. Children:

33. Reese Miller. resided on Buffalo Creek.

16. BENJAMIN SALYER, b. in Virginia in 1798 and d. in Johnson County, Kentucky, in 1872; m. in Floyd County, Kentucky, February 15, 1821, Frances Conley, b. 1800, daughter of Thomas Conley. See Conley Family). Children:

34. Henderson Salyer, b. September 30, 1822; m. September 17, 1849.

*35. Christine Salyer.

36. Elizabeth Salyer, b. April 13, 1826; m. Benjamin Castle.

37. Margaret Salyer, b. March 13, 1828; m. Lewis Williams.

38. Rebecca Salyer, b. March 14, 1830.

39. Eliza Salyer, b. May 29, 1832; m. Edward Stapleton.

40. Naomi Salyer, b. July 3, 1837; m. Jeff. Pelphrey.

41. Samantha Salyer, b. February 12, 1843; m. Joseph Stapleton.

*42. Benjamin Henderson Salyer.

17. JOHN SALYER, lawyer, of Johnson County; held a position for a time in a governmental department at Washington, D. C.; m. Margaret Sparks. Children:

*43. Benjamin F. Salyer.

18. SAMUEL SALYER was known as "The Legislator" to distinguish him from numerous other Samuel Salyers. He was perhaps the most noted of the Salyer family. Born in Scott County, Virginia, in 1813, and was brought to Johnson County, Kentucky, when five years of age. He was State Representative from Johnson County 1859-61, and through his influence the County of Magoffin was established (1860); and Salyersville, the county seat, was named in his honor. He d. in 1890 at the age of 73. Samuel Salyer married and had issue:

*44. Samuel J. Salyer.

19. ABNER SALYER, b. 1800, d. in Johnson County 1884; m. in Floyd County, July 17, 1821, Nancy Hale. Children:

*45. Abner B. Salyer.

20. SAMUEL SALYER, JR., was b. in then Russell County, Virginia, in 1793, and d. in Wise County that state in 1911 at the age of 117 years. Probably no other Salyer ever lived so long, the span of his life touching three centuries. He had no educational advantages during his youth and grew to manhood without an education. His wife taught him to read, write and "cipher" while he was recovering from fever. He had a remarkable memory and readily recalled many incidents and stories concerning his grandfather, Zachariah Salyer, who served under Washington at Valley Forge; and he had stored up a vast fund of authentic lore concerning the various branches of the family back to Benjamin K. Salyer, the planter of South Carolina. During the last fifty years of his life he was a Justice of the Peace for Wise County. He was captain in the Mexican War, and commanded a brigade of Home Guards during the Civil War.

Samuel Salyer, Jr., m. in 1834, Lydia Culbertson of Scotch Covenanter stock, daughter of Tyree Culbertson, b. 1788, and his wife Mattie (Vicars) Culbertson. Tyree Culbertson was a son of James Culbertson and his wife Mary (Kilgore) Culbertson whose

father, Charles T. Kilgore, had service in the Revolutionary War
and was in the Battle at King's Mountain. James Culbertson was a
son of Joseph Culbertson, a Revolutionary War soldier, who was a
son of Andrew Culbertson, Jr., whose father, Andrew, Sr., was b.
in Ireland before 1700, the son of a Scotch Covenanter who fled from
Roxburyshire, Scotland, on account of religious persecution. Andrew, the immigrant, lived at Shippensburg, Pennsylvania, and was
one of the wealthiest men of that section. He m. Janet Breckenridge
of the Virginia and Kentucky families of that name. Among their
most noted descendants were the late Senator Charles A. Culbertson
of Texas and Governor Cooper of South Carolina.

Children of Samuel Salyer, Jr., and his wife Lydia (Culbertson)
Salyer:

*46. Colonel Logan H. Salyer.
*47. Tyra T. Salyer.
*48. Drusilla Salyer.

22. SOPHIA SALYER b. in Russell County, Virginia, about 1839; m.
in Johnson County, Kentucky, April 21, 1856, Parker D. Hitchcock
of Western Kentucky. Children:

49. Martha Hitchcock; m. John Selvage.
50. Mary Hitchcock; m. Daniel Ward.
51. "General" Hitchcock; m. Mary Ann Frazier.
52. Benjamin Hitchcock; m. Ella Spradlin.
53. Elizabeth Hitchcock; m. James Blair.
Martha and Mary Hitchcock were twins.

23. LUCINA SALYER, m. Dr. Nat Pickle (Picklesimer). Children:
54. Malissa Pickle; m. James Lemaster
55. Anna Pickle; m. Frank Blair.
56. William Pickle; m. ―――― Howard.
57. Delila Pickle; m. Smith Pelphrey.
58. Emma Pickle; m. Ben Pelphrey.

25. MALISSA SALYER m. Levi Van Hoose, son of John Van Hoose.
Children:
59. Mary Van Hoose; m. ―――― Reed.
60. Almira Van Hoose; m. Lee Van Hoose.
61. Emma Van Hoose; m. Henderson Smith.
62. Minerva Van Hoose; m. John Horn, son of Thomas Horn.
63. Julia Van Hoose; m. Marion Stapleton.
64. Louisa Van Hoose; m. Mack Osborn.
65. David Jesse Van Hoose; m. Hester Auxier.
66. John Van Hoose was thrice married.

26. THOMAS SALYER, b. 1846; m., first, Mollie Caudill. Children:
67. David Jesse Salyer; m. Ellen Rice.
68. Alice Salyer; m. L. F. Van Hoose.
69. John M. Salyer; m. Ida Horne.

70. A. M. Salyer; m. Cora B. Rice.
71. Julia Salyer; m. Thomas Horne, Jr.
72. Clark Salyer; d. at the age of 20.
73. Lawrence Salyer; m. Ida Blair.

26-A. Thomas Salyer, m., second, Martha E. James of Lee County, Virginia. Children:
74. Frank Salyer; m. Mary Ward.
75. Myrtie Salyer; m. Jesse ———.
76. Bertha Salyer; m. Kirk Van Hoose.
77. Willie Salyer; d. at the age of 23.
78. Virgie Salyer; m. C. Van Hoose.
79. Russell Salyer; d. at the age of 20.

28. DAVID JESSE SALYER, JR., m. Martha Spradlin, daughter of Rev. James Spradlin. Children:
80. Rhoda Ann Salyer; m. John Ward.
81. Cynthia Salyer; m. Bud Frazier.
82. Fred Salyer; d. young.
83. Garfield Salyer; d. young.
84. Greenville Salyer; m. ——— O'Brien.
85. Milton Salyer; m. Adaline Caudill.
86. Blaine Salyer; m. ——— Van Hoose.

29. B. F. SALYER; m. Sarah O'Brian. Children:
87 Lucina Salyer; m. Albert Caudill.
88. David Salyer; d. young.
89. Felty Salyer; d. young.
90. James Monroe Salyer; m. Ella Van Hoose.
91. Mary Ann Salyer; m. Dan Ely.
92. Elizabeth Salyer; m. William Sturgill.
93. Alphonso Salyer; m. Lula Blair.
94. Lon Salyer; m. ——— O'Brian.
95. Martella Salyer; m. ——— Preston.
96. Ollie Salyer; m. Henry Clark.

31. WILLIAM SALYER m. ——— ———. Children:
97. Victoria Salyer; m. James Meek. (See Meek Family).
98. Wayne Salyer.
99. Bee Salyer.

35. CHRISTINE SALYER, b. April 5, 1824; m. in Floyd County. October 28, 1841, John Williams. Children:
100. Powell Williams.

42. BENJAMIN HENDERSON SALYER, b. July 23, 1845, m. in Johnson County, February 1, 1866, Margaret Williams; resided on Barnetts Creek, Johnson County. Children.
101. Victoria Salyer; b. April 23, 1868.
102. Milton Salyer; b. May 16, 1870.
103. Elzy Salyer; b. February 4, 1872.

104. Claude Salyer; b. March 9, 1874.

105. Rose Salyer; b. June 13, 1878.

106. Francis Salyer; b. September 21, 1882.

43. BENJAMIN F. SALYER, b. in Johnson County, August 15, 1829, d. April 21, 1908; was elected and served one term as Justice of the Peace of Johnson County and was thereafter known as "Squire Ben"; resided the greater part of his married life at Flat Gap, Johnson County, and his home there was a favorite stopping place for travelers, traders and emigrants. He m., August 13, 1848, Martha Easterling, b. April 15, 1829, daughter of James Easterling of Scott County, Virginia. Children:

107. Nancy Jane Salyer; b. November 6, 1849; m. Joseph Pelphrey, son of William Pelphrey.

108. Greenville Powell Salyer; b. August 14, 1853; m. Lydia Rice, daughter of George Washington Rice.

109. James Clinton Salyer; b. August 27, 1855; m. Sarah Jane Pelphrey, daughter of William Pelphrey.

110. Jesse Franklin Salyer; b. November 2, 1858; m. Theodocia McKinnon, duaghter of James McKinnon.

*111. William Hamilton Salyer; b. July 31, 1869; m. Sarah Elizabeth Williams, daughter of Dr. H. A. Williams.

44. SAMUEL J. SALYER, b. March 18, 1865, m. ———— ————.
Children:

112. Samuel J. Salyer.

45. ABNER B. SALYER; b. 1840 and d. 1901; m. Sarah Arnett, b. 1838 and d. 1883. Children:

*113. Benjamin F. Salyer.

46. COLONEL LOGAN H. SALYER, noted laywer and judge, was b. in Virginia in 1830, and d. at Whitesburg, Letcher County, Kentucky, in 1916 at the age of 86. He had service in the Confederate Army in the Civil War serving under Generals Lee and Jackson, and was with Gen. Lee at Gettysburg. He lived the latter part of his life at Whitesburg where he was a noted lawyer. He was judge of the United States District Court for the Eastern District of Kentucky, which position he was holding at the time of his death.

47. TYRA T. SALYER was a lieutenant in the Confederate Army during the Civil War, and was a minister of the Methodist Church in North Carolina for many years. Tyra T. Salyer m. ———— ————. Children:

114. Nattie Salyer; m. ———— Taylor.

48. DRUSILLA SALYER; b. in Virginia in 1842 and d. in 1921; m. Henry Frazier, son of James Frazier of Scott County, Virginia, who m. a Miss Hogg of Scott County. Henry Frazier d. in 1872 leaving his widow, Drusilla, and four small children. It is said that Mrs. Frazier not only reared the children properly but accumulated an estate of $100,000 in Wise County, Virginia.

Children:

*115. Martha Frazier.

*116. Henry Tyra Frazier.

111. WILLIAM HAMILTON SALYER, b. July 31, 1869, d. ———
———. He was a typical representative of the Salyer family and was devoted to the interests of his home city, Paintsville. For years he was a member of the School Board of Paintsville, serving as Chairman of the Board part of the time. He was Chief Accountant for the North-East Coal Company at Paintsville. He m. Sarah Elizabeth Williams, daughter of Dr. H. A. Williams. Children:

117. Mary May Salyer; teacher in the City Schools of Ashland, Kentucky.

118. Katharyn Salyer was employed in the office of the Sandy Valley Grocery Company before her marriage. She m. Harrison Wheeler, President and General Manager of that company. They had a son, Harrison Wheeler, Jr.

113. BENJAMIN F. SALYER, b. 1862, d. 1906; m. Mary E. Brooks; removed to Navasota, Texas. Children:

119. Edith B. Salyer.

115. MARTHA FRAZIER, b. 1869; m. David F. Beverly, son of John F. Beverly and his wife, Pheobe Jane Huff, daughter of Charles Huff and his wife, Polly Dotson, daughter of Thomas William Huff and his wife, a Miss Josephs. John F. Beverly was a son of Freeman Beverly and his wife, Polly Ramsey, a daughter of Joel Ramsey, a Revolutionary War soldier, and his wife, Polly Belcher. Freeman Beverly was a son of Elijah Beverly whose daughter Abigail married Jacob Butcher. Elijah Beverly was a weaver by trade and died at Castlewood, Russell County, Virginia, about 1835. He was living in Pike County, Kentucky, in 1814. It is said that his father, Robert Beverly, with brothers John and Elijah, fled from the Highlands of Scotland after the last uprising and final defeat of the clans in 1745. It is believed that all three of the first Beverly brothers were soldiers in the American Revolution. Children of Martha Frazier and David F. Beverly:

*120. Walter F. Beverly.

116. HENRY TYRA FRAZIER, a prosperous farmer in Lee County, Virginia; m. Emma Collier. Children:

121. Clark Frazier, teacher of agriculture in the high schools of Cumberland County, Virginia.

120. WALTER F. BEVERLY, a professional genealogist of Richmond, Virginia, was b. at Dorchester, Wise County, Virginia, September 29, 1889; m. in 1915, Martha Belle Pearce. Children:

122. Morgan Beverly; b. 1917.

123. W. F. Beverly, Jr., b. 1919.

124. Martha Belle Beverly; b. 1921.

125. Paul Baldwin Beverly; b. 1925.

SEATON FAMILY OF GREENUP COUNTY

Tradition and history declare that the Seaton or Seton family originated in Scotland. However, the family lived in England in early days as is evidenced by public records which bear the names, among others, of Richard de Seton, County Devon, 1273; Elena de Seton, County Devon, 1273; John de Seton, County Cumberland; John de Seton, Northumberland; Johannes de Sayton, Marchant, 1379.

Seaton is a place name—'Local of Seaton', parishes and townships in counties Cumberland, Devon, Durham, Rutland, York and Northumberland.

"Jon" Seaton probably was the first of the name to come to America. He apparently was a son of Sir David Seton of Parbroath and came from London to Virginia, August 7, 1635, on the ship Globe when he was 19 years of age.

The family was represented in New England by three brothers: James Seaton of Amherst, New Hampshire, came in 1727; John Seaton; and Andrew Seaton who came in 1740.

1. JOHN SEATON I was b. in Scotland and went from there to Ireland where he had lived for about 15 years when he came to America. He finally settled and lived at Amherst, New Hampshire. He m. Jane Edwards in Scotland and they were the American ancestors of the Seaton family of Northeastern Kentucky.

Issue:

2. Mary Seaton who m. John Mann.
3. James Seaton who m. Elizabeth Robinson.
*4. John Seaton II
5. Martha Seaton.
6. Samuel Seaton.
7. Elizabeth Seaton.
8. Jane Seaton.

4. JOHN SEATON II was b. in Ireland about 1724; m. October, 1744, his cousin, Ismenia Seaton, daughter of Samuel Seaton. He was deacon in the Congregational Church at Amherst when he m. and continued in that capacity until 1783. He d. in 1793.

Issue:

9. Elizabeth Seaton; m. Richard Godman.
10. Jane Seaton; m. Samuel Stanley.

11. Andrew Seaton.
12. Mary Seaton; m. Peter Robinson.
13. Margaret Seaton; m. Timothy Hortshorn.
14. Martha Seaton; m. Jesse Stephens.
*15. John Seaton III.
16. Ann Seaton.

15. DEACON JOHN SEATON III, b. at Amherst, New Hampshire, April 8, 1756; m. April 28, 1787, Rebecca Kendall, daughter of Nathaniel Kendall and Rebecca (Converse) Kendall. He became deacon in the Congregational Church at Amherst, 1795, and continued as such until his death in 1836, when he was over 80 years of age.
Issue:
*17. John Seaton IV.
*18. Nathaniel Kendall Seaton.
*19. Samuel Seaton.
*20. Ambrose Seaton.

17. JOHN SEATON IV was b. at Amherst, November 2, 1791. After a course in school he studied law with the intention of practicing. However, he and his family considered it a greater honor to be a deacon in the church—to follow in the footsteps of his father and grandfather. He d. in early manhood, on August 5, 1831.

18. NATHANIEL KENDALL SEATON, b. October 24, 1794; m. Nancy D. Richardson. He was an officer or employee in the Boston Custom House for about 12 years during the administrations of Jackson and Van Buren. In 1843 he removed to Greenup County, Kentucky, where his brother Samuel had settled. He engaged in merchandising here until his death, March 11, 1859, and was buried in the Seaton burying ground at Greenup. His widow went to Illinois but her remains were brought back to Greenup and buried beside her husband.

19. SAMUEL SEATON, farmer, teacher, lawyer, merchant, trader, legislator and iron master, was the immediate progenitor of all the Seatons of Northeastern Kentucky. He was b. at Amherst, New Hampshire, July 3, 1796. He was a student, devoting considerable time in preparing himself for teaching school and for practice of law —teaching as a stepping stone to the legal profession. He learned the printer's trade and also learned how to make hand-cards for carding wool and cotton. At about the age of 19, taking with him a testimonial from persons of importance in Amherst as to his good character, being a gentleman and scholar and of good mind, he began the trek Westward seeking his fortune. He stopped at Harrisburg, Pennsylvania, for a time where he taught school; from there he went to Ohio where he again engaged in teaching in Meigs and Athens counties. Later he went to Greenupsburg, Greenup County, Kentucky, where he continued teaching, organizing in that town Seaton

Academy, the first of such educational institutions in that section. In Greenupsburg some of Jesse B. Boone's children were his pupils and he lived for a time in the Daniel Boone old cabin. While engaged in teaching he commenced reading law under the instruction and in the office of the distinguished lawyer, John M. McConnell, of Greenupsburg; and about 1818 he went to Portsmouth, Ohio, where he continued his legal studies under a Mr. Clough, an attorney of that city. Subsequently he was admitted to the bar and practiced at Piketon, Ohio. 1819-1820; and in Meigs County, that state, for a time; and finally he returned to Greenupsburg where he practiced for a time after which he engaged in merchandising at Greenupsburg.

In the autumn of 1826, he, with his family, consisting then of his wife and two children, John and Rebecca, began a trip to New Orleans on a flat boat loaded with produce for sale along the route. The passage down the river to New Orleans was not without many dangerous and hazardous incidents, one of which was Mr. Seaton was thrown overboard and, being encumbered with his clothing and a large money belt he barely escaped from drowning.

From New Orleans the party sailed to Boston and from thence to Amherst for a visit to the old home.

Samuel Seaton and his family returned to Greenupsburg in 1827, when he entered upon his career as a merchant which he successfully managed until his death. As has probably been observed, he was engaged in many enterprises: In 1847 he constructed at a cost of $5,000 a large stone dam 12 feet high across the Little Sandy River at the falls one mile from the Ohio, and a large mill. In the same year (1847) he began the construction of a large charcoal iron furnace twelve miles westerly from Greenup on a tract of 20,626 acres—the Thomas Keith patent. The furnace was completed in 1849 at a cost of $50,000 and was named the New Hampshire, after his native state. At about the time the furnace began producing pig iron, he died of "lung fever" (pneumonia?) March 29, 1850, and was buried there by a small stream called "Undine" by his wife. Subsequently his remains were removed to the Seaton family burying ground at Greenup. He was universally regarded as a "friend of the poor' and an honest man.

During his very busy business career Samuel Seaton was interested in other activities, particularly in public affairs. In politics he was a Whig of the Clay-Webster faction. He represented Greenup County in the Lower House of the Kentucky Legislature in 1832, 1833 and again in 1845, 1847; and is the author of the Seaton Act, 1847, which secured to married women certain property inherited by or bequeathed to them separate from their husbands.

SAMUEL SEATON m. in then Washington County, North West Territory, August 22, 1822, Hannah Eddy, daughter of Nathaniel Eddy and his wife, Hannah (Shepardson) Eddy.

Issue:

*21. John Seaton.
*22. Rebecca Seaton.
23. Emily Seaton, b. May 7, 1829, and d. August 10, 1831.
24. Emma Seaton, b. November 1, 1831, and d. October 2, 1832.
*25. Samuel Seaton II
*26. Mary Peak Seaton.

20. AMBROSE SEATON, physician, was b. at Amherst, September 27, 1804, and d. at Maysville, Kentucky, April 9, 1866; graduated from college in 1825, and was Town Clerk, at Amherst in 1829; was a fine musician but chose medicine as his profession. He practiced medicine at Amherst, Boston and Maysville, Kentucky; m. in Amherst, November 12, 1828, Mary Rand Goss, b. March 25, 1804, and d. at Maysville, July 4, 1863.

Children:

27. Helen Augusta Seaton, b. in Boston, grew up in Maysville and came to greenup to teach school in 1857 where she met and m. Dr. Alfred DeBard in 1859.

28. Mary Elizabeth Seaton came to Greenup to live with her sister's family, Dr. and Mrs. DeBard. She was an accomplished musician and owned the first piano in Greenup. She taught the Spaulding and DeBard children.

21. JOHN SEATON, accountant, merchant, and sometimes public official, was b. in the Boone house near Greenup, July 25, 1823; was educated principally at home and in the local schools and attended the Boston and the Hingham (Massachusetts) schools, 1836-39. His early life was spent as salesman and bookkeeper in his father's store at Greenup. On election day, November 7, 1844, after having voted for Clay for president, he mounted his horse and rode to Grayson, Carter County, Kentucky, where he opened his stock of goods, previously shipped there, and began the business of merchandising. Subsequently he returned to Greenup and on Thanksgiving Day, Thursday, November 20, 1845, he m. Mary Elizabeth Rice, b. in Greenup County, October 26, 1825, daughter of John and Elizabeth Rice. The ceremony was performed at the home of William Biggs, the bride's uncle. After having been in business at Grayson for exactly five years, in the Autumn of 1849, he went to the New Hampshire Furnace in Greenup County, where he assisted in conducting the store and the office until his father's death. In July, 1850, he removed to Greenup where eight of his children were born.

Aside from his business activities, John Seaton was interested and active in public affairs, particularly in politics. He was a Whig and, after its organization, a Republican. He was a strong Union man and was elected county judge of Greenup County in 1862 on that ticket. Previously he had served as deputy County Court Clerk for some time; and was master commissioner of the Greenup Circuit

Court. He was a licensed attorney but did not actively engage in the practice of law.

Children of John Seaton and his wife, Mary Elizabeth (Rice) Seaton:

*29. Hannah Elizabeth Seaton.

30. Anna Seaton, b. at Grayson, February 16, 1849, and d. at Greenup, September 24, 1852.

31. Rebecca Seaton; b. 1849; d. 1852.

32. John Seaton, b. January 13, 1854, and d. August 10, 1854.

*33. William Biggs Seaton.

34. Nathaniel Eddy Seaton, b. October 11, 1857, and d. a month later.

35. Edward Eddy Seaton.

36. Mary (Mollie) Seaton, b. July 15, 1862; lived at Greenup; unm.

37. Dora Peck Seaton; lives on the home farm but not in the original house which burned some years ago. She is at an advanced age.

*38. Samuel Seaton III.

22. REBECCA SEATON was b. near Marietta, Ohio, March 2, 1826, and d. September 6, 1896 in the home of her son, Dr. Alfred Spaulding in New York City. She was educated in the schools of Greenup County, Kentucky, and at Bishop Smith's school at Kalorama, near Louisville, Kentucky. She m., in Greenup County, May 14, 1846, Dr. Alfred Spaulding, who was b. at Amherst, New Hampshire, in 1815, a son of Dr. Matthias Spaulding. After graduating from Yale, he completed courses in medicine at Dartmouth in New Hampshire and at the Medical College in Cincinnati. While a student in Cincinnati he visited the Seaton family at Greenupsburg and after receiving his M. D. degree he established himself, in 1843, at Greenup for practice of his profession and practiced there and in that locale for 34 years. He d. in 1878. Members of the family removed to and lived in New York City. Children:

39. George Atherton Spaulding, b. January 14, 1849; m. his cousin, Rebecca Davis, of Amherst, New Hampshire, September 4, 1878; resided and practiced medicine in New York City. Children:

38. Honora Spaulding, b. July 25, 1881, and 39. Mary Seaton Spaulding, b. July 8, 1883, and d. February 24, 1897.

40. Hannah Eddy Spaulding, b. November 2, 1853, and d. July 28, 1854.

41. Alfred Matthias Spaulding, physician; resided and practiced medicine in New York City.

42. Helen Hookaday Spaulding, b. October 30, 1860.

43. Rebecca Wentworth Spaulding, b. September 15, 1863; resided in New York City and afterwards in Asheville, North Carolina; author of many books about the pioneers and early happenings of

Greenup County, Kentucky, one of which, "Buttercups and a Silver Snuff Box", relates the journey of her grandfather, Samuel Seaton and family, down the Ohio River to New Orleans.

25. SAMUEL SEATON II was b. at Greenup, July 7, 1833. He was educated at home and at Marietta College, Marietta, Ohio, 1847-1849. In 1855 he went West to Comal County, Texas, to home of George Wilkins Kendall, his father's cousin who had established and was then editor and part owner of the New Orleans Picayune. After a short visit here he went to his uncle Nathaniel Eddy's home at Fort Worth, Texas. He engaged in teaching at Fort Worth and Dallas for several years and during this period he m. Lizzie Addington of Fort Worth. There were no children of this marriage.

Samuel Seaton II was a staunch Union man and when the Civil War broke out he returned to Greenup, Kentucky, where he remained teaching, clerking in store, etc., until the close of the war. In 1865 he was appointed postmaster at Dallas, Texas, by then Postmaster General William Dennison, ex-Governor of Texas. At the close of his term he went to Fort Worth where he purchased a farm and erected some business buildings.

He m., secondly, Jennie Pollard Johnson and they had one child; 44. Samuel Seaton, Jr., druggist, of Fort Worth.

He m., thirdly, November 10, 1886, Miss Lavora Patton of Senatobia, Mississippi. They went to Alabama and lived for a time at Decatur, at Anniston and at Mobile. Finally they returned to and resided at Fort Worth.[1]

26. MARY PECK SEATON; b. at Greenup, March 26, 1836; m. John Means, son of Thomas Williamson Means and Sarah (Ellison) Means and grandson of Colonel John Means who migrated from Spartanburg South Carolina, to Adams County, Ohio, in 1819, was b. at West Union, Adams County, Ohio, September 21, 1829. Settling in Greenup County, Kentucky, in early manhood, he soon entered upon a successful business career in the fields of manufacturing, mining, transportation and banking. In 1851 he took the position of book-keeper and manager of the Buena Vista Furnace; was one of the organizers in 1856 of the Portsmouth, Big Sandy & Pomeroy Packet Company, known as the White Collar Line; a director in 1856, of the Kentucky Iron, Coal & Manufacturing Company; one of the founders of the Bank of Ashland; one of the Organizers of the Lexington and Big Sandy Railway Company, later the Ashland Coal & Iron Railway Company; and a director and Treasurer of the Norton Iron Works.

He was trustee and councilman of Ashland for 30 years. He moved to Catlettsburg in 1855 and to Ashland in 1857 where he lived until his death.

John Means m., first, Harriet Perkins of Marietta, Ohio, and they had Thomas Hildreth, Harold, Ellison Cooke, Elizabeth Seaton, Lillian Maynard and Rosalie Ballard.

29. HANNAH ELIZABETH SEATON; b. at Grayson, Kentucky, August 7, 1847, and d. June 15, 1936; m., February 15, 1866, Jerome Bonaparte Secrest in her mother's home near Greenupsburg. Mr. Secrest was b. in Lewis County, Kentucky, September 28, 1843, a son of William Bogges Secrest, (b. in Virginia, November 23, 1804, and d. April 14, 1860) and his wife Katherine (Ingram) Secrest, (b. in Virginia, November 13, 1809, and d. September 21, 1881, at Concord, Kentucky) and a grandson of Hon. Joseph S. Secrest, (b. in Virginia, April 8, 1780, and d. at Flemingsburg, Kentucky, May 4, 1859) and Sarah Ann (Mershon) Secrest, (b. in Virginia, October, 1786, and d. October, 1830). Hon. Joseph S. Secrest was a prominent planter in Virginia and had service in the War of 1812 under General Nelson.

Jerome B. Secrest was an educator. He was educated, principally, at Flemingsburg (Kentucky) College and at National Normal University, Lebanon, Ohio, graduating from the latter institution. In early manhood he engaged in merchandising at Concord, Kentucky, for about six months when he entered upon a career as an educator which he successfully followed until his death in January, 1916. From Concord he went to Willard, Carter County, Kentucky, and taught the public school there; thence he went to Grayson, county seat of Carter County, and took charge of the public schools there. Leaving Eastern Kentucky, he went to the bluegrass section where he taught and organized academies and normal schools until his death. He was principal of the Henry Clay County School at New Castle; principal of the Normal College at Eminence; and in 1886 he organized and opened a Normal School at Pleasureville, Henry County, with an attendance of only three students which number increased to 110 the second year, with five instructors. This was considered to be one of the best schools of its class in the State. In addition to the usual English branches taught in such schools, courses in business— typewriting, telegraphy, etc., were taught. Finally he organized and conducted the Waddy Normal School for teachers at Waddy, Shelby County. He was also an instructor of teacher's institutes.

Professor Secrest was a scholar of considerable literary attainments; of pleasing and attractive personality; and exerted a powerful influence over his students. In politics he was a Democrat, a member of the Christian Church and affiliated with the Masonic fraternity.

Children:

45. Lyda Secrest; b. at Concord, Kentucky, January 23, 1868, and d. April 4, 1873.

*46. John Seaton Secrest.

47. Mary Seaton Secrest, b. at Concord, Kentucky, March 4, 1872, and d. June 22, 1873.

48. George Rice Secrest; b. at Greenup, Kentucky, April 7, 1874, and d. at Louisville, August 8, 1943; was representative of the Belknap Hardware Company of Louisville for many years; m. Elsie Paxton of Shelby County.

49. William Arthur Secrest; b. at Willard, Kentucky, October 5, 1878; m. Lillian Burton of Willisburg, Kentucky, daughter of Capt. John Burton; reside at Shelbyville, Kentucky.

50. Anna Secrest; b. January 10, 1882, and d. January 23, 1882.

51. Rebecca Secrest; b. at Grayson, Kentucky, April 16, 1883; m. William Smith Hackworth, lawyer, of Shelby County, Kentucky; reside at Shelbyville, Kentucky.

52. Sarah Secrest; b. at Eminence, Kentucky, August 18, 1886 and d. at LaGrange, Kentucky, April 4, 1909; m. Kirke Muse of Shelbyville, Tennessee, a U. S. railway mail clerk.[2]

33. WILLIAM BIGGS SEATON, businessman, was b. July 18, 1855, in his grandmother Hanna Eddy Seaton's home. He was well educated principally in the public schools. In March, 1872, he accepted a position as storekeeper, later becoming furnace clerk and assistant manager of Bellefonte Iron Furnace operated by Means, Russell and Means afterward incorporated as Means-Russell and Means. In 1882 he accepted position as manager of the Mount Savage Iron Furnace for Joseph S. Woolfolk, continuing for 2 or 3 years. Subsequently he went South with view of establishing car wheel works at Birmingham. Afterwards he turned his attention to banking and with Charles P. Mead and others organized the Charleston (West Virginia) National Bank in September, 1884, of which he became teller and later cashier. Returning to Ashland in 1886 he became bookkeeper and cashier of the Ashland Coal and Iron Railway Company; and at the end of the year he became manager of the Bellefonte Iron Furnce and continued as such as long as it was in operation. He was president and general manager of Russell & Means Iron Company after the death of the president. John Russell; was one of the organizers of the Citizens Telephone Company of Ashland and the Lawrence Telephone Company of Ironton, Ohio, and was president of both; was secretary and general manager of Kentucky Iron, Coal and Manufacturing Company; and a director of the A. C. & I. Railway Company.

WILLIAM BIGGS SEATON m., September 17, 1885, Miss Eliza Isabella Means, b. August 8, 1855, daughter of John and Mary Peck (Seaton) Means.

Children:

53. Harriet Hildreth Means Seaton; b. at Charleston, West Virginia, June 18, 1886; educated at Andover College; m. Mr. Peebles.

54. Isabella Seaton; b. at Bellefonte, Boyd County, May 17, 1888; educated at Andover College; m. Mr. Humphreys.

55. John Means Seaton; b. at Bellefonte, April 15, 1891; educated at Yale.

56. Kendall Seaton; b. at Bellefonte; February 26, 1893; educated at Yale; m. Grace Mary Watson. Children: Mrs. Mary Isabel Holt, who resided at Versailles, Kentucky; and Mrs. Mary Raines, who resided in Chicago.

57. Edward Everett Seaton; b. at Ashland, April 26, 1894; educated at Yale; m. Rebecca Todd of New York; resided in Ashland.

William Biggs Seaton was a Republican in politics and was a consistent member of the Christian Church.

38. Samuel Seaton III, businessman, was b. at Greenup, Kentucky, November 21, 1867, and d. May 15, 1927. For thirty five years he was connected with the Ashland Iron and Mining Company, serving that company in many and various capacities during which time he resided at Rush, Boyd County, Kentucky. After the Ashland Iron and Mining Company sold its interests to the American Rolling Mill Company he went with that company as superintendent of the Rush mines in which capacity he was serving at the time of his death.

At Rush on October 7, 1898, Samuel Seaton was m. to Miss Della Mae McNeal, b. June 23, 1882, and d. September 28, 1952.

Children:
*58. Vernon Seaton.
*59. Gwendolin Seaton.
*60. Margaret Elizabeth Seaton.
*61. Mary Rice Seaton.

58. VERNON SEATON; b. at Rush, Boyd County, Kentucky, December 8, 1899; educated in the Ashland (Kentucky) public schools and at Tennessee Military Institute at Sweetwater; was elected as a Republican and served as State Representative from Boyd County, 1944-45; was connected with the American Rolling Mill Company Ashland, Kentucky, as head of the real estate department for 17 years when he resigned to become a private coal operator in Boyd County; m., May 25, 1935, Virginia Sue Wright, who was b. in Pine Bluff, Arkansas, December 31, 1910. Children: Vernon Wright Seaton, b. at Ashland, April 6, 1936; James Langford Seaton, b. at Ashland, September 10, 1939; and Samuel Kendall Seaton, b. at Ashland, October 14, 1945.

59. GWENDOLYN SEATON; b. at Rush, October 2, 1903; educated in public schools of Ashland; at Mary Baldwin College, Staunton, Virginia; and at Ward Belmont College, Nashville, Tennessee; m. at Jeffersonville, Indiana, April 23, 1938, William Winston McGuire, b. July 25, 1891. Mr. McGuire had service in World War I in the American Expeditionary Forces under General Pershing. He is presently connected with the Chesapeake & Ohio Railway Company,

as engineer. Children: Edward Winston McGuire, b. at Ashland, February 14, 1939, and David Seaton McGuire, b. at Ashland, December 21, 1940.

60. MARGARET ELIZABETH SEATON; b. at Rush, November 5, 1905; educated in the Ashland public schools and at Berran College for Women, Gainesville, Georgia; m. at Ashland, October 6, 1933, Francis Tillman Watson, b. July 4, 1906, and d. July 17, 1950. Mr. Watson was the owner of the White Swan Laundry at Ashland. Children: Samuel Seaton Watson, b. at Ashland, April 22, 1934, and Robert Burgraff Watson, b. at Ashland, July 21, 1940.

61. MARY RICE SEATON; b. at Rush, November 25, 1921; educated in the Ashland public schools and at Ward Belmont College, Nashville, Tennessee; m. at Ashland, November 1, 1947, John Wallace Taylor. Mr. Taylor was b. July 24, 1916; had service in World War II in Europe as captain, 13th Armored Division and was recalled to active duty during the Korean War and served in the Office of the Assistant of Chief of Staff, Washington, D. C. Captain Taylor is presently a real estate broker in Huntington, West Virginia, and he and his family reside at 1659 Glenway Lane, that city. Children: Twins, John Seaton Wallace, and Thomas Wallace, b. in Washington, D. C., May 11, 1951.[3]

46. JOHN SEATON SECREST; b. at Concord, Lewis County, Kentucky, November 13, 1869; educated in the public schools of Carter County, Kentucky, and at Pleasureville (Kentucky) Normal School, graduating from the latter in 1892. Soon after graduation he located at Ashland, Kentucky, and became bookkeeper at Bellefonte Furnace for Means & Russell Iron Company. In 1895 he accepted a similar position with the Ashland Coal and Iron Railway Company, at Rush, Kentucky, and continued in that position for the succeeding 17 years. Returning to Ashland, he was bookkeeper for the Ohio Valley Mill & Supply Company of that city for eight years. In 1920 he went into business for himself, organizing a dairy business at Summit, Boyd County, which he successfully conducted until the Fall of 1925 when he was elected clerk of the Boyd County Court. After the expiration of his term as clerk, he returned to Summit where he conducted a poultry farm. He d. in 1934. He was a Republican in politics and was a member of the I. O. O. F. and Jr. O. U. A. M. fraternities.

On February 18, 1897, John Seaton Secrest was m. to Miss Emma Arnold, daughter of John and Catherine (Johnson) Arnold of Ashland.

Children:

62. Mary Elizabeth Secrest; b. at Rush, Kentucky, June 24, 1901; attended Marshall College, Huntington, West Virginia, University of Cincinnati where she was a member of Phi Mu Sorority, and Uni-

versity of Miami, Coral Gables, Florida; m., April 12, 1925, John Molsberger of Ashland, b. October 21, 1900, who has had a position with Ben Williamson Hardward Company of Ashland since October 1, 1924.

Children: Helyn Molsberger, b. May 8, 1926, assistant director of publicity for A. C. Neilson & Company, New York City, and John Molsberger, musician, b. December 11, 1927; graduated June 9, 1953, from Sherwood School of Music, Chicago, Illinois, with Bachelor Degree in Music (violin); played with Huntington Symphony, 1947-49, and with Sherwood Symphony, 1949-53; composer of invention for flute, violin and viola, a song using one of Shelley's poems and a sonata for piano.[2]

Lyda Secrest, Federal employee, daughter of William Arthur and Lillian (Burton) Secrest (See No. 49) was b. at Waddy, Kentucky, January 14, 1912; educated in the public schools of Estill County, Kentucky; entered the U. S. Government service in Washington, D. C., December, 1937, and is presently Librarian of Claims Division of the General Accounting Office; m. at New Albany, Indiana, November 2, 1935, H. H. Morris. Mr. Morris, a son of Joseph W. Morris, lately a member of the U. S. House of Representatives from Kentucky, and Mildred Morris, was b. at Carrollton, Kentucky, September 23, 1911; educated in the public schools of Carrollton and was graduated from the National University Law School, Washington, D. C.; became Secretary, January, 1932, to Virgil Chapman, U. S. Representative from Kentucky and continued in that capacity while Mr. Chapman served as U. S. Senator from Kentucky and until his death in 1949 when he was appointed Administrative Assistant to the Clerk of the House of Representatives in which position he served for the succeeding two years when he became Secretary to Thomas R. Underwood, U. S. Senator from Kentucky, serving until the expiration of his term when he became Secretary to John C. Watts, U. S. Representative from Kentucky, in which capacity he is presently serving.

1. JAMES SEATON, bookkeeper or accountant; b. at Medina, Ohio, December 13, 1834, and d. near Grayson, Carter County, Kentucky, March 16, 1916. He was a cousin (three times removed) of John Seaton III of Greenupsburg, Kentucky. (See No. 4), being a son of Reed Page Seaton (b. at Charlestown, Massachusetts, July 25, 1805, and d. at Medina, Ohio, July 13, 1877) and his wife, Frances Henrietta (Abbott) Seaton, a grandson of Andrew Seaton (b. November 4, 1762) and his wife Polly (Mary) Bowers (See No. 11), and a great grandson of John Seaton II and his wife Ismenia Seaton (See No. 4).

James Seaton removed from Ohio to Carter County, Kentucky and for many years was connected with various Iron Furnaces in Carter County, principally as bookkeeper. He served in the Union

Army in the Civil War as Adjustant on the staff of Colonel John Mason Brown of the 45th Regiment Kentucky Volunteers Mounted Infantry.

James Seaton m. Mary A. Womack, b. January 22, 1838, and d. August 25, 1937, a daughter of James A. and Susan Anne Womack (See Womack Family).

Children:

2. Mary F. Seaton; b. at Catlettsburg, Kentucky, December 12, 1866, and d. September 23, 1951; m. Warren B. Meeks at Covington, Kentucky, June 16, 1904.

3. Paul Seaton, an employee of C. & O. Railway Company, b. at Catlettsburg, October 16, 1867; d. June 15, 1939; unm.

4. Helen Seaton, teacher; b. at Star Furnace, Kentucky, October 5, 1870, and d. March 26, 1949; m. Robert F. White at Lexington, Kentucky, 1901.

5. Annie Seaton; b. at Star Furnace, December 21, 1872, and d. February 26, 1935; m. T. F. Rice at Evermans Creek near Grayson, Kentucky, October 28, 1891.

6. Lucy Seaton, teacher; b. at Coalton, Kentucky, October 13, 1875, and d. June 15, 1950; m. Rev. L. O. O'Nan at Pine Hill Church near Grayson, 1897.

7. Reed Seaton; b. at Rush, October 8, 1877; was an employee of the C. & O. Railway Company, at Winchester, Kentucky, for several years; m. Lula Crawford, 1905.

8. Kennie Seaton; b. at Rush, May 28, 1880; m. Ed. Rupert at Everman's Creek near Grayson, June 8, 1904. Mr. Rupert, a farmer and merchant, is a son of William Rupert (See Rupert Family). He was reared on his father's farm near Grayson which farm he afterwards acquired and operated for some time. After retiring from farming, he moved to Grayson where he operated a general store.

9. Emma Seaton; b. on Straight Creek, Carter County, Kentucky, August 15, 1884; m. William D. Jones at Lindsay Chapel, near Grayson, November 22, 1903. Mr. Jones is a son of Thomas D. Jones. (See Hord Family.)[4]

---

1 "The Seaton Family", by Oren Andrew Seaton, Editor, Topeka, Kansas, Crane and Company, 1906.

2 The Descendants of Hon. Joseph Secrest and His Wife, Sarah Ann (Mershon) Secrest (Manuscript), prepared by Rebecca (Secrest) Hackworth (Mrs. William Smith Hackworth), Shelbyville, Kentucky, 1953.

3 Samuel Seaton III and His Descendants (Manuscript) prepared by Mary Rice (Seaton) Taylor (Mrs. John W. Taylor), Huntington, West Virginia, 1954.

4 The Children of James Seaton and His Wife, Mary Ann (Womack) Seaton (Manuscript) prepared by Kennie (Seaton) Rupert (Mrs. Ed Rupert), Grayson Kentucky, 1950.

SCOTT FAMILY OF CARTER AND GREENUP COUNTIES

Scot was originally an English name, the designation of one who came from Scotland. The English medieval records, especially during the twelfth and thirteenth centuries, abound in such descriptions as le scot and le escot. A name like Scot would naturally not originate in Scotland where all were Scots. The Scots of the Highlands originally came into Scotland from England where the family name was "Escot".

The family was in England in very early times as shown by the Hundred Rolls which bear the names of:

Roger Le Scot, London, 1273.

Elias le Scot, Co. Salop, 1273.

Walter Scot, Co. York, 1273.

Johannes Scot, Co. Yorkshire, 1379.

Adam Scotte.

Several Scott families lived in Northeastern Kentucky in pioneer days. In Mason County, James Scott m. Margaret Simms, January 2, 1798, and Thomas Scott m. Mattie Ralston, February 26, 1799. David Scott and Thomas Scott were residents and heads of families in Greenup County in 1810 as shown by U. S. Census of that county for that year. James Scott and John Scot were tax-payers in Greenup County in 1811.

1. CAPTAIN THOMAS SCOTT was the ancestor of a large branch of the Scott family of Greenup and Carter Counties. The U. S. Census of Carter County shows that he was b. in Pennsylvania about 1781 and m. Elizabeth ———, b. in Virginia, 1784. Historians state that he was an early resident of Lexington, Kentucky, and afterwards became one of the first settlers in what is now Carter County, settling near present Grayson in 1808 and being interested in the salt works near there; and that he d. in 1870 at the age of 93 years.[1]

Children, among others:

2. Robert Scott; moved to Ironton, Ohio, and became connected with the Mt. Vernon Furnace in Lawrence County, that state. He purchased Laurel Furnace in Greenup County, Kentucky, in the 1860s.

Children:

3. Thomas Scott; resident manager of Laurel Furnace.

4. Fannie Scott; m. Mr. Spears; lived in Greenup and a daughter, Kitty, attended Greenup Academy.

*5. Nannie Scott.

6. Jennie Scott.

7. Nora Scott.

8. Rozzie Scott.

9. Harry Scott.

5. NANNIE SCOTT, while on a visit to Chicago met Marshall Field,

a young man engaged in mercantile business there. He visited the
Scott home and he and Nannie became engaged to be married. On
the eve of the wedding, a tragedy occurred in the home when Nannie
was seriously burned by the explosion of an oil lamp from a chande-
lier. The wedding was postponed for a time. They lived in grand
style in Chicago. He d. in 1905 and she, while traveling abroad, d.
at Nice, France.
Children:
*10. Ethel Field.
*11. Marshall Field, Jr.
10. ETHEL FIELD m. Lord Beatty of England; and resided in
England.

11. MARSHALL FIELD, JR., m. Albertine Huck of Chicago and went
to England, living on an estate adjoining that of Lord and Lady
Beatty. He d. in New York in 1906.
Children:
12. Marshall Field III; resided in Chicago.

Children:
13. Marshall Field IV; resided in Chicago and was interested in
publication of the *Sun* and *Times* of that city.
Other Scott families lived in Greenup and Carter Counties in
pioneer days, some of whom apparently were children of or related
to Capt. Thomas Scott, the pioneer, who settled near present Grayson about 1808:
14. Richard Scott, farmer, b. in Pennsylvania about 1794; m.
Mary ———, b. in Ireland, 1795.
Children living in the household and approimate dates of birth as
shown by U. S. Census of Greenup County for 1850:
15. John Scott; b. in Ohio, 1827.
16. Andrew Scott; b. 1828.
17. Stewart Scott; b. 1830.
18. May Ann Scott; b. 1832.
19. Mary J. Scott; b. 1834.
20. Richard Scott, Jr.; b. 1837.
21. Eleanor Scott; b. 1839.
22. Crawford Scott, farmer, b. in Pennsylvania about 1801; m.
Mahala ———, b. in Virginia, 1806.
Children living in the household and approximate dates of birth
as shown by U. S. Census of Greenup County for 1850:
23. Janus Scott; b. 1843.
24. Abraham Scott; b. 1845.
25. Elizabeth Scott; ;b. 1847.
26. ANDREW JACKSON SCOTT, farmer, b. in Kentucky, 1817; m. in
Carter County, April 5, 1846; Rhoda Morris, b. 1827, daughter of
John and Louanna Morris (probably).
(See Morris Family).

Children living at home and approximate dates of birth as shown by the U. S. Census of Carter County, for 1850, 1860 and 1870:

27. Delila Scott; b. 1847.
28. Nancy Scott; b. 1850.
29. Fannie Scott; b. 1855.
30. Rose Scott, b. 1857.
31. Eliza Scott; b. 1857.
32. George Scott; b. 1863.
33. Hattie Scott; b. 1867.
34. Henry Scott; farmer; b. in Kentucky, 1808; m. in Greenup County, December 19, 1829, Jane Bradford, b. in Virginia, 1813.

Children living at home and approximate dates of birth as shown by the U. S. Census of Carter County for 1850 and 1860:

35. Elizabeth Scott; b. 1830.
36. William Scott; b. 1834.
37. Sarah Scott; b. 1837.
38. Thomas Scott; b. 1839.
39. Jackson Scott; b. 1844.
40. Katharine Scott; b. 1849.
41. Mary Scott; b. 1850.
42. Alice Scott, b. 1853.

1. GABRIEL SCOTT was the ancestor of a branch of Scott Family of Carter County, Kentucky. He m., apparently in Greenup County about 1814, Esther ———, b. in Kentucky in 1796, whom the records would seem to indicate was a daughter of David Davis and Martha Davis, pioneer residents of Greenup County. In his will, executed September 9, 1868, and probated in the Carter County Court, September 13, 1869, Gabriel Scott mentions his wife, Esther, Sarah E. Jarvis and two children:

*2. Mary Offill.
*3. James Scott, only son and Executor.

In 1870 in the household of the widow, Esther Scott, aged 74, lived Martha Scott, aged 34; Mary Offill, daughter, aged 56; and Hervey ———, aged 35.

2. MARY LOUELLYN SCOTT was b. in Kentucky in 1814 or 1815; m. about 1832, James Offill, farmer and justice of the peace of Carter County, who was b. about 1798.

Children living in the household and approximate dates of birth as shown in the U. S. Census of Carter County for 1850 and 1860:

4. James P. Offill; b. 1833, school teacher.
5. John H. A. Offill; b. 1835.
6. Francis M. Offill; b. 1839; school teacher.
7. Martha J. Offill; b. 1842.
8. Louisa Offill; b. 1843.
9. Ellen Offill; b. 1846.

10. Amanda Offill; b. 1849.
11. Cordelia Offill; b. 1853.

CAPTAIN JAMES W. SCOTT, farmer, was b. about 1814. A staunch Union man, he had service in the Union Army during the Civil War, as Captain, Co. "D", 22nd Kentucky Vol. Inf.; mustered in at George's Creek, Kentucky, January 10, 1862, and resigned October 18, 1862.[2]

He m. about 1837, Jane Garvin, b. in 1815.

Children living in the household and approximate dates of birth as shown by the U. S. Census of Carter County for 1860:
*12. Calvin H. Scott; b. 1838.
*13. Mary Scott; b. 1841.
*14. Louisa Scott; b. 1845.
*15. Johnson Scott; b. 1846.
*16. Sarah E. Scott; b. 1848.
17. Simeon Scott; b. 1851.
*18. Winfield Scott; b. 1853.
19. John M. Scott;; b. 1857.

12. CALVIN H. SCOTT, dry-goods merchant at Olive Hill; b. January 11, 1838; m. Martha Ann James; b. August 17, 1843.
Children:
20. Martha Jane Scott; b. October 26, 1863; m. William Craycraft.
21. James W. Scott; b. December 26, 1865; m. Sidney ———.
22. John M. Scott; b. February 18, 1867, unm.
23. Sarilda Catherine Scott; b. January 24, 1869.
24. Mary Ellen Scott; b. January 24, 1869; m. Bert Benton. A son, Scott Benton, resided in Ashland.
25. William H. Scott, merchant at Olive Hill; b. September 1, 1872; m. Lillie King, daughter of Van B. King and Nancy (Counts) King.
26. Sarah Scott; b. January 12, 1874; m. John M. McGill, onetime merchant at Olive Hill; county judge and county attorney of Carter County; deceased.
27. Edward Scott; b. December 1, 1875.

13. MARY SCOTT; m. William Jarvis; reared a large family.

14. LOUISA SCOTT; m. ——— Gilbert.

15. JOHNSON SCOTT; m. Mary Jarvis; reared a family.

16. SARAH E. SCOTT; m. about 1867, James S. Jarvis, farmer and businessman of many activities; b. 1847.
Children:
*28. Bartola Jarvis.
29. Louisa Jarvis; b. 1870.
*30. Oney Jarvis; m. W. B. Whitt.

31. Hattie Jarvis; m. —— James.
32. Dr. Winfield Jarvis.

18. WINFIELD SCOTT, merchant at Grayson for many years and a
banker, was b. near Olive Hill, Carter County, February 5, 1853, and
d. at Grayson, July (?), 1920. He was one of the organizers and a
stock holder of the Citizens Bank of Grayson (now First National
Bank); was chosen its first president and served as such until his
death. He m., February 14, 1878, Sarah Rachel Alexander, b. March
4, 1858, and d. August 11, 1916.
Children:
*33. Grace Scott.
34. Albert Scott; b. at Grayson, June 27, 1894.
33. GRACE SCOTT; b. at Grayson, April 30, 1881; educated in the
public schools of Grayson and at Hamilton College, Lexington, Kentucky; m. John H. Culton.
Children:
35. Winfield Scott Culton.
36. Grace Scott Culton; deceased. Residence: 820 11th Avenue,
Huntington, West Virginia.

28. BARTOLA JARVIS; b. 1868; and d. 1906; m. in 1887, William
B. Whitt.

WILLIAM B. WHITT, businessman of many activities and sometime
public official, a son of Jack and Missouri (Cox) Whitt, was b. at
Whitt, now Corey, Carter County, Kentucky, September 17, 1867;
educated in the public schools of Carter County; at the age of 17
he took charge of his father's general store which he successfully
managed. He formed a partnership with James H. Kitchen which,
in 1898, was incorporated as Kitchen, Whitt & Co. wholesale grocers
of Ashland; capitalized at $100,000, of which he was chosen vice-
president. He also acted as general manager and filled these positions
until his death. He was also president and general manager of the
Watson Hardware Company of Ashland, Kentucky.

Mr. Whitt was a Democrat, a Knight Templar Mason and a
Noble of the Mystic Shrine. During his long business career, he
was interested and participated in civic and public affairs. While a
resident of Carter County, he was elected and served as State Senator
for one term 1906-1910. After he located in Ashland, Kentucky, he
served as a member of Ashland school board for four years; and in
November 1925, he was elected Mayor of Ashland and served as
such until his death on December 19, 1926. Children of William B.
Whitt and Bartola (Jarvis) Whitt:
37. Mrs. R. A. Kerkeek.
38. Mrs. Claude James.
39. Mrs. Van C. Underwood.

40. E. Russell Whitt.

41. W. P. Whitt.

Subsequent to the death of Bartola (Jarvis) Whitt and on May 15, 1907, Mr. Whitt m., secondly, Miss Bessie J. Sexton, daughter of A. J. and Laura Alice (Duncan) Sexton of Morehead, Kentucky. Their Children were:

42. Hazel Gladys Whitt, deceased.

43. William B. Whitt, Jr.

44. Jack Whitt.

45. James Seitz Whitt.

46. Alice Jean Whitt.

47. Arthur Francis Whitt.

("History of Kentucky" by Temple Bodley and Samuel M. Wilson, Vol. IV, page 1092.)

---

[1] "History of Kentucky" by Lewis Collins, Revised by his son, Richard H. Collins, 1877. p. 122.

[2] Report of the Adjutant General of Kentucky, 1861-1866, Vol. II, p. 106.

SILER FAMILY OF WHITLEY COUNTY

1. JACOB SILER was the ancestor of the Siler family of Southeastern Kentucky. He was of German descent, a farmer and came from North Carolina to Whitley County, Kentucky, in early days. His son

2. Adam Siler, farmer, was b. in Whitley County, 1795, d. in 1882; m. Polly Brock, who was b. in 1800 and d. in 1881. Their son

3. Terrell Siler, farmer, was b. 1835 and d. 1913. He was a Republican in politics and a member of the Baptist Church. He m. Mary Blakely who was b. in Whitley County, 1841.

Children:

4. William A. Siler, merchant at Pleasant Valley, Whitley County, d. in 1892.

5. Lillie F. Siler; m. Henry S. Jones, merchant.

6. John M. Siler; engaged in teaming at Packard, Kentucky.

7. Cynthia Siler; m. Ulysses S. Jones, wholesale grocer at Jellico, Tenn.

*8. Adam T. Siler.

9. Martin V. Siler, commercial traveler; resided at Jellico, Tennessee.

10. Dr. J. E. Siler, physician and surgeon at Lott, Kentucky; veteran of World War I, serving as first lieutenant, Medical Corps, U. S. A., on foreign service in France three months.

11. Ulysses S. Siler; resided at Packard; was purchasing agent for Mahan-Jellico Coal Company.

8. ADAM TROY SILER, lawyer, banker, businessman and public official, was b. on his father's farm on Tackett Creek near the village of Pleasant View, Whitley County, February 13, 1870; educated in the rural schools; was graduated from Cora Institute at Pleasant View, 1887; attended Glasgow (Kentucky) Normal School two years, 1888-9; and was graduated from the National Normal University at Lebanon, Ohio, with degree of B. S., 1892; taught in the rural schools of Whitley County, three years; was elected and served two terms, 1893-1901, as superintendent of public schools of Whitley County, in the meantime studying law under the preceptorship of J. N. Sharp of Williamsburg; admitted to the bar, 1898, and practiced with success as member of the firm of Tye and Siler, representing the Louisville & Nashville, the Southern, the Cincinnati New Orleans and Texas Pacific Railway Companies, the Western Union Telegraph Company and many important coal mining corporations in Southeastern Kentucky.

A staunch Republican, he rendered valuable services in the councils and campaigns of the party and served two terms, 1904-1911, as a member of the State Board of Railway Commissioners, being chairman during the second term. He was chairman of the Republican Executive Committee of the 11th Congressional District, 1908-1916; was a trustee of the Baptist Church of Williamsburg; and was affiliated with the Masons: a member of Williamsburg Lodge No. 490, F. & A. M., Kenton Chapter No. 148, R. A. M., Cumberland Commandery No. 40, Knights Templar, all of Williamsburg, and a member of the Kentucky State Bar Association.

Mr. Siler was identified with many business enterprises; President of the Bank of Williamsburg; president of the Jellico Grocery Company; president of the Kingsport (Tennessee) Grocery Company; vice-president of the wholesale grocery house of Mahan Company, established at Winchester and Hazard; vice-president of Lotts Creek Coal Company; and very much interested in coal lands in Harlan County.

He was m. at Campbellsville, Kentucky, December 1, 1898.

Children:

12. Lillian Siler; m. Clarence L. Aerni, general manager of the Jellico Lumber Company.

*13. Eugene E. Siler.

14. Irma Catherine Siler.

13. EUGENE E. SILER, Republican of Williamsburg, Kentucky, lawyer and judge; b. in Williamsburg, Kentucky, June 26, 1900; educated at Cumberland College at Williamsburg, and at the University of Kentucky at Lexington; served as an enlisted man in the U. S. Navy in World War I and as a captain in the U. S. Army in World War II; elected judge of the Court of Appeals of Kentucky, 1945, and served from 1945 until January 1, 1949; was the Republican nominee for Governor of Kentucky in 1951; elected Moderator of the General Association of Kentucky Baptists in 1952 and re-elected in 1953; elected to the Eighty-fourth Congress, November 2, 1954, and is presently serving as such.

Judge Siler is a Republican in politics and a member of the Baptist Church. He is affiliated with the Masons, I. O. O. F., Jr. O. U. A. M., and the American Legion. He is a trustee of Cumberland College, a director of the Bank of Williamsburg, of the Kingsport Grocery Company and of the Kentucky Mine Supply Company.

He is married.

Children:

15. Mrs. J. R. White of Sardinia, Indiana.

16. Mrs. O. D. Hungerford of Kingsport, Tennessee.

17. Caroline Siler, a student at University of Kentucky.

18. Eugene Siler, Jr., a student at Vanderbilt University.

SPARKS FAMILY OF LAWRENCE, CARTER AND ELLIOTT COUNTIES

The families of Sparks were well established in the United States when the Federal government was organized. The first U. S. Census (1790) and reconstructed censuses from tax-lists for those destroyed by the British Army when Gen. Ross captured Washington, D. C., and burned public buildings and destroyed records during the War of 1812, would seem to indicate that there were about 700 Sparkses, men, women and children in the United States as of that time. About 15% of the families were slave holders. The Maryland census reports a greater number of Sparks families than any other State; and then in order with respect to numbers are North Carolina, Pennsylvania and Virginia (same number), South Carolina, Connecticut, New York, Massachusetts and Maine and Vermont (same number), and Rhode Island. At this period Sparks families lived also in Georgia, New Jersey and what is now Tennessee.

John Sparks of North Carolina was the progenitor of a large branch of the family, members of whom migrated to and settled in Eastern Kentucky, circa 1820. He was a Revolutionary War soldier; and on the 30th day of October, 1832, he personally appeared in the Court of Pleas and Quarter Sessions of Wilkes County, North Carolina, and filed a declaration for a pension [1] based on such service wherein he declared, among other things, that he was a resident of Wilkes County, North Carolina, aged 79 years; that he was b. on the 25th day of February, 1753 in Rowan County, North Carolina, where he lived until 1772 when his father moved to Wilkes County, formerly Surry County; that he enlisted in Wilkes County in 1775 or 1776 in Captain Jesse Walton's Company of Minute Men that had volunteered for two years' service in the Revolution; that under orders of Captain Walton, he took command of a scouting party and scoured the country around in Wilkes and Surry Counties, suppressing the Tories or bringing in such as were supposed to be disaffected; that in this expedition he served two or three weeks; ;that after remaining at home some months he was ordered by Colonel Martin Armstrong to rendezvous at the head of the Yadkin River to prepare to march against the Cherokee Indians; that they rendezvoused at the head of the Yadkin until they built Fort Defiance during which time he was in command of Captain Walton's company, that officer having been appointed a major; that orders were received for the company to return home and prepare for an expedition against the Cherokees: that he and his company reported at Headquarters at Pleasant Gardens where they joined General Rutherford and that the company he was attached to was attached to the command of Captain Benjamin Cleaveland; that after organizing at Headquarters, the entire command marched to the Cherokee towns of Watauga, Cowee, Hiwassee, Big Chota, etc., during which expedition he was detached as a spy while in the Indian nation; that after destroying crops the army returned home and he was discharged after about three months' service; that subsequently he was called out and served in various short expeditions against the Tories; that when Cornwallis invaded North Corolina from the South, he was again called out and joined the command under Colonel Benjamin Herndon in pursuit of Cornwallis as he was on his march from Cowan's Ford on the Catawba to Guilford, which pursuit continued until they reached General Greene's army at High Rock on the Haw River where General Greene discharged them; and they returned home, having been gone at least one month.

1. JOHN SPARKS, Revolutionary War soldier, was b. in Rowan County, North Carolina, February 25, 1753, and d. in Wilkes County, that State, about 1840; m. (time and place not learned) Sarah Shores, daughter of Reuben and Susannah Shores.

Issue:

Second Generation

*2. Levi Sparks.
*3. George Sparks.
*4. Robert Sparks (Note: Although not definitely established that Robert was son, however, on the basis of family tradition, supported by some documentary evidence, it is probable that he was a son.)
5. Joel Sparks; b. about 1785.
6. John Sparks, Jr.; b. about 1787.
7. Reuben Sparks; b. September 26, 1799.
8. Colby Sparks; b. about 1801.
9. Sally Sparks; b. about 1793.
10. Polly Sparks; b. about 1780?

There were other children, a son and two daughters, who have not been identified.

Of these children, Levi, George and Robert migrated to and settled in Eastern Kentucky, circa 1820. The others continued to reside in North Carolina.

2. LEVI SPARKS, farmer, was b. in Surry County, North Carolina, October 2, 1778, and d. in Lawrence County, Kentucky, October 21, 1851; m., first, Miss Walsh, in North Carolina.

Issue:

Third Generation

*11. Garret Sparks.
*12. Sidney Sparks (daughter)
2-A. Levi Sparks m., secondly, Sarah Lyon.

Issue:

Third Generation

*13. Calvin Sparks.

*14. Wiley Sparks.
*15. Sinay Sparks (daughter).
*16. Sarah Sparks.
*17. Nelson Sparks.
*18. John L. Sparks.

3. GEORGE SPARKS, farmer, was b. in Wilkes County, North Carolina, November 9, 1796, and d. in Elliott County, Kentucky, May 11, 1879; m., first, a Miss Mainer (or Maynor).
Issue:
Third Generation
*19. Lucinda Sparks.

3-A. George Sparks, m., secondly, in Lawrence County, Kentucky, June 8, 1822, Nancy Short, b. in Virginia 1800, and d. in Elliott County, 1879.
Issue:
Third Generation
*20. John W. Sparks.
21. Cynthia Sparks; b. July 16, 1827; unm.
*22. Hugh Sparks.
*23. Nancy Sparks.
*24. Levi Sparks.
*25. Emma Sparks.
26. Colby Sparks.
*27. Mary Sparks.

4. ROBERT SPARKS; b. in North Carolina, about 1780, and d. previous to 1830; m., (probably) Margaret Rigg.
Issue:
Third Generation
*28. Wesley Sparks.
*29. Nancy Sparks.
*30. William Sparks.
31. Solomon Sparks.
*32. Joel Sparks.

11. GARRET (OR GARRED) SPARKS, farmer, was b. in North Carolina, September 15, 1802, and d. in Lawrence County, Kentucky, September 1, 1873; m. in Lawrence County, September 22, 1825, Elizabeth Boggs, b. in Virginia, December 27, 1808, and d. in Lawrence County, Kentucky, December 21, 1873.
Issue:
Fourth Generation
33. Reuben Sparks; b. February 8, 1829; m., first, —— Boggs, and secondly, Mary Curnutte.
34. Eleanor Sparks (twin to Reuben); b. February 8, 1829; m. William Lyon.

35. Levi J. Sparks; b. February 19, 1831; m. Mary Gambill.
36. Sarah E. Sparks; b. about 1832; m. Minyard Holbrook; no children.
37. Hugh Sparks; b. about 1834; migrated to Kansas; unm.
38. Bethany Sparks; b. about 1836; m. David Curnutte.
39. Nancy Sparks; b. about 1837; m. Isaac Lester in Lawrence County, February 4, 1858.
40. Jemima Sparks; b. about 1839; m. Berry Fugate.
41. Walter N. Sparks; b. about 1841; m. Rena Boggs?
42. Rebecca Sparks; b. about 1842; m. John Green.
43. David L. Sparks; b. about 1844; m. Thursa Curnutte; no children.
44. Phoebe J. Sparks; b. about 1845; m. Francis Parker.
45. Sidney D. Sparks; b. about 1848.
46. Lydia Sparks; b. about 1851.
47. Garrett Sparks, Jr., b. April 15, 1854; m. Mary Miller.
48. Elizabeth Sparks; m. Hack Griffith.
49. Lavina Sparks; m. "Bud" Berry.

12. SIDNEY SPARKS; b. in North Carolina; remained in that state; unm.

13. CALVIN SPARKS, farmer; b. in North Carolina, November 6, 1806, and d. in Lawrence County, Kentucky, February 26, 1894; m. in Lawrence County, June 19, 1828, Sally Lyon, b. in North Carolina, July 10, 1806, and d. in Lawrence County, August 29, 1876.
Issue:
Fourth Generation
50. Alfred Sparks; b. February 22, 1831; m. Mary Ann Green in Lawrence County, December 30, 1852.
51. Mary Sparks; b. about 1837; m. Harvey Lester. (Note: One "Polly" Sparks m. Thomas Lester in Lawrence County, May 11, 1854.)
52. Perlina Sparks; b. about 1840; m. Jackson Dobyns.
53. Nelson Sparks; b. June 1, 1845; m. Sarilda Holbrook.
54. Thomas Benton Sparks; b. about 1849; m. Galena Stegall?

14. WILEY SPARKS, farmer, was b. in North Carolina, about 1808 and d. in Lawrence County, Kentucky, sometime subsequent to 1880; m. in Lawrence County in 1832, Cynthia Holbrook, b. in North Carolina, about 1820.
Issue:
Fourth Generation
55. Nancy Sparks; b. about 1833; unm.
56. Mary Sparks; b. about 1834; m. Lewis Lyon in Lawrence County, January 2, 1854.
57. Lindsey Sparks; b. about 1839; m. Katie Skaggs.

58. George Washington Sparks; b. about 1843; m. Linnie Grizzell.
59. Matilda Sparks; b. about 1849; unm.
60. John M. Sparks; b. March 10, 1856; d. young.
61. William N. Sparks; b. August 13, 1860.
62. Nesbitt Sparks; b. about 1862; m. Elizabeth Sparks.

15. SINAY SPARKS; b. in North Carolina about 1812; m., September 5, 1833, Ira Ison.
Issue:
Fourth Generation
63. Nelson Ison; d. young.
64. Argalus Ison; d. young.
65. Sarah Ison; m. Braxton Adkins.
66. Emily Ison; m. Eli Adkins.
67. John Ison; m. Mary Waggoner.
68. Ira Ison; m. Mary Adkins.
69. Martin Ison; m. Mary Fraley.
70. David Ison; m. Sarah Kimbleton.
71. Doctor Ison; m. Parthena Fraley.

16. SARAH SPARKS; b. in North Carolina about 1814; m. Tillman Craft in Lawrence County, March 18, 1835.
Issue:
Fourth Generation
72. William Craft; b. about 1836.
73. Aaga? Craft, daughter; b. about 1838.
74. Henderson Craft; b. about 1840.
75. Elizabeth Craft; b. about 1842.
76. Mary J. Craft; b. about 1845.
77. Wiley Craft; b. about 1848.
78. Lydia Craft; b. June 22, 1853.
79. Surrilda Craft; b. December 27, 1855.

17. NELSON SPARKS; b. in North Carolina about 1819; m. Margaret Mauk in Carter County, Kentucky, March 16, 1843.
Issue:
Fourth Generation
80. Peter Sparks; b. about 1844; m. Julia Cox.
81. Pauline Sparks; b. about 1846; m. Corbin Lyon.
82. John E. Sparks; b. about 1848; m. Elizabeth Boggs.
83. Sarah Sparks; b. about 1849; m. George Bear (Bayer?).
84. Leander Sparks; b. about 1851.
85. Frederick M. Sparks; b. about 1853; m. Catherine Kegley.
86. Levi Sparks; b. June 2, 1855.
87. Louisa J. Sparks; b. January 22, 1857; m. Thomas Kelley.

88. Martha F. Sparks; b. December 25, 1860; m. John Binion.
89. George Sparks; b. April 9, 1862; m. Lucinda Sargent.

18. JOHN L. SPARKS; b. in North Carolina about 1820; m. Paula Hays.

Issue:

Fourth Generation

90. Surrilda Sparks; b. about 1851.
91. Sarah Sparks: b. February 25, 1853.
92. Levi Sparks; b. March 17, 1854.
93. Elizabeth Sparks; b. December 29, 1855.
94. James B. Sparks; b. March 15, 1857.
95. Milburn Sparks; b. July 15, 1859.
96. William Sparks.

19. LUCINDA SPARKS; b. in North Carolina, March 21, 1816; m. in North Carolina, January 13, 1838, James Hanks; continued to live in North Carolina and reared a family.

20. JOHN W. SPARKS; b. in Lawrence County, Kentucky, November 5, 1822, and d. in Elliott County, Kentucky, November 17, 1895; m. Alameda Green in 1845.

Issue:

Fourth Generation

97. Minerva Sparks; b. about about 1847; m. Washington Boggs.
98. Cynthia Sparks; b. about 1849; m. Arthur Prince.
99. Richard Sparks; b. July 6, 1852; m. Jane White.
100. Sarah Sparks; b. October 3, 1853.
101. Cena Sparks; b. about 1856; m. Wilson Tackett.
102. Susan Sparks; b. February 20, 1859; m. Claborne White.
103. Rachel Sparks; b. September 1, 1861; d. young.
104. Nancy Sparks; b. about 1865.
105. Mary E. Sparks; b. about 1867; m. Ison Flannery.

22. HUGH SPARKS; farmer, was b. in Lawrence County, Kentucky, May 21, 1829; m. in Carter County, Kentucky, April 10, 1852, Nancy Curnutte, b. in Kentucky about 1836 and d. 1913.

Issue:

Fourth Generation

106. Mary Elizabeth Sparks; b. April 18, 1853; m. Harvey Walker.
107. Marcia Frances Sparks; b. November 19, 1854; d. young.
108. James B. Sparks; b. November 18, 1855; m., first, Elizabeth Evans, and secondly, Mary Jane Taylor.
*109. Colby Sparks; b. September 22, 1857; m. Martha Chaffin.
110. George Sparks; b. July 10, 1860; m., first, Elizabeth Painter, and secondly, Gertie Satterfield.
111. Hugh S. Sparks; b. April 4, 1862; m., first Rhoda Burchett, and secondly, Jennie Chaffin.

23. NANCY SPARKS; b. about 1825; m. John N. Hutchinson in Lawrence County, Kentucky, March 21, 1847.

Issue:

Fourth Generation

112. James Hutchinson; b. about 1850.

24. LEVI SPARKS, farmer, was b. May 31, 1834, and d. May 20, 1911; m. Nancy Lawson in Carter County, Kentucky, July 7, 1860.

Issue:

Fourth Generation

113. Leburn Sparks; b. December 17, 1861; unm.
114. John Sparks; b. about 1862; m. ——— Waddell.
115. Alameda Sparks; b. about 1865; m. ——— Messer.
116. Ashby Sparks; b. about 1866; m. ——— Mauk.
117. Sarah Sparks; b. about 1869; m. ——— Boggs.
118. Juda Sparks; b. about 1871; m. ——— Holbrook.
119. Hansford Sparks: b. about 1873; m. Lula Holbrook.
120. Colby Sparks; b. February 25, 1876; m. ——— ———.
121. Nancy Sparks; b. about 1878; m. ——— Skaggs.
122. James Sparks; b. January 23, 1883.

25. EMMA SPARKS; b. about 1839; m. John Harper, December 28, 1861.

Issue:

Fourth Generation

123. Mary Ellen Harper; b. November 2, 1862; m. Sam Green.
124. James Harper; b. about 1864; m. Elizabeth Moore.
125. Nancy Harper; b. about 1867; m. John Leedy.
126. Sarah Harper; b. about 1872; m. "Coon" Moore.
127. Phoebe Harper; b. about 1873.
128. John Jacob Harper; b. about 1877.
129. Julia Ann Harper; b. about 1880.
130. Lucy Harper; b. about 1882; m. "Ell" Johnson.

27. MARY SPARKS; b. June 7, 1844 and d. April 27, 1902; m. John N. Lawson, July 12, 1864.

Issue:

Fourth Generation

131. Levenia Lawson; b. about 1866.
132. Nancy Lawson; b. about 1868; m. Willis Cox.
133. George Lawson; b. about 1870; m. ——— Fraley.
134. Ida E. Lawson; b. about 1872; m. ——— Boggs.
135. Amanda Lawson; b. about 1876; m. "Mid" Bowling.
136. James Hugh Lawson; b. about 1880; m. ——— Barker.
137. "Dell" Lawson.
138. Nora Lawson; m. ——— Walker.
139. Winnie Lawson; m. ——— Hanshoe.

28. WESLEY SPARKS was b. in North Carolina about 1805; m. Nancy Kesee in Lawrence County, August 22, 1835.

Issue:

Fourth Generation

140. Mary Sparks; b. about 1836.
141. Richard Sparks; b. about 1841.
142. Robert Sparks; b. about 1843.
143. Martin Sparks; b. about 1846.
144. Sena Sparks, b. about 1848; m. George Stevens.
145. Rilda Sparks; b. about 1849; m. Caney Stevens.
146. William Sparks; b. May 1, 1853; m. Malinda Stevens.
147. Hugh Sparks; b. April 23, 1856; m. Lady Gilbert.
148. Nancy Sparks; b. about 1859.
149. Rena Sparks; b. August 5, 1860; m. George Sparks.
150. Wesley Sparks, Jr., b. about 1863; m. Josephine Sparks.
151. Reuben Sparks; b. about 1865; m. Dova Whitt.

29. NANCY SPARKS; b. about 1810; m. in Lawrence County, Kentucky, Martin Ison, in 1829.

Issue:

Fourth Generation

152. Charles Ison; b. July 3, 1830.
153. William Ison; b. March ——, 1832.
154. Joshua Ison; b. May ——, 1833.
155. Brydine Ison; b. about 1836.
156. Reuben Ison; b. March 3, 1839.
157. Martin Ison, Jr., b. July ——, 1841.
158. Sidney Ison; b. October 13, 1844.
159. Nancy Ison; b. August 14, 1850; m. J. M. E. Sparks?

30. WILLIAM SPARKS; b. in North Carolina about 1812; m. Mary Lyon.

Issue:

Fourth Generation

160. Nancy Sparks; b. about 1835; m. Nelson White in Lawrence County, January 8, 1857.
161. Reuben Sparks; b. about 1838.
162. Isaac Sparks; b. about 1840; m. Polly Branham.
163. Joel Sparks; b. about 1842; m. Eliza J. Boggs.
164. William Henry Sparks; b. about 1844; m. Clarinda Harris.
165. George W. Sparks; b. about 1846; m. Louisa Creech.
166. Francis Marion Sparks; b. about 1847; m. Frances Wells.
167. Doctor Franklin Sparks; b. about 1849.
168. Solomon Sparks; b. about 1851.
169. James Milton Elliott Sparks; b. about 1852; m., first, Margaret Johnson and secondly, Nancy Ison.

32. JOEL SPARKS; b. about 1825; m. Mary Grow.
Issue:
Fourth Generation
170. Solomon Sparks.
171. George Sparks; b. about 1857.
172. John Sparks; b. about 1866.
173. Lydia Sparks.

109. COLBY SPARKS; b. in Carter County, Kentucky, September 22, 1857; d. in 1951; m., March 16, 1879, Martha Permelia Chaffin, b. 1862, d. 1927, daughter of George Washington and Margaret (Short) Chaffin.
Issue:
Fourth Generation
*174. James B. Sparks.
175. Nora Jane Sparks; b. October 2, 1882; m. Samuel J. Jobe.
176. Rose Emily Sparks; b. May 19, 1885; unm.
177. Flora Hulett Sparks; b. November 15, 1887; m. Lee Williams.
178. Georgia Belle Sparks; b. October 2, 1896; m. George W. Edwards.
179. Dewey Lee Sparks; b. August 28, 1898; m. Frank Graham.
180. Elwood Sparks; b. February 5, 1901, d. February 10, 1902.

174. JAMES B. SPARKS; b. January 18, 1880; m. November 2, 1905, Sarah Elizabeth Conley, b. at Willard, Kentucky, 1887, d. 1922, daughter of Isaac Redmond Conley (1859-1937) and Martha (Sexton) Conley (1858-1935) and granddaughter of Enoch Sexton (1841-   ) and Sarah (Mitchell) Sexton (1838-   ).
Issue:
Fifth Generation
181. Martha W. Sparks; b. February 3, 1907; m. Fred Davis.
*182. Paul Emerson Sparks.
183. Eva Virginia Sparks; b. November 12, 1912; m. Roy Fields.
184. James Edison Sparks; b. August 24, 1916; m. Leona Christian.
185. Hettie Conley Sparks; b. April 4, 1919; d. at age of four years.
186. Dorothy Sparks; b. January 31, 1922; m. Warren Murphy.

182. PAUL EMERSON SPARKS, teacher; b. in Lawrence County, Kentucky, January 17, 1910; educated in the public schools of Lawrence County, graduating from the Louisa High School in 1927; attended Akron (Ohio) University, 1927-1931; and was graduated from Morehead (Kentucky) Teachers College with degree of B. S., 1933; taught in the high schools at Webbville and at Blaine, Kentucky, 1933-1935, when accepted position in the Louisville schools, teaching in the junior high and elementary schools until 1938 when appointed principal of an elementary school. He was graduated from Northwestern University, Evanston, Illinios, with degree of M. A., while teaching

in Louisville; served in U. S. Army Air Corps, June 1942-February 1946; and took a sabbatical leave of absence from school principalship to return to Indiana University in January 1955, for a semester to complete requirements for doctorate.

Aside from his educational work, Mr. Sparks is deeply interested in genealogy and has made extensive research and prepared a manuscript on John Sparks, Revolutionary War Soldier, and His Descendants in Eastern Kentucky. He was one of the organizers of The Sparks Family Association and is presently the editor of The Sparks Quarterly, the official publication of that association. He is a lineal direct descendant of John Sparks, Capt. Henry Connelly, Abiud Fairchild, all of whom had service in the North Carolina Forces in the Revolutionary War. (See Connelly and Fairchild Families.)

On November 9, 1933, Paul Emerson Sparks was united in marriage with Miss Sue Miller, daughter of Anderson L. and Hattie (Pope) Miller. She was b. June 26, 1910; educated in the public schools of Rowan County and Morehead, Kentucky; was graduated from the Morehead Normal School, 1927, from Morehead State Teachers College, with degree of A. B., 1933; and from Indiana University with degree of M. A., 1955; has been employed as teacher in the Louisville Public Elementary schools since 1946.

Issue: Sixth Generation
187. Robert L. Sparks; b. October 21, 1944.

JAMES CECIL SPARKS, physician; b. April 4, 1875, near Martha, Lawrence County, Kentucky, on farm of parents, Reuben R. and Mary (Carnutte) Sparks; educated in the public school and at Blaine (Kentucky) Normal School and taught for nine years in the public schools of Lawrence County; graduated in 1906 from the Hospital College of Medicine (now a department of the University of Louisville); began practice of medicine at Sandy Hook, Kentucky, 1906 and continued there until 1910; practiced at Glenwood, Lawrence County, 1910-1913; at Van Lear, Johnson County, 1913-1919; at Paintsville Hospital, 1919-1923; and located at Ashland for practice of medicine in 1923.

A Republican in politics he was elected and served as mayor of Paintsville, 1919-1923. He affiliated with the Masons and was a member of the Boyd County, the Kentucky State and the American Medical Associations.

Dr. Sparks m. Miss Nora Holbrook, April 23, 1899. Their children are Clyde Cecil Sparks, b. May 24, 1903; graduated from Georgetown College, with degree of B. S., 1924; m., 1926, Mabel Coakley of Compbellsville, Kentucky; and Chiles Emory Sparks, b. October 10, 1909; educated at Georgetown College.

---

[1] Revolutionary War Pension Papers, The National Archives, Washington, D. C.
[2] John Sparks of North Carolina, Revolutionary War Soldier, and His Descendants of Eastern Kentucky (Manuscript and Family Tree) prepared by Paul Emerson Sparks, 155 North Hite Avenue, Louisville, Kentucky, 1952.

STAFFORD FAMILY OF JOHNSON COUNTY

According to reputable genealogists and historians the history of the Stafford family of America has been traced in England back to the reign of the Stuarts when Viscount John Stafford, who claimed the throne of England, was beheaded by order of James II. Lord Stafford left one son, John, who was kidnapped in England and deported to America. He, after a time, m. a lady in Virginia whose name has not been learned. One of their sons, John, removed to Maryland from whom the Staffords of Maryland and New Jersey are descended.

There are several branches of the Stafford family living in the United States; and there were branches of the family living in all the original thirteen colonies, except Maine, at the time of the enumeration of the first U. S. Census (1790). The male line of the family was extinguished in England with the death of Lord Stafford, and the family is now represented in the older female line by Sir Stafford Jerringham, and in the younger line by Sir Stafford Northcote.

The Stafford family is of Scotch-Irish descent and the first to America was Thomas, b. about 1605. He emigrated from Warwicksshire, England, to Plymouth in New England, in or about 1626. A few years later he removed to Providence, Rhode Island, and from thence to Warwick, Rhode Island, in 1652, where he died in 1677.

The founder of the noble house of Stafford was Robert, a younger son of Roger de Tonei, standard bearer of Normandy, whose name appears in the Doomsday book as the owner of one hundred and thirty-one lordships in the counties of Suffolk, Gloucester, Lincoln, Warwick and Stafford. William the Conqueror appointed him govenor of the Castle of Stafford, from which he assumed a new surname; and from him descended the dukes of Buckingham and several other noble houses.

The coat of arms of the Staffords has often changed to suit the varying rank of the family, and the motto likewise has not always been the same. At one time it was "Virtus basis vitoe;" at another "Frangas von flectes". The former, "Virtue the corner-stone of life," was probably the motto used by the family at the time the first immigrant arrived in New England. Other coat of arms of the Staffords reads: Or, a chevron gules between three saltiers of the same. In English this is—A gold field with a red chevron and three red crosses.

1. —— Stafford, m. —— ——.
Children:
2. Ralph Stafford.
3. William Stafford.
4. John Stafford, m. —— Mollett; settled at White House, now Johnson County.

*5. James Stafford.

The name of the father and/or the mother of these four brothers has not been learned. However it is known that the brothers emigrated from Staffordshire, England, and settled in Giles county, Virginia.

5. JAMES STAFFORD came to Floyd county, now Johnson county, Kentucky, about 1794. He acquired a large tract of land in Johnson county, now known as the F. M. Stafford farm which he transferred to his son, John, and which is now owned by descendants. He m. Abigail Davis.

Children:

6. James Stafford, lived in Giles county, Virginia; later removed to Lewis county, Kentucky, where he died.

7. —— Stafford.

*8. John Stafford.

9. —— Stafford, m. —— Blankenship.

10 Thomas Stafford, lived in Johnson county, but d. in Indiana.

11. William Stafford, lived in Lewis county, Kentucky.

12. —— Stafford, m. —— Stone.

13. Ralph Stafford, lived in Lewis county, Kentucky.

8. JOHN STAFFORD, farmer, b. in Floyd county, now Johnson County, Kentucky, December 15, 1804, d. in Johnson county, December 15, 1869; m. in Floyd county, April 8, 1825, Calista Nott, daughter of Dr. Arbeth Nott and his wife, Laura Allen Schofield b. April 15, 1808, d. February 25, 1865, who, according to family history and tradition, was a granddaughter of Capt. Ethan Allen who captured Ticonderoga during the Revolutionary War.

Children:

*14. James Stafford.

*15. Ralph Stafford.

*16. William Stafford.

*17. Jane Stafford.

*18. Irene Stafford.

*19. Lucina Stafford.

*20. Francis Marion Stafford.

*21. Malissa Stafford.

22. Thomas Stafford, b. June 14, 1843, d. in the Civil War.

*23. Mary Stafford.

*24. Jesse Stafford.

*25. Lydia Stafford.

14. JAMES STAFFORD, farmer, b. in Floyd county, now Johnson county, March 21, 1825, d. in Johnson county, January 2, 1911; m., in Johnson county, December 27, 1844, Cynthia Dixon, b. 1828, d. 1912.

Children:

26. John Henry Stafford, d. young.
27. George Stafford, m., first, Susan Turner, and, second, Mary Melvin.
28. William Stafford, killed by a horse.
29. Frank Stafford m. Laura Rule.
30. Martin Stafford, m. Mary Pyles.
31. Burns Stafford, d. young.
32. Mary Anne Stafford, m. Peter Mankins.
33. Manfred Stafford, drowned.
*34. Thomas R. Stafford, m. Sarah Litteral.
35. Charles Stafford, m. Belle Salyer.
36. Harry B. Stafford, m., first, Minnie Anderson; second, Betty Litteral, and, third —— ——.
37. Frederick Stafford, d. in infancy.
38. Tallie Stafford, m. Hiram Roberts.
39. Benjamin Stafford, m. Sarah Wireman.

15. RALPH STAFFORD, b. September 9, 1827, d. 1877; m. Amanda Hager.

Children:

40. Lucretia Stafford, m. John Keelin.
41. Susan Stafford, m. David Meeks.
42. Sophronia Stafford, m. John Kinds.
43. John Stafford, m. Alice VanHoose.
44. George Stafford, d. young.
45. Frank Stafford, d. young.
46. Lena Stafford, m. —— Burchett.
47. Dolly Stafford, m. Samuel Rice. (See Rice Family).

16. WILLIAM STAFFORD, b. December 25, 1829, d. February 22, 1892; m. Martha A. Hager, b. July 30, 1830, d. 1911.

Children:

48. Worth Stafford, m. Martha J. Spradlin, d. May 20, 1903.
49. Henry Stafford, m. Mollie Preston. (See Preston Family).
50. Nettie Stafford, m. George B. Rice. (See Rice Family).
51. Charley Stafford, m. Lizzie Preston. (See Preston Family).
52. Robert Stafford.
53. Martha Stafford, m. James Auxier. (See Auxier Family).
54. John Frew Stafford, bachelor, sportsman; lived in Paintsville, Johnson county during the summer and in Florida during the winter.

17. JANE STAFFORD, b. February 15, 1832, d. 1902; m. Henry Dixon.

Children:

55. Rhoda Dixon, m. George Baldwin.
56. Benjamin Dixon m. Nancy Prater.

57. Martha Dixon, m. James Henry Hager. (See Hager Family).
58. George Dixon, m. Sallie Wilson.
59. Mercy Dixon, m. Joseph Borders.
60. John Dixon, m., first, Minnie Bayes, and second, Della Walker Williams.
61. Mary Dixon, m., first, Frank Conley; second, —— Mayo; and third, —— Taylor.
62. Malissa Dixon, m. Bird Randolph.
63. Peter Cooper Dixon, m. Laura Conley.

18. IRENE STAFFORD, b. March 5, 1834; m., first, Henry Porter, and, second, J. H. Mahan.
Children of Irene Stafford and Henry Porter:
64. Mary Jane Porter, m. Barney Blackburn.
65. John Porter, m. —— Mobley.
Children of Irene Stafford and J. H. Mahan:
66. Susan Mahan, m. J. M. Clay.
67. Pauline Mahan, m. James McKenzie.
68. Cynthia Mahan.
69. Henry Mahan, m. Susan Turner.
70. Calista Mahan.
71. Lee Mahan, m., first, —— Sturgill, and second, ——— Gullett.

19. LUCINA STAFFORD, b. July 12, 1836, d. 1904; m. William Woods of West Virginia.
Children:
72. Wesley Woods.
73. Julia Woods.
74. Martha Woods, m. H. M. Gibbs.
75. Frank Woods, m. Laura Webb.
76. James Woods, m. Rose Butler.
77. Mary Woods, m. John M. Conley.
78. George Woods, m. Sarah Arrington.
79. H. B. Woods, m. Emma Estep.
80. Charles Woods, m. Emma McKenzie.

20. FRANCIS MARION STAFFORD, farmer, realtor and businessman, b. in Floyd county, now Johnson county, Kentucky, November 15, 1833, d. at Paintsville, Johnson county, May 16, 1924. He was an outstanding member of the Stafford family of Eastern Kentucky and was a well-known and highly respected citizen. By great industry and good business judgement he became a man of means. He was a man of exceptional business ability, possessed of a brilliant mind and remarkable memory and was a great conversationalist; was of a very sociable disposition but never ostentatious. He had a tender heart and a loveable disposition. His devotion to his family was great

and he spent what would be considered a modest fortune in the education of his children.

The county court records show that Mr. Stafford dealt extensively in real estate beginning in 1858 and continuing to about one year before his death in 1924, a period of sixty-five years. For many years he was president of the firm of F. M. Stafford & Company, consisting of Dr. I. R. Turner, John C. C. Mayo and himself.

On December ———, 1859, in Johnson county, Mr. Stafford m. Marietta Lavendar, b. June 28, 1845, d. ——— ———.

Children:
81. Aramintie Stafford, m. James Lyons.
82. Celista Stafford, m. R. A. Patrick. (See Patrick Family).
83. William Tecumseh (Son) Stafford.
84. Mary Frances Stafford, d. young.
85. Ella Stafford.
86. Hattie Stafford, d. at the age of 28.
87. Cora Stafford, d. at the age of 5.
88. Thomas Stafford, m. Sarah Ramey; d. at the age of 21.
89. Carrie Stafford. m. Rev. M. E. Stafford.
90. Dora Stafford. m. John L. Spears. (See Preston Family).
91. Ethel Stafford. d. at the age of 18.
92. Edna Erle Stafford, m. F. F. Smith.
93. May F. Stafford.
94. DeWill T. Stafford.

21. MALISSA STAFFORD, b. in Johnson county, July 8, 1840, d. January 21, 1915; m. in Johnson county, July 15, 1856, Thomas S. Williams, b. in Morgan county, Kentucky, December 1, 1838.

Children:
95. Frank Williams, d. in infancy.
96. John R. Williams, m. Elizabeth Tackett.
97. Walker Williams, m. Victoria Walker.
98. Milton Williams, m. Della Walker.
99. Wiley Williams, d. in infancy.
100. Bessie Williams, m. W. Stambaugh.
101. Jennie Williams, m. Frank Chandler. (See Chandler Family).
102. Barnes Williams, m. Fannie Murray.

23. MARY STAFFORD, b. in Johnson county, June 13, 1845; m. Jesse Rule.

Children:
103. Alice Rule, m. Wilk Witten.
104. John Rule, m. Minnie Estep.
105. Isola Rule, m. John McKenzie.

24. JESSE STAFFORD, sometime timberman, dry goods merchant at Staffordsville, Johnson county, and realtor at Paintsville, b. December 30, 1849; m. George Ann Turner, b. May 31, 1849.

Children:

106. Colista Stafford, b. July 7, 1869, d. young.

107. Rose Stafford, b. October 7, 1870; m. John W. Spradlin.

108. Mary Emily Stafford, b. April 12, 1872; m. Abel Pitman.

109. Flora May Stafford, b. January 14, 1874; m. William W. Swetnam.

110. Gillian Stafford, b. September 29, 1875; m. W. G. Franklin.

111. Henry Gordon Stafford, b. April 23, 1877; m. Ruth Burch.

112. Lucina Stafford, b. July 13, 1879; d. in infancy.

113. Ralph Stafford.

114. Clara Stafford, b. December 11, 1882; m. Sanford Stapleton.

115. Jesse Stafford, Jr., b. August 9, 1885; m. Grace Hitchcock.

25. LYDIA STAFFORD, b. in Johnson county, August 20, 1855; m. George Estep.

Children:

116. Ina Estep, m. ——— Meeks.

117. Mollie Estep, m. Epperson Ward.

118. Jesse Estep, m. ——— ———.

119. Colista Estep d. in infancy.

34. THOMAS R. STAFFORD, a progressive citizen and prominent merchant at Oil Springs, Johnson county; m. December 17, 1885; Sarah Litteral, sometime teacher in the public schools of Johnson county, b. March 20, 1868, d. July 4, 1927.

STEWART FAMILY OF LAWRENCE COUNTY

1. JAMES STEWART was the ancestor of a branch of the Stewart family who settled in the Big Sandy Valley in pioneer days. He was of Irish ancestry and his forebears lived in Ireland. Coming from Giles County, Virginia, in 1813, he settled in what is now Lawrence County, Kentucky, on the Big Sandy River.

Children, among others:

*2. Col. Ralph Stewart.

3. John Stewart; m. Miss Burgess.

2. COLONEL RALPH STEWART, farmer; was b. in Virginia, 1799; owned and operated a fine farm on Durbin Creek near Big Sandy River; prominent citizen; never held or sought public office but held many positions of honor and trust; m. in Lawrence County, July ——, 1829, America Canterberry, b. 1814, and d. December 27, 1886, daughter of Reuben Canterberry.

Children living in the household in 1850 and approximate dates of birth as shown by the U. S. Census of Lawrence County for that year:

*4. James E. Stewart; b. 1833.

5. Elizabeth Stewart; b. 1834.

6. Lafayette Stewart; b. 1836.

7. Jeremiah F. Stewart; b. 1839.

8. Albert Stewart; b. 1841.

9. Frances Stewart; b. 1843.

10. Gerard Stewart; b. 1846.

11. Emma Stewart; b. 1849.

4. HON. JAMES E. STEWART, b. in Kentucky, 1833; lawyer, judge and public official. On reaching his majority he studied law, was admitted to the bar and began the practice of law at Paintsville in 1855. A Southern sympathizer, for spoken words, he was arrested and imprisoned at Camp Chase for a year or two. On being released from prison he returned home and purchased a fine property at Louisa where he established his home. Subsequently he was elected and served as Commonwealth's Attorney for six years and Judge of the Circuit Criminal Court for 6 years.

Judge Stewart was a Democrat in politics and a member of the Methodist Church.

He m. in Johnson County, about 1861, Cynthia F. Mayo, b. 1841, daughter of Louis Mayo. (See Mayo Family).

Children living in the home and ages in 1870:

12. James L. Stewart, aged 8.

13. John W. M. Stewart, aged 6.

STRATTON FAMILY OF PIKE AND FLOYD COS.

Stratton is an English name of local origin, from Stratton in Cornwall. The name is derived from the old English straet (Strat stret): "Street, way, road, place, market". In this case the proper interpretation would seem to be "market town".

The Strattons came from Amherst County, Virginia, and settled in Floyd County, Kentucky about 1796. *1. Col Harry settled near the mouth of Toms Creek; *2. Henry, in whose home the first Methodist sermon was preached in the Big Sandy Valley, settled near the present Ival; 3. Tandy, who had m. in Amherst County, Virginia, Mildred Layne, sister to James Shannon Layne, arrived about 1796; and 4. Solomon, who had service in the Revolutionary War in Virginia State troops (General George Rogers Clark's Illinois Regiment), came in with his son, Richard.[1] Apparently Harry, Henry, Tandy and Solomon Stratton were brothers.

1. HARRY STRATTON I. Very little has been learned concerning him. The records would seem to indicate that he was a man of importance in the early affairs of Floyd County. He was tax commissioner of the county, 1808, and for many years served as a justice of the peace during the period 1808 to 1831. He d. about 1840 at Mare Creek, present Pike County.

It has not been learned when he m., but it is definitely known that he had children, among others:

*5. Harry Stratton II.

*6. Hiram Stratton.

7. Richard Stratton; migrated to Terre Haute, Indiana, when a young unmarried man.

*8. Tandy Stratton.

*9. Vina Stratton.

5. HARRY STRATTON II, farmer; b. in Floyd County, Kentucky, 1808, d. in Pike County, about 1890, and was buried in Pinson Cemetery at mouth of Joe's Creek, Pike County; m. in Pike County, January 26, 1829, Martha McGuire.

Children:

10. Nancy Ann Stratton, b. 1830 and d. about 1892; m. in Pike County, April 9, 1851, James Wingo of Morgan County, Kentucky.

11. Richard Stratton, b. 1832 and d. 1866; m. in Pike County, August 17, 1853, Susan Howard.

12. Mary Stratton, b. 1834 and d. about 1935; m. in Pike County, July 24, 1855, Albert Thompson.

13. Malden Stratton, b. 1836 and d. about 1905; m. in Pike County, ———, 1859, Jackson Clark.

14. William Harvey Stratton, b. 1838, and d. 1889 or 1890; m. in Pike County, May 23, 1861, Lucinda Ross.

15. Tandy Stratton, b. 1841 and d. about 1909; m. in Pike County, May 27, 1862, Millie King.

*16. Henry Stratton.

17. Margaret Stratton, b. 1851 and d. about 1938; m. in Pike County, first, William D. Ratliff, in 1875, and secondly, William Clevenger, in 1902.

16. HENRY STRATTON, farmer, was b. on Johns Creek, Pike County, December 23, 1843, and d. in Pike County, September 29, 1916; m. in Pike County in 1866 Malinda Syck, b. January 4, 1846. Both were consistent members of the Methodist Episcopal Church. He was a Republican in politics. Henry Stratton, two brothers and three brothers-in-law had service in the Union Army during the Civil War in Company "C", 39th Kentucky Volunteer Infantry, under Capt. T. J. Sowards.

Children:

18. Esther Stratton; m. Sam Blackburn of Pike County.

19. Martha J. Stratton; m. O. A. Stump, lawyer of Pikeville.

20. John T. Stratton; resided in Pikeville.

21. W. E. Stratton, lumberman of Town Creek, North Carolina.

22. Amanda Stratton; m. P. K. Damron.

23. Orpha Stratton; m. Robert Maynard.

24. Pemberton B. Stratton, lawyer, was b. in Pike County, April 30, 1874. He was educated in the public schools of Pike County; later was a student at Pikeville College; subsequently was a student at Bowling Green (Kentucky) University; and then for two years studied law at Valparaiso (Indiana) University.

In 1898 he was admitted to the bar and began general practice at Pikeville. In 1910 he formed a partnership with Mr. Stephenson (Judge E. D. Stephenson of Pikeville); and the firm gained an eviable reputation as civil lawyers and has been connected with some of the most important legal matters of their day and locality.

On July 12, 1900, Mr. Stratton m. Quinnie Hamilton, daughter of W. H. Hamilton of Millard, Pike County, who died February 22, 1914.

Children:

25. Marjorie Stratton.

26. Louise Stratton.

Mr. Stratton m., secondly, June 7, 1919, Miss Minnie Davis of Westplains, Missouri.

In politics Mr. Stratton is a Republican; in religion a Methodist. He is affiliated with the Masons and Odd Fellows.

6. HIRAM STRATTON, farmer, was b. in Floyd County, 1814, d. about 1900 in Pike County, and was buried on Joe's Creek, that county; m. in Pike County, September 2, 1834, Mary Pinson.

Children:

27. William Stratton, b. 1836; m. in Pike County, February 4, 1856, Nancy J. Helvey.

28. Alexander Stratton, b. about 1840 and d. about 1910; m. Marietta Weddington.

29. Sophia Jane Stratton, b. about 1845 and d. about 1900; m. 1866, D. M. Syck.

30. Eunice Stratton, b. about 1850; m. 1869, George W. Johnson.

31. Margaret Stratton, b. 1846; m. 1878, James Powell.

32. Thomas B. Stratton, b. 1855 and d. about 1935; m. 1884, a Miss Williams.

33. Mary E. Stratton, b. 1858 and d. about 1910; m. in 1884, M. L. Yeary.

34. Richard Stratton, b. about 1863.

35. H. J. Stratton, b. 1865 and d. about 1911; m. in 1886, Mary Ball.

8. TANDY STRATTON. Very little has been learned about him. He probably lived in the Mare Creek community, Pike County. He had sons:

36. Washington Stratton.

37. Wesley Stratton.

9. VINA STRATTON m. a Mr. Preece; descendants live in Martin County, Kentucky:

38. Jasper Preece, attorney, Inez, Kentucky.

39. W. H. D. Preece, attorney, Huntington, West Virginia.

2. HENRY STRATTON. The U. S. Census of Floyd County for the year 1850 bears the names: Henry Stratton as head of family, aged 76, farmer, b. in Virginia; Anna Stratton, aged 56, b. in Virginia, and Harvey Stratton, aged 43, b. in Virginia, living in the household.

Other Stratton families were living in Floyd County in 1850: Solomon Stratton, farmer, b. in Virginia about 1798; m. Jenny (Jane) Layne in Floyd County, November 20, 1820. She was b. about 1804.

Children living at home and approximate dates of birth as shown by U. S. Census of Floyd County for 1850:

40. John Stratton; b. 1828.

41. Lindsey Stratton; b. 1832.

42. Solomon Stratton, Jr., b. 1831.

43. Samuel Stratton; b. 1841.

44. Allen M. Stratton; b. 1846.

8. TANDY STRATTON, farmer, b. in Kentucky about 1799; m. in Floyd County, July 24, 1823, Mahala Lewis, b. in Kentucky about 1808.

Children living at home and approximate dates of birth as shown
by the U. S. Census of Floyd County for 1850:

45. Hezekiah Stratton; b. 1827.
46. Mary Stratton; b. 1829.
47. Margaret J. Stratton; b. 1832.
48. Hiram W. Stratton; b. 1832.
49. Lucinda Stratton; b. 1836.
50. Lorena L. Stratton; b. 1838.
51. Araminta Stratton; b. 1841.
52. Amanda Stratton; b. 1845.

Early marriages of members of the Stratton Family:

Floyd County

Charles Stratton and Hannah Lester, February 25, 1808.
Sally Stratton and William Whitley, March 27, 1811.
Solomon Stratton and Sarah Walker, September 17, 1812.
Tandy Stratton and Polly Preece, May 25, 1813.
Jenny Stratton and Wilson Mayo, September 24, 1818.
Levisa Stratton and Edward B. Miller, April 21, 1819.
James Stratton and Cassander Garrett, October 29, 1820.
Solomon Stratton and Jenny Layne, November 20, 1820.
Lovince Stratton and Alex B. Preece, October 24, 1822.
Tandy Stratton and Mahala Lewis, July 24, 1823.
Elizabeth Stratton and John Kelly, February 25, 1825.
Polly Stratton and William McGuire, July 25, 1827.
Thursa Stratton and John G. Hatcher, March 1, 1832.
Solomon C. Stratton and Elizabeth Stratton, December, 1834.
Polly M. Stratton and John N. Layne, October 22, 1836.
Milly Stratton and Anthony H. Martin, July 7, 1839.
Mary Jane Stratton and James Harvey Leslie, March 3, 1843.

Pike County

William Stratton and Dicie Spurlock, April 3, 1824.
Harry Stratton and Martha McGuire, January 26, 1829.
Milton Stratton and Martha B. Leslie, September 17, 1829.
Hiram Stratton and Mary Pinson, September 2, 1834.
Harry Stratton and Anna Adkins, December 21, 1843.
Emily Stratton and John Ramey, March 15, 1846.
Nancy Ann Stratton and James Wingo, April 9, 1851.
John S. Stratton and Malissa Ellen Burk, June 15, 1853.

Richard Stratton and Susan Howard, August 15, 1853.

Mary Stratton and Albert Thompson, July 24, 1855.

Hezekiah Stratton and Nancy A. Ross, October 18, 1855.

William H. Stratton and Nancy J. Helvey, February 5, 1856.

Malden Stratton and Jackson Clark, ————, 1859.

William H. Stratton and Lucinda Ross, May 23, 1861.

Tandy Stratton and Millie King, May 27, 1862.

Manda M. Stratton and William Scott, July 7, 1865.

Sixteen Strattons served as commissioned officers and/or enlisted men in the Virginia forces during the Revolutionary War,[2] and six had service in the Union Army during the Civil War in Company "C", 39th Kentucky Volunteer Infantry, under Captain Thomas J. Sowards.[3]

---

[1] Henry Preston Scalf, "Historic Floyd", 1800-1950.

[2] John H. Gwathmey, "Virginians in the Revolution", 1775-1783.

[3] Report of the Adjutant General of Kentucky, 1861-1865, Vol. II, pages 392-4.

STROTHER FAMILY OF VIRGINIA AND CARTER CO. KY.

The Strother family is an ancient one and is supposed to be of Scandinavian origin. The name is found in Sweden and Denmark at the present time. Whatever its remote derivation, the name in its present form has existed several hundred years. General David Hunter Strother says: "It was carried by the Danish rovers and planted in the county of Northumberland, England, sometime in the tenth century". In this county the name and family have been conspicuous for centuries. Its intermarriages have been with some of the most influential and prominent families in Northern England. Alan del Strother, Lord of Lyham, was High Sheriff of Northumberland from 1354 to 1357 and "warden of the border". His son, Alan del Strother, was also high sheriff and warden of the castle and shire of Roxburgh, and he in turn was succeeded by his son Henry. In 1440, William del Strother, a grandson of Lord Lyham, m. a daughter of Robert Wallington and lived at Castle Strother in Glendale.

The direct descent of the Strother Family is as follows:

Alan del Strother.

William, third son; d. in 1315.

Henry, Lord of Newton; d. in 1379.

John; d. in 1394; m. Mary, daughter of Sir Alan Heton.

William; d. in 1409.

Thomas, Knight; d. in 1440; m. ———— Swinbourne.

William, of Wallington; d. in 1470.

Thomas; d. in 1501; m. a daughter of Thomas Horton.

Richard; d. in 1530; m. Margaret Mere.

William; d. in 1549; m. Barbara, daughter of Sir Roger Grey.

William; d. in 1580; m. Agnes, daughter of Sir Thomas Grey.

William Strother, of Newton, who m. Jane Selby.

Lancelot Strother; d. in 1611; m. Elinor Congers (of many royal descents).

William Strother, of Northumberland; b. 1597; d. 1667.

William Strother; b. about 1627; d. about 1702, the immigrant to Virginia.

The records of the various branches of the family in England are preserved but the links of connection with the Virginia family are not definitely known. However, there is a great similarity of christen names and it is not improbable that the first immigrant to America was a direct descendant of some branch of the Northumberland family. Coming to Virginia, the early generations were loyal and active churchmen, as is attested by the old church records of King George, Stafford and Culpeper counties. They became large land holders, lived the life of cultivated planters of the time and inter-married with the leading families of the colony. Some of them were lawyers, physicians and ministers of the Gospel; many held positions of honor and trust in the government of the Virginia colony and state and the nation; and a relatively large number served as commissioned officers in the French and Indian War, the Revolutionary War, the War of 1812 and later wars.

WILLIAM STROTHER, 1 the first of the name to immigrate to America and the founder of the family in Virginia, is supposed to have immigrated from Northumberland county, England—date and particulars unknown. Arriving in Virginia, he settled in Cittenborne parish on the Rappahannock river, near the present Port Conway, then in Rappahannock, later in Richmond and now in King George county. His name appears on the records the first time when, on June 12, 1673, he came into a court of old Rappahannock county to designate the mark of his cattle. His will, probated in Richmond county, on Nov. 4, 1702, names his wife "Dorothey" and their six sons: William 2, James 2, Jeremiah 2, Robert 2, Benjamin 2, and Joseph 2, and grandson, "Will" Strother 3.

II   William Strother 2, m. Margaret Thornton.
       (2) James Strother 2, d. in 1716 and devised his property to his brother Joseph.
III   (3) Jeremiah Strother 2, m. Eleanor ———.
       (4) Robert Strother 2, m. Elizabeth Berry, daughter of a clergyman; resided in King George county where he d. in 1735, his will being probated November 7th, that year.
   Children:
       (1) Elizabeth Strother 3, m. twice, but d. childless.
       (2) Enoch Strother 3, m. Mary Key and d. prior to June 4, 1772, when she qualified as administratrix of his estate. After his death, in consequence of the annoyance of the British, she removed to Clarke and thence to Fauquier Co., where descendants subsequently resided.
       (3) John Strother 3; (4) Robert Strother 3.

(5) BENJAMIN STROTHER 2, m. Mary, daughter of Adam Woffendall; resided in King George county, where he d. in 1752, his will being probated May 5th that year. He was justice in Richmond

county and continued as such in King George county, where he was a vestryman of the Church, sheriff and a land proprietor. In his will he names children:

(1) Richard Strother 3, d. in 1761; will probated December 1761.

(2) George Strother 3, m. Mrs. Tabitha (Payne), widow of William Woffendall; resided in King George county. His will probated, December 13, 1761 names wife Tabitha and sons John Strother 4 and George Strother 4.

(3) Benjamin Strother 3, m. Anne ———. By deed executed in 1754, his mother Mary Strother gave him—then as of Hanover parish—the land given her by her father. July 20, 1758, Benjamin Strother and his wife, Anne, of the parish, executed a deed. In 1759 he was fined for not keeping a road in order to Port Royal.

(4) John Strother 3; (5) Samuel Strother 3; (6) Francis Strother 3.

(6) JOSEPH STROTHER 2, m. Margaret Berry, daughter of Grace and ——— Berry. He was a justice in Richmond county and continued as such in King George county, where he was a vestryman and sheriff. He owned and lived on a part of his father's old home place near Port Conway. His will was probated August 7, 1766, in which he names his children:

(1) Mary Strother 3, who m. William Wren.

(2) Margaret Strother 3, who m. ——— Clannahan.

(3) Dorothy Strother 3, who m. ——— Walker.

(4) Thomas Strother 3, who lived in Stafford county.

(5) Nicholas Strother 3, who d. in 1779.

(6) Joseph Strother 3, who m. ——— Berry and d. in King George county in 1762. As Captain Joseph Strother he was granted, May 28, 1748, lands lying partly in King George county and partly in Westmoreland county. His will names wife and brother-in-law, Benjamin Berry, as executors. An only daughter, Elizabeth Nicholas Strother 4, d. unm., and left legacies to his nephews, Nicholas Wren 4, William Clannahan 4, and Joseph Walker 4.

II WILLIAM STROTHER 2, (son of William Strother 1, the immigrant and Dorothy, his wife) was b. probably 1665-75. He was a planter and lived at the original seat of his father, now in King George county. On December 20, 1718, there were patented to him and three others 6,000 acres of land in St. Mary's parish, Essex county, now Spottsylvania county. He was a vestryman of Hanover parish and was sheriff of King George county. He m. Margaret Thornton, b. April 2, 1678, daughter of Francis Thornton, son of the first William Thornton, of Gloucester

county, and his wife, Alice, daughter of Captain Anthony
Savage, of Gloucester county. His will was probated on July 26
1726 and his widow qualified as executrix.

Children:

(1) Mary Strother 4, m. Colonel William Bronaugh, of London, England.

(2) Alice Strother 4, m., December 16, 1756, Robert Washington, b. June 25, 1729, son of Townsend and Elizabeth (Lund) Washington, of King George County. A son, Lund Washington, b. September 25, 1767, was the father of Colonel Peter G. Washington and Colonel L. Q. Washington.

(3) A daughter 4, m. Henry Tyler, who was clerk of Stafford county, in 1764, whose son, Thomas G. Strother Tyler 5, succeeded him.

(4) Anne Strother 4, m. John James and had a large family. The third son, Hon. Benjamin James 5, m. Jean Stobo, of Charleston, S. C., and their daughter, Susan 6, b. May 9, 1804, m. John Garlington, of Laurens county, S. C.

III JEREMIAH STROTHER 2, (son of William Strother 1, the immigrant, and his wife Dorothy), was a freeholder in Westmoreland county as early as 1702. Subsequently, he was a planter in King George county, where he resided probably as late as 1736, when he moved to Orange county, now Culpeper county. Here he d. in 1741. His will, probated March 26, 1741, devised all property to wife, Elener (sic) for life or widowhood, and after her marriage or death to son Christopher 3. Special legacies were made to sons James 3, Francis 3, Jeremiah 3, and Lawrence 3, and daughters Catharine 3, and Elizabeth 3.

Children:

(1) James Strother 3, m. Margaret French.

(2) William Strother 3, m. Mildred, daughter of Charles Taliaferro, in Spottsylvania county in 1729, and d. in Westmoreland county in 1749. In his will, executed in 1749, he names son William 4, who m. Winifred ———; Charles Strother 4, who d. at Charleston, S. C., in 1773, leaving sons George 5, is thought to have been son of William 3; George Strother 5, was a lieutenant in Marion's Brigade in 1781. Both he and William Strother 5, settled in old Cheraw District, Chesterfield county, S. C.

(3) Francis Strother 3.

(4) Catherine Strother 3.

(5) Elizabeth Strother 3.

(6) Lawrence Strother 3, m. Elizabeth ———, in 1742 they resided in Orange county.

(7) Jeremiah Strother 3, m. Catharine Kennerly; resided in Culpeper county and removed to South Carolina and settled on Saluda river. One son, John E. Strother 4, returned to Virginia and m. Anne Strother 5, daughter of Captain John Strother 4, and their son, George Strother 5, moved to Trimble county, Kentucky and was long a minister of the Gospel.

(8) Christopher Strother 3, m. Ann ———. In 1746 as of Caroline county, he executed a conveyance of 350 acres in Culpeper county; and in October 1749, as of Fairfax county, he conveyed to Captain Benjamin Strother "the lands in King George in Hanover Parish, given him by his father, Jeremiah Strother". About 1750 he removed to Edgecomb county, North Carolina, but was included in Franklin county upon the formation of that county. One daughter, Ann Strother 4, m. Garrett Goodloe, son of Rev. Henry Goodloe, of Caroline county, Virginia, and they had a son, James Kemp Goodloe 5, who m. Mary Reaves Jones (daughter of Daniel Jones, son of the first Edward Jones, early prominent in Granville county, N. C.); and they had a son, Colonel Daniel R. Goodloe 6, who resided in Washington, D. C.

IV WILLIAM STROTHER 3, (son of William Strother 2, and his wife Margaret Thornton, and grandson of William Strother 1, the immigrant and his wife Dorothy), was b. about 1700. After the destruction of the old mansion house of his grandfather the first William Strother, he sold his estate near Port Conway and in 1727 purchased lands on the river opposite Fredericksburg which was sold November 3, 1738, by his widow and executrix, to Augustine Washington, father of General George Washington. On May 26, 1727, he received a grant of 266 acres in King George county and on September 12, 1731, as "Captain William Strother", 372 acres in Prince William county. He was sheriff and justice of King George county and was vestryman of the parish. He m. Margaret Watts, who, on his death, m. (2) John Grant. He d. in 1732 and in his will directed sale of his lands in King George and Prince William counties and named his wife as executrix.
Children:

(1) Elizabeth Strother 4, m., November 9, 1738, John Frogg, of Prince William county, who subsequently moved to the Valley of Virginia, and resided near the families of the wife's sisters. A son, John Frogg, Jr., 5, m. Agatha Lewis 5 his first cousin, and was killed at the battle of Point Pleasant (October 10, 1774).

(2) AGATHA STROTHER 4, m. John Madison (a near relative of President Madison) who was the first clerk of Augusta county, 1745; member of the vestry and also of the Virginia House of Burgesses and House of Delegates. He d. in Botetourt county, March, 1784.

Children:

William Strother Madison 5, of Botetourt county, m. Elizabeth Preston, daughter of Col. William Preston; George Thomas Madison 5, lawyer, of Botetourt county, m. Susannah Henry, sister of Hon. Patrick Henry; Roland Madison 5, m. Anne Lewis, daughter of General Andrew Lewis, "The hero of the Point" (son of John Lewis, "the founder") and removed to Kentucky; James Madison 5, b. August 27, 1749, near Port Republic, then in Augusta now in Rockingham county, was an ardent patriot in the Revolutionary War and the first Resident—Bishop (1785) of the Episcopal Church in Virginia. He m., in 1799, Sarah Tate, of Williamsburg, and they had children: James Catesby Madison 6; and Susan Madison 6, who m. R. G. Scott, of Richmond; George Madison 5, soldier and sixth Governor of Kentucky (1816), m. Jane Smith, daughter of Major Francis Smith; Margaret Madison 5, m. Judge William McDowell, a son of Judge Samuel McDowell, of Kentucky, and had children, among others a daughter, Agatha McDowell, who m. Hon. James G. Birney, first Abolition candidate for President of the United States.

(3) MARGARET MADISON STROTHER 4, b. in King George county, m. (1) April 26, 1744, George Morton, who d. soon thereafter; (2) October 16, 1749, Gabriel Jones, "The Lawyer", who was b. near Williamsburg, May 17, 1724, son of John and Elizabeth Jones; prepared for the bar at London, England, and in 1745 was admitter as as attorney in Augusta county "as a fit person to transact his Majestic affairs". He and his brother-in-law, Thomas Lewis, represented Rockingham county in the Virginia Convention of 1788. He d. near Port Republic Rockingham county, in October 1796 and his wife d. near the same place in 1822, in her 97th year.

Children:

(1) Margaret Jones 5, m. Colonel John Harvie, of Albemarle county, a lawyer and signer of the Articles of Confederation. Of their seven children, Gabriella J. Jones 6, m. (1) Colonel Thomas Mann Randolph, and (2) Dr. John Brokenborough, who erected the "Jefferson Davis House" Richmond.

(2) A daughter 5, was the third wife of John Lewis (son of Fielding Lewis and Catharine Washington), who moved to Kentucky.

(3) A daughter 5, m. John Hawkins.

(4) Strother Jones 5, b. March 21, 1756, was a captain in the Revolutionary War; m. Fanny Thornton, daughter of Francis Thornton of "Fall Hill", and his wife Anne, who was a daughter of the Rev. John Thompson. Their only child, William Strother Jones 6; m. Ann Maria Marshall, daughter of Charles and Lucy (Pickett) Marshall.

(4) ANNE STROTHER 4, m., January 26, 1749, Thomas Lewis b. in Donegal, Ireland, April 27, 1718, the eldest of the distinguished sons of Colonel John Lewis, "the founder", and his wife Margaret Lynn. He was a man of cultivated mind, great ability and enterprise and rendered many important services to his country. He lived and d. near Port Republic.

Children:

(1) Thomas Lewis 5, d. in 1788.

(2) Margaret Ann Lewis 5, m. (1) ———— McClenahan and (2) William Bowyer.

(3) Agatha Lewis 5. m. (1) Captain John Frogg 6, her first cousin and (2) John Stuart.

(4) Jane Lewis 5, m. Thomas Hughes.

(5) Andrew Lewis 5, d. unm.

(6) Thomas Lewis 5, d. unm.

(7) Mary Lewis 5, m. John McElhany.

(8) Elizabeth Lewis 5, m. Thomas Meriweather Gilmer, of Rockingham county, Virginia; they removed to Georgia and were the parents of George R. Gilmer, author, member of Congress and Governor of Georgia.

(9) Anne Lewis 5, m. (1) ———— Douthat; and (2) ———— French, of Kentucky.

(10) Frances Lewis 5, m. Layton Yancey.

(11) Charles Lewis 5, m. ———— Yancey.

(12) Sophia Lewis 5, m. John Carthrae; they removed to Missouri.

(13) William Benjamin Lewis 5, m. M. Hite.

V FRANCIS STROTHER 3, (son of William Strother 2, and Margaret Thornton, his wife and grandson of William Strother 1, the immigrant, and his wife, Dorothy), was b. probably in Richmond county, now King George county. By deed executed August 1, 1727, Margaret Strother gave to her son Francis Strother, of Hanover county, certain slaves with reversion to her grandson, William Strother 4. On January 22, 1745, William Coleman conveyed to Francis Strother, of St. Martin's parish, Hanover county, 583 1/3 acres in St. Mark's parish, Orange county, near the county seat of the present Rappahannock county. Here Francis Strother removed and settled close to his son, John 4, and probably here he died. He m. Susannah Dabney, of the Hanover county family of that name, probably in that county, where it is known his son John 4, was born. He died in 1752 and his will, dated April 17, 1751, probated in Culpeper county, names his wife, Susannah, their five sons, three of whom were then under sixteen years, and four daughters.

Children:

(1) John Dabney Strother 4, b. in 1721, in Hanover county, m. Mary Willis Wade.

(2) William Strother 4, m. Sarah (Bayly) Pannill.

(3) Elizabeth Strother 4, m. James Gaines.

(4) Mary Strother 4.

(5) Behethland Strother 4, m. Oliver Walliss.

(6) Susannah Strother 4, m. Thomas Gaines, son of Henry and Isabella (Pendleton) Gaines. Their children were: Philip Gaines 5, m. ——— McGavock; James Strother Gaines 5, m. Judith Easley and they had among other children, John Strother Gaines 6, who m. Letitia Dalton Moore. Their daughter, Amanda M. Gaines 7, m. Charles A. Rice and they are the parents of Susan L. Rice 8, who m. John B. Clotworthy and resided at Hillman, Georgia. Richard Thomas Gaines 5; Elizabeth Strother Gaines 5; Susan Gaines 5; Henry Pendleton Gaines 5; Francis Gaines 5, m. ——— Cardwell; George W. Gaines 5, m. ——— Joyce, of North Carolina; and Francis Thornton Gaines 5.

(7) ANTHONY STROTHER 4, m. Frances Eastham; removed from Culpeper county to Hardy county, Virginia, now West Virginia.

Children:

(1) Robert Strother 5; John Strother 5; Francis Strother 5; Benjamin Strother 5; Philip Strother 5, a Methodist minister, removed to Eastern Kentucky and descendants live in Carter County, that state.

(8) GEORGE STROTHER 4, m. Mary Kennerly. He d. in Culpeper county in 1767.[1]

Children:

John Strother 5, who served in the Creek Indian War; George Strother 5, who had service in the United States Army, 1794-99, and resided in Tennessee; Margaret Strother 5. m. Colonel George Hancock, of Botetourt county, Virginia, who was a member of Congress, 1793-97. Their daughter, Caroline Hancock 6, m. Major William Preston, of Kentucky, U S. Army, afterward General, Confederate States Army, lawyer and statesman, son of William Preston and Caroline (Hancock) Preston, grandson of Colonel William Preston and great-grandson of John Preston, the immigrant. A daughter, Henrietta Preston m. General Albert Sidney Johnston Confederates States Army, who was killed at Shiloh, April 6, 1862 (dying in the arms of his father-in-law, General Preston) who were the parents of Colonel William Preston Johnston of New Orleans, Louisiana.

(9) FRANCIS STROTHER, JR., 4, m. Anne Graves and lived and d. Culpeper county. He served as a lieutenant of the militia of that county and rendered valuable service in the French and Indian War, 1756-59. His will, probated October 20, 1777, names his wife, Anne, and sons, John 5, Francis 5, Samuel 5, and George 5.

Children:

(1) Francis Strother 5, moved to Georgia with his uncle, Colonel John Gràves; his son, Charles R. Strother 6, was a laywer and a member of the Georgia Secession Convention, 1861.

(2) John Strother 5, was a seaman and d. in England.

(3) Samuel Strother 5, and (4) George Strother 5 d. in their youth.

(10) ROBERT STROTHER 4, m. Eizabeth ———. In 1771 he executed a deed to Charles Browning for lands in Culpeper county.

VI ANTHONY STROTHER 3, (son of William Strother 2, and Margaret Thornton, his wife, and grandson of William Strother 1, the immigrant, and his wife Dorothy), was b. August 1, 1710, and d. December 10, 1765. He was a merchant in Fredericksburg, resided across the river from the town, and the Fredericksburg ferry was on his land. On January 27, 1734, he received a grant of 600 acres in Spottsylvania county, on the "Goad Vine Fork". In 1739, William Thornton conveyed to Anthony Strother and Behethland, his wife, 250 acres below the falls of the Rappahannock river in King George county. His will, probated in October 1766, directed his property to be kept together as a whole for ten years and then sold and the proceeds equally divided among his widow and children. He m. (1) August 25, 1733, Behethland Starke, b. December 27, 1716 and d. after December 2, 1753; and (2) in 1754, Mary James, b. December 28, 1736. His widow, Mary, M. (2) Colonel Henry Smith (brother of Daniel Smith, United States Senator from Tennessee, and also of Enoch Smith, great-grandfather of James

Milton Bourne, of Louisville, Kentucky). Colonel Henry Smith and his wife removed to Russell county, Virginia. Children of Anthony Strother and Behethland Starke:

(1) William Strother 4, b. August 29, 1734 d. March 18, 1743.

(2) Anthony Strother 4, b. May 10 1736, m. ———— Kenyon, daughter .of Abram Kenyon. He was sheriff and also justice of King George county; and lived at the old home of his father.
Children:
George Strother 5, who inherited the family seat; Anthony Strother 5, m. ———— Newton and removed to the Valley; John Strother 5, m. ———— Price.

(3) Elizabeth Strother 4, b. September 22, 1738 d. August 3, 1745.

(4) Margaret Strother 4, b. September 23, 1740, d. February 4 1741.

(5) John Strother 4, b. February 11, 1742.

(6) Francis Strother 4, b. November 23. 1743, d. August 15, 1745.

(7) Alice Strother 4, b. January 18, 1744, d. March 18, 1744.

(8) William Strother 4, b. April 30, 1746.

(9) Betty Strother 4, b. August 8, 1747, d. September 10, 1748.

(10) Benjamin Strother 4, b. June 25, 1750 d. in 1805; entered the Virginia Navy in 1776 and served three years; subsequently he entered the Army and served until the close of the Revolution. He m. Kittie Price. He settled in Berkeley county, now Jefferson county, West Virginia and built "Park Forest," near Charles Town. Daughters: Mrs. Benjamin Pendleton 5; Mrs. J. M. Crane 5; Mrs. Cato Moore 5; Mrs. Richard Duffield 5. His son, John Strother 5, b. November 18, 1782, entered the United States Army and served from 1813 to 1815; m. September 7, 1815, Elizabeth Pendleton Hunter, sister of Hon. Andrew Hunter; was clerk of Berkeley county; and d. January 16, 1862. General David Hunter Strother 6, b. September 26, 1816; d. March 8, 1898, author and artist, known by the pen-name of "Porte Crayon", brigadier-general of West Virginia Volunteers in the Union Army during the Civil War and minister to Mexico, was a son.

(11) Starke Strother 4, b. April 12, 1752.

(12) Behethland Strother 4, b. December 2, 1753. Children of Anthony Strother 3, and his wife Mary (James):

(13) James Strother 4, b. November 19, 1755; served in the Revolutionary War; m. Elizabeth B. Morton; lived in

Fauquier county, and about 1807 removed to Russell county, Virginia, leaving descendants.

(14) Mary Strother 4, b. June 2, 1757; m. Benjamin Ficklin, of Fauquier county.

(15) George Strother 4, b. September 1, 1760; d. December 6, 1769.

(16) Betty Strother 4, b. July 20, 1763.

VII JAMES STROTHER 3, (son of Jeremiah Strother 2, and his wife, Eleanor and grandson of William Strother 1, the immigrant and his wife, Dorothy), lived in King George county; in 1733 was deputy under Benjamin Strother 2, sheriff; in 1741 was sheriff and a justice; in 1742 was appointed collector and in 1747 inspector at Falmouth (then in King George county). Subsequently, he removed to Culpeper county, where he d., intestate in 1761, leaving a large personal estate, which was divided among his children, his real estate passing to his eldest son, French Strother 4. He m. Margaret French, daughter of Daniel French, of King George county, and his wife, Margaret, who was a daughter of John Pratt and his wife, Margaret, of King George county. Daniel French was of the prominent family of that name of Roscommon county, Ireland.

Children:

(1) French Strother 4, m. Lucy Coleman.

(2) James Strother 4, d. unm., in 1764. His will, probated in Stafford county, leaves property to brother, French 4, and sister, Mary Gray 4.

(3) Mary Strother 4, m. George Gray and lived in Stafford county. Children: (1) George Gray 5, m. Mildred Thompson, daughter of Rev. John Thompson; in 1800 they removed to Louisville, Kentucky; he served in the Revolutionary War. Children: George Gray, Jr. 6; James Strother Gray 6,; French Strother Gray 6; Minor Gray 6; Anderson Gray 6; Henry Weedon Gray 6; all of whom lived in Kentucky. George, James and French served in the Army as commissioned officers.

(2) Daniel Gray 5, m. Mary Strother, daughter of Colonel French Strother 4, his first cousin.

VIII JOHN DABNEY STROTHER 4, of "Wadefield (son of Francis Strother 3, and his wife, Susannah Dabney, grandson of William Strother 2, and his wife, Margaret Thornton, and great-grandson of William Srother 1, the immigrant, and his wife Dorothy, was b. in Hanover county, in 1721; m. Mary Wade and soon thereafter removed to Culpeper county, settling near the town of Washington, where he d. in April 1795. He served as captain in the French and Indian War, 1756-7.

Children:

(1) Joseph Strother 5, m. Nancy Stewart and in 1800 removed to Jefferson county, Kentucky. A son, Benjamin Strother 6 had service in .the United States Army from 1792 to 1797 and d. at Warm Springs, Virginia. A son, William Strother 6, had a daughter, Harriet, who m. Rev. Horace Stringfellow.

(2) Susannah Strother 5, m. John Lawler.

(3) Mary Strother 5, m. Charles Browning.

(4) Sarah Strother 5, m. William Hughes.

(5) Lucy Strother 5, m. Francis Covington.

(6) Mildred Strother 5, m. William Covington.

(7) Anne Strother 5, m. John F. Strother.

(8) Elizabeth Strother 5, m. Captain John Browning, of the Continental Line, son of Frank Browning. D. P. Browning who lived at Lewisburg, Kentucky, was a descendant.

(9) John Strother 5, m. Helen Piper. He inherited "Wadefield" and d. in 1818. Among: his children, a daughter, Nancy Strother 6, b. November 20, 1784, m. in June 1799, William Pendleton, whose son, Albert G. Pendleton, m. Elvira Chapman, the parents of the wife of Judge Philip William Strother 7. William Pendleton was the son of Captain James Pendleton and Margaret Bowie, son of James Pendleton and Susan Clayton, son of Henry Pendleton and Mary Taylor (daughter of the first James Taylor), son of Philip Pendleton and Isabella Hurt.

IX WILLIAM STROTHER 4, (son of Francis Strother 3, and his wife, Susannah Dabney grandson of William Strother 2, and his wife, Margaret Thornton, and great-grandson of William Strother 1 the immigrant, and his wife, Dorothy), was b., probably, in Hanover county, about 1725. In 1749 he received a grant of 400 acres in Orange county. He was a large landed proprietor in Culpeper and Orange counties. He m., prior to February 20, 1752, (1) Mrs. Sarah (Bayly) Pannill, widow of William Pannill, who d. in 1774, and (2) Anne Kavenah (sic). Late in life he removed to Woodford county, Kentucky, where he d. in 1808.

Children:

(1) Susannah Strother 5, m. Captain Moses Hawkins, of the 14th Virginia Regiment, who was killed at the battle of Germantown (October 4, 1777). His children received a land grant for his services. They lived in Woodford county, Kentucky, and were: Sarah Bailey Hawkins 6, William Strother Hawkins 6, m. Katherine Keith; Moses Hawkins 6, m. a Castleman; and a daughter 6.

(2) William Dabney Hawkins 5, who, it is thought, was killed at the Battle of Guilford Court House (March 15, 1781) in the Revolutionary War.

(3) Sarah Hawkins 5, b. December 11, 1760, m. Richard Taylor, son of Zachary Taylor and Elizabeth Lee, son of James Taylor, II and Martha Thompson, son of James Taylor, the immigrant, and his first wife ——— ———. He was a lieutenant colonel in the 2d Virginia Regiment in the Revolutionary War.

Children:

(1) Hancock Taylor 6, m. (1) Elizabeth Hord; and (2) Annah Lewis.

(2) Zachary Taylor 6, General, U. S. Army, national hero, known as "Old Rough and Ready" and twelfth President of the United States, m., June 18, 1810, Margaret Mackall Smith (1787-1852) of Maryland. Their daughter, Sarah Knox Taylor 7, m. June 17, 1835, at the home of Mr. and Mrs. John Gibson Taylor, at "Beechland," Kentucky, Jefferson Davis, then lieutenant, U. S. Army, subsequently President of the Confederate States of America.

(3) George Taylor 6.

(4) William Dabney Taylor 6.

(5) Richard Taylor 6.

(6) Joseph Pannill Taylor 6, m. Evaline McLean.

(7) Elizabeth Lee Taylor 6, m. John Gibson Taylor.

(8) Sarah Taylor 6; m. French Strother Gray, son of colonel George Gray 5, son of George Gray and Mary Strother 4. daughter of James Strother 3.

(9) Emily Taylor 6, m. John S. Allison.

X ELIZABETH STROTHER 4, (daughter of Francis Strother 3, and Margaret Thornton, his wife, granddaughter of William Strother 2, and Susannah Dabney, his wife and great-granddaughter of William Strother 1, the immigrant and his wife Dorothy), m. in Culpeper county, probably about 1765-75, James Gaines, son of Henry Gaines and his wife, Isabella (Pendleton) Gaines. Subsequently they removed to North Carolina. Captain James Gaines had service in the Revolutionary War and was in the battle of Eutaw Springs (September 8, 1781) and other engagements and was a member of the North Carolina Convention which ratified the Constitution of the United States. He was a nephew of Edmund Pendleton who, for many years, was the presiding judge of the Court of Appeals of Virginia. He removed to Tennessee and d. at Kingsport, that state, in 1808.

Children:

(1) Edmund Pendleton Gaines 5, b. in Culpeper county Vir-

ginia, March 20, 1777; d. in New Orleans, Louisiana, June 6, 1849; m. (1) Frances Toulmin, daughter of Judge Harry Toulmin, Secretary of State of Kentucky in the administrations of Governor James Garrard, 1796-1804 and first Territorial Judge in the Alabama portion of the Mississippi territory; (2) Barbara Blount, daughter of Governor William Blount, first governor of Tennessee. A son E. P. Gaines, Jr., resided in Washington, D. C.; and (3) Mrs. Myra (Clark) Whitney, daughter of Daniel Clark.

He entered the United States Navy as an ensign, Jan. 10, 1799; served during the War of 1812, and was promoted major-general for services in defense of Fort Erie in 1814. He was commissioner to the Seminole Indians in 1816, and took command against them in 1817.

(2) George Strother Gaines 5, b. in Stokes county, North Carolina in 1874, d. in Alabama in 1873; m. Ann Gaines; was an early and influential settler in Alabama, then Mississippi Territory.

(3) Frances Gaines 5, m. Charles Lynn.

(4) James Gaines 5, m. Fanny Rogers.

(5) Agnes Gaines 5, m. Joseph Everett. Their daughter, Susan Dabney Everett 6, m. Joseph O'Brien and their daughter Eliza Ann O'Brien, b. September 25, 1819, m., September 11, 1835, William G. Brownlow (1805-1877), of Tennessee, who in early life was a Methodist minister, and for many years edited the *Knoxville Whig*. He strongly opposed secession and became known as the "Fighting Parson". During the war he was the center of the Unionist feeling in Eastern Tennessee, and was at one time imprisoned. He was Governor of Tennessee, 1865-1867 and United States Senator 1869-1875. They had seven children, one of whom Colonel John Bell Brownlow 6, soldier and historian, m. Mary Fouche, and resided in Washington, D. C.

(6) Patsy Gaines 5, m. —— Everett.

(7) Nancy Gaines 5 m. —— Asher.

(8) Lucy Gaines 5, m. David Childress.

(9) Elizabeth Gaines 5, m. Samuel Moore.

(10) Susanna Gaines 5, d. unm.

(11) Sarah Gaines 5, d., unm.

(12) BEHETHLAND GAINES 5, m. James Lyon, of Stokes county, North Carolina.

Children:

James Gaines Lyon 6, m. Rosanna Fisher, daughter of Colonel George Fisher, of Alabama, son of Frederick

Fisher and Ann McBride, of Rowan county, North Carolina; they removed to Alabama. One daughter, Sarah B. Lyon 6, m. Charles K. Foote, of Mobile, Alabama, and they had, among other children, Nellie G. Lyon Foote 7, wife of R. H. Clarke, of Mobile, Alabama, lawyer, and some time member of Congress; Francis Strother Lyon 6, b. in 1800 in Stokes county, North Carolina, removed to Alabama and resided at Demopolis. He was a lawyer and honored and respected citizen; m. Sarah Serena Glover, daughter of Allen Glover, of Goose Creek Parish, South Carolina, and they had, among other children, Mary A. Lyon 7, who m. William Henry Ross, a prominent citizen of Mobile Alabama, son of Jack Terrill Ross (the first treasurer of Alabama) and Anne Amelia Fisher, daughter of Colonel George Fisher, above. He was a son of John Ross and his wife, Temperance Terrill, of Franklin county, North Carolina. A daughter, Amelia L. Ross 8, m. James L. Abbott and resided at Little Rock, Arkansas; William Lyon 6; Kittie Lyon 6; Elizabeth Lyon 6, m. ———— Martin; Sallie Lyon 6, m. ———— Flippin; and Nancy Lyon 6.

XI FRENCH STROTHER 4, (son of James Strother 3, and his wife, Margaret French, grandson of Jeremiah Strother 2, and his wife, Elenor, and great-grandson of William Strother 1, the immigrant, and his wife, Dorothy), was b. about 1735, in King George county, Virginia. He lived on a handsome estate of 1,500 acres, lying on Mountain Run, on the Fredericksburg road between Culpeper and Stevensburg. He was a vestryman and warden of St. Mark's parish; represented Culpeper county for more than a quarter of a century in the General Assembly, before, during and after the Revolutionary War; was a member of the Virginia conventions of 1776 and 1788, opposing in the latter, with Patrick Henry, George Mason and others, the adoption of the Constitution of the United States. For his boldness and aggressiveness during the Revolutionary struggle, he was designated by Grigsby as "The Fearless". He d., intestate, in August 1800, and is buried at Fredericksburg. He m. Lucy Coleman, daughter of Robert Coleman, formerly of Caroline county. She was connected with the families of Clayton, Foster and Stevens.

Children:

(1) Margaret French Strother 5, b. in 1758, d. in 1849, m. Captain Philip Slaughter who had service in the Revolutionary War. They had many distinguished descendants.

(2) Gilley Strother 5, m. Colonel John Evans. Commander French Chadwick 7, U. S. Navy, was a grandson.

(3) Lucy Strother 5, d. unm.

(4) Elizabeth Strother 5, m. Nimrod Evans.

(5) Mary Strother 5, m. Daniel Gray, her first cousin.

(6) Daniel French Strother 5, m. Fannie Thompson, daughter of Judge John Thompson, of Louisville, Ky., son of Rev. John Thompson and his wife, Dorothy, who was widow of Governor Alexander Spottswood, of Virginia. They lived and d. at Louisville, Kentucky.

(7) George French Strother 5, m. (1) Sarah Green Williams, daughter of General James Williams of "Soldiers Rest", Orange county, and his wife, Eleanor, daughter of Moses Green, youngest son of Robert Green, the immigrant. General James Williams was the son of the second William Williams and Lucy, the daughter of Philip Clayton, of Catalpa, who was himself the grandson of the first Philip Pendleton. George French Strother 5, was a lawyer; member of the Virginia Assembly; and Member of Congress, 1817-20, when he resigned to become Receiver of Public Moneys at St. Lewis, Missouri, where he d. in 1840. He m. (2) Theodosia Hunt, daughter of John Hunt, of Lexington, Kentucky. They had two children: Sallie Hunt 6, and John Hunt 6.

James French Strother 6, son of George French Strother 3, and Sarah Green Williams, his wife, was b. at Culpeper Court House, September 4, 1811, and d. September 20, 1860; m. November 2, 1832, Elizabeth Roberts, daughter of John Roberts, of Culpeper county, who was commissioned a major in the Rev. War, on March 5, 1779. He was a lawyer; Member of the Virginia Constitutional Convention of 1850; and Member of Congress, 1851-53.

Children:

(1) George F. Strother 7, d. without issue.

(2) John Roberts Strother 7, m. ——— Payne.

(3) James French Strother 7, m. ——— Botts.

(4) William Strother 7, d. without issue.

(5) Judge Philip Williams Strother 7, lawyer and jurist, of Pearisburg, Virginia, now West Virginia, m. Nannie Strother Pendleton, daughter of Colonel A. G. Pendleton.

(6) Sallie Williams Strother 7.

(7) John Hunt Strother 7.

(8) W. Johnson Strother 7, m. ——— Shackleford.

(9) Lewis Harvie Strother 7.

(10) Charles Strother 7, d. without issue.

THE STROTHER FAMILY OF NORTHEASTERN KY.

*1. Philip Strother and *2. John R. Strother, his nephew, were the immediate ancestors of the Strothers of Northeastern Kentucky.

1. PHILIP STROTHER 5, a minister in the Methodist Church, a son of Anthony Strother 4 and Frances Eastham, a grandson of Francis Strother 3, and Susannah Dabney, a great-grandson of William Strother 2, and Margaret Thornton and a great-great-grandson of William Strother 1, and Dorothy ——— (surname not learned), was b. in Culpeper County, Virginia, in 1780; went with his father to and was reared in Hardy County, Virginia (now West Virginia), and d. at Pleasant Valley, Carter County, Kentucky, June 5, 1865, where he was buried and where he had lived for many years. He m., about 1812, Sarah Clemens, b. in Ohio in 1795, and d. September, 1868. She was buried beside her husband.

The Strothers were Baptists in religion but Sarah Clemens Strother was a Methodist; was possessed of many virtues and was a devoted Christian; and it was to her pious example that her husband ascribed his conversion to active christianity. He became a member and a minister of the Methodist Church and continued in the ministry until his death.

Mr. Strother became an itinerant in 1825; and after traveling the Nicholas, Big Kanawha, Kanawha, Burlington and Guyandotti Circuits (the latter for two years), all in the Kanawha (Virginia) District, he settled in 1831, (probably in the Big Sandy Valley) as a local preacher. His labors in the ministry may be partially described in the following tribute from the "History of Methodism in Kentucky" by Dr. Redford (Vol. III, page 416):

"Philip Strother and Stephen Spurlock will not only be remembered by the present generation (1870), but their names will be transmitted to generations yet unborn . . . . the good that he (Mr. Strother) accomplished can be estimated only in the light of eternity".

"A man of wonderful powers in the pulpit was Rev. Philip Strother who preached in the Big Sandy Valley for many years. He had a most captivating voice, was a man of true eloquence, and had superior descriptive powers. He was greatly beloved by the people and his name is worthily perpetuated in his gifted son, Hon. Joseph Strother, at this time judge of the County Court of Carter County. He was an old time Methodist".[2]

Philip Strother had service in the War of 1812. He was a man of strong convictions which is characteristic of his family. Living in a typical community of Southern sympathizers and slave holders in Carter County, he remained firm and steadfast in antagonism to slavery which institution had existed in the Strother families. His father, Anthony, had manumitted numerous slaves. He preached the funeral sermon of three Federal soldiers at Olive Hill on Sunday, June 4, 1865, and died very suddenly on the night of June 5th.

Children:

3. Hannah Strother, the eldest child; m., July 1, 1832, James Davis in Floyd County, Kentucky; d. early in life. Their children were: John, who m. but names of children, if any, not known; Fleming, who m., but names of children, if any, not known; and Catherine, who m. John Frazier, d. young and had two children, one of whom, Hannah, lived to maturity.

4. Frances Eastham Strother, the second child; m. James Ratliff or Radcliffe in Pike County, Kentucky, April 2, 1835. Their children were: Sarah, Marion, Meribah, Philip, William, America and Deborah. They removed to Carter County, Kentucky, and James Ratliff d. and was buried at Pleasant Valley, that county, beside his daughter America. His Widow Frances survived him many years and died during a residence with her daughter Meribah Boothe in Symmes Creek region of Lawrence County, Ohio.

5. Deborah Strother, the third child, m. Fleming H. Brown in Lawrence County, Kentucky, September 4, 1834.

*6. Joseph Haven Strother.

7. Anthony Strother; m. Aura (Aurena) Reeves in Carter County, November 10, 1850. Children: (a) John R., m. Rebecca Nethercutt and they were parents of George and Aura. John R. Strother resided in Galena, Kansas, where he d. in 1913. (b) Philip Strother, (c) Joseph Strother, (d) William Strother, (e) Green Strother and (f) Anthony Strother, Jr.

8. America Strother; d. young.[3]

The U. S. Census of Carter County for 1850 shows the following with respect to the members of the household of Philip and Sarah Strother: "Strother, Philip, 71, preacher, b. in Virginia. Strother, Sarah, 55, b. in Kentucky. Deborah Brown, 35, b. in Ohio. Sarah, 13, b. in Kentucky. Mary, 8, b. in Missouri. Melvin, 6, b. in Missouri. Frances, 5, b. in Missouri. Joseph, 3, b. in Missouri. James, 1, b. in Missouri. Sarah K. Davis, 13, b. in Virginia."

6. JOSEPH HAVEN STROTHER, the fourth child and eldest son, was b. in Pike County, Ohio, February 22, 1819; m., in Greenup County, February 22, 1843, Sari Anne Osenton, b. March 13, 1824, a daughter of Samuel and Emsy (Downs) Osenton of Greenup County, Kentucky. (See Osenton Family.) He d. March 17, 1907, and she November 29, 1904. Both were buried at Lindsay Chapel near Grayson, Kentucky.

JUDGE JOSEPH H. STROTHER was a man of great ability, broad information and strong convictions with the religious tendencies inherited by many of the descendants of Philip Strother. They resided for many years at Counts Cross Roads, Carter County. He was elected and served two terms as judge of Carter County Court, being at that time the only Democrat elected to that office since the Civil War.

Children—nine daughters and one son:

9. America Strother; b. December 6, 1843, and d. November 20, 1845.

10. Lucy Strother; b. November 25, 1845, and d. February 28, 1860.

11. Sari Emsy Henrietta Strother; b. June 17, 1848; m. October 5, 1870, Vivian Powell Meade, b. in Russell County, Virginia, in December, 1836, and d. May 26, 1898, a son of Richard and Letitia Meade of Russell County, Virginia. Vivian Powell Meade removed to Kentucky after the Civil War and was buried at Pleasant Valley.

Children:

Ethel Deborah Lausanne Meade, b. September 10, 1871; m., first, Stephen Jacobs of Carter County, when in her sixteenth year. They were parents of Luther, b. November 6, 1887, d. September 3, 1898, and John Augustus, b. February, 1902. Stephen Jacobs d. February 19, 1913, and he and son Luther were buried at Pleasant Valley. Mrs. Jacobs became a resident of Denver, Colorado. She m., secondly, Biretzinger and d. in the early 1900s.

John Strother Meade; b. October 25, 1873, d. at Portsmouth, Ohio, February 21, 1909, and was buried at Lindsay Chapel near Grayson.

Annie Meade; m. George Rose; resided in Portsmouth, Ohio. Children: Ruth and Ethel.

Gus Meade; m. Miss Black; resided in Portsmouth, Ohio.

12. Hannah Strother, b. about 1852; m. William Goble in Carter County, September 23, 1851. Children: Joseph Haven, Anna Sarah, m. ——— (name not learned). Children: Billy, Jennivere, Ephraim, Ruth, Frank, Loraine, Green and Alice Emily, m. ——— Justice. Children: Mattie Ruth m. ——— Barnhill, Garnet, Junior, Ralph, Mildred and Helen.

13. Alice Strother; b. about 1855; m. ———Harris. No children.

14. Geneva Strother; b. about 1857; m., first, ——— Virgin; no children; m., secondly, Stephen Easterling. Children: Philip Strother Easterling, Federal employee, Post Office Department, Washington, D. C.; m. Bernice Shaffer, teacher. Children: Philip II, who is married and has one child (son) Philip III.

15. Belle Strother; d. in infancy.

16. Mary Lousanne Strother; b. October 22, 1862; m. ——— Davis.

17. Philip Strother; b. about 1866; m. ——— Meade. Children

(a) Ella Sherman m. Jake Burton and they are parents of Beulah who m. ——— Stamper and they are the parents of M. H., Ella Mae, Phyllis and Bobby; Kathleen who m. ——— Kouns and they are parents of Ella Nora, Carolyn Kay, Douglas and Phyllis Ann; Harold who m. ——— Johnson; Tempest who m. ——— Everman; Philip; Shirley, who m. ——— Crawford and they are parents of Larry Patrick.

(b) Winnifred m. ——— Forrest and they had Agnes and Helen.

(c) William Meade m. Margaret ——— and they had Roger and Philip.

(d) Helen m. ——— Johnson.

(e) Beulah m. Mack ———.

18. Josephine Strother; b. about 1868; m. Allen Carter Beckwith, February 28, 1895. Children: (a) Arthur Lewis, b. January 2, 1897 ; m. Layce Gilbert, February, 1922. Children: Lillian Mae, b. April 17, 1923.

(b) Luther, b. May 12, 1900, d. in infancy.

(c) Warren Strother, b. August 13, 1903; children: Helen and Philip.

(d) Lola Osenton, b. April 17, 1906; m. ——— Rummel. Children: Phyllis Ann.

(e) John Carter, b. March 18, 1909; m. ———. Children: Sue Carter, Judy Ann and Jane Webb.'

2. JOHN RATCLIFFE STROTHER, a son of Robert Strother 5, Revolutionary War soldier of Culpeper County, Virginia, a grandson of Anthony Strother 4, and Frances Eastham, a great-grandson of Francis Strother 3, and Susannah Dabney, a great-great-grandson of William Strother 2, and Margaret Thornton and great-great-great grandson of William Strother 1, and Dorothy ——— (surname not known), was b. in Culpeper County, Virginia, in 1807, and d. in Cowley County, Kansas; m. about 1835, Ruth Shommaker, who was b. in Jackson County, Ohio, in 1814. They lived at Grayson, Carter County, Kentucky, for a number of years.

Children living in the household and approximate dates of birth as shown by the U. S. Census of Carter County for 1850, 1860, and 1870:

19. Martha J. Strother; b. 1836.

20. Robert S. Strother; b. 1840.

21. Nancy A. Strother; b. 1842.

22. George W. Strother; b. 1845.

23. Elizabeth D. (Jennie) Strother; b. 1847.

*24. John W. Strother; b. 1850.

25. America Strother; b. 1853.

26. Mary V. Strother; b. 1855.

27. William P. Strother; b. 1858.

24. JOHN WILSON STROTHER, physician and banker at Grayson; b. at Grayson, October 28, 1850, d. in the J. Q. Stovall Memorial Hospital, Grayson, January 8, 1935; educated in the public schools

of Carter County and engaged in teaching in those schools for a short time in young manhood; was graduated from the Miami Medical College at Cincinnati and was subsequently a "Horse and Buggy" doctor in the Grayson Area as long as he lived. He organized the Commercial Bank of Grayson, May 1, 1891, the first bank in the area; and was made first president and continued in that capacity until his death.

Dr. Strother was of pleasing personality, of good address, friendly and sociable and was withall a colorful figure. He was a Democrat in politics and a member of the Christian Church; and during the latter part of his life frequently preached in country churches that could not support regular preachers.

On September 2, 1877, he was united in marriage with Amanda Maud Horton, daughter of Elijah Sargent and Nancy (Cox) Horton. (See Horton Family.)

Children:

28. Jessica (Jessie) Strother; b. at Grayson, August 18, 1878; educated in the local schools and at Transylvania University, Lexington, Kentucky; was an employee of the Commercial Bank of Grayson for several years and became familiar with the banking business. A great reader and student, she studied law and medicine— not with any intention of engaging in practice—and then entered the field of literature. She has written much poetry and some poems were published in "Voice of Freedom" and "Voice of America". Recently she has had published a volume which has received favorable reviews by critics of lyric poetry, particularly the poems "The Convoy" and "Sunset Over Italy."

Miss Strother m. H. R. Dysard (See Dysard Family).

29. Gussie Strother; b. at Grayson September 5, 1880; educated in the public schools of Grayson and attended a private school in Winchester, Kentucky, m. Clyde Gaines.

Children:

John Strother Gaines; was graduated from the Staunton Military Academy, Staunton, Virginia; is presently holding a very responsible position with the L. & N. Railway Company; m., no children. Resides in Louisville.

Thomas Wickliffe Gaines; was graduated from the University of Louisville with degree of LL.B.; is cashier of the Lincoln Bank and Trust Company of Louisville; is m. and has two children: Wickliffe and Margaret Ann. Resides in Louisville.

W. C. ("Connie") Gaines; was graduated from University of Kentucky with degree of A. B. in engineering; was president of the Gaines Wood Preservative business at Harlan, Kentucky, and operated several saw mills in Harlan County; was killed in airplane accident about 1947.

Clyde Gaines, Jr.; was graduated from the University of Louisville with degree of LL.B.; is presently conducting the business of his deceased brother, Connie, in Harlan County.

30. BELLE ("BELLE TOM") STROTHER; b. at Grayson, September 22, 1882; educated in the public schools of Grayson; studied art and music in Grayson; taught music and was an employee of the Commercial Bank of Grayson for a time; m., August 31, 1915, Leslie Womack. (See Womack Family.)

Children:

Leslie Womack, Jr.; killed by a train when very young.

John Gaines Womack; was graduated from the University of Kentucky with degree of A. B.; is presently operating the J. W. Strother old farm near Grayson.

31.WICKLIFFE HORTON STROTHER, banker, civic leader and businessman; b. at Grayson, April 18, 1885; educated in the public schools of Grayson and Kentucky University (now Transylvania College) at Lexington; became connected with the Commercial Bank of Grayson early in life and has since served that institution in many capacities, except for about five years when he was cashier of the Bank of Carrollton at Carrollton, Alabama. He was serving as vice-president when the president of the bank, his father, died, and he succeeded him as president and is presently holding that position.

Mr. Strother is civic minded and has always been active in community affairs. He was instrumental in securing lights and water for Grayson, being one of the organizers and stock holders of both companies. When the Eastern Kentucky Railway became defunct and ceased to operate, he assisted in promoting and operating a transportation system ("the blue goose") over the railroad tracks from Grayson to Webbville.

Mr. Strother is a Democrat and a member of the First Christian Church at Grayson. He is a charter member of the Rotary Club at Grayson; sold War Bonds during World War II and is active in crippled children work and cancer drives.

He m., June 16, 1907, Miss Inez Blackburn Wilhoit, daughter of Col. E. B. and Anna (Blackburn) Wilhoit of Grayson. (See Wilhoit Family.)

Children:

Louise Strother; educated in the public schools of Grayson and at Brenau College, Gainesville, Georgia; m. Thomas Dudley Theobald, lawyer, at Grayson. (See Theobald Family.) Children: Jackie, student; attended Mary Baldwin Seminary, Staunton, Virginia, and University of Kentucky; Mary, student; and Robin, student.

Jack (John Wilson) Strother, banker; educated in the public schools of Grayson and was graduated from the University of Kentucky with degree of A. B. in commerce and banking. Upon graduation when 20 years of age, he became connected with the Commercial Bank of Grayson and has since served that institution when not serving in the U. S. Navy—having been made vice-president when his father was made president—and is presently serving in that capacity. He had service in World War II; was commissioned an ensign, U. S. Navy, 1942, and was stationed in Philadelphia for several months receiving training in Codes and Communications and subsequently served 18 months in the Pacific area. Returning to the United States, he was stationed in California until the close of the war when he resumed his position in the bank. He is married and has a son, Jack.

Bob (Robert Blackburn) Strother, physician and surgeon and Naval Officer; received his preparatory medical education at the University of Kentucky and the University of Alabama, and was graduated from the Medical Department of the University of Louisville; was an interne at the University of Iowa when in 1941 he was commissioned a lieutenant (j. g.) in the Navy; was graduated with the first class of flight surgeons that was graduated at Pensacola, Florida; sailed for foreign duty on the first converted aircraft carrier and had active service in both the Atlantic and Pacific areas until the close of the War. Returning to the United States, he reentered the U. S. Navy, a commander of the Medical Department, stationed at Philadelphia; subsequently was appointed Chief of Surgery of Guam and, with family, sailed for his new station in June, 1942. He is married. Children: Roberta, deceased; Robert and Myra Louise.

Inez Wickcliffe (Wick) Strother; educated in the public schools of Grayson, at Sullins College, Bristol, Virginia, and was graduated from the University of Kentucky with degree of A. B. in Commerce; m. John Stebbins Loomis, Jr., a graduate of Yale, son of John Stebbins Loomis, president of an investment banking business in Chicago with which John Stebbins Loomis, Jr., is connected. Children: Jack and Wickie. Residence Winnetka, Illinois.[5]

[1] "William Strother of Virginia and His Descendants", by Thomas McAdory Owen, Harrisburg Publishing Company, 1898.

[2] "The Big Sandy Valley", by William Ely.

[3] Philip Strother, a Virginian and His Descendants (Manuscript) prepared by Jessica (Strother) Dysard (Mrs. H. R. Dysard), Ashland, Kentucky.

[4] Profile of the Osenton Family, Edited by Dorothy Mary Wollin, 1946.

[5] Wickliffe Horton Strother and His Descendants (Manuscript) prepared by Louise (Strother) Theobald (Mrs. T. D. Theobald), Grayson, Kentucky, 1952.

STUART FAMILY OF GREENUP AND LAWRENCE COS.
STUART, STEWART

Stuart
Stewart

This illustrious name has been identified with the history of Scotland for many centuries. However, the Stuart family really originated with a Norman Knight named Fitz-Alan who accompanied William the Conqueror to England in the eleventh century (1066). As a reward for his military prowess he was given great tracts of confiscated lands, among them the grant of Aswestry, in Shropshire. His eldest son, William Fitz-Alan, became the ancestor of the Earls of Arundel, while his second son, Walter, went to Scotland and became prominent in the service of the King, David I, who bestowed upon him large territorial possessions, among them the barony of Renfrew. He became the lord high steward of Scotland which office became hereditary. His great grandson, Alexander, assumed Stewart as his surname, changing the last letter, "d" to "t". Thus it can be said that Alexander Stewart was the ancestor of the royal line of Stewarts. Mary, Queen of Scots, was the first to change the spelling to Stuart. Having been educated in France, she wrote her name in the French language, in the alphabet of which there is no "w". Her father, James V., however, wrote his name Stewart as did his son, James VI.

The crown of Scotland was brought into the Stewart family by Walter, the sixth lord high steward of the realm. He performed brilliant service in the battle of Bannockburn (1314) during the reign of Robert Bruce, and subsequently married the daughter of the great Bruce, thus originating the Stewart dynasty in Scotland.

The descendants of Walter Fitz-Alan (Stewart) formed a large Scottish clan, which through its younger members became very numerous. Representatives of the Stewarts emigrated to America in great numbers and descendants are now living in every section of the country.

Many Stuart or Stewart families lived in Eastern and/or Southeastern Kentucky in pioneer days, some of whom might have been related to each other.

MITCHELL STUART, SR., was the immediate ancestor of a branch of the Stuart family who settled and now live in the Plum Grove community near Riverton, Greenup County, Kentucky. His family emigrated from near Berthshire, Scotland, and settled near present Wytheville, Wythe County, Virginia, in pioneer days. From here members of the family migrated to the Big Sandy River region in Kentucky and settled in Lawrence County. From whence Mitchell Stuart, Sr., moved to the Plum Grove community in 1896, later returning to Lawrence County where he died. Among his children were Mitchell Stuart, Jr.

1. MITCHELL STUART, JR., farmer and for many years an employee of the Chesapeake and Ohio Railway Company as a maintenance man, was b. in Lawrence County, Kentucky, June 17, 1880; m. in Greenup County, Thanksgiving Day, November 26, 1902, Martha Hylton, b. near Willard, Carter County, Kentucky, August 1, 1882, and d. in Greenup County, May 11, 1951, a daughter of Nathan Hylton and his wife, Violet (Pennington) Hylton. (See Hylton Family.)

Children:
*2. Jesse Hilton Stuart.
*3. Sophia Stuart.
4. John Herbert Lee Stuart; b. October —, 1909, d. January —, 1914.
*5. Mary Stuart.
*6. James Mitchell Stuart.
7. Martin Stuart; b. March —,1918, d. April —, 1918.
*8. Glennis Juanita Stuart.

2. JESSE HILTON STUART, termed the "Robert Burns of the Kentucky Highlands" and "Poet Laureate of Kentucky"; sometime teacher and public official, farmer, lecturer, short story writer, poet and novelist, was b. on W-Hollow of the Plum Grove community near Riverton, Greenup County, Kentucky, August 8, 1907. In his youth he evinced a talent for writing, particularly poetry; was a voracious reader and resolved to acquire a good education. His parents being desirous of educating their children, approved and encouraged him in his ambition and objectives but they were poor and having a large family to support contributed practically nothing to his collegiate education. He taught school and engaged in manual employments with the savings from which he managed to complete his education in college and university.

Mr. Stuart is of English and Scottish ancestry. On the paternal side the Stuarts are Scotch. On the maternal side he is of English ancestry, being descended from the Hyltons or Hiltons, the Greenes, the Chandlers and the Prestons. He is a lineal (direct) descendant (sixth generation) of Nathan Preston, Revolutionary War soldier who came from Bedford County, Virginia, to Floyd County, Kentucky, about 1800. (See Nathan Preston Family); and of Thomas Chandler, Revolutionary War soldier who came from Surry County,

North Carolina, to near present Wayne Court House, West Virginia, about 1808. (See Chandler Family).

Mr. Stuart was educated in the one-room rural school in the Plum Grove community near his home; graduated from the Greenup High School and from the Lincoln Memorial University, Harrogate, Tennessee, with degree of A. B., 1929; did graduate work at Vanderbilt University, Nashville, Tennessee, 1931-32; and at Peabody College, Nashville, Tennessee, during summers equivalent to one year; has received honorary degrees of D. Litt., University of Kentucky, 1944; Doctor of Humane Letters, Lincoln Memorial University, 1950; D. Litt., Marietta College, Marietta, Ohio, February 22, 1952, and Doctor of Laws LL.D., Baylor University, Waco, Texas. The General Assembly of Kentucky at the session of 1954 conferred on him the literary title of Poet Laureate of Kentucky.

Mr. Stuart is not only a prolific writer but has been and is a prodigious worker in fields other than literature: For eleven years he was engaged in educational work: teacher in the rural schools of Greenup County; principal of the Greenup High School and of the McKell High School; teacher of remedial English in the Portsmouth, Ohio, city system; and superintendent of schools of Greenup County.

Mr. Stuart wrote his first poems on "pale poplar leaves" and has written and there have been published in magazines hundreds of sonnets and short stories together with eighteen volumes of poems and novels:

1. "The Man With A Bull-Tongue Plow", 1934, poetry, E. P. Dutton & Co.

2. "Head O' W-Hollow", 1936, short stories, E. P. Dutton & Co. (Note: These two books won for Mr. Stewart a $2,000 Guggenheim fellowship which supplemented enabled him to study and travel in Europe for fourteen months.)

3. "Beyond Dark Hills", 1938, autobiographical, E. P. Dutton & Co.

4. "Trees of Heaven", 1940, novel, E. P. Dutton & Co.

5. "Men of the Mountains", 1941, short stories, E. P. Dutton & Co.

6. "Taps for Private Tussie", 1943, novel, E. P. Dutton & Co. (Note: This book won the Thomas Jefferson Southern Award for 1943; was the Book-of-the-Month's December 1943 choice; and it is the consensus of opinion that it is Mr. Stuart's best book to date.)

7. "Mongrel Mettle", 1944, autobiography of a dog, E. P. Dutton & Co.

8. "Album of Destiny", 1944, poetry, E. P. Dutton & Co.

9. "Foretaste of Glory", 1946, novel, E. P. Dutton & Co.

10. "Tales from the Plum Grove Hills", short stories, E. P. Dutton & Co.

11. "The Thread that Runs so True", 1949, autobiographical—teaching, Charles Scribners' Sons.

12. "Hie to the Hunters", 1950, novel, McGraw-Hill Book Co.

13. "Clearing in the Sky", 1950, short stories, McGraw-Hill Book Co.

14. "The Good Spirit of Laurel Ridge", 1953, McGraw-Hill Book Co.

15. Kentucky Is My Land", verse, 1952.

16. "The Beatinest Boy", junior book, 1953.

17. "A Penny's Worth of Character", junior book, 1954.

18. "Red Mule", junior book, 1955.

Contemporaneous with these various activities, Mr. Stuart lectured in many sections of the country, operated his 600-acre farm and served as commissioned officer in the Navy during World War II.

In recognition of the many achievements of Mr. Stuart and the honor and recognition which he has brought to the Commonwealth of Kentucky, the Governor of the Commonwealth, Lawrence W. Wetherby, issued a proclamation of September 19, 1955, designating Saturday, October 15, 1955, as Jesse Hilton Stuart day in Kentucky.

On the day designated, October 15, 1955, great honor came to Jesse Hilton Stuart. His home town, Greenup, was invaded by thousands of Greenup Countians and others—probably the greatest number that had ever assembled in the town at one time—who came to honor him and to participate in and/or to witness ceremonies that had been carefully planned. There was a parade through the streets of the town, led by bands—mostly high school bands, floats and a number of show-horse riders. Addresses, lauding Mr. Stuart were delivered by Dr. Robert L. Kincaid, President of Lincoln Memorial University, and by Dr. H. L. Donovan, President of the University of Kentucky; and remarks by Mr. Stuart at the conclusion of which occurred the main event of the day: The Master of Ceremonies, Judge J. R. Sowards, presented a memorial marker of Mr. Stuart which had been erected at the northwest corner of the court house lawn which was unveiled by Mr. Stuart's only child, Jessica Jane.

The marker, which was sponsored by the Greenup Lions Club and financed by public subscription, is a bust of Mr. Stuart in Georgia granite, resting on an imposing pedestal, in all about nine feet high. The sculpture captured a youthful, dreaming Stuart as he perhaps looked when he made his fledgling literary flight with "Man With a Bull-Tongue Plow" (1934), which book is suggested by the incised figure of a plow directly below the statue. Beneath the statue, carved into the tablet, is the legend: "Jesse Stuart, Poet, Novelist, Educator"; and beneath the legend is this selection from Packinham Beatty's essay "Self Reliance."

"By your own soul's law,
    learn to live,
And if men thwart you,
    take no heed,
If men hate you,
    have no care;
Sing your song, dream your
    dream, hope
Your hope and pray your
    prayer."

Mr. Stuart was m. at Ashland, Kentucky, October 14, 1939, to Miss Naomi Deane Norris. Miss Norris was b. April 16, 1908, at Hopewell, Greenup County, a descendant of a pioneer family of that section; attended the rural school at Hopewell; went with her parents to Greenup in 1918 where she finished elementary and high school, graduating from the Greenup High School; was graduated from the State Teachers' College at Morehead, with degree of A. B., 1938, and taught for several years in the rural public schools of Greenup County and Greenup city schools.

Mrs. Stuart is a lover of all nature and is fond of out-of-door life; is interested in antiques; and in addition to giving material assistance to her husband in the steady flow of the voluminous manuscripts from his pen, she occupies the choice position of being the great inspiration in his life and works.

Children:

9. Jessica Jane Stuart, student; b. August 20, 1942.

3. SOPHIA STEWART, teacher in the public schools of Greenup County; b. September 3, 1903; was graduated from the Greenup High School and later was a student in college for two years; m. in July 1926, Henry Keeney, an employee of the Chesapeake & Ohio Railway Company.

Children:

10. Norma Jean Keeney, one time teacher; b. May 30, 1927; was graduated from the Raceland (Kentucky) High School; B. S., Lincoln Memorial University; M. T. (Medical Technician), University of Louisville, 1951, and presently employed by a hospital operated by the Shriners; unm. (1953).

11. Naomi Vivien Keeney, teacher; b. March 3, 1929; was graduated from the Greenup High School here she was chosen the Beauty Queen; attended Lincoln Memorial University where she is a senior; unm. (1953).

12. Walter Stuart Keeney; February 20, 1931; graduated from high school conducted by the U. S. Navy; now serving in the Navy;

13. Carroll June Keeney; b. December 23, 1933; was graduated

from the Greenup High School and presently (1953) a student in the Ashland (Kentucky) Junior College.

5. MARY STUART; b. August 7, 1912; educated in the public schools of Greenup County, graduating from the Greenup High School; m., first, Leonard Darby.

Children:

14. Betty Darby; teacher, b. December 4, 1930; graduated from Powells Valley High School, Claiborne County, Tennessee; student two years in Lincoln Memorial University; taught one year in rural schools; m., 1949, William Elmon Vaughn. Their child, Michael William Vaughn, b. August 9, 1951, d. October 23, 1951.

15. Leonard Eugene Darby; b. September 9, 1934; presently a student in Greenup Junior High School (1953).

16. Nancy Sue Darby; b. April —, 1939; presently a student in the Greenup Junior High School (1953).

5A. Mary Stuart, m., secondly, Oran Nelson.

Children:

17. Sandy Kay Nelson; b. July 4, 1947.

18. Stacey Ray Nelson; b. January —, 1949.

19. Regina Lee Nelson; b. February —, 1952.

6. JAMES MITCHELL STUART, teacher and sometime public official, was b. in W-Hollow of the Plum Grove community, near Riverton, Greenup County, August 11, 1915; was educated in the public schools of Greenup County, graduating from the Greenup High School at the age of fourteen years; was graduated from the State Teachers' College, Morehead, Kentucky, with degree of A. B., 1941; has had approximately fifteen years experience in teaching at different intervals; served in both World War II and the Korean War; was commissioned a lieutenant, senior grade, U. S. Navy; and is presently serving as superintendent of the Greenup City Schools (1953); m. November 23, 1940, Betty Stephens, teacher, who was graduated from State Teachers' College at Morehead with degree of A. B., and has had about fourteen years' experience in teaching.

Children:

20. James Stephens Stuart; b. 1947.

8. GLENNIS JUANITA STUART, teacher; was b. August 31, 1921; was graduated from the Greenup High School; finished Nurses' training at Marting Hospital, Ironton, Ohio, 1941, and for some time engaged in nursing; was graduated from Lincoln Memorial University with degree of B. S., 1948; engaged in teaching for four years; m., February 5, 1951, Herbert Liles, an employee of the C. & O. Ry. Co., at Russell, Kentucky. No children (1953).

SWETNAM FAMILY OF LAWRENCE COUNTY

1. NERI SWETNAM was the ancestor of the Swetnam family of Eastern Kentucky. He was b. in Virginia in 1778, and d. in Blaine, Lawrence County, Kentucky, in 1861. In 1818 he migrated with his family from near Washington, D. C., and purchased a large tract of land on Blaine, then Floyd County, now Lawrence County, Kentucky. Here he settled and here he died. The great landed estate of Mr. Swetnam has remained in possession of his descendants. He m. in Virginia, Mildred Cross, b. in Virginia in 1778, and d. in Lawrence County in 1859.

Mr. Swetnam was a man of wealth and he and his wife were cultured. They entertained in their home, among others, Methodist ministers on the circuit; and a majority of the lawyers and public officials, who so frequently in an early day passed through the Swetnam neighborhood on the road from Louisa to West Liberty and from the interior of the state to the Big Sandy Country, stopped at their home instead of lodging at a public inn.

Mr. Swetnam was a good man and true and his family came to honor.[1] Children: six sons and two daughters.

2. John Swetnam; removed to Bath County, Kentucky. One John J. Swetnam m. Rebecca Osborn in Floyd County, November 22, 1840.

*3. Claiborne Swetnam.

*4. Neri Swetnam, Jr.

*5. Elza (Elzaphan) Swetnam.

6. Zephaniah Swetnam; m. Charlotte Burgess in Floyd County, April 13, 1836; migrated to Iowa.

7. Louisa Swetnam; m. Robert Walter. (See Walter Family.)

8. ―――― Swetnam, a daughter; m. John Osborn; migrated to Arizona.

9. ―――― Swetnam, a daughter (the oldest).

3. CLAIBORNE L. SWETNAM, farmer and merchant; residence Blaine, Lawrence County, was b. in Virginia in 1806 or 1807; m. in Floyd County, April 27, 1837, Deresa or Theresa Wellman, b. in Kentucky about 1812.

Children living in the household and approximate dates of birth as shown by the U. S. Census of Lawrence County for the years 1850 and 1860:

10. Milton Swetnam; b. 1839.

11. Sarah J. Swetnam; b. 1841.

12. Emily A. E. Swetnam; b. 1843.

13. Mary E. Swetnam; b. 1845.

4. Neri F. Swetnam, Jr., farmer; residence Blaine, Lawrence County; b. in Virginia about 1814; m. Serena ———, b. in Kentucky, about 1834.

Children living in the household and approximate dates of birth as shown by the U. S. Census of Lawrence County for the year 1860:

14. John J. Swetnam; b. 1851.
15. William W. Swetnam; b. 1854.
16. Louisa R. Swetnam; b. 1857.
17. Joseph T. Swetnam; b. 1859.

5. Eliza Swetnam, farmer; residence on Blaine, Lawrence Co., was b. in Virginia about 1806; m. in Lawrence County, January 31, 1839, Cynthia Preston. b. in Kentucky in 1825.

Children living in the household and approximate dates of birth as shown by the U. S. Census of Lawrence County for the year 1860:

18. Serilda or Zarilda Swetnam; b. 1841.
19. Julia Swetnam; b. 1843.
20. Paulina Swetnam; b. 1845.
21. Neri Swetnam; b. 1847.
22. Leander C. Swetnam; b. 1849.
23. Trinvilla Swetnam; b. 1853.
24. Samantha Swetnam; b. 1856.
25. Hester A. Swetnam; b. 1859.

The 1870 Census shows additional persons living in the household as follows:

Margaret, apparently wife, b. in Kentucky, 1823.

Children, apparently:

26. John J. Swetnam; b. 1862.
27. Cynthia J. Swetnam; b. 1865.
28. Elza M. Swetnam; b. 1868.

---

[1] William Ely, "The Big Sandy Valley", pp. 84-5.

THEOBALD OF OWEN AND CARTER COUNTIES

Theobald

Theobald was originally an ancient Saxon name, being derived from two words meaning "God's Power". Applied to an individual, it assumed the meaning of a "bold leader". Many other surnames have sprung from Theobald—the old English name, Tibbals, Tibbald, Tipkins, Tippet, Tippets, Tibbs.

The coat of arms here displayed is that which was brought to America by the colonist Clement Theobald, and is traceable to the Theobalds of County Kent, England.

Clement Theobald arrived in Virginia in 1641 and established his home in lower Norfolk County. He was twice married. Some of his children moved to Kentucky and settled in Bourbon County. Their descendants scattered from that point into many other sections.

JUDGE THOMAS DUDLEY THEOBALD, lawyer and judge, was b. at Owenton, Owen County, Kentucky, March 29, 1856, son of Rev. John M. and Jane Thomas (Vallandingham) Theobald; educated in the public schools of Owen County and attended Harrodsburg Academy; studied law in the office of and under the supervision of Hon. Asa P. Grover; admitted to the bar March 31, 1877, and began practice of law at Owenton and continued for five years when, in 1882, he located at Grayson, Carter County, for the practice of his profession and where he practiced in the State and United States Courts, having a large and important clientele, until December 1, 1925, having been elected the previous November Circuit Judge of the 37th Judicial District, composed of the counties of Carter, Elliott and Morgan. He served as Circuit Judge for the six-year term, 1926-1932, after the expiration of which he resumed the practice of law at Grayson.

Judge Theobald was a Republican, a member and elder in the Presbyterian Church at Grayson, and a member of the Carter County, the Kentucky State and the American Bar Association.

He m., July 18, 1877, Miss Sarah Dale Ford, daughter of Col. Thomas Ford of Owen County. Children: *1. John M. Theobald and *2. Mary C. Theobald.

1. JOHN MAUEX THEOBALD, lawyer, at Grayson; b. in Owen Co., April 20, 1878; educated in the public schools of Grayson and select school conducted by Miss Stella B. Morton there; was graduated from Washington and Lee University, Lexington, Virginia, with degree of

LL.B., 1900; admitted to the bar at Grayson, 1899, and after graduation began the practice of law at Grayson in partnership with his
father under the firm name of Theobald & Theobald; and since has
practiced with success.

Mr. Theobald is a member of the Presbyterian Church at Grayson. A Republican in politics, he is an active party worker and a
wise counselor in local party affairs.

He m., first, Miss Minnie Jones, who d. January 22, 1919, daughter of Thomas D. Jones of Grayson, and m., secondly, Emma, daughter of J. C. B. and Mollie (Friend) Auxier of East Point, Johnson
County, Kentucky. There were no children by the second marriage.
Children (a) Mary Catherine, b. October 11, 1904; m. W. A. Wilson;
(b) Thomas Dudley Theobald, Jr., lawyer, at Grayson; b. at Grayson,
March 11, 1906; began the practice of law as an associate of Theobald & Theobald after which time the firm consisted of grandfather,
son and grandson—representing three generations—until December,
1925, when Thomas D. Theobald, Sr., was elected Circuit Judge.
Subsequently he has been associated in practice at Grayson with his
father, John M. Theobald, under the firm name of Theobald & Theobald. He m. Louise Strother, daughter of Wickliffe H. and Inez B.
(Wilhoit) Strother. (See Strother and Wilhoit families.) (c)
Martha V. Theobald; b. at Grayson, January 5, 1910.

2. MARY C. THEOBALD; b. in Owen County, September 7, 1879;
m. Luther Campbell Spangler, now deceased, who for many years held
responsible positions with the Chesapeake & Ohio Railway Company,
the last being superintendent of terminals at Newport News and
Norfolk. Children: Luther Campbell, Jr., b. May 22, 1911, and
Thomas Theobald, b. May 27, 1914.

Mrs. Spangler is presently residing in Grayson.

TURNER FAMILY OF JOHNSON COUNTY

1. Very little is definitely known concerning the ancestor of the Turner family of the Big Sandy Valley. Tradition has it that he emigrated from Ireland to America and was a Revolutionary War soldier. It has been definitely established that he had children.

Second Generation

2. Cuddith Turner.
*3. James W. Turner
4. George Turner.
5. William Turner.

3. JAMES W. TURNER was b. in Virginia, probably in Henry County, in 1799 and d. in Johnson County, Kentucky, September 15, 1872. He was brought to Kentucky about 1820 by his father who settled on Johns Creek, then Floyd County, where he became a wealthy agriculturist and slave holder. Subsequently James W. Turner moved to and established a home on Paint Creek about three miles west of present Paintsville which property has ever since remained in possession of the family. He was a very successful trader, operated a general store, was a member of the Christian Church and contributed liberally to religious and charitable organizations. He m. in Floyd County, January 2, 1820, Annie Waller, daughter of Jake Waller from Holland. They reared a large and respectable family and many of their descendants became prominent in the business and political affairs of Eastern Kentucky.

Children:

Third Generation

*6. George Washington Turner.
*7. Edwin Suddith Turner.
*8. Samuel Turner.
*9. Martha Turner.
*10. Priscilla Turner.
11. Mary Turner; m. Henry S. Vaughan. (See Vaughan Family.)
*12. Joseph Turner.
*13. Dr. Isaac Redmond Turner.
*14. Cynthia Ellen Turner.
*15. Rachel Emmaline Turner.
*16. John Wesley Turner.
17. Nancy Catherine Turner; m. Jasper VanHoose. (See Van-Hoose Family.)

6. GEORGE WASHINGTON TURNER, farmer; b. March 28, 1822, and d. March 21, 1849; m. Rachel Pelfrey.

Children:

Fourth Generation

18. James Turner; b. 1844; d. 1849.
*19. E. Washington Turner.
20. George Anne Turner; b. May 31, 1849; m. Jesse Stafford, Sr. (See Stafford Family.)

7. EDWIN SUDDITH TURNER; served in Union Army in Civil War; was mustered into the service at Catlettsburg, Kentucky, October 10, 1863, as first lieutenant, Company "C", 45th Kentucky Volunteer Mt'd. Infantry, and mustered out at Catlettsburg, December 24, 1864,[1] m. Mary Jane Rule.

Children:

Fourth Generation

21. Emma Turner; m., first, Luke Melvin and, secondly, Sanford McFarland.
22. Susan Caroline Turner; m. George Stafford.
23. George Turner.
24. James Turner; m. ——— Thomas.
25. "Sissie" Turner; m. ——— Nichols.
26. Ina Turner.
27. Mollie Turner; m. ——— Parker.
28. Rose Turner.
29. French Turner; d. in infancy.

8. SAMUEL TURNER; m. in Johnson County, April 12, 1853, Cynthia E. Rule.

Children:

Fourth Generation

30. Helen Turner; m. John Howes.
31. Louisa Turner; m. Nathaniel Bayes.
32. Edwin Suddith Turner; m. Elizabeth McKenzie.
33. Charley Turner; accidently killed.
34. Willie Turner; m. ——— Cheek.
35. Frank Turner; m. Rose Boyd.
36. Ellen Turner; m. Smith Osborn.

9. MARTHA TURNER; m. in Johnson County, March 13, 1848, James Stambaugh.

Children:

Fourth Generation

37. Jaques Henry Stambaugh; m. Lydia Van Hoose.
38. Garfield Stambaugh; m. Thursa VanHoose.
10. PRISCILLA TURNER; m. Green Rule.

Children:
Fourth Generation

39. Millard Rule; m. Alice Preston.
40. Laura Rule; m. Frank Stafford. (See Stafford Family.)
41. Kate Rule; d. young.
42. Mollie Rule; m. Powell Williams.
43. Addie Rule; m. Bascom Helton.

12. JOSEPH TURNER; m. in Johnson County, February 22, 1857, Mary J. Collins.

Children:
Fourth Generation

44. George Anne Turner; m. ——— Jennings.
45. Victoria M. Turner; m. Laban Love.
46. Henry Turner.
47. James Turner.

13. ISAAC REDMAN TURNER, physician; b., January 1, 1838, and d. August 27, 1920; was graduated from the Medical Department of the University of Cincinnati and thereafter practiced medicine at Paintsville. He was held in great esteem and had the confidence of the people of his section of the State. He was one of the most noted of the early physicians in Johnson County and distinguished himself professionally in the small pox epidemic on Beaver Creek, Floyd County, in 1883. He served in the Union Army during the Civil War as a private, Company "C", 45th Kentucky Volunteer Mt'd. Infantry; was mustered into the service at Catlettsburg, Kentucky, October 10, 1863, and was mustered out at Catlettsburg, December 24, 1864.[2] He m. in Johnson County, Mrs. Louisa (Hager) Preston, daughter of General Daniel Hager and widow of Moses Preston. (See Hager Family and Moses Preston Family.)

Children:
Fourth Generation

48. Ernest T. Turner; d. young.
*49. James W. Turner.

14. CYNTHIA ELLEN TURNER; m. William Nelson.

Children:
Fourth Generation

50. Annie Nelson.

15. RACHEL EMMALINE TURNER; m. Andrew Fox.

Children:
Fourth Generation

51. Mary Fox; m. Jesse Pelfrey.
52. James Fox; d. in infancy.

16. JOHN WESLEY TURNER; m., first, Frances Lyons.

Children:

Fourth Generation

53. Ernest Turner; m. Mollie Rice.
54. Nell Turner; d. young.
16A. John Wesley Turner; m., secondly, Lou (Wheeler) Colvin.

Children:

Fourth Generation

55. Ray Turner; m. Virgie Conley.

19. E. WASHINGTON TURNER; b. on Toms Creek, December 23, 1846; m. Nancy McKenzie, daughter of William A. McKenzie of Mud Lick.

Children:

Fifth Generation

56. Laurin Turner; b. February 16, 1872.
57. James Turner; b. January 14, 1874; m. Jennie Artripp.
58. Annie Turner; b. April 1, 1876; d. November —, 1921.
59. Nancy Jane Turner; b. April 23, 1878; m. Robert Butler.
60. Maude Turner; b. November 7, 1880; d. young.
61. Pearl Turner; b. 1884; d. young.
62. Hattie Turner; b. 1888; m. Joseph Lewis.
63. Harry Turner; b. 1891; m. Etta Bishop.
64. "Dotsy" Turner; b. 1895; m. Frank Mutters.
65. Rachel Turner; b. 1899.

49. HON. JAMES W. TURNER; lawyer, judge, businessman and civic leader, was b. in Paintsville, Kentucky, November 19, 1874; educated in the public schools of Paintsville, at Kentucky Wesleyan College, Wesleyan University, Delaware, Ohio, Harvard University and University of Boston where he pursued his law studies and was graduated with the class of 1899.

Locating at Bristol, Virginia, he became clerk and master of chancery there, but resigned at the end of two years and returned to Paintsville to assist in organizing the Paintsville National Bank with which he has been connected, being one of the largest stockholders. Being in close touch with the commercial, industrial, financial and economic conditions in Johnson County, he has worked with commendable zeal and marked ability to develop the natural resources of the county and to elevate standards generally.

In politics, Judge Turner is a Republican. He has held many offices and positions of honor and trust and filled all of them creditably and well. He was State representative, 1910; was the nominee of his party for Speaker and served during the session as minority leader. He was elected and served ably and impartially as circuit judge of his judicial district for several years. For many years he was a member of the Board of Trustees of Kentucky State University.

During World War I, he was Chairman of the Speakers Bureau in the Big Sandy Valley and made numerous speeches throughout the region in addition to doing other work in behalf of drives and movements of the Red Cross, Y. M. C. A. and Liberty Bond Loans.

Judge Turner is a member of the Methodist Episcopal Church. Fraternally he is a Mason (Knights Templar), a member of the Independent Order of Odd Fellows, the Knights of Pythias and Modern Woodmen of America.

James W. Turner was m. September 7, 1898, to Josephine L. Creed, a native of Brocton, Massachusetts. Mrs. Turner is one of the most distinguished ladies and a leader in the social activities of her home city. She is an unusual woman of extraordinary ability. Her sense of duty to her husband and family and the demands in time of making a home for them left very little time for other things; nevertheless her advice, opinion and companionship have doubtless been a contributing factor in Mr. Turner's success in life.

Children:

Fifth Generation

66. Ernest Redmond Turner; b. 1900; d. 1905.

*67. James Douglas Turner.

68. Chester Turner; d. at age of 7.

67. JAMES DOUGLAS TURNER; educated in the public schools of Paintsville; and was graduated from Centre College, Danville, Kentucky; is connected with the Paintsville National Bank; m. May 22, 1927, Sally Byington, daughter of Prof. W. M. Byington. Mrs. Turner is a graduate of Womens College, Danville, Kentucky, and is an accomplished and popular woman.

Children:

Sixth Generation

69. James Douglas Turner, Jr.; b. February 10, 1928.

---

[1] "Report of the Adjutant General of Kentucky, 1861-1866", Vol. II, page 446.
[•] "Report of the Adjutant General of Kentucky, 1861-1866", Vol. II, page 447.

VANHOOSE FAMILY OF FLOYD AND JOHNSON COS.

1. JAN FRANCE VAN HOESEN, a Hollander, was the ancestor of the Van Hoesens in America. He came to the Hudson River region of the New York colony about 1635 as Commissioner of Lands for the Dutch West India Company of which Kilean Van Rensselaer was the founder. He settled at Fort Orange and subsequently went to New Amsterdam, now New York City, where he d. in 1667. His son Jurian was appointed as administrator of his estate. Nothing has been learned of his marriage. However, he left children as follows:

2. Jurian Van Hoesen.
3. Jacob Van Hoesen.
4. Volkert Van Hoesen.
5. Anna Van Hoesen.
6. Styntje Van Hoesen.
7. Maria Van Hoesen.
8. Catherine Van Hoesen.
*9. Joannes Van Hoesen.

9. JOANNES VAN HOESEN m. Jeanette Jan De Ryck.
Children:
10. Jacob Van Hoesen; m. Rachael Hollenbeck in 1714.
Children:
11. Jurgen Van Hoesen.
*12. Valentine (Fealty) Van Hoesen.

12. The records show that VALANTINE VAN HOOSA (the name has been variously spelled as Van Hooser, Van Hase, Van Hoose) acquired lands in Philadelphia County, Pennsylvania, surveyed May 5, 1750. Although not definitely established by record, it would soom that Valentine Van Hoose disposed of his lands in Pennsylvania and with other pioneers he and his family trekked the way to North Carolina by way of the Shenandoah Valley over the route travelled by the Boones, the Bryans and others from Eastern Pennsylvania to North Carolina. From North Carolina he went to Bedford County, Virginia; and the records indicate that he and/or members of his family lived in Wythe and Montgomery Counties and in the Clinch River region of Virginia prior to the migration of members of the family to then Cabell County, Virginia, now Wayne County, West Virginia, and to Eastern Kentucky.[1] Nothing has been learned concerning his marriage.

Children:
*13. Jacob Van Hoose.
*14. John Van Hoose.
15. Abraham Van Hoose.
16. Isaac Van Hoose.

17. Valentine Van Hoose; m. in Wythe County, Virginia, January 31, 1799, Julianna Tucker.

The records would seem to indicate that Valentine Van Hoose had other children:

18. Esther Van Hoose; m. Joseph Wampler, 1793.
19. Isabel Van Hoose; m. David Chambers, 1794.
20. Jane Van Hoose; m. Hugo Dietz.
21. Mary Van Hoose; m. William Purcell.
22. Hezekiah Van Hoose; m. in Mason County, Kentucky, 1799, Sarah Clark.

13. JACOB VAN HOOSE, the eldest, was appointed administrator of his father's estate about 1790. He was living in Wayne County, Kentucky in 1811. It is believed he had children:

23. Priscilla Van Hoose; m. Gene Stout in Augusta County, Virginia, July 26, 1801.
24. Elizabeth Van Hoose; m. Francis Lambert in Augusta County, November 26, 1801.
25. Jacob Van Hoose, Jr., m. Sally Lambert in Augusta County, August 3, 1806.

14. JOHN VAN HOOSE, b. April 5, 1762, presumably in North Carolina, and d. in Johnson County, Kentucky, January 5, 1860; m. about 1788, Mary Bryan, daughter of William Bryan of North Carolina. He had service in the Revolutionary War in the Virginia State Troops, Clark's Illinois Regiment.[2] Migrating westward, he is believed to have been living at Point Pleasant, present Mason County, West Virginia in 1792. The records show that in 1807 he was granted 50 acres of land on account of military service located on Twelve Pole Creek, present Wayne County, West Virginia, adjoining lands of William Bryan, William Clark and Samuel Ferguson, Revolutionary War soldiers and all related by marriage. Disposing of his land in Virginia, he removed to then Floyd County, Kentucky, and in 1822 purchased 100 acres of land at what is now known as Hager Hill, comprising the Mounds there. "Colonel" Van Hoose was one of the trustees of the first Seminary founded in the Big Sandy Valley, "Prestonsburg Academy, established about 1820 pursuant to act of the General Assembly of Kentucky. In recognition of his services to his country his name, with others, is inscribed on a monument erected in the court house yard, Paintsville, Kentucky, by the Daughters of the American Revolution of Johnson County.

Children:

*26. James Van Hoose.
*27. John Van Hoose.
*28. Levi Van Hoose.
*29. Valentine Van Hoose.
30. Hannah Van Hoose.

*31. Elizabeth Van Hoose.
*32. Jesse Van Hoose.
*33. Reuben Van Hoose.
*34. Sarah Van Hoose.
*35. Thomas Van Hoose.

26. JAMES VAN HOOSE, farmer; b. in North Carolina, 1791, d. in
Johnson County, Kentucky, 1884; m. in Floyd County, Kentucky,
September 25, 1811, Elizabeth Preston, b. in Bedford County, Vir-
ginia, 1799, daughter of Nathan Preston, Revolutionary War soldier,
and his wife, Elizabeth (Vaughan) Preston. (See Nathan Preston
Family.)

James Van Hoose settled at mouth of Johns Creek and afterwards
lived on a farm on Big Sandy opposite mouth of Greasy Creek.
Finally he moved to Tom's Creek where the great majority of his
descendants reside.

Children:
*36. Jentz Van Hoose.
37. Wiliam Van Hoose; d. at age of 21.
*38. Valentine (Felty) Van Hoose; b. about 1820.
*39. Bracken R. Van Hoose; b. 1820 or 1818.
*40. James Van Hoose, Jr.; b. 1823.
*41. Moses Van Hoose; b. 1831.
*42. Nathan Van Hoose; b. 1829 or 1830.
*43. Levi Van Hoose; b. 1829.
*44. Jesse Van Hoose; b. about 1825.
*45. Henry J. Van Hoose; b. 1835.
*46. Eliphus P. Van Hoose; b. 1837.
*47. John B. Van Hoose; b. 1832 or 1833.

36. JENTZ VAN HOOSE; m. Robert Childers.

Children:
48. William Childers.
49. Marion Childers.
50. John Childers.
51. James Childers.
52. Owen Childers.
53. Hardin Childers.
54. Elizabeth Childers.
55. Sarah Childers.

39. BRACKEN R. (LIFE) VAN HOOSE, farmer; b. in Floyd County,
Kentucky, December 22, 1818; m. in that county, July 29, 1841, first,
Mary Pelfrey, b. June 9, 1820.

Children:
56. Nancy Van Hoose; b. April 29, 1842.
57. Elizabeth Van Hoose; b. February 18, 1844.

58. William R. Van Hoose; b. January 26, 1846, and d. April 9, 1852.

59. Sidney Van Hoose; b. February 13, 1848, and d. March 13, 1848.

60. Lydia Van Hoose; b. May 24, 1849.

61. James H. Van Hoose; b. April 23, 1851, and d. May 24, 1851.

62. Daniel Van Hoose; b. April 18, 1852, and d. April 19, 1852.

63. Eliphus P. Van Hoose; b. April 30, 1853.

64. Mary E. Van Hoose; b. May 17, 1855.

65. Lucinda Van Hoose; b. July 2, 1857.

39A. Bracken R. (Life) Van Hoose, m., secondly, in Johnson County, Kentucky, December 18, 1859, Anna Davis, b. April 14, 1830, daughter of Elias Davis.

Children:

66. Amanda Van Hoose, b. 1860; m. Burgess P. Randolph.

67. Malissa Van Hoose; m. M. L. Price.

68. David Van Hoose, m., first, Adeline ———, and, secondly, Addie Jackson.

69. Matilda Van Hoose; m. William Walker.

70. Noah Van Hoose, grocer at Paintsville and local politician; served as jailer of Johnson County for one term, 1910-1914.

71. Sarah Alice Van Hoose.

72. Henry Van Hoose.

40. JAMES VAN HOOSE, JR., farmer; b. 1823, m. in Johnson Co., first, Betsey Hays, b. 1822.

Children:

73. Marion Van Hoose; m. Emma Dixon.

74. Thomas Van Hoose; m. Lydia Stapleton.

75. Haska Van Hoose.

76. Hoesa Van Hoose.

77. Fanny Van Hoose; m. Bishop Price.

78. Sarah Van Hoose; m. Taylor Daniel.

79. Amanda Van Hoose; m. James B. Preston.

80. Matilda Van Hoose; m. Samuel Stapleton.

81. Dove Van Hoose; m. Valentine Daniel.

40A. James Van Hoose, m., secondly, Mrs. Castle, widow of Thomas Castle.

Children:

82. Bessie Van Hoose; m. Julius Daniel.

83. Julia Van Hoose; m. Jesse Daniel.

84. Lena Van Hoose; m. Scott Daniel.

41. MOSES VAN HOOSE, farmer; b. 1832; m. in Lawrence County, January 19, 1854, Mary (or Mariam) Hays, b. 1839, daughter of Zeal Hays.

Children:

85. Harvey Van Hoose m. —— Travis of Lawrence County, Kentucky.

86. Julia Van Hoose.

87. James Van Hoose; migrated to Missouri and became a millionaire leadmine operator at Leadville, that state.

88. Brook Van Hoose; served in the Spanish American War as photographer; was partner of his brother, James, in lead-mine operations at Leadville, Missouri, and became very wealthy; was kidnapped and held for purpose of ransom and, resisting, was killed by his kidnappers. His five carat diamond ring was still on his finger when his body was found by neighbors.

89. Trinvilla Van Hoose; m. James Music.

90. Malengthon Van Hoose; m. Laura Bays.

91. Zeal Van Hoose.

92. Sally Van Hoose; m. Jonathan Francis.

93. Lonnie Van Hoose.

43. LEVI VAN HOOSE; farmer; b. in Kentucky 1829; m. Mary or Nancy Dixon in Johnson County, January 11, 1851.

Children and approximate dates of birth as shown by the U. S. Census of Johnson County for 1860 and 1870:

94. Mary E. Van Hoose; b. 1853.

95. James Van Hoose; b. 1855.

96. Richard or Robert Van Hoose; b. 1857.

97. Moses D. Van Hoose; b. 1859.

98. William Van Hoose; b. 1861.

99. Julia F. Van Hoose; b. 1864.

100. Winfield S. Van Hoose; b. 1868.

38. VALENTINE VAN HOOSE, farmer; b. in Kentucky, 1820; m in Floyd County, June 11, 1840, "Leasy" (Louisa or Loucinda) Price, b. 1826. Children living in the household and approximate dates of births as shown by U. S. Census of Johnson County for 1850, 1860 and 1870:

101. William J. Van Hoose; b. 1843.

102. Martin Van Hoose; b. 1845.

103. Harrison Van Hoose; b. 1848.

104. Elizabeth Van Hoose; b. 1849.

105. Jesse Van Hoose; b. 1852.

106. Lyncha J. Van Hoose; b. 1854.

107. Lafayette Van Hoose; b. 1855.

108. Franklin Van Hoose; b. 1857.

109. Sarah H. Van Hoose; b. 1859.

110. Benjamin F. Van Hoose; b. 1858.

111. Alice Van Hoose; b. 1860.

112. John S. Van Hoose; b. 1862.

113. Rheuemima Van Hoose; b. 1862.

114. Julia Van Hoose; b. 1864.

41. MOSES VAN HOOSE, farmer; b. about 1832; m., in Lawrence County, January 19, 1854, Miriam or Mary A. Hays, b. about 1839.

Children living in the household and approximate dates of birth as shown by the U. S. Census of Johnson County for 1860 and 1870:

115. Elizabeth Van Hoose; b. 1855.
116. Julia Van Hoose; b. 1856.
117. Henry B. Van Hoose; b. 1860.
118. Basil Van Hoose; b. 1862.
119. James Van Hoose; b. 1864.
120. Trinvilla Van Hoose; b. 1866.

44. JESSE VAN HOOSE, farmer; b. about 1825; m. in Johnson County, November 29, 1845, Keziah Van Hoose, b. about 1825.

Children:
121. William Van Hoose; b. 1848.
122. Levi Van Hoose; b. 1850.
123. H. J. Van Hoose; b. 1853.
124. Angeline Van Hoose; b. 1855.
125. Major Van Hoose; b. 1857.
126. Mary J. Van Hoose; b. 1862.
127. Elizabeth Van Hoose; b. 1864.

42. NATHAN VAN HOOSE, farmer and Baptist preacher; b. about 1830; m. in Johnson County, June 30, 1852, Lydia Pelfrey, b. about 1838.

Children living in the household and approximate dates of birth as shown by the U. S. Census of Johnson County for 1860:

128. Matilda Van Hoose; b. 1854; m. Isom Daniel.
129. John B. Van Hoose; b. 1856; m. Louisa Boyd.
130. Nancy Van Hoose; b. 1858; m. Clark Castle.
131. Martin L. Van Hoose; b. 1859 or 1860.

Other Children:
132. Life Van Hoose; m. Matilda Daniel.
133. William Van Hoose; m. Margaret Music.
134. Josephus Van Hoose.
135. James Van Hoose; m. Sarah Music.
136. Sallie Van Hoose; m. Jackson Castle.
137. Elizabeth Van Hoose; m. Edward Preston.

45. HENRY J. VAN HOOSE, farmer; b. March 5, 1835, and d. December 29, 1905; m., August 6, 1865, Nancy Baldwin, b. February 1, 1844, daughter of Thomas Baldwin of Wise County, Virginia.

Children:
138. Elizabeth Van Hoose; d. at age of 12.
*139. Warren M. Van Hoose.
140. Josie Van Hoose; d. at age of 11.
141. William Edwin Van Hoose; d. young.

*142. Don C. Van Hoose.
143. Martha Van Hoose; d. young.
46. ELIPHUS P. VAN HOOSE, farmer and Baptist preacher; b. 1837 or 1838; m. Julia Price, b. about 1837.

Children:
144. Faris Van Hoose; b. 1861; m. Winnie Helton (Hylton), daughter of Nathan Preston Hylton. (See Hylton Family.)
*145. Bascom ("Bass") Van Hoose; b. 1864.
146. Matilda Van Hoose; b. 1863; m. James Van Hoose.
147. Manford Van Hoose; b. 1866; m. Nancy Fairchild.
148. Albert Van Hoose; b. 1869 or 1870; m. Letitia Boyd.
149. Louise Van Hoose; m. Jethro Preston.
46A. Eliphus P. Van Hoose; m., secondly, Freelove Bryant.

Children:
150. Millard Van Hoose; m. Ethel Walker.
151. Kenas Van Hoose; m. a Rice.

139. WARREN M. VAN HOOSE, accountant; b. December 23, 1872; lived for a time in Johnson County and was special accountant; was in the Revenue service for several years; served as Assistant Secretary of State of Kentucky for four years and was an inspector and examiner for the State; m., March 12, 1902, Erie Dixon, b. March 18, 1880, daughter of Isaac Dixon (See Dixon Family); resided on a farm on Route 2, Frankfort, Kentucky, reared and highly educated a family. Mr. Van Hoose was a staunch Republican.

142. DON C. VAN HOOSE, teacher, public official and businessman; b. November 29, 1884; taught in the public schools of Johnson County; served as clerk of the Johnson Circuit Court for one term; and was postmaster at Paintsville; m. Josie Stapleton, daughter of Samuel Stapleton of Paintsville.

Children:
152. Marsha Van Hoose.
153. Henry Fleming Van Hoose.
154. Robert Cecil Van Hoose.

145. BASCOM VAN HOOSE; m. Julia Helton (Hylton), daughter of Nathan Preston Hylton. (See Hylton Family.)

Children:
155. Edward Van Hoose, merchant, first at Toms Creek, afterwards at Paintsville and finally at Ashland; m. Emma Witten, daughter of "Bud" Witten.

Children:
156. Arthur Van Hoose.
157. Burns Van Hoose.
158. Charles Van Hoose.
159. Leslie Van Hoose.

160. Beulah Van Hoose.
161. Nellie Van Hoose.
162. Zelda Van Hoose.

47. JOHN B. VAN HOOSE; m. Nannie Brown, daughter of Thomas Brown of Paintsville; lived at mouth of Sycamore Creek on Toms Creek; served as jailer of Johnson County for one term.

Children:
163. George Van Hoose; m. Alice Daniel.
164. Charles Van Hoose; m. Sarah Castle.
165. Cyrus Van Hoose; m. Elizabeth Witten.
166. Harry Van Hoose; m. Cora Preston, daughter of Dr. J. M. Preston.
167. Emma Van Hoose; m. A. F. Van Hoose.
168. Walter Van Hoose; served as County Court Clerk of Johnson County; resided in Paintsville; m. Sola Witten.
169. Ida Van Hoose; m. Edgar Rice.
170. Alonzo Van Hoose; was in the Revenue service; resided in Frankfort, Kentucky.

27. JOHN VAN HOOSE; b. 1792, d. at Fayetteville, Arkansas; m. in Floyd County, March 24, 1813, Lydia Lewis, daughter of Zachariah Lewis.

28. LEVI VAN HOOSE, farmer; b. in North Carolina, 1796; m. in what is now Wayne County, West Virginia, 1815, Sarah Clark, daughter of William Clark.

Children:
171. Mary Van Hoose; m. Enoch Auxier in Floyd County, December 28, 1833.
172. Lydia Van Hoose; m. Robert Meade in Floyd County, May 16, 1837.
173. John Van Hoose; m. Almira Keesee in Greenup County, October 27, 1836.
174. Kesiah Van Hoose; m. Jesse Van Hoose, a cousin, in Johnson County, November 29, 1845.
*175. William C. B. Van Hoose; m. Minerva Barnhard (or Lee).
176. Elizabeth Van Hoose; m. Solomon Ward in Johnson County, January 27, 1847.

Levi Van Hoose owned land in present Wayne County, West Virginia, deeded by his father-in-law, William Clark "for one dollar and the love he bore him as father-in-law". After the death of his wife, Sarah, in 1828, Levi Van Hoose disposed of his land in what is now Wayne County, West Virginia, and took his younger children, John, William and Elizabeth, to Kentucky and placed them under the care of his brother, Valentine, who had no children.

28A. Levi Van Hoose; m., secondly, Emily Elizabeth (Saddler) Damron at Louisa, Lawrence County, Kentucky, November 23, 1828. Children:

177. Ann (Mary Ann) Van Hoose; m. Jesse C. Middaugh in Lawrence County, May 28, 1854.

178. Nancy Van Hoose; m., first, Isaac Lambert, and secondly, John Humberson Lyon.

179. Sarah Van Hoose; m. Matthew (or Madison) Meek in Lawrence County, November 2, 1854. Lived in Ironton, Ohio.

180. Lexetta Van Hoose; m. Henry Daniel.

181. Rachel Van Hoose; m. William Daniel.

182. Adeline Van Hoose; m. Mr. Basham of West Virginia.

183. Moses Van Hoose; m. Margaret Adkins of Morgan County.

184. Jefferson Van Hoose.

Moses Van Hoose lived at White House, Kentucky. He was a farmer; was superintendant of the coal mines at White House and represented his district in the Kentucky General Assembly for several years.

175. WILLIAM CLARK BRYAN VAN HOOSE; b. October 14, 1821, and d. 1902; left an orphan when seven years old, he was brought to Johnson County where he was reared by his uncle, Valentine Van Hoose. He taught school on Buffalo Creek, Johnson County, when in his early teens; migrated to Ohio where he was living in 1858 when he purchased a farm on Picke fork of Barnetts Creek, Johnson County, on which he afterwards lived; served in the Kentucky militia during the Civil War, stationed at Ft. Gay (Louisa); m. Minerva Lee.

Children:

*185. John Wesley Van Hoose.

186. Matilda Van Hoose; m. John G. Trimble, a farmer and stock dealer of Johnson County.

*187. Elizabeth Van Hoose; m. Shadrack Preston.

188. Elijah Van Hoose; m. Elizabeth Picklesimer. He was a minister of the Church of God; d. in Carter County, Kentucky.

189. Nancy Van Hoose; m. Nathaniel Trimble, a farmer and blacksmith.

190. Sarah Van Hoose; m. William ("Dodger") Trimble, a farmer.

*191. Henry Milton Van Hoose.

192. Mary (Molly) Van Hoose; m. William Blair, farmer and miller.

193. Lee Van Hoose, carpenter and farmer; m. Alice Salyer.

194. James Van Hoose, farmer; m. Betty Preston, resided near Lucasville, Ohio.

195. George Washington Van Hoose, carpenter, preacher and poet; m. Mary Witten. Three sons were ministers of the Church of God.

185. JOHN WESLEY VAN HOOSE, a minister of the Baptist (Missionary) Church; m. Elizabeth Baldwin. The U. S. Census of Johnson County, 1870, shows "John W. Van Hoose, age 21, and Elizabeth S. (Van Hoose) age 17."

187. ELIZABETH VAN HOOSE; b. about 1848; m., about 1866, Shadrack Preston, farmer, b. in Kentucky in 1841 or 1842. Apparently he was a son of James Preston and Sally Preston of whom the U. S. Census of Johnson County 1860 shows: "James Preston, 49, b. in Ohio. Sallie (Preston), 51, b. in Tennessee. (Children) Shadrack, 19, b. in Kentucky; Jesse, 16, b. in Kentucky; Eliphus, 15, b. in Kentucky; James, 9, b. in Kentucky; Wallis, 14."

Children of Shadrack and Elizabeth (Van Hoose) Preston:

196. Ella Preston; b. 1867; m. Sherman P'Simer.
197. Henry Preston; b. 1860; d. young.
198. Jesse Preston; m. Louemma Roland.
199. William R. Preston; m. Della McKenzie.
200. Julia Preston; m. Manford M. P'Simer.
201. Bird M. Preston; m. Mahala Trimble.
202. Cora Preston; m. a Pelfrey.
203. Hoadley Preston.
204. Guy Preston; m. Jennie Williams.

Shadrack Preston lived on a farm on the Caudill fork of Barnetts Creek, Johnson County. They entertained, lavishly, the related families of Preston, Van Hoose and Trimble and many others of Johnson County. It has been suggested that Shade Preston's father James Preston, is identical with James L. Preston, son of Eliphus and grandson of Nathan, the Revolutionary War soldier. However, the records are conclusive that they are not identical as James Preston, father of Shadrack, was b. in Ohio about 1811, and James L. Preston, son of Eliphus and grandson of Nathan, was b. in Kentucky in 1857. (See No. 32, Nathan Preston Family.)

191. HENRY MILTON VAN HOOSE, teacher and minister of the Gospel; m. Mary Agnes Cunningham, teacher, deceased, taught in the Johnson County public schools for several years; was a minister in the Church of God; organized many Churches of this denomination in West Virginia and Eastern Kentucky; and was State Evangelist of this Church at the time of his death. During the latter part of his life, he was a resident of Huntington, West Virginia, where he died.

Children:
*205. Neva Van Hoose.
206. Charlotte Van Hoose, teacher; m. Fletcher Cales; three children.

207. Augustus Milton Van Hoose, carpenter and builder; veteran of World War I (Navy); m. Mrs. Gladys (Bryan) Kay; no children.

208. Hubert Henry Van Hoose, deceased, long an employee of the Chrysler Corporation; m. Violet Pennington; three sons.

209. Elizabeth Van Hoose, artist; served in World War I as yoemanette; m. Woolsey L. Hurt, veteran of World War I; three children.

210. Raymond Van Hoose, employee of the C. & O. Railway Company; lost his life in an accident in the yards of the company at Huntington; m. Beulah Hanshaw; one child (son).

211. Ruth Van Hoose (twin to Raymond); m. Alden G. Lambert, electrical engineer, with Dupont Corporation at Charleston, W. Va.; three children.

212. Beulah Van Hoose; b. in Carter County, Kentucky; d. from effects of burns at age of three years.

205. NEVA VAN HOOSE, teacher, welfare worker, poet and writer, was b. June 14, 1885, on Mill Creek fork of Jennies Creek, near Paintsville, Johnson County, Kentucky; educated in the rural elementary schools of Johnson and Carter Counties, the Willard (Kentucky) Graded School, the Grayson (Kentucky) Normal School where she received teachers' training, the Boothe Business Collgee, Huntington, West Virginia, and Marshall College at Huntington; was granted a teachers' first class certificate by the Carter County (Kentucky) Board of Examiners in June, 1903, and began teaching in the rural schools of Carter County in July that year when barely 18 years of age; subsequently taught six years in the Carter County schools; two years in the Crawford County (Illinois) schools; in the Huntington (West Virginia) Independent School District system as teacher and/or attendance supervisor for about eight years; as principal of the Geneva Kent school, Huntington, five years; and in Greenup County (Kentucky) schools seven years (1949-1955). She was retired from teaching in June. 1955.

During this long period, 1903-1955, when not engaged in educational work, she was interested and engaged in many and various other activities: Soon after graduation from Boothe Business College and in 1912, she entered the business field and for the next eight years she was employed as bookkeeper and stenographer, sales lady and for four years as organizer and buyer for several chain stores in Kentucky, Ohio and West Virginia, terminating as buyer for seven months in New York City for "The When" chain stores. While employed in New York City she lived on the corner of Fifth

Avenue and had a good view of "The Little Church Around The Corner." Because of war conditions and absence from her two young daughters whom she left in Huntington, she terminated her connection with "The When" stores in 1920 and returned home.

In the 1920s while employed in educational work in the Huntington schools, her duties connected her with the Juvenile Court and she became the first woman probation officer of Cabell County. During the period she became a charter member of the Huntington Council of Social Agencies, serving as Secretary-Treasurer for two years; co-organized the Family Welfare Society, and was a member of the State and National Conference of Social Work.

The Huntington school teaching staff having been reduced by dismissal of 40 teachers due to the depression, her connection with the Huntington schools was terminated and in October, 1932, she again entered the field of Public Welfare work as Home Visitor; was advanced to County Supervisor under the old RFC set-up and served in Lincoln and Tyler Counties, West Virginia, and Lawrence County, Kentucky. In 1936 she was appointed County Administrator of Cabell County under the new State Welfare set-up and was serving in that capacity in 1937 when the disastrous flood occurred in the Ohio Valley.

In 1939 she severed her connection with the State Welfare Department and for the succeeding several years she was employed by the unemployment Compensation Department at Huntington and at Charleston, West Virginia. In 1949 she returned to Kentucky and resumed teaching in Greenup County.

During this long period she has written several narratives and shorter poems (not published in book form), historical sketches of the Tri-State region of Ohio, West Virginia and Kentucky (published in newspapers), and is presently engaged in genealogical research and family histories in which she is deeply interested and thoroughly conversant.

She is a member of the Kentucky Historical Society, the National Genealogical Society, Washington, D. C., the Eastern Kentucky Teachers and the National Educational Association. Residence: Russell, Kentucky.

On February 15, 1905, Neva Van Hoose was united in marriage with Nayanthan B. Forrest, farmer, of Deevert, Carter County, Kentucky, who d. February 22, 1908. Mrs. Forrest never remarried.

Children:
213. Blanche Nadine Forrest.
214. Clara Elizabeth Forrest.

29. VALENTINE VAN HOOSE, farmer; b. in Virginia 1797 or 1798, d. in Johnson County; m. Jemina Borders, b. in Kentucky, 1806, daughter of John and Elizabeth (Sellards) Borders.

Children living in the household and approximate dates of birth as shown by the U. S. Census of Johnson County, for 1850:

215. John Van Hoose: b. 1830.
216. Mary Van Hoose; b. 1835.
217. Juliana Van Hoose; b. 1837.
218. Vashti Van Hoose; b. 1845.

31. ELIZABETH VAN HOOSE; b. in Virginia, 1801, d. 1884; m. about 1830, Richard Price, farmer; b. in Virginia, about 1798.

Children living in the household and approximate dates of birth as shown by the U. S. Census of Lawrence County for 1850:

219. Lyncha Price; b. 1831.
220. Hannah Price; b. 1837.
221. Jane Price; b. 1841.
222. Elizabeth Price; b. 1845.

32. JESSE VAN HOOSE; b. 1804: m. Mary Brown in Floyd County, November 11, 1826, daughter of Francis Asbury and Edy (Preston) Brown. (See Brown Family of Floyd and Johnson Counties.)

33. REUBEN VAN HOOSE, farmer; b. in Kentucky, about 1807; m. in Lawrence County, June 4, 1827, Leodocia Pack, b. in Kentucky about 1808 (believed to be a daughter of James Pack, Revolutionary War soldier).

Children living in the household and approximate dates of birth as shown by the U. S. Census of Lawrence County for 1850:

223. William Van Hoose; b. 1831.
224. Elizabeth Van Hoose; b. 1833.
225. Valentine Van Hoose; b. 1838.
226. Julian Van Hoose; b. 1840.
227. Thomas Van Hoose; b. 1845.
228. Martin Van Hoose; b. 1847.

34. SARAH VAN HOOSE; b. in Kentucky about 1809; m. in Lawrence County, August 20, 1829, Moses Price, farmer, b. in Kentucky about 1809.

Children living in the household and approximate dates of birth as shown by the U. S. Census of Lawrence County for 1850:

229. Charlotte Price; b. 1833.
230. James B. Price; b. 1835.
231. Detroit Price; b. 1836.
232. Mickworth Price; b. 1838.
233. Lumey? (female); b. 1840.
234. Martin V. Price; b. 1842.
235. Morgana (female); b. 1844.
236. Cleveland Price; b. 1846.
237. Molenthian Price; b. 1849.

35. THOMAS VAN HOOSE, farmer; b. in Virginia, 1812; m. Elizabeth Damron in Floyd County, January 4, 1832.

Children living in the household and approximate dates of birth as shown by the U. S. Census of Johnson County for 1860 and 1870:

238. Lucinda (either a daughter or second wife, probably the latter); b. in Kentucky, 1834.

239. Julia Van Hoose; b. 1851.

240. Lydia Van Hoose; b. 1853.

241. Malinda Van Hoose; b. 1854.

242. Major V. Van Hoose; b. 1856.

243. James B. Van Hoose; b. 1857.

244. Henry J. Van Hoose; b. 1859.

245. Thursa Van Hoose; b. 1861.

246. Lafayette Van Hoose; b. 1864.

247. Cynthia Van Hoose; b. 1866.

---

[1] "The Van Hoose Family of Eastern Kentucky", (Manuscript), prepared by Mrs. Neva (Van Hoose) Forrest, Russell, Kentucky, 1952.

[2] "Historical Register of Virginians in the Revolution, 1775-1783", by John H. Gwathmey, 1938, page 791.

VAUGHAN FAMILY OF JOHNSON COUNTY

This surname originated in the old Welsh word "vychan" meaning small in stature, corresponding to other names having the same significance, such as Petit, Bassett, Littlo.

There were several branches of this ancient family, but the records bear out the fact that the house of Vaughan was one of the foremost in shaping England's destiny. The families were numerous in England in early days as is evidenced by the Hundred Rolls and other records which bear the name of:

William Vachan, county Salop, 1273.

Adam ap Thewely Vachan, county Cardigan.

Owen Vaghan, county Salop, 1273.

Davey Watkyage Vaghan, county Gloucester.

Evan Vaughan, county Salop.

Jenkin Vaughan.

Jerworth Vachan.

The Vaughans of Burlton Hall, County Salop, trace descent from the renowned Tudor Trevor, the common patriarch of a number of noble and gentle families.

The Vaughans were prominent and were numerous in both Northern and Southern Wales. The old manor, Trawscoed, which came into possession of the family in 1200, is still standing and is used by descendants now the title of Viscount Lisburne and that of Lord Vaughan.

One branch of the family descended from Sir Roger Vaughan, who was slain at Agincourt in 1415, and from his son of the same name, who was beheaded in 1471 for his allegiance to King Edward IV in the War of the Roses.

Many distinguished men have borne the name of Vaughan. Richard Vaughan was Bishop of London in the reign of Queen Elizabeth; Sir Henry Vaughan and his nephew, Richard Vaughan, championed the cause of Charles I in the Civil War in England, and commanded the Royalist troops in Wales.

Families of Vaughan and/or Vaughn lived in all the original thirteen colonies in early colonial days.

The Vaughans of the Big Sandy Valley trace their ancestry back to England from whence they came in a very early date, settling in Halifax county, Virginia.

1. STEPHEN VAUGHAN of Welsh descent, lived in Halifax county, Virginia, near the North Carolina line. He m., presumably in that county, but the name of his wife has not been learned.

Children:

*2. John Vaughan.

2. JOHN VANGHAN, m. Isabella Griffin, daughter of Lewis Griffin

of Halifax county, Virginia, who owned considerable land and slaves. According to family tradition the bride's parents bitterly opposed the marriage on account of the financial status and social position of the groom and disinherited the daughter. However, relenting before his death, the father shared his estate with his daughter, the proceeds from which she purchased a farm on Mud Lick Creek, Johnson county, where descendants live.

John Vaughan was b. in Halifax county, Virginia, in 1801 and d. at Paintsville, Kentucky, in 1885. He was a pioneer carpenter and builder of Paintsville where he located in 1844, and where he continued to live during the remainder of his useful life. His wife, Isabella (Griffin) Vaughan, was b. in Halifax county, Virginia, in 1810, and d. at Paintsville in 1883.

Children:
  *3. Henry Stephen Vaughan.
  *4. Rebecca E. Vaughan.
   5. Sandy Vaughan b. September 5, 1838, d. February 18, 1911.
   6. William (W. W.) Vaughan, b. February 22, 1826, d. February 9, 1901.

3. HENRY STEPHEN VAUGHAN was b. in Halifax county, Virginia, in 1826 and d. at Paintsville in 1910. In 1844 he removed with his parents to Johnson county, Kentucky, locating at Paintsville and assisting in building the town. He became a man of prominence; acquired large farming interests, and during the last years of his life devoted himself exclusively to farming. Early uniting with the Methodist Episcopal Church, he continued a zealous member until his death. and for years was a local preacher. He was equally earnest in living up to the ideals of the Masonic fraternity, of which he was a consistent member. In politics he was a staunch Republican and firmly supported the cause of the Union in the dark days of secession. He served as county tax collector in the early sixties; and was elected and served as judge of the Johnson County Court, 1866-1870.

Henry Stephen Vaughan m., first, Mary Turner, b. at Paintsville in 1825, d. in that city in 1865, and, secondly, Mary E. Burgess, b. in Lawrence county, Kentucky, in 1840.

Children of Henry Stephen Vaughan and his wife, Mary (Turner) Vaughan:
   7. George Bascom Vaughan, m. Louisa Jane Davis (See Davis Family).
   8. Martha Vaughan, m., first, John Brown (See Brown Family) and secondly, Bee Dixon.
   9. Jessie Thornton Vaughan, m. Daniel M. Hager (See Hager Family).

Children of Henry Stephen Vaughan and his wife Mary E. (Burgess) Vaughan:

10. Mary A. Vaughan, m. W. P. Williams, farmer. She d. at Flatgap, Johnson county, at the age of fifty years.

11. Alexander G. Vaughan, farmer, Howard Lake, Minnesota.

12. Lou Emily Vaughan, m. W. H. Muncy, a Methodist clergyman. They resided at Scottsville, Allen county, Kentucky.

13. Jennie P. Vaughan, m. James Marion Williams (See Williams Family.)

14. Fred A. Vaughan was one of Eastern Kentucky's most distinguished men: He was one of the most active men in educational as well as political matters in the state. In concentrating his energies upon the development of better educational facilities for his home town, his country, and, later his state, Mr. Vaughan advanced in popular esteem, and his fellow citizens recognizing his capabilities, selected him for one office after another, desiring to have him conserve their interests and represent them in important matters.

Fred A. Vaughan was b. at Paintsville, Johnson county, December 8, 1876, and d. suddenly in 1927. He attended the public schools of Paintsville and then became a student in the Kentucky State College, now the State University at Lexington, and remained there through the Sophomore year, but left college in 1896 and for the subsequent ten years was engaged in teaching in Johnson county, the last year of which he was instructor in the Sandy Valley Seminary, predecessor of the John C. C. Mayo College, at Paintsville, resigning in 1906 to engage in politics. During eight of the ten years he was engaged in teaching, he was a member of the Board of Examiners for teachers' certificates for Johnson county; and for ten years was a member of the Board of Regents of the Eastern Kentucky State Normal School.

In politics Mr. Vaughan was a Republican. In 1906 he became chairman of the Republican Campaign Committee of the Tenth Congressional District and carried the district for John W. Langley for Congress in November 1906, although ordinarily the district was Democratic and had been electing congressmen of that politics for a number of years. He was secretary to Congressman Langley, 1906-1908, and was connected with the Census Bureau at Washington, D. C. for a year.

Mr. Vaughan was a State representative from the Johnson-Martin district in the General Assembly of Kentucky from 1904 to 1906, during which period he was especially active in educational matters and served on the Educational Committee and also on the committee having in charge the A. & M. College at Lexington, now the State University. He was elected as County Judge of Johnson county for two terms and served from January, 1914 to January 1, 1920, when he resigned; and was elected and served as Secretary of State of Kentucky for one term, from January, 1920 to January, 1924.

Mr. Vaughan was a member of the Methodist Church and was always active in church work and a teacher in Sunday School. Fraternally he was a member of Flat Gap Lodge No. 616, A. F. and M.; Flat Gap Lodge, I. O. O. F., and Frankfort Lodge, Loyal Order of Moose.

In 1914 Mr. Vaughan m. at Bardstown, Kentucky, Mary Muir Halstead, daughter of Col. Nat W. Halstead, distinguished attorney, and his wife Susan (Muir) Halstead of Bardstown. Mrs. Vaughan was educated in Nazareth Academy, at Bardstown. They had no children.

15. Isabella Vaughan, d. at the age of 34 years, unm.

16. Maud Vaughan.

*17. Roscoe Vaughan.

4. REBECCA E. VAUGHAN, b. October 28, 1845, d. February 6, 1926; m., April 12, 1864, Judge John Wesley Walker, b. 1840, d. September 26, 1926.

Judge Walker had service in the Union Army in the Civil War. He was always interested in public affairs and it has been said that he held every county office in Johnson county at some time or another during his life. The records indicate that he was county attorney for Johnson county from February 12, 1886 to April 1891; and again county attorney from 1898 to 1902.

Children:

18. William F. Walker, m. Matilda VanHoose (See VanHoose Family).

19. Ida Walker, m. Morrell Preston. (See Preston Family).

20. Pauline Walker, m. John W. Preston. (See Preston Family).

*21. Stella Walker.

22. Theodore G. Walker.

17. ROSCOE VAUGHAN resided in Paintsville and was employed by the North-East Coal Company at Thealka, Johnson county; m. ———— ————.

Children:

23. Dora Vaughan, m. Dona Wheeler.

21. STELLA WALKER, m. Dan W. Ward, businessman of Paintsville and a member of the firm of Copley, Ward and Preston.

Children:

24. Freeda Ward, m. C. P. Willoughby of Richmond, Kentucky.

25. Eugene Ward, businessman and cashier of the Paintsville National Bank; m. ———— Ecklere, of Catlettsburg, Kentucky.

26. Pauline Ward, m. James A. Ramsey, businessman of Pikesville, Pike county.

VINCENT-PEAY OF CARTER COUNTY

1. JOHN F. VINCENT, farmer and mechanic, was the ancestor of a large and prominent family of Vincents of Northeastern Kentucky. He was b. in Shenandoah County, Virginia, July 27, 1785, and d. at his home at Vincents Switch in Carter County, Kentucky, December 29, 1854. He m., first, in Virginia, Miss Nancy Renick by whom he had five children:

2. Sarah Vincent, m. Mr. George, lived in Virginia.
3. Allen Vincent.
4. Joseph Vincent.
5. Susan Vincent.
6. Lutilla Vincent; m. Mr. Surbaugh; lived in Virginia.

1A. After the death of his first wife, Mr. Vincent m., secondly, June 21, 1827, Sarah Hoke, who was b. in Monroe County, Virginia, now West Virginia, October 12, 1806, and d. in Carter County, Kentucky, April 15, 1882. They were parents of nine sons and two daughters.

Mr. Vincent came from Virginia to Carter County, Kentucky, with his family in 1846. He purchased the Lewis Stewart and the George M. Davis farms which included the Vincent Switch on the E. K. Railroad and the land at E. K. Junction (now Hitchens). He was a slave holder and left a large estate out of which each of his numerous children received a good home. He was a member of the Presbyterian Church and quietly lived his religion.

Children:

7. John H. Vincent; b. May 1828, d. 1872; m. Lucy Mary Roberts, January 15, 1852.
8. Christopher Hoke Vincent; b. March 1830, d. 1897; m. Julia F. Horton, March 30, 1852. (See Horton Family.)
*9. Delilah Vincent; b. July 29, 1832.
*10. James A. Vincent.
11. Henry W. Vincent, b. July 20, 1838.
12. Francis Marion Vincent; b. February 24, 1840.
13. Michael A. Vincent; b. April 8, 1845.
*14. Lewis Stewart Vincent; b. March 19, 1845.
15. Emily Alice Vincent; b. May 8, 1847; m. John William Richards, February 13, 1873. (See Richards Family.)
16. Thomas C. Vincent; b. January 14, 1850.
17. William C. Vincent; b. August 29, 1852.

9. DELILAH ANN VINCENT; b. July 29, 1832, d. February 1893; m. in Carter County, William Kendall Elliott. (See Elliott Family.)

Children:

18. John Charles ("Bogue") Elliott; b. May 23, 1856; migrated to California early in life and married there.

19. Sarah Jane Elliott; b. 1858.
20. Mary Alice Elliott; b. 1860; m., first, Samuel Thomas, and, secondly, John Zimmerman.
*21. Willie Hamilton Elliott.
9A. After the death of her husband, Delilah Ann (Vincent) Elliott m.. secondly, Andrew J. McClung.

Children:
22. Laura McClung, deceased; m. Worth Burns.   They were parents of three children: Earl. a veteran of World War I, deceased; Milton, who resides in California and m. there; and Thelma, who m. Dr. Clarence W. Warnock. (See Warnock Family.)   They were parents of three children: Dr. Clarence W. ("Jack"), a surgeon in Miami, Florida, who is m. and has three children, Marjorie, who m. James Mathney. They are parents of three children; and Don, unm., who is presently serving in the Air Forces in Japan.
23. George McClung, deceased.
24. James McClung; resides near the James F. Vincent homestead.

21. WILLIE HAMILTON ELLIOTT; b. in Carter County, in 1862 or 1863—probably the latter year, d. at Willard; and was m. in Carter County, June 21, 1877 to William George Peay.

WILLIAM GEORGE PEAY, jeweler, was a son of Elias Claiborne Peay (1795-1870) and Virginia (Fox) Peay and a grandson of George Peay, of King William County, Virginia. George Peay had other children: William, Nancy and Matilda. William Peay migrated to Kentucky early in life and it is thought that the Peays in Western Kentucky and Tennessee are descended from him.

According to family two brothers Peay of England, enroute to America, were shipwrecked off the coast of Bermuda.   Later one of the brothers reached America and settled in Tidewater, Virginia where he acquired vast landed estates.   He was ancestor of the family of Peay in Virginia.

William George Peay was b. in King William County, Virginia, August 21, 1848, d. at Willard, Carter County, Kentucky, May 4, 1935. At about the close of the Civil War he left King William County, Virginia, and came to Carter County, Kentucky. For a time after marriage he resided on a farm he had purchased at Vincent Switch but later removed to Willard where he lived until his death.

Both Mr. and Mrs. Peay were buried in the Vincent cemetery near Vincent Switch on the Little Sandy River.

Children:
*25. Maybel Elliott Peay.
26. Oscie Peay; b. December 26, 1883, d. January 9, 1948; m. Albert Theodore Engdahl, May 25, 1909. No children.
27. Kyon Peay, teacher, b. February 23, 1885; educated in the

Willard Graded and High School and Grayson Normal School; m. Charles Northcott Gee, June 10, 1914. See Gee Family.)

25. MAYBEL ELLIOTT PEAY, teacher, civic, church and social leader, was b. at Vincent Switch, Carter County, Kentucky, May 9, 1879; educated at Willard (Kentucky) High School, Kentucky University at Lexington, Eastern (Kentucky) State College at Richmond; and at National Kindergarten College, later National College of Education, Evanston, Illinois; began teaching in the Carter County school early in life and continued as teacher in the rural and graded schools for several years. Later going to Paintsville, Kentucky, she engaged in teaching in the public schools of that city for a time. Here she met Mr. Everett James Evans to whom she was married in her father's home at Willard, Kentucky, on June 21, 1913. No children.

Mrs. Evans has always been deeply interested in the welfare of the people of her home city and has always been an active worker and leader in its church, civic and educational affairs. She has been equally interested in the exploration and development of the coal, oil and gas industries in Eastern Kentucky in which her husband was one of the outstanding developers and operators. Present home address, Court Street, Paintsville, Kentucky.

Everett James Evans, developer and operator of mineral resources and businessman, was b. February 1, 1882, at Gallia, Gallia County, Ohio, and d. at Paintsville, Johnson County, Kentucky, September 24, 1951. He was a son of Rev. and Mrs. W. R. Evans of Welsh ancestry, and was of a family of twelve children. Rev. W. R. Evans was b. in Gallia County, Ohio, in 1843 and d. in 1918. Everett Evans grew up in Gallia County where he attended the public schools. Soon after leaving the farm on which he was reared, he became associated with the late Henry LaViers in what was then known as the Wellston Drilling Company. He came to Eastern Kentucky in 1907 to prospect for coal for the late John C. C. Mayo. His first core drill hole was drilled on Greasy Creek in Johnson County. Continuing in prospect work he gained wide knowledge of coal resources throughout Eastern Kentucky and was considered an authority on coal in the section. He was also interested in the production of coal, having been one of the original stockholders of the South East Coal Company in its development on the Kentucky River. He became one of the largest prospectors and drillers in Eastern Kentucky. His purchase of 46,000 acres of land in Breathitt and Knob Counties added to holdings which were already very large. Through his efforts great material resources of the State were located and developed, resulting in enrichment of both himself and the State and providing a means of livelihood for many people.

During the slump in the coal industry in the early 1920s, Mr. Evans switched to the oil and gas business, first as an oil broker for the Ashland Oil & Refining Company and other refineries. About

1925 he began oil development and production in the Blaine section and these leases are still producing now under the firm name of Evans & Turner, Judge James W. Turner being his partner. He also pioneered in the oil development in Western Kentucky and oil is being produced in that area. In 1932 he formed his own corporation, the Evans Oil and Gas Company. In 1931 he organized the Blackog Oil & Gas Company of which he was president, with gas production in Martin County. He was a director of the Kentucky Oil & Gas Association for many years.

About 1941 Mr. Evans again became interested in coal and was instrumental in acquiring and leasing the coal lands now operated by Princess Elkhorn Coal Company in Floyd County and Pond Creek Pocahontas Company in Breathitt County. The town of Evanston in Breathitt County was named in his honor.

Aside from his many and varied business activities, Mr. Evans, was deeply interested in and was active in civic and educational affairs. He served as regent of the Eastern Kentucky State College at Richmond; was a director of the Lonesome Pine Council, Boy Scouts of America; served on the Postwar Planning Commission of Kentucky. He purchased the Mayo estate in Paintsville in 1936, having in mind the idea of the establishing of a school by the State which would furnish vocational education free of charge to the young people of Eastern Kentucky. The Governor of Kentucky became interested in the idea, and to further the project Mr. Evans sold part of the estate at a sacrifice to himself, and the school was established by the State. It is a free institution, with a large and increasing enrollment, fills a very real need in the community and the thousands who have attended it have learned skills and occupations which have made them more valuable citizens and gave them the means of enjoying fuller and richer lives. Thus Mr. Evans was instrumental in developing human resources just as he was instrumental in developing the natural resources of the State.

Mr. Evans was active in several fraternal organizations: He was a Mason, a member of the Benevolent and Protective Order of the Elks and of the Rotary Club. He helped in organizing the Country Club and the building of the clubhouse in Paintsville. He was a Republican in politics and a member of the First Christian Church of Paintsville.

He was buried in the Vincent cemetery near Vincent Switch on Little Sandy River, in Carter County.

10. JAMES A. VINCENT, farmer and miller, was b. in Greenbrier County, Virginia, now West Virginia, November 29, 1835, and d. at Vincent Mill, near Grayson, Carter County, Kentucky, July 23, 1902. He came to Kentucky with his parents when in his youth. On November 6, 1870 he m. at "Walnut Grove" near Soldier, Kentucky, Susan ("Sue") Rebecca Richards, daughter of Jeremiah P.

and Amanda S. (Elliott) Richards. (See Elliott Family.) Mr. Vincent became a member of the Christian Church in 1871 and was a constant worker for all that was good until his death.

SUSAN REBECCA RICHARDS was b. at "Walnut Grove", near Soldier Kentucky, August 16, 1845, and d. at Vincent Mill, near Grayson, Kentucky, in 1935, at the advanced age of 90 years. She grew to womanhood in Kentucky. At the age of sixteen she went with her parents, Jeremiah P. and Amanda S. (Elliott) Richards, to Illinois. Here she was converted and became a member of the Christian Church in which she was a consistent member and active worker until her death. She was m. to James A. Vincent on November 6, 1870.

Mrs. Vincent was a cultured, literary woman, a great reader and fond of poetry. She was charitable and hospitable. For many years she taught in the public schools of Carter County. She was a member of Grayson Chapter Order of the Eastern Star.

Children:

28. James Vincent; m. Miss Gertie Prichard, daughter of Green Prichard. (See Prichard Family.)

29. Elliott Vincent.

30. Carlisle Vincent; m., March 17, 1910, Miss Gertrude Bayley.

31. Amanda S. Vincent; m. Robert H. Garvin; reside at Hazelton, Kansas.

14. LEWIS STEWART VINCENT, farmer and merchant at Soldier, Kentucky, was b. March 19, 1845; m., first, Julia Richards, daughter of Jeremiah P. and Amanda S. (Elliott) Richards. (See Elliott Family.)

Children:

32. Nellie Vincent; m. William Ferrell.

33. Reba Vincent; m. M. F. Christian.

34. Julia Vincent; m. Rev. C. M. Summers.

35. Jerry Vincent.

36. Frank Vincent; m. Josie Patton.

14A. L. S. VINCENT; m., secondly, on April 27, 1894, Miss Mollie Fleming, a teacher, of Willard, Kentucky, who was b. June 15, 1865, and d. January 9, 1945.

Children:

37. Jennie Vincent; b. May, 1898; unm.

38. Loraine Vincent; b. August 1900; m. Pierce Madden.

39. Paul Vincent; b. January, 1901; m. Pearl ———.

40. Russell Vincent; b. April, 1903; m. Nina Underwood.

VINSON FAMILY OF LAWRENCE COUNTY

Vincent is Norman-French (St. Vincent), a local name in Normandy; and the family Vincent is of French Huguenot origin.

James Vinson was the progenitor of the prominent and influential family of Vinson in Eastern Kentucky and Southern West Virginia. He was a South Carolinian and when on his way from South Carolina to the Big Sandy River section of Kentucky, he fell in at the "Gap Mountains" with Benjamin Sperry, Peter Loar and William Artrip, three brothers-in-law, and their families from the Shenandoah Valley in Virginia, who were also on their way to the Big Sandy River country to settle and establish homes. All the parties proceeded on their way and settled near present Cassville, West Virginia and Louisa, Kentucky, about 1800.[1]

1. JAMES VINSON m. in Floyd County, Kentucky, in 1812, Rhoda Sperry, b. in Virginia, 1796, daughter of Benjamin Sperry.[2] They settled on the Virginia (now West Virginia side of the Big Sandy River above present Louisa. Here they girded themselves to endure the vicissitudes of pioneer life on the frontier. James Vinson began the reclamation of and opened up a large farm.

From this marriage sprang the house of Vinson in Eastern Kentucky and Southern West Virginia, a family destined to attain a high place in the history of the section. Among its members have been successful and distinguished men in all walks of life: in business, in politics, in public office and in the law, members of the latter class having been distinguished at the bar and one of them became Chief Justice of the United States.

James Vinson and Rhoda (Sperry) Vinson were the parents of six sons and two daughters:

Second Generation

*2. William Vinson.
*3. Samuel Sperry Vinson.
*4. Lazarus Vinson.
5. Lafayette Vinson; b. about 1836.
6. ———— Vinson, a son.
7. ———— Vinson, a son.
*8. Nancy Vinson.
9. Rachel Vinson; b. about 1833.

2. "COLONEL" WILLIAM VINSON was b. in Virginia, now West Virginia, in 1816, and d. at Louisa, Lawrence County, Kentucky, in 1883. He was an extensive farmer, engaged in the timbering business and filled many positions of trust. He was an ardent Whig in politics and generally voted the Republican ticket after the formation of that party. Being a staunch Union man, he gave valuable as-

sistance in recruiting the 14th Kentucky Volunteer Infantry but on account of ill health, he was unable to perform service in the field. In the latter part of his life he united with the Christian (Disciples) Church and d. within its pale.

William Vinson was brave, noble and just. He possessed the usual Vinson characterictic: "Quick to resent an insult but as ready to do a kind act or charitable deed to any one who might stand in need."[3]

William Vinson m. in Lawrence County, Kentucky, September —, 1835, Jane Chambers, b. in Kentucky, 1820, daughter of Richard Chambers and his wife Mary, "Polly", (Garred) Chambers. (See Garred Family.)

Issue:

Third Generation

*10. Richard F. Vinson.
11. Zauriah Vinson; b. about 1842.
12. Tennessee Vinson; b. about 1844.
13. Zattoo C. Vinson; b. about 1846.
14. Mary Jane Vinson; b. about 1848.
15. Pharaoh ("Farrow") Vinson; b. 1849.
16. Sarah Vinson; b. about 1853.
17. Nancy Vinson; b. about 1857.
18. Elizabeth Vinson; b. about 1859.

3. SAMUEL SPERRY VINSON, farmer; b. in Lawrence County, Kentucky, April 14, 1833, and d. in Wayne County, West Virginia, June 19, 1904. He went with his family to Wayne County, West Virginia, when two years old and, except for eight or nine years spent in Lawrence County, he lived in Wayne County until his death. He resided on a large farm two miles above Ceredo, West Virginia; was senior member of the firm of Vinson, Goble and Prichard, Timber Trading Company at Catlettsburg. At the peak of his affairs, he owned 10,000 acres of land on or near the Ohio and Big Sandy Railroad in West Virginia and Kentucky.

He was a Democrat in politics and a member of the Christian (Disciples) Church, having been one of the founders of that church in Wayne County in 1882. He cast his fortunes with the Confederacy and had service in the Confederate States Army; enlisted in June 1861, in the 8th Virginia Cavalry, in which he commanded a company with rank of first lieutenant; served until March 1865, when cautured by guerillas and taken to Lexington, Kentucky. Having taken an oath not to take up arms against the United States, he was parolled and returned home just before the surrender of Lee at Appomattox, April 9, 1865.

Samuel Sperry Vinson was one of the picturesque pioneers of his region. He possessed great natural ability, great energy and reckless courage. He was dominant in manner and intense in his friendships and hates, though withall a devoutly religious man and generous to a fault. It is no exaggeration to say that he was typical of the early American pioneer stock such as has made this great nation.'

Samuel Sperry Vinson m. Mary Damron a daughter of Samuel and Vashti (Jarrell) Damron.

Issue:

Third Generation

19. Tennessee Vinson; b. June 4, 1853.
*20. Zachary Taylor Vinson.
21. Josephine Vinson; b. February 10, 1862.
22. William Vinson, b. January 1, 1866.
*23. Ida Belle Vinson.
24. Lynn Boyd Vinson; b. September 25, 1871.
25. Lindsay T. Vinson, physician, Huntington, West Virginia; b. August 28, 1874.
26. Mary Vinson; b. February 16, 1878; m. Donald Clark.

4. LAZARUS VINSON, farmer; was b. about 1825 on his father's homestead in West Virginia on the Tug River above Louisa. He m. about 1850, June Ratcliff, b. about 1825, daughter of William Ratcliff and his wife, Nancy (Garred) Ratcliff. (See Garred Family.) After his marriage he moved over to the Kentucky side of the Tug Fork of the Big Sandy River above Louisa and obtained a large tract of land on both sides of the river. For many years he was actively engaged in the timber business in connection with which he cleared the timber from much of his land and made the property available for cultivation. He was one of the honored and respected citizens of Lawrence County at the time of his death in 1895. He was robbed and murdered while on a business trip to Catlettsburg. His tragic death was deeply deplored in the county that had long represented his home and the stage of his productive activities. His wife d. in 1873.

Issue:

Third Generation

Persons living in the household, apparently children, and approximate dates of birth as shown by the U. S. Census of Lawrence County for 1860 and 1870:

27. Daniel Vinson; b. 1850.
28. Isabella Vinson; b. 1853.
29. Millard F. Vinson; b. 1855.
*30. James Vinson; b. 1856.
31. Winfield Vinson; b. 1859.
32. Lucy F. Vinson; b. 1862.
33. William Vinson; b. 1863.
34. Lafayette Vinson; b. 1868.
35. Albert F. Vinson; b. 1869.

8. NANCY VINSON; b. about 1803; m. William Ratcliff, farmer; b. in Virginia about 1802. Children living in the household and approximate dates of birth as shown by the U. S. Census of Wayne County, West Virginia, for 1860:

36. Garred C. Ratliff; b. 1839.
37. Sarah A. Ratliff; b. 1836.
38. William D. Ratliff; b. 1845.
39. Nancy E. Ratliff; b. 1848.
40. Albert Ratliff; b. 1853.

10. RICHARD F. VINSON, lawyer, judge and public official, was b. in Lawrence County, Kentucky, in 1838, and d. at his home at Louisa, Kentucky, in July 1910; attended the public schools and through self-study acquired a liberal education; studied law, was admitted to the bar and for many years was one of the leaders at the Louisa bar; served as clerk of the Lawrence Circuit and County Courts from 1858 to 1872; and served as judge of Lawrence County Court.

Judge Vinson was a Democrat in politics; and was long affiliated with the Masonic fraternity. He m. Georgia Ann Randall, b. 1840, d. April 1902, daughter of Dr. Perres M. Randall, who came from the state of Maine and became a prominent pioneer physician in Eastern Kentucky.

Issue:

Fourth Generation

41. Victoria Vinson; b. 1860; m. R. J. Prichard; residence, Louisa.

42. Jennie Vinson; b. 1863; m. Arnoldus J. Garred. (See Garred Family.)

*43. George R. Vinson.

44. Dora M. Vinson; b. 1868; m J. T. Groover; residence, Louisa.

45. Jay A. Vinson; resided at Garrett, Floyd County, Kentucky, where he was postmaster.

20. ZACHARY TAYLOR VINSON, lawyer, was b. December 22, 1857, on his father's farm in Wayne County, Virginia, now West Virginia, and d. in Huntington, West Virginia, January 30, 1929; educated in the public schools of Wayne County and at Bethany College from which he was graduated in 1878. His legal education was received at the University of Virginia and at the Boston University Law School; was admitted to the bar in 1886 and a short time thereafter he located in Huntington, West Virginia, where he became a partner with Judge Thomas H. Harvey in the firm of Harvey, Vinson and McDonald. Judge Harvey having gone on the bench, the firm became Vinson, Thompson and McDonald in 1892.

Aside from his law practice, he became interested in coal lands and transportation. He had a material part in and realized a substantial sum in the construction of the Huntington & Big Sandy

Railroad which subsequently became a part of the Baltimore & Ohio system. About 1900 he negotiated the sale of a boundary of coal lands in Logan County, West Virginia to the Island Creek group; and subsequently he dealt in coal lands.

Mr. Vinson was a good lawyer, a most plausible advocate and a powerful figure in State affairs. He m., June 19, 1901, at Richmond, Virginia, Mary Chafin, daughter of Richard and Sarah (Harvie) Chafin, who is a descendant of Colonel John Harvie, member of the Virginia Convention of 1775 and a colonel in the Virginia forces during the Revolutionary War.[5]

Issue:

Fourth Generation

46. Taylor Vinson, Jr., lawyer; b. February 7, 1904; educated at Bethany College and at the University of Virginia; admitted to the bar, 1930; m. Betty Jane Nelson, daughter of C. P. Nelson.

Issue:

Fifth Generation

Z. Taylor Vinson, named for his grandfather.

23. IDA BELLE VINSON, b. July 30, 1868; m. James Anthony Hughes.

James Anthony Hughes a Representative in Congress from West Virginia, was b. near Corunna, Ontario, Canada, February 27, 1861; attended the public schools; moved with his parents to Ashland, Ky., in July 1873; completed preparatory studies; was graduated from Duff's Business College at Pittsburg, Pennsylvania, in 1875; employed as bank messenger, 1879-1881 and as a traveling salesman in 1881 and 1882; moved to Louisa, Kentucky, in 1883 and engaged in dry goods business; member of the Kentucky House of Representatives, 1888-1890; moved to Ceredo, West Virginia, in 1891 and engaged in the timber business; moved to Huntington, West Virginia, in 1892 and engaged in real estate business; served in the State Senate, 1894-1898; delegate to the Republican State Conventions in 1896 and 1898; delegate to all the Republican National Conventions from 1892 to 1924, inclusive; served as postmaster at Huntington 1896-1900; elected as a Republican to the Fifty-seventh and to the six succeeding Congresses (March 4, 1901-March 3, 1915); because of ill health was not a candidate for renomination in 1914; resumed the real estate business in Huntington, West Virginia; again elected to the Seventieth and Seventy-first Congresses and served from March 4, 1927, until his death in a sanitorium at Marion, Ohio, March 2, 1930; interment in Spring Hill Cemetery, Huntington, West Virginia.[6]

30. JAMES VINSON, timberman and public official, was b. on his father's farm on the Tug River in Lawrence County, Kentucky, March 27, 1856. He was actively identified with the timber in-

dustry in the Big Sandy River section from early youth until he was 30 years of age; was elected and served as jailer of Lawrence County, 1885-1895; again engaged in timber business until 1906; engaged in contract work for two years on the Tug River Division of the Norfolk and Western Railroad; served as City Marshal of Louisa, 1895, and from 1909 to 1913 when he engaged in livery business at Louisa. A Democrat in politics, he affiliated with the Masonic fraternity and the Independent Order of Odd Fellows and was a member of the Baptist Church.

James Vinson m. Virginia Ferguson, b. December 8, 1860, daughter of Samuel Ferguson, long one of the influential citizens of Wayne County, West Virginia.

Issue:

Fourth Generation

47. Lourissa (Lou) Vinson; residence Louisa; unm.
*48. Robert W. Vinson.
49. Georgia Vinson; m. Joseph Merchant of Ferguson, West Virginia.
*50. Frederick Moore Vinson.

43. GEORGE R. VINSON was b. at Louisa, Kentucky, December 7, 1869; educated in the public schools of Louisa supplemented by attendance at the Agricultural & Mechanical College (now Kentucky University) at Lexington. He also completed a commercial course. He was prominent and influential in connection with the business and civic affairs of his home city, Louisa. He became bookkeeper in the Bank of Louisa at the time of its organization and was chosen cashier in 1893 and continued in this position since the reorganization of the institution as the First National Bank; became identified with the development of the oil and gas industry in his section of the state; and was liberal and public-spirited as a citizen and man of affairs.

Mr. Vinson was a Democrat in politics but was essentially a businessman and never sought public office. He was affiliated with the local Blue Lodge and Chapter of the Masonic fraternity. He m. in 1904, Emily Burchett, daughter of Major D. J. Burchett.

Issue:

Fifth Generation

51. Helen Vinson.
52. Frances E. Vinson; d. in infancy.

50. FRED M. (FREDERICK MOORE) VINSON lawyer, congressman, Secretary of the Treasury, jurist and Chief Justice of the United States, was b. at Louisa, Lawrence County, Kentucky, January 22, 1890; educated in the public schools of Louisa; graduated from the Kentucky Normal School at Louisa in 1908; was graduated from

Centre College, Danville, Kentucky, with degree of Bachelor of Arts in 1909, being awarded the Armond-Beatty Alumni prize; and was graduated from law department of Centre College with degree of LL.B. in 1911, his record as a student having gained him a scholarship in the college of arts. In college he was a member of "Ye Rounde Table", an honorary scholarship fraternity, and was also a member of Phi Delta Theta fraternity; was admitted to the bar in 1911 and commenced practice at Louisa; served as City Attorney of Louisa 1914 and 1915; had service in World War I, entering the U. S. Army, August 30, 1918; assigned to the Infantry and was in training for a commission at Camp Pike, Arkansas, when the armistice was signed; was honorably discharged December 6, 1918; commonwealths attorney for the thirty-second district of Kentucky, 1921-1924; elected as a Democrat to Sixty-eight Congress to fill the vacancy caused by the resignation of William J. Fields; reelected to the Sixty-ninth and Seventieth Congresses and served from January 12, 1924, to March 3, 1929; unsuccessful candidate for reelection in 1928 to the Seventy-first Congress; resumed the practice of law at Ashland, Kentucky; again elected to the Seventy-second Congress and to the three succeeding Congresses and served from March 4, 1931, to March 12, 1938, when he resigned having been appointed by President Franklin D. Roosevelt an associate justice of the United States Court of Appeals for the District of Columbia and subsequently designated by Chief Justice Stone on March 2, 1942, as Chief Judge of the United States Emergency Court of Appeals; served in each capacity until his resignation, May 27, 1943, to become Director of the Office of Economic Stabilization in which capacity he served until March 5, 1945; served as Federal Loan Administrator from March 6, to April 3, 1945, and as Director of War Mobilization and Reconversion from April 4 to July 22, 1945; appointed Secretary of the Treasury by President Harry S. Truman and served from July 23, 1945, to June 23, 1946; appointed and took the oath of office as Chief Justice of the United States on June 24, 1946, in which capacity he served until his death on September 8, 1953.[7] Interment, Pine Grove Cemetery, Louisa, Kentucky.

Judge Vinson m. at Louisa, ——— Roberta Dixon, daughter of Robert L. Dixon and his wife, Sallie (Borders) Dixon. (See Borders and Dixon Families.)

Issue:

53. Fred M. Vinson, Jr., lawyer; b. April 3, 1925, at Louisa, Kentucky; was graduated from Washington and Lee University with degrees of A. B. and LL.B.; and is presently engaged in general practice of law in Washington, D. C.

54. James Robert Vinson; b. September 1, 1929, at Louisa, Kentucky; educated at Washington and Lee University and at Centre College; m. Margaret Russell of Stanford, Kentucky; presently serving in the U. S. Army.

Issue:

55. James Robert Vinson, Jr.

[1] William Ely, "The Big Sandy Valley," pp. 156-159.
[2] Benjamin Sperry was b. in Connecticut in 1767, being 83 years old in 1850 as shown by the U. S. Census of Wayne County, Va., for that year.
[3] William Ely, "The Big Sandy Valley", pp. 156-159.
[4] George Selden Wallace, "Cabell County Annals and Families", p. 507.
[5] John Hastings Gwathmey, "Virginians in the Revolution, 1775-1783" p. 358.
[6] "Biographical Directory of the American Congress, 1774-1949", p. 1345.
[7] "Biographical Directory of the American Congress, 1774-1949", p. 1957-8.

VIRGIN FAMILY OF CARTER AND GREENUP COS.

The name Virgin probably was given to someone who had taken the part of the Virgin Mary in one of the Miracle Plays. The family is of English extraction and lived in England in early times. William Virgyn of County Essex, m. Lettice Sheppie in London in 1851; John Virgin of County Somerset was enrolled as student at Oxford University in 1587; John Vergine and Margaret Barrows were m. in 1610; John Virgin and Lena Warrington were m. in 1637.

Three Virgin brothers—Ebenezer, Samuel and Jeremiah, of Scotch-Irish extraction, emigrated from England to America in early Colonial days. Ebenezer, with one hundred families settled at Concord, New Hampshire; Samuel, a sea captain, was drowned at sea; and (1) Jeremiah settled in Virginia. He was the progenitor of the Virgins who finally settled in Northeastern Kentucky. Very little has been learned concerning him. However, it is definitely known that he had a son-

2. Jeremiah Virgin, Jr., who m. Lucy Dickinson in Virginia or Pennsylvania about 1735 and they had children:
*3. Reason or Rezin Virgin.[1]
*4. Nellie Virgin.
*5. Brice Virgin.
6. Kinsey Virgin.
*7. John Virgin.
*8. Thomas Virgin.[1]
*9. Clara Virgin.
*10. Jeremiah Virgin.
*11. Lucy Virgin.

3. Captain Rezin Virgin was commissioned a captain in the Virginia (Ohio County) militia in 1777. The records disclose that he settled on a 400-acre farm in Washington County, Pennsylvania, in 1780. He m. in Virginia or Pennsylvania Jemima Arnold, b. in Virginia, daughter of Jonathan and Rachel Scott) Arnold, b. in Talbot County, Maryland. Capt. Virgin d. at Old Town about 1816.

Children:
12. Rachel Virgin; b. 1771; m. David Enslow.
13. Kinsey Virgin; b. 1773; m. Hannah Tygart; they migrated to and settled in Scioto County, Ohio.
14. Eli Virgin; b. 1775; m. Nacka Hyatt.
15. Cassandra Virgin; m. Hezekiah Lyons.
16. Rebecca Virgin; m. John E. Wells in Greenup County, Kentucky, July 25, 1806.
17. Hannah Virgin; m. Ephraim Goble in Greenup County, November 2, 1808.
18. Eleanor Virgin; m. Moses Everman.
19. Rezin Virgin, Jr.; m. Polly Ann Lyons.

4. NELLIE VIRGIN; m., first, Col. Van Swearingen of Fayette County, Pennsylvania. They resided at West Liberty, Ohio County, Pennsylvania (now West Virginia). She m., secondly, a Mr. Newhouse. Col. Van Swearingen was of the party of twelve who assisted in the rescue of the citizens at Fort Henry being beseiged by the Indians.

5. BRICE VIRGIN; served as a lieutenant in the Virginia militia in the Revolutionary War. In 1790 he accompanied his parents and sister Lucy to Limestone (now Maysville) Kentucky, and in 1792 he and Lucy went to present Cincinnati (then Fort Washington). He lived for many years in that part of Ohio.

7. JOHN VIRGIN; had service as a private in the Revolutionary War. He sold his lands in Washington and Fayette Counties and probably settled in Berks County, Pennsylvania.

8. THOMAS VIRGIN; settled at or near present Cincinnati about 1800. He had service as a private in the Revolutionary War; had service in many Indian Wars and the War of 1812. He migrated west as the country was settled. A grandson, J. M. Virgin, of Pleasant Grove, Iowa, in a letter written in 1877, states that about 1807 or 1808 he sold his land in Cincinnati, allegedly ten acres embracing the site of the Burnett House, and with his wife, five sons and one daughter, he settled near Hamilton, Ohio; that leaving his family in Ohio, about 1816, he went to St. Louis where he joined the St. Louis Fur Company and made two or three trips to the Rocky Mountain region for furs; that on the third trip he and party of about 120 men attempted to cross the mountains to present Washington state but were ambushed by Indians on the headwaters of Yellowstone River and all killed but two.

9. CLARA VIRGIN; m. a Stuart; settled in Southern Ohio.

10. JEREMIAH VIRGIN, the youngest son, was too young to serve in the Revolution. He had an attack of congestion of the brain when six years old and upon recovery was speechless and remained so until the happening the following incident: He brought a terrapin into the house and placed it on the hearth by the fire. Becoming hot, the terrapin started to travel and touching his foot he kicked it off, shouting "Damn the thing!" Afterwards he talked. He d. and was buried in Greenup County; unm.[3]

11. LUCY VIRGIN, b. September 17, 1769, near Uniontown, then Beesontown, in what is now Fayette County, Pennsylvania, d. at Old Town, Greenup County, Kentucky, in 1847, was the first white child b. of American parents west of the Alleghany mountains. In 1790 she migrated with her parents and other members of the family to Limestone, (Maysville), Mason County, Kentucky, and thence in 1792, to present Cincinnati, Ohio, then Fort Washington, where she was m., September 20, 1800, to one John Downs[2] under a marriage license issued by General Arthur St. Clair, Governor of the

territory of the United States north of the Ohio River. She and her husband removed to and settled at Old Town, Greenup County, about 1807. Her parents and other members of the family had preceded her and settled there about 1800.*

20. REZIN VIRGIN, grandson of Captain Rezin Virgin (3), m., first, Lydia Meadows of Tygart Valley, Greenup County.

Children:
21. Henry Virgin.
22. Robert Virgin.
23. Elza Virgin.
*24. Butler Virgin.
*25. Virgil Virgin.
26. Lucy Virgin.
27. Laura Virgin.
28. Tempa Virgin.
20A. Rezin Virgin; m., second, Ann Nichols.
Children:
29. Catherine Virgin.
30. Rosa Virgin.
31. Florence Virgin.
32. George Virgin.

25. VIRGIL VIRGIN; lived all his life on the original Virgin farm at Old Town and several other members of the family lived in that vicinity. He m., first, Dolly Bays.

Children:
33. Orin Virgin; m. Sadie May.
*34. Martha Virgin; m. Victor Wells.
35. Mary M. Virgin; m. John Allen.
36. Fay Virgin; m. Don Oney.
25A. Virgil Virgin; m., secondly, Della Bays, sister to first wife.
Children:
37. Harry Virgin; m. Martha Hicks.
38. Charles Virgin; m. Minnie Fannin.
39. Clotine Virgin.
40. Howard Virgin; unm.
41. Vera Virgin; unm.
42. Billy Virgin; m. a Miss Scott.
34. Children of Martha Virgin Wells and her husband, Victor Wells:
43. Mrs. Dorothy Major.
44. Mrs. Norma Wright and
45. Robert Wells, all of whom resided at South Shore, Greenup County.

24. BUTLER VIRGIN; m. Perla Burton; resided at Old Town for many years, later removing to the western section of Greenup County.

Children:
46. Ben Virgin; m. Fannie Belle Morton; resided in Ashland, Kentucky.
47. Edward Virgin; m., first, Eva Lamblin, and, secondly, Emma Taylor, resided in Ashland.
48. Reason Virgin; m. Gladys Wells; resided in Ashland.
49. Mamie Virgin; m. Terry Skaggs of Indiana.
50. Sylvia Virgin; m. Thomas Bailey; resided in Washington, D. C.
51. Oscar Virgin; m., first, Virginia Burns, and, secondly, Ada Swamberger; resided in Portsmouth, Ohio.
52. Flora Virgin; m. Everett Hitchcock; resided in Ashland.

LAMACH (LAMECH) VIRGIN, farmer, was b. in Greenup County, Kentucky, 1808, a son of Thomas Virgin of Greenup County (See Virgin Family.) He was one of the wealthiest farmers of his time and section of the State. He listed for purposes of taxation in 1860, $10,000 in real estate and $4,500 personal property. He was the grantee in the first deed recorded in Carter County. When he d. he owned approximately 2,000 acres of land, a plat of the division of which is of record in the office of the Circuit Court Clerk of Carter County. A parcel of 550 acres set aside for his widow and a daughter was inherited by and is now in possession of a great-grandson, Henry Rupert Wilhoit, attorney, at Grayson.

Children living in the household and approximate dates of birth as shown by the U. S. Census of Carter County for 1860 and 1870:
Catherine Virgin; b. 1846.
Nancy E. Virgin; b. 1848.
Laura W. Virgin; b. 1851.
Thomas Virgin; b. 1853.
Miriam Virgin; b. 1855.
Reason (Rezin) C. Virgin; b. 1859.
Martha Virgin; b. 1862.
Belle Virgin; b. 1869.

---

[1] The U. S. Census of Greenup County, for 1810, show that Kenzie Virgin, Rezin Virgin and Thomas Virgin were heads of families in that county as of that time.
Vital Statistics of Carter County for the period 1852-1862, show that one Rezin Virgin, born in Bourbon County, Kentucky, about 1804, died in Carter County, April 13, 1853, aged 49 years, was a son of Thomas Virgin and his wife, Eleanor Virgin.
[2] John Downs was probably the first of the name to settle at Old Town. He and his wife, Lucy Virgin Downs, had issue: Emzy, who married Samuel Osenton (See Osenton Family.), Sarah, Jeremiah and Nellie.
One Henry Downs, probably a relative of John Downs above referred to, came from Central Kentucky to Old Town where he married Polly Ann Lyons. Their children were: (a) David Downs, who married Nancy Kouns Gibbs and had Bertis of West Virginia, and Addie, a well-known school teacher in Greenup County, now retired; (b) Henry Downs, who married Nancy Kouns Gibbs, a widow with two children: Emma, who married Scott Warnock, and Sallie, who married Elexious Riffe.
The records show other families of Downses in Greenup County: Matilda Downs m. Henry Hardwick, January 31, 1832; Thomas G. Downs married Matilda Davis, 1836; James Downs, married Polly Ann Virgin, 1844.
[3] Profile of the Osenton Family, Edited by Dorothy Mary Wollin, 1946.
[4] History of Kentucky, by Lewis Collins, 1847. (See Greenup County therein.)

WARD OF JOHNSON COUNTY

Ward

The well-known English ward represents a survival of Old English weard ("a protector, watcher. guardian"). The name Ward corresponds to the French "Garde". Sometimes Ward may be a shortened form of Warder ("Church warder") or abbreviated from any of the many names having ward as the last component, for example: Steward, Howard, Hayward, Woodward. There is another possible source for Ward in the Welsh Bhard ("a singer").

THE WARDS OF BIG SANDY VALLEY

This branch of the family came to the valley soon after the first settlement on Sandy. James Ward was the pioneer of the family. He settled on Rockhouse Creek, then Floyd, now Martin and Johnson Counties. The family is one of the most numerous in Eastern Kentucky. They have all along been noted for quiet dispositions and good citizenship. The pioneers were noted hunters, having been trained in Indian warfare. Among them have been preachers, professional men and public officials. In religion they are generally Baptists; in politics Democrats. A notable characteristic was the naming of their children for their ancestors. Of "Jim" Wards there have been a large number and in order to distinguish them they were given nicknames. Hence, there were Big Foot, Nine Toes, White Head, Bit Nose, Jimper, Little Jim, Jim's Jim, etc.[1]

Other authorities state that:

1. LEMILL WARD was the ancestor of this branch of the Ward family who settled on Rockhouse Creek, present Martin County; that very little has been learned concerning him; that he is said to have m. Sallie Osborn.[2]

Children:
*2. James Ward.
*3. Shadrack Ward.
*4. Solomon Ward.
*5. William Ward.
*6. —— Ward.

2. JAMES WARD; lived on Rockhouse Creek, present Martin County. It is not certainly known whom he married. However, one James Ward m. Lucinda Meek in Floyd County, April 13, 1820.

*7. Nathan Ward.

8. Emmanuel Ward; had service in the Union Army in Civil War and was killed in action.

One Emmanuel Ward m. Matilda Moseley in Lawrence County, August 25, 1858.

*9. Wells Ward.

10. Washington Ward; migrated to New Mexico.

11. ——— Ward, a daughter; m. Freeman Copley.

12. Elizabeth Ward; m. James Delong in Lawrence County, June 1, 1834.

3. SHADRACK WARD; m. Vina Hilton.

Children:

*13. James A. Ward.

14. John H. Ward.

15. Sally Ward; m. Isaac Meek in Floyd County, June 19, 1828.

16. Exer Ward; m. in Floyd County, July 30, 1837, Greenville Preston, son of James (Cobe) Preston and his wife Levina (Murray) Preston. (See Moses Preston Family.)

17. Jesse Ward; m. Mary Wheeler in Floyd County, July 30, 1837. (See Wheeler Family.)

*18. Levina Ward.

19. Julia Ward; m. Calvin Walter in Floyd County, May 13, 1830. (See Walter Family.)

*20. Jeff Ward.

4. SOLOMON WARD; m. ———.

Children:

*21. James (Whitehead) Ward.

22. Hezekiah Ward; m. Elizabeth Bowen in Floyd County, November 13, 1822.

23. Hiram Ward; m. Polly Johnson in Floyd County, December 3, 1830.

24. Shadrack Ward; m. Hettie Daniel.

25. Sarah (Sally) Ward; m. Drewry Castle.

26. Solomon Ward, Jr.; m. Nancy Ann Kidd in Floyd County, June 22, 1828.

27. Nancy Ward; m. ——— Bowen.

5. WILLIAM WARD; m. in Floyd County, January 11, 1816, Elizabeth Meek, daughter of James Meek. (See Meek Family.)

Children:

*28. James Ward.

*29. William Ward.

*30. Solomon Ward.

*31. Jonathan Ward.

*32. Stephen Ward.

33. Ali Ward; migrated to Ohio.
*34. Shadrack (Shade) Ward.
*35. Andrew Jackson Ward.
36. Susan (Suka) Ward; m. Jeff Price.
37. Malelia Ward; m. Ranson Lyons.
*38. John M. Ward.
39. Anglie Ward; m. Harman Harris.

6. ——— WARD, daughter, m. William Chapman, Sr.
Children:
40. ——— Chapman: m. ——— Williamson. They had a son,
41. Rev. James Williamson.

7. NATHAN WARD; m. ——— ———.
Children:
42. Nathan Ward, Jr.
43. Jane Ward; m. ——— Warnock.
44. Beecher Ward.
45. John C. Ward, resided at Offut.
46. ——— Ward. daughter; m. Harrison Conley.
47. William Ward.
48. David Ward.

9. WELLS WARD; m. in Lawrence County, August 31, 1843, Sarah
Preston, daughter of Henry Preston and his wife, Betty Cains. (See
Moses Preston Family.)
Children:
*49. Arthur Ward.
*50. Wells Ward, Jr.
51. Jane Ward; m. F. W. Price.
*52. Elizabeth Ward.
*53. Monterville Ward.
*54. Stephen Ward.

13. JAMES A. WARD was School Commissioner (County Superintendent) of Johnson County, October 15, 1854-April 1, 1855, and
from July 7, 1857, to June 6, 1858, and sheriff of Johnson County
from January 3, 1859, to May 19, 1862. One James Ward m. Jane
Wheeler in Floyd County, January 31, 1839.
Children:
55. Apperson Ward.
56. Shade ("Tackett") Ward.
57. Colista Ward; m., first, James Clayton Preston, son of James
(Cobe) Preston and his wife, Levina Murray, (See Moses Preston
Family.) and, secondly, Press Jennings.
58. ——— Ward, daughter; m. "Wal" Preston.

18. LEVINA WARD; m. Joseph Davis.

Children:

59. Zina Davis; m. Henry Meade.

20. JEFF WARD; m. ———.

Children:

*60. Shade Ward.

*61. Jeff Ward, Jr.

62. Laura Ward; m. "Ted" Preston.

63. Vina Ward; m. McClellan Preston, son of William Preston and his wife, Susan Murray. (See Moses Preston Family.)

64. Jennie Ward; m. John B. Wells.

21. JAMES ("WHITEHEAD") WARD; m. in Floyd County, April 13, 1820, Lucinda Meek, daughter of James Meek, Jr. (See Meek Family.); lived on Greasy Creek.

Children:

65. Cynthia Ward; m. Alfred Osborn in Johnson County, October 26, 1848.

66. James Ward; m., first, Mariah Viers in Johnson County, February 28, 1858, and, secondly, ——— Perry.

67. Nancy J. Ward; m. Sylvester Webb in Johnson County, February 5, 1857; lived on Greasy Creek.

68. Jack Ward; m., first, Clarinda Webb in Johnson County, February 15, 1856, and secondly, ——— Stepp.

69. Susie Ward; m. "Liss" Mollett.

70. Owen Ward; m. ——— Cannady.

71. Julia Ward; m. Pleasant Crum in Johnson County, September 11, 1845.

72. Jonathan Ward; m., first, ——— Spears; secondly, ——— Stapleton; and, thirdly, ——— Crum.

73. Mary Ward; m. Calvin Osborn in Johnson County, August 13, 1849; lived on Greasy Creek.

74. Squire Ward.

75. George Washington ("Cuby") Ward; m. Martha Wolfe.

28. JAMES WARD; m. ——— Lyons.

Children:

76. Ransom Ward; m. Elizabeth Meade.

77. Elliott W. Ward; m. ——— Van Hoose.

78. Alifair Ward; m. ——— Gambill.

79. Sallie Ward; m. James Spears.

80. Polly Ward. One Polly Ward m. George W. Daniel in Johnson County, November 6, 1845.

81. Elizabeth Ward; m. John C. Welsh.

29. WILLIAM WARD; m. Lucinda Lyons.

Children:
82. Corbin Ward; m. Emma Begley.
83. Colby Ward; m. in Johnson County, November 1847, Nancy Preston. (?)
84. John Ward; m. Julia Stafford.
85. Sallie Ward; m. —— Draper.
86. —— Ward, daughter; m. Shade ("Tackett") Ward.
87. Fanny Ward; m. Shade Preston.

30. SOLOMON WARD. One Solomon Ward, Jr., m. Lucilin (?) Porter in Lawrence County, August 3, 1843.

Children:
88. Ali Ward, prominent minister in the United Baptist Church.

31. JONATHAN WARD; m. Pricie Crum.

Children:
89. Moses C. Ward; lived near Tomahawk, Martin County.
90. —— Ward, daughter; m. —— Perry.

32. STEPHEN WARD; m. Polly Lyons.

Children:
91. William Ward.
92. John Ward

34. SHADRACK ("SHADE") WARD; m. —— Mollett.

Children:
93. "Az." Ward.
94. Green Ward.
95. T. Ward; lived at Chestnut, Kentucky.
96. Columbus ("Lum") Ward.
97. Johnson Ward.

35. ANDREW JACKSON WARD, prominent citizen and widely known as a minister of the United Baptist Church; lived near Oil Springs, Johnson County; d. at the age of 93 years; m. in Johnson County, February 27, 1858, Lydia Litteral.

Children:
*98. Ashley Ward.
*99. Zollie C. Ward.
100. Emma Ward; m. G. B. Stapleton.
*101. Angie Ward.
*102. Harry Ward.
*103. Katherine Ward.
*104. William Ward.
105. Elizabeth Ward; d. at age of 16.
106. Archie Ward; d. in his youth.
*107. Henry Ward.

38. JOHN M. WARD; m. Perlina Meek in Johnson County, August 2, 1853.

Children:

108. William A. Ward; m. Mintie Borders.
109. ——— Ward; m. ——— Borders.

49. ARTHUR WARD; m., first, ——— ———.

Children:

110. Edward Ward.
111. Matilda Ward; m. ——— Harmon.

49A. Arthur Ward; m., secondly, America Taylor.

Children:

112. Hamilton Ward.
113. George W. Ward; Editor of the "Big Sandy Advertiser."
114. Sherman Ward; merchant at Ironton, Ohio.
115. Benjamin Ward; physician and surgeon, Chicago, Illinois.

50. WELLS WARD, JR.; m., first, ——— Cassidy (?).

Children:

116. Alwilda Ward.
117. Sena Ward.
118. Jacob Ward; lives in Virginia.

50A. Wells Ward; m., secondly ——— Delong; a resident of Martin County; he served as sheriff for one term.

52. ELIZABETH WARD; m. Asa Williams.

Children:

119. George M. Williams; m. ——— Copley.
120. Joseph M. Williams; m. ——— Preston.
121. Sena Williams; m. ——— Dingess.
122. Sarah Williams; m. ——— Preston.
123. Ada Williams, m. Reuben Copley.
124. Dosia Williams, m. ——— Mills.

53. MONTERVILLE WARD; m. Lucinda Maynard; lived in Martin County.

Children:

*125. W. B. Ward.
126. Albert Ward.
*127. Maud Ward.
128. Elizabeth Ward; m. Sam Davis.
129. Edna Ward.
130. Grace Ward; m. ——— McGinnis (?).

54. STEPHEN WARD; m. ——— McGinnis(?).

Children:

131. Travis Ward.
132. Foster Ward.
133. German Ward.

60. SHADE WARD; m., first ——— Mollett; lived on Pigeon Roost Fork of Greasy Creek. He was a Democrat in politics and prominent in local affairs.

Children:
134. Manda Ward.
135. Benjamin Ward.
136. Jefferson Ward.
137. Shade Ward.
138. John C. Ward.
139. Laura Ward.
140. Nancy Ward.
141. James Ward.
60A. Shade Ward, m., secondly, ——— Music.

Children:
142. Sarah Ward.
143. Jennie Ward.
144. Russell Ward.
145. Lou Ward.
146. Edgar Ward.
147. Rose Ellen Ward.
148. Joe D. Ward.
149. Irvin Ward.
150. Evelyn Ward.

61. JEFF WARD, JR., farmer and lawyer; veteran of World War I; lived for a time at mouth of Greasy Creek, later moving to Thelma and afterwards locating at Paintsville; and finally located on a farm near mouth of Buffalo Creek; m. ——— ———.

Children:
151. Vina Ward; m. Nollis Meade.
152. Heber Ward; m. Malta Sublett.
153. Laura Ward.
154. Shady Ward; m. Evelyn Welch.

98. ASHLEY WARD, farmer and businessman; prominent in the affairs of Johnson County; sheriff of Johnson County, 1902-1906; connected with many business enterprises; lived near Oil Springs, later at Paintsville and finally on a farm near Concord Church where he lived at date of death which occurred about 1916; m. Katherine Reed.

Children:
155. Maude Ward, b. August 10, 1890, d. May 30, 1927—lost her life in storm that swept over Johnson County; m. Dr. T. B. Bailey, December 22, 1918.

156. Walter Ward; d. July, 1924; unm.

*157. Della Ward.
158. Dewey Ward.
159. Blanche Ward; m. Dr. Paul B. Hall.
*160. Golda Ward.

99. ZOLLIE C. WARD, merchant at Mud Lick; lived in Paintsville; connected with business enterprises; m. ――― ―――.
Children:
161. Josie Ward; m. Hopkins Preston.
162. Jettie Ward; d. young.
163. Arch Ward.
164. Stella Ward.
165. Scott Ward; d. young.
166. ――― Ward.

101. ANGIE WARD; m. Bryant Fannin; lived near Oil Springs. Mr. Fannin was deputy clerk of the Johnson County Court for a time.
Children:
167. Tobe Fannin.
168. Elsie Fannin.
169. Clyde Fannin; lived in Paintsville; was deputy clerk of the Johnson County Court for a time; veteran of World War I; d. in Veterans Hospital, Dayton, Ohio, March 12, 1927, and buried in U. S. cemetery there; m. ――― Stamper.
170. Henry Fannin; m. Callie Collins; lived in Paintsville and d. there.
Children:
171. Martha Fannin.
172. LeRoy Fannin
173. Walter Fannin.
174. Ernest Fannin.

102. HARRY WARD; m. Rose Hilton.
Children:
175. Dennis Ward; m. ――― Atkins.
176. Mary Ward; m. Carl Crase.
177. Eva Ward; m. Sanford Frazier.
178. Beecher Ward; d. young.

103. KATHERINE WARD; m. Dr. F. M. Witten; reside at Oil Springs where Dr. Witten is a prominent citizen and local leader.
Children:
179. Clara Witten; m. Charles Mahan.
180. P. French Witten; m. Hazel Risnor.
181. Emma Witten; m. Taylor Meade.
182. Thelma Witten.
183. Neva Witten; deceased.

104. WILLIAM WARD; m., first, Hattie Estep; resided at Concord for a number of years and then removed to Ashland, Kentucky.

Children:
184. Beulah Ward; m. "Pit" Witten; lived at Oil Springs; interested in early development of oil industry.
185. Dona Witten.
186. Lydia Witten; m. Fred Lemaster.
104A. William Ward; m., secondly, Hannah Blair.
Children:
187. "Jim" Ward, (a daughter).
188. Virginia Ward.

107. HENRY WARD; sheriff of Johnson County, 1910-1914; m. Stella Williams.
Children:
189. Lillian Ward; m. Paul Hilton.
190. Florence Ward.
191. Arbie Ward.
192. Langley Ward.

125. W. B. WARD, educator; b. in Martin County, Kentucky; taught in the public schools and in many other educational institutions of Eastern Kentucky: Instructor in the Sandy Valley Seminary; Superintendent of the Paintsville High School for many years; head of the Elkhorn High School; also conducted Teachers' Institutes and Summer Schools; m., first, Hattie Cline.
Children:
193. Oscar Ward; served in U. S. Army in World War I.
194. Olive Ward, teacher.
195. Georgia Ward.
196. Corrine Ward.
197. W. B. Ward, Jr.

127. MAUDE WARD; m. Granville Sitser; resided in Ashland, Kentucky.
Children:
198. ——Sitser, daughter.
199. —— Sitser, daughter

157. DELLA WARD; m. Levy R. Peters, businessman at Paintsville for a time; later went to Ashland where he was connected with the C. & O. Railway Company.
Children:
200. Katherine Peters.
201. Walter E. Peters.

160. GOLDA WARD; b. in Johnson County, December 14, 1900; m. July 10, 1925, Carl H. Fraim, b. August 12, 1896, son of W. S. Fraim of Ohio County, Kentucky.

1 William Ely, "The Big Sandy Valley", p. 155.
2 Mitchel Hall, "History of Johnson County, Kentucky, 1928" Vol. II, p. 582.

THE WARDS OF LITTLE SANDY VALLEY, CARTER CO.

Several Ward families lived in Northeastern Kentucky in pioneer days. They were principally farmers and slave holders; some were professional men; others held public office; some were prominent in the early affairs of Greenup and Carter Counties; and many of them were regarded as wealthy in their time. Of these families, four brothers, *1. Joseph Russell Ward, *2. Thompson Ward, *3. James Ward, *4. Abram Ward and their sister. *5. Malinda Ward, came to that part of Mason County which was subsequently (1804) established and organized as Greenup County. They constituted all the children of the family and were b. near Richmond, Virginia. They were brought to Kentucky by their father at an early day who settled in or near present Mt. Sterling, then Bourbon Co., living in a fort that had been erected for protection of the settlers against the Indians. Later they migrated to what is now Greenup County.

1. COL. JOSEPH RUSSELL WARD, lawyer and public official, was b. near Richmond, Virginia, January 1, 1799, and d. near Grayson, Carter County, June 17, 1851. He was buried in the cemetery on the hill above the Green Prichard farm on Little Sandy River, a short distance above Grayson.

Joseph R. Ward was well educated, an able lawyer and practiced on a large circuit which embraced several counties. He was the first clerk of Lawrence County, having been appointed clerk pro tem by the court, March 25, 1822, when Lawrence County was organized. It is related that on the day appointed for laying out the county-seat town (Louisa) he was late in returning to his office from the noon-day meal, giving as a reason the birth of a daughter whom they had named Louisa. Thereupon one of the commissioners, probably John M. McConnell, a brother-in-law, suggested that the county-seat town be named Louisa for the new-born daughter, which suggestion was approved by the commissioners.

Leaving Louisa Mr. Ward purchased a tract of land on the Cats Fork of Blaine, Lawrence County, and moved to and resided there a year. Selling the farm to one Dave Large, he moved to Carter County and established his home near Grayson in 1834. When Carter County was organized in 1838, he was made clerk of the County (the first) and served as such from May 1838 through 1850, or until date of his death.

Joseph Russell Ward m., presumably in Greenup County, about 1820, Adelaide Bragg Lewis, b. about 1803, daughter of Charles Nelms Lewis I and his wife, Elizabeth (Bragg) Lewis. (See Lewis Family.)

Children:

6. William Ward.

*7. Louisa Ward.

*8. Charles L. Ward.

 9. Dr. Lafayette Ward.

*10. Harriet Ward.

11. Susan H. Ward, b. 1841; m. Ben Wallis.

12. John Butler Ward, b. 1845; killed in the Civil War; buried at Greenup, Kentucky.

13. Milton L. Ward; b. 1850; d. young.

14. Sidney Ann Ward, b. 1837; m. Edwin R. Fry, May 2, 1865.

15. Joseph Ward; d. young.

16. —— Ward, daughter; d. young.

17. —— Ward, daughter; d. young.

2. THOMPSON WARD, lawyer; deputy clerk of the Greenup County Court; lived on the Little Sandy River below Old Town; m. Sally ——. He is said to have gone West and become governor of his adopted state.

Children:

18. George Ward; d. young.

(Note: One Thompson Ward, probably not identical with No. 2 here, was one of the most prominent citizens of Greenup County in pioneer days. He was a farmer and slave holder; b. probably in the 1770s as the U. S. Census of Greenup County for 1820 shows that he was then over 45 years of age. He was a lawyer and practiced at the Greenupsburg bar, 1815-1830; was State representative from Greenup County, 1815, 1818, and 1830; State senator, 1820, 1826; and was a captain in Poage's Regiment in the War of 1812.)

3. JAMES WARD. Very little is definitely known of him. He lived three score years and ten.

Children:

19. George Ward; clerk of the Fleming County (Kentucky) court.

20. —— Ward, daughter; m. Dr. Belt. Both resided in Flemingsburg, Kentucky.

(Note: There were other James Wards in Greenup County in pioneer days. One James Ward, farmer and slave holder was b. about 1775, as the U. S. Census of Greenup County, 1850, shows that he was then between 70 and 80 years of age. A James Ward was justice of the peace of Greenup County, 1813-1818; deputy sheriff of the county under Charles Nelms Lewis, 1810-11; sheriff of the county, 1827. A James Ward m. Elizabeth (Bragg) Lewis, widow of Charles Nelms Lewis I.)

Their children were:

21. George T. Ward; d. in infancy.

22. Harriet Ward; m. Richard Womack. (See Womack Family.)

4. ABRAM WARD; migrated and settled in Tenneseeee.

5. MALINDA WARD, a teacher in the Greenup County Schools.

7. LOUISA WARD was b. in Lawrence County, Kentucky, February 15, 1823(?), and d. in Ashland, Kentucky, April 27, 1913; m. at Grayson, Carter County, in 1839, Jackson Brown Ward (no relation), farmer, b. in Kentucky, 1817, and d. in 1884. After the close of the Civil War they moved to Catlettsburg, Kentucky.

Children who reached maturity:
*23. James Ward.
*24. Mary Adelaide Ward.
*25. George W. Ward.
*26. Eliza (Lyda) Ward.
27. Robert L. Ward; b. 1840, m. Lucy Anglin in Carter County; migrated to Kansas where they reared a family.

8. CHARLES L. WARD, farmer; b. in Kentucky, 1825; m. in Carter County about 1843, Nancy ———, b. in Kentucky, about 1826.

Children living in the household and approximate dates of birth as shown by the U. S. Census of Carter County for 1850:
28. Benjamin Ward; b. 1844.
29. Joseph Ward; b. 1846.
30. Charlie Ward; b. 1850.

10. HARRIET WARD; b. in Kentucky, 1833; m. in Greenup County, about 1852, Henry McAllister, farmer, b. in Kentucky, 1824.

Children:
31. Temperance J. McAllister; b. 1853.
32. James T. McAllister; b. 1855.
33. Christopher C. McAllister; b. 1857.
34. Joseph McAllister; b. 1860.
35. John McAllister.
36. William McAllister.
37. Nancy Amanda McAllister; m. Silas Singleton.
38. Clara McAllister; m. Joseph Vincent.
*39. Erie Adelaide McAllister.
40. Madison D. McAllister; m. Sallie Jones of Grayson, Kentucky.

23. JAMES WARD; b. at Grayson, 1844, and d. November ———, 1867; m. at Louisa, Kentucky, May 17, 1864, Katherine Burns. He was buried on the George Prichard farm, now owned by Dr. J. Watts Stovall, overlooking the town of Grayson.

Children:
41. Louisa Ward; b. at Grayson, February 20, 1865; m. Andrew Daniels at Ironton, Ohio, April 27, 1887. She resides at Kenova, West Virginia, and he d. April 18, 1936, and was buried in Spring Hill Cemetery, Huntington.

Children:
42. Katherine Daniels.
43. James Daniels.
44. Frances Daniels.
45. Yeland Daniels.
46. Vivian Daniels.
47. Charles Daniels.
48. Margaret Daniels.
49. Leland Daniels.
50. Franklin Daniels.

24. MARY ADELAIDE WARD; m. William Oliver Hampton. (See Hampton Family.)

25. GEORGE W. WARD; b. in Carter County, September 11, 1854, and d. March 23, 1931; m. Lizzie Sweeney.
Children:
51. Ethel Ward; m. Will Gates; no children.
52. Ella Ward; m. Charles Pugh; no children.
53. Clotine Ward; killed by train; unm.
54. Oliver Hampton Ward; m. Clara White of Cincinnati, Ohio.
Children:
55. Oliver Hampton Ward, Jr.

26. ELIZA (LYDA) WARD; m. David L. Williams of Catlettsburg, Kentucky. Both d. in Atlanta, Georgia.
Children, among others:
56. Mamie Williams; resides in Atlanta, Georgia; unm.
57. Aleene (Williams) Weekly, widow; resides in Atlanta, Georgia.
Children:
Mary (Williams) ———, m. ——— ———.
Charles Williams; m. ——— ———.
Betty (Williams) ———, m. ——— ———.
58. Sally Kate Williams; m. W. A. Harris, now deceased. She resides in Atlanta, Georgia.
Children:
Lyda Frances (Harris) ———; m. ——— ———.
Maurie (Harris) ———; m. ——— ———.
Arthur (Harris); m. ——— ———.
59. Louisa Williams; m. J. C. Reynolds, now deceased. She resides in Tampa, Florida.

39. ERIE ADELAIDE MCALLISTER was b. at Grayson, Carter County, Kentucky, in 1877; educated in the public schools of Carter County and for many years was a teacher in the common and graded schools of the county; m. at Grayson, January 3, 1900, Hardin Gilbert. She resides at 108 West Second Avenue, Medicine Lodge, Kansas.

HARDIN GILBERT, physician and surgeon, one-time teacher and public official, son of Oliver Gilbert, tobacco farmer, was b. at Gratz, Owen County, Kentucky, February 20, 1873. The family moved to a farm near Grayson, Kentucky, when he was a youth. Plagued with ulcers since childhood, he did not attend school until in his teens when he determined to secure an education. During the next several years he was an assiduous student in the public schools of Carter County; at the Willard (Kentucky) Normal School; at a select school at River, Johnson County, Kentucky, conducted by Prof. John B. Wheatley; and at the National Normal University, Lebanon, Ohio. Being thoroughly prepared for the teaching profession, he was granted a teachers' certificate and for several years taught in public schools of Carter County, the last years as principal of the Grayson Graded School.

A staunch Republican and active party worker, he was elected on the Republican ticket in 1901 as Superintendent of Public Schools of Carter County; was renominated by his party and reelected in 1905 and served until his resignation in 1908. Finally choosing the medical profession as a career, he attended the Medical College of Kentucky University, at Louisville, while still holding office and was graduated therefrom in 1906 as valedictorian of his class. He immediately began the practice of medicine at Grayson.

In the Spring of 1908, Dr. Gilbert resigned his position as Superintendent of Schools of Carter County and located at Medicine Lodge, Kansas, for the practice of his profession, where he continued practicing for forty years, or until his retirement in 1948. Here he became one of the most colorful and influential figures in the community. He held many positions of honor and trust. He served as coroner of the county, county health officer, member of the school board, president and charter member of the Lions Club; one of the organizers (1919) of the Barber County Building and Loan Association, of which he served as director for a time and was president at time of his death; also he established, in 1932, the first hospital ever organized in Medicine Lodge.

Dr. Gilbert d. in 1952 at Medicine Lodge Memorial Hospital at the age of 78; interment in Highland Cemetery, Medicine Lodge.

Children:

60. Oliver Hardin Gilbert, Colonel, U. S. Army, retired, was b. in Grayson, Carter County, Kentucky, January 29, 1906; educated in the public schools of Medicine Lodge, Kansas, and at the U. S. Military Academy, West Point, New York, graduating from the latter in 1929; was commissioned a lieutenant upon graduation and by successive promotions attained the rank of lieutenant-colonel when retired from the service in 1944, by reason of physical disability; residence Quincy, Massachusetts; m., upon graduation from

the Military Academy, Florence Beers, daughter of Frederick Beers, then president of the National Biscuit Company.

Children:

61. Patricia Gilbert; m. Staffan Rosenborg; residence 1315 12th Street, N. W., Washington, D. C.

62. Oliver Hardin Gilbert, Jr., student, senior class, Massachusetts Institute of Technology.

WALTER

1. ISRAEL WALTER was the progenitor of the Walter family of Eastern Kentucky. He lived in North Carolina, probably at Walterboro, in the early days. He was a noted Baptist minister. In 1805 he migrated with his family to Russell County, Virginia, where he d. about 1818. He m. ―――― Holbrook and soon after his death his widow and children moved to Blaine, Lawrence County, Kentucky.[1]

Children: Three sons and four daughters:

Second Generation

2. William Walter, farmer and physician; b. in North Carolina about 1798; m. in Floyd County, June 13, 1830, Elizabeth Woods, b. in Ohio about 1798. They left no descendants.
*3. Robert Walter.
*4. Calvin Walter.
*5. Elizabeth (Betty) Walter; m. Winfred Holbrook.
6. Sarah (Sally) Walter.
*7. Mary (Polly) Walter.

3. ROBERT WALTER, farmer; residence—Blaine Creek, Lawrence Co., was b. in North Carolina and d. in Lawrence Co., November 26, 1878, aged 79 years, 5 months and 27 days; m. in Lawrence County, February 26, 1824, Louisa Swetnam, b. is Virginia and d. in Lawrence County, August 18, 1877, aged 72 years, 6 months and 20 days, a daughter of Neri Swetnam, Sr. (See Swetnam Family.)

Children according to authorities[2] and/or the U. S. Census and approximate dates of births:

Third Generation

8. Edford Walter, b. January 31, 1827, and d. August 2, 1913; unm.
9. Swetnam Walter; migrated to and d. in the West.
10. Marion Walter; migrated to Kansas about 1855 and d. at his home at Latimer, that State.
*11. Emily Walter.
12. Rebecca Walter; b. in Kentucky; m. William Woods, a prominent farmer and stock-trader of Western Lawrence County.
13. Lou Ann Walters; m. John Sturgill of Kansas.
14. Neri Walter; b. 1830.
*15. Trinvilla Walter; b. 1833.
16. William W. Walter; b. 1835.
17. Louisa Ann Walter; b. 1838.
18. John C. Walter; b. 1840.
19. Robert L. Walter; b. 1844.
*20. Madison Monroe Walter; b. 1846.
21. Paulina B. Walter; b. 1849.

4. CALVIN WALTER, farmer; b. in Virginia, 1810, d. in Johnson County, Kentucky, in August, 1880; came to Lawrence County with his mother; lived near mouth of Greasy Creek, Johnson County; m., first, in Floyd County, May 13, 1830, Julia Ward, daughter of Shadrack Ward and his wife, Vina (Hilton) Ward. (See Ward Family of the Big Sandy Valley.)
Children:

Third Generation

*22. Shadrack ("Shady") Walter.
*23. Winfrey H. Walter.
*24. John M. Walter.
4A. Calvin Walter m., secondly, Sally Gambill.
Children:

Third Generation

25. Paris Walter; resided at Dockery, North Carolina.

5. ELIZABETH (BETTY) WALTER, b. in North Carolina, 1804; m. Winfrey Holbrook, farmer and miller, b. in North Carolina, 1802.

Children living in the household and approximate dates of birth as shown by the U. S. Census of Lawrence County for 1850, 1860, and 1870:

Third Generation

26. Calvin Holbrook; b. in Kentucky, 1829.
27. Robert Holbrook; b. 1833.
28. Elisha Holbrook; b. 1836.
29. William Holbrook; b. 1844.

7. MARY (POLLY) WALTER, b. in Virginia, about 1809; m. James Graham, farmer; b. in Kentucky, 1806.

Children living in the household and approximate dates of birth as shown by the U. S. Census of Lawrence County for 1850, 1860 and 1870:

Third Generation

30. Louvinia Graham; b. 1829.
31. William W. Graham; b. 1832.
32. Lafayette Graham; b. 1834.
33. Martin V. Graham; b. 1836.
34. Greenville A. Graham; b. 1838.
35. Larkin M. Graham; b. 1840.
36. Emily Graham; b. 1844.
37. James K. P. Graham; b. 1847.
38. Marcus N. Graham; b. 1848.

11. EMILY WALTER; b. about 1825; m., first, ———— Grubb.
Children:

Fourth Generation

39. Scott Grubb.

40. Genoa Grubb.

11A. Emily (Walter) Grubb; m., secondly, James Riley Dean, farmer and public official, b. in Kentucky, about 1826. Mr. Dean could neither read nor write when he m., but possessing great natural intelligence and encouraged and assisted by his wife, he acquired an education sufficient to anable him to carry on his personal affairs and to perform his official duties creditably. He served as surveyor of Lawrence County; was judge of the Lawrence County Court; and represented his district in the State House of Representatives at Frankfort.

Children, according to authorities:

Fourth Generation

41. Gus Dean.

42. Belva Dean; m. a minister of the Gospel at Barbourville, West Virginia.

Children living in the household and approximate dates of birth as shown by the U. S. Census of Lawrence County for 1860 and 1870:

Fourth Generation

43. Mary J. Dean; b. 1856.

44. Stanton F. Dean; b. 1857.

45. Leander B. Dean; b. 1859; prominent physician in Lawrence County.

46. Robert M. Dean; b. 1863.

47. William R. Dean; b. 1866.

48. Effie J. Dean; b. 1846.

49. Pennelia B. Dean; b. 1868.

50. Infant; b. October, 1869.

15. TRINVILLA WALTER; b. in Kentucky, 1833; m. William Ely, minister of the Methodist Episcopal Church, South. He was the author of "The Big Sandy Valley"; and resided at Catlettsburg, Kentucky. They were the first couple to have a "church wedding" in the Catlettsburg area.

Children:

Fourth Generation

51. Eugene Cary Ely, steamboat clerk on steamboat which ran from Catlettsburg to Pikeville; d. at Catlettsburg on his twenty-eighth birthday, December 15, 1879.

52. William Wirt Ely; engaged for many years in steamboating on the Big Sandy and the Southern waters; d. in 1882.

53. Iuka Ely; went to Herrington, Kansas; m. and had a daughter, whose name is unknown and who was connected with a newspaper in Kansas City.

54. Everett Ely; resided at Herrington, Kansas.

20. MADISON MONROE WALTER, farmer; was b. at Blaine, Lawrence County, in 1846 and d. on his farm there in 1935; m. Ann Patrick, b. in 1856 and d. in 1934 a daughter of Reuben and Amanda Patrick of the Burning Fork of Licking River about four miles from Salyersville, county seat of Magoffin County. (See Patrick Family.)
Children:

Fourth Generation

*55. Luther Mason Walter.

56. Lena Walter, teacher; b. May 20, 1878; educated in the public schools of Lawrence County and Blaine (Kentucky) Normal School; resides in Louisa; m. Dr. David J. Thompson.

David J. Thompson onetime teacher and a physician, was educated in the public schools of Lawrence County; at Blaine (Kentucky) Normal School; and was graduated from the Medical Department of the University of Louisville; resided at Webbville, Lawrence County, and practiced medicine in that area for a number of years; deceased. Interment in Webbville Cemetery.

Children, Fifth Generation: Irene, Walter and Monroe.

57. Roscoe Franklin Walter, lawyer and Government official, was b. at Blaine, Lawrence County, Kentucky, March 23, 1880; educated in the public schools of Blaine and was graduated from Vanderbilt University with degree of LL.B., 1908; admitted to the Tennessee State Bar; entered the Government service in Washington, 1909, as attorney in the Interstate Commission, and later served with the Bureau of Safety, resigning as chief attorney in 1921; rejoined the Interstate Commerce Commission in 1927 and later was an attorney and examiner for the Civil Aeronautics Administration; retired from the Government service in 1943. He d. April 24, 1955, at the Memorial Hospital, Lynchburg, Virginia. Interment in Fort Hill Park there.

In 1908 Mr. Walter was m. to Addie Pearl Callihan. To this union three children were b. (fifth generation): Charlotte, who m. Ronald MacDonald of Arlington, Virginia; Ann, who m. Verne Payne of Oakland, California; and Isabel, who m. Glen Snider.

58. Amanda Walter; b. at Blaine, Lawrence County, Kentucky, August 24, 1882; m. Curtis L. Thompson, onetime teacher and dentist at Webbville, Kentucky, (brother of Dr. D. J. Thompson). Children (fifth generation): Eloise, who m. Herbert Martin of Shelbyville, Kentucky.

59. Pearl Walter; b. at Blaine, Lawrence County; m. Dr. Ben Vaughan of Port Arthur, Texas. Children (fifth generation): A daughter, Mildred, who m. Stanley Hidalgo. They are parents of three children (sixth generation).

60. Edford Walter; killed in airplane accident, 1935.[2]

61. A. Henry Walter, lawyer and Government official, was b. at

Blaine, Lawrence County, Kentucky, April 19, 1899; attended the Blaine public schools and was graduated from George Washington University, Washington, D. C., receiving the degrees of LL.B. in 1923 and LL.M. in 1924; admitted to the Washington, D. C. Bar, 1923, and practiced his profession in Washington and New York City, 1926-37. Entering the Government service in Washington, he was Attorney and Examiner for the Interstate Commerce Commission, 1937-1948, Director, Bureau of Inquiry, 1948-1954; Director, Bureau of Inquiry and Compliance, 1954 to the present time.

Mr. Walter is a Republican in politics, a member of the Methodist Church and is affiliated with the Masons. He belongs to Washington Golf and Country Club.

He was m. to Melissa Boyer, May 18, 1951. Home—Route 2, Herndon, Virginia. Office — Interstate Commerce Commission, 12th Street and Constitution Avenue, Washington, D. C.

55. LUTHER MASON WALTER, lawyer, was b. at Blaine, Lawrence County, Kentucky, March 2, 1877; educated in the public schools of Kentucky; National Normal University, Lebanon, Ohio, Bachelor of English, 1896; graduated from Columbia University, now George Washington University, Washington, D. C., LL.B., 1901; Master of Laws, 1902; Doctor of Civil Law, 1903; and Master of Diplomacy, 1904.

Mr. Walter was engaged in teaching in the public schools of Lawrence County, 1892-99; studied law and was admitted to the bar at Louisa, Kentucky, April, 1898. Entering the Government service, he was clerk of the Census Bureau, Washington, D. C. 1900-1902; member of U. S. Board of Pension Appeals, 1903; law clerk, examiner and attorney, Interstate Commerce Commission, 1903-1910; special assistant to the Attorney General, 1908-1910; assistant director, Public Service and Accounting, U. S. Railway Administration, 1918.

While a clerk in the Government service, Mr. Walter completed his law education and began service with the Interstate Commerce Commission in September, 1903; and under directions of the Secretary of Commerce began prosecutions for enforcement of safety appliance acts; secured favorable interpretations of statutes through U. S., D. C., in various District Courts, U. S. Circuit Court of Appeals and the Supreme Court of the United States; was made attorney for the Interstate Commerce Commission in suits brought to set aside orders of that Commission and secured judicial interpretations of the Act. Severing his connection with the Government, in 1910 he went to Chicago as commerce counsel for Morris & Company, packers and formed partnership with M. W. Borders, then general counsel of Morris & Company; specialized in cases relating to common carriers and public utility matters.[3]

Mr. Walter was a member of the American Bar Association, Illinois State Bar, Kentucky State Bar, Chicago Bar, Trade and Commerce Bar Associations and Association of Practitioners before the Interstate Commerce Commission. He was a Republican, a Methodist and a Mason and a member of many clubs: Union League (Chicago), University Club (Washington), Olympia Fields Country, South Shore Country, Traffic Club (Chicago), Washington Golf and Country Club (Washington) and Country Club (Chevy Chase).

Mr. Walter was m., December 12, 1901, to Miss Anna Bradbury of Arlington, Virginia. Children (fifth generation): Paul Bradbury Walter and Helen (Walter) Munsert.

Mr. Walter d. June 30, 1948. Mrs. Anna Bradbury Walter resides at 9615 Glencrest Lane, Kensington, Maryland.

22. SHADRACK W. WALTER, farmer; lived on Greasy Creek, Johnson County; m., in Johnson County, April 2, 1853, Elizabeth Litteral.
Children:

Fourth Generation

62. John C. Walter; m. —— Arrowood.
63. George M. Walter; m. Marier (Mariah?) King.
*64. Dr. Winfrey L. Walter; resides in Winchester, Kentucky.
65. William M. Walter; m., first, Julia Davis and secondly, Emma Hodge.
66. Paris Walter; m. —— Watkins; resides in Bluegrass region of Kentucky.
67. Mahala Walter; lives at Auxier, Kentucky.
68. Juda Walter; m., first —— Arrowood and secondly, Preston Jennings.
69. Perlina Walter.
70. Sarah Walter; m. —— Elliott.
71. Louisa Walter.
72. Vina Walter.

23. WINFREY H. WALTER, farmer; b. August 22, 1833, d. April 1, 1914; m. in Lawrence County, October 11, 1854, Elizabeth Preston, daughter of James (Cobe) Preston and his wife, Levina (Murray) Preston, (See Moses Preston Family) lived in Johnson County.
Children:

Fourth Generation

73. John M. Walter.
74. James P. Walter.
75. Vinton Walter.
76. Shadrack W. Walter; lived at Malla, Kentucky.
77. Vina Walter.
*78. Dr. W. Jefferson Walter.
79. Juda Walter.
80. Rev. Ulysses S. Walter; resided on Blaine for a number of years where he conducted a general merchandizing business; later

he moved to a farm on Toms Creek and afterwards purchased the Preston farm at Thelma where he lived. He was a prominent citizen, a member of the United Baptist Church and one of its most ardent workers.

81. Rev. Lafayette Walter, minister of the United Baptist Church; lived for a time in Ashland, Kentucky, and also in Pikeville, Kentucky, and finally purchased the Davis farm near White House where he made his home.

82. Elizabeth Walter.

83. Dr. Edward P. Walter, physician; resides in Pikeville, Kentucky.

84. Exer Walter; m. Hansford Preston, son of Jeff Preston and his wife, Mary (Williams) Preston. (See Moses Preston Family.)

85. Mary Ellen Walter.

86. Clara Walter.

87. Susie Walter; m. James L. Preston.

24. JOHN M. WALTER; m. ———— ————?
Children:
Fourth Generation
*88. Ernest Walter.

78. DR. W. JEFFERSON WALTER, physician; b. in Johnson County, December 3, 1867; m. July 12, 1900, Mary Elizabeth Syck, b. April 28, 1871. They located in Pikeville, Kentucky, in 1900 where he practiced his profession. He acted as health officer of Pike County and was considered as one of the leading citizens of the Eastern section of the State.

Children:
Fifth Generation
89. Daniel G. Walter; b. May 24, 1901, d. February 13, 1902.
*90. Walter P. Walter.
91. William Robert Walter; b. June 3, 1905.
92. Amanda C. Walter.
93. Edith M. Walter; b. September 25, 1908.

88. ERNEST WALTER; m. ———— ————.
Children:
Sixth Generation
*95. ———— Walter.
*96. ———— Walter.

90. WALTER P. WALTER; b. May 4, 1901; m. Judith Fitzpatrick.
Children:
Sixth Generation
97. Dan Houghton Walter; b. June 5, 1925; resides in Pikeville.

95. ——— WALTER; m. Arrowood.

Children:
Sixth Generation
98. Clara Belle Walter.

96. ——— WALTER; m. ——— Dutton.

Children:
Sixth Generation
99. Eula Lee Walter.[4]

---

[1] William Ely, "The Big Sandy Valley", pp. 398-9.
[2] The Walter Family of Eastern Kentucky (manuscript) prepared by Roscoe Franklin Walter, Lynchburg, Virginia, 1954.
[3] "Who's Who in Kentucky", 1936._____
[4] Mitchel Hall, "Johnson County, Kentucky", pp. 578-81.

WARING FAMILY OF GREENUP COUNTY

The surname Waring is a derivative of the Latin word "Verus" meaning true. The Anglo-Saxon word "Wear", meaning a covenant or an oath, was undoubtedly the first form used by English-speaking peoples.

There were several branches of the Waring family that settled in America during the early days of colonization.

The New England branch was represented by Christopher Waring; the Virginia and Maryland Warings were founded in 1643 by Sampson Waring who came from England to Lower Norfolk Conty, but later moved to Calvert County, Maryland, where he established his estate at the Clifts. He was a prominent lawyer and a member of the Council of the colony.

The Carolina and Georgia Warings were founded by Benjamin, who came from Lea, near Wolverhampton, Staffordshire, England. He settled at Pine Hill, South Carolina, and became a distinguished colonist.

Descendants of the early settlers are living today in practically every section of the United States.

1. THOMAS WARING was the progenitor of a branch of that family in Northeastern Kentucky. He was b. in Prince George County, Maryland, in 1752, a son of Major Francis Waring and his wife (Hollyday) Waring, who was a direct descendant of Leonard Hollyday, one-time Lord Mayor of London. He m. Lydia Walton, daughter of Roger Walton of Philadelphia. He had service in the Revolution as lieutenant and captain of the Maryland Militia. Migrating with his family to Kentucky in 1784, he purchased a 1000-acre tract of land within a few miles of Limestone (Maysville), Mason County. Here he built Waring's Station for protection and defense against the Indians, and here he was joined by several brothers and their families in the 1780's, among whom were James Haddock Waring and Leonard Waring. In 1799 he purchased from the government a 1000-acre-tract of land near present Lynn, Greenup County, where he established his home, being probably one of the earliest settlers in that section.

Thomas Waring held many public positions of honor and trust in Kentucky: He was a justice of the peace while Kentucky was still under the jurisdiction of Virginia; a member of the Constitutional Convention that formed the first constitution of Kentucky; and was very active and influential in formulating plans for the formation and organization of Greenup County. He was a member of the commission that laid out Greenupsburg, the seat of justice; was a justice of the first Court of Quarter Sessions, organized February 20, 1804; and was an assistant (associate) Judge of the first Circuit Court, organized March 6, 1806, and served also as such judge in 1811 and 1815.

Judge Waring was buried in the Waring Cemetery on the original farm at Lynn and the inscription on his tombstone reads: "In memory of Hon. Judge Thomas Waring. Born in Prince George County, Md. Emigrated to Kentucky in 1784, and d. in Greenup County, January 15, 1818, in his 67th year."

The Warings were people of education and refinement and their influence was always for good. These traits have been outstanding in the family even to the present generation.

Children of Judge Thomas Waring and his wife Lydia (Walton) Waring:

2. Francis Waring.
3. James Waring; m. Lydia W. Waring in Greenup County, February 3, 1808.
*4. Roger W. Waring.
*5. Thomas Truman Greenfield Waring.
*6. Basil Waring.
7. Mary Hollyday Waring.
8. Dorcas Waring.
9. Lydia Waring.
10. Sarah Whitehead Waring.

4. ROGER W. WARING; d. in Ohio, 1816, and his daughter, Mary Hollyday Waring, b. in 1808, was adopted by her uncle and aunt, Francis and Mary Hollyday Waring (2) who lived on Tygarts Creek.

5. THOMAS TRUMAN GREENFIELD WARING b. in Maryland, 1778; m. in Mason County, Kentucky, April 25, 1799, Nancy Mefford, b. in Pennsylvania in 1783, daughter of George Mefford. He served as field officer in the Kentucky Militia, 1802-1818, and in 1815 he is borne of the records as major. He was State representative from Greenup County, 1819-21, and was sheriff 1830-31. In his will dated ————, 1865, he mentions children:

*11. Basil Waring.
12. James Waring.
13. John Waring.
14. Truman Greenfield Waring.
15. George Waring.
16. Leonard Waring.
17. Thomas Waring.
18. Nathan Waring.
19. Francis Waring.
20. Lydia Waring; m. William Fuqua (See Fuqua Family); migrated to Missouri. A grand-daughter, Mrs. Emma Kidd Hulbert, author of children's books, resided in Oak Park, Illinois.
21. Mary Waring; m. Richard Fuqua. (See Fuqua Family.)

22. Dorcas Waring; m. Charles Barrett.
23. Sarah Ann Waring; m. James H. Waring.
24. Martha Waring; m. Edmund L. Phillips.

11. BASIL WARING, farmer, b. in Kentucky about 1801; m., 1827, his cousin, Mary Hollyday Waring, b. in Ohio, 1808. He was State representative from Greenup County, 1840-41; school commissioner, 1841-43; and was sheriff 1846-47.
Children:
*25. Francis Waring.
*26. Basil Alvin Waring.
27. Roger T. Waring; m. Frances Van Bibber.
28. Martha Waring; m. Richard Dupuy.
29. Mary Hollyday Waring, b. about 1843; m. Rev. C. C. Armstrong; migrated to Texas.
30. Jane Waring; b. about 1836, m. Van Bartlett.
31. Ella M. Waring; unm., b. about 1850.

25. FRANCIS WARING; b. about 1830; m. Jennie Stewart.
Children:
32. Lucy Waring.
33. Leona Waring.
34. Margaret Waring.
35. Ada Mefford Waring.
*36. Francis B. Waring.
*37. Edward Taylor Waring.
38. Agnes Waring.
39. Jennie M. Waring.
40. Lawrence Waring.
41. Mary Waring.

36. FRANCIS B. WARING; resided in Piqua, Ohio.
Children:
42. Mrs. Nellie Killen; resided in Piqua, Ohio.
43. James Waring; resided in Piqua; leader in Young Men's Christian Association activities.

37. REV. EDWARD TAYLOR WARING; m., first, Etta Smith, a teacher in the Greenup County schools.
Children:
44. Charles Edward Waring; resided in Baltimore, Maryland; an executive in the Davvison Chemical Corporation, that city.
37A. Rev. Edward Taylor Waring; m., secondly, Louverna Hill Bennett, cousin to first wife. He was pastor of several large Methodist Churches in Ohio, and was retired and resides in Lakeland, Fla.

26. BASIL ALVIN WARING; b. about 1846; m. Nancy Bell; resided in Portsmouth, Ohio for a number of years and afterwards removed

to Lynn, Greenup County, Kentucky, where he conducted a general store.

Children:

45. Ida Waring; m. Edward Howland. She is the last Waring to own a part of the original large farm in Tygarts Valley acquired by the pioneer, Judge Thomas Waring.

46. Clarence Bell Waring; m. Daisy Laura Wood.

47. Maurice Waring; m. Elizabeth Greenslate; resided in Greenup County.

6. BASIL WARING; had service in the War of 1812 from August 6, 1813, to November 6, 1813, as a private in Captain Gaines' Company of Colonel John Poage's Regiment of Kentucky Mounted Volunteer Militia; was a justice of the peace of Greenup County at an early day; m., first, Sarah Mackoy, daughter of John Mackoy of Siloam; secondly, in Greenup County, December 28, 1829, Jane R. McCall, probably from Adams County, Ohio; and thirdly, January 1, 1834, Tabitha Mackoy, daughter of John Mackoy of Mason County.

The inscription on his grave stone reads, "General Basil Waring, b. Mason County, Kentucky, May 11, 1794, d. in Greenup County, Kentucky, August 21, 1844." The circumstances under which the appellation "General" was bestowed are not known. Probably by reason of his service in the War of 1812.

Children of Basil Waring and his wife, Tabitha (Mackoy) Waring:

48. Mary Lovina Waring; m. Thomas Lee Jordan. Their grandson, Robert Pearce, is a resident of Crestwood, Kentucky.

49. James Edward Waring; d. young.

50. Agnes Basil Waring; m. Stephen Carnegy; resided on the Basil Waring homestead on Tygarts Creek.

51. Sarah (Sally) Lydia Waring; m. W. Boyd Wilson, one-time publisher of the Louisville Courier Journal.

Children:

52. Mary Wilson; m. Rev. John E. Travis; resided at Anchorage, Kentucky.

53. Agnes Mackoy Wilson.

Other pioneer Warings lived in Northeastern Kentucky:

1. JAMES HADDOCK WARING, JR., b. in Maryand, son of James Haddock Waring, Sr., and his wife, Ann (Boone) Waring, who migrated to Mason County, 1786, m. in Greenup County, February 3, 1808, his cousin Lydia Walton Waring, daughter of Judge Thomas Waring (1). He was a successful farmer, and built a large brick dwelling at Lynn.

Children:

2. Ann Boone Waring; m. ——— Newcomb.

3. Eliza Lydia Waring; m. Thomas J. Stewart, August 1, 1836.

4. Thomas Waring; m. Mahala Howland.
*5. Roger Walton Waring.
6. James H. Waring; m. his cousin, Sarah Ann Waring, daughter of Thomas T. G. Waring (5).
*7. Sarah Waring.
8. Frances May Waring; m., first, John King, and secondly, William Flowers.
*9. Henry Ellis Green Waring.
10. Leonard Waring; m. Pricilla Stephenson.

5. ROGER WALTON WARING, deputy sheriff of Greenup Co., for several years and sheriff in 1851; m., first, in 1844, Eliza Phillips; no children; secondly, in 1848, Amelia Ann Phillips; no children; and thirdly, in 1852, Mrs. Mary Eliza Carnegy Phillips. Children, probably among others:
11. Mary Walton Waring; m. Wilbur S. Tinsley.

SARAH WARING; m. James Mackoy of Mason County. Their daughter, Mary Virginia Mackoy Grossenback, resides in that county.

9. HENRY ELLIS GREEN WARING; m., first, Louisa Hanks, daughter of Abraham and Poly Ann Wigglesworth Hanks; settled on the old homestead on Tygarts Creek.
Children:
12. Agnes Waring.
13. James Marshall Waring.
14. Mary Ann Waring.
15. Louise Nutter.
9A. Henry Ellis Green Waring; m. secondly, in 1868, Mary Ann Fox, daughter of Patrick and Eliza Tierney Fox.
Children:
16. Frances Mary Waring; m. Andrew Jackson Henry Lewis; resided in Ashland.
17. Albert Thomas Waring; d. in infancy.
18. Eliza Lydia Waring.
19. Edward Stephen Waring.
20. Sarah Nancy Waring; m. Frank Alexander Livingston; resided in Columbus, Ohio.

1. CLEMENT H. WARING. Very little has been learned concerning his antecedents. He was head of a family in Greenup County in 1810 and enumerated the U. S. Census of that county, for that year. He served as justice of the peace, 1839-45, and was sheriff, 1844-45. He was one of the three men who organized the Greenup Union Presbyterian Church. Inscriptions on gravestones in the Brick Union Cemetery read: 'Clement H. Waring, b. June 24, 1781, d. May 28, 1853." "Mary Waring, b. August 7, 1783, d. January 21, 1861."
In his will Clement H. Waring mentions children:

2. James Lawrence Waring.

3. William Waring.

4. Hollyday Waring.

5. Melvina Waring; m., first, in 1833, John P. Powell, and, secondly, Obadiah Fuqua Mackoy. She was buried in Brick Union Church Cemetery.

6. Thomas Waring.

7. Barton Waring.

8. Richard Waring.

9. Elizabeth Waring.

This family lived on Gray's Branch, Greenup County, and members of the family migrated to Illinois.

WARNOCK FAMILY OF GREENUP COUNTY

This family is of Scotch or Scotch-Irish ancestry and has been traced in Scotland back to the seventeenth century when three brothers took up arms with many others to defend the Presbyterian form of church government. They were bitterly persecuted and fled to Ireland where they found refuge. James, one of the brothers, became a merchant of prominence in Inneskillen, County Tyrone, where he d. in 1667.

Attracted by the promise of religious freedom several Warnock brothers emigrated to the American Colonies prior to the Revolutionary War; and it is claimed that some of them served in the American Army during that war. Members of the family settled in Pennsylvania, Maryland, Virginia, North Carolina and probably other colonies. Among these was:

1. WILLIAM JAMES WARNOCK who came to North Carolina. He was b. in County Tyrone, near Londonderry, Ireland, and m. Elizabeth Carlisle of that county.

Historians state that he was of Daniel Boone's party of six families and forty men who, on September 25, 1773, began the trek from the Yadkin River in North Carolina to Kentucky for the purpose of making settlement and establishing homes. However, William James Warnock did not reach Kentucky at this time. When the party neared Cumberland Gap, a number who had fallen in the rear were fired upon by Indians and six killed, including one of Boone's sons, which disaster changed their plans and the entire party retraced their steps to the settlement on the Clinch River where they remained for some time.

William James Warnock subsequently passed the barrier of the mountains and settled in what is now Greenup County, then Mason County, Kentucky, before the establishment of Greenup County in 1803. When the town of Greenupsburg was plotted he purchased eight of the sixty-four lots sold, two of which have always been owned by members of the family.

Children of William James Warnock and his wife Elizabeth (Carlisle) Warnock:

Second Generation in Kentucky

*2. James Warnock, Jr.
*3. Johnson Warnock.
*4. William J. Warnock.
*5. Samuel Warnock.

2. JAMES WARNOCK, JR., a farmer and slaveholder; b. in Virginia about 1781; owned a large plantation called Warnock on the upper reaches of Tygarts Creek. He was poetical and sometimes

wrote poems for his own and his family's pleasure, one of which was a tribute to Robert Burns in the poet's own style and dialect. Some of his descendants inherited his literary and artistic tastes.

He m. in Greenup County, Rebecca Howe, b. in Kentucky in 1784 or 1785, daughter of John W. Howe, Revolutionary War soldier. (See Howe Family.) In his will, probated in the Greenup County Court in 1856, he mentions children:

Third Generation

*6. John W. Howe Warnock.
*7. William Howe Warnock.
*8. Matthew Warnock.
*9. James Wesley Warnock.
10. Sallie Warnock who m. James Alexander.
11. Cynthia Warnock; unm.

3. JOHNSON WARNOCK; m. in Greenup County, June —, 1813, Betsy Forester; built a dwelling house on Lot No. 12 in Greenupsburg the same year and probably went to housekeeping there. In his will he mentions children:

Third Generation

12. Carlisle Warnock.
13. Robert Warnock.
14. James Warnock.
15. Martha Warnock; m. her cousin, James Warnock.
16. Lavina Warnock.
17. Malinda Elizabeth Warnock.

4. WILLIAM J. WARNOCK. Very little has been learned concerning him. He m. Lucy Forester, probably a sister to his brother Johnson's wife.

Children:

Third Generation

18. Andrew Warnock; m. Miss Colter.
19. James Carlisle Warnock; m., first, Miss Hunt and secondly, —— ——.
20. Ann Warnock; m. George Howland.

5. SAMUEL WARNOCK, farmer and slaveholder. In his will, probated in the Greenup County Court, December 6, 1843, he mentions his wife, Rachael, and children:

Third Generation

21. Andrew Jackson Warnock.
*22. William L. Warnock.

23. James Carlisle Warnock.
24. (Mrs.) Mahala Reaves.
25. Mary Warnock who had m. William Brown in Greenup County, December 23, 1829.
26. Elizabeth Warnock who had m. Solomon Huffman in Greenup County, January 20, 1829.
27. Sarah Warnock who had m. Allen Huffman in Greenup County, November, 1829.
28. Jane Warnock who had m. Robert Bradshaw in Greenup County, February 11, 1833.
29. Lavina Warnock who had m. Sanders Crawford in Greenup County, December 21, 1836.
30. Teresa Warnock.

6. JOHN W. WARNOCK, farmer; b. in Kentucky about 1811; m. in Greenup County April 1, 1833, Grace Guilkey, b. in Kentucky, about 1816. They lived in Greenup County, Kentucky many years. He was very active in the affairs of the county; was part owner of the Laurel Furnace; and was of literary tastes and possessed a library of many books.

Children:

Fourth Generation

*31. James (Red James) H. Warnock.
*32. Edward G. Warnock.
*33. Matthew Warnock.
*34. William W. Warnock.
*35. Benjamin Franklin Warnock.
36. Betsy Ann Warnock who m. her cousin, Basil Warnock.
37. Rebecca Warnock who d. young.

7. WILLIAM HOWE WARNOCK, farmer, b. in Kentucky, about 1813; owned large tracts of land on Tygarts Creek in Greenup County, and in Carter County on which the Carter Caves are located; m. in 1835, Emma Duzan Ratcliff, b. about 1817, daughter of Samuel Ratcliff.

Children:

Fourth Generation

*38. John Wesley (John Dock) Warnock.
*39. Samuel Price Warnock.
*40. Richard Matthew Warnock.
*41. James Warren Warnock.
*42. Francis Marion ("Slick") Warnock.
*43. William Lindsay Warnock.
*44. Taylor ("Whig") Warnock.
45. Julia Warnock Hall.

Three other children d. in infancy, and are not listed here.

8. MATTHEW WARNOCK, SR., farmer, b. in Kentucky about 1807; m. in Greenup County, April 5, 1828, Lydia Warnock, b. in Kentucky about 1810, daughter of William Warnock.

Children:

Fourth Generation

46. Elizabeth Warnock; m. James Clifton.
47. James (Black Jim) Warnock; m. Miss Bradshaw.
48. Polly (Mary) Warnock, b. 1838; m. Dr. Charles W. Secrest, b. in 1829.
49. Margaret Warnock, b. 1838; m. James Warnock, son of John W. H. Warnock.
50. John W. Warnock, b. about 1840; m. Kate Eifort.
51. Bazil Warnock, b. about 1842; m. Betsy Ann Warnock, daughter of John W. H. Warnock (6).
52. Charles W. Warnock, b. about 1844; m. Cassie Roberts.
53. America C. Warnock, b. about 1846; m. Benjamin Franklin Meadows.
54. Matthew Scott Warnock, Jr.

9. JAMES WESLEY WARNOCK, farmer; m. his cousin Martha Warnock, (15), daughter of Johnson Warnock (3); resided on a farm at Bennetts Mills, Greenup County.

Children:

Fourth Generation

*59. Robert Johnson Warnock; m. America Batman.
*60 Scott Warnock; m. Miss Batman.
61. Price Warnock; unm.
62. J. C. Warnock; m. Mabel Gannon.

31. JAMES H. WARNOCK; b. about 1835; m. his cousin Margaret Warnock, b. about 1838, daughter of Matthew and Lydia Warnock (8).

Children:

Fifth Generation

63. Winfield Warnock.
64. Willard Warnock.
65. Catherine Warnock; m. —— Holbrook.
66. Grace Warnock; m. Dr. John Sowards.
67. Mary Warnock.
68. Lulu Warnock; m. Walter Greenslate.

32. EDWARD G. WARNOCK, farmer, b. about 1837; lived on Tygarts Creek; served with his cousin, "John Dock" Warnock, as road commissioner and made possible good roads throughout the county, including Raccoon Hill which was given special attention and over which a good road was constructed; m. Mary Mearns.

Children:

Fifth Generation

69. Cora Brady.
70. Maud Heisel.
71. Ernest Warnock.
72. Frank Warnock.
73. Grace Huffman.

33. MATTHEW WARNOCK; b. 1839; served as sheriff of Greenup County, 1893-94; m. Elizabeth Breeding.

Children:

Fifth Generation

74. Grace Warnock; d. in childhood.
75. John Denny Warnock; served as Mayor and as Police Judge of Greenup; was affiliated with the Masonic fraternity and was secretary of Greenup Lodge No. 89 F. & A. M. for thirty-six years; m. Lyde Fullerton, a teacher, daughter of Harvey and Mary Terrell Fullerton.
76. Fannie Warnock; m. Elwood Kinner of Greenup.

Children:

Sixth Generation

77. Matthew Kinner; m. Mabel Curry Womack, daughter of Ward and Gertrude Curry Womack of Old Town and Florida.

34. WILLIAM W. WARNOCK; b. about 1841; m. May (Molly) Deering.

Children:

Fifth Generation

78. Dr. Horace H. Warnock.
79. Edward T. Warnock.
80. Nannie Warnock who m. Dr. Ernest Sellards.
81. Wirt Warnock.
82. Bessie Warnock.
83. John W. H. (Herbert) Warnock.

35. BENJAMIN FRANKLIN WARNOCK, b. 1844; served as sheriff of Greenup County, 1875-78, and was a State representative from the county, 1880-82. M., first, Faith Fraley and secondly, Mary (Mollie) Ellis Ramey.

Children of B. F. Warnock and Faith Fraley:

Fifth Generation

84. Finley Warnock.
85. Elwood Warnock.
86. Harry Warnock.
87. Alfred Warnock.
88. Paul Warnock.

89. Grant Warnock.
90. Ella Warnock; migrated to Texas.
   Children of B. F. Warnock and Mary Ellis Ramey:
Fifth Generation
91. Jessie Warnock; unm.
92. William Warnock; m. Elizabeth Fraley.
93. Sallie Warnock; m. Carl Finney.
94. Lorena Warnock; m. Cyrus Van Bibber.
95. Faith (Fay) Warnock; resided in Portsmouth, Ohio.

38. JOHN WESLEY ("JOHN DOCK") WARNOCK, farmer, b. about 1836; m. Martha Clark in Lyon County, Kentucky, in 1864. They lived in the Warnock neighborhood on Tygarts Creek until 1897 when they removed to Fullerton and built a dwelling in the eastern part of that village.
   Children:
Fifth Generation
*96. Clark Warnock.
97. Walter Warnock; unm.
*98. Lyman Warnock.
*99. Elizabeth Warnock.
100. Fred Warnock; unm.

96. CLARK WARNOCK; m. Margaret Meadows of Tygarts Valley.
   Children:
Sixth Generation
101. Ward Warnock.
102. Wade Warnock.
103. Eunice Warnock; m. Nichols; resided in Easter Greenup.
104. Blanche Warnock; resided in Fullerton.

98. LYMAN WARNOCK; m. Edith Roe.
   Children:
Sixth Generation
105. Raymond Warnock.
106. Ruth Esnor.
107. Helen Griswold.
108. Edith Smith.

99. ELIZABETH WARNOCK, a teacher in the schools of Greenup County many years; m. Charles Holbrook.
   Children:
Sixth Generation
109. Lloyd Holbrook.
110. Dana Holbrook.

39. SAMUEL PRICE WARNOCK; b. about 1838; m., first, America

Alexander and, secondly, Mary Nancy Morton, daughter of Henry Clay Morton.

Children:

Fifth Generation

*111. Nellie Warnock.
*112. Charles R. Warnock.
*113. Samuel B. Warnock.
 114. Sallie Warnock.
 115. Albert Warnock.

111. NELLIE WARNOCK; m., first, Edward Meadows and secondly, Arthur Winkler.

112. CHARLES R. WARNOCK; m. Lucy Montgomery.

Children:

Sixth Generation

116. Richard Warnock.
117. Eugenia Vincent.

113. SAMUEL B. WARNOCK; m. Hattie, daughter of Henry Sloan and Emma (Riffe) Curry of Hopewell.

Children:

Sixth Generation

118. Verna Clay Warnock of South Carolina.
119. Phineas Glen Warnock of South Carolina.

114. SALLIE WARNOCK; m. George Wear.

Children:

Sixth Generation

120. Virginia Rush.
121. Charles R. Wear.
122. Marynelle Literal.
123. Olive Lindeman.
124. Morton Wear; m. Nina Lou King.

40. RICHARD MATTHEW ("DICK MATT") WARNOCK; b. about 1840; m. Adeline (Addie) Morton, daughter of James Morton.

Children:

Fifth Generation

125. Alvin Morton Warnock; m. Ruby Helen Withrow, daughter of William Withrow.
126. Emma Warnock; m., first, Shannon Taylor, and secondly, Dan Withrow.
127. Lillian Warnock; m. John Ratcliff.
128. Lovina Warnock.
129. Nancy Warnock; m. Leslie McGinnis.
130. Elmer Warnock; m. Lillian Abdon.

131. Leslie Warnock.

132. Allen Warnock; m. Willie Womack.

Children:

Sixth Generation

133. Howard Warnock.

134. Louise Warnock.

41. JAMES WARREN WARNOCK, b. 1841; m. Julia Bartlett Morton, daughter of Henry Clay Morton.

Children:

Fifth Generation

*135. Allen Bartlett Warnock.

*136. Bess Warnock.

137. Don Warnock; d. young.

138. William Warnock; m. Margaret Harper of Siloam.

135. ALBERT BARTLETT WARNOCK; m. Zona Wolfe of Mason County.

Children:

Sixth Generation

139. Audrev Warnock; m. Harmon Hammond.

140. Paul Warnock; m. Bertha Dotson.

141. Don Warnock; m. Nellie Majors.

136. BESS WARNOCK; m. Price Taylor. They have three sons and two daughters, names not learned.

42. FRANCIS MARION ("SLICK") WARNOCK; b. about 1844; lived at Tygart Valley for a time and later in Greenup. Served as post-master for twenty years; and for several years was deputy County Court Clerk of Greenup County; m. Sarah Jane Breeding.

Children:

Fifth Generation

142. Ury Warnock; decs'd.

143. Elizabeth Warnock; m. Edward Womack (See Womack Family.)

43. WILLIAM LINDSAY WARNOCK; b. about 1845; m. Susan Taylor.

Children:

Fifth Generation

144. David Warnock.

145. Nora Warnock.

146. Amanda Warnock.

147. Agnes Warnock.

148. Addie Warnock.

149. Henry Warnock.

44. TAYLOR ("WHIG") WARNOCK; b. about 1849; m. Catherine ("Kit") Morton, daughter of Richard and Martha (Garrett) Morton.

Children:

Fifth Generation

150. Myrtle Belle Warnock; m. John Plymale.
151. Lulu Warnock; m. Dahl Green of Adams County, Ohio.
152. Edith Warnock; m. Bert Trickler.
153. Elby Warnock; m. Laura Fultz.
154. Dr. Clarence Woodson Warnock; m. Thelma Burns; resided in Huntington, West Virginia.
155. Etta Morton Warnock; m. Albert Hilliard.

22. WILLIAM L. WARNOCK, farmer; b. about 1824 m. in 1846, Ann Littleton Craycraft, b. about 1830; lived on a farm at Bennetts Mills.

Children:

Fourth Generation

156. Lydia or Louisa Warnock; b. about 1847; m. William Lee.
157. Ada J. Warnock; b. about 1850; m. Dock Stepter.
*158. John William Warnock.
*159. Samuel Lakin Warnock.

158. JOHN WILLIAM WARNOCK; b. about 1856; m. Sarah or Sadie Nickell.

Children:

Fifth Generation

160. Charlie Byron Warnock; m. May McClave, daughter of Claude and Ella (Hill) McClave; resided in Portsmouth, Ohio.
161. Amy Warnock; m. Chester Imes; resided in Sciotoville, Ohio.
162. Louise Warnock; d. in childhood.

159. SAMUEL LAKIN WARNOCK; b. about 1859; m. Martha Morton, daughter of Henry Clay Morton.

Children:

Fifth Generation

163. Lowery Morton Warnock; m. Hattie Wear.
164. Nathaniel Guinn Warnock; m. Etta Pitts.
165. Fannie Warnock; m. Lafe Jordan.

54. MATTHEW SCOTT WARNOCK, JR.; b. about 1848; m. Emma Gibbs.

Children:

Fifth Generation

166. Clara Kinner of Louisa, Kentucky.
167. Edith Kinner of Greenup.
168. Earl Warnock.
169. Doris Warnock.

59. ROBERT JOHNSON WARNOCK; m. America Batman.
    Children:
                    Fifth Generation
*170. John Wesley Warnock.
*171. Ella Virgie Warnock.
172. Alma Warnock; m. first, Dave Holbrook and, secondly, Thomas Swearengen.
*173. Margaret Warnock.

170. JOHN WESLEY WARNOCK; m., first, —————— ——————.
    Children:
                    Sixth Generation
174. Dennis Warnock.
175. Ralph Warnock.
176. Hubert Warnock.
177. Elma Warnock.

170A. John Wesley Warnock; m., secondly, Lora Swearengen.
    Children:
                    Sixth Generation
178. Millie Warnock; m. Newton McGinnis.

171. ELLA VIRGIE WARNOCK; m. John Miller in 1854.
    Children:
                    Sixth Generation
179. Robert O. Miller.
180. Glen Earl Miller.
181. Madge A. Miller.
182. Russell O. Miller.

173. MARGARET WARNOCK; m. Owen Hopkins.
    Children:
                    Sixth Generation
183. Homer Hopkins.
184. Robert Hopkins.

WEDDINGTON FAMILY OF PIKE COUNTY

*1. Henry Weddington and *2. Jacob Weddington, brothers, were the ancestors of the Weddingtons of Eastern Kentucky. They migrated from Russell County, Virginia, and settled on Shelby Creek, Floyd County, now Pike County, Kentucky, in 1790. The family originally lived in North Carolina. They were not educated, but were men of good minds, practical common sense and very intelligent. They succeeded in all their undertakings.[1]

1. HENRY WEDDINGTON was a merchant. He d. in 1836 and was buried on Shelby Creek where the family had first settled. He m. in Floyd County, in 1800, Elizabeth Jarrell,[2] b. in North Carolina in 1780 and d. in 1860 at the home of her son, William Weddington, about seven miles below Pikeville, where she was buried.

Children, among others:
*3. James Weddington.
*4. William Weddington.

3. JAMES WEDDINGTON, farmer, b. in Kentucky in 1804; m. about 1828, Katie Meade, b. in 1806.

About 1866, when an old man, he left home for the West and was never heard of again. It is supposed he was murdered.

Children living at home and approximate dates of birth as shown by the U. S. Census of Pike County for 1850:
5. William M. Weddington; b. 1829.
6. James M. Weddington; b. 1831.
*7. Henry Weddington; b. 1834.
8. A. Jackson Weddington; b. 1839.
9. Kenas Weddington; b. 1841.
10. Thomas J. Weddington; b. 1843.
11. Susan Weddington; b. 1844.
12. Nancy Weddington; b. 1845.
13. David Weddington; b. 1847.

4. JUDGE WILLIAM WEDDINGTON, farmer, was b. in then Floyd County, Kentucky, 1807, and d. in Pike County in 1878. He served in the Union Army during the Civil War as 2nd lieutenant of Company "D" 39th Kentucky Volunteer Infantry.[3] He served as judge of the Pike County Court. He m. in Pike County, January 27, 1828, Polly (Mary) Meade, b. in Kentucky in 1809, daughter of Rhodes Meade.

Children, among others:
14. Martin Weddington; m. Miss Tipton; migrated to Arkansas.

15. Nannie Weddington; m. A. J. Scott of Pike County.

*16. Lucinda Weddington; m. Dr. S. M. Ferguson.

17. Amelia Weddington m. Washington Cloud of Pierce City, Missouri. He was editor of the Pierce City Democrat.

Children living at home and approximate dates of birth as shown by the U. S. Census of Pike County for 1850:

18. James M. Weddington; b. 1831.

19. Rhoades M. Weddington; b. 1832, migrated to Texas.

20. Elizabeth P. Weddington; b. 1835; m. in Pike County, February 6, 1865, John L. Hatcher. (See Hatcher Family.)

*21. Robert M. Weddington.

22. Harrison (Harry) Weddington; b. 1839; businessman of Pikeville.

23. Mary K. Weddington; b. 1840; m. James A. Porter of Johnson County. (See Porter Family.)

24. Angeline Weddington; b. 1842; m., July 30, 1860, Thomas Layne.

25. Colbert C. Weddington; b. 1844; migrated to Arkansas.

26. Alpha S. Weddington; b. 1847.

27. Debora A. Weddington; b. 1848.

28. Nancy Weddington; b. 1849.

29. Ailsey Weddington; b. 1851.

2. JACOB WEDDINGTON, farmer and stock dealer was b. in Virginia. He was thrice m. and reared a large family, members of whom m. into some of the prominent families of the Big Sandy Valley. A daughter m. John Hargis and they were the grandparents of Thomas F. Hargis, Judge of the Court of Appeals of Kentucky.'

Nothing has been learned about Jacob Weddington other than what is disclosed by the census and marriage records. One Jacob Weddington was living in Pike County in 1840 as head of household. He was between 60 and 70 years of age, and his wife was between 50 and 60 years of age. His son at home was between 15 and 20 years of age. He m. Jane ——— (surname not known).

Children, among others:

*30. Jane Weddington; m. Thomas Hargis.

31. Martha Weddington; m. Reuben Meade of Pike County, October 12, 1837.

32. Abigail Weddington; m. Jesse P. Meek in Pike County, September 28, 1839. (See Meek Family.)

33. Louisa Weddington; m. James Williams in Pike County, March 28, 1839.

34. Jacob Weddington, Jr., farmer, (believed to be the son of

2. Jacob Weddington), was b. in Virginia about 1805; m. Nancy ———, b. in 1805.

Children living at home and approximate dates of birth as shown by the U. S. Census of Pike County for 1850:
35. Jacob Weddington; b. 1829.
36. Mary J. Weddington; b. 1831.
37. John T. Weddington; b. 1836.
38. James H. Weddington; b. 1844.

7. HENRY WEDDINGTON; m. Susanna Ratliff, in Pike County, July 3, 1800. Children living at home and approximate dates of birth as shown by the U. S. Census of Pike County for 1870:
39. Theodore H. Weddington; b. 1861.
40. Henry Weddington; b. 1864.
41. Alphonzo Weddington; b. 1867.
42. California Weddington; b. 1870.

16. LUCINDA WEDDINGTON; m. in Pike County, May 5, 1847, Dr. S. M. Ferguson, who came from Virginia to the Big Sandy Valley in 1843. Dr. Ferguson was one of the outstanding physicians in the Big Sandy Valley. He was a man of great energy and became wealthy. A staunch Republican in politics, he served in the Union Army during the Civil War as lieutenant-colonel, 39th Regt. Kentucky Volunteer Infantry.

21. HON. ROBERT M. WEDDINGTON, lawyer, was b. in Pike County, 1837. In 1883 he and J. K. Leslie, a lawyer, founded and published at Prestonsburg, the *Banner,* a Democratic newspaper. He m. in Floyd County, about 1856, Elizabeth Harkins, b. about 1839, daughter to Hugh Harkins. (See Harkins Family.)

30. JANE WEDDINGTON; b. 1812; m. in Pike County, June 28, 1818, Thomas Hargis, farmer, b. in Virginia in 1809.

Children living at home and approximate dates of birth as shown by the U. S. Census of Pike County for 1850:
43. Elizabeth Hargis; b. 1834.
44. John P. Hargis; b. 1836.
45. Jacob Hargis; b. 1838.
46. Samuel Hargis; b. 1840.
47. James K. Hargis; b. 1841.
48. Louisa Hargis; b. 1843.
49. Nancy Hargis; b. 1845.
50. Jesse Hargis; b. 1849.

Thomas Hargis and his wife, Jane (Weddington) Hargis were

the grandparents of Hon. Thomas F. Hargis, Chief Justice of the Court of Appeals of Kentucky.[5]

The influential families of Weddingtons of Morgan and Elliott Counties are descendants of the Big Sandy Weddingtons.

---

[1] William Ely, The Big Sandy Valley, page 151.

[2] After the death of Henry Weddington, his widow, Elizabeth, m. a Ford and they had three sons: Jackson Ford; William Ford, captain Company "B", 39th Kentucky Volunteer Infantry, who entered the service at Peach orchard, Kentucky, February 16, 1863, and d. November 24, 1864; and Harrison Ford, captain Company "K", 39th Kentucky Volunteer Infantry, who entered service at Peach Orchard, February 16, 1863, and resigned August 21, 1863, by reason of ill health. He d. in 1880, leaving a widow and several children: sons Moses, S. King, and John. A daughter m. J. Crittenden Cecil. The widow m. Mr. Phergo, a journalist. (Ely, The Big Sandy Valley, pages 151-3.)

[3] Report of the Adjutant General of Kentucky, 1861-1866, Vol. II, page 366.

[4] William Ely, The Big Sandy Valley, pages 151-53.

[5] Judge Thomas F. Hargis, lawyer, and jurist, was b. in Breathitt County, Kentucky, June 24, 1842; removed to Rowan County, Kentucky, in 1856; enlisted in the Confederate Army in 1861 as private in the Fifth Kentucky Infantry, C. S. A., under Colonel, afterwards General, John S. Williams; promoted to captain, January 7, 1863, Company "E" 10th Kentucky Cavalry; was captured in Luray Valley, Virginia, in November 1864, and held a prisoner of war until the close of the War.

'Judge Hargis' education was meager. Returning home to Rowan County at the close of the war, he devoted himself to the study of English and the law. He was admitted to the bar in April 1866; removed to Carlisle, Kentucky, 1868, and entering politics was elected to several offices soon thereafter. He was elected and served as judge of the Nicholas County Court in 1869 and 1870 and was State Senator, 1871. He was defeated for Circuit Judge in 1874; elected judge of the Criminal Court in 1878 by a majority of 2214; elected judge of the Court of Appeals in 1879 by a majority of 3355 for the term ending 1884; voluntarily declining to be a candidate for re-election he removed to Louisville and resumed the practice of law

Judge Hargis acted as Chief Justice in Judge Cofer's stead and acted as Chief Justice for two years by his own succession.

WELLS FAMILY OF JOHNSON COUNTY

Wells

This surname was evidently affixed to one who resided near a well or spring. "John at the Wells"—John Wells. A bishop's see in Somersetshire, England, was so called from the springs there. One of the most powerful houses in Normandy and Provence, France, as far back as the eighth century was known by the name of Vaux, the French equivalent for Wells. With this surname some of the knights accompanied William the Conqueror to England (1066). In the thirteenth century the English family name was known as De Vallibus, and Welles or Wells, became a corrupted form of this name.

The Hundred Rolls and other Records of England bear the names of —
Gilbert de Welles, County Norfolk, 1273.
William de Welles, County Lincoln, 1273.
Hervy del Wells, vicar of Mendham, County Norfolk, 1320.
Johannes del Well, 1379.
Anthony Welles, County Sussex 1583.
John Welles m. Joane Vicarries in London, 1617.

William Wells of Norwich, England, came to America about 1639 and settled at Southhold, Long Island, in 1640, and immediately became active in the colony, serving as Sheriff at New Yorkshire, now Suffolk, New York. He was b. in Norwich and d. in Southhold in 1671.

David Wells, a son of William served in the American Revolution.

The Welles family of New England was prominent from the beginning of the settlement. Thomas Welles, b. 1598, was Governor of the Connecticut Colony from 1655 to 1658, and held other high offices. John Welles, b. 1621 d. 1659, was an active colonist, of Connecticut, serving as Representative, magistrate and justice. Robert Wells, b. 1648, d. 1714, was captain of Connecticut military forces from 1687 to 1701.

Wells families were numerous in the Southern colonies in early colonial days. In Virginia there were many of them particularly in the counties of Middlesex, York, Warwick and Chesterfield.

1. According to reputable genealogists and historians GENERAL JAMES WELLS was the progenitor of the Wells family of Eastern Ken-

tucky. He lived at Baltimore, Maryland, and m. ——— ——— presumably in that province, but nothing has been learned of his wife.

Children:

*2. Richard Wells, Sr.

3. ——— Wells, m. ——— Carr and settled in Missouri.

4. George Wells served in the Revolutionary War as surgeon in General Pulaski's Legion, and was killed at the siege of Savannah in October 1779. He had resided at Augusta, Georgia.

5. Hannah Wells, b. December 10, 1724, m., first, William Holmes and, second, Richard Brown.

6. Alexander Wells, b. March 15, 1727.

2. RICHARD WELLS, SR., b. in Baltimore, Maryland in 1715, d. in 1808; m. first, Nancy Brown, daughter of George Stevenson and his wife Nancy Stevenson, and, second, Mary Stevenson.

Children of Richard Wells, Sr., and his wife, Nancy (Brown) Wells:

7. Alexander Wells, had service in the Indian Wars under General St. Clair. He was killed by the kick of a horse at Ft. Washington, now Cincinnati, Ohio.

*8. Zachariah Wells.

*9. Moses Wells.

10. Aaron Wells, lived on Wells Creek, Mason county, Kentucky.

*11. Nathaniel Wells.

12. Edmond Wells, lived near West Liberty, Morgan county, Kentucky.

13. George Wells, b. 1745, d. 1831.

14. Mary Wells, b. 1748; m. Dr. Doddridge(?).

15. James Wells, b. 1751.

16. William Wells, lived near West Liberty, Morgan county.

17. Robert Wells, migrated to Kentucky, place not known.

*18. Thomas Wells.

19. Patience Wells, b. 1759.

*20. Richard Wells.

Children of Richard Wells, Sr., and his wife, Mary Stevenson.

21. Charles Wells.

22. Bazil Wells.

23. Hugh Wells.

8. ZACHARIAH WELLS, lived at Big Stone Gap, Virginia; m. ——— Osborne. (?)

Children:

*24. Jeremiah Wells.

9. MOSES WELLS, a hunter; had service in the War of 1812; lived on Wells Ridge and on Twelve Pole Creek, now Wayne county, West Virginia; m. Sarah Ratliff.

Children:
25. William Wells, went West.
26. Joe Wells, left Wayne county after the Civil War.
27. Caroline Wells, m. and went West.
28. Buck Wells, lived on Twelve Pole Creek, Wayne County.
29. Elizabeth Wells, m. and went West.
30. Mary (Polly) Wells, m. and went West.
*31. Mahala Wells.

11. NATHANIEL WELLS, b. 1765, d. at Eminence, Henry county, Kentucky, 1862; lived, in early life, in Bullitt county, Kentucky; removed to Carrollton, Kentucky, where his descendants lived; m., name of wife not known.

Children:
32. Richard Wells.
33. Elizabeth Wells.
34. Grayson Wells.
35. Nellie Wells.
36. Nathaniel Wells, Jr.
37. Celia Wells.
38. Nancy Wells.
39. Rebecca Wells.

18. THOMAS WELLS, b. 1758, d. May 6, 1839; removed to Mason county, Kentucky, in 1794 and remained there until 1804 when moved to Strodes Run in Shelby county where he lived until 1836 and where he was buried. It has been said that Captain Thomas Wells was a noted hunter, trapper, and Indian fighter. He m., first, in 1780, Sarah Scott, and, second, Nancy Davis, b. 1768, d. December 29, 1835.

Children of Thomas Wells and his wife, Sarah (Scott) Wells:
*40. James G. Wells.
41. Alex. Wells, m. Polly Chance and removed to the American Bottom. opposite St. Louis, Missouri. He served with credit in the Black Hawk War, and d. at Jacksonville, Illinois.
42. Ann Wells, m. —— McCarty and d. in Clay County, Missouri.
43. Rachel Wells, m. John Shepherd.
*44. Thomas Wells.
45. John Scott Wells, m. Cynthia Wilson.

Children of Thomas Wells and his wife Nancy (Davis) Wells:
46. Sarah Wells.
47. Mary Wells.
48. Samuel Wells.
49. Patience Wells.
50. Richard Wells.

20. RICHARD WELLS was b. in Philadelphia, Pennsylvania Feb-

ruary 11, 1760, and d. in Floyd county Kentucky May 18, 1838. He had service in the Revolutionary War, having enlisted in the latter part of 1778 as an orderly sergeant in a North Carolina regiment under Captain Paine and Colonel Jackson. He was in the Battle of Stono (June 20, 1779), and was honorably discharged in July following his enlistment, having served six months. He enlisted again in September 1779, under Captain Lowry and Colonel Harris, and had three month's service. In May 1780, in Washington county, Virginia, he enlisted as an Indian spy under Captain Snoddy and Colonel Smith, and ranged the frontiers of Virginia until discharged in May, 1781. After the close of the war, he settled on an estate in what is now Scott county, Virginia and from there he removed to Floyd County, Kentucky, in 1820, where he lived until his death.

On September 28, 1797, in Scott county, Virginia, Richard Wells m. Susannah Hutchison, who d. in 1862.

Children:
*51. George Wells.
*52. Andrew Wells.
*53. Moses Wells.
*54. Elizabeth Wells.
*55. Rosa Wells.
*56. Peter Wells.
57. John Wells, m. Nancy Ann Webb; removed to Ohio in 1863.
58. Agnes Wells, m. Samuel Auxier (See Auxier Family).
59. Martha Wells, m. William Webb, Jr.
*60. Dr. William Green Wells.
*61. Mary Wells.

24. JEREMIAH WELLS, m. Elizabeth Culbertson.

Children:
*62. James Wells.

31. MAHALA WELLS, b. in what is now Wayne county, West Virginia in December, 1818, and d. at Fort Gay, Wayne county, January 13, 1927, at the extreme age of 108 years. She m. September 5, 1869 James Huff, Captain, Camp's Company, Virginia Militia, War of 1812, who d. February 10, 1879. She was allowed a pension from February 11, 1879, as widow of the late Captain Huff; and for many years was the oldest widow whose name was borne on the Government's pension rolls.

40. JAMES G. WELLS, m. Margaret Watts.

Children:
64. Sally Wells.

44. THOMAS WELLS, b. February 13, 1789, d. April 20, 1847; m. Nancy McIlvain; removed from Mason county, Kentucky, to Shelby county, that state, and settled on Clear Creek in 1825.

Children:

65. James Wells, b. April 6, 1812, d. July 28, 1843; m. Margaret Watts. (?)

66. Hannah Wells, b. January 12, 1814.

67. Selinda Wells, b. May 18, 1815.

68. Sarah Wells, b. February 23, 1817.

69. William Wells, b. March 31, 1821.

70. Harriet Wells, b. February 14, 1822.

71. Alex. Wells, b. November 3, 1824.

72. Thomas Wells, b. December 10, 1826.

73. George W. Wells, b. January 16, 1828; m., in 1860, Virginia Harris, daughter of Jordan Harris and his wife, Kitty Harris.

74. Alfred P. Wells, b. January 26, 1831.

75. John S. Wells, b. November 10, 1834.

51. GEORGE WELLS, b., March 22, 1800, in Scott county, Virginia, and d. in Johnson county, Kentucky, December 14, 1887. He came to Kentucky about 1828; m., first, Elizabeth Delong and second, Nancy Butcher.

Children of George Wells and his wife, Elizabeth Delong.

76. George W. Wells.

77. James Wells.

78. Hiram Wells.

79. David Wells.

80. Allen Wells.

81. Martha Wells, m. Alexander Webb.

Children of George Wells and his wife, Nancy Butcher:

82. Green Wells.

83. ——— Wells, m. Steve Ward.

84. Bert Wells.

85. ——— Wells, m. John Porter.

86. Noah Wells.

87. Scott Wells.

88. ——— Wells, m. Jacob Burchwell.

89. Theodore Wells.

90. John Wells.

91. Louis Wells.

52. ANDREW WELLS, m. ——— Hite (Polly Mobley?).

Children:

92. Morgan Wells.

93. William Wells.

53. MOSES WELLS, m. Margaret (Peggy) Hillman. Apparently he lived on Daniel's Creek as he was superintendent of the construction of a road on that creek.

Children:
94. Louisa Wells, m. Thomason Coates.
95. John Wells.
96. ——— Wells.
97. William Wells.
98. Mintie Wells, m. G. L. Porter of Floyd county, Kentucky.
99. Henry Wells.
100. ——— Wells, m. Garrett Arrowwood.
101. Morgan Wells.
102. Nancy Wells, m. William Arrowwood. Their descendants lived in Minnesota.

54. ELIZABETH (BETSY) WELLS, m. John Hillman, son of William Hillman. Their descendants lived in Virginia. The records indicate that William Hillman came to Scott county, Virginia, from Pennsylvania, and that his wife, Nancy Burton, was b. in Holland and when very young came with her parents to Pennsylvania.

Children:
103. Thomas Hillman.
104. Wesley Hillman.
*105. James Monroe Hillman.
106. William Hillman.
107. Isaac Hillman.
108. Henderson Hillman, lived at Dungannon, Virginia.

55. ROSA WELLS, m. Spencer Spears and their descendants reside in the Big Sandy Valley, mainly in Lawrence County.

Children:
*109. Morgan Spears.
*110. Wiley Spears.
*111. Susan Spears.
*112. Ruthie Jane Spears.
*113. Wallace Spears.
*114. John W. Spears.
*115. Agnes Spears.
116. Thomas J. Spears, m. Sarah Ellis.
*117. George W. Spears.
*118. Moses Spears.

56. PETER WELLS, m. Mary Hager; and their descendants settled in Boyd county.

Children:
119. Andrew Jackson Wells, m. Rebecca Howell.
120. Eizabeth Wells, m. Pleas. Craft.
121. Amanda Wells, m. Samuel Rons.
122. Martha Wells, m. David Morgan.
123. George Wells, m. Louisa Brown.
124. Perry Wells, m. Rebecca Litteral.

125. Samuel Wells, m. Jane Craft.
126. Richard McDonald Wells, unm.
127. Mary Wells, m. Hamilton Colegrove.
128. (Infant).

60. DR. WILLIAM GREEN WELLS, physician and surgeon. He and his family were members of the Methodist Church and religion and service in the name of Christ was the passion of his life. The home of Dr. Wells and the generous hospitality of his wife were the boon and comfort of the traveling Methodist ministry of those early days. In 1838, Dr. Wells m. Mary Butcher, b. in Scott county, Virginia, daughter of Jacob Butcher and granddaughter of Elijah Beverly of Tazewell county, Virginia. Twelve of their thirteen children grew to maturity and were citizens of fine character, fully sustaining the distinguished lineage of the family.

Children:
*129. Richard M. Wells.
130. Moses Wells, m. Mrs. Mintie Clark.
*131. Aaron Wells.
*132. William A. Wells.
*133. Susannah Wells.
*134. M. L. K. Wells.
*135. Sarah Wells.
*136. Nancy J. Wells.
*137. John P. Wells.
138. Chares J. Wells.
139. Mary Wells.
140. Julia Wells.

61. MARY WELLS, m. William Butcher.
Children:
*141. John W. Butcher.
142. Lewis Butcher.
143. Susan Butcher, m. Aaron Meek.
144. George D. Butcher.
145. Simon Butcher.
146. M. L. Butcher.
147. Mary Butcher.
148. Henry Butcher.
149. R. E. Butcher.

62. JAMES WELLS, m. Jeanetta Elliott.
Children:
150. Ellington Wells.
151. Brickey Wells.
152. David Wells.
*153. Judge Tazewell Gallington Wells.
154. Nancy Wells.

155. Della Wells.
156. Winfield Wells.

63. HENDERSON WELLS m. Laura Workman.
Children:
157. Minnie Wells, m. William Thompson.
158. Ruth Wells, m. John Bobbitt.
159. Carrie Wells, m. Rudolph ———.
160. Willis Wells, m. Millie ———.
161. Irene Wells, m. Thomas Thompson.
162. Tymage Wells.

105. JAMES MONROE HILLMAN, m. Elizabeth Stollard (Stallard).
Children:
163. Martha Hillman, m. ——— Carico; lived at Herald, Virginia.
164. Elizabeth Hillman, m. ——— Carico; lived at Coeburn, Virginia.
165. Thomas Benton Hillman, lived at Lakeland, Florida.
166. James Monroe Hillman, lived at St. Paul, Virginia.
167. Luther M. Hillman, lived at Herald, Virginia.
*168. Benjamin F. Hillman.

109. MORGAN SPEARS, m. Sarah Robinson.
Children:
169. Alex. Morgan Spears.
170. Jennie Spears.

110. WILEY SPEARS, m. Elizabeth Ann Crider.
Children:
171. Alafaire Spears.
172. Francis Marion Spears.
173. Jane Spears.
174. Elijah Spears.

111. SUSAN SPEARS, m. John Robinson.
Children:
175. Garfield Robinson.
176. Cordelia Robinson.

112. RUTHIE JANE SPEARS, m., first, James McGuire, and, Second, John M. Fraley.
Children of Ruthie Jane Spears and James McGuire:
177. Sarah McGuire.
178. Rosa McGuire.
179. Sarah McGuire (?).

Children of Ruthie Jane Spears and John M. Fraley:
*180. James C. Fraley.
181. Wallace C. Fraley, m. Jeanette Castle; no issue.

*182. Joe L. Fraley.

*183. Laura B. Fraley.

John M. Fraley came to Johnson county from Russell county, Virginia, when a young man. Previous to his marriage to Ruthie Jane Spears he m. Lucy Lauhorn and reared a large family.

113. WALLACE SPEARS, m. Mary Robinson.
Children:

184. Greene Spears.
185. Mary Frances Spears.
186. George Spears.
187. Rosa Spears.
188. Thomas Spears.
189. Florence Spears.

114. JOHN W. SPEARS, m. Irene Hannah.
Children:

190. Angeline Spears.
191. Etta Spears.
192. Martin Spears.
193. Maude Spears.
194. Grover Spears.
195. Walker Spears.
196. Walter Spears.

115. AGNES SPEARS, m. Rev. M. T. Burris, who had a retentive memory and took much interest in his family history; resided at Buchanan, Lawrence county, where descendants reside.
Children:

197. Sarah Agnes Burris, m. J. O. Black.
198. Rosabelle Burris, m. J. M. Hatten. She d, May 10, 1928.
199. John Tevis Burris, m. Maggie Kendrick.
200. George Thomas Burris, m. Laura Kendrick.
201. William Stanton Burris, m. Ella Chapman.
202. May Louise Burris, m. Frank Black.
203. Robert Fox Burris, m. Nellie Gates.
204. Marcus L. Burris, m. Estelle Boyle.
205. Maud Miller Burris, m. Dr. William Stidham.
206. Ada Olive Burris, m. Durward Hurt.

117. GEORGE W. SPEARS, m. Matilda Clark; resided at Odds, Johnson county.
Children:

207. Alvertie Spears.
208. Alex. Morgan Spears.
209. John T. Spears.
210. Hansford W. Spears.
211. Laura Spears.

212. Ella Spears.
213. Kelly Spears.

118. MOSES SPEARS, m. Sarah Crider.

Children:
214. John M. Spears, m. Hettie Hamilton.
215. William Wesley Spears, m. Luch Hamilton.
216. Rosa Spears, m., first, Charles Adkins, second, George Maxil.
217. Mary J. Spears, m. Elliott Hamilton.
218. Thomas J. Spears, m. Mary Lewis.
219. Andrew Jackson Spears, m. Leota Adkins.

129. RICHARD M. WELLS, m. Susan Meek; lived on Greasy Creek, Johnson County.

Children:
220. Richard Wells, Jr.
*221. William G. Wells.
222. Jane Wells, m. George Akers.
223. Dollie Wells.

131. AARON WELLS, m., first, Lousina Ward, and, second, ——— Porter.

Children of Aaron Wells and Lousina (Ward) Wells:
224. Marcina Wells.
225. Mary Wells.
226. Catherine Wells.
227. Jennie Wells.
228. Susanna Wells.

Children of Aaron Wells and his wife, ——— (Porter) Wells:
229. George Wells.
230. Viola Wells.
231. Dowe Wells.
232. Emma Wells.
233. Canada Wells.
234. Green Wells.

132. WILLAIM A. WELLS, m. Mary Hicks, daughter of Isaac Hicks of Greasy Creek Johnson County.

Children:
*235. W. G. Wells.
236. Jenny Lee Wells, m. Charles Davis (See Davis Family).
*237. Isaac S. Wells.
238. C. J. Wells, m. Victoria Pack.
*239. Malissa Wells.
*240. Sarah Wells.
*241. Moses A. Wells.
*242. Dr. J. A. Wells.
*243. Elizabeth Wells.

*244. Richard Grover Wells.
*245. John L. Wells.
*246. Elbridge D. Wells.
*247. German C. Wells.

133. SUSANNAH WELLS, m. Samuel Clark.
   Children:
248. J. Blaine Clark, onetime State Senator from the Johnson-Martin district and commonwealth's attorney for the same district (circuit), m. Lutie Exer Delong.
249. Logan Clark.
250. —— Clark, m. Samuel Richmond.
251. —— Clark, m. Alex Wells.
252. —— Clark, m. Kelly Spears.

134. MARCUS L. K. WELLS, sometime teacher, surveyor and merchant was b. on the old homestead farm of his father near the present post office hamlet of Odds, Johnson county, on December 5, 1848, and d. at Paintsville, Johnson county in 1927. He was head of one of the largest and most influential branches of the Wells family in Eastern Kentucky. He attended school near the home as a boy, and he was but fourteen years and eight months of age when, on September 18, 1863, he enlisted (enrolled) as a soldier in Company "C", Forty-Fifth Kentucky Volunteer Mounted Infantry, for one year, and was mustered out at Catlettsburg, Kentucky, December 24, 1864, a corporal to which he was appointed soon after enlistment, being probably the youngest corporal in all the Union forces during the Civil War. He participated in the engagements at Cynthiana (June 12, 1864), at Kings Salt Works (October, 1864) and at Mount Sterling (June 9, 1864), where he was slightly wounded by a minnie ball. His loyalty to the Union is more remarkable evidence of his patriotism in view of the fact that his father and most other members of the family, as well as family friends, were in sympathy with the Confederacy. In his youth Mr. Wells thought and reasoned for himself, and this he continued to do in all the relations of life during an active and productive career. Marrying at the age of eighteen, he thereafter advanced his education by studying at home by judicious reading particularly in the fields of science and literature, becoming a man of broad information and sound judgment. After his marriage he established his home on a farm near Boons Camp, Johnson county. He was soon elected justice of the peace (magistrate) and served one term; was an efficient notary public and deputy county court clerk; conducted a general mercantile business at Ward City, now Offutt, for four years, and at Boons Camp with his son, William G. Wells as partner, for eight years; was appointed and served as postmaster at Ward City and at Boons Camp for periods aggregating fourteen years; did considerable land surveying; and was associated with

the late John C. C. Mayo in the purchase of land and opening of coal mines in the vicinity of his residence.

Mr. Wells and his wife were earnest members of the Wells Chapel Methodist Episcopal Church, South, named in honor of the Wells family; and he was a member of the board of trustees of the church. He affiliated with the Masons in early manhood and was a member of the David Auxier Post, Grand Army of the Republic, while that organization was active. In politics he was a Democrat. In 1916 he removed to Paintsville where he lived until his death.

Mr. Wells m. Exer Meek, b. near Offutt, September 6, 1849, d. —————— ——————, daughter of Isaac Meek and his wife, Sallie (Ward) Meek.

Children:
*253. Sallie Wells.
254. William G. Wells, m. ——— Austin.
*255. Paulina Wells.
256. Shadrick Wells.
257. Dr. J. P. Wells.
258. Marcus Lynn Wells.
259. Edmund Wells.
260. Zephaniah Wells.
261. Goldie Wells.

135. SARAH WELLS, m., first, Solomon Porter, and second, Eli Hinkle.

Children of Sarah Wells and Solomon Porter:
262. ——— (?) Porter.

136. NANCY J. WELLS, m. J. H. Mollett.

Children:
263. Mary Mollett.

137. JOHN P. WELLS, lawyer, sometime teacher and public official b. in 1854. He became a successful teacher in the public schools of Johnson county; admitted to Kentucky bar in 1877; state representative from the Floyd-Johnson district, 1884-86; represented Johnson county at the Southern Exposition at New Orleans, 1884. In politics he was a Democrat. He was influential in community affairs, progressive and public-spirited as a citizen, gained much prestige as a real estate attorney and was very popular in the county. He m. Julia (Howes) Buckingham.

Children:
264. J. Kendrick Wells.
265. Virginia Wells.
266. Walter S. Wells.
267. Hubert Wells.
268. Geneva Wells.
269. Byron Wells.

141. JOHN W. BUTCHER, was b. at Odds, Johnson county, in 1860; m., first, in 1881, Julia Davis, b. 1864, d. 1902, daughter of Joseph Davis. He was a minister in the Baptist Church; served as justice of the peace (Magistrate) of Johnson county for eight years, and was judge of the Johnson County Court, 1926-1930.

Children:

270. Jeff. Butcher, b. 1882; m. ———, in 1903.
271. Alice Butcher, b. 1887; m., first, Jesse Daniel, and, second, James Perry.
272. Atley Butcher, b. 1893.
273. Grace Butcher, b. 1899; m. Earl Marcum.

141A. John W. Butcher, m., second, Rachel Phelps.

Children:

274. Herschel Butcher, b. 1904; m. Lorena Roberts.
275. Glenn Butcher, b. 1905.
276. Maxie Butcher, b. 1911.
277. William Butcher.

153. JUDGE TAZEWELL GALLINGTON WELLS, m. Mary Fugate.

Children:

278. ——— Wells, m. R. B. Bruce.
279. ——— Wells, m. O. B. Gilly.
280. Sarah Elizabeth Wells.
281. Patrick Wells.
282. ——— Wells, m. ——— Richardson.
283. ——— Wells, m. ——— Lipps.
284. Nancy Wells, m., first, James Dorton, and second, ——— Eddington.
285. ———Wells, m. J. O. Carpenter.
286. ——— Wells, m. C. W. Tunes.
287. Dr. Fugate Wells.

168. BENJAMIN HILLMAN, m. Nancy Susannah Grear.

Children:

288. Bessie Hillman, m. ——— Dingus of Coeburn, Virginia.
289. Charles Wesley Hillman of Coeburn, Virginia.
290. Etta Elizabeth Hillman of Bristol, Virginia.
291. James Noah Hillman, sometime president of Emory and Henry College, Emory, Virginia.
292. Leslie Wise Hillman of Coeburn, Virginia.

180. JAMES C. FRALEY, m. Julia Johnson.

Children:

293. Effie Fraley.

182. JOE L. FRALEY, progressive farmer of Johnson county, m. Mary Johnson.

Children:
294. James W. Fraley, m., first, Edith Childers, and, second, Alice Childers.
295. Wallace W. Fraley.

183. LAURA B. FRALEY, m. Garland Hurt.
Children:
296. Everett Hurt, m. Josephine May.
297. Joe Hurt.
298. Thursten Hurt.
299. Mabel L. Hurt, m. Alonzo Lacy.
300. Sallie Hurt, m., first, —— Howard, and, second, ———— Howard.

221. WILLIAM G. WELLS, lawyer; b. in 1870; admitted to the bar, May 10, 1895, and practiced his profession in Paintsville; made an unsuccessful race for circuit judge in his district in 1927; m. Emma Burgess, daughter of John Burgess.
Children:
301. —— Wells.
302. —— Wells.
303. —— Wells.
304. —— Wells.
305. —— Wells.
306. Alton Wells.

235. W. G. WELLS, m., first, Mollie Mars.
Children:
307. Bernard Wells.
308. Charlie Wells, businessman, in Paintsville; m. Musette Sowards.
309. Anna Lee Wells.
310. Elizabeth Wells, businesswoman in Paintsville.
311. Sarah Wells, teacher.
312. William C. Wells, businessman in Paintsville.
235A. W. G. Wells, m., second, Malva Penix.
Children:
313. Pearl Wells, teacher in the public schools of Paintsville; m. Edward Short.
314. Myrtle Wells.
315. Allie Wells.
316. George Wells.

237. ISAAC S. WELLS, m. Mary Dutton, daughter of William Dutton of Greasy Creek.
Children:
317. Chloe Lee Wells.
318. Mary Malissa Wells.
319. Sarah Ellen Wells.

239. MALISSA WELLS, milliner in Paintsville for a number of years, m. George C. Perry, who, for a number of years, was connected with mercantile estabishments in Johnson county.

Chidren:

320. Abert W. Perry, resided in Beckley, West Virginia.
321. Elva Perry, m. Levi C. Heltze, July 7, 1927, and resided at Cisco, Texas.
322. George C. Perry, Jr., m. Eulah Preston.
323. Charles Perry.

240. SARAH WELLS, b. April 4, 1878; m. May 5, 1898, Ulysses G. Welch, b. April 25, 1872, a prosperous farmer and one of Johnson County's best citizens.

Children:

324. Dewey Welch.
325. Ulysses S. Welch, b. July 29, 1900, d. November 2, 1918, was well educated and was prepared to enter the business field but died in the prime of life.
326. Elbridge D. Welch, accountant; a graduate of the Bowling Green (Kentucky) business school; b. February 6, 1902; m. Bernice Mae Chandler, February 22, 1927.
327. Fanny Welch, sometime teacher in the public schools at Thealka and at Van Lear, Johnson County; b. January 13, 1904; m. Ernest D. Neal, April 9, 1928.
328. William T. Welch, engineer, a graduate of the University of Kentucky; b. January 23, 1906.
329. Mary May Welch, b. May 19, 1916.

241. MOSES A. WELLS, b. March 17, 1874; m. first, Ellen Walters, d. January 13, 1903, daughter of John C. Walters; and, second, on June 6, 1915, Ella Oboyle, daughter of Bernard Oboyle of West Virginia.

Children of Moses A. Wells and Ellen (Walters) Wells.

330. Lawrence Wells, b. 1902, d. at the age of six months.

Children of Moses A. Wells and Ella (Oboyle) Wells:

331. Clarence B. Wells, b. April 18, 1916.
332. Ruby Alice Wells, b. September 18, 1917.

242. DR. J. A. WELLS, b. May 5, 1883, physician, practiced at Betsy Lane, Floyd county, for a number of years, and later moved to Paintsville where he was connected with the Golden Rule Hospital; m. Lillian James, b. March 29, 1888.

Children:

333. Alice May Wells, b. March 25, 1912.
334. James Dennis Wells, b. December 2, 1914.
335. Robert Wells, b. October 16, 1916.
243. ELIZABETH WELLS, m. George W. Walters.

Children:
336. Elmer Walters.
337. Ulysses Walters.
338. Shady Walters.
339. Gertrude Walters.
340. George W. Walters, Jr.
341. Bernard Walters.

244. RICHARD GROVER WELLS, m. Vina Arrowood; conducted the Home Furniture Store at Pikeville, Kentucky.
Children:
342. R. G. Wells, Jr.
343. Walter Ray Wells.

245. JOHN L. WELLS, traveling salesman; resided in Paintsville; m. Theo Long.
Children:
344. Chester Wells.
345. Mary Ruth Wells.
346. Shirley Heith Wells.
347. Roger Heith Wells.

246. ELBRIDGE D. WELLS, m. May Price.
Children:
348. Willa Mae Wells.

247. GERMAN C. WELLS, merchant in Paintsville; local politician in the Democratic party and county leader; b. December 5, 1890 at Boons Camp, Johnson county; m., August 1, 1916, Cora Blair, b. June 13, 1894, daughter of F. P. Blair.
Chidren:
349. Frank Allen Wells, b. June 13, 1917.
350. E. D. Wells, b. March 5, 1919.
351. Mary Catherine Wells, b. March 30, 1925.

253. SALLIE WELLS, b. September 1, 1868, d. March 19, 1927; m. in 1887, John P. Delong, of Inez, Martin county, onetime state representative from Martin County.
Children:
352. Lutie Exer Delong, m. J. B. Clark (See No. 248, Wells Family).
353. Hubert Delong.

255. PAULINA WELLS, m. M. L. Robinson, lawyer, in Paintsville, sometime teacher in the public schools of Johnson county.
Children:
354. Doras Robinson.
355. Gypsie Robinson.
356. Exer Robinson.

357. Homer Robinson.
358. Dewey Robinson.
359. Lillian Robinson.
360. Aubra Robinson.
361. John Bruce Robinson.

256. SHADRICK WELLS, farmer, resided at Boons Camp, Johnson county, for a number of years and subsequently removed to Paintsville; m. Amanda Ward, daughter of Shade Ward.

Chidren :
362. Exer Wells.
363. Margaret Wells.
364. Perlina Wells.
365. Robert Wells.
366. Sallie Laura Wells.
367. Nancy Jane Wells.
368. Shady Wells, Jr.

WHEELER FAMILY OF JOHNSON AND LAWRENCE COS.

The genealogy of the "Wheeler" family would be incomplete, for example, if it did not include also the records of the "Wheler" and "Whaler" families. The name first appears in history in the eighth century when one of the Saxon chieftains is recorded as bearing the name "Wielher". As the work shows progressive changes from that date onward, there is no great difficulty in tracing the character of that change. Thus, in the great Domesday Book of William the Conqueror, the name appears as "Weleret", the holder of the name being recorded as a landowner, "Hugh Le Welere" is mentioned on the One Hundred Rolls in 1273 and "Richard le Whelere" on the Close Rolls in 1348. The spelling "Wheeler" does not appear until later.

The early spelling "Wielher" is evidently a compound of two Anglo-Saxon words "wel" or "weil" meaning "prosperous" or "fortunate" from which derivation the modern word "weal" and "wealth" may be traced; and the Anglo-Saxon word "hari" or "heri" a warrior, a root traceable in the modern word "hero". The present spelling of the family name "Wheeler", therefore, is a spelling of words which in their modern form would be "Weal-Hers", or in the Anglo-Saxon words "well-hari". The meaning of the family name, therefore, is "the lucky warrior" or "the prosperous hero."

In colonial records alone there were twelve or more variations in spelling the old "wel-hari" name. However, the bearers of these names may be reasonably sure of tracing back their ancestry to a Teutonic origin, and may rightfully think of their forbears as having been men and women of a rugged war-like race, fortunate upon the battle-field and prosperous upon their home estates.

The Wheelers in America.

In America, prior to 1650, the Wheelers were numerous and were not exceeded in numbers by many other families. The principal reasons for their emigration from England were similar to the causes which led to almost all the emigration of that period. The Wheelers appear in Massachusetts, Maryland, Virginia, Connecticut and Pennsylvania as early as 1629. Everything would seem to indicate that they were well-to-do when they arrived at Concord, Massachusetts.

The Wheelers of Eastern Kentucky.

The Wheelers are scattered all over Eastern Kentucky. The pioneer of the family settled near the present-day Paintsville, John- son county, and members of his family settled on the Hood's Fork of Big Blaine, that county. The pioneers were nearly all Baptists and there were many preachers of that faith among them. Generally they were farmers but there has been and are now many businessmen, lawyers, doctors and ministers among them.

Jesse Wheeler was the progenitor of the Wheeler family of

Eastern Kentucky. Probaby he was b. in Southwestern Virginia and was m. there. However, nothing definite has been learned with respect to these matters.

1. JESSE WHEELER, m. ———— ————.

Children:

*2. Stephen Wheeler.

2. STEPHEN WHEELER, farmer, b. in Virginia, October 15, 1780 d. in Floyd county, Kentucky, April 6, 1835, m. in Floyd county, January 9, 1805, Catherine Remy (Ramey), b. May 26, 1786, d. November 27, 1852, daughter of William Remy. Stephen Wheeler lived on a farm opposite the mouth of Buffalo Creek on the Big Sandy River in Johnson County.

Children:

3. Dorcas Wheeler, b. November 22, 1805, d. January 4, 1902, unm.

4. Elizabeth (Betty) Wheeler, b. June 14, 1807, m., in Floyd county, James Daniel.

*5. Anna Wheeler.

*6. William Remy Wheeler.

7. Jesse Wheeler, b. June 2, 1811, m., in Floyd county, January 13, 1840, Susanna Nott.

8. Eleanor Wheeler, b. October 6, 1812, m., in Floyd county, April 19, 1832, Joseph Lemaster.

9. John Wheeler, b. February 11, 1814, d. August 25, 1854, m. in Floyd county, March 18, 1838, Mary Davis.

10. Jemima Wheeler, b. July 15, 1815, d. September 28, 1875, m. in Floyd county, June 28, 1840 John Davis.

11. Lydia Wheeler b. October 18, 1816, d. December 18, 1818.

*12. Daniel Wheeler.

13. Jane Wheeler, b. November 16, 1819, m. in Floyd county, January 31, 1839, James Ward.

14. Mary Wheeler, b. March 17, 1822, m., first, in Floyd county, July 30, 1837, Jesse Ward, and, second, Rhode Murray.

5. ANNA WHEELER, b. in Floyd county, January 18, 1809, d. in Johnson county, February 2, 1849; m. in Floyd county, May 3, 1835, James F. Preston, son of Eliphus Preston, Sr., and his wife, Anna (Pelphrey) Preston, and grandson of Nathan Preston, Revolutionary War soldier (See Nathan Preston family).

This family lived near the present-day town of Offutt, Johnson county.

Children:

15. Jesse Preston.

16. Eliphus Preston.

17. Shadrack Preston.

6. WILLIAM REMY WHEELER, farmer, surveyor and Baptist

preacher, was b. in Floyd county, February 15, 1810, d. in Johnson county, September 12, 1896; m. in Floyd county, in 1829 or 1830, Eizabeth Borders, d. 1875, of Georges Creek, daughter of Hezekiah Borders.

William Remy Wheeler lived on the Hood's Fork of Big Blaine Creek, Johnson county. He was the father of nineteen children.

Children:
*18. John Borders Wheeler.
19. Daniel Wheeler.
20. Stephen Wheeler.
21. Isaac Wheeler.
22. Dorcas Wheeler.
23. Jemina Wheeler.
24. Mary Wheeler.
25. Lousina Wheeler.
26. Emeline Wheeler.

12. DANIEL WHEELER, prominent citizen, a well-to-do farmer and coal operator, was b. in then Floyd county, February 25, 1818, d. in Johnson county, in February, 1888; m., in Floyd county, November 22, 1840, Elizabeth Hager, b. in September, 1821, d. in August, 1885, daughter of John Hager (See Hager Family).

DANIEL WHEELER lived on the old home-farm at the mouth of Buffalo Creek and is buried there.

Children:
*27. Samuel Wheeler.
*28. Amanda Wheeler.
29. Eleanor Wheeler, m. Lafe Preston (See Preston Family).
30. Mary Jane Wheeler, m. Dr. J. F. Hatton of Rockville.

18. JOHN BORDERS WHEELER, farmer and Baptist preacher, was b. in then Floyd county, in 1825; m. in Johnson county, in 1848 or 49, Nancy Wheeler; lived on the Hood's Fork of Big Blaine.

Children:
*31. Martin Van Buren Wheeler.
32. Franklin Wheeler, m. Levisa Salyer.
33. Amanda Wheeler, m. Shanklin Salyer.
34. Catherine Wheeler, m. David Harris.
35. Elizabeth Wheeler, m. Wiley Craft.
36. Eliza Wheeler.

27. SAMUEL WHEELER, a well-to-do farmer; sheriff of Johnson county, 1873-76; devout member of the Methodist Church; was b. in Johnson county, and d. at Paintsville, that county, in December 1900; lived on the old-home farm near Concord nearly all his life; m. Maria Van Horn, daughter of John Van Horn of Boyd county, Kentucky.

Children:

37. Charles Wheeler, b. September, 1877, d. August, 1885.
38. Fred Wheeler, d., unm.
39. Ellen Wheeler, d., unm.
40. Daniel Wheeler.

28. AMANDA WHEELER, b. at Paintsville, Johnson county, September 9, 1843, d. January 29, 1919; m., December 15, 1868, George W. Syck, b. January 4, 1839, d. October 10, 1915, son of Jacob Syck of Pikeville, Pike county, Kentucky.
This family lived at Paintsville.

Children:

41. William Syck, b. October 3, 1869, d. October 27, 1872.
42. Mary Eizabeth Syck, m. Dr. W. J. Walter. (See Walter Family.)
43. Samuel Crittenden Syck, b. August 25, 1873, d. May 15, 1879.
44. Daniel J. Syck, b. July 15, 1877.

31. MARTIN VAN BUREN WHEELER, b. August 28, 1850, m., in 1869, Sarah Justice, b. April, 1844, daughter of Samuel L. Justice. This family lived on the Hood's Fork of Blaine.

Children:

*45. Columbus B. Wheeler.
*46. Casbianca Wheeler.
47. Lora Alice Wheeler, b. February 7, 1874, d. at age of sixteen years; m. D. J. Wheeler.
*48. John Wesley Wheeler.
*49. Wiley Harrison Wheeler.
*50. William Franklin Wheeler.
*51. Jasper Clinton Wheeler.
*52. Julia Wheeler.
*53. Nancy Louise Wheeler.
*54. Martin Oscar Wheeler.
55. Samuel Laney Wheeler.

45. COLUMBUS B. WHEELER, lawyer and judge, b. in Johnson County, November 2, 1870; educated in the rural schools of Johnson County, the Blaine (Kentucky) High School and the law department of the University of Louisville from which he was graduated in 1891; admitted to the bar and practiced his profession at Paintsville for a number of years, next at Ashland for seventeen years and finally at Prestonsburg where he resided the latter part of his life. He held many public offices of honor and trust and filled all of them with credit to himself and to the satisfaction of his constituents. He served as police judge of Paintsville for five years, was State representative from Johnson and Martin Counties and was Circuit Judge of the Floyd-Knott district. He m., first, on March 4, 1890, Elizabeth Walter, b. July 8, 1874, d. April 12, 1902, a daughter of W. H. Walter. (See Walter Family.)

Children:

56. Esta Wheeler; b. April 16, 1891; d. March, 1894.
57. Zella Wheeler; b. July 8, 1894; d. January 1896.
*58. Elizabeth Essie Wheeler.
*59. William Henry Wheeler.
*60. Madeline Wheeler.

46. Casbianca Wheeler, physician; was graduated from the Louisville Medical School and practiced his profession in Johnson and Lawrence Counties; m., first, Allie Ramey.

Children:

61. Ora Wheeler.
62. Allie Wheeler.

Dr. and Mrs. Wheeler resided on Hood's Fork of Blaine at time of Mrs. Wheeler's death. Dr. Wheeler m., secondly, Amanda Swan of Lawrence County.

Children:

63. Alka Wheeler.
64. Lora Wheeler.

Dr. and Mrs. Wheeler resided at Louisa and at Hazard, Kentucky.

48. John Wesley Wheeler, lawyer, judge and public official; b. on Hood's Fork of Blaine Creek Lawrence County, December 4, 1875; educated in the public schools and was graduated from the Paintsville High School, after which he taught in the rural schools of Johnson County for eleven years; commenced reading law at the age of eighteen and admitted to the bar soon after he had passed the age of twenty-one; commenced the practice of law at Paintsville in partnership with his elder brother, Columbus B. Wheeler, which partnership was dissolved when his brother removed to Prestonsburg. Subsequently he was associated with his younger brother, M. O. Wheeler in the practice of law at Paintsville. He was owner and publisher of a newspaper, the Paintsville Post, from April, 1915, to March 13, 1918, retiring from the newspaper field on the latter date when his press, office and law library were destroyed by fire. He has held many public offices of honor and trust and his performance of duty in all of them was creditable. He served as Circuit Court Clerk of Johnson County, 1904-1909, inclusive; Judge of the Johnson County Court, 1910-1914; Commonwealth's Attorney for the circuit composed of Johnson and Martin Counties, 1922-1927, inclusive, and subsequently served as a Commissioner of the Court of Appeals of Kentucky, after which he resumed the practice of law at Paintsville.

On December 23, 1896, he was m. to Dora Walker, who d. September 4, 1926, a daughter of J. F. (Foss) Walker.

Children:

65. Bruce Halstead Wheeler; b. November 24, 1898; d. July, 1901.
66. Lora Blanche Wheeler; b. November 9, 1900; d. October, 1904.

67. Hermalee Wheeler; b. November 24, 1904; m. Eugene Adams, a civil engineer; resided in Richmond, Virginia, where Mr. Adams was connected with a railroad contractor. Judge Wheeler is a Republican and a Baptist. He is affiliated with the I. O. O. F., the local F. & A. M. Lodge and the Ashand Chapter and Commandery.

49. WILEY HARRISON WHEELER, physician, at Ashland; b. in Johnson County, October 11, 1877; m. Rosa Williams.

Children:

68. Edra Wheeler; m. Scott Earl Roberts.

Children:

69. Kent Earl Roberts.

50. WILLIAM FRANKLIN WHEELER, farmer; b. October 12, 1879, in Johnson County; m., first, Elizabeth Lemaster; resided on a farm on Hood's Fork of Blaine; served on the Johnson County Board of Education.

Children:

70. Arville Wheeler, who was graduated from Centre College with degree of A. B. and was an instructor in the Paintsville High School.

71. Vivian Wheeler.

50A. William Franklin Wheeler m., secondly, Lizzie Fairchild.

Children:

72. Roy Wheeler.

73. John Martin Wheeler.

51. JASPER CLINTON WHEELER, physician, at West Liberty, Kentucky; b. in Johnson County, October 2, 1881; m. Gypsie Spencer.

Children:

74. Lucille Wheeler.

75. Hallard Wheeler.

76. Godfrey Wheeler.

52. JULIA WHEELER, m. Aide Dempsey; reside at Wellston, Ohio.

Children:

77. Edgar Dempsey.

78. Elaine Dempsey.

79. Francis Dempsey.

53. NANCY LOUISE WHEELER; m. E. D. May; resided at Salyersville, Kentucky.

Children:

80. Robert Wheeler May

81. Wendall May.

54. MARTIN OSCAR WHEELER, lawyer; was b. on Hood's Fork of Blaine, April 13, 1890. His early boyhood was spent on the home farm during which time he attended the rural public schools. At the age of fourteen he made his home with his brother J. W. Wheeler at Paintsville who assisted him in securing an education and pre-

pared him for his chosen profession, the law. He attended the Sandy Valley Seminary, now the John C. C. Mayo College, from which he was graduated in 1912. For four years he taught in the public schools of Johnson County and in 1913, he entered the law department of the University of Kentucky where, on account of his previous study and great diligence, he was able to complete three years work in two years. On being admitted to the bar, he joined his brother, John W., in 1915, and has since engaged in the practice of law at Paintsville.

Mr. Wheeler is regarded highly by the citizens of his home town. He is a republican in politics and has served as Chairman of the Republican Committee for Johnson County.

On December 19, 1914 he was m. to Maye Stafford, a teacher in the Paintsville city schools.

Children:

82. Mary Jo Wheeler; b. August 21, 1920.
83. Helen Martyn Wheeler.

58. ELIZABETH ESSIE WHEELER; b. in Johnson County, March 23, 1896; m. Harvey R. Bixler, then connected with the local American Railway Express office at Frankfort, whom she met when she was an employee of the State Compensation Board at Frankfort.

Children:

84. William Harvey Bixler; b. June 22, 1923.
85. Elizabeth Marguerite Bixler; b. December 29, 1925.

59. WILLIAM HENRY WHEELER; b. January 13, 1898; m. Betty ———; had service in World War I; resides in Los Angeles, California.

Children:

86. William Henry Wheeler, Jr.

60. MADELINE (MADGE) WHEELER; b. September 8, 1899; m. Sterling Berger; reside at Catlettsburg.

Children:

87. Jack Sterling Berger.

PETER TAYLOR WHEELER, lawyer, son of James L. and Mahala (Sparks) Wheeler, was b. at Flat Gap, Johnson County, Kentucky, 25, 1873, and d. near Slade, Powell County, Kentucky, August 24, 1945, as result of automobile accident; interment in Lexington Cemetery, Lexington, Kentucky. He was educated in the public schools of Elliott County, Kentucky, and at Blaine (Kentucky) Normal School, where he received training for teaching, and was graduated from Central Normal College, Danville, Indiana, with degree of LL.B., July 31, 1899; and on the following day was admitted to practice law in the Supreme Court of Indiana. He engaged in teaching in the public schools of Elliott County for six years.

Immediately after graduation in law he went to Grayson, Kentucky, where he was associated with Thomas D. Theobold, lawyer, for a time. In March, 1901, he went to Hazard, Kentucky, for the practice of his profession and for a time was associated with F. J. Eversole and later was a member of the law firm of Miller, Wheeler, and Craft at Hazard but subsequent to 1917 he devoted himself exclusively to the interests of the Kentucky River Coal Corporation which he represented as attorney for many years.

Mr. Wheeler was a member of the various organizations of his profession. He was one of the organizers of the Perry County State Bank and various coal companies; also one of the organizers of the Hazard Leader, a Republican newspaper and its first president. He was a Republican in politics but never sought public office. Fraternally he was a member of Hazard Lodge No. 676, F. & A. M. He was a Baptist. He was active in all civic matters, particularly those pertaining to improvement and progress.

On June 30, 1904, Mr. Wheeler was united in marriage with Miss Leora Obra Aulick, daughter of H. M. Aulick of Campbell County, Kentucky. Mrs. Wheeler is a graduate of Georgetown (Kentucky) College, Class of 1902. In the year of her graduation she taught at Wasioto, Bell County, Kentucky, and in 1903 and 1904 in the Hazard Baptist Institute. She is a member of the Baptist Church in the work of which she takes a constructive and active part. Residence: 317 Kingsway Drive, Lexington, Kentucky.

Mr. and Mrs. Wheeler are parents of five children, all of whom are living, graduates of Hazard High School and members of the Baptist Church:

Glenna Lee Wheeler was b. at Hazard, Kentucky, September 28, 1905; m. at Hazard, July 18, 1923, C. J. Fitzgerald of Cynthiana, Kentucky, a farmer, now retired. They are parents of five children —four sons and one daughter, and presently, reside in Miami, Florida.

Verdie Bliss Wheeler; b. at Hazard, January 4, 1907; attended Georgetown College for four years, graduating in June, 1927; m., June 23, 1927, William E. Boswell of Cynthiana, Kentucky, a teacher in Harrison High School and subsequently judge of the Harrison County Court. Children: two daughters and one son.

Maurice Aulick Wheeler, dentist at Lexington, Kentucky; b. at Hazard, September 17, 1908; attended Fork Union Military Academy in Virginia, Georgetown (Kentucky) College and Louisville School of Dentistry, graduating from the latter in 1934; served three and one-half years as dentist in World War II at Camp Walters, Texas; m. October 6, 1936, Helen Brashear of Hazard. Children: two daughters and one son.

Le Obra Taylor Wheeler; b. at Hazard, June 26, 1914; attended Carson-Newman College in Tennessee for three years and subsequently Georgetown College one year, graduating from the latter in 1934; was employee of the Citizens State Bank of Hazard for several years and afterward manager of the Collection Department of the First National Bank of Louisville.

Nadine Wheeler; b. at Hazard, March 28, 1920; attended Carson-Newman College for one year and then Western (Kentucky) State College at Bowling Green for three years from which she was graduated in 1942; was a chemist for Dupont Powder Company, Charleston, Indiana, until close of World War II and since has been employed as calculator for the Burley Cooperative Association, Lexington, Kentucky, where she resides at home with her mother.

WHITE FAMILY OF CLAY COUNTY

The Whites were among the most enterprising, prominent and influential pioneer families of Southwestern Virginia and Southeastern Kentucky. They were of Scotch-Irish origin and the first known ancestors were 1. John White and his wife, Isabella, who emigrated from Ireland and with sons 2. Hugh and *3. William, settled at Harrisburg, Pennsylvania.

3. WILLIAM WHITE was b. February 4, 1743, and d. December 20, 1813. He m. Ann Lowery in Lancaster, Pennsylvania, January 8, 1769.[1]

Children:
*4. James White.
*5. Hugh L. White.

4. COL. JAMES WHITE, "trader", businessman and manufacturer, was b. at Carlisle, Pennsylvania, February 22, 1770. When quite a young man he became a clerk in the business establishment of Talbot, Jones and Company of Baltimore, Maryland, with whom he remained for two or three years. This firm advanced him a small stock of goods with which he made his first trip to Southwestern Virginia.

He m. Miss Eliza Wilson, January 4, 1798, and they settled at Abingdon, Washington County, Virginia. Here he became a citizen of prominence and influence and amassed considerable wealth. He was a colonel (quartermaster) in the army of Gen. Cox of Tennessee whose duty it was to protect the white settlers on the frontier. He operated iron furnaces in Washington County, Virginia, and Johnson County, Tennessee, and carried on an extensive trade in the West. While on a "shopping" trip at Lexington, Kentucky, he first heard of the production of salt in Clay County and hastened to and purchased some land on which "salt licks" had been located. Subsequently he became identified with the development of the salt industry there.

Col. White became the wealthiest man in Washington County, Virginia. At date of death, October 20, 1838, his estate was valued or estimated at three-quarters of a million dollars. He left a large and distinguished family of children,[2] of whom a son—

6. Addison White (cousin of John White) a Representative in Congress, was b. at Abingdon, Washington County, Virginia, May 1, 1824; received an academic education; was graduated from Princeton College in 1844; engaged in agricultural pursuits and cotton raising; elected as a Whig to the Thirty-second Congress (March 4, 1851 -March 3, 1853); during the Civil War served in the Confederate Army; moved to Huntsville, Alabama, and resumed agricutural pursuits; d. in Huntsville, Alabama, February 4, 1909; interment in Maple Hill Cemetery.[3]

5. GENERAL HUGH LOWERY WHITE, salt manufacturer and one-time public official, was b. in Pennsylvania in 1777 and d. in Clay County, Kentucky, in 1857. He m. Catherine Cain who was b. in North Carolina in 1780. He entered into an agreement with his brother, 4. Col. James White, for the development and operation of the salt industry in Clay County, Kentucky, pursuant to which, in the Spring of 1804, he brought his wife and four children from Tennessee to Clay County and took charge of the Outlaw Salt Works which he afterward purchased and turned over to his son, Alexander. He established another furnace near his home at the forks of Goose Creek, which was called Goose Creek Salt Works.' He continued in the salt industry until his death.

General White was one of the outstanding citizens of his section of the state. He grew wealthy in lands and personal property including thirty-five negro slaves.

In addition to his business activities, he was interested in civic and public affairs. He was commissioned by the Governor as an assistant judge of the Clay County Circuit Court and qualified as such on April 13, 1807, when the county was organized. He was brigadier-general of the Kentucky militia. He reared a large and prominent family of children.

Children:

*7. Alexander White.

8. Margaret White. One Margaret J. White m. Lyne S. Kenningham in Clay County, March 14, 1817.

*9. John White.

10. Susan White. One Susan C. White m. C. W. White in Clay County, November 8, 1820.

*11. Daugherty White.

*12. James White.

*13. Hugh L. White, Jr.

14. Ann White. One Ann White m. William Letcher in Clay County, December 21, 1824.

15. Amelia C. White.

16. Sarah White.

*17. William W. White.

*18. Ben F. White.

*19. Daniel G. White.

7. ALEXANDER WHITE, farmer, salt manufacturer and sometime legislator, was b. in Tennessee in 1793; represented Clay County in the State House of Representatives, 1825-6 and 1861-3; and in the State Senate, 1847-1850; m. apparently in Clay County, Amelia ———, b. in Maryland in 1801.

Children living at home and approximate dates of birth as shown by the U. S. Census of Clay County for 1850 and 1860:

20. James White; b. in 1836.

21. Catherine White; b. in 1837.

9. JOHN WHITE (cousin of Addison White and uncle of John Daugherty White) a Representative from Kentucky; b. near Cumberland Gap (now Middlesboro, Kentucky) February 14, 1802; received a limited schooling; studied law; was admitted to the bar and commenced practice in Richmond, Madison County, Kentucky; member of the State House of Representatives in 1832; elected as a Whig to the Twenty-fourth and to the four succeeding Congresses (March 4, 1835-March 3, 1845); served as Speaker of the House of Representatives in the Twenty-seventh Congress; appointed judge of the nineteenth judicial district of Kentucky and served from February 8, 1845, until his death in Richmond, Kentucky, September 22, 1845; interment in the State Cemetery, Frankfort, Kentucky.[5]

11. DAUGHERTY WHITE, farmer and salt manufacturer, was b. in Clay County, Kentucky, in 1812 and d. in that county in 1875; m. October 8, 1846, Sarah A. Watts, b. in Fayette County, Kentucky, in 1824, daughter of David Watts.

Children living at home and approximate dates of birth as shown by the U. S. Census of Clay County for 1850, 1860 and 1870:

22. Frances White; b. in Fayette County, Kentucky, in 1847.
*23. John D. White.
24. Catherine White; b. in 1851.
25. Louisa White; b. in 1853.
26. Sarah White; b. in 1855.
27. Lizzie White; b. in 1862.

12. JAMES WHITE, farmer and salt manufacturer, was b. in Clay County in 1806; m. Mary J. ———, b. in Clay County in 1820.

Children living at home and approximate dates of birth as shown by the U. S. Census of Clay County for 1850, 1860 and 1870:

28. Margaret White; b. in 1844.
29. Mary J. White; b. in 1846.
30. Helen G. White; b. in 1848.
31. Sally A. White; b. in 1851.
32. Lucy C. White; b. in 1852.
33. James C. White; b. in 1854.
34. Letitia White; b. in 1856.
35. Thomas White; b. in 1857.
36. Emily M. White; b. 1861.
37. Leslie White; b. 1859.
38. Jennie White; b. 1869.

13. HUGH L. WHITE, JR., merchant and salt manufacturer, was b. in Clay County in 1827; m. Mary ———, b. in Virginia in 1826.

Children living at home and approximate dates of birth as shown by the U. S. Census of Clay County for 1850:

39. Alexander White; b. in 1849.

The record would seem to indicate that Hugh L. White m., second, Lucy W. ———, b. in 1839.

Children living at home and approximate dates of birth as shown by the U. S. Census of Clay County for 1860 and 1870:

40. Susan White; b. in 1857.
41. Olevia White; b. in 1859.
42. Stephen White; b. in 1860.

17. WILLIAM W. WHITE, farmer, was b. in Clay County in 1816; m. Eliza ———, b. in Kentucky in 1822.

Children living at home and approximate dates of birth as shown by the U. S. Census of Clay County for 1850:

43. James White; b. in 1839.
*44. William White; b. in 1841.
45. Daugherty White; b. in 1842.
46. Catherine White; b. in 1844.
47. Hugh White; b. in 1845.
48. Aderin (?) White; b. in 1848.
49. Francis White; b. in 1850.

18. BENJ. FRANKLIN WHITE, farmer; b. in Clay County, November 16, 1817, and d. November 9, 1855, when taking a boat loaded with salt down the river; m. December 31, 1836, Alabama Taylor, b. in Alabama about 1821, daughter of John E. Taylor of Chattanooga, Tennessee.

Children living at home and approximate dates of birth as shown by the U. S. Census of Clay County for the years 1850 and 1860:

*50. John E. White; b. January 27, 1838.
*51. Dillian White; b. in 1839.
52. Catherine White; b. in 1841.
*53. Beverly White; b. in 1842.
*54. William White; b. in 1844.
55. Ann White; b. in 1846.
56. Ellen White; b. in 1849.
*57. Letcher White; b. in 1844.
58. Frank White; b. in 1851.
59. Paralee White; b. in 1853.
60. Hugh White; b. in 1855.

19. DANIEL G. WHITE, salt merchant, was b. in Clay County in 1820; m. June 20, 1843, Mildred D. Morgan, b. in 1827, daughter of Gen. Daniel Morgan of Fleming County.

Children living at home and approximate dates of birth as shown by the U. S. Census of Clay County for 1850:

61. Daniel White; b. in 1844.
62. Hugh White; b. in 1846.
63. John White; b. in 1848.

64. Henry White; b. in 1849.
65. Catherine White; b. in 1850.

23. Hon. John Daugherty White (nephew of John White) a Representative from Kentucky; b. near Manchester, Clay County, January 16, 1849; attended a private school until 1865 and Eminence (Kentucky) College and the University of Kentucky at Lexington until 1870; was graduated from the law department of the University of Michigan at Ann Arbor in 1872; also attended the medical department of the same institution; declined a nomination for clerk of the Court of Appeals of Kentucky, in 1874; was admitted to the bar by the Kentucky Court of Appeals in 1875 and practiced law; elected as a Republican to the Forty-fourth Congress, (March 4, 1875-March 3, 1877); declined to be a candidate for renomination; chairman of the Republican State Convention at Louisville in 1879; member of the State house of representatives in 1879 and 1880; resigned in 1880; endorsed and reelected without opposition during the sitting of the legislature; chairman of the Kentucky delegation to the Republican National Convention at Chicago in 1880, which nominated James A. Garfield, of Ohio, for President, and Chester A. Arthur, of New York, for Vice-President; unsuccessful Republican candidate for the United States Senate in 1881; elected as Republican to the Forty-seventh and Forty-eighth Congresses (March 4, 1881-March 3, 1885); declined to be a candidate for nomination in 1884 and resumed the practice of law in Louisville; unsuccesful candidate of the State Prohibition Party for Governor in 1903; unsuccessful candidate of the Progressive Party for Judge of the Kentucky Court of Appeals in 1912; d. near Manchester, Kentucky, January 5, 1920; interment in the family burying ground near Manchester, Clay County, Kentucky.[6]

51. Dillian White, farmer, was b. in Clay County in 1830; served in the Union Army during the Civil War as sergeant and second lieutenant of Company "E", 24th Kentucky Volunteer Infantry; promoted from sergeant to 2nd Lieutenant December 20, 1862; resigned November 5, 1863;[7] m. Mary ———, b. in 1843.

Children living at home and approximate dates of birth as shown by the U. S. Census of Clay County for 1870:
66. John White; b. in 1862.
67. Beverly White; b. in 1865.
68. William White; b. in 1867.

53. Beverly P. White; b. in Clay County in 1842; served in the Union Army during the Civil War as lieutenant and captain of Company "E", 7th Kentucky Volunteer Infantry; promoted from 1st lieutenant to captain, June 3, 1863, at Vicksburg, Mississippi; honorably separated from the service at Louisville, Kentucky, October 5, 1864;[7] Judge of the Clay County Court, 1870; m. Helen G. ——— ———, b. in 1848.

Children living at home in 1870:
69. James White; b. in 1869.

50. JOHN E. WHITE, farmer, businessman and public official; b. in Clay County January 27, 1838; d. in 1915; m., March 31, 1859, Elizabeth Garrard Brawner, b. 1843, and d., 1922, daughter of Luther and Maria (Garrard) Brawner; engaged in mercantile business, at first near his home and later about two years after the close of the Civil War with his brothers in Manchester, continuing until about 1900; served as School Commissioner of Clay County for several terms; also had large timber interests.

Children living at home in 1870 and approximate dates of birth as shown by the U. S. Census of Clay County for that year:

70. Mary E. White; b. 1863.
71. Daugherty W. White; b. 1865, and d. in November, 1928; elected and served as clerk of the Clay Circuit Court from 1891 to 1903; was county judge, 1906-1910, and sheriff, 1922-1926. During the periods while not holding elective office, he held appointive offices. He was admitted to the bar in 1906 but did not engage extensively in the practice of law.

He m. October 27, 1887, Lucy House (Howes), descendant of Charles Howes, a pioneer settler of Clay County. Charles Howes was also the ancestor of Elexious Howes, the founder of the Howes family of the Big Sandy Valley. (See Howes Family.)

Children:
*72. Roy R. White.
73. Walter R. White; b. October 5, 1891; m. Roberta Burchell, 1915; d. during the influenza epidemic, October 12, 1918, while attending Officers' Training Camp at Camp Taylor. They had one son, First Lieutenant Walter R. White II, a pilot of a B26 Bomber who was shot down over the Aegean Sea in 1943; body never recovered.
74. Lyle B. White; b. November 10, 1893; d. July, 1933; m. Lillie Gambrel.
75. John E. White; b. November 5, 1895; m. Tenny White.
76. Charles W. White; b. January 4, 1900; m. Nora Sizemore.

72. ROY R. WHITE, civil engineer, was b. at Manchester, Clay County, October 29, 1888; educated in the public schools of Manchester, finishing the equivalent of a high school course; student at the Agricutural and Mechanical College (predecessor of Kentucky University), at Lexington, 1904-5; and pursued a course in engineering at the Ohio Northern University at Ada, 1908-9; accepted a position with the Colorado & Santa Fe Railway Company, and was in the service of that company in Texas during the winter of 1909-10 when he returned to Clay County and was employed until 1911 by his father and grandfather who were engaged in a large

timber operation; accepted a position as land surveyor and did surveying until the Fall of 1913 for a company that had large mineral acreage in Clay County; engaged in farming in Ohio for two years; accepted a position with the Pittsburg Crucible Steel Co. at Midland, Pennsylvania and was in the employ of that company as assistant foreman, foreman and general foreman until August 1917, when, having been accepted as a candidate for a commission in the Second Officers' Training Camp at Fort Benjamin Harrison, Indiana, he entered the U. S. Army; was commissioned a second lieutenant, F. A., and assigned to the 326 F. A., at Camp Taylor; had service overseas in France from September 1918 to February 1919, when returned to the United States; discharged March 31, 1919.

Subsequent to his discharge from the Army, Mr. White was employed for a time by the Firestone Tire and Rubber Company, Akron, Ohio. Returning to Clay County he was engaged for the next several years in engineering work. The Ford Motor Company had acquired large acreage in the Clay County area and he was employed by that company as land and mine surveyor from 1923 to 1929 when he resigned to superintend a mine in Clay County of which he was part owner. From 1933 to 1935, he was supervisor of a relief organization and in the latter year he accepted a position as engineer in the Civilian Conservation Corps, Forestry Service, and continued until the beginning of World War II when he was employed as engineer in charge of construction work through 1942. Returning to his home in Clay County, he was again employed by the Ford Motor Company from the Spring of 1943 to January, 1949 when he resigned his position.

Mr. White is a Republican in politics and a member of the Presbyterian Church, serving as Elder. He is a member of Manchester Lodge No. 794, F. & A. M. and has served as Master twice and Secretary for several years. He is a member of the American Legion and has served the organization as Post Commander twice and as District Commander once.

While a student at Ohio Northern University, Mr. White met Miss Jeanette Haney of Wapakoneta, Ohio. They were m., September 5, 1908. Mrs. White d. in January 1949.

Children:

77. Dorothy White; b. July 5, 1909; m. John Manning, 1925. They had two children of whom the older, Robert, had service for two years in the U. S. Navy in World War II.

78. Robert E. White, coal operator at Manchester; b. November 27, 1911; m. Ruth Marcum. Three girls were born to them. He had service in U. S. Army in World War II.

79. Elizabeth White; b. April 28, 1914; m. Benjamin Sevearagen; reside in Orlando, Florida.

80. John D. White, lawyer; b. October 28, 1915; educated at Kentucky University and at University of Louisville Law School; served

in CIC in World War II; m. Juanita Mills. They have three children.

81. Walter J. White; b. October 29, 1917; served as second lieutenant, Air Corps; (pursuit pilot), World War II; m. Dorothy Mae Hensley; reside in Lexington, Kentucky, and is presently employed by the Department of Revenue. Two children.

82. Marshall White; b. October 5, 1920; served as first lieutenant, Air Corps, (pursuit pilot), in World War II; m. Mildred Road; resides in Lexington, Kentucky, and is presently employed by the Herald-Leader Newspaper. Two children.

83. Ann White; b. June 26, 1926; m. Lee R. Hensley; reside at Clarksville, Indiana. Four children.

84. Hugh L. White; b. June 26, 1828; entered U. S. Army October 1945; m. Joyce Hunt. Two children; reside at Manchester.³

Mr. White is deeply interested in and thoroughly conversant with the history of Clay County and its people. He has prepared a history of the county (manuscript, unpublished); and has written and there has been published, an interesting and factual article on the salt industry in that county.

---

¹ The Whites of Clay County as Salt Makers, by Mrs. Bessie White Hager, The Register of the Kentucky Historical Society, July, 1952, Vol. 50, No. 172, pages 242-247.

² History of Southwest Virginia, 1746-1786, Washington County, 1777-1870, by Lewis Preston Summers, 1903, p. 793.

³ Biographical Directory of the American Congress, 1774-1949, page 1999.

⁴ The Salt Industry of Clay County, Kentucky, by Roy R. White, The Register of the Kentucky Historical Society, July 1952, Vol. 50, No. 172, pages 238-241.

⁵ Biographical Directory of the American Congress, 1774-1949, p. 2002.

⁶ Biographical Directory of the American Congress, 1774-1949, pages 2002-3.

⁷ Report of the Adjutant General of Kentucky, 1861-1866, Vol. II, page 180_1.

⁸ The White Family of Clay County (manuscript), by Roy R. White, Manchester, Kentucky.

WILHOIT FAMILY OF BATH AND CARTER COUNTIES

The Wilhoit family of Kentucky is of German origin. The first of the family of whom there is any available record was 1. Adam Wilhoit, a native of Germany. His son, 2. Phillip Wilhoit, immigrated to South Carolina. He had children, among others:

3. John Wilhoit who migrated to Madison County, Virginia. John Wilhoit was an agriculturist and merchant. He, his wife Nancy and their children migrated to Montgomery County, Kentucky. He d. in Bath County, that State. Their son,

4. James Alfred Wilhoit, farmer, preacher and sometimes local public official, was b. in Madison County, Virginia, 1816, and d. near Willard, Carter County, Kentucky, 1873.[1] Coming to Carter County when a young man, he m., August 11, 1841, Matilda A. Boggs, b. in Virginia, November 2, 1820, and d. in Carter County, at an advanced age—nearly 100 years. She was a daughter of James Boggs.[2]

JAMES A. WILHOIT was a practical stone-cutter and was a justice of the peace in Carter County for 16 years. He was a strictly moral and religious man and for many years was a consistent member of and a preacher in the Baptist Church.

Children:

*5. Ephraim Boggs Wilhoit.
6. Frances A. Wilhoit.
7. Nancy Wilhoit; b. 1847.
8. Jane Wilhoit.
9. Ellen Wilhoit; b. 1849.
10. Mary Wilhoit; b. 1852.
11. John Wilhoit: b. 1854; m. Miss Armstrong; migrated West.
*12. James B. Wilhoit.
13. George W. Wilhoit, b. 1860, merchant at Olive Hill, Kentucky; m. Miss Armstrong.
14. Matilda or Myrtle Wilhoit; b. 1862.

5. COL. EPHRAIM BOGGS WILHOIT, lawyer, was b. near Willard, Carter County, Kentucky, September 19, 1842, and d. at Grayson, Kentucky, in 1919; educated in the public schools of Carter County and at the Seminary, Mt. Sterling, Kentucky. A staunch Union man, in 1861, he enlisted in Company "I", Twenty-second Regiment, Kentucky Infantry, and served to the close of the war. He studied law and in 1866 was admitted to the bar at Grayson, Kentucky; and was one of the outstanding lawyers of his time in the State, practicing in the State and Federal Courts for more than fifty years with distinction and success.

Mr. Wilhoit was commissioned by the Governor of Kentucky, Hon. Luke P. Blackburn, as aide-de-camp on his staff with rank of colonel and served as such for four years. He served as county attorney of Carter County, 1873-7. He was a Democrat in politics and a member of the Episcopal Church. Fraternally, he was a member of the Independent Order of Odd Fellows, a Royal Arch Mason and a member, serving as Master, of Trimble Lodge No. 145, F. & A. M., at Grayson.

Mr. Wilhoit m., first, on August 30, 1867, Miss Alice Frizzell, b. 1845 and d. about 1881, a daughter of Maj. Alfred H. and Eliza (Scott) Frizzell.

Children:

15. Alfred Frizzell Wilhoit, lawyer, b. 1868; m. Naomi Holcomb; no children.

16. Edward Wilhoit; b. about 1870.

17. Eustace Wilhoit; b. about 1872.

5-A. Col. E. B. Wilhoit m., secondly, on September 19, 1882, Miss Anna Blackburn of Atlanta, Georgia, a highly educated and accomplished lady, who was a daughter of John C. C. Blackburn, of Atlanta, a physician, an officer in the Confederate States Army and a cousin (twice removed) of the late Jo. C. S. Blackburn, U. S. Senator from Kentucky. John C. C. Blackburn was a son of John Lowe Blackburn physician, who was b. at Newberry, South Carolina, December 23, 1792, and d. July 11, 1856, at his home, built in 1848, on his plantation about 40 miles southwest of Atlanta.

Mrs. Wihoit was a member of the Episcopal Church. She d. at Grayson at an advanced age—about 96 years.

Children:

18. Marie Wilhoit; b. at Grayson, Kentucky, January 9, 1884; educated in the public schools of Grayson and at Hamilton College, Lexington; m. Dr. Fulkerson. They had one child, Heman Fulkerson, who was educated in the Grayson Graded and High Schools; was graduated from Eastern (Kentucky) State College with degree of A. B., and from University of North Carolina with degree of A. M.

19. Inez Blackburn Wilhoit; b. at Grayson, June 3, 1886; educated in the public and a private school, Grayson, and at Mary Baldwin College, Staunton, Virginia; m., 1907, Wickliffe H. Strother. (See Strother Family.)

*20. Calhoun Blackburn Wilhoit.

21. Junius Wilhoit; b. at Grayson, August 16, 1894; m. Helen Burns of Ashland.

Children:

22. Gordon Wilhoit; resides in West Virginia.

20. CALHOUN BLACKBURN WILHOIT, lawyer; b. at Grayson, December 17, 1888; educated in the Grayson Graded and High Schools; studied law in the office of father; admitted to the bar and for a number of years practiced his profession at Grayson in partnership

with his father. Subsequently retiring from active practice on account of ill health, he has devoted himself to the management and operation of his farm at Pactolus.

Mr. Wilhoit m. Miss Irene Rupert, daughter of Henry C. and Louella (Virgin)Rupert. (See Rupert Family.)

Children:

23. Henry Rupert Wilhoit, lawyer; b. at Grayson, Kentucky, September 28, 1912; educated in the public schools of Carter County and Grayson, graduating from the Prichard High School at Grayson in 1928; was a student at Georgetown College, Georgetown, Kentucky, for two years and then entered the University of Kentucky at Lexington from which he graduated with degree of LL.B., in January, 1934; admitted to the bar in March, 1934, and since has continuously practiced law at Grayson (except when serving in the U. S. Navy). his practice extending over the several counties of northeastern Kentucky in which he is counselor for a great number of casualty and fire insurance companies.

He was commissioned a lieutenant (J. G.), U. S. Navy, and entered on active duty September 15, 1943; served in the European Theatre of Operations and was released from duty in November, 1945.

Mr. Wilhoit is a member of the Bar of the Court of Appeals of Kentucky, the United States District Court for the Eastern District of Kentucky, and the United States Court of Appeals for the Sixth Circuit. He is a member of the Carter County, the Kentucky State and the American Bar Associations, and the American Judicature Society. When in the University he was a member of Kappa Alpha, social fraternity and Phi Delta Phi, legal fraternity. He is a Republican in politics and a member of the Methodist Church.

December 18, 1933, Mr. Wilhoit was united in marriage with Miss Frances Kathryn Reynolds, b. April 20, 1913, daughter of H. E. Reynolds of Cave City, Kentucky. She was educated in the public schools of Barren County, Kentucky, at Ward-Belmont College, Nashville, Tennessee, and at University of Kentucky from which she graduated in June, 1934. She has been prominently identified with many organizations: the Kappa Kappa Gamma sorority, Daughters of the American Revolution, Garden Clubs of Kentucky, American Federation of Women's Clubs, the American Cancer Society. She is a Methodist.

Children: Henry Rupert Wilhoit, Jr., and Michael Brady Wilhoit.

12. James Buchanan Wilhoit, lawyer; b. near Willard, Carter County, Kentucky, March 6, 1857; educated in the public schools of Carter County, suppemented by a course of study at Kentucky Normal College, Carlisle, Kentucky, where he was trained for teaching; taught for 12 years in the schools of Carter County and adjoining counties, in the meantime studying law; admitted to the bar in

Greenup County in 1880 and practiced for the next three years at his home town of Willard when he located at Grayson, where he main tained his home and practiced his profession for the next 15 years. In 1898 he was appointed Supervisor of Forestry by President Mc-Kinley and in connection with his duties passed two years in New Mexico. In January, 1900 he located and resumed his practice of law at Greenup, Kentucky, entering into a partnership with Col. William J. Worthington, the firm doing business until 1902, when, in October of that year, he established his home at Ashland, Kentucky, where he soon built up a large and lucrative practice. He was a versatile and skilled trial lawyer and was retained in many important cases in both State and Federal Courts.

Mr. Wilhoit was a staunch Republican and for many years was active in party affairs. He held many public offices of honor and trust and filled all of them with credit to himself and to the satisfaction of the public. He served as County Attorney of Carter County for five years; was elected commonwealth's attorney for the 20th Judicial District, 1907, to fill an unexpired term of two years and was reelected, 1909, for the six year term; was Republican Presidential elector for the 9th Congressional District, 1896, and elector at large, 1904; resumed practice of law at Ashland after expiration of term as commonwealth's attorney in 1915.

Mr. Wilhoit m., first, in 1881, Miss Callie Bowman (or Boldman).

Children:

26. James LeRoy (Roy) Wilhoit, lawyer; was rate clerk of the Kentucky Railroad Commission for a number of years; practiced law at Pikeville and Vanceburg, Kentucky, and is presently practicing law at Ashland and Catlettsburg, Kentucky. Residence, 501 Fourteenth Street, Ashland.

27. Willie Wilhoit, druggist, at Maysville, Kentucky.

12-A. J. B. Wilhoit, m., secondly, Mrs. Marguerite (Rupert) Osenton. (See Rupert Family.) No children.

---

1 Kentucky, A History of the State, by W. H. Perrin, J. H. Battle and Kniffin. F. A. Battey & Co., 1888.

2 James Boggs was a native of Virginia and a son of John Boggs. He settled in then Lawrence County, Kentucky, on the Little Fork of Little Sandy River probably in the Hitchens-Willard area in the early 1820's, where he became a large land owner. The records would seem to indicate that his wife was Frances ———— (surname not known), born in Virginia in 1792 and died in Carter County within the period 1850-1860. Their children other than Mrs. James A. Wilhoit, were Eleanor, born 1826; married Milton Kennedy, born 1820; Rebecca, born 1827; m. William Jason Fields (See Fields Family.); Elihu, born 1829; married Temperance ————, born 1832; John, born 1832; Hannah, born 1833; m. Isom Ison, born 1829.

WILLIAMS FAMILY OF JOHNSON COUNTY
WILLIAMS FAMILY OF THE OIL SPRINGS VICINITY, JOHNSON COUNTY, KENTUCKY

James Williams was the founder of this branch of the Williams family of Eastern Kentucky. He migrated from North Carolina to Scott County, Virginia, and from thence to Big Mud Creek, Floyd County, Kentucky.

1. JAMES WILLIAMS; m., first, ——— Spears.
   Children:
   2. Jacob Williams.
   3. Isaac Williams.
   4. Abraham Williams.
   *5. James Williams.
   6. Patience Williams.
   7. Jackson Williams.
   8. Malinda Williams.
1-A. James Williams; m., secondly, ——— Yates.
   Children:
   9. Harris Williams.
   10. George Williams.
   11. Thomas Williams; resided near Asa, Johnson County.
   12. Riley Williams.

5. JAMES WILLIAMS; b. in Floyd County, 1826; m., first, 1845, Margaret Meade, daughter of Robert Meade (See Meade Family). He, in company with Robert Meade, removed from Floyd County to Johnson County and purchased lands near Oil Springs.
   Children:
   *13. Alexander Williams.
   *14. Samuel P. Williams.
   *15. C. C. Williams.
   *16. Polly A. Williams.
   *17. Catharine Williams.
   *18. John Williams.
   *19. Sukey J. Williams.
   *20. Sophronia Williams.
   *21. Joseph Williams.
   22. Margaret S. Williams, m. Sherman Trimble.
5-A. James Williams; m., secondly, Nancy Reed Lemaster.
   Children:
   23. James Polk Williams, b. 1872, d. 1896.
   24. Lorenzo D. Williams, b. 1874, d. 1895.
   25. Patience Williams, m. Grant Trimble; resided near Ivyton, Magoffin County.

13. ALEXANDER WILLIAMS, b. 1846, d. 1923; m. Susan Bayes.

Children:

26. Theodore Williams; m. Berta Williams.
27. L. D. Williams; m., first, Julia Bayes and secondly, Phoebe Lemaster.
28. Charley Williams; m., first, Rachel Williams and secondly, Lulu Colvin.
29. Millard Williams; m. May Reed.
30. Floyd Williams; m. Elizabeth Meade.
31. John Williams; m. ———— Williams.
32. James Williams; m. Alka Reed.
33. Taylor Williams; m. ————Frazier.
34. Thomas Williams; m. ———— Lemaster.
This family resided near Oil Springs, Johnson County.

14. SAMUEL P. WILLIAMS, b. 1848; m., first, Sadie Reed, and, secondly, Georgia (Davis) Williams; resided in Oil Springs section of Johnson County.

Children of Samuel P. Williams and Sadie Reed:

35. Alexander Williams, Jr.; m. Elizabeth Davis.
36. Ida Williams; m. George W. Reed.
37. Manda Williams; m. Charles Trimble.
38. Fred Williams; m. Kate Meade.
39. Prudence Williams; m. W. D. Huffman.
40. Herbert Williams; m. Susie Thomas.
41. Winnie Williams; m. May Horn.
42. Winfred Williams.
43. Lexie Williams; m. Hammie Williams.

15. C. C. WILLIAMS; m. Alcey Virginia Cuddy.

Children:

*44. James A. Williams.
45. John Williams; m. Anne Roberts.
46. Joseph Williams; m. Lillie Litteral.
47. Dixie Williams; m. W. H. Roberts.
48. Ben Williams; m. Bertie Coones.
49. Charles Williams; m. Mattie Byrd.
50. Jack Williams; m. Oneida Howes. (See Howes Family.)
C. C. Williams removed to Wolfe County, Kentucky, in 1876 and all the family lived in that county other than James A. Williams, who lived in Johnson County.

16. POLLY A. WILLIAMS; m. Daniel Reed; resided near Oil Springs.

Children:

51. C. C. Reed; m. Rissie Blanton.
52. Mason Reed; m. Lulu (Salyer) McKenzie.
53. Alonzo Reed; m. Vertrice Smith.
54. Dock Reed; m. Alice Helton.

55. Bessie Reed; m. William Fairchild.

17. CATHERINE WILLIAMS; m. N. M. Cantrill; resided near Ophir, Morgan County, Kentucky.

Children:

56. Versie Cantrill; m. Ben Hamilton.
57. Frazie Cantrill; m. Wince Smith.
58. Janie Cantrill; m. Buck Smith.

18. JOHN WILLIAMS, b. 1856, d. 1888; m., first, Julia Williams.

Children:

59. Dollie Williams; m. Arch Lewis.
60. Alice Williams; m. Warnie Wollums.
61. Mancie Williams; m. G. W. Difenbach.
62. N. Kendrick Williams; m. Bessie Rice.
63. Sue Williams; m. John Stephenson.
64. Lucy Williams; m. ———— Nowlin.

John Williams, m., secondly, Lucinda Reed and, thirdly, Nannie Asbury.

19. SUKEY J. WILLIAMS, b. 1858, d. 1898; m. Logan Salyer.

Children:

65. Carrie; m. John Wireman.
66. Lora; m. John Collins.
67. Shella; m. Fred O'Brian.

20. SOPHRONIA WILLIAMS, b. 1860, d. 1900; m. Mason Cantrill.

Children:

68. Oscar Cantrill; m. ———— Farley.
69. Dixie Cantrill; m. Amos Cantrill.
*70. Joseph C. Cantrill; m. Linnie Litteral.
71. Myrtle Cantrill; m. ———— Cantrill.
72. James Cantrill; m. ———— Cantrill

21. JOSEPH WILLIAMS, b. 1864, d. 1895; m. Lena Fulks.

Children:

73. Chester Williams; m. ———— Johnson.
74. Flossie Williams.

44. JAMES A. WILLIAMS, sometimes teacher and businessman, was b. in Floyd County in 1872. After obtaining a common school education he engaged in teaching in the public schools of Wolfe County for a number of years. In 1895 he removed to Johnson County and continued teaching school until 1905 when he accepted a position as teller in the Paintsville National Bank. He continued in the service of the bank for seven years and subsequently was cashier of the bank of Wayland for two years and cashier of the Paintsville Bank and Trust Company for six years.

A Republican in politics he was Republican County Chairman

of Johnson County for twelve years and was delegate to Republican National Convention in 1916; was deputy collector of United States Internal Revenue for three years; and was judge of the Johnson County Court, 1920.

Mr. Williams m. Flora Penley, only child of Thomas J. Penley, onetime assessor of Johnson County.

Children:

75. Ethel Williams.
76. May Williams.
77. Annie Williams.
78. Luzelle Williams.
79. James Thomas Williams.

70. JOSEPH C. CANTRILL, oil development business; m. Linnie Litteral who d. February 18, 1926, daughter of Judge W. E. Litteral; resided in Johnson County for a number of years and then at De-Land, Florida where Mrs. Cantrill died.

Children:

80. Dixie Cantrill.
81. William Cantrill.
82. Irene Cantrill.
83. Pauline Cantrill.
84. Martha Alice Cantrill.

WILLIAMS FAMILY OF THE MUD LICK VICINITY, JOHNSON COUNTY, KENTUCKY

Samuel Williams was the progenitor of this branch of the Williams family.

1. SAMUEL WILLIAMS; b. in Scott County, Virginia, in 1811, d. 1877; m. presumably in Scott County, in 1834, Katherine Kimbler, b. 1812, who resided near Hill, Scott County.

Samuel Williams and his three sons were imprisoned in a Confederate prison prior to their having been drafted into the Confederate Army. One son escaped from prison.

Children:
*2. Preston Campbell Williams.
3. Melvina Williams; b. 1837.
4. Billy Williams; b. 1839, d. 1863, in Confederate prison during the Civil War.
5. Asbury Williams, b. 1842, d. 1911; m. ———, 1865.

2. PRESTON CAMPBELL WILLIAMS, b. in Scott County, Virginia, in 1835, d. in Johnson County, Kentucky, 1902; m., presumably in Scott County, in 1859, Winnie Lark, b. 1843, d. 1922, daughter of Michael Lark of Virginia.

PRESTON CAMPBELL WILLIAMS fled from Virginia to Kentucky through the "Breaks of Sandy", to evade being drafted into the Confederate Army and afterwards enlisted in the Kentucky militia in 1864. His wife, with their two children followed him to Kentucky in the summer of 1864 and after his discharge from the service at the close of the war of 1865, they settled on a farm on Mud Lick Creek near Volga, Johnson County, where their descendants reside.

Children:
*6. James Marion Williams.
7. William Patton Williams.

6. JAMES MARION WILLIAMS, b. in Scott County, Virginia, in 1860; d. in Johnson County, Kentucky, 1927; m. in Johnson County, April 30, 1891, Jennie P. Vaughan, b. 1873, daughter of Judge Henry S. Vaughan and his wife, Mary E. (Burgess) Vaughan. (See Vaughan Family.)

Children:
8. Cova Maud Williams.
9. Jessie Gladys Williams.
10. U. D. (Uhl Dover) Williams.
11. Hazel Gaynell Williams; m. Harry Davis.
*12. John Fred Williams.
13. James Sankey Williams, b. 1907, single.
14. Cyrus Coke Williams; b. 1911, single.

12. JOHN FRED WILLIAMS, educator and one-time public official; highly educated; was engaged for a number of years in educational work in Eastern Kentucky; elected on the Republican Ticket and served as Superintendent of Public Instruction of Kentucky from December 1943 to December 1947; unm.

WOMACK OF GREENUP COUNTY

Womack is an old Virginia family and was spread over all parts of that colony in Colonial days, being particularly numerous in the Tidewater region, as is evidenced by the first U. S. Census (1790) which shows about twenty Womacks as heads of families in that area.

The first Womack to migrate and settle in Eastern Kentucky was Archer Womack who settled near present Old Town, Greenup County, probably about the time the county was established (1804). He was a son of James Tignal Womack who came with his family and slaves from near Farmville, Prince Edward County, Virginia, and settled about 1812 on a large tract of land, afterwards known as the Virgin farm on the Little Sandy River nearly opposite present Pactolus, Carter County. Son Archer and a negro slave had built a log cabin and raised a crop on the land before James Tignal Womack and family came in from Virginia.

1. JAMES TIGNAL WOMACK was the ancestor of the Womacks of Northeastern Kentucky. He was one of the prominent pioneers and was considered wealthy in his time and place. In his will he devised, among other property, twenty-three slaves to his family. Nothing has been learned concerning his wife. Children (Second Generation):

*2. Archer Womack.

3. Polly Womack; m. a Mr. Hatchett in Virginia; never came to Kentucky.

*4. Allen Womack.

5. Eliza Womack; m. David Kibbey in Greenup County, September 1, 1828; migrated to the West.

6. Nancy Womack; m. William ("Buck") Kouns in Greenup County, November 5, 1836 (See Kouns Family).

7. Martha Womack; d. before reaching womanhood.

8. Clarinda Womack; m. Reason or Režin Virgin (See Virgin Family).

*9. Samuel Womack.

*10. Richard D. Womack.

*11. William Womack.

*12. James Allen Womack.

2. ARCHER WOMACK, farmer; b. on a farm near Farmville, Prince Edward County, Virginia, 1798; m. in Greenup County, Kentucky, July 4, 1823, Mariam Kouns, b. in Kentucky, 1804, daughter of Major John C. Kouns of Greenupsburg. (See Kouns Family.)

Children:

Third Generation

Children living in the household and approximate dates of birth as shown by the U. S. Census of Greenup County for 1850 and 1870:

13. George Womack; b. 1826.

14. Samuel Womack; b. 1832; m. Emily McAllister.
15. Elizabeth Womack; b. 1830.
16. Thompson Womack; b. 1834.
17. Charles Womack; b. 1836.
18. Watson Womack; b. 1838.
19. Mariam Womack; b. 1840.
20. Mildred B. Womack; b. 1842, m. James Wilson.
21. Benjamin Womack; b. 1845, m. Dortch.
22. Archer Womack, Jr.; b. 1856.
23. Alfred Womack; b. 1859.
24. Andrew Womack; b. 1861.
25. Charles W. Womack; b. 1862.

Other children:
*26. William Archer Womack.

Archer and Mariam (Kouns) Womack established their home on the Little Sandy River about two miles south of Greenupsburg.

4. ALLEN L. WOMACK, farmer; b. in Kentucky, 1815; m. in Greenup County, May 20, 1842, Lucy Jane Osenton, b. October 20, 1821, at Old Town, d. January 20, 1884, and was buried in the Old Town cemetery near the church. She was a daughter of Samuel and Emzy (Downs) Osenton. (See Osenton Family). Children (third generation) living in the household and approximate dates of birth as shown by the U. S. Census of Greenup County for 1860 and 1870:

27. Samuel T. Womack; b. 1845.
*28. James W. Womack; b. 1849.
*29. George H. Womack; b. 1854.
30. Emily Womack; b. 1857.
31. Henry Womack; b. 1859.
32. Josephus Womack; b. about 1860.
33. Jefferson Davis Womack; b. about 1861.
34. Sarah Daisy Womack; b. 1866.

Other children:
*35. "Bud" Womack.

9. SAMUEL WOMACK; m. Susan Ferries (Farish?); settled at West Liberty, Morgan County, Kentucky.

Children, among others (third generation):
36. Andrew J. Womack, farmer and for many years a justice of the peace in Carter County, was b. in Morgan County, October 15, 1846, and d. in Carter County, November 27, 1937; m., March 10, 1872, Mary Everman, b. July 21, 1846, and d. March 29, 1933.

Children (Fourth Generation):
37. Willis T. Womack, sometimes merchant and for many years cashier of the Commercial Bank of Grayson, was b. in Carter County,

January 27, 1873, and d. at Middletown, Ohio, June 4, 1930; m., March 20, 1895 Mary S. Womack, who d. March 10, 1931.

Children (fifth generation):

(a) Mariam Womack, b. August 5, 1905; m. Barr Irwin, February 18, 1927. Children (sixth generation): Domie Barr Irwin.

(b) Easter Clay Womack, b. February 16, 1896; m. Rem Nickels, December 23, 1926. Children (sixth generation): Barbara Jean Nickels, b. July 6, 1928.

(c) Winnie Lee Womack; b. March 10, 1899; m. Arch Bales, September 21, 1922. Children (sixth generation): Mary Lee Bales, b. February 21. 1923; W. T. Bales, b. November 4, 19—; and Houston Bales, b. February 23, 1928.

(d) Russell W. Womack; b. September 8, 1902; m. Gladys Hall, November 11, 1928. Children (sixth generation): Geraldine Womack, b. July 1, 1930, and Bobby Womack, b. September 2, 1933.

(e) Wickliffe T. Womack; b August 12, 1903; m. Mayble Robeson, June 8, 1929; no children.

(f) Marguerite Womack; b. January 15, 1915; m. Ferd Kissner, June 6, 1935.

38. Ernest B. Womack; b. November 27, 1875, and d. December 19, 1880.

39. Lewis P. Womack; b. January 19, 1877, and d. April 4, 1953; m. Belle Sexton, October 22, 1915. Children (fifth generation): Watts P. Womack, b. September 21, 1918; Jack A. Womack, b. September 2, 1920; and Owsley S. Womack, b. December 4, 1922.

40. Leslie S. Womack, architect and contractor, b. April 19, 1879, and d. November 22, 1937; m. August 31, 1915, Belle Strother, daughter of Dr. J. W., and Amanda (Horton) Strother. (See Strother Family.) Children (fifth generation): Samuel Leslie Womack, Jr., b. July 7, 1916, and d. July 19, 1920; and John Gaines Womack; b. August 21, 1918; m. Margaret Gwendolyn Stephens, October 2, 1940. Children (sixth generation): Karen Leslie Womack, b. December 24, 1942; and John Gaines Womack II, b. June 20, 1950.

41. Annie Womack; b. August 8, 1886; m. Lawrence Martin, May 31, 1908. Children (fifth generation): Irene Martin, b. December 26, 1910; Mildred Martin, b. April 27, 1913; Frances Martin, b. June 21, 1918; and Helen L. Martin, b. June 15, 1922.

42. Lucy Womack; b. June 5, 1881; m. Ben Burnett, December 24, 1915. Children (fifth generation): Homer Burnett, b. October 5, 1916.

43. Homer Womack, merchant at Grayson; b. January 14, 1884; m., November 5, 1916, Doris Avis Hall, teacher. Children (fifth generation): (a) Zachary Taylor Womack, b. September 21, 1917; m. Nan Adelaide Farmer, March 24, 1940. Children (sixth generation): Nan Taylor Womack, b. August 4, 1946, and Zachary Andrew Womack, b. June 15, 1949.

(b) Homer Baxter Womack, b. October 18, 1923; m. Annabelle Evans, June 15, 1944. Children (sixth generation): Ann Baxter Womack, b. November 30, 1946, and Homer Thomas Womack, b. March 27, 1949.

44. Strother Womack; b. March 4, 1889; m. Jennie Rupert, November 17, 1914. Children (fifth generation): (a) Carrie E. Womack, b. July 30, 1916; m. Palmer Lancaster, March 20, 1946. Children (sixth generation): Palmer David Lancaster, b. March 8, 1948.

(b) Mary E. Womack, b. December 24, 1917.

(c) James B. Womack, b. December 24, 1920; m. Edna Ellenbourg, August 3, 1946. Children (sixth generation): James Stephen Womack, b. September 5, 1949 and Deborah Ann Womack, b. February 5, 1952.

(d) Virginia R. Womack; b. January 19, 1923; m. Harry Griggs, June 4, 1945. Children (sixth generation): Jennie Lee Griggs, b. August 26, 1946, and Arthur Walter Griggs, b. July 16, 1953.

(e) Ann Lee Womack, b. September 9, 1927.

10. RICHARD D. WOMACK, farmer; b. near Farmville, Prince Edward County, Virginia, 1812 or 1813; m. in Greenup County, Kentucky, February 28, 1833; Harriet B. Ward, b. in Greenup County, 1818, and d. at Reedville, Carter County, at an advanced age. She was a daughter of James Ward and Mrs. Eliza (Bragg) Lewis Ward, widow of Charles Nelms Lewis I. (See Lewis Family and Ward Family of Carter and Greenup Counties.)

Children (Third Generation) and approximate dates of birth as shown by the U. S. Census of Carter County for the years 1850 and 1870:

45. James A. Womack; b. 1836.
46. Adelaide Womack; b. 1838.
47. Tignal Womack; b. 1841.
48. Lavina Womack; b. 1843.
49. Nancy E. Womack; b. 1845.
50. George J. Womack; b. 1846.
51. William Womack; b. 1849.
52. Samuel W. Womack; b. 1850.
53. Charles Nelms Womack; b. 1852.
54. Mary Womack; b. 1854.
55. John B. Womack; b. 1857.

11. WILLIAM WOMACK, farmer; b. near Farmville, Prince Edward County, Virginia, 1809; m. in Greenup County, Kentucky, December 29, 1829, Jacintha Kibbey, b. in Greenup County, Kentucky, 1812, daughter of Moses Kibbey.

Children (Third Generation) living in the household and approximate dates of birth as shown by the U. S. Census of Carter County for 1850 and 1860:

56. Nancy Womack; b. 1831.
57. Moses Womack; b. 1833.
58. Martha Womack; b. 1837.
59. Archy Womack; b. 1839.
60. Egbert Womack; b. 1841.
61. James Womack; b. 1844.
62. Sally Womack; b. 1847.
63. Ephraim Womack; b. 1849.
64. William Womack; b. 1852
65. Richard Womack; b. 1854.

William and Jacintha (Kibbey) Womack lived on the old home farm near Pactolus.

12. JAMES ALLEN WOMACK; served as clerk of the Greenup County Court and was a charter member of Trimble Lodge No. 145 F. & A. M., at Grayson. It is said that his funeral was the first in the vicinity of Grayson that was conducted by that fraternity. He m. in Greenup County, October 29, 1833, Susan Ann Lampton.

Children, among others (third generation):
66. Mary A. Womack; b. January 22, 1838, d. August 25, 1937; m. James Seaton. (See Seaton Family.)
66a. Kennie Womack; m. R. C. Burns of Catlettsburg, Kentucky. (See Burns Family.)
66b. James Tignal Womack; m. Fannie Collier of Steubenville, Ohio; removed to Minneapolis, Minnesota, with his family where he lived until his death.

Children (fourth generation): William, Robert, Mary, Sarah, John and Frank. Two children d. in infancy.
66c. Susan Lampton Womack; m. John B. Connelly. Children (fourth generation): Annie, who m. Robert Talbert and lived in Pelican Rapids, North Dokota; Nellie, who m. Charles W. Hill. Their daughter, Florence, m. George Tutoit; James m. and migrated to Oklahoma; and Susie, the youngest.

The Connelly Family lived in Cincinnati, Ohio, and Mrs. Connelly d. at birth of daughter, Susie. The older children were placed in orphan's home but Susie was reared by her grandmother, Susan Ann (Lampton) Womack. Sometimes both of them lived in the home of R. C. Burns and Kennie (Womack) Burns in Catlettsburg and at other times in the home of James Seaton and Mary A. (Womack) Seaton near Grayson. At the time of death of Susan Ann Womack in 1896, they were living in the Seaton home where Susie Connelly continued to live until she began teaching school. She taught in the public schools of Carter County for many years, principally in the primary department of the Grayson Graded School.

26. WILLIAM ARCHER WOMACK, farmer and merchant, b. 1828; m. in Greenup County, Ann Elizabeth Lyons, b. 1835; lived at Old

Town the greater part of their lives. In 1853 they, with son James Watt, than a baby, moved to Three Prong of Tygarts Creek, where they lived until 1863. Mr. Womack was taken a prisoner by the Home Guards during the Civil War on account of being a secessionist and was confined in Camp Chase, Ohio, for almost a year. When released, the family moved to Greenup where Mr. Womack was engaged in merchandising until 1867. Later the family moved to Old Town where the Womack children grew to manhood and womanhood. Here Mr. Womack engaged in merchandising with his brother-in-law, William ("Billy") Kouns, and operated a grist mill and tannery. The store was operated by Cardinal F. Stark in 1845 and has been in the Womack family ever since and is now being operated by Walter Orin Womack.

Children (fourth generation):

*67. James Watt Womack.

68. Elizabeth Womack; m. Joshua Keely of Laurel Furnace.

69. Charles Womack.

70. Mary F. Womack; m. Robert A. E. Leslie. (See Leslie Family.)

71. Frances Womack.

*72. John Thompson Womack.

73. Millie May Womack; m. John Bowers; resided in Houston, Texas.

74. Alma Ann Womack; m. Dr. William Morris of Fullerton.

75. Benjamin Ward Womack; m. Gertrude Curry of Hopewell; migrated to Florida.

76. Walter Orin Womack; m. Mary Carnahan of Old Town.

77. Edward Reason Womack; m. Elizabeth Warnock of Tygarts Valley; reside in Greenup.

Two children, Alice and Emma, d. young.

67. JAMES WATT WOMACK, merchant and sometimes pubic official b. at old Town, Greenup County, Kentucky, November 24, 1852; removed with parents when six weeks old to farm on Three Prong, Greenup County, where they lived until 1863 when they removed to Greenup; attended the Greenup schools until 1867 when the family removed to Old Town; returned to Greenup to attend school; subsequently was a clerk in the general store of Womack & Kouns at Old Town, and for a year held a similar position in the Laurel Furnace store.

Mr. Womack was a life-long and staunch Democrat in politics, always voting a straight ticket. He held many positions of honor and trust, and served his country creditably in all of them. He removed to Greenup in 1874, having been appointed deputy sheriff under Basil F. Warnock, Sheriff of Greenup County, which polition he held from 1875 to 1878; served as deputy sheriff under J. W. Kouns, Sheriff of Greenup County, 1879-1882; served as sheriff of

Greenup County 1883-1886; State representative, 1890-1892; and judge of the Greenup County Court, 1912-1918.

Contemporary with performance of his official duties, Mr. Womack was the active senior member of the firm of Womack Brothers, merchants, at Greenup, his brother, John Thompson Womack, being the junior member after whose death in 1946, James Watt Womack decided to dispose of the business after sixty-three years of honest dealing.

Mr. Womack was a Mason, having been made a member of F. & A. M. Lodge No. 89, at Greenup, April 8, 1876. He held at one time or another every position or office in the lodge. He d. June 9, 1951, at the venerable age of 98 years, six months and 16 days.

Mr. Womack m. Miss Ida Mae Osenton of Wheelersburg, Ohio, b. February 16, 1860, and d. July —, 1930, daughter of John Thomas Osenton and his wife, Katherine (Cameron) Osenton. (See Osenton Family.) They had no children but reared Mrs. Womack's niece, Mabel Osenton, who m. O. W. Stennett of Russell with whom James Watt Womack lived during the latter part of his lifetime.

70. JOHN THOMPSON WOMACK, merchant and sometimes public official was b. on Tygarts Creek, Greenup County, January 26, 1863; and d., 1946; moved with his father's family to Greenup when a young man; served as deputy sheriff of Greenup County under W. Butler Taylor, 1887-1890; was sheriff, 1891-1892; m., 1887, Lydia Connor Biggs, daughter of Thomas Naylor Biggs and his wife, Ellen (Humphreys) Biggs. (See Biggs Family.)

They lived in the William Kouns house, lower Main Street, Greenup.

28. JAMES W. WOMACK; b. 1843 and d. 1919; m. (but name of wife not learned). Children (fourth generation):
78. H. E. Womack; b. 1886; resides at Dover, Tennessee.
35. "DUD" WOMACK; b. 1845; went to Arkansas; m. Miss Long.

Children (fourth generation):
79. Pearl Womack; m. Dr. Robb.
80. Allen Womack; m. but name of wife unknown. They had a daughter, name unknown.

29. GEORGE H. WOMACK; b. 1848 and d. April —, 1910; interment, Huntington, West Virginia; m. Alice Wertz Jones.

Children (fourth generation):
81. David H. Womack; m. Mayme Hays. They have one child (fifth generation): Mrs. Ruth (Womack) Beard.
82. Frank Womack; m. Ethel Smith. They have two children (fifth generation): Aldene and Fern.

32. JOSEPHUS WOMACK; b. 1858 and d. 1917; m. Mary A. Anglin.

Their children are (fourth generation): Clyde, Lucy, Anna, James, Kenneth, Iona, Owen and Alton.

33. JEFFERSON DAVIS WOMACK; b. 1860 and d. 1926; m. Effie Taylor, b. 1873. Their children (fourth generation): Alta, Edna, Lucy Lee and Mary Elizabeth.

34. SARAH DAISY WOMACK; b. June 20, 1866, and d. October 25, 1924; m. April 23, 1884, Travis Kendall, b. February 15, 1862 and d. December 13, 1928. Both are buried in the Anglin Cemetery at Hopewell, Greenup County. Children (fourth generation): (a) Lonnie Penn Kendall; m. Ida Freeman. Their children are (fifth generation): Morris, Mildred, Hubert, Madeline and Walter.

(b) Travis W. Kendall; m. Dorothy Dempsey. Children (fifith generation): Dorothy Marie and Travis Joe.

(c) Owen C. Kendall; m. Bess Van Bibber. They have one child, (fifth generation): Robert Owen.

(d) Vernon V. Kendall; m. Mary Dene Norris. Children (fifth generation): Mary Lucille and Charles Brooks.

(e) Lucy Virginia Kendall; m. Jack McDonald. She had service in the W. A. C.'s in World War II.

(f) Daisy Marie Kendall; m. Barr B. Irwin. Children (fifth generation): Gene Frederick, Virginia Ann and Barbara Marie.

(g) Allen Wick Kendall; had service in World War II as ensign, U. S. Merchant Marine; m. Fern Womack.

WORTHINGTON FAMILY OF GREENUP COUNTY

Worthington

The surname Worthington is derived from an old Saxon word signifying court yard, farm or any other place of possession.

The Worthington family is of English extraction; and the progenitor of the distinguished Maryland family from which many of the same name in various sections of America claim descent was Francis Worthington of Lancastershire, England. His son, Captain John Worthington, was b. in Lancastershire in 1650, emigrated to America in 1673 and settled in Maryland. He acquired a large tract of land on the shores of the Severn River opposite Annapolis which he called "Pendennis."

Nicholas Worthington was the New England representative of the family. He emigrated from England to America in 1649 and settled in Saybrook, Connecticut. He was a freeman in Hartford in 1668 and later removed to Hatfield, Massachusetts where he d. in 1683.

Three brothers, *1. William Jackson Worthington, *2. John Worthington and 3. Charles Worthington were the immediate ancestors of a branch of the family in Greenup County, Kentucky.

1. WILLIAM JACKSON WORTHINGTON, farmer, ironmaster, public official and lawyer, was b. in Pennsylvania, near Johnstown, in November, 1833, and d. in Greenup County, Kentucky in 1914. He was educated in the public schools of Pennsylvania and Ohio; and while a comparatively young man, he became the manager of an iron furnace but later engaged in farming in Greenup County, Kentucky, having come to that state with his parents. He was a staunch Union man and at the outbreak of the Civil War he enlisted and became captain of Company "B" Twenty-second Regiment Kentucky Vounteer Infantry; was promoted to lieutenant-colonel and at close of the war was offered but declined a commission as brigadier-general, U. S. Army.

Colonel Worthington held many public offices of honor and trust. He served as State senator from Greenup and Lewis Counties, 1865-1869; State representative from Greenup County, 1884-86, and again from 1902-06; judge of the Greenup County Court, 1866-70; and was elected and served as Lieutenant-Governor of Kentucky, under the administration of Governor William O'Connor Bradley, 1895-1899. Continuing his farming operations until 1873, he then became part owner and the manager of an iron furnace which position he held for about ten years. The remaining active years of his life after the expiration of his term as Lieutenant-Governor were spent in farming and the practice of law at Greenup, he having been admitted to the bar in early manhood.

In politics, Colonel Worthington was a Republican, and his sympathies were with the Methodist Episcopal Church.

Colonel Worthington was twice married. He m., first, Catherine Steele, b. in Washington County, Virginia, in 1835 and d. in Greenup County, Kentucky, in 1888.

Children:

4. Anna Worthington; b. about 1858; m. Charles Dickey, of Greenup. They migrated to Montana.

5. Agnes Worthington; b. about 1859; m. George Callahan of Danleyton, Greenup County.

6. Finley Worthington; b. 1860, went to Alabama when a young man.

7. Thomas Worthington; b. about 1861, went to Alabama when a young man.

8. William Worthington, lawyer, was b. in Greenup County, Kentucky, February 2, 1869; received his elementary education in the public schools of Greenup County after which he was a student in the University of Kentucky. Subsequently he completed a course in a business college and then accepted the position of stenographer with the law firm of Breckenridge and Shelby of Lexington, Kentucky, with whom he remained for about seven years, serving one year as private secretary to Colonel Breckenridge. During that period he gave serious attention to reading law and also attended law school at Georgetown University, Washington, D. C. Admitted to the bar in 1897, he at once established an office in Lexington where he has practiced continually since. For more than twelve years he was U. S. District Court Referee in bankruptcy of the district composed of the counties of Clark, Fayette, Mason, Scott and Jassemine, after which and in November, 1921, he was elected Circuit Judge of the Twenty-second Judicial District. He d. at St. Joseph's Hospital, Lexington, May 29, 1922.

Politically, Mr. Worthington was an earnest and warm supporter of the Republican party; in religion he was a Presbyterian.

Mr. Worthington m., May 4, 1898, Addie Swift Norwood, b. in Fayette County, daughter of Dr. Edward M. and Pricilla W. (Downing) Norwood, natives respectively of Massachusetts and Kentucky.

Children:

9. William N. Worthington.

10. Frank F. Worthington.

1-A. Colonel William J. Worthington m., secondly, Lucy York of Hunnewell, Greenup County.

Children:
*11. Nancy Worthington.
  12. Mrs. James Collins of Greenup.

11. NANCY WORTHINGTON m., March 15, 1911, Patterson Anderson Williams, a merchant at Russell, Kentucky. He was b. April 4, 1890, and is one of nine children of Henry Arnstead and Margaret (Patterson) Williams, the former of whom was a resident of and a contractor at Russell.

Mr. Williams was educated in the public schools at Advance, Greenup County and at a business college in Ironton, Ohio.

His first position was that of car repairer in the shops of the C. & O. Railway Company at Russell. By conscientious application to his work he soon merited and was promoted to the position of foreman of the shop and continued in that capacity until he opened a store at Raceland, Kentucky, which he operated for two years when, in 1918, he entered the field of contracting. He was joined by his father in 1920 and they continued in the business until 1922 when they acquired the stock of the Russell Hardware Company. After the death of his father, he continued the hardware business; and was president, treasurer and general manager of the company. He was also a director of the First National Bank and the Peoples Bank.

Children: Patterson, Lucie, Margaret and Adelaide.

Mr. Williams is a Republican in politics and is active in party affairs. He is affiliated with the Masons.

2. In the early 1880's JOHN (JACK) WORTHINGTON built a home at the Falls of Little Sandy and here the family lived for several years.

Children·
13. Ona Worthington; m. David Vallance.
14. Sarah Worthington; m. Mr. Davvison.
15. Nancy Worthington; m. George Thom.
16. Tempa Worthington; m. Uhl McCoy.
17. James Worthington.
18. John Worthington.
19. Charles Worthington.

3. CHARLES WORTHINGTON; m. Nancy Holbrook of Tygarts Valley, Greenup County. He was a merchant and the family still owns and operates the business.

Other Worthington families lived in Greenup County, who probably were of the same family as Colonel William J. Worthington (1).

20. James Worthington, collier, b. in Pennsylvania, about 1803, m. Eleanor ———, b. in Pennsylvania about 1809.

Children and approximate dates of birth as disclosed by the U. S. Census of Greenup County for the years 1850 and 1860:

21. James Worthington, collier, b. in Pennsylvania, 1828.
22. Nancy Worthington, b. in Pennsylvania, 1831.
23. Orlando Worthington, b. in Pennsylvania, 1834.
24. Isabel Worthington, b. in Pennsylvania, 1836.
25. Charles Worthington, b. in Ohio, 1839.
26. Rinalda Worthington, b. in Kentucky, 1849.
27. Audria Worthington, b. in Kentucky, 1854.
28. James S. Worthington, collier, (Oldtown District), b. in Pennsylvania about 1830; m. Elizabeth ———, b. about 1836.

Children and approximate dates of birth as disclosed by the U. S. Census for Greenup County, for the year 1870:

29. Aurelia Worthington, b. 1855.
30. Laura Worthington, b. 1857.
31. Virginia Worthington, b. 1859.
32. John Worthington; b. 1861.
33. Nancy Worthington; b. 1865.
34. Mary Worthington; b. 1868.

THE END

INDEX